Falling Up

Carlisle Floyd, 2011. Portrait by Jesse Guess, Denver, Colorado.

Falling Up

The Days and Nights of Carlisle Floyd

The Authorized Biography

Thomas Holliday

With a Foreword by Plácido Domingo

Syracuse University Press

The generous assistance of the following is gratefully acknowledged:

Furthermore:
a program of the J. M. Kaplan Fund

The William C. Fleming Educational Unitrust

Mary Selden Evans

Syracuse University Press
Syracuse, New York 13244-5290

First Edition 2013
13 14 15 16 17 18 6 5 4 3 2 1

∞ The paper used in this publication meets the minimum requirements of the American National Standard for Information Sciences—Permanence of Paper for Printed Library Materials, ANSI Z39.48-1992.

For a listing of books published and distributed by Syracuse University Press, visit our website at SyracuseUniversityPress.syr.edu.

ISBN: 978-0-8156-1003-8

Library of Congress Cataloging-in-Publication Data
Holliday, Thomas.
Falling up : the days and nights of Carlisle Floyd : the authorized biography / Thomas Holliday ; with a foreword by Placido Domingo. — 1st ed.
p. cm.
Includes bibliographical references and index.
ISBN 978-0-8156-1003-8 (cloth : alk. paper) 1. Floyd, Carlisle. 2. Composers—United States—Biography I. Title.
ML410.F645H65 2012
782.1092—dc23
[B] 2012038544

Manufactured in the United States of America

For Sheila, for her days and nights of love, support,
forbearance, proofreading, editing.

My dancers never fall to simply fall.
They fall to rise.
—Martha Graham, *Blood Memory*

Thomas Holliday has a performing background in brass instrumental and vocal music, and has directed multiple productions of over fifty operas, operettas, and musicals in Europe and the United States. He has also worked as a composer-arranger, conductor, opera educator, writer, and lecturer on operatic subjects. His published and performed output includes articles for Lyric Opera of Chicago's *Season Companion* and *The Opera Journal,* twenty-five English performing translations, fifteen supertitle translations, and two original opera libretti.

Contents

Illustrations

Foreword

PLÁCIDO DOMINGO

What has always enticed me about Carlisle Floyd's music is how it captures the essence of American life, as demonstrated with subjects such as *Susannah* and *Of Mice and Men*. His musical language is so unique that one immediately knows it is written by Carlisle Floyd. I have presented both *Susannah* and *Of Mice and Men* (in a coproduction with the Bregenz Festival) at the Washington National Opera in my capacity as general director. This is part of my administrative philosophy of producing an American opera each season.

My interest in *Susannah* came first, having heard so many of the opera's virtues over the years, from its original starring performers Phyllis Curtin and the late Norman Treigle, and later from its current exponents Renée Fleming and Samuel Ramey. Thank God that we have stars who make it a priority in their careers to sing this country's great music. Which of us has not marveled at the achingly beautiful vocal line of "Ain't it a pretty night," or has not witnessed and been strongly affected by the hypnotic revival scene of the preacher Olin Blitch?

What is so admirable about Carlisle Floyd is that he is what one might describe as self-taught, and has in turn spent so much of his career as a splendid pedagogue.

Acknowledgments

Carlisle Floyd lived in towns with smaller populations than the number of people it is my pleasure to thank. All have manifested friendship, communication, and hospitality without borders. This is above all a mark of the esteem in which Carlisle Floyd is held by all who have known, worked with, or simply heard of him. Any factual inaccuracies, misinterpretations of information, individuals, or incidents, or omissions are my sole and regretful responsibility. As my father used to say with regard to media citations, "You'll never know how much they get wrong until they write about you."

Above all I thank the Floyd family. The subject himself, Carlisle Floyd, has set new records for generosity, patience, kindness, and good humor, throughout dozens of interviews, phone conversations, and e-mail exchanges, without which this study would not have a ghost's chance at truth, intimacy, or the *lived* details that make a biography more than metafiction. His late wife, Kay Reeder Floyd, graciously relinquished her husband to my persistence and curiosity. His sister Ermine Floyd Matheny, her husband Billy Matheny, and their daughters Jane Floyd Matheny, Harriett Matheny, and Martha Matheny Solomon have involved themselves in Carlisle's life in heroic ways, and welcomed me into theirs. Cousins Helen Harris, Marjorie Manning, the late Henry Bascom Floyd (the family genealogist), and the Ellerbe brothers of Latta, Hazel Earle "Bud" and Frank, contributed a wealth of personal detail.

Special thanks to Plácido Domingo for the foreword to this book; to his agent Patrick Farrell, who enabled the contact; and to my friend, Renaissance man/visual artist Jesse Guess, for his wonderful frontispiece portrait of the subject.

Thanks to friends, colleagues, Floyd students, cocreators, and interview subjects: Mark Adamo; Marshall Bialosky; Craig Bohmler; Lew McSwain Brandes; Rick Brown; Ian Campbell; Judith Christin; Jona Clarke; Frank Corsaro; Phyllis Curtin; Nancy Smith Fichter; Mark Flint; Dana Gioia; Dr. Joseph Glatthaar, University of North Carolina, Chapel Hill; David Gockley; Linda Golding; Dr. Charles Hausmann, Dr. James Pipkin, Buck Ross, David Tomatz, Dr. David Ashley White, University of Houston; Jake Heggie; Polly Holliday; Paula Bailey Hulslander; the late Cecelia King of Bethune, South Carolina; Henson Markham; Leonard and Norma Mastrogiacomo; William Mayer; James Medvitz; Susanne Mentzer; Henry Mollicone; Donald Mowrer; Marni Nixon; Jack O'Brien; the late Julian Patrick; Harold Prince; Samuel Ramey; Donald Rand; Ned Rorem; Glen Rosenbaum; Julius Rudel; David Small; Robin Stamper; James Staples; Edward Thomas; Peggy Tapp Turman; Carl Vollrath; Sheryl Woods Olson; and Ellen Taaffe Zwilich.

Academic, government, and civic administrators: Betty Aumann, Kate Rivers, and Amber Thiele, Music Division, Library of Congress; Ben Bolden, College Music Educators Association (CMEA); Bobray Bordelon; Princeton University Library, holders/publishers of CPANDA, with its complete set of online issues of *Central Opera Service Bulletin,* 1959–1990; Bill Bugg, Samford University; Dr. John Burt, Brandeis University; Don Gibson, Dean, College of Music, Florida State University; Dee Beggarly, Sarah Gross, Wendy Smith, Dan Clark, Mark James Froelich, Sarah Cohen, Brad Brock, Timothy Hoomes, Kathleen Harvey, and Dr. Robin Sellers, also of Florida State University; Thorne Compton, University of South Carolina; Nicolette A. Dobrowolski, Syracuse University Library;

Diane Ducharme and Moira Fitzgerald, Beinecke Rare Book and Manuscript Library, Yale University; Henry Fulmer, and assistants Graham Duncan and Rose Thomas, Manuscripts Division, South Caroliniana Library, University of South Carolina; Jane Gottlieb and Jeni Dahmus, Juilliard School; Robby Gunstream, College Music Society; Dave Knapp, Opus II, Kitchener, Ontario, Canada; David Low and Ann Guthrie Hingston, National Endowment for the Arts; Cindy Hurbutt, City of Spartanburg, South Carolina; Donna E. Kelly, North Carolina Office of Archives and History; Helen Moody, Dillon County Library, South Carolina; Lynn B. Lamkin, Joan O'Connor, Moores School of Music, University of Houston; Brenda and William McNeiland, Jacksonville University; Sarah Mazur and Stephanie Krolick, Aspen Festival; Lee Mitchell, South Carolina Department of Natural Resources; Jim Neal, Michael Ryan, and Elizabeth Davis, Department of Music, Columbia University; Raymond Neal, Jacksonville Public Library; Sara Pitcher, Coe College; Chris Prom, Lisa Renee Kemplin, University of Illinois Libraries; Edgar Loessin; Hope Mizzell and Wes Tyler, South Carolina Office of Historical Weather Records; A. Sandy Neiman, Paul Stuart, Inc., New York; Steve Parrott and Bea Fields, Kershaw County Public Library, South Carolina; Adrienne Rose and Cathy Hurd, Coker College; Ralph Rosinbum, University of Washington, Seattle; Anna L. Scott, Aspen Historical Society; Maureen Breed, Marietta Dooley, Kyle Harris, and Mary O'Brien, Syracuse University; Dr. Phillip Stone, archivist, Wofford College; Drs. Elmer Thomas and Earl Rivers, College-Conservatory of Music, University of Cincinnati; Susan Thoms, Spartanburg County Public Libraries, South Carolina; Steve Tuttle, South Carolina Department of Archives and History; Dr. Jeffrey Willis, Beth Lancaster, Sarah Spigner, Susan Stevenson, Converse College; Michael Williams, Wortham Theater Center, Houston; Dr. Blake Wilson, Malinda Triller, and Debbie Ege, Dickinson College; Theresa Wood, Records Office, Spartanburg (South Carolina) High School;

Arts administrators and journalists: John Allison, editor, *Opera;* Jack Belsom and Carol Rausch, New Orleans Opera Association; Sarah Billinghurst, Metropolitan Opera; Robert Wilder Blue, USOperaWeb; Ann Branton, *The Southern Quarterly;* Garnett Bruce, Opera Omaha; Chad M. Calvert, Opera Carolina; Max Carlson, Schubert Club, St. Paul, Minnesota; Stephanie L. Challener, publisher, *Musical America Worldwide;* Averil Cook, Calgary Opera; Jonathan Dean, Seattle Opera; Lois Duplantier and Jack Gardner, Louisiana Philharmonic Orchestra; Michael Egel, Des Moines Metro Opera; Gerald Ensley, *Tallahassee Democrat;* Ernest Gilbert, Allan Altman, Video Artists International; Carolyn Gordanier and Virginia M. Long, Lyric Opera of Kansas City; Mark Gresham, *Chorus! Magazine;* Ray Hammond, EMI/Virgin Records; Dr. Robert Hansen, National Opera Association; Naomi Havlen, *Aspen Times;* Patti Humphrey, Michelle Krisel, Marina Stiajkina, Washington National Opera; Amy Jo Inskeep, *Louisville Courier-Journal;* Tim Jerome, National Music Theater Network; Monte Jacobson, Seattle Opera; Althea Katona, Kentucky Opera; Liz Keller-Tripp and Peggy Monastra, G. Schirmer, Inc.; Mary Kiffer, John Simon Guggenheim Memorial Foundation; James K. McCully, Jr., Opera Music Theater International; Mike McMurray and Terry Brown, Houston Symphony; Albanela Malavé, Holly Mentzer, Joe Rubinstein, Catherine Rice, Steven Swartz, Eddie Whalen, Boosey & Hawkes; Sarah C. Mieras and John "Jeep" Jeffries, Opera Grand Rapids; James Meena, Opera Carolina; Ava Jean Mears, Brian Mitchell, Houston Grand Opera; Sean Moores, *The Augusta Chronicle;* Deborah Morrow and Valerie Hamlin, Central City Opera; Idelle Nissila-Stone, Ford Foundation; Michael Nutter, Capitol City Opera; Karen Olinyk, Canadian Opera Company; Suzanne Palmer, *St. Petersburg Times;* Leslie Parsons, Albany Records; Eric Price and Gemma Wilson, assistants to Harold Prince; Kitty Reagan and Kathy DeLoach, Augusta Opera; Dr. Michael Remson and Amanda Fisher, American Festival for the Arts; Rental/Performance Department of Theodore Presser Co.; David Sander, Minnesota Opera; Todd Schultz, Old Globe, San Diego; Marc Scorca, Opera America; Bill Higgins, Alexa Antopol, Melanie Feilotter, Adam Gustafson, Opera America; Richard Sherwin,

Tallahassee Little Theatre; Matthew Shilvock, San Francisco Opera; Alastair Sutherland, *The Mirror,* Montreal; Brett Surguine, Arizona Opera; Kathleen Trocino and Kathleen Kienholz, American Academy of Arts and Letters; F. Paul Driscoll and Adam Wasserman, *Opera News;* Amanda S. Wilborn and Cristina Vásconez Herrera, Atlanta Opera; Paul Witkowski and Alan Hopper, Jacksonville Symphony Association; and Susan Woelzl, New York City Opera.

Good Samaritans: Peter Alexander, the Avant family of Tallahassee; Ellen Wendt Bacon, widow, and Sam Farrell, grandson, of Ernst Bacon; Joan Kaye Barrow, the Blackmon family, Florence, South Carolina; Jeff Bretz of BretzTec in Denver, the computer guy who has saved our bacon so many times in the last six years; Heather Cole, Houghton Library, Harvard University; Pandora Douglas, Bethune, South Carolina; Sherri Feldman, Random House; Doug Foster, Louisville, Kentucky; John Freeman, photographer; Desmond C. Gates, photographer, Seattle; Mike and Patty Griffey of the gracious Abingdon Manner in Latta, South Carolina, who are acquainted with everyone of consequence in the composer's birthplace, including Brenda Lloyd, the Floyd House's owner in 2006; Martha L. Hart, photographer; Howard Hensel, photographer; Mary Marshall, assistant to Ned Rorem; Janice Mayer; Jill Michnick, Los Angeles Opera; Robert Quarles, Florence, South Carolina; Robert E. Quarles, Jr., Florence, South Carolina; Richard Schwent and Keith Anderson, Denver; Rev. Barbara R. Segars, Bethel United Methodist Church, Bethune, South Carolina; Anita J. Stanton, artist; Evon Streetman, photographer; N. Donn Talenti, Patricia Windrow-Klein, artist; and Mark Shulgasser.

And thanks to the long list of agents and publishers who rejected this project, allowing me to find the right ones at Syracuse University Press: my editors, Mary Selden Evans, Marcia Hough, Mary Petrusewicz, Kay Steinmetz; Kelly L. Balenske, editorial assistant; Mona Hamlin, Lynn Hoppel, and Lisa Kuerbis, marketing and design staff; and Erica Sheftic, office coordinator.

And, far from least, but apparently last, thanks to Jean Kellogg and Jesse Gram, Lyric Opera of Chicago. It was their assignment to me in 2002–2003, for pieces on *Susannah* for Lyric's *Season Companion,* that allowed me to meet and interview Carlisle. Gram also volunteered to read the entire prepublication manuscript and still liked it, as did Stephen Fiol and Harold Kafer.

With one exception, there are no examples of Floyd's music, and I have paraphrased or drastically truncated most reviews and articles because of copyright restrictions, denial of permissions, demands for licensing fees—including, inexplicably, Floyd's publisher, Boosey & Hawkes—or delays in responding by deadline dates. I encourage the reader to seek out the sources listed in the bibliography or footnotes. I have included most of the nonoperatic poetry set by Floyd, again excepting copyrighted material. As my wife says, "Don't take it personally: it's about money." (For the same reasons, there are not as many pictures as I had hoped to include.)

Music professionals and specialized readers will know the meanings of the tempo and interpretative markings included, most in Italian; for definitions, any edition of *The Harvard Dictionary of Music* will provide clarification.

Finally, the appendix offers an extended genealogy of the Floyd and Fenegan families.

Introduction

Carlisle Floyd is bored. In the endless dark cold of a Syracuse winter evening, this rare idle moment is downright uncongenial. He huddles, shivering, in his room on Beacon Road, doodling. He scans a returned paper on Robert Penn Warren's poetry, written for a major American poets class, to see how it might have been better. On the title page, Professor Cady had scrawled, "A+: Best student paper ever!" Carlisle transforms doodles into an imitation of Cady's handwriting, a gift he has always used with admired teachers. The copied script is indistinguishable from the original, and the world's deep pockets will grow safer on the day that Floyd chooses music over forgery.

The preceding is an imagined, however truth-based, theatrical vignette; everything that follows is scrupulously factual, within limits dictated by my reliance on so many memories communicated in so many interviews. Floyd was and is a Renaissance man, talented in visual arts, writing, piano performance, composition, stage direction, public speaking, teaching. His third opera, *Susannah,* premiered just weeks before his twenty-ninth birthday, created an overnight sensation when New York City Opera unveiled it a year later. Manhattan critics not known for their charity fell all over their thesauri to express admiration for this unknown southerner: "Some of the most powerful pages in American opera," "a towering crescendo of music and mood unlike anything else in American opera," "a triumph of spare strength and bold vitality," "a Verdian flair for extracting the last drops of dramatic juice," "the most moving and impressive opera to have been written in America—or anywhere else—since Gershwin's *Porgy and Bess."*

Trained as a concert pianist, Floyd became a master teacher of that instrument as well as of composition. His catalogue spans thirteen operas, including first settings of John Steinbeck's *Of Mice and Men* and Robert Penn Warren's *All the King's Men,* orchestral works, music for one and two pianos, art song, song cycles with piano and orchestra, and large- and small-scale choral music. As mentor to composers like Mark Adamo, Craig Bohmler, and Jake Heggie, his vision lives on.

Floyd has received most of the awards and honors available to American composers. The Music Critics Circle of New York anointed *Susannah* as the best new opera of 1956, and the work showcased American culture at the 1958 Brussels World's Fair. Floyd went on to win a Guggenheim Fellowship, Ford Foundation commissions, Opera Music Theater International's Lifetime Achievement Award, the National Medal of Arts, and membership in the American Academy of Arts and Letters. At eighty-two, he became one of four individuals from varied backgrounds in opera to win the National Endowment for the Arts' first Opera Honors Awards.

So why have many of you never heard of Carlisle Floyd? Related anecdotes give hints. At an early interview, I noticed that he wore no socks with his soft loafers—the style is Florida casual, or a preppy thing. He's a sharp dresser.

Then I learned that he had worried to a friend, the nuclear chemist Gregory Choppin, "Tom's doing all this work on my genealogy."

Gregg said, "Carlisle, that's what biographers do."

After initial pleasantries before the next interview, Floyd said, "Now that I know you intend to write this book about *me* and not just my operas, I feel that I have to confess things to you. Well, I just hate wearing socks."

A *confession?* Floyd is highly conflicted about having his closely kept life mirrored while he lives it. The thought of even *having* a biographer makes him squirm.

Why *should* we care about Carlisle Floyd? His is the story of every individuated human being on the planet, only on a more, well, *operatic* scale. The great tenor Plácido Domingo, artistic director of the opera companies of Washington, DC, and Los Angeles, answered the question, why Floyd?, in October 2001: "He is not only a living maestro, he is also a living American Dream. . . . We should look at this life and realize that America offers opportunity to anyone who is willing to grasp his dream and work for it."

Actors know about the sensation of "falling up." In that split-second transition that ignites an entrance from the wings, they inhabit a new and different character, and the character inhabits them. It is an unwilled ascent to a different mode of being, an in-body experience that overlays preparation, opportunity, or chance. I also use the expression as a metaphor for the uncanny human ability to rise from seeming disaster in rebirth—a literal renaissance, especially when it involves the generation of operas, either spontaneous or, more often, hard-won. Carlisle Floyd's life is marked by a regular succession of such moments, be they soars, stumbles, slides, or wrenches, in a delicate balance of dark and light, day and night.

Floyd's story is one of triumph over odds. His path from the unlikely cradle of Latta, South Carolina, through a childhood maze of family complexities and religious revivals, to the world of academia that molded his young adulthood, to the world's great opera houses, is an odyssey in the classical mold.

In spring 2006, having researched and written about *Susannah* and *Cold Sassy Tree* for company publications in Chicago and Charlotte, I asked Floyd's opinion about my undertaking a book on his operas. He responded graciously that he was collaborating on that very book with Doug Fisher, the head of Florida State University's opera program, but wondered how I might feel about a biography. Having no need to ponder, I responded, "Sign me up." This book is nonetheless all about music, because that is who Carlisle Floyd is and what he makes; however, with the exception of his considerable nonoperatic catalogue, I have left the musical exposition of his operatic oeuvre to the composer and to Fisher, whose study, *The Operas of Carlisle Floyd in the Composer's Words* (a working title), is in preparation.

Love of family, the singular quest for independence, personal freedom of expression and living, and the acquisition and perfection of resources form the through line of Floyd's life. The face he presents to the world is anything but that of intrepid explorer, much less cause combatant. He has at times put himself forward, but the effort exacts a price: from childhood on, getting noticed was hazardous to his health and sanity. The interstices between *Susannah, Of Mice and Men,* and *Cold Sassy Tree* coalesce as years of inner searching and growth, after processing criticism ranging from intelligent and well-meaning to petty and vicious, and turning his back on what brought him early success. *Susannah* continues to be performed worldwide, dozens of times each year, by professional opera companies, colleges, conservatories, even high schools. Its composer was once approached by an adoring soprano who told him that the heroine's first aria was "our national anthem."

Years of success, security, physical and psychological trauma, deflation, rebirth, and personal sacrifice define the Floyd mix. Though none of it kept him from amassing a body of important work, the combination explains in part why Carlisle Floyd does not (yet) have the name recognition of Samuel Barber, Aaron Copland, or, a more exact parallel, Gian Carlo Menotti.

If this telling of Floyd's story seems at times discursive, the reader should know that creating opera or any other musical form rarely pursues a linear path. More often than not, Floyd worked on several projects simultaneously, most without holidays from his teaching career. And while excursions into matters monetary, contractual, and otherwise practical and mundane in a composer's workaday life may impede the story's through line, I have included them as confirmation, solace, and warning for those contemplating or pursuing musical careers. In Floyd's eighty-five years of life, sixty of them in the world of opera, teams and totals are crucial; but if the reader finds lists yawn-inducing, please feel free to glide over the enumeration of productions, casts, and reviews—the last of which indicate less stone-hewn judgments than the serendipitous (in)disposition of a given listener's eyes and ears. Yet there were weeks, months, entire years in this extraordinary life when our subject had little else in the way of encouragement or nourishment.

Independence is the core of Floyd's life, an independence sought early, hard-won, and nurtured throughout his long succession of days and nights. His protagonists may be different, outsiders, an interpretation that has gained currency in Floyd criticism, but remaining different and outside is always their *choice.* They achieve that status through independence from restriction, false values, dishonesty, bigotry, outmoded traditions, and societal pressures. From the beginning, Floyd's characters were strong, independent explorers, like slandered Susannah against her crabbed fundamentalist community; Cathy and Heathcliff of *Wuthering Heights,* fighting for identity as a couple; George's day and Lennie's night in *Of Mice and Men.* Floyd's creations are a pantheon of vital, *essential* characters, voices from a better world. And the music? Seeking, challenging, touching, accessible melody, haunting the brain and heart. At his thorniest, Carlisle Floyd remains an unapologetic romantic.

Floyd has always struggled with his Janus faces: The consummate professional and the fellow who always expected someone to approach him with the challenge, "Boy, why don't you just go home?" He is a certifiable genius, but abashed by the characterization; a tireless worker who bests Sisyphus, rolling dwarfing great rocks uphill on the slippery slopes of the classical music world, to positions of permanence; the husband who felt guilty reading or listening to a recording, much less playing the piano or composing, because they abstracted him from caring for his wife of half a century.

Floyd hates being called a southern gentleman, but he's the real deal: southern to a fault and a gentle man. And gentleman. Neither critic nor even biographer can tarnish that, because all these Floyds, all paradigms of determinism, are so lovable. None lives on the Internet, or in *The New Grove Dictionary of Opera*—though he's all over both. Still, the man is not a little worried that his eighty-five years of life and accomplishment are not interesting enough to make a biography.

You decide.

Abbreviations

B & H	Boosey & Hawkes
FALOC	Floyd Archive, Library of Congress; cited locations as of October 2008.
FASCL	Floyd Archive, South Caroliniana Library, University of South Carolina, Columbia; cited locations as of July 2011.
FF	Ford Foundation
FFA	Ford Foundation Archives
FSU	Florida State University
HGO	Houston Grand Opera
JRP	Juilliard Repertory Project
NEA	National Endowment for the Arts
NOA	National Opera Association
NOI	National Opera Institute
NYCO	New York City Opera
OMT	Opera/Music Theater Program (NEA)
SU	Syracuse University
SUSC	Syracuse University Special Collections
UH	University of Houston

Falling Up

1

The Cradle

Latta, 1926–1932

The clock's hands pass midnight, and the calendar turns to June 11, 1926. Expectant father Carlisle Sessions Floyd, known to all as Jack, a month shy of twenty-two, works days as a teller at Farmers and Merchants Bank, manages family farm affairs, and sells the annual tobacco crop.

Ida Fenegan, Jack's bride of nineteen months, is just two months into her twenty-first year. She'd much rather be where she was days earlier, sitting in the back porch shade, fresh peach juice dripping down her chin. South Carolina's late spring steams in the nineties as rain falls across much of the state. Ida and Jack swelter in their little bungalow, a few doors from both family houses on Latta's Marion Street, catty-corner from the big brick Methodist church. The stage is set for the arrival of Carlisle Jr., whose name today appears in every shred of literature into which the town, county, and state can work it.

The esteemed Dr. Henry Arthur Edwards and his nurse share the perspiration. Ida's father, Oscar Fenegan, keeps peeking in to ask, "Why have it on the eleventh? The tenth sounded so much better!"[1]

The first in a long succession of reviews.

At 12:05 a.m., Jack becomes Carlisle Sessions Floyd Senior, the child named like his daddy: Carlisle for James Carlisle, Civil War hero and president of Wofford College; Sessions for Grandma Floyd, and one of the lines allied through marriage with the Floyds.

Daddy mutters, "I do not ever want to be called Old Jack."

Following birthing and bathing, the mercury will vault to just shy of a hundred on Carlisle Junior's first day.

THE SOUTH in general, and Ida Fenegan Floyd in particular, kept "baby books" that recorded details of a child's emergence and early expressions. The family's oral history preserved Carlisle's greeting the world with the umbilical cord wrapped around his neck. His first breaths took an anxious while in coming, but soon the room vibrated with the lusty squalling of the future composer of so much vocal music.

Most of the family thought he was scrawny, just six and a quarter pounds at birth. Only Ida and her sister

1. Carlisle Floyd at c. 6 months. Quarles Studio, Florence, South Carolina. Floyd collection. By permission of Robert E. Quarles Jr.

Mary Kate, "Bunny," expressed the minority opinion that he was a pretty baby. Carlisle Floyd has no particular first memory, but Ida recalled that his first word, just shy of his first birthday, was "dat," for "daddy," an imitation of her call to her husband. In *Baby's Record,* she recorded "Baby's First Journey":

> One hot July night when Carlisle was about a month old, we decided to take granddaddy's car and ride to Dillon. We thought it would be refreshing to us all, but lights went out, a tire went flat, and we hope Carlisle's life will never be so imperiled again as it was when we missed a truck by a few inches.[2]

No one had an inkling of the conditions of life in the serious music world, but it would seem that he entered his world with defensive skills:

> Little Carlisle has a great notion of waking at five o'clock every morning and seeing to it that his mother and daddy are properly entertained by his cooing . . . not so pleasant to others. He especially enjoys pulling hair, and biting too, since his teeth appear so useful.[3]

Carlisle Floyd's paternal grandmother, Ermine Mercer Sessions Floyd, living in the family home at 309 North Marion, survived her grandson's birth by just two months, dying on August 15, 1926. She joined husband Giles in Mt. Andrew Cemetery, beneath a stone reading, "A faithful wife and a loving mother."

Jack and Ida lost little time in moving back into the big house, joining his sisters Doris, twenty, and Hazel, sixteen, the former preparing to leave for college. Carlisle adored Hazel, nicknamed "the Countess," and her soulful qualities, as perhaps the most beautiful woman on whom his eyes ever rested. Even in her sixties, Latta elected her queen for its homecoming parade.

On the other hand, Doris gained a certain notoriety for quirkiness, and in midlife flirted with the notion of becoming a lawyer. She might invite the Floyds to visit, but no sooner had they arrived than she sighed, "There is nothing more difficult than having company." In the same vein, when everyone gathered in her kitchen during meal preparation, she'd shoo them off, grumbling, "The hardest thing in the world is being a housewife, having to cook for people."

Jack's eleven-year-old brother, Bascom Lorraine, or "Sonny," also still at home and in grade school, rounded out a family population of six. Elder brother Giles Roberts Jr., known as "G. R.," was already away at college.

Ida discovered inherent tensions in sister-in-lawhood, new motherhood, and sharing space with these relative strangers. Hazel had a sweet, gentle disposition, but Doris was tactlessness personified, and those two sisters were often at each other's throat. The environment was less than soothing, even for a newborn who retained no conscious memory of ambient discord; but the world of music theater would feel like home.

Jack and Ida had a time of it, claiming moments of peace and privacy, but find it they did, at least around Columbus Day 1926. Jack's diaries make it clear that he never lost his strong physical attraction to his smart, delicate, pretty, musical wife. That they had plans for a substantial family became clear around the Christmas holidays, when Ida was again expecting.

On July 29, 1927, they were blessed with a healthy daughter, Katherine, named for Ida's mother, and Ermine, for Jack's; only Ermine stuck. As we shall see in a broad cross section of Floyds and Fenegans, family names fell no farther than apples from the proverbial tree.

Carlisle grew reed-slender and Ermine tall and strong. With just a year separating them, many outside the family thought them twins, and their lifelong friendship and parallel interests and talents made them the closest of siblings. Carlisle remembers no life without Ermine; Ida recorded one of his first sayings: "Mama, ain't Ermine a sweet little girl?" But the household's increase to seven did nothing for domestic tranquility.

Southerners tend to be particular about names, and, unlike their father, the Floyd children were proud of their givens. In letters to closest friends and family, Carlisle used the affectionate "Ermie" for his sister, but as both say, "There is not much you can do with the name 'Carlisle.'" Uncle G. R. was outraged that any parent would so burden a child, maintaining that henceforth he would call them "Gus" and "Lucy."

To his parents, Carlisle was just "Son."

IDA'S PARENTS, Oscar Fenegan and his Kate, were far from idle, but less than profitable since 1924. When she discovered the chest empty of funds, Kate swept her mother and the children off to Laurinburg, North Carolina, just across the state line, thirty-eight miles from Latta, in an area where Cottingham kin farmed outlying lands. U.S. Highway 15 ran through Laurinburg, making it a convenient resting place for tourists.

On September 30, 1927, Kate sold the Latta house to Sam Edwards, cobbled together the down payment on a rambling 1910-vintage white frame house next to Laurinburg's Methodist church, and proceeded to equip it as both Fenegan nest and tourist home-cum-boarding house, the Shamrock Inn. She hired a cook, and pressed daughters Bunny and Lucile into service for housework, bed making, and other chambermaidenly duties. Soon after the turn to 1928, the inn opened for business, swiftly liquidating its mortgage and replenishing empty family coffers.

Carlisle and Ermine remembered the Shamrock as their maternal grandparents' home, and the one constant between their own dwelling places for many years.

After selling the farm, Oscar rejoined the family in Laurinburg in 1928. Thanks to the kindness of a local businessman, the fifty-one-year-old began clerking at Cox Hardware. History repeated itself, but with a positive twist. No one remembers whether he quit or was fired, but Oscar had the storied Irish luck: a job as caretaker of the local cemetery materialized. Fit and strong from years of farm labor, he loved working the earth. With a single black helper, he flourished, developing a reputation for keeping the grounds immaculate.

Oscar enjoyed and became so good at his job that he kept it, and was kept in it, well into his eighties. One of the perquisites of efficient groundskeeping was hours of free time, during which he indulged his facility with verse. For children and grandchildren, he wrote poems by turns amusing, touching, and philosophical.

Yet there were still obligations to people in Latta and Laurinburg: grocers and other merchants all expected timely payment. Like her husband, Kate had no use for idleness or false pride. She supplemented Shamrock profits by baking and selling fruit cakes in any place where they still owed money, until repayment of the last penny of debt.

JACK AND ELDER BROTHER G. R., coadministrators of their mother's estate, paid $950 to settle the Marion Street house on May 19, 1927. Their arrangement left both house and farm in Jack's care, with the understanding that each Floyd sibling would share alike in proceeds from crops and property sales, but Jack was "chairman."

G. R. had embarked on studies in English literature at schools all over the country, beginning at Wofford College and progressing to slightly more liberal environments. He specialized in the Elizabethan era at Vanderbilt, the University of Chicago, and the University of Iowa, where he completed his doctorate with a dissertation on "Ben Jonson's Manservant," before leaving to teach at colleges in Tennessee, South Dakota, Ohio, and North Carolina. In short, G. R. could have cared less about property in South Carolina; it would be Jack's as long as he needed it.

Around 1910, their father had built his plantation-style, single-story home, between 3,000 and 3,500 square feet, in Latta. It sat on a handsome lot of one and two-tenths acres of sweeping green lawn. A generous porte cochere blossomed off the south end, and living quarters lay behind a deep porch with six stately columns. To the right of the wide shotgun hallway, front to back, lay the front parlor, dining room, and kitchen; to the left, bedrooms.

The children's release from cribs coincided with their immersion in endless family, what one scholar has termed an "extended, dense tribalistic network"[4]: Floyds, Fenegans, Sessionses, Cottinghams, Mannings, Robertses, Legettes, Betheas, Waynes, and Trezevants, to name just a few. Carlisle soon learned that he was related to most everyone in Latta. The liberal and inventive appendage of surnames as strings of given names made it no easier to tell who belonged to, was married to, or related to whom.

Ermine remembers both Lorraine Trezevant Sessions Jr.[5] and his cousin Percival,[6] sons of Civil War veteran brothers, and known as "uncle Trez" and "uncle Percy," "smelly old men with beards."

The spacious backyard of the Floyds enclosed a kitchen garden, chicken coop, and stables. Jack kept a pony there in his childhood, and the Floyds quartered horses for other families in the late twenties. Carlisle and Ermine soon had a pair of pet rabbits: fluffy, white, soft, pink-eyed, and kept caged in the stable. They shuddered with horror to learn that "Grandmammy" Cottingham, still living with the Fenegans, had *eaten* rabbit. The unblemished whiteness of these creatures gave them protected pet status, but they grew so large that their care became a chore, then a nuisance. More to the point, they began to devour Ida's vegetables, and were lucky to escape the stew pot.

2. Top: Ida Fenegan Floyd, Katherine Cottingham Fenegan. Bottom: Ermine, Ida Legette Bennett Cottingham, and Carlisle, c. 1932. Courtesy of Carlisle Floyd.

Of the town itself, Carlisle recalled Kornblut's dry goods store, already a local legend and downtown's most substantial business. Streets were not yet paved, and Latta was slow, peaceful, safe. No one locked doors. Though neither child yet read, Ida emphasized to them that the town had the last library built with Carnegie funding. The addition of Highway 301 to the country's burgeoning road system did the most to keep Latta from sharing the withering fate of many of the other small towns where the Floyds lived in years to come. The even smaller village of Floydale, named for forebears, lay eight miles distant, and another three miles from the family tobacco farm.

FLOYDS AND FENEGANS were for the most part healthy and long-lived, even if the men often outlived the women. The most dramatic inherited condition was the bronchial asthma of the Floyds. In the throes of an attack, chests constricted by invisible but inexorable steel bands, these otherwise strong men and women needed several days of enforced bed rest; school and work absences were followed by days of gasping for breath.

Jack and his sisters were chronic sufferers, and at about age three Carlisle's condition manifested. Ermine was spared. His would be a childhood and adolescence with many friends, but none closer or more needful than the arcane devices, techniques, and medications to open bronchial passages. As late as 1929, the condition still baffled the medical community and lay people alike. Episodes could be triggered by seasonal allergens, cold air, warm air, moist air, exertion, or emotional stress. Carlisle spent his first six Christmases, most on visits to Laurinburg, in bed.

Both Floyd children were physically active, and their high-spirited running, skipping, and jumping distressed Ida. Time plodded when Carlisle recuperated in bed and other boys were out having fun. Until he read, spring and summer droned on endlessly, as he longed to be up and about with friends and cousins, Daddy or Ermine, tossing the ball, exploring, playing with the rabbits, watching the chickens. He internalized his childhood self as skinny, anemic, and ugly, an evaluation that is utterly belied by the photographic record.

Ida, at the best of times nervous and overprotective, became the identified caregiver of father and son; her solicitous attention appears to have reinforced the disease's psychic side effects, which manifested early: inhibition in expressing anger and self-assertion, setting of unattainable goals, impaired self-confidence, and the exacerbation of separation anxiety would plague Carlisle Floyd in later life. In the opinion of one physician,

> The asthmatic child appears to be over-dependent upon his mother, and he is valued by her only when he is sick . . . the allergic child is unable to express his hostility toward his parents. He tries to repress it, but . . . repression only partially relieves his inner tensions . . . The growing child is . . . conflicted by his need to develop independence and maturity, while being constantly threatened by controlling parents. The engulfing parent manipulates every act of the child. Rejection may arise when the mutual engulfment fails to satisfy the parental needs.[7]

As she nursed two asthmatics, Ida's watch swung from worry to wary to prohibition. She applied a long list of "Thou shalt nots" derived from folk wisdom rather than medical certainty: no breaded or fried meat, nothing greasy. Carlisle ate uncoated steak served almost raw. Going out with a wet head was definitely taboo. Fretting dominated Ida's character: in place of such vulgar demonstrations as loving touches, hugs, or other signs of empathy, she limited affectionate behavior to quick pats on greeting and leaving.

Later, in Carlisle's adolescence, spending time together in the same room as his father grew difficult; but at the boy's sickbed, Jack related as a fellow sufferer. In the throes of an attack, Carlisle might fear for his life, but a gentler Jack perched on the edge of the mattress, brows knitted, nodding or shaking his head, saying, "You could not get much tighter, could you, son?" He always wanted to know how bad it was, how far down Carlisle could breathe.

Then he left.

The children heard that one never died from asthma, that adrenaline "kicked in" first; and Jack's certitude on that score consoled. Ephedrine sulfate became available in most Western countries only after 1932, and the Floyds used this treatment only in extremis, in tablet form. On rare occasions, family doctors might administer morphine. Carlisle watched his aunts with their omnipresent "squeezers," early atomizer/inhalers; he acquired his own unwieldy gray plastic Asthmafedrin appliance just before leaving for college in 1943. Ephedrine's associated tachycardia, the racing and pounding of the heart, seemed a small price to pay for breath.

SOUTHERN SPIRITUAL AND SOCIAL LIFE, then as now, centered on church. Jack had vowed to dedicate his life to God if he won Ida Fenegan's hand, and with the Methodist church across the street, the children were soon immersed in the rites and rhythms of southern Protestantism. The Marion house served as home and classroom, a training ground for family and society. The Golden Rule, "Do unto others as you would have others do unto you," filled their ears from the beginning.

Sundays were "bespoke": church school for children and adults, some classes taught by Jack, and morning and evening services. Wednesday or Thursday night prayer meetings were augmented by one or more summer revivals, requiring full weeks of twice-daily services. Within established church edifices, town or rural, visiting evangelists exhorted the faithful to rededicate their lives by coming to the rail and emptying their pockets of specie.

Carlisle and Ermine learned old-school southern manners and customs. Parents were addressed as "Mama" and "Daddy"; noon and evening meals were dinner and supper. Ida policed conduct, and the children's ears rang with the admonitions "Do not put your arms on the table," and "Chew with your mouths closed." Boys always stood when adults entered the room, and shook hands. One always addressed others as ma'am and sir. If Carlisle answered an adult with a simple yes, he heard about his rudeness. Men always opened the door for ladies, and the lady always entered first; outdoors, failure to walk on a lady's curb side guaranteed a sharp reprimand.

The children's infractions received responses both oral and gestural. Terse words of correction, exasperated sighs, eye rolling, and dagger looks were usually enough to discipline hypersensitive Carlisle, born with antennae fine-tuned for the tiniest hint of disapproval. Punishment for the repeat offender was usually a switching; added humiliation came from the switchee cutting off his or her own long twig, usually willow.

At age two or three, Carlisle once called for water after he'd been put to bed for the night. Jack obliged, then snapped, "do not do that again." No sooner had Daddy gotten back between his own sheets than Son tested the waters and repeated the request. Jack administered a spanking.

Years later, Jack bolstered his grandiosity by chuckling, "I knew you all were watching me around corners"; but from such trivial incidents, Carlisle's shyness toward and fear of his parents waxed, as trust waned: "If you can't trust *them,* where do you start?"

The worst infraction was not minding Mama, disregarding or disrespecting her requests. Forgetting to say ma'am, or whining that you did not want to do something amounted to disobedience. Ida usually supervised punishment and administered light spankings. After one lecture about "abridging the law," followed by a switching, Carlisle and Ermine crawled like bugs beneath their beds. The nostrum that punishment hurt the punisher more than the recipient struck them as absurd from the first; both behaved as well as they could.

Though Jack and Ida never systematically spelled out southern mores, the children nonetheless intuited that the region and its people were different. Ask anyone today about Carlisle Floyd, and the words "southern gentleman" spill from every lip. Carlisle himself grew weary and scornful of the characterization as somehow emblematic of a milquetoast personality; yet, inescapably, he is both southern and a gentle man.

The Floyds were only too aware that a scant sixty years separated their children's lives from the Civil War's trampling of old ways. Many South Carolinians still refer unsmilingly to the conflict as "the war of northern aggression." In the twenties and thirties of the last century, one might encounter, and be expected to honor, Confederate veterans; and the Floyds would grow close to one in a few years.

Besides practicing gallantry toward women, one avoided contradiction. It is still with the greatest reluctance that Carlisle Floyd approaches outright disagreement. One did not blurt out questions about a family's wealth or poverty, and certainly one never used a crass word like "rich." Ida advised, "If you *must* ask, say 'Are they *wealthy*?'" But she preferred that economic status not be mentioned at all. If one had to comment on the behavior or attitudes of others, it should be prefaced by the softening phrase "I hate to sound judgmental." Individuals or families with whom one was not to associate were "not our kind of people."

Carlisle was taught that Yankees were rude, loud, and hyperaggressive; in other words, socially unacceptable. Ida and her sisters had been raised with Mother Kate's constant admonition, "Moderate your voices, girls."

Music and poetry flowed in the Fenegan bloodline. They were great readers and often hosted family hymn sings and spelling contests. Yet Ida remained high-strung and nervous about everything, prompting Jack's principal admonition on southern manners: "Our role as males is to take care of the women." From an early age, Carlisle accepted the personal responsibility of improving his mother's emotional lot; and his greatest joy came from making her smile or laugh, or from overt approval from either parent. Yet for decades after his youth, when people showered Ida with compliments on her brilliant son, her stock response was, "We're glad he's ours."

THE FLOYD CHILDREN grew enmeshed in a dense web of tensions separating them from Jack and Ida, exacerbated by a lack of physical affection from either. Jack and sister Doris behaved with notorious tactlessness, speaking without filtering their thoughts. As a role model for southern behavior, Jack left much to be desired, and his narcissism devastated old and young alike. Confused and conflicted, Carlisle took it all personally, although Ermine was blessed with an easygoing nature. When brother marveled at sister's endurance of Jack's thoughtlessness or tongue-lashings, Ermine declared, "Mama and Daddy are just silly!"

In Jack Floyd's diaries, we meet the former farmer and bank teller who gained a pulpit from which to share his faith. This earnest, limited man strove to do the best he could. His religion was sincere, with nothing of the charlatan or rabble-rouser about him; but of emotional content in any aspect of life we find only the barest hints in his daily entries. Verbal attacks and insensitivity were facets of his darker side; but his early wonder at Carlisle's abilities comes almost as a surprise. Though unequipped to express himself emotionally, in later life he often thanked God for "my famous family."

Jack projected vibrant bonhomie and competence, striking up conversations with perfect strangers anywhere. He could build or fix anything around the house, do anything mechanical with ease; but the children watched their mother work herself dog-tired at the real business of keeping house and home together. Added to her musical skills, she was a proficient cook and seamstress, and made most of her own clothes, all of Ermine's, and some of Carlisle's, until he turned six or seven. Ida excelled at these domestic accomplishments, but they were simply expected. The Floyds were comfortable by comparison to many neighbors; however, no African American mammy helped rear the children, nor did maids, cooks, or washerwomen appear. With Jack at the bank, Ida did it all, including keeping chickens and a kitchen garden at most of their homes until late in life.

Carlisle helped feed the fowl—both he and Ermine were avid egg collectors—and did yard and garden chores. Jack built the coops, and wrung the necks when supper was poultry; but Ida plucked, simmered, boiled, breaded, fried, baked, broiled, and served. Until the children were a little older, she did most of the cleanup.

Taught her mother's culinary accomplishments, Ida cooked southern style. Her table regularly bore platters of chicken, the occasional steak, and fish fresh from local waters, often Jack's catches. Unless one of the men ailed with asthma, meats were breaded, country fried, and served with white gravy; fresh poultry and eggs came from just the other side of the threshold. Her kitchen gardens included field peas, butter (lima) beans, okra, corn, and greens. Vegetables were invariably well-cooked, the longer the better, with flavorings of bacon, sausage drippings, or fatback. Homegrown tomatoes abounded: sliced, stewed, and fried. Grits and hominy, cornbread, dumplings, biscuits with gravy emerged from her oven and stove; and her lard- or butter-rich pies, cakes, and puddings awakened the future composer's sweetest tooth. Ida cooked well, but got little enjoyment from it.

Wine, beer, any other alcoholic beverage, or tobacco, found no welcome in Floyd and Fenegan homes. Great quaffs of sweet tea and Coca-Cola washed down the mountains of solid southern cookery.

The family blessing over meals began as a simple incantation that Carlisle later recorded in his short story "The Woman and the Romans": "Lord make us thankful for these and all other blessings, for Christ's sake amen." Once invested with ministerial authority, Jack's blessings grew more elaborate.

DENSE TIERS of Carlisle's people had lived, worked, and intermarried in the Pee Dee region for centuries, never thinking of going elsewhere; yet children are not that interested in kinfolk per se. Most of all, Carlisle and Ermine dreaded the annual Cottingham summer reunion in the nearby hamlet of Little Rock. Scores of old people fussed, cooed, and clucked over them, kissing them at every turn. The one exception to the tedium of such events was the groaning board, a table laden with every sort of southern delicacy, like dripping canned pineapple rounds on white bread, squishy with mayonnaise.

At family socials and reunions, music played a great role. From the Fenegans came a fine old Kingsbury upright piano that had belonged to Carlisle's great-grandmother Cottingham.[8] Built around the turn of the century, the instrument accompanied the Floyds, at considerable effort and expense, on four moves around South Carolina, and played a central role at the frequent clan gatherings. Ida or her sister Lucile gravitated to the keyboard to accompany rounds of hymns and favorite folk and popular songs. Granddaddy Oscar, untrained but brimming over with music and words, harmonized impromptu. His lovely clear voice graced the Baptist church choir, and in the closest family circle he might produce his harmonica or even dance a step or two. Though present, his stern and musically disinclined wife did not join in the singing, which she thought unladylike.

Oscar's occasional harmonica excepted, the Floyd house boasted no other instruments. They did not consider the guitar a serious, much less a classical component, and Ida scorned its identification with country efforts as "wang-doodle music."

THREE WAS AN AUSPICIOUS AGE for Carlisle. In partial compensation for displaying the Floyd asthma, a first interest in music blossomed. Ida had few opportunities for diversion at the keyboard, but at odd moments, out came volumes of light classical salon music. Anton Rubinstein's *Melody in F,* Gustav Lange's *Flower Song,* or Massenet's *Elégie* were sweet delight. Carlisle wanted to make such magic, and asked Ida to teach him.

Excited, Ida ordered a sheaf of instructional methods for the young from such publishers as Theodore Presser;[9] but listening to Mama play and doing it himself were quite different things. This was *work,* and Carlisle, like any three-year-old, just could not be bothered. He was an awful student, and his musical urges took a dive for another six years.

Yet precocity peers from the pages of *Baby's Record:* "Carlisle is four and one-half years old now and we think he's smart to know all his letters at sight and can write some of them. He also knows birthdays of every member of Floyd and Fenegan family."

LATTA LIFE held many attractions for a growing boy, like trips in Jack's Model A Ford. Carlisle Junior inherited his father's love of high-performance automobiles, and he shared Daddy's palpable excitement at the annual unveiling of new models. The family's life between world wars unfolded as a sequence of frequent road trips, and a day's holiday might sweep them sixty-three miles up to North Carolina's Lake Waccamaw, the second largest natural freshwater lake east of the Mississippi. Jack began teaching the children to swim, an exhilarating change of pace from the daily activities in Latta.

More common were ten-mile jaunts to the farm in Floydale. Despite Jack's ban on tobacco consumption in the family, he saw no ethical conflict in owning a farm that produced the stimulant weed. Day-to-day management of the twelve-month, labor-intensive process of growing, harvesting, and curing the crop was entrusted to the capable African American Baker Campbell, born in 1882 and a World War I veteran.[10] Respected by two generations of Floyds, the Campbells had a lively ménage: wife Laura, who had been Jack's mammy; three young boys, Sam, A.G., and Lemon; and a complement of three daughters, Louise, Carol, and Annie. The latter child, nicknamed Coupé, became a playmate on Floyd visits. The Campbell house, with its typical broad porch, had been home to generations of Floyds before the move in to Latta.

With his accountant's eye, Jack oversaw the entire tobacco process, but especially relished the final marketing. Auction season presented a theatrical phenomenon, hallmarked by the auctioneer's breakneck patter. The crucial phase of taking the product from simple plant to intoxicant began each year around the end of July, and Jack turned up to exercise his formidable people skills. Once the crop was sold, he received payment from the warehouse and made distributions to his foreman and any creditors.

Baker Campbell came to Marion Street to discuss farm news or problems; and after church on Sunday, the Floyds might pile into the Model A and motor out to inspect fields and buildings, or ramble to the Pee Dee or Little Pee Dee rivers.

Carlisle was the first Floyd or Fenegan to enter the world as anything but a future farmer. From the age of three or four, at the end of the rutted dirt road from Floydale, he and Ermine inhaled the pungent drying tobacco in the barns. Baker gallantly called

Ermine "Mr. Jack's china doll," but that never warded off parental scolding when she soiled her dress with farm dirt. Carlisle's apprehension on these early trips betrayed his fear that they would run out of gas. Standing on the front seat, he peered anxiously at the dashboard, worrying his father about having enough fuel to get home; and if the car drowned out, stalled after running through a mud puddle or shallow creek, he began to cry, convinced that their end was nigh.

The family held an idiosyncratic and complex position on race. The Methodist Church, even its conservative southern wing, had condemned slavery and had become an early and influential advocate of emancipation, education, and equality; but the south was still the south, with too recent an experience of a devastating war that forever obliterated a centuries-old order based on slave labor. As Carlisle grew, he found no racial crossover in church attendance; and schools took another thirty years to desegregate.

Within the family, sentiments, actions, and politics were mirrored in parallel ways. Jack, at least a closet liberal, voted for as rarefied a Democrat as Adlai Stevenson in the fifties; but Ida was an "I Like Ike" lady, loving a man in uniform.

Carlisle's uncle G. R., the family's intellectual, and his wife, Fredrika Knight (aunt Freddie),[11] a Latta schoolteacher, stood at one ideological pole. Though South Carolinian, she spent most of her adult life in the north, in social work. She had assisted Jane Addams at Hull House in Chicago,[12] but her popularity with some members of the family fluctuated when she voiced her core opinion on racial matters: in the south, she believed, blacks were despised as a race, but loved as individuals, with stances reversed in the north. The rest of the Floyds were, by and large, *tolerant*, a word Carlisle grew to dislike in this context. Yet the 1930 census was the first to show a Caucasian majority in South Carolina's population, 54.3 percent to 45.6 percent African American.[13] In other words, in Carlisle's youth black people were everywhere, turning up at the family's door, looking for work or food: omnipresent but still, in most ways, invisible.

Carlisle saw little anti-Semitism in South Carolina's smaller towns; but excepting major Jewish communities in cities like Charleston, there simply were not that many Jews in the south. The most prominent families often owned and operated community dry goods stores, like the Kornbluts in Latta or the Basses in North. Carlisle felt an immediate bond with the quick-witted, talented, motivated Bass boys, with whom he attended high school in the latter city. The Finkelsteins, owners of the largest such store in Florence, produced Carlisle's eventual piano teacher, Sidney Foster, né Finkelstein.

FOR THE FLOYDS, family was *the* priority, and drives to Laurinburg and the Shamrock Inn began as soon as upstairs rooms were appointed. Room 3 was Jack's and Ida's usual headquarters; the children were fit into any untenanted spaces. The parents took an adults-only holiday to New York in the Model A in 1931, leaving the children with the Fenegans.

The venerable white clapboard house sported two tall front columns. One side of the broad porch had a two seat swing in which Carlisle and Ermine spent many hours. Eight bedrooms lay upstairs; hallways both up and down were punctuated with curtained alcoves that struck Carlisle as sinister. At hall's end lay a small balcony whose height made Carlisle giddy, his horror and fascination enhanced by parental injunctions against going out onto it; and there were bats, one of his few phobias.

Furnishings were dark, heavy, fusty in the British sense, and the house seemed to lack defining color. By a stroke of good fortune, another Kingsbury upright came with the place, a treat for family and guests. The downstairs parlor featured an old Chesterfield sofa much prized by Mr. Oscar, but which Carlisle found cruelly uncomfortable. Also downstairs were a spacious kitchen and dining room, a family sitting room, and separate bedrooms for Mrs. Kate and Mr. Oscar.

The front public rooms excepted, it all seemed functional but unwelcoming. For winter conditions, each bedroom had a small coal or wood-burning heater that began to "dance," threatening to explode when fully stoked; the children often preferred to huddle shivering in the cold beneath piles of blankets and quilts.

3. Pen and ink drawing of the Shamrock Inn, Laurinburg, North Carolina. By permission of the artist, Anita Jones Stanton.

Yet for all its discomforts, Carlisle loved visiting the Shamrock and his grandparents. Some months, some years, the Floyds came every weekend, from wherever they happened to live. The inn was the one constant in Carlisle's life until he moved into his first house in Tallahassee almost thirty years later.

Forty-nine-year-old Baker Campbell died on the last day of 1931,[14] leaving a widow of forty-one, daughters of twenty-one, eighteen, fifteen, and sons of nine, seven, and four.[15] Considering the two-generation bonding of families, Jack would never have ousted the survivors from their home; in fact, his diaries record continued visits to the family on later trips to Floydale, until Laura's death in 1963. Yet the succession of land management fades at this point. Perhaps a neighboring farmer or cousin—it was, after all, *Floydale*—filled that gap.

Jack faced other complications in life and work. Well before the October 1929 stock market crash, rural community banks, especially in southern agricultural regions, struggled. Now they began to fail, and the boom in agricultural land prices far outstripped farm income. The market crash merely capped a decade of speculative bubbles, of which the Carolina farm economy was symptomatic. From a Dow Jones high of 381 on September 3, 1929, the market plummeted by fits and starts, the worst on Black Thursday, October 24. It reached a low of 230 on the 28th, and America's Great Depression officially began with widespread bank failures and farm foreclosures. Many banks saw runs; depositors stormed the premises to retrieve their cash. Some institutions simply closed their doors, and some never reopened. Images of stockbrokers and bankers jumping to their deaths from office windows on and near Wall Street are still embedded in the memories of many elder Americans.[16]

The same events that savaged banks likewise devastated tobacco farmers. Between 1920 and 1927, prices for market-ready cured tobacco remained fairly constant at around 20 cents per pound. Prices dropped to 17.3 cents in 1928, 12 cents in 1930, and a catastrophic 8.4 cents in 1931.[17]

With the failure of the bank of neighboring Lake View in January 1931, Dillon County's seven financial institutions—as of 1920—shrank to three. Jack Floyd was one of the luckier of his colleagues: Farmers and Merchants, one of the region's oldest banks, and managed by a Bethea cousin, held on, perhaps because of the area's heavy investment in tobacco rather than staple grains; but on one Monday morning in November 1931, Farmers and Merchants failed to open its doors in Marion and Latta. Dillon County was down to two banks, and Jack Floyd had neither job nor workplace.[18]

Were it not for this scenario, the Floyds might still be in Latta. Late in 1931, they were for the first time a family divided by a national crisis: G. R. pursued graduate work at the University of Chicago; aunt Hazel and the youngest Floyd uncle, Sonny, tagged along with G. R. and Freddie to the Midwest. Around 1932, Hazel married Latta native Frank Ellerbe, a former professional baseball star, scion of an old Marion/Dillon county planter family and son of the state's eighty-sixth governor, William Hazelden Ellerbe.[19]

Frank's courtly yet imperious manner and his father's reputation caused his baseball teammates to nickname him "Governor"; the family called him Lord Chesterfield. Several years after marrying, he purchased the Floyd House on Marion Street, convinced that it would gratify Hazel to return to her childhood home as chatelaine; but Hazel, far from pleased, set about remodeling at once, transforming it into Ellerbe House.

Also in 1932, the elder Floyd daughter, Doris, married John W. Moore, and they soon moved to Asheville, North Carolina. Generous uncle J. W. had studied law, but went into restaurant management and supply, running into tax and other legal problems by importing cartons of whiskey; North Carolina was still a dry state.

The next year, Ida Fenegan's sister Mary Kate, "Bunny," tied the knot with Yates Gamble, a North Carolina insurance salesman and soon-to-be executive, in Laurinburg. Also an accomplished seamstress, during the war years she ran Dillon County's rationing board.

Lucile Fenegan remained a spinster to the end of her life, at first teaching school and then working as a bank teller in Laurinburg; and the family's baby, James, was still too young to do anything but excel at school.

NEWS FROM THE FINANCIAL AND TOBACCO WORLDS was disaster enough for the Floyds, but another quite literal stroke of fate brought further complications. Each family member has a slightly different recollection of the incident, but common to all versions, athletic Jack was playing his favorite sport, baseball. Whether beaned by a fast pitch, or from falling and striking his head, he was knocked unconscious, taken home to bed and attended by the family doctor for two or three days. Spells of verbalized dreams and fantasies punctuated his state, and Carlisle heard his father "talk out of his head," which he found by turns hilarious and terrifying. Ida did her best to comfort and reassure the children. Never having worked outside the home, she speculated that, were Jack not to recover, she might find work as a laundry seamstress.

Jack regained consciousness and had a wakeup call in the form of a vocational Call. The children were often told that he had vowed to devote his life to God, if their Mama would just be his; but they also sensed that this may have been a fiction for edification and flattery. Ida took it as both; but Jack now planned in earnest, at twenty-eight, to complete his education and ordainment as a Methodist minister. Clergy were hardly at the top of the wage-earning pyramid, but even if banks failed, people still needed the guidance and reassurance of organized religion.

Ida experienced religion as something internal, quasi-mystical, and undogmatic, alongside Jack's easy assumption of clerical trappings. Were this the only thing that would make their father happy, she told the children, she would support his decision. For the two years it took Jack to finish an undergraduate degree at Wofford College, and ever after, Ida cooked, sewed, and cleaned for the four of them and others, becoming a model minister's wife.

It would take her a while to fully realize what this involved. Though her refined, high-strung temperament and musical soul paid a price, she nonetheless took a certain pride in housewifery. A good cook, she remained largely indifferent to the blandishments of cuisine as anything more than subsistence, but she *did* enjoy the immediate gratification of keeping a clean and tidy house. Money was tight, but they would make do with whatever the farm brought in.

In the Latta years, Ida zealously insisted on having a photographic record of her children's growth. The in place for family portraits was the Quarles Studio in Florence, and just before moving to Spartanburg, and the subsequent leaner years, she had a final set of studio poses recorded. We see a shy six-year-old Carlisle, beside five-year-old Ermine, he struggling with interior notions of his ugliness. He saw his slight build as emaciated, at best skinny. He had long since resigned himself to chronic asthma, thanks to Christmas bed confinements and his father's reinforcement. He celebrated the day when he gained enough weight for Ida to make him pairs of short pants held up with belts rather than buttons. Swayed by her fretting, he felt physically insecure, more often inferior. Ermine remembers him as "a tenderhearted, anxious little boy" who cried at the least mortification, real or imagined.

4. Carlisle and Ermine, c. 1932. Quarles Studio, Florence, South Carolina. Floyd collection. By permission of Robert E. Quarles Jr.

Yet Ida predicted, "When Carlisle is a grown man he may like to know that he was an unusually good little boy and if he is as thoughtful of his mother then, she'll be a lucky one."[20]

Carlisle Floyd was no conservatory baby with preternatural musical abilities manifesting along with walking and talking. Yet precocious he surely was: his parents soon noticed and encouraged his gift for drawing. At age three or four, he sketched a face of Christ on the cross that seemed to capture the agony of those final moments. Jack and Ida saw revealed in their boy a keen sensitivity to people and emotions, and an ability to translate feeling into concrete, focused aesthetic forms.

Years later, Carlisle thought about that drawing, not as an eruption of little-boy religious fervor, but as something technical whereby intensity was conveyed in the slant of the eyebrows. So by three, he already intuited levels of feeling beyond appearances and possessed the embryonic technique to depict more than his intellect understood. There was always more than met the eye, and with tact and circumspection, he began analyzing motives and modes of behavior. What became strengths in his creation of words and music began as drawn character studies that laid bare emotional extremes. For years after, he watched Jack carry that tiny Christ sketch folded in his Bible or wallet. The praise he received faded soon enough, but its very brevity made this early memory vivid and precious.

Drawing anticipated Carlisle's music by years, and it seemed so easy. He used pencil, plain and colored, charcoal and colored chalk, but never ventured into watercolor or oils. Drawing was fun, but it never touched his soul; yet the rest of the family marveled at this quiet, sensitive child, skilled at recording from both nature and imagination. No one suspected the depths of his inner life spiraling in all directions. He had already intuited lessons that no school save life teaches, like the self-defense of keeping one's counsel though sensing one's differences of intellect, interest, and ability. In the case of asthma, though he had no vocabulary to express it, observing Jack and his aunts taught him the realities of genetic predisposition: it was just something that happened. It was modeled for him that, whatever happens in life, if you fall into a hole, you do whatever it takes to climb out.

2

Where's Daddy?

Spartanburg, McClellanville, Jordan, 1932–1936

When Jack Floyd reentered Wofford as a sophomore in the fall of 1932, enrollment totaled just 385. Despite financial constraints, he was excited and expansive: for the first and only time, he hired a professional mover for the two-hundred-mile trip from Latta.

Spartanburg sits at 875 feet, close enough to the southern end of the Blue Ridge to keep summer temperatures moderate, compared to many South Carolina locales. Yet the town sizzled on the June day when the van pulled up to the rented bungalow at 205 Evins Street. Carlisle watched one of the movers collapse on the front lawn from heat stroke.

Spartanburg's embodiment of the genius of independence—a 1781 victory over seasoned British regulars in the Battle of Cowpens, fought in a pasture just north of town, which marked the turning point of the southern Revolution—would have been emphasized to first- and second-grader Carlisle in months to come. In 1930, the city held 28,723 souls.[1] Carlisle felt that they had moved to the Big City, and the Floyds kept no chickens or kitchen garden here.

Their side of Evins Street, just north of downtown, and bordering the Wofford campus, featured one-story bungalows housing middle-income families; the Floyd's was a cream-colored frame, on a tiny lot. Half inside, half outside, a screened-in sleeping porch opened off the master bedroom, the latter occupied by three Wofford student boarders. They paid room and board, Ida cooked for everyone, and Jack and Ida almost broke even. With this arrangement and crop income supporting a family of four, the tobacco calendar became a fixed priority, integrated with Jack's school rhythms.

He needed to keep closer watch over the farm after Baker Campbell's death. The first semester, with emphasis now on religious studies, began September 21, coinciding with tobacco harvest, curing, and storage. Founder's Day on October 19, then the Thanksgiving holidays, necessitated more trips back to Floydale. Jack took exams between December 16 and 23, before Christmas swept the family off to the Shamrock Inn.

The second semester began hard on New Year's Day. The planting of indoor seed beds inaugurated the farm year, between the second week of February—coinciding with Washington's Birthday, and exams from March 4 through 11—and the third week of March. Seedlings were transplanted into fields around May 1, just in time for Wofford's holiday in honor of founder Dr. James Carlisle's birthday on May 4. Summer break awaited the weary farmer/student after finals from May 26 through June 2. Auction time loomed at the end of July, and the Model A's odometer rolled up thousands of miles in these years.

The cycle began anew on September 20 in 1933. With tobacco prices unstable, Jack buckled down to his studies to complete his degree in the shortest possible time. Plagued with frequent asthma, and always overworked, he compressed his final three years of degree work into two.

He accrued sizeable debts to fulfill his vows to God and Ida and provide for his little family, as the early thirties brought tobacco another bear market. When creditors or stomachs pinched, Jack answered by driving the 183 miles back to Floydale and selling a farm mule, other livestock, or a piece of machinery. The grocery on Evins Street was a godsend too. The kind owners recognized in the Floyds a struggling, devout, devoted family, and they let Jack run up sizeable tabs. His lived his clergyman's life close to the margin, but paid back every cent of borrowed money or credit over the ensuing three years.

Perhaps because they had come from a place where they either knew or were related to everyone, in Spartanburg the children made friends easily with their neighborhood peers, racing on tricycles the Floyds had hauled from Latta. The nearby downtown might as well have been Manhattan: Main and Pine Streets were lined with impressive buildings, especially churches.

In an era without home or portable electronics, games assumed great importance. Carlisle had a set of marbles, and an accompanying board punched with holes with different numerical scores. Ensconced on the floor, he and Ermine played for hours on end, shooting from increasing distances. Jack joined in when not submerged in Wofford coursework, predictably besting his children.

Just as Spartanburg's summers were more temperate than Latta's, its winters were fiercer. Carlisle dowsed a well of compassion for his father, as Jack did his dogged best to fend off asthma. Carlisle watched Daddy hunch over, or trudge backwards across campus, in December and January winds howling from the Blue Ridge.

That same fall and winter, Carlisle began his own formal education at the neighborhood school. His preschooling in Latta had been limited to the abortive piano lessons three years earlier; but reading and speaking skills had been encouraged and lauded by the Fenegan grandparents, aunts, and uncle G. R., future professor of English Literature.

The old Fremont Grammar School building at 600 Magnolia Street seemed enormous. It was less than a half mile from home, and Carlisle walked. First grade left him with few memories other than an aversion to his stern teacher, Mary Johnson. From the beginning, he found mathematics and science unpleasant obligations; yet up he fell into the alphabet, writing, spelling, and reading, opening windows onto shimmering new worlds, a lifetime of voracious consumption of the written word, and eventually his own writing.

The years 1910 to 1924 had seen great ferment in the science of reading. Theorizing led to extensive testing, proving beyond doubt that early reading affected all brain and motor functions, individual motivation and advancement. The most popular new basal readers were Zena Sharp's *Dick and Jane* series. Dick and fellow characters Jane, Spot the dog, and Puff the cat had a series of simple adventures that promoted whole-word reading. At the end of each exciting school day, Carlisle found Ermine waiting on her trike at the foot of the hill, eagerly wishing him home.

He contracted bronchial pneumonia in 1933, and the porch served as sickroom for three months that spring and summer. Seven-year-olds have little concept of death's reality, but in adulthood he reckoned this spell as his first intimation of mortality. Aunt Bunny came from Laurinburg to nurse him, as Ida had her hands full with husband, household, and lodgers. Ida was the calmest Fenegan sister; Bunny saw Jack as controlling, and disliked Ida's putting up with it. As her daughter Helen Harris says, "Mama would just tell you the way things were."[2] To improve matters, Jack hired a black laundress for the household. When Carlisle emerged from his ordeal, he was so weak that walking required relearning.

Spells of illness continued to be opportunities for Jack to show a nurturing side, a pattern that sent disturbing messages in later years. But once when Ida sat on Carlisle's sickbed and took his hands in hers, she started at their coldness. She enforced the children's use of face stockings, constrictive masks of elastic gauze thought to prevent chills and the spread of infection. Jack felt his son's misery, and finally demanded the garment's removal. Ida relented, and Carlisle remembered this as one of the only times his father failed to indulge Mama's fretting.

That fall, second grade brought a new teacher, Miss Camilla Tatum. Hers was the kind of attention any boy would love, and Carlisle relished his first but far from last stint as teacher's pet. Tatum, warm and genial, gave him extra time, recognizing a gifted student, and his every pore absorbed her praise and encouragement.

His artistry continued to develop, as he willed his handwriting to change, and often. Beginning with aunt Lucile in Latta, if he liked or idolized an elder or teacher, he pored over blackboard script or other scraps of writing. Scanning notes, letters, or comments and grades on his papers, he copied them in his own hand, using pencils with different leads, pens with different-colored inks, different nibs.

Once he had learned to write, he carved Ermine's name in tribute on the slick top of Ida's vanity table. Ermine was of course punished, whereupon Carlisle burst into tears and confessed. Further retribution was suspended, but he felt this was about the worst thing he ever did.

Rigor dogged the Floyds' two Spartanburg years. Carlisle watched his parents scrimp, save, and sacrifice, providing the best they could, without complaint or whining. Three of the composer's most practiced words about life, work, and personal effort are "expected," "standard," and "inevitable."

By the time Jack graduated from Wofford on June 4, 1934, he had achieved distinction in all his classes. He had also sold more than the occasional mule to buy food for four: the farm itself was gone, sold to the farmer-builder W. H. Benton, and the proceeds divided between the quintet of Floyd siblings. But beneath his cap and gown, Jack carried something even more prized than his sale share: the papers for his first ministerial appointment, or charge, as a supply preacher for the village of McClellanville, South Carolina.

Carlisle's memories of his preclerical father soon reached the vanishing point. Only one faded photograph, in subsequent years enlarged and given a place of honor on the composer's home studio desk, remains: the boy is about three, in Latta. He has one arm around his father: "Maybe it was posed for the picture, but it looks much warmer than it got later."

Methodist supply preachers are not yet *effective*, that is, active, members of the annual conference, but are often appointed as seminarians, to complete the term of a retired or deceased minister. Conference is the Methodist governing body, composed of representatives from states in a given region. Church advancement continues with probationary membership in Conference and a two-year period of call testing at a local church. McClellanville was the beginning of Jack's climb.[3]

5. Ermine, Ida, Jack, Carlisle. Latta, c. 1929. Courtesy of Carlisle Floyd.

Methodist ordination has four steps, beginning with a Call. Jack must have satisfied this requirement during his first year at Wofford, as he was licensed to preach in 1924. What we may term a "True Call" blazoned forth after the baseball accident in Latta. The superintendent of the seaside district north of Charleston appealed to his bishop for an urgent replacement when McClellanville's incumbent pastor died that spring of 1934. Jack's appointment actually began in April, while he was still in school. He piloted the Model A 254 miles—at the car's top speed of sixty-five, at least a four-hour trip—each way at least once a week, preaching on Sundays and getting back that night for class first thing Monday morning.

The trip was its own kind of test, threading the car through the ten-foot-wide unshouldered lanes of treacherous Grace Bridge over Cooper River, one of Charleston's waterways.

Those who heard Jack Floyd preach had little praise for his oratory. Cousin Marjorie Manning of Latta gives perhaps the kindest assessment: "I've heard him twice, and he was not a good speaker. There was a shyness, I saw him almost groping for words at times."[4] But Mrs. Manning confirmed what many others said about Jack's strong suit: "Every town where he served, people all loved Jack. Really *loved* him." In other words, he was a poor preacher but a model pastor. He and Ida worked *hard.* His people skills were legendary, and he relished being a minister. Carlisle remembers, "My father never saw a stranger, he would talk to anybody, anywhere." Ida was chronically appalled.

Jack's work took him away from home for more time than he spent in it. Of course he needed to provide for his family; but the new position also flattered his grandiosity as an admired authority figure. Despite Carlisle's and Ermine's perpetual wondering where Daddy was, Jack modeled and reinforced behavior that served Carlisle admirably when he needed to sequester himself for the solitary work of composing.

MCCLELLANVILLE boasted a population of 502 in 1930. Today, on turning off coastal highway 17, a little less than forty miles north of Charleston, scrub pines give way to live oaks festooned with Spanish moss. The Francis Marion National Forest at our backs, a mile later we enter a molasses-paced artist's colony with galleries, a nature conservancy, and ancient glossy leafed magnolias and palmettos ranged about rambling old homes with verdant lawns.

On June 8, 1934, three days before Carlisle's eighth birthday, it was a sleepy fishing village. Oysters, crabs, and shrimp formed the hamlet's economic backbone, producing the sweet-rot effluvium that competes for attention with heady salt air. Local blacks sold their catches door to door. Boats packed the saltwater creek, or inlet, and the only things between the town beach and Morocco's coast were 4,120 miles of Atlantic Ocean. Ida took Carlisle to the small public library to exercise his new reading skills.

The McClellanville United Methodist Church sits in its coat of gleaming white at the corner of Dupre and Pinckney Streets. The rambling two-story, decrepit-genteel white frame parsonage no longer exists, but it introduced the Floyds to this mode of housing, half sanctuary, half transient hotel. Jack and Ida took certain pieces of their own inherited or hard-bought furniture from place to place; but their initial tour guide at each successive church property pointed out local sacred cows: the chair that some totemic Aunt Ella had cherished and donated, and so on, iconic pieces that held the sweat and toil of generations of preachers and their families. The master bedroom in each Floyd parsonage held a single double bed. Jack and Ida always slept together, but never in anything larger.[5]

This parsonage's primitive yard showed clumps of grass struggling atop sand and oyster shells, a combination that supported no kitchen garden. None of this seemed to faze a dense population of snakes, of which Ida was terrified, in and out of the house. Because the plumbing stood outdoors, no one sat around long enough to learn whether any were poisonous.

Jack, flushed with his first assignment, saw no deficiencies. His bride would sometimes be in church near the pulpit, providing music on piano or pump organ, if the regular player was indisposed or on holiday. Weekly services and annual revivals at Ocean Grove, McClellanville's satellite church in Awendaw, eleven miles south, further stoked young Reverend Floyd's excitement.

Next door stood the lovely old Graham House, home of Carlisle's playmate Mitchell Graham, also born in 1926. In later years, Graham, nicknamed Mitch, became to state civic leaders what Carlisle would be to American composers.[6]

McClellanville's great allure for Carlisle, Ermine, and their friends was the sea, virtually across from their new home. Cracked oyster shells paved all walks and streets. One of Ermine's playmates shared with them the fun of collecting live oysters and smashing them open with bricks, and the pleasure of eating them raw.

Jack decided it was time for his children to learn real swimming. He taught them to keep their toes on the sandy bottom close to shore, to practice their crawl stroke, and to tread water. When those results proved less than satisfactory, he put a fatherly hand under their midsections to help them float, then kick, with proper head rotations.

Meanwhile, Ida applied cool damp cloths to her worried brow. She made light of her pathological fear of water by joking that it was a good thing that she and Jack quit college and married when they did, because she could never have passed swimming. Though she never masked her anxiety with much success, she trusted Jack and suffered his helping the children to acquire an important skill; after all, he had in his own boyhood almost drowned in the Pee Dee River. Swimming was often the only thing to which the children could look forward in torrid summer weeks.

Besides the Atlantic, Carlisle's most vivid memory of McClellanville was a case of the boils, accompanied by anemia. In most instances, this staphylococcus inflammation of hair follicles, bettered by warm compresses, passes within four to ten days. Once the painful lumps drained, Ida woke him early each morning to bandage his legs before he hiked to school. Both he and Ermine were already nauseous from bottles of cod liver oil, but now Ida got him to force down other revolting concoctions for the attack's duration.

While Carlisle swam, ate raw oysters, read everything he could understand, and tried to stay healthy, the church was right there. And there was Jack, present at only the best and worst of times, while Ida, clever, an excellent manager and economist, stewed and made do. Jack gave her twenty-five dollars each week to buy food for the whole family, and she prided herself on saving out a certain amount that became *her* money, generally spent on the children.

She had never dreamed of being a preacher's wife, and only now began to learn why.

At the annual three-to-five-day Conference in each district, in these years in October or November, the bishop installed and moved ministers like chess figures. Carlisle's third and Ermine's second grades began that fall of 1934 in another large brick building. Both looked forward to new books on the first day of school; yet just five months after moving in, with school in session only during September and October, the Conference found a more pressing test of Jack's skills and sincerity at a smaller church in an even smaller community: Jordan, in Clarendon County, population ninety-five.

Into a borrowed truck the family threw their belongings, which had barely acquired a glaze of sea salt. On a November day they motored northwest through pinewoods and rolling meadows. Jack voiced his new ministerial mantra: he was "marching under orders"; and Carlisle learned that nothing was permanent.

BY THE WINDING BACK ROADS the Floyds would have taken, Jordan lies seventy-eight miles north and west of McClellanville. Today this crossroads—for years it was not on any map—lies just north of a serpentine arm of 110,600-acre Lake Marion, an important source of hydroelectric power for the region and a state recreation area. This project existed only on paper when the Floyds moved, but it became the largest land-clearing operation to that date in American history; groundbreak was in April 1939.

The lovely old town of Manning, six-and-a-half dirt road miles north of Jordan, must have given the Floyds hope that they were moving up; but Ida's heart and jaw dropped when she saw what passed for a town: a scattering of weathered farm buildings, rough frame houses, a general store and school, and, of course, a Methodist church, at the intersection of state road 260, Moses Dingle and Bonanza Crossing roads. The surrounding flatland held clumps of trees huddling in swampy hollows; cotton, corn, and sugar cane struggled in their fields in the hot months. Carlisle's short fiction "A Lengthening Shadow" paints the picture:

> From the high ground you could see for several miles around and everywhere there was the barren expanse of sand and weak, powdery soil, dotted by scrub oaks and occasional tall pines. There were poor hapless men who tried fiercely to till this soil and bring something out of it; who spent blood money year after year on fertilizer and on seed and there was never any return. Here was a stricken country, doomed to poverty and the unalterable reign of sandspurs.[7]

Only a coat of white paint offset the clapboard frame church from its drab neighbors: Jordan had not a single brick structure. The parsonage was as charmless as the rest of the place, a dilapidated one-story raw wood cabin with hard-packed dirt for a yard. Mama was appalled.

The good news: chickens and a garden were once again possible. The bad news: there are more people buried in Jordan Methodist Church cemetery than ever lived there at any single moment in history. And more good news: no one died on Jack's watch. A few months into his thirtieth birthday, he learned that he had three other facilities in his charge: Bethlehem Methodist, three miles west, in even tinier Davis Station. Two additional homely facilities at Oak Grove and Union kept Reverend Floyd in constant motion; a harried and delicate wife and two children were left alone in the heat, longing for Daddy.

6. Ermine and Carlisle, Jordan, c. 1935. Courtesy of Carlisle Floyd.

Although the Methodist *Book of Discipline* does not specify ministerial terms, the annual district conference reviews each appointment. The church has a marked tradition of frequent change of assignments, suggesting that policy rather than chance accounts for Jack—now the Reverend C. S. Floyd—having variable tenures for the rest of his career. To speed his scaling the ladder of church accreditation, from supply to minister to elder, he began taking correspondence courses from Atlanta's Emory University. When not at one of his churches—Sunday services, Sunday school, revival weeks at all three—Jack, pitied by the children, bent over his studies by smoky kerosene lamplight.

Jordan's original white frame Methodist church has been bricked over, a far cry from the primitive structure Carlisle knew. It held at most a hundred, but the congregation was never close to that; the parsonage has long since been demolished. Its interior consisted of a small parlor, where the massive Kingsbury upright held pride of place, providing the sole links to beauty and culture. Across the hall, the entire family slept in a single bedroom, Carlisle and Ermine in one bed, their parents in the other. Without screens on the windows, every sort of insect, and Carlisle's nemeses, bats, hurtled through the house. While Ida and the children hid beneath covers, Jack flailed at the intruders with shirts, rags, or brooms; but even if the airborne mammals got back outside, the mosquitoes fed.

Behind the sleeping space lay a dining room. A separate kitchen behind the house was connected by a covered breezeway. Cooking was done over a wood-burning stove, of which the female protagonist of Carlisle's story "The Woman and the Romans" says, "The smokin' an' soot gets 'em black an' potty."[8]

At the windows fluttered lace curtains, but the house had neither electricity nor indoor plumbing. The only light after sundown came from kerosene lamps, which had to be carried from room to room, and the house reeked of the fumes. Someone once placed a lamp too close to the parlor's lace curtains, and, more than seventy years later, Carlisle and Ermine both still insist on taking blame for the resulting blaze, which Jack snuffed out.

All water came from a back porch pump. If anyone took a bath, it needed heating on the kitchen stove. Most personal hygiene happened at a washstand, filled with cold pump water from pottery pitchers. Old Sears and Roebucks catalogs suffered their inevitable rural fates as outhouse toilet tissue.

As a first regular chore, eight-year-old Carlisle split kindling wood. This exempted him from drying dishes, which fell to Ermine. Though the hard-packed dirt yard required no mowing, it did need to be swept of the thickest dust, leaves, and blown-in refuse with a type of rustic reed broom. Most locals observed this custom, particularly if Reverend Floyd and his family came to dinner after services.

Jack replenished Ida's stock of chickens, and their new garden produced hardy winter vegetables, collard greens, and turnips. Augmenting the family table were food gifts from parishioners, making the minister's life somewhat more comfortable. Jack appeared home from pastoral calls with jugs of versatile sugar cane syrup, and what the locals called "fresh," pork that a few hours before had been on the hoof.

SOON AFTER ARRIVING in this swampy country, Ida succumbed to the first of several bouts with malaria, and an inexperienced young doctor in Manning put her into hospital there in the fall of 1934. Carlisle and Ermine had no idea what was wrong, but they knew that Mama was very, very sick when aunt Lucile came from her teaching job in Hyman to nurse Ida and care for the children, the house, and Daddy.

Bright spots in otherwise dismal winter months came when anyone received a letter or poem from grandfather Oscar Fenegan. On November 9, 1934, by which time Lucile had left, he posted an envelope to her, in Hyman. The letter typifies his prolific output, testimony to his sense of humor, creative wordplay, and keen ear for regional accent, all of which Carlisle inherited. The deviant phonetic orthography is intentional:

> Sunday a.m., 8 o'clock
> Dear Lucile,
>
> Cain't rite much cause they ain't nutthin to rite. This has sho been a purty day hain't it? Yore Ma and me, both of us went to preachen this mornin but we didn't go no whur the evenin. We had cumpony the evenin. . . . U reckun me and your ma wood-a went off sum whur if ita hatten a cum, but I don't know whur we wood a went. Grandma bumpt her hed on a chur post tothur da an maid a sooter bad soar on it but hits gittin olrite now. Hunny we shore duz mis you. Seams lak yu ben gon seben er ate muntz, an yu hain't ben gon but jes won weak.[9]

Jack grew pessimistic, morose and testy. As wife and mother, Ida strove to avoid unpleasantness or confrontation, and expressions of anger were not part of her vocabulary. When irritated with Jack, when frustration outpaced speech, she withdrew into distant silence or burst into tears; but they never fought in front of the children or showed the smallest crack in their united front.

Five decades later, in his libretto for *Willie Stark,* Carlisle had Sadie Burke boast, despite her frustrating relationship with the protagonist, that they were a team.[10] And for better or worse, this was how Jack viewed their marriage. Despite his overwhelming physical attraction to Ida, confirmed by his diaries, the most extreme display of affection that Carlisle ever saw between his parents might be a peck on the cheek when Jack came home at day's end. Overheard conversations seemed curt and impersonal. When Jack and Ida spoke on the telephone, calls ended abruptly, without "goodbye," much less "I love you." Yet some mysterious intuition seemed to guide the relationship, a language of looks, gestures, and shared assumptions.

As far back as Latta, Carlisle adopted, however unconsciously, the Oedipal stance of rescuing his unhappy but submissive mother. Ida and the children were comfortable companions, talking like friends; but to gain parental approval, Carlisle strove to appear more advanced than his actual nine-year-old self. One day as he lay on the floor drawing, Ida tending to her housework, he thought to enlighten her with a fresh-minted sort of worldly wisdom: "Mama, I have a new proverb."

Admiring Ida's tidiness and industry, he wanted to make just the right encapsulation: "Well-made things show up well." Ida offered neither argument nor affirmation.

Alone with Jack, wretched because of that and hungry for Daddy's attention, Carlisle found his emotional world anything but safe. Jack's ministerial persona evaporated on entering the parsonage, and most exchanges involved pedantic instruction on the best way to do something or browbeating Carlisle for carelessness. (Jack's diaries are peppered with references to his own carelessness, often confessed at rededication services. In these early days of his ministry, excitement caused him from time to time to lose sermons before preaching to a full church.)[11] As absurd as anyone meeting Carlisle Floyd finds the notion of carelessness in reference to him, the accusation injected potent toxins under the boy's skin. Jack had no reticence in broadcasting opinions and criticisms, acting out frustration by sulking, or worse, by ignoring Carlisle altogether.

Jack's religious beliefs, though sincere, could be cryptic. Unlike many of his more evangelistic colleagues, he rarely if ever preached on the Second Coming, the Rapture, or the End of Days. He obsessed about converting others to Christianity's promise of a personal savior, mistakenly assuming that *his* congregations had already achieved salvation. In prayer, he intoned, "Make us sensitive souls," perhaps addressing that lack in himself. He fixated on "thinking towards Eternity," but what child understands *that* concept? Carlisle's sensitive soul feared what he felt in Daddy's; but at least he never found Jack's *church* words frightening.

The boy could not wait to be given something to do, something as simple as going to the store for a quart of milk. Jordan's two streets and all its pathways were sand covered, and he loved the feel of the warm fine grains pushing between his bare toes.

IDA frowned at Jordan's educational deficiencies. It had no library, and the children resumed their interrupted education in a literal one-room schoolhouse. A large bare chamber held seven rows of desks, each row a different grade. First grade held down the front, closest to teacher's desk, with seventh grade at the back. Ermine was one of three pupils in second grade, Carlisle one of five in third grade. Two teachers divided grades between them, simply walking to each row in turn, discussing lessons, and leaving them to their work. The total group, compact, homogenous, and well behaved, had few disciplinary problems; but there was little challenge or incentive to excel.

Jack and Ida had solid academic records, and good schooling for their time and place. Ida, thanks to her Fenegan heritage, had a high regard for learning, and in particular for the written and spoken word, as well as for music's charms. Once in Jordan, aunt Lucile asked Carlisle to spell the word "sarcastic." It was a new word for him, and actual sarcasm was never tolerated in the family; but he spelled it phonetically and correctly, to praise from the women and silence from his father.

Jack nonetheless displayed a certain contempt for education. He often paraphrased a statement of Booker T. Washington's, to the effect that "Education so unfits a man for work."[12] Jack's own spelling, writing, syntax, and punctuation were idiosyncratic. In letters, sermons, and his diaries, he capitalized odd words to emphasize their importance, and the rest of the family saw this as willful. Carlisle, genuinely curious, asked why, but received only glares in response.

Ida lamented, "I wish your Daddy read more, studied more." Reverend Floyd may have won distinction in his classes, and would never have admitted disdaining intellectual pursuits; but historically and intrinsically, the Floyds were farmers, despite Jack's work at banking and preaching. The Fenegans were poets who earned livings as farmers.

Other inner balances shifted as Carlisle's artistic sensibilities settled into an aesthetic. Living by his proverb, he developed an aversion to anything not "well made." In Laurinburg, the Shamrock's unadorned walls and worn furniture advertised that no special care had been taken, and on one visit he pulled a face, or shuddered. When Mrs. Kate asked what was wrong, Carlisle answered without subterfuge (or tact), "Grandmammy, it's all so plain." The family thought that very funny, and the remark dogged him for years.

Early in 1935, Carlisle heard a popular song, "A Little Bit Independent," lyrics by Edgar Leslie, music by Joe Burke. The performer could have been Rudy Vallee, Fats Waller, or Eddie Cantor, all of whom recorded this jazzy tune in cut time, with infectious repeated triplets and dotted and syncopated figures.

It is one of those songs of which Mark Twain observed that only passing it to someone else stops it from devouring the brain.[13] Carlisle's method of exorcism, many months before his first real piano lesson, was puzzling out the melody and bluesy harmonies on the Kingsbury. His persistence finally irritated Jack and Ermine to the point of teasing and then berating him, with much rolling of eyes and despairing sighs, "Oh no, not old In-de-pen-dee again!" Jordan boys did not play much piano, much less by ear; but Ida, though never a stage mother, encouraged, "Son, if that is what you want to do, you do it."

For all its catchiness, "Independent" offers neither great poetry nor music, but it exerted undeniable allure on nine-year-old Carlisle Floyd, even though it took years before he felt called to music as a vocation; however the irresistible, verbalized *notion* of independence tugged at him. No wonder Jack felt irritated.

One of Jordan's more numerous, impoverished clans were the next-door Richburgs. The forty-year-old father, Oscar, attracted Carlisle's attention with a given name that duplicated his grandfather Fenegan's. The wife, Sue, was five years younger than her husband; but Carlisle thought her thirty-five looked more like ninety-five,[14] and the family roused his pity. Their old house was little more than a shanty, and Sue dropped new babies with astonishing regularity. Ermine's memory is that she was "just a sack of bones," drained of life and joy, incapable of cooking fast enough on a wood stove to feed her growing brood. Her meager kitchen staple was sweet potatoes, and Carlisle became quite attached to the luscious and blessedly healthful tuber. The Richburg boys included Freddie, eleven, and Ernest, six, and both became Carlisle's inseparable playmates. He supposed that they must have had church clothes—"wash pants"—but otherwise they dressed in nothing but tattered denim overalls.

Carlisle recalled his sister in Jordan as a "pepper pot." After taking a serious dislike to a redheaded schoolmate, and full of knowing disdain, Ermine explained to her mother, "Her name is Wanita, and she spells it with J-U." One of Ermine's teachers came to Ida and announced, "Your daughter will do anything rather than blank a question. I asked her, 'What is the great crop of Kansas?' And Ermine said, 'Collards.'"

It was one of the few times the children heard Ida laugh, and it encouraged them to keep trying.

Differences between siblings grew more pronounced, though neither became the stereotypical preacher's kid.[15] Ermine may have thought Mama and Daddy "silly," but both parents frightened Carlisle. One day, after dragging in a particularly heavy load of wood, smarting from the injustice of having so many more chores than his sister, his frustration reached a critical mass. He decided to follow the time-honored boyhood challenge of running away from home. Independence!

Of course, failing to tell anyone what he was doing, much less *why*, may have declawed the action. No one came in pursuit or to rescue him. He got a block or two away, tramping through a field toward the woods; paused, reflected; and slunk back home, where he was astonished at how nice Daddy and Mama acted about his being away. There were no harsh words, no punishment. No one indicated that he had been missed. Both parents casually mentioned that they were glad he had decided to return.

As Carlisle's passion for reading grew, he felt the absence of a library. He spent solitary hours maneuvering a set of metal toy soldiers into attacks in complicated battle formations he had drawn. Shooting was fun; was war not supposed to be fun? Or he pored over newspaper cartoons, his favorite funny papers,

Dick Tracy, Little Orphan Annie, Boots and Her Buddies. Shortly after Parker Brothers introduced its board game Monopoly in 1935, the Floyds acquired one, and Carlisle was hooked.

Summer and holiday visits to Laurinburg became all the more hotly anticipated on all sides. The elder Fenegans had a set of *Compton's Encyclopedia,* and soon after arriving, when not sketching, Carlisle pulled out a volume and began reading it from cover to cover. Though the family seemed to take it all in stride, Oscar Fenegan watched his grandson with pride.

Meanwhile, Carlisle enlisted Ermine in another ill-fated end run for independence: Ensconced in the Shamrock Inn that August in stern aunt Lucile's charge, they languished in dog days, Ida at her sister's house across town assisting a midwife with Bunny's daughter's birth. The children sensed something big in the offing. Confident that they knew the way, they crept out of the inn, making it as far as the corner church a block away. Seconds later, Argus-eyed Lucile, looking most displeased, pulled up in her enormous blue Dodge and ordered the truants inside. Though not present at the birth, they soon enough became enamored of their new cousin, Helen Gamble, whom Carlisle thought the family's real star.

Carlisle's wardrobe reflected growing maturity. In Jordan, his parents presented him with his first store-bought suit with full-length trousers. New clothes dependably began to show up at Christmas and birthdays, selected, bought, or made by Ida. In the fall of 1935, he moved to the schoolhouse's fourth-grade row, staring at Ermine's third-grade back.

Jack and Ida had every intention of adding brothers and sisters for their two maturing children, a second generation. It proved fortunate, however, that Carlisle and Ermine had graced their first years of marriage. For the next eight, Ida suffered chronic poor health. She had in all five miscarriages, a reminder of South Carolina's early years when the average family had seven children. Typical pregnancies averaged eighteen months apart, and around 25 percent of infants failed to survive past the age of five.[16] During Ida's Jordan pregnancy, her doctor in Manning administered a series of injections subcutaneously rather than intravenously, and she miscarried, with massive internal bleeding, and lay near death.

Jack sank into his own crisis of conscience and confidence. He considered leaving the ministry, and even contemplated suicide.[17]

Ida had never masked her dislike for Jordan. In small matters, Jack's wishes and intentions usually prevailed. Ida's hot-tempered sister Bunny once told him with steel-cored humor, "You surely married the right Fenegan girl"; but in a charged emotional impasse, Jack caved in to keep the peace. He took his despair to the district superintendent and bishop, but would have to wait for November's conference.

Ida sank. After the children spent September in new grade rows, Jack again yanked them from school and drove the family to Laurinburg and better medical care for Ida. Compared to Jordan, the Shamrock Inn seemed a luxury hotel, even without indoor plumbing. Ida recuperated over the last three months of 1935, while Carlisle and Ermine played, read, and drew, never dreaming how serious their mother's crisis was to warrant such a disruption. Instead, Carlisle mused over grandfather Oscar's morning shave at a cold-water basin.

But the boy had learned Jordan's lesson: "This too shall pass." Though longing for more contact with his father, he had dependable friends in his mother and Ermine. Even away from formal schooling, the world of books and music beckoned with siren songs of independence.

November's conference confirmed Jack's appointment to Bethune, South Carolina, and Ida rejoiced: Bethune lay just fifty-five miles northeast on US 1 from the attractions and culture of the state's capital, Columbia. Better yet, Ida's sister Lucile found a new teaching position at a small public school in Cassatt, just six miles from Bethune.

Alone in Jordan, Jack bided his time, packed for the move, and said the family's farewells to the community in which they had spent less than ten months. Never afraid of a road trip, he drove the 188 miles from Jordan to Laurinburg as often as he could. On one visit, he took Carlisle for barbering, which was botched so badly that the family women gave a blistering lecture. Ida patted Carlisle and whispered, "Son, it always grows out." Jack tried to make amends by visiting one of the better local clothing stores, buying his boy a shaggy wool sweater.

Ida and her sisters thought it looked dreadful.

3

Golden Days

Bethune, 1936–1939

If Jordan represented hell to Ida and her children, Bethune approached her vision of heaven. Reverend Floyd celebrated his new posting by buying a used 1934 Ford, moving by himself just after Christmas 1935; he collected his family from Laurinburg in January. The unfamiliar vehicle fascinated the children, who thought it snazzy. It sported the recent innovation of a heater, which channeled both warmth and a miasma of fumes.

Bethune looked familiar and comfortable when they rolled in, its size, layout, and railroad presence much like Latta's. The streets were full: people walked, drove, bustled from one business to the next. Paradise continued to open with a well-proportioned brick ranch-style parsonage only a few years old, a spotless environment for their cherished pieces, and the odd preordained "Aunt Ella's chair." It seemed a mansion, with front and back yards of healthy grass and towering chinaberry trees. Carlisle appreciated the beds of many-hued spiraea exuding sweet perfume. Great fat bumblebees invited capture in glass quart jars. After repeated stings, still fascinated by the whole natural universe, he grew more adept at the pastime. On hot summer nights he and Ermine filled jars with lightning bugs, riveted by their pulsing luminescence, coordinated like the chirping cricket orchestra. The yard had room aplenty for garden beds, and Jack built a new chicken coop. By 1936 standards, the kitchen was modern, meaning that the stove burned wood; Ida had ample room for flour and sugar canisters. Even though Carlisle and Ermine still shared a room, the house had guest quarters, occupied more than empty, by visiting family or summer revival preachers.

And the plumbing: porcelain toilets indoors, water running hot and cold; yet the house still had no telephone. For calls made or taken, Jack trotted over to an ever-beckoning auto emporium, a Chevrolet dealership and garage owned by Mr. Doug Mays, or across the street to the King Davis Hotel.

BETHUNE, KERSHAW COUNTY, lies in South Carolina's Sandhill region,[1] its landscape a striking change from the amorphous swamps, struggling fields, and back-country isolation of Jordan. The county seat, Camden, South Carolina's oldest inland town, offered rich Revolutionary War history, with more than a dozen battles for independence fought in its vicinity. The fifty-five-mile route from Columbia climbs gently but steadily into a land of scrubby pines, weeds, and rocks. And sand.

The Seaboard Railroad, competing with the Atlantic Coast Line that made Latta, arrived around the turn of the twentieth century. Descendants of Scottish settler Daniel Murdock Bethune granted right-of-way across their farmland, changing the town's name from Lynchwood to Bethune in 1900.

Though only 283 feet above sea level, the town sits in a sandy bowl. As in many southern villages, the central business area featured a bisection of two main streets lined with storefronts. Across pavement and sidewalks, wisps of cotton, the local crop of preference, drifted into tiny piles. In 1930, the oily tang of ginned cottonseed made Carlisle's ten-year-old eyes water. Bethune was home to 522 persons[2] and, over the next decade, it acquired about ten new citizens each year, thanks in part to its situation on US Highway 1, forerunner of today's I-95, facilitating commerce and exposure to the rest of the country.

The town's prosperity, consequently the Methodist church's, was guaranteed by three wealthy intermarried families of Mayses, Kings, and eponymous Bethunes. The Boykins, another prominent Methodist clan, boasted descent from Mary Boykin Chesnut (1823–1886), whose diaries tell of South Carolina life during the Civil War.

Thanks to the county's rich deposits of natural clay, local ceramics had already appeared in native American and colonial cultures. In 1920, Oscar Brumbeloe, whose work would be shown in museums, founded and operated a kiln and showroom that became Bethune Pottery, on the town's north side.

Directly across from the parsonage stood Bethune's school building, a two-story brick structure, since demolished, but Carlisle's educational home for four years. Each class of between twenty-five and thirty students, grades one through seven, had its own room and teacher. Long desks held up to four young bodies each, and Carlisle became dear friends with his mates, Johnny Watts Smith and Bobbie Gardner.

From the moment they arrived in January 1936, Carlisle and Ermine scrambled to catch up. Fortunately, South Carolina had standardized textbooks for each grade, so most makeup work involved reading. Fourth grade marked the transition between short and long division, and arithmetic plagued Carlisle. The teacher was Miss Louise Tiller. He admired everything about her, except her strong backhand writing, one of the few teacher scripts he never sought to imitate; but his grades improved, and Jack gave nickels for good report cards.

Among close neighbors were the prosperous Clyburns, but Carlisle heard that only the Bethunes, Kings, and Mayses had *real* money. McNeal Clyburn, a year older and a grade ahead of Carlisle, became his best friend. The family kept cows in the backyard, and Mrs. Lula Clyburn, one of Jack's flock, did the milking, which she sold for profit. The father, T. M., a master builder in the county, also sold corn for the town's chickens and coal for its heat.

Lula had competition from Mrs. Helen Best, another Bethel Methodist parishioner. The two women were archrivals in home-dairy commerce, and the sons delivered fresh milk each morning. Miz Lula would accuse Miz Helen of watering her milk, and so forth, and Reverend Floyd trod a delicate line. More than dairy was at stake in such a small community, where milk acquired political relevance.

Other connections came through Carlisle's brief membership in Children of the Confederacy,[3] sponsored by local women in the United Daughters of the Confederacy. Members were young people from infancy to age eighteen, descended from Confederate military veterans whose memory, deeds, and high principles they were enjoined to honor and perpetuate. Carlisle came to realize that dignifying the Bethune chapter as an organization misled: no more than three or four children attended a few meetings, and he recalled only their pathetic attempts to sing "Tenting Tonight on the Old Camp Ground."[4]

As at all their homes, Carlisle and Ermine acted as magnets for the town's youth. The parsonage yard buzzed with noisy children in constant motion, leaving bicycles strewn across Jack's manicured lawn. Ida, always undone by noise and commotion, strove to keep Carlisle's horde outdoors.

The town's confluence of families was represented in the person of Miss Cecelia King, who reached the century mark in 2008. In the years before Mays Chevrolet moved to Camden, Miss King kept the firm's books, and Carlisle remembers her as handsome and beautifully dressed. Her sister Alice was chairwoman of the Methodist Board of Stewards, and Kings and Mayses were all Floyd intimates.

As someone who knew and interacted with Carlisle in his early years, King offered glimpses of the community's reception of the new family:

> Mr. Floyd was the resident preacher; Carlisle was a natural. In those days, right across from the parsonage, there was a diamond where the boys played baseball. Mr. Floyd loved baseball, he wanted Carlisle to play. And Carlisle says, 'Daddy, you love baseball, I love music. I'll keep my music, you keep your baseball.' Even then, he was serious about his music. It was a disappointment to Mr. Floyd; but Carlisle had the

> talent, determination, and the will to go through with whatever it took; and he did it!
>
> In my mind, as a young boy, Carlisle is slender, dark-haired, kind of an olive-complexioned young man, nice looking. He had a pleasing personality, and a pleasing presentation of himself. He was charismatic, able to present his own image of who he was. We saw a lot of the Floyds when they were here. They were good people; and Miz Floyd was a lady, all the way.
>
> Carlisle was a good boy, and Ermine a good girl. Never in my life did I know them to get into any kind of trouble. And Carlisle at the piano: he played beautifully, everybody was excited about his playing. It was rather unusual, we did not have other boys in town that were musically inclined. That was a first, and it was something that everybody respected, and looked up to. So Carlisle was revered from the time he was a little boy. He had the acceptance of his peers because of his ability.
>
> We asked the Floyds to come to our house every Sunday that we could. We had live-in help, our dining room table sat twelve. The whole family came.[5]

The parsonage sat just a block from Bethune's center. At the corner of Main and King (US 1) stood King's General Store, founded by George S. King (1853–1923).[6] In the thirties, the owner-operator was George's son Lonnie, a dour Methodist pillar and Reverend Floyd's confidant. Carlisle was sent for loaves of bread, or quarts of milk when the cows of the neighbor ladies had a low-volume day.

With Jack spending more time away from home, Carlisle's chores multiplied. The day began with splitting soft-pine stove wood, hauling coal, and laying fires; he then helped Mama manage the chickens. "Setting a hen" involved one person lifting an aging layer, while another put eggs beneath her. Carlisle hoped that it had not rained, which meant wet feathers in the coop or at the sink from Ida's plucking.

Ida also expected him to help weed and hoe the garden, in Bethune replete with tomatoes, butter beans, corn, and Irish potatoes; and the canned volume fed the family well into winter. Carlisle so pitied Mama that he pitched in with cleaning chores; he then mowed the lawn and raked leaves, with their enduring scents of boyhood autumns. Delivering weekly church bulletins gave less pleasure.

There were also plum trees in the yard, but Carlisle never cared that much for their tart fruit, not when a string of parishioners brought baskets and bushels of delectable peaches and pears. Many afternoons and evenings were spent at the family farm of Johnny Watts Smith, with its scuppernong grape arbors. The thick ropy vines invited climbing and reclining, and big fun came from picking and gobbling the sweet cool fruit for hours. Carlisle brings such Jordan and Bethune scenes bubbling back to life in *Cold Sassy Tree,* of walking barefoot on sandy lanes and lying in the embrace of scuppernong vines.[7]

Toward summer's end, Carlisle and Ermine earned eighty-five cents a day for the Epworth Orphanage in Columbia, when Jack drove them out to blistering hours of cotton picking on local farms. The only relief came from quart jars of ice water they brought along, eyes smarting from the musty bleach smell of the plants and the fiber-packed bales. The black farmhands awed them, working like well-oiled machines, gathering hundreds of pounds to their pitiful fifty or sixty; but they knew intellectually that centuries of practice had enforced these skills under the cruelest conditions.

Ida, back in form after her Jordan illnesses, became Jack's equal partner in his ministry, serving on women's committees, playing the organ when needed, and running one of Kershaw County's better kitchens. The Clyburns sold feed corn, the Floyd's coop stood right out back, and Carlisle inhaled Ida's fried chicken. He loved the macaroni and cheese she made as a kind of pudding; but desserts were the best of all. Each year for his birthday she produced his favorite yellow cake with white coconut frosting.[8] She also whipped up dense frosted pound cakes and "stickies," cinnamon buns held together with caramelized sugar, treats that made getting home from school a special occasion.

During leisure hours, the chinaberry trees invited climbing and swinging, despite their soft wood; the tiny, inedible yellow fruit caused a spectacular mess if tracked into Ida's clean house. June bugs—fat buzzing scarab beetles—abounded, and tying a string around their bodies and watching them fly on leashes proved fine sport; and between King's store and the parsonage lay a no-man's-land of weeds and bushes where Carlisle and Ermine played explorer. With friends they tramped and hunted in the woods with slingshots, improvising forts from piles of rocks, sticks, branches, and leaves, dividing into sides and attacking each others' bastions. In this sandy soil, team fights, often between factions of the church boy's club, were waged with cottonseed from the gins, and sandspurs, the latter a common weed with stems studded with spiked burrs. Never mind that both did Carlisle's asthmatic lungs no good; and a sandspur in the eye could cause real trouble.[9]

Diversions gained importance, as it dawned on him that a minister's child lived by different standards than most of his peers. Still, Bethune's was an independent life that parents and children today can only regard with nostalgia; children wandered miles out into the country or explored the railroad tracks. As long as no one asked Ida, fear scarcely existed.

JACK HAD STRUCK a Pyrrhic bargain to escape Jordan. In Bethune, he had charge of not only Bethel's congregation and church school but also a bouquet of smaller churches in the surrounding countryside, with evocative names like Concord, Providence, Sandy Grove, St. Matthew's, Lucknow, and Bethany. Never did they all operate simultaneously; but in staggered weeks, at least two or three offered Sunday services, church school, and summer revivals, plus regular duties at the home church. Sunday mornings and afternoons were dense with sequential worship for the whole family, and evenings found Jack and Ida at prayer meetings at the Baptist or Presbyterian churches, and/or choir rehearsal at Bethel.

Days overflowed with chores at all seven churches: posting hymns, changing bulletin boards, cutting and running off stencils, delivering church newsletters and bulletins, meeting committees, officiating at weddings, funerals, and baptisms, making calls on laid up parishioners at home or hospitals, and depositing offerings. Special events required quasi-dramatic presentation, hence extra rehearsals. The choirs needed weekly practice for Sunday services, seasonal ceremonies, and special cantata performances (seasonal choral concerts).

This combination of responsibilities would be more than enough for one man in a thriving, growing town, but Jack still carved out chunks of time for reading and writing long papers for Emory University. Carlisle did not really understand what he was doing, but knew it was hard work. Each course involved ten or more papers, and Jack was dutiful in their execution. He also attended at least one annual session of pastor's school at Columbia College, and these labors resulted in his ordination as deacon, then elder, in Bethune.

The greatest benefit in this multiplication of effort was his elevation as The Minister in Town, whose responsibilities were balanced by power, prestige, influence, and sheer ego gratification.[10] Carlisle saw his popular parents making friends easily, even while maintaining boundaries and distance, calling close acquaintances "Mr. King," "Mrs. (Miz) Mays," and the like. (For that matter, Jack never called his in-laws anything but "Mr. Oscar" and "Mrs. Kate.")

Outside the parsonage, he strove, with marked success, to please everyone in the community. Despite the accident in Latta, his activities outside church walls included umpiring church and Bethune school baseball games, to which he brought ecclesiastical overtones. Though Jack wore no special collar or other distinguishing garb, Carlisle rarely saw his father without coat and tie. In summer, that might be a white linen suit and Panama hat; but all such garments outside the sanctuary substituted for vestments, ministerial propriety taking precedence over comfort in summer's deadliest heat. Jack's teams and their families teased, and glee erupted if they ever coaxed him down to vest and shirt. From observing such behavior, Carlisle saw elements of character crystallize, in a very theatrical sense, as close to home as the baseball diamond.

Jack's natural extroversion made his parishioners adore him, and he grew to become his ministerial persona. Carlisle's developing ability to read people helped him see Jack's evolution as a kind of unholy trinity: first a minister, second a man, and only third a husband and father. In part because Ida could not deal with tension or confrontation, the duration of Jack's dark moods increased. During stressful times he rarely shouted, but complained and pouted. He rarely retreated into silence, and subdued anger inflected his words, whether the predominant emotion was impatience, frustration, or disapproval.

With her genius for sewing, Ida had always been fashion conscious. Now, as The Minister's Wife, she described her passion for clothes as her "besetting sin." In moments of exasperation, she might sigh to the children, "Your father is the most insensitive of men." Niece Helen Harris recalls tuning out Jack's Sunday sermons "when they got all emotional"; yet no sooner had he pronounced the benediction than Helen saw him "really looking forward to being asked to Sunday dinner. He had a healthy appetite, and aside from the food, he felt like a king."[11] As course followed course, Carlisle watched his parents negotiate how long to stay after the meal. Bethune loved Jack, from which he extrapolated that everyone lived to spend limitless hours in his company; but the hosts might grow as visibly impatient as Carlisle and Ermine. Ida, keenly attuned to appearances, always noticed; but Jack stayed on. And on. She might whisper, "Jack, it's up to *you* to announce we have to leave," the children adding nods; instead, Jack slew the faithful with a few more choice groaners. Even this taught Carlisle lessons of theatrical timing.

The popularity of the Floyds bore fruit in numerous ministerial perks, including substantial gifts of food and services. During summer revival season, the whole family accompanied Jack to social events before and after each service. A new custom to which Bethune introduced them was the "pounding." Far from a physical hazing, groups of parishioners gifted the minister and his family with literal pounds of all types of foods and supplies.[12]

BETHUNE'S CENTRAL LOCATION in the state, and the renewed closeness to Ida's parents and siblings of both families, proved a tonic for everyone. The tiny hamlet of Cassatt was around six miles south on US 1. Lucile Fenegan taught school there, and spent many weekends in Bethune. Latta and Laurinburg were each just sixty miles apart, and the Chevy stayed in constant motion to both, sometimes two or three times a week. Asheville, where Jack's sister Doris and husband J. W. Moore lived, was a slightly more ambitious trip of 202 miles each way; but the family again became a coherent nucleus, its shape and consistency maintained by constant driving. Jack often tallied a day's round trip of 400 miles or more, ending a diary entry of one such long drive with the comment "feel good."[13]

Carlisle enjoyed listening to the living room wrangles on philosophical and moral issues and watching his father squirm to make points. Doris had embraced Christian Science, and she and Jack once debated concepts of truth. Looking to deliver a crushing blow to her brother's ego, Doris began, "From the standpoint of a Christian Scientist. . . ."

Jack interjected, "And a Methodist!"

Doris: "Truth. . . ."

And, while she formulated her thought, a moment of silence ensued, just enough for droll, skeptical J. W. to interject, "Is a very scarce commodity."

Besides Lucile, Jack's youngest brother, Bascom Lorraine, Carlisle's uncle Sonny, often visited for extended periods, and became the boy's mentor. Sonny adored boxing, and taught Carlisle how to position his fists and make effective uppercuts and jabs. Carlisle practiced with ardor, and Sonny gave him a bodybuilding device, a broad rubber strap with handles on both ends, to strengthen chest and arms. Carlisle made himself a sand-filled punching bag that he and Jack hung from a chinaberry tree.

It seems a peculiar occupation for a gentle boy with musical interests coming to the fore, but Jack longed to see Carlisle spar with his peers. In the Bethune schoolyard, rowdy country children, the "bus kids," looked for and found trouble, but they occupied the periphery of Carlisle's circle. The single time he put boxing skills to the test involved his best friend, McNeal Clyburn, who was enamored of Ermine. A few swipes and hits to the face ended with a cut lip for Carlisle, and both boys dragged home in tears. Ida, predictably undone, could still give no comfort, but wanted instead to know, "What did *you* do to *him*?!"

Jack sent unhelpful double messages by observing, "Son, you never get into fights. That's just not boylike!"

The town's living statue, its venerated Civil War veteran, emphasized contrasts of time and place. Mr. Gilliam King, patriarch of a family that had owned as many as forty slaves,[14] served as another pillar of Bethel Methodist. He and Jack spent many earnest hours conversing about philosophy, life experiences, and history, especially Reconstruction. King's dress and grooming were textbook Southern Aristocrat: white linen suits, string ties, broad-brimmed hats, and natty goatee. Mr. Gilliam made no secret of loathing everything about the Yankees who had destroyed the old ways of southern life and culture.

On frequent visits to Latta, the Floyds stayed in the family house with Jack's sister Hazel and Frank Ellerbe, who affected external gallantry; but Jack had difficulty spending much time in his brother-in-law's company. Frank liked his bourbon before supper, making him voluble and vehement in his opposition to Methodist unification, one of Jack's passionate causes. The question of race was not open to discussion, unless one deliberately sought angry words. Carlisle squirmed.

Race relations in Bethune bore the double standard of philosophical lines in the sand and fluid accommodation. Most black women worked as maids, cooks, washerwomen, and childcare givers; the men, as farm workers, handymen, and mechanics. Schools, churches, hospitals, restaurants, and other public facilities were still completely segregated.

Despite cultural obstacles, at home the Floyd children saw a great deal of a young black man with the unlikely name Judybell Murphy, orphaned son of a local handyman. About fifteen to Carlisle's ten, Judybell followed parental footsteps, doing odd jobs and occasional yard work for the Floyds during Jack's asthmatic periods. For the children, to expand their "explorer" game, Judybell dug caves in the parsonage's back yard, and built playhouses in the chinaberry trees. The age difference posed no problem: Judybell was just their friend, bigger and stronger, and full of more life than anyone they knew. Community tongues wagged, but matters stopped with Jack and Ida. She was not crazy about Ermine going into the caves, though: it was not ladylike.

Racial issues may have been taboo in certain segments of the family, but human anatomy and sex posed even greater obstacles. Grandmother Kate had married from the starchy Cottinghams into an earthy, scatology-prone Irish clan. Devout Baptist that he was, granddaddy Oscar peppered his narratives with occasional vulgarisms; but sex was different, and Oscar displayed as much reticence as his wife. Public displays of affection went the way of hens' teeth. When an unmarried pregnant woman visited the elder Fenegans in Laurinburg, Mrs. Kate thundered, "Where is the *perpetrator* who did this to you?!"

For his part, Jack practiced obsessive modesty. Once Ermine burst in on him when he was changing clothes, and Jack raised the roof, not the wisest course with his feisty daughter. She found Carlisle, and fumed, "Does he think I *want* to look at him?!"

Carlisle soon realized that neither of his parents had any vocabulary for the physiology and protocols of reproduction, and that they had probably had no guidance before their marriage. Despite her usual fragility, Ida was more Fenegan than Cottingham, thus more forthcoming on the subject than Jack, and, around the time of the Bethune move, essayed a "birds and bees" talk with the children. To her bright brood, this made no sense: she got as far as "Daddy plants his seed," but then fell silent on further aspects of one of creation's greatest mysteries. Carlisle and Ermine remained unenlightened.

One day, digging a new cave in the yard for Carlisle, Judybell used a strange term, the quintessential four-letter expletive, whether as noun or verb is lost to memory. Carlisle had never heard that sturdy Anglo-Saxon word, much less a clinical description of the act for which it stood. As far as he was concerned, his friend now spoke a foreign language, so he asked for translation. Judybell obliged, birds and bees escaped nest and hive, and Carlisle fell up closer to the portals of adulthood. Though his parents had always bathed him and Ermine together, neither was clear about the anatomy of the opposite sex; but Judybell's unvarnished clarification made crude sense. Because the siblings kept no secrets from each other, Carlisle found Ermine and shared the new information. Both were still shocked and puzzled, but it was a start. Thanks to acquaintance with Judybell, the ten-year-old who came to Bethune a complete innocent would leave better informed than many peers.

Another singular character turned up around 1938: Wayne Martin, Carlisle's senior by eight years. Wayne claimed distant kinship, and he and Jack somehow puzzled out the degree of cousinage. The boy, who struck Carlisle as a "wild street kid," had run away from Epworth Orphanage, the Methodist charitable institution in Columbia for which Carlisle and Ermine had picked cotton. No one was clear about where he had otherwise lived, and Ida fretted about "bad influences." Wayne never wore shoes, and in the house tucked his filthy feet under the rug; but even barefoot, with arch alone he punted a football farther than anyone Carlisle had ever seen. Wayne rarely appeared when or where he said he would be, but he turned up now and again to replace Judybell for the odd yard or house chore. Jack negotiated with the orphanage to take Wayne back, or to place him in a trade school. The family lost track of him after leaving Bethune, but between Wayne and Judybell, Carlisle gained a fuller view of life.

Owing to Bethune's situation on Highway 1, the Great Depression swept a steady procession of homeless and jobless through from all directions. Jack received tramps, migrants, and drifters seeking a future, or just looking to get out of the weather, for meals and a night's lodging. On November 28, 1938, "a Mr. Brooks from California asked for some food."[15] On December 2, a "hobo by the name of Frost" spent the night, ate supper and breakfast the next morning, and continued his trek to Kansas.[16] The wildness of these dispossessed unnerved Ida. One, an unemployed circus performer, delighted the children by performing a repertoire of odd tricks, like sticking long nails up his nose. Jack reluctantly sent him off when Ida blanched at the hardware.

Carlisle had scant experience with losing family members. His paternal grandfather Giles had died eleven years before his birth, and his grandmother Ermine Mercer Sessions Floyd died when he was a month old. Though both of Ida's parents were role models for longevity, Carlisle was about to learn empathy with adult suffering.

On a car trip, a few months after getting to Bethune, he overheard a peculiar parental conversation with agitated overtones: something was driving Ida's mother crazy. Jack declared, "Mrs. Kate is just not rational!" Over succeeding days, once Carlisle realized that the concern was his grandmother's *mind*, he and Ermine pieced together the horrifying story of a car accident in Laurinburg: Mrs. Fenegan had struck a young black man, who died from his injuries. Grandmama would never get over her guilt.

Now a fresh disaster enveloped the Fenegans: Oscar and Kate's youngest child, James, whom Carlisle idolized, had earned high honors in French studies. Toward the end of May 1937, the night before his final exam, nineteen-year-old James was about to take a ship for graduate study in Paris. His roommate at the University of North Carolina woke to the sound of loud groans, and ran for help. When the parties returned, James was dead of complications from childhood rheumatic fever.

The Floyds drove to the funeral in Laurinburg, to inaugurate the Fenegan burial plot. With the family sitting around the Shamrock's living room, the sight and sound of Granddaddy Oscar's sobbing stunned Carlisle. Did grown men cry like that? The Fenegans puzzled Carlisle with their apparent disunity as a couple: in her staid, stiff matriarchy, Grandmama eschewed outward signs of affection to her husband. Granddaddy was just Granddaddy: ever sweet and gallant, bestowing kisses on the top of Kate's head after meals. He executed shenanigans to amuse her, courting her good graces. No one ever breathed a word about Oscar's financial missteps, but some degree of tension existed between the couple, and they kept to separate bedrooms.

The Shamrock also brought great joy to three-year-old cousin Helen. After Carlisle terrorized her with tales of bats in the attic, she begged him to play one of his new piano pieces, *The Wedding of the Painted*

Doll.[17] Carlisle groaned, but play he did; and with Helen perched on that notoriously uncomfortable horsehair couch, he drew for her, creating generations of paper dolls.

ON JANUARY 7, 1938, Jack began the diary he kept for forty-eight years, the first volume covering 1938 to 1941. The space allotted for daily entries is three-and-five-eighths inches by one inch, and his tiny handwriting cannot be comfortably read without magnification. Most days produced dry listings of baptisms, marriages, funerals, sermon topics, pastoral visits; monies received and disbursed, household chores and trips, meals eaten, family chitchat, and mentions of conversations: form without content. He avoided committing most emotional issues to paper, but as a strict chronicle it is a biographer's boon.

After Jack's investitures as deacon and elder, the diary became part of a grander new persona. With a great show of keeping daily recording time sacrosanct, he sequestered himself behind closed doors. He often declared how handy these journals were for birthdays and anniversaries, and as a kind of backup financial ledger; but he also took much ribbing from his nearest and dearest about what they believed affectation or addiction. Carlisle saw his father most comfortable as the Reverend C. S. Floyd, surrounded by adoring parishioners rather than by those who had known him as just Jack. He did not take kindly to the teasing of skeptical elder brother G. R., prone to asking, "How's the Great Divine today?" The diary acquired an aura of mystery through isolation as Jack pursued his ministry.

On Thursday, February 10, 1938, something strange and painful exploded behind closed doors at the Bethune parsonage. Jack's diary has scrawled across the day's space two words, "Forever Blank." The next day, Ida drove off with the children to Laurinburg, leaving Jack to fend for himself. That evening, on the way to a basketball game in Bishopville, he occupied the front passenger seat of his Presbyterian colleague Frank Morse's car when they collided with an oil truck. Unconscious, Jack was ambulanced to the hospital in Camden, where x-rays showed six broken ribs and a concussion. He spent ten days in hospital, surrounded by bouquets and floral sprays from parishioners, but remembering little of what had happened. Ida, Carlisle, and Ermine drove back on Saturday, only to learn of Jack's second closed-head injury.

He returned home on February 21 to a "juice shower"—a welcome home featuring copious quantities of fruit juices without alcohol—from his flock. When leg pain did not lessen after almost two weeks of home recuperation, he returned to the hospital. X-rays showed that the leg was indeed broken, and he hobbled for weeks with a cast. Carlisle came down with asthma and flu the day after Jack rose from his bed. Well aware of his father's mortality, he now heard new tones of pessimism as Jack ended discussions with, "Well, the world's in God's hands." He expected the worst. If the family took a car trip, Jack anticipated at least two flat tires, if not a fatal wreck; and toxic anxiety rarely dies with the elder generation.

Asthma and other respiratory ailments continued to devil both father and son. Hardly a week passed without one having an attack, or else colds or influenza that sidelined them for three to five days. Nearing adolescence, Carlisle manifested more of the emotional traits of asthma sufferers.[18] Each of his Bethune episodes showed close ties to family stressors, performances, or school events. A good example was the first mention Jack made in his diary of a possible move away from Bethune, at the end of October 1938: Carlisle fell literally breathless.

Perhaps to spite the disease, life in Bethune saw a quantum increase in his outdoor activity. Excepting the occasional figure like the Australian Percy Grainger, composers are not known for athletic prowess; but then Carlisle waited another twenty years before deciding to be a composer. Part of his longevity and general good health derives from his early and continuing interest in sports: in Bethune he played baseball and football, rode his bicycle many miles weekly, worked alongside Jack in the parsonage yard and garden, ran for groceries, and delivered church bulletins. In cold weather, he continued to split kindling, haul coal, and lay fires in the home stoves.

Cooling off in South Carolina's summers prompted short trips to Big Springs, a natural effluence on the west bank of Lynches River. In 1914, a Mr. Maynard had founded the Big Springs Resort Company, which had its own railway station, hotel and restaurant, bathhouses, concession stands, and picnic areas. Of course, there was also an outlet for the site's bottled mineral water, thought to ameliorate rheumatism, chronic indigestion, Bright's disease, and other kidney and bladder problems. In addition to diverting the waters into swimming pools on the grounds, the company shipped its product nationwide in the first decades of the twentieth century. At a constant temperature of fifty-seven degrees, the water flowed at more than three hundred gallons per minute. One company proprietor advertised what some might think a liability as an asset: "You don't need ice in this water."[19] The swimming offered a treat for Jack and the children, some weeks more than once. That the water turned Carlisle's thin flesh shades of blue posed a minor hindrance; but this colorful metamorphosis only reinforced Ida's anti-water tirades, regardless of restorative properties.

Though Ida had taken physical training at Coker College in the twenties, she remained indifferent to all sports. Jack had given her proof of what might happen. If he, a gifted athlete, were prone to injury, she anticipated the maiming or killing of her children. Organized by Jack, however, team sports with friends and family filled Carlisle's life; frequent touch football enhanced evenings and weekends. The sport became such an obsession that his most extravagant fantasies in Bethune focused on becoming a star quarterback like his idol, Duke University's Clarence "Ace" Parker. Daydreaming brought pleasure, but by this time Carlisle's wariness never let him retreat too far into imaginative ether.

On Easter Sunday 1936, he came home from an egg hunt, dashed not to have found a single specimen. Later that afternoon, he lay on his bed, weeping, wanting someone to comfort or at least acknowledge his disappointment. His parents happened upon him like this, and Ida limited her sympathy to asking the reason for his tears, assuming that he missed the Richburg boys, his Jordan playmates. That night, still crying, Carlisle overheard her say, "He is such a strange, sensitive little boy. What can we get to make him feel better?"

It was hardly the first and surely not the last parental watering of the seed message of Carlisle's hypersensitivity. Jack seemed to place an odd premium on this quality; but like asthma or defeat at anything, it bolstered his grandiosity at Carlisle's expense. Many times over many years, Carlisle writhed to hear from his entire family, "You were always such a sensitive little boy." Ida's answer to the current dilemma smacked of genius: a new baseball glove. Not only did Carlisle feel better, but Bethune also gained a new second baseman on that diamond across from the parsonage. Despite Cecelia King's recollection, some of his best childhood memories were simple rounds of catch, just tossing the ball back and forth with Daddy and Ermine, pure delight at hand-eye coordination. In Bethel's boy's club, Methodists played Baptists and Presbyterians, town boys, or teams from other nearby villages. Jack dutifully recorded scores in his diary, and Bethel's lads won more than they lost. The club met every Wednesday night, attendance hovering between seven and eleven. Jack counseled, took them on camping, fishing, and hiking trips, and supervised community building projects and athletic contests, investing each activity with as much religious content as they could absorb or tolerate. Carlisle attended irregularly, mainly for sports. He lacked confidence in his abilities at second plate, and his baseball ambitions were relatively short-lived. Though he never felt that he *had* to play, he *wanted* to, with more desire than skill. He was in fact something of a triple threat, practicing if not excelling at basketball, baseball, and football, in their appropriate seasons. Sports, as he said of this phase of his southern upbringing, were "expected."

Even in these years before serious hostilities erupted between father and son, whatever encouragement Jack provided did little to counter Carlisle's diffidence; and indeed, the thought of Daddy calling balls and strikes behind him at bat inspired little confidence. Carlisle recalled no stunning double plays, no home runs; but on a dash toward first after a base hit, the ball thrown for the out struck his head instead. Unlike Jack, he was neither knocked out nor sent to a doctor, but gained deeper respect for the risks of the game.

Swimming and team sports formed but the iceberg's tip of Carlisle's outdoor activities as he raced between ten and twelve to "the very top of boyhood."[20] It is no wonder that he retained an indelible love for this little town as the place where he was most often happy.

He and Ermine had long since abandoned their battered tricycles. For Christmas 1937, Jack mail-ordered new bikes from Sears Roebuck, for twenty-six dollars each. They arrived in the nick of time, and he and Ida's brother-in-law Yates Gamble assembled them on Christmas Eve. The next morning, they gleamed beside the parsonage's tree, "From Santa Claus." Carlisle's was black, Ermine's blue, both with balloon tires, and the proud owners became one with these incomparable new symbols of mobility. They rode everywhere, ranging miles from home, through high grass and weeds, hot shifting sandbars, gravel, mud, and smoking tar on the roads.

Ermine went on to star in women's basketball in high school and college; but despite Carlisle's continued play at all available sports, his dreams of an athletic career "died a-borning." Ermine perceived her brother, with all of his music, drawing, and writing, as an absolutely average boy: "He played basketball, football, baseball, we had tree houses. With all of his talents, he was just normal."

CARLISLE REAPED BENEFITS from the calendar's even division between his birthday and Christmas, as he most often requested—and got—fresh reading matter. He never lost his fascination with encyclopedias, but interest in the funny papers waned. In 1938, Jack subscribed him to the monthly magazine *The Open Road for Boys.* The typical issue featured articles and short fiction about hunting, nature, military combat, Western and Oriental adventure, exploration, and sports. Advertisements appeared for products like Cocomalt, because "a baseball player needs plenty of strength and pep," or Kellogg's Corn Flakes, because—above an illustration of two grappling football players—"it takes drive and energy to win!" Carlisle was drawn to all the sports stories in which the little guy's brains defeat brawn.[21]

Bethune's branch of the Kershaw County Library provided other adventures. Its founder, Miss Mary Arthur, a Yankee spinster relocated to Bethune and a church schoolteacher at Bethel Methodist, became another of Carlisle's mentors. Ida promoted visits to the tiny library, making the children feel like fashionable adults, especially when Carlisle got his own card. Arthur suggested reading appropriate for young minds; Reverend Floyd in the back of hers. Carlisle haunted the facility, and one classic after another fell into his hands, beginning with Dickens's *Oliver Twist.* To a ten-year-old it seemed like a very big book, but Ida kept urging him to finish it. If either child ever complained of boredom, Mama countered, "With all the good books there are to read?" Carlisle persevered, and moved on to Mark Twain, whose memorable characters, humor, strong plotting, and vivid language never left him.

A natural outgrowth of Carlisle's athletic enthusiasms was a torrent of reading the twenty-three inspirational-motivational sports novels for boys written by the indefatigable Harold M. Sherman between 1926 and 1932.[22] Miss Arthur set each aside for Carlisle, who thrilled at the athletic triumphs that eluded him on Bethune's playing fields.

Sherman's *Goal to Go!* (1931) made a deep impression, inspiring him to greater efforts in his own games and fuel for fantasies: a boy like Carlisle was Sherman's target audience. His characters strove to please, to succeed, to break through. Every Sherman message brimmed with aspiration, the hero triumphing at the last moment through the combination of personal effort, skill, and luck. Buoyed by such motivation, the things Carlisle most wanted, from music to acting in plays, to sports, seemed more realistic and doable.

Around his eleventh birthday, Miss Arthur, to Reverend Floyd's ardent approval, urged the boy to read the books of New York author Grace Livingston Hill (1865–1947), whose prolific output ran to more than one hundred volumes of Christian romances. Carlisle identified with any figure divided against him- or herself, as Hill's inevitably were, and he read at least thirty of her books, later considering this a strange detour from typical boyhood fare. Yet Hill had a simple but effective formula: no matter the time, place, or permutations of trial and tribulation in the face of ridicule and scorn, the hero or heroine achieves a glorious conversion by each book's final chapter, complications and contradictions resolved in a rosy nimbus of salvation.

LIFE AS A MINISTER'S SON defined Carlisle as it set him apart, and that dichotomy remained in constant flux throughout his life. He studied his father's unique position in the family and community, the bedrock of his power and self-esteem; yet certain aspects of Jack's personal theology were enigmatic. On the one hand, he urged strict acceptance of the literal truth of the Bible's every word, and unquestioning compliance with its basic doctrines. Though emphasizing the need to prepare for eternity, he shied away from embracing a literal hell and its attendant pyrotechnics. Jack's religion was, for his time and place in the south, moderate to liberal. Despite their eventual estrangement, Carlisle admired his father's ability to suppress private prejudices and inbred bigotries by listening to what prayer told him. Ida emphasized, "Your father is very good, he carries out the work of the church very well, even if he is not the world's greatest preacher."

Ida's simpler spirituality eclipsed that of her husband the ordained minister. A dutiful wife, she often said, "If I just do what I already know I have to do, that will keep me very busy." In public meek and docile, privately she spoke out against women's subservience. Her religious convictions remained personal, sound, and deep, unorthodox in unexpected ways. She never forced her beliefs on her children, but gave them the feeling that religion had most to do with one's relation to others. If one showed people respect, compassion, and kindness, things would work out for the best: the Golden Rule in action.

Other family influences on Carlisle's religious convictions stood out during the Bethune years. His Floyd aunt Doris avidly embraced Christian Science, as did his maternal grandmother Fenegan and aunt Lucile. Uncle Sonny Floyd turned to Seventh Day Adventism late in life, after returning from the South Pacific in World War II. He began reading the Bible over and over, cover to cover, and Jack came to believe that Sonny knew more about the Book than he did.

Jack prepared sermons and church school lessons on Saturdays, and family rhythms centered on Sundays. The Sabbath was inviolable, the one off-limits time for sports. Jack expected the whole family to attend each service at each church. Until well after devotions, even the funny papers could not be read, making them naturally all the more delectable.

Besides Methodist, Presbyterian, and Baptist interpretations of Christianity, Carlisle gained eclectic exposure to other varieties of southern Protestantism. Some ultrafundamentalist sects seemed exotic, like Washfoot Baptists, who bathed one another's feet as a gesture of humility and identification with Christ. In the thirties, South Carolina had other sects like Truelights and Disciples, whom Carlisle would use as figurative Montagues and Capulets in the blighted romance of his short story "A Lengthening Shadow,"[23] in turn the basis for his first opera, *Slow Dusk*, in 1949. In the Floyds' travels all over the south, he was riveted by signs that these groups posted on roadsides. Some urged repentance, some promised damnation; others, the world's end and the Rapture.

In any event, beginning in Jordan, congregations at rural Methodist churches constellated a stratum new to Carlisle. The blunt-spoken ladies in particular made a stark impression on him, with their Depression-straitened circumstances and diminished expectations; already at age ten, Carlisle interpreted their mode as a minimum of social striving and a maximum of plain speaking. At the whirl of social events attached to summer revivals, he saw little of the pleasantry affected by more affluent middle- or upper-class families in Latta, Spartanburg, and McClellanville. He was already honing his ear for speech, gaining insights into character and motivations. Judgmentalism flourished as a byproduct of deprivation, together with suspicion of anything beautiful or sensual; a cult was made of plainness. Carlisle tells an anecdote about two country women at an exhibition of dried flower arrangements: One turns to the other and says,

"Well I declare, I guess that was pretty when it was fresh."

Ida kept her delicate good looks for decades beyond many of her peers. Years later, she and Jack attended a reunion with many country families they had known in the thirties. An acquaintance approached and declared, without apparent malice, "Rev'rend Floyd looks about the same; but my, Miz Floyd, you've done broke."

A similar dynamic manifested at the senior Floyds' fiftieth wedding anniversary in November 1974 when another such lady wound down the reception line and stopped by the now-famous composer, then close to fifty: "Why Carlisle, you've grown up to be an old man." He knew that these folk never meant to wound; but they nonetheless showed a basic disconnect with the sensitivities of others. He felt a fundamental level of anger in people so long so impoverished, which he encapsulated in *Susannah*'s supporting cast.

There had been revivals in McClellanville and Jordan, but nothing on the scale mortared into Bethune's multiple churches. Since the first years of the nineteenth century, the Methodist Church sought to increase congregational fervor and attract new converts, and it held these annual events in July or August. The typical Methodist revival took a week, in the sponsoring church's sanctuary. The denomination disdained presentations that smacked of the primitive backwoods, such as outdoor tents or baptism by immersion. Unless demonstrably ordained, Methodists scorned such officiants and sacraments.

In Reverend Floyd's case, some summers saw as many as three or four revival weeks, at any combination of the Bethel home church and its satellites, with morning or afternoon and evening services for the duration. The format was simple but effective: Jack invited a revival specialist from outside the community, renowned for hellfire and brimstone oratory. If no such man could be engaged, Jack himself might preach, or do so at other churches as a favor to colleagues. His discursive, soulful delivery, though, was never the true revivalist's meat. Each service's main event was the sermon, its intent to inspire visceral emotion in the congregation, repentance of sins and renewal of faith. A typical week's schedule might include, as it did in August 1939, a sequence of sermon titles like "Repentance," "Fearing Burdens," "The Thief on the Cross," "To Know God is Life Eternal," "Glorying in the Cross," and "Confessing Christ." At event's end, inspired old members and strangers alike made public gestures of rededication by approaching the altar rail to kneel and be blessed.

Offerings were crucial, because most guest preachers received a portion of the week's receipts as compensation. Cecelia King served as church treasurer in those years and recalled Reverend Floyd's sanctuaries packed to overflowing, standing room only, with sweating bodies pressed against side and back walls; but good attendance was no guarantee of cash flow, and sometimes the combined offerings of all the Bethune churches amounted to a few dollars and change. Twenty years later, Carlisle wrote for *Susannah*'s evangelist Olin Blitch a memorable exhortation to fill the offering plates with bills rather than coins.[24]

It was not enough for Jack to make an appearance at every service of each set of revivals: the minister's whole family was expected to attend all services and social components. Carlisle dreaded those weeks, "a lot of preaching and a lot of eating," with services typically followed by trips to more groaning boards of country food, both dinners and suppers. The formidable church ladies vied to outdo each other in showcasing their special dishes, and to avoid offending anyone, everything had to be sampled and praised. Carlisle ate himself close to nausea on many a steamy southern evening; but despite enforced consumption, he was blessed with slenderness and high metabolism. Yet it is no wonder that dining al fresco, sharing meals in the heat with ambient insects, has held no charms for him as an adult.

His youthful exposure to religion represented more than a figurative trial by fire, with the stifling closeness of so many unventilated small spaces in South Carolina's summers, and endless hurled threats of damnation. By this time, he and Ermine had insulated themselves with exemplary behavior. Any tussling or picking at each other was reserved for the back seat of the family car. They may have been just ten and nine, but there was no note passing, eye rolling or whispering.

Carlisle was a far more serious child than his sister. In the dark of night, after a long day of being preached at, and stuffed with starches and country-fried meats, the siblings talked over what they had heard and felt. If Ermine failed to see the point of something, she might sigh, shrug, or fume, "How in the world do you get *saved*? You don't want to go to Hell, and they're telling us that's the only alternative. That's just silly."

But Carlisle, convinced of missed links in the chain of their logic, took it all very personally. There he sat in some tiny chapel, sweat pouring down through his clothes, packed against other bodies in varying states of heat and rising mass intoxication. Mama might be playing the pump organ at Sandy Grove, and they had to be role models. The walls had hundreds of eyes. Carlisle might fantasize making that star quarterback touchdown pass, or, eventually, playing a stunning recital, bowing before a cheering, stamping audience; but even then, he could not compass descriptions of eternal flames licking at the edges of consciousness, obliterating pleasant reverie, scaring him half to death. Imagine something a million times hotter than summer in Bethune, with no such thing as spring, fall, or winter: "You know you've done something, but can't quite put your finger on it. And you're going to Hell for it, unless. . . ."

The floor all but rumbled, matters of life and death absolute, immediate and very literal. Personal memory informs the stage directions for *Susannah*'s revival scene, during which a few cowed teenagers trudge like zombies to the altar.[25] Several times, Carlisle and Ermine were those young people. He was developing an uncomfortable sensitivity to mass coercion in this "violently mysterious life-and-death proposition. You simply bend the knee without question, the basis of any totalitarian society."[26] He and Ermine knew what they were expected to do, and they did not disappoint; but lingering doubts and guilt over motivation and sincerity bred festering cankers in his childhood's core.

During those intense weeks, escape was not an option with guest preachers living at the parsonage. Just after sunrise, Carlisle might observe the visitor's severe devotions; and the stranger's presence increased the family's obligation to attend every service. Coming home with his head buzzing with horrific images, Carlisle prayed late into the nights that he would be spared the agonies of the damned. He was a good boy, respectful of his elders, diligent in duties and studies. In time, this atmosphere provoked resentment at what felt like focused attempts to shackle his spirit.

JACK AND IDA continued to marvel at their son's drawing. He saw nothing remarkable in these skills or its products, but adored finding coloring books and pencils beneath successive Christmas trees. Up to his tenth birthday, in laughing hours of flying pencils with his sister or cousin Helen, he played magazine illustrator, dashing off one alluring sketch after another. He thought them whimsies, but Ermine declared them every bit as good as the beautiful people of famed commercial artist Jon Whitcomb.[27]

One episode of art making caused violent ripples in the family. Carlisle had drawn and cut out elaborate sets of paper dolls for years, for Ermine and Helen, but now he asked for a real doll. Jack was horrified, especially as his tomboy daughter had never shown interest in such things. All of hers seemed pitiful, shabby, bedraggled; but Jack's very resistance inflamed Carlisle, and a doll suddenly seemed essential. On a visit from childless aunt Doris and husband J. W. Moore, this uncle saved the day by laughing, "Oh Jack, just get the boy the doll," and he and Ida finally did. It turned out that all Carlisle wanted was to paint its face, for Ermine as much as for himself. Above and beyond the art, he had no idea what to do with it, and the beautifully made-up plaything languished.

At the same time, cowboy gear seized his interest, the snap-pop of cap pistols ringing in his ears. With the family sitting around the Christmas tree, a box of new dress-up clothes for church or visiting relatives offered little fun; but when a football jersey, Western shirt, or set of leather chaps emerged from tissue paper, the metamorphosis from Reverend Floyd's good boy to star quarterback, Wild Bill Hickok, or Hopalong Cassidy was quick and satisfying.

Model ships and planes also became passions. The great Cunard ocean liner *Queen Mary* embarked on its maiden voyage in May 1937, and a scale model kit turned up under the tree that Christmas. A few weeks later, Jack recorded that he was still "helping Carlisle with his boat."[28] After Pan American's Giant Clipper made its first flight in 1938, Carlisle spent hours cutting precise slivers of balsa wood with razor blades and gluing them together for his replica.

The great world entered the Floyds' home on March 17, 1938, when well-heeled parishioner James King gave Jack a used Atwater Kent Tombstone console radio, and the instrument took pride of place in the parlor. Ringed about in a breathless hush, the family listened to transatlantic voices crackle over sputtering static, as Adolf Hitler shrieked from Germany. Nightly news gave anything but reassurance, though commentators like Edward R. Murrow and Lowell Thomas did their best to soothe. Carlisle felt terror in September 1938 when Jack explained prime minister Neville Chamberlain's speeches: England had caved in to Germany's invasion of Czechoslovakia, another sobering preview of things to come. Jack's diary entry for November 21 reflected his newspaper reading "about [the] raw deal German Jews are getting." Carlisle watched trains shuttle soldiers back and forth to the opposite of certain life, and it was time to put away the military toys. Family emotions ran high, and Carlisle had an asthma attack the next day.

More relaxed Floyd rituals found the laughing family at comedy programs like *Lum and Abner.*[29] This duo of Arkansas country wits, voiced by comedians Chester Lauck and Norris Goff, ran a general store in Pine Ridge, their grandiose schemes carrying them to the brink of regular disaster. Clear parallels between these riotous characters and Olive Ann Burns's Rucker Lattimore and his cohorts would inform Carlisle's *Cold Sassy Tree* in another sixty-two years.

Another favorite was *Amos and Andy,*[30] spawned from minstrel show traditions of Caucasian performers in blackface. White comedians Freeman Gosden and Charles Correll played all the male roles, in the misadventures of two farm workers from Georgia who moved to Chicago and launched a taxi company. Though this perennial favorite of many American families relieved a few wartime horrors, it left no discernable traces in Carlisle's operas. His black character Nicey in *The Passion of Jonathan Wade* is anything but a stereotype.

When the radio was not on, Carlisle loved board games like Pollyanna and Monopoly. Chinese checkers was another particular favorite, and Jack's diaries record family tournaments. Reverend Floyd even tolerated certain nonwagering card games, like Lexicon, a forerunner of Scrabble, in which each card was marked with a letter, and players built words. Also popular were Old Maid, Rook, Authors, Bang Bird, and Battle, which Carlisle thought the world's least sensible card game. When other amusements paled, or weather or sickness discouraged outdoor activity, Jack fitted their round dining room table with a net for ping-pong. Many mornings, Carlisle and Ermine played before walking to school. Ida had no interest in joining in, but Jack could never resist. Most games ended with him trouncing the children.

Jack had a conflicted view of popular entertainment, and his ministerial persona alternately disdained, suspected, and craved motion pictures. Bethune had no theater, but Camden and Hartsville, both twenty miles from home, and Bishopville, sixteen miles afield, did. Jack censored, but in an era when the Hays Office oversaw most of Hollywood's family-appropriate output, opportunities abounded to see most anything new on a nearby screen. The children nagged, and thrifty Ida put enough aside for regular cinematic indulgences. She found the more genteel actors with anglicized elocution gratifying. Leslie Howard and Ronald Colman epitomized her ideal male; Clark Gable's overt sensuality struck her as a little raw. Carlisle found the cartoons moderately entertaining, but prized *News of the Day* and previews. Events and personalities in Europe seemed terrifying, riveting accidents from which he could not look away, especially the ranting little German lunatic with the brush mustache.

Carlisle and Ermine played movie star, acting out scenes as Robert Taylor and Jeannette McDonald, and as screen partners like Eleanor Powell, Irene Dunne, or Nelson Eddy. They spent hours re-creating scenes they had heard or seen from shows like the Screen Guild Theatre's radio production *A Song for Clotilde.* McDonald and Eddy played exiled royals who meet and fall in love, unaware of the other's lineage.[31] Or, after inhaling *Magnificent Obsession* (1936), Carlisle strode back and forth under the backyard chinaberry trees, declaiming Taylor's speeches as Dr. Robert Merrick:

> MERRICK. Take this back to the cook and tell her that if she brings it back again, I'm gonna buy this hospital and fire her and everybody else in it. I want some decent breakfast.
>
> NURSE. It's the same breakfast we serve all the patients.
>
> MERRICK. Yeah, but I am "The Special."

Director Frank Capra's 1937 film of James Hilton's novel *Lost Horizon,* with Ronald Colman, Jane Wyatt, and Sam Jaffe, made another lasting impression. A group of travelers finds its way into Shangri-la, a utopian kingdom hidden deep in the Himalayas. Toward the end, some of the new arrivals and longtime residents head back to civilization. The beautiful Maria, played by the Mexican American actress Margo, falls exhausted in the snow: once outside Shangri-la's enchanted borders, she reverts to her actual advanced age. Carlisle found this scene so terrifying that he almost bolted from his seat in the Hartsville theater. Decades later, at a Kennedy Center Awards program in Washington, he still felt uneasy astonishment at beholding the living Margo, the object of his childhood terror, now a woman of almost seventy.

Music filled both the movies and Carlisle's head, and he picked out new tunes on the Kingsbury. He latched onto melodic lines with some ease, but his harmonizations left much to be desired. A lame self-defense that he was simply being original failed to impress Ida. She demanded, "If you insist on playing the piano, you've got to learn the notes." In other words, learn to read music. Now a sixth-grader at school, he was drilled in pitches, key, and time signatures by Miss Sarah Proctor. Ermine had already begun private piano study with Mrs. Augie Foster, wife of Bethune school superintendent J. C. Foster, and Jack insisted that Carlisle follow suit.

Even so, at no time during their youth did Jack or Ida give either child an inkling of any career path they thought might be best, much less how they felt about music as a life's work.

Ermine recalled Mrs. Foster as dignified and proper, citing that as one reason why she failed to learn much from her: "It was never any fun." But not so with Carlisle: After his first lesson, Mrs. Foster called on Ida with an encouraging report: "Carlisle's moving so fast that I'd like to give him an additional lesson a week." At no extra charge. Mrs. Foster taught him better music-reading skills, and disciplined him to observe dynamic markings and correct fingerings in scales and arpeggios. Other than that, for the two years he studied with her, "She pretty much gave me my head." Still, she expected him to practice at least a half hour each day.

More music in the house and Carlisle's hands created a firmer bond with his mother. He asked her about composers, and she shared the extent of her knowledge, augmented by Theodore Presser Company's 1925 *Little Lives of the Great Masters.*

Trained musician that she was, Ida's experience and opinions had their limits. She shared the time's prevailing wisdom that one played Bach only for technical exercise; Mozart was a stranger. Romantics like Chopin won her heart and praise, as did sentimental light classics of such composers as Anton Rubinstein, Massenet, Grieg, Godard, and MacDowell. Yet in the end, "Mama gave me my head as much as my other teachers did."

Carlisle began performing in public during sixth grade in the fall of 1937, but not as a pianist. Toward the end of the first week of May 1938, he succumbed to asthma, probably from rehearsal-induced anxieties; but by May 20 he was well enough for Bethune's public to hear him and Ermine in a musical version of the Snow White legend. Grandmother Fenegan, aunts Bunny and Lucile, cousin Helen, Ida and Jack watched them sing and act *Snow White and the Seven Dwarfs* at the schoolhouse.[32] Bethune sixth-graders traditionally got the leads, so fifth-grader Ermine was thrilled to land the title role. Carlisle played Carl the Huntsman. Neither remembers the experience, save feeling special in Ida's handmade costumes. Ermine loved her blue dress and bodice, and swirling an elegant, gleaming red chintz cape. In his hunter green outfit and peaked Tyrolean hat, sporting an enormous turkey feather, Carlisle felt jaunty.

In scene 2, Carl leads Snow White into the dark forest, where the wicked stepmother-queen has ordered the huntsman to kill the girl. Snow White laments that Carl robs happy young creatures of their lives; he answers by declaring, "Your highness, close beside the prosperous life you speak of stands Death, waiting to claim his own." He sings a song as sporty as his hat, "Old Death, he goes roving the wide world o'er,"[33] before confessing his dire mission. When Snow White reminds Carl that she once saved his child from a charging horse, he relents. Carlisle/Carl and Ermine/Snow White sang the duet "Good-bye my Princess/Farewell, thou huntsman good, May all good fairies guard me/thee," and the piece rushed headlong to its happy ending. Jack diarized, "Ermine and Carlisle did grand."[34]

Though it took Carlisle years to compose music of his own, *Snow White* places him in a rare category of composer, like Rossini, Gounod, and Samuel Barber, who gained some renown as singer-performers, if not in operatic venues. Carlisle never studied singing, and disparaged his vocal efforts; but as with sports, so the stage: desire trumped endowment, and for several years he was a passable singer of popular tunes. He also realized that Bethune offered no serious competition: if a boy wanted to be on stage, there he was. Ermine, far more extroverted than her brother, had most of the family's vocal talent; but Carlisle's devotion to stage performances continued into his twenties. By the time the Floyds left Bethune, he knew that he wanted to be a pianist; but when he began to write dramatic texts and music, he literally preached what he had practiced.

Fresh from *Snow White,* Carlisle was laid low by the most severe asthma attack he ever experienced. Jack dropped Ida and the children off for a visit to Doris in Asheville on June 20, and drove on to pastor's school in Columbia; but a terrifying escalation of symptoms convinced Carlisle that he hovered near death. Doris, though a Christian Scientist, also suffered from the malady and kept a store of "asthma cigarettes,"[35] inhaling the smoke, then puffing it out around Carlisle. Despite the foul odor, its effectiveness kept him reliant on this cure until adulthood.

But this time was different, and he continued to worsen. Ida wrote Jack to come take them home, which he did on June 29. Carlisle already felt better, but this again portended abstinence from Mama's fried chicken, replaced by a white diet of custards. Jack believed that plain grits had therapeutic properties to cure any ailment, and Carlisle went through plate upon bland plate. Thereafter, for the most severe attacks, ephedrine tablets were available and administered; otherwise, heated bourbon—the only permissible liquor in the house—lemon juice, and honey proved both salutary and pleasant.

BY SEPTEMBER 1938, Jack and Ida felt that times had improved, and decided to try for another child. Whether she conceived or miscarried, Jack did not record. The family's relative affluence also resulted in more frequent trips to the movies, purchases of a new watch and books for Carlisle, and, for Ida, a new Frigidaire refrigerator. Finally, and best of all, a spanking new black two-door Chevrolet 1939 Master Deluxe Town Sedan rolled fresh from the Mays showroom, sending Kershaw County the message that Reverend Floyd, in his first charge lasting more than a year, had arrived.

Carlisle completed seventh grade in 1938–1939. His class teacher, the most influential of a growing list, and also grammar school principal, was Herbert Fincher, a handsome, somewhat distant and formal man of parts, born in 1913. On his 1943 draft registration card, his profession is listed as "photographer and retouching artist."[36] Carlisle lionized him, emulating his handwriting with pride.

Fincher had mastered every subject but music, taught that year by Sidelle Ellis, who seemed a bit out of place in that setting, "what we'd call 'spacy' today, with an 'arty,' otherworldly air." When Ellis discovered that Carlisle took piano lessons, she singled him out as a prodigy and role model. One day she asked him to conduct the class in a song; then, to his mortal embarrassment, taking his hands in hers, declared, "Look how artistically Carlisle does that!"

The year 1939 began with even better financial portents for the Floyds. Jack continued to manage the Floyd holdings, selling the Latta house to his brother-in-law, Hazel's husband Frank Ellerbe, and dividing the proceeds between his siblings.

It rained a great deal that winter, bringing more than the usual flurries of colds, influenza, and asthma. Jack bought a new stove from Mr. Lonnie King, and Carlisle split more kindling and hauled more coal. There was heated family conversation about an entrepreneur's attempt to give Bethune its first liquor store. Jack prayed against the proposal for hours, always ending with "May God's will be done."

On April 7, Carlisle and Ermine performed in "Amateur Night in Dixie" at the schoolhouse: "What on earth prompted me to do that, why I thought I could or should perform, I do not know." His choice was the 1934 hit tune "Isle of Capri," with words by Jimmy Kennedy and music by Wilhelm Grosz, aka Hugh Williams. Though Carlisle remembered all three verses, someone else won.

With the onset of adolescent hormonal storms, Carlisle's problems with Jack grew more pointed, and reading and music brought escalating disapproval. No matter where Carlisle was or what he did, his father thought it the wrong place, the wrong activity. He wondered whether his father disliked him. Beginning early in 1939, such tensions were mirrored in Carlisle's absence from the usual Chinese checkers matches.

Even sibling rivalries erupted: Ermine adored her brother, and they were inseparable. He included her in his circle of friends, which was much more interesting to her than little girls; but when nettled, she had no hesitation in taking advantage of his constitutional anxiety. One day, on a detour home from school, they walked along the tracks when a long train pulled into town. Rather than trekking all the way to the end and back, they stood for a moment in the broiling afternoon sun, shifting their books from one arm to the other, debating what to do.

Exasperated, Ermine said, "I'm just going to crawl under it." Near panic, Carlisle watched his sister perform with the greatest of ease a maneuver they had been ordered never to contemplate, much less attempt. Although already a big boy, as Ermine observed with rue, Carlisle burst into tears. Seventy years later, she confessed, "I knew it would upset him; but it was just my way of getting at him."[37]

The last Bethune years also saw friction with aunt Bunny's husband Yates Gamble. Yates played practical jokes—he once gave Jack a cigar for Christmas—and bullied. He delighted in startling and frightening Carlisle by jumping out from hidden corners. Carlisle's insatiable curiosity about people made him turn around in church pews and stare at any given object of interest, letting his bottom jaw drop. If Yates was there, he lost no opportunity to humiliate by likening Carlisle to Willie Willis, a comic strip "goony boy."[38] As late as his thirties, Carlisle told Jack of the discomfort his uncle had caused him. Jack responded placidly, "I always meant to talk to Yates about that." Frequent asthma attacks before, during, and after Laurinburg visits reflect time spent around this uncle.

On May 26, the school promoted its twenty-nine seventh-graders to high school. Carlisle led his class in academics, graduating from what we think of today as middle or junior high school; yet aspects of the children's education nettled Jack and Ida. Ermine came home from a sixth-grade class one day, declaring, "Miz Castin says that in the objective case, first-person singular is 'to I.'" Wary of damaging confidence in a teacher, Ida corrected gently, "No, Ermine, you say 'to me,'" then lamented, "Your language, your speech, your grammar! You've picked up all the worst habits of the children around you."

Sixteen years later, such incidents drifted back to Carlisle, who realized that even educated people stray from proper usage. After his sermon in *Susannah*'s revival scene, Blitch invites his congregation's sinners to approach the altar, in much the same distortion of the objective case.[39] Far from excusing or ennobling poor grammar, Carlisle Floyd's characters simply speak the language of the men and women around whom he was raised.

That August, a deteriorating family situation coincided with world news exploding from the radio. On August 3, Jack records that it looked "as if Hitler will take Danzig; Japan continues to rape China." Carlisle heard Ida moan, "I don't know why good doesn't triumph over bad."

In summer's last weeks, Carlisle and Ermine pooled what money they had saved for an exciting Floyd first, a family trip to Washington, DC, arriving at a tourist home on August 23. The next four days of forced march may explain why the Floyds never took another family holiday of this scope. A guide showed them all the famous sights and sites, beginning with Ford's Theatre, witness to Lincoln's assassination, which Carlisle commemorated thirty-three years later in his multimedia choral work *The Martyr.* On August's last day, Jack got them up at six and drove back to the Washington Monument for photographs. By 9:40 that night, they reached Bethune, to the pleasant surprise that church ladies had cleaned and dusted the parsonage and laid a new living room rug.

The next day, September 1, Hitler's armies invaded Poland and the world was again at war, as Carlisle moved to a new classroom at the Bethune school to begin his first year of high school, eighth grade. On November 12, Jack attended District Conference in Orangeburg, and learned from Bishop Purcell that he was being moved to North, South Carolina.

The stunned family began saying goodbyes. Carlisle was devastated. At thirteen, he had formed attachments that might be supplemented but never replaced. Spending four years in the same town had created an emotional home in which the physical structure played the smallest role. Ever after, Bethune represented idyllic green summer, light and color, a golden, carefree time of growth, discovery, and independence. One of Floyd's recurring dreams is of Bethune: "For so long, I kept returning to something that was obviously very important. And I'm still not quite certain what's going on in my dream, except the idea of pleasure at going back: I can detour over *here,* and get *there.*"

Bethune helped him get to other places. He learned the dynamic of adult relationships and psychology, and basic intellectual knowledge about human sexuality, if not its practices. Four years of vigorous physical exercise had kept him strong and healthy, better at coping with the onslaughts of asthma. His observation and participation had caused him to question much of the religious activity in which he had been immersed, without destroying his core belief in a supreme guiding intelligence; and without those summer revivals, it is impossible to imagine *Susannah.*

Reading took him from boyhood entertainments across the threshold of great literature; and the movies had hooked him. Bethune's soil had saturated his observations and experiences of people, motivations, events, institutions, and history; and it is there that seed-themes were sown that informed the operas that would make him famous.

DURING ONE DAY'S RARE LEISURE, Ida leafed through her piano albums, paused, and shaped her fingers to Chopin's Etude in E Minor, op. 28, no. 4. Wherever Carlisle was, whatever he was about, he stopped: this was a different kind of music, with its endless transparent right-hand melody rising and falling like a litany of sighs, the left hand's minimalistic chords shifting in subtle chromatic increments. It spoke to some reserve of emotion beyond the boy's vocabulary: "It pushed me into music: Here was an art form that expressed something absolutely beyond words, but still very real."

For the first time, he grew aware that he had fallen up *into music.* From humble beginnings, the worm of excitement from performing had begun to turn. The practical experiences of using his voice on stage, feeling what was grateful or not to sing, the timing that got laughs from line readings and physical comedy, what pleased audiences, instilled a love for singing and singers: the high-performance vehicle that took Carlisle Floyd to that life in music of which he dreamt.

Another poem of Oscar Fenegan's from this period offers a Janus-headed past/future reflection on much that unfolded in Carlisle's life. Away from Mrs. Kate's severe eye, Oscar sat on his manicured lawn in the Laurinburg cemetery, surrounded by tombstones old and mossy, his son James's all too new. Clouded by grief, his words exhaled loss and the ravages of time.

His customary fine hand shook a bit on the page that came down to Carlisle in more ways than one:

> Youth is not—a time of life—
> it is a state of mind.
> It is a temper of the voice, a quality
> of the imagination, a vigor of the
> deep springs of life.
> Nobody grows old by living a number
> of years. People grow old by deserting
> their ideals.
> You are as young as your faith, as
> old as your doubt,
> as young as your self-confidence, as
> old as your fear;
> as young as your hope, as old
> as your despair.
> In the central place of your heart
> there is a wireless station.
> So long as it receives messages
> of beauty, hope, cheer, grandeur,
> courage & power from the
> earth, from men and from
> the Infinite, so long are you young.[40]

About to spend his last night in Bethune, Carlisle pondered his enjoyment of time and place. Sixty-seven years later, America's most famous living composer of opera set his jaw and stated the simple fact, "Then things turned darker."

4

Dark Adolescence

North, 1939–1943

Thanksgiving 1939 brought cold shivers at North's parsonage, which smelled the grayish white of old plaster. On Tuesday that week, Frank Morse, Jack's Presbyterian counterpart in Bethune, helped pack and load Mr. Loring's truck with cherished pieces of furniture, family piano, chickens, and new Frigidaire. The ninety-mile trek from Bethune down Highway 1 began at six a.m. They discovered a sign of things to come when water couldn't be shut off in their new home.[1]

North, in the heart of South Carolina's limestone area, was home to about 730 persons in 1939. Today, driving south from Columbia, the road slips over a rise, and suddenly it's upon you: a strip mall of dead and dying storefronts. In 1939, a movie theater glimmered mecca, the first such in-town oasis on any of the Floyds' Methodist caravan stops.

Blackwater forms the town's southern boundary, a swampy creek off the Edisto River's north fork. With its inevitable bisecting railroad tracks, the town's money lives on the west side, in fine old homes on shaded lots, though conditions may have been different during the Floyds' residence. Today, other streets are spotted with ghost cottages old when the Floyds moved in; overstuffed couches and other discarded comforts molder in the rain. North's older, better-educated citizens—compared to Bethune's—had marginal tolerance for high-spirited children. In their four years here, Jack and Carlisle often fell ill; and Reverend Floyd held a higher proportion of funerals than at most of his pastorates.

On the east side of Main, at the corner of Salley Road and Dogwood Drive, sits the imposing North United Methodist Church.[2] A white dome lends its architecture a Byzantine flavor, but the edifice looms severe. Though Jack had just one satellite church, Limestone, about a ten-mile drive toward Orangeburg, the county seat, his weekly calendar remained packed. In addition to all the chores practiced at earlier assignments, the Sabbath brought morning church school and services at both facilities, Sunday evening services, and Wednesday prayer meetings. Frequent thirty-mile trips to hospitals in Columbia, and nineteen to Orangeburg, plus the constant to-and-fro of family visitations, added wear and tear on bodies and car.

But Jack had moved up; he had an annual salary of $1,500 and a supplementary operating fund of $600. He could now ease Ida's load by hiring a black washerwoman/housekeeper/cook, Catherine Govan, soon a family favorite. Once, when Catherine arrived at the back door, he told her, "You come in the front. You do more for us than any white person I know." The scent of clothes washed in Ivory soap each week bubbled from iron cauldrons in the backyard.

North brought Carlisle four years of escalating stress, coinciding with the natural cycle of puberty. As his self-importance ballooned, Jack seemed puzzled. His narcissism conflicted with Carlisle's longing for role modeling and nurture, but Reverend Floyd remained oblivious of his own affect. Constitutional tactlessness produced wounding sarcasm, and taking down the easiest target, Carlisle, heightened Jack's sense of omnipotence.

The gaunt white frame parsonage filled Carlisle with dread, despite having two stories, a family first. Indoors smelled of that dirty-plaster mix of mold and must. Combined with the mothball odor wafting from Ida's cedar chest, it made eyes water.

The structure offered space devoid of comfort or central heating, much less cooling: the downstairs parlor and dining room, and the kitchen behind, drew heat from fireplaces. The parental bedroom lay on the ground floor as well, adjoining a single bathroom that the whole family used, with scant, malodorous heat trickling from a kerosene appliance. Water again came from an outdoor pump, requiring stovetop warming for baths.

For a brief time, Carlisle and Ermine relished the novelty of second-story bedrooms, separated by a hall; but unlike Bethune's parsonage, when guest preachers rolled into North for revival weeks, Carlisle faced eviction to a couch or floor pallet downstairs, or a neighbor's house.

The structure has been gone for years, but the yard is still tree-filled, as in the composer's short fiction "Which Shall Not Perish from the Earth": "The weeds were tall and thick. . . . They were dying. Everything seemed transient—nothing stable and immobile."[3]

Besides a chicken coop, the yard allowed a garden plot about thirty feet square, larger than any they had farmed. The family's love of fresh vegetables guaranteed hot months of toil for Carlisle.

As with all of Reverend Floyd's postings, both church and personal mail had to be picked up from post office boxes; but in the hall hung a new and formidable convenience, a hand-crank telephone. Carlisle had never been, nor sought to be, adept with things mechanical. Given Jack's natural abilities, and the growing friction between father and son, the former could never have tolerated any degree of competition from the latter, and Carlisle had his terror of the apparatus reinforced for months. When it rang, he ran through the house to find someone, *anyone,* to answer it; his using it for outgoing calls remained beyond the pale.

Ridicule and self-recrimination made him a quick study, though, as adolescence struck. His voice had begun to change in Bethune, but in North it reached that awkward stage when the larynx can't seem to choose between soprano and baritone. When his heritage of dark, hirsute Welshness manifested, he began to shave; and once begun, there was no mediation or truce with that beard. True to form, jokey uncle Yates, now a successful broker for Metropolitan Life in Laurinburg, found his nephew's new toilette hilarious. Yates and irrepressible Granddaddy Oscar gave the boy no peace, much less pride, about this normal masculine development.

When darker storms brewed, Carlisle took solace in a roomy porch swing for secure conversations with Ermine, wound licking, reading, study, homework. From a sawmill on the town's outskirts wafted the sweet-pungent resinous odor of "lightwood," pine kindling, as he sat absorbed in the sparkling language and madcap plots of Booth Tarkington's *Penrod* and *Seventeen,* featuring boys who could and did behave independently, apparently not an option for Floyds.

AS JACK ABSTRACTED HIMSELF in the transition from Thanksgiving to Christmas, the children scrambled to catch up at the newer, more populous and competitive two-story brick school. Overall enrollment that fall was about one hundred, Carlisle's eighth grade around fifteen, and he walked the half mile from home across the railroad tracks. In cases of torrential rain, winter cold snaps, or serious respiratory infection, Jack piled them into the Chevy.

Almost fifty years later, one of Carlisle's teachers, Margaret Morgan, recalled him that first year: "Besides teaching math, I used to work in the library and [Carlisle] would help me with bulletin boards. We used to argue about it. He once said to me, 'If you were doing a bulletin board about the Ten Commandments you'd do it in red, white, and blue.' He wanted it to be more soft and tasteful."

But the lady had no idea what was in this boy's future: "You can't tell what a seventh-grader's going to do."[4]

Yet Mrs. Morgan described a confident, assertive Carlisle, in a comfort zone surrounded by books and art. In a matter of weeks, his musical and linguistic gifts pulled him into dedicated paths, just as his nimble hands and feet brought him to school sports. At home, Jack, Carlisle, and his friends again played touch football. With spring's bloom-bursting, Jack suffered such terrible allergy and asthma attacks that Carlisle had to hose down the front yard and adjacent dirt street to keep dust and pollen out of his father's sinuses and lungs, as well as Ida's pin-neat house.

As Christmas approached, the family drew close around the fire, playing Pollyanna, a track-pursuit board game derived from Parcheesi, or Monopoly. Escalating war in Europe broadcast terror from the radio. On December 27, after delivering gifts to the Epworth Orphanage in Columbia, the Floyds watched seven thousand soldiers parade through the city.

The year's turn to 1940 brought a nasty cold streak, rain, and snow. A troop of parishioners "pounded" the Floyds with eggs, milk, butter, quail, fish, ham, and sausage. Jack bought a ton of coal in mid-January, and Carlisle's chores again included hauling fuel, cutting kindling, starting fires, helping his mother with the garden and chickens, hoeing weeds from shrubbery beds, mowing and raking the park-sized lawn, and delivering weekly church bulletins.

Some compensation came from increased moviegoing; yet the higher Jack climbed on the clerical ladder, the more conflicted he grew about popular entertainment. As late as 1943, a classic like *Casablanca* found no favor with him: "Not much picture. Too much drinking."[5] When Carlisle or Ermine begged to go to Saturday matinees, their father's first response was negative. Carlisle developed a tactic, claiming that the film was based on a book, even if that source was a Western by Zane Grey. Eventually, perhaps thirty or forty minutes into the feature, Jack might change his mind, spoiling any chance of their seeing the entire picture. Also, with allowances of twenty-five cents, compared to the thirty-five-cent price of admission, the children could only go on alternate weeks.

On January 26, the mercury plummeted to ten degrees, and every body of water in the region froze. Ida sickened for weeks with a new pregnancy in February. Jack was elated: between running back and forth to Bethune to conduct funerals there, he declared, "The child has already been dedicated to God."[6]

Meanwhile, North High drafted Carlisle to accompany the mixed glee club's populist music on the piano.

The Dougherty family—Mrs. Imogene played organ at North Methodist—occupied roles of increasing importance in Carlisle's musical and social life. On February 23, these new friends took him to Columbia to hear Spanish pianist-conductor José Iturbi's recital.[7]

With spring's thaw, Jack and Carlisle worked the garden, preparing beds and planting six rows of corn and three of butter beans. Some years they set out as many as one hundred tomato plants. Yet winter lingered on, and March 26 saw the coldest temperature recorded there for this day, twenty-six degrees. Jack wrote that he "helped" Carlisle with coal and wood chores, the preacher's euphemism for telling his son he was doing everything wrong.

Ida's pregnancy began to show, and her illness worsened. While Jack sat at the bedside, uncle Sonny used the parsonage as a base for selling Bibles and magazine subscriptions, and drove Carlisle and Ermine to Orangeburg to see the first run of *Gone With the Wind* on March 30. Max Steiner's symphonic score lingered in Carlisle's memory as a veritable southern hymnody.

In the middle of the night between April 5 and 6, Ida awoke in searing pain, bleeding. Jack summoned Dr. Fort, and at 5:30 that morning he and Sonny took her to hospital in Orangeburg. A hundred days into her pregnancy, the baby was lost.

Ida and Jack now traded supine positions: under doctor's orders, he took to bed with a vicious asthma attack. Ida drove Carlisle and Ermine to school on the evening of April 19 for their next theatrical venture, *The Blue Fairy.* North High was too small to boast an instrumental ensemble. French teacher Betty Weber, also a skilled pianist, provided keyboard accompaniment for musicals, and Carlisle assisted either her or Miss Minni Walker with the staging. Ermine played the eponymous Blue Fairy, a character prominent in retellings of the Pinocchio story, responsible for the boy's transformation from puppet to human. This was actually the operetta *The Adventures of Pinocchio,* with book by Theodosia Paynter and music based on Italian folk songs by Canadian composer George Alfred Grant-Schaefer (1872–1939).[8]

By the end of April, Jack was up again, and "helping" Carlisle mark off a rudimentary tennis court between trees in the parsonage's backyard. Tripping a grotesque jig to avoid gnarled roots, they played their first three games early the next month, igniting another of Carlisle's lifelong passions.

A week later, on May 10, Hitler's *Wehrmacht* invaded Holland and Belgium, and Neville Chamberlain resigned as Britain's prime minister. Jack's diary reads, "The war is terrible. *What will stop Hitler?*" The next day, British forces narrowly escaped annihilation at Dunkirk.

Just before turning fourteen, Carlisle looked down a short tunnel of years to draft age should America be drawn into the European crisis, still unthinkable from the fastness of rural South Carolina. For that June 11 birthday, Jack gave him a dollar, and took him and Ermine for a swim at Haley's Pond. The next day, the minister wrote, "Poor France!" On June 21 and 22, that country surrendered to Hitler in the same railway coach in which the World War I armistice so humiliating to Germany had been signed. Carlisle found nothing funny about Hitler's celebratory jig in movie newsreels.

In mid-July, Carlisle and new best friend Sam Dougherty, Imogene's son, boarded the bus for Methodist Camp Forest. The rustic facility, 121 miles distant (in present-day Cheraw State Park), on Lake Juniper, offered a week of healthy outdoor activity without parental observation, all for $1.25. Meals for up to one hundred twenty boys in the dining hall, inevitable worship services, swimming, boating through cypress wetlands, hiking, and nature watching became annual events. The day he and Sam got home, they wished they were still swimming, as it reached 108 in North's shade; but camping offered Carlisle welcome relief from world news, not to mention the first round of Jack's 1940 revivals.

Education focused at summer's end, when school superintendent Nathan Lynch approached Jack and Ida with a plan to push Carlisle up from the path trod by many of his classmates. With the state's economy still dominated by agriculture, Future Farmers of America remained the typical boy's most prestigious extracurricular activity. Lynch observed that a little rule bending seemed in order for one of Carlisle's talent: Why saddle him with agricultural or wood- or metal-shop courses when it was apparent that French was a subject that he might actually use one day? With Jack's salary raised to $1,600, he dutifully rolled to Orangeburg to purchase the required text, as school doors opened on Carlisle's ninth-grade (sophomore) year.

Summer waned, weeds filled the shrubbery beds, and Carlisle took up his hoe. Jack "helped": "Son, you missed a patch." There always seemed to be errant strips of lawn that Carlisle hadn't mowed. Pecans needed picking and shelling, and Carlisle shinnied up the trees to shake them from branches, Jack's pedantic exhortations spoiling an otherwise pleasurable challenge.

At the same time, adolescent plagues of bolting, gangly growth, and pimples descended, as well as a ten-day resurgence of the boils he had suffered in McClellanville. Yet Carlisle went on to win election as sophomore class president, junior vice president, and senior treasurer, and induction into the Beta Club, a scholastic honor society. This spiraled into work as graphic arts editor of the school newspaper, the mimeograph machine's fumes an intoxicating elixir. He wrote editorials, cut stencils, drew cartoon illustrations, assisted by his mentor, superintendent Lynch.

Carlisle had taken no piano lessons since leaving Bethune the previous fall, and again felt music's tidal pull. The best teacher North offered at the moment was his French teacher, Betty Weber, with whom he studied for the next year. Ida also thought it time to introduce him to opera, that sublime but daunting combination of all the arts. Columbia's NBC affiliate reached North with the Metropolitan Opera's Saturday broadcasts, and on December 14 they tuned in to Verdi's *Un Ballo in Maschera,* with Zinka Milanov as Amelia and Jussi Björling as Riccardo.

Later, sitting around the kitchen table, Ida asked the children their opinions on the music of a composer whose name she pronounced as "Vairdee," with the "r" properly flipped. Carlisle and Ermine rolled their eyes and retorted, "Oh Mama, everybody knows that's *Vurr*-dee."

Ida disabused the children, but Carlisle was still too focused on the piano to take much notice of this strange new medium, even if his ear for languages picked up his mother's insistence on proper pronunciation. In those days he caught only bits and pieces of Met broadcasts, but found them oddly intriguing.

Over the holidays in Laurinburg, world news was anything but encouraging: London lay in ruins from German bombing, and the Floyds heard Edward R. Murrow's signature line: "This is not a Merry Christmas in London. . . . I should like to add my small voice to give my own Christmas greeting . . . [with] the current London phrase: So long and good luck."[9]

The more acclaim Carlisle accrued, the more complicated the relationship with his father became; and 1941 marked a new beginning. As the mature composer later observed, "Child rearing and nurture was left to other people; but you can't explain that to a child. Then a boy turns eighteen or twenty-one, and Daddy sees, 'Oh, I have a son'; and you go from being ignored to being a rival. Interesting and devastating."

Jack's idea of father-son bonding in those months involved Carlisle in a chapter of the Methodist Epworth League youth group that he tried to establish at Limestone, in effect pressing his son between stained glass windows. A year or so of Boy Scout membership, once he learned to tie the knots, proved more enlightening and enjoyable.

Jack loved preaching. To further distinguish, he loved *having* preached, being himself worshiped: emotional transubstantiation, even without a reliable barometer for content or effectiveness of public utterances. His ego was never better-fed than when greeting parishioners after services, and the children soon learned that if they sought favors or permissions, that was the time to ask.

At home, the inevitable separation of child from parent, the mythical paradigm of wars of independence, unfolded by fits and starts. Jack's professional absorption and Ida's continuing miscarriages coincided with more frequent and severe asthma attacks for both father and son. Carlisle now found that his father's attention came with scolding for any manifestation of negligence, real or imagined. It put the boy in a familiar bind: he couldn't make a right choice. Only the shared activity of playing catch gave any pleasure. If Jack walked in while Carlisle practiced piano, a hard knot formed in the pit of the boy's stomach, and he stopped. His father invariably asked whether he'd fetched the coal yet. Had he split kindling? Any hint of defiance or contradiction in Carlisle's answers elicited Jack's dismissal to go help Ida with *her* mountain of chores.

Reverend Floyd brooked no anger or disobedience in his household. Outdoors, the badgering intensified: the volume of trees meant weeks of leaf raking into piles for burning. Jack hectored, "No, son, you should've made two piles instead of one big one." No right way existed, and the boy's resentment crystallized into a lump of cold but silent fury. The sun had set, chill suffused the dank air, but Carlisle refused to come indoors. Well before psychology popularized the concept of "acting out," Carlisle grew adept at epitomizing his emotion, despite eliciting little comfort from anyone.

The inescapable conclusion that Carlisle drew from these calcifying patterns was that his father simply didn't like him, that Jack would have been happier without his son in sight; so Carlisle did his best to stay invisible.

Before and after resuming formal piano instruction, he received inspiration from two unrelated teachers with the same surname, Marvene and Minni Walker. The former, from an old aristocratic Savannah family, had earned the distinction of a master's degree and taught history; but it was English teacher Minni who captured the lion's share of Carlisle's attention.

When Orangeburg County's library truck visited school, students had no access; but Minni Walker charged aboard to select volumes to guide Carlisle's reading. Augmenting Dickens and Twain, Minni pulled him up into the twentieth century with popular and controversial writers like Louis Bromfield (1896–1956), who peopled his worlds with sophisticated, brittle cosmopolitans, living out tense family dramas about changing generational mores.

And then, Sinclair Lewis (1885–1951); Jack wasn't at all sure about him, affirming, without having read a word, "I don't like that fellow Lewis"; but then he wouldn't, given Lewis's treatments of small-town, class-oriented life in *Main Street* (1920), *Babbitt* (1922), *Arrowsmith* (1925), *Dodsworth* (1929), and especially his exposé of corrupt revivalists in *Elmer Gantry* (1927). However unconsciously, Carlisle's future priorities are encapsulated in Lewis's acceptance speech as America's first Nobel Prizewinner for Literature in 1930:

> In America most of us . . . are still afraid of any literature which is not a glorification of everything American.

With each of Carlisle's reading enthusiasms, the interplay and variations of usage, the magic of words in the mouths of earthy characters, took him to finer places; and he never lost sight of how writers achieve their effects. If he stumbled over a word, he added it to a growing vocabulary list for memorization.

Gentle subversion enhanced his reading in 1942: uncle G. R., professor of English, whom we have seen eager to puncture younger brother Jack's grandiosity, sent Carlisle a new and scandalous book, *Kings Row* (1940), by Henry Bellamann.

Bellamann (1882–1945) for a time served as literary editor for Columbia, South Carolina's *State* newspaper, but his first profession was music, which he taught on the faculties of Juilliard and Vassar. He became one of the few critics of his generation to write about music without condescension, and without treating it as an alien activity.[10]

One wonders at G. R.'s daring in picking this book for his nephew. It achieved some notoriety because of its frank eroticism and exploration of homosexuality. Like Bellamann and Carlisle, the protagonist, Parris Mitchell, is a musician and poet who grows aware of concentric circles of self.

In addition to steering Carlisle's reading, Minni Walker directed the school's plays and operettas. North High's theatrical ventures offered independence from the repression of selfhood that life with Jack required; and, like most fourteen-year-old boys, Carlisle had a streak of the show-off. On February 21, 1941, voice fully changed to tenor range, he appeared as Nanki-Poo in an adaptation of Gilbert and Sullivan's *The Mikado*. (Ermine sang one of the female roles.) His principal solo, "A Wand'ring Minstrel I," with its Italianate line and turns, gave first-hand exposure to the bel canto that would later influence his vocal compositions.

Jack's diary attests, "Carlisle and Ermine did well"; but he rewarded both with weeks of renewed labor in the garden, planting corn, green and butter beans, okra, squash, and peas.

Carlisle continued his obligatory half hour of practice each day, with extra time devoted to his flashiest piece, *Tam o' Shanter*. Just after receiving a special-order copy, and dying to tear into it, he rushed into the living room, where Jack lay on a couch, wheezing from asthma: "Daddy, I got *Tam o' Shanter*!" Rain on this modest parade fell from Jack's baleful glance, as he sneered with disgust, "Oh, Carlisle."[11]

Jack moderated his antipathy when he reported Carlisle's participation in a school recital on May 8: "Carlisle played real well." Outside the church, superlatives were never Reverend Floyd's forte.

In the senior class play, Charles George's *Bringing Up Mother* (1935), again directed by Minni Walker, Carlisle shifted aesthetic gears as the school year rushed to its conclusion. This time he acted the witty, acerbic butler Marmaduke, in George's droll treatment of inept American social climbers in England. The character may have been minor, but his lines and actions are pure comedy, teaching vital lessons of timing and delivery. In the final scene, menaced at gunpoint by rough-and-ready Idaho Ike, Marmaduke collides with a pretentious lady in search of status, who orders him, "Look where you're going." Chagrined, but faced in the direction of the armed cowboy, Marmaduke bows, "I'm so sorry Madame—but I can hardly go where I'm looking."

The best Jack could do was, "Carlisle played the part of the butler."[12]

With school out, health issues took the front seat as allergies and a deviated septum brought Carlisle to a Dr. Truluck in Orangeburg. The physician's name proved anything but auspicious: his treatments involved clamps to hold the nasal cavities stretched and immobile, followed by multiple injections to interior surfaces, all without anesthesia. Carlisle's fifteenth birthday gift was surgery by Dr. Truluck to correct the anomaly; but treatments continued until mid-September.

Attending camp or going to Columbia for piano lessons spared Carlisle most of the North and Limestone revivals; but August 1941 brought a veritable southern Savonarola to the parsonage: long-lived Henry Bennett (1909–2002), whom Carlisle found ascetic and severe, practicing such disciplines as fasting and solitary prayer before preaching. Bennett displayed no traces of humor or lightness. With sermon titles like "All Are Sinners," "Repentance," and "Strive to Enter In" reflecting a fire-breathing, narrow-lipped focus, Bennett provided direct inspiration for *Susannah*'s tormented Olin Blitch.

Carlisle allowed school, housework, and yard work to supplant piano practice, and Ida put her foot down. It was high time to temper his *Tam o' Shanter* enthusiasms and focus on more refined, rigorous training, with Bach *Inventions* and Haydn sonatas; and he needed a different piano. On Monday, September 8, the whole family drove to Columbia, arranged a $55 trade-in on the Kingsbury, and bought a $450 Howard, Baldwin's budget trademark.

Organist Imogene Dougherty's daughter had studied with the state's best private piano teacher, Margarette Richards in Columbia.[13] Ida, at Jack's astonishing insistence, arranged Carlisle's audition for this formidable, well-dressed maiden lady, who taught lessons through and at Columbia College, where Jack attended pastor's school each spring. Added to monthly payments of $18.17 for the new piano, the biweekly lessons and drives to Columbia were enormous commitments for the family. Once gasoline rationing was imposed in May 1942, Jack justified his preacher's exemption by visiting sick parishioners in the city's hospitals, or attending to Epworth Orphanage business. His salary grew to $1,700 that fall, and Carlisle's practice time increased to a minimum of an hour daily.

Carlisle saw at once the breadth of the leap from the pedagogies of Augie Foster and Betty Weber to that of Richards, which was based on scales and arpeggios. Her French school of playing emphasized raised, strengthened fingers for better articulation, and playing octaves from the end of the wrists. To Carlisle, Richards, in reality just forty-one that year, seemed ancient.

His eagerness to perform advanced repertoire met a solid wall: "She held my feet to the fire. Miss Richards told *me* what I wanted to do." He suffered a week-long asthmatic attack after his third lesson. Richards either thought little of his talent, or withheld any hint of approbation. Ida, frustrated, tried numerous strategies to ferret out Richards's assessment; she reinforced the sacrifice they were making, but the most she ever elicited was the cryptic—and, one senses, *practiced*—statement from Richards, "He certainly seems to love it."

Initially, the piano formed a bond between Carlisle and his mother; but once the Richards lessons began, Carlisle played repertoire Ida didn't know, and music slipped from family conversations. His teachers, school and private, replaced the emotional component lacking at the parsonage.

By November 1941, Carlisle alternated basketball with play practice for another butler role—but this time adding the spice of acting a jewel thief—in *The Marlenburg Necklace* by James C. Parker.

Basketball duplicated some of his Bethune experiences with baseball, enthusiasm unequaled by skill; but the sport's intense hand-eye coordination had enormous value, especially since Jack wasn't coaching. At home, under their hoop, Jack was a favorite with his children's friends; but even here, he strove to defeat Carlisle.

North's boys won about as many as they lost. Once during a game, Carlisle sprained his right wrist after a fall. For weeks, lessons, practicing, and playing for the glee club were not improved by bandages down to the first knuckle of the injured appendage.

Outside school, North offered few distractions, and class plays, operettas, and sports counteracted Carlisle's lack of confidence. These activities were among the last in which he would engage for sheer delight, for the thing in and of itself.

Everything screeched to a halt with news of Japan's attack on the United States naval base at Hawaii's Pearl Harbor. The next day, President Roosevelt issued his declaration of war, characterizing December 7 as "a date which will live in infamy." In school, Carlisle and his peers heard reminders that neither Japan nor America had ever lost a war; but abstract fears now yielded to reality. Speculation about the future was rendered moot: uncle Sonny enlisted in the Army Air Corps and would soon be on his way to New Guinea in the South Pacific. Carlisle had two and a half more years until his eighteenth birthday.

After a family Christmas in Laurinburg, on New Year's Eve Jack and Carlisle drove Sonny to Ft. Jackson outside Columbia for examination and induction. The three ate dinner in the mess hall, as Carlisle craned around to assess his likely future.

CARLISLE SAW HIS FIRST OPERA in early 1942, a production of *Carmen* by the Charles L. Wagner touring company in Columbia. Framed by flimsy soft-goods sets and moth-eaten costumes, Bizet's gypsies and soldiers provoked little more than aversion in the future composer of thirteen musical dramas.

More to his taste was a solo recital at Columbia College on January 16 by the Russian pianist-composer Sergei Rachmaninoff (1873–1943). The great man, equally renowned for virtuosity and funereal deportment, already suffered from the cancer that would end his life a year later. He plodded onto the stage with such deliberation, adjusting his cuffs while waiting out the audience's restless ovation. Jack delighted in imitating the scene for years to come. The program included Liszt's transcription of Bach's Prelude and Fugue in A Minor, the Liszt chestnut Liebestraum no. 3 in A-flat Major, and, inevitably, Rachmaninoff's own famed Prelude in C-sharp Minor, op. 3, no. 2.

Carlisle found this introduction to rubato galvanizing, without knowing the term or its meaning: literally, robbing a strict tempo by slowing the pace, which was repaid by balancing acceleration. On his next trip to Rice Music in Columbia, he plunked down allowance coins for a copy of Rachmaninoff's ubiquitous Prelude, but his attempt to learn it elicited little more than the incredulity and scorn of Miss Richards, and a certain amount of unfocused noise from the young pianist.

In March, Carlisle rehearsed his final North class play, Anne Coulter Martens's *Don't Darken My Door,* a domestic comedy about alliances and misalliances among the northeastern upper class.[14] Aside from the fun of playing a clueless Brahmin, confirmed bachelor Roger Kent, the involvement kept Carlisle away from home for a few more welcome hours.

Conflicts arose from wanting the acclaim that might come with acting, and from striving for parental demonstrations of affection, notice, and approval. During the rehearsal process, Miss Walker aroused Carlisle's resentment by accusing him of inattention or, much worse, carelessness in preparing or executing his role. Furious, he threw his script to the floor, stalked out and home, in tears. Out came Ida from the kitchen, more curious than concerned. Carlisle climbed upstairs to his room, weeping even more bitter tears, craving a shred of consolation; but Ida didn't have it in her to ask what was wrong, and acted as though the fault was his.

Carlisle swallowed his grief and slunk ignominiously down the back stairs and into the solitary porch swing; but on April 2, the show went on, and he absorbed more theatrical lessons. Once he began to practice his own sleight of hand at turning everything from the Apocrypha, Brontë, and Robert Penn Warren into opera librettos, he would not ignore or forget Martens's skills at such translations of books into plays.

Following this latest thespian turn, singer Ermine and accompanist Carlisle were bused to radio station WIS in Columbia for their first live broadcast performances.[15]

In this hive of home and school activity, garden to keyboard, church to stage, balance came from Carlisle's friends and attempts to carve out personal space. Busy at her chores, Ida again shook her head at the pack of young folk drawn to the parsonage, groaning, "Why don't they go somewhere else?" But there sat bosom friend Sam Dougherty on the porch, waiting each morning for Carlisle. Enough older and a year ahead in school, Sam was smart-minded and -mouthed, with a supercilious air, and Carlisle admired his knowing attitude and attention. Most afternoons after school, Sam turned up to play football, basketball, or tennis on the improvised backyard court. Jack encouraged the relationship because of sports, but Ida wasn't so sure. She'd roll her eyes and ask, "Why don't you play with your other friends?"

Then Carlisle and girls discovered each other. For some months, he nurtured a crush on a classmate, Myrtiss Beacham, for perhaps the sole reason that she barely acknowledged, much less encouraged or returned his interest. Yet even this dead end bore fruit, sixty years later: the character of Myrtis in *Cold Sassy Tree*, with one less *s*, turns up as an example of a rural southern name, sweet witness to a tenth-grade infatuation.

The end of junior year brought a junior-senior, North's version of a prom, a dress-up reception with punch and finger foods sans dancing. Good preacher that he was, Jack took a dim view of tripping any weight of fantastic; this was no burden for Carlisle, who would remain indifferent to dancing. Carlisle's date was Carolyn Bethune, whose family managed the King Davis Hotel in their former town.[16] She had been his and Ermine's playmate and classmate for those four years, but Carlisle worked hard to convince himself of a romance budding at fifteen that wasn't and didn't.

With summer's advent, Jack participated in a volunteer air watch program, on a shift from two to eight a.m. With his head to the sky, he seemed blind during daylight hours to his son on the ground, digging Irish potatoes, working the tomatoes, pushing the lawnmower. Jack tolerated no appearance of idleness, and drafted Carlisle and Ermine as church janitors. Leaks needed patching, windows sealing, walls and trim, painting; but the first job was spraying the church for flea infestations. This work occupied all of every Saturday and Sunday morning. After laying and starting the parsonage fires, Carlisle vacuumed the church while Ermine dusted; in winter, church fires needed starting as well. As fall approached, Jack found the children's work lacking, and accompanied Carlisle "to show him how to clean up."[17]

Reverend Floyd's euphemisms for shaming were but another prelude to Carlisle's asthma attacks that fall; but the advantage of now being employed was the children's progress from a weekly twenty-five-cent allowance to a salary of fifteen dollars per month, ample subsidy for their movie addiction, and books and music for Carlisle.

With college just over the horizon, he began saving. It looked like he would study music, hence would not observe the family tradition of Floyd men attending Wofford; but Spartanburg boasted the state's best music school, Converse College.

BY THE END OF MAY 1942, Ida and Carlisle agreed that the relationship with Miss Richards had pretty much run its course, and wartime economy discouraged the trips to Columbia. When they cast their glance about North to continue his training, the answer sat under their noses: Imogene Dougherty, church organist and mother of Sam.

Gene (pronounced Jeanie) was indeed as her name sounded, a warmer guide than the dour Richards. Born in 1890, thus much older than either of Carlisle's parents, she may not have challenged him, but she encouraged, and allowed him to play whatever he wanted: "It was a way to keep me practicing." And the Doughertys lived just across town, perhaps a half-mile walk from the parsonage.

At home, emotions veered from frayed to torn. Carlisle realized that he posed an unintentional threat to his father's very profession in the house *because* he played the piano. His talent was a different animal than Ida's, who had never pursued a career; but despite her inability to encourage, music still formed a mother-son bond to which Jack was an eternal outsider. When Carlisle looked to her for defense against his father's resentment and hostility, she sighed, "I wish you loved your father more and me less"; or, "It's so hard for your Daddy to be good." In the privacy of their home, Jack had no curbs on selfish impulses, acting out, doing and saying hurtful things that he would later rue.

If *any* divisive or unpleasant subject lay submerged, Jack brought it up; tempers flared, wounding feelings. The frequency and severity of *his* asthma attacks mirrored his subsequent remorse, exacerbated in turn by Ida's contradictions. Carlisle came to expect his father's disapproval, but such intellectual armor proved flimsy when Jack's anger disintegrated into sheer pettiness. One of his lifelong prerogatives was collecting the mail from each town's postal boxes. Once in North, Carlisle thought to surprise his parents and save them the trip. He started to hand the envelopes to Ida, but Jack snatched them away.

Carlisle declared, "But it's for Reverend *and* Mrs. Floyd!"

Jack had the last word, "Whose name came first?"

Carlisle's best defense lay in exemplary behavior; yet he internalized an ongoing debate of who he truly *was,* who and what he would *become,* which affected his father like a saddle burr. Uncle Yates used to observe that whenever Jack was upset, he'd pull his nose constantly; and the North years gave him ample opportunity to resemble Pinocchio.

As with asthma attacks, so with Carlisle's discouragement: Jack pounced on any opportunity to assure him, "Son, don't let it get you down." These were the better moments when Carlisle felt noticed. The children never caused their father public embarrassment, and Ermine gave as good as she got; but Carlisle became the identified scapegoat, suffering in silence, dreading Jack's lurking animosity. Carlisle gave him nothing overt of which to complain; but Reverend Floyd's suspicion, hardening to conviction, of Carlisle's difference was well-founded, thus offering further incitement.

Precious moments of escape came from career-directed daydreams. He'd been accused of such "wastes of time" for years by his father and uncle Yates. He had gathered enough evidence that professional athletics afforded no option. He'd had just enough success at the keyboard, however, and with words, crayon, and pencil. Windows opened onto the arts. His and Ermine's role-playing movie games incubated his theatrical ethos; yet even his fantasies, aimed at eliciting praise and acceptance, focused on modest goals. When he envisioned success as a concert pianist, he never saw it unfold at Carnegie Hall, but rather at Township Auditorium in Columbia, where Rachmaninoff had performed.

The root of Carlisle's oedipal struggle with Jack, aside from the eternal drama of sons superseding and surviving fathers, was his closeness with Ida. Despite her constitutional inability to bestow the praise he craved, she had a gentle soul: at least Carlisle had one parent who demonstrated concern for his welfare. Ermine observed, "My memories of North aren't as dark as his, but Daddy didn't treat me the way he did Carlisle. He was jealous of Carlisle as an adolescent, critical of the things he did: fathers and sons."[18]

At school, Carlisle added typing and bookkeeping to his practical skills. He drew inspiration from reading Marjorie Kinnan Rawlings, *The Yearling* (1938), the saga of a Florida boy who adopts a deer as pet, which he is forced to shoot when the animal destroys the family's crop. Carlisle's inborn tenderness toward animals made him an ideal subject for devastation by this tale, and the bitter father-son crises spoke to his present experiences.

He next became obsessed with the works of George Eliot,[19] in particular *Silas Marner* (1861), *Adam Bede* (1859), and *The Mill on the Floss* (1860). The combination of newly acquired music lore and his ugly duckling self-image drew Carlisle to this author, whom composer Franz Liszt reportedly characterized as the least attractive woman he had ever seen. Carlisle was also the target audience for Eliot's preoccupation with country life, marginal figures persecuted for their differences, and alienation from organized religion.

Inspired, he embarked on a "violently romantic" visionary novel of his own, *Eternal Winter,* to immortalize his bleak teen tragedies. He shared it with no one, not even Ermine, and got perhaps two chapters into the story before history repeated itself: as with his desire at three to study piano, so with the epic novel. Finding it too much work, he discarded the manuscript as "pretentious beyond belief."

Though from time to time he toyed with the notion of writing as a career, the craft, like drawing, never acted on him like music; then one day a tune wove its tendrils through his brain. Its simplicity was striking, rich with possibilities for development, and Carlisle wished for the technique to write it down. How did composers transcribe what they hear? Despite his growing assurance at playing and interpreting the sophisticated musical thoughts of others, this remained a mystery. The tune would follow him from North through the rest of his years.

THE YEAR 1943 began uncertainly: uncles Sonny and Yates served in the Pacific theater, and Guadalcanal and New Guinea saw some of the most brutal combat. At North's parsonage, Jack's diary confirmed other wars being waged: "Went over to church to see that Carlisle and Ermine did everything right."[20]

In February, Carlisle got his volumes of Chopin Nocturnes and Preludes, and began to dissect the Opus 28, no. 4 that had enchanted him in Bethune. It crystallized sadness, yet there seemed to be a confluence of other emotions, and he longed for the technical means to express its tantalizing complexity. Already tonalities affected him synesthetically with colors: B Major suggested ruby red. Other favored keys like D flat and G flat came across as "luxurious blue," a rich brownish red, and so forth. With a virtually photographic memory, memorizing music came easily. His sense of pitch was not perfect, but it was keen enough to improve over time.

As senior year's final exams approached, family conversation turned to careers. Ida was content to wait and see which path her son would take, confident that it would be in one of the arts, and hoping that it would bring him pleasure and fulfillment. Expectant parishioners always asked Jack whether Carlisle Jr. might follow in Daddy's clerical footsteps. To Reverend Floyd's credit, he shrugged off such flattering inquiries, never giving his boy the feeling that he was under *that* obligation. Jack wanted Carlisle to be a professor of something: history, art or music, whichever promised the best college scholarship.

On the cusp between sixteen and seventeen, despite the town's lack of gathering places for youth, Carlisle's social life improved. His first real romance was with Jean Hutto, blond and the prettiest girl at school, and the first to teach him the shivers of kissing. Carlisle and Jean took the literal backseat on a double date with Ermine and her beau, but this involved nothing more than a lot of "smooching."

At get-togethers in the parsonage parlor, Carlisle might take his place at the keyboard to play his version of popular dance tunes to gratify Ermine; but to her, they still sounded classical.

Dissatisfied with Carlisle's progress with Imogene Dougherty, Ida got Jack to replace him with a different church janitor, to allow him more practice time. Through a combination of musical and church grapevines, she learned that a supposedly noted pianist, Dr. Frederick Manchester, had taken up residence in nearby Orangeburg. On January 14, Ida took Carlisle to play for him: Manchester characterized Carlisle's runs as "muddy." One more lesson on February 20 clarified this as another dead end.

Unfortunately, Ida repeated Manchester's criticism to Jack. From then on, whenever he found Carlisle practicing, he taxed him with "muddy runs."

Yet increased practice produced results. Converse College announced a scholarship competition in March, and Carlisle was eager to try his skills. Ida discouraged him, wringing her hands over his having skipped so many basic pianistic disciplines, like Bach's *Inventions* and Czerny and Hanon exercises, and groaned over his lack of background. But Carlisle had a mission: to win recognition as a concert pianist; he would neutralize his father's demeaning treatment by proving him wrong.

Whatever the motivation, one of the great ironies and, ultimately, upward falls of Carlisle's life was Jack's insistence that his son follow through with the competition. On Friday, March 5, the family drove to Spartanburg and checked into the Franklin Hotel.[21] That alone betokened adventure; and the next morning, after meeting an assortment of Converse luminaries, Carlisle's playing won him a $125 scholarship. Two other awards would cover expenses other than board: a work-study grant for clerical chores in the music office, and one of the school's special awards for ministers' children, with a 10 percent tuition reduction.

For once, his and Jack's dreams seemed to coincide; but allowing Carlisle to experience celebrity was outside the family vocabulary. The new church janitor didn't work out, and Carlisle again sprayed for fleas, swept, and lit the fires, Jack dogging his tracks to see whether they were burning. The usual spring outdoor chores brought days of asthma between concerts at school and church. On graduation day, June 2, temperatures soared into the mid-nineties, and Jack had Carlisle paint three posters for vacation Bible school before giving the salutatory address, receiving the history medal and a certificate for highest scholarship.[22]

NO LONGER CONTENT with having his children in sight at church, Jack now insisted that both get jobs. With Daddy away at pastor's school in Columbia, Carlisle applied his typing and bookkeeping skills to an office job with a small-time defense contractor brought in to build North's army airbase.

The manager may have been a parishioner or family friend, but Carlisle had no clue why they hired him. He found it unique, if easy, to practice a nonmusical skill, a different coordination. Sweating through days in the flimsy prefab onsite building, he lived in fear that some blunder in tabulation would land him behind bars.

He had driven the family car under parental supervision for about two years. Ida was quite comfortable behind the wheel, negotiating the drive to Laurinburg and back; but Jack was, after all, *the* designated driver. Carlisle's drawing, reading, writing, and music might exist in their own magic boxes; but Mama reinforced her son's sense of mechanical incompetence. Still, for personal and social independence, he needed to get his license, that clerical job being well beyond walking distance. On July 7, both children took their first driver's tests in Jack's 1939 Chevy, with its balky shift; they failed the written component, but a week studying South Carolina's rules of the road helped them to pass their second effort.

Carlisle's driving habits often puzzled his family. Aunt Bunny thought him "too good for his own good. He's always late because he's doing something for somebody else. Somebody needs help, so he helps them. It's always something for somebody else."[23] Cousin Helen Harris tells the tale of Carlisle's car breakdown one night some distance from the parsonage. Rather than disturb anyone, and risk the paternal carelessness tirade, he left the car locked at the roadside and walked miles back through town: "He always seemed willing to do what people expected of him."[24]

Short-term office work at an end, he was back spraying the church, mowing the lawns, and attending revivals through the end of August. That year's guest, Reverend B. C. Gleaton,[25] received $63.55 for his week's work, and gave Carlisle $10 of it for the college fund earning interest in his new bank account. Jack added $140, and busied himself assembling a kit for the scholar: suitcase, blankets, pillows, and new clothes.

On the evening of September 13, Jack climbed the stairs to Carlisle's room and supervised the last details of packing. Carlisle froze, wondering what was coming; Jack sat on the bed, fidgeting, pulling his nose.

"Son," he finally said, "you're going to be in a school with a lot of young girls."

Carlisle had been in high school with girls, and had even kissed a few. He may not have practiced Judybell's Bethune illuminations, but he'd done reading that filled in blanks. He had no idea what Jack was driving at, which was more or less par for any "tender subject." Ida may have put him up to it, but Jack spoke his piece.

Carlisle thought, "It's a little late in the day for this production." Sex Education 101.

"I know, Daddy, I know."

He'd need a good night's sleep before gaining a lot more independence tomorrow.

5

Escape

Converse College, Spartanburg, 1943–1945

Tuesday, September 14: After Carlisle loaded his trunk and new suitcase stuffed with clothes, music, books, and drawing board into Daddy's car, the family drove off; Ermine and a friend wanting to look over campus buildings and boys made a party of five. They hit Spartanburg just after noon. Carlisle registered and got a hearty welcome from college president Edward Gwathmey and dean of music Ernst Bacon before auditioning for placement with a piano teacher.

He was bowled over when Bacon rhapsodized over his performance, "There was such an intensity about what you did; it could almost be called *passionate*!" Unfamiliar praise from Caesar. Jack wrote, "Dr. Bacon . . . made us feel mighty good about Carlisle's playing." He paid the treasurer sixty-four dollars for two months' board, the other expenses covered by scholarships; he would send Carlisle ten dollars each month for incidentals.

Carlisle roomed at the cavernous 1908 home of Mrs. Howard Carlisle[1] and her daughter, campus librarian Louisa, at 151 North Fairview Avenue. The location was ideal, directly across from Twichell Auditorium, site of the School of Music's larger performances. Each year a few rooms in the Carlisle house were offered to students at a modest fee, but this cost was covered by Carlisle's taking care of the monstrous old furnace.

He lay down to sleep that night, seventeen, escapee from North, and on his own for the first time.

CONVERSE WAS A LOGICAL and peculiar choice for Carlisle's undergraduate education. Founded as a women's school in 1889, and named for the Spartanburg textile magnate Dexter Edgar Converse (1829–1899), within its first decade it established a reputation as one of the country's finest professional music schools.[2] In 1943, it boasted an enrollment of around 350, of whom 50 or 60 were pianists. Jack's nearby alma mater, Wofford, was used during the war years as a military training center, and Converse became temporarily coeducational in 1943 and 1944. With its still-larger proportion of women students, it is no wonder that Reverend Floyd was concerned for his son's moral welfare.

In addition to Ernst Bacon, Converse's music program had a multitalented faculty with national, even international, reputations, including N. Irving Hyatt, graduate of the Leipzig Conservatory and pupil of Carl Reinecke. He served as Converse's dean of music from 1933 to 1937, before becoming dean emeritus and professor of piano and composition. Edwin Gerschefski (1909–1992), Phi Beta Kappa from Yale, had studied piano with Tobias Matthay and Artur Schnabel, and composition with Joseph Schillinger.[3] Gerschefski's wife, Ina, also from Yale, taught piano, music theory, and child pedagogy. Lionel Nowak, piano student of Edwin Fischer and Walter Gieseking,[4] had studied composition with Roger Sessions and Quincy Porter. The pianist Walter Spry, a Leschetitzsky pupil in Vienna, was a composition student of Henri Rousseau's in Paris; and the voice teachers Glenn Stables and Radiana Pazmor both had extensive European backgrounds.

Converse was still small enough that the faculty knew most of the students, and vice versa. When Carlisle won his scholarship in March, he was assigned to Walter Spry; but the school's guiding light, star, and dean, the pianist-composer Ernst Bacon, had been away on one of three Guggenheim fellowships. At Carlisle's placement audition, Bacon recognized the boy's superior talent and cornered Jack and Ida in his office, finessing their agreement that *he* was Carlisle's ideal teacher.

Bacon, born in Chicago in 1898, child of an Austrian noblewoman and an American doctor, led many charges toward an authentic American music. In 1917, as a precocious nineteen-year-old, he published a treatise, *Our Musical Idiom,* in the philosophical journal *The Monist,* taking to task the then-popular notion that Richard Wagner had exhausted traditional harmony. Bacon demonstrated polemic gifts in his explication of the mathematics of half steps in harmonies and scales:

> With our twelve equal notes of the octave I have found it possible to construct precisely *350 separate and distinct harmonies* (barring inversions, transpositions, and varieties of open and close position), making it possible to form 1,469,650 different progressions of but two successive harmonies, or over 6,000,000 progressions of three successive harmonies. We can also make out of this same chromatic system some 1,490 scales, none of which employ an interval larger than the largest used in the harmonic minor scale, namely, the augmented second. If we were to go into quarter-tones or sixth-tones . . . then these figures would swell to even more indigestible dimensions.[5]

7. Ernst Bacon, by Arthur Bacon. Courtesy of Sam Farrell and Ellen Wendt Bacon, Ernst Bacon Society.

First trained as a concert pianist and conductor, Bacon's composition catalog includes more than 250 art songs and four symphonies, the first of which (1932) won a Pulitzer Prize; a Piano Concerto, String Quintet, Piano Quintet, sonatas for cello, violin, viola, and trios for different instruments; two operas, a musical comedy, two ballets, and incidental music for plays; solo and four-hand piano music; dozens of works for chorus; and two influential books, *Words on Music* (1960) and *Notes on the Piano* (1963). Though he liked to present himself as self-taught, Bacon had studied composition with the Austrian Karl Weigl and the Swiss American Ernest Bloch.

Bacon first taught at the Eastman School of Music in Rochester, New York, from 1925 to 1928, then at the San Francisco Conservatory. While in California, he founded and conducted the Carmel Bach Festival. He then became supervisor of the Works Projects Administration Federal Music Project in San Francisco, and conductor of the group's orchestra. He began as dean and professor of piano at Converse College in 1938, never accepting more than two or three pianists in a given semester.

Of his enormous output, Bacon is today best remembered for his songs and a handful of piano and choral pieces. His personal mission was to forge a militant American aesthetic in music reflecting history, literature, poetry, folklore—especially black and Appalachian—and even the country's very geography. In his own music and that of his students, he fulminated against traditional Italian tempo and dynamic markings. His musical language was tonal and melodic. Nothing was too insignificant for his attention: alongside eloquent settings of serious poetry by Dickinson and Whitman, many of his compositions bear homely titles like "The Chewing Gum Song," "The Telegraph Fugue," and "Flop-Eared Mule."

Bacon's flamboyance blended the cosmopolitan and bohemian. As Converse's Resident Genius, he wore floppy hats, scarves, and took long walks. Friend and photographer Ansel Adams, who shared Bacon's love of the outdoors, found him "like the clear dawn wind in the midst of the foul smogs of contemporary cultural decay."[6]

One of the vehicles with which Bacon hoped to further his American manifesto was a "music play in two acts," *A Tree on the Plains,* with libretto by the poet-novelist Paul Horgan, commissioned by the League of Composers for its Composers' Theater Plan. This project promoted operas written specifically for colleges, conservatories, and community theaters. It had modest technical and musical requirements, an agenda that impressed Carlisle Floyd.

Tree premiered at Converse College on May 2, 1942, the year before Carlisle's arrival; but his awareness of the event and Bacon's espousal of American causes had drawn him to Converse. The event was important enough, and Bacon such a tireless promoter, that *The New York Times* sent composer Henry Cowell to review it. Bacon would have been gratified by his colleague's admiration for the music, and his feelings that the opera contained great moments; but he would have raged at Cowell's notion that it abounded with wild imperfections.[7]

AS TIME PASSED and Carlisle's awareness deepened—his own composing still in the future—he admired Bacon's aesthetic, noting also its mixed success. Although by turns drawn to and repelled by his teacher's grand manner, Bacon's talk of the American opera scene as it percolated in New York excited the novice, who longed for the day when he might achieve something similar.

Bacon's personal life matched his musical profusion: by the time of his death at ninety-one in 1990, he had married four increasingly young women, of whom we shall hear more. The first wife that Carlisle met was the cellist Analee Camp,[8] also on Converse's faculty.

In all his extended periods away from home and family, Carlisle remained the dutiful son, remembering birthdays and anniversaries, writing and calling regularly. He attended church, because he knew he would be asked, and chose Episcopal services; but what an eye-opener: the priests served real wine for Communion, and attached no opprobrium to drinking.

Though just 135 miles from North, he corresponded several times weekly; but Jack could not resist reinforcing the myth of his son's carelessness. The day after depositing Carlisle at school, he wrote that he "went all over town looking for Carlisle a razor," finally finding one in the washstand drawer of the parsonage bathroom.[9] Another time, he dispatched a scolding message that the scholar must remember to turn off the lights when leaving his room. But Carlisle existed elsewhere; now free in most ways, he pursued his dream of success as a concert pianist. His two years' study with Bacon at Converse was confined to piano, and Bacon became a surrogate father.

Bacon's pedagogy was of a different stripe than any Carlisle had experienced, exciting but contradictory, and ranging from grand and archromantic to slovenly. On the first page of *Notes on the Piano,* Bacon claimed: "My credentials are in part a lingering amateurism; that is to say, a love that resists too much learning."[10] Carlisle's first weeks of lessons were devoted to exercises of Bacon's devising, aimed at relaxing the pianist and using the fingers and hands with greater muscularity. As Bacon put it: "Weakness and strength must be equalized, or else utilized for unequal ends . . . relaxation [is the] base from which, and toward which, all operations should proceed. . . . Gravity gives all the power the piano will take."[11]

Carlisle later came to see that this brilliant man wrote more lucidly than he taught, that his best rests in his two slender books. He recognized and appreciated his teacher's intent; but as Bacon himself maintained: "The teacher's hardest lesson is to limit his explanations to the minimum. . . . In aiming to enlighten, too much mechanical self-knowledge mostly confuses. Piano playing will never be a science. If it were, it would cease to be an art."[12]

In Carlisle's case, Bacon offered too *little* of a good thing. Exercises were never integrated into, much less coordinated with, repertoire study and performance. The closest Bacon came was general admonitions, like, "You are not relaxed enough." And Carlisle, at a stage where intensity was what he most valued, learned to doubt: one cannot play the piano at all if *totally* relaxed.

Carlisle found that Bacon lacked patience to follow through on his best intentions. In the words of composer and fellow Bacon student Marshall Bialosky: "He was not much interested in real teaching; he was more interested in staying out of your way, letting you do what you wanted to do."[13]

Bacon's personality matched his technical instruction in idiosyncrasies ranging from formidable, stern, or sardonic, to warm and encouraging. He was a great believer that American universities and conservatories fostered a hothouse climate in which "too much . . . teaching is by encouragement, too little by provocation."[14] He was "all for exposing every student to some torrid or arctic weather."[15]

A cold front blew in at one of Carlisle's first lessons. While playing Chopin's Prelude in A-flat Major, op. 28, no. 17, a shocking dialogue ensued when he struck one too many wrong notes. Bacon was at his most unsmiling: "I do not know how many misreadings you have made. Again!"

Carlisle played, but Bacon bristled at persistent errors: "This time you still had thirty-six! Again!"

Shaken and shaking, Carlisle tried again: "Two less, but still too many. Again!"

After the next attempt, Bacon bolted up. "When you have looked at every note three or four times in your practice room, then you can come back to me and I'll listen to you."

He stormed out: end of lesson.

Yet in performance class the atmosphere could just as abruptly thaw and become embarrassingly nurturing. Carlisle gave his first public performance outside a teacher's parlor that fall, with Chopin's Preludes in A-flat Major and G Minor, op. 28, nos. 17 and 22. Though paralyzed by stage fright, desire propelled him onstage. Once seated at the keyboard, routine and reflex took over, and he played as if in a trance. With lessons absorbed from Rachmaninoff, he applied judicious rubato to his playing of romantic repertoire. He cringed as Bacon enthused to envious peers, "See how Carlisle has developed a wonderful sense of timing?!"

Bacon's finest gift was his ability to bring encyclopedic cross-cultural influences to bear in *talking* about and kindling inspiration for music and its allied arts. In other words, he was a coach who offered insights that enriched musical experiences rather than precise technique. His ego matched his intelligence and intuition, but unfortunately these qualities had little foundation in discipline, in either teaching or his own playing. Routines were his downfall. Carlisle might walk into the studio, and Bacon would say, "I do not feel like teaching today. Do you want me to teach when I do not feel like it?"

"No, Mr. Bacon, I don't believe I do."

But then, sometimes at night, the dean prowled Converse's halls and practice rooms. More than once, he found Carlisle at work at nine in the evening, and insisted on giving him a spontaneous lesson.

In discussing the work of contemporaries, Bacon's disdain tended to be withering. When Carlisle expressed admiration for José Iturbi, Bacon sneered at his competitor's Hollywood experience by declaring, "He has too much 'film quality.'"

Yet he could just as easily catch students off guard with unexpected or unorthodox views that validated. Once while strolling Converse's grounds—Bacon prized Beethovenian long nature walks—Carlisle confessed with embarrassment that he loved Tchaikovsky's music, a highly unfashionable stance at a time when serialism began to dominate American academia.

Bacon stopped short and declared, "I love everything the man wrote," vindicating Carlisle's freshman judgment.[16]

Bacon's manner of playing was as divided as his teaching. When Carlisle first saw Willy von Beckerath's 1896 drawing of Brahms seated at the keyboard, cigar in mouth, the magisterial ruler of his realm, he recognized the quintessential Baconian attitude. Everything might be moving along, but when things started going wrong—usually when Bacon had not practiced or learned the piece—he began to snort audibly, standing upright while continuing to play.

CARLISLE'S CONVERSE YEARS were mostly play-free work. One of his classmates, the Alabama pianist Margaret Guy, had placed second in the scholarship competition the previous spring. Carlisle admired her skill, intelligence, and composure, and fancied himself in love with her, writing to her after the competition. To no avail: those first experiments with the opposite sex that began in North were for the time being suspended and limited to platonic friendships, as Carlisle began experiencing Mistress Music's inherent jealousy.

Students took meals in the college dining room in a formal atmosphere. Every woman was expected to dress for supper, in church or cocktail dresses; for the few men, coat and tie were de rigueur. "Miss G.," the facility's presiding spirit and captain, bestowed favor with invitations to her table at the front, but Converse men ate at their own separate table.

Despite her intelligence, Louisa Carlisle, a confirmed spinster and college librarian, had her peccadilloes: Bacon never tired of telling how he combed the library for Baudelaire's *Fleurs de mal* (Flowers of Evil), only to be informed by Louisa that she had catalogued the volume as botany. Meanwhile, Carlisle reckoned with a "wild and wooly" roommate, in most ways his polar opposite: C. Jules Douglas, a science major, and Carlisle's senior by about ten years. In every area in which Carlisle had been sheltered, Douglas had worldly experience, especially with the ladies. Tall, blond, and muscular, he appropriated Carlisle's prized drawing board for homework. While expounding on women who were "after him," he doodled, played tic-tac-toe, and carved his name into the wood; but Douglas treated his naive roommate as a younger brother.[17]

IN THE MUSIC OFFICE, Carlisle worked as secretary to the dean's secretary, Anna Margaret Williams. A Latta native, she had taught both Ida and Jack in school there, and her brother Herbert had been one of the Floyds' Wofford boarders in the thirties. Carlisle filled out report cards, filed, and amassed weekly hours of every kind of busy work. It took him no time to realize that Bacon was as disorganized in office as in studio, and that Anna Margaret wielded power behind the throne. In addition to efficiency, she provided Bacon with pointers on the southern way, especially what would give offense.

Carlisle's work-study also involved studio accompanying and recital setup: moving pianos on and offstage, placing stands and music, setting and operating concert lights. Accompanying taught him the basics of opera and art song repertoire, instilling further love and respect for singers and their art; and concert hall duties let him rub shoulders with music world greats on the school's Artist Series, like Jeannette McDonald, Artur Rubinstein, Gladys Swarthout, and Blanche Thebom. While these and others waited, paced, or fretted backstage, Carlisle devoured their talk. McDonald, for so many years an idol, and still gorgeous, revealed herself to be not such a role model in person, grousing to her accompanist during a pause between song groups, "This audience is impossible! They're trying to decide if these are my real teeth!"

In academic studies Carlisle was inconsistent or indifferent, slogging through basic curriculum requirements. The school stipulated a year of either French or Spanish, and because Carlisle had taken the former at North, and still regarded it as *the* language, he resented receiving a C in the latter. His grades were sent home: two As (Piano and English); three Bs (General Theory, Ear Training, Speech); four Cs (including Spanish and Counterpoint, the latter from Lionel Nowak); and a pass in Physical Education (tennis). Jack wrote, "Guess it's as good as I could have done."[18]

But English with Elizabeth Bearden, "a maiden lady in every aspect," proved the exception; she ignored students until they demonstrated their worthiness, thereby provoking Carlisle. He had scored high enough on entrance exams to place in advanced English, moving directly to creative writing. Bearden offered timeless injunctions: be vivid, one good active verb is worth a hundred piled-on adjectives, and watch out for smacks of cliché. When Carlisle pondered his upbringing, with its upheavals from frequent moves, he hit upon dramatizing his own history. He had always been most touched by stories and accents of acquaintances from strata less economically favored than the Floyds, and easily picked up the need for unsparing self-criticism of his writing. At first, none of Carlisle's weekly themes rated anything better than a C+, but she returned his papers covered with editorial marks and notes to "See me about this."

When Bearden learned that Carlisle's reading tastes ran to Louis Bromfield, she dictated a purging with Thomas Mann. For his first term paper, she assigned him Mann's first three *Joseph* novels,[19] a long read at seventeen; but the result was his first Bearden A-.

Now he had her attention. To keep it, he produced his first fiction since the abortive *Eternal Winter.* The new piece had autobiographical inspiration: fear for his uncles in the South Pacific, where intense fighting raged for all of 1943, and accelerating claustrophobia about his rapidly approaching eighteenth birthday. The result was "Which Shall Not Perish from the Earth," two pages of concentrated angst. Set in a North-like town, and featuring a large yard with a grove of trees, its protagonist, like Carlisle, is just seventeen. Panicky about bad news from the war, and abandoning "exterior braggadocio," he agonizes over whether he is a coward to prefer his own charted course to enlistment. (The boy's uncle is also stationed in New Guinea.) The trees, the soil of home, and the stars reassure him that, no matter what happens, "These things are eternal." As he walks back to "the gaunt white house," Abraham Lincoln's words, "which shall not perish from the earth," offer solace and benediction.

Bearden again awarded him her top A-, and placed the piece in two campus publications: an informal fall anthology, *We, the Freshmen,* then in the more rigorously juried *The Concept.*[20] This also swept Carlisle into Converse's writing society, Wild Thyme; yet his just-begun career with words met with less than unanimous success. Rosalyn MacEnulty, one of his music theory teachers and the wife of the theory-composition teacher John MacEnulty, commented scathingly on Carlisle's "frantic effort to be polysyllabic"; but Elizabeth Bearden continued as mentor and champion, even after he left her class the following spring.

ON OCTOBER 29, Jack learned at Conference of his reassignment to Holly Hill, a prosperous town of around 1,100, about fifty miles closer to Charleston. Moving day was set for November 10 and Carlisle felt palpable relief at leaving North's depressions. His first visit began in a driving sleet storm that turned to snow over the night of December 15–16. Jack built a fire in the living room, and Carlisle played for the family. Five days later, enough snow had melted for Jack to hand both of his children rakes to clear the yard of fall leaves. The expansion of horizons in college was not always an advantage, and Carlisle's attempts to meld his new world with the family's met with minimal success. From then on, he brought records, books, and work home to pass otherwise deadly hours.

Ermine, finishing senior year in North, wryly confessed that she had missed his "glacial moods" with their father, but she had finally "told Daddy off," letting him know that the one thing she'd learned thus far was how *not* to raise the children she planned to have. After Christmas with Bunny, Helen, and Yates home from the war, Carlisle took the bus back to Spartanburg on January 4, with a new sport jacket, an overcoat donated by a wealthy parishioner, and expense checks for the next month.

As he settled into second-term routine, striking and subtle changes tinged his days and nights. Away from home, he had few asthma problems, and he peppered his letters with remarks that he was getting As. Bacon was so pleased with Carlisle's playing that he assigned Liszt's Piano Concerto no. 2 in A Major, seemingly unaware that it was far beyond his student's actual abilities. At his most expansive, Bacon enthused, "This is theater music, but it is the *greatest* theater music!"

Carlisle's music history course required pleasant hours of listening in the library, and more creative writing blossomed. He wrote two articles for the campus newspaper, then called *Parley Voo.* For Bearden's class, and published in the March issue of *The Concept,*[21] he produced "Low-Country Town." Set in a village blended with traits of and characters from North and Holly Hill, it offers a warm, wise, good-humored dissection of life in such places. The narrator's father is the minister, "about the biggest man in the town."

Carlisle stayed so busy, and was in such a perpetual hurry, that he fell trying to take a flight of steps outside the music building three at a time. The resulting right-ankle sprain crimped his piano pedal action, not to mention his tennis game, that spring.

On February 29, the book world erupted with Lillian Smith's *Strange Fruit*,[22] about an interracial love affair and its horrific end with a lynching in a small Georgia town in the twenties. It became the best-selling fiction of 1944, and its banning by booksellers in Detroit and Boston only piqued the nation's interest, including Carlisle's. He read it as soon as he could get his hands on a copy, and connected with Smith's outrage at such blatant social injustice.

Back on campus, *The Concept* that May offered a virtual Carlisle Floyd issue, beginning with his turn as *Wild Thyme*'s student-critic.[23] For the "Laurels" page, a dissection of the most successful works published within, he wrote a sympathetic analysis of a classmate's one-act play; and further contributed three new pieces: "Thought," a young man's fervid meditation on the mind's abilities to enslave and liberate; "Tschaikowsky's Sixth," a one-page sketch of a group of students listening to the eponymous symphony; and "The 'Pounding,'" a lightly fictionalized account of a phenomenon Carlisle had observed since his Jordan days, the gifting of food and household goods to a minister and his family.

He may not have dated at Converse, but he certainly thought about the opposite sex: Millicent, one of his "Tschaikowsky" characters, seems to have a vivid moment of release reacting to "these magic sounds" that "had us all," music that would leave its listeners "exhausted physically; uplifted, regenerated spiritually."[24]

His other grades, particularly in music theory, improved. The instructor was another 1943 Bacon hire, Alia Josephine Ross, young, good looking, and strict.[25] Carlisle and his male peers stood in awe of her, and a little enamored. Late in her long life, Ross wrote a memoir, *A Journey of a Thousand Miles*, recalling Carlisle as: "A fine student, and he said he did his first writing [i.e., composition] for me. Everything he wrote seemed to have the background of his father's being a minister in the South. . . . He was a fine student at all times. I taught him piano harmony. . . . What theory I did with him was in scales, chords and harmony, mostly beginners material. In those days the classes were large, with at least 20 in each freshman class."[26]

He began to understand music's inner workings, as opposed to the simple fact of notes on a printed page; then he discovered that music theory had given him the tools to write down that theme skittering through his brain since high school like a caged squirrel. From the first, composing came with a sense of receiving transmissions. His inner ear produced shapes and sounds in much the same way that his inner eye prompted him to draw; but music fed his soul. As a class assignment, he set about composing his opus 1, *Theme and Variations*, a piano quintet. Alia Ross organized a program of original compositions by freshmen at Twichell Auditorium at 2:15 on the afternoon of Friday, May 12, 1944, and Carlisle's quintet took pride of place as the grand finale of twenty-two short peer works.[27]

This first effort appears to have vanished. Floyd recalled it as a simple, primitive theme and variations lasting several minutes, "a pathetic little piece." The score that he reconstructed in 2011 for inclusion in this book begins with a sweeping chordal folklike theme in F Minor. Its first variation employs syncopation and dotted eighth-sixteenth note figures in the left hand that Carlisle used to imitate the forties boogie-woogie dance craze, and assigned to the cello in his string complement. The assertive Ross spared no efforts to obtain the best possible performance: string players included faculty members Claire Harper as first violin and Bacon's wife Analee Camp as cellist. Camp stopped at the boogie-woogie figuration and waxed mock-indignant: "And *this* is what you give the king of instruments to play?!" Both piece and performance were afterward blanks for the composer, who participated as pianist; but this was early Floyd, with miles to go before taking himself seriously as a composer.

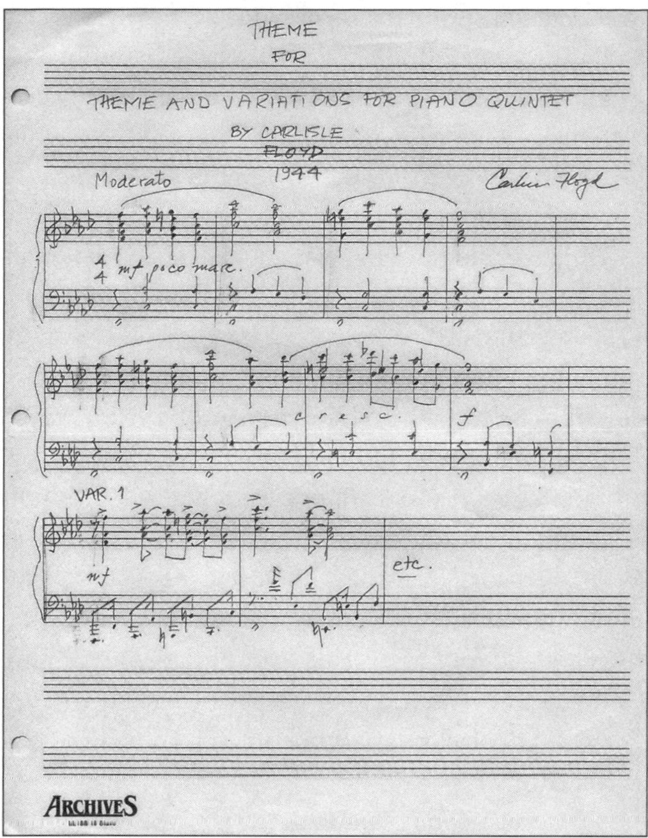

8. Theme and Variation 1, from Floyd's Quintet for Piano and Strings, op. 1. Courtesy of Carlisle Floyd (reconstructed from memory, 2011).

It seemed so easy, gave such pleasure; and his grades had improved enough to make him runner-up for the School of Music's highest grade point average.

SETTLING INTO the Holly Hill parsonage for the summer, Carlisle attended Ermine's high school graduation on May 26. At the end of the month, he received Elizabeth Bearden's letter telling him that "Tschaikowsky's Sixth" had won a five-dollar prize.

The war in Europe preoccupied everyone. On June 6, at 3:30 a.m. eastern time, Operation Overlord, the D-Day invasion, began. Jack's diary enumerated, "13,000 planes and 4,000 ships."[28]

Five days later, on June 11, Carlisle turned eighteen, facing a murky future. Cousin Helen's visit that summer at least provided distraction. The daily breakfast table ritual had grown longer and more leisurely. Reverend Floyd read the day's meditation from *The Upper Room,* with frequent nose-pulling stops to ponder, "Hmm . . . you think God really thought that?" No one ever answered. He proceeded with a more than usually elaborate blessing. Helen recalled: "Ida would have cooked breakfast, it would sit on the table getting cold while we went through this devotional; but you didn't even think about eating before he was through with all that."[29]

One morning, Carlisle sat cutting out paper dolls for Helen. Jack walked into the room, saw his son wasting time with "sissy stuff," grabbed the dolls and tossed them into the fireplace. Carlisle then turned his efforts to safer paper silhouettes, or drawings of Helen, Mickey Mouse, or Katherine Hepburn, and a set of illustrations of young women in the style of Jon Whitcomb.

On Jack's fortieth birthday, July 21, the day's mail included the Selective Service's envelope with Carlisle's 1-A classification, that is, "available immediately for military service." Jack recorded, "He took it like a man."[30] Carlisle conveyed stoic acceptance of his lack of choices. Later that day, the family heard President Roosevelt's fourth-term acceptance address, and that Count von Stauffenberg's plot to assassinate Hitler had failed. The military establishment was in for the long haul; only Carlisle's role remained undetermined.

Ermine had meanwhile decided that she wanted to follow in Carlisle's footsteps as a Converse music major, and Jack and Ida deposited both children in Spartanburg on September 18. After Ermine's placement audition for the voice faculty, she was assigned to resident diva Radiana Pazmor, for whose studio Carlisle had accompanied for a year.[31] Ermine's subsequent college career was predictably brilliant: as basketball star and student body president, she soon realized that she was not meant to be a professional musician, and switched her major to history, with a minor in voice. It was only when Carlisle heard his mother exult over Ermine's triumphs that he supposed that she must have been proud of him too.

Carlisle's sophomore year had barely begun when the expected army induction summons arrived, ordering him to report on October 3 for a physical at Fort Jackson outside Columbia. Though terrified, on the

9. Ermine and Carlisle, Converse College, c. 1944. Courtesy of Helen Harris.

trip from Elloree he was put in charge of the boys on his bus. Gossip flew about how the Nazis would invade Mexico on their approach to America, as they had done with North Africa and Russia. Carlisle met girls whose fiancés were dying overseas. One told him in tears that her fellow's plane had been shot down, and asked him to imagine what it would be to see the earth rushing up to meet you, knowing that your life was measured in seconds of pain and flame.

When he returned to Holly Hill on October 4, his stories of induction protocol overflowed with astonishment, shame and relief. From the bus he had watched German prisoners of war on work detail behind barbed wire. After a thorough physical, the medical officer declared him unfit for service for three reasons. He had always been thin, a condition unchanged by college food (Ermine teased him with the epithet "starving Europe"). At 118 pounds on his 5 feet 10 inch frame, he fell just below the army's minimum requirement of 120 pounds. More seriously, there was his asthma.

A psychological battery probed such issues as his closeness to his father and mother. He realized, "The questions were so loaded, they knew what they wanted was not me." Real humiliation came from a determination that he showed "neurotic tendencies." The baffling term could mean anything and nothing. Still, he knew it was bad, and kept his relief to himself, both at Fort Jackson and later at home; but secret joy carried a backlash of guilt at selfishness for wanting to pursue a music career. The grizzled induction sergeant had told him, "Fall on your knees and thank God right now that you don't have to go! If I had a home at Fort Jackson and one in hell, I'd sell the one at Jackson."

In days to come, Jack took the neurotic label quite personally, assuming that Carlisle would do the same. For weeks, he clipped newspaper and magazine articles about great neurotics like Napoleon, and forwarded them to Carlisle at school.

THE YEAR 1945 got off to a peculiar start: first, he was moved to a room the size of a broom closet in the Carlisle house, just large enough for a single bed and dresser. At least he would not have to fight C. Jules Douglas or another roommate for his drawing board; and the solitude ensured that he could indulge his passion for reading everything of Thomas Wolfe's that he could beg, buy, or borrow. A fellow southerner, Wolfe came from Asheville, where aunt Lucile and uncle J. W. lived. He had made an enormous splash in New York, and Carlisle inhaled every volume of this intense personal writing, especially *Of Time and the River.*

Henrietta Browning, in charge of physical education, decided that she wanted no more of that Floyd boy playing tennis with *her* girls, and banished Carlisle from the courts. She assigned him to walk a fixed number of miles each week, which he hated; but he strode the campus perimeter and kept a precise log.

Converse required a certain number of ensemble credits for pianists, and Bacon, never a stickler for administrative niceties, invented a duo-piano course for Carlisle and Anne Halley, a student from Georgia. They met a few times, became friends, but never really explored the four-hand literature. He would later describe her as "about my best friend at Converse."[32]

Since Carlisle's quintet, Analee Bacon had been friendlier, and she and Ernst now invited him for the occasional meal. Despite a background of wealth and privilege in Chicago, Bacon's aesthetic tended to early hippie, and Analee's menus featured such delicacies as celery soup, leaves, stalks, and all.

Guilty relief at his draft status sent him to the campus playhouse, where casting was underway for Lillian Hellmann's 1941 play *Watch on the Rhine,* about the insidious growth of fascism. The role of the family's young son was open, and Carlisle begged the director in vain to let him act it.

Things were looking up in Alia Ross's theory class, and Carlisle turned more assignments into finished pieces. Hoping to interest a women's choral ensemble, he wrote a four-part setting of Carl Sandburg's World War I poem "Among the Red Guns,"[33] a reflection of the young composer's ambivalence about war: legions of soldiers dead, "running free blood," to a quasi-ironic refrain, "Dreams go on." It struck him as a sympathetic expression of grief for women who had lost husbands, sons, and fathers.

In 4/4 time, marked "Slowly," the piece adopts a chromatic style reminiscent of Frederick Delius's *Part Songs,* and tending to C Minor resolutions. As with the poem, the setting is a simple rondo, each stanza beginning and ending with "Dreams go on," on a diminished seventh chord on D, with added C-natural. The second verse has a broken-chord accompaniment, giving way to a bass line of tolling chimes. For the final stanza, Carlisle paired chordal vocalization with a half-step ostinato eighth-note figure, to much the same effect as Mussorgsky's for the Simpleton's aria in *Boris Godunov.* The piece ends quietly on open fourths and fifths that prefigure Carlisle's later expansion of quartal and quintal harmonies. Though his first vocal work, it has never been performed.[34]

As fall semester progressed, Carlisle, sponsored by Elizabeth Bearden, expanded his creative writing. She persuaded one of her influential friends, J. Mitchell Morse,[35] an associate editor of *The Nation,* to critique issues of *The Concept,* and Carlisle's work did not escape his keen editorial eye or ear. For the November 1944 issue, Morse dissected Carlisle's *Ode* on the "Laurels" page, explaining that the poem had "The three movements of the classic Greek ode. But technically only that far the likeness goes. The meter, rhyme scheme and tone are modern and his own. Using a personal idiom and molding rhythm to moods, Carlisle has objectified an emotion and anchored it."[36]

The movements are "Dilemma," "Revelation," and "Resolution." Under the spells of Hart Crane and Thomas Wolfe, *Ode* reflects a young man's tumultuous inner search for emotional handholds against his soul's dissolution, "Only a dimly lighted life of void/ In smoking, swirling gas!" Imaginative Wolfian language heightens the pessimism of *Ode:* The gentle spit of meshy rain on your face . . . a sky, smutty with black clouds. . . . The unutterably frantic ecstasy of landscape!"[37]

Ermine's short fiction "Embers" appeared in the same issue.

In *The Concept* for February 1945, Morse expanded on *Ode,* that it "belongs to a type of poetry that has always baffled me. I read it and read it and read it, and always come out by the same door where I went in." Yet he allowed that "Mr. Floyd can handle a familiar poetic property in a fresh and interesting way, thereby making it his own."[38]

Carlisle got much the same criticism from his aunt Lucile, always interested in his writing. After reading *Ode,* she told him, "I never thought I'd feel illiterate."

His parents drove from Holly Hill for a student recital on November 16. Jack wrote that his son "did well," playing Brahms's Rhapsody in G Minor, op. 79, no. 2. Push had come to shove, and Carlisle had gotten over the worst of his stage fright; but for years to come, he experienced a destructive postrecital pattern: disappointed and depressed at not playing up to his expectations. Later, after his first major successes, he steeled himself for someone to approach after a performance, pat him on the head, and say, "Sonny, go back home, you don't have what we're looking for"; but up against the wall, he never quit.

The winter holiday proved as much a blur as recitals: within two days of getting to Holly Hill on December 19, he came down with a bad cold. Despite the whole Fenegan Laurinburg contingent invading the parsonage on Christmas Eve, Carlisle brought home several manuscripts in progress. On New Year's Eve, he completed his first solo song, William Butler Yeats's 1893 mystical invocation of lost love, "When You Are Old."[39]

When you are old and grey and full of sleep,
And nodding by the fire, take down this book,
And slowly read, and dream of the soft look
Your eyes had once, and of their shadows deep;
How many loved your moments of glad grace,
And loved your beauty with love false or true,
But one man loved the pilgrim soul in you,
And loved the sorrows of your changing face;
And bending down beside the glowing bars,
Murmur, a little sadly, how Love fled
And paced upon the mountains overhead
And hid his face amid a crowd of stars.

As became his habit, he composed at the keyboard, mostly for pitch confirmation. This far past singing in public, he tried out vocal parts as he wrote, and felt his voice settling into a raucous croak. This required solitude: the parsonage had to be empty, or he might seek out a piano at his father's church.

Carlisle's interpretation of the poem, anchored in a somber but sensuous E-flat Minor, "Slowly and Nostalgically" in 4/4, begins with an ostinato chordal trudge with a tenth-span in the left hand, marked "softly yet distinctly fading—an echo—drowsily." The voice enters in the fifth measure in a monotone chant, lifting, as the chords rise chromatically, enharmonically, "wistfully," to a first climax in D Major, the voice soaring to high A on "the soft look your eyes had once." The second stanza employs a more impassioned melody that wavers between the relative major of G-flat, then D-flat, returning to the E-flat Minor "chant" theme for stanza three, and ending with the piano's lowest and highest E-flats. Throughout, rumbling bass sonorities underline the song's timeless images.

In the seven months that separate Carlisle's quintet from "When You Are Old," his tonal language graduated from kindergarten to middle school. His love for the voice would always take inspiration from literary texts; but his choices had to surpass mere word painting with affects more emotional than cerebral. The Library of Congress manuscript bears a double inscription: a completion date of December 31, 1944; but beside that, "For Nancy who doesn't know why, January 5, 1944." Nancy Steele was a singer and Ermine's Converse roommate, on whom Carlisle had "a very temporary and imaginary crush," but one strong enough to make him forget to write the correct year, 1945.

Back at Converse, he put finishing touches to a longish poem, "Transcendency," another callow, impassioned musing on life's futility and "the endless desolation of the sky." The poet longs for "Love . . . All consuming, that disembodies thoughts/That throttles wills, devours ambitions . . . that can sublimate one moment into an eternity!" Bearden put "Transcendency" into the February issue of *The Concept*, along with Carlisle's first attempt at drama, a one-act play, *Too Dear, the Price*.[40]

Set in a living room with a homely chintz-covered divan, in a middle-class house in an unnamed southern town, its three protagonists are forty-five-year-old Elizabeth Duckworth, twenty-one-year-old Helen Singleton, and Sam Duckworth, Helen's fiancé, returned from the war's Italian campaign physically and psychically scarred. Sam is very close to his mother, and loves to sing. Elizabeth invents any excuse for her boy's odd behavior, observing, "He has quite a range; up there like a woman now." Helen fears that Sam's experiences, rather than deepening him, have made him "light and changeable." Sam enters wearing a summer uniform, limping, with empty chatter about everything from baseball games to Chekhov and Cézanne, before losing his train of thought. Elizabeth leaves the two alone, but Sam falls into distracted silence, then bursts into unprovoked rage at Helen. Elizabeth tries to intercede, but the confrontation ends with Sam slapping Helen and calling her a liar. He attempts a lame apology, blaming his behavior on encroaching madness. Lapsing into even more convincing histrionics, he runs upstairs, "sobbing brokenly." Helen casts their relationship in the past tense, declaring, "I was so proud of that mind—*so* proud!" The curtain falls as Sam begins singing again, offstage, "in a light falsetto." His mother "stands absolutely rigid," as Helen stares "granite-like" at Elizabeth.

Ernst Bacon read all of Carlisle's published pieces and encouraged each such creative manifestation. He overlooked the play's mannerisms, praising "The son, the son! So Ibsen!"[41] In *The Concept* for May, Morse found the play "well constructed as a drama," but tore into Carlisle's dialogue. He wondered whether "people really talk in complex sentences? Do you really hear such a high proportion of words of Latin derivation in the speech of real people, especially under stress? . . . Listen to the speech of the boys and girls on the campus. Then write another play."[42]

Unfortunately, this one was never staged; but Carlisle learned his lessons. *Too Dear, the Price* would remain a minor footnote to his career, except for serving five years later as the germ for his second (and likewise abortive) opera.

Converse had no formal opera workshop in these years, but Bacon tried to program at least one opera—once including his own—in the annual Spartanburg Music Festival. Over the course of Carlisle's education, school and local papers occasionally asked him for reviews or commentary. For the campus newspaper *Parley Voo,* he contributed an elaborate puff in "Music Notes" for the school's upcoming production, Gilbert and Sullivan's *Iolanthe,* for which Bacon had appointed him coach-accompanist and assistant musical director. Carlisle touted the school as "continuously bustling," claiming that the rush of rehearsals was "more fun than work."[43]

Carlisle rarely risked sharing enthusiasms with his parents, but this was opera (almost), which his mother had encouraged him to sample beginning in North. He brought the program home for discussion, comment, and the status the exotic medium conferred. In March, he paid his five-dollar entrance fee for a contest held in Columbia by the National Federation of Music Clubs. As the nation was swept with optimism over the news from Europe—American armies crossing the Rhine and advancing toward Berlin—Carlisle played three new pieces on April 7: J. S. Bach's Partita in C Minor; a set of Chopin Variations; and Charles Tomlinson Griffes's demanding Scherzo, the third of the Fantasy Pieces, op. 5. Three judges recorded comments. Perla F. Sumner suggested a slower tempo for greater clarity, less pedal in Bach and Chopin, but praised Carlisle's "nice touch." Hugh Williamson also cautioned against overuse of pedal, and felt that the tone was forced. Carlisle could only have winced to read a hated word on the judging sheet: "Clean up technique in Griffes—too careless." But Williamson also reassured, "Interesting pianist. . . . Very musical boy—has a flair for making his playing interesting."

The third and best-known judge, the Vienna-born conductor-teacher Carl Bamberger, after cautioning Carlisle to "avoid hurrying of phrases," complimented the "light easy technique, smooth phrasing, colorful playing!"[44]

Carlisle's classmate Anne Halley left that day with first prize.

THE END OF SOPHOMORE YEAR brimmed with sad news and good news: on April 12, Franklin D. Roosevelt died in Warm Springs, Georgia; three days later, American forces liberated Nazi concentration camps; and on the last day of the month, Adolf Hitler and his mistress Eva Braun committed suicide in their Berlin bunker.

By the end of his second year, Carlisle tallied the highest grade point average of any music student. He and Ermine both won the college's highest awards for English in their respective classes; and despite Morse's reservations, Bearden awarded Carlisle another prize for "Transcendency." He promptly turned the check over to his father.

Jack drove his children home on May 21. Carlisle brought with him the manuscript for a long story, "The Woman and the Romans," which he polished that summer. Reverend Floyd viewed this as indolence, and it was a matter of days before Carlisle was back at his usual house and garden chores, planting peas between rows of corn his father had already sown.[45]

On his nineteenth birthday, June 11, the *Upper Room* devotional before breakfast urged, "Thy will be done." *Jack's* will mandated toughening Carlisle, and bringing another wage into the house. That afternoon, without consulting Ida or Carlisle, he drove out to the Holly Hill Lumber Company, where the manager, parishioner "Brother Cooler," assured him of a summer job opening. The next day, Cooler put Carlisle on the payroll and instructed him in grading lumber, which soon expanded to carrying, stacking, and minor carpentry. Carlisle was miserable, his pianist's hands bleeding and bruised, full of splinters.

He continued working until July 2, when Ida put down her foot, and he was free to get back to his new story. The following week, Jack fretted, "Don't see why Carlisle and Ermine could [*sic*] get some job, but Ida thinks they should stay at home."[46] At least he had the satisfaction of putting his boy back to work in the church and parsonage yards.

Since the previous winter, Carlisle had done much spiritual thinking, processing early and ongoing experiences with his father and defining his own beliefs. Reverend Floyd's diaries refer to a sequence of "good letters" about religion.[47] Carlisle's natural extroversion, tempered by familial inhibitions, left his adapted inner child guarded and cautious. He remained curious about people and the world, and came to question the "sensitive artist" characterization reinforced by his parents; yet he respected the feelings of *others,* not least because he had so often heard his mother describe his father as "the most insensitive of men." He found himself attracted to those more introverted than he, relishing the challenge of discovering their true identities. Supported by school peers and mentors, relying on their astute criticism and praise for his words and music, he began to trust intuitions that rarely failed him in years to come.

Raised with a creed based on the word "don't," which rubbed out life's joys, he saw his father, the minister, as an overgrown child, guilty if he enjoyed himself at the movies, more concerned with his family as a reflection of himself in the community than for themselves; and Carlisle knew early that he could not in good faith call himself a Christian, in the sense of regular church attendance or endorsing any dogma. In "Which Shall Not Perish from the Earth," he had written, "God knew what he was doing"; but Carlisle experienced the most frequent users of His name doing so to divide, conquer, punish, and deny. In Carlisle's vocabulary, "no" became the most hated word; but he embraced Deism as supreme logic: "It seems inconceivable that there is not a Divine Intelligence. I have no idea why what happens, happens; but if there is another level, perhaps it will be explained. But it is all a mystery. If you accept the fact of our birth, and how that happened, you can accept almost anything; and needless to say, you cannot dismiss anything."

On his evolving path, connections between science, art, and religion grew clearer, all parts of the same Intelligence. Great art of any kind was proof enough of divinity in the universe; and proof against attempts to keep Carlisle Floyd down.

On a purely external level the 5,800-word story "The Woman and the Romans" reflects the Floyds' transition from Jordan to Bethune. Carlisle transcribed the regional dialect his inner ear dictated. The story features a boy, Jamie; his sister, Willie Sue; and their mother, who craves an oil stove to replace the family's troublesome, filthy wood-burning appliance. They have moved from country to town, whose inhabitants are the title's Romans, and Mama aspires to live a little more as they do. Daddy is absent at a menial grocery clerk job, and gives his wife ten dollars each week for household expenses. Mama displays some of the existential anger Carlisle saw in Ida, but his fictional character is sharper-tongued and more confrontational than her real-life model. The Woman hovers close to the breaking point, emotionally and materially. When

Willie Sue hesitantly broaches the subject of a new dress for her school commencement, Mama snaps: if she gives in to the girl's vanity, she'll never get that new stove. Daddy shows up only to eat and trudge off to bed. The next morning, the spirit of O. Henry peeks around the story's edges: Mama tells Willie Sue simply that she will have her commencement dress. The stove can wait, and she knows she has made the right choice.

Any child of emotional abuse would find wishes fulfilled in this simple tale of defiance and maternal bonding. On the first page, Carlisle typed *ATLANTIC FIRST,* meaning to send it off to *The Atlantic Monthly,* of which nothing came.

DESPITE ERNST BACON'S administrative ineptitude, Syracuse University (SU) wooed him away from Converse, with a more powerful and lucrative position as director of their school of music, and Edwin Gerschefski succeeded Bacon at Converse. Bacon took with him as many gifted Converse students as he could, including Carlisle, by offering scholarships and grants to cover private lessons and tuition.[48] Carlisle looked forward to escaping the narrow confines of Converse, to having a "room in a dormitory and . . . some friends of the male sex for the first time since high school!"[49]

Bacon had auditioned another South Carolina pianist, Mozelle "Peggy" Camp (no relation to wife Analee), and invited her to join the party in Syracuse, appointing Carlisle as her guardian and companion. Visits from and to the Camps in nearby Bamberg ironed out the particulars of Carlisle's new charge: Carlisle viewed Peggy, two years younger and a gifted pianist, as a charming if outlandish sister or niece. On July 22, he wrote to Bacon, "Peggy seems to be sincere and unaffected. She played some for us and showed quite a facile finger technique. She also has not a little sensitivity and approaches her music in the right way."[50]

Peggy's aggressive stage mother—Carlisle described her as "an interesting and amusing conversationalist—if untiring"—dressed her daughter in Mary Janes, two-tone little girl's shoes, and made her a wardrobe of billowing skirts evocative of *Alice in Wonderland.* Peggy spoke with an outrageous Geechee accent, the Low Country white equivalent of black Gullah dialect.[51]

During July's third week, Carlisle turned again to song composition, with Christina Rossetti's poem "Remember Me":[52]

> Remember me when I am gone away,
> Gone far away into the silent land;
> When you can no more hold me by the hand,
> Nor I half turn to go, yet turning stay.
> Remember me when no more day by day
> You tell me of our future that you plann'd:
> Only remember me; you understand
> It will be late to counsel then or pray.
> Yet if you should forget me for a while
> And afterwards remember, do not grieve;
> For if the darkness and corruption leave
> A vestige of the thoughts that once I had,
> Better by far you should forget and smile
> Than that you should remember and be sad.

In a July 22 letter to Bacon, Carlisle wrote a first creator's manifesto, speculating that the new song

> may or may not have merit; at this stage, I can't appraise it unbiasedly. It is the largest song that I've done yet, both in scope and actual time duration. . . . [Rossetti] has attracted me since I first came into contact with her work. She has a brooding, elegiac element . . . that is fascinating, knowing the unhappy circumstances of her life. I began the song at school for Hannah Walker.[53] I had promised to write one for her and finally we mutually agreed on the poem. With her voice in mind, I wrote it . . . for mezzo-range. Before the summer's over, I want to do a suite of piano pieces or a suite for voice, and if for voice, compose the words myself. I've found out, however, that you can't force composition in the least or you'll turn out utter banalities (this is of course the amateur's revelation!) . . . but always there's the fear of being too emotional (thanks to Gerschefski's influence), of appearing sentimental by using harmonies which are not "different"

or stridently dissonant. I can't justify what musical instincts I may be endowed with to composition via the Schillinger method. At the beginning of the summer, I had a recurrence of those characteristic periods of self-doubt which you are so familiar with. Nothing came when I tried to play and my technique seemed hideously deficient. When I tried to compose, likewise nothing came and I despaired of that overpowering, sterile feeling. There was no confidence and worlds of ambition. Always . . . I have the fear of mediocrity which I despise. Small-town life is seething with it, they see no difference between mediocrity and genuineness. In composing, I am afraid of being too imitative, which certainly tends to mediocrity. . . . But then I suppose somebody *has* to be mediocre, eh?[54]

"Remember Me" begins in 4/4, "Moderately," with rippling two-hand triplet chords in C-sharp Minor, the song's harmonic glue, together with repeated intervals of perfect fourths and tritones in the vocal line, marked "very *legato* throughout." After a rhapsodic swerve to E Minor for its middle section, and a climax on high B (*ossia*, i.e., optional, G for mezzo-soprano) at "Only remember me," the line builds, "always smoothly," in escalating sequences at "you understand it will be late/To counsel then or pray," with a second culmination at "A vestige of the thoughts that once I had." The triplets return in the home key for a quiet coda on the poem's final two lines.[55]

Summer's end witnessed the detonation of America's two atomic devices over Hiroshima and Nagasaki, and Japan's surrender on August 15. After spending the next week with family in Asheville, and receiving and returning Syracuse's application forms, Carlisle wrote to Bacon on August 16:

For the last weeks I have been living in a very undesirable state of indecision. The last week in July I was feverishly making plans for school and practicing very diligently when I received my second orders to report to Ft. Jackson for a re-examination. That, of course, "took the wind out of my sails," and put a stop to all plans for the future until *after* August 13th, the day I reported. I am back from Jackson now and as yet, do not know the verdict of the examining doctors. They had to write to a former doctor of mine to get his statement that he had treated me for asthma; so until all that is settled, I won't definitely know whether I'll go back to school or not. . . . Of course, there is the imminent possibility that I *will* be accepted for the Army and *that* certainly will alter things unless they order a cessation of induction which the officers at Ft. Jackson seem to think probable.[56]

Carlisle had other unsettling news of no campus rental vacancies from Syracuse's housing office, dashing his dream of dormitory life. After receiving the army's acknowledgement that his asthma still classified him as 4F, while packing his trunk, he consulted a university-approved list of town housing. Despite worries over his financial situation, the summer of 1945 produced a few carefree moments. During another of cousin Helen's visits, when Jack was off preaching revivals, Carlisle and Ermine seized a Sunday evening's leisure to drive Helen to a black church outside of town for the music making. Not even Ermine made bold enough to go inside, but the three sat in the car, grooving to real gospel singing. The fun continued the next day: with Helen posted as a sentry to warn against the approach of parental figures—Jack would have deemed it a profound sacrilege—Carlisle played and Ermine sang in a thoroughly inauthentic interpretation of soul style.

Solemnity ruled the morning of August 29 at the Floyds' breakfast table. After reading the Twenty-third Psalm, things turned "All sort of quiet because of Carlisle's going away to Syracuse."[57] Carlisle wired Bacon that he would need a room upon arrival the following night. Money was on everyone's mind, but immediate worries were soothed by a visit to Mr. Sam McCoy, president of Farmers and Merchants Bank and chairman of the board of stewards at the Methodist church. Mr. Sam assured them that a timely loan was theirs for the asking. The whole family drove to Columbia, with time to spare to see Nelson Eddy in *Knickerbocker Holiday*. Jack bought Carlisle's ticket for $25.25; Carlisle checked his trunk and boarded the train at 7:30 that evening.

Mrs. Camp had considered sending Peggy with Carlisle "by plane and train from Columbia. She has a certain aggressiveness that really accomplishes things";[58] but the two young pianists met on the train, and Jack never considered that his boy was making an overnight trip with an unmarried nubile female. Two days later, Reverend Floyd received a "nice letter" from Mrs. Camp saying that their children had found good seats.[59]

6

Swimming with Yankees

Syracuse University, New York, 1945–1946

Somewhere between Columbia and New York, Carlisle had seeds of competence watered. Someone needed taking care of: Peggy Camp, who with friends in large groups loved to indulge her narcissistic streak. Bound for New York, Carlisle's southern training kicked in. With the war over, and trains overrun with homeward-bound soldiers, the crowds posed novel, uncomfortable challenges. Peggy hung on for dear life, and Carlisle used his suitcase as a battering ram, cleaving a path through a sea of shouting Yankees at Penn Station to the crosstown train to Grand Central and transfer to Syracuse. They arrived on Thursday, August 30.

Returning servicemen also contributed to the scarcity of campus housing. That fall, Syracuse University admitted 3,190 students, 326 of them fine arts majors. Peggy walked into a university-sponsored arrangement whereby students were assigned to faculty homes in exchange for chores or minding children. Ernst Bacon himself sponsored Peggy, and managed to secure a room for Carlisle on fraternity row, at the Sigma Nu house at 711 Comstock Avenue. He did not need to join the fraternity and found his nonmusician roommate, Ralph "Dutch" Ressler, congenial for his very differences. Bathroom facilities were communal, and Carlisle took most meals at a university cafeteria run by the home economics department. Sigma Nu, just three blocks from campus, had location on its side in Syracuse's arctic winter.

Methodists founded Syracuse University between 1870 and 1871, so of course the denomination occupied its chapel, one reason why Reverend Floyd agreed to his son's decamping. The distinctive "Old Row" of administration and classroom buildings displayed the era's Romanesque Revival architecture, and the college of visual and performing arts became the nation's first higher educational institution to offer a bachelor of fine arts degree in 1874. In 1889, construction was completed on Crouse College to house those disciplines. The work of architect Archimedes Russell, Crouse was and is a four-story brownstone pile of turrets and soaring bell tower. The interior glowed with dark wood like vampire castles of the imagination, its main staircase boasting a replica of the Winged Victory of Samothrace. The campus, colloquially, The Hill, has Crouse College at its summit, overlooking the rest of the city. Its basement warren of practice rooms, however, left much to be desired: students frequently had to walk through each other's etudes to get to their own.

Everything about the new environment stimulated and challenged; and Carlisle had "the ignorant confidence of being eighteen."[1] Converse had its share of gifted students, but most came from well-to-do families with boarding school backgrounds. Once graduated and married, many had no thought of music except as a household ornament. Syracuse plunged Carlisle into different social strata and different nationalities and ethnicities, especially black and Jewish; and into a dedicated career orientation in all the arts. He soon made friends in departments other than music. The exciting, ultrabohemian art students roamed the halls, peering through doors at classes with nude models. Carlisle attended just enough Methodist chapel to satisfy his father's grilling.

It did not take long to notice peer perceptions of *him*. He had, after all, never been farther north than a few days in Washington, DC, and South Carolina's accent and code of conduct suffused his very DNA. Many new acquaintances assumed that southern speech meant that he was just a bit slow. Southern protocols, with elaborate courtesies before getting to points, drove these Yankees crazy; but Carlisle and several compatriots set out to prove them wrong. He heard his polite concern for women's comfort denigrated as "monkey manners": opening doors, walking on the street side, holding chairs and coats, addressing others as ma'am and sir. When treated to such consideration, though, the women themselves did emotional double takes, and rewarded him with, "Ooh, that is so *sweet*!"

Peggy Camp was another matter, delighting in the attention her Scarlett O'Hara dresses, headbands, and speech provoked. On bus rides downtown, Carlisle saw other passengers fall silent as she "took stage," exaggerating her outrageous accent; but he embraced the new environment and adapted. Without apologizing for his origins, he let his own speech acquire "edges."

He began experimenting with pleasures that his family regarded as vices, if not outright sins: drinking, smoking, and strong language. His funds did not allow for much of the first two, but once he tasted his first gin and tonic, whiskey sour, and Tom Collins, he acquired a lifelong taste for sweet-tart beverages with a buzz, beginning at The Orange, the group's pub hangout on Crouse Avenue. Part of Carlisle lived in terror of his father learning the truth, and the rest of him fumed at the hypocrisy that aunt Hazel's smoking was excused. (His mother averred that Hazel's social set expected it, but Ermine took up the habit as well.) Everyone in the movies smoked, and Carlisle thought it "cool." With Syracuse just 250 miles from the center of America's music industry in Manhattan, he scraped together enough money to travel twice to hear his latest hero, child prodigy and matinee idol William Kapell, play at Carnegie Hall.[2] Just four years older than Carlisle, Kapell was the first great artist with whom he identified; and one of the pianist's later concerts introduced him to a showpiece that Kapell's subsequent recording made wildly popular, Aram Khachaturian's 1936 Piano Concerto in D-flat Major.

Carlisle began composing for voice again, over inner protest that he was squandering keyboard practice time. Though he had little faith in such efforts—he had yet to take a formal composition lesson—instinct propelled him. With Rainer Maria Rilke's "Love Song," in translation by M. D. Herter Norton, he listened to his internal dictator, who was also a brilliant pianist. The manuscript is for the moment missing in action.[3]

Loans from two parishioners enabled Reverend Floyd to send room and board of $236 each semester, and $100 for tuition. Carlisle determined to equal his father's educational history at Wofford and reduce the family's debt by compressing two years of study into one, despite enormous class loads each semester. Bacon assured him that the combination of composition and pianism would stack the career deck in his favor, and Carlisle took the necessary proficiencies and auditions to be declared a senior. He longed to enlist one of the school's star sopranos, gorgeous Priscilla Gillette,[4] as his literal mouthpiece. Bacon took the matter into his own hands, approached Gillette and cajoled, "Help this good fellow out." She agreed, and two pianist-composer judges were impressed by Carlisle's showing at a Tuesday afternoon student recital. With the new Rilke song, and his chestnut "When You Are Old" from Converse, senior status was his.

As at Converse, it took him a while to get serious about academics. New classes, new personalities challenged, but not always for the right reasons. His uninspiring theory teacher, William Naylor, practiced dry sarcasm. One day, demonstrating a harmonization at the piano, he noticed Carlisle yawning, and commented, "Sleep is good for that." Carlisle never rose to the bait, but felt himself the bane of Naylor's existence; the professor made repeated references to "certain members of the class with distinguished talents who do not seem to find theory interesting" while making specific eye contact with young Mr. Floyd. A first-semester C confirmed the animus.

Even less successful was his study of the organ. He despised the whole gestalt, finding its technique foreign and unpleasant, though he subsequently used it in several of his father's churches. He believed that he had pulled the wool over the eyes of Belgian professor Leon Verrees. Verrees remained jovial and agreeable until grade time, when Carlisle's reward was a first-semester B, which fell to C during the event-packed second term.

Perhaps even more than Syracuse University's career orientation, Carlisle's social contacts stimulated. He saw at once that his northern peers had been exposed to the arts earlier and longer than he, and that he lacked their levels of sophistication and worldliness; but as always, he proved a quick study. Crouse's arts crowd coalesced in support as he worked and played with painters, actors, and singers. He hit it off at once with a fellow pianist, witty, elfin, erudite Don Rand, much amused by the southern drawl.

Carlisle was changing; but since Converse, Ernst Bacon had not. Syracuse was a larger pond, the director's position more complex, there were more claims on his time and no assistant comparable to Anna Margaret Williams. Gone were the nights of practice-room stalking, but Carlisle's lessons grew ever more erratically scheduled and taught. First semester, they returned to Liszt's Piano Concerto no. 2, and a student recital performance took place with Bacon playing the orchestral reduction. He usually practiced just enough to get "in finger," but this time struggled to sight-read Liszt's accompaniment. The rest of the piano faculty frowned, particularly as Bacon was new to his job. Carlisle had plenty to do with his own part, and Bacon consoled, "Don't worry about all the notes"; yet throughout, Carlisle heard the telltale huffing, puffing, and snorting.

Don Rand describes Bacon's "Beethoven Complex": "He was totally self-focused, theatrical, and played it up: wearing capes, sitting by himself in the balcony and glowering, that sort of thing. He commanded lots of personal attention, and some antagonism from other faculty members. He had the most dramatic studio in that tower, a big round room."[5]

Priscilla Gillette, nicknamed "Woo" by her circle, came to Syracuse to study poetry but sailed through Crouse's vocal program. Despite talent and looks, she seemed ill-starred: one week she might be hard at work, then vanish for two or three days and return looking much the worse for wear. Despite terrible depressions, Gillette alternately fascinated and appalled everyone with her ready laughter at anything serious. Once her friendship with Carlisle deepened, she asked why he spent so much time at the piano when he could compose. He naturally took it to mean that she thought him untalented, but she clarified, "Anybody can be a pianist; you can write!" The piano had fed his soul in times of starvation with quantifiable, immediate personal expression. With its physical dimension of body connected to instrument, the piano was safe, and he was loath to abandon it. The puritanical streak bred into him dictated that composing was easy, playing the piano was hard, and he fought his guilt over doing what came naturally or gave pleasure.

Don Rand and his peers reacted to Carlisle's artistry and work ethic: "He worked harder than any of us; and he had ambition, a desire to make a name for himself. We respected his dedication and pianism."[6]

One day a bizarre personal scene erupted: Carlisle showed up at Bacon's tower warren for a lesson, and a stern, unsmiling teacher beckoned him in, "I have something very serious to talk with you about."

Carlisle gulped, "What have I done?"

Grave and distant, Bacon continued, "We've gone to all this trouble to get Peggy here, and now she wants to go home. Analee and I are upset, and *very* angry with you."

Two and two approximated four: Ernst had rhapsodized to Carlisle about Peggy's collection of billowing skirts and winter white knee-length boots; but despite her full-time residence with the Bacons, she had complained to Carlisle about irregular and insufficient lessons. Carlisle had suggested that she confront Bacon: if she remained unhappy, then she *should* go home. But that was not her southern way: she had told their teacher that Carlisle had advised her to retreat to South Carolina, and Carlisle wondered whether she was trying to eliminate him from the Bacons' affections.

When Carlisle explained himself, Bacon backed down, but with the caution, "You'd better not come to the house for a while, you would not get a very cordial reception from Analee." Carlisle stalked back down past Winged Victory, staring daggers at the waiting, bereft Peggy, whom he ordered to set things straight. In a few weeks, the Bacons forgave him; but questions lingered: What was really afoot in that house?

CARLISLE'S ENERGIES and positive emotions ran so high that he almost forgot asthma; but when long winter descended on Syracuse on the heels of Labor Day, and snow began to fly, the condition reasserted itself with the fury of a scorned lover. Reverend Floyd, long a disciple of multivitamins to cure everything from colds to cancer, sent bottles of Abdol; but still Carlisle gasped, staying indoors as much as possible when winds howled in dark and subzero chill by three in the afternoon. His gaunt frame carried just 140 pounds.

Fascinated as he was by Woo Gillette, it was to her best friend, the actress Jona Heimlich, that Carlisle, in another melding of music and drama groups, first gave his whole heart. During that first semester, he saw her act the title role in Rose Franken's 1941 comedy *Claudia,* and he tumbled like the proverbial hod of bricks. For her part, Jona, with separated parents, was drawn to Carlisle's closeness to his family; but it was his attention to detail and person that won her love. Once on the street, when she wore a dress with pointillist squares of white and multishaded blues, Carlisle reacted with artist's eye and hand, took the material between his fingers, and enthused, "That is the most beautiful blue fabric I've ever seen." This was not the ordinary run of men Jona had known.

Within his means, Carlisle dressed impeccably. Their violinist friend Libby Withrow commented with admiring irony once on his appearance in coat and tie, "Doesn't Carlisle look *purda*?," and the nickname, Carlisle's first, stuck. When flush with more than change, and Jona had no rehearsal, they met the gang at the Cosmo or College Spa, the latter a Greek restaurant on Marshall Street. Carlisle regaled this constellation with his wicked quick humor and gift for mimicry, imitating his southern family and friends. If Peggy Camp turned up, she could not help providing a textbook example; and Don Rand imitated both to their faces.

Jona encouraged Carlisle's movie addiction. The two of them, or the whole group, might plow through the snow, on foot or by bus, to see *Now, Voyager* or *Casablanca* for the sixteenth time. In straitened weeks, they attended student recitals and drama productions, or formed a Bloomsbury-style salon, neither pretentious nor dissolute, at Jona's mother's apartment at 311 East Castle Street or in the parlor of Priscilla's Gamma Phi Beta sorority house. On weekend afternoons, Carlisle might amuse the group with his forger-perfect handwriting imitations. They drank tea, talked to all hours, listened to Saturday Metropolitan Opera broadcasts, or to whatever records people might bring, especially Debussy, Ravel, Fauré, and Delius. Carlisle began visiting Olmstead's record store, adding Stokowski's *Tristan und Isolde* orchestral synthesis to his own modest collection.

Don Rand, a gifted improviser from his part-time work playing at silent movie screenings, would hold forth at any available keyboard, creating imaginary operas, singing all the parts, keeping everyone in laughing tears. Sometimes more free fun was to be had wandering the halls of Crouse College after hours, stopping at the door of a practice room to listen to Don practicing Liszt's Sonata; and there were those modeling classes.

With Carlisle and Jona alone together, entwined on the sofa in the front room of his apartment, the south came alive for her, as he enthralled her with hours of talk of his parents, Ermine, aunts, uncles, galaxies of extended family. Many if not most of Carlisle's romances were colored by a lack of faith in the unconditional love he had never fully experienced from his blood family, except Ermine. Though cautious and circumspect, with Jona he experienced the aliveness and enlargement of having affection returned without possessiveness. Jona was in turn drawn by his vulnerable goodness. Demonstrative, tender, and passionate in his attentions, it was still the forties: regardless of how much he might fantasize, Floyd boys did not "go all the way" before marriage.

WITH CHRISTMAS APPROACHING, Ida bustled about the parsonage, cleaning, cooking special treats for the returning Yankee conqueror. His grades could have been better: A in only Chorus and Aesthetics, and B in Piano, Ensemble, Piano Teachers Training, Organ, American Literature since 1890 and History of Fine Arts. Holly Hill parishioners contributed more money toward travel costs. Carlisle, shepherding Peggy Camp, missed their Manhattan connection and arrived at Orangeburg a half-day late. Jack lay abed with asthma, and Ida drove to meet Carlisle. For the entire holiday, she pointed out to everyone his addition of very unsouthern "ings" to the ends of all his gerunds. Jack may have thought, "He looks thin and tired,"[7] but it was not long before his comment, "You never have asthma anymore," took on an accusing tone. As late as 1984, Reverend Floyd connected his son's qualities with their shared disease: "He is such a thoughtful fellow, like he was when he was sick with asthma."[8]

Carlisle longed to share excitement about his new Syracuse work, but the problem lay in finding someone safe. In Laurinburg, he confided to his aunt Lucile that, more than anything, he wanted to be a real artist, a great artist. Like the rest of the family, she simply took it in and nodded; but Carlisle's exuberance and Lucile's Christian Science met at a wall: with raised eyebrow, she asked, "Does your father know how often you use the Lord's name in vain?"

Everyone played lots of Rook over the holiday.

Turning the corner into 1946 and back in Syracuse, Carlisle rented a private room in a university-owned house at 724 Comstock, just down the street from Sigma Nu, for $29 per month.[9] Though he had made the honor roll, he faced Naylor again in the classroom; but the new subject was orchestration. Carlisle enjoyed this, and his grade climbed from C to A. The teacher's bromides were the Berlioz and Rimsky-Korsakov treatises, but Carlisle never found much in either that stuck. Naylor's official text was Arthur Heacox's aging *Project Lessons in Orchestration,* which at least laid out the basics in an orderly fashion.[10] Needing piano pedagogy credentials, Carlisle took Elvin Schmitt's course and taught small children who came to the university for inexpensive lessons.[11]

Too much time had passed since working with Bearden at Converse, and Carlisle now responded to an advertisement for an extracurricular writing seminar, limited to ten, taught by one of the English department's young lights, Daniel Curley.[12] Carlisle submitted selected Converse pieces for admission, and Curley accepted him.

A prolific novelist and short story writer, Curley had graduated from the University of Alabama and, two years younger than Carlisle, was still pursuing his own aggressive career. In professional critique group style, Curley might read someone's work and ask, "Should that be sent to *Esquire*?," followed by class discussion. Carlisle was thankful that he'd had Bearden first. Whereas she urged him to use heightened language, especially active verbs, to evoke settings and emotional states, Curley offered drier pragmatic guidance. If he or a student mentioned an unfamiliar author, Carlisle headed to the library after class, to look up Frank O'Hara or Ellen Glasgow.[13] Glasgow, a fellow southerner, appealed for her penetrating social and intellectual content, and stories of family dynasties that echoed the Floyds and Fenegans.

Another Curley student, Bernard Barrow, Jona Heimlich's speech and drama peer—they acted together in *Claudia*—was already a centerpiece of Syracuse's arts clique. A bright, funny Manhattanite, he wrote poetry, mostly for women for whom he had fallen. For Priscilla Gillette, he dashed off a schoolboy verse, "I am a beggar on a lonely hill." The theater was Barrow's true love and the source of his ultimate success in television and film.[14] Carlisle was not the only class member who begged him to perform class readings of poetry and prose: Barrow's voice made anything sound good; and, like Carlisle, Barrow had love on his mind. When Woo showed Carlisle the "Beggar" poem, he was touched by its bittersweet humor and filed it away for future use.

Carlisle produced both prose and poetry for Curley. That spring, the university's literary journal *Tabard* published his poem "Resolution," another Wolfean cry of pessimism against the futility of life. As a final project, he wrote a five-thousand-word story, "A Lengthening Shadow." Following tried and true advice to write about what one knew, his thoughts went back to the barren sandhills, "a stricken country, doomed to poverty." Families strove there to wrest marginal crops of cotton and corn from the sand, and opposed fundamentalist sects erected barriers to young lovers forging independent lives.

The "Shadow" girl's romantic involvement with a boy from a different religious group mirrors *Romeo and Juliet* in South Carolina garb, set in an amalgam of Jordan and Bethune. Maternal grandmother Katherine Cottingham and grandfather Oscar Fenegan had braved enmity between Methodists (later, Christian Scientists) and Baptists. Having experienced religion as the bastion of southern women, sibyls who sniped at any order that strayed from theirs, Carlisle recalled the doom-promising roadside billboards of Washfoot Baptists, True Lights, and Disciples of Christ. Though he never cultivated friends from these groups, Bethune's school had its contingent of "bus kids" from such families, driven in from outlying farms. For his denouement, Carlisle summoned up years of long country rambles and sinister dark ponds masking gnarled tree roots, of which Ida warned him.

The lovers are Micah Hatfield, nineteen, of a Truelight family, and Sadie Kinsey, seventeen, raised Baptist, and intent on finishing high school. Micah and Sadie agree to marry, and Sadie heads home to tell the Kinsey materfamilias Aunt Sue, while Micah goes fishing. Away from Micah, Sadie feels a heaviness descend, but the thought that her love will come tonight to ask for her hand lifts the pall: "She knew that the shadow could only be completely lifted when she was with him." Aunt Sue forbids the union, religion her justification, and Sadie storms away to walk off her fury. When she returns, her brothers wait in the front room to deliver a dire message: Micah snagged his hook on a submerged stump, dove in to free it, and drowned. Carlisle had Sadie walk back to confront the night pond, the "murderer" on whom "there was no revenge." We see a woman alone, battered by forces larger than she, but gaining survival skills to confront the rest of her life. It is also Carlisle's first exposition of religion as a divisive force.

Meanwhile, he wrote home about Jona. His mother in particular, never having offered relationship advice, was thrilled by their involvement; and Reverend Floyd wrote, "Carlisle seems right much interested in Jona."[15] He and Ida cooked and wrapped candy to send north; then Ida made a very southern gesture. On a February day, plodding home through a blizzard, Jona pulled back the screen door of her mother's apartment and discovered a florist's box on the doorstep. Unwrapped, it held a bouquet of South Carolina camellias.

Bacon encouraged Carlisle to produce new songs for his upcoming senior recital; and now he had an in-house exponent, Priscilla Gillette. Art song was Bacon's forte, and the path by which many composers approach the voice before attempting opera, but Carlisle always had difficulty finding poetry to set. Each of his own verse efforts led a separate, subjective life, and, despite his comment to Bacon the previous summer, he never set any of his own verse as an art song. The poetry of others provided objectivity, but it had to suggest a *need* for music. Love preoccupied him, and he responded to fervid verse that might invite musical extension. Building on Rilke's "Love Song," he edited, revised, and recopied his setting of Christina Rossetti's "Remember Me" for Gillette. He dated the new manuscript February 25, 1946, "For Ermine, with best love," and the poem itself would seem to be a gesture of homesickness for her company.[16]

Next, at Jona's suggestion, he turned again to Yeats for "The Fairy's Song," from the Irishman's 1894 drama, *The Land of Heart's Desire:*

> The wind blows out of the gates of the day,
> The wind blows over the lonely of heart,
> And the lonely of heart is withered away.
> While the fairies dance in a place apart,
> Tossing their milk-white arms in the air,[17]
> Shaking their milk-white feet in a ring,
> For they hear the wind laugh and murmur and sing
> Of a land where even the old are fair,
> And even the wise and merry of tongue
> But I heard a reed of Coolaney say:
> "When the wind has laughed and murmur'd and
>   sung,
> The lonely of heart is wither'd away.

Carlisle pushed his harmonic envelope, experimenting with more quartal and quintal harmonies, and the Orientalism of the so-called gypsy scale, with a lowered second on descent. The short song in 6/8, "Very Moderately, airily and softly throughout," anchors in F-sharp Minor. Rapid descending scales in the left hand suggest the wind of the poem's first line. The vocal line is "to be sung in half-voice throughout, simply and wistfully," with an open, ethereal effect.[18]

CARLISLE HAD HOPED to finish school in April, but saw now that his plan had been too ambitious: it would take the summer session to prepare a senior recital. His father wired money for the trip home, and Carlisle landed in Holly Hill on April 20. Between such chores as addressing envelopes for church assembly delegates and attending revivals that his father preached, he kept busy making music. On May 8, visiting Ermine at Converse, he found himself close to peer acceptance by former teachers, and played his new songs for pianist-composers Lionel Nowak and John MacEnulty. He admired both men, but feared what such followers of Hindemith would think of his postromanticism; yet the doyens found his work very fresh. MacEnulty even praised one piece as "something honest."[19]

Bacon, believing that Carlisle had exceeded his teaching, arranged an audition at the Curtis Institute. During Carlisle's April visit to Converse, he had played his audition pieces for Lionel Nowak, who pronounced that he had "tamed down considerably" in his year at Syracuse.[20] On May 8, Carlisle and Ermine rode the rails to the venerable Curtis Institute on Philadelphia's Rittenhouse Square, which struck him "as having more the appearance of a morgue or an old mansion relic of the Nineties." To Isabelle Vengerova and Josef Hoffmann he offered Bach's Prelude and Fugue in C-sharp Minor, from volume 1 of *The Well-Tempered Clavier;* the first movement of Beethoven's Sonata in E Minor, op. 90; and a Chopin Etude; but he came away with little more than the image of the legendary Vengerova's size:[21]

> They were very kind and courteous to me and . . . my whole stay in the building couldn't have amounted to more than a half hour. My playing time must not have consumed ten minutes. I played as well as I ever have although I realized when I left that I had almost no chance of getting in. Nevertheless, I did my best . . . [but] I simply don't think my best was good enough. The competition was very keen. . . . Ten minutes seems like a very inadequate length of time to decide whether a person is capable of becoming a professional in his field. . . . Nevertheless, we can always say it was good experience; that seems to compensate for almost anything.[22]

On May 16 he concertized for the Holly Hill Book Club; and on June 3, he and Ermine gave a recital for friends and family in Latta that included three of his recent songs. Carlisle turned twenty on June 11, about to launch into the world with no visible future except indebtedness to family and their friends: his idea of life in hell. On June 21, he and his mother drove to Red Springs, North Carolina, where he interviewed for a faculty position at Flora MacDonald Women's College. Failing to receive an offer heightened concern about the future once he had gotten his Syracuse bachelor's degree, but the weeks before returning north flew by as he memorized his recital. To thank Priscilla Gillette for supporting his music, and in particular for agreeing to sing in his upcoming program, he wrote her a short improvisation, "Who Has Known the Panic," in the style of their beloved Thomas Wolfe. In a single page, neither submitted nor published, he concentrated the urgency of his creative process and conflicts over his relationship with Jona:

> And in the vast aloneness of a man's soul is the fierce, impatient illusion of greatness. And the creative urge is tempered by these two things: the desire of a man to perpetuate his spirit, the core of himself, for the future, and the violent terror of an uncompromising Time. And between these, there is the fury of existence.[23]

Such verbal creativity stimulated new music, a setting of southern musician and poet Sidney Lanier's "An Evening Song" (1876):

> Look off, dear Love, across the sallow sands,
> And mark yon meeting of the sun and sea,

How long they kiss in sight of all the lands.
Ah! Longer, longer, we.
Now in the sea's red vintage melts the sun,
As Egypt's pearl dissolved in rosy wine,
And Cleopatra night drinks all. 'Tis done,
Love, lay thine hand in mine.
Come forth, sweet stars, and comfort heaven's heart;
Glimmer, ye waves, round else unlighted sands.
O night! Divorce our sun and sky apart
Never our lips, our hands.[24]

He wrote Bacon, lamenting the "period of temporary sterility which has ensued ever since I have been home. . . . I have thought a great deal about my composing this spring and read a good bit regarding the work of Debussy and Delius, both of whom I admire tremendously. I feel constantly the urgency of developing an idiom for myself which will be instantly recognizable when my music is performed. I am not content with the rampant emotionalism of the late Romantics nor am I satisfied to any great extent by the barren mechanism of Schillinger and his gang. Somewhere in between, I hope to find myself. You seem to have done it, Mr. Bacon; I hope I am able."[25]

All Floyd song accompaniments employ maximal pianism, with resonant pedal bass and full right-hand chords at extreme keyboard ranges, and the Lanier setting overflows with such contrasts. Nominally in E Major, much of its melody and harmony involves accidentals, the overall effect reminiscent of the early work of Schönberg, Berg, and Webern. Emotional intensities shift and shimmer like Lanier's evening light. The vocal line challenges: one note per syllable, with ascending and descending tritones, fourths, fifths, sixths, sevenths, and octaves. Floyd again creates a kind of post-Wagnerian endless melody, with emotional and sonic climax on a high B at "Never our lips." (He offered an *ossia* of G sharp for Gillette's problematic upper register.)

In all his vocal writing, he emphasizes natural speech rhythms and accents. Melodies avoid the obvious, but the entire miniature structure of each song intensifies a complete story, providing a satisfying emotional experience. All of his songs remain unpublished; Ernst Bacon was, however, impressed enough to recommend them to the prestigious Philadelphia firm of Theodore Presser.

ON JUNE 29, Ida drove him to Bamberg, and Mrs. Camp saw Carlisle and Peggy off on their Syracuse-bound train from Columbia. The cars still teemed with returned soldiers sleeping in seats and corridors. As long as he could guide Peggy to her reserved place, Carlisle was content to sit on his suitcase and lose himself in reading.

Jona awaited his return with open arms. Bacon had worked in Carlisle's behalf during the break, nosing out a faculty vacancy at the University of New Hampshire, though no interview materialized. With the senior recital date looming, the elder Floyds and Ermine picked up Lucile Fenegan in Laurinburg on August 2, and arrived in Syracuse the next day. Reverend Floyd, with his ever keen eye for the ladies, offered his stamp of approval: "Jona surely is a sweet girl."[26] She and Carlisle took them on the obligatory campus tour, after which Ermine spent the night at Jona's.

Recital day was Sunday, August 4. First, though, Reverend Floyd insisted on everyone attending Methodist services at Hendricks Chapel, after which he treated a party of ten to lunch in the Onondaga Hotel's dining room. Carlisle offered a varied, ambitious program at eight that evening in Crouse College Auditorium: Bach's Prelude and Fugue in C-sharp Minor; Brahms's Sonata in F-sharp Minor, op. 1; his own four songs ("Love Song," "Remember," "The Fairy's Song," and "Evening Song"), with Priscilla Gillette; Chopin Etudes in C-sharp Minor and B Minor, op. 25; and Debussy's *Les sons et les parfums tournent* (Préludes, Book 1) and *L'isle joyeuse.* As he set his music and adjusted the bench, Bacon approached him on stage. As they shook hands, he acknowledged that Carlisle had not been his easiest student: "You hoe your own row."

With no reference to his son's compositions, Reverend Floyd wrote, "Carlisle did *real* well and we are proud of him."[27] On her salary as a hospital phone receptionist, Jona's mother hosted a party at her apartment, attended by the Floyd contingent and Analee and Ernst Bacon.

The next morning, Carlisle and family piled into the 1939 Chevy, its radiator now predictably overheating. They played tourist at Niagara Falls, enjoying the novelty of crossing into Canada, submitting to their first immigration and customs inspections. Back in Syracuse that evening after the 340-mile round trip, they stopped for Jona, and everyone dined Italian at the Savoy Restaurant.

Carlisle finished the year in strength: A in Piano, Music Theory, Ensemble, University Chorus, and Creative Writing; B in Piano Teachers' Training, History of Fine Arts, and Musicology. After early breakfast on Tuesday, the family visited Bacon, "who made us feel very proud of Carlisle and said that he would give him $400 scholarship and give him a job as [*sic*] tutoring, which would pay $600."[28] Curious as to Bacon's beliefs, Jack broached the topic of religion. Bacon confided that his father had been a Baptist, his mother, a Catholic; the Reverend later told Carlisle, "No wonder he is agnostic."

Bacon was tempting Carlisle to return to Syracuse for a master's degree without a break, and any hint of funding was music to Reverend Floyd's ears. He, Ida, Ermine, and Lucile left that afternoon, but Jack was so flushed with the experience that he sent Carlisle a postcard from Gettysburg telling him "to come home via air if he cared to."[29]

By now the family had accepted Jona as The One for Carlisle, and they prepared to welcome a daughter-in-law-elect for her first visit to South Carolina. Jona snagged a ride with Peggy Camp and her mother, anticipating Carlisle's arrival on August 14 by two days. The next sixteen were packed with feasting, visits to friends and relatives in Latta and Laurinburg, impromptu Carlisle/Ermine concerts, swimming, touring to Charleston and the immense Santee-Cooper Dam project.

Yet all was not well. The most telling indication of Carlisle's emotional state was his first serious asthma attack in months. Jona was attuned to the siren songs of marriage and parenthood, but Carlisle was not ready for either. From the moment he arrived, Jona felt him distanced, and distracted. In a parsonage packed to the rafters with parents, aunts, and uncles, Jona sharing a bed with Ermine, and Carlisle wheezing through nights on the parlor settee, the lovers found scant chance for intimacy or communication. Finally, over the weekend, they drove off in the old Chevy and parked and talked. Carlisle broke from pressures of commitment and expectation, and tears fell: a beautiful, intelligent woman admired him, was good to him, and expected things of him; but he, still working toward a music career, had no prospects, no independent means of supporting a wife, much less a family. Better to end matters now rather than lead Jona on. For both, it was a moment of loss and sorrow; when Floyds married, it was for keeps.[30]

The romance over, Jona spent a marvelous second week. She and Carlisle could simply be themselves: fond friends enjoying a new and different closeness, realizing that their investment in each other would never be misplaced. Looking forward to a lifetime of friendship struck both as preferable to the specter of a problematic marriage.[31]

BARELY TWENTY, Carlisle now found himself stranded in the Holly Hill parsonage. His world had changed, but without providing the means or desire to integrate his parents into it. He had saved them thousands of dollars with scholarships that allowed him to finish undergraduate school in three years; but Reverend Floyd exacted a different price, with constant reminders about the $600 in outstanding loans that Carlisle had no means to repay. Too young to be given serious consideration for academic positions, he embarked on nine months of self-imposed exile, "going quietly crazy." As he wrote Bacon during winter's bleak months, "It is difficult to get down to one's most intensive and serious efforts with nothing particular in view towards which to work. . . . There was, of course, all the time I wanted for practice and I availed myself of it, trying . . . to work up repertoire. The almost total absence of distractions was of course a major element in any progress I may have made and although that same absence . . . can at the same time become a little maddening, it is very much in contrast to my life the last three years. I cannot say that it is a blessed state, however."[32]

He caught up on reading, mostly Ellen Glasgow; practiced piano for hours each day, played church services when his mother fell ill; took the bus for long visits to family in Laurinburg and Asheville, and the Camps in Bamberg; did yard work, washed the car, drew in chalk, crayon, or colored pencil with neighbor "Gene" Wiggins; contacted all of Holly Hill's piano teachers in an effort to snag a few students; and had his father borrow a typewriter to copy his last three pieces of unpublished fiction. Whenever opportunity arose to concertize, he seized it, usually for the women's book club.

It was fortunate for him that Reverend Floyd was so absorbed in his job, and in preaching revivals around the state. The two had relatively few unpleasant path-crossings, but Carlisle sensed that his very presence provoked his father, who could not understand why his son was not out earning a living. Once when he and Reverend Floyd began to wrangle, Carlisle stood his ground, perspiration pouring down his sides, terrified of retribution that threatened like distant heat lightning but never struck. Anxious as ever, Mrs. Floyd took him aside, heaving, "I can't stand it when you and your father fight!"

Mrs. Floyd showed more concern for putting meat on her son's bones, getting him to a weight of 130, a figure no one in the family thought they would ever see. Ida's sister Lucile memorialized this success on one of Carlisle's Laurinburg visits by taking him to a photographer.

In September, Carlisle fell up on meeting Isobel Lyons when she visited relatives in Holly Hill. A chemistry professor at Florida State College for Women in Tallahassee, Lyons gave him an insider tip on the college's dramatic expansion and added teaching positions in most areas. On September 19, Carlisle wrote the enterprising music dean, Karl Kuersteiner,[33] and enclosed a brief résumé. He emphasized both piano and composition, claiming that Ernst Bacon had coached him in the latter; that Carl Deis at the venerable New York music house of G. Schirmer was considering publishing one of his songs; and that he was currently at work on an instrumental trio.[34]

Kuersteiner replied on October 28 that one of the school's theory and piano teachers would leave on January 1, 1947, creating an instructorship vacancy. In addition to piano, Carlisle would teach one to three sections of freshman theory, including harmony, solfeggio (sight singing) and keyboard harmony. Unbeknownst to Carlisle, Kuersteiner had determined to assemble a faculty of performer-composers, hence his interest in Carlisle's burgeoning composition catalogue. He asked for recommendations, added information on Carlisle's personal qualifications, and a photograph.[35]

The downside was salary: the position paid just $1,800 for the school year, of which only $1,200 might be dedicated to Carlisle, from January 2 through June 9.[36] Reverend Floyd, in his belief that Carlisle had a firm offer, wrote in his diary for October 31, "Do hope he gets job. . . . Carlisle beat me 6 games to 4 in table tennis."[37] Carlisle masked elation in his response of November 1: concerned about practice time, he asked how many weekly hours he would be expected to teach. He sent Kuersteiner transcripts from Converse and Syracuse, emphasizing honors in creative writing and accompanying opera repertoire, and supplied three sources for recommendation: Ernst Bacon and George Mulfinger at Syracuse, and Alia Ross Lawson at Converse. His father gave him $19.50 on November 18 to have a new studio portrait taken.

On November 20, Kuersteiner wrote to specify that Carlisle's private lessons would not exceed twenty-five hours per week, the school's maximum. The dean also asked his prospective new hire's exact age, provided in Carlisle's response of November 22.

Carlisle was not surprised to learn that Ernst Bacon had been removed as dean at Syracuse University and moved to a position created for him as composer-in-residence and professor of piano and composition. Bacon's recommendation, dated November 21, contains nuggets of perception in his characteristic bluff manner: "Concerning Carlisle Floyd, I can only speak in terms of the highest praise. He has an exceptional musical talent, perhaps not fully disciplined but of a nature that one could say borders in a small sense on genius. He is no less interesting for his talents as a composer than as a young pianist, and I am not even sure that his talents as a writer are not equal to either of his musical talents, as a result of plays, poems, and other writings of his which I have run across. In addition, he is a boy of the very finest character. . . . Certainly his lack of experience is much over-balanced by his gifts and his excellent human qualities. If I did not feel that he needed a change of influences I would see that he gets something with us, but I am quite convinced that he needs to knock around elsewhere."[38]

A SETBACK ARRIVED with Kuersteiner's letter of December 6: added to concerns about Carlisle's youth, there had been a blanket raising of existing faculty salaries. The consequent shortage of funds discouraged new hires, and a returning army captain had been given priority with the theory instructorship; yet the school found itself in the odd position of having more demand for piano instruction than it could meet, so jobs would still be available either for spring quarter at the end of March or summer quarter in June. Kuersteiner asked Carlisle to set an on-site interview.[39]

After recovering from an asthma attack, Carlisle and Ermine concertized at Holly Hill High on December 20, but his condition reasserted itself on Christmas Eve. On December 26, Reverend Floyd drove him to aunt Doris and uncle J. W. in Asheville, and wrote, "Carlisle sat in front with me all the way."[40] The topics of their conversation en route are matters for speculation, but one suspects that Jona Heimlich headed the list. For the first time, that evening Carlisle turns up in his father's diary prayer lists. The next day, on the solitary drive back to Holly Hill, Jack "thought about what a good boy Carlisle had always been."[41] Meanwhile, Doris and J. W. took Carlisle on to New Orleans for that year's Sugar Bowl. Wheezing his way through New Year's Eve at the Edgewater Park Hotel, Carlisle got little sleep, much of his floor occupied by the University of North Carolina's football team, that year playing the University of Georgia; but aunt Doris had brought her supply of asthma cigarettes and ministered as well as she could.

With the figurative death of his romance with Jona, and learning of the recent passing of his bosom friend McNeal Clyburn in Bethune, more of Carlisle's childhood had evaporated; but he had held his own with Yankees in Syracuse, in fact finding the place a prod to creativity. Now the problem was not coming home, but getting away from it again. On December 5, he earned $34 for playing a concert in Allendale, repeating his senior recital program plus Scriabin's *Nocturne for the Left Hand*, which Reverend Floyd considered the pinnacle of his son's pianistic accomplishment. With Christmas approaching, Carlisle still had Jona on his mind. To commemorate their relationship, he settled on a book by their mutually beloved poet Rupert Brooke. One of the verses, "The Hill," held special meaning for both, as the title was also the nickname for Syracuse University, cradle of their romance:

Breathless, we flung us on the windy hill,
Laughed in the sun, and kissed the lovely grass.
You said, "Through glory and ecstasy we pass,
Wind, sun, and earth remain, the birds sing still,
When we are old, are old. . . ." "And when we die
All's over that is ours; and life burns on
Through other lovers, other lips," said I,
—"Heart of my heart, our heaven is now, is won!"
"We are Earth's best, that learnt her lesson here.
Life is our cry. We have kept the faith!" we said;
"We shall go down with unreluctant tread
Rose-crowned into the darkness!" . . . Proud we were,
And laughed, that had such brave true things to say.
—And then you suddenly cried, and turned away.[42]

Youth had ended for Carlisle Floyd.

7

Young Professor Floyd Writes an Opera

Florida State University, Syracuse Again, Slow Dusk, *1946–1949*

The trip to New Orleans marked Carlisle Floyd's first venture anywhere *south* of his various South Carolina homes, and he expected semitropical weather. Instead, gasping for breath between puffs on Doris's asthma smokes, he found "rain, heavy fog, and wet cold, unexpectedly severe."[1] At least he had the pleasure of watching North Carolina defeat Georgia 20 to 10 in the Sugar Bowl on New Year's Day. Back in Holly Hill on January 7, desperate to end his exile, Floyd welcomed Karl Kuersteiner's letter of January 8, suggesting a meeting at Winthrop College in Rock Hill, South Carolina, on January 15.

Kuersteiner seemed cordial and well-disposed, but the encounter proved inconclusive; yet Floyd seized any hand that might pull him up from Holly Hill. That fall, Bacon had offered him another scholarship to return to Syracuse in the fall of 1947, and he wrote Bacon on January 19 about his Florida State University prospects:

> I think I can have a position on their faculty beginning in June (after I'm 21!), if I decide that that is what I want to do. It is really hard to know what is best for me: I don't think I am being obstinate in still hoping and working towards a career as a pianist. If, after I've been in New York and see that I don't "stack up" or simply lack whatever it takes to have a career, I think I'll be content to go into teaching permanently, but *only* after I have agreed with myself, so to speak, that whatever ability I may have had better be channeled towards a teacher's career rather than that of an active performer.[2]

To that end, he hoped that a June audition at the Juilliard School might prove more productive than his Curtis experience the year before; but he spent the next two months twiddling his thumbs, personally and professionally, longing, as he had written Bacon, for "the companionship of congenial associates, [which] has become very precious to me, here where there is none."[3] Instead, he ran errands, did more house and yard chores, attended local basketball and baseball games, visited nonmusical friends. On February 20, he played again for the Holly Hill Book Club; and, on March 24, wrote Kuersteiner that he would be happy and honored to join their faculty either in June or the following September.

Floyd sought isolation in the church choir room or sanctuary, any space with an instrument. He was composing again, his first solo piano literature, *Soliloquy and Phantasm.*[4] Driving intensity and dotted sixteenth-thirty-second figures in melodies and syncopated bass lines connect these short pieces, both modified rondos, the opening material varied and ornamented in chromatically or enharmonically related tonalities. "Soliloquy" is grounded in A Minor, 4/4, A*dagio, molto cantabile.* Pedal A-natural three lines below the bass staff tolls in thirty-four of the piece's seventy-one bars, as an ascending stepwise melody and dotted-note figure suggest an emotional hiccup. The middle section of chordal triplets in 3/4, *molto espressivo,* returns to the tonic. A second theme has the character of an augmented retrograde of the original theme. This acquires intensity, *appassionato e marcato,* in yet another rhythmic augmentation, with accidentals, triplet accompaniment, and a jazzy flat seventh. As in Floyd's earlier songs, quartal and quintal openness, and quick sequential figures in distant keys, convey notes of distress in this meditation, ending with recapitulation of opening material and abrupt modulation to the home key.

The companion piece, 40-bar "Phantasm," is in the distant key of B-flat Minor, again in 4/4, *Allegro non troppo, molto cantabile.* As in his song accompaniments, Floyd uses great handfuls of notes, both left and right. He establishes a rhythmic pattern of quarter-quarter, two sixteenths-eighth, eighth-two sixteenths, against an ostinato left-hand syncopation. Two statements of the opening theme lead to a transposition to E-flat Minor, followed by A-flat Minor, C Minor, then F Minor, with a flat seventh functioning as dominant. He varies the return to the original theme in B-flat Minor by fragmenting the melody from one hand to the other, building, *rallentando,* to a shattering climax, *L'istesso tempo ma largamente.* The manuscript expands to three staves, with the two lowest octaves of unison B-flat as a pedal to the end and an unresolved unison shriek on the keyboard's three highest A-naturals.

Despite their brevity, both pieces require hand-spans of at least a tenth, and archromantic virtuosity in rhythmic precision and unrelieved emotional intensity. Although never published separately, *Soliloquy and Phantasm* will make later appearances in this chapter.

FLOYD LEFT COLLEGE knowing that a composer had to pick his camp: Schönberg and dodecaphony; the measured neoclassicism and *Gebrauchsmusik*[5] of Hindemith; the idiosyncratic harmonic-rhythmic gestures and preserialism of Stravinsky; or American, embracing the multiplicity of that term, broad as the land itself, and exemplified by the openness and spare diatonic harmonies of Bacon and Copland. When Floyd read of Copland's conscious stylistic shift away from his jazz-influenced Piano Concerto (1926) and abstract Piano Variations (1930) to greater simplicity and audience-friendly subjects and sounds, he took it as a serious hint.[6] This was not to say that Floyd embraced composers' pandering to their public, but his credo became "give them what they expect, then more." The study of Mozart's operas opened his eyes to how the great musical dramatist had pleased his public, who at the same time had little conception of the totality of his offering.

Finally, Kuersteiner's letter of April 16 settled matters, offering Floyd a summer appointment as piano instructor, to "get better acquainted": in other words, an extended audition.[7] He was to appear in Tallahassee by June 16, by which time he would have turned twenty-one. The summer term ended July 24, and the salary for this period of about five weeks would be four hundred dollars. At least he would be spared the drudgery of teaching freshman music theory, but continued employment was contingent on his earning a master's degree as soon as practicable. With Bacon's offer of a scholarship and assistantship, Floyd refocused his sights on Syracuse, but first accepted the Tallahassee offer without qualification on April 22. Five days later, perhaps as penance for glee, or sheer thanksgiving, he played the new organ—an instrument he still loathed—at his father's church in Holly Hill.[8]

The following week, he received Kuersteiner's outline of the facilities at his disposal; meals for the entire summer term would be around $40, housing $12 or $13. The dean urged his new instructor to plan a summer recital early enough for inclusion in the school's calendar of events, and suggested June 20, confirmed by Floyd in his letter of May 7. On May 6 he gave an ambitious warm-up concert for Laurinburg's St. Cecelia Club, repeating the Chopin, Brahms, and Debussy from his senior recital, Scriabin's Nocturne from his Allendale concert the previous December, and adding Grieg's Ballade in the Form of Variations on a Norwegian Folksong, op. 24.

Floyd turned twenty-one on June 11. Short of funds as the long-awaited day of departure for Tallahassee approached, he borrowed $125 from parishioner-banker Sam McCoy. The three Floyds headed south at 5:45 on the morning of June 12, arriving in Tallahassee the following afternoon.

Floyd's career engine had idled since Syracuse, and now slipped into first gear. Except for discrete periods of an occasional few days at a time, this marked the end of his leisure but also the beginnings of real independence. At their first campus meeting, Kuersteiner told Floyd that his official title would be assistant instructor, with music theory a part of his teaching load after all, at least form and analysis. Weighted to

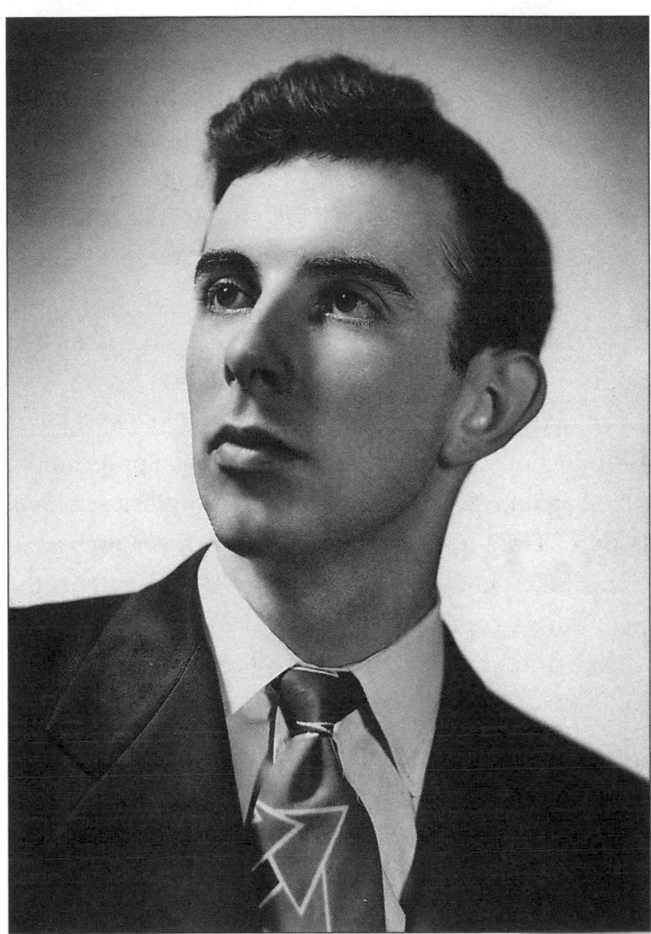

10. Young professor Floyd, 1947. Avant Studios, Tallahassee, Florida. Floyd collection. By permission of Gayle C., David, and George D. Avant.

the dissection of fugues, Floyd's training had been from William Naylor at Syracuse, hence dry and boring. He promptly pulled appropriate books out of the music library and equipped himself for this less than appealing prospect by staying several chapters ahead of his students, many older than he. Floyd and his parents then settled him into a small, hot room in a private home on West Call Street, where they left him to unpack, study for his first classes, and contemplate the bliss of his first paycheck.

With classes beginning on June 16, Floyd first worked the music registration tables. Still under the impression that his employer was a college for women, he gaped at the flood of male former military personnel streaming through the doors. A colleague told him that the college was now coeducational, renamed Florida State University. That summer, the music department was housed in a tiny deconsecrated and relocated white frame church. Although his west-facing studio channeled Florida's summer heat, and had neither climate control nor soundproofing, he soon discovered a great love for teaching. When a good talent appeared, the hour sped by; at other times it was just work. The typical first lesson began with a thirty-year-old man coming through the door looking sheepish and out of place. Floyd asked why he wanted to play the piano, to which the answer was usually a variation on "It's something I always thought I'd like to do." Floyd reached over to his thick pile of beginners' technique books, and they'd be off. From noon to five, sweat-drenched, he demonstrated and drilled basic hand placement and fingering for scales, arpeggios, and easy tunes, for more than twenty-five hours each week.

Still, by inclination and training, he worked even harder with less gifted students, finding their minimal progress more exciting than that of better but less-motivated talents. He discovered joy and pride in being a good teacher, and would not fail through lack of effort. In each discipline he would teach, Floyd learned far more on his own, one day at a time, than he had ever been taught by any instructor, at any school. Absorbing new skills and literature in order to pass them on appealed to his voracious intellectual appetite, and he appreciated the differences between college and reality: learning only what has been *assigned* is a pitiful excuse for education.

Four days in, he played his FSU debut recital, repeating his Brahms, Chopin, and Debussy, and adding a Haydn Sonata in C Major and his own *Soliloquy and Phantasm.* The *Florida Flambeau* praised Floyd's Haydn for its delicate precision. The first-ever press notice of his own music pronounced *Soliloquy and Phantasm* abstract and psychological: "Soliloquy" internal, and "Phantasm" turbulent and restless.[9]

One senior faculty member voiced the old guard's refreshingly surprised attitude, enthusing, "It was very enlivening!" Floyd began repaying debts to his father with his entire first check of $128.45. With spare change from the McCoy loan, for Reverend Floyd's forty-third birthday on July 21, he sent Harry Emerson Fosdick's 1943 book, *On Being a Real Person.*[10]

Kuersteiner rewarded Floyd's performance by hiring him for the second summer term for another four hundred dollars. Floyd continued sending most of his salary home, as well as repaying Sam McCoy with his first August check. On August 30, he splurged by flying to Charleston. His mother and Ermine met him and drove him back to Holly Hill for a two-week stay of sleeping and reading.

THE FIRST ORDER OF BUSINESS after returning on September 14 was moving into new housing, a converted barracks at the former Dale Mabry airfield about five miles west of town.[11] Renamed West Campus, this barracks included studio and eating facilities—a former mess hall—but it lacked air conditioning. Floyd was one of six piano instructors—the other five older than he—who lived and taught at the site, sharing a single bathroom and shower area. Makeshift walls of papery wood-fiber beaverboard separated the various studios. At first, the entire building had no heating system, but administrators relented in October, installing a single pot-bellied stove at one end of the communal hallway, onto which each studio's door opened. Inner doors had to be left open to admit any heat, negating the minimal sound insulation, so Floyd taught in his overcoat, watching his students' icy fingers while listening to lessons given by each of his neighbors. Still without his own transportation, bus trips to meetings or performance events on the main campus, or shopping in downtown Tallahassee, had celebratory airs.

In these early years, money never ceased to be an issue. Floyd continued sending the bulk of his $2,800 annual salary to his father for deposit in Holly Hill, and to repay Holly Hill parishioner Carlisle Harvey's $1,500 loan. There was just enough left over to mail Ermine $10 each month during her final year at Converse, "to have cinnamon toast." By the end of the academic year, all five of Floyd's piano instructor colleagues had resigned. Older faculty were mainly entrenched female instructors, headed by Floyd's supervisor and eventual friend, Mary Winslow. Everyone seemed amused by Floyd's youth as much as his pianism, and treated him like a younger brother or nephew.

For fall term, Kuersteiner embarked on a campaign to hire as many artists of national and international reputation as the state's budget would allow, but progress was slow. Soprano Elizabeth Ellison, alto Betty Jane Grimm, tenor Walter James, and bass Herman Gunter taught voice. Another 1947 hire was the composer John Boda,[12] also housed in the West Campus barracks; the senior composer was Walter Ruel Cowles.[13]

Floyd's teaching load now included Music 110, Introduction to Music, or general music appreciation. Once again, the subject required familiarity with a body of literature he had never heard, for orchestra, chamber ensembles, solo instruments other than the piano, and opera. He quickly took up the latest edition of Martin Bernstein's lively *An Introduction to Music,* for the six or seven years that he taught the class.[14]

Alongside the usual slog of beginner students in the fall of 1947 came the occasional supernova like Ryan Edwards, of Quincy, Florida, who had worked with other faculty at the school since early childhood.[15] Now just eleven, he wanted to study composition, which Floyd had yet to teach. Kuersteiner had the instinct to place Edwards with his youngest faculty member, and Floyd introduced his prodigy to score analysis; soon the teacher's Beethoven sonata scores were filled with the boy's scrawl.

Edwards finished high school two years early, at fifteen or sixteen, and tested out of so many basic college requirements that Florida State invited him to begin as a junior. He declared that he wanted no preferential treatment, and meant to undergo the same process as his peers. His five years with Floyd proved a sequence of magical feats: Edwards might attend a movie, come to his lesson the next day, and play the score from memory. His composing over the next years produced songs, chamber and dance music, and a short opera, *See the Wind.*[16]

Floyd's recital at University Auditorium on October 17 set in motion a revolving door of fall performances. Teaching agreed with him, and he pulled out all the stops with some new repertoire: Beethoven's Piano Sonata in E Minor, op. 90; a Chopin group:

Etudes in E-flat Minor and C Minor, op. 10, Nocturne in E Minor, op. 72, and Ballade in G Minor, op. 23; closing with Ravel's *La vallée des cloches* and *Alborada del gracioso,* from *Miroirs.* Three weeks later, on Halloween, he partnered faculty soprano Elizabeth Ellison in songs and arias of Handel, Sarti, Donaudy, Massenet, Schumann, Debussy, Dittenbauer, Carpenter, Wolf, Vaughan Williams, and Leonard Bernstein's satirical *I Hate Music.*

He was also composing again, *Odyssey for Piano and Cello,* for colleague Owen Sellers. They unveiled the work on November 4, just four days after the Ellison recital, at the thirteenth annual state music teachers association convention, at Miami's McAllister Hotel. In its six minutes, *Odyssey* showcases the extremes of the cello's rich low and mordant upper registers, connected by a cantabile theme, varied by augmentation and diminution in rhythm and harmony. Pianistic brilliance and accompanimental variety again figure prominently. Circling a B-minor core, piano and cello alternate and imitate each other's running triplets and long-limbed central theme, suggestive of Chopin's Etudes and Preludes. Never less than shamelessly romantic, *Odyssey* echoes Floyd's Wolfen prose like "Who Has Known the Panic?," making one wish that he had delivered on past and future intentions to write more chamber music.[17]

That fall, Jona Heimlich, engaged to a fellow student in Syracuse, visited Floyd twice. Determined to keep the friendship alive, she and Floyd's family attended a November 14 faculty composition recital divided between Floyd and John Boda. Floyd played *Soliloquy and Phantasm,* and accompanied Ermine in "Love Song," "Remember," "The Fairy's Song," and "Evening Song." Ermine recalled, "It was hard for me to learn the intervals, so the music stuck; but I couldn't dwell on singing something that intimate, by and with someone with whom I'd shared so much life. I was just hoping to get through those songs."[18]

CHRISTMAS BREAK and New Year's 1948 in Holly Hill and Laurinburg took its asthmatic toll. Floyd flew back to Tallahassee on January 2 and checked into the infirmary at the same former barracks where he slept and ate. Doctors loaded him with morphine for two days, and he joked that he would find any excuse for the drug's legal use. Then, on January 10, sick with flu, but hardly relishing more infirmary time, he spent two nights at the home of his colleague Roy Will.[19] Will's wife, Martha, expecting her third or fourth child, found caring for one more convalescent a natural activity. Floyd recovered just in time to accompany Owen Sellers in his faculty recital on January 16, including *Odyssey*'s Tallahassee premiere.

On February 21, Floyd wrote Bacon his decision to return to Syracuse that fall for his master's degree. Aware that he needed a stricter technician and taskmaster than Bacon, he proposed piano study with Lionel Nowak, and asked Bacon for a letter of recommendation to Syracuse University's scholarship office: "I have pondered the matter of studying next fall at great length. . . . I had thought of going to New York for some time but financially it would be almost impossible. . . . I have great faith in Nowak's ability as a teacher and I really think he is what I need at the moment. And if teaching becomes my livelihood (and that is hardly *un*likely) I shall need a master's degree if I do anything in that field at all. . . . Teaching has given me a great deal . . . and I think I shall return to studying with quite an altered point of view."[20]

The stage called again, and Floyd could not resist another acting turn, as soda jerk Frank Lippincott in FSU's April theater department production of *My Sister Eileen,* a 1940 comedy by Joseph A. Fields and Jerome Chodorov.[21] May brought a trip to Spartanburg for Ermine's graduation from Converse, and composer-ethnomusicologist Henry Cowell's weeklong visit to the Florida State campus. Floyd also reveled in his first hearing of Russian American mezzo-soprano Jennie Tourel, whom he recognized as a total artist. The bus trip to Pensacola made the event a kind of pilgrimage to reconnect with Tourel's level of commitment: "Enormous temperament reined in by terrific intelligence; but the temper was always right there on the edge, pushing, giving everything she did such immediacy and involvement."[22]

By May 18, Floyd had repaid all of his Holly Hill loans, and Reverend Floyd sent his son a Farmers and

Merchants checkbook, to divert portions of each paycheck to build a Syracuse fund. Jona Heimlich and Bruce Cooper Clarke were married on June 14 in Syracuse.[23] Floyd, preparing to teach that summer and give more recitals, could not attend, and wrote Jona, "Well, a week from tomorrow and you end your twenty-two years of celibacy. . . . Your last letter was overflowing with "joie de vivre" and if that is what *anticipation* of your marriage is doing for you, what will the actual thing be? . . . You know I'm wishing for you two very dear friends everything that's beautiful and happy and long-lived and by everything that's decent and right you should have it. Give Bruce's hand a warm and hearty shake for me, Jona, because he's getting one of the most extraordinary—if not the most extraordinary—girls I've ever known. And have him kiss the bride for me, will you, in token of very great love and admiration."[24]

Not to be outdone in the romance department, Floyd proceeded to confess his latest infatuation: "I'd like to announce that I think I've really found somebody. Or at least I should say that I have all the symptoms of an adolescent in the first throes and I feel like a fool and love it. I dated her for the first time after admiring her from afar all year Friday night. She's beautiful and I mean that *physically* (was up for May Queen and all that). She reminds me very much of Gillette and did the very first time I saw her—only a much smaller edition."[25]

This was Betty "Skippy" Shirley, a petite brunette actress with gorgeous brown eyes. Floyd commented to Jona, "God, I can't find anything else it seems."[26] Betty was about to depart for summer stock work in Vermont, and planned to move to New York in the fall. As usual, Floyd was undone by the combination of physical beauty, talent, and intelligence; Betty failed to reciprocate his level of interest.

The summer's whirl of classes and concerts began on June 30. Floyd and soprano Elizabeth Ellison, together with the university chorus, performed three of Dvorak's *Biblical Songs* on July 18. On August 5, he gave his next recital of all-new repertoire: Bach's Partita and Fugue in F-sharp Minor; Mozart's Sonata in F, K. 280; Chopin's *Fantaisie* in F Minor, op. 49; *La terrasse des audiences du clair de lune* from Book 2 of Debussy's Préludes and *La danse de Puck, Des pas sur la neige,* and *Ce qu'a vu le vent d'Ouest* from Book 1; finishing with the complete Khachaturian Piano Concerto in D-flat Major. The "orchestra" was Margaret Dunn, a mutual friend of Floyd and the Clarkes.

In the summer's course, Floyd learned that Lionel Nowak would leave Syracuse for Bennington College in Vermont. On August 7, Floyd wrote humbly to Bacon "to ask if you will accept me as a student this fall. . . . Mr. Nowak's leaving of course rather confused my plans for study next year, but . . . I had no other thought but to go back to you. . . . It has become increasingly evident to me in my teaching how difficult a student I must have been in many ways; however, what with being thrown on my own these last two years and through teaching, I think I can assure you of an appreciable change of attitude in many directions."[27]

Floyd enclosed the program from his two-day-old recital, "which constituted by all odds the best playing I believe I have ever done—certainly in public. For the first time, I think I am beginning to learn how to play the piano a little. At any rate the program was a source of some genuine satisfaction to me and that is, for me, very rare . . . [but] my need for instruction, I feel, is acute."[28]

Despite Floyd's quasi-defection, Bacon responded graciously. Still flushed with his recent success, Floyd wrote the Clarkes in a similar vein: "This recital was in every way the most successful one I have ever given; the principal satisfaction being . . . that it partially pleased *me.* For the first time that I can remember I didn't cringe backstage at the things I left undone and did wrongly. I hope it marks some sort of a pivotal point in my development (be that what it may) . . . all of which probably sounds ridiculously highflown but I say it with all seriousness."[29]

On August 14 he played another recital for Elizabeth Ellison, accompanying her in Rachmaninoff's "In the Silence of the Night" and Hugo Wolf's "Weather Forecast," and playing the second movement of the Khachaturian. On August 18 he accompanied the university chorus and music camp chorus summer concert in a program of folk and cowboy songs, spirituals, and short works of Stephen Foster, Alec Rowley, Aaron Copland, J. S. Bach, and Lindsay Norden. Just two nights later, on August 20, he returned Margaret Dunn's earlier favor by playing second piano for her Brahms Piano Concerto no. 2 in B-flat Major, op. 83.

With no way home between summer school and fall term, Floyd called his father to "come after him."[30] During the next three weeks, he assembled his Syracuse kit and strove to stay out of Jack's way. True to form, Reverend Floyd delighted in bringing up unpleasant or controversial topics. On August 31, he "had quite a long talk with Carlisle about Negro question and social problems. He has good grasp on right attitude."[31] On September 2, Floyd and Ermine performed for Orangeburg's Music Club, repeating "Love Song," "The Fairy's Song," and "Remember," Chopin's C-sharp Minor Etude, the first movement of the Brahms Sonata, and two Debussy pieces from his Syracuse senior recital. The *Orangeburg Observer* praised Floyd's "musical understanding" and "excellent degree of technical development," exalting him as a "young virtuoso."[32]

ON SEPTEMBER 3, Floyd sorted possessions and thoughts. His mother was making a wardrobe for Ermine's upcoming October wedding, but found time to produce a wine-colored corduroy Eisenhower jacket for her son. He wrote the Clarkes of his FSU work, "I am really strongly attached to many friends there but Tallahassee—the city and its climate—fails to excite me." He had ordered reams of new repertoire and taught himself to play it, including such hurdles as Ravel's *Gaspard de la nuit* and Prokofiev's Piano Sonata no. 3 in A Minor, op. 28: "They will doubtless keep me busy for quite a while." He still had no room reserved in Syracuse, but his parents waved goodbye as the train pulled out of Columbia on September 16.

Thanks to another loan from Carlisle Harvey for the year's expenses, above and beyond the graduate fellowship Bacon had arranged to cover his tuition, he found a second-story room in a private home, listed in Syracuse University's directory as 196 Beacon Road, about three and a half miles from campus. Enrollment that fall tallied 4,894, 1,700 more than in 1945. Music students made up 76 of the 366 fine arts majors. One of the latter was Peggy Camp, in her final undergraduate year, still living with Analee and Ernst Bacon. If Floyd invited Peggy to join his social group, she might put in an appearance, but never with a date. She seemed otherwise friendless, the practice room her entire world.

Jona, now Mrs. Bruce Clarke, still lived in town; and Don Rand was finishing his master's degree. With a newly serious attitude and less socializing, Floyd meant to make all As. He had a graduate recital to prepare, a music history treatise to write; and he learned that he would perform Khachaturian's Concerto with the Syracuse Symphony, conducted by Syracuse University faculty violinist Andre Polah. For a short time, thinking the habit debonair, he took up smoking a pipe, but abandoned it when he could not stop inhaling.

During Floyd's absence between degrees, Ernst Bacon had established one of the earliest permanent opera workshops, taught as a drama course. As its director he hired Ruth Ives, who had studied and taught voice at Converse College, and worked as production manager of the Spartanburg Lyric Opera, which had performed Bacon's *A Tree on the Plains* in 1942. Attractive and vivacious, and an accomplished singer, Ives specialized in Gilbert and Sullivan. Her energy and imagination as a stage director made an immediate impression on Floyd, and he accompanied her workshop's "Ballatella" scene from Leoncavallo's *I Pagliacci,* and the Mimi-Rodolfo aria and duet that conclude act 1 of Puccini's *La bohème.*

As before, Floyd took as many English courses as he could fit into his master's curriculum; from sheer credit hours, he could have earned an English degree as well. One such class was major American poets, taught by Edwin H. Cady. Floyd wrote his term paper on the poetry of fellow southerner Robert Penn Warren, and Cady awarded it an A+, appending a note that he had never before encountered work of such intelligence and insight from any student.

Reverend Floyd married Ermine to John William "Billy" Matheny in Holly Hill on October 12, and Floyd spent six days there for the event. With both sides of the family attending the ceremony, Floyd played the organ: "An event never to be forgotten! Everyone was so pretty."[33]

Back in Syracuse, Floyd immersed himself in the university's creative hotbed and worked on two new songs. For the first, he turned to a poem by Bernard Barrow, his friend from Daniel Curley's writing seminar. "I Am a Beggar on a Lonely Hill," one of Barrow's laments for lost love, uses rhymed couplets that refuse to take themselves too seriously:

> I am a beggar on a lonely hill,
> Mine is the sorrow of a whippoorwill,
> Mine is the picture of a woman's face
> Standing in silence on that barren place.
> Mine is the memory of a woman's cry
> As the night winds murmur and the night winds
>   sigh.
> Mine is the longing for a woman's lips,
> Yearning for the burning of the world's eclipse.
> Come sorrows, come onions, come longing,
> Cover me with ashes from the great Until,
> I am a beggar on a lonely hill.[34]

In 4/4, without tempo or dynamic indications, or sharps or flats in its key signature, the song's tonal center suggests E Minor; but through accidentals and enharmonics, it ends in B-flat Minor. Neither accompaniment nor vocal line repeats until the return of the opening line; yet Floyd maintains a strict unity with a persistent rhythmic phrase: quarter note, four-eighth notes, dotted quarter–eighth-half note. On its surface, it seems a respectful, solemn realization, but overt jazzy syncopations, and major and minor seventh, ninth, and eleventh chords betray Floyd's tongue in musical cheek.[35]

For a companion piece, Floyd turned to the symbolist-influenced poetry of controversial, short-lived Hart Crane: "Old Song," from the poet's unfinished 1926 collection *Key West*.[36]

As much as its images of loss and longing, Floyd appreciated the sheer beauty and unexpected associations of Crane's language. Professor Cady himself declared that Crane might emerge as the last century's finest poet. Floyd's setting in B Minor for high voice opens with an ostinato bass half-note figure followed by three quarter notes, and the voice sings its pain in interval leaps of sixths and sevenths. The only thematic repetition is brief, by transposition to open A-sharp Minor and B-major chords below and above a running triplet filigree, the melody a half-step lower than its first statement, returning to the home key in the song's final measures.[37]

Floyd's antiwar sentiments next found reflection in the raw emotions of Wilfred Owen's sonnet "Futility"; Floyd named his rendition by the first line of the verse:[38]

> Move him into the sun—
> Gently its touch awoke him once,
> At home, whispering of fields unsown.
> Always it awoke him in France,
> Until this morning and this snow.
> If anything might rouse him now
> The kind old sun will know.
>
> Think how it wakes the seeds—
> Woke, once, the clays of a cold star.
> Are limbs so dear-achieved, are sides
> Full-nerved,—still warm,—too hard to stir?
> Was it for this the clay grew tall?
> —O what made fatuous sunbeams toil
> To break earth's sleep at all?

Floyd's rough draft manuscript[39] offers a complete setting for high voice in A Major. After a two-bar introduction of descending even eighth notes, the first hymnlike septet has a simple chordal accompaniment. The second grows agitated and dissonant, with an ostinato rhythm of eighth note–two sixteenths, eighth rest, six sixteenths, a diminution of the introductory figure, emphasizing the bitter futility of Owen's vision. The final rhetorical question returns to held chords, a tolling bass chime, and descending vocal line that refracts the introduction, which, repeated, closes the song in F Minor.[40]

There was no verifiable professional performance of any of these three songs. The composer recalled a single hearing of the first two in a student recital by

Priscilla Gillette, visiting fresh from her triumph in 581 performances of the original *Brigadoon* on Broadway, and her romantic interest of the moment, baritone Warren Schmall.

Bacon took note, and nudged Floyd to expand his vocal writing into opera and to add composition to his class schedule next semester, for which he would need a graduate project in lieu of thesis. The subject that fell into Floyd's lap was his own short story, "A Lengthening Shadow," from Daniel Curley's 1946 seminar. To test the waters of a medium of which he was suspicious, he excerpted a moment from the story, envisioning it as an arietta: Sadie's first attempt at turning her lover Micah's thoughts from farming to a shared future. Floyd had yet to set a line of his own poetry,[41] but narrative fiction seemed more objective.

> She glanced at his hands and saw them unseeing, and then her vision became real and suddenly she saw them as she had never seen them before: they were thick and wide, and although she knew he had scrubbed them before he had come to meet her, there was dirt caked in the wrinkles of his knuckles and the calluses in his palms were not to be scrubbed clean. Slowly, she turned and looked at her own hands and saw them red and hard and shiny on the back and there was a crescent of dirt at the end of her fingernails. She looked at him and suddenly there was in her a new part to her love: a pity—an overwhelming pity for both of them.[42]

Eliminating descriptive passages of locale and the like, he found that turning literature to song did not after all pose such a hurdle. His first attempt at an opera libretto acquired a sandhill accent, and Floyd's free verse transformed the focus onto a coup de théâtre on the separation of hands and souls.

Bacon saw a winner, urged Floyd to continue, and secured Ruth Ives's commitment that Syracuse University's workshop would produce the finished product in the coming spring.

Meanwhile, Bacon and Floyd recalled that conductor Carl Bamberger, who had complimented Floyd's playing at the contest in April 1945, now led the North Carolina Symphony in Raleigh; and Floyd had a Liszt concerto ready for orchestral accompaniment. He made a quick trip to New York at the end of November to audition for Bamberger, without the desired result.

In December's first week, Floyd read through the Khachaturian Concerto with Andre Polah and the Syracuse Symphony, the showy work shimmering with romantic-Oriental colors. When he played it for Bacon, the teacher effused, "Just when I thought I was going to simplify my style of writing, make everything thinner, here you come with *this*!"

On December 13, Floyd saw Syracuse University's opera workshop perform Otto Luening's relatively new work *Evangeline*. (At its first complete production at Columbia University that May, critic Olin Downes found that both libretto and score lacked emotional propulsion.)[43] Floyd told himself, "OK, Carlisle, the first rule of opera is Don't Be Too Subtle."

Over Christmas in Holly Hill, he found his father more amenable than usual. Of a conversation with both children about their finances, Reverend Floyd marveled, "Carlisle has done right well so far."[44] What time remained between feasts of Ida's southern cookery—fried oysters, turkey with all the trimmings, pies and cakes of every description—and nightly board games, Floyd read sources for a term paper on music criticism for musicologist William Fleming's music history and appreciation class:[45] M. D. Calvocoressi's *The Principles and Methods of Music Criticism* and Eduard Hanslick's *The Beautiful in Music*.[46]

Floyd's paper has three parts: "An Historical Sketch of Musical Criticism," "An Estimate of Musical Criticism and the Critic, His Necessary Background and Qualifications," and "The Music Critic Today." Considering Floyd's eventual experiences with critics, the document is eerily prescient:

> I doubt . . . that critics are as aware of their responsibility as they are of their power. The critic must have authority obviously, or what good would his criticism be? But there must be a curbing somewhere and this authority must not needlessly make havoc of careers. . . . The critics, through their compactness and uniformity of opinion generally (more particularly in

> the drama), have gained a strangle-hold on modern music and its makers.[47]

Not even Fleming's solid A could neutralize the holidays' usual toll, and Floyd spent a couple of nights in Syracuse University's infirmary, which he judged inferior to Florida State's, as no morphine was offered. The best tonic was performing Khachaturian's Concerto at Lincoln Auditorium. As Floyd played the first astringent chords, Jona Clarke recalled a German friend whispering to Mrs. Heimlich, "Chosephine, dot piahno iss oudt of tune!"[48] Coordination problems arose: Bruce Clarke noticed a moment in the second movement when soloist and orchestra began to travel different paths, and conductor Polah strove to pull things together. The stress showed: Floyd directed a very vocal, annoyed grunt at the erring players, but forged serenely ahead, as though no problem had ever arisen.[49]

Critic Thola Tabor Schenck had not read Floyd's paper on her discipline, and had no such caveats, rhapsodizing over his technical mastery, and "cascades of notes . . . in a maze of color and tone."[50]

Floyd celebrated by moving a week later to a room closer to campus, in a Mrs. Clark's (no relation to Jona's husband) house at 317 University Avenue, with a new roommate, Lon White. That winter Floyd's visits to Bacon's studio grew more frequent as he submitted his compositional skills to a more experienced brain and set of ears.

As prolific a composer as Bacon was, his tutelage in the discipline was even looser than his piano pedagogy. He assigned Floyd no exercises, fugues, themes and variations, or experiments with writing in other styles; he offered no extended dissections of work submitted. In short, Bacon said nothing of pure theory, or the workaday technique of *how* a composer facilitates or improves his internal dictator's communications. Though he declared Verdi the greatest figure in nineteenth-century music—a point not lost on Floyd—Bacon avoided references to other composers' solutions of specific problems.

Bacon's convictions were antidoctrinaire, and he disparaged separating music into either/or categories of serious or popular. He reserved special wrath for the serialism of Schönberg and his disciples, and the newer schools of electronic *musique concrète,* mocking their products as "music totally abstracted from its human sources."[51] This suited Floyd, who found such literature repellant. Already enthralled by the theater, he could not imagine using the newer idioms to reflect genuine emotion or character.[52] Bacon's interest in Floyd's prose and poetry helped convince him that the word, the libretto, had to precede music. Bacon might have had Floyd in mind when quoting Verdi's dictum: "If you terrify the man of genius with your wretched measured criticism, he will never let himself go, and you will rob him of his naturalness and his enthusiasm."[53]

Bacon identified with Floyd's idiosyncratic natural talent, especially his lyric gift for vocal writing, and had no intention of straitjacketing Floyd with "isms" or modernist schools: "Write what you want to write" was Bacon's push toward independence, but perhaps not all one needs when one has never had a composition lesson. Yet their conversations on music theater's ethics sparked Floyd's determination to broaden the medium's base: to tell stories about real people, in their language, and redress perceived imbalances between music and drama.

TO ADAPT "A LENGTHENING SHADOW," Floyd sketched a scenario for his musical play in one act, retitled *Slow Dusk.* Its forty minutes unfolds on and in front of a simple farmhouse porch in sandhill country like Bethune. For his seventy-measure introduction-cum prologue, Floyd reached back to his two-year-old piano piece "Soliloquy." Aunt Sue Kinsey (mezzo-soprano), a rough middle-aged survivor, sits in a rocker shelling peas on a sweltering May morning. Sue is raising her nephew Jess (baritone), a twenty-something naïf (a conflation of Willie and Jess in the original story), and her niece Sadie (soprano). Jess shuffles onstage from plowing, fanning himself with a straw hat. The two discuss Sadie, the only one of the family to pursue an education, and about to finish high school. They worry that she spends a great deal of time these days with a neighboring farmer, Micah Hatfield (tenor). Sue thinks it bad enough that Micah ended his schooling with eighth grade, but the real stumbling block is the Hatfields' status as Truelights, and the Kinseys' as opposed Disciples.

Sue goes into the kitchen to fix supper, and Jess returns to plowing, just before Micah walks Sadie home from their tryst by the pond. After musing on locality and agrarian life—including sandspurs—the conversation swells to a mutual declaration of love, and Micah's marriage proposal. Sadie vows to be a good partner and wife, to work as an equal in the backbreaking farm chores, and then to relax into retirement. In other words, together they will rise to independence from the strictures of family, church, and poverty. Micah leaves to fish the pond, promising to come back that night.

Sadie gathers courage to declare her plans to Aunt Sue, confessing that her spirit lives in endless shadow without Micah. In their inevitable confrontation, Sadie holds her own, despite the older woman's trump card, religious difference. Sadie leaves to walk off her frustration and grief. Literal slow dusk falls during an impassioned interlude (the repurposed 1947 "Phantasm"). When Sadie returns, Jess and Aunt Sue break the disastrous news that Micah has drowned while trying to free his snagged fishing line. Sadie screams and runs off toward the pond.

After Aunt Sue and Jess go in for the night, Sadie returns, dazed, and begins her lament as an inarticulate wail; when she finds words, she surrenders to the hope-quenching shadow of her earlier vision.

With no real background in the medium, in fact fighting an early distaste for it, Floyd worked from pure instinct. Creative writing had taught him how to structure a good story: a climax toward which everything moved, followed by a swift denouement. That now suggested harmonies and musical forms, a series of episodes with a climactic event that changes everything. He defined his gift for writing programmatic music that furthers or intensifies a dramatic situation. He first sketched key dramatic moments and emotional states, the piece's sine qua non, thematic material that could be used in many guises. His developing technique consistently employed such elements, more in the sense of Puccini's "logical reminiscences," and his *motivo di prima intenzione,*[54] than in Wagner's *Leitmotiven.* Floyd's relationship to Wagner became increasingly complex, and inevitable comparisons between these librettist-composers became thorns in the American's side. Floyd saw Wagner as a world unto himself: for a librettist, a marvelous composer. The fact remains that the two share more commonalities than discrepancies, both were autodidacts with minimal formal training.

The process Floyd established with *Slow Dusk* has served him, with few exceptions, for his entire composing career: words first, music later;[55] and piano accompaniment always preceded orchestration. He wrote *Slow Dusk* in rough pencil draft, then a final clean copy for rehearsal material, later edited for the published vocal score.

From the first, Floyd dedicated himself to keeping music theater's technical apparatus in scale with its human elements, focusing on clear, effective communication between characters and between characters and audience. He knew The Sound when he heard it; it was never un-conscious.

For each composition lesson with Bacon, he brought new sections that he played on the piano. His teacher offered neither specific criticisms nor suggestions, only general praise for Floyd's theatrical flair.

FLOYD STILL DEFINED HIMSELF as a pianist who composed. During the *Slow Dusk* winter into spring of 1949, he continued studying the instrument with Bacon, but learned valuable lessons from concert artists brought in for Syracuse University's Artist Series. American soprano Eleanor Steber nourished his growing absorption with vocal writing and his love for Debussy, performing all of the *Proses lyriques.* Floyd admired Steber's total mind-body immersion in serving as the composer's voice, coupled with formidable intelligence and musicality;[56] but Rudolf Firkušný's pianism elicited Floyd's greatest admiration, the Czech American's trademark musical integrity, modesty, and, again, total emotional involvement. Firkušný had earned some colleagues' enmity with a reputation for impeccable accuracy. Floyd gravitated to this musical personality and his modesty in the service of the music he played: the kind of pianist Carlisle Floyd meant to be.

While crafting *Slow Dusk*'s libretto and music, Floyd prepared a graduate recital with minimal guidance from Bacon. His teacher paid him a backhanded compliment when he commented on the difficulties of Chopin's D Minor Prelude, one of Floyd's new pieces: "I will have to die without playing that." Better assurance came in a letter from Kuersteiner at the end of March, offering Floyd a contract for 1949–1950, with a salary increase to $3,700.

The Fenegan contingent announced its arrival in Syracuse for the recital, without Reverend Floyd, an unheard-of departure for Carlisle's mother Ida; but she would be with sisters Lucile and Bunny, uncle Yates Gamble, and niece Helen; and Floyd saw his mother more cheerful without his father. His program on March 31 was Bach's *Capriccio on the Departure of a Beloved Brother,* BWV 992; Mozart's Sonata in F Major, K. 280; a Chopin group (Prelude in C-sharp Minor, op. 45, Prelude in D Minor, op. 28, no. 24, Etude in E-flat Minor, op. 10, no. 6, and *Fantaisie* in F Minor, op. 49); Wallingford Riegger's *Blue Voyage* (1926), with its overtones of Debussy, from a composer better known for serialism,[57] and a grand finish with Prokofiev's Sonata no. 3 in A Minor, op. 28. Reverend Floyd, holding down the Holly Hill parsonage, wrote, "Ida called from Syracuse at 11:00—she said Carlisle did well."[58]

With an Everest of work remaining to ready *Slow Dusk* for performance in a month, Floyd did not visit home that spring, but moved to a different rented room on Euclid Avenue. Practicing the piano, he could shut down his mind and simply perform; but if he entered such states as a composer, no notes found their way onto the page. Syracuse practice rooms were anything but soundproof, and Bacon gave Floyd a key to his turret studio with its two Steinway grands.

By 8:30 p.m. on May 2, Floyd's circle buzzed with excitement over the premiere of *Slow Dusk* at Crouse College Auditorium. The program's epigraph—and the opera's title—came from Wilfred Owen's 1917 poem "Anthem for Doomed Youth":

What candles may be held to speed them all?
Not in the hands of boys but in their eyes
Shall shine the holy glimmers of goodbyes.
The pallor of girls' brows shall be their pall,
Their flowers the tenderness of patient winds,
And each slow dusk a drawing down of blinds.[59]

Ruth Ives's workshop cast included Floyd's fellow-pianist and mezzo-soprano Margaret Dunn as Aunt Sue, baritone Lou White as Jess, soprano Eleanor Bailey as Sadie, and tenor Grant Williams as Micah. Evangeline Straver designed and built costumes; the sets—a doorway, steps, a rocking chair, and a few hand props—were built by SU's workshop techniques classes. Syracuse Scenery Company provided lights and curtains for the challenging Gothic auditorium space, complete with its immense pipe organ as backdrop.

The program listed Floyd as accompanist and conductor. Apparently only the first is true, though he coached each singer in his or her role. From his place at the keyboard, his recollections of the premiere are understandably vague: the accompaniment, especially the repurposed *Soliloquy and Phantasm,* required all the virtuoso skills at his disposal. The response, albeit from a large audience of music, drama, and speech students and family, was an emotional aphrodisiac. Jona Clarke remembered, "That is when we all knew." Ernst Bacon pumped Floyd's hand, enthusing, "If there were an award for the number one graduate student at Syracuse University, it should go to you!" Floyd's mother did her best with the comment, "I was certainly glad to see that young man come back on stage," meaning Mr. Williams, for his curtain call, following his offstage drowning.

Still, Mrs. Floyd's pleasure in the event warmed her son and established a pattern for the next forty years. She may never have acquired the vocabulary of praise that Floyd craved, but her eager anticipation—buying or making new clothes for a premiere, before a long trip to some distant city—and her simple attendance spoke clearer than words.

A few days later, Floyd was summoned to the studio of the formidable pianist-composer George

Mulfinger,[60] who proclaimed that Floyd had a true gift for the lyric and tragic. Syracuse's *Herald-Journal* echoed this, describing Floyd as an already skilled composer with a bright future, and praising *Slow Dusk* as suspenseful and "action-filled, with no lagging moments . . . a vivid picture."[61]

Astonishingly, Bacon gave Floyd a B for his operatic thesis, but public response was overwhelming enough that he and Ives scheduled a second performance on June 3, attended by all the Floyds. Everyone dined at Edwards Department Store, where Jona Clarke worked as a bridal consultant. Reverend Floyd wrote, "Sat and watched and listened to Carlisle's opera *Slow Dusk.* Large audience!"—always one of his criteria for success—"Surely am proud of my boy!"[62] Thola Tabor Schenck, a Floyd devotee since the Khachaturian Concerto, commented more explicitly in the *Syracuse Post Standard* that the reprise of *Slow Dusk* held the audience's rapt attention with its "fine script and melodic content." Schenck pronounced the work "a well executed and polished contribution to American music."[63]

Peers and mentors alike began to regard Floyd as the next Puccini, a flattering but uncomfortable mantle for any twenty-two-year-old. His parents drove him back to Holly Hill, and he graduated from Syracuse in absentia, in order to return to Tallahassee in time to teach summer school.

FLOYD'S HANDFUL OF LESSONS with Bacon embodied his first and last formal instruction in composition, reinforcing lifelong insecurities about his skills. Bacon's greatest gift lay in brilliant conversation, and Floyd acquired the bulk of his education in composition independently. When young composers came in future years to his studio, the strengths and weaknesses of what Bacon had given him seemed outlined in black and white. Bacon's method constituted an *ethos,* not a technique: What do you hear? If one's music is a faithful transcription of that hearing, there can be no argument with the product, beyond subjective love or aversion. Students might bring Floyd music that he abhorred; but had they truly *heard* it? Much later, Floyd incorporated the core of Bacon's instruction into his own teaching of young composers: "We can fiddle with it, we can tweak it, we can find out what is good or not so good; but you cannot quarrel with the basic language. Just be sure it furthers what really comes out of the inner ear."

In other words, continuing self-education led Floyd to personal discoveries toward which he could only point his students. He felt that his greatest strength as a teacher of both piano and composition was diagnostic, especially in the latter:

> Either the student is gifted, or it's pulling teeth. Which it most often is. When you get right down to it, can [composition] be taught? I felt that anybody could learn to write stage music, or light music for the theater, until I started working with composers. I could get a good libretto out of them, by holding their feet to the fire, but that did not do it. As soon as they started setting it to music, they did not have the impulse for furthering it musically. If you have the instinct for the stage, if you love the whole collaborative atmosphere, that is one thing; but a great many composers do not.

Floyd refined his teaching process by asking the right questions: What is the prevailing emotional color of this scene? Which character's point of view will you take? Will you make an "omniscient" musical comment on emotions or situations?

It was no coincidence that sustained outbreaks of asthma became put-aside childhood things. Floyd fell deeply and passionately in love with music for the theater, and with acolytes of both disciplines. *Slow Dusk* became Floyd's highest fall yet: no one told him he could not do this.

8

Women, and Other *Fugitives*

Tallahassee, 1949–1953

Under unfamiliar pressures to complete and perform *Slow Dusk,* Floyd came out to his family in Syracuse about drinking. In months to come, he appeared regularly in his father's diary prayers, as though in need of special help. Floyd wanted his father to treat him as another adult man, but the religious grilling continued: "How many people were at Sunday school last week? Why don't you go to church?" Deciding that his son needed to be taken down a peg from his recent successes, Jack opened a wider breach in their relations: One night at the supper table, he declared that Floyd would never be the musician his mother was. Ida huffed and sighed, but no matter how keenly he felt the put down, Floyd refused to take this bait. After four days of parsonage life, he wrote the Clarkes in Syracuse, echoing Thomas Wolfe's perceptions about going home: "Our trip home was comparatively quick and pleasant; I spent most of the time immersed in sleep . . . with the bed-pillow and the rest of the time [I] was pretty glum company. For some reason I was totally indifferent to the rigors (and pleasures) of the trip and . . . I have yet to rouse myself out of this very strange state in which very little matters: I simply can't get concerned over when or what I eat . . . where or how I sleep . . . or whether or not I am nice to people here. All this sounds alarmingly like one of Ellen Glasgow's hapless heroines but seriously I don't know what to attribute it all to—whether it's general fatigue or reluctance to leave something to which I can never return."[1]

The farthest he got for the next six months was back to Tallahassee, on June 26, for summer school. His rented room for the summer, in a private home on West Tennessee Street, was near the new state-of-the-art music building. He slipped back into teaching and practice routines, now fully credentialed and headed for tenure, in his own studio, 310, in what is today the Kuersteiner Building.

By the end of Syracuse's academic year, two more Florida State University piano positions had opened, and Floyd successfully proposed his friend Don Rand for a fall instructorship. On July 15, FSU president Doak Campbell announced that the other vacancy would be filled by the concert pianist Sidney Foster. Unbeknownst to Floyd, Foster was a native of Florence, South Carolina, born there as Sidney Finkelstein in 1918, son of the dry goods merchants. Just eight years Floyd's senior, Foster seemed to have done everything in the highest ranks of the classical music world. Graduate of the Curtis Institute, student of Isabelle Vengerova and Josef Hoffmann, he won the first Levintritt Prize in 1940. The award brought a debut appearance with the New York Philharmonic, and an equally successful Carnegie Hall debut later that year, followed by triumphs with most of America's major orchestras. At just thirty-one, Foster, also a composer, already had a reputation as a master teacher and pianist's pianist. Adding him to Florida State's roster was another Kuersteiner coup in his quest for performing faculty to match other giants like Juilliard and Indiana University.

Floyd invited Foster to his recital on August 1, repeating the Bach, Chopin, and Riegger sections of his Syracuse program; impressive additions were Ravel's *Gaspard de la nuit,* Aaron Copland's *Passacaglia* (1922), and Poulenc's *Toccata* (1928). After adjourning to colleague Wiley Housewright's for coffee and pie with Reverend and Mrs. Floyd in tow, Floyd sought Foster's opinion. The latter insisted, "No pianist really wants to hear what another thinks."

Floyd cajoled further, and Foster shook his head, "I think you are amazing"; but he continued, "It's scandalous how you can play with such stiff wrists." Dashed but intrigued, Floyd asked Foster to take him on as student, and still claims the result as one of his life's two proudest accomplishments. With Foster's help, he undertook a fundamental relearning of his entire pianistic technique. He had grown secure with a certain level of accomplishment and had amassed a large repertoire. Facility, inattention, or impatience had exacerbated the haphazardness of what Bacon and previous teachers had taught him, which was inadequate for the virtuoso works that drew him. Foster's very dissatisfaction spurred him to move ahead. After all, this was the first successful concert pianist he had gotten to know—Floyd was impressed that Foster had known William Kapell—and he deferred to his new teacher as he never quite had to Bacon: this man knew exactly what virtuosity meant and required. The process unfolded with Foster's trademark sarcasm and analytical brilliance over the fall quarter of 1949. When Don Rand arrived in Tallahassee with his master's degree that year, Floyd located better and larger rooms for the two of them in a widow's house at 210 Woodward Avenue, just south of the College of Music. Like Floyd, Rand studied with Foster.

Between 1948 and 1949, FSU hired so many new faculty that the collective came to be known as "the Forty-Niners." Kuersteiner lured further imports to his growing coterie of stars, beginning with the Polish American pianist-composer Franciszek Zachara;[2] but the most famous Forty-Niner, Hungarian conductor-pianist-composer Ernst/Ernö von Dohnányi (1877–1960), has a riveting story too involved to consider here.[3] His Piano Quintet in C Minor, op. 1, had won the approval of Johannes Brahms, who helped spread the young composer's fame in Vienna. Owing to wartime difficulties, Dohnányi had fled to Argentina, and was exported from there thanks to Karl Kuersteiner's dealings with Edward Kilenyi, an army captain and pianist of Hungarian extraction, serving as the postwar music control officer in Bavaria for the United States military government. When Dohnányi arrived in Tallahassee, his résumé embraced an international concert career, four operas, three symphonies, and a great deal of popular chamber and solo literature. He was seventy-two that fall, and Zachara became his self-appointed proselyte.

Floyd's relationship with both men remained cordial and complex. He found Dohnányi affable, sweet, gentle, wearing a perpetual smile, and enjoyed the old fellow's anecdotes of Rachmaninoff and others; but Sidney Foster's presence and Floyd's alliance with him acted as an irritant to Zachara, who at end-of-quarter piano juries might lean over to Foster and needle, "Sidney, do you think you're as good a musician as Dohnányi?" Foster's impeccable response: "I have to respect myself first." Zachara persisted, "You think you're as important as maestro?"

Dohnányi could be just as rude, but somehow gentler, with age, his eternal smile, and European bonhomie. During juries or recital hearings, he often strolled in late, midmovement, as some young pianist sweated bullets, and promenaded to shake each colleague's hand, chatting amiably in raised tones. In many ways, Dohnányi never adjusted to either the American clock or standard academic deportment.

FLOYD'S PIANISTIC DEMOLITION and reconstruction began with Foster's weight technique. He traced the method all the way back to Beethoven, teacher of Carl Czerny, who taught Liszt, one of whose innovations was a higher piano chair, facilitating better engagement of the arm's weight. Liszt passed the technique to Theodor Leschetitzky, who in turn taught it to Isabelle Vengerova, from whom Foster inherited it at Curtis. The technique required a quasi-isometric engagement of the *relaxed* weight of the upper arm and shoulders with a supple, flexible wrist, creating famously strong fingers. Rather than arching, the finger pads established greater contact with the keys, dividing the weight and energy of the entire upper body *between* the fingers, and freeing the hand, wrist, and elbow, all especially prone to tension. (Some called the fluid alternation of raising and lowering the fingers off and onto the keys "drop flex.") Using Hanon[4] and Czerny[5] exercises, beginning at maximum volume, Floyd learned to shape sound through sophisticated muscular control, a skill as much mental as physical.

This overhaul, though a constant sequence of discovery and application, often disheartened, and always exhausted, from undoing and redoing, analyzing, diligently plowing through week after week of Czerny. Foster's only comment might be, "Not there yet." Ernst Bacon, sensing in Floyd a kindred soul, had let him get away with pianistic murder, believing that encouragement was all it took to nurture Floyd's natural gift; Sidney Foster was the teacher who brought this talent to heel and gave it spine.

Once Floyd began to comprehend and assimilate, the individual in whom he confided was his utterly unmusical grandmother Fenegan in Laurinburg. Taking new information, much less enthusiasm, home to his parents was entrusting chickens to foxes; but when he demonstrated the differences to "Mrs. Kate," regardless of her grasp of pedagogical concepts, she listened, validated, and encouraged his excitement.

And once acquired, like swimming or cycling, Floyd never lost Foster's technique, and passed it on to his own students. He began a weekly studio piano class, a common event today, but one that raised eyebrows at prefifties FSU. The stimulating exchange of ideas and technical information began to attract other teachers' students, flattering but not always comfortable attention in the hothouse of academia. Floyd grew so fascinated with the physiology behind Foster's work that he contacted the school's director of physical education for women, the kinesthesiologist Dr. Katie Montgomery. She watched him play, and validated the scientific accuracy of the method's pianistic application. When Floyd launched into a Liszt or Rachmaninoff barn burner, Montgomery verified, "That's no work at all." She gratified him with her pronouncement that the first rule of accuracy was to use the smallest muscles closest to the point of work, that is, the fingers, supported by the upper torso, now more productive through relaxation. Floyd increased his daily practice time to at least three or four hours, restricting himself to problem areas. Extended passage work—runs—had always been his bête noir, but Foster's new tools brought a thorough if not quick fix.

That October, Columbia University's opera workshop director Willard Rhodes wrote Floyd that the group had chosen *Slow Dusk* for study. Ruth Ives would direct, with Albert Rivett's musical direction, for an invited audience.[6]

Years would pass before Floyd had an agent or publisher, but this expression of interest, clearly spearheaded by Ives, made another dream come true: Bacon had dazzled him with Columbia's reputation as an incubator for new music theater since the early forties. Rhodes further requested several copies of the score in order to begin rehearsals.[7] Floyd replied that he was pleased to have his opera chosen,[8] and sent a score to Ruth Ives for copying in New York; and Ives expressed enthusiasm about the cast and musical director.

Despite Floyd's uncertainty about whether this event materialized, and a corresponding lack of archival confirmation,[9] colleague-composer Jack Beeson, long associated with Columbia, reminded Floyd that he had met him in New York around this time and that *Slow Dusk* did in fact receive an in-house showing, thus becoming, less than a year after its premiere, the first performance of *any* Floyd work without the composer's direct involvement.

As long as the Foster/Floyd dynamic stuck to technique, the relationship flourished and Floyd was welcomed as extended family into Foster's home, with wife Bronja[10] and children Lincoln and Justin. When it came to interpretation, though, teacher and student collided as fall quarter drew to a close. Once as Floyd played Debussy, Foster stopped him, snarling, "Oh, you play that like a lily."

Floyd snapped back, "Don't you ever play pianissimo?" By that time, he was secure enough in his concept of good pianism and exposed as little repertoire as possible to Foster's acerbic wit. Also, Floyd's position on the faculty, and the fact that *he* had approached Foster, heightened his vulnerability. Foster's own performing career had waned, and Floyd recognized this as a partial source of the man's sarcasm and bitterness. He appreciated Foster's objectivity, but grew disenchanted with the concomitant emotional detachment. Though Foster championed contemporary music—especially that of his friend Norman Dello Joio—and performed some of his own jazz-influenced, dissonant compositions at FSU, he scorned or ignored Floyd's efforts. Once at a party, in a group of colleagues, Floyd overheard Foster say, "Well, if Carlisle were just more original"; and only Floyd's reluctance to think of himself as a composer salvaged the association. He attended each Foster recital, and praised his teacher's superlative artistry.[11]

AT THE END OF OCTOBER, Floyd's parents were reassigned to Saluda, South Carolina; but before they left Holly Hill, Floyd wanted to buy a first car, and had his father begin negotiations with the town's Ford dealership. He continued to send at least fifty dollars from his monthly check to repay Sam McCoy's Syracuse loans, and now set aside even more for the Ford purchase.

Meanwhile, between his return in the fall of 1948 and the summers of 1949 and 1950, Floyd anchored a new circle of students and faculty. The choral director Wiley Housewright played bridge avidly, and in barter for piano lessons, his wife Lucy (Lucilla) instructed Floyd in the game's convoluted rules and quirks.

As ever drawn to those whose work and persona combined music, movement, words, and the stage, another group included dancers, actors, and artists. Many of these relationships began at beach parties at which wealthy townspeople and creative types met and mingled, swimming, talking, telling jokes, playing cards and other party games, drinking. Floyd kept a swimsuit packed, always ready to make the hour's drive south to the Gulf to recapture the childhood feel of sand between his toes. The new group included Nellie-Bond "Bondie" Dickinson, head of FSU's modern dance program, and her leading light, dancer Nancy Warren Smith.[12] Dickinson was in many ways the dancer's antithesis: stocky of frame, almost masculine, with a reddish, pockmarked complexion. Her professional manner tended to the dictatorial; but a ready laugh and bawdy sense of humor recommended her to Floyd.[13]

Most significantly, Floyd now acquired a patroness, Hazel Richards, a local woman of fortune as large as her personality. Born into the socially prominent Moren family of Minneapolis in 1901—she frequently sallied that Queen Victoria had to die before she could be born—Hazel was an only child of wealth and culture, whose father helped found the Minneapolis Symphony in 1903. An ardent feminist and civil rights activist, a commanding presence in figure, voice, and intelligence, Hazel married Harold Richards in Wisconsin in 1924. He became head of FSU's physics department the next year,[14] and Hazel taught American history at Leon High School. The couple soon became a fixture in Florida's capital, hosting festivities at a beach home at Carrabelle, south of Tallahassee. Passionately interested in and involved with the local arts scene, Hazel was known for adopting new protégés, going after, and usually getting, whatever or whomever she chose to acquire. She threw famous parties, at the beach and at a town mansion on Country Club Drive, and it was at one of these that she first met Floyd, who on the spot became her new project.

Hazel became increasingly involved in Floyd's life and career. It seems clear that she fell in love with his talent and person, but, despite wagging tongues, the relationship never turned amorous. Still, her Floyd worship was less than pleasing to husband Harold. Floyd's next roommate, Donald Mowrer, observed, "This was really a love relationship, but not a romantic love; this was purely son and mother, nothing oedipal, nothing sexual."[15]

Many felt amusement or jealousy at Hazel's attentions to Floyd. Don Rand answered the door one morning when Floyd was out, practicing for a recital that evening. Eyes shining, Hazel asked, "Is he here?"

Gadfly Rand countered, "You mean He, with a capital H?"

Hazel became the most pervasive presence besides music in Floyd's life.[16] She turned up at his dwellings, cleaned, washed dishes, cooked, and served as party hostess. Richards establishments were open at all times and hours to Floyd, his circle, and guest artists for evening receptions or Sunday morning postperformance breakfasts. When other Floyds came to town, visits became mandatory.

Floyd began having the quintessential stage creature's dreams: sitting down to play recitals without a note of music in hands or head; striding onstage during a play performance not knowing his lines. Another friend, the petite blonde Kathryn Reece Haun, a well-off theater and operetta diva,[17] had introduced Floyd to Hazel, and now tempted him back onto the stage with one of the Florida capital's latest cultural adornments, the Tallahassee Little Theatre. For the second offering of its first season, the group produced Ferenc Molnar's 1910 farce, *The Guardsman,* and Floyd stepped forward with only a gentle nudge from Haun, who played a flirtatious stage moth provoking her husband's jealousy.[18] Directed by Airey Mays,[19] rehearsals and performances on December 12, 13, and 14, 1949 were held at an old Floyd haunt, the university's West Campus (Mabry Air Field) Little Theatre. A *Tallahassee Democrat* puff gave plot details and then some, describing Floyd's role as "an old friend" who played the piano onstage and, in the mold of Mozart's *Così fan tutte,* helped the husband prove his wife's fidelity.[20]

The same paper's review of opening night made the generic observation that "Carlysle [*sic*] Floyd . . . added to the evening with [his] . . . supporting role."[21] The day after the play closed, he boarded the train for New York. Theater addiction and friendship motivated such visits, usually involving meetings with Priscilla Gillette. Floyd discovered the Woodstock Hotel, at 127 West 43rd Street. Just around the corner from Times Square, and a quick stroll from Town Hall, it offered a reasonably clean, affordable crash for Broadway show and concert nights. Tennessee Williams's *A Streetcar Named Desire* had played the Ethel Barrymore Theatre since December 3, 1947, and Floyd saw one of the final performances of Elia Kazan's production, starring Jessica Tandy, Kim Hunter, Marlon Brando, and Karl Malden; and he took in Arthur Miller's *Death of a Salesman,* with Mildred Dunnock, Cameron Mitchell, Arthur Kennedy, and Gene Lockhard.

On December 21, the train dropped him in Columbia for a rainy drive to Saluda, and Christmas with his family. Exhaustion and stress prompted Floyd's first asthma in months; at least the family's games had progressed to canasta and Ghost, at which Floyd and his partners usually won. On New Year's Eve, he played the church organ, attracting early admiring parishioners. His parents drove him to Augusta, Georgia, for a flight back to Tallahassee on January 2 of the new year and decade.

No sooner did classes resume than Floyd began composing again, albeit on a small scale. Speech and drama's innovative new director, George McCalmon, a specialist in historical drama,[22] reached out to involve all campus arts in his productions, and enticed Floyd to write about ten minutes of incidental music for his production of Euripides' *Iphigenia among the Taurians.* (Floyd would later practice recycling decades before it became environmental policy, as he did with *Slow Dusk:* one of *Iphigenia*'s four movements, "Lamentation," would resurface sixteen years later, after which the earlier score vanished.)

The *Tallahassee Democrat*'s report hints at Floyd's musical aesthetic, an atmospheric recreation of music in the ancient Greek theater, with its "model [*sic,* instead of "modal"] character" and spare, open harmonies, to reinforce the play's startling, "even terrifying" nature.[23] The *Democrat*'s brief review of the two-piano performance by Floyd and his student Cortlandt Morper referred to the score as "mood music."[24]

Bondie Dickinson devised choreography, the title role played by temperamental, dynamic Julie Storm, with whom Floyd fell promptly in love during rehearsals. He pursued her intermittently but intensely—when he was not doing likewise with another actress, Jayne Gardner—over the next year. After the experience with Jona, he craved the feeling of aliveness and ego reinforcement that love offered if reciprocated. Not for Floyd the oceanic merging of personalities: he had first to know the wind's direction, admitting his own fundamental lack of trust.

On February 13, idol Jennie Tourel gave a Florida State University Artist Series recital. Floyd believed that he learned more about musical phrasing from Tourel than from any teacher or other artist. Bronja and Sidney Foster hosted the after-party, and Floyd and Don Rand chatted casually with the guest of honor, a larger-than-life paragon of all they found essential in art. Almost sixty years later, Floyd testified, "I still don't know any artist I admire more than Tourel, in terms of musical intelligence and sensitivity. Her degree of immersion transported me. You can't imagine how often I think about her, the way she sang, the things she did with Rachmaninoff. It opened up a whole new idea of expressivity in singing, still within wonderful limits."

The rest of the winter spun, beginning with Don Rand's concert on February 17, and proceeding with a University Chorus concert on February 20, assisted by Dickinson's modern dance group; Floyd played an arrangement of Irving Berlin's "Let's Take An Old-Fashioned Walk" to Bondie's choreography, danced by Nancy Smith. February 24 brought a Sidney Foster recital. On March 10 Floyd played his own recital of Norman Dello Joio's Sonata no. 1; Beethoven's Piano Sonata in A Major, op. 101; and the Khachaturian Concerto, with Don Rand as second pianist. The *Democrat* lauded Floyd's powerful technique and original interpretation in this "prodigiously exacting" concerto.[25]

In a rare burst of self-congratulation, Floyd described this concert to Jona Clarke as "the best piano recital I think I have ever given, due chiefly to working with Sidney Foster, who has been wonderful for me."[26] On March 15, Floyd landed with his family in Saluda for spring break, and continued to discuss buying his first car. When Floyd asked his father to sign a note for monthly payments, Reverend Floyd asked for collateral. By this time, Floyd had won financial independence by paying off every loan, and felt himself a safe investment; beside himself with fury, he stalked upstairs, followed by his distraught mother, urging him to let Reverend Floyd cosign the note, with a familiar refrain: "I just can't stand it when you and your father fight." With Ida's intercession, another Carlisle Harvey loan was secured, and the note to the Holly Hill dealership executed; but father still knew how to punch son's buttons. Attending a concert of the American pianist Byron Janis in Columbia on March 17 minimally doused this new blaze. The car, a new Sunland beige Ford convertible, was ordered after Floyd huffed back to Tallahassee on March 21. He and Don Rand returned to retrieve the vehicle eight days later, rolled into Saluda like kings, and trounced Billy Matheny and Reverend Floyd at canasta that evening. Floyd began liquidating the new debt at once.

The time had arrived to introduce FSU to the *other* Carlisle Floyd, composer of opera. With student and faculty singers, staged by Bondie Dickinson, overall dramatic supervision by George McCalmon, and Floyd himself as pianist, *Slow Dusk* played on May 10, 11, and 12, 1950, as the closing half of "An Evening of Experimental Theatre" at the Augusta Conradi Theatre.[27] Paula Bailey [Hulslander], Sadie, secured a private vinyl pressing of a dress rehearsal recording that she donated to Florida State University College of Music in 2007. Beneath the expected surface noise and primitive technical conditions, the bones of a singular experience emerge strong and clean. It remains a moving document of time, place, and Floyd's first operatic effort, just a year after its creation. The composer's pianism in the "Phantasm" interlude rises to the virtuoso caliber of Rachmaninoff or Horowitz.

11. Floyd with Sunland beige Ford convertible, c. 1950. Courtesy of Donald Mowrer.

The *Democrat* found the piece to be "haunting" and "well-knit," reserving special praise for Floyd's playing.[28] The Floyd parents, aunt Bunny, cousin Helen, Hazel Richards, Dickinson, and the Fosters attended the second performance together. Reverend Floyd recorded, "Gee! The audience gave Carlisle a great ovation. He was wonderful! Sure was proud of my boy."[29] The school paper's review, typos, solecisms, and all, predicted a bright future for Floyd, comparing him favorably to "Vincent Minotti" [*sic*], presumably Gian-Carlo Menotti.[30]

As we have seen from his diary entries, Reverend Floyd rarely commented on what his son actually created; but Floyd derived real pleasure from subsequent discussion of *Slow Dusk* with grandfather Oscar Fenegan. The old gentleman, all admiration, declared poignantly that the situation of family opposition because of religious differences had taxed his courting of "Miss Kate." Ida concerned herself more with Hazel Richards, almost apologizing to her son that something must be wrong with them, that Hazel supported him more than they; Reverend Floyd was in his way more clear sighted, admitting that they had done everything for Ermine but nothing for Carlisle.

Floyd's considered response is instructive and defining: "I grew up to be very independent because of that." Then, with characteristic self-deprecation, "Too much so, probably." His family always told him that he responded to affection but didn't invite it. Ermine unhinged his jaw with the observation that everyone she had ever loved had loved her in return; and that everyone she had *wanted* to love her, had. In Floyd's eyes, this most important friend and second self enjoyed independence, and was happy to ask for, even expect, support and assistance, whereas he grew self-sufficient from necessity; yet aspiration to that level of independence shaped his life, relationships, and career.

ON MAY 15, Floyd ended spring quarter by accompanying faculty tenor Walter James in a program of Handel, Vaughan Williams, Poulenc, Duparc, Anes, Cowell, Diamond, Presser, and Floyd's own "Fairy's Song." After juries and finals, Floyd and Don Rand spent a few days visiting and nightclubbing in St. Augustine with Barbara Manford, one of *Slow Dusk*'s Aunt Sues, and actress Jayne Gardner, whose family lived there. Floyd needed this preparation for two weeks in Saluda and Laurinburg between June 10 and 24.

On May 25, war broke out in Korea, and Selective Service mistakenly summoned Floyd to another induction exam in August. In the following weeks, Reverend Floyd had records showing the earlier 4-F determination forwarded to Tallahassee, and Floyd found the attendant examination in Pensacola almost pleasant, confirming the earlier verdict.

Fueled by the success of *Slow Dusk*, Floyd's urge to create a second opera reasserted itself that summer, and he winnowed new subjects. One of the first, George Eliot's novel *Adam Bede* (1859), centered on a love triangle, class conflict, and out-of-wedlock pregnancy, which Floyd soon rejected. As before, he found a better subject closer to hand, his one-act Converse play *Too Dear, the Price*. Remembering Mitchell Morse's criticism about writing another play, he began a sweeping adaptation for his new libretto, *Fugitives*, in three short acts.

The earlier work's Duckworth house becomes the Davis home, "in one of the lower middle-class residential sections of a large Southern town."[31] Sam Duckworth becomes Dan (baritone), still narcissistically incapable of relating to others; Helen is now Claire Pinckney (soprano);[32] and Sarah Davis is Elizabeth Duckworth, still a "grayingly beautiful,"[33] powerful mother (mezzo-soprano or contralto). There are added roles for a neighbor (soprano), and Josie, a mute. Floyd's viewing of Menotti's groundbreaking opera *The Medium* in New York, with its similar character Toby, influenced his inclusion of a vocally challenged sidekick, as did his friendship with dancer Jean Forhan, who created Floyd's role.[34]

In the opera, Mrs. Davis is dying of leukemia. Dan has grown attached to Claire, daughter of one of the town's wealthiest families, invited for supper that evening. Claire arrives before Dan, who works at the local cemetery (reminiscent of Floyd's grandfather Oscar Fenegan), giving the two women a chance to get acquainted. Claire observes, in words that Jona Clarke might have spoken of Floyd, "I've never seen a boy so completely devoted to his mother, you are his whole world. . . . He's completely untouched by the world, and it's a good sort of *independence* because it hasn't been acquired" [my emphasis]. Action centers on Mrs. Davis's efforts to see Dan happy and settled before she dies. She confesses her illness to Claire, extracting a promise that she will take care of Dan; she then tells Dan before leaving for the hospital to die.

By act 3, Mrs. Davis has been gone for two weeks, and Dan's mute friend Josie looks after him. Claire did not attend the funeral because, as she says, "I loathe private grief made a public way." She is shocked by the condition into which Dan has let himself fall, the same depression and incipient madness that plagued Sam in *Too Dear.* Claire tells Dan that she will not marry him, "Because I would simply be a substitute for your mother. . . . I could never take your mother's place, nor would I want to." Dan attempts to verbalize, then make physical, his love for her, and she declares their relationship over, precipitating an argument. Claire analyzes, "You have a great gift for searching out the ills of other people. But when it happens to you, you are lost!" Wanting "to belong somewhere, to be needed, but for myself," she begs Dan's forgiveness, and leaves him, "a silhouette of loneliness and dejection as the curtain falls," both embodying the title's fugitives.

AFTER SUMMER VISITS to Saluda and Holly Hill, Ermine pregnant with her first child, fall sped in. Floyd chased his two actresses, Julie Storm and Jayne Gardner, both part of a growing clique of English and drama majors. Julie was "a fierce and ferocious energy, very demanding, a force of nature," but without Jayne's more disciplined talent; yet both worked on Floyd as emotional stimuli. He wrote to Jona Clarke, "I have an undeniable weakness for the dramatic type. . . . She's [Jayne] the first girl I have dated more than three or four times in the past four years: that should be indication enough of my feelings toward her."[35]

Sidney Foster urged Floyd to enter the Leventritt competition, and at the end of September the two men drove to New York. Floyd, nurturing his ambition to prepare a New York recital in the next couple of years, described the resulting competition as "glaringly unsuccessful. . . . I had been warned by Sidney that the contest was a grab-bag, and it really was sort of a farce." But the trip bore other fruit: "soul-splashing" with Priscilla Gillette for three hours, drinking and ending up high.[36] He also saw the first stage production of the Carson McCullers play *Member of the Wedding,* its all-star cast featuring Julie Harris, Ethel Waters, and Brandon de Wilde; and Menotti's *The Consul,* anchored by singer-actress Patricia Neway as Magda Sorel.

That fall, Floyd was invited into a group that seemed created just for him, the Possums (as in "playing possum," seeming other than what one in fact is). These were established Tallahasseans, not necessarily connected with FSU, but passionate theater lovers. Each month, *Theatre Arts Magazine*[37] contained one or more complete new play scripts; and the Possums, which included LeRoy and Mary Call Collins, Florida's future governor and first lady,[38] composer Walter Ruel Cowles and wife Elfrieda, ceramicist William Watson, and, of course, Hazel Richards, gathered at different members' homes for readings. Floyd's participation continued for the next seven years, with plays like William Inge's *Come Back, Little Sheba* (November 1950),[39] F. Hugh Herbert's *The Moon Is Blue* (January 1952), Louis Coxe and Robert H. Chapman's *Billy Budd* (February 1952), *The Country Girl* by Clifford Odets (May 1952), John Van Druten's *Bell, Book, and Candle* (June 1952), Inge's *Picnic* (April 1954), and Jean Kerr and Eleanor Brooke's *King of Hearts* (July 1955). In the fifties, the use of profanity by well-bred women was still blushworthy, and the proper Mrs. Collins inevitably wound up cast in hellion roles with all the "damns," making her redden to her hair's roots. Considering the personalities involved, entertainment was guaranteed, and it was a means of staying informed about the latest in good theater when the calendar or finances ruled out New York junkets.

Meanwhile, Ermine bore her first daughter in Holly Hill, Martha Katherine Matheny, and uncle Carlisle visited over Thanksgiving while working feverishly on the *Fugitives* libretto. Back on campus, he accompanied faculty tenor Woodrow Pickering in a concert of Hahn, Ravel, Fauré, Debussy, and Britten.

ON NEW YEAR'S DAY 1951, Floyd got back to his University Avenue apartment and studio piano; he had most of *Fugitives* to compose before its April premiere. As with *Slow Dusk*, he planned only piano accompaniment, reducing the time it took to complete the three short acts, which would last slightly less than an hour. On February 2, he played in a Delius memorial concert for Tallahassee's Friday Musicale; and on March 15 he addressed the Newcomers' Club for faculty wives on "Why and How a Musical Theater is Different from an Opera," illustrating with scenes from *Slow Dusk.* Two days later, the senior Floyds received his letter, "saying he was head over heels in work with his opera,"[40] and close to delivering completed scores to the cast. His setting experimented with complex meters like 11/8, 13/8, and 9/8, stretching rhythmic and tonal horizons, mixing singing and spoken declamation, with influences of Hofmannsthal's and Strauss's conversational manner in *Der Rosenkavalier.*

12. *Fugitives*, 1951. Barbara Manford, David Lowe, Mary Ellen Warner. Courtesy of Florida State University College of Music, Dr. Don Gibson, Dean.

Floyd's parents attended the premiere of *Fugitives* on April 17. Floyd directed and accompanied a student cast with Barbara Manford as Mrs. Davis, Mary Ellen Warner as Claire, David Lowe as Dan, Virginia French as the Neighbor, and Jean Forhan as the mute Josie. Anthony Terenzio created the minimal sets, Ann Kirn designed the costumes, Joan Owen headed the props crew, and Julie Storm was the house manager. Reverend Floyd said nothing to his son, but wrote, "It was very moving and received fine response from large audience."[41]

Ida, on the other hand, gave an honest but daunting review: "Son, I couldn't understand a thing that girl was saying, but I knew she was in trouble." Floyd sensed that he had written too much talk and too little music. The after-party at Bronja and Sidney Foster's was even worse; the paucity of meaningful comment from friends and colleagues—including Foster—was more eloquent than overt criticism. The *Florida Flambeau* provided the sole surviving press reception, which emphasized Floyd's use of "song dialogue" or "music conversation" to obliterate false divisions of music and drama. Floyd told a reporter that the new work depicted a forcible refusal to accept conscious and subliminal loneliness, and the struggle, however unsuccessful, to find a partner with the same needs with whom to share a life.[42]

The piece received two more performances on April 18 and 19 before Floyd put it aside forever. He soul-searched for months, highlighting painful mistakes never to repeat: opera and psychodrama were antithetical, especially when they consist mainly of talk, which he pronounced "emotionally uninformed words," between three miserable people. The psychology now struck him as "hokey, sophomoric, gloomy," as he studied the writer's lesson of the fundamental difference between telling and showing: Stage presentation has no virtue unless clear dramatic *situations* establish a discernible theatrical context to which plot and characters are viscerally connected, and which they carry forward. In years to come, Floyd described *Fugitives* as "the biggest mystery in my life. On the impetus of success from *Slow Dusk*, I wrote something

I can't imagine *ever* having written: totally interior, talky, violating every rule of what you should put on the opera stage."

Though riding his own roller coaster of romantic relationships, and still rebuilding his piano technique with Sidney Foster, Floyd denied any conscious autobiographical element in *Fugitives*. He thought male protagonist Dan a "weak reed," an unestablished personality. When Floyd signed publishing contracts five years later, he refused to let anyone see *Fugitives;* a half century later, donating his manuscripts to the Library of Congress, he wanted to say of the piece, "Take it, but don't ever let anyone see it." After assessing his failed creation, he shook himself free from impulses to retreat, equating *Fugitives* with his abortive juvenilia *Eternal Winter*. Lesson learned: theatrical efforts, though intensely personal, may never evolve into true drama.

WITH JAYNE GARDNER out of the picture, Floyd and Julie Storm had been a hot item since January.[43] What he craved above all was a partner of intelligence and magnetism, and Julie had both. The day after *Fugitives* closed, Floyd drove her to Saluda for a weekend visit with the family. Ermine, Billy, and baby Martha joined the party, and parsonage plumbing picked the least convenient time to malfunction. On April 21, Reverend Floyd reported, "Children late getting up for breakfast." Everyone sat around listening to recordings and dissecting *Fugitives*, and finally went to the movies in Greenwood. Floyd and Julie left in his convertible in a downpour the next afternoon.

On the pianistic front, Sidney Foster experienced friction with his employer. He fulminated over the conundrum of Kuersteiner's hiring of distinguished artist-faculty, then feeling threatened by them. Floyd, though fully supported by the administration, always knew who was boss, and the dean decided not to retain Foster, who left at the end of the 1950–1951 academic year.[44]

During summer school, Floyd acquired new talented students, like Lew McSwain[45] and James Staples, who would partner their teacher in years to come in duo-piano performances with Nellie-Bond Dickinson's dance program. Floyd's teaching load had grown to between ten and fifteen students, plus music appreciation. McSwain found in Floyd a wonderful corrective for her shyness and Florida small-town naïveté. The first time she played for him, he declared, "You are a diamond in the rough!" As with many students, with down-to-earth intelligence, humor, and kindness he guided her both into and outside of music, wanting to stimulate her intellect, and suggested literature of which she had never heard, much less read. He also included such students in extracurricular social activities, like Richards parties and beach trips. Evenings often began when a group assembled around practice rooms and decided to go out for Cokes, or to someone's apartment to cook spaghetti, eat, talk, laugh, play bridge, listen to music: meaningful learning that bears no course number.

A natural beauty, McSwain entered FSU in the summer of 1951 with Peter Pan collars as her most sophisticated sartorial accessory. At parties, a group of peer women might take her aside to teach her makeup tricks or how to smoke, or have her try on clothes (hand-me-downs, perhaps) light years removed from her habitual dress. Floyd, always a sharp dresser, once took McSwain on one of his clothes-buying expeditions, giving pointers on what to look for in a good Harris tweed jacket, rep tie, or men's loafers.

In addition to incorporating the Foster weight technique, Floyd introduced McSwain to his own pedagogical devices:

> Say you have a scale passage starting on middle C: he'd have me play C-D, C-D-E, C-D-E-F, till you could play the entire length of whatever it was, just a method of thinking as you played it. In technical passages, you often get lost because you only know the first four notes, and that was one of the things he had me fix. Or say you're going to play the C-major chord with your right hand, and you need to bring out one note more than another. He taught me to play that note a split second before I played the rest of the chord. Pretty soon, when I got used to that, I could play it without the anticipation. And with the weight technique, it

> didn't matter if you weighed 75 pounds or 200. With this arm weight, you could play a beautiful triple-forte chord; it had to do with the drop from the shoulder with total relaxation.[46]

The expansion of her world shook McSwain. On trips home, she shocked her conservative family with a new-found sense of humor, openness, and perspective. It was natural and typical of many Floyd students that McSwain fell a little in love with her teacher, who had a gift for putting his charges in touch with their talents and attractions. McSwain's recollections of social Floyd mirror those of her peers: "His students were very close-knit. We'd go to movies with him, maybe have supper someplace. Having been brought up in the south, I learned not only music, but how to think in a less prejudiced way than I'd been taught. Carlisle was one of the highlights of my life, a wonderful teacher, a wonderful man; he didn't have a student who didn't think the world of him."[47]

FSU HOSTED an annual summer music camp for precollege-age students. James Staples, a high school junior from Fort Lauderdale assigned to Floyd that summer, came to be another close associate and friend in years to come: "I was a real novice. I had a good potential technique, but I was very stiff, and not very expressive. My idea of playing soft was using the left pedal! Carlisle had worked with Sidney Foster, and introduced me to the weight technique. As a pianist, he freed me up quite a bit, but his contributions were even more about musicality. My competitors were people like Ryan Edwards: I had to keep up with Ryan, Carlisle always inspired me to do that. The things he assigned me always pushed me forward. I have taught now for more than forty years, and I have never imposed on my students the kind of literature that he did on me, but he never asked more of me than I could do. He simply said, "All right, you have this talent, let's make the most of it."[48]

Once Staples entered FSU as a freshman in the fall of 1952, his repertoire began featuring Beethoven and Brahms concerti, with Floyd playing second piano; his senior recital included Ravel's *Gaspard de la nuit* and Liszt's Sonata in B Minor. Floyd motivated Staples to enter competitions, and even drove him to Atlanta and Miami for National Association of Music Clubs events. For the prestigious Leventritt, Floyd took Staples to New York, guiding him through the mazes of city and contest; and inclusion in Hazel Richards's social milieu was another perk. Staples found Floyd unfailingly cordial, generous, and supportive, without displays of temper, even when students disappointed him: "I considered him a hero, someone to be emulated in all respects."[49] In Staples's case, this even included taking up smoking because his teacher did.

By the end of July, things still seemed to be going well with Julie; but to Jona Clarke, Floyd confided that his twenty-fifth birthday was a trying milestone: "To be perfectly honest, I was no little frightened by it. I suppose I'll never be one of these people who 'grow old gracefully': I heartily resent any encroachment of age—probably because of the inevitability of feeling a certain irony attached to the process. . . . When I think back to when I first met you even and realize what I expected of myself by the time I was twenty-five then it is a thoroughly disheartening affair. However I realize that I've grown immensely towards being the artist I one day hope to become, but even so there is something invariably defeating about stacking yourself up against your ideals. . . . You know me—the perennial malcontent."[50]

Of Julie, he wrote, "I'd like very much for you all to know each other. We've . . . had wonderful times together—and long serious times as well. As for our present status, it would be difficult to say. We're still seeing each other all the time and making the best of the short space of time we have before she hikes off to the Univ. of Illinois for her master's in English. She's a very brilliant, violently enthusiastic or unenthusiastic blonde with all the earmarks of a born leader. She's alternately gloomy or 'zingy' . . . and loves to the point of fervor music and literature. In a word, I'm crazy about her in spite of multiple serious differences in personality, background, etc., but I don't imagine that we'll ever marry."[51]

Just as Floyd had intuited human situations since childhood, he had this one pegged: the relationship with Julie cooled that summer, and he fell up into intense new friendships. One was the artist Evon Streetman, studying painting at FSU, which she later transposed into photography, founding a highly esteemed art and portrait studio in Tallahassee. Her work and Floyd's would soon grow more and more intertwined.

On one of their last dates, Floyd and Julie strolled into a favored local hangout, The Sweet Shop. Sitting there were Julie's two roommates, the pianist Joan Owen, who had worked props on *Fugitives,* and a young lady of whom Floyd had heard a great deal but never met, another brainy English major, Margery Kay Reeder, from Jacksonville. Kay, five years younger than Floyd, was a senior. After entering FSU in the fall of 1948, she won election to Phi Beta Kappa in 1949. She had taught herself to read at three, and later to play the piano. Her interests were oceanic, and she knew more musical literature than Floyd, mostly through recordings. Yet the combination of high-strung temperament, pathological shyness, and impulsiveness made her tender a withdrawal from the university in the first week of July 1950. Julie now introduced the brilliant and accomplished Carlisle Floyd. Kay said little that first evening, but confided her impressions years later in an interview: she was more than peripherally aware of handsome young Floyd, as were all her female English-circle friends from Jacksonville.[52] Neither was immediately smitten, but both grew intrigued; Kay stayed to finish her bachelor's. Kay and Julie both had ferocious intellects, but in temperament, reserved Kay seemed dynamic Julie's polar opposite. The dancer Nancy Smith had known Kay casually in high school in Jacksonville, and described her as "extremely bright, very nervous, high-strung, and not gregarious. On a one-on-one basis, discussing something she had read, she could talk for hours. She always had impactful ideas."[53]

FLOYD AND DON RAND advertised their desire for more living space. Julie and her roommates had a second-floor apartment in a house on West College Avenue, and convinced the two men to move in across the hall when a roomy unit became available: three bedrooms, living room, kitchen, and bath, large enough to serve as a kind of salon for the music and drama crowd. Floyd's eventual roommate Don Mowrer found it "nicely decorated, but a little archaic."[54] As neighboring tenants vacated, Floyd gave congenial students insider tips, until most of the building was occupied by musicians, actors, and dancers. Hazel Richards turned up everywhere, tidying, dusting, doing laundry, washing dishes, both hostess and guest. Don Rand indulged his fancy for decoration, painting one wall black, surprising no one more than their landlady. Kay Reeder meanwhile taught herself to play the flute, and Floyd's evening strolls back from campus, or attempts to take weekend naps, were often accompanied by her plaintive efforts.

After spending time in such close proximity, in succeeding weeks Kay and Floyd discovered shared passions for music, movies, bridge, psychiatry, and sports, especially tennis.

Taking a break before fall quarter, after driving Julie Storm to Chicago,[55] Floyd looped up to Syracuse to visit friends, then stopped off in New York, where he took a lesson from Sidney Foster, who gave him the key to composer Norman Dello Joio's temporarily vacant apartment. Floyd lost himself again on Broadway, first with Tennessee Williams's *The Rose Tattoo* with Maureen Stapleton, Eli Wallach, and Martin Balsam. His reading of the play had left him unimpressed, but he now found that "it comes to life with quite a bang on the stage and really has some of the quality of a good lusty Elizabethan comedy."[56] Of Otto Preminger's production of *The Moon Is Blue,* which the Possums had read the previous winter, he wrote, "The other little item was 'nothing but fun' . . . and of course I mooned over Barbara Bel Geddes."[57]

A two-week family visit to Laurinburg and Saluda gave him time to practice four hours daily, sleep, and read, prompting his first mention of Emily Brontë's *Wuthering Heights,* "which I marveled over. Actually. . . . it was a pretty unpleasant experience because the characters were too real not to let their behavior affect me. I am still interested in making an opera out of the first half—before Heathcliff turns out to be so completely unsympathetic—but that would require a good librettist and I don't know where one is to be found."[58]

He chain-smoked, at least around his mother. On a car trip to Laurinburg, Ida fretted, "Son, you just had a cigarette, why are you having another one?"

Floyd laughed, "Mama, I don't know how I take care of myself when you're not around."

Ida thought this hysterically funny, and repeated the anecdote for years. Floyd knew that seeing her children become adults made his mother happy, and he wanted nothing more than treatment as a friend and near-contemporary. Reverend Floyd offered neither: outwardly proud of his son's gifts, he remained a seething mass of contradictions and envy. Ida confided, "You wanted your father's approval so much as a child; now he wants *your* approval."

When Floyd drove away from Saluda, he revealingly left both his asthma medicine and atomizer behind; Reverend Floyd had to use both a week later.

Back in Tallahassee by September 14, Floyd was not yet ready to tackle *Wuthering Heights;* but, itching to compose again, he turned to a classical form he had yet to try, with *Theme and Variations* for two pianos. His characteristic style began to gel as early as 1944, with the song "When You Are Old": establishing one tonality, then stacking others atop the basis to disguise it. Polytonality, bitonality, broad use of accidentals served as forms of heightened concealment, and became his musical grammar. This was no intellectual exercise, but rather what his inner ear dictated: packing tonalities, before a final resolution into glowing consonance, drawing strength from and relieving accumulated harmonic tension.

In *Theme and Variations,* Floyd's two-measure core motif outlines D Minor, in 4/4, without key signature, its B-natural suggesting mixolydian mode. Characterized by ascending and descending open fourths, fifths, and sevenths, its brevity and economy were rife with Beethovenian possibilities. Its seven variations cover harmony, rhythm, texture, and function: melody, accompaniment, diminution, augmentation, fragmentation, with tonal centers of D, F, F-sharp; a dirge, march, even a modified tango in 6/4. Floyd first conceived this nine-minute piece for dancing; the manuscript in his Library of Congress collection is headed "Opus 7," and peppered with notations for eventual orchestration.[59]

Theme and Variations shows influences of music that Floyd had been studying, teaching, and playing, especially Prokofiev, Poulenc, Debussy, Ravel, perhaps Respighi and Copland; but the totality is quite distinctly his own. For the premiere performance, he wrote, "As a theme shows its full potentiality through its variations, so a personality shows its total self through its many facets."[60]

Around the same time, he composed a second two-piano dance score, *Lost Eden.* Lasting about twenty-five minutes, its three sections begin with "The Cleavage," a chord-stacking rhapsody centered on A Major/Minor. This is followed by "The Innocence," a related theme and six variations traveling through major keys of E, G, C, and F, with a triumphant return to E. The final movement, "The Temptation," uses fleet fragmentation and augmentation of the principal theme. A triple-*forte* coda on pedal bass D, with dissonant G-sharps, ends on the original open A/a tonality without major or minor third. Floyd had also composed "Aubade" and "Dance," two occasional pieces that never found their way onto any dance or recital program.

Floyd's September 28 recital tested his fingers, newly strengthened from the Foster-cum-Vengerova school of Russian pianism, though retaining the good points of Ernst Bacon's Viennese Romantic manner. He taught himself Liszt's monumental Sonata in B Minor, pairing it with Mozart's Sonata in F Major, K. 332, and a closing sequence of virtuoso showpieces: *Le gibet* and *Ondine* from Ravel's *Gaspard de la nuit,* Debussy's *La terrasse des audiences du clair de lune* from Book 2 of *Préludes,* and Prokofiev's Toccata in D Minor, op. 11. Such feats earned Floyd a reward as unexpected as it was cherished: after the Liszt, Ernst von Dohnányi came back at intermission, embraced Floyd, kissed him on the cheek, and exclaimed, "How remarkable, my boy!" Compliments from fellow pianists at the university were anything but the norm.

RYAN EDWARDS's switch to piano study with Floyd that fall posed a pleasant challenge; but the constant routine of lessons and recitals meant that writing his own music could only be done weekends or evenings at his studio. If parental or other visits intervened, practice grew more elusive, and he felt guilty and agitated; winding down came only from equally stolen social hours. Kay Reeder still piqued his interest, but expanded work with Dickinson's dancers brought him in closer contact with Nancy Smith, and their warm friendship developed. He was further impressed to discover that she was the niece of author and civil rights activist Lillian Smith, author of *Strange Fruit.*

Born in Jacksonville, Nancy Smith belonged to a circle that included Kay Reeder and Julie Storm. She began study with Dickinson in 1948, before a formal dance program existed.[61] Earlier work with Martha Graham and Louis Horst had shifted her aesthetic from ballet to modern dance, which thrived best on new music; and for a time in the fifties, dance and music administrations were housed together. Smith's first exposure to Floyd came when friends whispered about a mysterious new pianist-composer. Her expectations were confirmed on hearing *Slow Dusk* in May 1950. "I was so interested in and enthralled by him, but just devastated by his pianistic talent; and then later by his music, whether dance literature or other."[62]

Both found becoming "just good friends" a deep experience, though it skittered at the edges of romance, which Floyd referred to as "closet dating." And regardless of location, afternoons or midnights, Kay Reeder typically appeared as a member of their fluid group. Over the years, Floyd, Smith, and the others ate out, cooked together, exchanged books, went to movies old and new: *An American Tragedy, A Place in the Sun, Camille, A Streetcar Named Desire, An American in Paris, Picnic;* and two-hour films inevitably led to six hours of conversation. One frigid midwinter night after a movie date, Floyd living in his first independent house, they rushed back with the latest movie magazine. Like a scene from *La bohème,* it was so cold that their fingers could not turn the pages. Floyd dialed up the gas oven, pulled chairs over, and they devoured fan news in growing comfort as their bodies thawed. If Smith made light of their movie addiction, Floyd reminded her that it was a part of their work: composition, image, enjoyment. As a companion, she found Floyd "very affectionate, attentive, and wanting to know what you thought about everything. Not in a pushy way, he was just so interested in what you thought. What he was *not* was distant. The quality of his attention was wonderful, a rare commodity. And fun . . . fun*ny*! There is in him a kind of naïveté, but he's very canny and savvy. I think he still has a capacity for wonder."

Over the years, she observed Floyd as a fellow creator: "He has certain protean qualities. I have always deplored a hard and fast separation between the literate and the artistic, because each informs the other, they're all a function of the mind, and I think he's such a good example of that. His orchestration amazed me, because it's what people are trying to do with dance notation now, combining, clarifying, unifying many voices and energy components. Our friendship was one of my most gratifying, significant experiences. Getting your aesthetic feet wet, talking about everything, about what you're trying to do in the arts, something you have seen or read, that was nonstop, natural and spontaneous."

FOR HOLIDAY BREAK IN 1951, Floyd brought Don Rand and Bondie Dickinson home with him to Saluda. Everyone filled up on Ida's good home cooking, and Dickinson regaled Reverend Floyd with her outrageous experiences in SPARS, a women's coast guard reserve organization in World War II. On December 26, Ida gave her son fifty dollars for trip expenses, and Floyd rode the Silver Meteor north, joining Rand and Dickinson for six more days of socializing and theater in New York. He saw one of *South Pacific*'s 1,925 performances, with Mary Martin and Ezio Pinza; and his all-time favorite musical, Frank Loesser's *Guys and Dolls,* with its original cast including Robert Alda, Vivian Blaine, Isabel Bigley, and Sam Levene.

This theater infusion inspired Floyd's participation in another FSU speech department production, in cooperation with the art department and university museum. Its experimental series presented Henri Becque's *La Parisienne* (The Parisian Woman) on

January 8, 9, and 10, 1952,[63] in Jacques Barzun's translation. Directed arena style by Roger Busfield,[64] Floyd played Lafont, one of the flighty (but married) female protagonist's lovers, rejected because he behaves too much like a husband. The *Florida Flambeau* praised him for "ably supporting" in a wholly enjoyable play.[65] With the exception of recitals and curtain calls after Floyd premieres, this marked his last stage appearance.

Floyd's creativity now churned as never before. Less than a week after *La Parisienne,* on January 14 and 15, Dickinson's Theatre Dance Group presented "An Evening of Dance" at FSU's Music Hall. The program included choreographed music of Barber, Britten, Chopin, Dohnányi; and first performances of Floyd's *Lost Eden,* danced by Nancy Smith as Eve, and *Theme and Variations,* featuring Dickinson herself, Smith, and Jean Forhan. Floyd and Lew McSwain accompanied both pieces, supporting Dickinson's choreography. When a suitable Adam for *Lost Eden* could not be found, Floyd and Dickinson pressed student Donald Mowrer into service.

McSwain's head spun to make music with her teacher: "I was so flattered to be asked. I'd never seen modern dance before. It was so wonderful to be playing with them, and him. Those two pieces were in the same vein as *Susannah:* poignant, haunting melodies and harmonies . . . so lyrical, but also deep, moving."[66]

The *Florida Flambeau* thought the event superb, *Lost Eden* the highlight of a successful unified experiment.[67]

Don Mowrer's recollections are less reverent; but college dance programs prize virtually any male volunteer: "All I remember was Miss Dickinson telling me how to raise my arms. I was very good in jitterbug, I loved dancing. I didn't know anything about modern dance, and why they ever let me do that is more than I know. Dancing with Nancy was very good. I don't know what the reviews were, but I didn't care for the piece."[68]

On April 4, Floyd presided over a program devoted to his compositions: *Theme and Variations,* played by the composer and McSwain, and the first performance of a new work for tenor Walter James, *Nocturne for Voice,* based on Walt Whitman's "Out of the Cradle Endlessly Rocking," a paean to love, loss, and death

13. *Theme and Variations,* 1952. Nancy Warren Smith, Nellie-Bond Dickinson, Jean Forhan. Courtesy of FSU College of Music, Dr. Don Gibson, Dean.

as stimulants to poetic awakening. Floyd's manuscript bears the dates March 5–10, 1952, and demonstrates his professed lack of seriousness about composing at the time. The vocal score is a bare-bones sketch for accompanist Floyd; crossed-out first thoughts and measures of simile marks indicate ostinato passages. For James, he produced a clean vocal "lead sheet," with *tempi* and accent marks, but no harmonic indications.[69]

Floyd rode Whitman's waves of ecstatic wordplay, extracting a center slice of this long poem, from "Soothe! Soothe! Soothe," to "We Two Together No More."[70] He used no key signature, and the meter expands the lessons of *Fugitives,* mirroring the accents of Whitman's free-form verse, back and forth between 12/8, 9/8, 4/4, 5/4, and 6/4. After a four-bar introduction on left-hand pedal D-A-E, *Molto sostenuto,* the right hand adds a few open chords pointing to D Major. The singer's entrance on "Soothe" is a clarion call: descending major third, F-sharp to D, to a major tenth leap to top-line F sharp for the tenor, on the word's third iteration. Melodic leaps of major and minor sixths and sevenths, octaves, and tenths unify the work's seven and a half minutes like crashing surf, each wave different, yet the same, in *tempi* from *Allegro agitato* to *Molto moderato.* The form is a broad ABA, with the voice mostly *parlando,* but covering the staff. The opening figure returns for "O Brown Halo in the Sky," as the voice soars in wide leaps for the final anguished eulogy, "O past! O happy life! . . . we two together no more."

The program ended with the complete *Slow Dusk,* the cast of students and faculty including Walter James as Micah and Kay Reeder's roommate Joan Owen as Aunt Sue. The *Tallahassee Democrat* made no mention of *Nocturne,* but praised Floyd's versatility as pianist and composer, for his flawless text setting.[71]

THAT SPRING, Floyd read in either *The New York Times* or *Musical America* that New York's Mannes College of Music held a competition for new operas, and thought that he might like to enter something of his. First, though, opportunity arose to have the university symphony play *Theme and Variations,* meaning that it would need orchestration, Floyd's first. Out came the Naylor class notes from Syracuse, and Heacox's *Project Lessons,* and his music gained space and transparency as it inhabited different instrumental families. Performances on the ensemble's twenty-fifth anniversary concert on May 22 and 26, again with Dickinson's choreography, were the work's first and last.

For summer, Floyd trained his sights on Colorado's Aspen Institute of Music, in its second year of existence. The two Ernsts, Bacon and Dohnányi, as well as Sidney Foster, wrote recommendations, and Floyd was accepted as one of four or five students by Rudolf Firkušný, whom he had idolized since the Czech American's Syracuse recital. Tuition was $250, practice fees $15, and room and board $25 per week, all payable in full by June 30, the first day of the nine-week session. Floyd estimated his school and trip expenses at six hundred dollars, and his father loaned him half that amount.

Kay Reeder graduated with her bachelor of arts, cum laude, on June 7. She'd had enough of school for a while and returned to Jacksonville, taking an office job with Prudential Insurance. After bidding her reluctant farewells, Floyd spent two weeks in Saluda, then, on June 22, after church, and his last southern fried chicken for at least two months, he put the convertible's top down and headed west. Stopping en route to see the Fosters in Bloomington, Indiana, he pulled into Aspen on June 29.

Having lived his entire life close to sea level, Aspen's 7,980-foot elevation posed challenges. His summer home was the Prince Albert Hotel,[72] pressed into use for student housing, like every space in town with four walls. Meals were served cafeteria style at the Roaring Fork dormitory. The facility's guiding spirit was a masculine Tugboat Annie character named Florence, whom the music students predictably dubbed Firenze, for the Tuscan city. She dressed in men's all-white work clothes, and no one picked fights with Firenze.[73]

Any space in town with a door and a piano served as a practice room, and competition was fierce; the summer-empty high school was a favorite. Aspen itself, its Victorian charm fast yielding to international tourism, had been founded in 1879. The area's economy stood on its silver mines, the state's most productive, until the gold standard for American currency was upheld in 1893. Jerome B. Wheeler, half owner of Macy's department store in New York, and one of Aspen's first and largest investors, opened both the Wheeler Opera House and the plush Jerome Hotel in 1889.

By the 1930s practically a ghost town, Aspen had dwindled to about four hundred from its heyday population of seventeen thousand, Colorado's third-largest city at the time and the first with electric lighting. Enter Chicago industrialist Walter Paepcke and his wife Elizabeth, whose vision of a "Salzburg in the Rockies" began as a two-week Goethe bicentennial convocation and music festival in the summer of 1949. The Paepckes meant to demonstrate that Germany had more to offer than two world wars: great musicians, poets, playwrights, philosophers, theologians, and scientists from all over the world swept the tiny mountain mining town back into the world's attention. A two-month 1950 Aspen Festival sprang from this seed, destined to become a thriving summer tradition. By 1952, the artist faculty included singers Leslie Chabay, Herta Glaz, Mack Harrell, and Martial Singher, the last also director of the program's opera studio. Firkušný and duo pianists Victor Babin and Vitya Vronsky rubbed shoulders and instruments with violinists Szymon Goldberg and Roman Totenberg, conductor Joseph Rosenstock, and composers Darius Milhaud and Charles Jones. Although there strictly as a pianist, Floyd cautiously signed up for Jones's composition class.

Firkušný, regularly praised for the noble warmth and elegance of his performances, was born in Moravia-Czechoslovakia in 1911. A child prodigy, from ages five to fifteen he studied general music, and some composition, with his country's seminal figure, Leoš Janáček. He then worked with Vilém Kurz, Alfred Cortot, and Artur Schnabel (piano) and Josef Suk (composition), concertized extensively in Europe, and emigrated to the United States in 1940 after the Nazis occupied Czechoslovakia. Firkušný became an American citizen in 1948. Although best known as an interpreter of the music of his countrymen Dvořák and Martinů, he had a wide repertoire that ranged from Mozart to the French impressionists to contemporary American works. A great believer in long and regular practice, he emphasized Bach, "not only for the music, but also for the concentration . . . because you can't hide anything."[74] Firkušný's own practice included analysis of a piece's harmonic, formal, and dynamic structures, to establish a unique shape in his mind and, only after that, to address technical details.

One of the distinctive aspects of his performing was that his very touch "somehow expresses most of your ideas."[75] Floyd found him stylish, elegant, and poetic. Exposed for the first time to lessons on the European model, he experienced Firkušný more as a style and interpretation coach in the Bacon mold rather than as a dogged technician like Sidney Foster. One played a great deal of repertoire, typically an entire concerto and sonata in each session, never to be repeated. After Floyd's performance, Firkušný leafed quickly through the music, pausing only with his eyes on a phrase to say, "Perfect, perfect." He taught in his Aspen home, and they began with Chopin's *Fantaisie* in F Minor, op. 40. The amount of conversation surprised Floyd: "It wasn't teaching per se, more of an exchange of information about the shaping of a phrase at the opening, how we'd justify it different ways."

But Firkušný's personality and talk, his urbane bons mots, most impressed Floyd. Of Ravel's *Ondine*, its beginning dynamic marked *ppp*, Floyd remarked, "It's fiendish to execute with one *p*." Firkušný insisted, "I don't want to hear it begin . . . be very nocturnal." Floyd sat there thinking, "OK, buddy, you do it!," before realizing that Firkušný actually could. He encouraged Floyd with whispers, "*Fantaisie . . . fantaisie*," eliciting more poetry, more rubato, the vague images somehow freeing Floyd's imagination.

Lessons were weekly, but Firkušný left early, after six or seven meetings, and Floyd ended the summer with Victor Babin. The Russian's methods revealed a different European model in which lessons included the entire roster of students perched on every available surface, encouraging student-teacher badinage. Floyd had an unusually long fourth finger, and used it to play trills. Babin, acerbic but not malicious, remarked, "Ooh, I see Mr. Floyd can do those trills with [fingers] two and four." Floyd's dander rose; Babin smiled, "Then I'm going to wear you out."

Without a pause, Floyd shot back, "Not before I wear you out," to good-natured general laughter. Floyd found Babin's ear keener, and his technical guidance far stronger than Firkušný's, and his advice on Chopin's *Fantaisie* helpful. Babin insisted on absolute precision in dotted rhythms, whether playing them as written, or exaggerating with "double dotting." Floyd nonetheless found the theatricality of his teaching a little suspect.

At the second student concert in the Wheeler Opera House on August 6, Floyd was less than pleased with his playing of Ravel's complete *Gaspard de la nuit;* yet flutist Albert Tipton showered him with compliments: "What are you doing in Aspen? You are no *student*!" For the first time, Floyd realized the quantum expansion of his pianism, and a wider musical universe radiating from this mountain-girt nook. This further encouraged him to seek out the most difficult pieces in the pianist's repertoire. Everything before this had been academic; Aspen represented the profession.

Each piano lesson brought exponential growth; but Charles Jones dampened his compositional spirits.[76] Floyd attended one group lesson, and played his *Theme and Variations.* Jones, an ardent protégé of Milhaud, who in turn treated Floyd coolly, listened and examined the score, filled with simile marks. His judgment stung: "I think you need to compose more measure to measure," meaning fewer ostinati, and greater thematic concentration and development. In time, Floyd took the advice to heart; but that was his last Aspen composition class. His pianism showed far greater sophistication than his composing; measuring what he had written against what he could now perform, he had to learn to translate comparable musical intuitions onto staff paper.

But it was not all work: there were talkfests beside the Hotel Jerome pool, with its breathtaking mountain view; cheap meals at the Red Onion, whose upstairs had been a brothel a few decades earlier; and pastries at the Epicure Shop. Some of his new friendships would last Floyd a lifetime: Marleen Forsberg, so impressed with his playing that she followed him back to Tallahassee to become his student, and rented an apartment in the "arts building" on West College; and Catherine Murphy, whose unlikely dream at thirty-six was to become a concert singer, but whose true calling was as a professional student. Floyd marveled at her indomitable drive and her defiance of obstacles, shaking her fist at the road's bumps. Murphy, with a serious crush on Floyd, moved from Oklahoma that year to begin a music education doctorate at FSU.

Aspen's regular concerts and special events opened Floyd's eyes and ears: Firkušný playing Chopin's Sonata in B Minor, op. 58, and Mack Harrell singing Wolf's *Michelangelo-Lieder* on July 6; or Firkušný, Totenberg, Marjorie Fulton, Samuel Lifschey, and Nikolai Graudan in Dvorak's Quintet in A Major on July 12. Programming tended to attract connoisseurs, as in the August 3 evening of Virgil Thomson's *Five Songs from William Blake,* sung by Harrell; Milhaud's song cycle *Alissa,* with Herta Glaz accompanied by Brooks Smith; and Firkušný soloing in Mozart's Piano Concerto in B Major, K. 456, Rosenstock conducting. Comedienne Anna Russell's one-woman show on August 6 left other indelible impressions.

This rich blend was topped with Monday night films, from the Museum of Modern Art's collection, at the 360-seat, faux-Egyptian Isis Theatre: *Morocco, The Tramp, The Thief of Bagdad, Anna Christie, Beau Geste,* and *The Thin Man* figured among 1952's offerings.

Floyd left Aspen on September 1, arriving back in Saluda, famished, three days later. After an unsuccessful attempt to arrange a concert in Columbia, and shopping for clothes for fall quarter, he was in Tallahassee by midmonth, writing checks to repay his father's Aspen loan. On September 19, Floyd and star pupil Lew McSwain passed back through Saluda on the way to Floyd's audition for Benjamin Swalin and the North Carolina Symphony in Raleigh, playing Schumann's Piano Concerto in A Minor. No concert materialized, but Lew turned Reverend Floyd's head: "Lew is very attractive."[77]

Floyd had missed Kay Reeder while she typed and filed memos in Jacksonville. Nancy Smith, Bondie Dickinson, and Hazel Richards kept him occupied in Tallahassee; but with Don Rand leaving to continue study with Sidney Foster in Indiana, the need for a new roommate pressed. Floyd settled on speech and drama student Donald Mowrer, an acquaintance since *Iphigenia* in 1950, and *Lost Eden* the previous January.[78] Rand was a compact pixie, but Mowrer, tall, thin, and athletic, measured over six feet; and he owned a phonograph. Despite different fields of interest, they were compatible and congenial, and Floyd's vibrant social circle never excluded roommates.[79] He soon learned Mowrer's unconventional musical tastes: Though anything but a connoisseur of serious music, Mowrer's favorite early morning listening was Marie's Bible-reading scene from Alban Berg's *Wozzeck.* Floyd would have welcomed a Haydn symphony, and tried to explain his incapacity for listening to music in the same way as others; but he was in fact incapable of *not* listening to *any* music.

Mowrer found Floyd kind, modest, agreeable, tidy and calm, a diligent if unskilled cook who shared all aspects of household upkeep and never domineered or antagonized. Single-minded in his professional focus, however, he offered unabashedly authoritative expositions on music, art, and the theater. Mowrer saw the apartment fill with small groups of friends and school people of all ages and disciplines, including Nancy Smith and Dickinson. He thought Floyd "a very loving individual who made even strangers feel at home."[80] Nonstop talk covered everything from ancient history and philosophy to music, theater, dance, and the plastic arts. The women from across the hall, Floyd's new student Marleen Forsberg and Joan Owen, might walk in at any time, and the conversation and laughter continued. Hazel Richards further enlivened these sessions with her outrageous presence. Mowrer recalls, "She blended in almost like a giddy young student, fun to be around. No stick-in-the-mud, she! She'd try anything, including tearing around town on the back of my motorcycle."[81]

14. Hazel Richards with Don Mowrer's motorcycle, c. 1952. Courtesy of Donald Mowrer.

Floyd's maternal grandmother Katherine Cottingham Fenegan died on November 13, and the family met in Laurinburg for the next day's funeral, held at the Shamrock Inn. No one, including Grandfather Oscar, seemed unduly distraught, as "Mrs. Kate" had suffered from dementia in her final years and was hospitalized since the end of October. She had reached a point familiar to Alzheimer's families, regularly packing a suitcase and waiting on the front porch for the ride that would never take her home.

On December 2, Floyd gave a lecture and demonstration on theme and variations, using his own so-named piece as example; he and Lew McSwain played, Dickinson and Smith danced. During the Saluda holiday visit from December 19 to Christmas Day, Reverend Floyd pressed his son to explain and justify his apparent lack of religiosity. On December 26, Floyd boarded the Silver Meteor in Columbia for a two-day theater binge in New York, including Arthur Laurents's *Time of the Cuckoo,* directed by Harold Clurman and starring Shirley Booth and Geraldine Brooks. NBC Opera Theatre had produced and televised operas since Menotti's *Old Maid and the Thief* on March 16, 1949, and Floyd paid serious attention to whatever the Italian-born composer was doing. Menotti's *Amahl and the Night Visitors,* the first opera written *for* television, had debuted on NBC on Christmas Eve 1951. This year's visit with Woo Gillette included serious brainstorming about adapting *Slow Dusk* for television, of which nothing came.

Dickinson's new "Evening of Dance" for January 1953 reprised *Theme and Variations,* and Floyd appeared as pianist on FSU's television series *At the Piano,* on WMBR-TV in Jacksonville. With Dickinson, Reverend and Mrs. Floyd attended their son's next solo recital on March 20, a ninety-minute program of Mozart's *Fantasia* in C Minor, K. 475; Schubert's *Moment Musicale* in A-flat, op. 94, no. 6; a Bach Toccata in D Minor; then Chopin's Sonata in B-flat Minor, op. 35; Debussy's *La soirée dans Grenade* and *Jardins sous la pluie,* from *Estampes;* and closing with Balakirev's challenging Oriental fantasy *Islamey.*

Floyd had promised to be home for Easter, but a singular opportunity arose for him to accompany

Dickinson to New York, where she took classes with Martha Graham. Thanks to his experience writing ballet scores for FSU, Floyd hoped to attract Graham's attention at a class he attended; but no special introduction or conversation developed.[82] He was nonetheless content to bask in her presence, and listen to Dickinson's critique of the current group's work: "Martha, I don't see personalities coming out of the class as I remember it." Graham responded in sepulchral tones about the work being prepared, "Well, I don't blame them: it's the Crucifixion."[83] On the way out, Nellie-Bond advised Floyd, "Keep your works current"; but Floyd never submitted a score to Graham.

With Don Mowrer's graduation that spring, Floyd decided that a private house would suit him and his work better than revolving roommates and a perpetual salon. When his operetta-actress friend Kathryn Haun got wind of this, she offered a property that she owned, a one-thousand-square-foot green clapboard cottage at 503 West Call Street, across from Old City Cemetery. At fifty-six, Haun, retired but still her girlish self, had proven an astute investor, even if the little green house had nothing to call interior decoration. From the front porch, Floyd walked directly into a living room, behind which lay a small kitchen, and one tiny bedroom and a three-quarter bath. That it was just blocks from the music building, and that rent was only sixty dollars a month were compensatory pluses; but best of all, when the door closed behind him, it was his alone: independence. Except for out-of-town trips, it was the last time Floyd would live in rented rooms. For the first time, neither family nor roommate had to be accommodated; he had solitude, silence, room to think, space to create. 503 West Call became the gathering place for Tallahassee's dancers, photographers, artists, writers, and laughter. Envious others dubbed it "Snob Hill."

9

"The Old Girl," *Susannah*

Tallahassee, 1952–1955

In the quiet of Floyd's green cottage, piano and composition migrated to opposite poles. Both required a keyboard; but playing brought the drudgery of practice, whereas writing music, despite gaps in his training, tempted with guilty, *easy* pleasure.

Floyd fell up into opera in a quintessentially American way: initial distaste, modulated to simple aversion, then suspicion of Dr. Johnson's "exotick and irrational entertainment."[1] A decade would pass before he classified a work with anything but the Wagnerian nomenclature "musical drama"; but tentative beginnings led to seduction, as opera intimated ranges of the human condition not possible in spoken theater. Transcending the burden of work—the Latin term *opera,* literally a "collection of works," is the plural of *opus,* a singular work—Floyd discovered independence akin to the body's when anaerobic heaviness kicks into runner's high.

He had always loved the theater, acting, even writing a play and two musical dramas; he had tasted love with actresses, dancers, and musicians. Now, enmeshed in a bubbling fleshpot of creativity with like-minded students and peers, his true passions emerged: the operatic medium, its singers, text, and music in their alchemical marriage.

ONCE ASPEN FRIEND Catherine Murphy established herself in Tallahassee, her apartment became a magnet for Floyd. Murphy's teenage daughter Judith had yet to become Judith Moore, author of the thinly veiled shrieks of anger disguised as memoir, *Never Eat Your Heart Out* (1997) and *Fat Girl* (2005);[2] but if a fraction of her detail about those Florida years is accurate, her life there was nightmarish. She alleged belt lashings from her mother, and endless taunting about her weight. Floyd thought Judith stocky but not obese, and did his best to intervene in the mother-daughter uncivil war. In calmer moments, as Judith struggled to learn the violin, Floyd taught her the intricacies of two-against-three rhythms. Without naming Floyd, Judith reported that she told one of Catherine's friends about the belt thrashings, and Floyd suspected it may have been he. Regardless, the beatings ceased.[3]

A brighter side of life at the Murphys' involved food, Floyd a frequent guest, sometimes with Nancy Smith at his side. Once Catherine served rabbit, which Floyd, remembering his childhood pets, had never eaten. The hostess advertised it as chicken, but in midbite confessed its true identity. Floyd convulsed the table by putting on a horrified face, and pantomimed pulling rabbit fur from his mouth. Even Judith laughed.[4]

In the spring of 1953, new factors at Florida State University made Floyd's life less comfortable. The first and easiest lasted longer: the faculty appointment of pianist-composer Edward Kilenyi, who hit the ground running as Ernst von Dohnányi's paladin.[5] As we have seen, Kilenyi had used his army position to get Dohnányi out of Europe, and to FSU. The entrenched celebrity now returned the favor, and Dean Kuersteiner hired the protégé when a position opened. Although Floyd's relationship with Dohnányi remained cordial, Kilenyi imagined that Floyd never showed his idol proper respect; but this one-sided rivalry spurred Floyd to forbid his students to participate in Dohnányi's master classes.

Though limited to the decade between 1947 and 1957, two other personalities, champions of the witch hunts for Communists and sexual deviants, exerted influences more systemic and toxic: Joseph McCarthy (1908–1957) on the national scene, and his Florida counterpart, Charley Eugene Johns (1905–1990).

McCarthy gained national prominence as a Wisconsin senator in 1946, just as the House Committee on Un-American Activities (HUAC) began investigating Hollywood's motion picture industry. That curtain rose on a sideshow of "friendly witnesses" like Ronald Reagan, Walt Disney, and Gary Cooper.[6] The suspect Hollywood Ten, including director Edward Dmytryk and scriptwriter Dalton Trumbo, "took the Fifth,"[7] which was interpreted as an admission of guilt. The blacklisting of artists cast a pall over such greats as Bertolt Brecht, Lee J. Cobb, Lillian Hellman, Sam Jaffe, Burgess Meredith, Zero Mostel, Clifford Odets, Ayn Rand, and Edward G. Robinson. Many musicians who became Floyd's elder peers landed on "gray lists": Marc Blitzstein, Leonard Bernstein, Aaron Copland, Lotte Lenya, Kurt Weill, Jerome Robbins, and Roger Sessions most prominently. The term "McCarthyism" became a synonym for a decade of Cold War-fueled mass hysteria, paranoia, and suspicion tantamount to guilt, accusation to conviction.

Charley Johns used his two years (1953–1955) as Florida's governor, and eleven subsequent years in the state senate, as forums for his crusade, wryly nicknamed the Johns Commission, against Communists, civil rights advocates, and homosexuals. Students and faculty in Florida's state universities and public schools became special targets; and Doak Campbell, FSU's president from 1941 to 1957, withdrew support and even employment from anyone who incurred the suspicion of Johns.[8] By 1963, more than a hundred teachers and deans, and as many students, had resigned or been dismissed. At least one professor known to Floyd attempted suicide following an accusation of homosexuality.

Though no charges arose against Floyd, he found himself enmeshed in the tribulations of colleagues and students in a miasma of anxiety and fear. After all, the performing arts, then as always, attracted their share of "sensitives," and music and drama loomed in the crosshairs of Johns's crusade. Bad enough that one of Kay Reeder's roommates was expelled for suspected lesbianism, and that a music faculty colleague was lured into a compromising sexual situation in the men's room of the Greyhound bus station; but Floyd's particular ire rose when piano student Lew McSwain, who had no comprehension of the idea, much less the practice, of lesbianism, faced grilling by university authorities. She and her roommate *had* played bridge with an expelled gay pianist, hence were deemed guilty by association. The school required its faculty to sign loyalty pledges, attesting that they did not personally advocate, or belong to organizations that advocated the overthrow or subversion of the United States government.[9] All of it smacked to Floyd of pressures at revival meetings. Just that spring, during a visit to his family in Saluda, his father wrote, "Talked with Carlisle about Jesus being God's Son. Wish he would accept Him. I have made a terrible mistake with him somewhere."[10]

KAY REEDER stayed in Jacksonville, and she and Floyd drove back and forth for occasional visits. The Mannes School's opera competition, with its one thousand dollar prize and premiere performance, kindled his ambitions and he lobbied friends about libretto subjects. Nancy Smith's roommate Barbara "Bal" Goleman asked one of her brainy pals to go over to Floyd's for a chat. With McCarthyism imposing coercion to confess and conform, when a knock came at the door of Floyd's house one late spring evening, the contagion of suspicion was very much on his mind.

Nathan Samuel "Sam" Blount, three years younger than Floyd, was working on a master's in English at FSU, and Goleman thought the two might make a good creative team. Blount had seen *Slow Dusk*, and the two men shared interests in music, art, and cooking; but Floyd found him an "odd duck," moody and prone to lapse into dark uncommunicative spells. As they sat at the kitchen table, Blount asked whether Floyd knew the story of Susanna and the elders, and her vindication by the prophet Daniel, from the biblical Apocrypha. Though most printings of the King James Bible omitted these chapters,[11] decades in a church family had given Floyd the gist, and his youth coincided with the rise of a literature exposing religious hypocrisy. He had read or knew of Theodore Dreiser's *An American Tragedy* (1925), Sinclair Lewis's *Elmer Gantry* (1927), and Erskine Caldwell's *Journeyman* (1935), with its serial-seducing preacher, the action taking place in a Wednesday to Monday span, ending with a revival scene.

Sam Blount was in fact less familiar with the Apocrypha than Floyd, but they compared notes on the source story: a party of lustful elders espies innocent Susanna bathing in a stream. When she rejects their sexual propositions, they accuse her of adultery. She appeals to and is vindicated by the prophet-hero Daniel. Influenced by the recent McCarthy and Johns investigations, Blount proposed updating the action to the present day, with a final stage picture of the heroine dispersing an outraged populace with derisive laughter. Floyd thought to Americanize the heroine's name by adding a final "h," to distinguish her from the chambermaid-bride in Mozart's *Le nozze di Figaro*. Discussion ensued with a series of what ifs, ending with the understanding that Sam would draft a libretto, despite showing muted enthusiasm for the project.

With Floyd, the material struck sparks, but no word came from Blount. If they ran into each other socially, Floyd might probe, but they had no further discussions, and the composer finally scratched an itch to write his own libretto. He already had, twice; and if Menotti could do it, why not? *Susannah*'s dramatic kernel, unlike that of *Fugitives*, could "be externalized through action and visible situation and still retain absorbing, multi-dimensional characters."[12]

The story's human motives and behavior good and bad further reflected the McCarthy madness.[13] Fragments of the discussion with Blount coalesced when Floyd envisioned an isolated Tennessee mountain setting. Memories of the stifling midsummer heat of revival weeks and their picnic suppers had potent resonance and relevance for him. He saw no need for a Daniel-rescuer, but transformed the male protagonist into a visiting preacher who becomes embroiled in the community's friction with Susannah. The revival week in turn suggested the inevitable baptismal creek, in which the elders espy Susannah at her bath; and the revival meeting would be the hinge, culminating in Susannah's ostracism and the preacher's eventual death in that very creek.

In an even more significant departure from the story's roots in the Apocrypha, Floyd dramatized the grotesque tyranny and narrowness of Puritanism against authentic Christian teachings of compassion and forbearance. He took Blount's present day backward to the Depression years of the thirties, with the existential anger and minimal social skills he had experienced firsthand. The irony of the name Floyd chose for his community, New Hope Valley, belies its residents' inbred suspicion of anything or anyone beautiful.

Floyd's early immersion in southern Christianity shaped *Susannah*'s ethical core: beware any entity whose "faithful" seem to have all the answers, who don armor against life and beauty, who practice cruelty and coercion as institutional priorities, and who make of religion a redoubt from whose ramparts they hurl devastating judgments. As Floyd observed of his heroine, "It doesn't turn her into a cruel person, but I don't think at the beginning of the opera we'd have ever thought she had a cruel instinct. But we all have that capacity, if we are tormented to that point."[14]

As always, the southern-accented words came first, distilling Floyd's memories and life experiences to date. Some characters' names, preempted for their rural or onomatopoeic feel, have roots in family circles. Over the course of three evenings, he chose these, and determined the opera's spine. A Gleaton had served as one of Reverend Floyd's guest revivalists in North, and became one of the libretto's elders. In another branch of the Floyds, the given name Bascom traveled generations, shared by Floyd's great-uncle Henry Bascom Floyd Sr. (1858–1943). With the middle name commonly shortened to "Bat," his son H. B. Floyd Jr. (1897–1963) became "Little Bat."[15] For his preacher's given name, Floyd drew Olin from the South Carolina politician Olin D. Johnston,[16] then changed the character's original surname, McKnight, to the more grating, Dickensian Blitch. Although Floyd recalled no Blitch family in Holly Hill, Reverend Floyd recorded one in his diary;[17] and considering the initial conversation with Blount, naming Susannah's brother "Sam" is at least a remarkable coincidence.

Blitch's early line about ascetic practices[18] reflects memories of severe North revivalist Henry Bennett. Floyd had seen his own father adopt such a ministerial persona, pride swelling from success and adulation, and this now served as the perfect tool to collapse Susannah's resistance. Olin Blitch, though a man of real convictions, has grown inflated by *becoming* his trade, with glad-handing and superficial extroversion; at heart he is humorless, guilt-ridden, and conflicted. Floyd relaxed into happier memories with the "Jaybird Song," which his grandfather Oscar Fenegan had sung;[19] and he'd heard aunt Bunny describe the night sky as Susannah's diamond-stitched velvet blanket.

Within ten days, he drafted a complete libretto, sixty-six pages in pencil in a spiral binder,[20] without consulting the Apocrypha again. Between first and final versions, he added or modified a wealth of detail; even Susannah's best-known aria began life as "Shore is a pretty night."

Floyd's two acts, each with five scenes, display the mix of forms that became his customary practice: verses blank and free, with iambic and dactylic stress patterns, and metric feet with four, five, and six beats, tailored to natural speech rhythms. He employs assonance, alliteration, and outright rhyme for the folklike songs, hymnody, and some scenes with elders and wives—the McLeans (baritone/mezzo-soprano), Gleatons (tenor/soprano), Hayeses (tenor/soprano), and Otts (baritone/contralto)—especially their negative observations and maxims. Struggling with the notion of traditional grand opera, he called the work a musical drama in two acts.

Floyd's dramatization plunges us at once into its rural origins: On a sultry Monday night in New Hope Valley, Tennessee, square dancers fill the churchyard, passing time before the revival preacher's arrival. One uncommonly beautiful young girl, Susannah Polk (soprano), conspicuous in her brightly colored dress, radiates excitement.[21] The four elders' wives brand her as shameless, and her brother Sam as an irresponsible drunkard. Meanwhile, their husbands jostle to dance with Susannah. Reverend Blitch (bass-baritone) enters, states his week's agenda, and joins the dance with fair Miss Polk.

Later that evening at the Polk cabin, Susannah sings to the McLeans' challenged son, Little Bat (tenor), of her dreams and aspirations. Her rough-edged brother Sam (tenor) returns from hunting, and Susannah asks him to sing a favorite song, "Jaybird," to lighten the mood.

On Tuesday, the elders look for a baptismal site to cap revival week. They find a creek near the Polk cabin, but it is occupied by Susannah, bathing. Cloaking their lust, they declare satanic influences in her behavior. Unlike their apocryphal sources, they never proposition Susannah: New Hope's mores forbid elders to share or confront their true impulses: making Susannah an easy target sublimates their own low desires.

Gossip spreads, and that evening at a picnic supper—Floyd's memories of groaning boards—the church folk ostracize Susannah and tell her that she is no longer welcome in their midst.

Back at the cabin, Little Bat confesses to Susannah his inadvertent compounding of her problem: he bowed to parental pressure and told them that she had made love to him. She explodes with anger, chases Little Bat off, and begs Sam to sing "Jaybird" again.

Act 2 opens on Friday morning. Sam counsels Susannah to swallow her pride and go to that night's revival: nothing will change unless she makes a public confession. Before heading back to the woods, he leaves her a rifle, just in case.

At church, the revival gets under way with Susannah seated on the rearmost bench. Blitch exhorts the faithful to make a generous contribution. His unscripted sermon uses the story of a sinner consumed by hellfire before confessing. With clear references to Susannah's alleged transgression, he invites the faithful to the altar. At the last moment, seeing a smile of triumph on Blitch's face, Susannah screams and runs from the church.

Later, alone and disconsolate at the cabin—Sam is still away hunting—Susannah sings a ballad about an unwed mother deserted by her lover. Blitch strolls in for the last measures, and attempts a personal conversion. Susannah defends herself, but the week's stresses have taken their toll, and she collapses, drained. Blitch, touched, places his hands on her shoulders. Suppressed desire, incubated in his lonely profession, flares up. Learning that the house is empty, he leads her inside. Exhausted, Susannah surrenders her will to fight.

The following morning, Blitch prays alone at church for forgiveness for the wrong he has done Susannah. Elders and wives gather, but the preacher fails in his attempt to exonerate Susannah. Blitch begs her to forgive him, but she has forgotten that practice.

At sundown Saturday evening before the baptism, Sam returns with his sack of game. Susannah reveals what Blitch did to her the previous night, and Sam charges off in search of the preacher, rifle in hand. A shot rings out—Floyd's first comment on America's disastrous love affair with guns—and the mob spills in, meaning to force Susannah out of the valley, and to have Sam arrested for Blitch's murder. She defies them with Sam's other rifle, and the crowd slinks off, muttering threats.

Little Bat stays behind, and Susannah pretends seduction. At the last moment, she gives him a vicious slap, and he skitters away to the sound of her derisive laughter. Susannah remains alone, strong and resigned to her fate, and her future path will never lead out of the mountains. Instead, she will spend the rest of her life as the community's eccentric, scarred but not destroyed: independence at a price. Floyd forces his heroine, along with his audiences, to discover unattractive truths about themselves: though not innately hurtful, when tormented past endurance, the capacity for cruelty seeps like a dark pool up to the surface of thought and action.

WITH HIS FIRST TWO OPERAS, Floyd had fine-tuned his recipe. In *Susannah,* as at the curtain of *Slow Dusk,* a lone woman holds the stage, her dreams dashed, meaning only to survive. The earlier opera's much younger heroine has decades of life to work through depression and loss; with Susannah, we are not so certain.

Within days of its completion, Floyd held a libretto reading at Hazel Richards'. His friend Del Hansen[22] played Sam; other actors and actresses from FSU speech and drama took the remaining roles. Without a note of music, *Susannah* scored her first triumph, but now other questions arose: Floyd wanted a full evening's event, but not the three or four hours of so many operas. Each moment of each fast-paced scene had to be pared to essentials. He sought to blend elements of Greek theater, Italian verismo, and Hollywood, everything imbued with rural southern colors, to create a totality all his own. His spare text needed an equally taut, evocative score, and he set to work without pause: summer school would begin in just weeks, and each moment had to count. More than a half century later, Floyd recalled, "I had a card table set up to put the score on. . . . It was so hot that your hand would stick to the paper."[23]

For the title character, he thought first of Priscilla Gillette, whose career was soaring, and whose voice filled his inner ear as he wrote Susannah's two arias. That August he jumped into his new jet-black Ford convertible with red interior and sped west with his arias to St. Louis, where Gillette was singing at the Municipal Opera. Following a performance of Sigmund Romberg's *Blossom Time,* the composer threaded his way backstage to the dressing rooms, music in hand; but the star behaved as a queen receiving lowly subjects. Without inviting him to sit down, much less asking him to give or send her the pieces, Gillette made it clear that she had no time.

Disappointment evaporated in the course of Floyd's extended road trip to Bloomington to see the Fosters, then to New York to see William Inge's *Picnic* with Paul Newman and Kim Stanley. There were quick visits with the Clarkes in their new Virginia home, and Nellie-Bond Dickinson in Wilson, North Carolina, to discuss the year's dance projects. By August 22 Floyd arrived in Saluda, where his father "helped" tighten screws in the car's doors. Back in Tallahassee by September 5, Floyd prepared to teach his raft of pianists and finish *Susannah* for the Mannes competition.

The professional music fraternity Sigma Alpha Iota (SAI) now approached him with a small but urgent request. Since 1941, during the school's years as the State College for Women, its recreation association had published an annual volume of "favorite camp, patriotic and university songs." With changes wrought by FSU's coed status, the association hoped "to stimulate school spirit and to give us a picture of life on our campus today,"[24] and enlisted SAI to convince faculty composers to write new entries.

To verses by Ralph Bellamy, head of FSU's sociology department, and no apparent relation to the like-named actor, Floyd's contribution, "Our Hearts Leap Up," appears on the booklet's fourth page:

Our hearts leap up to hear the call
Of golden sun on garnet wall,
Of garnet wall and golden sun,
The home of work, the land of fun.
Garnet and gold, Garnet and gold,
Our hearts leap up as in days of old,
To spread thy glory and praise.

Floyd's setting in C Major, 4/4, in solemn four-part hymn style, has nothing outlandish about it. The vocal ranges are unexceptional, taking the soprano no higher than top line F-natural; yet the melody never goes quite where one expects at phrase endings. Mild dissonances through passing tones in the bass line, and enharmonic cadences through added G-sharps into relative A Minor make it unlikely that this modest little anthem got much play at football games or assemblies.

BEFORE, BETWEEN, AND AFTER LESSONS, Floyd drafted most of the piano score for *Susannah* in twelve weeks between September and December 1953, all in his university studio, in his enthusiasm often sharing just-finished numbers from the opera with piano students arriving for lessons. Added to the sonic world established in his early songs and first two operas, a new sustained lyricism defined New Hope Valley's populace. As Floyd found music for the picnic supper (act 1, scene 4), emotion surged up in him, creating an inner dialogue of resentment toward the wives of the elders, "For God's sake, *somebody* come forward and speak up for Susannah!" At the revival meeting, the congregation accepts that God speaks through Blitch; but two scenes later, when the preacher proposes Susannah's exculpation, they want *not* to hear, and assume that Blitch is speaking, not God.

Though Floyd scorned every aspect of *Fugitives*, time's pinch made convenient the occasional recycling from that earlier opera. In the first scene of act 2 of *Susannah*,[25] the 6/4 measure of chromatic buildup to a resounding E-flat Minor statement underscores Susannah's wondering to Sam how she has deserved such treatment at the community's collective hands; it is appropriate in its anguished search for one of the darkest keys in music's night sky. He kept the rest of the score entirely his own, with deft imitations of square dance, folk ballads, and hymnody. He consciously assumed Copland's spare manner for the opera's ending, and realized later that a few Hollywood film score mannerisms had crept into his Appalachia.

Two Floyds, Carlisle and a recently acquired cat, Herbert, arrived in Saluda on December 19 with a carload of dirty laundry and dry cleaning. As Reverend Floyd habitually observed, "Ida in better humor since Carlisle came."[26] Her hearty southern dishes, as well as those of Ermine's cook Hermie in Holly Hill, and aunt Lucile's at the Shamrock in Laurinburg, proved antidotes to the eighteen-hour work marathons at Call Street and FSU. Floyd spent New Year's Eve with Kay in Jacksonville before returning to Tallahassee.

Jumping without pause into 1954, Floyd completed *Susannah*'s piano-vocal score for Mannes on March 7.[27] This took in all about five months, even with interruptions. For the January 13 and 14 "Evening of Dance," Floyd and dance faculty member Lester Bruch shared musical direction, and *Lost Eden* scored a triumphant reprise; the *Flambeau* admired the fusion of Floyd's musical and Dickinson's choreographic ideas.[28]

On February 4, the elder Floyds and aunt Bunny arrived for their boy's latest piano recital, and Floyd spent the night before a gargantuan program on his own living room couch. The day of, February 5, saw a dizzy whirl of activity, with guests and a frantic city-wide search for formal collars and studs, before Floyd located the set he thought lost. That night marked his final solo recital at FSU: Beethoven's late Sonata in A-flat Major, op. 110; Prokofiev's Sonata no. 7 in B-flat Major; and Mussorgsky's *Pictures at an Exhibition.*

Reverend Floyd wrote, "Listened to Carlisle play for an hour and half and he has never played as he played tonight." Everyone attended an elegant postconcert reception at the home of old-society Tallahasseeans Gladys and George Henderson,[29] whose butler George Hall would make an unexpected appearance, in name only, in a Floyd work twenty-seven years later.

The *Tallahassee Democrat* made a point of remarking Floyd's consistency, intensity, precision, and creation of appropriate moods and "immense architectural shapes."[30]

On March 19 and 20, the Florida Composers' League held its tenth annual forum at FSU, with visiting composer-pianist-author Halsey Stevens. Floyd and Jim Staples played *Lost Eden*, with Dickinson's choreography, danced again by Nancy Smith and her new partner Jack Holmes. At the end of April, Floyd judged pianists at the Florida Vocal Association's annual festival in Tampa; yet the composer had *Susannah* in legible condition by May's third week and mailed her off to Mannes. He rewarded himself with the illusion of "sleeping forever"[31] on a visit to Saluda and Holly Hill, interspersed with long family Scrabble tournaments, and a celebration of his twenty-eighth birthday on June 11.

15. Phyllis Curtin, c. 1955. Photograph by Gene Cook. Courtesy of Phyllis Curtin.

FLOYD'S CAREER PATH took other decisive twists that summer. Mannes promptly returned *Susannah*, letting the composer know that they had decided not to bestow an award that year; but they had selected three entries, including his, for honorable mention. Floyd presented Kuersteiner with this distinction, and the dean agreed to stage the world premiere of *Susannah* the following year.

Kuersteiner further empowered Floyd to engage professionals to create the roles of Susannah and Blitch. Floyd had already planned a return to Aspen, for more study with Firkušný, in lieu of teaching a second summer term. A friend from two years earlier, pianist Phyllis Rappeport, wrote a glowing report of two singers on Aspen's faculty, soprano Phyllis Curtin and baritone Mack Harrell, and Floyd decided to approach them.

Curtin, née Phyllis Smith in Clarksburg, West Virginia, in 1922,[32] began musical training as a violinist, changing her Wellesley College major from political science to music. She made her first important public appearance in 1946, in the American premiere of Benjamin Britten's *Peter Grimes* at the Tanglewood Festival. Following engagements with the New England Opera Theater, Aspen invited her to join its faculty in the summer of 1953. That fall witnessed the beginning of her reign as a New York City Opera diva, after her company debut in Gottfried Von Einem's *The Trial* (*Der Prozess*). Phyllis Rappeport had touted the soprano's phenomenal musicianship, and Curtin had built much of her career on contemporary music.

Marrying historian Philip D. Curtin in 1946 allowed her to change her maiden name, Smith, deemed unpromising for opera; and her husband spent the summers of 1953 and 1954 with her in Aspen. Floyd saw him removed from music; and indeed, in his memoir, Curtin referred to his "nine-year involvement on the fringes of the music business . . . another world." When Curtin began teaching at Swarthmore College, he groused that the beginning of his wife's career required "a lot of practice at home."[33]

Mack Harrell (1909–1960) had probably the biggest reputation on Aspen's vocal roster. He had won the Metropolitan Opera Auditions of the Air in 1939 and sang with the company until 1958, with other engagements at New York City Opera, Lyric Opera of Chicago, and San Francisco Opera. He taught at the Juilliard School from 1945 to 1956, and recorded much of his operatic and concert repertoire.

Floyd invited Kay and his student Peggy Tapp to accompany him on the drive west, and the trio left on August 7. Peggy had no experience with maps, and when Kay handed her one with a request to navigate, the party had a few driving adventures. Though they discovered no pleasant or fast route through Kansas, they arrived in Aspen on August 10, a fine time to be in Colorado rather than Florida or South Carolina. Floyd checked into the Prince Albert, the two women into the Roaring Fork dormitory, along with college-age Aspen students. In addition to taking in festival concerts and films, the three met for communal meals at the Roaring Fork cafeteria, beneath "Firenze's" baleful gaze.

At twenty-eight, Floyd was one of Aspen's older students, and especially popular because he had a car. Firkušný's lessons continued to stimulate. Floyd most treasured his extraordinary teacher-coach's praise, "You have such a mastery of style. If it is Mozart or Chopin, it *sounds* like Mozart or Chopin." At one of their repertoire-intensive sessions, Floyd played all four Chopin *Ballades*. Firkušný was puzzled: "The A-flat does not have your usual personal imprint." Floyd had studied that one with Sidney Foster.

Weighing *Susannah*'s options, Floyd evaluated musical personalities at concerts: on August 14, Phyllis Curtin and Martial Singher performed Pergolesi's *La serva padrona*, conducted by William Steinberg; meanwhile, Kay and Peggy saw the sights and sunbathed in Colorado's high country. Finally, around August 20, Floyd screwed up his courage and called the diva. When he said that he would like to show her an opera he'd written, she was at first nonplussed; her rooms were scattered with stacks of new music to learn. But as long as Floyd could come right over to her little red house—Philip Curtin described Aspen's accommodations as "gentrified miners' cottages"[34]—and play it for her, certainly she'd listen.

Thanks in equal parts to her fresh voice, good looks, and trim athletic figure, Curtin had just scored a triumph as Strauss's Salome at New York City Opera that March. Critics were still agog at seeing the role sung by an artist who actually *looked* like a teenager, and who executed the "Dance of the Seven Veils" without embarrassing herself or the audience. Even more scandalous, photographs of her costumed for the role had appeared in *Life* magazine's April 12 issue, leading to public censure from Clarksburg's church pulpits; meanwhile, matters compounded when the soprano and *Life* photographer Gene Cook fell wildly in love.

Thus the plight of Floyd's good girl framed as bad touched her. He began by roughing out the opera's plot, then sat at the keyboard and played through Susannah's two arias, with Curtin following over his shoulder, growing excited. He asked whether she would care to hear more, and she answered that she had heard all that *she* needed; but, flipping back and forth through the score, she told Floyd, "There's a role in here that Mack should sing." She phoned Harrell at his cottage.

Miracles do happen: Harrell was game, and the party of two became a grand crowd of three. *Susannah*'s story and music also resonated with Harrell, a Texan with his own experience of fundamentalism. Floyd explained that he had been authorized to contract them for an FSU premiere in February 1955, and it chanced that both singers had the same two weeks open.

On August 21, Floyd called his parents with the good news, "saying that his opera was to be at FSU with Met stars."[35] Later that evening Curtin, accompanied by Brooks Smith, sang Samuel Barber's *Hermit Songs.* She reinforced Floyd's impressions of her theatricality by appearing in a burlap gown ordered from a local seamstress: she could not imagine offering these intense, personal songs without visually reinforcing the stark lives of ascetic monks.

The next day Curtin, Harrell, and other colleagues performed Darius Milhaud's *Les amours de Ronsard,* conducted by the composer. Atop a busy teaching schedule, the soprano was exhausted from the week's earlier performances. Floyd was touched when this extraordinary artist broke down in tears after singing, feeling that sheer facility had led her to be taken advantage of. She had failed to maintain her personal standard in the Milhaud, which she had practically sight-read. Floyd put his arm around her as they walked across the field outside the performance tent, consoling and reasoning with her as a peer. In championing *Susannah,* Curtin knew that she had made a wise choice to help a good and compassionate man, as well as a promising composer.

On August 25, Floyd, Kay, and Peggy headed down the mountains and east. He arrived back in Saluda two days later; his father "talked with him about his opera and Jesus."[36]

KAY REEDER tolerated no boredom, and Prudential offered plenty. Having decided to earn a master's in English, she enrolled at the University of Wisconsin, Madison. Floyd knew her well enough by then to feel something deeper than friendship; but Kay set her courses without discussion. Already a great letter writer, for the next nine months Floyd discovered a new language of endearment.

Otherwise he was hardly at loose ends: with school underway, he began orchestrating *Susannah.* For four days, he worked at Nancy Smith's parents' home on St. John's River, and discovered in himself the headstrong confidence of a young composer with nothing to lose in this strange new world of opera.[37] Orchestration consumed the next three months, then he and Jim Staples extracted parts for what became the standard Floyd orchestra of about sixty: two flutes, one doubling on piccolo; two oboes, one on English horn; two clarinets, one on bass clarinet; two bassoons, one on contrabassoon; four horns, two trumpets, three trombones, tuba, timpani and other percussion, celesta, harp, xylophone, and a string component of about sixteen violins, eight violas, eight cellos, and four double basses.

Working with pianists, as in his own playing, Floyd continued to emphasize technique, but in service to artistry. He gave students a form of creative visualization: a performance must *look* as the player wishes it to sound. Reaching this point requires analysis of form, shape, and balance, those essentials so rarely taught in tandem with the mechanics of playing. This would be the meeting ground of Floyd's inner pianist and composer: diagramming the piece helped the brightest students, like Ryan Edwards or Jim Staples, to identify peaks of tension and valleys of repose, just as it guided composer Floyd with opera's massive architecture. Frustration, sometimes defeat, came when he had to admit that integrating skills, to say nothing of emotional apprehension and capacity, were in large part unteachable.

His experiences with singers and dancers emphasized global correspondences between breath control and phrasing: thinking of the diaphragm as the focal point of musical intensity could transform any performance. Nellie-Bond Dickinson once compared two concertizing violinists: the one literally on his toes far outpaced the flat-footed player. Floyd learned to watch conductors' midsections, which he had heard Martha Graham call "the dynamic middle."

FSU'S ACADEMIC COMMUNITY had retained vestiges of McCarthyism. Suspicious of Dean Kuersteiner's commitment to *Susannah,* university president Doak Campbell asked to read the libretto. Floyd sat working in his studio one day when Kuersteiner tapped at the door, looking grim as death: it seemed that Campbell's wife, Edna, a straitlaced Mississippian whom Hazel Richards dubbed "the unreconstructed Southerner," a self-appointed custodian of campus morality, had had her turn with Floyd's text. Kuersteiner confided that

Campbell refused to release student funds earmarked for costumes and sets, terming the opera "a very questionable enterprise," even though Curtin and Harrell had already been contracted for a Spartan $1,500.

Kuersteiner expressed visible relief when Floyd offered to confront the ogre in his lair. After arriving at the president's office, the composer was surprised to learn that he had written a "trashy dirty" story. Campbell and his Mrs. had agreed that Blitch must have impregnated Susannah during their night of illicit passion, thus the entire opera concerned nothing but gratuitous sex. The production's cosponsor, the Service League of Tallahassee, a branch of Junior League, would not take kindly to anything so explicit.

"Pregnant?" Floyd gasped. "You do understand the dramatic purpose of this so-called seduction?"

Campbell huffed, "Well, it's just sex."

When Floyd pointed out that this was how Blitch discovered Susannah's *innocence,* Campbell began to back down, growling, "We'll reread it."

During the span of days it took the Campbells to reassess Floyd's morality, the composer related the incident to Nellie-Bond Dickinson. She laughed, and told Floyd that every year before the "Evening of Dance," Mrs. Campbell approached her with the ultimatum, "Nellie, I trust you are not doing anything *risqué* this year."

Kuersteiner reappeared at Floyd's studio in September's third week, all smiles: the composer had been vindicated; student funds would be released, meaning that Susannah and friends would appear clothed and housed.[38] The university began issuing publicity statements, announcing the world premiere for February 24, 1955 as the State Symphony of Florida's second program of the season, Kuersteiner conducting. Much space was given to the résumés of Curtin and Harrell, together with Eugene Cook's pictures of the diaphanously clad soprano as Salome. The *Tallahassee Democrat* of October 31 showed Mary Call Collins, wife of Governor Leroy, purchasing the first ticket. In a happy coincidence, the United States Senate announced plans to censure Senator Joseph McCarthy on November 5.

On November 26, Curtin wrote Floyd that the score had arrived safely: "It is clear to read and there should be no major problems that I can see."[39] On November 9 *Flambeau* had seized on the fact that Curtin and Harrell would work in Tallahassee for a salary equivalent to three hours' service in New York. Curtin reassured Floyd, "Rejoice (though privately) that there is money and interest to produce the opera at all. . . . Most schools, opera companies and theaters are afraid to spend anything at all on works they are not certain are standard enough to catch the big audience."

During the holiday break, Floyd spent a frantic nine days in South Carolina, including the first inspection of his parents' latest home in Florence, where his father had been reassigned to St. Paul Methodist Church. While Kay Reeder visited her family in Jacksonville, Floyd typed a long letter to "Dearest Pigeon" on December 20, clearly disappointed to not finagle a visit:

> This fall and winter have been about the busiest . . . and certainly the happiest I have ever known. There has hardly been time for anything except the old girl (*Susannah*) but as a consequence all the stolen moments have probably been sweeter. . . . We're into musical rehearsals on S. and have gone all the way through it with orchestra and singers which, believe me, has been a thrilling experience. . . . I can't wait for you to hear the orchestration; I'm mightily pleased. The singers have done an excellent job of learning their parts and frankly, my dear, I don't see how we can lose on this one. . . . The set [by Franklin Adams] is designed and although it isn't at all what I had imagined, I like it very much. [Director Lynn] Orr will do marvelous things with the staging and lights.[40]

Floyd considered Orr, FSU's current speech and drama head, an accomplished professional in all areas of the theater, if not a musician. To give him a better feel for the score, Floyd taped the entire piano reduction. Orr called one day and announced that the hearing had changed his entire production concept: he would not use any three-dimensional scenery, but do it all with ramps and parallel platforms, very simple, very stark.

On Christmas Day the composer gave himself the luxury of flying to Washington for a quick visit with the Clarkes, "to divulge the events of the fall,"[41] and on to New York for the usual week of plays and Menotti's new opera *The Saint of Bleecker Street* on Broadway; and, perhaps, to tell Priscilla Gillette of his coups with Curtin and Harrell, with whom he also planned to rehearse.

In tandem with Orr, and Catherine Murphy, who was cast as Mrs. Gleaton and who would also build all the costumes, Floyd scrambled to finish the musical preparation and approve staging and lighting. With a costume budget of $50, he accompanied Murphy to McCrory's five-and-ten-cent store to buy all the fabric remnants they could afford: the entire production, excluding the guests' fees, could not exceed $1,500.

The pivotal role of weak-minded Little Bat McLean had gone to the nonsinging speech and drama student Eb Thomas,[42] whom Floyd helped devise a kind of *Sprechstimme* deviating from written pitches. The faculty tenor Walter James was cast as Sam; elders and wives would be sung by students: Harrison Fisher and Martha Kay Willis (McLeans), J. Dayton Smith and Joan Meador Nichy (Hayses), Ken Nelson and Catherine Murphy (Gleatons), Lee Liming and Bette Jo Armstrong (Otts). Pianists Ryan Edwards and Jim Staples satisfied accompanying scholarships by dividing staging rehearsals.

The production had originally been scheduled for a single performance on February 24 for $3 a ticket; but with student activity funds paying so many of the bills, the school added a second student night on February 25 with $1 general admission. On January 21, Curtin wrote Floyd that she would gladly sing the added performance for an additional $250. She also confided her difficulties with the repeated climactic phrases in her second aria:[43] "The first time I tried to sing [it] I was totally unable to keep from weeping. This presents a problem, plus the fact that it is a very difficult thing to sing the high B-flats convincingly in the style. . . . I love the opera and am convinced that it is a really great work."[44]

Virtually every soprano who has essayed the piece will sympathize. Curtin solved the problem with her New York voice teacher Joseph Regneas, who observed, "You cannot sing anything but an open 'ah' at that point!" They continued to vocalize on the vowel sound alone until the rough edges were smoothed.[45] Floyd wanted a high keening sound, and when he heard that Curtin could actually *do* that, he responded inwardly, "To hell with it, everybody else will just have to do it their own way."

For five days around the weekend of January 22 and 23, he flew to New York for rehearsals with Mack Harrell at the baritone's home in suburban Larchmont. On February 13, a plea appeared in the *Democrat*, asking the general public to donate costume pieces and props, especially hats, hair pieces, and shoes, and to drop these off at the city's Bargain Box.[46] Curtin and Harrell arrived on February 15 for rehearsal, and stayed respectively at the Floridan and Seminole hotels.

Meanwhile, other wheels turned: in Florence, Ida fretted over making a new dress for her son's big night. From New York, Curtin received an invitation to a reception for the British composer Benjamin Britten from his publisher, Boosey & Hawkes. Curtin respectfully declined, mentioning that she was in Tallahassee, rehearsing a new work by a composer she'd met in Aspen. Robert Holton, one of Boosey's New York agents, had never heard of this Floyd; but that Phyllis Curtin would work almost *for free* for two weeks in *Florida* was quite a recommendation. Curtin told him, "Somebody from your place ought to see this opera."[47] Holton asked her to pass on a summary of his publishing credentials, and for Floyd to send him a score. "She did, he did, and I did—and so it began, for I was thrilled with the work and its potential."[48]

Music publisher, entrepreneur-agent, and composer, Holton exerted enormous influence as mentor and personal friend to the younger generation of Boosey & Hawkes's roster of composers. His exuberant promotion of talents like Floyd, Lee Hoiby, Ned Rorem, Stanley Hollingsworth, and Conrad Susa would in time include free access to his apartment in New York, a courtesy warmly reciprocated by Floyd whenever Holton might be within range of Tallahassee.

With Curtin and Harrell in place, rehearsals proceeded quickly, with ten days till opening night.

Although both appeared with parts learned and memorized, Floyd spent two or three intensive hours with each, reinforced by sessions with Edwards and Staples, both of whom the singers later hired as concert accompanists. Floyd marveled at Curtin's musicianship, honed through her background as a violinist and enhanced with perfect pitch.

Orr planned his staging in meticulous detail and established immediate rapport with both guests. Accustomed to students' overacting, he expressed quiet amusement at Curtin's and Harrell's "marking" (rehearsing without the total emotional investment or full voices they saved for orchestra rehearsals and performances). Floyd explained, "Phyllis is riding technique today."

16. Phyllis Curtin, Mack Harrell, *Susannah*, Florida State University, 1955. Courtesy of FSU College of Music, Dr. Don Gibson, Dean.

In conversation outside rehearsal, Curtin and Harrell asked the composer whether he'd written other works, and he laughed off the thought that anything he'd done before *Susannah* might be worth saving. Referring to his dance scores, he confessed, "I have them sketched out, but never took the time to edit or copy them." (He copied nothing in those days.) The guest professionals rode him about making readable scores, and Floyd began for the first time to consider that he might really be a composer.

A potential sour note sounded when Edna and Doak Campbell informed Kuersteiner that they would not attend the opening; but that changed when Floyd received an engraved invitation: "Governor and Mrs. LeRoy Collins request the pleasure of your company at a reception honoring Miss Curtin, Mr. Floyd, Mr. Harrell, at 10:30 p.m. at the Governor's Mansion."[49]

Mary Call Collins, one of Floyd's playreading Possums, came through in the clinch, and the Campbells' other commitment vanished as abruptly as it had appeared. A small army of Floyds converged on Tallahassee on February 23: Reverend Jack and Mrs. Ida, Ermine and Billy Matheny, Doris and J. W. Moore, Freddie and G. R. Floyd. Ida and Ermine attended dress rehearsal at Westcott Auditorium, joined later by Reverend Floyd and Billy. At one point, Floyd ran down the aisle calling out that one tempo was too slow, and even Reverend Floyd knew that something was afoot: "The orchestra did not seem to get the time right, so Carlisle corrected them. I do hope it all works out for the best."[50] With the Call Street house overflowing with family, the composer phoned to tell them not to wait up, that he needed to take Curtin and Harrell out for a late supper. That night, Floyd again tossed and turned on his living room couch, while his father prayed for *Susannah*'s success.

February 24, a Thursday, dawned cloudy. Hazel Richards dropped by with fresh-cut camellias from her garden, agog over the governor's reception. Reverend Floyd took his son's Ford to a station for gas and put on 1955 license plates. Floyd taught a normal day of lessons and classes, and his parents stayed home to answer phone calls and receive telegrams from Hazel and Frank Ellerbe in Latta, Jona and Bruce Clarke in Washington, and Mrs. Dougherty in North. While Floyd took Curtin and Harrell out for an early supper at the Silver Slipper, Tallahassee's finest steak house, Reverend Floyd polished his son's shoes. Rain began falling at six that evening, before the eight o'clock curtain.

At the theater, the elder Floyds found themselves centers of attention, sitting in a special roped-off box with the Campbells and Collinses. The performance itself took everyone by surprise. The *Democrat*'s reportage, sandwiched between photographs of the city's movers and shakers milling about the lobby, crowed that Floyd had put FSU and himself, "a man to be reckoned with in setting American grass-roots traditions to effective words and music," on the operatic map, predicting a bright future for native operas as long as they were "nourished in rich American soil."[51]

Reverend Floyd wrote, "watched and heard *Susannah* and was made to feel most proud of my boy. It was wonderful."[52] Hazel Richards put Floyd off by

17. Phyllis Curtin, *Susannah*, Florida State University, 1955. Courtesy of FSU College of Music, Dr. Don Gibson, Dean.

steamrolling ahead of everyone to get to him backstage after the performance; but he brightened at her observation of FSU's first family, the Campbells, preening in the governor's company: "You would have thought they wrote it themselves."

When his parents met him at the governor's mansion, their reaction was the muted approval he had come to expect. Mrs. Floyd watched Richards's attentions and later told her son, "I guess I should be more like Hazel." Ida might be proud of his accomplishments, but she deplored female acquaintances who gushed tastelessly about their miraculous progeny. She wanted people to know what *hers* had done, but not through her having borne the news: people should read about it in the newspaper. If anyone enthused, "You must be so proud," Ida Floyd offered a stock response: "We're glad he's ours." She also made no secret of liking "pretty music," automatically provoking her son's suspicion of anything of his she might praise.

Despite Reverend Floyd's habitual grandiosity, he seemed overwhelmed by the Collins reception: "Seems like I am in a fairy land, can not get used to so much ovation! Last night we entered Gov's Mansion, the Gov., Dr. Campbell and others applauded. I surely felt funny."[53]

The next morning's *New York Times* left no doubt that Floyd had made a mark. As a state capital, Tallahassee supplied a local stringer who trumpeted that *Susannah* had played before a near-capacity crowd in the 1,600-seat auditorium. Floyd did not see this validating notice until over a half century later, and was much amused by evidence that the reporter had left before the opera's conclusion: After giving a brief cast list and plot sketch, he/she wrote that Susannah and Blitch fall in love at the happy ending.[54]

For the most part, Floyd's colleagues held their peace about his success. Dohnányi said nothing, but his mouthpiece Kilenyi showed disdain, shrugging theatrically to others behind Floyd's back, "Well, what can you say?" Members of the production team fretted that the story or its presentation may have given offense. On Monday morning, Floyd walked into the music office expecting a wrist slapping from

18. Floyd, c. 1955. Photograph by permission of Evon Streetman.

conservative Methodist secretary Frances Pemberton. A lady given to voicing outrage, she declared, "Anybody who's offended does not understand it!"

Floyd always found it curious that Sam Blount had never stepped forward between their Call Street kitchen meeting and *Susannah*'s premiere. Their mutual friend Bal Goleman told him later that she'd spoken with Blount, who professed astonishment that Floyd had proceeded with "his" idea. Goleman retorted, "What do you mean? Carlisle's too much of an artist to just let something like that drop." And that was the end of Blount.[55]

Floyd had made tentative peace with opera. On his many New York visits, he had avoided the medium, instead seeking out the best legitimate theater, sharpening his dramatic instincts. Yet he remained keenly aware of currents swirling toward a serious American musical theater, neither musical comedy nor Eurocentric grand opera, but a form suitable for performance in the venues of both. In the vanguard, Menotti offered *The Medium, The Consul,* and *The Saint of Bleecker Street* in populist Broadway houses. At Columbia University, Douglas Moore produced operas of Ernst Bacon, Otto Luening, and Jack Beeson, all of whom shared Floyd's goals. *Susannah*'s composer had thrown his hat into a very busy ring.

10

The Short, Fast Fall to Fame

Susannah *in New York, 1955–1956*

Susannah's gestation took somewhat longer than the average human's, but now Floyd could watch the child grow. Curtin and Harrell beat the underbrush in New York in Floyd's and "their" opera's behalf, but the composer had no time to preen, much less rest; Nellie-Bond's "Evening of Dance" performance fell on March 1, five nights after *Susannah* closed. As musical codirector, he supervised two works. Nancy Smith and colleagues reprised *Theme and Variations* with Staples and Edwards as the orchestra.

Incredibly, Floyd also unveiled *A Woman Sings*, a four-movement piece choreographed and danced by Smith; but the composer forgot or ignored his colleagues' injunctions about finished scores. *Woman* eschews key signatures and most dynamic indicators; tonalities are suggested by accidentals, repeats by simile marks. The first movement, "Love Lyric," marked Lento, is a 6/8 *Sicilienne*, in melodic and harmonic sevenths, with a tricky sixteenth-note left-hand chordal accompaniment, resolving in E Major after just twenty-six measures.

For the second movement, "Lament," *Molto moderato*, in 5/4, Floyd sketched thirty-two measures of a choralelike theme, with rich bass sonorities in both hands, centered on C Minor. The third movement, "Cry of Fear," fifteen measures of 6/4, offers a spiky rhythmic theme of four descending sixteenths, quarter note, three quarter-rests, then an alteration of the sixteenth pattern, while the left hand anchors the music more or less in B-flat Minor. These tricky variations require three staves. For his pianists, Floyd marked the fall of beats above measures one through ten. The final movement, "Song of Rest," has eighteen measures of rich, dignified Adagio in D-flat Major.[1] Nancy Smith Fichter recalled, "His music touched me so; and I think that would have happened even had we not had a personal relationship."[2]

A week later, Floyd drove Jim Staples to Chicago to play in the National Federation of Music Clubs' annual student contest. Finally, on March 17, he wrote the Clarkes his considered response to the *Susannah* experience:

> It was, I am told, a tremendous success and well it might have been with what amounted to a beautiful production and four notable performers. . . . The orchestra was only so-so but . . . thoroughly respectable. . . . Curtin and Harrell were magnificent and a joy to work with. . . . I can't remember a pleasanter or more rewarding association in my life. They unfortunately did the two roles so well and so convincingly that I can't imagine at this point that anybody else will ever be able to equal them. Their interest and belief in *Susannah* has been very humbling and something I shall always be grateful for and they are the kind of people who when they say they believe in something and intend to push it, carry out their threats![3]

To wit, Floyd planned a New York trip over Easter weekend, April 8–10, "to peddle the work with Mack and Phyllis." The singers contacted such theatrical powers as Chandler Cowles and Lincoln Kirstein, hoping to fix *Susannah*'s professional debut on Broadway. In any event, such a boost far exceeded the usual neophyte's introduction to New York: "I feel that I am in a unique situation having the projected two stars of my show pushing it and also willing to sing the audition for it for a producer."

At some point during these weeks he finally read the Apocrypha, but saw no need for revision to make the opera conform: he had scored his intended points. Floyd and company covered much ground: to cap his recent flow of good news, he visited Robert Holton's office at Boosey & Hawkes at 10 West 57 Street, just steps from Carnegie Hall. He was quite aware that Boosey's roster of composer-clients included Bartok, Britten, Copland, Delius, Elgar, Finzi, Holst, Ireland, Kodaly, Prokofiev, Rachmaninoff, Richard Strauss, and Stravinsky.[4] Holton, an enterprising collector of young composers,[5] treated Floyd to lunch at the opulent Russian Tea Room. Curtin had done an admirable job as the composer's pro tem public relations manager, and Holton persuasively outlined the benefits of being a Boosey & Hawkes composer. In the event, it took little convincing: Holton had examined *Susannah* closely and recommended it to his superiors. The firm expressed doubts that it would ever exert more than a limited regional appeal; but Holton looked beyond its "pre-*Down-in-the-Valley* atmosphere," to "the personal moving tragedy which follows the folksy beginning" of "rustic square dance."[6]

Holton did what he did better than anyone else in the business, one of the last agents of a kind depicted in Hollywood films of the thirties and forties: career builders, enterprising for and passionate about themselves and their hopeful, needful clients. His intelligence and energy allowed creative artists to sleep better at night. He truly loved opera, the form and its people, and he and Floyd shared a theatrical aesthetic. Holton convinced his employers to take *Susannah* "on agency," with no guarantee of publication, but to promote and place it with any and all respectable performing organizations.

With Holton's help, Curtin used her position at City Opera to arrange an audition for the company's general director, Joseph Rosenstock,[7] whose three-year tenure was in crisis. The hopeful trio tracked the harried conductor to City Center's dingy backstage, located a piano, and sang through as much of *Susannah* as Rosenstock had the patience to hear. The man's bluntness was proverbial: he rose and barked, "No, I won't do it. I haven't the funds."

Their next contact, Chandler Cowles,[8] a Broadway wunderkind since 1946, was the son of Floyd's former Florida State University colleague Walter Ruel Cowles.[9] Chandler welcomed Floyd, Curtin, and Holton to his apartment, along with impresario, writer, balletomane, and famously bisexual Lincoln Kirstein, Curtin's admirer since her 1953 City Opera debut. Harrell could not make this audition, so Curtin sang all parts, including chorus, again to the composer's accompaniment.

Kirstein had just resigned as City Center's managing director.[10] Though controversial and temperamental, he knew everything and everyone around New York's cultural scene, and seemed impressed; but Cowles mused, "It is so grim, so bleak, unrelieved." A strange judgment from a backer of Menotti, whose *Consul* heroine ends by putting her head in a gas oven. Kirstein corrected his colleague, "I think that is probably its strength," and remained *Susannah*'s champion.

Though *Susannah* never found a Broadway home, Curtin and Holton pursued other leads. For Floyd's last day in town, Kirstein and Cowles arranged a third hearing, for NBC Opera Theatre's founder and artistic director, Samuel Chotzinoff,[11] and the conductors Herbert Grossman and Peter Herman Adler, the group's music director.[12]

NBC had televised hour-long condensations of operas since 1949, beginning with the crowd-pleasing last act of Puccini's *La bohème*. With four offerings the following year, the medium reached an audience of millions, whereas the average opera house held at most two to three thousand. Chotzinoff and NBC, who had already aired Menotti's *The Old Maid and the Thief*, commissioned the Italian American to write the first opera specifically for television, *Amahl and the Night Visitors*, in 1950–1951. Chotzinoff held the passionate belief that television offered opera its only hope of persistence in America, and the network's initiative in fact paved the way for PBS *Live from the Met* broadcasts beginning in 1977.

After the audition in Adler's NBC office, Chotzinoff and Grossman seemed interested; Adler had reservations. Grossman took Floyd aside, sugarcoating a bitter pill by first complimenting him on the opera's ending, then asserted that the piece would never appeal outside a few southern states. He even suggested that Floyd rewrite the libretto to create a sexual relationship between Susannah and Little Bat. To Curtin, Grossman reworded his concern: "There's no boy meets girl." The meeting ended with *Susannah*'s NBC fate in limbo, but Holton's potent advocacy kept the door to production open a crack; most important, the agent maintained an unshakeable belief in Floyd as an opera composer.

ON APRIL 15, Floyd played a recital for tenor Walter James: Buxtehude and Schütz, for which Floyd did a turn on harpsichord; Barber, Cowell, Mussorgsky; and Britten's *Serenade for Tenor, Horn, and Strings,* in Floyd's keyboard reduction. A week later he confirmed his growing reputation when a request came from the American Music Center's Marion Andersen for a work list and biographical data: AMC had already received numerous queries about Floyd's catalogue.[13]

Kay Reeder had meanwhile had enough of Wisconsin. Her first year of master's work included student teaching in Madison's school system, and she recoiled out of constitutional shyness. The mandatory thesis proved the final straw, with its tedious hours of library research, and she returned to Jacksonville and another job with dependable but boring Prudential Life. She and Floyd drove back and forth for quick visits. He had smoothed the way with FSU administrators for a transfer of her credits to complete her degree in Tallahassee with a graduate assistantship; but she delayed moving back.

Floyd had always been drawn to strong women, beginning with his mother and aunts on both sides, but also the Priscilla Gillettes, Jona Clarkes, Jayne Gardners, Julie Storms, and Phyllis Curtins. When Kay first met the senior Floyds, she intuited Floyd's preference with characteristic bluntness: "Many of your problems come from the women being the interesting people in your family."

Floyd grew ever more fascinated with the originality of Kay's mind. Despite her reluctance or inability to produce a tangible body of work, he thought her greatest skill might be as an essayist in the intellectual mold of Diana Trilling.[14] He had more in common with Kay than with any woman he had met, beginning with their twin passions for music and literature. She had taken piano lessons as a child, and loathed the experience; as an adult she learned the flute and retaught herself piano, becoming an excellent sight reader and player of literature from Bach to Chopin, Rachmaninoff, and Scriabin. The broth took on added spicing from the recent innovation of television. Kay's parents were the first set owners that Floyd knew, and he soon became addicted to the medium.

Kay had survived a childhood far more dysfunctional than Floyd's. Her father Guy Wilton Reeder had no formal education past the sixth grade, yet taught himself navigation and astronomy. During World War II he had served on a Merchant Marine tanker, leaving Kay to be raised by her mother, Marguerite ("Gundy"), née Nelson, who hungered to be anything but a housewife, cook, or parent, and worked as a Western Union operator. The Reeders retained a housekeeper, Mrs. Rakestraw, whom Kay called "Wawa," and who showed the girl more love than either parent. Threatened by the affection between the two, Gundy summarily fired Mrs. Rakestraw, surgically removing Kay's sole source of empathy; Gundy went on to preempt and possess each new friend that Kay made.

As a child, like Floyd, Kay reaped praise for sensitivity, brilliance, and gravity. Her father took charge of her extracurricular education, giving her advanced books and recordings, fetishizing her intellectual growth; Gundy watched from the sidelines, competing at every turn. Kay skipped first grade. Both parents saw that her education had surpassed her social skills, yet they pushed her, little more than a toddler, to frequent reading performances in her second-grade class. They took her to be examined, evaluated, prodded, and poked by experts, who declared that her precocity would eventually cause psychological damage. Later, when Kay earned election to Phi Beta Kappa, Gundy appropriated the honor: "*We're* 'Phi Bates' now."

Most damaging, when Guy returned from a cruise, he regaled Kay with lurid detail of his sexual escapades in distant ports, and the girl became a shuttlecock in parental warfare. Floyd identified with anyone who had survived two adults mired in their own emotional childhoods. Though Kay had no history of expressing or resolving her anger, Floyd detected in her a certain purity of soul; both were fascinated by what made people most themselves.

When Floyd shared his romantic interest in Kay with Jim Staples, the latter experienced a hero worship of his teacher so deep that he too began to feel romantic toward Kay: "It's not so much that I was in love with her; but anything Carlisle ever said or did, *I* wanted to do."[15]

ON MAY 29, after two South Carolina nights of his own family drama, his parents put him on the train to New York to follow up with NBC and to coordinate a possible production there with his FSU schedule; but the network kept him on tenterhooks. He wrote the Clarkes, "The wheels of such ventures turn slowly. I do know that they have been extremely interested and the staff there knows the show almost as well as I do! So if it isn't done there I will know that it has had great consideration."[16]

He spent more productive time in the audience at Tennessee Williams's latest, *Cat on a Hot Tin Roof,* with Burl Ives, Barbara Bel Geddes, Ben Gazzara, and Mildred Dunnock, directed by Elia Kazan. Holton assured him that things were going well, and Floyd returned to Florence on June 2. He practiced at the church, and, in the parsonage, impressed his father by cooking "pigs in a blanket." Countering Reverend Floyd's astonishment, the composer asserted that every man ought to be able to take care of himself.

Boosey's contract to represent *Susannah* arrived on June 10. Reverend Floyd, for once sheepish about his son's business affairs, thought that he should check with Hazel Richards before signing; but the next day, Floyd's twenty-ninth birthday, his father witnessed the document, and bade his son farewell with a dim sense of losing him to an alien world.

A quiet first summer term gave Floyd time to begin composing a work more ambitious than anything outside his operas: *Pilgrimage,* a twenty-minute, five-movement solo cantata on serious biblical texts, for low voice, conceived for and dedicated to Mack Harrell. The cycle spans a tonal world of D Minor/D Major, with a carefully constructed emotional arc. The first movement, *Adagio molto sostenuto,* 3/4, sets Job 14, verses 1–2 and 7–12, one of the more positive statements in that prophet's grim assessment of humanity; it opens with "Man that is born of a woman is of few days and full of trouble." Both hands begin in bass clef, with open parallel fifths and fourths in gentle syncopation: quarter-half in the right, dotted quarters in the left suggest the opening vocal line's contours with rising half steps, intimating that all is not right with the world as we know it. Brief surprise glints from "There is hope of a tree," underscored with radiant B Major; but the general pessimistic view of life's hollowness returns with repetitions of the stark opening D Minor superimposed on and clashing with E-flat Minor. Hope of literal and figurative harmony reappears in A Major, "Yet through the scent of water it will bud"; but respite proves illusory, and dissonance pulls back the original sentiment and thematic material, plus the singer's fortissimo threefold "Where is he?" With a falling version of the syncopated rhythms, now in E Minor/B Minor, Floyd slides chromatically, stacking D Major and E-flat Minor, back to barren D Minor homeland. The singer finishes on repeated low A, toward the bottom of his range of articulation.

Movement two, from Psalm 69, verses 1–3, 14–17, and 20, establishes an altogether more anxious mood. This intense prayer for release from spiritual malaise proceeds in 4/4, *Andante e molto largamente,* with the eighth note at metronomic 100. The piano flourishes up to E Major, stacked with raised B-sharp fifth and C-sharp Minor. The syllabic vocal line uses triplet sixteenths, two tied eighths, two sixteenths and syncopated sixteenth-eighth-sixteenth. A new ostinato—half note, two eighths, dotted eighth-sixteenth—underlines the singer's plea, "Save me, O Lord," rising toward the top of his range. A second theme uses another ostinato rhythm: two thirty-second notes, dotted eighth-tied eighth, *Allegro non troppo, molto marcato,* almost a doubling of the initial tempo, with the quarter note now at 96, conveying the urgency of "Deliver me out of the mire." The meter shifts to 3/4, *Molto meno mosso,* quarter note 69, with the vocal line returning to the initial rhythmic device for "Hear me, o Lord, for Thy loving kindness is good." The pianist's left hand mirrors the text's agitation, with open fourths and fifths, articulated in jagged sixteenths, eighths, and rests, marked *sempre agitato,* and a relentless crescendo to "Hear me speedily," with stacked chords based on C sharp and E. The song's final page returns to the first song's rhythmic and melodic devices, in 4/4, grave: "Reproach hath broken my heart." A new and more lyrical theme outlines G-sharp Minor, modulating to F-sharp Minor with melodic passing tones, intensifying the pathos of the line "And I looked for some to take pity but there was none," ending in thirdless C-sharp Minor.

If the first two songs suggest a grouping of "sin and expiation," the third, verses 1–4, 6–10, and 23–24 of Psalm 139, balances the cycle, as the singer makes peace with himself before God. Predominantly in 4/4, andante, and centered on F Major and B-flat Major, the vocal writing is still syllabic, but far more lyrical, a return to *Susannah*'s tonal world. A climax with the line "Such knowledge is too wonderful for me. It is too high," takes the baritone up to high F sharp. An interlude of three-stave pianism follows, with soaring permutation of the vocal melody, leading to calm F Major acceptance of God's omnipresence. The last two pages combine the singer's ecstasy and the interlude's pianistic splendor, in resounding B-flat Major.

Songs four and five embrace acceptance and repose. The fourth uses verses 1 and 2 of Psalm 146, and 2 and 3 of Psalm 148, a short, exultant paean to God in unambiguous F-sharp Major. In 4/4, *Allegro deciso,* Floyd demands three-stave virtuosity in the keyboard's central half. The vocal writing displays confidence in Harrell's ringing top, and keeps the singer much above the staff, with stentorian F sharps at "Praise the Lord!" The return to Psalm 148 is mirrored in ABA fashion by restating the striding initial theme, with elaborated accompaniment.

The cycle concludes *Largo, molto tranquillo,* with verses 38 and 39 from the eighth chapter of St. Paul's *Letter to the Romans.* Both hands play open fifths of the D Major triad, in octaves in treble clef, followed by a gentle rippling from D to G and A Majors, with brief excursions to unrelated tonalities. Conditioned by church hymnody, the music drifts back into an idyllic *Susannah* mood, all torment and searching drained away; anything, in fact, as the text affirms, that might "separate me from the love of God." The setting makes free-form variation on keyboard themes, sometimes underlined by a mild but insistent pulse of dotted quarter-eighth pedal on D in the left hand. The conclusion reaches gently back to Numbers 6, verses 24–26, the Aaronic benediction: "May the Lord bless you and keep you"; but Floyd personalizes the request by substituting "me" for each "you." He confirms his harmonic and rhythmic "family," together with the ostinato left-hand pulse, finding repose on an unadorned single-line recapitulation of the entire cantata's principal building block: D-A-D-D, open D chord, low D, adding the major third F sharp.

If accidental, the near-complete *soggetto cavato* D-A-D-D-(Y) nonetheless provokes, reinforcing as it does the composer's longing for male parental approval. Unparalleled in Floyd's output, *Pilgrimage* hints at mysteries behind its somber facades. For months, Reverend Floyd had placed two close relatives in his daily diary prayer lists. The first, his younger brother "Sonny," had lifelong alcohol-related problems; but why Reverend Floyd feared that his son needed special help from the Almighty remains a mystery. He knew that he smoked and drank, and that he did not subscribe to orthodox religious doctrines; but the diary offers no explanation of why Floyd appears so regularly and insistently on that list. Floyd's letters to others contain no hints of emotional crises; but *Pilgrimage*'s dark drama, no less than conflicts bared earlier in *Fugitives,* suggests otherwise.

THOUGH FLOYD had by now based two works on biblical themes or texts, he never approached his father for input or praise. He exercised similar restraint in shielding Kay Reeder from his family until their relationship had advanced. The first reference to Kay in Reverend Floyd's diary appears in a remark that his son called her in Jacksonville on August 30, 1955, four years after they met.

Toward the middle of July, Hazel Richards, vacationing in the West, sent Floyd a card advising him of

Curtin's and Harrell's upcoming performance of *Susannah* excerpts at Aspen. Kay was not available, but Nellie-Bond Dickinson, who had enjoyed getting to know the singers during February's production, had never seen the Rockies, and they set forth on July 27. Floyd found Dickinson an amusing companion, with her insistence on regular afternoon siestas, for which she clambered into the back seat, while Floyd steered them across the Great Plains. On their next-to-last day, he glanced at his rearview mirror, hearing growls of discontent. Dickinson sat up, hair plastered to head, and asked, "Where are we? Hell?" It was only Kansas. They arrived at the Prince Albert, on the much cooler banks of the Roaring Fork, on the evening of July 29. The old Aspen gang's dynamic made the trip worth its discomforts. Phyllis Curtin was housed in one of the town's plum decorator apartments that became headquarters for a fluid group of vocalists and instrumentalists that included the festival's executive director, Norman Singer, and prize Floyd students Edwards and Staples, imported by Curtin and Harrell to play lessons and recitals.

Singer, a Manhattanite nonmusician, raised Floyd's hackles by pontificating on matters aesthetic. Curtin sang a group of Liszt songs on July 23, and Singer pronounced the Hungarian composer a panderer in Romantic drivel. Floyd called his bluff by expounding on Liszt's processes of thematic transformation. Curtin pulled Floyd aside, urging, "Don't let Norman irritate you; just think Rockaway Beach."

Another festival participant that year, the pianist-conductor Paul Berl, had overseen the Mannes School's 1954–1955 competition for new operas. At a cocktail party, he confided to Floyd that *Susannah* had done better than an honorable mention. It had in fact *won* hands down, but the school had run out of funds, hence the ambiguous cancellation.

On August 2, Floyd played for his two stars at Aspen's schoolhouse, *Susannah*'s first exposure outside Tallahassee and New York audition venues. Curtin asked Floyd to orchestrate his Whitman Nocturne for her future orchestral appearances, emphasizing connections with the Philadelphia Orchestra; and violist Walter Trampler requested a string quartet for the New Music Quartet. Floyd and Dickinson began the drive home on August 23, arriving back in Florence three evenings later.

Adding to the restorative properties of a month in the Rockies, brainstorming friends now urged Floyd to investigate one of the era's great sources of financial support for scholars and creative artists, the John Simon Guggenheim Memorial Foundation. On August 27, he requested an application packet. Summer drew to its humid close with Bob Holton's predictions of *Susannah*'s success all over America, and abroad in England, France, Germany, and Australia. Boosey was also looking over *Theme and Variations, Lost Eden,* and *Slow Dusk,* the last of which Floyd planned to orchestrate for a proposed St. Louis production. He reported to the Clarkes, "I am no more portly than I was in December, although I have since then resigned myself to a 32-inch middle. A few more gray hairs came into view during and after the production of *Susannah* but I still consider them appallingly out of place."[17]

In the same letter, he revealed the germ of a new operatic project already begun in Florence, and called *Independence Day:* a young man intervenes in a bitter struggle between a mother and a daughter, and wages peace, in the process dissolving his very compulsion to succeed. In addition to ample firsthand experience of parental conflicts, the subject reflected Floyd's involvement with Judith and Catherine Murphy. In his Guggenheim application, he elaborated:

> The opera will be in a sense experimental . . . an opera whose book could be considered independently on its own merits and construction as a straight play; that type of play which is essentially psychological and philosophical in content and in which the emphasis is on the interior lives and problems of the characters, rather than the play of external circumstances. It will require decided experimentation in the combined techniques of the spoken word, *Sprechstimme,* and pure song, with an almost continuous musical accompaniment. The orchestration as presently envisioned would be small and designed to facilitate the singer-actors in being heard at all times, since the impact of the opera relies as heavily on what is being said as what is objectified in action.[18]

A half century later, embarrassed that he ever entertained such a project, Floyd denied awareness of its autobiographical origins. He got as far as a first-draft libretto, but, realizing its likeness to *Fugitives,* found it "personal without being dramatic" and abandoned, then destroyed it.

A letter from Sylvia Goldstein, Boosey's director of business affairs, awaited Floyd's return to Tallahassee, with a contract for the firm's representation of *Slow Dusk.* As he had told the Clarkes, summing up every composer's dilemma, "I have been extraordinarily lucky and it is particularly heartening to know that one is not composing in a vacuum but that what one writes stands an excellent chance of being performed at least once if not more."[19]

In the course of twelve days in South Carolina, he found that time out of the south had increased his sensitivity to racism. His father proved the point on September 3 with a visit to Florence's Firestone dealer for tire adjustments. Reverend Floyd habitually called all black men either "boy" or "uncle," depending on their age and station; but at the garage, he addressed the mechanic as "Shine," visibly offending the worker and his own son. On their way back to the parsonage, Floyd gave his father a piece of his mind. When Reverend Floyd swore that he had meant nothing by the term "Shine," Floyd conveyed the mechanic's displeasure. Reverend Floyd let his son out at home, drove back to the garage, and apologized. Over supper he declared breezily, "He forgave me," and switched the conversation to Floyd's need to replace his convertible's leaky top.

After getting back to Florida on September 8, a conversation with Nancy Smith aroused Floyd's empathy for more of the world's disadvantaged, and he subscribed to the Foster Parents Plan for War Children.[20] His designee was twelve-year-old Francesca Ponza, child of a farmhand and olive picker in a small village near Rome. She suffered from malnutrition, and Floyd sent fifteen dollars each month for two years.

On September 27, though his FSU salary had risen to a yearly $5,450, Floyd submitted his Guggenheim application for a year off from teaching to focus on composing. During the fellowship year, he projected working on the pieces he had discussed with Curtin and Trampler in Aspen, plus completing *Pilgrimage* for Mack Harrell, two new dance scores, and text and music for a unnamed "new music drama" (*Independence Day*) that he expected would occupy the summer and fall of 1956. He requested a monthly stipend of $300 for living expenses, travel reimbursement for performances, interviews and auditions, duplication of scores, copyists' fees, and purchase of manuscript paper and ink.

He assembled a distinguished group of references: Ernst Bacon, Phyllis Curtin, Rudolf Firkušný, Sidney Foster, Mack Harrell, Robert Holton, and Karl Kuersteiner. On September 29, after a lapse of six years in their communication, he advised Bacon that the foundation would be contacting him, "if you feel that you can pen some sort of recommendation on my behalf without inordinately perjuring yourself!" He continued: "Suffice it to say that more and more time has been going into composition and from the looks of things . . . that will continue . . . for some time to come. I feel certain that you are acquainted with the difficulty of teaching full time, composing, and practicing simultaneously. In the past two years the practicing has of necessity been forced to give way. Of course teaching piano to some twenty students keeps you very actively engaged in the re-creative end of the art and I wouldn't take anything for the joy and satisfaction that continue to come in teaching. For the past three or four years I have had really superlative students."[21]

He gave Bacon the bare details of *Susannah*'s successful premiere, the excerpts in Aspen, and prospects with NBC: "The latest word is that they won't get to it before next season if they decide to take it. Also Chandler Cowles and Lincoln Kirstein have shown a decided interest in the idea of producing it commercially in New York but there is nothing definite on that yet since such a production from them seems contingent on the television performance. I have been a very fortunate fellow."

Phyllis Curtin's statement to the Guggenheim Foundation concluded, "This sounds more effusive than reasonable. And yet I have the greatest confidence in Mr. Floyd's ability to produce art of high and lasting value."[22] Harrell endorsed Floyd's talent as "thoroughly disciplined and his musical intelligence quite extraordinary . . . given the opportunity he can contribute material of lasting and outstanding value, not to mention unusual originality." And the ebullient Bacon wrote that Floyd had "a very refined, sensitive musical nature—poetic and intellectual, both. He may become a leading operatic writer (both text and music)—comparable perhaps eventually with Menotti. A worthy risk, it seems to me. One of the best of younger men, as I know them."

In a Christmas note to the Clarkes, Floyd described Kay Reeder, accompanying him for her first visit to New York, as "a very dear friend." He had completed *Slow Dusk*'s orchestration, and was still at work on *Pilgrimage.* His five-day Christmas trip to South Carolina included a visit to Hazel and Frank Ellerbe in Latta. Frank imbibed a quantity of bourbon, and the topic of race arose. Floyd gave curt, tight-lipped "yes" and "no" answers to his uncle's increasingly inflammatory questions; but Ellerbe finally confronted his nephew outright, "You wouldn't bring some nigger gal home, would you?"

Aunt Hazel did her best to intervene: "Now Frank, Carlisle may have had different experiences than ours." Floyd vented his liberalism, Ellerbe ordered him from the house, and the Floyds could not leave soon enough. On the drive to Laurinburg, Reverend Floyd took Frank's side, accusing his son of exacerbating the situation, while Ida strove to make peace. Hazel tamped down the home fires, and Frank sent his nephew a conciliatory Christmas tie; but for Floyd, this remained a serious family wound.

The relationship between Reverend Floyd and his son's music remained uneasy. One day when Mrs. Floyd asked about his latest project, he described *Pilgrimage,* with its biblical text. Ida brightened, observing that the church had the best piano, and asked her son to play the new work for her. Once there, she sat beside Floyd on the bench as he read through the last radiant song of conciliation and reassurance. Meanwhile, Reverend Floyd strode into the sanctuary, went straight to the pulpit and arranged Bible and papers. He began whistling, and continued for the remainder of Floyd's playing, as though on a stroll down a carnival midway. Ida had nothing to say.

Following gift exchange on Christmas Day, Floyd boarded the Champion for New York, where the staff of NBC continued to sit on *Susannah* as though incubating an egg. In February, *The New York Times* announced Chandler Cowles's appointment as general manager of NBC Opera.[23] Although encouraging to Floyd, this also explained a reason for *Susannah*'s continued deferral: Chotzinoff, still a power, had long dreamed of using NBC as the nucleus for a repertory company, and now its mission embraced an ambitious touring schedule under the direction of Cowles, in cooperation with Columbia Artists.[24] Contemporary repertoire was not part of the plan.

Floyd enjoyed more productive visits with Woo Gillette and Phyllis Rappeport. When he enthused about his works in progress, Rappeport thought him a beam of southern light, and tantalized him with the convenience and delights of living in New York, should the Guggenheim come through.[25] On Broadway, Floyd's reconnection with spoken theater included Michael V. Gazzo's *Hatful of Rain,* with Ben Gazzara, Shelley Winters, Anthony Franciosa, Harry Guardino, and Henry Silva. This also gave Floyd his first exposure to the direction of Frank Corsaro, with whose career his would soon be entwined.

In February, Floyd sent off a packet of materials to support his Guggenheim application: the libretto and piano-vocal scores of *Susannah, Pilgrimage,* a two-piano score of *Lost Eden,* and a recording of the latter that he made with Jim Staples. On March 1 and 2, he fulfilled his promise for new dance scores for Nellie-Bond Dickinson's "Evening of Dance." The program included a new Ryan Edwards piece, *Man Alone,* played by the composer and Staples; and a reprise of *Lost Eden,* danced by Nancy Smith and Jim Fadigan.

Floyd's first new item, *Frame of Remembrance,* featured Nancy Smith in Dickinson's choreography, Floyd accompanying. Dickinson took her inspiration from Graham Greene: "A story has no beginning or end—one chooses that moment of experience from which to look back or from which to look ahead."[26] Scenery consisted of a single door frame, taken from a recently demolished century-old country house. Despite Floyd's best intentions, this latest effort wound up in rough draft in the pencil manuscript book containing the end of *Susannah*.[27]

Frame is an overtly Romantic ten-page ABA arc from F-sharp Minor to E-flat Minor and back. In 6/4 and 3/4 and marked *Molto sostenuto,* its dynamic extremes range from *pianissimo, molto teneramente,* to *fortissimo, sforzando,* and back down. The first section sways on an eerie chordal motive, both hands playing high in treble clef. Sixteenth-note filigrees pass from hand to hand, creeping into a nostalgic middle section, with texture dense enough to require the three staves of most Floyd dance scores. About halfway through, runs and trills of Lisztian bravura lead to fragments of the main theme, climaxing in a full high chordal statement of the melody. This subsides back into the opening's rocking, and a pensive finish.

The composer and Jim Staples also played Floyd's second new piece, *Be Still, My Soul,*[28] another theme and variations for nine student dancers executing Valda Mock's choreography. As with all Dickinson productions, choreographers supplied titles and content, and Floyd's contributions were limited to a set number of measures with a particular emotional coloring. In its journey from torment and uncertainty to praise and confident reflection, *Be Still* echoes *Pilgrimage*'s religious preoccupations; but unlike *Frame,* this work displays some of Floyd's thorniest music to date, and it is a leap in his compositional technique.

A reader spoke biblical texts before and between each section, beginning with the line "And they shall wander from sea to sea, and from the north even to the east; they shall run to and fro to seek the word of the Lord" (Amos 8:12). In extreme high and low octaves, both pianos play a unison eight-bar theme in 3/4, *Poco adagio,* in mirrored symmetry and rhythms, repeated and varied with stacked dissonances for another eight measures. The reader interpolates Ecclesiastes 8:6: "Because to every purpose there is time and judgment, therefore the misery of man is great upon him. For he knoweth not that which shall be; for who can tell him when it shall be?" Marked *Più mosso* and *Dirge,* tonalities shift and converge in dissonant half steps for another twenty-four measures. The spoken interruption, "Hush! Only wait for Him!" is probably an adaptation of Lamentations 3:25. This precedes, *Agitato, più vivo,* twenty-eight measures of fragmentation of the octave theme, traded between treble and bass. From Job 4:5, the reader intones, "But now it is come upon thee, and thou faintest, it touchest thee and thou art troubled." The score heats up into a four-hand showpiece, thirty-two measures of syncopation, dissonant contrary motion, and flashing sixteenth- and thirty-second-note runs.

Then Floyd returns to the world of *Pilgrimage*'s fourth song, beginning with a reading from Lamentations 3:41: "Let us lift up our heart with our hands unto God in the heavens." Both pianists continue in fleet virtuoso mode for twenty-four measures of pounding rhythms, the original theme in fragmented diminution, ending on an open chord of octaves of D sharp and G sharp. To illustrate Revelation 22:13, "I am the Alpha and Omega, the beginning and the ending, saith the Lord," Floyd wrote a simple seventeen-measure melodic augmentation of his principal motive, in cloudless, at times playful, F Major.

WHILE FLOYD crafted music for dancing, Holton, Curtin, and Harrell plied their own steps in New York. Holton sent *Susannah* to City Opera's new general director, Erich Leinsdorf, who felt enough interest to schedule an audition over Easter weekend.

For more than two years, hostilities at City Center had swirled around Kirstein and Rosenstock. The modernist season of 1952—*Wozzeck, Amahl and the Night Visitors, The Consul,* Bartók's *Bluebeard's Castle,* and Ravel's *L'heure Espagnole*—had left the company with a fifty thousand dollar deficit, close to an equivalent half-million dollars in 2012 funds. In 1953, Kirstein resigned to focus on ballet operations, keeping that division of the company afloat with his own money, and friction with Rosenstock increased. Without consulting the conductor, Kirstein personally commissioned Menotti's *The Saint of Bleecker Street* and Carlos Chavez's *The Tuscan Players,* committing 25 percent of available season funds.

In spring 1954, Rosenstock fired three Kirstein appointees while Kirstein was out of the country. Despite publicity generated by Phyllis Curtin's Salome that spring, the fiscal situation deteriorated. Kirstein opposed extending Rosenstock's contract, and proposed Menotti for the job. The board voted to keep Rosenstock, and Kirstein turned increasingly critical, in very public ways, of the hands that fed him. After mixed results in the 1955 spring and fall seasons, Rosenstock resigned at the end of the 1956 spring season.

City Opera's board reached beyond company ranks to Austrian-born Erich Leinsdorf, who had conducted at the Met since 1938 and had been the music director of the Cleveland and Rochester orchestras, the last of which he was eager to leave.[29] Leinsdorf's agent Arthur Judson warned him of City Opera's parlous state of affairs: "You will be on the thinnest layer of ice and you may fall through if it breaks; but if enough people have seen you skate, it may be worth while."[30]

When the job was offered, Leinsdorf strapped on the figurative blades. Mack Harrell and Leinsdorf were neighbors in Westchester County's tony suburb of Larchmont, and *Susannah*'s audition took place in the conductor's living room on March 31. When Harrell, Curtin, Floyd, and Holton showed up that afternoon, Leinsdorf was meeting with the tenor turned general director of the Royal Swedish Opera, Set Svanholm,[31] who stayed to hear this American novelty. Curtin and Harrell, with Floyd at the piano, repeated their sing-through of the entire opera, choruses and all, while Leinsdorf's wife, the former Anne Frohnknecht, sat in the background. Leinsdorf listened quietly, and at the conclusion seemed impressed. After hearing the dreaded words, "We'll be in touch," Floyd flew back to Tallahassee; but later, as Floyd learned from Harrell and Curtin, Mrs. Leinsdorf had been even more moved by *Susannah* than her husband, and urged its acceptance.

Floyd had barely unpacked before he and Kay tuned in on April 11 to a televised Screen Directors Playhouse production of *Markheim,* based on Robert Louis Stevenson's eerie novella. Ray Milland played the eponymous dissolute nobleman who murders from greed, with Rod Steiger as the mysterious Stranger. Floyd thought it might make an interesting opera subject, but *Susannah*'s fate was too much on his mind to act on this interest.

Two days later, he received notification from James F. Mathias, Guggenheim's associate secretary, that he had won his year of grace, to begin that September, with a bare-bones stipend of three thousand dollars. Floyd called his parents in Florence, and Kay in Jacksonville. Not given to gushing, she pleased Floyd by admitting, "Of course I know what a Guggenheim is! I just never knew anyone who *had* one!" On April 17, he penned a grateful acceptance, after arranging his FSU leave of absence, and salved Kuersteiner's anxiety by arranging a replacement, his Aspen and New York friend Phyllis Rappeport.[32]

Leinsdorf saw his opportunity to give City Opera "a shot in the arm,"[33] with a season of unusual repertoire, believing that a sprinkling of contemporary music would attract younger audiences. He proposed opening with Offenbach's *Orpheus in Hell* (*Orphée aux enfers*), "to bring in the cash customers," along with selected house staples: *La traviata, Mignon, Die Fledermaus, Carmen, La bohème* and *Rigoletto.* His most daring choices were Frank Martin's setting of Shakespeare's *The Tempest,* about to receive its premiere in Vienna that June; and Carl Orff's 1950 revision of *The Moon* (*Der Mond*), oddly paired with *Susannah.* Emerson Buckley was announced as the conductor of the double bill.

Leinsdorf proposed aggressive money-saving measures, most dramatically his hiring of German émigré Leo Kerz,[34] to design a revolving unit set for the entire season, the acting areas defined principally by lights and the nonrealistic background architecture supplied by projections. Kerz himself would direct all new productions, and adapt existing sets to his turntables for repertory productions. When he made strenuous objection to the Orff/Floyd combination, Leinsdorf linked *The Moon* with City Opera's first performances of Stravinsky's *L'histoire du soldat. Susannah* would have her own "pretty night," and Bob Holton called on April 28 with the glad tidings of City Opera's official announcement of *Susannah*'s three performances on September 27 and 30 and October 17, 1956; Leinsdorf himself would conduct. Curtin would repeat her title role, and Floyd's year of waiting was at an end. He jumped in to save the company tidy sums on costumes and staffing with FSU's loan of Catherine Murphy's clothes for women principals and chorus. Chotzinoff and Co. at NBC had remained silent, and only now did Floyd realize how lucky he'd been that the Mannes project had fallen through. On several later occasions, Floyd ran into Peter Herman Adler, and the subject of NBC's inaction arose. Adler swore, "I really wanted to do *Susannah,* but Chotzie . . . I couldn't get him."

PHYLLIS CURTIN'S MARRIAGE had been troubled for some time: she had lost her heart to photographer Eugene (Gene) Cook, born Gino Cocca, who called her "The Lark," and had made her a national media celebrity with his *Salome* photographs.[35] On May 6, the day after finalizing her divorce from Philip Curtin, she married Gene in Las Vegas, "a bizarre place, to be sure, but *quite* magical too."[36] Curtin had established a professional name during her first marriage, and kept it, despite frequent homonymic misspelling as "Curtain." The depth of the new couple's friendship for Floyd glows from a note penned just two days after the wedding, addressing the composer in classic southern manner as "Dearest Cousin." Away from New York, she noted, "We will be collapsing to hear news of *Susannah.*"

For eleven days, Floyd sped between Florence and Holly Hill, setting the families abuzz with his news, fueled by a mounting avalanche of newspaper coverage. Reverend Floyd swelled with pleasure when journalists began contacting *him* for interviews about his progeny's boyhood.[37]

Floyd learned of City Opera's difficulty in casting Little Bat and arranged an audition for Eb Thomas. As the young student was about to be thrust into a national spotlight, Floyd accompanied him on the train to New York on June 11, Floyd's thirtieth birthday, and upgraded his accommodations from the Woodstock to the Great Northern, at 118 West 57th Street, just minutes' walk to both Boosey & Hawkes and City Center on 55th. In years to come, his professional life centered on this hotel, as well as Riverside Drive, at Bob Holton's apartment at 210, and the Cooks' at 110. Nancy Smith spent time in town taking more Martha Graham classes, and she and Floyd socialized with the Cooks, who offered the composer housing during his post-*Susannah* Guggenheim weeks.[38]

Over supper one evening, Floyd met with Leo Kerz, who elaborated his Brechtian aesthetic of epic theater: *Verfremdungs-Effekt,* or distancing. This involved prompting the audience to judge between *ideas* proposed in a drama. Essential to the dialectic, characters were presented as archetypes of opposing principles; there was scant illusion of representing real people. At all costs, arousing emotional involvement had to be avoided. With Leinsdorf's full backing, and having devised his nonrepresentational set, Kerz declared that, were he to get his way, he would put the orchestra onstage. Floyd breathed deeply, swallowed hard, but saw no reason to take issue with this experienced man of the theater; besides, knowing opera singers as he did, Floyd intuited that he may have director-proofed *Susannah.*

Youthful ardor also prompted Floyd's offer to serve as rehearsal accompanist at no additional compensation. Not imagining that he would be taken advantage of, he reasoned that he'd always be on hand to let everyone know proper tempi. A more serious situation arose when Leinsdorf and Mack Harrell failed to come to terms on the baritone's fee.[39] The company next tried to sign Cornell McNeill, who proved unavailable,[40] but Leinsdorf coaxed the extraordinary Norman Treigle from an engagement in his hometown, New Orleans.

Many likened this singing and acting phenomenon, born Adanelle Wilfred Treigle in 1927, to a kind of male-voice Maria Callas. Bringing a quasi-demonic intensity to all his portrayals, he excelled in roles as different as Mozart's Figaro, the three villains in Offenbach's *Les contes d'Hoffmann,* and the Mephistopheles of both Gounod and Boïto. He had sung at City Opera since the spring of 1953 with Curtin in Von Einem's *The Trial.*

After hiring Eb Thomas to reprise Little Bat, the company filled the other roles with Jon Crain (Sam), Arthur Newman and Irene Kramarich (Elder and Mrs. McLean), Gregory Miller and Sarah Fleming (Gleatons), John Druary and Olivia Bonelli (Hayses), and Joshua Hecht and Mignon Dunn (Otts). Margaret Hillis prepared the chorus, Anna Sokolow the choreography, and Leo Van Witsen designed the men's costumes.

ON JULY 15, the composer sequestered himself in his sweltering Tallahassee cottage. While teaching that summer, he made a clean conductor's score from the pencil copy of *Susannah* that Kuersteiner had used the year before. Hazel Richards took pity and installed an air conditioner, and by the middle of August Floyd had the fresh volume completed, bound, packed in a Campbell's soup carton, and shipped, together with the year-old orchestra parts, to City Opera. On July 16, he advised Jona and Bruce Clarke about ordering tickets, and the best place to sit: right orchestra, at a top price of $3.80, made it truly the people's opera. He acknowledged his good fortune in securing the Guggenheim: "I am still happily trying to absorb the fact that I have a year ahead of me in which I don't have to do anything or be any place unless I want to. This may sound a little selfish but after all I have been at this business since I was pretty young and a year off after nine years of such routine is nothing short of a godsend. . . . I am frankly still a little awed at being in the company of such people as Carson McCullers, Aaron Copland, Hart Crane, and the like."[41]

Floyd boarded a New York-bound train on August 24 with a year's worth of clothing, books, and music, after installing Jim Staples as house sitter on Call Street. Moving into the Great Northern, he began musical rehearsals, only to encounter Priscilla Gillette. "Woo" had already sung with City Opera—Alexandra Giddens in Blitzstein's *Regina* in the 1953 spring season—and Leinsdorf had cast her as Miranda in Martin's *The Tempest.* The role was minor enough that the conductor awarded her a consolation prize as Curtin's Susannah understudy.

Though Gillette had dismissed the opera in 1953, Floyd now met her in a City Center practice room to go through the part, only to discover that his old friend lacked the vocal equipment or technique to sing what he had written with her in mind. Gillette had studied with a German-trained professor at Syracuse and now worked with another Teutonic coach in New York, both of whom encouraged a tense throat technique. The Floyd songs that she had performed on his senior recital rarely exceeded A natural, and he had written an optional G sharp in "Evening Song" because of her problems with his high B; Susannah's *tessitura* now lay quite beyond her. Fortunately for Gillette, Floyd, and *Susannah,* Curtin never missed a rehearsal or performance. Floyd strolled one day from City Center with two striking Susannahs on his arms, thinking, "Boy, this is really high cotton."

City Opera scheduled a photo shoot for Gene Cook and Phyllis Curtin with a spur-of-the-moment jaunt back to South Carolina with the composer. Reverend Floyd gleefully scouted authentic locations: old country churches, weathered cabins, and a bathing stream. On August 31, Reverend Floyd and Ermine met the travelers at Florence's tiny airfield, and a *Florence Morning News* photographer captured him greeting the party. Mrs. Floyd cooked a late lunch for everyone, after which the Reverend drove them eleven miles south to inspect his revival church site, St. Paul's, at Effingham, then to a nearby water locale at Cockfield's Landing, before depositing Phyllis and Gene at Florence's Gasque Hotel.

The next morning, Floyd and his father collected the Cooks at seven, and began the shoot at Cockfield's Landing. Phyllis donned a discreet swimsuit, hit the water, and Gene shot "Susannah bathing." Reverend Floyd reddened, discreetly turning his back when the soprano lowered shoulder straps; but he clearly loved being in on the event. Hunters came by looking for a lost hound, then two equally bemused fishermen floated past in their boat; at St. Paul Church, Gene put Phyllis through other poses. Back in Florence, Mrs. Floyd spread a lavish noon meal of ham, peas, corn, and candied yams. Later that afternoon, the composer

19. Floyd and his father. Florence, South Carolina, 1956. Floyd collection. Photograph by Gene Cook. Courtesy of Phyllis Curtin.

drove the Cooks back out to the country farmhouse his father had spotted, for cabin shots. The long day ended with another southern feast and games of Scrabble.

Cook's efforts appeared with newspaper reviews, and in Boosey's first edition of the vocal score, Floyd's first printed music. The composer especially prized one of Curtin sitting in Effingham's church, alone in a pew beneath a bare light bulb, for its suggestion of desolation; a large print still hangs in his home.

The party flew back to New York on September 2 to begin staging. Floyd volunteered to coach each singer in his or her part, and did so each time one approached with questions or problems. Even Mignon Dunn, whose career was sprinting ahead, asked him to help with Mrs. Ott, a relatively minor role. Playing for rehearsals made Floyd a member of the company, and he relished lunches at Francine's, a traditional hangout, getting to know his interpreters as people.

One day during a full company staging, mezzo-soprano Irene Kramarich, Mrs. McLean, repeated a rhythmic error, doubling the length of a set of quick syncopated notes. Leinsdorf, a volatile combination of

20. Floyd and Curtin, 1956. Floyd collection. Photograph by Gene Cook. Courtesy of Phyllis Curtin.

21. Curtin as Susannah, Cockfield's Landing, 1956. Photograph by Gene Cook. Courtesy of Phyllis Curtin.

22. Curtin as Susannah, 1956, St. Paul Church. Photograph by Gene Cook. Courtesy of Phyllis Curtin.

high intelligence and Teutonic impatience, corrected her sternly, "In cor-rect rhythm."

Kramarich tried and stumbled again. The room's temperature rose as Leinsdorf barked "Again!" and the singer repeated her learned mistake.

"Again!" Perhaps five times, "Again!"

Kramarich dissolved in tears, and Floyd offered to take her to a practice room to amend the minor but irritating misstep, if Leinsdorf would proceed. Alone with Floyd, Kramarich, still weepy, confessed that she did not read music, and had learned her part by rote, facts that she could not admit to a roomful of colleagues. Floyd's gentility carried the day, and Kramarich became letter-perfect.[42]

At another rehearsal, Floyd addressed the conductor by his given name, Erich, which was repaid with an autocratic frown; ever after, it was "Mr. Leinsdorf." Their working relationship never ripened into friendship, but remained cordial and supportive. Though a virtuoso conductor, Leinsdorf erred in his concept of *Susannah* through vertical execution, rather than allowing the music to flow across bar lines. Excepting the Khachaturian Concerto in Syracuse, keyboardist Floyd had never needed to follow anyone else's beat. Intent on the music unfolding as he heard it, he played with virtually no cues from Leinsdorf, who used the opportunity to learn a new score from its composer. He later assured Floyd that he'd gladly look at future works.

Momentary hiccups aside, all continued smoothly. The singers' naturalistic acting put to rest any fears the composer had about Kerz enforcing his aesthetic. By September 6 they had reached Blitch's part, and Curtin and Floyd made inevitable comparisons between Treigle and the role's creator, Mack Harrell. Both men were southerners, but resemblances ended there: Harrell was rotund, almost cherubic, with a smiling, plump-cheeked face, upturned nose, expressive eyebrows, and sandy-blond hair. He made a genial preacher with a subdued twinkle in his eye. Rail-thin Treigle played a dark and tortured character, with a certain menace foreshadowing his doom. Floyd pondered how two such different temperaments could both be perfect for this complex role. Treigle enlarged the character, investing Blitch with nuances that had never occurred to dramatist or composer Floyd. He began by underlining Blitch's aloneness and self-denial of luxury or pleasure, which Floyd recognized from the more extreme revivalists of his youth. In person compulsively tidy, Treigle kept every hair in place, in an elaborate grooming ritual that the composer often watched in the singer's dressing room. He wore his fine black hair slicked back, but before going onstage for the revival, shook his head to dishevel his appearance. The dynamic between the character's outward affability and severe asceticism made his unmasking of fleshly urges in act 2 almost too personal to watch. He gave Blitch the tragic stature of ancient Greek drama, and Floyd came to regard Treigle's interpretation as the standard by which all others would be measured.[43]

Floyd also learned just how challenging he had made the role for baritones *and* basses. Once talents like Curtin and Treigle proved their ability to bring off extraordinary dramatic and vocal effects, Floyd assumed that others could too; but Treigle cautioned that a drop from high F sharp down to low A sharp in the revival scene "separates the men from the boys."[44] He joked further, "For baritones those low notes are just air." Floyd made mental notes to temper his writing in extreme ranges; but the chocolate-velvet of Treigle's sound also conditioned future works for this favorite vocal type. The two men struck up a warm friendship, and subsequent Floyd operas, excepting the monodrama *Flower and Hawk,* contain prominent roles for voices much like Treigle's, and two of them *for* Treigle.

Curtin also took the measure of her first two Blitches: "Norman was also easy and affable at first, but the physical difference made you have a different feeling about him. . . . In the church scene, when he's trying to convince the congregation of poor Susannah's innocence, Mack's heartbreak absolutely tore you up. You felt more sorry for Mack, because he seemed more like us, while Norman was such an individual; he broke your heart as well, but for a different reason."[45]

She offered good advice to future generations of singing actors: "Find your own Blitch; don't look for it in anybody else."[46]

Treigle wrote his wife Loraine on September 6, "Yesterday I rehearsed *Susannah* . . . and it's coming along okay. Floyd is a great guy and easy to work with. . . . I look like Wyatt Earp in this Blitch suit."[47] The bass wrote home almost daily, claiming that everyone complimented his work: "It is gonna be great and I'm real flipped with it as is everyone. It should be a big hit . . . Phyllis is terrific in it."[48]

There was little time for socializing, but Floyd went out of his way to advise Eb Thomas, also lodged at the Great Northern, on résumés and auditions. As opening night approached, Floyd received checks for tickets for the South Carolina and Florida contingents coming to cheer him on. On September 18, Bob Holton sent Floyd a copy of the printed libretto of *Susannah,* with a note declaring this one of the more satisfying moments in his years at Boosey, together with hopes that this represented just the beginning of Floyd's larger career.[49]

Once Leinsdorf began rehearsing the orchestra, he and his players spat abuse at the condition of the Floyd/Staples parts: there were two hands of variable legibility, from pianists with no attention paid to orchestral page turns, no measure or sectional cueing numbers or letters, and a host of errors. The conductor complained bitterly to Holton, but Floyd had had neither time nor funds to pay a proper copyist. After Tallahassee, Curtin wished that a few parts had been *lost,* pacing herself not to compete with what she considered Floyd's thick orchestration.[50]

Once in the theater, Kerz's two concentric turntables provoked alternate mirth and ire: the company called them the "Lazy Susan." Another Austrian-born conductor, Julius Rudel, described the Polk cabin as "a kind of Scarsdale house with a nice little white fence.

Kerz really had no relationship with America; of the Appalachians, the back roads, he had no idea."[51]

On September 23, Curtin, Treigle, Jon Crain, and Floyd were booked to visit CBS television studios for a *Camera Three* program devoted to *Susannah.* City Opera naturally expected Floyd to accompany, of which he thought nothing. Pleased and excited, when he informed Bob Holton of the event, the publisher/agent demanded, "Did you discuss *fees*?" The program proceeded with Leinsdorf at the keyboard.[52]

In Florence, Mrs. Floyd sewed up a fresh storm and drove her son's convertible around town; Reverend Floyd borrowed a friend's tuxedo for the big night. On September 26, after a 680-mile drive, they arrived at the Great Northern with Floyd's aunt Bunny, while the composer watched rehearsal. His parents eventually found their way backstage at the theater, where they met City Opera's administrative director, John White,[53] and watched the remainder of the final dress rehearsal. Afterward, Floyd and Nancy Smith ate dinner with them at the Three Crowns Smorgasbord. Anything but a world traveler, Reverend Floyd commented, "What a meal—and what a price," and gave his son ten dollars toward the tab. From his parents' hotel room, Floyd called his cast with encouraging words. Reverend Floyd wrote, "Am so proud of him. He looks right tired."[54]

On premiere morning, September 27, New York awoke to rain. Floyd shuttled back and forth between theater and hotel, while Reverend Floyd shined his son's shoes, and the family gathered in the parental room: aunts Bunny and Freddie, Ermine, Billy, and friends from Holly Hill. Tallahassee's contingent included Ryan Edwards, Jim Staples, Evon Streetman, Nellie-Bond Dickinson, and Nancy Smith. Jona and Bruce Clarke came from Washington.

But there were two conspicuous absences: Hazel Richards, invested emotionally and financially in Floyd, had been given an ultimatum by husband Harold: Carlisle or me. Despite several weeks in France, it killed Hazel to miss this. And Kay Reeder's aversion to travel kept her at home in Jacksonville.

The dressed-up Floyds hopped into a taxi headed downtown "in wind and mud."[55] The cabbie inquired about their home:

"South Carolina."

"Whatcha doin' in New York?"

"We're going to City Center, where our son's opera is being performed."

Incredulous laughter from the front seat: "So tell me another one!"

In place in the first balcony, Reverend Floyd turned critic: "It was very good, but moved rather slow at times. Phyllis and Treigle did their parts well."[56] Backstage teemed with well-wishers, including conductor André Kostalanetz, soprano Lily Pons, Boosey's English-born managing director David Adams, and, of course, Robert Holton, whose prediction had come true: Floyd was suddenly a hot property. Curtin and Cook held the reception at their Riverside Drive apartment, and everyone piled into cabs in still-driving rain. Inside, liquor flowed. Despite Reverend Floyd's abstention, he managed to get into the party spirit; and Floyd drank in front of his parents for the first time.

The next morning, reviews rolled in broadcasting a major triumph. Most critics praised Floyd's libretto, with cavils for the music. *The Times'* Howard Taubman, despite highlighting *Susannah's* minor weaknesses, offered warm praise for the opera's earnest power and youthful ardor, and predicted a glowing future for Floyd as a fearless melodist born to write operas.[57]

Louis Biancolli, even more enthusiastic in the *World-Telegram,* found Floyd's "towering crescendo of music and mood unlike anything else I know in American opera . . . a triumph of spare strength and bold vitality."[58]

THE ELDER FLOYDS drove back to South Carolina on September 30. Floyd checked out of the Great Northern and moved his belongings to the Curtin/Cook guest room on Riverside, where he spent the next six weeks as house sitter; Phyllis and Gene were often away for concerts and City Opera tour performances. One day when Floyd walked in off the street, he discovered Curtin on her hands and knees scrubbing the floors. Mirth succeeded embarrassment after Floyd declared, "Ah, the diva."

Meanwhile, Bob Holton applied his foot to the pedal of Boosey's publicity machine: anything to get

Floyd's name in the papers. He brought Leontyne Price to sit with him and the composer at the second performance on September 30. Backstage, Rudolf Firkušný surprised Floyd with a visit, asking his former Aspen student to write him a piano sonata. Holton even schemed with Cook to arrange, without success, a PR date for Floyd with *belle du jour* Julie Andrews, playing to wild acclaim in Lerner and Loewe's *My Fair Lady* since March 15.

Time ran "Discovery in Manhattan," placing Floyd's name for the first time before the entire country and expressing wonder that so young a prodigy should appear from South Carolina with such singable, audience-friendly music: "Floyd has a Verdian flair for extracting the last drops of dramatic juice."[59]

In addition to postulating a rivalry between young Floyd and Menotti, the uncredited writer may have underestimated attendance: conductor Julius Rudel called *Susannah* "the only success of the whole Leinsdorf season."[60] Martin Sokol wrote, "On the artistic side . . . the major event was the premiere of *Susannah,* considered by many to be the finest American opera to date. . . . Norman Treigle became a superstar overnight . . . and Phyllis Curtin . . . reinforced her status in the title role."[61] In his season summary Biancolli urged Floyd and his country to regard *Susannah* with pride, as "proof that America no longer takes a back seat in operatic composition."[62]

Meanwhile, City Opera fell into turmoil: other productions had not fared so well and the company ended up cancelling eight of its scheduled thirty-nine performances. The rest sold at just 57 percent of house capacity, and the season ended on November 3 with a staggering loss of over $157,000.[63] Leo Kerz took much of the blame: his turntables were cumbersome, noisy, and distracting, and audiences complained of the season's unrelieved drabness. The board fired Leinsdorf without his contracted pay; he took no legal action, but resolved to never again accept a position in opera administration. The board appointed Julius Rudel general director in January 1957, and cancelled its spring season, including projected performances of *Susannah.*

Monthly journals, whose writers attended more performances than critics for dailies, began to appear. In *Saturday Review,* Irving Kolodin pronounced Floyd a man to watch, with the caveat that final judgments had to await successive operas; but for a first effort—at this stage, no one outside Syracuse and Tallahassee knew Floyd had written anything else—this was absorbing drama, and reasonably well-written for the voices. He thought Floyd's orchestration challenging for singers, and admitted that the composer had much to say but needed to learn much more about how to use his vocabulary.[64]

Ronald Eyer took a somewhat cooler approach in October's *Musical America,* calling Floyd "a hitherto little-known American composer of arresting talent, if not genius (one wants to hear more of his music before pronouncing any final benedictions)." But Eyer found *Susannah* itself a "gripping, flesh-and-blood drama." Floyd took particular note of the critic's reasoning that "the score is unself-conscious and unstylized in any particular way. While cognizant of contemporary harmonic and rhythmic devices, it is not widely dissonant and depends frequently upon frank lyricism."[65]

Letters and telegrams of congratulation poured in from friends old and new. On October 9, Florida Governor Leroy Collins wired that "Mary Call and I are extremely proud of you and *Susannah.*" On October 25, Bernard Barrow, now teaching at Brooklyn College's Department of Speech, wrote, "The price of fame is that your friends of yesteryear appear out of the cobwebs and silence—to say how nice, how really wonderful . . . you must accept the consequences of fame."[66]

On October's last day, Bob Holton finessed another treat for Floyd, and the composer signed an exclusive contract with Boosey & Hawkes, renewable in five-year increments. He still questioned whether he had the goods; but now, with a powerful international firm behind him, the gates to success and financial security flew open. The contract's terms were generous beyond Floyd's most extravagant dreams: he assigned Boosey the copyright for *Susannah,* to make and sell, rent or otherwise distribute copies of the music, to prepare derivative works like concert suites from the original score; to license public performances, whether to opera producing or recording companies; and to print and sell librettos and vocal scores. Floyd would receive 10 percent of the retail price of sheet music sales in the United States, 5 percent of foreign sales, and 50 percent of net receipts for licenses to broadcast or record the work. Mechanical rights to the entire work or substantial excerpts constituted "grand rights," for which Floyd's cut would be 66 and 2/3 percent. Smaller sets of excerpts, that is, those that taken together do not tell the opera's entire story, were "small rights," 50 percent going to Floyd. The composer would also receive 33 and 1/3 percent of rentals, that is, the hire of materials, such as conductor's score, orchestra, and chorus parts, and 50 percent of any subpublications, such as arias or other excerpts in anthologies. Finally, Boosey agreed to pay royalties within ninety days of December 31 each year, for the preceding twelve months, except for foreign performances subject to unexpected delays.

Wary of signing any legal document on the spot, Floyd asked Sylvia Goldstein whether he ought to have a lawyer review the contract. Goldstein laughed, "Anybody in publishing might be willing to take advantage of a lion. Nobody would of a lamb, but suit yourself."

City Opera took *Susannah* on tour to Michigan State University in East Lansing on November 6 and to Detroit's Masonic Auditorium on November 11. Floyd tagged along, jubilant at audience responses. He thought nothing of being asked to speak at Michigan State, unaware that having composers on road trips was also novel for the company. The *Detroit Times* reported a "deeply stirred" audience, praising Floyd's music as "irrevocably committed to the words . . . immediate, exciting and always legitimate. *Susannah* gets to you fast."[67]

Tenor Richard Cassilly joined Floyd's circle of favorite interpreters as Sam. A tall, burly man, he internalized Floyd's words and music in ways already familiar to Curtin and Treigle. In a spontaneous theatrical moment at the end of act 1, Susannah, devastated by rejection, begs Sam to sing "Jaybird" again. Cassilly swept Curtin up in his arms and walked offstage carrying her, real tears streaming down his face.

Back in New York on November 16, Boosey amended Floyd's contract to represent everything it wished to publish that he had written to date, and *would* write, topped with a five hundred dollar advance against future royalties. In Florence for Thanksgiving between November 17 and 20, and fearing that he had missed something in the thicket of legalese, Floyd showed his father the still unsigned contract. The minister glossed over his perplexity by suggesting that Floyd show the forms to Mrs. Richards: Margarette Richards, his piano teacher of fifteen years earlier. The composer decided to trust his new associates at Boosey & Hawkes. Reverend Floyd meanwhile adopted an irritating habit that the composer recognized as a form of diminishment, by referring to the publisher as "Bosey and Hawks." Floyd's correction received a standard response of wounded innocence, "Oh, I didn't know that."

When Floyd returned to Tallahassee for a quick visit, he picked up *The New Yorker*, which contained Winthrop Sargeant's summation of the critical community's perspective on *Susannah:* "the most moving and impressive opera to have been written in America—or anywhere else . . . since Gershwin's *Porgy and Bess.*" He thought the opera's shortcomings minor when compared to its "dramatic sweep . . . the heartening sincerity of its musical style" and its "enthralling intensity."[68]

11

The Climb to *Wuthering Heights*

New Forms, Marriage, 1956–1959

Floyd holed up to finish *Pilgrimage* for Mack Harrell. Composition had by this time pushed his keyboard activity into the shadows. Although he continued to accompany special colleagues, he never agonized over dropping solo pianism as a career. Realization sank in that work as an opera composer meant collaboration with hundreds of different people on each project. Kay Reeder visited at least once from Jacksonville, and friendship became romance. In the Call Street house, they kissed for the first time and declared their mutual feelings.

Bob Holton lost no time in capitalizing on *Susannah*'s triumph, rushing the vocal score into production in the winter of 1956/57, with a centerfold of Gene Cook's photographs and a cover designed by Floyd's Tallahassee artist-friend Evon Streetman. Floyd dedicated the volume to his parents, who never told him how they felt about this.

Holton had also been approached by two prominent Broadway producers, Edward Padula and Emmett Rogers,[1] who wanted to know whether Floyd might consider Dubose Heyward's 1929 novel *Mamba's Daughters,* adapted as a play in 1939, as an opera subject. After all, Heyward was a South Carolinian, and so was Floyd; *Susannah* was being favorably compared to Gershwin's *Porgy and Bess,* based on Heyward's 1925 novel and 1927 play version,[2] so why not another Heyward musical? *Mamba's Daughters* tells the story of an uneducated black woman breaking racial barriers and class lines in Charleston to improve her daughter's chances for a singing career. Floyd read and considered, before deciding that another southern subject at this point in his career would calcify stereotypes, and said thanks, but no thanks.

Familiar with *Susannah,* the producers, through Holton, offered another property to which they held rights of adaptation, Esther Forbes's bizarre, seductive novel *A Mirror for Witches,* first published in 1928.[3] From an old Massachusetts family, Forbes was steeped in and moved by the seventeenth-century Salem witch trials, and her novel magnifies this phenomenon—the viral self-delusion of Satanic possession fostered in repressive puritan societies—also treated by Arthur Miller in *The Crucible (1953).* Forbes's complete title is a précis of the subject in antiquarian format: *A Mirror for Witches in which is reflected the Life, Machinations and Death of Famous Doll Bilby, who, with a more than feminine perversity, preferred a Demon to a Mortal Love. Here is also told how and why a Righteous and Most Awful Judgment befell her, destroying both Corporeal Body and Immortal Soul.*[4]

Holton scheduled a meeting with the producers, and Padula gave the composer a copy of Forbes's book; but on their way out, Floyd wondered why they wanted *him.* In later negotiations, Holton voiced his client's concerns: "Floyd doesn't do thirty-two-measure hit tunes." Padula and Rogers reminded him that they had seen *Susannah,* and wanted *exactly* what Floyd did.

In interviews for the October article in *Time,*[5] Floyd had pinpointed America's Puritan tendency to equate nonconformity and sin; and Frank Merkling's review of *Susannah* in *Opera News* offers added perspective with the observation that "Susannah's small-minded neighbors . . . almost succeeded in remaking her in their own image."[6] Thus we see Floyd drawn to

Forbes's story as a virtual sequel to *Susannah*'s final curtain. Also, Phyllis Curtin ached to do this role. On the basis of Floyd's eventual seven-page scenario the producers commissioned his book, lyrics and music, for out-of-town tryouts in Boston and Philadelphia in September 1957, and a Broadway opening that November 7.[7] Morton DaCosta, who had staged *No Time for Sergeants,* was proposed as director, Franz Allers and Hanya Holm to conduct and choreograph.[8]

The financial prospect enticed, but the producers offered no advance money. Floyd would be working on spec, and had his doubts, but Curtin rejoiced and auditioned for the producers, singing something jazzy/blues-y, quite out of her usual repertoire. Yet Floyd felt bullish enough to secure Dean Kuersteiner's permission to extend his leave of absence without pay for another year, agreeing to resume teaching in fall 1958.

Meanwhile, the composer blossomed in the energy and competition of New York. He had always appreciated fine clothes, and now had the wherewithal to acquire some. Paul Stuart became his store of choice, at 45th and Madison Avenue[9] and later at its Chicago branch.

Back from touring, Curtin insisted on introducing Floyd to Gian-Carlo Menotti, whose work he had admired for years, and who strove to alter America's perceptions of opera. Meeting at a downtown Italian restaurant, the charming Menotti demonstrated that he had read the *Time* piece, exclaiming as he shook Floyd's hand, "Ah, my rival!" They developed a cordial friendship over subsequent years, although Menotti's partnership with composer Samuel Barber made any closer acquaintance unlikely.[10]

During these six post-*Susannah* weeks, Floyd met other successful composers who treated him as a colleague and friendly rival. Among these was Ned Rorem, born in Richmond, Indiana, three years Floyd's senior, and one of the first Americans to make a living exclusively from composing. Rorem began writing seriously in the early forties, excelling at art song, but in time working in every musical form: chamber music in all combinations, and concertos, choral, keyboard, and symphonic works of every dimension and description. Over the years, he gained notoriety by keeping and publishing his confessional diaries. By the time he and Floyd met, Rorem was one of Holton's "golden boys" at Boosey. Like Floyd, Rorem longed for success with opera, but found mixed results in the medium. He had been in France during City Opera's *Susannah* premiere, working on his own second opera, *The Robbers,* but caught up with later productions of Floyd's hit.[11] Phyllis Curtin was one of Rorem's favorite interpreters, and one night while Floyd was at her apartment the soprano rehearsed Rorem songs with their composer at the keyboard. He glanced at one point to Floyd to say, "I'll take the lyric and leave the dramatic to Carlisle." Subsequent meetings were always friendly, surpassing mere politeness.

With spoken theater available as never before, Floyd drank deeply at the well of drama, taking in Eugene O'Neill's *Long Day's Journey into Night,* with Frederic March, Florence Eldridge, Jason Robards, Bradford Dillman, and Katherine Ross, and Shaw's *St. Joan,* with Siobhan McKenna, and produced by Roger Stevens, who would assume a crucial role in Floyd's career in years to come.

Another sobering call to attention met Floyd in February's *Musical America,* with another Ronald Eyer piece on *Susannah,* the most comprehensive consideration of the work to date.[12] Hypersensitive to criticism in any guise, Floyd took to heart Eyer's qualified but still admiring description of *Susannah* as "a straightforward, unadorned story . . . of almost scriptural simplicity of language and characterization." For this article, Eyer had even solicited Floyd's personal aesthetic, giving the composer a chance to speak for himself, printed as the "Composer's Credo":

> My first consideration in attempting an opera is whether . . . the subject is one in which the emotional, psychological, and philosophical conflicts of the story can be externalized through action and visible situation and still retain absorbing, multi-dimensional characters. For the very reason that opera must be primarily externalized, we have erred too often . . . in favor of situation, leaving character development in a rather primitive, elementary state . . . it is time that we . . . attempt to make some commentary on timeless

human problems in a contemporary way, and that it is not inappropriate that an opera have a "theme," so long as it is not tiresomely didactic.

Yet Eyer's comments on *Susannah*'s music provoked the composer to undertake a transformation of style akin to his reconstruction of piano technique with Foster. Eyer specified:

The musical structure of *Susannah* is, for the most part, simple, not very difficult of execution and quickly communicable. There are no polyphonic developments and, while dissonance and even polytonality are employed to project the dramatic content of certain scenes and situations, the music is anchored in tonality and in traditional patterns of rhythm and meter. Liberally applied in the interest of unity is the device of thematic transformation which the composer chose as a happy Puccinian compromise between the leitmotif method of Wagner, the formal designs of Berg and the recitative-and-aria system of the 17th and 18th centuries.[13]

Floyd took all this to mean that his future work needed greater complexity to compete: more modulation, contrapuntal textures, extension of material over longer arcs of time. This would involve turning his back on the overt tunefulness and diatonic harmony that had brought him overnight success.

For a man whose southern metal (and mettle) shone from its centuries-old patina, Floyd took stock of his new life in larger cultural contexts. Important critics were taking him seriously, approving and encouraging what he had to offer, and had yet to do. As he listened to the latest from Copland and Stravinsky, both experimenting with serialism, Floyd sensed that these older masters had somehow lost themselves; yet despite his resolve to adopt a new style, the pitfall he most dreaded was loss of individuality. Though staying true to his roots, he had to transcend and purify them; at all costs, he had to avoid postmodern stereotyping, which in music meant atonal/serial, random, or electronic/synthesized schools. All composers felt enormous pressure, radiating outward from academe's groves, to conform to these trends. As early as 1958, Milton Babbitt argued for the supremacy of university over concert hall as the proper home for all that is "'complex,' 'difficult' and 'problematical'" in music, and that an evolution based on mathematics rather than emotion superseded obligations to any hypothetical or real musical audience.[14]

Floyd could have written any kind of music he wished, but knew that affecting another's style would offer neither pleasure nor excitement nor aesthetic satisfaction just to prove that he could. Many New York friends pressed him to turn his back on the south, to give up that bill-paying university job and move to the city, the Mecca of the classical music world, but Floyd knew that Eudora Welty, Flannery O'Connor, and William Faulkner had done or were doing just fine on home territory.

On Floyd's Tallahassee turf, excerpts from his operas began appearing on student and faculty concerts, with or without his presence. On December 13, soprano Edith Kaup included two arias on a Phi Mu Alpha campus composer's concert, alongside Ryan Edwards's new theater piece *See the Wind*. The following May 14, soprano Mary Jane Marriott offered "Wail and Lament," that is, Sadie's lament, from *Slow Dusk*. Even in New York, Floyd items began to pop up, as with "The Dirge," yet another name for Sadie's lament in Ethel Colt's Town Hall recital on March 31, 1957.[15]

Back from touring, Phyllis Curtin wondered aloud whether Floyd might write a concert aria for her upcoming Town Hall recital. He was not sure, but Curtin reminded him that being an opera composer had never stopped Mozart from writing such pieces for his singer friends. The notion took root when Floyd recalled Jona Clarke's telling him that actresses favored an audition monologue drawn from *Wuthering Heights*, beginning with "Nelly, do you never have queer dreams?" from volume 1, chapter 9 of Emily Brontë's novel of 1847.[16] Female protagonist Catherine Earnshaw explains to companion Nelly her torture over accepting the love of either decent Edgar Linton or stooping beneath her station to favor wild Heathcliff, already her soul mate. She connects her situation to a dream in which angry angels cast her out of heaven. Floyd mooted this to Curtin, and floodgates opened: she had adored and identified with the story as a teenager. She had even had one beau who called *her* Cathy, after the novel's heroine, and gave her a ring with a dedication to "Cathy" engraved inside.

The train from New York deposited Floyd and his satchel, most prominently stuffed with Brontë's novel, in Florence at 3:10 a.m. on December 23. This year's eleven days of Christmas were nothing more nor less than he had come to expect. Everyone had read all the post-*Susannah* press. Mrs. Floyd now sent her husband out for every week's Sunday *New York Times;* but it was the national exposure of *Time* that most impressed the family. His mother marveled, "Son, you didn't expect this much so soon, did you?" It was about the closest to a compliment that Floyd would ever hear from a parent. Her inability to jump with joy onto her son's speeding bandwagon came not so much from any feeling that his success was undeserved, as from her fears that disappointment might overtake him.

Reverend Floyd had taken up golf, and Floyd gifted him with a fine set of clubs, then applied himself to Curtin's aria for the remainder of the stay, finding most of the novel's dialogue usable as written. Brain still teeming with *Bilby's Doll,* he completed a shapely six-minute vehicle, which he called simply "The Dream." Profiting from criticism of *Susannah*'s thick orchestrations, he wrote the vocal line as much as a third higher than he otherwise might, to give the voice a better cutting edge. With memories of Priscilla Gillette's huskier soprano quite faded, he now tailored his writing to Curtin's higher *tessitura.* Pricked by Ronald Eyer's call to complexity, he filled his new music with plentiful counterpoint, modulation, and more ambiguous (and ambitious) harmonic language. He did not exaggerate in his Christmas card to the Clarkes: "Things post-*Susannah* have been mounting unbelievably and I am . . . deluged with work."[17]

After stopping in Jacksonville to see Kay on January 2, Floyd returned to New York to deliver "The Dream" to Curtin and her accompanist Brooks Smith. At the end of the piece, imagining effects that most voices could not produce, the composer had written a trill on high B-flat. When he accompanied Curtin to a lesson with her vocal guru Joseph Regneas, after introductions Floyd sat down to play and Curtin sang "The Dream" straight through. At the end, no one spoke. Curtin and Floyd looked expectantly at Regneas, who finally said, "Well, my dear, whoever wrote this piece certainly has no idea about the human voice."

Of the composer's reaction, Curtin said, "He just looked very Carlisle."[18]

When Bob Holton learned of the project, he leapt into impresario mode with the suggestion that Floyd attempt a complete *Wuthering Heights* opera. The composer laughed, "I can't put my neck on the block with something that well-known"; but when Curtin held that it would confound critics who had pigeonholed him as an "Americana" composer, Floyd listened.

He also had a seventy-one-page *Bilby's Doll* libretto, imagining Curtin as the doomed heroine.[19] His substantial apparatus ran to fifteen scenes in three acts, with fifteen principal roles and another eleven smaller characters drawn from a chorus of fifteen to twenty, and ten to twelve dancers to execute Doll's demonic hallucinations. With a Broadway run in mind, his eight different settings reflected designs that had impressed him, especially Jo Mielziner's multilevel environments, and even Leo Kerz's *Susannah,* in which lights alone cause acting areas to advance and retreat from awareness.

He had compressed as much as possible of Forbes's book into his libretto, and his dramatic points are subtle and double-edged. The audience might first believe this a supernatural story, but the truth is that Doll has been sold a colossal bill of goods by a society even more repressive and hysterical than that of *Susannah*'s New Hope Valley. *Bilby's* offered Floyd's sharpest indictment of how a religious culture may punish what it most fears in itself: Doll's only fault is accepting that she is what people say she is. The story is both a continuation of and an alternative to *Susannah*'s theses; but Susannah lives, strong and unrepentant, while Doll dies, victim of her own gullibility.

While Floyd whipped "The Dream" into shape in South Carolina, the New York press began announcing the Padula/Rogers coup: first the *Times* on December 30, then the *Daily Mirror* and *Daily News* on New

Year's Eve. Bob Holton passed the completed *Bilby's Doll* libretto to the producers. On January 3, 1957, they, Floyd, and Holton met the proposed production staff, and Padula played the role of staunch defender, declaring that Floyd had given the theater one of its great characters with Doll Bilby. Choreographer Hanya Holm was not so sure. Scanning Floyd's demonic fantasy sequences, so removed from the *My Fair Lady* world that she had helped create, she shook her head, seeing nothing for her in the new vehicle. Rogers confided that CBS, one of *My Fair Lady*'s backers, was interested in Floyd's piece, but the producers wanted Floyd to play them a few of his hit tunes. His back up, the composer reminded them that he did not work that way; when Rogers insisted that Floyd devise a happy ending to replace Doll's death, the composer envisioned a Holm sequence of jolly witches' barn dances or pirate hornpipes.

With *Bilby*'s future in limbo, he returned to Tallahassee to determine whether the work could be salvaged, to organize the remainder of his Guggenheim projects, to work on his Piano Sonata for Firkušný, and to spend any free moments with Kay in Jacksonville. The Sonata became a template for the new sounds he planned for *Bilby's Doll.* Its idiom would veer boldly away from *Susannah*'s romanticism, but still incorporate traditional structures: sonata-allegro for the first movement, fugato for the second, and rondo for the third.

Phyllis Curtin urged him to expand his work on *Wuthering Heights.* Having family roots in the East Anglia region of England, she sent Floyd a clipping from the *Manchester Guardian* about the survival of witchcraft in that backcountry as late as 1933 and 1934. She circled the item, scrawling the words "Tallahassee Alchemist" across the page.[20]

At Boosey & Hawkes, Bob Holton lobbied to acquire Floyd's other works besides *Susannah;* and on January 11 and 12, 1957, Augustana College's opera workshop in Rock Island, Illinois, performed *Slow Dusk* on a double bill with Seymour Barab's *A Game of Chance.*

On January 17, Julius Rudel was appointed general director of New York City Opera and one of Rudel's first thoughts was of a new and improved *Susannah.* On February 3, news that Padula and Rogers were abrogating the *Bilby's Doll* agreement came almost as a relief. The property had gotten under Floyd's skin, but Padula and Rogers still owned it.

On February 11, for one dollar each—a standard contractual stipulation—Boosey acquired rights to *Slow Dusk, Lost Eden, Nocturne, Theme and Variations for Two Pianos,* and the as yet unperformed *Pilgrimage,* with publications projected between the end of 1957 and 1959. Only *Pilgrimage* and *Slow Dusk* appeared, in 1957, the latter with cover photography by Evon Streetman and a dedication to Hazel Richards.[21] When Harrell received his copy of *Pilgrimage,* he told Floyd, "You've done it again." The baritone had exclusive rights to the piece's first performance, planned for the 1958–1959 season.

Phyllis Curtin's Town Hall recital on February 24 featured Handel's solo cantata *Lucrezia, Eight Epitaphs* of Theodore Chanler, six of Debussy's Verlaine settings, Rachmaninoff's *Vocalise,* and, closing the first half, the premiere of Floyd's *The Dream.* The composer was not present, but the performance gained enhancement with a few astute technical effects. Bob Holton sent Floyd a program with a note enthusing, "The audience got cold chills, and gasped at the lighting—and loved it!"[22] Yet the *Times* bestowed anything but compliments, speculating that Floyd might be toying with setting Brontë's entire story to music.[23] Louis Biancolli more positively heard "a powerful, soaring soliloquy . . . as strikingly rendered . . . as . . . the gripping music of *Susannah.*[24]

In the Town Hall audience sat San Francisco Opera's general director, Kurt Herbert Adler, who made a beeline backstage to ask Curtin what the rest of the opera was like. She could only laugh, "There is no 'rest of the opera,' this is it." But Holton hovered, and for his next brainstorm contacted John Crosby, about to found the Santa Fe Opera that summer on his New Mexico ranch. With Curtin's backing, Floyd's burgeoning reputation, and a detailed scenario to back it up, Holton extracted a commission for summer 1958, and Floyd breathed sighs of relief at the promise of income for his post-Guggenheim year, having just lost *Bilby's Doll.* Boosey always negotiated Floyd's commissions, but in this instance Holton *generated* the project. The terms were advantageous: $4,500, more than his entire Guggenheim stipend, but in three installments—one-third on signing the contract, another third on delivery of the vocal score, and the last on delivery of the orchestration.

With Floyd back in Tallahassee working on his Sonata, Curtin wrote him details of the concert and her backstage visitors. She confided that she had done her best with that high warble at the end, but ultimately chose discretion, giving her audience a solid B-flat sans trill.

GIUSEPPE VERDI had referred to his middle "Galley Years,"[25] when he turned out one opera after another without pause to reflect or worry; and Floyd, already a fervent Verdian, was reaching for the oars on his own vessel. His resolve got a boost from Robert Sabin's admiring commentary on "The Dream":

> The Brontë text lent itself very well to Floyd's purposes and he has set it with a vivid sense of dramatic effect. The startling high phrases, the abrupt clashes of dissonance, the verbal rhythm and emotional surge of the music all reveal a practiced hand. In style, the piece is neo-romantic, with a spicing of modernism in its harmonic treatment, but if its materials are unimpressive, their treatment is expert and imaginative. Only a virtuosic singer could do justice to the work, and Miss Curtin gave a thrilling performance of it.[26]

Floyd read and reread Brontë, struggling to transform the diffuse story into valid contemporary drama.[27] Other composers had tried to make operas of *Wuthering Heights,* with mixed success. In the 1920s, Frederick Delius contemplated but failed to realize a series of "pictures" from the novel.[28] Bernard Herrmann, using a libretto by his first wife, Lucille Fletcher, agonized over his setting between 1943 and 1951; he considered it his magnum opus, but did not live to see it staged. To friends he wrote, "The only thing I ever did do that was foolhardy was to write an opera. . . . Franz Liszt said that you have to have the soul of a hero to write an opera and the mentality of a lackey to have it produced."[29] The English firm Novello published Herrmann's score in 1965, and the Unicorn-Kanchana label released a studio recording the following year, conducted by the composer. Portland Opera gave the work, heavily cut, its world stage premiere in November 1982.[30]

Besides the novel, Floyd knew only the 1939 Goldwyn/Wyler film scored by Alfred Newman, and its focus on the passion of Cathy and Heathcliff and the love triangles with Edgar and Isabella up to Cathy's death.[31] Concentrating the epic scope of the novel into an event-rich unit of reasonable dimensions posed the first obstacle; then there was the challenge of "translating" Brontë's Victorian diction, which he had already tackled in "The Dream," into something timeless, and that swept credible human characters into an incredible milieu.[32] The book's doom-laden Gothic ambience, its very soul, tended to swallow up individuals, and Floyd had to preserve atmosphere and sharpen characterization, had to temper Brontë's wildly irrational behavior with the next century's Freudian and other psychological findings. The character Cathy dies without admitting that she has destroyed more than one life, so Floyd had her experience a tragic enlightenment; and he would have to draw Heathcliff out of his violent, brooding self-absorption and bitterness to express recognizably human emotions.

Crafting his text, with Kay never far from his side, he handed her new pages for comment. She made tiny, often illegible jottings in the margins that nonetheless expressed shrewd judgments about a literature she knew well; she had an uncanny ability to see past his blocks. The depth of his growing passion for Kay took dramatic form in the tempestuous relationship of Cathy and Heathcliff, and his dedication of the opera to her came naturally. He moved the action forward from the eighteenth century to the mid-nineteenth and told the story in a series of cinematic flashes backward and forward. He adhered to Brontë's plot, and created a prologue and three acts in seven scenes that covered a span of four years. To make productions affordable, Floyd specified that the two principal houses that host the entire action, Wuthering Heights and Thrushcross Grange, should share the same outline, varied through shifting inner walls, drops, and décor.

The prologue opens on a stormy winter's evening at crumbling Wuthering Heights in 1835. Lockwood (tenor), tenant at the nearby Grange, also owned by Heathcliff (baritone) and his wife Isabella (soprano), begs housing for the night, having been stranded outdoors by weather. The Heathcliffs receive him with minimal courtesy, offering an overnight place by the fire. Isabella gives him reading material, and Lockwood opens a diary kept by Catherine, née Earnshaw (subsequently Heathcliff and then Linton). When an outside shutter bangs against the sill, Lockwood tries to fasten it. A ghostly arm reaches through to grasp his, its owner proclaiming that it is Cathy, who has lost her way on the moors.

A brief confrontation with Heathcliff sets the stage for the first flashback to the winter of fifteen years ago, 1820. Act 1, scene 1 reveals the living room and kitchen of Wuthering Heights, owned by the aged and infirm Mr. Earnshaw (bass). His two natural children, Cathy (soprano) and Hindley (tenor), form a dysfunctional family with a rescued orphan child, the plowboy Heathcliff. Cathy teases and torments Heathcliff, who clearly loves her, much to the disapproval of housekeeper Nelly (mezzo-soprano) and servant Joseph (tenor). Hindley rightly sees that his father prefers Heathcliff to him, and threatens the boy with dire reprisals should anything happen to the old man, who conveniently dies at scene's end.

Scene 2 unfolds three months later, with Joseph reading scripture to Cathy, Heathcliff, and Hindley, the last now lording dominion over everyone and ordering the other two from the house. Nelly wryly congratulates Hindley on this punishment; her motivation is made clear as we see the two on the heights outside, singing a rapturous love duet filled with references to the natural world engulfing them and heightening their passion.

Lighting effects transform the house into neighboring Thrushcross Grange, owned by the Lintons. Cathy twists her ankle on the rocks. Edgar (tenor), Isabella, and their mother come out and offer hospitality during Cathy's healing process. Enjoying Edgar's attentions, Cathy happily accepts; stoking Heathcliff's jealousy flatters her vanity. The act ends with Heathcliff's plaintive calls after her.

The first scene of act 2 returns to Wuthering Heights, four weeks later. The Lintons have driven Cathy home in their carriage, and she introduces her benefactors to Nelly. Hindley summons Heathcliff from the kitchen, and Cathy's teasing provokes his rage. Nelly advises Heathcliff to apologize for his outburst, then prepares tea while Cathy shows the Lintons the new Earnshaw colts. Heathcliff strives to fit in, but Edgar comments on the boy's lack of manners. Heathcliff hurls the contents of his teacup at the guest and storms out, and Hindley follows, to whip Heathcliff. Before the Lintons leave, Edgar promises to call on Cathy soon. Heathcliff stumbles back inside, and Cathy is horrified that he is bleeding. He ascribes his submission to Hindley to wanting to be near her.

Scene 2, another month later, finds Cathy primping, expecting Edgar. Heathcliff awkwardly confesses his love and jealousy, and bolts out. Edgar arrives, proposes marriage to Cathy, and she accepts but then confesses to Nelly her misgivings, which are prompted by odd dreams she has had (the rightful place of *Dream* in the larger structure): Cathy believes that she was never meant to be happy, and the act ends with news that Heathcliff has run away.

Act 3 opens three years later at Thrushcross Grange, with a party in progress. Cathy is mistress of the house, but shows signs of boredom as Edgar's wife. Unseen by the hosts, Heathcliff enters in cape and evening dress. He has revenged himself on Hindley by winning the Earnshaw house and grounds in a card game, and asks Nelly to bring Cathy to speak with the new owner of Wuthering Heights. Cathy, flushed in party mood, hungers to see Heathcliff. She dismisses her brother's plight, but Edgar is not so cheerful to see their guest. On the other hand, Isabella Linton is much taken with this new Heathcliff, who asks Cathy to dance. She declares that they must waltz, and they begin as other couples drift away. Heathcliff himself leaves, promising to call again if he is welcome. After Edgar turns in for the night, Cathy and Nelly discuss the about-face in Heathcliff's situation: it is now

Edgar who has cause for jealousy. Cathy is thrilled to have her old friend back in their circle, and Nelly sees darker events looming.

Scene 2, again at the Grange, jumps ahead four weeks. Isabella, clearly falling in love with Heathcliff, quarrels with Cathy, jealous of Cathy's renewed interest in the former plowboy. Cathy lists every reason why he is the worst man for Isabella, but the two women seem bent on rivalry. Heathcliff enters with Hindley, now a broken man. Cathy cheerily asks Heathcliff to clear the air with Isabella, but the women's competition escalates. Heathcliff turns the tables on Cathy, making her wretched through his involvement with Isabella and his observations that Cathy's feeling for Edgar is mere pretense. Cathy tries to enlist Edgar in this coldest of wars, but Edgar refuses to sully himself with physical violence; Cathy screams at Heathcliff to get out, that she never wants to see him again, and vents her bitter self-reproach to Nelly.

The final scene, seven months later at the Grange, shows Cathy pregnant but ailing, wishing to be outdoors again. Heathcliff, now married to Isabella, pays a visit, and Cathy asks whether he will remember her once she is gone. They revisit their tortured past and the deadly game that has destroyed both their human cores. They reprise their love duet from act 1, and Cathy dies. The opera ends as Heathcliff flings venom at the universe, defying Cathy to haunt him for the rest of his life.

IN *WUTHERING HEIGHTS,* Floyd latched onto another subject with two rebels, Cathy and Heathcliff, flailing to gain independence but losing the battle through codependency. While dwelling on the moors, the composer's stock hit a new high on March 4 when the Music Critics Circle of New York picked *Susannah* as the best new opera of 1956, winning over William Bergsma's *The Wife of Martin Guerre* and Frank Martin's *The Tempest.* After reminding Floyd that Kurt Herbert Adler had not forgotten "The Dream" after Phyllis Curtin's recital, Bob Holton opened negotiations with San Francisco, competing with Santa Fe for the world premiere of *Wuthering Heights;* and NBC's Peter Herman Adler asked about developing the new work for television.[33]

Floyd interrupted work on *Wuthering Heights* with occasional visits to his once and future employer, Florida State University. On April 10, he spoke to the University Wives Music Club on "Opera Today and Yesterday." In May, Boosey considered substituting Floyd's forthcoming Sonata for Theme and Variations in their publication lineup. Firkušný had an option on the premiere, originally set for the fall of 1957, but no date had been announced; and Holton, David Adams, and Sylvia Goldstein opted to wait for a tape before reaching a final decision on a piece of abstract instrumental music from a composer identified exclusively with opera. With a complete *Wuthering Heights* in view, Floyd requested that "The Dream" not be published separately. As for the opera itself, Boosey wanted a complete manuscript score by April 1, 1958, for which they set a copyist budget of $1,500.

Beginning in 1958, the firm also published seven excerpts from *Susannah* for voice and piano or with orchestration: Susannah's two arias, Blitch's prayer for forgiveness, his aria before Susannah's seduction, Sam's sad music on the lamentable state of mankind, "Jaybird," and the entire revival scene. Between 1958 and 1964, the publisher also had Floyd arrange "Jaybird" for unison voices and mixed chorus.

With his Sonata complete, Floyd wanted to hear it played before delivery to Firkušný. He had considered performing it himself, but saw that he had written a virtuoso piece that would take too much time away from composing to learn and perform. He gave it to his star pupil Ryan Edwards, who "played the hell out of it" on his senior recital on May 13.

Floyd's Sonata spans about eighteen minutes in three movements, fast (*Allegro risoluto*), slow (*Lento assai*), and fast (*Deciso*). The first takes sonata-allegro form, with clear exposition of three contrasting themes, development through diminution, contrapuntal imitation, fragmentation, and augmentation; and recapitulation, though much elaborated, and coda. Heralded by a sixfold fanfare, its tonal center is D; but Floyd masks determination of minor or major by studiously avoiding obvious thirds. His signature open fourths and fifths lend a sense of Dorian modality, the so-called Phrygian second, in this case a B-flat/A device, used both melodically and harmonically. Despite frequent alternations of 4/4, 3/4, 2/4, and 5/4, the principal theme, with its dotted eighth-sixteenth pattern, and finishing run of sixteenths, resembles Chopin's mazurkas and polonaises. Confident of Firkušný's elegant performance, abundant bravura gestures include crossed-hands passages, grace notes, and roulades. The sheer size of the piece swells aurally and visually, as Floyd goes to the three-line format of his dance scores. With its dense textures, despite some extended passages in bare octaves, a great deal happens with inner voices.

The slow movement, a fairly strict fugato in 6/8 and other triple meters, centers on E-flat, with persistent two-against-three syncopations, and a central contrasting *Andante con moto* on an ominous ostinato bass line of adjacent seconds. The blurring of tonality acquires the feeling of Chopin's familiar funeral march, within the larger context of theme and variations. A shattering climax and resolution dwindle to a stark high chord of E-flat, B-flat, the E-natural and E-flat making an imperfect octave in the right hand.

The concluding movement opens with a different set of fanfares of dotted and running sixteenth-notes skirting D, clashes between natural and sharp thirds, and new mazurka references. The main theme in 4/4, *Allegro con brio,* establishes a modified rondo on three themes: a rhythm of four sixteenths, sixteenth rest, three sixteenths and half note, accruing complexity and density through imitation, then highly chromatic unison-octave running sixteenths. A second, more legato motif with a quasi-Alberti bass figuration leads to alternation of the sixteenth patterns and the original fanfare, elaborated into a more lyrical arioso, before returning to the agitation of the initial material, imitated in the left hand in parallel thirds. The concluding two-part coda varies all the movement's themes, alternating fanfare, mazurka, and sixteenths, arriving at a syncopated measure of unison D in high and low octaves, and a final crash on open D-A-D. This reminiscence of *Pilgrimage*'s concluding song may be accidental, but Floyd dedicated it to another paternal figure, Rudolf Firkušný.

Some have compared Floyd's Sonata to similar large-scale works by Barber and Bloch.[34] There is just as much of Hindemith in some of Floyd's elements; but detection of overt or submerged influences leads to the realization that his music sounds like nothing but itself.[35]

ON MAY 23, the National Association of American Conductors and Composers awarded its citation of merit for *Susannah,* describing Floyd as hitherto little-known, young, creative, and highly gifted as an opera composer.[36] That same week, FSU's chapter of Phi Mu Alpha Sinfonia, the national men's professional music fraternity, gave the composer honorary membership. Yet despite accomplishment and honors, Floyd succumbed to an onrush of disillusionment and depression. He had realized every young composer's fantasy: overnight operatic success in New York, the Critics Circle's accolade, and a contract with one of the world's most prestigious music publishers. Yet the voids kept open by old lying voices could still drag him down. He had to talk sense—his first realization of a need for therapy—with someone, and drove to Kay in Jacksonville. Once he began confessing his feelings that the empty places were still empty, the tears flowed and did not stop for three days. His threnody with variations was Reverend Floyd's abandonment of him to the family's women. Kay listened patiently: she wanted to know everything there was to know about him. Without coddling, she offered sympathy and intelligence, and Floyd drove home with certainty's cold comfort that his career activity was and would always be "what it was."

Though not yet back on FSU's payroll, Floyd always found time to help needy students. Jim Staples hoped to earn a master's degree at Juilliard, but would need a generous scholarship; and he had enlisted in the army to avoid being drafted. Floyd knew Irwin Freundlich, the Juilliard teacher with whom Staples wanted to study, and contacted the man on behalf of Staples.

Floyd's word proved recommendation enough, and two years later, when Staples had completed his service, a two-year scholarship was waiting.

In June, Floyd gathered a bouquet of thirty-first birthday presents: Bob Holton called to say that Edward Padula, having severed his association with Emmett Rogers, wanted the composer after all to realize *Bilby's Doll.* Holton advised Floyd to ask this time for advance money; but Floyd already had enormous servings on his plate, and Padula could not meet the new demands. City Opera then announced that it would take *Susannah* as one of America's cultural showpieces to the Brussels World's Fair in 1958. Finally, on June 10, New York radio WNYC broadcast the University of Southern California Opera Workshop's West Coast premiere of *Susannah,* staged and conducted by Walter Ducloux.[37]

Kay Reeder decided to return to Florida State that fall to complete her master's degree, and she and Floyd agreed to marry around Thanksgiving. They had been romantically involved for more than two years, and he had yet to introduce her to his family. On June 17, Floyd shared their plans with his father on a drive around Florence, and the best Reverend Floyd could offer was, "Well, it's about time." Despite Ermine's production of four grandchildren, the minister was pleased by his son's news: he would do the marrying, come November.

Susannah received another West Coast performance on August 1 and 2, at the Montalvo Summer Music Festival in Los Gatos, California, by a cast of Bay Area singers. Floyd also received his final Guggenheim check on August 1. Three months later, he wrote the foundation a formal letter of thanks, summing up the year as the most significant of his life. In addition to participating in City Opera's *Susannah* production, he had written two libretti, a piano sonata, and begun work on *Wuthering Heights;* but even more important was "the time it allowed me for intensive artistic reflection . . . and personal exploration of a very exhaustive nature. These are the things which seem to me vitally necessary in the last analysis to creative growth. To free the artist from the exigencies of external living so that this process of contemplation and assessment can occur in its proper atmosphere seems to be the greatest of many services the Foundation does its Fellows."[38]

A friendly response from Guggenheim's James Mathias two days later emboldened Floyd to ask whether the fellowship might be extended; but the deadline for such application had long since passed, and Floyd dropped the matter. A lean year was in the offing, but thrifty ways and commission money from Santa Fe enabled him to save $1,200 to see him through until delivery of the vocal score of *Wuthering Heights.*[39]

On August 24, with some dread, Floyd introduced Kay to his parents. To welcome her prospective daughter-in-law, Ida roasted a twelve-pound turkey and baked a cake; Reverend Floyd ordered six carnations from a local florist. After supper, the proud parents displayed photo albums of Carlisle's Converse and Syracuse years. Though Reverend Floyd wrote little about Kay in his *Diary,* a decades-long dynamic began that evening. Both parents admired Kay's mind, and liked her, with reservations: Kay had never learned the art of small talk and shunned social events that might require it. Since childhood, she took what others said literally, and her intellect cut through facades. Mrs. Floyd found in Kay an ally and confidante, and prized her reserved nature and smoky low speaking voice. In time, Ida admitted to Floyd, "I'm so glad you married Kay rather than Phyllis." Not that such an option had ever been contemplated; but Mrs. Floyd simply found Kay more approachable than the opera diva. With Kay, Ida openly discussed personal travails and family secrets that she had never or never *would* have shared with her own children, and that Reverend Floyd would have considered disloyal. One such confidence was that Carlisle had been the most consistently thoughtful of her, and she embraced Kay as another daughter.

Reverend Floyd would have preferred someone who flattered his grandiosity. Kay had been raised by atheists, and Floyd had warned her about his father's dogmas. When the reverend regularly and predictably baited her about beliefs, she shifted focus by saying that she had received little religious education and knew little about the Bible. This, of course, gave *him* the opportunity to preach without leaving the parsonage; he insisted that prayer did the pray-er more good than it did God, and thus did Floyd learn more about his father's convictions. Reverend Floyd once told Kay, "I really like you because you are so interesting to talk to." Floyd thought to himself, "He has no choice: she's marrying me."

One of the supper-table conversations in Florence contained the revelation, never before voiced to Floyd, that his father had been so offended by *Susannah*'s revival scene that he had almost walked out in Tallahassee. Kay, seeing her fiancé's rising emotions, filled the void by saying, "Yes, I can see how you might feel that way." Kay later told Floyd that she liked his mother better than his father, whom she thought a bit of a fool. Although Reverend Floyd's ploys fell flat with her, she contrived enough pleasantry to make family visits tolerable, and Floyd warmed to see his mother blossom in Kay's company; but the couple nonetheless stayed away from church the next morning.

When he called Ermine to tell her to expect them on August 26, she expressed surprise at the marriage news. Floyd explained, "I have finally met someone smarter than I." Ermine was not so sure and established little common ground with Kay, besides their love for Carlisle. Their relationship remained cordial though guarded; but Ermine's daughters stood in awe of the exotic new sophisticate who wore pants, smoked, discussed Freud and Jung. As Kay resumed FSU classes in September and a graduate assistantship, the composer buckled down to finishing his *Wuthering Heights* libretto, relying frequently on her keen eye and ear.

Floyd packed again for New York and approaching rehearsals for City Opera's new *Susannah* conducted by Julius Rudel. A four-day visit to his parents from September 21 to 25, less than a month after his last, suggests curiosity about their reaction to his upcoming marriage, as well as stress over the new opera and fears of burnout. His father commented that Ida was worried "about Carlisle's not feeling up to par;"[40] but her solid

23. Floyd and nieces, 1955: Martha, Nancy, Harriett, Jane. Courtesy of Carlisle Floyd.

meals, including his favorite coconut cake, restored at least the appearance of health. Between frequent visits to the church to compose, he listened to his father's rants about President Eisenhower sending troops to Little Rock to enforce segregation.[41] Reverend Floyd was televising sermons on WBTW-TV, and on September 25 introduced his son around the studio. The station manager extracted the composer's promise to help with a future program, and the Floyds drove their son to the station to catch his train at 10:30 that night.[42]

Floyd stayed again at the Curtin/Cooks' in New York for the next weeks. City Opera had assigned a staff accompanist to play rehearsals, all of which Floyd nonetheless attended. Marcella Cisney directed the new production, with sets by Andreas Nomikos and choreography by Robert Joffrey. Phyllis Curtin reprised the role she had created, to Norman Treigle's Blitch, Richard Cassilly's Sam, and Eb Thomas's Little Bat. Half of the Elders and their Wives had been replaced, including Irene Kramarich, who had seen the end of her City Opera career.

Floyd discovered in Rudel an ideal interpreter, prizing his dynamic yet precise style, his ability to control balances between stage and pit and to elicit subtle inner vocal and instrumental lines. Between his work on *Wuthering Heights* and meetings with Santa Fe's John Crosby, who unfortunately answered few questions, Floyd had more than enough to occupy his waking hours away from City Center. Bob Holton had negotiated Floyd's contract directly with Crosby, whose shyness and taciturnity made communication difficult. Crosby and Floyd now discussed scoring for a small orchestra based on Santa Fe's pit restrictions. Crosby never asked for a libretto or score, and never inquired about the composer's rehearsal needs, and Floyd left their encounters with little more than premiere dates in July 1958.[43]

On October 8, Holton/Boosey acquired and agreed to publish *Pilgrimage* and *Piano Sonata* in 1958 and *Wuthering Heights* in 1959.

JULIUS RUDEL meant to display *Susannah* as a gem without Kerz's gloomy agenda, but his new director Cisney seemed determined to outdo Kerz at every turn, regardless of appropriateness, beginning with the notion that Blitch came onstage in act 2 *planning* to seduce Susannah. Her approach alarmed Floyd, who came to loathe directors' attempts to portray the preacher as a kind of country cousin to used car salesmen. He pointed out that Blitch stumbles into this situation, and that Cisney's determination robbed him of every shred of vulnerability, humanity, and integrity. Treigle took the composer's side. His star power was unquestioned: he'd had an enormous success with the role, took great offense at Cisney's concept, and let the director know that he had no intention of doing what she had asked. Rehearsals moved forward.[44]

To lend the opening extra sparkle, Rudel coordinated a citywide event: Mayor Wagner proclaimed the second week of October "New York City Opera Week," and *Susannah*'s opening on October 10 was announced as a United Nations salute. The company invited U.N. representatives from more than twenty-five nations and Secretary General Dag Hammarskjöld to the premiere, followed by a block party on West 55th Street.[45]

Reverend and Mrs. Floyd and her sister Bunny checked into the Great Northern on the afternoon of October 9; once again, Kay's travel phobia and school responsibilities kept her in Tallahassee. The composer and Eb Thomas met Floyd's parents at City Center's stage door, and Floyd took his father to Boosey & Hawkes to meet Bob Holton.

On the afternoon of the premiere, without telling anyone in his party, the baseball-hungry minister took the D train to the Bronx for the final game of the 1957 World Series. He had to leave before seeing the Milwaukee Braves defeat the Yankees 5–0, but he had left his family in considerable confusion.

At City Center that evening, the Floyds sat in a row with U.N. delegates from Belgium and India. Reverend Floyd found the performance "not up to what I thought it was last year,"[46] but Howard Taubman of the *Times* differed. He thought that Rudel's conducting lacked the crispness of Leinsdorf's, but then turned a corner on his earlier assessment of Floyd after a year of better acquaintance with the score. Like some of his colleagues, he now thought Floyd a born opera composer: "The hot blood of life beats through it."[47]

The United Nations after-celebration that Floyd and his family enjoyed featured live music, and female principals from City Opera hawked refreshments from sidewalk booths.[48] The company's celebration moved to Bob Holton's apartment. Despite the free-flowing liquor, the urbane agent charmed Floyd's parents, who later relished telling everyone back home his latest joke or bit of Manhattan gossip.

After a short night's sleep, the family collected reviews. Floyd lunched with Don Rand, then the Cooks treated all the Floyds to an Italian supper at the Red Devil. An ardent drinker of copious draughts of weak coffee, Reverend Floyd was unprepared for espresso.

On the morning of October 12, the composer and his parents left for South Carolina after stopping by the *Times* for an advance copy of the October 13 issue containing an article about the commissioning of *Wuthering Heights.* Another piece in that issue announced the Ford Foundation's plans to award grants of $860,000 over the succeeding two years to spur growth in education and the humanities. One such infusion of $105,000 would go to City Center, allowing Rudel to realize his ambition of an all-American season in 1958.

In Florence for the next three days, Floyd kept his promise to his father's TV producer and taped an interview on October 15; he was back in Tallahassee three days later. As the year drew to an end, Floyd's champion Mack Harrell strove to make up for missing City Opera's *Susannahs.* On the faculty of Southern Methodist University in Dallas, Harrell imported Phyllis Curtin and stage director Lynn Orr to reprise their shared Tallahassee triumph. Under the aegis of Southern Methodist Community Opera Guild, the school's orchestra, conducted by Paul Vellucci, and a mixed cast of faculty and students gave two performances on December 13 and 17. Floyd earned critical kudos for his "exquisite taste" in adapting the apocryphal story and in conveying an impression of "profound, elemental tragedy."[49]

NOW IT WAS TIME for Floyd to get married. Most of the composer's friends were surprised to learn that he had at last, and it seemed to them suddenly, chosen a life partner. Nancy Smith, who had known Kay since high school in Jacksonville, popped by Floyd's Call Street house. The composer was glad to see her, but Nancy thought she was missing something when he kept constantly referring to Kay. Nancy asked, "Carlisle, are you and Kay . . . ?," and Floyd finished her sentence, "Oh yes, we're getting married next Thursday."[50] Jim Staples, unaware at that point that Kay and Floyd had dated seriously, much less embarked on a romantic relationship, felt shock that Floyd was marrying at all. Staples had always found Kay somewhat distant, fragile, moody, easily provoked, and reclusive, unlike Floyd's positive, forward-looking nature.

Kay next appears in Reverend Floyd's diary on November 2, when Floyd called to say that they planned to marry on Thanksgiving. He had also told the Cooks in New York, and Curtin wrote on November 7 to "Dearest Cuzn Carlisle," gushing, "We are completely thrilled with the prospect of acquiring a new cousin and hope that Kay will accept such outlandish but affectionate relationships."[51]

Over the years, the two couples saw each other often, spending work, vacation, and travel time together, and corresponding; yet Curtin puzzled, "I never knew Kay very well at all. I liked her a great deal, and we always had interesting table conversation, much of it literary. I have always felt that she and Carlisle admired each other tremendously, but I never felt much of a physical connection between them. I had the feeling that they were always very interested in each other's company, but not passionately *in* each other's company. It seemed to me that Kay always thought she was smarter than Carlisle. Not in any offensive way, just kind of the last-word way."[52]

On November 23, the National Association for American Composers and Conductors gave the first concert of their silver jubilee season at Grace Rainey Rogers Auditorium at the New York Metropolitan Museum of Art. On a program of new works by Paul A. Pisk, Eli Krul, Godfrey Schroth, Harry R. Wilson, Werner Josten, and Heskel Brisman, composer Paul Creston introduced Floyd's *Lost Eden, Music for the Dance of the Same Title,* performed by duo-pianists Esther Fernandez and Stephen Kovacs. Floyd of course had other things on his mind and could not attend, but the *Times* found it accessible, and likened the work's joyous rusticity to Percy Grainger's music.[53]

Floyd and Kay arrived in Florence late on November 26, amid the bustle of wedding preparations, and showed off the new luggage set Floyd had given his bride. Kay's mother, Gundy, arrived the next night. Of the hours before the wedding on Thanksgiving Day, November 28, Reverend Floyd wrote, "Carlisle had sick spell and Kay was ill too"; but the couple and their guests from Holly Hill and Latta rallied, and Reverend Floyd "performed the double ring ceremony for my only son, who married a very fine girl."[54] Following the service, everyone watched televised football, had a traditional turkey dinner at the Colonial Hotel, and opened wedding gifts at the parsonage. The Floyds gave them china, the Reeders, a Tiffany silver service. A mark of Floyd's rising fame was *The New York Times* November 30 announcement of the wedding. There was neither time nor funding for a proper honeymoon: Floyd had an opera to write, and the couple sped back to Tallahassee.

The libretto of *Wuthering Heights* drafted, Kay continued to offer editorial suggestions. If the process distressed Floyd, or if he struck Kay as too full of himself, she gave him the "two or three heads are better than one" lecture, as the couple settled into domestic routines. Kay, as it turned out, was considerably less charmed by the little green house than her husband, and longed to move as soon as possible. The first chunk of Floyd's savings went for a used upright piano for $250 for their living room, as Phyllis Rappeport was still teaching in his FSU studio.

Kay marveled at his discipline and focus, his spending so much time alone at desk and piano. Though she was trained to write, Kay never discovered an inner voice to express, and Floyd could only have nodded to read Diana Trilling's comment that writers embody what they write and also do *not* write.[55] Kay remained supremely private, and that included reluctance to commit her thoughts to paper. Yet released from her dark childhood, she longed to pursue anything that piqued her interest, and now transformed herself into a passionate amateur in an astonishing

24. Wedding Day, 1957. J. W. "Billy" Matheny, Ermine, Martha Matheny, Ida, Reverend Floyd, Carlisle, Kay, Marguerite "Gundy" Reeder. Floyd collection. Photograph by Blackmon Studios, Florence, South Carolina.

range of subjects: nature, science, religion, philosophy, and Jungian psychiatry. Like most artists, she and Floyd shared liberal political views, and both craved movies, theater, and music. Yet the fit of "Mrs. Carlisle Floyd's" shoe often pinched; there were his endless mornings, noons, and nights of solitary work, and extended production weeks away, which she had no interest in sharing.

An interviewer once queried Floyd, "And what does your wife do?" at which the composer laughed, "Well, right now she's interested in volcanoes." At another point, she became obsessed with meerkats. Her reading tended to the esoteric, along the lines of Julian Jaynes's *The Origin of Consciousness in the Breakdown of the Bicameral Mind.*[56] At the beginning of their marriage, Floyd had neither time nor money to travel, except in connection with work; and Kay's disinclination grew with time into agoraphobia. Fortunately, they remained interested in sports, especially tennis, which both played, as Floyd disclaims, "passionately if not well." Both began lessons soon after marrying.

Growing up, Floyd never felt comprehended. He had been no prodigy, nor did his family or friends treat him as one, so his early passion for music had made him something of an oddity; but he felt that Kay "got him." The longevity of their relationship as a couple took grounding from their ability to pursue individual goals to satisfaction and somehow meet back in the middle, to share the fruits of intellectual curiosity and his work ethic. Kay had no role modeling for tenderness, but now Floyd saw a different, exuberant Kay relishing her new status. She most prized wit, and admired quick ripostes and laughter. In private, they delighted in acting silly, making faces; and Floyd, with decades of joy from making his mother laugh, found his wife a new challenge. This took the form of word games, and in seeing and pointing out situational absurdities. Floyd, rarely taken seriously by his family, developed a grave mask for the outer world and came to take himself quite seriously as a musician; now, sharing hilarious moments with a partner put him in touch with his own razor-edged wit and ready laughter.

Domesticity was hardly Kay's long suit, but she and Floyd shared an interest in good food, mainly Southern and French, with an accent on sweets, and she became a skilled cook. Once Floyd rejoined FSU's faculty in the fall of 1958 and had a new measure of financial security, the couple threw frequent dinner parties for ten or twelve.

Hazel Richards now proved an ongoing source of stress. Floyd's FSU colleagues alternately teased and sniped that the wealthy patroness was smitten with him, that she had never attended school events before his arrival; and Hazel made secrets of nothing. Her stentorian assertions on anything to do with Carlisle Floyd, and her continued lavish gifting, put the composer in an awkward position with wife and peers. Once Kay moved into Call Street, Hazel began excluding herself from their circle. She disapproved of the marriage in strong terms, lapsing into illogical demands that he should have married someone younger, like Ermine! (Ermine was four years older than Kay.) It seemed clear to everyone that Hazel wanted Floyd for herself; he feared that his colleagues saw him as "a horse that Hazel had bid on." She demanded some kind of daily visit, and when he proposed a more modest schedule, Hazel snapped, "I would not be interested." Kay's repeated invitations, even for Hazel's birthday, met with icy refusals. When the Floyds attended an event at a local country club and saw Hazel, Kay approached and said, "Hazel, enough of this, let's be friends," but Hazel's silence and public turning of shoulders lowered the temperature permanently, despite Floyd's dedication to her of *Slow Dusk* later that year.

The pleasures and pressures of adapting to marriage, the realignment of his social life, finishing *Pilgrimage,* and the deadlines of his first commission, found their way into *Wuthering Heights,* as turbulent, dissonant, and angular as anything Floyd had written to date. He knew that this setting needed very different aural clothing than *Susannah*'s, something more organically constructed and idiomatically consistent.[57] Above all, he had to avoid Americanisms; and each scene would derive from a single motive stated at the opera's beginning. Having first written *Susannah* with

Priscilla Gillette in mind, he had concentrated the leading role's *tessitura* in middle soprano range; now, with intimate knowledge of Curtin's instrument, he counted on her apparently endless supply of top B-flats and Cs.

As Christmas approached, the Houston Symphony Orchestra and the Houston Grand Opera collaborated in performing scenes from *Susannah* on December 16. The sopranos Frances Yeend and Nancy Swinford and Floyd veterans Richard Cassilly and Norman Treigle performed Treigle's staging of the revival scene, conducted by Walter Herbert. During family visits, Floyd composed *Wuthering Heights* at St. Paul Methodist, scribbling penciled notes onto manuscript paper as fast as he could give them stems and bodies.

He and Kay boarded a train for New York at 11:40 p.m. on December 27. Pinching and stretching their pennies that year, Floyd wanted to introduce Kay to the Cooks—Santa Fe had cast Curtin as Cathy—and to play for them what he had written of *Wuthering Heights.* They began to sing through the score, and, after about eighteen minutes, when they reached the end of Hindley's aria in act 1, scene 1, Curtin turned the page, found empty paper, and gaped at Floyd. "That's it," he shrugged. He still had two hours of opera to compose, the opening night at Santa Fe just seven months away.

THE YEAR 1958 opened with another honor: *Theatre Arts Magazine,* the source of the monthly play scripts read by the "Possums" in Tallahassee, devoted its January opera issue, now a collector's item, to Floyd's complete *Susannah* libretto, together with a generous selection of Gene Cook's photographs. To accompany these, Floyd interrupted his round-the-clock frenzy of composing to write his first essay on the librettist's art. He proposed that the words, the play, come first. "Immediate and provocative human situations" must form the drama's crux; opera militates against discursiveness. The librettist must "construct his play almost skeletally . . . amassing dramatic tension kaleidoscopically."[58]

As summer approached, Floyd and Kay offered to share Santa Fe housing with the Cooks. John Crosby asked Floyd about directing the new work—which Floyd ultimately declined—and Curtin wrote practical advice that every novice stage director should memorize: "Just keep the running and leaping to a minimum before the big singing—and get the general *mise-en-scène* clearly in mind apropos chorus—and everything will work beautifully. I shall try to be as unquarrelsome as possible."[59]

As he progressed with the score, Floyd used sophisticated musical devices like a fugato at the beginning of act 1, scene 2. When he reached the end of act 2, scene 2, he experienced an eerie déjà-vu in the seamless join of "The Dream" with material before and after. When it came time to orchestrate, he kept instrumental colors both transparent and somber, to mirror Brontë's cold, dark world.

Within a few months of resuming master's degree work, Kay decided once and for all that academic life was not for her and left school; Floyd agreed that she did not have the personality to be a teacher. Already in Wisconsin she had been unable to discipline unruly students; and despite her interests in the most challenging and arcane literature, graduate school in the pre-PC and Internet era meant unacceptably long research hours in libraries. For the time being, she seemed satisfied with reading, tinkering at the piano, and above all playing tennis and cooking, all of which made her life less structured than her husband's.

FEBRUARY 1958 proved one of the coldest on record in the south, with freezing weather and as much as three inches of snow as far south as Tallahassee. The *Wuthering Heights* premiere was set for July 16 in Santa Fe. The Ford Foundation planned to send Floyd with City Opera's troupe for the World's Fair *Susannah* performances in June.[60] In the thirteen weeks since his wedding, Floyd had put final notes into his *Wuthering Heights* pencil score and delivered it to Boosey for the copyists; and Santa Fe's second $1,500 installment ended his immediate cash shortage.

Pianist-conductor-composer Walter Hendl,[61] between positions with orchestras in Dallas and Chicago, approached Bob Holton about creating an orchestral suite from *Susannah.* Holton pounced on the notion, but Floyd had no time for the task, and Hendl extracted a nineteen-minute selection of big moments: the opening square dance and choral sequences, Blitch's entrance, Susannah's two arias, Blitch's aria of repentance, excerpts from the revival scene, and the closing moments.[62] The premiere took place at the Coe College fine arts festival, and Floyd took a working vacation for three days of panels, workshops, and concerts on that campus in Cedar Rapids, Iowa. On March 18, the composer, with pianists William Masselos and Herbert Melnick, gave a workshop discussion and demonstration of contemporary piano literature, including Floyd's *Lost Eden.* The next day, Floyd gave a solo workshop on composing for the voice, and on March 20, with soprano Dorothy Warenskjold, a vocal techniques workshop focused on opera and recital performance.

Floyd's chance meeting with the Iowan poet-writer-novelist-editor Paul Engle would bear fruit in another decade.[63] The festival's crowning event was a concert on March 24, with the Cedar Rapids Symphony premiere of the *Susannah* Suite. Floyd could not spare more time after the final workshop and headed back to Tallahassee on March 21 without hearing the piece.

An unpleasant discovery welcomed the composer home: his 1953 convertible had been stolen from Call Street. Police located the car, undamaged, in northwest Tallahassee's Frenchtown neighborhood; but a glove not belonging to either Floyd or Kay was found on the front seat, leaving both with eerie violated feelings.

With the premiere in four months, *Wuthering Heights* now had to be orchestrated. During nine days in Florence, on Call Street, and on later trips to Kay's parents in Jacksonville, Floyd voiced his score with his usual complement,[64] and finally saw light on the moors. It was not without envy, though, that he sat at the Reeders' kitchen table, pencils flying, while the others laughed and watched television.

April 23 was a big Floyd day: *Slow Dusk* made its New York debut with the Lyric Festival Company, which was managed by Virginia Card and Dorothy Raedler, who also directed *From Here to There, a Bill of Three Musicals* at the Sullivan Street Playhouse.[65] The third offering, *A Real Strange One,* written by Robert Holton, did not fare well; but the next morning's *Times* praised the emotional power of *Slow Dusk.*[66]

On April 23, 25, and 26, the University of Hartford Hartt College of Music Opera Theater presented

25. Floyd at work on *Wuthering Heights,* 1958. Photograph courtesy of Evon Streetman.

Susannah, staged and designed by Elemer Nagy and conducted by Moshe Paranov. *The Hartford Times* called Floyd "a growing genius," and the writer indicated Floyd's contribution to a bright future for American opera.[67] Next in line on the *Susannah* express came opera workshops at Tufts University in Medford, Massachusetts, on April 25 and 26; Washington University in St. Louis on May 16, 17, and 18; and Nashville's Circle Theatre, to an accompaniment by Floyd's student Peggy Tapp, whose husband, Jay Turman, designed the production.

In the meantime, thanks to the Ford Foundation, Julius Rudel was preparing a dazzling and insanely ambitious spring season of all-American opera at City Center: Douglas Moore's *The Ballad of Baby Doe,* Mark Bucci's *Tale for a Deaf Ear,* Leonard Bernstein's *Trouble in Tahiti,* Kurt Weill's *Lost in the Stars,* Vittorio Giannini's *The Taming of the Shrew,* Marc Blitzstein's *Regina,* Menotti's *The Old Maid and the Thief* and *The Medium,* and Robert Kurka's *The Good Soldier Schweik.* The final offering of this amazing venture was what Rudel hoped would be the definitive *Susannah:* an unprecedented third production of a new work, three seasons running, and which City Opera would take to the Brussels World's Fair in June. Rudel reached out to New York's legitimate theater directors to invigorate the season's dramatic component, and for *Susannah,* Frank Corsaro grasped the brass ring.[68]

26. Frank Corsaro, c. 2000. Courtesy of Frank Corsaro.

Corsaro, born in 1924, and as of this writing still working as a director, novelist, and opera librettist, rose to prominence in the midfifties and was affiliated with the Actors Studio. Descended from the Group Theatre of the twenties and thirties, the studio was founded in 1947 by Lee Strasberg, Harold Clurman, Cheryl Crawford, Robert Lewis, and Elia Kazan; it set the bar for theatrical authenticity with its adaptation of the Stanislavsky Method of acting.[69] Corsaro's involvement with the studio began in 1952 and intensified with his production of Michael V. Gazzo's *A Hatful of Rain,* which Floyd had seen during its Broadway run in 1955/56. Strasberg soon appointed Corsaro one of his moderators for acting classes and play development with young authors; and in 1957, Rudel approached him for City Center. Though Corsaro's Italian American childhood was filled with opera, *Susannah* was his debut as a director of the medium in which he was to make his greatest impact. Corsaro saw Cisney's production that fall, which struck him as "a little old hat,"[70] but the impact of Curtin and Treigle was another matter, and Corsaro had wanted to dive into opera for some time.

As with Cisney, Treigle at first posed a stumbling block for Corsaro over costuming: Corsaro did not see Blitch as quite so dark and tortured, and wanted him to appear in seersucker. Treigle put his foot down, declaring that he'd either wear his regular suit, or else; and in the end, "or else" turned out to be the bass's acceptance of work in Houston and Minneapolis that spring. While Floyd orchestrated *Wuthering Heights* at his in-laws' kitchen table in Jacksonville, William Chapman sang two Blitches, on April 30 and May 4.

Rudel made other sweeping changes in both cast and staff: Curtin and Cassilly anchored, but Chapman, Keith Kaldenberg as Little Bat, and several Elders and

Wives were new, as were Paul Sylbert's multiunit sets, kept to a budget of one thousand dollars.[71] By and large, the production slowly gained favor. The *Times* praised Chapman's Blitch and Corsaro's dramatically unified staging.[72] *The New Yorker*'s Winthrop Sargeant found much to criticize in both singers and staging, but confirmed his opinion of *Susannah* as "one of the finest operas ever to come from the pen of an American composer."[73]

Corsaro's production, which Floyd did not see until the World's Fair (with Treigle as Blitch), would stay in City Opera's repertoire until fall 1971. Floyd himself felt even more strongly about its assets: "Corsaro's version was really new, dynamic, and immediate, in a sense, an 'Actors Studio version.' The European presses were so taken that American singers acted and sang at the same time. They were in no way 'operatic,' just wonderful theater people, as well as singers."

FLOYD PUT FINISHING TOUCHES on the orchestration of *Wuthering Heights* by the end of May's third week, in time for a quick trip to New York to collect his final $1,500 and to deliver his materials to Boosey's copyist, Arnold Arnstein. Dubbed by the *Times* as the ultimate master of his craft,[74] Arnstein impressed Floyd at once as a strict taskmaster for young composers. Though he submitted *Wuthering Heights* proofs to Floyd with red marks everywhere, he told Holton, "Carlisle learns fast: tell him something once, he has it." Over the years, Arnstein taught Floyd what composers ought not to do a second time: with respect to notation, this ranged from the correct direction to face note-stems to repeating accidentals in each measure, except in cases of tied notes. After *Wuthering Heights,* even though Floyd wrote around strong tonal centers, his habit of stacking tonalities called for a profusion of accidentals, and he came to find, despite the extra strokes for himself and copyists, that it saved time where it counted most, in orchestra rehearsals.

Most important, one had to center measures. For instance, a bar with four beats, divided quarter, dotted quarter, quarter, eighth, might confuse a player or singer at first reading; but a simple change in notation to quarter, eighth tied to a quarter, then quarter, eighth guides the eye to the bar's middle. Arnstein stressed the human factor of believing what one first reads on the page: correcting learned errors is always harder than perceiving correctly at first glance. Many orchestral players take a kind of perverse pride in argument and questioning, and Arnstein pursued the goal of making the first ensemble session a real *rehearsal* and not a note-fumbling exercise. Such particularity explains both Arnstein's legend in the hermetic world of music copying and the fees he charged for his work. When Boosey's *Wuthering Heights* vocal score rolled off the presses, incorporating all of Floyd's eventual revisions and corrections, it had Evon Streetman's atmospheric line drawing on black background as cover design and bore the composer's dedication "To Kay, my wife."

At the same time, Holton convinced Floyd that *Susannah*'s original thick orchestration, about which many singers had complained, was no longer viable; and the American Pavilion's pit in Brussels would hold no more than twenty-five or thirty players. With Floyd's approval, Holton contracted the composer-arranger Hershey Kay for a reorchestration, bartered for a set of Boosey & Hawkes scores rather than a fee, while Floyd scaled *Wuthering Heights*.[75]

Resigned to Norman Treigle's somber Blitch suit, Corsaro staged the singer into the Brussels-bound cast. With daily performances at the American Pavilion between June 25 and 29, touted by the press as America's entry in a "cultural cold war" with the Soviet Union,[76] Rudel double-cast the two principal roles, Lee Venora alternating with Phyllis Curtin, Treigle with William Chapman.

Though Floyd had no chance to attend rehearsals in May, he lunched one day with Bill Butler, a stage director at work on City Opera's Menotti double-bill.[77] Butler declared that Floyd was the first contemporary composer he had known New York critics to take seriously in many years. Floyd hurried off to Champaign-Urbana, Illinois, as a panelist at the University of Illinois humanities and arts program conference on music on May 23 and 24. Phyllis Curtin, composers Norman Dello Joio and Leon Kirchner, violist-conductor Milton Katims, and pianist György Sándor, who later played Floyd's Sonata, were all fellow panelists. Proceedings were recorded by W. McNeil Lowry, the Ford Foundation's vice president and director of its arts and humanities program, and who became a vital Floyd supporter.[78]

Floyd needed to apply for his first passport for the European trip and, on May 28, asked his father to mail his birth certificate; three days later, another package arrived, containing the composer's tuxedo and dress shirt. The Ford Foundation allocated two thousand dollars to cover Floyd's expenses in attending this event. Even Kay decided to make the trip, their first to Europe, but other arrangements pressed before they could leave Tallahassee. They had contracted the purchase of their first home, a modest one-story brick bungalow of 1,300 square feet, at 1605 Redwood Drive. To avoid paying rent at Call Street during their European sojourn, they planned to store their belongings with Kay's parents in Jacksonville. When she asked Mrs. Reeder to clear a large closet, Gundy temporized, "Well, I don't know; I have a lot of things in there now." Floyd discovered that his mother-in-law's perverse dynamic was to first deny any request; but Kay knew her mother better: when she displayed righteous anger, her mother wilted, and the closet was theirs.

On June 12, Carlisle and Kay left New York and toured Paris, Rome, and Vienna. In the latter city, they attended *Tosca* at the Staatsoper, and Floyd realized one difference between most American and European singers: The Austrian soprano Leonie Rysanek sang the title role beautifully, but acted in a style Floyd thought semaphoric. The Italian tenor Eugenio Fernandi inhabited Cavaradossi that evening, but his respectable vocalism was compromised by a stolid stand-and-deliver presentation. The malign Baron Scarpia was bass-baritone George London,[79] whose singing, musicianship, and in-depth characterization overshadowed that of his colleagues.

The Floyds reached Brussels for *Susannah* rehearsals around June 20. Director Corsaro recorded his first impressions of the composer:

> The last thing you would imagine him to be is a composer—a teacher, the proprietor of a sporting goods store, maybe an airline captain—for there is something deceptively square about him. He is almost down-home folk—affable and obliging, with just the right touch of taciturnity. . . . The other side of the Janus head reveals a nature of guarded, even feral, circumspection that belies his usual bonhomie . . . for Carlisle cannot quite quit on the notion that Southern men are not supposed to be composers. Yet Carlisle finds that . . . he is one—and in that fraternity he is almost nonpareil in his pursuit of the theme of brotherhood, and the ineluctable musical passion he brings to that vision. This combination of old flapjacks and tender grapes is both unexpected and endearing.[80]

One of the facts of life at a World's Fair pavilion was the parade of preperformance visitors looking in: On June 21, Monaco's Prince Rainier III and his glamorous American wife, the actress Grace Kelly, stopped by, and rehearsal predictably ground to a halt until the royals took their leave. On another occasion, Floyd had a pleasant conversation with England's Princess Margaret and her paramour Captain Peter Townsend. On opening night, June 25, the two-time Democratic presidential nominee Adlai Stevenson and his wife sat in the audience. Floyd's former student Jim Staples, on army leave, also found his way there.

Between May 1 and October 13, the American Pavilion Theater offered the country's finest entertainment. The wide-ranging performance schedule included jazz concerts by Benny Goodman and his orchestra, the folk singing of Harry Belafonte, chamber music concerts and solo recitals by Yehudi Menuhin, Leontyne Price, George London, Eleanor Steber and John Browning. Audiences heard orchestral concerts by the Philadelphia Orchestra under Eugene Ormandy, the Juilliard Orchestra conducted by Jean Morel, and the National Symphony Orchestra conducted by Howard Mitchell; and saw the American Ballet Theatre and Jerome Robbins Ballet. New York's City Center presented Rodgers and Hammerstein's *Carousel* and Bernstein's *Wonderful Town*, and the NBC Opera gave the world premiere of Menotti's *Maria Golovin*.

But City Opera's *Susannah* gambit won the greatest acclaim. *The New York Times* confirmed that so quintessentially American a work appealed to open-minded European audiences and was rewarded with frequent spontaneous applause.[81]

Even the Flemish newspaper *De Standaard* of Brussels marveled that Americans were producing such unique musical works.[82] On June 27, Treigle wrote his wife, "Everyone did a great job and I did as good as ever, maybe a bit better. . . . They seemed to really like the opera and everyone was flipped with me. It was a good audience considering only about 1/4 of them understood English and they really tore the house down for us. . . . [Stevenson] said I was another Raymond Massey."[83]

Back on American shores, the train from New York deposited Floyd and Kay in Florence at 3:35 a.m. on June 28. At the first opportunity, he tabulated how much of his travel allowance he had actually spent, and, seeing a substantial amount remaining, returned the balance of several hundred dollars to the Ford Foundation. When he reported this to Bob Holton, the agent branded Floyd as overly principled, reminding him of all the expenses that he could legitimately deduct from this or from his tax obligation, but Floyd never felt comfortable with other people's money.

Just three days and loads of laundry and dry cleaning later, he and Kay left for Santa Fe. In the course of that two-and-a-half-day trip, after a decade of nicotine addiction, they decided, for the first but not last time, that they needed to give up their favorite mentholated Winstons and Newports. The issue had complex layers, but Floyd eventually realized that his equation of smoking with relaxation after work reinforced the addiction. It had permeated every aspect of a life that seemed empty without a cigarette as a hand extension, and going cold turkey just before a premiere was doomed to failure. Shortly after moving into the adobe house the company provided them, a few miles from Crosby's ranch, Kay lit up first, and Floyd gratefully followed suit.

The staging rehearsals with Canadian director Irving Guttman[84] were pleasant. The cast included, besides Curtin (as Cathy), Robert Trehy (Heathcliff), Regina Sarfaty (Nelly), Loren Driscoll (Edgar), Mildred Allen (Isabella), Davis Cunningham (Hindley), John Macurdy (Earnshaw), Nico Castel (Joseph), David Dodds (Lockwood), and David Beckwith and Elaine Bonazzi (Mr. and Mrs. Linton).

The twenty-nine-year-old Guttman had been staging operas for just five years, and *Wuthering Heights* marked his American debut. Whenever Floyd attended rehearsal, the sweet-tempered gentleman seemed so eager to please that he often interrupted work by turning to the composer for feedback. When word got back to Crosby, the assistant director Robert Askart approached Floyd and asked whether he would mind *not* coming to these rehearsals. The composer was less than pleased, but Kay and Phyllis convinced him that it was for the best; as the opening approached, orchestra rehearsals called for closer attention to such a difficult new work.

On July 12, Norman Treigle staged and sang *Susannah*'s revival scene with Crescent City Concerts Association in New Orleans, his wife Loraine playing

27. Phyllis Curtin, Robert Trehy in *Wuthering Heights*, Santa Fe Opera, 1958. Photograph by Gene Cook. Courtesy of Phyllis Curtin.

a nonsinging Susannah. The performance was taped by WDSU-TV, and later transferred to the Bel Canto Society's video collection "Six Great Basses."[85]

The New York Times of July 13 ran Floyd's two-column analysis of his adaptation of Brontë;[86] then, in a *Time* interview he mentioned his consideration of Hawthorne's *The Scarlet Letter* and Wharton's *Ethan Frome* as opera subjects.[87] (He abandoned the first as too close to what he had already attempted with *Bilby's Doll,* and the second because he could not solve the problem of staging the book's crucial sledding accident.)

The July 16 opening night of *Wuthering Heights* proved a qualified success.[88] One local critic saw the work's challenges, with "mixed reactions of awe and uncertainty." While noting that audiences would probably not leave the theater humming Floyd's tunes, he predicted that the new opera would in time equal *Susannah*'s popularity.[89]

Floyd's fellow-composer Marvin David Levy[90] found the libretto short on lyricism, and the vocal writing monotonously intense, with climaxes cancelling each other. Broadcasting mixed signals, he called it "an exciting stage piece . . . moving and powerful," and praised Curtin's stunning vocalism but explicitly denied it classification as an opera as opposed to a play with music.[91] Even more significantly, Levy asserted that the orchestrally dense third act, which he found harmonically static and musically undistinguished, needed rewriting.

None of this bitter pill was untasted by Floyd. Warnings had already sounded when such a complete musician as Curtin had unprecedented difficulty in learning act 3. Working together in a practice room, after repeated musical stumbles, Curtin shook her head, "I just don't get it: I learn everything so well, even Schoenberg's *Second String Quartet;* but not this."

Two other visitors at opening night reinforced Floyd's impressions. The Ford Foundation was underwriting another season of all-American opera in the spring of 1959 with grants to City Opera of $310,000, and Julius Rudel flew out from New York to scout. Though feeling that Floyd needed to tighten the new work, especially act 3, he saw that an East Coast premiere of *Wuthering Heights* would be a strong addition to his assembly of firsts: the world premiere of Hugo Weisgall's *Six Characters in Search of an Author;* the first City Opera productions of Menotti's *Maria Golovin,* Weill's *Street Scene,* Robert Ward's *He Who Gets Slapped,* Dello Joio's *The Triumph of Saint Joan,* Lee Hoiby's *The Scarf* (also a U.S. premiere), Douglas Moore's *The Devil and Daniel Webster;* and revivals of *The Ballad of Baby Doe, The Medium, Regina,* and *Susannah.*

Rudel's loyalty to Floyd never wavered, but the relationship had its complexities. Rudel felt that Floyd tended to overmeticulousness rather than allowing audiences a few mysteries to ponder. *Susannah* had impressed the conductor with its conciseness, every note participating in the drama's essence, but *Wuthering Heights* struck him as verbose and diffuse.[92] In his teens in Vienna, Rudel had composed two short operas,[93] and as his personal and professional relationship with Floyd developed, his desire for collaborative input intensified. Rudel rushed back to New York, where he took City Opera on tour to the Chautauqua Opera Association for *Susannah* performances on July 18 and 21, with Lee Venora in the title role, Joshua Hecht as Blitch, and Robert Moulson as Sam.

Then Mack Harrell, on a break from teaching and performing at Aspen, took Floyd aside at the Santa Fe Opera. Polite but practical, he allowed that the third act was not up to the other two. Painful as this was, Floyd had to agree with his critics: Kay was right, two or three heads *might* be better than one, and he resolved to listen to anything anyone had to say, to take it all seriously, but make his own final determination. He could not wait to get home to work on act 3, but Phyllis Curtin and Gene Cook prevailed on the Floyds to join them in Aspen for a ten-day holiday, where Curtin finished the summer alongside Harrell. The party of four got into Floyd's convertible on the afternoon of July 23, bound for even higher country, sparking a new crisis. The scenic route spanned three hundred miles, about six and a half hours of two-lane roads, in part unpaved, narrowing to a single lane crossing Independence Pass at an altitude of 12,095 feet. When Kay learned of this route, it was nothing doing: she suffered from vertigo at such altitudes. She much preferred driving the three hundred miles northeast to Denver, and veering back west another hundred and fifty miles to Aspen, adding four hours to the day's trip.

Curtin gave Floyd the high sign for the high road, got into the back seat with Kay, and magpie chattered for the entire trip to distract her charge. Floyd had taken the pass on previous Aspen trips, but as they neared, dusk began to fall. Approaching headlights meant that one driver had to pull over onto a narrow shoulder without railings for the other to proceed, but as long as Kay could not see what lay below, she seemed fine, as Curtin taxed her conversational repertoire. As they pulled in well after dark, quid pro quo for the Cooks sharing their New Mexican adobe was free housing for the Floyds at Phyllis and Gene's Aspen cottage. Four short days later, on July 27, Curtin sang the female protagonist in Handel's *Apollo and Dafne*. For Floyd, it was a purely social visit, laughing and catching up with old friends; but when they picked up the new *Time* with its review of *Wuthering Heights,* they puzzled over praise for Floyd's "sweeping, intricate score" that "pulsed with moments of moving lyricism," compromised by condemnation of the libretto.[94]

A better reward arrived with a glowing review in *The Musical Courier,* the country's oldest musical periodical, which reported shouted "bravos" for the performers and a "constant awareness of intense musical drama . . . the result of painstaking scrutiny and admirable fidelity . . . a scrupulously honest and compelling interpretation of one of the most powerful tales of all time."[95]

DURING FLOYD'S succeeding two weeks in South Carolina, his Mannes and Aspen acquaintance Paul Berl presented *Slow Dusk* on a double-bill with Douglas Moore's *Gallantry* at the Cleveland Institute of Music summer opera workshop in Peninsula, Ohio. On August 8, Floyd and Kay slept through breakfast; but that afternoon, Reverend Floyd took his son along to speak at Florence's Lions Club luncheon. The *Diary* tells one version of the story. "My son in whom I am well pleased. . . . Carlisle gave a résumé of his European tour and the attitude of Americans at World's Fair."[96]

But what Floyd remembered of that day was his father's bizarre introduction of his son to the town's leading businessmen: "I don't have much to say about him, because he was much closer to his mother than to me." Despite worldly success, Floyd retained a wounded core, resentful that his rearing *had* in fact been left to women. He recalled, "I did not speak very well, for obvious reasons; and the first thing Daddy said to his Lions afterward was 'Carlisle can do better than that.'"

Floyd and Kay returned to anything but a haven of calm in Tallahassee on August 18. In the days before he resumed teaching, he set about revising and recomposing act 3 of *Wuthering Heights.* After his and Kay's third attempt to abandon smoking, Floyd quit for good; it took Kay another eighteen months to accomplish that feat. After two years of Guggenheim independence, Floyd's lighter teaching schedule allowed more time for composing, which was one of his incentives to return to FSU. Without applying for extended leaves, he arranged with Kuersteiner for time off to attend productions in other cities, as long as lessons were somehow made up; yet he had to tread a careful path with colleagues, who managed to cloak most of their envy. Another reward was a larger studio, room 312, in what would be named the Kuersteiner building.

The dean asked him to begin teaching composers, at first rarely more than two or three. As he had with piano, Floyd learned anew that pedagogy clarified processes and priorities, but composers either have dramatic sense or not. Core aspects of composing were nonnegotiable and largely unteachable: timing, shaping, structuring large forms. One never simply arrived at a curtain. He also created a course devoted to problems shared by librettists and composers. His teaching load sank to ten or twelve piano students, he taught no more music appreciation and accompanied no more choral concerts or summer music camps; but thanks to the school's excellent music library and record collection, Floyd now set himself the goal of learning the operatic repertoire as thoroughly as he had that of piano and symphony. Aside from the few operas he had seen in New York, he was familiar with *La bohème* and *Madama Butterfly,* and now began to study scores of everything from Monteverdi to Berg, to stage works of his own contemporaries. Late Verdi spoke to him in profound ways of sheer workmanship and ethos.

In the midst of retrieving possessions for their move, Floyd got down to the task of completely reformulating act 3. He assigned paramount importance to colorful, poetic prose in a realistic framework, as well as to deintellectualizing and heightening his two larger-than-life protagonists.[97]

The first two acts needed only minor word changes and cuts. Throughout, he clarified and compressed the opera's time scheme: the new prologue begins in winter 1835; act 1, scene 1 flashes back to February, 1817; scene 2 to two months later (April). Act 2, scene 1 moves four weeks ahead, to May; scene 2, to June. The three scenes of act 3 play, respectively, in August 1820, one month later (September), and end seven months later, in April 1821. He eliminated the minor characters of Mr. and Mrs. Linton at the end of act 1. The latter role had been offered to the character mezzo Elaine Bonazzi, who had sung the role in Santa Fe and now found herself without a contract at City Opera that spring.

One major *expansion* came with Cathy's effusion on lapwings, toward the end of act 1. This Floydian meditation on independence, for which the ill-fated lovers pine, brought twenty-one measures of rhapsodic new music for Curtin; then in act 2, scene 2, Floyd added an impassioned fourteen-line/thirty-nine-bar proposal aria to make Edgar a more impactful suitor.

He completely rewrote words and music of the first two scenes of act three. In its first scene, a party is still in progress at Thrushcross Grange, but now Floyd devised his first choral showpiece, as the guests speculate on the identity of the mysterious stranger (Heathcliff) who ruins his old enemy Hindley at the gaming table. Cathy exults when these two appear, and dances an ecstatic waltz with Heathcliff; Edgar's reception is understandably cooler. Heathcliff explains to Cathy his transformation from plowboy to gentleman, and proposes that she run away with him. Hindley interrupts, asking to gamble again, putting Wuthering Heights up as his stake. To breathless interjections from the chorus, Heathcliff annihilates Hindley, adding the ancestral home to his portfolio. As guests begin to leave, Heathcliff suavely courts Edgar's sister Isabella, precipitating an argument between Edgar and Cathy. Nelly fails to persuade her mistress that Heathcliff's return is an unhappy occasion.

For scene 2 at Thrushcross Grange, Floyd added a new sequence for Nelly and Isabella, the latter having fallen for Heathcliff. Nelly's remonstrations do no more good with Isabella than they had with Cathy, now pregnant with Edgar's child. Cathy bursts in, declaring that she too loves Heathcliff, who arrives to twist the knife of Cathy's jealousy, bidding a joyous Isabella to pack and leave with him. He and Cathy trade insults, then in torment he pours out his unslaked passion for her. Edgar and Nelly enter, and Cathy orders her husband to throw Heathcliff out. Floyd then devised an impassioned canonic quartet on new text on the only principle on which these four can agree, the binding quality of their shared doom, in a strong closed musical and theatrical unit that concentrates pages of talk from the first version. The scene ends with Heathcliff's departure. Cathy clutches Nelly, shrieking that she cannot live without her soul-bond with Heathcliff.

FLOYD INTERRUPTED this torrent of revision to move to Redwood Drive on October 1. At the same time, he traded in his $250 bargain piano on a new ebony Steinway upright with which he'd fallen in love, and plunged ahead with *Wuthering Heights* revisions. After Call Street, the new house seemed luxurious; it had two baths and three bedrooms, of which Floyd claimed one as studio. Mortgage payments, taxes, and insurance left enough to purchase a hilltop lot on Lakeshore Drive, with the idea of eventually building a custom home.

Reverend and Mrs. Floyd arrived for their first visit on October 20, bowled over with the growth of Tallahassee and FSU, and their son's prosperity. Ida had her hands full with helping the newlyweds make a home of their house, sewing new curtains on a machine borrowed from Nellie-Bond Dickinson. Food became a focus, and Kay and her husband showed off recently acquired culinary skills.

Given his upbringing, Floyd had rarely, if ever, felt anything but aversion to religion. It came as a great surprise, considering Kay's recent introduction to the elder Floyds' theocentric life, that she now wished to explore a middle ground between the atheism of her rearing and the unpleasantness of her husband's early immersion in Protestantism. Floyd had attended Episcopal services during his Converse years, and the denomination seemed to embrace a more liberal worldview. Dickinson, an ardent Episcopalian, introduced the Floyds to local rector Frank Pisani, whom they found personable, attractive in all senses, intelligent, and unauthoritarian, hence worlds apart from Reverend Floyd. Floyd and Kay attended Episcopal services until at least the end of 1959,[98] but soon Kay's interest in religion, like most of her enthusiasms, waned. Floyd continued solitary attendance for another six months, making a number of new friends on Sundays.

Even as Floyd continued recomposing *Wuthering Heights, Opera News* lauded Santa Fe's production, making by far the most favorable comment on the original version:

> Many who had read the Brontë novel or seen the motion picture wondered whether the music would live up to the story. It did more: it often dominated the story. The very first measures of the Prologue establish an ominous mood sustained throughout the work. There are many unforgettable passages . . . the music lives in the memory after only one hearing.[99]

Ida Floyd had stayed behind to help "the children" get settled in their new home. On October 29, she took the bus to Columbia, where Reverend Floyd had received his most prestigious posting to College Place Methodist. She reported to her husband, "I think that Kay is selfish about Carlisle."[100] Soon thereafter, the newlyweds began seeing therapists to work through separate and joint childhood issues.

In October, *The Musical Courier* published the original version of the complete and unrevised *Wuthering Heights* libretto, with a selection of Gene Cook's photographs; and on November 2 and 14, City Opera reprised Corsaro's World's Fair production of *Susannah.* Lee Venora sang the title role, and Joshua Hecht replaced Treigle, both to great acclaim.[101] November 6 found Floyd in New York to discuss his *Wuthering Heights* revisions with Erich Leinsdorf between the conductor's spring and fall seasons at the Metropolitan Opera. Bob Holton had sent Leinsdorf a prepublication copy of the score to stimulate interest in possible productions. Leinsdorf complimented Floyd, with one caveat: Cathy's high *tessitura* courted shrillness, not to mention reducing the effectiveness of necessary high notes for emotional climaxes. Though Leinsdorf never championed the opera, Floyd took his advice and eliminated many unnecessary above-the-staff pitches, and also authorized transposition of "The Dream" from its original B-flat a third down to the darker emotional ambience of G-flat.

Floyd moved on to Boston to supervise lightly staged and costumed *Susannah* excerpts with Lee Venora and William Chapman and the Springfield Symphony on November 11;[102] and from November 18 through December 13, Cleveland's Karamu Theatre presented the complete opera in a multimedia production by Benno D. Frank and William Jean.

Floyd and Kay made a quick Christmas visit to Columbia, and the composer spent every free moment scoring at College Place Church. They continued on to New York on December 26, and Floyd dropped off his revised vocal score and orchestrations.[103] He had borrowed twenty dollars from his father for the trip, repaid swiftly after their return on New Year's Eve.

THE PREMIERE of *Wuthering Heights* was set for April 9 at City Center. By the time Hawaii became America's fiftieth state on March 13, Floyd and Kay were ensconced with the Cooks at 110 Riverside Drive, with rehearsals underway. To give his latest Ford-sponsored productions extra glitter, Rudel had hired renowned motion picture and Broadway directors, including John Houseman, José Quintero, and Herman Shumlin. On Gene Cook's recommendation, Rudel contracted film and television director Delbert Mann for *Wuthering Heights.*[104] Lester Polakov designed sets, Patton Campbell costumes; once again, Robert Joffrey devised the revision's more extensive choreography.

Besides Curtin as Cathy, the cast featured Jack De Lon (Lockwood), Grant Williams (Joseph), Jack (not yet John) Reardon (Heathcliff), Jacquelynne Moody

28. John Reardon, Phyllis Curtin, *Wuthering Heights*, New York City Opera, 1959. Photograph by Gene Cook. Courtesy of Phyllis Curtin.

(Isabella), Patricia Neway (Nelly), Arnold Voketaitis (Earnshaw), Jon Crain (Hindley), and Frank Porretta (Edgar). From the first staging rehearsals, the principals vented dissatisfaction. As often happens when film directors translate their vision to opera, that largest of all stages, Mann did not help matters by looking through a figurative lens. Occasional cast insurrections placed the composer in triangulated mediation with the director.

Floyd asked his publisher to remove *Lost Eden, Theme and Variations* and *Nocturne* from their production schedule, in return for which the firm agreed to publish the orchestrated *Slow Dusk* as soon as he could deliver a score.[105] Lighter moments, likewise courtesy of Boosey & Hawkes, provided other relief. On April 8, the firm received a request for Floyd materials from a master's degree candidate at the Eastman School of Music, Robert Dowden, who was writing a musical and textual analysis of *Susannah*'s revival scene, the first but far from last such distinction accorded the thirty-two-year-old composer. Boosey's Sylvia Goldstein typed a note with Dowden's request, congratulating Floyd on falling up into the elite world of scholarship, alongside Stravinsky, Prokofiev, Copland, and Britten.[106]

Reverend and Mrs. Floyd, Ermine, and the minister's sister Doris drove to the Great Northern Hotel on the afternoon of April 8, by which time Floyd and Kay had checked in, leaving the Cooks to their necessary solitude. After storing the car and unpacking, Reverend and Mrs. Floyd saw the last two acts of dress rehearsal, and the whole family had supper at the Continental Tea Room.

On premiere day, April 9, Floyd delivered the family's tickets after supper, and everyone headed for City Center at 7:40. Reverend Floyd wrote, "The performance was wonderful, the applause was tremendous. . . . Many curtain calls, Carlisle received ovation."[107]

Bob Holton hosted opening night festivities with typical flamboyance at the Cub Room, the inner sanctum of the fabled Stork Club on East 53 Street. Founded by former bootlegger Sherman Billingsley, the site had fallen into decline since its heyday in the thirties and forties. Columnist Walter Winchell once described it as "New York's New Yorkiest Place,"[108] and it still exuded glamour, however faded. The Floyds rolled back to the Great Northern at one the next morning.

Reviews ran the gamut from heartening to devastating. Most critics gave the cast and production staff high marks, but composer Floyd learned that second New York premieres carried no guarantee of success. Paul Henry Lang, one of the city's most respected critics, was the kindest, recognizing that Floyd had kept the promise of *Susannah* and shown maturity. He thought Floyd an operatic natural, even if he was a "curious mix of the professional and the homegrown amateur," and had overlooked many dramatic opportunities; but he hailed the composer for eliminating folk elements from his vocabulary, for adding continuity, complexity, and a more modern tonal language while preserving his "almost Puccinian suavity."[109]

So far so good: Lang, famed for his magisterial *Music in Western Civilization* (1941), went on to praise Floyd's treatment of the solo voice in arias, but then disparaged his ensemble writing, deficiencies of color and balance in the orchestration, and his use of leitmotifs as somewhat "obvious and . . . too much according to the book."

What really brought the composer up short, after Lang's assertion that "from first to last the familiar story is handled in a manner that compels attention and strong sympathy," was the critic's conviction that "teaching in a provincial college" was "no place for an opera composer raring to go."

Howard Taubman offered neither analysis nor praise. Despite complimenting Floyd on his growth, demonstrated by his crafting of a powerful, straightforward libretto from Brontë's dense prose, Taubman's dominant opinion was that "Floyd's reach has exceeded his grasp."[110]

Despite a few mixed impressions, Miles Kastendieck noted that Floyd, despite continuing to struggle with the medium, had made a significant contribution. The opera's musical stridency and emotional intensity, he felt, underlined Brontë's obsessive drive, and translated "dramatic dialogue into sound which is woven out of . . . one fabric."[111]

As the family passed newspapers from hand to hand, the composer realized that his determination to strike out from *Susannah*'s more listener-friendly world had achieved at best a qualified success. Outdoors, rain poured all day. Everyone ate a lunch that Reverend Floyd found awful and scandalously expensive, and matters went from bad to worse. They went to the Cort Theatre to see Dory Schary's play *Sunrise at Campobello,* about President Franklin Roosevelt's struggle with polio at Warm Springs, Georgia. Their second-balcony seats, which Reverend Floyd as usual thought too costly, proved unsatisfactory, and the play itself irritated him, as "just another advertisement for the liquor interest."[112]

After an even more disastrous supper for seven wet, stressed travelers, misunderstanding arose over taxis back to the hotel. Floyd hailed one for Kay and his mother-in-law, and got in beside them, leaving Reverend Floyd to fend for his wife, sister Doris, and daughter Ermine. When the two carloads reassembled at the Great Northern, Reverend Floyd seized the moment to take his famous son down another peg. In front of the family's women, he began a classic rant: "I don't know how you can treat your mother that way," meaning that Floyd should have bundled all the women into the same taxi and accompanied his father home. When the composer observed that he had merely tried to care for Kay and Gundy, Reverend Floyd exploded, taking his son to task for rudeness, depicting Ida as the victim of neglect. Mrs. Floyd sprang up from the bed, burst into tears, and fled the room.

The composer, Kay, and Ermine, livid, retreated to Floyd's room. After a few minutes came the predictable knock: Reverend Floyd, penitent, swore that he'd never do anything to hurt his children. Ermine had none of it, spitting out, "That won't do!" Reverend Floyd burst into tears, and Floyd followed suit, submitting to his father's blubbering hugs. Though mortified to still be such an easy mark for his father's abuse, Floyd found himself consoling remorseful Jack.

The situation remained unresolved. Floyd's mother later told him that this was the worst thing that had ever happened in the family. Reverend Floyd always felt out of his element in New York, and taking that out on his son reclaimed a tiny strip of familiar ground. Ida was furious at herself and lacked words to express anger at the embarrassment her husband had caused her. Reverend Floyd's befuddlement, reflected in his *Diary,* offers proof positive of his unregenerate narcissism: "It was raining when we got out [of the play]—almost got wet again, but got back to hotel in taxi at 11:30—all in a stew. Prayed for God to control me and make me do right. Carlisle and Kay came in for a while."[113]

After handing his son $7.75 for their opera tickets, Reverend Floyd and his female entourage left the next morning in the frostiest of atmospheres, Ermine driving most of the way to Columbia in the rain. Reverend Floyd prayed not to be "such a pusher," and suffered through a week of asthma.[114] It is to Floyd's credit that he, on the other hand, breathed free, despite grim residues of the production and of his family, as he and Kay boarded a train for Florida later that day.

12

The Grand One

The Passion of Jonathan Wade, *1959–1962*

As train steel bore them back to Floyd's routine teaching, Kay displayed more anger than her pensive husband over the previous night's events. Floyd meanwhile wrestled with what ifs, prompted by Paul Henry Lang's conviction that he belonged in New York, not on a Florida college campus. Floyd wrote Boosey's David Adams that he had gotten past the "bugaboo" of a second New York opera, "and that, as a consequence, there will be no lost ground to be won back on the third one which is what . . . so often happens on second novels, Town Hall debuts, or what not."[1]

He fretted that City Opera's box office receipts might prevent Rudel from reviving *Wuthering Heights* that fall; and indeed, the three performances had drawn just 40 percent of capacity.[2] The situation only worsened as monthly journals weighed in over the next weeks. In his *New Yorker* column, Winthrop Sargeant rued his young hero's stumble. Though praising Floyd's libretto,

29. Floyd in studio, c. 1959. Courtesy of FSU College of Music, Dr. Don Gibson, Dean.

City Opera's cast and production, he found *Wuthering Heights* the antithesis of *Susannah:* "overcomplicated, full of self-conscious mannerisms, and apparently incapable of rising to the heights of lyricism that the story demands." Though he scolded Floyd for abandoning his southern roots, and prescribed the study of scores by Wagner, Puccini, even Menotti, Sargeant predicted that the thirty-two-year-old composer would proceed in more fruitful directions.[3]

Irving Kolodin's *Saturday Review* observations, though more encouraging in dispelling the notion that Floyd "might be a one-opera composer," also took issue with a lack of invention, variety, harmonic color, and contrapuntal technique in the music to keep the audience interested in his characters.[4]

Floyd had no way of knowing that his critics had yet to roll out their heavier-bore field pieces, but opera criticism, like contemplation of any manifestation of beauty, rests in the eye and ear of the beholder. Floyd had to wait for support from Robert Sabin in *Musical America;* and Sabin might as well have had a copy of Ronald Eyer's 1956 *Susannah* review at hand, or have been critiquing a different opera than his colleagues:

> Mr. Floyd has now found his own musical language; he has vastly increased his command of the orchestra and the devices of writing for the stage; and above all, he is inspired, he has something urgent to say. The work . . . took hold of the audience with the sort of hypnotic power that any successful operatic treatment of this wild, relentless, and fantastically penetrating novel must have. . . . Mr. Floyd follows the path of Richard Strauss and others in setting much of the dialogue in a flow of sung speech rather than the set pieces and formalized recitative of older opera. But, like Strauss, he continually broadens into lyricism. . . . Equally notable are the ensembles. . . . Here we see how far Mr. Floyd has developed as a contrapuntist and harmonist since *Susannah.*[5]

May 3 witnessed a veritable Carlisle Floyd Day at City Opera, despite the composer's absence. At the matinee of *Susannah,* Lee Venora sang the title role. Phyllis Curtin, *seeing* the opera for the first time, sat in the audience with composer Ned Rorem (his first *hearing* of the work); Rorem remarked that Curtin displayed obvious jealousy.[6] Though perhaps envious of Floyd's success at receiving notable commissions and performances, Rorem later gave eloquent testimony to his colleague's service to the profession: "I've seen most of Carlisle's operas . . . all of which I admire. In the main, nobody was writing operas until he did it, because they couldn't get them produced; but he more or less put opera back on the map, after Menotti paved the way."

In an attempt to lift Floyd's spirits, Bob Holton typed Floyd a note on May 4: "Last night's performance of *W.H.* was cheered and screamed! Act III really pulled together into the form you must have intended. It was great. Not a largish house—but truly a *standing ovation*! . . . Phyllis, Gene and I are pouncing on Julius [Rudel] to keep *W.H.* in repertoire. Cheers, Bob."[7]

Floyd had at least as great a horror of confrontation as his mother, but Kay insisted that he write his father a letter to get the figurative elephant off the roof and vent his outrage and frustration at the Great Northern fiasco. Floyd saw this incident as an encapsulation of the entire father-son relationship, but knew that it would take some time to order his thoughts, to purge himself of years of unexpressed fury.

At least one exciting new project sat on the horizon: on March 10, the Ford Foundation had announced a $130,000 program of grants to enable ten concert artists, nominated by a control group of 450 arts-affiliated experts, to commission new showcases for their instruments.[8] Performances with three different orchestras were guaranteed each pairing: Adele Addison/Lukas Foss, Leon Fleisher/Leon Kirchner, Joseph Fuchs/Walter Piston, Irene Jordan/Vittorio Giannini, Jacob Lateiner/Elliott Carter, Seymour Lipkin/Harold Shapero, William Masselos/Ben Weber, Michael Rabin/Paul Creston, and Leonard Rose/William Schuman.[9] Phyllis Curtin, the tenth nominee, knew that Floyd could use a push, rather than turning to any of the better-established creators with whom she had worked, like Copland or Rorem. Floyd received a letter dated March 6, from Ford's Joseph M. McDaniel, Jr., notifying him that he would receive $3,000,[10] with a possible added $1,000 for materials and extraction/copying of parts; $1,500 would arrive on receipt of Floyd's countersigned copy of the letter, and the final half on delivery of the finished product to Curtin and the foundation.[11] The first check, mailed on March 24, awaited Floyd's sorting of accumulated mail in Tallahassee.

The composer began scouring libraries for texts, wanting to write something specifically feminine and feminist. Kay sped to the rescue with a volume containing verses on motherhood by Chilean poet Gabriela Mistral, translated by Langston Hughes.[12] Knowing Curtin's devotion to family and her love of children—later that year she would be pregnant with her only child, Claudia Madeleine—Floyd looked no further. To avoid the complications of the copyrighted version by Hughes, he asked his bridge-playing friend Anita Fleet, a member of Florida State University's Spanish faculty, to translate a cohesive group of five items.

Mistral's 1950 collection *Poemas de las Madres* (The Mothers' Poems) provided the first four of Fleet's sources: "Me ha besado" (He has kissed me), a woman's meditation after conception; "La dulzura" (Gentleness), an address to the growing, sleeping child within; "Al esposo" (To my husband), a plea for understanding in late pregnancy; and "El amanecer" (At dawn), leading up to the actual moment of birth. The final poem, "Meciendo" (Rocking), the mother's lullaby to her child, came from Mistral's 1922 collection *Desolación* (Desolation).[13]

Though Floyd's take on organized religion lay somewhere between skeptical and hostile, he had always marveled at the awesome process of bringing new life into the world, and the new cycle's title came easily: *The Mystery.* Snatching what time he could from teaching at the end of the spring session, he began composing for Phyllis and orchestra.

It was also time to act on Kay's prompting to write his father. He asked Reverend Floyd how he would have felt in his son's shoes, at the age of thirty-two, humiliated before the family's important women. He reminded his father how often he had asserted, "However low you sink, I'll be there to pick you up": a lovely sentiment, rarely practiced. Floyd observed that the offer worked both ways. Reverend Floyd received the letter on May 6, and sent a terse response five days later, taking great issue with the picking-up comment. He told his son that his letter was "very hard," and signed it formally, "C. S. Floyd."

On June 3, while Floyd and Kay visited her mother in Jacksonville, Reverend Floyd attended a relative's funeral in that city. After dinner at Mrs. Reeder's house, the two men negotiated an uneasy truce, ending with the minister's declaration, "I'll never meddle in your business or try to run your life again."

ON JUNE 23, the Vocal Art Trio and Ottawa Chamber Players offered Canada's first *Slow Dusk.* At month's end, Floyd sent Curtin his volume of Mistral—Fleet had yet to complete her translations—to which the soprano responded, "We are both greatly moved by these poems. I have only the regret that we aren't Spanish speaking and setting the original language which I feel certain must be more musical than Mr. Hughes and English. . . . I feel confident that the few clumsy things will be more than compensated for by your enthusiasm for the poems."[14]

Julius Rudel already knew that he would not revive *Wuthering Heights* at City Opera. Box-office losses and even worse critical reception of another world premiere, Hugo Weisgall's setting of Pirandello's *Six Characters in Search of an Author,* mandated a season of crowd-pleasers like *Madama Butterfly, Die Fledermaus, The Mikado, La bohème, Carmen, The Merry Widow,* and *La traviata;* but as consolation to Floyd, Rudel muscled through a second *Wuthering Heights* production by that summer's Chautauqua Opera Association, of which he was music director. Curtin reported to Floyd of the new stage director, "I've had a few hours with John [Daggett] Howell. . . . He disagreed with certain of Del's [Mann's] ideas. . . . He is convinced that Cathy and Heath. have sexual relations after the hair down scene. He explained the calendar scene as partly motivated by the fact that that one time left Heath. wanting more, naturally, and Cathy bewildered, a little frightened & afraid of H's sexuality. . . . I don't believe things are much different if they *didn't* have sex. I don't think they did. The trouble with applying Freud to everything is that one applies 20th c. Freudianism to 19th c. isms and conventions and abnormal people & that is nonsense. . . . Well, *do* tell me. Did they or didn't they?"[15]

On June 30, Floyd visited Europe for a second time, for *Susannah*'s first German production at the Städtische Bühnen Oberhausen, a modest city of around two hundred thousand in West Germany's Rhine-Westphalian region, about twenty miles north of Düsseldorf.[16] The stage director Dr. Viktor Warsitz had also done the German performing translation, but local critics found little to like or even comprehend, especially Floyd's conservatism. Frankfurt's *Abendpost* thought *Susannah* "an operatic thriller," and Floyd's music "patched together from some old family recipe," with banal echoes of Puccini, Lehar and Menotti, divorced from the dramatic action.[17]

The *Düsseldorfer Nachrichten* sang a refrain that would plague most European Floyd productions, referring to *Susannah*'s music as "very loud massed-sound film music."[18] The *Hamburger Abendblatt* found the action naive and inadequately psychological, attributing the work's deficiencies to America's inexperience with opera. Floyd, as a university-trained musician, had demonstrated his familiarity with the European repertoire, and combined those traditions "with elements of Negro and folk music"; but "alongside our operas, it is sketchy, like a painted woodcut."[19]

FLOYD FARED BETTER at home that summer: The Cincinnati Summer Opera offered *Susannah* on July 10 and 14, with Rudel conducting and Dino Yannopoulis directing veterans Curtin, Treigle, and Cassilly. Gene Cook wrote that both houses had given Curtin standing ovations. Treigle's throat was inflamed on July 14, and he had cut one of his arias, but "Phyllis was at her best vocally . . . sounding rested and free-soaring as a lapwing."[20]

On July 30, Rudolf Firkušný finally got around to premiering Floyd's Sonata at that year's Vancouver Festival as an out-of-town tryout before its New York premiere. Floyd and Kay attended Chautauqua's *Wuthering Heights,* featuring City Opera regulars Curtin (Cathy), Grant Williams (Joseph), Patricia Neway (Nelly), John Druary (Hindley), and the Canadian baritone David Atkinson as Heathcliff.[21] Rudel also imported Giannini's *Taming of the Shrew.* Both operas sustained financial losses, and the press showed no change in its reception of Floyd's latest.

Patricia Neway rode back to New York with the Floyds, sounding them out for better ways to stay before the public than in City Opera *comprimaria* roles. She had made earlier impacts on Broadway in Menotti's *The Consul* and *Maria Golovin,* and longed to return to those venues in similarly unusual vehicles.

Floyd resumed teaching at FSU with a new composition colleague, Harold Schiffman.[22] As with John Boda, the relationship was friendly and respectful without intimacy, though Schiffman and his wife Manon were for a time reliable tennis partners/opponents.

On October 9, the Ford Foundation announced its latest juggernaut to promote higher American culture with a grant of $950,000 shared by the Metropolitan, Chicago Lyric, San Francisco, and New York City Opera companies for commissions for new works.[23]

Rudolf Firkušný gave his Carnegie Hall recital on October 13, with a program of Schubert, Schumann, Debussy, Martinů, Smetana, and the professional premiere of Floyd's Sonata. It was just as well that the composer was occupied in Tallahassee, as most critics found little to like. Harold C. Schonberg thought the music more calculated than inspired, lacking emotional resonance, and "even more difficult than it looks."[24]

Louis Biancolli, on the other hand, thought the sonata "complex and proclamative . . . forceful and individual in idiom," and likely to enter the repertoire alongside other major American works. He urged Floyd to make future contributions in this vein.[25]

By the time his column appeared in *The New Yorker,* Winthrop Sargeant had decided that Floyd's search for a "new musical vocabulary" was going less well than hoped. While complimenting Floyd's "genuine musical ideas," the critic felt a lack of "technical machinery," and looked forward to an integration of Floyd's new manner with the innate lyricism of *Susannah*.[26]

After Floyd's return to FSU, on October 16 new faculty member and soprano Charlotte Reinke included his Yeats "Fairy's Song" in her recital; the next evening, for Phi Mu Alpha's campus composers' concert, Reinke, accompanied by the composer, repeated the song, and added his Hart Crane "Old Song," as well as Cathy's aria, "Heathcliff has shattered my life," from *Wuthering Heights*.

The Metropolitan Opera Council sought Floyd out that fall to write a keynote article for the first issue of its *Central Opera Service Bulletin*. He contributed an "Apologia for Composers of Opera," in which he turned the tables on his critics, stating that America was still playing catch-up with Europe's centuries-old operatic culture. Quite naturally, he looked into the future when predicting that "an informed public will . . . be able to see our contemporary operatic strivings in historical perspective and will understand that many poor or mediocre efforts inevitably precede the final emergence of a great work."

He put his finger on how film and television were shaping audience demand for immediacy and close-up realism, compared with larger-than-life grand opera traditions. With a certain note of defiance, he and his colleagues were thus

> trying to evolve a new and workable aesthetic and rationale for opera in light of new learning in other disciplines and changes in attitude on the part of society. Consequently I think we, with ample justification, can expect a certain permissiveness and even encouragement from the music public while we are moving through our cultural adolescence to a proud time of musical maturity.[27]

Unbeknownst to Floyd, *Time* publisher James Linen III had nominated him for a United States Junior Chamber of Commerce (Jaycees) award, as one of the nation's ten outstanding young men for 1959. At the end of November's second week, word came that he had been selected, along with Hawaii Senator Daniel Inouye, Assistant United States Commissioner of Education Dr. Homer D. Babbidge Jr., *Newsweek* editor Osborn Elliott, and Dr. Harry Prystowsky, chairman of obstetrics and gynecology at the University of Florida. At the attendant press conference in Hartford, Connecticut, that January—awards were presented at the city's armory on the 16th—the composer declared that intellectuals might do well to descend and step away from their "ivory towers." His citation congratulated him, at thirty-three, for already having made memorable contributions to the "dauntingly rigorous" medium of opera.[28] Throughout the first months of 1960, Floyd reaped abundant praise for this award, receiving fulsome letters of congratulation from Vice President Richard M. Nixon and Florida Senator George A. Smathers.[29]

An intense focus on pregnancy and childbearing lay in the forefront of the composer's mind while working on *The Mystery*, and it rubbed salt into the wound of his and Kay's childlessness after more than two years of marriage and many fruitless visits to Tallahassee specialists. Dr. Prystowsky, whom Floyd had just met as a fellow Jaycees award winner, offered whatever help the University of Florida's Shands Clinic might provide, and the couple headed to Gainesville. After both submitted to every test available in 1960, the determination was made that Kay was one of that 2 percent of women between the ages of fifteen and forty-five—she was about to turn twenty-nine—with premature ovarian failure, and hence incapable of conception. Floyd, pragmatic about his own sense of loss, ached at Kay's despair: Would children have validated her compromised youth as an only child? Would her pursuit of so many intense enthusiasms, without consideration for the time or feelings of others, have allowed her time and inclination to focus on a child? When Floyd saw her nurture their cats, though, all such questions were blunted.

Though Ermine diligently provided four granddaughters, on a visit to the Columbia parsonage his father grilled Floyd about his and Kay's family plans, giving the questioning an accusatory twist. Floyd exploded, finding it easier to spring to Kay's defense than to his own: Was this not trying to run his life? Did his father have any comprehension of what Kay had been through over this?

NEW YORK CITY OPERA reprised *Susannah* in its abbreviated spring season—February 11 to 21—with Rudel conducting Curtin, Cassilly, and Treigle.[30] Critics marveled that the opera had appeared for five consecutive seasons. Gene Cook wrote Floyd that when Phyllis appeared for rehearsal, no choreographer had been engaged. To save money, the company had decided that chorus members could execute the square dance, rather than professional dancers. Rudel turned to the soprano and asked her to stage the dance: "And of course, she doesn't remember the dance, any one of the four or five she has done. She remembers her part vaguely, but never tried to memorize what everyone else was doing. And so last night [February 11] for precisely one hour she went over it with her stand-in, Helena Scott, doing the Susannah, and Phyl is calling the turns from the notes she had made in the score. . . . Great bit to have on her mind—the choreography—with all she has to sing. . . . Next week, I trust the Met will present [Zinka] Milanov in *Gioconda,* not only singing, but also choreographing the "Dance of the Hours," and dancing at least one hour, say 9 o'clock???"

In the same letter, Cook reported the anticipated birth of Norman Treigle's daughter, whom the bass named Phyllis Susannah Treigle, for his costar and Floyd's opera.[31]

In the meantime, Floyd put finishing touches on *The Mystery.* Though little in the settings has overt Latin American flavor, "He Has Kissed Me" flows, Andante, between 3/4, 4/4, and 5/4; but triplets, septuplet, and sextuplet flourishes and outbursts of "Ah" nonetheless honor Mistral's ethnicity. Floyd returned to his impressionistic polytonal, quartal/quintal style in a world without key signatures. An initial quiet cluster of G-sharp, A-natural, C-sharp, and D-sharp outlines both harmonic and melodic contours of the song's tonal world, with frequent shifts from sharps to naturals. "He Has Kissed Me" reflects the woman's wonder and exaltation at the discovery of her pregnancy.

The cycle's remaining four songs reinforce a sense of rocking and cradling, with triple meters of 6/8, 12/8, and syncopations of two-against-three. "Gentleness," according to Floyd, describes the wife's heightened awareness of the being growing within her, and her kinship with all childbearing women. The song relies on pedal tones on A, E-flat, E-natural, and F-natural, with an impassioned outburst in the accompaniment after the central word "mystery."

In "To My Husband," the loving woman asks her husband to treat her patiently and gently. The setting relies on quick syncopated off-beat pickups, and Floyd had no worry about giving Curtin a solid high B to express the woman's longing to give birth. The middle section in slowly syncopated 5/4 suggests the mother's heaviness, and ebbs away in a prayerful *Lento, molto sereno,* with a return to the original rhythmic figures, ending in quiet E Major.

"At Dawn" finds the woman actually *having* her child, quasi- delirious yet blissful to bring this new life into the world. Marked *Allegro deciso,* the song employs a restless dotted eighth-thirty- second figure and rolling sixteenth-note sextuplets in the accompaniment, to chords transposed from the original cluster to E-F-A-B, a vivid depiction of the mother's labor. Incorporating the signature flourishes in octuplets and septuplets, the woman summons the child about to be born, culminating in the actual moment of delivery on a high B-natural "Ah!"[32]

In "Rocking," the mother cradles her newborn, likening her action to the millions of similarly moving waves in the sea, the action of wind in fields of grain, and finally, God rocking his thousands of worlds in silence. Quarter-eighth and triplet figures in 6/8 and 5/8 introduce a gentle lullaby, building and broadening to 5/4 and 6/4, to a great outcry of triumph.

Experimenting with lighter instrumental colors and textures, Floyd wrote for an orchestra of strings, pairs of flutes, oboes, clarinets and bassoons, four horns, and pairs of trumpets and trombones. There is no tuba, but exotic accents sound from timpani, percussion, harp, and celesta. Curtin had her copy of *The Mystery* by the middle of February,[33] and Boosey acquired the work on March 3. Orchestration took another month, and Arnstein charged Floyd $977.62 for extracting parts, proofreading, and vocal scores. By mid-May, Floyd received his remaining $1,500, plus reimbursement for Arnstein's fees. Ford sent scores to the three conductors whose orchestras had contracted to play the work in the coming year: Victor Alessandro in San Antonio, who gave the world premiere on November 26, Leopold Stokowski in Houston,[34] and William Steinberg in Pittsburgh.[35]

By March, City Opera was in the second week of a tour, to nine northeastern and ten midwestern cities, of *Susannah* (nine performances), *The Ballad of Baby Doe* (twelve), *Six Characters in Search of an Author* (two), and *Street Scene* (seven), all underwritten by Ford grants. With Floyd tied down at FSU, Phyllis Curtin and Gene Cook kept him informed and titillated with day-to-day items from this odyssey, their letters hilarious exposés of life in the trenches of the operatic road. Cook, like Holton, delighted in entrepreneurship, taking an intense interest in everything Curtin did, and in the process becoming something of a stage father to Floyd, who soon realized that such strengths had their weaknesses. In the fury of new creation, though, it was essential that the composer have a sympathetic and intuitive ally in rehearsal or in the audience, when everyone from singers to stagehands triangulated Floyd in their interactions with administrators, usually over complaints.

The tour's Washington performances ignited a controversy with *Washington Star* critic Day Thorpe, who fulminated that Floyd's Southern dialect did not deserve Ford Foundation respect, much less support. Cook mounted a surreptitious counterattack with a sarcastic letter signed "John E. Walker," and even convinced Julius Rudel to write the newspaper a defensive statement.[36] As often happens, however, the critic had the final dissenting word, dismissing *Susannah* as "a good production of a dull opera."[37]

When Rudel complained of Cook's intrusions to Floyd, and the composer transmitted the conductor's dissatisfaction, Cook swore that he would henceforth act *con sordino*.[38]

FSU's new president, Robert Manning Strozier,[39] had earned a PhD from the University of Chicago in 1945, and insisted that Floyd travel to American opera's "second city" for the March 4 performance of *Susannah*. Floyd might have saved himself the trouble: in the *Chicago Tribune*, the notoriously viperish Claudia Cassidy thought *Susannah* "a small house libretto and a big house score."[40]

A second local critic, Don Henahan—in the days before he graduated to Donal—began a long and acrimonious relationship with Floyd, finding *Susannah*'s score "embarrassingly derivative," far from great opera, and not even particularly good.[41]

In the privacy of a Pullman car on the train back to Florida, Floyd, devastated by his latest press, declared that he wanted to disown everything he had written, especially *Susannah*, much less any future operas, and that he would reject any royalties from these performances. Kay calmly asked who would then receive this income. Her voice of reason may not always have offered the comfort Floyd craved, but it now snapped him back to reality, and the conversation turned to Ford's new program of subsidies to generate operas, City Opera being one of the four recently announced recipients.

As the train pulled them away from *Susannah*'s pans, the Floyds brainstormed new subjects. The composer had been intrigued by Robert Penn Warren's *All the King's Men* long before he had started writing operas,[42] but Kay posited a different kind of southern story: a high-principled Union officer in South Carolina during Reconstruction, caught between poles of love and duty in personal life and political currents. This notion swept the board clean: Floyd appreciated his wife's instinctual knowledge of what opera should be, more so than many librettists or composers, much less critics.

In the back of his mind lay a favorite author, Louis Bromfield, whose 1941 novel *Wild Is the River* told a kindred story:[43] Tom Bedloe, a Union officer serving in New Orleans as a collector of port revenues with the army of occupation, is a very un-Floydian ladies' man, seduced by the city and its people. Like Bedloe, the character Floyd developed sees both sides of most issues:

> He was aware of the resentment . . . which came from the injured pride of the conquered. . . . At heart he was a reformer, a builder, a colonizer, a creator. He wanted to change things, to alter them for the better.[44]

On more than one occasion, Bedloe does his gallant best to protect an elderly southern autocrat from persecution and prosecution; and Tom dies by shooting at book's end, the victim of a former lover. Many of Bromfield's characters, white and black, began to color Floyd's vision of Reconstruction, amplified by childhood memories of Bethune's Civil War veteran Gilliam King.

Floyd wrote the Cooks about the project, and Gene jokingly referred to it as "the war bride," before mentioning one of his many show business connections, Tom Ryan, an assistant to the film director Otto Preminger. Ryan thought that a new one-act play of Tennessee Williams, *Portrait of a Madonna,* might offer a promising operatic subject.[45] Ryan had earlier suggested Floyd to Preminger, to compose the score for the 1960 film *Exodus,* about Israel's founding, but, as Cook reported, that honor went to Ernest Gold after Preminger scoffed, "What does a southerner know about Hebraic music?"[46]

Phyllis Curtin, in Tennessee for *Susannah* with Treigle on April 12, wrote the Floyds, wittily cribbing the text of her most popular aria, "Here I am just being sure of which direction it is to Nashville, Asheville and Knoxville." Floyd still smarted from critical slaps at *Wuthering Heights,* and Kay had alarmed Phyllis by writing that her husband intended never writing another diatonic melody.

Curtin, while not budging from friendly empathy, summed up the strengths of *Wuthering Heights* more astutely than any critic: "You say the mass audience hasn't ears for it yet. . . . The . . . *audience* was always enthusiastic. *Critically* was where the trouble came. Actually, I found *W.H.* more melodic than *Susannah.* . . . The fact that *W.H.* was not repeated had no relation to its audience response . . . [and] Chautauqua is not what I'd call a listening audience . . . to consider them a test group would be a mistake."[47]

THE WORLD lost its chance to hear Mack Harrell fulfill his exclusive option on *Pilgrimage*'s premiere with the baritone's tragic early death in Dallas on January 29, 1960; but Floyd and Holton found an appropriate venue: the composer's alma mater, Syracuse University, with Norman Treigle as guest soloist with the University Symphony Orchestra, conducted by Louis Krasner. Floyd caught up with his mentor Ernst Bacon, still composer-in-residence there, and introduced Kay to a couple who had made such an impact on his life. Peggy Camp's years of living in close proximity to Bacon and his second wife Analee had bred anything but contempt, and she became the third Mrs. Bacon in 1952. Floyd learned that Peggy's mother had fulminated about paying so dearly for her daughter to go to Syracuse and wind up a dishwashing housewife, but the Bacons welcomed both Floyds when they arrived for the Syracuse festival. Peggy seemed to have matured, and adored Kay; but Floyd was shocked to hear her call her formidable husband "Ernie." Bacon seemed humanized by the marriage, and he invited Floyd, after almost twenty years of acquaintance, to call him by his given name.

On April 22, Floyd spent the day lecturing: on "Theory and Composition" at ten in the morning, "Opera in the United States" with Triegle at two, and "The Composer in America: His Art and Milieu" at four. The concert on April 24, dedicated to Mack Harrell, scored a great success, opening with Bacon's *Ford's Theatre, A Few Glimpses of Easter Week, 1865.*[48] *Pilgrimage* followed, with Floyd keenly aware of Treigle's comments about his middle and high voice writing, as the central three songs stressed the bass's upper resources.[49] Soprano Joan Aceto, a senior voice major, next joined Treigle in the twenty-six-minute concert suite of five scenes from *Susannah.*

The press gave Floyd much-needed reinforcement, calling *Pilgrimage* "inspired, colorful and emotional."[50] Elsewhere, Floyd's former professor William Fleming described *Pilgrimage*'s "inexorable . . . cumulative momentum," and "compelling power and pathos . . . obviously an outgrowth of deep personal feeling."[51]

Before leaving Syracuse, Floyd donated a copy of *Pilgrimage*'s manuscript to the university's library.

Floyd itched to work again. A Ford Foundation memo of a phone conversation between the program officer Edward F. D'Arms and Julius Rudel on April 28 confirmed that Rudel hoped to plug City Opera into Ford's new grant program and do the opera that Floyd had in mind for the fall of 1961.[52] D'Arms spoke with Floyd on April 29, and learned that the composer had completed a scenario that he would send to Rudel, set in early Reconstruction days following the Civil War, grander than anything he had written to date. Floyd believed that he could complete this by the fall of 1961 by devoting the next two summers to it.

Anxious to know from Rudel and Ford whether these hopes would materialize, Floyd needed to inform FSU of his availability to teach during those summers. His annual nine thousand dollar salary was not raised for 1960 and 1961, and not teaching summers would incur a loss of about two thousand dollars each year. This shortfall would require compensation, in addition to travel funds for New York consultations with Rudel and libretto research. Floyd also raised the issue of part extraction from the full score; but he had the impression that Rudel wanted the opera, with performance all but guaranteed.

Floyd wrote D'Arms on April 30 to clarify his financial needs: $3,000, to cover four months' leave of absence from FSU; between $2,500 and $3,000 for extraction of parts, duplication, and proofreading; $800 for travel to New York for meetings; and living expenses during the rehearsal period. He needed $200 for manuscript paper for vocal and orchestral scores. The total projected expenses were between $6,500 and $7,000. On May 15, Floyd informed D'Arms that Arnstein's copying of a full-length opera would add between $4,000 and $4,400 to this budget.

Meanwhile, Floyd supervised FSU's *Wuthering Heights,* directed by Richard Collins, conducted by Robert Sedore, and performed on May 13 and 14. He, Kay, and his South Carolina family took a quick break to attend the Spartanburg Music Festival's *Susannah* on May 6, and to be feted by local Jaycees as one of their previous year's Ten Outstanding. Driving around town, the Floyds were surprised to see that their home from 1932–1934 had been demolished.

Between May 4 and 15, Bob Holton kept in touch with D'Arms about final arrangements for the new opera, and payment for Arnstein's copying bill for *The Mystery.* On May 18, Rudel wrote the Ford Foundation arts and humanities director W. McNeil Lowry, who had entered Floyd's life in 1958, to formally request $4,500 to commission Floyd's new opera for City Opera, with the understanding that the company would pay Floyd's fee from their grant money.

Ford's Secretary Joseph McDaniel duly informed City Center of the foundation's approval on June 3, suggesting that the composer's payments be made in a minimum of two installments owing to the broad expanse of two summers. D'Arms passed this information to Floyd in a letter of June 7, and Ford sent a check for $4,500 to City Center's director, Newbold Morris, on the 20th.

FLOYD NEEDED to immerse himself in the post–Civil War period of Reconstruction and its personalities, but first had to complete two smaller but time-consuming projects. Bob Holton had arranged a commission from Brown University's glee club in Providence, Rhode Island. Its conductor Erich Kunzel had been impressed by *Susannah* and *Wuthering Heights,* which motivated him to seek a work by this rising composer.[53] Floyd selected Joseph Auslander's "Death Came Knocking," from the poet's 1924 collection *Sunrise Trumpets*—another prompt from Kay—and Boosey & Hawkes scurried to secure rights from publisher Harper.[54]

Auslander's copyright had been renewed in 1952, and Sylvia Goldstein informed Floyd on June 7 of Harper's terms: a fifty dollar advance against monies received from Floyd's publication and subsequent performances or recordings.[55] With some trepidation, Floyd agreed to the terms on his birthday, June 11. Along with advice to choose poems in the public domain in years to come, Goldstein assured him that the fifty dollar advance would be deducted from future royalties, so the entire commission fee of fifteen hundred dollars would be his without deductions.

Floyd's setting of Auslander's macabre vision of Death approaching in the night to claim his latest victim is unlike anything else in his catalog. In 3/4, *Allegro non troppo, ben marcato,* with an accompaniment based on pedal C at the piano's lowest octave, it imitates Death's knocks on several levels: ostinato Cs, a rolled triad of C-F#-G in high right-hand octaves for two introductory measures, then a syncopated thirty-second-eighth pattern that could be a heartbeat or a knock, appearing at irregular intervals throughout. Basses enter in bar twelve with an augmented variant of this last material, the "knocking" always accented, and the other voices enter fugally at two-bar intervals. Unrelieved dissonance, with Floyd's signature "stacked" harmonies, open fourths and fifths at phrase endings, and consistent, tight rhythms and harmonies converge in a terrifying portrait of Death everywhere: persistent, monomaniacal, patient.

For the work's premiere on April 5, 1961, at that year's national convention of the Canadian Music Educators Association at McGill University in Montreal, Floyd wrote the following program note:

> The poem . . . was chosen primarily because . . . it would afford me an almost perfect text from which to construct an arresting choral piece, unmistakably dramatic in concept. . . . I found the poem to be direct yet strongly evocative and . . . beautifully formed. The composer's job (as I believe to be the case with all good program music) was simply to match the various tension levels of Mr. Auslander's perfectly wrought structure and to heighten with music the atmosphere of anxiety, terror, and release from terror.[56]

With the premiere unreviewed, Kunzel wrote that he considered "Death Came Knocking" a most exciting and difficult work, requiring psychological preparation on the part of performers to properly interpret both words and music.[57]

Boosey printed the work in 1964, in editions for male chorus (TTBB) and mixed chorus (SATB). Holton also had Floyd craft his own orchestral suite from *Wuthering Heights* as a companion piece to the November premiere of *The Mystery* in San Antonio. The composer quickly assembled a twenty-two-minute symphonic poem from segments of the opening music, the love music of Cathy and Heathcliff, themes of the violent Hindley, the gentle, well-born Edgar and Isabella, and lifted intact the minuet and waltz from act 3. In his program note, the composer wrote that he intended the suite as a symphonically integrated work, logical, balanced, and above all suggestive of the desolate moorland of northern England, rather than as a potpourri of the opera's content.[58]

Before returning to the historical period of South Carolina's Reconstruction for his new opera, Floyd met the latest addition to FSU's star faculty, mezzo-soprano Elena Nikolaidi, who became a magnet for superior students, and Floyd's close personal friend and colleague. As her operatic career transitioned to concert work, Kuersteiner lured her to the university for an interview before she had ever taught a single voice lesson. On a sweltering August day, Floyd met Nikolaidi's flight at Tallahassee's old airport, another former military base. Following rounds of conversation and demonstration teaching, she revealed that she had booked a lengthy tour to Australia and the West Coast; but when Kuersteiner extended his offer, she nodded, "I think I'll try it."

In the course of the next seventeen years at FSU, and a subsequent decade at the University of Houston, "Niki" fell in love with her new calling. Until her retirement in 1994, she was a master teacher of singers like sopranos Jan Grissom, Erie Mills, and Linda Zoghby; mezzo-sopranos Denyce Graves, Suzanne Mentzer, Robynne Redmon, and Stella Zambalis; tenor Bruce Ford, baritone Richard Paul Fink; and bass-baritone Eric Halfvarson.[59] But pedagogy had its price: in 1994, Nikolaidi told Floyd of Kuersteiner's approach after students had complained to him of her inflexible standards and brutal honesty:

> KUERSTEINER. "Please don't scare the students."
> NIKOLAIDI. "I don't scare anybody. I just tell them they cannot be singers."
> KUERSTEINER. "You can't do that!"

NIKOLAIDI. "Dean, I cannot put in anybody's throat a voice. I am not a god."

For Niki, Floyd played recitals until the summer of 1974. Their first concert, on June 13, 1960, included Mozart's concert aria "Ch'io mi scordi di te," Schumann's *Frauenliebe und Leben,* a group of Greek folk song settings by Fauré, Ravel, and Spathy, and three Richard Strauss songs.

AT THE END OF APRIL 1960, Floyd sent Rudel a twenty-page handwritten synopsis of his new opera in three acts.[60] From childhood conversations with Bethune's Civil War veteran Gilliam King, Floyd recalled that enforced loyalty pledges had been a sticking point with proud southerners during Reconstruction. This in turn reminded the composer of the oaths that he and his colleagues had been forced to take during the McCarthy era, which prefigured *Susannah,* and he decided that the "ironclad oath" would occupy a central position in the opera; above all, honor, dignity, and independence became the core of the work.

The Union army of occupation viewed South Carolina as the cradle of insurrection after Charleston shore batteries—a Floyd ancestor possibly among them—fired on the Union's Fort Sumter on April 12, 1861. Much of Gilliam King's bitterness toward the Yankees concerned the intense damage that the state, particularly its capital, Columbia, sustained during Sherman's march to the sea in the last two months of 1864.

Following Robert E. Lee's surrender to Ulysses S. Grant at Appomattox Court House on April 9, 1865, and Lincoln's assassination less than a week later, the South found its economy in a shambles. Some northern politicians strove to ensure equal rights for former slaves, and supported Lincoln's plan to rebuild the South with federal monies; but the radical Republicans, a powerful Congressional subgroup, sought to punish the South for starting the war and believed that the free black vote would ensure permanent Republican dominance. The radicals in time swayed the party's moderate wing; they planned to remove anyone formerly associated with Confederate government from power and distribute the property of the wealthy to former slaves. Unified Republicans created the Freedmen's Bureau, intended to help blacks move from slavery to freedom with schools and labor laws, families reunited, and a guarantee of civil rights. At state and local levels, political appointees merely executed the policies of higher-ups.

Idealistic as its origins were, the program soon dissolved into a morass of corruption, and Union forces had to remain as occupiers. Military commanders were required to take orders from local Freedmen's Bureau officials rather than from their own superiors, creating obvious conflicts of interest; and into this poisoned swamp Floyd dropped his protagonist Jonathan Wade.

Just as racial equality took center stage in both Reconstruction and Floyd's tale of Jonathan Wade, the period between 1960 and the opera's 1962 premiere reinforced Floyd's agenda with daily reports of violence surrounding the civil rights movement, which was then centered in Mississippi and spread to all southern states, even Ohio, Illinois, Delaware, and Maryland's eastern shore.

The world witnessed the anything but peaceful desegregation of the University of Georgia and the University of Mississippi in October 1962, less than a month before the premiere of the new opera. President John Kennedy dispatched tens of thousands of national guardsmen and army soldiers to restore order. Freedom Riders attempting to desegregate interstate transport held sit-ins, while others held rallies and voter registration and literacy drives, seeking to abolish the separation of the races at drinking fountains, and in rest rooms, waiting rooms, and eating facilities. The Ku Klux Klan, often operating covertly and in concert as "night riders," met most of these actions with brutal reprisals, including lynching, and were frequently aided and abetted by local law enforcement officials.

Against this contemporary background, Floyd turned for his nineteenth-century research to the diaries of Mary Boykin Chesnut, born into a well-connected South Carolina political family in 1823 and married to the wealthy planter James Chesnut Jr., aide to the Confederacy's President Jefferson Davis and a brigadier general in the Confederate Army. Mary's diary from February 15, 1861 through August 2, 1865 focuses on her impressions of the war and its aftermath. Her descriptions of southern society, relationships, the duties of men and women, and the grim realities of slavery made her book a best-seller; it was published in 1905, 1949, and 1981.

Chesnut assigned a leading role to Wade Hampton III, a South Carolinian later familiar to every schoolchild, and the source of the Wade surname in Floyd's libretto.[61] On visits to his family in Columbia that August, Floyd stopped at the University of South Carolina library to research Hampton.[62] Though Floyd's Jonathan had different priorities and antecedents than the historical figure, Hampton's ethos suffused the eventual operatic character. When offered nomination as South Carolina's governor in 1865, Hampton declined, feeling that the northern victors would mistrust a former Confederate general in high political office. Throughout his service, he sought to tamp down extreme radical policies and promoted conciliation with freed blacks.

The Chesnut family patriarch and Mary Boykin's father-in-law, James Sr., was a colonel; and Floyd's title character's given name may have been inspired by the many Johns and Jonathans in four generations of Chesnuts. Mary's description of Colonel Chesnut found its way into Floyd's character Judge Townsend: "Partly patriarch, partly grand seigneur, this old man is of a species that we will see no more. . . . He is a splendid wreck. His manners are unequalled still, and underneath this smooth exterior—the grip of a tyrant whose will has never been crossed."[63]

Added to Floyd's personal memories of archetypes like Gilliam King, Chesnut gave the composer insights into many of his dramatic situations: the burning of Columbia, Union forces occupying and looting southern homes, black servants remaining faithful to former masters, the wreck of the South's economy and the attendant debts and tax consequences, despised political figures like President Andrew Johnson and Charles Sumner, and the enforcement of loyalty oaths.

Floyd's villain Lucas Wardlaw also appears in Chesnut's milieu, where he is "a lazy gentleman who will scarce move unless it be for a fight, a dance, or a fox hunt."[64]

Wardlaw, though it was the *given* name of a lovely parishioner of Reverend Floyd's from North's well-to-do Culler family, became another relic of the composer's years of anger and frustration in that town.[65] Even his first scene of impetuous love for Jonathan and Celia Townsend is suggested by a similar encounter in Chesnut;[66] and numerous Townsends lived in Latta, Spartanburg, Manning, Bethune, and North. Some of Floyd's character roles—J. Tertius Riddle and Enoch, later Ely Pratt—had onomatopoeic origins evoking a particular species of New Englander.

Subsequent visits to FSU's library produced other books that gave Floyd an even more solid historical framework for his epic tale: Hodding Carter's *The Angry Scar: The Story of Reconstruction;* James S. Pike's 1873 study of Reconstruction in South Carolina, *The Prostrate State;* and Harold M. Hyman's *Era of the Oath: Northern Loyalty Oaths during the Civil War and Reconstruction.*[67] Carter in particular detailed the radical Republican agenda, including the replacement of white judges and other officials with black counterparts, the Freedmen's Bureau, the Union League, the Ku Klux Klan, the selling of pardons, and the riotous behavior of black state legislators. Floyd's starchy character Ely Pratt seems a conflation of the historical General Oliver Otis Howard and the vindictive South Carolina preacher James W. Hunnicutt; and the pardon-seller Riddle has Franklin J. Moses as a historical prototype.

Also from Carter came the verbatim declaration, "Oh, I'm a good old rebel," which Floyd gave his three ne'er-do-wells in the episode dividing scenes 2 and 3 of act 1; the loyalty pledge Jonathan administers to a group of sandhillers and dirt farmers in act 2, scene 1;[68] and the Klan song, "Thodika, stevika!"[69] Even the name "Nicey" peered from between Carter's pages.[70]

IN THE WEEKS that saw America's initial descent into the maelstrom of Southeast Asia, Floyd's thoughts about his new tale reawakened pacifist leanings. The realities of World War II—Hitler ranting from the living room radio, uncles in harm's way, trains shuttling armless and legless soldiers back and forth, German prisoners of war at Fort Jackson, newsreels unveiling the Holocaust, his own brushes with induction—forever blasted away any illusion about war's glamour, and Floyd grounded his Reconstruction with antiwar sentiments. This forged an ironic new bond with Reverend Floyd, who shared with his son a horror of militarism and violence. In years to come, whenever the topic of ethical choices arose, Reverend Floyd invariably capped the discussion with, "Just like Jonathan Wade."

Floyd never set out to write a grand opera per se, but his new project grew into the incontestable result: three acts, eight scenes, and five episodes, or scenic interludes played before a scrim, to cover set changes while adding period flavor. Floyd's first draft libretto features nine principal roles, six *comprimari,* and an enormous choral and supernumerary component of emancipated blacks, Ku Klux Klansmen, Union and Confederate soldiers, people of Columbia, and party guests. This earliest sketch would have taken at least another hour to perform than any subsequent version, and served as a theme for later variation.[71]

In addition to his usual orchestra of paired and doubled flutes/piccolo, oboes/English horn, clarinets and bassoons, four horns, two trumpets, three trombones, tuba, timpani, harp, and strings, a rich percussion component reflects Floyd's experimentation in *The Mystery:* snare drum, cymbal, glockenspiel, xylophone, tambourine, gong, bass drum, wood block, and triangle. To match and enliven an apparatus of this size, the libretto employs all modes of operatic discourse: "Recitative, declamation, sung dialogue and the set piece, in which I include ensembles and solos. . . . I realized that because of its length I would have to calculate very carefully how each of these techniques was to be used . . . in order to achieve the maximum variety."[72]

Act 1 opens in May 1865 in the burned ruins of Columbia. The chorus intones a litany of the city's destruction, and a refrain states their status as survivors. Mood and content show the influence of Floyd's study of Verdi, in particular the chorus of Hebrew slaves from *Nabucco,* and that of the refugees in *Macbeth.* Northern victors herd Confederate prisoners onstage, and women seek sons, husbands, fathers. Judge Brooke Townsend (bass-baritone), accompanied by his daughter Celia (soprano), greets Union commander Colonel Jonathan Wade (baritone). Wade proclaims amnesty, moderation, and the preservation of southern honor. Townsend invites Wade to his home for a brandy.

The first episode juxtaposes Jonathan, a wounded Confederate (tenor) surveying the ruins of his formerly beautiful city, and a young black man (boy soprano) celebrating his freedom.

Scene 2 moves to the Townsend home interior. Proud Celia's initial hostility throws Jonathan into consternation, and he hotly maintains that the war has affected him as well. The two young people effect more than reconciliation: it has after all been many months since Jonathan has been this close to a young woman, and he and Celia melt into a passionate kiss and embrace. After promising to meet again soon, Jonathan leaves, and Celia sings of her conflict at feeling love for an enemy, which is dissolved by an awareness that they both have suffered.

Episode 2 focuses on the dark side of Reconstruction: the corrupt pardon-seller J. Tertius Riddle (bass-baritone) offends Judge Townsend by offering connections in Washington; and three dissolute young blades led by Lucas Wardlaw (tenor) mock Riddle with their rebellious song.

Scene 3 takes us back to a party at the Townsends'. The judge complains to Jonathan about pardon-selling and Washington's corrupt political establishment. When Jonathan defends the right of blacks to vote, Wardlaw scorns the illiteracy of the former slaves. Jonathan counters by comparing freed blacks to the region's ignorant sandhillers. Townsend toasts the discipline of Jonathan's men. The black servant Nicey (mezzo-soprano) answers a knock at the door and admits Ely Pratt (tenor), the Freedmen's Bureau commissioner, and his mousy wife, Amy (mezzo-soprano). Pratt defends his bureau and asks Nicey whether she prefers education to bondage. Incredulous and amused, Nicey explains that Townsend long ago taught her to write, that she's now too old to learn more, and that she has no notion of what bondage might mean: she has been free for more than two years. Pratt, offended by the resulting laughter, denounces the group and trumpets that the Yankees will crush rebellion in peace as in war. When Pratt asks Jonathan where he stands, the colonel reaffirms his priorities: compassionate justice and every citizen's freedom of choice; and he says that he is an officer, not a politician. The act ends in discord, with the late President Lincoln denounced as a lunatic by Pratt and as a tyrant by the southerners.

Act 2 begins a year later, in the spring of 1866, in Jonathan's barracks office, as he administers the loyalty oath to a group of sandhillers and merchants. Wardlaw sneers from the sidelines, complaining that he wants compensation for a vanished black tenant farmer. Jonathan advises him to treat his workers more fairly. Pratt complains that the Episcopalian rector omits prayer for the president from his services, and Jonathan agrees to investigate. When poor blacks gather outside in confusion over voting practices, Jonathan is about to advise them, but Pratt intervenes, claiming this as a bureau rather than a military matter. When Jonathan characterizes blacks as the true victims of Reconstruction, Wardlaw hints at Ku Klux Klan reprisals.

In the next episode, another rabble-rousing "hoaxer" (tenor) hawks bogus land certificates, promising forty acres and a mule to a group of blacks: the radical government will confiscate plantations and redistribute them in forty-acre plots to the freedmen.

Jonathan begins scene 2 by upbraiding the hoaxer. A courier (baritone) interrupts with an order from the military government. Jonathan summons Pratt: Judge Townsend, too proud to take the oath, is being replaced, and by a black judge. Pratt defends the order, threatening Jonathan with court-martial if he impedes its execution. Jonathan implores his conscience to sleep, but also to allow him to fulfill his duty as an officer. When he informs Townsend of the decision, the judge is outraged; Jonathan tells Celia the latest events, and she begs him to use his authority to effect a different solution. Grief stricken, Jonathan confesses that he loves Celia and has long wanted to ask for her hand. When she begs her father for his blessing, his implacability forces Celia to choose love for Jonathan over family loyalty. Townsend declares that he hopes to never see Celia or Jonathan again, and stalks off. Acting on their love, Jonathan decides that they be married on the spot, and sends for the rector: they confirm their independence by finding it in and with each other, come what may. Nicey consoles Celia, and goes off to the college gardens to gather roses for a bridal bouquet and a piece of mosquito netting from Jonathan's bed as a veil. The rector (bass) marries the couple, and Nicey's friends sing in counterpoint to a distant but ominous Ku Klux Klan song while the couple exchange impassioned vows.

Act 3 leaps forward three years to a late summer evening in 1869, Jonathan's quarters softened by Celia's domestic touches. Jonathan tells their young son a story, and cautions him about guns. Nicey, appalled by her visit to the legislature, describes the behavior of black and white participants alike, and predicts that the toxic combination of Radicals and carpetbaggers will one day leave blacks vulnerable to reprisals by low-minded whites. Amy and Ely Pratt arrive to invite the Wades to a Union League meeting, but Jonathan refuses. Pratt accuses him of obstructing Republican efforts because of his southern wife's influence. Celia lashes out, ridiculing the notion, and chides Pratt for his associations with a corrupt government. Pratt, suspecting that Jonathan will refuse to obey an order about to arrive from headquarters in Raleigh, enlists the sentry Patrick (tenor) to spy on Jonathan.

Scene 2 finds Jonathan at his desk later that evening. Patrick delivers the order for the confiscation of Judge Townsend's furniture to settle unpaid taxes. Jonathan knows that this will devastate and enrage Townsend, and tells Celia that his only options are court-martial or desertion. At the distant sounds of a Klan song, Jonathan sends the eavesdropping Patrick in pursuit of the outlaws. Jonathan chooses the lesser of several evils, desertion, in order to do the least harm: He plans to escape with Celia to the West Coast and thence to South America. They will leave that very night in a carriage they ask Nicey to arrange. Celia agrees reluctantly, wishing that they could have lived at any other time than the present.

The last episode shows a disheveled Townsend presiding over a commemorative tableau depicting states of the former Confederacy in progressive stages of the South's punishment. Townsend broadcasts his disillusion, relating how Union officers have removed bedroom furniture and his deceased wife's piano from his home, and his anger builds to threats of vengeance.

In the final scene, Jonathan asks Celia how this latest disaster could have struck without his knowledge: he is the only one who has seen the order, and he gave no command for its execution. Celia and Nicey have finished packing, and the carriage will arrive as soon as dark falls. Amy Pratt comes to warn them of the Klan's latest activities; but she is interrupted by the arrival of Patrick, who announces that three Klansmen, including the leader, have been captured. Jonathan orders their hoods removed, and their leader, Wardlaw, laughs defiance. The carriage arrives. Jonathan goes to the door at the sound of distant rebel yells. A shot rings out, and Jonathan staggers back into the room, clutching his chest. The room fills with more captured Klansmen and Union soldiers now led by Pratt. Celia calls for a doctor, but Jonathan dies in her arms. As Pratt ineffectually demands to know the perpetrator's identity, the broken Judge Townsend staggers in, carrying a smoking gun, muttering of Jonathan's betrayal and dishonor. Celia reveals that Jonathan was in the process of deserting to prevent the order of confiscation from being carried out. When Townsend tries to make amends, Celia tells her father calmly that she has never known him, and orders Patrick to take the old man away. Nicey places a widow's veil on Celia's head, and the room slowly empties, while Celia holds her son's tiny hand. Pratt assures her that Jonathan will be given a funeral befitting his rank and record. Celia remains in the empty room, kneeling by her husband's body, and tells her son that tomorrow they will leave this hateful place forever. She pulls the veil over her face, and stands in place, arms crossed over her chest, sobbing, as the curtain falls.

Besides expressing ethical and regional concerns, Floyd wanted to give City Opera a box-office success with a title to stimulate the public's imagination. This was the era of grand historical novels (and their eventual cinematic adaptations) that stirred the emotional pot, like Irving Stone's *Lust for Life* (1956) and *The Agony and the Ecstasy* (1961), about big artists with big personalities and big ethical concerns. Floyd, whose sympathies clothed his male protagonist like chain mail, chose *The Passion of Jonathan Wade*, its subject, treatment, and title further emblems of their time. He later stated:

> The word "passion" is used in its archaic sense of suffering and martyrdom, but Jonathan is more active than a Christ-figure. . . . I wanted to tell a story about a human being in an unconscionable situation. Jonathan is basically just a good and decent man. . . . My aim . . . was to create a libretto in which no one would know whether the author was Southern or Northern. And yet inevitably there is a certain amount of swaying towards the people who have been destroyed by the war. It's the only war we have ever had in which a . . . culture was destroyed, quite deliberately . . . [engendering] a perpetual feeling of victimization.[73]

In Floyd's theater we have already seen guns take center stage as instruments of destruction. As in *Susannah*, the fatal bullet for Wade flies from offstage, but the consequence is visible and visceral compared to Blitch's slaying. Despite Floyd and Fenegan origins as rural farmers, the influence of religion seems to have stigmatized guns on both sides of the family. It was considered a mark of honor, morality even, that doors were never locked: guns were unnecessary, even déclassé, to the Floyds. (The sole exception was the Ellerbe household in Latta; Frank ("Lord Chesterfield") hunted quail as a planter-class adjunct.) Floyd's childhood enjoyment of cap pistols and toy soldiers having long since faded, the composer was shocked to discover firearms owned by his in-laws, the Reeders. In widowhood, Gundy even had a license to carry a pistol, which she dubbed "Susie," in her car's glove compartment.

BY THE TIME fall classes began in 1960, a close circle of inquisitive, brainy friends had coalesced around the Floyds. A husband and wife duo-pianist team, Norma and Leonard ("Lenny") Mastrogiacomo had moved from New York to join the faculty of FSU, and the two men bonded at their first meeting. Lenny found Floyd "modest to a fault, a gracious southern gentleman. No matter where he goes, he fits in, people are drawn to him. I'd meet Carlisle in public markets, and he'd talk just as easily to the clerk as he did to the governor."[74]

When these newcomers learned that their furniture would arrive ten days late, they gratefully accepted the Floyds' invitation to share quarters on Redwood Drive until the vans pulled in. Lenny and Floyd agreed on technical points of pianism and pedagogy. Even though Lenny's new friend was also a distinguished opera composer with a national reputation, when the Mastrogiacomos' son Joel was born at three in the morning in 1962, it was Floyd and his old friend from Aspen days, Catherine Murphy, who sat with the nervous father at Tallahassee Memorial Hospital.

The Floyds discovered shared tastes and a sense of outrageous humor with a group that called itself The Four, or The Clique: the Mastrogiacomos; Alabaman William (Bill) Rogers, a specialist in southern history, and his wife, Miriam; and New Orleans native and nuclear chemist Gregory (Gregg) Choppin and his wife, Anne. Elena Nikolaidi and Catherine Murphy, together or separately, often joined the lively symmetry of the four couples. Movie nights proved great favorites, and subsequent hours of enthusiastic analysis. The Floyds hooked Lenny on tennis, and with Kay's friend Nelda Kittle joined the Rogerses and Choppins for mixed doubles. With Kay's new cooking skills, the Floyds gave legendary New Year's Eve parties. At regular gourmet feasts at rotating houses, games included bridge, poker, Clue, and especially Monopoly. Lenny usually won, but everyone felt the joy of reviving pastimes that had brightened their childhoods. The group attended FSU football games together, dressed for the occasion in their Sunday best. Catherine Murphy, who knew next to nothing about the sport, invariably appeared with just-styled hair, and off they'd go to Campbell Stadium, hilarity and high spirits reigning. The only qualifications for inclusion in this brain trust were an utter lack of pretension or stuffiness, and an ability to laugh at life's absurdities; that everyone shared liberal political views formed an added bond.

Lenny echoed other observers on the Floyds as a couple: "Carlisle adored Kay, it was very apparent. Not what you usually think of between husband and wife; but there was a great respect."[75] Above all, the clique gave Floyd a much-needed balance to his solitary hours of work, and, for Kay, compensation for her husband's prolonged unavailability. During the first years of their marriage, the first thing to go was socializing with students, but his campus studio became the center for private discussions of professional and personal matters with students. Floyd's studio gained added sparkle that fall with the addition of a student from Jasper, Alabama, Polly Dean Holliday, who remained close to her teacher, despite a career switch from music to acting after just two semesters at FSU.[76] Floyd translated his experience with Aspen's master classes into a weekly event in Tallahassee, as pianists from other studios began to attend a forum anything but cosmetic: Floyd guided young minds and ears in their discovery of new means of verbalizing what they heard.

LESS THAN THREE WEEKS after John F. Kennedy's election to the presidency, on November 26, 1960, Floyd found himself in Texas, as Phyllis Curtin and the San Antonio Symphony, conducted by Victor Alessandro, gave the world premieres of *The Mystery* and the *Wuthering Heights* Suite. Local press thought this "an event of considerable importance in the history of American music";[77] *The Mystery* won a standing ovation; the reviewer wished, after the Suite, to hear the complete opera in its proper context. Another critic approached the poetic in describing the "clean lines and astringent harmonies" of *The Mystery*, Floyd's capture of deep feeling, and the Suite's evocation of the "harrowing novel."[78]

Floyd could not attend the other performances of his new cycle,[79] but Curtin sang it in Pittsburgh on December 29 and 31, conducted by William Steinberg, and in Houston on February 19 and 20, 1962, under Barbirolli. When Curtin arrived in the first city for orchestra rehearsal, she learned that Steinberg had programmed *The Mystery* as a kind of curtain-raiser to Mahler's gigantic Symphony no. 7. When she asked the conductor whether he wanted everyone to forget Floyd's piece, Steinberg seemed irritated at having agreed to participate in the project, snarling, "This piece was old-fashioned when I was in knee pants."[80] The *Christian Science Monitor* begged to differ, finding Floyd's settings "logical, imaginative, inspiring and communicative."[81]

Amid rumors that City Opera might not have a 1961 spring season, the *Times* reported that things were not as bad as they seemed. Thanks to the Ford Foundation—City Opera had had Floyd's first $4,500 in its coffers since the previous June—the commissioning of two new works was now formally announced. Rudel hoped that at least one would be ready in time for next fall's season; and the first, by the librettist Bernard Stambler and the composer Robert Ward, made that deadline: *The Crucible*, based on Arthur Miller's 1953 play about witch hunts, opened in October 1961. Floyd's commission, still nameless as far as the general public was concerned, would center on "conflicts of allegiance" during Reconstruction.[82]

Early that winter, Bob Holton played a tape of the San Antonio *Mystery* for Patricia Neway, and she approached Floyd with a request to write something for her with beautiful sonorities similar to those he had given Curtin. Neway, famed for her histrionic abilities, still dreamed of returning to Broadway by renting an intimate theater seating no more than a thousand. Emulating the late Ruth Draper, who wrote and delivered entire programs of character-driven monologues and monodramas in similar venues,[83] Neway hoped to add the twist of sung monologues.[84] Floyd agreed, and wrote his own text, set in a deep, sunlit wood in midsummer.[85] A young pregnant girl in her late teens runs onstage and falls to her knees in the grass, crying bitterly to God to destroy the life growing within her. The lover for whom she professes hatred and disgust—Floyd gave him tattoos to indicate his lower social class—has deserted her, and her family has rejected her for disgracing them. Pounding the ground with her fists, her despair turns to nostalgia at the scents of jasmine and honeysuckle: she remembers lovemaking on this spot with her coarse wooer four months earlier. When the child stirs within her, her face turns luminous. She proclaims love for the unborn being, prays that the baby ripen within like darkening corn-tassels, and vows that she will strive to be worthy of both her child and its birth.

Aside from its relevance to the Floyds' personal drama of childlessness and *The Mystery*, this subject and Floyd's treatment have much in common with Richard Dehmel's 1896 poem *Verklärte Nacht* (Transfigured Night), appropriated by Schoenberg as a program for his like-named *String Sextet* of 1899 and expanded in 1917 for full string orchestra: A young woman and her sweetheart walk through a moonlit forest, she shamed, pregnant by another man. After receiving his text back with Neway's annotations and suggestions in the margins, Floyd completed a thirty-two-page setting, in much the same jagged polytonal idiom as *Wuthering Heights*. Repeated devices of trills, running sixteenths, and dotted eighth-sixteenth, or, conversely, sixteenth-dotted eighth rhythms, depict the girl's agitation; Floyd set a phantom tonic center of G minor disguised by frequent melodic and harmonic tritones and harmonic minor scale fragments. He had second thoughts about the middle section's lyricism and added lines to heighten the girl's disgust at her present situation and memories, the scent of jasmine identified with desertion. Nowhere do melody or harmonic underpinning relax into repose, much less pleasure, and even her final triumphant outcries are for a love-child.

Bob Holton adored the whole idea, and discussions between him, the composer, and Neway had advanced enough by February 1961 to specify orchestration: string quartet plus string bass, woodwind quintet (flute, oboe, clarinet, bassoon, horn), piano, and a single part for timpani and other percussion;[86] Neway agreed to pay for part extraction. When Floyd sent his manuscript to Holton that September, the publisher filed it away as "Neway's Dream," a tongue-in-cheek reference to the concert aria for Phyllis Curtin that became *Wuthering Heights*.

As it turned out, Neway's project never materialized, and Floyd grew disenchanted with what he had written in haste; but this was just so much spilled ink as he pressed on with *Jonathan Wade*, which he came to think of as "my *Don Carlo*." Like Verdi's 1867 masterpiece of political intrigue and emotional crisis, Floyd's opera demanded grander clothing of words and music than anything he had written.

His and Kay's two-day Columbia visit at the end of February, with their latest cat, Heathcliff, would be the only time he saw his family for the rest of 1961; and that trip had been motivated by an all-Floyd program at the Columbia Art Museum on March 1. A group of local singers performed *Slow Dusk* and *Susannah*'s two arias; and Mme. Gertrude Tremblay-Baker played his Sonata. During family meals on this quick visit, Reverend Floyd pried as usual about Carlisle's and Kay's religious views. The day after they left, he speculated in his diary, "Maybe Carlisle and Kay are right and the Bible is wrong—who knows."[87]

With Floyd back in Tallahassee drafting the libretto for *Jonathan Wade,* letters and even phone calls to family dwindled to a trickle, yet he always managed to steal time for Elena Nikolaidi. In mid-April, the mezzo was invited to sing for one of Elsa Maxwell's legendary parties, for the high society of Mobile, Alabama.[88] She and Floyd drove over, and he accompanied her in "Mon coeur s'ouvre à ta voix" from Saint-Saëns's *Samson et Dalila,* a Greek shepherd's song, and "Una voce poco fa" from Rossini's *Il barbiere di Siviglia.* They made quite a splash in the local press: when questioned about having never sung any of Floyd's operas, Nikolaidi quipped that, because he wrote opera in English, he must want only native speakers.[89] Floyd had his own bon mot for Maxwell: opera is never a concert; if it tries to be, it has no place in the opera house.[90] Three days later, the *Press* ran a long feature article that characterized Floyd as a young "businessman type" and "no-punches talker," and articulated his thoughts about the potential of opera to be wide-open, flexible art.[91] When the reporter asked whether opera composers had the same opening night jitters as others, Floyd replied that he still got edgy: At least pianists have the material in their hands at recitals, but so much in opera depends on others.[92]

VARIATIONS ON THIS THEME also colored Floyd's thoughts on teaching the utterly dissimilar disciplines of piano and composition. Like the cycles of pregnancy and childbirth that so awed him, music posed no less a puzzle; but all these forms and processes shared a sense of divine order. Floyd, having once taught pianists scarcely older than he, now began teaching composition from a base of four complete operas and a respectable quantity of songs and abstract music. Yet the nature of musical ability impressed him as the heart of a Churchillian enigma-wrapped mystery: Every musical gift teeters on a razor's edge between endowment and application; but the pianist's or singer's core talent can be molded, extended, focused. Floyd's pianistic experiences with Ernst Bacon and Sidney Foster served as perfect examples, and to the present day he professes to know more about teaching piano than anything else.

Composition posed quite a different ball of silly putty: For reasons already suggested, Floyd never resisted his gift of taking dictation from a mysterious internal source. He saw keenly that a student who wanted to compose either had the instinct or did not. Ryan Edwards did, most others did not.

Once Floyd determined levels of ability and instinct, his teaching might work on very primitive levels to get results: Can we agree that what's wanted is a happy tune? What does this suggest in terms of tempo? Slow? Fast? Medium? What about pitch? The most gifted students came to him with materials to make their points; however, although Floyd's methods could not guarantee results, students with more modest instincts might be impressively engaged. As with all teaching, he had to trigger basic thought processes that led to wider vistas; but some gifts may have lain undeveloped, or been abandoned or bred out. Still, why choose this particular meter or tempo, for this particular movement or scene? What is the student trying to convey here, or further dramatically, in purely *musical* terms?

Three student composers, two from the sixties and one a decade later, offer good examples of the nuts-and-bolts techniques Floyd developed to implement the intangible. The first, Carl Vollrath, a music education major, worked with Floyd in 1963 and beyond on a young peoples' opera, *The Quest.* Vollrath remembered Floyd as unfailingly cordial, friendly, professional, and impeccable in dress: "It was a very particular style. I don't mean overdone; but he always had a jacket, a wonderful shirt with the right color tie, everything like that."[93]

Floyd first addressed the essence of Vollrath's project by cautioning the student that future performances would be unlikely, as professional opera companies tend to shy away from children's choirs or amateurs of any kind. With that behind them, they began, as Floyd himself did, with the libretto. Vollrath spent the better part of a year ferreting out literature for adolescents, with disappointing results; then one day in a bookstore he happened on a volume about the Children's Crusade of 1212, and knew that he'd found his subject. Floyd next urged the creation of an antagonist: Vollrath had a story, but no plot; once he made his youthful protagonist's father the dramatic obstacle, the rest fell into place.

The next hurdle came in deciding whether to write a children's opera or an adult opera with children in the cast. Vollrath wrote tuneful music that children could learn and sing, and Floyd said, "You are not going to be able to keep that up for very long," that is, Vollrath should beware the librettist's and composer's greatest sin, boredom. Floyd urged his student not to write a junior-high opera for a junior-high band: "Don't keep it so simple that you limit what you can say."

Their work had just begun when Vollrath came to him with a line about money. Floyd pointed out that he was writing about the Middle Ages and needed something more evocative: gold or silver, perhaps; musical ideas depended on the right choice of words. When Vollrath proposed a two-minute dance sequence, Floyd cautioned that two minutes in stage time might as well be two hours in an operatic frame; if he really needed dance, fine, but keep it short. Vollrath learned, as had Floyd, that teaching composition had an oxymoronic essence. Much of their work involved observation: "This is good; but you can make this a little better over here." The real miracle to which Floyd led him consisted of a musical theme capable of development throughout the entire opera.

The Quest had two performances in June 1966, and after Vollrath accepted a teaching position at Troy University, he stayed in touch with Floyd. When a former friend spread rumors that Floyd had himself written the piece, Vollrath learned that his teacher had completely debunked the charge by saying that he had only pointed the way to a few ideas.

In 1961, Ellen Taaffe, a young violinist studying composition in the years before she married the violinist Joseph Zwilich,[94] learned that her regular professor, John Boda, would not be teaching summer school and she enrolled in Floyd's master class. Zwilich describes herself at the time as "unformed, very immature; I didn't get myself together until my thirties."[95] Yet she found Floyd's methods complementary to Boda's: in an intimate but informal group, each student could learn as much from discussion of one another's work as from their own. Most important for Zwilich was Floyd's insistence on organic musical development. She had immersed herself in the philosophy of Alfred North Whitehead, who, years before the discovery of the double helix structure of DNA, used the analogy of the acorn as oak-seed, and the concept of all of earth's systems as interrelated parts of an organic whole. Thus Floyd exerted a profound influence, however brief, by relating Whitehead's concepts as key to this student's musical lock. Zwilich dates her maturing focus from this period, as well as the trademark clarity and logic of her compositional textures and structures, which reflected another Whitehead *dictum*, "Art is the imposing of a pattern on experience, and our aesthetic enjoyment is recognition of the pattern."[96]

Rick Brown's work with Floyd took parts of three years that led to a master's degree.[97] Having decided that he wanted to compose, but having no background in the discipline, and minimal keyboard facility, he registered for summer school in 1971 and was assigned to Floyd, the only faculty composer teaching that session. As he seemed to reap a preponderance of criticism over praise, Brown felt that he never impressed Floyd; but his teacher's patience and attention to detail floored him. Unfailingly tactful, Floyd never pulled punches: here's what's wrong and here's how you fix it. One of his most frequent observations was that Brown abandoned good ideas without proper development, that he could extend a fruitful two-line idea into three pages.

One of Brown's favorite efforts was a florid polyphonic choral piece; but Floyd isolated a pattern of four repeated notes far stronger as thematic material than all of Brown's other "noodling." Something clicked: Brown, better at exposition than development, found resemblances between his motive and the famous opening of Beethoven's Fifth Symphony, realizing its potential for expansion and variation. Like most Floyd students, pianists, and composers, Brown pinpointed his teacher's greatest strength as "zeroing in on whatever was weak."

Floyd had discovered that all musical talent demonstrates elasticity when provoked by thought. The process and its tools often reduced themselves to pure intellect, by turns exhausting or exhilarating; but the more light Floyd could shed by stimulating consciousness, the more fluent the student became. From his own work, Floyd knew that getting stuck meant that he was working without adequate emotional content, living in a vacuum, light years from any connection to opera. The fact remained: dull, undeveloped, or ignored emotional receptors never suggest living music.

AS THE CALENDAR TURNED TO MAY, and Allen Shepherd became the first American in space, Floyd's *Wuthering Heights* was in rehearsal for its Chicago premiere on May 15 and 16. In a production sponsored by the Musicians' Club of Women, at the city's Eleventh Street Theatre, the cast of young singers included twenty-six-year-old Sherrill Milnes as Heathcliff.

In New York, the day after his thirty-fifth birthday, Floyd signed a five-year renewal of his contract with Boosey & Hawkes, guaranteeing him most of the same royalties and percentages for the sale of sheet music and mechanicals; but three short pages from 1956 swelled to eight long ones, with a plethora of "whereases," "wherefores," and "therefores." Boosey knew that they had a winner in Floyd, and added language covering the use of his music in films or television. A few percentages dropped: 25 percent of rental fees instead of the original 33 1/3 percent, and 50 percent for grand rights, down from 66 2/3 percent. Another substantial difference, in light of the two suites crafted from existing material, lay in Boosey's acquisition of the right, subject to Floyd's consent, to make changes, editions, translations, and arrangements of both existing and new works; and that if Floyd wished to make any changes to existing printed scores, that is, revised editions, it would be done at his expense. To relieve Professor Floyd's chronically empty pockets, the publisher contracted to advance him $1,250 each year—more than $9,110 by 2010 standards—against royalties collected. The new agreement extended until December 31, 1966, renewable after that date by mutual consent.

Floyd's other 1961 birthday gifts were the appearance of the vocal score of *Wuthering Heights* with another handsome cover by Evon Streetman; and finalizing the contract to write, compose, and score *The Passion of Jonathan Wade* for City Opera, Rudel urging its completion by spring 1962.[98] Released by terms of his Ford Foundation agreement from teaching FSU summer sessions, Floyd completed his grand tapestry of words in sunrise-to-midnight marathons. At the end of June, he finally told his parents of the new project,[99] work on which erased the usual South Carolina holiday visits this year. By Christmas he had sent Curtin and Gene Cook his libretto, and the soprano tugged at the reins to learn whether Rudel planned to cast her as Celia.[100] Floyd lost no time beginning composition, and the work helped to blunt the news of his grandfather Oscar Fenegan's death on January 30; he did not attend the funeral two days later. Oscar was laid to rest in the cemetery he had so lovingly tended, beside his Mrs. Kate and their beloved son James.

Death touched Floyd again when he read in the newspaper that Hazel Richards's husband Harold had died in a fire at their beach house in Carrabelle, under conditions suggesting suicide. The composer and Kay remained estranged from his difficult patroness; but Hazel kept in touch with Reverend and Mrs. Floyd, bombarding them with invitations to the new house she was building on Old Plank Road: anything to keep a tie to her beloved protégé.

Floyd's work on *Jonathan Wade* had progressed far enough as winter gave way to spring 1962 to undertake two new ventures. Venerable choral conductor Hugh Ross, director of the New York Schola Cantorum,[101] approached Bob Holton with a request that Floyd revise *Pilgrimage* for full chorus and solo baritone, and the composer found it easy and grateful work, alternating unison and four-part writing in the most dramatic sections of the first and third movements. Chorus alone declaimed the ebullient fourth song, "Praise the Lord, O My Soul," with *divisi* parts for altos and basses, and the soloist returned for the final affirmations of the fifth movement, "For I Am Persuaded." The refurbished work, with baritone McHenry Boatwright, premiered on March 27, 1962 on a program with Brahms's German Requiem and excerpts from Schumann's *Paradise and the Peri.* Paul Henry Lang slammed Floyd as "self-made," and his orchestra as speaking "the equivalent of basic English."[102]

Miles Kastendieck, though he too found *Pilgrimage* dated, thought the work interesting enough to wish for a second hearing, and confirmed that Floyd knew how to fuse words with meaning.[103]

NORMAN TREIGLE was playing impresario with his hometown company, the New Orleans Opera, which had scheduled its first *Susannah* for that spring. When the bass asked Floyd in the summer of 1961 to direct, he demurred, thinking the requisite skills too far outside his ken; but Treigle insisted: an opera director's most important assets were knowledge of and sensitivity to the music, and who better than the composer to further both? Sandwiched into his *Jonathan Wade* research and libretto writing, Floyd read as much as he could about directing, especially on general principles of how to dress the stage. Fresh perspective allowed him to see the chorus as the true antagonist of the work; both Susannah and Olin Blitch were destroyed by it. He accepted that his greatest task in New Orleans would be acquainting the chorus with their essential role in the drama.[104]

Encouraged that his maiden directorial voyage would be crewed by Treigle, Curtin, and Cassilly, Floyd arrived in New Orleans for rehearsals in mid-March. The performances on March 29 and 31, conducted by Knud Anderson,[105] took this bastion of traditional opera by surprise. The first act produced reactions of cautious pleasure, but "the dramatic impact of the steadily mounting tension of the second act" prompted "cheers and thunderous applause. . . . *Susannah* is . . . music-drama in the Wagnerian sense with American mountain accent," and Floyd won plaudits for his staging.[106]

A second critic considered that the company had made history by presenting contemporary opera in New Orleans. Though he sniffed at a homegrown opera by a university teacher, he conceded that *Susannah* was "artfully conceived and theatrically effective."[107]

The principal singers all reaped praise, and Treigle's wheels began turning on other initiatives involving Floyd. New Orleans remained a very small town in this regard, and Treigle approached the opera's board, asserting that he could deliver a new opera by Floyd, with himself in the leading role, subject and dates to be determined.

On April 15, Floyd and Kay took a train to New York—she usually refused to fly—for City Opera meetings. Reverend and Mrs. Floyd seized their only opportunity for a visit, their first since March of the previous year, by dropping in at the Seaboard depot in Columbia, where the four chatted between trains; it would be another six months before they saw their famous son again.

Gene Cook had recommended to Rudel a brilliant young designer, Will Steven Armstrong, born in New Orleans. Just four years younger than Floyd, a graduate of Louisiana State and Yale, Armstrong came to New York in 1957 as assistant to Jo Mielziner, Donald Oenslager, and Boris Aronson. Floyd may have met him in 1958 at the Brussels World's Fair, where Armstrong designed the color television studio at the American Pavilion; and his designs for Bob Merrill's and Michael Stewart's *Carnival* had just appeared on Broadway.[108] Rudel hired Ruth Morley to design costumes for *Jonathan Wade,* and Allen Fletcher to direct.[109] After reading the libretto, Fletcher's only comment to Floyd was, "I can't tell whether these people are men or women." At least Armstrong gave the composer everything he could wish for in a scenic frame.

In Tallahassee, Floyd was chained to his studio piano, composing, then scoring, when not teaching a full load of young pianists and composers, and attending evening student and faculty recitals, many featuring excerpts from his operas. At Phi Mu Alpha Sinfonia's American composers concert on April 28, Hedi Svendsen and Joy Davidson sang the Cathy-Nelly duet from *Wuthering Heights.*

At home after supper there would be none of the accustomed reading, listening to music, or watching television or movies, and Floyd left Kay to her own devices far into the night.

A libretto draft serves only as template for what appears in a final score; but Floyd's changes to *Jonathan Wade* ranged from cosmetic to sweeping away about one-third of the overall length, mostly repetition or overexplanation, and alteration of many details of plot and character. In early exchanges between various citizens and Townsend, Floyd changed the judge's given name from Brooks to Gibbes. He trimmed the first scene's cast to a single girl (soprano) awaiting her brother's return, and inserted a brief reprise of the opening chorus. He made ruthless cuts in Jonathan's speeches to Townsend and Celia, and halved Townsend's explanation of Celia's hostility.

He then truncated Townsend's and Celia's listing of war calamities in scene 2, while devising Jonathan's new introduction to Nicey, adding an actual laugh line when that family retainer observes that the colonel approximated a human personage with the exception of his Yankee uniform. The thawing and courtship between Jonathan and Celia was halved, and Celia's subsequent aria shortened by a quarter.

In the episode of pardon-selling, Floyd cut enough to add another verse of Riddle's bouncy spiel; and, in scene 3, he curtailed Townsend's rant against such abuses and the wrangling between Jonathan and Wardlaw. As they altered over the years, several of the opera's moments seem to have plagued or intrigued Floyd, such as Pratt's sermonizing at the Townsend party.

At any rate, only half of this found its way into music. The final moments of act 1 underwent similar transformation; Floyd gave a more dignified tone to the guests' defiance of Pratt, and new *obbligato* solo writing for Celia, Amy Pratt, Jonathan, and Townsend.

In act 2, scene 1, Floyd realized that he could profit by raising his curtain on the latter half of Jonathan's administration of the loyalty oath, focusing on the emancipation of former slaves. Following the confrontation with Wardlaw, about half of the talk with Pratt hit the cutting-room floor. Celia's appearance to take the oath is never realized in any version; but several large text abridgements were replaced with a new focus on her father's perceptions of her growing relationship with Jonathan. Minor nips and tucks dot the remainder of the scene, until Lieutenant Patrick delivers the denial of Jonathan's appeal against Townsend's replacement. Floyd moved the greater part of the ensuing and much-cut discussion between Jonathan and Pratt to act 3, scene 1. Once Townsend is summoned, accompanied by Celia, Floyd had Jonathan personally inform him of his replacement; he halved and rewrote most of the confrontation, arriving much sooner at Celia's taking sides with Jonathan, and their wedding ceremony. In the process, he telescoped several pages—most of the deliberation about flowers for the bride and Nicey caring for the Judge—into a few short lines; and then sharpened the postwedding duet by eliminating at least half of the ensuing dialogue between Celia and Jonathan, getting far more efficiently to the dramatic counterpoint between Nicey's spiritual and the Ku Klux Klan song, and keeping only a quarter of the act's concluding love duet.

For the opening of act 3, three years later, Floyd eliminated Jonathan's gun lecture to his two-year-old son. Nicey puts the child to bed, and Floyd wrote an entirely new aria for Celia, complaining of rampant corruption in Columbia. The curtain now rose midway through the argument between Jonathan and Pratt; but by the time Floyd's text assumed its final shape, the music had almost written itself. His process is clear in Pratt's scorn for his wife's anxiety, and his enlistment of Lieutenant Patrick to discredit Jonathan, both scenes drastically cut or rewritten.

Between first draft and full score, Floyd invented a new episode to follow act 3, scene 1, in which two carpetbaggers (tenor/bass) bribe a black senator (bass). This sets up the vital cameo role of Judge James C. Bell (baritone), the Freedmen's Bureau replacement for Townsend. Bell expresses disgust for such abuses, and the intervening curtain rises on scene 2, as Bell informs Jonathan that he has asked to be replaced. Patrick's delivery of the order to confiscate Townsend's household goods follows, but cut by two-thirds, as are Jonathan's scene with Celia and his resolve to desert.

Floyd struck the first half of the next episode, with its cumbersome pageant of defeated Confederate states, in favor of Townsend's dedication of a monument to southern dead and a straightforward vow of vengeance.

In the final scene, he cut two pages of dialogue between Jonathan, Celia, and Amy Pratt, along with lengthy deletions from the confrontation with Wardlaw, and the preparations for Jonathan and Celia's departure. Most significantly, Floyd realized that, in order to preserve sympathy, dignity, and tragic dimension in Judge Townsend, as well as eliminating maudlin and distracting melodrama, he needed to keep the assassin's identity ambiguous: the shooter's identity was less important than the air of violence in that time and place. And finally, Floyd wisely deleted three full pages of back and forth between Celia, Townsend, Nicey, Pratt, and Patrick *after* Jonathan's shooting, in favor of a simple refrain of her longing to have lived in a different time.

Floyd's dramaturgy embraced the wisdom that if an opera has three acts the last should be the shortest and build relentlessly but quickly to its denouement. As it was, the work would last more than three hours.

ON MAY 1, Curtin reprised *The Mystery* with the Syracuse Symphony Orchestra, conducted by Karl Kritz. The seemingly imperishable Ernst Bacon served as critic for the occasion, praising in his ever-vivid prose Floyd's resistance to "all recent anti-lyrical, hyper-cerebral, post-serial, randomist tendencies and cults," together with memories of his exceptional writing and exquisite pianism.[110]

On May 15, the University of Tulsa presented *Susannah* with Norman Treigle as guest artist, and Floyd supervised FSU's production of *Slow Dusk* on July 21 and 23. *The New York Times* announcement of the world premiere of *The Passion of Jonathan Wade* on October 11, 1962 showed that Rudel had cast from strength: Phyllis Curtin (Celia), Norman Treigle (Judge Townsend), and baritone Theodor Uppman in the title role. Though the paper gave away no more of the plot than its basis in Reconstruction in the South,[111] it marked the first public appearance of the work's title.

Harmless as it may seem, the *Times* announcement raised the curtain on a comedy of errors between Floyd and fellow composer Dominick Argento. By the time Argento signed with Boosey & Hawkes in 1957, he had written a handful of songs, instrumental music, and two one-act operas, *Sicilian Limes* and *The Boor,* both to libretti by John Olon-Scrymgeour. Argento's *Catalogue Raisonné as Memoir: A Composer's Life*[112] relates his version of the origins of his first full-length opera, *Colonel Jonathan the Saint,* begun in 1958 and completed in 1961, to another Olon-Scrymgeour text, and bearing the subtitle *A Comedy of Reconstruction in Four Acts and an Interlude of Waltzes.*

Following the destruction of Lyonnaise, a great home in the Tidewater region of Maryland during the Civil War, Colonel Jonathan Gilmourin, who led a wartime raid that fired the structure, is in residence as a guest in the recently opened hotel on the premises. The building's owner, Sabrina, away in search of her presumably dead Confederate husband, rejoins her Aunt Allegra, manager of the new hotel. Jonathan falls in love with Sabrina, around and between a number of anecdotal relationships between other guests, who, as the subtitle suggests, dance a great many waltzes. By the opera's end, several years have passed. Though Sabrina and Jonathan have in the meantime married, her first husband's *ghost* returns and the two swear everlasting love across the spirit world's boundaries, leaving her future relationship with Jonathan in considerable but undefined confusion.

Aside from the extraordinary coincidences of the appearance of the name "Jonathan" in both titles, and the character's rank of colonel, Argento's plot and characters could not be farther from Floyd's saga of Reconstruction that actually treats the aftermath of the Civil War. In his memoir, Argento maintains that Boosey & Hawkes arranged an audition at which he played the first act of his *Jonathan* for Julius Rudel and Phyllis Curtin, with a view to Curtin performing Sabrina. This hardly sounds like the event described by Curtin in a letter to Floyd of February 18, 1960. She had caught cold following a performance of *Susannah* on February 12, and attended a later rehearsal for the upcoming City Opera tour to watch Helena Scott be staged into the role: "Listened to our opera, following a talk to the Ford group of composers and librettists, by a composer named Argento. The man has all the right kind of ideas for setting his libretto, but no variety of expression. A curious situation. He has a most interesting imagination about what to do with the music—but just no vocabulary."[113]

By the time that Argento and his librettist read the *Times* announcement of *The Passion of Jonathan Wade,* they had completed their own opera. They speculated that either Curtin or Bob Holton, citing friendship with and favoritism of Floyd, had mentioned Argento's project to his competitor, who then appropriated the subject for himself. To his credit, Argento never directly accused Floyd of plagiarism; yet Olon-Scrymgeour descended on Boosey & Hawkes in high dudgeon, demanding to see Floyd's libretto. Argento claimed that the story of *Jonathan Wade* was virtually identical to theirs; Olon-Scrymgeour favored bringing suit, citing nineteen specific resemblances to his libretto, but Argento discouraged legal action after examining Floyd's score, convinced that it would fail.

At eighty-six, Curtin, still incisive, may be forgiven for slim recollection of an event of which she made no mention of anything but Argento *speaking,* almost a half-century before her incensed response in 2007: "I was NEVER asked to read, sing, look through [Dominick Argento's] or ANY score with Julius Rudel. Not ever. I never heard of any such *Jonathan* till I received Carlisle's score. I don't think I ever discussed the opera with Bob Holton. This is a false story in every way."[114]

When asked for his memories of the events Argento describes, the conductor Julius Rudel offered, "I have absolutely no memory of such an audition, with or without Phyllis Curtin, as Argento put into his book, or even that he'd written such an opera. Argento may have imagined it, or perhaps it's some form of wish fulfillment; at the very least, it's pretty far-fetched, as I've always known Carlisle to be a total straight-shooter."[115]

Floyd remained blithely unaware of the tempest swirling about him in the summer of 1962: Bob Holton had in fact mentioned in passing, well after Floyd had finished his own opera, that Argento was writing one with a protagonist named Jonathan. Floyd thought it a peculiar coincidence; but had he been up to a knock-off, he would surely have given his protagonist a different first name and rank.

THE OPERATIC POT IN NEW YORK was similarly aboil that summer: Robert Ward won a Pulitzer for *The Crucible;* Douglas Moore had retired from Columbia University to devote more time to composition, and addressed the American Symphony Orchestra League on the stagnation of opera in this country. He believed that America would never achieve musical selfhood without a native opera tradition, performed in English and with heightened dramatic content.[116]

But violence was in the air, and contemporary news deflected attention from such noble cultural goals: the abortive Bay of Pigs invasion of Cuba (April 17–19, 1961), the subsequent Marxification (December 2, 1961) and America's embargo of that island nation (February 3, 1962); the construction of the Berlin Wall (August 13, 1961); the dispatching of American military advisors to South Vietnam (November 18, 1961) and the ignition of full scale war in Southeast Asia (December 11, 1961); and the Cuban missile crisis (October 14–November 20, 1962). Yet as Floyd's October premiere approached, all of New York's dailies gave *Jonathan Wade* astonishing advance publicity and respectful analysis.

On October 7 the *Times* even ran the composer's "Story of '*Jonathan,*'" a two-column exposition of themes and southern history. Rudel studied the new score, and identified a burden of too-regular musical phrases. In *Susannah,* this had not bothered him, as it grew organically from the subject and its folksong influences; and he could mitigate Floyd's predisposition to symmetrical patterns by phrasing across bar lines. On the one hand, he had always found in Floyd an ideal collaborator:

> He was very modest, quiet. I never heard him say anything negative. He was helpful, whenever need

> arose to clarify; that's his way. He was the ideal creator, because he listened. We could talk freely and openly about anything: phrasing, emphasis, accent, whatever. He was always open and available, he'd listen to anything you had to say. We'd talk about it, and then he'd usually make it his own, if he accepted the premise; which, I must say, most of the time he did. It was always two artists, working together toward a common goal. We wanted the same thing, spoke the same language.[117]

By August 25, Rudel felt that their relationship would survive his nine-page typed letter to Floyd, which cited 174 details in text and score that he felt needed attention. He included both sweeping generalities and minutiae of prosody, tempo, *tessitura*, dramaturgy, and characterization: "I shall call you in two or three days but thought it wise to send you some of the problems in writing to give you a chance to think them over. I'm not going to pull any punches as I take it for granted that you know how I feel about you and that every criticism is intended to be a positive rather than a negative statement."[118]

The conductor's principal concern was Floyd's symmetrical lines; and, through Rudel, even director Allen Fletcher added his two cents' worth: "[Though] not musically trained, [he] has noticed the frequent regularity of rhythmic cadence. . . . You must go through the entire opera with a fine tooth comb and adjust many of these eight-bar phrases that are so evenly split up in two-plus-two and two-plus-two."

After complimenting Floyd on the beauty of the opening chorus, Rudel went on to "page 3, last line, second bar—have you considered changing the second eighth note of the soprano to C natural to get a kind of follow-up effect to the second bar of the second line of page three?"

Floyd penciled the word "OK" in the margin, as he did with most of Rudel's suggestions; but he also held his ground and wrote "No" or "Why?" beside other comments. Most of the conductor's points were well-taken, arising as they did from his long experience of singers and operatic literature: "Norman Kelley has gone through the role of Pratt and finds it uncomfortably high. I . . . think it would be too high for anyone. Also Uppman finds several spots high, and again I agree. There's a point of diminishing returns in writing high phrases. I hate to bring in other examples, but notice what register Puccini always uses. No tenor sounds good singing constantly in the crack around F and G."

Where Rudel felt that Floyd had missed opportunities to shine, he encouraged: "Page 43—end of third line: For God's sake, keep going! You've got something, now carry it further, don't cut back again. Spin the line. You've got a beautiful melodic germ there—let it germinate (to mix flora and fauna)." The conductor concluded, "After you get through sticking pins into my image and have had a chance to mull over the few points I raised, I think it better that you call me. Make it person-to-person and reverse the charges, that is, if you'll still talk to me."

Floyd's private reactions veered between practicality and exasperation. He implemented many of Rudel's ideas to the work's benefit, knowing that the conductor simply wanted the best for everyone. With Rudel's annotated letter in hand, Floyd made the proposed call a few days later. For the better part of two hours, he paced his bedroom on Redwood Drive as far as the phone cord allowed. In a moment of irritation, he asked Rudel, "Why don't you just write your own opera?" Rudel stammered about his inability to do any such thing, and backed off, for the moment. Though he continued calling at irregular intervals with new criticisms and brainstorms, the two remained the best of friends and colleagues. Floyd had the good fortune to work with at least two generations of superb colleagues in the pit, such as James Conlon, John DeMain, Mark Flint, Robert LaMarchina, Kent Nagano, and Patrick Summers; but Julius Rudel, standing apart from the alphabetized names, heads Floyd's list of favorites.

By the beginning of September, changes effected, Boosey sent scores to the principal singers. Gene Cook wrote Floyd that he and Curtin were both "moved and gripped." Ryan Edwards, by then established in New York, and Curtin's regular accompanist, "played through the first two acts of it for us. . . . He even sang much of it, and that *Wade* could survive that is really a tribute . . . Phyllis . . . likes her *tessitura* and this time has no doubt that she will still be standing at the end."[119]

During the final weeks of revision, Floyd received a call from a Miss Julia Ribet, representing North Carolina's Tercentenary Commission. To cap the state's celebration, just a year away at the end of 1963, it seemed that the organization wanted to commission Floyd to write a piece based on some unspecified incident in the state's colonial history. With a clear idea of the trajectory of the coming months, Floyd declined, but not without giving the young woman contact information for Ryan Edwards and colleague Lee Hoiby.

JONATHAN WADE rehearsals began in New York in mid-September,[120] and Floyd and Kay again occupied the Cooks' guest room. When the composer arrived, Curtin voiced concern: "There was a big stretch of it [beginning with her act 1 aria] that was all about a third too high. Celia is so normal, and it changed her personality, it wasn't the right thing for that woman. I never asked him to change anything, just to listen when he came. We sang through it, and he agreed absolutely, and said, 'It didn't sound that way in my head.'"[121]

Because company manager John White maintained that weekend performances—excepting Sunday matinees—of new operas never sold, City Opera scheduled just two *Wade*s that season, on October 11 and 28. The company had otherwise spared no expense and effort on a beautiful and well-cast production: besides Curtin, Uppman, and Treigle, the singers included mezzo-soprano Miriam Burton (Nicey), and house character singer-actors Paul Ukena, Frank Porretta, and Norman Kelley as, respectively, the malicious Riddle, Wardlaw, and Pratt. Even the smallest roles were filled with such promising young talents as soprano Patricia Brooks (Amy Pratt), tenor Harry Theyard (Lieutenant Patrick), and baritone Richard Fredericks as a Confederate soldier. All became City Opera stars in coming seasons.

Teaching commitments had kept Floyd in Tallahassee during initial rehearsals, long enough for the cast to descend on him with grumbling discontent, playing the parental triangulation game. As always, the stage director provoked the most grievances. With a solid background in legitimate theater, Allen Fletcher was a competent professional, but distanced himself from the cast, perhaps discomfited by the singers' different priorities and attitudes. During staging, when things came to a halt, Fletcher sat apart, pondering in silence for long spells. The cast waited, growing understandably impatient, given City Opera's limited rehearsal hours. As Floyd knew, singers *want* direction, and they were not getting enough of it: "You're lucky to have people as competent as Phyllis, Norman, and Ted Uppman, but they want a reaction from the stage director: 'Is what I'm doing OK? Is this what you have in mind?' But Fletcher didn't seem to work that way. There was something phlegmatic, much too severe about him . . . but he got the job done."

Fortunately, Floyd loved the fluid, flexible use Armstrong's sets made of the stage; and he anticipated with the usual mixture of trepidation and excitement the phalanx of family and friends about to arrive: Reverend and Mrs. Floyd, Kay's mother, Gundy, aunts Doris, Hazel, and Bunny; Ermine, Billy, and a handful of Holly Hill friends; Jona and Bruce Clarke, Jim Staples, Priscilla Gillette; and, from Tallahassee, Elena Nikolaidi, Nellie-Bond Dickinson, Evon Streetman, and Catherine Murphy.

City Opera's mood waxed ebullient: at final dress rehearsal on October 10, John White rushed up to Floyd, effusing that the opera would win not one Pulitzer, but two.[122] Ned Rorem attended this rehearsal, and wrote with witty acid that he found it challenging to wish Floyd success, as his own new opera, probably the contemplated *Charade,* created a rivalry.[123] Rorem later amplified, "He's a major opera composer, and I wish he'd composed more. I approve of his lean language, especially then, when everyone was writing twelve-tone music, which doesn't really work in opera, or vocal music at all."[124]

Also on October 10, Gene Cook plied his entrepreneurial skills in synergy with Bob Holton, and sent the publisher Tom Ryan's film script for Carson McCullers's *The Heart Is a Lonely Hunter,* with Ryan's appended note asking for Floyd's feedback. On the street, Cook met *New Yorker* critic Winthrop Sargeant, who asked whether Floyd would be offended to receive a direct communication with constructive suggestions from Sargeant, who had also attended the dress rehearsal of *Wade*.[125]

The October 11 premiere was even headier than all that had gone before it, and it had a rapt and demonstrative audience: as in traditional Italian "number opera," spontaneous applause erupted after individual arias and ensembles. At the final curtain, cast and staff were called out six times; when Rudel and Floyd appeared, the audience leapt to its feet.

The next morning, Floyd's mother rushed out to the newsstand for papers; the composer had already read them by the time he arrived to say goodbye, before his family threaded their way south through that year's Columbus Day parade. Ross Parmenter wrote in the *Times* of the audience's enthusiasm, and that City Opera had performed another good service for American opera, but concluded that, although the opera had its strong moments, "Mr. Floyd had bitten off more than he could chew."[126]

Floyd was dashed, alive only to the qualifications. Paul Henry Lang wrote favorably of the opera's serious and sensitive elements, the liveliness of its plot and the delicacy with which Floyd had drawn his characters; yet he felt that "both text and music suffer from professional weaknesses," chiefly a failure to differentiate the needs of opera and spoken theater that remained unredeemed by the music. Despite a strong lyric gift, "rhetoric, or a kind of verbal and emotional sententiousness, is Mr. Floyd's weakness." Floyd had matured, but had "not yet found himself."[127]

Usually a staunch Floyd supporter, Louis Biancolli maintained that *Jonathan Wade* suffered from diffuseness, sermonizing, and a failure to realize this grand historical tapestry in human terms: Excepting "random vignettes," he thought it "contrived and self-conscious."[128]

The criticisms stung worse because of unfavorable comparisons with *Susannah*. Support came in the form of a letter from Floyd's elder colleague Douglas Moore, who found *Jonathan Wade* absorbing, suspenseful theater, and musically attractive, the kind of success of which American opera needed more; and he predicted that Floyd would deliver just that in coming years.[129]

Only weeks later might the composer have seen a more sympathetic account in *The Washington Post*, which, despite cavils about the music's lack of personality, emphasized that the opera ratified the promise of Floyd's earlier works, "in a style that is shaping up as the American operatic idiom."[130]

After the second performance on October 28, this *Passion of Jonathan Wade* disappeared forever from the repertory. Kay, who had given Floyd the germ of the opera, expressed disappointment even more bitter than the composer's. Rudel had set Floyd's bar high by preceding *Wade* with daunting competition: City Opera's all-contemporary spring 1962 season included Ward's aforementioned *Crucible*, and the company's first *Porgy and Bess*.

Even more prejudicial in Floyd's critical Armageddon, but far less obvious, was unrest within New York journalism itself. In 1960, Rudolf Bing had excluded the press from the Met's dress rehearsals. That company's season narrowly escaped cancellation in fall 1961 by direct intervention from the Kennedy White House; but in the interim, many of the greatest international artists had accepted contracts elsewhere.

New York's music critics, along with the rest of their newspaper colleagues, were living and writing in an atmosphere of rumor, skirmish, and open warfare that finally erupted on November 9, 1962, when the Newspaper Guild went on an eight-day strike against the *New York Daily News*. The remainder of the city's major news organs—the *Journal American*, The *Times*, the *World-Telegram and Sun*, the *Daily Mirror*, the *Herald Tribune*, and the *Post*—followed suit on December 8, until settlement 114 days later. Considering this atmosphere of anxiety and hostility, paired with inflammatory national and international news—a pacifist opera with America's Vietnam adventure underway, and perhaps a saturation of focus on civil rights—it should hardly surprise that Floyd and *Jonathan Wade* became collateral victims.

THE BITTER FOOTNOTE to *L'affaire Argento* was that composer's *Schadenfreude* over Floyd's "flop," as he termed it;[131] but when Argento later attempted to interest the Metropolitan Opera in his opera *Colonel Jonathan the Saint,* John Gutman objected that Carlisle Floyd had written that same story, and Argento found the door locked behind him. His work eventually premiered in 1971 at the Denver Lyric Opera, and Argento spread blame for the failure of his *Jonathan* on the fledgling company's poor publicity and bad food at a New Year's gala performance. *Colonel Jonathan the Saint* received just one other production, at the University of North Dakota in 1976, before being relegated to the shelves at Boosey & Hawkes.[132]

He who falls up will, now and again, fall down; Carlisle Floyd knew just enough up to tell the difference.

13

At the Oars

Mollie Sinclair *to* Markheim, *1962–1966*

After a glum lunch with Bob Holton, strategizing ways to profit, or at least learn from, *Jonathan Wade*'s disaster, Floyd and Kay lugged their bags aboard the Southern Atlantic train on October 13, 1962. This was as close as he'd come to realizing his worst fear of being told to go home, that he lacked the elusive *It*. His relationship to critics approximated that with his father: nothing made the bashing nicer, but he matured emotionally by gradually releasing more of his need for external affirmation. To gain his father's approval or any demonstration of affection, he had to plummet into a subordinate vacuum into which Reverend Floyd could leap like a caped crusader and offer the sage advice, "Don't let it get you down." Experience taught Floyd that getting up for round two with Daddy usually opened the door to worse put-downs; but he really had no choice with critics, and opera would never disappoint there. Floyd's wit had not recovered enough to allow him to reach his own good-humored formulation of Ned Rorem's dictum on the music critic, whom he compared to a professional marriage counselor who has never felt the emotion of love.[1]

Holton, a more positive paternal figure, encouraged the composer not to throw babies out with polluted bath water: get some rest, set some time aside for himself before seeking a full understanding of what had gone wrong. Holton had taken a call that morning from the North Carolina Tercentenary Commission's dogged Julia Ribet, approaching anew to snag Floyd for their celebration piece.

The composer asked Holton to extract him from the Tercentenary obligation, and the publisher dutifully relayed to Ribet that Floyd wished not to be considered. After almost two years of wrestling with *Jonathan Wade,* Floyd needed to unwind. Holton cannily anticipated that the North Carolinians may have seen the opera's negative press, and went on to describe the audience's delirious response to the work, stating that Floyd was returning to Florida triumphant, though cheated by the press from feeling the buoyancy of the reception of *Wade*. Holton wrote that Floyd now had to take a few weeks to normalize his life, which included reacquainting himself with Kay, his friends, and his students; and asked that the Tercentenary Commission act on his earlier suggestions to find another composer for their assignment. Yet Floyd had also authorized Holton to tell Miss Ribet, in the event that she could not find an alternate composer, to phone him in two or three weeks, by which time he would have breathed deeply and caught up on sleep.[2] In the absence of usable press, Holton extracted a testimonial from conductor André Kostalanetz, declaring *The Passion of Jonathan Wade* a brilliant American operatic milestone, a masterpiece.[3]

With Floyd away from New York, Gene Cook beat the bush for new projects to divert his friend's attention. He wrote Floyd to promote Thomas Ryan's *The Heart Is a Lonely Hunter* script as a possible stimulus for a film score or libretto, but to no avail.[4] Cook also prepared Floyd for an extraordinary letter from Winthrop Sargeant's *New Yorker* offices, seizing the opportunity to break down traditional barriers between critic and composer, and to make a suggestion. Sargeant repeated his admiration for Floyd's talent, and hoped that the composer would not find the communication presumptuous; but, he asked, why not employ a technical trick he had yet to notice to any extent in

Floyd's work, but one that the greatest opera composers, from Verdi to Wagner to Puccini had used, at times even in great climaxes: let the orchestra occasionally carry the main burden of Floyd's beautiful melodies, while the singer sings his or her part in a monotone or simple inner voice.

As far as he could at such a dark moment, Floyd took this in good humor; but Sargeant made even more important observations about criticism per se, hoping that nothing would deflect Floyd from his pursuit of opera, his métier, for which Sargeant affirmed Floyd's great gifts. The composer should never internalize hostile, or worse, condescending criticism, and remember how many unsuccessful, or only partially successful, operas Verdi had written before he really hit his stride. Sargeant looked forward with great anticipation to Floyd's next work, and praised the many magnificent moments in the second half of *Jonathan Wade.* He objected only to the opera's excess of preamble before Floyd got around to the simple action and passion that propelled the opera from the marriage scene on.[5]

FLOYD AND SARGEANT never met face to face, but the composer soon realized that concerned personal feedback from a powerful and articulate critic was as rare as the teeth on his mother's hens; but now it was time for the influential monthlies to weigh in. Irving Kolodin accused Floyd of short-changing emotion in *Wade,* but liked the love music and wedding scene; yet once Floyd strayed into political and social elements, Kolodin scorned it as "an inept opera of ideas," and thought that Floyd's quest for identity had "led him into a kind of musical Everglades."[6]

Not even Robert Sabin's encouragement could dispel the gloom that settled onto Redwood Drive: "Granted that there are too many characters and subplots; that the orchestration is still weak and uneven; this is, nonetheless, a powerful and heartfelt work, well worth European attention. Its characters live, breathe—and sing!—convincingly, in a language that the average opera-goer can understand immediately. Is this a crime? One might almost think so, to hear our avant-garde talk . . . the Ford Foundation . . . money [was] well spent, and the production was handsome."[7]

Floyd always took Sabin's criticism to heart, and began a decades-long study of scores of virtuoso orchestrators, not to imitate, but simply to learn how others achieved their textures, colors, and combinations. Delving into Ravel's arrangement of Mussorgsky's *Pictures at an Exhibition* proved to Floyd that even he could not hear in performance half of what lay behind that brilliant instrumentation; he also analyzed the works of Stravinsky, beginning with *The Rite of Spring;* Prokofiev's *Romeo and Juliet;* and Copland's *Appalachian Spring.*

Settling back into Tallahassee's academic groove without much confidence necessitated fundamental lifestyle changes. Kay had had her fill of weeks on the road, and long dark hours alone at home. She stipulated that there were to be no more late-night work sessions after full days of teaching, and Floyd arranged his schedule to concentrate his pianists and composers in the mornings. After lunch, uninterrupted home studio time stretched before him until supper, and evenings were reserved for more convivial pursuits with Kay and friends.

But the dauntless Julia Ribet surprised Floyd one day by appearing at his front door. The Tercentenary Commission had found no other composer for its showpiece. Now panicked over time constraints, they thought a one-man combination of librettist and composer essential, but there were not many of those floating about. They were looking for a one-act piece of an hour or less, and offered a hefty $2,000 fee—$14,200 in 2010 purchasing power. Floyd's thoughts turned to reliable old friends, debating whether he might adapt his *Monologue* for Patricia Neway, or discussing subjects with Norman Treigle. The composer simply could not disregard such a salary boost; and with artists and friends like Treigle and Neway, how could he go wrong?

The contract limited the orchestra to sixteen players from East Carolina University in Greenville, most of them students with no experience in contemporary musical idioms. Floyd would need a hero in the pit, and, in weeks to come, Julius Rudel agreed to conduct, which seemed a further guarantee of success for whatever Floyd might conjure. And as for that, the closest

Miss Ribet and the commission came to suggesting subject matter or historical sources was the general topic of prerevolutionary Scottish settlers. Once she had extracted Floyd's commitment, she sent a modest stack of books on the state's history. Speeding through three centuries of dry statistics and genealogies, the slim volume that seized the composer's fancy was Duane Meyer's *The Highland Scots of North Carolina, 1732–1776.*[8] Floyd grew intrigued by the state's eastern settlements, where the social structure and native customs endured but where residents nonetheless defied the hated Stamp Act,[9] their respect for tradition coexisting, however uneasily, with simmering revolutionary sentiments. Floyd, still smarting from criticism that his presentation of a historical era lacked humanity, now saw how he might heighten that element with the conflict of two vehemently opposed *personal,* character-driven points of view.

Two new protagonists took shape, inspired by the ferocity of Treigle and Neway: a vainglorious, aging Scottish laird, determined to maintain the old ways in his blindly obedient insular community; and a Scottish woman somewhere between *lass* and *carlin,*[10] who leads a ragtag band of disorganized but ardent protestors against British authority in the port city of Wilmington.

With more than three hundred years of historical incident from which to choose, Floyd followed his instinct to write about independence from Britain and from neurotic old ways. The pièce de résistance is the blossoming of love from the least promising soil, and gentle humor sprang from situation and character. Floyd never set out to produce a comedy, but with laughter he transcended the trials of *Jonathan Wade.*

The Floyds' agreement about abandoning night work had to be suspended, but at least they knew that this could not last more than a year. Meyer's little book provided most of the research and historical frame the composer needed. From an appendix of family names,[11] Floyd chose McDougald for Treigle's role; and what could be more Scottish than *Dougald* McDougald? Though most of the McDougalds Meyer named were men (recipients of land grants or land purchasers), there is a Jenny among them, so Floyd's Dougald got a daughter of that name. The same table contained a complement of Sinclairs, and Pat Neway would be Mollie, Treigle's antagonist and eventual love interest.

Meyer's observations on the decay of the ancient clan system gave Floyd his thesis: "Before 1745 the chief was the unquestioned ruler of his clan. His word was law and absolute discipline was demanded. Life or death, war or peace, awaited his command. The clansman rejoiced to share his name, religion, and his dangers. . . . Bound together by common devotion to a chief [Floyd's Dougald] the clan was an integrated family which prospered and suffered together, worked and warred together, lived and died together."[12]

Between 1730 and 1775, between twenty thousand and thirty thousand Highland Scots emigrated to America, and many settled in the Cape Fear region of the southern tip of North Carolina. Its sandhills and longleaf pines reminiscent of Bethune, Cape Fear lay across the border with South Carolina, close to Floyd's native Latta. His own blood being English-Irish-Welsh-Scottish, he would, in a sense, be re-creating family.

The curtain rises on the exterior and front yard of a plantation house on Cape Fear River, and the song of slaves working the fields. Jenny MacDougald (soprano) jousts verbally with young Lachlan Sinclair (tenor), who longs to marry her. Their sparring accelerates, reminding us that their respective families are anything but friendly: her father, the laird and chieftain Dougald MacDougald (bass-baritone), deplores Lachlan's assertive, forward-looking mother, Mollie (mezzo-soprano), while Mollie thinks of Dougald as a (barely) living fossil. The two young people are in love, but Jenny says she'll marry Lachlan only if he can last two months without other female companionship. Meanwhile, crusty old Dougald waits impatiently, in full Highland regalia, for clansmen and bondsmen to arrive to celebrate his sixtieth birthday. A self-defined "sojourner," or temporary resident, he sings of homesickness (after twenty years of life in America) for his native Isle of Skye. Lachlan has the bad sense to repeat his mother's opinion that Scotland presents terrible land for farming, sparking another Dougald tirade against Mollie. Jenny distracts her father by reminding him that he has forgotten to raise the British flag and sing "God Save the King."

Alone with his sweetheart, Lachlan reveals that his mother is organizing a brigade of young people to march on Wilmington to defy the Stamp Act. Dougald returns with the flag, flies it, and sings the British anthem. The kinsmen arrive to pledge their honor and respect, stoking Dougald's yearning for Scotland. To divert their laird's nostalgia, the kinsmen dance to the counterpoint of approaching marchers, as Mollie Sinclair and her ragtag band of protesters enter. Dougald thinks it is a raiding party, and orders everyone to hide; and no one is as astounded—and angry—as he to behold the very object of his animus. Floyd describes Mollie as a handsome, energetic middle-aged woman with a motley army of ill-clothed males of all ages. Mollie remarks that Lachlan told her of a party in progress, and Dougald summons his kinsmen back, announcing Mollie to be merely a broomless witch. He demands that she state her business and be on her way, railing that she is an ill-omened betrayer. Mollie in turn brands Dougald as an extinct species and an impediment to future accomplishment. The two spar on the pros and cons of revolution. The Scots had historically taken the losing side against the British crown, but Mollie cuts to the quick, pointing out that freedom's lure had less to do with their emigration than the promise of wealth on the new continent. In the process, Mollie rouses Dougald's indignation with news that British warships have seized two colonial vessels that refused to buy the new stamps. The kinsmen plead for his guidance, but the old fellow is still shy of rebellion. Mollie shames the lot by "baaaing" like sheep, to the applause of her pitiful troops. Dougald needs time to think, and storms into the house.

While the slaves reprise their work song, Jenny urges Mollie to show Dougald a more tender side. Mollie agrees to try, calling inside to Dougald to summon up a shared feeling: anyone who insists on living out myths of the past forfeits both present and past, much less a joyous tomorrow. After a long silence, the Spokesman (baritone) asks Mollie whether she still wrestles Indian-style, which she answers by defeating the strongest of the kinsmen. Dougald trudges back out, a sorry figure in shirt and breeches, having put aside his laird's regalia. Still trying to save face, he declares that Mollie is right. Despite loud protests from his kinsmen, he renounces all rights and claims to lairdship, urging them to make up their own minds to either join Mollie or return to their farms. The group disperses with subdued repetition of birthday wishes to Dougald, and some of the men join Mollie's brigade.

Following one last exchange of pungent insults, Mollie observes that Dougald might yet improve with a woman's care. Calling her forces to attention, she asks Dougald to ponder her words—she is rarely this emotionally open—and with a stalwart command she and her band step off toward Wilmington. Lachlan reaffirms his love for Jenny, and gets their monogamy bargain whittled down to two weeks. Dougald confesses to Jenny that when he left Skye, he vowed to return, and that with all the living that he has done in America—Jenny's birth, his wife's death—he has always felt himself to be a visitor, a sojourner, but his confrontation with Mollie has changed all that, and now he doubts whether he *could* go back. He sheepishly confesses that Mollie would make a handsome wife. To show his change of heart, while Jenny takes down the British flag, Dougald returns from the house with a pirate flag as a warning to George the Third.[13]

Remembering lessons from *Jonathan Wade,* in a later interview Floyd emphasized the opera's historical foundation: "But I hope it's sugar-coated."[14]

It must have come as a relief to spend November 30 and December 1 in Mobile, Alabama, as the featured speaker at a dinner for the Southeastern-Gulf Regional Convention of Central Opera Service. Richard Collins, Florida State University's director of opera theater, led a discussion, "Is Opera Drama?" and graduate students Ethel Donaldson and Phyllis DeKalk performed arias from *Jonathan Wade.* During a four-day Thanksgiving visit, the couple's first to Reverend Floyd's latest charge in Walterboro, South Carolina, Floyd and Kay were treated to the minister's sexist distinctions between parallel male and female conditions: "Kay surely has gotten fatter, Carlisle also is stouter."[15]

FROM START TO FINISH for text and music, *Slow Dusk* had taken Floyd a little less than seven months to compose, November 1948 to May 1949, *Fugitives,* about ten months, from June 1950 to April 1951; but for both pieces he adapted his own writing, rather than others' literature or theater. *Susannah,* from first draft libretto (June 1953) to orchestration (December 1954), required about eighteen months; *Wuthering Heights* for Santa Fe, a year and three months (March 1957 to July 1958), and its revision for New York City Opera another nine months (August 1958 to April 1959). From commission to premiere of *Jonathan Wade* spanned a year and five months (May 1960 to October 1962); but nothing had prepared him for the quick turnaround for *Mollie,* almost exactly a year from a slow start in November 1962 that included selecting and researching the subject, plus the usual libretto writing. He began composing in January 1963.

On January 20 and 21 Phyllis Curtin performed *The Mystery* with the Louisville Orchestra conducted by Robert Whitney. Though Floyd's academic obligations and *Mollie Sinclair* prevented his attendance, the piece was recorded and released on the orchestra's First Edition series. Despite a cool review,[16] Curtin wrote the Floyds, "Last night we did *The Mystery* here to a very pleased audience . . . they were curiously unresponsive while I sang—but beautifully responsive at the close. . . . Whitney . . . is very fond of the work and has studied it well. . . . I'm keeping my part as closely knit as I can, but I feel a bit like little Eva crossing on those ice cakes—I'd love a *solid* floor."[17]

To local press Floyd confided his consideration of one new subject, the 1951 Tennessee Williams play *The Rose Tattoo,* and one older source, Edith Wharton's *Ethan Frome.*[18] Since taking in the original Broadway production of the former, Floyd thought it a perfect vehicle for Elena Nikolaidi, as Williams's larger-than-life, Sicilian-American protagonist Serafina delle Rose. Niki embodied for Floyd "another stage personality like Norman [Treigle]: she came onstage, and . . . mmm!" Niki loved the notion, even if she insisted on calling the play *The Rose of Tattoo,* but Floyd tempered his enthusiasm with caution: "It required a Sicilian color that would have been duck soup for Puccini, but I didn't think I could make it sound really authentic. Still, it is a ready-made opera libretto, it calls out. I don't know why someone hasn't done it, except the content is a little heady."

And of course there was the practical question of gaining rights. *Ethan Frome* remained stillborn as well, as Floyd was too occupied with *Mollie Sinclair* to solve the logistics of Wharton's sledding accident: "It has to happen offstage in the stage version, and how can you have an opera whose big scene isn't visible?"[19]

Good news came in a letter from Sylvia Goldstein, with Floyd's contractual advance royalty of $1,250 for the year, and the firm's commitment to publish *Jonathan Wade,* but only when the work reached its final revised form.[20] On January 31, Boosey acquired the rights to a separate publication of two of the opera's hit tunes, "Free as a Frog" and the spiritual "Down in Galilee."

On the same day, the North Carolina Tercentenary Commission sent Floyd its check for his entire two thousand dollar commission fee. Julius Rudel also called, inviting him to direct City Opera's *Susannah* revival in three months.[21] The Floyds' social pot bubbled as well: Hazel Richards, installed in her new house after her husband's death the previous year, was lonely and bored. She had gotten far enough past her jealousy of Kay to seek reconciliation with Floyd, but rather than contact him directly, she invited the composer's parents to visit. As luck would have it, Floyd invited his parents to visit *him* five days later.[22]

The entire spring of 1963 gave Floyd scant time to breathe, much less write much new music. On March 15 and 16, the composer Roger Sessions held a guest consultancy at FSU.[23] Floyd's colleague Harold Schiffman, a Sessions pupil, brought news that the visitor was eager to meet Floyd. Floyd was puzzled: they could not have been farther apart aesthetically, but a pleasant meeting ensued at a party at the Schiffmans', with the inevitable social chat about the name "Sessions" being a part of each of their lines; but the conversation seemed to go nowhere past such trivia.[24] Later campus visits by composers Krzysztof Penderecki and

Malcolm Williamson occasioned similar but more substantive encounters.

Also that March, the University of California, Los Angeles, approached Floyd: composer Lukas Foss had just accepted an offer from the State University of New York at Buffalo to leave UCLA to become the first director of Buffalo's Center for Creative and Performing Arts.[25] Foss suggested that UCLA administrators explore Floyd's interest in the ensuing vacancy. Floyd had never visited Los Angeles, but numerous colleagues told him that it was not a place they (or he) would care to live, so Tallahassee remained home for the foreseeable future.

Reverend and Mrs. Floyd received another invitation from Hazel Richards, and arrived at Redwood Drive on April 18, less than a week after Boosey & Hawkes accepted the composer's new arrangements of *Susannah*'s "Jaybird Song" for publication. Though guaranteeing stress and overwork, Floyd's commissions and *Susannah* productions brought him undreamed-of prosperity. He took his parents on the inevitable city tour, including a new house he would buy for thirty-five thousand dollars at the beginning of May, in Tallahassee's Waverly Hills neighborhood. For the remainder of the visit, Floyd sequestered himself to work on *Mollie Sinclair.* His parents entertained themselves until the composer took the evening of April 20 off, and both generations paid an awkward, formal call on Hazel Richards.

Jack and Ida left shortly after dawn the next morning, while Floyd and Kay packed bags for New York and the Great Northern Hotel, for City Opera's sixth revival of *Susannah,* the first without Phyllis Curtin.[26] With Rudel in the pit and Rhoda Levine in her company debut as choreographer,[27] Floyd delighted in petite Lee Venora's Susannah, and of course welcomed the opportunity to work again with Treigle. In Paul Sylbert's 1958 sets, Richard Cassilly repeated his Sam, and Harry Theyard his Little Bat. Otherwise, Floyd found it to be a rather routine revival, with less than two weeks to slap things together, a common fact of City Opera life in those days; but Robert Sabin continued to encourage, with praise for Floyd's theatrical instincts, and for his characters, who "live and are movingly portrayed in his music. He can create a world of illusion without self-consciousness or stiffness." (Sabin thought that *Wuthering Heights,* which he considered Floyd's best work to date, should interest British audiences, and that *The Passion of Jonathan Wade* proved that America's Civil War was a conflict still in progress.)[28]

On a day off, Floyd took Kay to the Actors Theatre production of O'Neill's *Strange Interlude,* with an all-star cast including Jane Fonda, Ben Gazzara, Pat Hingle, Geraldine Page, and Franchot Tone, directed by José Quintero. Despite its cramped rehearsal period, *Susannah* opened strongly on May 3. Venora and the veterans, including Rudel, reaped their usual plaudits, and Floyd carried the day as both director and composer.[29]

IF MOVING sixteen years of music, books, recordings, and personal papers could be termed a holiday, the Floyds had one as they left Redwood Drive to establish themselves that June on Middlebrook Circle.[30] It was their largest home yet, and their first new construction, almost three thousand square feet and not quite finished. A huge family room adjoined a guest bedroom that the composer claimed as his studio. He traded in his old upright, which had heard everything from *Susannah* on, for a lusted-after new Steinway studio upright in black satin, on which he set about finishing *Mollie Sinclair,* just as summer school began. City Opera's *Susannah* had put him behind on his deadline. Still intrigued by the different challenges of comedy, by the first week of June he had composed only the first half of the music.[31]

Growing fame followed him back to FSU, setting political waters a-roil. He was summoned to the vice president's office one day and told of his promotion to full professor by the dean of faculties, fait accompli, over Kuersteiner's head. There were no immediate repercussions from colleagues, but Floyd's most serious difficulties with the institution date from this period: he had the title, but his salary still suffered from the conditions of his 1947 hire.

One pleasant fall surprise came from his strong list of student composers, including George Bew, James Woodward, and Carl Vollrath, whom we have already met. Still in the fury of composing *Mollie Sinclair,* Floyd eagerly prompted his students to undertake operas, both libretto and music, and landed on Woodward as the most likely candidate. It seemed natural to begin with a piece of modest dimensions, but Floyd was too preoccupied to research subjects. Kay, whose background in English literature remained broader than his, reminded him of Robert Louis Stevenson's 1885 short story "Markheim," and the Screen Directors Playhouse adaptation they had seen ten years earlier. When Floyd read the source, he found its blend of virtue, vice, guilt, terror, and pungent whiff of brimstone ideal for a one-act opera. Woodward nibbled, but got nowhere with it. The story remained at the back of Floyd's mind, as did visions of Norman Treigle as the murderous protagonist. Besides, Floyd had written *Mollie Sinclair* with Treigle in mind, and now he contemplated a double bill, one comic, one serious, both with leading bass roles.

Professional events gave other satisfaction toward the end of September: Victor Alessandro of the San Antonio Symphony Society hired Curtin, Treigle, and Cassilly to sing, and Floyd to direct *Susannah.* Treigle arrived later than the other principals, and Floyd decided to play a joke on his friend. At the first revival scene staging, Treigle rushed in straight from the airport, just seconds before his first vocal entrance, and stepped into place without greeting anyone, shaking the rafters with his exhortations in this great showpiece. The scene concluded, Treigle strode out to Floyd at the production table and asked cockily, "How was I?"

Straight-faced, Floyd said, "Well, Norman, it was fine, given that you were marking."

The nonplussed basso demanded, "What do you mean, man? *Marking*?"

Floyd enjoyed his imposture, and finally got to the unflappable Treigle: "We know it wasn't full voice, just coming in off the street like that; but terrific anyway."

When the singer at length caught on from surrounding grins and giggles that Floyd was pulling his leg, he glowered, then joked, "Look, man, I want you to stay healthy and writing till the end of my career. After that I don't care."

Relationships grew even stronger, and the production scored another hit for all concerned. During free moments, Floyd intrigued Treigle and Cassilly with thoughts about another project, an operatic adaptation of John Steinbeck's 1937 novella *Of Mice and Men.* From his earliest moments of conceptualization, he had Treigle in mind for George, and Cassilly for Lennie; neither singer did anything to discourage, but Treigle pressed him for something sooner, for New Orleans, as the company now thought of composer and basso as a creative team.

By mid-October, newspapers around the country announced the December 2 premiere and three subsequent performances of *The Sojourner and Mollie Sinclair* at Raleigh's Little Theatre.[32] The Tercentenary Commission had planned a subsequent videotaping for distribution to North Carolina public television stations in Asheville, Charlotte, Greensboro, Greenville, Raleigh, Wilmington, and Winston-Salem, to be shown during December's last two weeks. Floyd still had the end of the opera to write, but at FSU he directed a student-faculty cast in *Susannah* for the school's opera theater, now calling itself the State Opera Association of Florida. Performances on October 17, 18, and 19 were conducted by Robert Sedore and choreographed by Nellie-Bond Dickinson. Catherine Murphy sang Mrs. McLean, a step up from her Mrs. Gleaton and one-woman costume department at the work's 1955 premiere.

In a final spurt of creativity, Floyd finished *Mollie* on November 1, dedicating it to his sister Ermine. Boosey mailed scores to Neway, Treigle and locals and students in Raleigh who needed every spare second to learn it.

The *Times* gave the Louisville Orchestra's recording of Curtin's performance of *The Mystery* a dismal review;[33] but on November 16 and 17, Robert Shaw conducted the Cleveland Orchestra, the Oberlin College Choir, and the baritone Leon Lishner in *Pilgrimage.*

MOST AMERICANS past infancy on Friday, November 22, 1963 recall precisely where they were that afternoon. After two nights of exhaustion at the parsonage in Walterboro, Floyd and Kay climbed into separate cars after an early breakfast that morning. She drove to her parents' home in Jacksonville, he to Greenville, North Carolina, via Holly Hill. During a pause for lunch at Ermine's, Billy Matheny's mother burst into the house a few minutes after 1:30, gasping, "The president's been shot." By the time Floyd resumed his trip, he knew that John F. Kennedy was dead in Dallas from Lee Harvey Oswald's bullet. Not far out of Holly Hill, a wave of terrible sadness overtook him, and he began to weep, a reaction familiar to many who recall that day.

In *Susannah,* Sam's out-of-mind rage powers his rifle, albeit offstage, then Jonathan Wade dies in an assassin's sights. Kennedy's killing reinforced Floyd's horror of such irrational violence. *Mollie Sinclair*'s musket-toting bumpkins play at war, as had Floyd with childish tin soldiers, but in half of Floyd's subsequent stage oeuvre, death flies from gun barrels.

With ten days to *Mollie*'s opening night, it was just as well that his role was supervisory. Though the prevailing mood was anything but comedic, director Edgar Loessin had the production well-staged.[34] Neway and Treigle were at their best, and even the college students Alison Hearne Moss (Jenny), William Newberry (Lachlan), and Jerold Teachey (Spokesman) pleased the composer.

Not so the orchestra: Julius Rudel had no previous experience with academia, and the student players drove him to distraction. He pulled Floyd aside, moaning, "Why did I ever agree to take this job?" But chemistry between Neway and Treigle proved everything Floyd had hoped. Unlike situations in which two enormous stage personalities negate each other, or descend into destructive competition, these two singing actors honored each other's gifts and process. Neway, a dedicated method actress, engaged Loessin in long, detailed discussions of character and motivation, while Treigle, canny, instinctual, and private, waited calmly, chain-smoking unfiltered Kools. Floyd took special delight in watching Treigle play off Neway's ferocity with his natural abilities as comedian and mime, using his hands, torso, and legs to express astonishing nuance and depth. Floyd described the result as "totally devoid of operatic artifice. . . . It more than justified the stress I had felt in undertaking the commission simply to have witnessed Treigle and Neway . . . together: two of the finest actor-singers of their generation, heralded for stunning dramatic portrayals, revealing true comic flair that was at the same time always combined with touching humanity."[35]

For the opening on December 2, Floyd and Kay were joined by Ermine and Billy, his parents, aunts and uncles, Catherine Murphy, Elena Nikolaidi, and Bob Holton. Floyd had written to the latter, "The sound of the orchestra leaves a great deal to be desired, although Julius has done an excellent job of making them play accurately and on pitch. The orchestration itself pleases me and sounds, I think, remarkably rich for so few instruments. . . . The stage director [Loessin] . . . is first-rate and a pleasure to work with, and his contribution is conspicuous for its quality. . . . I am very happy with the piece itself and relieved, since I've long since given up prognostications about new works of mine. The opera moves well, is genuinely comic, I feel, and I hope we have a winner."[36]

Floyd then let on that great plans were afoot: he had reread *Of Mice and Men,* and asked Holton to look into securing rights; and *Mollie Sinclair* came off without major hitches. By the following morning, he had made cuts to keep the piece within television time restrictions, a little less than fifty-two minutes. On December 3, most of the local papers praised the opening and described the audience's quasi-ecstatic applause thus: "Floyd . . . has given us words of significance heightened by the excitement of the music."[37]

The New York Times sent a stringer whose byline described the audience and the approaching videotaping, but neglected plot, libretto, or music.[38] A Winston-Salem critic found Neway "top drawer," thought that Treigle overacted, but complimented Floyd on writing an upbeat, tuneful work that had a future with colleges and civic music groups.[39]

In an interview the next day, when asked about his next work, Floyd replied, somewhat ingenuously, that there was "nothing, I'm happy to say."[40] Pressed to return to FSU, the composer could not stay for final performances or studio sessions; nevertheless, the televised extension of *Mollie Sinclair* enjoyed great success through the rest of December.

FLOYD NOW UNCHARACTERISTICALLY cooled his heels with teaching. Despite his fascination with *Of Mice and Men,* he had no commission in sight, and *Bilby's Doll* had taught him to never undertake uncontracted operas. Creative solace, a remedy for idleness over the next nine months, came from *Episodes,* two volumes of piano pieces written for his own pleasure, an American alternative to Bela Bartók's *Mikrokosmos* (from the Greek for "small world"). Regarded by many as Bartók's magnum opus, this massive work consists of two and a half hours of 153 solo piano pieces spread across six volumes, arranged in an ascending order of aesthetic and technical complexity.

Floyd's project, with a dedication to his friend Catherine Murphy in the scores that appeared in 1965, was modest by comparison: twenty-seven pieces, edited and fingered by the composer. None has a key signature, and dynamic markings are at first limited to simple *crescendi* and *diminuendi,* and remain at first in the range from *pianissimo* (*pp*) to *forte* (*f*), with a few simple interpretive markings like *dolce, espressivo,* or *lontano* (distant). Like Bartók, Floyd intended to make learning amusing and challenging. Volume 1 contains fifteen pieces, opening with "First Lyric Piece," a simple two-part *andante* invention in G Major, fourteen bars of fairly strict contrapuntal imitation in 4/4. A similar sixteen-bar "Second Lyric Piece" centers on F Major, in 3/4, demonstrating somewhat more of Floyd's tonal evasiveness. In two parts, *Allegretto,* imitation alternates with contrary and parallel motion. "Scherzino," just eight measures of *Allegro giocoso* in C Major/Minor, combines features of the preceding elements with gentle fragmentation. The "Third Lyric Piece," twenty *allegretto* measures more clearly in C Major, has a melody with accompaniment, the tune passing from right to left hand and back, with excursions to distant tonalities of A-flat and G-flat Majors.

A more challenging section of longer and harmonically complex pieces opens with "Fourth Lyric Piece," a twenty-six-bar *Allegro moderato* in C Major. It is the collection's first example of a distinct (and Chopinesque) melody in the right hand and chordal accompaniment, with harmonic excursions forth and back from C to B-flat, A Minor, G Minor, A-flat Major, G-flat Major, and so on, finishing with a D-flat Neapolitan sixth cadence to C, with typical Floydian omission of the third. The following "Marching Hymn" is shorter and faster, *Allegro moderato,* returning to two-part format. In cut time, again in C, the right-hand melody, in mostly *legato* half notes, is alternately mirrored and supported in the left in rhythmic diminution: rests followed by *staccato* quarter notes, a pianistic equivalent of simultaneous head-patting and tummy-rubbing.

The seventh piece, "An Ancient Air," gains complexity with three distinct lines. It returns to Floyd's beloved Chopin mode: *Andante sostenuto,* in 6/8, with a running triplet melody in the right hand, pedals on G and E in the left. In the course of its nineteen measures, cadences occur on unexpected accidentals of A-sharp, G-sharp, C-sharp, and so forth, ending with a sly Straussian half-tone harmonic slide in the final measure. "Arietta" follows, something of a breather in that it returns to two parts; but although it centers on G Major, the accidentals are less predictable, and both melody and accompaniment employ jagged lines with wider finger-spans. With no. 9, "Lullaby," Floyd embarks on longer units to stretch young memories and fingers. Twenty-three measures in 6/4, *Lento mosso,* employ a wide-ranging melody with wider leaps, and left-hand triads spaced octaves apart. No. 10, "Chorale," ten bars in C Major and cut time, *Maestoso,* is almost exclusively chordal; but occasional moving lines in both hands complicate with switches of treble clef to bass and back in the right hand. The player is challenged to decide which of the three or four simultaneous tones wants melodic emphasis.

No. 11, "Ballad," assigns the pianist twenty-four two-part measures, with tricks and surprises: in 6/8 and C, *Allegretto poco sostenuto,* the right-hand melody features more complex dotted eighth-sixteenth rhythms, the left-hand accompaniment switching from a legato off-beat/even eighth-note syncopated pattern, and a more staccato eighth-note figure, always against the beat. No. 12, "Pavane," *Andantino,* has a single melodic line and harmonic underpinning switching back and forth from 3/4 to 4/4. In its eighteen measures, nominally in C, Floyd uses more left-hand clef-switching. That hand's accompaniment first establishes a strong quarter-rest/two-three rhythm in gentle syncopation with the melody, changing midway to a strong left-hand downbeat.

With no. 13, "Serenade," thirty bars of *Allegro moderato, cantabile,* the composer combines and shuffles all elements previously introduced: a mostly three-part melody and accompaniment, augmentation, diminution, syncopation, leaps, more challenging fingerings, more subtle dynamic and rhythmic indications. No. 14, "Wind Song," throws the young pianist a rhythmic curve ball with its 5/8 meter, *Allegretto grazioso.* At thirty-six measures the set's longest piece, centered in F, Floyd returns to just two lines; but both have melodic characteristics that span consistently larger intervals, with unpredictable rhythmic variations, harmonic turns, and quicker, subtler shifts in dynamics and volume.

The final piece of volume 1, "Burletta," has just sixteen measures, but Floyd's challenges daunt: *Allegro vivace,* 5/4 alternates with 6/4 and 7/4, and a disjunct right-hand melody with tritone and third intervals, irregular melodic and rhythmic groupings. Left-hand silences alternate four- and three-beat rest patterns, with dissonant wide-spaced triads as upbeats/downbeats, leading to more rests, then choralelike chords, as the augmented right-hand melody switches from treble clef to bass.

Jane Magrath describes volume 1 as "Mostly one-page intermediate teaching pieces from a leading contemporary American composer. Found here is linear writing that is highly pianistic within a tonal but contemporary idiom. . . . Level 4 [on a scale of 1 to 10]."[41]

For volume 2, Floyd progressed to twelve far more complex pieces of escalating difficulty, all adding emotional characters suggested by their titles: "Fanfare," "Waltz," "Processional," "Siciliano," "Dialogue," "Bagatelle," "Jig," "Night Song," "Caprice," "Impromptu," "Morning Song," and "Dance." Throughout he emphasizes syncopation and contrast, extremes of gentleness and vigor, fleet melodies passing from one hand to the other, and increasing textural density.

The last two, having begun their lives in the early fifties as "Aubade" and "Dance," though not thematically connected, were the composer's special favorites. "Morning Song," in C Major, *Andante moderato* in lilting 6/8, is far more challenging than its ABA structure at first appears. It begins with running left-hand parallel thirds in sixteenths and eighths, joined in bar three to a long-limbed, eminently vocal melody in the right, an augmentation of the original left-hand figure, functioning now as accompaniment. After a four-bar excursion to E-flat Major, tonic C reappears, with melody and accompaniment reversing hands. After progressing through B-flat Major, A Major, and D Major, an extended dominant-tonic cadence in bars twenty-four and twenty-five returns us to C, and the original configuration of melody and accompaniment, ending with a brief graceful coda and deceptive turn from A-flat Major back to G and C.

No. 12, "Dance," is a jolly rustic affair in A major, 4/4, *Allegro vivace,* with four running sixteenths, two eighths and two quarters in the right hand accented on the last two beats of the measure by staccato eighths in the left. Running sixteenths against syncopated eighths lead to another hand switch for the entire thematic complex, and a tricky contest of two sixteenths and an eighth playing against each other for the central two bars; then a mad dash of running sixteenths in octaves to a deceptive cadence on C, and an off-beat finish in the final measure.

Magrath understated when observing that these twelve pieces, with their "strongly defined characters are slightly more difficult and somewhat longer than those in Volume I. . . . Better of the two volumes. Level 7."[42]

Small wonder that the composer took such pleasure in the variety and playful sophistication of these sets; he felt commensurate disappointment when they failed to sell in any quantity. But as with most inevitables in Floyd's life, he took this one stoically, realizing that, regardless of his decades as a pianist, he had been "pegged" as an opera composer. His two best payoffs from *Episodes* came at intervals of two and nineteen years: on April 2, 1966, one of Edward Kilenyi's students, Bonnie Ann Bromberg, programmed "Morning Song," "Night Song," "An Ancient Air," and "Dance." Floyd was unable to attend what was in all likelihood a premiere; but later this usually spiky colleague knocked on his studio door and blurted out, "I just wanted to tell you, you are very talented!"

Decades later, in the summer of 1984, Floyd received a testimonial letter from Dr. Marion Weide of Whittier, California. Together with a group of thirteen students, she had selected both *Episodes* volumes as a studio project because the pieces *looked* reasonably easy and accessible; but on closer acquaintance the group found each phrase of each piece suggestive of far more, satisfying aural and emotional interests.[43]

Episodes remains in print from Boosey, mostly to gather shelf-dust. Floyd's quotidian life during this period demonstrates that composing is anything but glamorous; evenings of applause and bows are separated by long stretches of mundane chores, correspondence, and phone calls. He reaffirmed his promise to Kay to give up night work when he *did* begin a new opera, and also determined never to accept another commission that involved working through summers without a break. Yet no matter how work-focused, Floyd never missed picking up the phone or sending a card or telegram for Mother's Day, Father's Day or family birthdays.

On the heels of his successful 1962 New Orleans staging of *Susannah,* new directing offers arrived from San Antonio, New York City Opera, San Francisco Opera, and Cincinnati. In his Christmas letter to the Clarkes, he mused on the benefits of directing his own works. "This has become a very pleasant by-product of writing operas, and I have my friend Norman Treigle to thank for pushing me into the business of directing. I had all kinds of misgivings but he wouldn't take no for an answer. . . . I find it a very stimulating business and frankly being involved in this way wards off a certain amount of boredom which, inescapably, is part of my reaction to *Susannah* these days. Fortunately, other people don't respond in the same way: it looks as if the opera may have its biggest year yet this coming year."[44]

IN ITS WINTER EDITION, North Carolina's *Tercentenary News* rectified the lack of a thorough and perceptive review of *The Sojourner and Mollie Sinclair* with this analysis of its music and drama by an unidentified writer: "Floyd was not writing music to be tucked away on a shelf until future generations might come to understand it. . . . There is music here that laughs and . . . builds up to profound feeling. . . . The fascination of Floyd's work and its challenge is his forthright though not overlavish use of the dissonant musical idiom of our time, with its new beauty intermingling with light-flecked tone colors and the wonderful flexibility of his music-writing style. His music is alive with the mood and meaning of his plot. The music gives the story whatever credence it has."[45]

The article further boasted that the opera's total cost of more than twenty thousand dollars for commission and production had been raised exclusively from private donations rather than state funds. At the National Opera Association's ninth annual meeting in Detroit, the commission got additional publicity from *Mollie*'s showing via closed-circuit television on December 27. Floyd pored over minutiae, beginning with his annoyance at a discrepancy of eighteen dollars still owed Arnold Arnstein for manuscript paper for his work on the piece. Cincinnati Summer Opera had offered Floyd an absurdly low fee to direct *Susannah,* but Bob Holton negotiated a fairer sum, even though the production was only allotted one week of staging rehearsal that July.

Floyd also sent San Francisco Opera's general director Kurt Herbert Adler a set of *Susannah* ground plans to be used in that company's production, which Floyd would direct, along with suggestions for casting and conductors. In Tallahassee, the mezzo-soprano Joy Davidson, one of Nikolaidi's star students, programmed a transposed *Mystery,* and Floyd grew entranced with the lower sound. He queried Holton whether Boosey might care to bring out versions for both soprano and mezzo, but wondered in his next sentence exactly when *any* publication of the cycle would appear.[46]

Finally, it seemed that his creative dry spell—all of a month—had ended. Bass-baritone James Pease,[47] teaching at the University of Texas in Austin, approached Floyd with the idea of writing a one-act opera for the school. Floyd responded enthusiastically, proposing another vehicle for Neway and Treigle.[48]

Though Pease dropped the matter, the idea of another one-act was more firmly planted.

Holton wrote that the Carolina Charter Administration had sent a check for $1,100 for December's *Mollie Sinclair* telecasts;[49] at the same time, Florida State Opera gave two tour reprises of Floyd's *Susannah* production in high school auditoriums in Clearwater and St. Petersburg. Floyd reestablished contacts with the professional world when Norman Treigle and his wife, Linda, visited from January 22 through 29; Treigle had been hired for a St. Petersburg recital with Floyd as accompanist in a program of excerpts from *Faust*, a group of traditional spirituals, and, as an encore, "Il lacerato spirito" from Verdi's *Simon Boccanegra*.

Arnstein let Holton know that he had still not received Floyd's corrected full score for *Mollie Sinclair*, and vocal score masters still awaited the composer's corrections.[50] On January's last day, Floyd gave Holton good and bad news: Treigle had accepted less than his usual fee for Blitch in San Francisco, but Adler had hired, of all people, Herbert Grossman to conduct. Floyd had not forgotten Grossman's slighting of the work during the abortive NBC negotiations in the fifties, and was now filled with misgivings about an imminent collaboration. The proofs of *The Mystery* had arrived before the Treigles, and sat stacked on Floyd's desk; Holton reassured the composer in a letter of February 18 that Grossman was anything but hostile to *Susannah*. By February 20, Floyd was back on familiar ground at Converse College as the featured guest at the school's festival of contemporary music. Following his address on "The Isms of the Twentieth Century" that afternoon, he met his parents, aunt Doris, Ermine and Billy Matheny, and their two eldest daughters Martha and Jane, at Spartanburg's Pine Street Motel. Reverend Floyd wrote, "He looked well but a bit tired."[51] Following supper at the Holiday Inn, the entire group moved to Twichell Auditorium for the second production of *The Sojourner and Mollie Sinclair*, staged by John McCrae and sung by Hugh Egerton (Dougald), Toni Hochstein (Mollie), Sandra Parker (Jenny), and George Bitzas (Lachlan). The next day, between panel discussions on "The Contemporary Lyric Theater" and "The Art Song Since the Turn of the Century," Floyd met with the dean of music and *Mollie*'s conductor, Henry Janiec, who proposed commissioning a small-scale orchestra piece.

During that winter Floyd studied *Susannah* pencil design sketches and ground plans based on his specifications, by the San Francisco Opera's technical adviser, T. L. Colangelo Jr. North Carolina's Tercentenary Commission strove to recoup *Mollie Sinclair*'s expenses by scheduling more performances than had originally been contracted. The success of Converse's production led the organization to take East Carolina's staging to the Music Teachers' National Association conference in Greensboro, and to give repetitions on home turf at East Carolina. To make possible wider distribution of video and audio tapes, the commission sought to have Boosey & Hawkes and Floyd execute a quitclaim on media rights. Bob Holton responded that the commission itself had stipulated restrictions of such activity in the original contract; besides, Boosey had just one set of performance materials, making simultaneous productions impossible, and the commission's exclusive lock on rights expired at the end of December 1964. Holton's generous counter was that Floyd and Boosey split a one-time $500 payment to the commission to terminate the agreement immediately, that Boosey take over negotiations for future performances; and to reproduce any materials lost since the first production. The quitclaim was another matter: Holton suggested that the commission charge $150 for each showing of the tape, pay Boosey the agreed-upon $100 apiece, and keep the profit; but he insisted that this clause would also expire in December 1964.

By mid-March, Floyd corresponded with Boosey's Gertrude Smith about Arnstein's charges for eighty-one hours, $364.50,[52] contractually the composer's expense, but which he thought excessive, for transferring corrections to *Mollie Sinclair*'s masters for scores. Smith and Holton discovered that Arnstein, whom Floyd described as "unabashedly expensive,"[53] had expended 155 hours on similar corrections to *Jonathan Wade* and 205 for *Wuthering Heights*, and the new charges stood.

Better news came with Sylvia Goldstein's April 3 letter, which contained the royalty statement for 1963 and a check for $598.57. Boosey had scheduled print runs of the unison first version of "Jaybird Song" and "Free as a Frog." Floyd looked forward to receiving proofs, and his portion of the $1,000 from telecasts of *Mollie*.[54]

That spring he reaped another honor in Tallahassee, as FSU's eighth distinguished professor. His citation from Dr. Laurence Chalmers, assistant dean of faculties, emphasized benefits to the university rather than Floyd's professional accomplishments.[55] The award bore a five hundred dollar honorarium, and recipients were asked to give an "address to the future," a kind of last lecture. Floyd titled his remarks "Society and the Artist," first acknowledging that American artists had become more respectable in the last century, although our country's pioneer origins militated against the survival of any form of superficial embroidery. The nation's single-minded pursuit of stability and wealth tended to foster the peculiar snobbery that American art was somehow inferior:

> When American orchestras, singers, and instrumentalists are considered . . . to be the finest in the world, when American composers, writers, painters and playwrights enjoy the esteem of foreign audiences, such a point of view seems not only incomprehensible but exasperating. Nevertheless the American public to this day still tends to accept its artists only after they have been certified by Europe. . . . [W]e are continuing to operate in artistic matters like unlettered country cousins whose city cousins across the water have been blessed with some Divine Right in matters of art which it would be impertinent of us to question, much less hope to have for ourselves.[56]

Floyd attacked the myth of the artist as spoiled child, characterized by "endowment of arrogance, eccentricity, and symptoms of general emotional instability"; he pinpointed "society's concept of the artist . . . [to be] something of an outsider" who must "be indulged and excused as a person not entirely grown-up or responsible." The fault, he believed, was trisected between history, an undereducated public, and the artist himself. He then proposed that mankind has a dualistic need: first, the essentials of food, clothing, and shelter, then

> the vicarious experience to provide his own life with illumination, continuity and enrichment, and the crucial element for him in this second life of art is . . . recognition and identification. All the arts of the theater, painting, poetry, and the novel supply him with this in a very tangible form and I suspect that music provides him with an externalization of his unconscious self.

This would happen only if society mandated that art in all its forms was accepted as a necessity rather than a luxury:

> The view of history is long and pitiless and I don't think it is merely coincidental that our most intimate contact with civilizations long since dust has been through the art that has survived them. This is no caprice of Providence but is . . . as it should be, for what more accurate, more immediate access do we have to the hearts and minds of men than through what they reveal of themselves and their age in art, for art, after all is said and done, is revelation.

The Tercentenary staff soon reached agreement with Boosey, as demonstrated by the next performance of *Mollie Sinclair* in Greenville on April 30. Floyd arrived a day early to speak before the open dress rehearsal. Except for Neway and Treigle, the cast duplicated the previous December's.[57] Floyd repacked and left for San Francisco around May 1, checked into the Hotel El Cortez, and began staging the Spring Opera's *Susannah.* The day after he arrived, Kurt Herbert Adler invited the composer into his inner sanctum and proposed a commission through the Ford Foundation on some John Steinbeck subject. Floyd confided that he had been thinking for some time about *Of Mice and Men* as a vehicle for Treigle and Richard Cassilly.[58] Adler was delighted: of all of Steinbeck's writings, *Of Mice and Men* was the only one he had *not* considered; and he suggested that Bob Holton secure rights (already in progress) while Adler initiated the Ford process.

After eleven years of *Susannah,* Floyd marveled that anyone regarded it as a new work; but he thought this its best production to date, with staunch allies in Lee Venora in the title role, Cassilly and Treigle in theirs, and Herbert Kraus as Little Bat. The collaboration with Herbert Grossman proved congenial and productive. Floyd, for whom intimacy became an honor sparingly bestowed, found the conductor "a friend . . . flexible, quick, and very alert to both musical and dramatic values." The two men tinkered with the still-thick orchestration, making it more transparent and singer-friendly. Neither mentioned their previous acquaintance. Floyd was thrilled with Colangelo's designs and the costumes: "The set is a beauty and the costumes are coordinated . . . everything sepia, black, and off-white except for the principals' . . . I don't think it's an exaggeration to say that I have been happier working here than with any place I have ever been connected. They have treated me wonderfully and the facilities for production seem limitless. At this point, before I even leave, I am hoping to come back—and soon."

FLOYD AND TREIGLE continued to discuss a New Orleans commission: in his May 9 letter to Holton, Floyd reported for the first time, besides Adler's *Of Mice and Men* offer, his desire to compose *Markheim.* Treigle outlined to Floyd his negotiations with the New Orleans board, presenting the arrangement as a certainty. Owing entirely to Floyd's friendship for and gratitude to Treigle for so many years of partnership, *Markheim* would be Floyd's first—and only—opera written without a contractual guarantee of a premiere.

Floyd was accustomed to working quickly and in rapid sequence after *Susannah*'s New York debut, completing two substantially different versions of *Wuthering Heights* between 1957 and 1959, and *The Passion of Jonathan Wade* from 1960 until October 1962. Producing *The Sojourner and Mollie Sinclair* in the year between November 1962 and 1963, he resembled a man determined to have a large family: one growing, another in the basket, and a third in planning stages. Back from San Francisco, he wrote Holton a long, informative letter, fixing the Steinbeck commission as his highest priority.[59] He had the streamlined orchestration that he and Grossman devised incorporated into *Susannah*'s instrumental parts and full score by Boosey, for its next outing with the Cincinnati Summer Opera. Pleased with *Episodes* but disappointed by their reception after Boosey's publication in 1965, Floyd switched gears in his reminder to Holton. "You once said that before I began a new opera, either one-act or full length, you wanted me to consider revising *Jonathan Wade.* I am willing to do this, but is there any particular point in it unless there is a definite performance in the offing? I have thought about some revisions and also re-writing, both on a fairly extensive scale, but of course this also depends upon what, if anything, B. & H. is agreeable to investing in changes. If Julius wants to revive the opera and if you all are willing to make the revisions we all agree are to the benefit of the opera, then I am ready to plunge in."

Thus Floyd had yet to begin either *Markheim* or *Of Mice and Men* by the summer of 1964. At FSU, Dean Kuersteiner approached retirement, and Floyd's colleague, choral director Wiley Housewright, stood next in line. *Of Mice and Men* would demand the composer's usual intensive work periods over the next summers; but Floyd, Housewright, and the composer Norman Dello Joio proposed a program for librettists and composers of operas for high schools for summer 1965, with Ford Foundation backing. If San Francisco came through, Floyd knew that Ford would not countenance any duplication of fees, and told Holton that he much preferred the opera commission; thus *Markheim*'s future also depended on Adler. Floyd's contingency plan, in case San Francisco fell through, or if Steinbeck denied rights, would be to concentrate on *Markheim,* even without a commitment to perform; should New Orleans fall through, Treigle assured Floyd that San Antonio's Victor D'Alessandro would premiere *Markheim* on a double bill with *The Sojourner and Mollie Sinclair.* Finally, after further conversation with Converse's Henry Janiec, Floyd turned down their five hundred dollar commission for a chamber orchestra piece.

With no forward motion on either opera project, Floyd approached summer 1964 with trepidation.

Then Holton, in touch with the Metropolitan Opera stage director Michael Manuel, wrote that the Met's new National Company would open their first season, 1965/66, with *Susannah.*[60] President John F. Kennedy had announced on October 11, 1963 that the National Cultural Center in Washington, DC, soon rechristened the Kennedy Center for the Performing Arts, would cosponsor the Metropolitan Opera's new permanent national company, to bring musical theater to communities otherwise without access to the medium and to showcase America's young talent.[61]

The Met's board president, Anthony Bliss, strongly supported the plan, to the acute discomfort of his general manager, Rudolf Bing, who feared that the new operation would divert funds and attention from the parent company's operations, especially its annual national tours. The new entity's artistic leadership was first offered to the German stage director Walter Felsenstein, to mount productions of unusual repertoire or of familiar works in new interpretations; but because of Felsenstein's association with East Berlin's Komische Oper, identified in turn with the country's Communist dictatorship, he was denied a visa to enter and work in the United States. The Met next coaxed the American mezzo-soprano Risë Stevens out of retirement to serve as the National Company's artistic director, and British-born Michael Manuel as the administrator.[62]

As the season took shape, twenty-eight young singers from all over the United States and Canada assembled for a full fifty-two weeks of employment, including three months of pretouring rehearsals; there were 260 performances in seventy-two cities in North America and Mexico, to audiences totaling more than a half a million. Robert LaMarchina became the group's first music director and principal conductor, of Rossini's *Cenerentola,* Puccini's *Madama Butterfly,* Bizet's *Carmen,* and, as it indeed turned out, Floyd's *Susannah.* Manuel confirmed reduced orchestration as imperative for the tour's unpredictable venues. In the course of a phone conversation with Holton on June 11, Floyd agreed, as long as Boosey assumed the expense of printing the changes he had already written into his score and San Francisco's parts, in which he had further corrected myriad errors in notation, dynamics, and tempo. Between Hershey Kay's work for the 1958 Brussels production and the new Floyd/Grossman changes, it would be a favor to all to arrive at a single orchestration for future productions. To assist in this substantial effort, Holton enlisted the services of the young conductor Ross Reimueller, to edit *Susannah*'s new vocal score, already a big seller for Boosey. Floyd met Reimueller a number of times in New York, and had subsequent phone sessions with this diligent scribe; he described Reimueller as a "musical watchmaker" who ferreted out the tiniest inaccuracies. Their work was and still is the basis of every *Susannah* vocal score that rolled off Boosey's presses after 1967.[63]

When Holton hired a money-saving copyist in Mexico for part extraction, Floyd agreed to take 25 percent of rental fees rather than his contracted 33 and 1/3 percent. Manuel planned to attend the Cincinnati production, directed by Floyd, and let the composer explain the reorchestration in detail. As it turned out, Hershey Kay's orchestration was kept as a first option, and the Floyd/Grossman revisions as a second, for companies with larger pits and budgets.[64] Also that June, FSU band director Robert T. Braunagel requested and received Floyd's permission, through Boosey, to make a band arrangement of *Susannah* excerpts.[65]

FLOYD'S PLATE may have been fuller than ever in 1964, but all was far from well at Boosey & Hawkes, beginning with its head of serious music, Robert Holton. One of the firm's last founding family members, Ralph Hawkes, had died in 1950, and his brother Geoffrey's tenure as chairman almost forced the company into bankruptcy in 1960. When the other name partner, Leslie Boosey, retired in 1964, the company engaged in an almost literal round of musical chairs for its principal administrative positions. David Adams, managing director of the New York office, with whom Floyd had solid relations, received a summons back to the London home office as director of music publishing. W. Stuart Pope came from the firm's South African office in early 1964 to succeed Adams, and it soon became apparent to many that this model expat Englishman, with a performing background in English boy choirs and later as an organist, was experiencing difficulties. Even the eminently agreeable Floyd remembered Pope as stiff and formal, and felt that Holton's encyclopedic contacts with composers, performers, managers, agents, and company directors threatened the new boss.[66] At any rate, Holton moved that summer to another venerable New York firm, G. Schirmer, Inc., of whose rental department of symphonic and operatic repertoire he took charge.

Cincinnati Opera performed Floyd's *Susannah* production twice in July, with Joy Clements and Norman Treigle, and conducted by Julius Rudel. In Bob Holton's July 21 letter to Floyd, the last in Boosey's files, he told the composer that he had flown back to New York with Rudel, and tried—unsuccessfully—to enlist the conductor for a double bill of *Mollie Sinclair* and the as-yet-unwritten *Markheim.* Rudel, however, felt bound to revive *Jonathan Wade* at City Opera as early as 1965/66, and Holton urged Floyd to begin revising,[67] but Floyd's wounds were still too fresh for such an immersion that was further complicated by the two new operas in process. Though he had signed a five-year renewal with Boosey in 1961, the question of whether to follow Holton, an able and motivated champion and personal friend, nagged at him, but Holton described his new job as a stop gap until he could find a better arena for his skills and ambition. In fact, when Holton left Schirmer in 1967 to become head of Theodore Presser's New York office,[68] Floyd told him, "When you decide where you're settling down, then we can talk."

Floyd wrote Sylvia Goldstein of other concerns: "I am looking forward to a few weeks away from the University and its unending claims on my time. I can't be too hard on my employer, however, since I am provided with a good livelihood for these claims!"[69]

ON AUGUST 18, Reverend and Mrs. Floyd, and Ermine's two eldest daughters Martha and Jane, arrived in Tallahassee for a visit. Jane has piquant memories of this visit, and provides a rare view of the serious composer at his relative ease:

> "Idy [Ida], with her pin-curled hair, drove their big old black preacher's Ford, while Nandy [Reverend Floyd] wore his skimmer hat holding down a handkerchief on his neck so the air wouldn't hurt his asthma. Martha and I were in the backseat, with me playing my guitar and us wailin' Beatles songs with our legs sticking out of the windows since it was hot as hell, before the age of car AC! We always loved entertaining at Carlisle and Kay's house. We taught them how to do the "dirty dog," and sang Beatles and Dylan songs and basked in the attention of our elders and groovy aunt and uncle."[70]

Reverend Floyd, despite his asthma, wrote of this visit, "Carlisle surely is a wonderful son and strong man. He is so thoughtful of everyone, no wonder he was voted the most distinguished professor at FSU this year. I thanked God for him."[71]

Floyd never received this sentiment in any direct form.

When the Met finally announced *Susannah* for the National Company's first season, Stuart Pope wrote Floyd—the two men had yet to meet—that the company planned twenty-five performances, for which Pope reduced the royalty fee to $250 for each, or a guaranteed total of $6,250, the 2007 equivalent of almost $42,000.[72] Floyd had hoped to get to New York that fall, to meet with the Met's announced stage director Edwin Sherin;[73] but in the meantime that job had been reassigned to José Quintero, whose Broadway productions of contemporary plays Floyd had admired since the late forties. The two had rubbed shoulders during Quintero's direction of Weill's *Lost in the Stars* at New York City Opera in 1957, and Norman Dello Joio's *The Triumph of St. Joan* in 1960.[74]

On November 3, Floyd accompanied Elena Nikolaidi at an FSU concert in "He Has Kissed Me" and "Rocking" from *The Mystery,* in the lower transposition he had done for Joy Davidson. Winter's end and spring 1965 were packed with stressors: Boosey without Bob Holton experienced such difficulties as the late delivery of Arnstein's *Mollie Sinclair* vocal score and the firm seemed perplexed by what to do with the four different orchestrations of *Susannah* currently in their files.[75] On March 12, Floyd lectured and participated in a panel discussion at the Florida Composers' League twenty-first annual convention at the University of Tampa. That afternoon he and Nikolaidi repeated the complete *Mystery,* minus its second song, "Gentleness," and the University of Tampa Madrigal Singers performed the "Jaybird Song" from *Susannah.*

At the end of March, New York City Opera revived *Susannah,*[76] in Paul Sylbert's 1958 sets, but this time directed *and* conducted by Julius Rudel. Joy Clements sang the title role, Treigle and Cassilly repeated their now all but mandatory characterizations, and Julian Miller sang Little Bat. With the opera in its second decade, critic Miles Kastendieck found that it was "wearing well," and that it had in fact "deepened first impressions of its worth."[77]

BEFORE IMMERSING HIMSELF in Steinbeck's California, Floyd had to complete *Markheim,* on which he had been working since at least the beginning of the year.[78] Robert Louis Stevenson's source story gleams as an example of his skill with concentrated forms; it made its first appearance in a Christmas periodical.[79] In a brief life—1850 to 1894—plagued by a complex of bronchial ailments, Stevenson honored and rebelled against his Scottish Presbyterian heritage; he excelled at historical adventure (*Treasure Island, The Master of Ballantrae, Kidnapped*) and terror (*Strange Case of Dr. Jekyll and Mr. Hyde*), the works linked by extremes of human good and evil and the consequences of both. With his asthmatic background, Floyd could empathize with the writer's medical history. The composer's own background in short fiction, plus Stevenson's ambivalence toward organized religion, made *Markheim* a natural choice for Floyd's seventh opera.

Only with *Wuthering Heights* had he adapted existing literature; even with *Susannah,* the Apocrypha provided the loosest of frames. Stevenson's greatest strengths—sharply observed nuances, meditations on character and its mirror to and on environment—created obstacles for librettist Floyd. No matter how keen the writing, music could substitute for only so much narrative description or inner monologue.

Stevenson's tale is clean and simple. Influenced by Dostoevsky's *Crime and Punishment,* the tales of Edgar Allan Poe such as "The Tell-Tale Heart," and Dickens's *A Christmas Carol,* it is told from the protagonist's point of view. Markheim, a dissolute nobleman, visits an antique store/pawnshop on Christmas Eve, pretending to look for a present for his fiancée. When the sarcastic proprietor shows him a mirror, Markheim is terrified by his own reflection. The dealer turns his back to look for more goods, Markheim knifes him to death and rifles the corpse for keys to the man's cashbox. Then, betraying a debt to both Goethe's and Gounod's *Faust,* a man, clearly of supernatural origin, appears in the doorway, asking, "Did you call me?" and offers his services. Markheim believes the stranger to be the devil, but others have seen him as an angel or a manifestation of Markheim's conscience. For the remainder of the story, the two characters hold a metaphysical discussion of good, evil, and the waste of Markheim's life. With the dealer's servant about to return, Markheim decides to redeem himself: though he may have lost the love of good, he still hates evil. The stranger disappears, the servant appears, and Markheim tells her to call the police.

Floyd saw that he could never have entrusted such tricky material to a student, and its problems provoked new solutions. He began by giving Stevenson's anonymous dealer a Dickensian name, Josiah Creach, and whereas Stevenson places the murder quite early in his story, Floyd needed more time to establish character and motive. He invented lively dialogue between Markheim and Creach to replace Stevenson's string of quasi-Handelian aria-monologues. The brooding Markheim would be for Treigle's bass-baritone; both slimy Creach and the Stranger would be tenors; and Floyd all but invented the servant's role, a lyric-coloratura soprano he named Tess. An offstage group of carolers provided bookends to establish the Christmas setting and to provoke Markheim's reminiscences of innocent childhood, briefly mentioned by Stevenson. Whereas Stevenson had Markheim go upstairs to rummage for money, Floyd renovated the shop as a one-floor unit set below street level and installed a doorway from upstairs through which the Stranger appears.

After these fundamental changes, the libretto unfurled smoothly and quickly. Following the initial carol, Markheim flings through the shop door. Attired in going-to-shabby black cape and top hat, sporting a cane, Floyd makes him somewhere between thirty-five and forty, dissipated and pallid: right up Treigle's alley. Creach shoos away the holiday celebrants, veiling his sarcasm to Markheim in thin courtesy, but the two men have done business before. Markheim, wishing to recapture his childhood innocence, reminisces about sunnier Christmases past, but is undone when Creach's numerous clocks chime at once.

The maidservant Tess takes her leave, but not before flirting with Markheim. This prompts Creach's fresh insults, and further revelations from his dissolute client, who faces danger from cuckolds and fathers; from the law, for drug use; and from former friends he has blackmailed. Now in urgent need of cash, Markheim tries to soften Creach's hostility by claiming that he is being hounded for gambling debts, only spurring the dealer to new taunts. Markheim reveals a supposed heirloom to pawn, a statue he claims is the final remnant of his father's collection; Creach recognizes the piece as stolen goods, goading Markheim to confess that he is indeed the thief. The seeming vigilance of the clocks intensifies his pathetic entreaties, but Creach overplays his hand, pointing out family items that Markheim has pawned with him over the years, turning a hand mirror—inspired by the device Stevenson used at the beginning of his tale—to show his visitor what a liar and thief looks like. Finally, a little more than halfway through his score, Floyd has Markheim strangle Creach with his bare hands, whereupon all the room's clocks chime eleven.

Markheim ruminates on having added murder to the list of his vices, and the sound of sleigh bells outside reawakens longing for his youthful Christmas Eves. The guilty man now believes that someone is in the house, and drags Creach's corpse behind the shop counter. He seizes a fat ring of keys and searches for his victim's cashbox. We hear steps descending from above; Markheim stares in mute terror as a figure looking and dressed much like a younger Markheim appears, only elegant and immaculate. The Stranger asks Markheim whether he would like to know the location of Creach's money. The two conduct a dialogue much like Stevenson's from this point on, tension building as the Stranger reminds Markheim of Tess's presence just blocks away. Markheim pretends that Creach was already dead when he entered, but the omniscient Stranger laughs, declaring that he has had his eye on Markheim for years, and offers his assistance, urging haste, as Tess approaches the shop. He hints that a life of sensual luxury awaits the murderer, but at a Faustian price. They veer from Markheim's odd protestations that he has yet to completely embrace evil, to the Stranger's seductive urgings, which turn to taunts and threats. When the doorbell rings, in a breathless rush the Stranger tells Markheim to kill the maid, the final link to Creach's murder. At the last moment, Markheim throws open the door, and, between the maid's perplexed queries and the Stranger's agitated promptings, finally confesses. Tess screams for the police, the clocks strike midnight, and Markheim laughs and cries in relief, singing a final reprise of the carol with the offstage chorus.[80]

WUTHERING HEIGHTS, *The Mystery, Jonathan Wade,* and *Mollie Sinclair* demonstrate Floyd's forcible progress to greater complexity of form and harmonic language; now *Markheim* guided him to an even more mature style, weeks before he turned forty. For this most rational and least superstitious of men to have recourse to a supernatural element seems ironic; but Floyd regarded the Stranger, as do numerous commentators, as a surreal projection, Markheim's double. Stevenson provided dramatic concision that allowed Floyd to use his very orchestra as a protagonist. Percussion instruments serve as clocks, intensifying the press of time, furthering the musical storytelling, and helping to clothe the seventy-minute work in Floyd's most organic, sophisticated text and music to date. After the haste in which he composed *Jonathan Wade* and *Mollie Sinclair,* he determined to never again provide critics an opening to smite him for unsophisticated orchestration.

To the press he explained this as the first opera he had written expressly for an individual, and without a commission; it was also the first stage work that he dedicated to a singer, Treigle, of whom he was still thinking for George in *Of Mice and Men*.[81] The lack of advance money from New Orleans meant that Floyd's only compensation would come from royalties, rentals, sales of sheet music, and mechanical rights. Boosey charged New Orleans $500 for the first performance and $300 for the second; rentals were similarly graded at $250/$150. At 50 percent of grand and small rights, and 25 percent of rentals, this means that Floyd's initial earnings for more than a year's work on *Markheim* came to around $500.

To Martha Baxter, who had taken over Holton's function as Floyd's agent at Boosey, the composer expressed panic to finish the new score and have it copied and delivered to New Orleans; he promised to send "sixty-odd pages" for Arnstein.[82] Thanks to FSU's trimester system, he saw two free months ahead to complete the piece, tentatively scheduled for performance on August 26 and 28. He agreed to serve as stage director; but having finished the opera without a firm premiere date, he wondered whether Boosey might negotiate the premiere production with a different company. Finally, on May 28, he phoned Treigle to see what was really going on, and learned that *Markheim* had been announced for March 31, 1966.[83]

The *Tallahassee Democrat* reported Floyd's citation by the editors of *Who's Who in the South and Southwest*, selected from fifteen thousand nominees, for single-handedly and brilliantly rescuing American opera from oblivion.[84] A few days later, Treigle visited the Floyds to coach *Markheim* with the composer,[85] who proceeded to finish his orchestration around mid-July.[86]

For the remainder of the summer, Floyd drafted his *Of Mice and Men* libretto, sending it off around the second week of September to Annie Laurie Williams, one of Steinbeck's agents, for the writer's approval: the composer wanted to embark on his next journey with a clear mind. The Met's National Company had chosen to inaugurate their tour season in the country's heartland, in Indianapolis, with *Susannah* on September 20. Arriving five days early, Floyd attended final dress rehearsal at Butler University's two-year-old Clowes Memorial Hall.

He was at first disconcerted: At the end of act 2, scene 4, as the elders and wives snubbed Susannah as they left the church picnic supper, Floyd noticed that four of his measures had been lopped off. When he corralled an assistant and asked what had happened to those bars, he was told, "Oh, they couldn't think of anything to do there"; but otherwise, director José Quintero's work excited him. Setting the work at the turn of the century rather than in the Depression years gave it a gentle lyricism that Floyd found quite theatrical. He was much taken with David Hays's efficient but atmospheric sets, and the strong cast that included Maralin Niska and Mary Munroe alternating in the title role, Vern Shinall and Arnold Voketaitis as Blitch, Chris Lachona and Robert Bennett as Sam, and Robert Cowden as Little Bat, conducted by Robert LaMarchina.

Another perk of this trip was reunion with Bronja and Sidney Foster, whom he visited in Bloomington. With opening night seats reserved for invited VIPs, Foster did not attend, but nevertheless ferried his former student back and forth in an enormous vintage Cadillac. Although Foster headed Indiana University's piano department, conversation inevitably turned to the school's extraordinary opera program. The brainchild of university president Herman B. Wells, who hired Canadian-born Wilfred C. Bain as music dean in 1947, Indiana University unveiled its first modest opera production that summer. In fewer than twenty years, this unlikely rural entity earned the envy of most other colleges, conservatories, and professional companies worldwide; but Wilfred Bain guarded his golden hoard like Siegfried's dragon. Always courteous to Floyd whenever they met at symposia and conferences, Bain seemed determined *not* to produce *Susannah*. This had nothing to do with the score's qualities, challenges, or technical requirements, and Floyd smiled to hear Foster's explanation: Bain simply refused to give a rival like Florida State an iota of credence or publicity.[87]

Though Foster had slighted Floyd's compositions during their work together at FSU, the Met event elevated Floyd to a different level. Foster enthused, "Norman [Dello Joio] always wanted to write a Great American Opera, and here *you've* done it!"

On the street, Floyd met Rudolf Bing, who, in a rare amiable mood, stopped and introduced himself.

Risë Stevens and Michael Manuel went out of their way to include Floyd in all functions around the event, and opening night had all the glamour for which the Met was famous. *Time* reported the hoopla, from searchlights to a limo parade with protopaparazzi, and touted *Susannah* as "a gripping tragedy of man's inhumanity to man in the name of religion." The magazine called the event "a resounding success on all counts."[88]

FLOYD RETURNED HOME as *Episodes* went into print. He wrote Sylvia Goldstein, "The Indianapolis performance . . . was excellent, as you have doubtless heard by now, and was by all odds the most gala event I have ever witnessed. I hope the Company fares well at Lincoln Center next month."[89]

Floyd was referring to an ironic twist of the tour: Following a two-week residency in Indianapolis, the company performed in Fort Wayne, Cincinnati, Cleveland, and Detroit. From November 1 through 20, they landed, not at the old Met downtown at 1423 Broadway, where the parent company was rehearsing Donizetti's *L'elisir d'amore,* but at New York City Opera's new home turf, the New York State Theatre, uptown at Lincoln Center. And Floyd need not have worried: *The New York Times* reported that the opera "fits the . . . National Company like a glove."[90]

A footnote to the tour of the National Company came with its performances in Guadalajara, Mexico. Irving Kolodin, a selective Floyd enthusiast, reported his emotional response to hearing "the surge of life that coursed through the music [of] . . . Floyd's freshly felt, deeply motivated work for the first time in a foreign country."[91]

Another indication of Floyd's acceptance in the higher reaches of the professional world came with the soprano Eileen Farrell's first New York solo recital in five seasons, on December 4, 1965, at Hunter College's Assembly Hall. Her aria group included one of the arias from *Susannah*—the *Times* review failed to specify which—and the feisty, outspoken soprano actually caused an incident. The critic reported audience applause following one particular high note, whereupon Farrell good-naturedly observed that she didn't think the tone all that good; "'And I haven't finished.'"[92]

AFTER PROCESSING STEINBECK'S FEEDBACK and altering his *Of Mice and Men* draft, Floyd flew to Ohio for a brief residency at Oberlin College in December's second week. Awaiting him in Tallahassee was a letter from Norman Dello Joio, whom the Juilliard School had asked to approach colleagues for its new Repertory Project (JRP), an initiative in the works since November 1963. In August 1964, a grant of $308,310 from the United States Office of Education enabled Juilliard to assemble or generate high-quality works.[93]

This effort would involve commissioning leading American composers to write works for different age groups. Subsequent JRP directors, the composers Vittorio Giannini and Roger Sessions, were charged with administration, and Dello Joio coordinated contemporary music. He recruited nineteen composers of vocal music including, besides Floyd, Jack Beeson, Mark Bucci, Nicholas Flagello, Morton Gould, Lee Hoiby, Ulysses Kay, Daniel Pinkham, Ned Rorem, Peter Schickele, and Robert Starer.

In his response to JRP's associate director, Arnold Fish, Floyd wrote, "I am very interested . . . in it, and find its aims and objectives wholly admirable. I have nothing I can submit to you from a backlog of compositions since everything that might be suitable is currently in print. Therefore I would like to think in terms of a few songs, either unison or two-part."[94] The composer also understated when asking about financial arrangements and deadlines: "With present commitments"—meaning *Markheim* and *Of Mice and Men*—"this would have some bearing on my being able to participate."

Fish replied on February 11 that he thought Floyd's suggestion perfect. The initial fee would be fifty to seventy-five dollars for each unison or two-part song, in return for a license to test the works in seven school districts throughout the country. If chosen for JRP's anthology, Juilliard would ask Boosey to pay similar amounts for outright purchase of the pieces; and if the anthology saw more than one printing, further payments would be negotiated. For grades K-3, each piece was to last one minute or less; for grades 4–6, two minutes or less. The form was to be simple and clear, and contain intervals of no more than a fifth for

K-3, the ranges from middle C to third-line treble D. Rhythms should be strong and invite body movement, and texts should appeal to a child's imagination and be cleared if copyrighted. For K-3, "Monody is mandatory; in third grade, some easy two-part pieces were possible, including rounds and canons at the unison; some two- and three-part writing, including canons, were acceptable for 4–6, with even a few canons at the fifth. Composers should write simple piano accompaniments, or descants for other instruments."[95]

FLOYD AND KAY arrived in New Orleans in the first week of March for stagings of *Markheim*. Their housing arrangement was quintessential Treigle: maneuvering through an arcane labyrinth of hometown acquaintances, he settled on the childhood home of New York agent Muriel Francis, née Bultman, a sprawling antebellum mansion in the heart of the city's Garden District. The structure actually incorporated two joined buildings; one housed the Bultman family, the other, the venerable House of Bultman funeral home, had conducted final rites for such diverse clients as Confederate President Jefferson Davis and the actress Jayne Mansfield.

Bultman père, A. Fred, was known to accept fine antique furniture and other artifacts in lieu of specie for his services, and both buildings were furnished entirely in nineteenth-century splendor. Floyd found their quarters, which had fifteen-foot ceilings and looming armoires, "a little spooky," and Treigle thought the whole arrangement hilarious: "You'd better watch out that those undertakers don't mistake you for a body." Each morning, Floyd and Kay made their way to the cavernous kitchen, and tucked into Creole breakfast fare and chicory coffee, under the scornful eye of Muriel Francis. As Floyd observed, "She weighed all of eighty pounds, and simply despised people eating; but we disregarded her and ate heartily."

Besides Treigle, the cast of *Markheim* included tenor William Diard as the Stranger and soprano Audrey Schuh as Tess.[96] Librettist-composer Floyd's alter ego as stage director saw an immediate problem: Canadian tenor Alan Crofoot,[97] singing the role of Creach, topped the scales at well above three hundred pounds, and Floyd had specified that Markheim—the cadaverously thin Treigle—drag the corpse behind Creach's shop counter. Treigle joked that this stage business gave him hemorrhoids for life, but that Floyd lived up to his publicity is confirmed in a Treigle interview in which the bass praised the composer's "fantastic mind for drama."[98]

Ermine and Billy Matheny made the trip from Holly Hill, as did a clutch of about thirty friends from Tallahassee, including the Mastrogiacomos and Choppins; but for once, probably because Reverend Floyd was dealing with preparations for Holy Week, the composer's parents did not attend. The world premiere performances on March 31 and April 2, conducted by the company's artistic director, Knud Andersson, on a double bill with the Paul Dukas ballet *La Péri*, proved all that the company and Treigle had hoped.[99] Floyd won high praise for his adaptation of Stevenson, without "a note . . . that isn't meaningful in the creation of atmosphere, and the revelation of character . . . in a logical, believable and gripping manner."[100]

For once, national monthlies glowed for Floyd. *Opera News* enthused, "as staged by the composer the opera built to a moving climax. Floyd has not charted new musical paths with *Markheim* but has provided a taut score . . . that underlies the onstage drama and at times reflects the lyric expansiveness of his *Susannah*. Vocal dialogue occasionally gives way to extended monologue or *arioso*, while the orchestra is used throughout to heighten the tension as Markheim's self-destruction is played out. In his adaptation . . . Floyd has successfully transformed a metaphysical tale into gripping theater."[101]

High Fidelity went even further, declaring *Markheim* "a work at least equally worthy of success [as *Susannah*], one which should excite and satisfy every audience. . . . Floyd's skill as a composer proved equal to the challenge. . . . He eschews Wagnerian symphonicism, virtuoso vocalism, and any other device that would detract from maximum concentration of dramatic effect."[102]

The production's tour to San Antonio on November 17 then played at the University of Texas twenty-fifth annual fine arts festival on November 18 and 20, reaping similar unqualified good press.[103]

The end of the spring trimester found Floyd coaching his student composer Carl Vollrath through the first production of *The Quest,* Vollrath's opera about the Children's Crusade of 1212, conducted by Harry Dunscombe on June 10 and 11. Floyd celebrated his fortieth birthday on the latter date; Bob Holton visited and as always sounded out the composer as to whether he could be lured away from Boosey & Hawkes. Holton attended Vollrath's performance and gave the student valuable advice: "You've got to interest people in the first ten minutes after the curtain goes up."[104]

At the end of the 1965–66 school year, Karl Kuersteiner retired as dean of music, but continued to teach until 1971. Floyd served on a national search committee, and after interviewing numerous candidates, the school chose one of its own, the choral director Wiley Housewright. Floyd was concerned for his friend, knowing the pitfalls of rising to a high administrative position from the ranks. He personally experienced no difficulty, but felt great discontent from the rest of the music faculty.

He was right.

14

Of Mice, Men, Martyrs, Flowers, Hawks

1963–1972

Late in life, Carlisle Floyd confirmed that his two proudest accomplishments began with the demolition and reconstruction of his piano technique with Sidney Foster. The second is his invention and reinvention of what is, after *Susannah,* his most popular opera, *Of Mice and Men.* Foster's intervention took most of a year; the Steinbeck odyssey, seven:

> No other work of mine has been as problematic, as trying, and occasionally as disheartening as *Of Mice and Men.* . . . I have never before invested what seemed . . . the endless amount of time required to complete [it]. To be fair . . . as is sometimes the case with difficult and willful children, no other opera gave me as much pleasure once it was finished.[1]

But, as he continued, "this is all getting ahead of the story."

WITH THE APPEARANCE OF *Of Mice and Men* in 1937, John Steinbeck began to taste real success. His previous novels and short stories had received mixed criticism and minimal attention.[2] Only with *Tortilla Flat* (1935) did he strike sparks with the reading public and some reviewers. His situation paralleled Floyd's in certain respects: by the time the latter turned thirty, he had written three operas, of which the third brought overnight fame. Although he and Steinbeck could hardly have differed more in personality and character, a casual scan of the writer's biography presents a few startling correspondences: shyness, inferiority about personal appearance, and, particularly, complex feelings about both parents that contributed to alternating patterns of compulsive productivity, crippling insecurity, and depression.

On the positive side, Steinbeck and Floyd both preserved a confidence in their gifts that was borne out by early excellence at reading and writing; both mined their own lives, cultures, and societies for creative ore; and both remained thorough professionals, passionate about their work, at times to the exclusion of their health and relationships. To co-opt a phrase of Ralph Waldo Emerson's, cited by Jay Parini in his biography of the writer, Steinbeck and Floyd were exemplars of "Man Thinking," absorbing and pondering all that the physical world, history, literature, poetry and their allied arts offered; whose resulting thoughts and perceptions exist in a constant state of evolution, and who engage with the world, milking "experience for what it was worth in imaginative value."[3]

Steinbeck's 1962 acceptance speech for the Nobel Prize for literature captures much of Carlisle Floyd: The writer, Steinbeck felt, has a duty to expose the shortcomings of individuals and societies; to expose, in the name of improvement, our dark natures and fantasies to the light of day; and to examine, promote, and celebrate the human spirit in all its conditions.[4]

As early as summer 1920, Steinbeck worked on ranches that raised cattle and grew sugar beets, hay, and alfalfa in California's Salinas Valley. He rubbed shoulders with "bindlestiffs," Depression Era drifters from one temporary job to another, and real-life models for George and Lennie in *Of Mice and Men.* Steinbeck based Lennie on an actual ranch hand who killed a boss for firing a friend, resulting in his incarceration in a California asylum in 1937: "Stuck a pitchfork right through his stomach. I hate to tell you how many times. . . . We couldn't stop him until it was too late."[5]

By 1936, convinced that the traditional novel was dead, Steinbeck imagined writing a children's story based on his bindlestiff acquaintances. This turned into the notion of an experimental play for reading, in three acts of two chapters each, accounting in part for the novel's preponderance of dialogue over narrative, and the ease with which the author turned it into a play. In about two months, Steinbeck wrote the story of smart George and dim Lennie, and their failed dream of a place of their own. At just 31,000 words, he called it his "new little manuscript,"[6] structuring it with "is-thinking," the nonjudgmental presentation of human situations. He kept the working title *Something That Happened* until a friend, no doubt swayed by the scenes of Lennie and his mouse, recalled the verse of Scottish poet Robert Burns, "To a Mouse." "The best laid schemes o' mice an' men/Gang aft agley" (dialect for "often go awry"). Shortly after the book's publication in February 1937, it sold 117,000 copies; it and *The Grapes of Wrath* (1939) continue to sell as Steinbeck's most popular works.

The novella soon attracted attention on Broadway and in Hollywood. Encouraged by his agent, Annie Laurie Williams, and the playwright-director George S. Kaufman, Steinbeck made his own theatrical adaptation. *Of Mice and Men* played for 207 performances at New York's Music Box Theatre, beginning in November 1937. Directed by Kaufman, Wallace Ford played George, Broderick Crawford played Lennie, and Will Geer, Slim. The book's first film treatment came two years later with music by Aaron Copland. Directed by Lewis Milestone, the cast featured Burgess Meredith as George and Lon Chaney Jr. as Lennie. It reaped four Academy Award nominations.

AS EARLY AS NOVEMBER 1963, while Floyd completed *The Sojourner and Mollie Sinclair,* Bob Holton saw a Great American Opera in their future, and nudged Floyd to reread Steinbeck. As the composer visualized Treigle and Cassilly as his protagonists, and a Ford-sponsored San Francisco commission in the works, he found himself "struck by its play-like qualities in addition to its memorable characters and theatrical scenes. Not knowing at the time that Steinbeck had very successfully dramatized his book for the stage . . . I thought I detected act-endings and scenes that built to curtains. . . . I frequently experienced that particular excitement reserved for books, plays, or whatever, that seem ideal for conversion into operas."[7]

At the end of 1963, Kay recalled a doctor friend who knew Steinbeck. Holton prodded the composer for the address, preferring to approach the writer directly rather than deal with literary agents or Steinbeck's publisher, Viking.[8] Kay learned that it would be best to write to Steinbeck at general delivery, Sag Harbor, Long Island, New York; but Floyd had read that the writer was traveling in Europe, and did not bother to send the information to Holton.[9] Holton learned that Steinbeck's representative was not a mega-agency, but rather the small firm of McIntosh and Otis, specifically Annie Laurie Williams and Lucille Sullivan. Holton exercised his usual charms and soon made fast friends of the two women, obviating any need for letters to Sag Harbor. (Holton could not ignore that Williams had been Margaret Mitchell's hard-nosed agent for *Gone With the Wind,* selling the rights to Selznick International Pictures in 1936 for a handsome fifty thousand dollars.)[10]

Floyd longed to work with Steinbeck, but the novelist remained unavailable and apparently disinterested. A complex of health problems headed the list of reasons: excruciating back pain, from which a debilitating surgery in late 1967 would provide only partial relief, emphysema, and a long sequence of strokes resulting from atherosclerosis. Legal battles with Gwyn Conger, his second wife and mother of his two sons, and the deaths of personal friends, business associates, and political figures exhausted and depressed him. His involvement with President Lyndon B. Johnson, whose advocacy of civil rights Steinbeck (and Floyd) admired, led to an officially sanctioned three-month trip to Vietnam, Thailand, and Laos in 1967. Seeking to build a core of support for Johnson's conduct of the war, Steinbeck wrote fifty-two columns for New York's *Newsday,* but the venture brought disillusionment that paralleled the rest of America's. He returned home in the summer of 1967 a broken man, and attempted to convalesce in the Sag Harbor house.

In short, Floyd never had a chance to get to Steinbeck. Earlier, when the composer learned that Steinbeck had written his own theatrical adaptation—and which Steinbeck later thought that Floyd should use—the campus and Tallahassee libraries turned out not to have a copy, and Holton sent one.[11] When Floyd read both versions, he found the play to be an almost verbatim transcript of the novel, and proceeded to strategize his own version for the different medium of opera.

On November 12, 1964, Steinbeck agreed that Floyd might adapt his novel and play for the opera stage, further certifying that he would not authorize any other musical theater production based on the work earlier than two years hence; and, for opera, three. Floyd countersigned on November 19.[12] He was to submit the final draft libretto for Steinbeck's approval, care of Annie Laurie Williams; copyright of the final work would be held jointly by Steinbeck and Floyd. Steinbeck agreed to 25 percent of future royalties for stage performances and sales of music and libretto; the remaining 75 percent would be Floyd's, for all media. The sole exception was the potential use of Floyd's music and text in motion pictures, in which case separate negotiations would be necessary; but Steinbeck assigned Floyd 100 percent of any income generated by performances of any portion of music without words.

Things now began to happen quickly: Holton informed San Francisco's Kurt Herbert Adler that rights had been secured, and passed this information to the Ford Foundation. On December 22, declaring ambiguously that his company would *consider* premiering Floyd's new opera in the fall of 1966,[13] Adler requested a Ford grant of ten thousand dollars to commission Floyd. This was later raised to twelve thousand when the composer asked for additional funds to defray travel expenses.

After completing the full score of *Markheim* in July 1965, and having a few free weeks, Floyd cleared his desk for *Of Mice and Men*. He confided to Martha Baxter that Adler had been clamoring for the libretto for three months, and that he hoped to deliver it by October.[14]

This included the time that it would take Steinbeck, as per their contract, to respond. Floyd wanted his treatment to reflect the novel's sharp punch, and saw that Steinbeck's story "derived a great deal of its power from its almost total lack of diffusion. . . . Lennie, in order to allow me to deal with him musically, would be characterized primarily as a child: a physical giant with the self-image, as Frank Corsaro put it, of a small and rather helpless mouse. I wanted to de-emphasize the empty-eyed, slack-jawed conception . . . which is where some actors begin and end their portrayal . . . and I felt I had Steinbeck in my corner since he has George frequently refer to Lennie as being 'just a kid.'"[15]

Though not favorably disposed to Steinbeck's play, Floyd's study of it was closer than his disdain might lead us to believe. As in the play, the libretto unfolds in three acts of two scenes each, in much the same sequence and settings. In many particulars, especially in Floyd's act 1, as much as 10 percent of the dialogue reproduces Steinbeck's, in a regional dialect not far removed from *Susannah*.

In the opera's act 1, scene 1, on the banks of the Salinas River, the curtain rises on George Milton (baritone) hectoring his companion, the huge, lumbering Lennie Small (tenor), whom our politically correct age would term developmentally challenged. Both are on the run because of Lennie's molestation of a young woman. George has promised Lennie's aunt Clara that he will care for the kid, whom he now berates for insisting on capturing small, soft animals and literally petting them to death. Lennie's current victim is a dead mouse. The hold George exerts over Lennie is the promise of a brighter future: they plan to take jobs on a nearby ranch to earn money to buy their own house.

Act 1, scene 2, and act 2, scene 1 both unfold in the bunkhouse of the ranch of which Curley (tenor) is foreman, and Floyd transposes elements from one Steinbeck scene to the other. George and Lennie try to fit into a motley group of ranch hands: Candy (bass), a bent, worn elder reduced to menial chores; tall, strong, dignified Slim (baritone); and the big portly extrovert Carlson (tenor). Soon Curley's Wife (soprano)—like Steinbeck, Floyd gives her no name—a tawdry blond wearing too much makeup—roams the bunkhouse, supposedly looking for her husband. Curley's reputation as a mean-tempered popinjay precedes him, as does his wife's as a predatory tart. An argument breaks out over Candy's dog, as decrepit as its owner, and Carlson takes the animal outdoors and shoots it offstage while the ranch hands attempt to break the tension by ridiculing the Curleys. After Carlson's shot rings out, a ballad singer (tenor) passes by, singing of the wanderer's loneliness. The scene ends as Lennie begs George to get him one of Slim's puppies to pet.

Act 2 opens in the bunkhouse the following evening, with some of the ranch hands pitching horseshoes outside. Lennie sneaks in, obviously concealing something: the puppy Slim has given Candy to replace his dead animal. Furious and fearful, George orders Lennie to take the animal back out to the barn. The men are naturally curious about this new odd couple, and George relates how they most recently became fugitives from the law. Slim announces his intention to go into town the next night to Louella's, the local whorehouse. George and Lennie long to own a plot of land and a house, and Candy eagerly proposes joining them, setting up a Floyd trio. At the height of articulating their dream of independence, Curley's Wife again appears in the doorway, looking for cheerful company. Calling her a tramp, George orders her out, paving the way for a lengthy aria in which she complains of loneliness since marrying Curley. The boss himself shows up this time, and a quarrel develops after George orders him to keep his wife away from the bunkhouse. Curley picks a fight with George, and Lennie sniggers. Enraged at being laughed at, Curley makes the mistake of goading Lennie, whom George now sics on the foreman. Curley is lucky to get away with a mangled hand, and George, Lennie, and Candy realize that getting their own place may now be a necessity.

Steinbeck set his act 2, scene 2 in the separate quarters of the stable's black groom, Crooks; but Floyd found this redundant, and knew that present-day audiences would find Crooks an offensive racial stereotype. Eliminating the character, Floyd set about creating a female component to vary Steinbeck's action: his act 2, scene 2 explodes at Louella's, which he eventually changed to the more ethnic name "Rosita's." After a satirical chorus on five sets of initials of Roosevelt's relief programs, and the president's initials, F.D.R., Slim and George enter and are approached by Rosita's girls; and Floyd wrote a grand character role for the madam (mezzo-soprano). To strengthen George's character, both Steinbeck and Floyd have him refuse to buy female company: he and Lennie are saving up for their land purchase. The mere concept of a ranch hand settling down provokes the women's ridicule, but George sings a long aria, vowing fulfillment of his will.

Act 3 opens in the barn with tall piles of hay. While the men play horseshoes outside, Lennie, alone, laments over the puppy at his feet, dead like all the objects of his uncontrolled love. Curley's Wife strolls in, and Lennie is terrified that George will find them together. The Wife soothes his anxiety by spelling out her extravagant plans for the future, prompting Lennie's own exposition. Then she invites him to stroke her hair, and the inevitable happens: when Lennie's treatment turns rough, the Wife begins to scream. Lennie smothers and shakes her violently, finally snapping her neck, then covers her with hay and creeps away. Candy and George enter and discover the badly hidden corpse. George, unable to let anyone hurt Lennie, sees only one course: he misdirects the others, who rush off in pursuit of the killer, then takes Carlson's gun and goes to the hiding place he and Lennie set in act 1.

Act 3, scene 2 returns us to that spot by the river. Lennie knows that he has ruined his and George's chances. When George arrives, he comforts Lennie, acting as though nothing has happened to alter their plans. As Lennie intones his child's mantra of house, property, and domestic animals, George stands behind his enormous companion like a ministering angel. After directing Lennie's sight across the river to visualize their dream of paradise, George, devastated, fires into the back of his friend's head. In a brief coda from the novella that Steinbeck omitted from his play, the ranch hands rush in and fall silent before the reality of another death by gun, this one in full view.

Floyd wrote his libretto almost as quickly as Steinbeck had produced his novella. It ran to seventy-five pages, almost the length of its source. The composer then boarded his plane for Indianapolis and the Met National Company's production of *Susannah* on September 15 with an easier conscience.

FLOYD WAS SURPRISED by Steinbeck's minimal feedback later that fall via Annie Laurie Williams: the writer agreed with Floyd's decision to omit Crooks. His sole criticism of Floyd's new whorehouse scene was of the "chorus of initials," on the grounds that it kept the piece time-bound. Floyd agreed, cut the number, and started composing. He had already told Adler in May 1964 of his wish to cast Treigle and Cassilly; and having just created *Markheim* specifically for Treigle, he naturally pitched George for bass-baritone. The composition flowed. Alongside preparing to direct *Markheim* in New Orleans and teaching his regular classes, by the spring of 1966 his pencil manuscript of act 1 filled several volumes of Passantino spiral staff paper.[16]

On February 9, 1965, the Ford Foundation approved the full twelve thousand dollars that Adler had requested, and sent a check on February 23 with the stipulation that San Francisco pay Floyd in no fewer than four installments: on signing the contract, after delivery of the vocal score and full score in turn, and after the premiere. San Francisco announced the commission ten days later; but on March 10, Adler again hedged his bet by adding that he would "consider" the opera for San Francisco's 1966 season.[17]

The San Francisco Chronicle reported the commission, stating that Steinbeck would assist with preparing the libretto and that Floyd would devote the next ten months to completing the score.[18] Bob Holton entered these facts in the March/April 1965 *Central Opera Service Bulletin,* listing the premiere date as spring 1966; but Floyd already knew that this had been postponed to fall 1967, as reported in the *Markheim* article of April 2 in *Opera News.*

Adler, looking at a premiere eighteen months in the future, kept pestering Floyd about the music, and the composer flew to San Francisco in April's third week[19] to sign his contract, collect three thousand dollars of his commission fee, and audition act 1. Adler did not like what he saw or heard, and gave Floyd a polite but equivocal response: in its present state, he informed the Ford Foundation, he found *Of Mice and Men* unsuitable for a San Francisco production, but stated that if Mr. Floyd cared to rewrite the score, he would be willing to listen to it again.[20] Having received a mid-August 1967 deadline from Adler for new music,[21] Floyd returned home in logical agitation, and without a check, despite the amount of completed work; the Ford Foundation's money had earned interest in San Francisco's coffers since February.

IN THE SHIFT FROM 1966 TO 1967, the nation, the world, and the composer's family entered a synchronous period of strife and disillusionment: By that spring, American casualties in Southeast Asia had climbed into the thousands, and Mao's cultural revolution was reaching its height in China. That April 18, Reverend Floyd learned of his transfer to Cherokee Place Methodist Church in North Charleston. Though Floyd had little contact with his parents during the coming year, Ermine kept him informed of their mother's undiagnosed clinical depression and Parkinson's disease, symptoms of which had appeared as early as 1957, and of her eventual nervous breakdown. Reverend Floyd found increasing comfort, revealed in his diary, by thanking God "for my famous family,"[22] meaning his composer son. Floyd visited North Charleston just once, without Kay, over Christmas 1966.

Sylvia Goldstein wrote on May 21, 1966 that *The Mystery* was finally in print. In time to meet Adler's deadline for a revised score, Floyd plunged back into *Of Mice and Men,* and finished the new libretto and music of acts 1 and 2 by summer's end. He later wrote, "The libretto had gone so smoothly and quickly that I had vague misgivings which, had I heeded them, might have saved me a great deal of time and grief. However, I attributed them to a residual Puritan distrust of anything that was achieved without great labor. The composing of the music also went quite smoothly, although I was concerned somewhat with the excessive length of the opera at that point (another warning signal I failed to acknowledge)."[23]

The time had arrived for an enforced break from Floyd's seventeen years on the opera treadmill. As Juilliard's Arnold Fish reminded him in a letter of June 13, he had promised to deliver four choral pieces for their Repertory Project. There is nothing surprising about Floyd's appeal to the intellects of young singers with quality literary texts and re-creations of natural speech rhythms as meticulous as anything in his operas. His recent *Markheim* immersion in Robert Louis Stevenson extended to an appropriation of two of the Scottish master's verses, "Where Go the Boats" and "Rain." Like Floyd, who was sickly as a child, Stevenson loved playing with toy boats and watching the rain from indoors:

"Where Go the Boats"
Dark brown is the river.
Golden is the sand.
It flows along forever,
With trees on either hand.
Green leaves a-floating,
Castles of the foam,
Boats of mine a-boating—
Where will all come home?
On goes the river
And out past the mill,
Away down the valley,
Away down the hill.
Away down the river,
A hundred miles or more,
Other little children
Shall bring my boats ashore.[24]

Following the guidelines for grades K-3, Floyd used no intervals larger than a fifth; yet his canny sophistication walks a fine line between complexity and easy grasp of the melodic lines, based on sequences and repetition. His near-exclusive focus on opera created distaste for such choral techniques as fugal imitation, which tends to obscure text. His melodies here are always reinforced in the accompaniments, but Floyd's setting of "Where Go the Boats" challenged and surprised with chromatic-enharmonic slynesses, returning to the dreamy, almost Delian feeling of his earliest choral music.

Testing in 1967 garnered mostly enthusiastic results from young singers and teachers at schools around the country. Of "Where Go the Boats," one supervisor for grades 4–6 noted, "I consider this the best setting of this particular poem. . . . The children find it difficult, but I am sure that they will grow to love it as their knowledge of the music progresses." The tester for grade 5 wrote, after two fifteen-minute rehearsal sessions, "We were just getting to the place where the students were beginning to see the beauty of this piece."[25]

"Rain"
The rain is falling all around,
It falls on field and tree,
It rains on the umbrellas here,
And on the ships at sea.

The nine measures of "Rain" seem even trickier, but its compact sequences of thirds, fourths, and fifths would be taught one interval at a time, without Floyd's piano accompaniment, a witty ostinato staccato in octaves. This occasionally gives way to brief legato ties, suggestive of pattering, sliding rain, mirrored in the vocal line's staccati. One assessor explained, "This was taught completely by rote, and as an exercise for matching tone and hearing intervals. It is difficult but likeable."[26]

For his two-part settings for grades 4–6, Floyd turned first to Christina G. Rossetti, whose sonnet "Remember" he had set in 1945/46. Her 1872 collection *Sing-Song: A Nursery Rhyme Book,* in its 1893 reprinting contained 126 poems. Floyd chose:

"Who Has Seen the Wind?"
Who has seen the wind?
Neither I nor you.
But when the leaves hang trembling,
The wind is passing through.
Who has seen the wind?
Neither you nor I.

But when the trees bow down their heads,
The wind is passing by.[27]

The economical setting, just two pages marked *Allegretto,* calls for keener musicianship than the Stevenson songs. As with most of Floyd's nonoperatic output, there is no key signature, and meters dance from 5/8 to 2/4 and 3/4. Tonality flickers around D Major, but intervals are larger, and unison yields to two-part harmony, mostly in open fifths, thirds, octaves, and even tritones. The overall impression, with an angular keyboard "wind motive" mirrored by the voices, evokes the desolate landscape. One tester stated the obvious: there are "some rather difficult intervals."[28]

For his final piece, Floyd chose an anonymous Christmas carol text that also uses wind as a central image:

"Long, Long Ago"
Winds through the olive trees softly did blow,
Around little Bethlehem long, long ago.
Sheep on the hillside lay whiter than snow,
Shepherds were watching them, long, long ago.

Then from a happy sky, angels bent low,
Singing their songs of joy, long, long ago.
For in a manger bed, cradled we know,
Christ came to Bethlehem long, long ago.[29]

Here Floyd's music, modal in feeling, and toying with B-flat as a tonal center, takes us back to *Susannah*'s Appalachian roots, and religious elements untainted by threats of hellfire. After a two-bar introduction with a fanfare motif, Floyd alternates 3/4 and 2/4, setting the first two lines in unison, then splitting into canonic imitation after one bar in the third line, the rhythmic variants bringing the lines together at the end of line four. The second stanza displays a transposed variant of the main tune in D Major. After lines five and six, a brief interlude reprises the introductory motif, and lines seven and eight repeat the canonic imitation heard in three and four.

All four schools that tested "Long, Long Ago" reported positive results: "This type of piece meets with being unfavorable at first, but I believe it is the type of composition that will grow on the students."[30]

Bob Holton sent Floyd's completed pieces to Juilliard in mid-September 1966,[31] and the composer received his three hundred dollar check around July 1, 1967. All four works were chosen for JRP's anthology, published by Canyon Press of Cincinnati, Ohio, in 1969/70. "Rain" appeared in volume 2 of the Canyon vocal performance edition, the other three in volume 3. Throughout the period of active distribution of these publications, vocal editions outsold instrumental between two and ten to one.

Holton handled some of Floyd's Juilliard communication, and after the anthology's initial release, Boosey published Floyd's settings in October 1967. Floyd was stunned that "Long, Long Ago" sold like hotcakes, not realizing that such a market existed for choral music. All four Juilliard pieces are still performed occasionally, as on an all-Floyd concert at Rhode Island College in Providence in May 2007. "Long, Long Ago" was released as part of Arsis Recordings' 2000 collection *A Christmas Album.*

STILL PROCESSING his San Francisco dilemma, Floyd now welcomed an immersion in abstract music. No other commissions arose, and he began to tinker, just to please himself, with a modest piano piece. Even before his new ideas had evolved, the music director of the New Orleans Philharmonic Symphony Orchestra, Werner Torkanowsky, asked whether Floyd might be interested in writing a short orchestral work.[32] Having just assessed New Orleans's orchestral players in *Markheim,* Floyd wanted his first complete orchestral work—roughly a quarter-hour's worth—to be attractive, colorful, and accessible to the average concertgoer, straightforward in emotional appeal, with a clear and cohesive design.

To economize, he dug out his 1950 incidental music to Euripides' *Iphigenia among the Taurians,* whose sinuous slow movement seemed too good to ignore, and a portion of the new work became that early work's only survivor. Floyd described this musical germ that he called "Aria" as an extended *cantilena,* with the melodic lines passed between solo instruments and entire orchestral families. Building musical tension and instrumental weight to a climax, the movement relaxes into a final mournful statement of the main theme.

Adding two bookend movements that evolved from the piano piece mentioned above completed his new symphonic commission, *Introduction, Aria, and Dance,* reminiscent of his work with Nellie-Bond Dickinson's students in the fifties. He conceived each section as an independent statement; a fleeting hint of the "Introduction" provides the only cyclic element bridging "Aria" and "Dance." "Introduction" functions as extended declamation with a contrasting lyrical section. The opening material returns, reaches its climax, and subsides into the "Aria," after which the bridge of "Introduction" material leads into the final movement, a scintillating, pulsing "Dance" in large arch form, leading to a brilliant finish for full orchestra, with a reminiscence of the "Introduction" theme.

Floyd completed the piece that fall, and scored it as winter moved toward 1967. Bob Holton was about to join Theodore Presser's staff, and Floyd, floating between publishers, turned his first piece *not* for Boosey over to Holton.[33]

BISECTING HIS FAMILY CHRISTMAS VISIT to North Charleston, Floyd flew to New York for two days on December 28. Over lunch at the Russian Tea Room with Stuart Pope, he discussed his situation at Boosey, and tracked Arnstein's progress on the vocal score of *Markheim,* only to find that the copyist had never received Floyd's corrected manuscript. Staying at Bob Holton's apartment, the composer caught up with his champion's latest water-treading career plans. Floyd and Pope failed to reach long-term agreement, for which Floyd compensated by assigning Boosey his four Juilliard pieces. On January 5, 1967, he wrote Pope, "The air was cleared on many counts. I especially appreciated your candor and feel that much forthrightness in discussing your difficulties and mine should make for increased ease in our future dealings."[34]

Around the middle of January, Floyd received a sad letter from Ernst Bacon: his third wife, Moselle "Peggy" Camp, had died in Contra Costa, California, on December 30, "frail and thin with merciful suddenness." Bacon continued, "My only rescue will be prodigies of work, and a seeking for healing in sound that comforts with the terrible beauty of love and even of loss."[35]

On January 19, Floyd wrote his condolences: "As I am sure you expected, I was stunned and saddened to hear of Peggy's death. When you were here last year you mentioned the fact that her health was somewhat precarious but of course I had no idea that whatever was wrong was really serious. I do hope that her final illness was not a painful one. Needless to say Peggy will always be a vivid part of my college years and I like to think that, from the beginning when she was assigned to me as a sort of younger sister, we had a very special relationship: certainly we spent many happy times together and consoled each other . . . in those [times] that were less happy."[36]

On January 25, Pope sprinkled a dash of vinegar on Floyd's peace offering, writing that he found the four Juilliard songs delightful, but that they might prove difficult for the targeted age groups. Because two were unison and the others two-part, his solution was to pair the *Two Stevenson Songs* and issue the others separately. Pope further thought that Floyd should write more Christmas pieces to expand "Long, Long Ago" into a collection, informing the composer that such works sold well and widely, and that Floyd had captured the right atmosphere. Pope reminded Floyd that he would be attending a meeting in Miami at the beginning of March, and thought it opportune to include a stop in Tallahassee to discuss future plans.[37]

For Elena Nikolaidi's faculty recital at the end of January, Floyd and Leonard Mastrogiacomo shared accompanist duties for the great mezzo in an esoteric program of Brahms, Chausson, Rimsky-Korsakov, Berlioz, Ravel, and the four lower songs from Floyd's *The Mystery.*

A somewhat awkward meeting with Pope did occur on February 27, despite Pope's insistence on taking up one of Floyd's full Monday teaching afternoons.

Floyd had forewarned, "I think it only fair to tell you that I am still of the same mind as I was at Christmas time regarding signing a new contract with B & H or any other publisher."[38]

Yet he successfully championed Evon Streetman's cover art for *The Sojourner and Mollie Sinclair* and *Markheim* scores, and Pope never raised other contractual matters. On March 3, Floyd journeyed as a guest composer-lecturer to the sixth annual contemporary music conference at Sam Houston State University in Huntsville, Texas. He spoke that afternoon on "The Problems of Composing Contemporary Opera" before a performance of *Slow Dusk*.

FLOYD'S ONGOING REWRITE of the first two *Of Mice and Men* acts only increased Kurt Herbert Adler's impatience to hear what he, or rather the Ford Foundation, proposed to buy, with the premiere now just nine months ahead. Claims on Floyd's time increased; there were piano lessons, composition classes, and recitals—one of his most gifted pupils at the time was George Darden[39]—and frequent performances of excerpts from his operas, *Pilgrimage* and *The Mystery* on student and faculty vocal concerts. Between spring trimester and summer school, Floyd threw together a group of Florida State University faculty, including the opera director and baritone Richard Collins as George, at the Middlebrook house to record sections of the new work and dispatched the tape, libretto, and vocal score to Adler. Toward the end of August, Adler's response addressed concerns more political than musical; he claimed that his latest reservations sprang from criticism in the local press for handing a plum commission to a non-Bay Area composer, and that San Francisco's cultural cliques were hostile to music as conservative as Floyd's. Adler left the door open, however, suggesting that Floyd return to San Francisco to show him the revised score and play it for the company's musical staff.

In the meantime, Bob Holton kept Julius Rudel apprised of the opera's progress, and the conductor declared that he wanted it for City Opera. San Diego Opera tossed its hat into the ring as well, stating its willingness to guarantee a production soon.[40] On August 28, Holton called Ford's project director, Edward F. D'Arms, to request funding for Floyd's next trip to San Francisco, and to rehash the opera's history to date. Despite the offers from other companies, the composer felt obliged to honor his original commission, and flew to San Francisco in September's first week to play through the revised score. After returning home, on September 6 he applied for and was granted a travel reimbursement by the Ford Foundation of $411.02. The trip had accomplished its purpose, he believed: Adler and company had heard the opera and conferred about producing it the following year; he was to give Floyd a final decision in about a week.[41]

Adler's final written rejection and release of premiere rights arrived around the middle of September,[42] and Bob Holton sprang into action. He wrote D'Arms on September 18, thanking the foundation for its support of Floyd, and hoped that the composer's recent trip would settle *Of Mice and Men*'s premiere situation within ten days, preferably at City Opera under Rudel.[43]

Floyd was devastated. Three years' work in vain, compensated by just one-fourth of the Ford Foundation's commissioning fee. He and Kay sat in their living room with Adler's letter between them. She had no advice about scrapping the opera or starting over, but suddenly jumped into the breach, suggesting that Floyd invite a group of trusted friends over to listen to him explain and play through the two finished acts: six or eight heads are better than two are better than one. The piano-duo Mastrogiacomos, the scientist Choppin, the historian Rogers, Catherine Murphy, and, of course, Kay beside her husband at the piano, saturated the room with formidable brainpower. When Floyd reached the end of what he'd written, he faced blank looks. Kay broke the tension by handing Floyd the judgment every composer fears. In his own words, "The reaction was unanimously negative, the general feeling being that, despite some attractive or effective moments, the opera as a whole was a bore. The verdict of dullness was . . . the death sentence, and, once given, I frankly never tried to circumvent it. I realized that I had two alternatives: give the opera up once and for all as an unsuccessful project, or start all over again. I chose the latter."[44]

At least Rudel still wanted it and could offer some guidance. Adler forwarded the foundation's remaining nine thousand dollars to the City Center board chairman Morton Baum on September 22, 1967; but before Floyd could resaddle Steinbeck's horse, he needed a breather. Even Kay advised him to take some time and get some distance. He dealt with Boosey's publication of the Juilliard songs, acted as middleman in the firm's confusion over Evon Streetman's fees for *Mollie Sinclair* and *Markheim* cover designs, and saw Opera Repertory Group's *Slow Dusk* in Jacksonville.

Of Mice and Men now acted as a midlife sandspur: he had faced career bumps aplenty, but this was a vehicle-swallowing sinkhole. He refused to let Adler's rejection be the final word and thought, "I'll show them." Around October, he closed the studio door behind him and started over. Opening his manuscript, he saw a two-act torso, based on a seventy-five-page source, approaching the proportions of *Götterdämmerung:* "I started from the absolute beginning, as though I'd never touched it. I made conscious everything I knew about libretto writing, getting it down to what I call the through-line. I started with a simple outline, reducing it to the irreducibles."

In other words, he did that without which nothing else is possible:

> I assumed that Steinbeck had done the work for me: it was a "novella," and with that extreme compression, I thought something could be missing. That is why it assumed such enormous length, diffused through literalism and detail, and utterly failing to observe the needs of the lyric theater.
>
> I realized that this was a suspense story, a thriller of its kind. The basic premise had to boil down to twenty-five words or less: George's frantic efforts to keep Lennie out of trouble, until he can get him away from society, in a home of their own. What feeds into that through-line, we'll use. Nothing else. I did a simple one-page outline, and every scene had to have that through-line, or it was not going to get in there.
>
> And somehow freed, I started writing again. The whole opening scene was the chase, none of it in the book; but I was off the book and it gave me the dramatic thrust into the story. Next I needed an encounter between the antagonists, in scene 2 between Curley and his Wife, to show the audience the volatile environment George and Lennie had stumbled into: explosive personalities and situations that led to ultimate tragedy. I wanted all the focus on George and Lennie instead of on the outsiders. The real antagonist is Curley's Wife, whose role I enlarged considerably, and to a lesser degree Lennie himself.[45]
>
> The drama . . . is a study of human attachment in an environment of harsh personal isolation and despair, and . . . what Steinbeck is saying throughout is that even George's unsatisfactory but nevertheless tender relationship with a slow-witted man-child is preferable to the loneliness and rootlessness of his fellow ranchhands.[46]

Floyd's twenty-three-word spine embraced protagonists, antagonists, and obstacles. Later additions grew organically from his new freedom: a want ad at the beginning of act 2 became George's tangible prop to concretize their dreams. This tiny detail heightened suspense for characters and audience; the dream was made visible.

Before getting too far into revision, Floyd headed north at the end of the Christmas holiday. Rudel corralled one of his new directors, the Argentinian Tito Capobianco, slated to direct *Of Mice and Men*,[47] and the three men read through Floyd's completed two acts at Bob Holton's apartment on Riverside Drive. Though Capobianco took the lead hesitantly, he made his point. Floyd had adhered too slavishly to Steinbeck's book, he needed to *never* read it again, and to tell his own version of the story. "This diagnosis, more poetic than precise, summoned my own critical faculties and brought into service, really for the first time, whatever experience I had gained in writing the libretti for six previous operas."[48]

Rudel offered sound musical advice. By shortening note values in the act 1 curtain music, Floyd could increase the agitation of George's and Lennie's plight. Floyd had written the interlude before the final scene of act 3 as a *toccata,* one of whose features is a single note value throughout. Floyd's choice had been the eighth-note; Rudel urged him to vary rhythms, again to heighten tension and suspense.

Once Floyd acted on these suggestions, he could not imagine having written it any other way, and thus took his next steps toward the definitive *Of Mice and Men*. The new libretto's length told the story in more ways than one. In all, Floyd retained less than one-fourth of version 1: Lennie's aria and the duet with George in scene 1, the Ballad Singer's piece and chorus at the end of act 1, and the act 2 trio, all with rewritten orchestral accompaniments. When the time came to find new music, the economy of the score had to re-create the *spirit*, if not letter, of Steinbeck. Version 1 was musical illustration, as opposed to illumination: Floyd had not found specific musical equivalents for his characters' emotions, or had failed to summon up the precise dramatic atmosphere in a given scene.[49]

He now focused above all on sharp musical characterization. George's extroverted emotional states presented few problems; but coming up with music for Lennie, a physical giant with the mental age of five, was another matter. The audience had to care about him within the first five minutes after the curtain rose; otherwise, why would *George* take such pains for and with him?

Curley's Wife would be a lyric soprano with coloratura extensions: runs, leaps, and trills would highlight her flirtatious or wiseacre tendencies; his music to project anger and yearning to escape her wretched lot as Curley's chattel would be more straightforward.

Action sequences provided further thrust, like the opening chase and act 2 fight. As Frank Corsaro later pointed out, Steinbeck had handed them a strong component of violence, between the shooting of Candy's dog, the fight, and two murders in act 3. At final curtain, the audience had to feel overwhelmed by compassion for George, who has destroyed his friend out of love.

Floyd studied Berg's *Wozzeck* and Britten's *Peter Grimes* at length, as examples of character-illuminating music that also furthered a complex dramatic dynamic. Floyd's musical challenges were twofold. The first requirement was for "music essentially simple and direct in its emotional appeal; the second, music sufficiently sophisticated in idiom to underscore a scene as grotesque and terrifying as Lennie's murder of Curley's Wife. The challenge then was to fuse . . . these disparate . . . demands into an overall musical language that would encompass them both."[50]

Directed by Capobianco, Norman Treigle and Beverly Sills sang in Orlando Opera's *Faust* on February 9, 1968. Floyd attended to support his friend, and to discuss *Of Mice and Men* revisions.[51] Sills's strengths as Marguerite prompted not only some of the Wife's vocal embellishments, but also a proposal that "Bev," City Opera's established star since 1966, undertake Floyd's new role. The three met again at another Capobianco production, New Orleans Opera's *Tales of Hoffmann* on April 25. *Of Mice and Men* was still slated for City Opera's fall 1969 season, but Sills declined Floyd's offer.

While plaster ceilings cracked and the roof leaked at Middlebrook Circle, Floyd completed the new score in early spring 1968 and played it for the same group of adviser-friends, who now found it anything but dull. Over the next year, he continued cutting, revising, and rewriting, eliminating another quarter of the opera's total length, receiving nothing more than travel money from the Ford Foundation's nest egg.

On March 20, Stuart Pope wrote that *The Sojourner and Mollie Sinclair* had been printed, and that everyone loved Evon Streetman's cover.[52] Floyd even urged entering the score in a printer's contest for graphic excellence; but Pope instead pressed Streetman to send artwork for *Markheim*.[53] On April 23, the New Orleans Philharmonic Symphony Orchestra finally played *Introduction, Aria, and Dance*. Floyd was too buried in *Of Mice and Men* to attend, but Hazel Richards did, and kept favorable press for the composer and his parents: "It held together splendidly and was quite an impressive piece."[54]

SPRING, SUMMER, AND FALL 1968 were among the most turbulent in modern American history. The nation rocked with widespread protests against the Vietnam War—by the end of June, more than twenty-six thousand Americans had died. Lyndon Johnson's declaration on April 1 that he would not seek reelection made headlines, as did the assassination of Martin Luther King on April 5, and of Robert F. Kennedy on June 5. Just five days after the nomination of Richard M. Nixon and Spiro T. Agnew by Republicans in Miami, Russian tanks rolled into Prague to end Czechoslovakia's heady spring of liberalism. As fires raged in many urban centers, FSU's usually peaceful campus became a hotbed of protest and riot. School President John E. Champion summoned the faculty to meet with concerned students at a general assembly at the administration's Westcott Hall. Student behavior, though not overtly violent, was vocal and disruptive, and there were sit-ins at Champion's office.

Music being its hermetic self, Floyd, preoccupied with *Of Mice and Men,* was still jerked into this different reality when student protests filled Ruby Diamond Hall, the site of so many Floyd performances. "It felt like everything was coming apart at the seams, things you have taken for granted all your life. I remember vividly being so unsettled by the angry students. I'd never been in that kind of atmosphere."

September's second week came as a great burst of freedom. Floyd met again with Holton, Rudel, and Capobianco in New York,[55] and their approval resounded in City Opera's scheduling *Of Mice and Men*'s world premiere for fall 1969. Just as Floyd had hoped when San Francisco was still in the picture, Norman Treigle and Richard Cassilly would be his two male protagonists. Floyd and Steinbeck had, through their respective agents, agreed to meet at the premiere.

It was thus with a lighter heart that Floyd played another Nikolaidi recital on October 4: arias and songs by Handel, Strauss, Debussy, Verdi, and a scene and aria from *The Sojourner and Mollie Sinclair.* Floyd flew again to New York on October 9 for Ginastera's *Bomarzo* at City Opera. The next evening, which Floyd did not attend, featured another Ford Foundation commission premiere, Hugo Weisgall's *Nine Rivers from Jordan,* to a libretto by Denis Johnson and scenery by the designer of *Jonathan Wade,* Will Steven Armstrong. It proved one of City Opera's worst gambles, as the work was placed by more than one critic at the head of the list of worst operas ever written. The public did not like it any better and stayed away in droves. Between *Nine Rivers* and another Ford Foundation commission, Vittorio Giannini's *The Servant of Two Masters* in its 1967 spring season, City Opera lost more money than any grant could compensate; and more serious, the tolerance and goodwill of much of their audience. Rudel observed, "I felt particularly bad because I wasn't involved in the choice of libretto; and of course that turned out to be the big problem. I was so mad at Weisgall because he killed his own clarity of singing speech by orchestrating so heavily. Nobody understood what was going on."[56]

Floyd, staying at Bob Holton's apartment, answered when the phone rang on October 11. It was Weisgall, one of Holton's composers at Theodore Presser, now seizing the moment to harangue his younger colleague about everything wrong with City Opera's production, singers, and orchestra. Floyd observed on his way back to Florida, "If I was ever inclined to try to shift that kind of blame, living with Kay took care of that."

Immediately following the season's final New York performance on November 17, Rudel took the company for a fourteen-performance tour to the Dorothy Chandler Pavilion in Los Angeles. Within a few days, Floyd's home phone rang: Rudel claimed that City Opera's season deficits necessitated *Of Mice and Men*'s postponement until spring 1970; Capobianco would direct and Ming Cho Lee would design the sets.[57]

Floyd wondered whether he or his opera, or both, bore curses. Rudel pleaded for understanding: he had to have a real hit with his next new piece, and deferment would give them time to build a success. Floyd demurred, and a rift of years opened with Rudel. His and Adlers's defections devastated then provoked Floyd to fashion the improved form in which we know the opera today; but Boosey offered him no powerful and involved ally like Bob Holton. Rudel's call made him see that his greatest lack was a real business manager to get *Of Mice and Men* onto the right stage, or onto *any* stage.

Floyd's ongoing five-year arrangement with Boosey had expired in January 1966. He was in no way disposed to grant Rudel another postponement, but without a more proactive agent at Boosey he had let his contract lapse for four years, during which he

30. Floyd, 1969. Floyd collection. Permission courtesy of the photographer, John W. Freeman.

wrote only the four Juilliard choral pieces, still represented by Boosey. However, *Of Mice and Men* was almost as much Holton's child as Floyd's. Though the composer maintained cordial and frequent relations with Boosey—after all, they had joint custody of *Susannah, Slow Dusk, Wuthering Heights, Jonathan Wade, Mollie Sinclair,* and *Markheim*—it was now to Holton that Floyd again turned. Within a few weeks, they had a contingency plan: Cincinnati's wealthy arts patrons Patricia A. and J. Ralph Corbett had long supported Norman Treigle's career and were instrumental in backing a year-round Cincinnati Opera. The summer company had been a Treigle redoubt, and the new entity now expressed interest in *Of Mice and Men*'s world premiere as their inaugural presentation in the fall of 1969.

JUST BEFORE CHRISTMAS, *Markheim* appeared in print. Floyd suggested to Pope and to Henson Markham, now Boosey's director of serious music,[58] that the firm send complimentary or approval scores of both *Mollie* and *Markheim,* together with the glowing press from *Opera News* and *High Fidelity,* to all companies that had done *Susannah.*[59] No record exists that this was done or seriously considered. Unbeknownst to Floyd, as he sat typing his letter to Pope, his chances to meet John Steinbeck vanished; the writer died at 5:30 that afternoon.

A little late, Pope wrote Floyd that Markham had tried without success to contact him on Christmas Eve, having learned from Seattle that Rudel had postponed *Of Mice and Men,* and that Seattle expressed serious interest in premiering the work there. Pope further told Floyd that the publishing rumor mill whispered that Floyd had placed the opera in Bob Holton's hands at Presser.[60]

Holton was indeed onto Seattle Opera, whose founder, Glynn Ross, agreed sight unseen to present

Of Mice and Men's world premiere, guaranteeing at least five performances. Rather than asking for extra production and promotion costs, Ross sounded the Ford Foundation for its thoughts about designing a production that could be shared with other companies.[61] The next day, D'Arms summarized his interview with Holton, which touched on the Floyd-Holton relationship, Rudel's offer of postponement, Floyd's refusal, and Rudel's cancellation. Holton had told him of the collapse of Cincinnati's interest, and Ross's desire to produce the work in Seattle. He estimated a need for $7,500 to extract and reproduce parts and full score, and to defray Floyd's travel expenses to confer with Ross in Seattle.[62]

The foundation's board agreed unanimously on February 5, relieved that Seattle was on the cusp of making history; and Floyd had a real agent again. By the time rehearsals began, Ford had pried its much-mailed $9,000 away from City Opera. Inflation being its inexorable self, Glynn Ross coaxed out another $20,500 for Seattle Opera, and Floyd could claim more of his commission fee.[63]

GLYNN ROSS, born in Nebraska in 1914, worked as a stage director in Italy after World War II, and then for various companies in the United States. He founded Seattle Opera in 1963, and his vigorous innovations earned him the nickname "the P. T. Barnum of Opera." He used controversial—for the time—promotional techniques like skywriting, bumper stickers, and slogans designed to attract a younger crowd.[64]

Before 1970, America's professional opera-producing entities had no effective central organization. Beginning in the early fifties, the Metropolitan Opera Council used its Central Opera Service (COS) to act "as liaison among community enterprises across the country," and as a data-gathering organization of industry news and performance schedules.[65] The council published the *Central Opera Service Bulletin* from 1959 until 1990, as the company's guild did *Opera News,* a mélange of articles, interviews, and reviews of performances at home and abroad, and of recordings and books. The National Opera Association (NOA), founded in 1955 "to promote a greater appreciation of opera and music theater, to enhance pedagogy and performing activities, and to increase performance opportunities,"[66] confined most of its activities to the realm of opera education, and published *The Opera Journal.*

Arguably, Glynn Ross's greatest contribution to the medium of opera was his brainchild, Opera America. He scheduled the entity's first annual conference in Seattle for 1970, hosting "sixteen opera directors representing companies of similar size and type of programming . . . to explore possibilities of joint planning for greater efficiency, better economics and higher artistic achievement."[67]

Ross rightly saw the world premiere of Floyd's *Of Mice and Men* as embodying his dream of and for American opera; but for Floyd, the only regrettable part of this premiere date and site was losing his connection to Norman Treigle and Richard Cassilly. Treigle had in the meantime accepted a *Faust* engagement in February 1970 with San Diego Opera, and Cassilly had since 1965 been a house *Heldentenor* at Germany's Hamburg State Opera.[68]

In January 1969, Ross set about assembling his own dynamic cast and staff, pending Floyd's approval: Frank Corsaro would direct, Anton Coppola conduct, and Allen Charles Klein design. As George, Ross cast the baritone Julian Patrick, summoning him that month to New York's Ansonia Hotel to sight read parts of the score. According to Patrick, "parts of the score" turned out to be a complete read-through of the role. "A few days later, Mr. Ross asked me to create the role in . . . an event [that] culminated a year later in the most exciting theatrical experience with which I have ever been associated."[69]

One day that February, tenor Robert Moulson stood by the stage door of the opera house in Frankfurt, Germany, when an attendant handed him a telegram from Ross, offering him the role of Lennie, in all ways the opera's greatest challenge. Moulson had performed Sam in City Opera's 1958 *Susannah* with Corsaro, who, with Floyd, thought him an ideal replacement for Cassilly. The cast received copies of Floyd's score that summer, and Moulson soon discovered the child in the character: "I was immediately impressed by . . . the beautiful, direct, but musically complicated melodies. . . . I soon learned that the pure singing of the part, with its extremely high tessitura, would challenge me to keep in character and not yield to the desire to 'belt.'"[70]

For the other roles, Ross chose Carol Bayard, who had sung leading roles at City Opera since 1964, for Curley's Wife; other cast members would include Harry Theyard (Curley), Archie Drake (Candy), Kerry McDevitt (Slim), Erik Townsend (Carlson), Elaine Bonazzi, (Rosita the whorehouse madam), and Gerald Thorsen (the Ballad Singer).

With Treigle out of the picture, George's median pitch level rose. In the months that followed, at musical rehearsals in New York and Seattle, Floyd and Patrick isolated the important climaxes that might have been perfect for Treigle, but sat too low for the baritone, and Floyd added optional high notes. The final vocal score reflected the shift between original inspiration and a finished product that specified many such *ossia* (optional) passages, allowing for a variety of lower male voices.

The first months of 1969 boiled with activity at FSU, postponing further work on the opera. On February 7, friend and colleague Leonard Mastrogiacomo played Floyd's Sonata: "The music is so intense and dramatic, so lyrical, you can tell that he is an opera composer. The shape and content of the line is so right, so inevitable. Why has this piece not been picked up more? Fírkušný played it, other people have; but contemporary American sonatas are not being played much."[71]

On February 22, Floyd accompanied a new faculty member, Donna Jeffrey, in a program of excerpts from Weber's *Der Freischütz,* Shostakovich's *Katerina Ismailova,* songs by Britten and Rachmaninoff, and Cathy's aria, "The Dream," from *Wuthering Heights.*[72]

Bob Holton explained to Floyd the latest obstacles convulsing the Ford Foundation and Seattle Opera during these weeks: Glynn Ross's funding demands for part extraction and shared productions exceeded Ford's guidelines, confirmed in a letter of February 25 from a new project officer, Richard C. Sheldon.[73] Shaken, Ross responded three days later that he had already signed a contract with Floyd and preferred not to buy him out. Reviewing the opera's rocky road to date, Ross understated that another cancellation would damage and demean Floyd, and he offered to eliminate plans for the shared production.[74]

The stresses showed, and the Floyds expanded their drinking and even sampled marijuana: "It never did anything for me that it was supposed to do; and what it did, I did not like. For a composer, the manipulation of time is about the worst experience you can have. Once I'd been out smoking with a friend, and thought I'd never get home! I doubt that I smoked six joints in all, and that over a long period; but Kay, being Kay, wanted to try everything. She made some brownies once, and that was that. Thank God she didn't get into LSD! Your daily dreams are a bad enough trip. And booze: the biggest deterrents were the hangovers, of which I may have had two or three; but you want to die, I didn't think anything was worth that. And I wanted to be able to work the next day."

EVERYDAY LIFE settled into a familiar pattern: early to rise, with an hour or two of writing, composing, and orchestration between breakfast and school; back home for lunch, a brief "toes up," then more composing until suppertime. In all but the most pressured situations, night work became a thing of the past, but expanded studio hours inevitably crept in. Around the beginning of February, Floyd began teaching *Markheim* to FSU students, abetted by the role's creator, Norman Treigle. Treigle and wife Linda stayed with the Floyds for the weeks of rehearsal and performance, enjoying guest of honor status at Clique parties. Treigle kept his hosts up until their cutoff time, about one a.m., after which he and Linda continued drinking, talking, and laughing until three or four. The next day, the walking skeleton that was Treigle emerged around two p.m., subjecting anyone in the house to weird vocalizations: "Nay, nay, nay. . . . Nothin'!"

Yet Treigle's consummate professionalism made this anything but a vacation. At his insistence, the school programmed a double bill with Puccini's *Gianni Schicchi,* with Treigle performing both title roles. Floyd staged *Markheim,* Florida State's opera director Richard Collins the companion piece. One day in rehearsal, Treigle injured his knee on a corner of the set, and Floyd rushed him to Florida State's football trainer Don Fauls for immediate therapy. The star quarterback Bill Cappleman stood nearby, and the cadaverous Treigle, pants leg rolled up, repaid the care he was given by mugging excruciating pain while Cappleman and Fauls looked on. Though mildly hobbled for the remainder of the production, and despite his specialization in portraying gloomy, tormented characters, Treigle demonstrated equal comedic skills as Puccini's sardonic trickster.

Floyd's celebrity as a composer makes it easy to lose sight of his parallel work as a piano teacher in these years; and the more he saw of the music world's ferocity, the more demanding a pedagogue he became. Though it went against the grain, he discovered the uses of sternness, discouragement, and reverse psychology in the studio. For six years during the sixties and seventies, one of his more brilliant students was Stephen Hess. Pursuing a double major in mathematics and music—his father headed the university's meteorology program—Hess brought little technical aptitude to his keyboard study, and Floyd despaired of making anything of him. "Many times I'd say, "Stephen, honestly, you'd probably be happier in math. I don't think you're likely to develop in piano." And he'd say, "Don't give up yet." I knew that he was intellectually precocious, but he'd been physically damaged by being assigned music too difficult for him, and had to play it any way he could. So I put him through a real technical regimen, undoing bad muscular problems and replacing them with things that worked. But he is the only one at that level on whom I gave up, and several times."

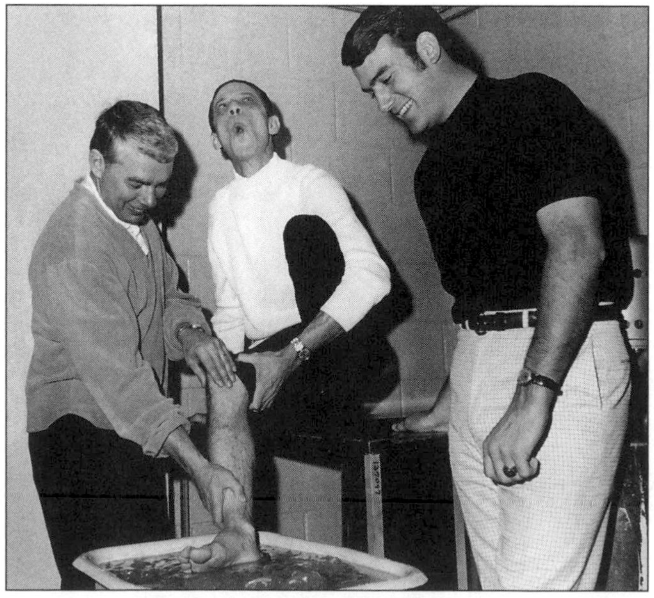

31. Norman Treigle "in extremis." Don Fauls, Treigle, Bill Cappleman, FSU, 1969. Photograph by Ken Richards. Courtesy of FSU College of Music, Dr. Don Gibson, Dean.

Then Hess gave a breakthrough graduate recital, playing Book 2 of Debussy's *Préludes,* and went on to become not only a superb student but also a prominent opera coach in Frankfurt, Vienna, Stuttgart, and Berlin.

Bob Holton's ship came in, the job for which he'd lusted, waited, and angled, at Belwin-Mills, in the fall of 1969.[75] Floyd was appalled, as the firm was known mostly for publishing children's music and jazz; but Holton reassured him that Belwin meant to elevate its profile, with him as head of classical music.

With Seattle's *Of Mice and Men* Manhattan rehearsals just nine months off, it was time for Floyd to orchestrate. He had studied Verdi's *Otello* and *Falstaff* as models of balance between pit and stage, and his instrumental palette had acquired shimmer and lightness, creating new space for intelligibility.

ON JULY 20, as Apollo 11 made history's first moon landing, Bob Holton mailed the vocal score piecemeal to Seattle's principal singers as fast as it could be copied. By the end of the month, Canyon Press announced the inclusion of Floyd's four Juilliard choral songs in its anthology. Following a quick trip to his parents in Barnwell, the elder Floyds' latest assignment, Floyd and Kay boarded the Silver Meteor on August 31 to spend eight days in New York to hear Julian Patrick and to confer with Glynn Ross and Ford Foundation officials. He also observed three days of musical rehearsals of the opera with Coppola, Corsaro, Patrick, Moulson, Bayard, and Theyard.

Patrick recalled, "My first impression was of [Floyd's] timidity and shyness: that kind of nervous laugh he has that makes you think he is not quite sure of himself. Even so, he was very friendly, very nice, but retiring, a southern gentleman. He grows on you as you get to know him. The next time you see him, if you become friendly, it is like picking up again where you left off. Then when he sat down and played rehearsals for us, or coached us, you realized there was something else hiding down there. The musical and vocal difficulties seemed insurmountable, but, with the composer there to explain and clarify, most problems came into perspective by the end of the third day. He was an extraordinary pianist. I have seen him upset at the way orchestras would play, but with singers he had the greatest patience and kindness."[76]

As Patrick studied the role of George, he found some of Floyd's devices vocally challenging, as his instrument lay that much higher than Treigle's. With time, he discovered that Floyd knew exactly what he had done. The role took Patrick from lyric baritone repertoire to greater depth and weight, dramatic territory that proved to be the right career move at the right moment as he reached his early forties.

Carol Bayard wrote eloquently of the cast's early bonding, "When we were singing through the score together for the first time, I remember the looks that passed between us. We were all swept up in the music and the drama . . . but there was even more—there was a mutual respect and affection between the cast, the composer, the conductor and the director."[77]

Visiting Kay's family in Jacksonville on September 9, an ebullient Floyd was interviewed by *Musical America:*

> This is the most dramatic, the most operatic of the works I've written so far . . . the trouble with so many contemporary operas—and I've been guilty of this myself, so I feel that I can point the finger—is that so often there isn't anything really vocal. . . . It's all gray and the voices just go along for the ride, sort of an *obbligato* for the orchestra. . . . When I read *Of Mice and Men* back in 1963 I thought this would be an easy book to make a libretto from because it reads like a scenario . . . but it turned out not to be so easy.[78]

Of his friends' judgment of the first version, he declared,

> I'd rather be melodramatic or bloodcurdling, but not dull. . . . I make George into an almost fanatical figure. . . . The one thing on his mind is to buy his piece of land. In the book . . . the property itself . . . is vague. Does it really exist or doesn't it? In the libretto I have George see an advertisement which he tears out of the paper. This becomes the symbol of the search for a house, an end of loneliness, which is what the whole thing is about. At the end, when Lennie is shot, George pulls out the ad and puts it into his hand.

On the subject of sharpening Steinbeck's drama, Floyd rhapsodized about opera's uniqueness, and his and Corsaro's production plans:

> Frank . . . uses headlights coming right out at the audience. You go straight into the action. Everything is very tight, and it moves. . . . There's no padding—the vocal parts really characterize the people. There is so much you can do in opera that you simply can't do in any other form. For instance, just before the murder of Curley's wife, when Lennie is sitting with her in the hay, each of them fantasizes about [their] own dreams. She sings about the career she's going to have in Hollywood, and he's singing about the land he will share with George. Each has [their] own kind of vocal line, and they weave in and out while they remain independent. This is something you can't do in any other medium.

After accompanying another Nikolaidi recital at FSU—Donaudy, Brahms, Theodore Chanler, De Falla, and Tchaikovsky—Floyd left for Shreveport, Louisiana, for whose Symphony Repertory Opera Company, conducted by John Shenaut, he directed *Susannah.* Before performances on November 24, 25, and 26, he managed to finish orchestrating *Of Mice and Men* in his hotel room, and dedicated the work to Elena Nikolaidi.

In New York, Corsaro coached the singers, identifying character identities through physical and psychological means. Julian Patrick recalled,

> Simplicity and honesty were the key words. . . . No operatic clichés for this production. I remember . . .

going to Frank's apartment to talk about the drama and George's character. . . . I had already come to think of George as a tough man, basically intelligent but lacking schooling. . . . Frank agreed. . . . In working on the score I had been perturbed by the beautiful lyric lines Carlisle had composed for George throughout. . . . They seemed to deny the hard-nosed individual I wished to portray. Frank then pointed out that *Of Mice and Men* is basically about non-communication and non-caring. The needs and thoughts expressed by the characters are seldom comprehended by the person to whom they are spoken. . . . George can, therefore, rightfully express hopes and plans in beautifully lyric melodies, Lennie celebrating only that which applies to him, leaving George's innermost hopes and dreams, sadly, still his alone.[79]

Corsaro began staging the principals at the end of December's second week, with Floyd in attendance at an Upper West Side studio. In the interest of a true ensemble performance, the vigilant director interrupted his singers each time their histrionics became grand or melodramatic: "That's too operatic! Simpler—just a look will do! No grand gestures! Let's keep Bobby Baritone, Samantha Soprano, and Terence Tenor out of this opera!"[80]

Corsaro staged completely against the tired operatic grain, asking Moulson to sing a high B-natural seated, with legs hanging off a board fifteen feet above the stage; and, for his principal aria, he lay on the floor, curled up "like a scared baby."[81] In a matter of hours, each seasoned professional became so involved in the work of their colleagues that they arrived early and stayed late to watch one another. Carol Bayard, a passionate knitter, more than once let yarn and needles fall from her lap, and each learned every line and staging detail of all parts. Floyd attended all rehearsals, jumping in to make changes when needed, but, as Moulson wrote, "only if they concurred with his ideas and only if they fitted what came before and after. Never was a change made just to make things easier."[82]

By week's end, Corsaro had staged everything except the brothel sequence with character mezzo Elaine Bonazzi. Corsaro thought the scene itself unnecessary, and he encouraged Floyd to cut it. The composer was adamant, and Corsaro enlisted Kay's and Bob Holton's support. Floyd met Corsaro at his Riverside Drive apartment, a fifth of Jack Daniels bourbon between them, and Corsaro attacked: "Carlisle, we'll go into rehearsal out there and waste a lot of time. We really have to consider this and decide what is best."

Floyd had already explained that he had added the scene to lend variety to a dark, male-dominated opera, and extra dimension to George's character. The composer set his jaw and said, "Besides, it's all so spare."

CORSARO: First of all, the spareness is what you really must concentrate. You have enough material here, you don't need a scene to explain something you could say in one line. Never mind worrying that the audience needs to be entertained by a bunch of bosoms!
FLOYD: Frank, they're doing the set for it as we speak! And they've contracted Elaine for the role!
CORSARO: They could have the Pope singing, I wouldn't care.[83]

Floyd wanted to get Glynn Ross on the phone, but Corsaro dissuaded him, and refilled their glasses. The composer said he wanted to think about it, and stalked out into the December night. He suspected that Corsaro was right: the dynamic was stronger with a solitary woman, Curley's Wife, as the catalyst for this particular group of stressed men. He even smiled to think, knowing opera singers, that he'd never met a soprano who minded being the only woman onstage for an entire evening. Ten minutes later, he returned, submitted, and they called Seattle. Ross was undone, but calmed when he realized that the set was still in its early stages; if anything spoke to this impresario, it was *not* having to spend money. Though buying Elaine Bonazzi out of her contract proved doable, Floyd regretted that this was the second of his operas in which this had happened.[84] Aside from the disappointment of Seattle's chorus ladies, eager for any chance to play rowdy loose women rather than the usual staid courtiers, no one noticed the scene's omission. Floyd moved Slim's and George's arias to the beginning of act 2, where he and everyone else thought they made a great deal more dramatic sense.

Floyd viewed his function at rehearsals as a resource "to talk with the set designer, the stage director, the conductor, any participant who wants my response: Is this what I had in mind, or do I see another way to go about something? It's a collaboration of professionals, because they are free to make suggestions to me. Frank wanted me there all the time, so we sat together. He'd say, 'You like that, Carlisle?' 'No, Frank, I really don't,' and he'd let out this falsetto shriek. The whole cast loved it, they knew what we were talking about, they were in on it from the beginning."

Corsaro, his observation honed by years of psychological study, and no mean writer himself, did not miss what Floyd was up to:

> Carlisle had been quite explicit in his stage directions, but as a true professional he knew such to be grist for the director's mill. Allowing me and the actors free rein, we often improvised and sought fresh solutions for each scene before making any definitive choices. Sometimes these possibilities had not been conceptualized by Carlisle, but once they met his approval he would revise bits of music and text to accommodate them.[85]
>
> Carlisle next became an actor—changing, rethinking his material as the individual artists assimilated and translated it into living terms. This is a dangerous gift. I have seen similarly gifted playwrights unconsciously distort intention in order to help maintain rehearsal harmony. Carlisle's on-the-spot compromises and elisions were made with an ever vigilant eye on the sparrow—or mouse, if you'll have it. The basic vision never altered. . . . [H]is range of flexibilities . . . is non-pareil among his contemporaries. It's a kind of "savvy" one encounters more often in musical comedy—a comparison not pejorative to either side of the musical zodiac.[86]

While Floyd worked, Kay kept mostly to the hotel, reading. Even in New York before Christmas, she was never a big shopper, and Floyd recognized that she was rarely comfortable around opera's close-knit, noisy world. On occasion she might appear at rehearsal for two or three hours, and Corsaro enjoyed her intelligent support of his solutions, but Kay's experience of Floyd's career environments had taught her all too well the evanescence of success, and the proportion of chance or sheer luck that predominated in the mix, and she surrendered further to agoraphobia.

With initial blocking complete, the composer tied up loose ends at FSU and flew to Seattle after Christmas. They had three full weeks on the set, rather than with folding chairs, tape-marked walls, and levels in a rehearsal room, quite the luxury in these early days of regional opera. Their hosts, Georgianna and John Theodore, became bosom friends, and a large family contingent—Ermine, Billy, aunts Freddie and Bunny, Reverend and Mrs. Floyd—planned their Seattle travel. Floyd saw to everyone's hotel arrangements and performance tickets.

As the calendar flipped to 1970, Holton convinced Floyd that he'd found his publishing niche. With *Of Mice and Men*'s premiere finally in view, Floyd signed with Belwin-Mills on January 10, during Seattle rehearsals. Boosey understood that they would continue to represent all of his earlier works; but *Of Mice and Men* inaugurated his Belwin years.

In his piece for *The Opera Journal* special issue, Holton wrote of his relationship with Floyd as "an extremely close collaboration in which we concentrated not only on the music, but also on the man, his needs

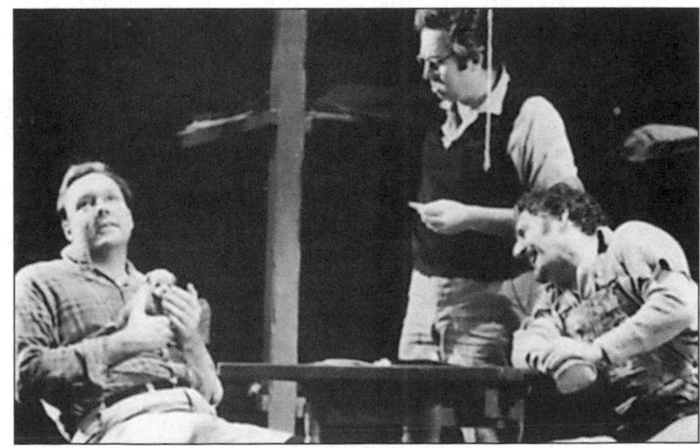

32. *Of Mice and Men*, Seattle Opera, 1970. Robert Moulson, Julian Patrick, Archie Drake. Permission courtesy of the photographer, Desmond C. Gates.

as an artist and his musical and theatrical goals. . . . In planning a career, the composer needs a sounding board as to the commerce of our industry, assistance in realizing realistic and equitable commissions, guidance in the area of public relations, contractual advice and, not to be laughed at, moral support. . . . There is no doubt in my mind that composers' needs greatly exceed the actual act of publication."[87]

Holton tailored their new contract generously: *Of Mice and Men* now Belwin's property, the high expense of part extraction, and the portion owed Steinbeck's estate—neither sum covered by the Ford grant—were offset by allocating Floyd 12 percent of the sheet music sales and 50 percent of rentals. Even better, Holton eased the part extraction situation that had alarmed Ford, and that had taxed Floyd for years, by agreeing that Belwin would cover anything above and beyond $1,250, to be deducted from Floyd's royalties. Holton had grand dreams for a long Broadway run following the Seattle premiere. Floyd's royalty share would have increased to 52.5 percent, with 22.5 percent going to Steinbeck Interests. Such hopes grew when producers Roger Stevens and David Merrick expressed interest; but Floyd suspected that his work struck such Broadway mavens as too riskily operatic.[88] Though he retained his previous percentages of royalties and other income after *Of Mice and Men*—50 percent of performance and mechanical rights—Floyd now had the right to compel Belwin to publish up to three new works each year.[89]

Belwin's contract also intimates that Floyd was already thinking of two new projects. Thanks to Cincinnati Opera's 1964 *Susannah* production, and the financial backing of the Corbetts, a commission was in the works for a large-scale choral work, *The Martyr*, based on Herman Melville's 1866 eulogy on the death of Abraham Lincoln. And South Carolina's Tricentennial Commission had sought out their native son to provide an *Overture for Orchestra* for the state's celebration in November 1970.

DESPITE FLOYD'S CERTAINTY that his orchestration skills had improved, when Anton Coppola began rehearsing the Seattle players, well-prepared by the company's regular music director, Henry Holt, he still found the scoring too thick in places. Julian Patrick attended an orchestra session during which Coppola put his baton down and addressed this or that player: "Here, for these three bars, you can play *forte;* but here you have to come down to *pianissimo* for six bars; then loud for two more bars; and here, bring it down to *pianississimo* [*ppp*]."[90]

Coppola sifted the entire score to gain such dynamic refinements, still managing to achieve Floyd's full orchestral effect. Floyd, present at each reading, solved other balance issues by repositioning the players outside their usual groupings. Heavier instruments—violas, cellos, horns, trumpets, and trombones—found themselves seated in new and unaccustomed places, and grumbled as players will; but, as Corsaro wrote, "At the final dress rehearsal all clouds lifted, and everyone was a genius."[91]

Once the cast began working with orchestra in the theater, they typically gathered in the wings for one another's big moments, especially the long duet between Lennie and Curley's Wife leading up to her murder. One of Julian Patrick's favorite moments was Floyd's act 3 orchestral interlude, which he believed "the finest orchestral construction I have heard from any contemporary composer in years."[92] Patrick managed to keep himself together emotionally until after firing into the back of Lennie's head; but then, thanks to Floyd's *not* writing anything more for George, the baritone inevitably found himself a "blubbering idiot," tears rolling down his cheeks.[93]

Still, the cast remained lighthearted, convinced that they were headed toward a triumph. They managed to ignore minor inconveniences, like real and quickly decomposing corn stalks; Corsaro directed Moulson to pile real hay onto Bayard after the murder, while the soprano had to remain motionless and restrain herself from sneezing. Curtain calls invariably found her with vegetal matter still in her hair; and there was Candy's very real dog, prone to turning Bayard's act 1 aria into a duet.

The day before the premiere, Floyd's family, Hazel Richards in tow, descended, and he installed them on the thirty-seventh floor of the Plaza Hotel, with its stunning views. In the next twenty-four hours, between Floyd's interviews with local newspapers, *Time* and *Newsweek,* and meetings with Bob Holton, the family absorbed the city's sights and sounds, and aunt Bunny finished Kay's dress for opening night. For the occasion, January 22, 1970, Kay's date for the evening, arranged by Corsaro, was the dancer Edward Villella. Floyd and Corsaro sat together, enjoying the whole experience. This and each Seattle performance elicited standing ovations, the only aspect of the opera that made it into Reverend Floyd's diary. It was Floyd's biggest and most immediate success.

Julius Rudel sent John White as his representative, to see what they had missed. Floyd described White as "almost Dickensian, kind of a Uriah Heep; but he could also be your enemy, because he always had the ear [of higher ups]. He was one of those survivors who knew where all the skeletons were."

33. *Of Mice and Men,* Seattle Opera, 1970. Robert Moulson, Carol Bayard. Permission courtesy of the photographer, Desmond C. Gates.

Floyd recalled White later saying, in his nasal Austrian accent, "Well, it's not *Susannah.*" At final curtain, Corsaro could not wait to ring up Rudel in New York, and tell him, "Ya blew it, baby!"[94] At the dinner party following the premiere, to Floyd's right sat the *San Francisco Chronicle* critic Robert Commanday, whose first question of the composer was, "How much of this piece did Adler see?" Most West Coast reviewers fell over themselves: "The best new American opera to come along in many, many years."[95] "Picks you up and shakes you hard, then drops you drained and overwhelmed . . . an artwork of stunning impact."[96]

Commanday was somewhat more reserved, admitting that Floyd had come a long way stylistically since *Susannah,* but he criticized the composer's romantic blunting of Steinbeck's harshness; yet he allowed that *any* good theater is always welcome, "and *Of Mice and Men* promises to be around for some time to come."[97]

Floyd intended to return to Tallahassee at once, but Ross asked him to stay on to observe the workings of Opera America and meet more press representatives; nor did having the composer of the work that put Seattle Opera on the map hurt Ross's cause. Floyd stayed for all five performances, on January 22, 24, 28, 30, and February 1, and found the idea of a national opera producers' organization intriguing, but viewed it initially as "an old boys club." He spoke with local press of his next as-yet-to-be-defined operatic project to explore the dichotomy between an "important person's" public and private lives; as a lifelong movie fan, he dreamed of utilizing the media resources of film or closed-circuit television.[98]

The national journals weighed in, with plaudits and predictions of a brilliant future for Floyd's "straightforward and consistently portentous score . . . and often soaring lyrical evocation of . . . everyman's struggle against loneliness."[99] *The New York Times* reprinted Commanday's review on February 1; but this and other lackluster voices were put to shame by a *Time* notice, which echoed praise for *Susannah* in 1956, comparing *Of Mice and Men*'s emotional impact to that of *Porgy and Bess,* and predicting the new opera's enduring popularity. The uncredited writer praised Floyd's revelation of human situations, with music that elevated the characters' "foolishness, vanity and ambition to the level of high tragedy. . . . Floyd's opera has calluses on its hands and hot blood in its heart."[100]

Glynn Ross claimed that fifteen thousand people had seen the opera, including Opera America's fifteen general directors.[101] Within a few weeks, with Bob Holton's energetic promotion, companies in Central City, Kansas City, St. Paul, and Cincinnati had scheduled productions. Floyd returned from Seattle with two commissions in the works; and *Musical America* named him "Musician of the Month" in its February 1970 issue.

WHETHER OWING TO the simple fact of having more disposable income, or Kay's increasing aversion to Floyd's professional life, the lasting effects of early abuse, or her lifelong interest in psychology, she now began Freudian couch analysis. Floyd sought closure with his own issues and followed suit in Freudian therapy with a different analyst, whom he found intelligent and well prepared. Their relationship lasted about three years, and subsequently expanded into group therapy with Transactional Analysis (TA).[102] The first practitioner Floyd saw, a medical doctor who had branched out into psychiatry, ran an "attack group," intended to get patients in touch with their anger. During one weeks-long phase, the gentleman began ignoring Floyd completely, not even looking at him: "It really hurt my feelings. Of course, I had no idea what was going on, and only found out quite belatedly, when he said, 'I had to do that, because if I'd acknowledged you, you and I would have controlled the group.'"

In coming months, a female therapist in Tallahassee seized an apparent monopoly on TA with professionals in various fields prosperous enough to afford her. One of her exercises for Floyd involved crumpling or tearing to shreds any negative review and tossing it into a wastebasket; yet the lady was jealous of her position and prerogatives. Once when Floyd offered an observation about a fellow-patient, she observed, "Oh, look at Carlisle playing psychiatrist." Yet work with the so-called Karpman Drama Triangle, invented in the midsixties by Dr. Stephen B. Karpman, made a great impression on Floyd. It designates roles of "persecutor," "victim," and "rescuer," and uses therapist-guided demonstrations of how role switches mirror or duplicate the transactions that Floyd knew so well from his family. For instance, when Reverend Floyd belittled and criticized (persecutor), Floyd was usually a victim. Sometimes his mother or Ermine might be a rescuer; but if the children ever teased their father, his response might be, "You all will just say anything to hurt me," donning the victim's mantle. In his relationship with Kay, Floyd, fearing that he might lose her, usually became the guilty party (victim) in any disagreement.

SOUTH CAROLINA had trouble organizing and executing its Tricentennial observation. As reported by state senator Eugene N. Zeigler Jr., "I persuaded the commission to get South Carolina native Carlisle Floyd to compose an overture."[103] Zeigler, a native of Florence, was known for his promotion of the fine arts, and succeeded in scheduling the musical celebration in his hometown. The state's needs for this event proved much simpler than the needs of its neighbor to the north had: Floyd was to write a short piece in celebratory mode, already in the works by the time he signed with Belwin-Mills.

In this ten-minute overture for his usual orchestral complement plus harp, Floyd chose a ternary structure. A solemn introduction, *Maestoso*, 3/4, in D Major—despite the expected tone-stacking throughout—consists of a syncopated fanfare motive, leading to a flowing quarter-note theme in 6/4, centered on D Major, augmenting and fragmenting some of the introduction's rhythmic, melodic, and harmonic features. A second theme revisits *Susannah*'s world with a warm folkish tune in G Major that also varies previous material. This climaxes on a triumphant return of the principal D Major tune, further developed before recapitulation of the introduction, and concludes with a spicy coda.[104]

On April 22, Floyd accompanied Elena Nikolaidi's next FSU recital, for which they performed all five songs of *The Mystery*. Two days later, the school hosted an event for Gian Carlo Menotti, but as playwright rather than composer. Floyd's elder university colleague Walter Ruel Cowles had been dead since 1959, but his son, the New York producer Chandler Cowles, called in favors to reserve the university's Fine Arts Theater for the event. Menotti had written one earlier play, *A Copy of Madame Aupic;* but his most recent effort, *The Leper,* was altogether more ambitious. Set in a kingdom bordering on the Byzantine Empire in the thirteenth century, a young leprous prince defies the kingdom's moral and social codes and is put to death by order of his mother the queen. Biographer John Gruen quotes Menotti, "My life is an open book; however, I don't like to leave it around."[105] Yet *The Leper* is as close as Menotti had come to exposing conflicted feelings about his homosexuality. Cowles, acting as producer, knew that the play needed an out-of-town tryout before putting it onto any New York stage. The cast of FSU drama students was headed by two "ringers": in the title role, actor-figure skater Francis Phelan, whom Menotti adopted as his son in 1974; and, as the Queen, the redoubtable Patricia Neway. Menotti as director found the theater's acoustic impossible and left for ten days in the middle of rehearsals. The cast, hoping to profit from his theatrical brilliance, received only entrances, exits, and other basic blocking.

Making matters worse, Cowles invited a private planeload of about a hundred movers and shakers from New York's cultural world, including Lincoln Kirstein, Virgil Thomson, and Menotti's life partner, composer Samuel Barber. On opening night, April 24, 1970, Floyd sat in the packed house. He agreed with most of the audience—and *all* of the critics—that the play left much to be desired. At a lunch the next day he spotted Barber, whose music he had admired for decades, across the room. Floyd had been told that Barber could be cool; but after introducing himself and voicing appreciative sentiments, Floyd was nonplussed to meet with cold silence from a personal hero. He got the snub of his creative life.

Moments later, in a curious juxtaposition with the Barber experience, Virgil Thomson bustled up to Floyd, blurting out his own species of encouragement: "Continue to be fecund." A few months later, in his review for *The New York Times* of Patrick J. Smith's *The Tenth Muse,* a history of the opera libretto, Thomson wrote oddly and somewhat deprecatingly that the operas of Britten, Floyd, and Ginastera all shared descent from *opéra-comique,* "the amorous pastoral, the comic skit, the cruel joke," particularly in their use of speech to project over the orchestra.[106]

Of Mice and Men's second outing scored eighteen performances at Central City, Colorado, between June 27 and July 25. Moulson reprised the role of Lennie, double cast with Allen Cathcart; Julian Patrick, Robert Trehy, and Mark Howard alternated performances as George; Gerald Thorsen, the Ballad Singer in Seattle, was promoted here to Curley, together with Joaquin Romaguera; and Carol Bayard and Alexandra Hunt shared the role of Curley's Wife. Corsaro again directed, with Thomas Martin conducting.[107] Floyd impressed Martin as "a young-looking man with trim hair, resembling a well-groomed, distinguished math professor . . . wearing a handsome blazer with a Florida State emblem . . . everyone was impressed by his calm, strong presence."[108]

As in Seattle, Floyd helped his conductor shuffle the orchestra into unfamiliar seating in Central City's tiny pit. As always with animals on stage, procurement and disposition posed problems: the company went to a local pound to find a suitably dilapidated dog and tranquilized it before performances. When Colorado's SPCA protested, the drug was withheld; but at one point during a performance, the canine, also fond of singing along, walked offstage. Moulson retrieved it unobtrusively during a few bars of rest. Later animals became concerns, not to say thorns, an element in which company prop masters and mistresses took special interest; they always assured Floyd, "Have we got a dog for you, the saddest creature you've ever seen!" One solution to onstage mishaps lay in costuming the animal's owner or trainer as a ranch hand, and letting him—or, in one case, her, dressed as a man with a slouch hat pulled down over her forehead—sit in the shadows behind Candy's bunk.

Of the opera, Denver's *Rocky Mountain News* expressed a majority opinion: "Gripping, intense, dynamic . . . subtle, touching . . . poignant, moving."[109] Floyd's Seattle hosts Georgie and John Theodore had already brainstormed the extended Broadway run anticipated in the composer's Belwin-Mills contract; but when they turned up for a Central City performance, the project seemed closer to realization when the couple offered to serve as producers.

As school resumed in Tallahassee, Floyd's interview in FSU's quarterly *Research in Review* appeared that August, summing up his midcareer position. He defined his greatest gift as "revealing smaller situations, personal relationships." The pomp and grandeur he had attempted with *Jonathan Wade* he felt "tended to overwhelm and diffuse the personal drama that was the heart of the story." With both *Wuthering Heights* and *Mollie Sinclair,* he had allowed historical detail to get in the way of "the human element, the emotional element." *Of Mice and Men,* he felt, offered a corrective, in which "the characters, their relationships, and the dramatic situations . . . evolve naturally." Floyd expressed politic gratitude for the university's support and time allowed off-campus, and for the college/conservatory opera workshop that offered composers opportunities beyond most professional company budgets. Higher education was successfully extracting opera from New York's stranglehold, and he credited teaching as "a wonderful way to grow and to stay fresh and . . . have one's musical ideas and precepts constantly challenged."[110]

In September's third week, Floyd flew to Kansas City to see the first *Of Mice and Men* ensemble that had no carryovers from Seattle's cast,[111] conducted by Russell Patterson and Ward Holmquist, and staged by Ian Strasfogel. Far more important than any aspect of the production was Floyd's first meeting with producer Roger Stevens. Chairman of the Kennedy Center from its inception in 1961,[112] Stevens proposed the opera's extended Broadway run. In 1967, three years before the center's public opening, Stevens offered Julius Rudel the position of artistic director. Rudel declined, but in January 1968 agreed to serve as musical advisor, in which capacity he remained until 1975.

On July 21, 1970, Stevens announced the formation of the National Opera Institute (NOI) with Rudel as chairman. A private corporation closely allied to the Kennedy Center, and also headquartered in Washington, DC, NOI began with an annual budget of $475,000 and the mission of encouraging the growth and development of American opera. As such, the organization assumed many of the functions previously addressed by the Ford Foundation: subsidizing productions of new or unperformed operas; commissioning new operas; providing grants for the training, coaching, and living expenses of young singers; and funding touring opera to regions of the country without access to the medium.

Floyd's name came up sooner rather than later: Rudel, still ruing City Opera's *Of Mice and Men* forfeit, had put Stevens onto its creator's work. After the opera's opening night in Kansas City, Stevens met Floyd and expressed passionate interest in *Of Mice and Men.* Even better, at a meeting on September 22, Stevens broached the subject of privately commissioning a new Floyd work through the Kennedy Center Foundation, to demonstrate America's native operatic talent to the world.

Also that fall, Floyd tempered some of his praise of academia with a piece for *College Music Symposium 10: The Composer in Academia.* Its keynote was Igor Stravinsky's caution, "A composer is or isn't; he cannot learn to acquire the gift that makes him one."[113] Stravinsky believed that the young composer who teaches tends to wilt on the vine without ever blossoming. Floyd's twenty-two colleagues in this collection included Milton Babbitt, Elliott Carter, Paul Creston, George Rochberg, and Hugo Weisgall. Floyd both agreed and disagreed with Stravinsky's premise, stating that "one of the greatest hazards that confronts composers in universities is the danger of becoming doctrinaire. . . . [Academia] fosters thought over feeling, cognition over instinct . . . the opposite pole from the artist's impulse to self-expression." On the other humble hand, he reaffirmed appreciation for the students themselves, and his experience of FSU's atmosphere of "support and sanction."[114]

On October 20, 23, and 25, *Of Mice and Men* continued its march across the country with a production by the St. Paul (Minnesota) Opera Association, conducted by Igor Buketoff and staged again by Ian Strasfogel with another new cast: William Neill (Lennie), Robert Paul (George), James McCray (Curley), and Alexandra

Hunt (Curley's Wife). Roger Stevens continued to show interest in Floyd's work by sending his assistant Charlotte Woolard to confirm his impressions of the opera. Floyd stayed just long enough for the opening, and to read the local press's positive reception, some of which contained neither the first nor the last review to list the composer as "Floyd Carlisle."[115]

WHEN JACKSONVILLE SYMPHONY conductor Willis Page called, Floyd learned that the city was about to celebrate its sesquicentennial; and the orchestra, rebounding from a year's hiatus, wanted a new Floyd work for the occasion. The commission fee for a piece lasting between thirty and sixty minutes would be two thousand dollars, and Floyd said he would think about it. Since the days of the abandoned *Monologue* for Patricia Neway, the notion of a semitheatrical work for a single voice and orchestra had intrigued him, and he turned to Frank Corsaro and to Phyllis Curtin, whose performing career had begun to wind down.[116] Corsaro suggested Eugene O'Neill's 1916 monodrama, *Before Breakfast,* but rights had already been granted to the Scottish composer Erik Chisholm.[117] When Floyd approached Curtin, the soprano had a suggestion ready: As early as November 1957, while down with the flu and hoping to make it through the next evening's City Opera *Susannah,* she read Amy Kelly's *Eleanor of Aquitaine and the Four Kings:* "First of all, the author was housemistress of my residence at Wellesley. . . . And now I have read every word, and adored reading about [Eleanor's] . . . castles and strongholds in that glorious country around Poitiers and the Dordogne Valley, and being totally swept up in the 12th Century. I'm thinking of giving up singing (after *W.H.*) and becoming a *savante* in all matters of that period in France and England."[118]

This remarkable queen, who lived from 1122 until 1204, first married her cousin, Henry VII of France. She had that union annulled, and weathered a tempestuous second marriage to Henry II Plantagenet of England (1133–1189). The final two kings to whom the title refers were Eleanor's and Henry Plantagenet's contentious sons, Richard I, the Lionheart (1157–1199), famed for his exploits during and after the Third Crusade; and his younger brother John (1166–1216), best remembered for his reluctant signing of the Magna Carta the year before his death. At first, Henry encouraged Eleanor's full and able partnership in forging an English empire; but then, during a period of marital estrangement, she kept her own court in Poitiers, at the center of the troubadour culture of chivalric love. When she supported John's and Richard's rebellion against their father, Henry had her imprisoned in Salisbury Tower for almost sixteen years, while he dallied with a mistress, Rosamond Clifford.[119] Upon Henry's death, Eleanor emerged as regent for Richard during his absence in the Holy Land and the continuation of King John's endless war with France.

Kelly's only book took her twenty years to complete and sold briskly, inspiring numerous theatrical and fictional interpretations, including James Goldman's 1966 play, *The Lion in Winter.*[120] To the larger world Kelly seemed a prim, strict, but good-hearted woman, not above showing one of Curtin's admirers, who had missed the last train back to Boston at the height of a snowstorm, to a couch for the night in the reception area of the Wellesley dorm. Curtin, one of the many who found *Eleanor* inspiring, wrote Kelly her appreciation, and tucked the author's return letter, which maintained that she had always known that Phyllis would make something of herself, into her copy of the book. Approaching fifty, Curtin had always been able to sniff out a great role in the making, and posted a copy of *Eleanor* to Floyd. Curtin echoed an earlier declaration of Floyd's, "What soprano doesn't love a vehicle in which she has no competition onstage?"[121]

NOVEMBER 9 began Floyd's marathon of family visits to Barnwell, Laurinburg, Latta, and Floydale, ending in Florence for South Carolina's "Musical Tricentennial" at Moore Auditorium, and the premiere of Floyd's new overture *In Celebration.* The composer's commission was $1,500; Belwin-Mills had already acquired the work, and sought other performance venues. The composer's father had grown more confused and narcissistically separated from the rest of the world; the best appraisal he could give *In Celebration,* the only purely orchestral composition by his son that he ever heard, was, "It was okay."[122] The event's chronicler, Eugene N. Zeigler Jr., seemed to agree, writing sadly, "It was largely ignored, although the symphony orchestra did play it in one of its concerts."[123]

Floyd's 1971 began with *The Opera Journal* issue devoted to *Of Mice and Men.* Plans for an extended run at Broadway's Anta Theatre were still under discussion while Floyd supervised the opera's FSU debut, duplicating the original experience as closely as possible. Frank Corsaro came as guest director, and Julian Patrick, Robert Moulson, and Carol Bayard sang their Seattle roles on Klein's sets. The rehearsal period found Bob Holton paying one of several visits to the Floyds, with much fast, furious talk about the proposed Theodore-financed Broadway run. One morning, passing by the guest bathroom door, Floyd thought he smelled an odd, alcohol-like substance. He knocked discreetly, then felt shock to see Holton wielding a hypodermic syringe filled with the odor's source. Holton, always seeking the latest health fad, hoisted his needle, boasting that *everyone* in New York was injecting themselves with pregnant women's urine. As Floyd says, "That's just how Bob was, and we indulged him. As they say in New York, *whatevah.*"

On January 29, Floyd sped the 326 miles across and down the state to Sarasota for the Turnau Opera Company's production of *Susannah* at the Asolo Opera Theatre, before *Of Mice and Men* played FSU on February 4, 5, and 6, then toured to St. Petersburg's Bayfront Theatre on February 9 and 10. The press effused, "Those who rant about the lowly state of American opera had better catch this show before their ignorance overtakes them."[124] Mary Nik Shenk, interviewing for the *St. Petersburg Times,* and to a degree smitten with Floyd, took a vivid snapshot of the composer in these days:

> Apparent ease is . . . Carlisle Floyd's hallmark. He's a modest, handsome brunet of medium stature, who moves easily and fluidly, his longish sideburns distinguished with new gray. Neat and orderly, he dresses impeccably, generally in matched browns and golds. His brown eyes sparkle, even when he is serious. . . . His intensity and concentration never wane, whether he's teaching, writing, composing, playing tennis, a game of bridge, reading medieval English history and archeology or working in his rose garden. It's difficult to imagine a frivolous bone in his body; even his laughter is solid and meaningful.[125]

The reference to English history pointed to his study of Amy Kelly's *Eleanor;* gardening, a new and fleeting passion, arrived courtesy of rose plants and cuttings from his father-in-law Guy Reeder. To Shenk, Floyd mused on the interface of genius and effort, "I haven't considered myself a genius since I was 15. . . . You simply can't just start out and write. . . . You have to sweat it out. Seventy per cent of creation is a technical problem. There may be inspiration, but most of it is training and preparation which allows an idea to take shape. *Susannah* was a fluke of raw talent. . . . Now, after 15 years and several musical dramas . . . I feel I've got the necessary materials to write." As for teaching, the tumult of the late sixties had left him admiring students' independence: "The new generation won't pay lip service to what they don't believe in, and I admire them for it. . . . I don't try to look and act like my students. They don't want a middle-age[d] hippie for a teacher. I'm 44 and can only be myself."[126]

In Barnwell, Floyd's father, now in his late sixties, arranged with his district superintendent to retire from the spin cycle of appointments and returned to Holly Hill. Meanwhile, his son received new accolades. On February 22, Florida Representative Don Fuqua read a statement of appreciation into the *Congressional Record:* "There are very few American-born opera composers, and Carlisle Floyd is, in my opinion, one of the best . . . an outstanding American."[127] In a similar vein, on April 16, the Florida legislature unanimously adopted a resolution of appreciation of Floyd.

In New York, the Anta Theatre *Of Mice and Men* run collapsed when the Theodores failed to assemble a team of fundraising partners; City Opera had announced its latest *Susannah* revival, but Corsaro, committed to directing *Jesus Christ Superstar* on Broadway, was unavailable, as he said, to "complete Floyd's 'Conquest of New York.'"[128] Rudel turned to another Actor's Studio luminary, Robert Lewis.

In mid-April 1971 Floyd directed *Susannah* for Orlando Opera. Phyllis Curtin and Norman Treigle allowed themselves to be cajoled into their signature roles, and Robert Moulson played Sam; but the soprano had reservations about the amount of white showing in her hair, and designated this production as her farewell to the opera, with performances on April 23 and 25.

On the day of the opening, the *Orlando Sentinel* interviewed Kay for the paper's "Action/Society" column, which offers a rare sketch of the couple, especially of reclusive Kay away from home and enjoying their life. The reporter found her beautifully tanned, racket in hand, dressed in a short white tennis outfit, on her way with Floyd to a match at the Orlando Country Club.

Following a brief recap of their meeting at FSU, and her graduate work at the University of Wisconsin, Kay confided that Floyd had picked her. A self-described musical amateur, she played music from his scores-in-progress. Though she had immersed herself in the study of English literature, she realized that becoming "a real writer" exceeded her self-discipline; in fact, knowing her husband to be a highly sociable man, she failed to understand how he could sequester himself for as many as ten hours at a time to compose. She admitted helping with the selection and development of some of his opera librettos; and while Floyd composed away, she played piano and tennis, read, and, to Floyd's particular delight, indulged her culinary skills. The interview ended with her assertion that they socialized with both musicians and business people who brought different interests and experiences to the encounters.[129]

34. Kay Floyd, c. 1971. Courtesy of Carlisle Floyd.

Though the Orlando *Susannah* proved bittersweet for everyone, it allowed Curtin and Floyd time to discuss the Jacksonville monodrama, sponsored by not only the Jacksonville Symphony Association but also by the Florida Fine Arts Council and the National Endowment for the Arts.

On April 23, Floyd, his parents, aunt Doris, and Bob Holton drove to Sadler Elementary School to watch a group of children perform *Susannah* excerpts. Reverend Floyd believed it "one of the most moving presentations I have seen."[130]

For the title of Curtin's piece, Floyd landed on *Flower and Hawk*, writing that it originated with Eleanor's seal, a part of the Louvre's collection, which shows her standing, holding a hawk and flower in separate hands, suggesting a duality in her nature.[131]

As always, focus and condensation became problems in adapting Kelly's 387 informative, atmospheric pages into a one-woman vehicle. Floyd's first libretto was ambitious and somewhat long: twenty-six pages containing six scenes and an epilogue. His adaptation relied heavily on projected scenery, and on pantomime characters filling the roles of Prince/King Louis; courtiers in the French throne room and the great hall of Eleanor's palace at Poitiers; a nobleman who consults her about family wedding plans; and the English throne room, where Eleanor dissects the relationship of Henry and Rosamond Clifford. Floyd then took a trip backward in time for Richard's death, and leapt forward to a final scene of old-age reminiscence.

By the time he trimmed this down to sixteen pages, Floyd's music would run to about fifty minutes.[132] The entire action shifted to a sparsely furnished Salisbury Tower.[133] After almost sixteen years of confinement, Eleanor (soprano) relives her time in sunless England, wondering whether she is remembered. She believes that death is preferable to more years of imprisonment. Her reminiscences expand outward like pond ripples to encompass her glamorous life as queen of France, the bitter separation from Louis, the death of her favorite son, Richard, the romantic escapades at her "Court of Love" at Poitiers, and the nightly visits of a troubadour lover. Reproaches to her unseen husband, Henry, for flaunting his lover Rosamond at court, drag Eleanor back to the overwhelming tragedy of her life, the death of her son Richard. After alternately praying for his soul and berating God for cruelty and injustice, she reaches epiphany in exhaustion: Richard had sought death as she has always craved life. As she intones the Latin *Requiem,* bells toll offstage: Henry is dead; Eleanor at last free.

ON MAY 13, Floyd drove to Jacksonville University to see a student production of *The Sojourner and Mollie Sinclair,* directed by Richard Bunting and conducted by William McNeiland. Before the year was out, Bob Holton rushed *Of Mice and Men*'s vocal score through Belwin's presses with another Evon Streetman cover design: the blended silhouettes of George and Lennie form a giant shadow hand holding a dead white mouse in the foreground. Horrified to learn that Floyd intended having every Seattle stage direction printed alongside his music, Frank Corsaro shrieked, "No, no! Then it becomes holy writ: The First and Original Version, the only way to do it!"[134] Floyd included only the most cogent of Corsaro's instructions. Having dedicated the opera to Nikolaidi, Floyd rewarded Corsaro by acknowledging those staging details that he incorporated into the score.[135]

Cincinnati Opera hired the composer to stage *Of Mice and Men* for two summer performances,[136] with Emerson Buckley conducting veterans Patrick and Moulson, Grayson Hirst as Curley, and Sylvia Cooper as the Wife. Kay had been complaining since Seattle and Central City of Corsaro's staging of the bunkhouse fight in act 2, scene 2, where Curley "fights" with only a riding crop. Now Floyd, the most peaceful of men, became his own fight choreographer in a scene wanting angry violence: he asked Moulson to turn his broad back to the audience, thus covering most of Hirst's fist action.

The critic John Ardoin felt that Floyd had made great strides since *Susannah,* and had particular praise for the opera's compelling theatricality, "coupled to some highly shapely and effective music."[137] On opening night, Floyd added another champion to his roster of personal and professional friends: David Gockley, who had big plans as the general director-designate of Houston Grand Opera. As an undergraduate at Brown University, he had sung in glee club; and as an apprentice at Santa Fe Opera for the summers of 1965, 1966, and 1967, he had gained an introduction to Floyd through hearing *Susannah*'s ubiquitous arias. Marriage to the soprano Patricia Wise, whose repertoire included *Susannah,* cemented Gockley's interest. He had seen *Of Mice and Men*'s world premiere in Seattle, and Bob Holton had sent him a tape as a reminder. Knowing something of Floyd's extensive background in academia, Gockley approached the composer with the idea of a state-of-the-art training center for young singers, conductors, and pianist-coaches, and, finally, about a bicentennial commission.

Gockley's first impression of Floyd was by now an oft-told tale: "Very dapper, beautifully dressed, very natty in a blue blazer; and very congenial, very direct. Also, in those days he'd travel with a bottle of "Black Jack" Daniels in his suitcase."[138]

Late that night they sat in Floyd's hotel room, bathroom glasses filled with the amber liquid, "getting more and more congenial as time went on." Floyd thought that Gockley, just four days shy of his twenty-eighth birthday, looked like a perennial college freshman, a trait the administrator carried with grace into his middle years. Gockley strategized Floyd's introduction to Houston like a military campaign, beginning with the known commodity, *Susannah,* as soon as it could be programmed, followed by *Of Mice and Men,* and then the bicentennial commission piece. A new opera had, in fact, been on Floyd's mind, at least since his *Seattle Times* interview in January 1970; and here was the perfect opportunity, after two decades of solid experience, to close the circle with *Susannah*'s logical successor, *Bilby's Doll.*

Floyd summarized Esther Forbes's tale, which he first approached in the fifties. Although Gockley expressed interest, he thought, "I did not know much about commissions at that point. I did not have a process like the one I have developed over the years, whereby a composer/librettist, or a partnership, submits a kind of scenario, an act/scene structure, and how the music might break down into substructures. But we talked about the story, and I was convinced that it could be a good work. Carlisle was so prominent, and I was not questioning whether this or that was appropriate, I let him run with it. He knew how he created a piece, writing the libretto with a musical structure of arias, duets."

Just as Curtin had provided Floyd with the source of *Flower and Hawk,* the composer now sent Gockley a copy of Forbes's *Mirror for Witches.* His other Cincinnati coup was finalizing details of the $1,500 Corbett Foundation commission for *The Martyr,*[139] to open the Patricia Corbett Pavilion at the University of Cincinnati on April 11, 1972. He would write for a large chorus of mixed voices, two trumpets, piano, and a battery of exotic percussion: timpani, celesta, chimes, vibraphone, xylophone, cymbals, suspended cymbal, snare drum, tenor drum, bass drum, whip (a musical solution for gunshots), tambourine, and gong.

The Jacksonville Symphony *Flower and Hawk* premiere was set for just a month off, on May 16; but now Floyd entered an uncharacteristic fallow period after finishing Curtin's monodrama. As he rode his lawnmower around the Middlebrook house that spring, he racked his brain to fashion an effective setting of Melville's dramatic poem, with its equation of Lincoln with Christ:

Good Friday was the day
Of the prodigy and crime,
When they killed him in his pity,
When they killed him in his prime
Of clemency and calm—
When with yearning he was filled
To redeem the evil-willed,
And, though conqueror, be kind;
But they killed him in his kindness,
In their madness and their blindness,
And they killed him from behind.

There is sobbing of the strong,
And a pall upon the land;
But the People in their weeping
Bare the iron hand:
Beware the People weeping
When they bare the iron hand.

He lieth in his blood—
The father in his face;
They have killed him, the Forgiver—
The Avenger takes his place,
The Avenger wisely stern,
Who in righteousness shall do
What the heavens call him to,
And the parricides remand;
For they killed him in his kindness,
In their madness and their blindness,
And his blood is on their hand.

There is sobbing of the strong, [etc.].

Floyd turned again to the theater for solutions. Thanks to exchanges with Frank Corsaro, who was involved in a series of multimedia opera productions with the designer Ronald Chase at City Opera, Floyd first thought of moving images on film; but logistics forced a shift to still slides of Lincoln, his death, and his funeral. In a preface to the published score, Floyd encouraged the use of dramatic lighting, with the chorus dressed all in black.[140]

The musical realization, running to about fifteen minutes, is, in the words of one critic, "muscular."[141] After two measures of chimes tolling on C-sharp, Floyd establishes his signature pandiatonic, polytonal clash, with the piano playing an ostinato of F-sharp Minor and B-flat Major. Trumpets proclaim a syncopated tattoo between piano and chorus, singing in unison, octaves, or four-part harmony, traditional in appearance, if not function, and supported by the keyboard ostinato. Throughout, Floyd tailors ever-shifting meters, tempi, and phrase lengths to the service of text, conveying each intonation of "weeping" with sixteenth-eighth syncopations, and later, for "in his kindness," a chromatic sixteenth-note keening figure echoed by trumpets.

Floyd telescoped Melville's four stanzas into three main sections, and recurring harmonic and rhythmic devices create the impression of a rondo. For the second stanza, a more legato rhythmic augmentation builds to a tremendous climax with chimelike use of voices, on "Bare the iron hand." Symmetrical recurrence of musical materials involves textual repetition, with an angry, vengeful conclusion. Floyd dedicated the score to his colleague, the choral conductor Wiley Housewright, FSU's new dean of music.[142]

At the end of July, the University of Iowa (Iowa City) became *Of Mice and Men*'s first academic host since FSU. Herald Stark, director of Iowa's opera program, sent Floyd a sheaf of reviews, all enthusiastic, even if one bore the unfortunate headline typo characterizing the opera as a "Gusty Earthy Opera."[143]

As the new school year began, Ermine's second daughter, Jane, joined her elder sister, Martha, at FSU, and studied voice with Elena Nikolaidi. On October 8, Floyd accompanied Nikolaidi's next recital: Ravel, Mahler, Canteloube, and a repeat performance of *The Mystery*.

On October 31, City Opera unveiled its new *Susannah,* staged by Robert Lewis in Ming Cho Lee's sets, and conducted by Rudel. Floyd attended, after playing through his pencil manuscript of *Flower and Hawk* with Phyllis Curtin. The soprano, despite scaling back her performances, had lost none of her phenomenal musicianship, sight-reading her way through the entire score in one sitting. After the triumphant E Major finish, with Eleanor exulting on a high B-natural, Curtin burst into tears from the effort. Floyd remembered her similar breakdown almost twenty years earlier in the meadow at Aspen; but now, as Curtin dried her tears, she observed, "I didn't find any color, I was just reading pitches; I hope to find out what this sounds like some time."

In the wake of City Opera's *Susannah,* Donal Henahan, elevated to *The New York Times* since 1967, bashed both Floyd and Treigle, calling the opera insubstantial and cartoonish.[144] Niska's Susannah drew praise; Lewis incurred wrath by staging her bathing scene seminude, but with her back turned to the audience on an obviously dry stage. Niska, Treigle, Harry Theyard (Sam), and David Hall (Little Bat) gave two more performances on November 2 and 14. A fairly clean tape of the former found its way onto pirated vinyl (that is, a "private recording not for sale"), the opera's first for fans and fanatics.

During that same performance, a stagehand carrying a bench during a scene change collided with Treigle, who then needed surgery. This resulted in performance cancellations and a consequent loss of income, placing even greater stress on the basso's relationship with City Opera. Yet the singer's loyalty to Floyd remained unimpaired: at the end of November, Treigle's recital with Judith Somogyi as accompanist at California's El Camino College included *Pilgrimage*'s three lower songs, which he then recorded with the New Orleans Philharmonic on December 7, conducted by Werner Torkanowsky. The eventual commercial release was reviewed in 1981: "Carlisle Floyd's songs . . . are of such artistic significance. They are beautiful . . . dramatic, and . . . magnificently set forth by this vocalist."[145]

THE YEAR 1972 loomed as another period of Floyd firsts and seconds: On April 6, the Florida Symphony Orchestra,[146] under the baton of the Croatian conductor Pavle Despalj, performed *Introduction, Aria, and Dance* at Orlando's Municipal Auditorium. On April 11, Floyd attended the premiere of *The Martyr* by the University of Cincinnati College-Conservatory of Music, conducted by Elmer Thomas. Press reception belied the composer's insecurities about the work, calling it remarkably beautiful, alternately lyrical and disjunct, with its "layered effects . . . strikingly modern and ruggedly individual."[147]

The Martyr was performed just once more, at the University of Houston in the eighties; but Floyd never felt disposed to revise it as he did his operas, and discouraged the work's inclusion on a retrospective concert at Rhode Island College in 2007.

Toward the end of May's first week, Floyd joined Phyllis Curtin and Frank Corsaro, whom the composer had asked to stage *Flower and Hawk,* in Jacksonville. The premiere on May 16 scored a triumph, sharing the program with Duke Ellington's *Celebration* and Howard Hanson's *Dies Natalis.* Floyd was surrounded for the occasion by Kay, the Choppins and Mastrogiacomos from Tallahassee, and he insisted on everyone accompanying him to an opening night party thrown by the event's wealthy patrons. Walking up to the mansion, Floyd, for whom such society events were anathema, growled to his friends, "We're gonna have a good time if it kills us."

The English journal *Opera* complimented Floyd on "the development and maturing of a talented composer of the American opera stage who knows how to weld his music to his own text into one homogeneous unit." Yet the critic took Floyd to task for resisting his natural melodic urge; finding that promising themes were "arbitrarily dissolved by a set of dissonant chords."[148] VAI's Ernie Gilbert managed to retrieve a tape of the premiere from Curtin, but various difficulties have prevented its commercial release.

Lloyd Evans had designed his minimal set for touring, and the orchestra packed cases for performances at the Kennedy Center on May 18, and at New York's Carnegie Hall the next evening. *Washington Post* critic Paul Hume had little good to say of either libretto or music, but found Curtin "marvelous."[149]

Floyd had planned to attend and slip in a visit to the Clarkes; but stresses at FSU seep from his Christmas 1972 message to them: "My Dean here [Wiley Housewright] quite unexpectedly developed a concern that his faculty were off-campus too much. . . . I was able to make the New York performance, which didn't involve missing teaching, but not the Washington one, which did."[150]

The New York Times praised the balance and variety of Floyd's vocal writing and Curtin's "emotional range." Despite this critic's characterization of Floyd's musical ideas as lackluster, he thought the opera's "theatrical shrewdness . . . will probably win a wide number of performances."[151]

Floyd's most sympathetic and knowledgeable listener may have been his composer-colleague Lee Hoiby. "Dear Carlyle [*sic*], I tried to get back stage to see you last night, but they wouldn't let me through. I wanted to tell you how much I admired your *Flower and Hawk*—it was beautifully made and very moving. I would like to hear it again with the text in hand, for one always loses words. The orchestration is masterful—how you have added to your technique since *Susannah!* Bravo!"[152]

Flower and Hawk has appeared in such disparate locations as North Carolina's Long Leaf Opera in 2003, Millsaps College in Dallas, the University of Delaware in 2007, WordStage Vermont and Boston's Goethe-Institut in 2008, and France's DiVivreVoix in Vivonne; but laurels in Carlisle Floyd's life and career rarely offer resting places. With Roger Stevens in Washington, and David Gockley in Houston, Floyd faced a mountain range of important new projects.

15

Completed Circle

Houston and Bilby's Doll, *1972–1976*

David Gockley kept his word, and on May 24, 25, and 29, 1972, *Susannah,* directed by Patrick Bakman and conducted by Charles Rosekrans, played Houston Grand Opera's (HGO) populist—no admission charged—summer venue, the Miller Outdoor Theatre in Hermann Park. Karan Armstrong sang the title role, with Michael Devlin as Blitch, Harry Theyard as Sam, and David Hall as Little Bat. Floyd's part, in Gockley's words, was "to come over from Tallahassee to supervise the last bit of rehearsals, and do his *shtick*": rounds of press conferences and interviews.[1] Thus, modestly, began an era in which Floyd fell up into a different kind of artistic home and creative independence. Affiliated with one of the country's fastest-growing and forward-looking opera companies, he overflowed with creativity, finishing four new operas as well as song cycles and choral works.

Floyd's Houston sequence began with a "whodunit" story of a murder committed within a wealthy landowning south Georgia family in the 1880s. An enterprising Brinks Agency detective was hired to investigate, but found himself summarily dismissed by the family's matriarch, sent back to Boston, and pulled from the case without explanation. Floyd adopted the working title *O'Brien,* and actually sketched a libretto on the skeletal secondhand story.[2]

Around this time he also contemplated adapting André Gide's 1919 novella *La symphonie pastorale* (The Pastoral Symphony).[3] As a student in Syracuse, he had seen the 1946 film directed by Jean Delannoy, starring Michèle Morgan and Pierre Blanchar, and scored by Georges Auric. With overtones of the legendary triangle of Theseus, Phaedra, and Hippolytus, the story also resembles Danish author Henrik Hertz's play *King René's Daughter,* which became Pyotr Ilyich Tchaikovsky's last opera, *Iolanta,* in 1892.

Gide's male protagonist, the Huguenot pastor of a mountain village, adopts a blind girl, Gertrude, to the discomfort of his long-suffering wife and five natural children. Over the course of years, the Pastor undertakes Gertrude's education. This includes a concert during which Beethoven's Pastoral Symphony is played, and the Pastor explains this music as proof of "the world as it might have been . . . without evil and sin."[4] As Gertrude's womanhood flowers, the Pastor falls in love with her, using every tool of sophistry to justify his involvement. When his son Jacques also falls for Gertrude, the Pastor sends him away, and the lad converts to Catholicism. The village doctor suggests an operation that restores Gertrude's sight. Her blindness over, she now realizes that the world is not the Eden the Pastor had described. By this time, he is an old man, whereas young Jacques embodied her mind's image of a beloved. She attempts suicide by jumping into a river, contracts pneumonia, and dies, after confessing to both Father Jacques and his father the Pastor.

The subject's interiority with interwoven threads of blindness—Gertrude's literal and the Pastor's figurative—and the multifaceted sins permeating each character, soon led Floyd to drop it without sketching a scenario. In the meantime he, Bob Holton, Roger Stevens, and Robert Penn Warren hammered out the tortuous details of a project that began as *The Man in Shirtsleeves,* which metamorphosed into *Grandboy* before Robert Penn Warren's *All the King's Men* became Floyd's *Willie Stark.*

THE conductor Walter Herbert worked as a kind of operatic Johnny Appleseed, founding New Orleans Opera in 1943 and Houston Grand Opera in 1955. By the time Gockley took the company reins in Houston, performances were held in the square-block-large Jesse H. Jones Hall. Gockley's arrival and Houston's oil boom years elevated the company to international prominence. Thanks to corporate support from such industry giants as Armco Steel, Atlanta Richfield, Shell, Tenneco, and United Energy Resources, and years of heavy subsidies from National Endowment programs, one of Gockley's lasting innovations was a series of five American premieres between 1975 and 1984, and thirty-nine world premieres by the company's various arms between 1974 and 2009. Besides Floyd's, this included works by composers Mark Adamo, John Adams, Leonard Bernstein, Daniel Catán, Philip Glass, Ricky Ian Gordon, Jake Heggie, Henry Mollicone, Thomas Pasatieri, Michael Tippett and Stewart Wallace; and three from this list would in time become Floyd protégés.

Another cornerstone of Gockley's dream, for which he sought Floyd's participation as codirector, was the Houston Opera Studio, "geared to the advanced young musician on his or her way to full professionalism."[5] Floyd knew that he was making the right move, even if it meant severance from Florida State University, his employer of almost thirty years; at least he had four years to prepare the dislocation.

On July 1 and 7, Yale University gave *Of Mice and Men* its northeastern premiere in Norfolk, Connecticut, with a student cast directed by James Crabtree, and conducted by Gustav Meier. Floyd confirmed that the students were not up to his vocal challenges, but he was pleased by his first exposure to the scenic designs of Michael Yeargan.[6]

Donal Henahan lambasted the opera as a populist version of Berg's *Wozzeck*, and took Floyd to task for too-regular metric stresses (shades of Rudel on *Jonathan Wade* almost a decade earlier). He tossed a bone by stating that *Of Mice and Men* had gained orchestral sophistication over *Susannah*'s folk elements, which tended to obscure Floyd's "awkward scoring." Henahan heard "no . . . memorable tunes" or musical character definition, then unwrapped his choicest bonbons, asserting that Floyd aimed at low common denominators: "Popularization is one thing; crudeness is another," branding the composer "a master of the obvious."[7]

Frank Corsaro sheds light on the dogged animus with which Henahan attacked Floyd for the next decade: "Henahan was anti-gay, and I think he had some notion about Carlisle being gay. He once said something a little odd to me about it; but he hated everything Carlisle did, and tore it up, even after people declared it a masterpiece."[8]

Bob Holton did his best to defuse this animosity by writing Henahan about Floyd's disappointment with the young singers, including the sweeping revision of the part of Lennie, which involved the singer taking his lines down as much as a third. No one had forewarned the press of this situation, out of optimism that critics would notice things amiss. Holton went on to ask Henahan to reevaluate the opera for his own information, not for printing a retraction but simply to visit Boosey's offices for lunch and listen to Seattle's performance tape. To that end, Holton sent the critic a complimentary vocal score.[9]

Henahan replied that he could only review productions that he actually saw, and that Floyd was misguided to believe that any critic could experience an unfamiliar opera with such clairvoyance. He thanked Holton for the score, especially as City Opera was still contemplating a New York production.[10] Holton posted a copy of Henahan's letter to Floyd, with a note regretting the critic's uncompromising response, but counseled patience.[11]

The day after the Yale performance, Floyd gave *High Fidelity/Musical America* a long and amusing interview, mostly about *Of Mice and Men*. The journalist, perhaps in fun, suggested that Luciano Pavarotti "would make a marvelous Lennie" if the opera were performed in Italy. Floyd told her that on his way back to Florida he would stop in New York to speak with Frank Corsaro about "the libretto he had just finished for his next opera." This was *Grandboy*, Roger Stevens's commission for the Kennedy Center, of which more in its place: "[Stevens] wanted it for 1972! I said

I needed two years. He said 'fine.' It was like taking candy from a baby." Floyd then revealed that *O'Brien* would be his bicentennial piece for Houston.[12]

ON JULY 21 AND 23, a student cast revived *Slow Dusk* at FSU, following which Floyd made his quick trip to New York to catch a rehearsal and give interviews for City Opera's *Susannah* revival. On September 3, Rudel conducted Maralin Niska (Susannah), William Chapman (Blitch), Harry Theyard (Sam), and Joaquin Romaguera (Little Bat). Ross Reimueller conducted a different cast on August 12: Nancy Shade, Michael Devlin, Theyard, and David Hall. The company performed *Susannah* on tour in Los Angeles on November 26; this would be Norman Treigle's last appearance as Blitch.

Floyd and Kay had their first look at his parents' custom-built home in Holly Hill on August 24, and Reverend Floyd described their reaction as "carried away."[13] In September Floyd and Kay took a rare actual vacation of several days to New York and Massachusetts to see the fall colors and to visit Emily Dickinson's home and grave in Amherst.

Fall 1972 ended with Richard Nixon's defeat of George McGovern on November 7. The next weeks brought Floyd a financial windfall, with a two thousand dollar stipend from the American Society of Composers, Authors, and Publishers (ASCAP), based on tallies kept by composers of performances of their works. In addition to City Opera's *Susannah* revivals, most of Floyd's output was finding a permanent place in America's repertory: *Susannah* was enthusiastically received at performances on October 27 and 28 by the Colorado Springs Opera Association. On November 17, Columbia College (South Carolina) performed *Slow Dusk*, unfortunately reviewed locally as *Slow Duck*.[14]

The first weeks of 1973 saw performances of *Susannah* by the Turnau Opera Company at Sarasota's Asolo Theatre, and *Of Mice and Men* by New England Regional Opera in Boston.[15] On February 12, Floyd and Elena Nikolaidi gave another of their famous FSU recitals: arias from Handel's *Giulio Cesare* and *Serse*, Schumann's *Frauenliebe und Leben*, three Rachmaninoff songs, and the *Seven Spanish Folk Songs* of De Falla.

The next installment of Floyd's introduction to Texas came with HGO's *Of Mice and Men* on February 20, 23, 24, and 25, 1973. Gockley had asked Frank Corsaro to direct, but at the last moment, the inveterate Manhattanite chose not to spend even a winter month in Houston and the production fell to Patrick Bakman, with conductor Charles Rosekrans. Julian Patrick, Robert Moulson, and Carol Bayard repeated their Seattle roles, with Brent Ellis and William Neill alternating as the two male leads. Carl Cunningham heralded the work as a rare specimen of "mature viable American opera," clothed in a tuneful, accessible, vocally grateful score.[16]

The Floyds looked over their prospective new city, and attended a lunch at a local restaurant with Gockley and members of the opera board to discuss the bicentennial project. One gentleman proposed that Floyd adopt a subject from Texas history: the semilegendary "Yellow Rose of Texas," a mulatto serving girl whose dalliance with Mexican General Santa Ana facilitated Sam Houston's 1836 victory at the Battle of San Jacinto. Kay jumped to her husband's rescue with an amusing digression: Because she and Floyd had lived so long in Florida, she asked the board member how he would feel about an opera based on Osceola, chief of the Seminoles. The topic was dropped, and lunch proceeded without further dramaturgical excursions.

A rare *Wuthering Heights* revival opened at the Rittenhouse Opera Society in Philadelphia on March 29 and April 1. Thanks to Marco Farnese's conducting, Michael Donahue's staging, and the cast of Maria Cocuzzi-Dawson and Janice Bryson (Cathy), George Mackes (Heathcliff), Jane Shaulis (Nelly), Doris Schmauk and Irma Snyder (Isabella), and Richard Camhi (Edgar), one critic thought better of the work than most earlier colleagues, praising both the drama and music.[17]

For most of the spring and summer of 1973, America thought little about opera, as the Watergate conspiracy unraveled in Washington. In Holly Hill, infirmity continued to wreak its relentless havoc with Floyd's mother, as it had since the sixties. Mrs. Floyd spent much of the next year in and out of doctors' offices and hospitals for batteries of tests, still with no identification of her condition. As Floyd prepared for FSU's fall term, Bob Holton, Roger Stevens, and Robert Penn Warren wrestled with the William Morris Agency over rights to *All the King's Men;* but with this major project held in suspension, Gockley enlisted the support of Nancy Hanks, the National Endowment for the Art's current chairperson, for Floyd's bicentennial opera. *O'Brien* had not worked out to the composer's satisfaction, but Holton learned from Esther Forbes's publisher, Houghton-Mifflin, that the rights to *A Mirror for Witches* were no longer encumbered, enabling Floyd's complete reworking of *Bilby's Doll.* The straightforward contract, dated August 31, 1973, assigned the Forbes estate 25 percent of proceeds from performances and subsequent sales of librettos and scores, and Floyd the remaining 75 percent, as well as 100 percent of rental fees or royalties from performances in which any of Floyd's music might be performed without words.

Thanks to Gockley's efforts, an NEA Arts Fellowship Grant and additional funding from Houston's Cullen Foundation and the National Opera Institute allowed the new work a budget of $250,000, a staggering amount for a regional company in the seventies. Even though the *Central Opera Service Bulletin* waited to announce the world premiere until its fall 1974 issue,[18] and *The New York Times* until November 17, 1974, Floyd set to work on *Bilby's Doll* in September 1973.[19]

From his first exposure to Forbes's novel, the very title lured him, oxymoronic in its pairing of witches with a mirror, and a clue to Doll's delusion, in that most witches, like vampires, supposedly cast no reflection. The very question of identity—the freedom to be who and what one truly is—molds the heart of Floyd's new story. As the piece's villainess Hannah remarks with certainty, Doll will in time reveal her true nature, so all must remain watchful. Doll herself insists at crucial moments that she does not yet know herself, or what she may become, and often begs higher (or lower) powers to send her signs. As director David Pountney put it, "She learns to comprehend good in the language of evil."[20]

Yet this strange, half-feral child-woman appears in the mirror beside Susannah: orphaned young, embodying difference—in Doll's case, witchcraft—as parental introject. Before the opera begins, she has watched both father and mother burn at the stake, and about halfway through she loses her adoptive father, the only other human to offer selfless love. Through insatiable loneliness and longing, in her final ecstasies she claims her heritage of beauty, romance, and fantasy, everything that had perished in the witch-burning fires of her native Brittany. The soprano Catherine Malfitano, hired for the title role by HGO, saw eye to eye with Floyd on the character's psychology: "Doll . . . contained all the dramatic possibilities I could have wished for in a role. I love to explore that particular period of time in a female character's development—the age of 15 or 16 when she is verging on womanhood—a very exciting time in a woman's life. Doll was similar to Butterfly and Salome in that regard."[21]

Floyd's perceptions of mass coercion had sharpened in the decades since *Susannah.* He invents a plague of witch hunters in crabbed Cowan Corners; and with so easy a target as Doll at hand, the conventionally faithful remain free to ignore their own failings. Conversely, if genuinely good people can be "proven" evil, what is the relative worth of good?[22]

Everything that drew Floyd to this material was the antithesis of Broadway hit fodder; and Gockley felt a similar fascination. For his article in HGO's program book, Floyd gave clues to his passionate devotion to the subject, some of them autobiographical: "I choose a subject not for polemical reasons, but because it contains vivid characters in highly charged dramatic situations. . . . Doll Bilby lived in a world firmly committed to the creation of whatever was functional and of practical use: the products of men were judged ultimately in terms of their utility. Consequently, the Puritans proscribed the arts and suspected all manifestations of human imagination, spirit, and need. Doll Bilby, irrevocably committed to precisely these same manifestations, was doomed to collide with such a society and in the end she became its victim."[23]

Applying this to America's historical attitude to art and artists, Floyd maintained that "we still encounter echoes of Henry James' businessman in *The American* who equated artists with 'women and other impractical people,' and we have paid a bitter price . . . the stunting of our own cultural growth through devaluing and discounting of our artists. . . . The view of history is long and pitiless and . . . our most intimate contact with civilizations long since dust has been through the art which has survived them. . . . Can we afford to permit Doll Bilbys to live and flourish among us or, more to the point, can we afford not to?"[24]

A reexamination of his 1956/57 libretto convinced Floyd to restart from scratch, and, as with *Of Mice and Men,* to swear off reliance on the literary source for further guidance. As before, his biggest job now involved development of characters that Forbes had merely daubed in: Pirate Shad, Goody Goochy, sweet, long-suffering Titus Thumb, and especially Hannah Bilby. Even the smallest roles, like Silas the barkeep and the Bilby twins, profited from Floyd's decades of practical experience.

The new treatment is far more concise and direct. Act 1 has just two scenes, the first set in Cowan Corners Tavern, May 1671. With a minimum of words, we hear scorn and envy from Deacon Thumb (tenor) and Tavernkeeper Silas (baritone) that Jared Bilby's trunk, laden with dresses for his adopted daughter Doll, has arrived from London. Titus Thumb (baritone) has just returned from Harvard College, where he is studying for the ministry. Seconds later, Bilby (bass) comes for his trunk, and the two Thumbs engage him with a proposal of marriage between Titus and Doll. Bilby is emotionally unready to give up his adopted daughter, but his musings are interrupted by a jeering crowd hauling the latest "witch," Goody Greene, off to prison. Titus explodes in frustration at this madness of finding witches in every nook and cranny, countered by the village clergyman, Mr. Zelley (bass-baritone). A spell of faintness and shortness of breath reminds Bilby of his mortality, and he invites Titus to call on Doll that afternoon. As the crowd continues to urge Goody Greene's hanging, Bilby mutters that gossiping tongues represent true evil here.

As a new connective device, Floyd added a series of interludes reminiscent of his episodes in *Jonathan Wade:* the Town Crier (tenor) adds details of period life that heighten atmosphere or foreshadow events: whose animal has escaped, who is ill, who is in the stocks, and so forth.

Scene 2 reveals interior-exterior views of Bilby's house, with Doll (soprano) sitting on the front steps, singing the Thumb twins Labour and Sorrow (sopranos) a song about a woman who takes a demon husband. Doll's nemesis, the piece's wicked stepmother Hannah Bilby (mezzo-soprano), sends Doll to her room to pray and to prepare for Mr. Zelley's religious instruction. When the clergyman arrives, Hannah spews resentment of Doll, describing her as evil, and believing, or at least claiming, that Doll cursed her recent lost pregnancy. Bilby arrives home shortly after Zelley leaves, and presents Doll with the trunkful of elegant clothes. After Hannah vows to make Doll's life a living hell if Bilby predeceases her, Bilby draws his wife away to facilitate Titus's courtship of Doll. Titus wastes no time in declaring that he has loved Doll since first sight, and asks for her hand. Doll gently refuses, but says that Titus would be her choice among mortal men. She observes that someone about to become a preacher ought to marry a native-born woman, not a shunned outsider. Puzzled and disturbed, Titus presses her to explain, prompting Doll's outburst that her parents had been witches, and that she is destined to follow in their footsteps. She relives the scene of her parents' arrest in Brittany, their burning as witches before her eyes, and how the seafaring Bilby rescued her, treated her with love and compassion and brought her back to America as his daughter.

Act 2 has four shorter scenes, the first in Cowan Corners cemetery on a bleak winter's day eight months later. Bilby has died and Zelley conducts the burial. Hannah declares that her husband was felled by Doll's curse, which the village doctor, Kleaver (baritone) contradicts. As the coffin is lowered, Zelley and Goody Goochy (contralto), an eccentric who places iron rings on her fingers to prevent the dead man's soul from entering her body, escort Hannah away. Left alone beside the fresh mound, Doll mourns the loss of the single human who has shown her love. Zelley, who has lost his own son, returns and offers himself as a substitute father. Doll blurts out that she has prayed to both heaven and hell, which Zelley interprets as proof of her bereavement.

Scene 2 returns to Bilby's house, as Doll prays for a messenger to end her loneliness, while Hannah entertains two suitors. A servant boy shouts that the Thumbs' barns are on fire. The stage clears, and a stranger, Shad (tenor), appears. Dark, tanned, muscular, bare-chested and barefoot, he wears a medallion around his neck, a silk scarf around his head, and seaman's trousers. Doll acts out her fantasy: Shad is the demon from hell come to end her misery. He falls without apparent effort into this new character, and vows to spend ten nights in her bed before leaving for his usual haunts.

In the next interlude, the Town Crier announces that a pirate ship has moored off Boston, and the outlaw crew are at large.

Scene 3, ten nights later, takes us to Doll's bedroom, where she has bedded with her exotic stranger. She proposes that they conduct their own wedding service, pricking wrists and drinking each other's blood. Shad complies; the two vow eternal love before he vanishes through the window.

In another interlude, the Town Crier proclaims that the pirates Calico Jack and Bloody Shad have been caught and hanged in Boston.

Scene 4 jumps forward to August 1672, at the Thumbs' house and yard. Sick to their stomachs, the twins Labour and Sorrow moan and whimper. Mrs. Thumb has summoned the clergyman Increase Mather (bass) to examine them for signs of witchcraft. Son Titus argues with his mother that Hannah has poisoned her against Doll, but now Hannah finds straw poppets that Doll has made for the children. When the twins confess that they have eaten the pumpkin-seed eyes and cornsilk hair, Mrs. Thumb wails that Doll has cursed them, giving them their own internal organs as food. An examination by Doctor Kleaver and Mr. Mather leads to a pronouncement of witchcraft. They formally accuse Doll and order her arrest; Titus Thumb rages at his mother while Doll is led off, and Hannah exults.

Act 3, scene 1 shifts to the meeting house in Salem, the center of witchcraft prosecution. Zelley fears that Doll has been ill-treated, yet *her* concern is for the twins' health. Kleaver and Mather overhear her declaration that their affliction must have been the work of *another* witch, and Zelley sees that Doll's case is lost. Titus urges her to recant, so he can marry her and leave Cowan Corners forever; but Doll recedes deeper into fantasy, revealing that she *is* married, and carrying her demon lover's child. When Zelley dismisses her story as fantasy, she pulls out Shad's medallion, which Zelley recognizes as his son's. Close to his own breakdown, he reviews Shad's pirate career and how he disowned him years earlier. Before Shad's capture and hanging, he had begged his father for shelter, and taken advantage of opportunities to observe Doll and learn her story. Shaken, Doll first denies that Zelley's son could have been her husband, begging him not to deprive her of this joy. Mather's insistence that she has been duped by a mere mortal crushes her, yet she refuses whatever comforts religion might offer, wanting no part of either Satan's or God's worlds. Judges enter the meeting room, and the scene ends with a hymn.

In the final interlude, the Town Crier proclaims that Doll has been sentenced to hang as a witch.

The last scene in February 1673 reveals Doll in her cell, very pregnant. Hannah comes to ask Zelley to give her the about-to-be-born child, and Goody Goochy arrives as midwife. Titus and Zelley have a final mournful encounter with Doll, who declares, much like Susannah before capitulating to Blitch, that this waiting has exhausted her. Zelley overrides his inclinations and allows the girl to die with hope and to feel loved. He encourages her to speak of her husband, structuring the conversation by describing "his son" with features diametrically opposed to those of the Shad who seduced Doll. In a final burst of loving energy, the dying girl prepares to rejoin her lost parents and husband in a dimension free from terror and coercion. Doll breathes her last, as Zelley and Titus pray for her and for themselves.

OCTOBER 15, 1973 brought another Nikolaidi/Floyd recital, with a program of Haydn, Brahms, and Wolf, the lament from Purcell's *Dido and Aeneas,* and a "Scene and Aria" from *Flower and Hawk* (Eleanor's prayer over her son Richard's body). Nikolaidi's transposition forced Floyd to relearn the piece pianistically, as he had done with all performances of his music originally written for Curtin's much higher voice; yet given Eleanor's age and imprisonment, not to mention Nikolaidi's passion and musicality, Floyd found her rendering appropriate and thrilling.

The Manhattan Theater Club kept Floyd's name before the New York public with performances of *Markheim* on October 18, 20, 25, 26, and 27. David Shookhoff directed, Ethan Mordden served as musical director and pianist, with Michael Riley (Markheim), Douglas Perry (Creach), Neil Rosenshein (Stranger), and Sarah Sager (Tess). Robert Jacobson contributed a generous appraisal for *Opera News:* "[A] first-rate specimen of its genre. The characters are engrossing, the dramatic situation is expertly built (as is the musical structure), the English language . . . is intelligently set, and the lyrical score carries the story along on a swell of arioso, proving that melody has not outlived its usefulness in the theater."[25]

It was only a matter of time before *Of Mice and Men* joined *Susannah* in the repertoire of European theaters. Germany's Stadttheater Augsburg lodged Floyd in the eighteenth-century Zum weißen Lamm, leveled by bombs during World War II, but rebuilt in its original form in 1949. Though it had housed such past travelers as Mozart and Goethe, Floyd shivered at the ineffective heating, and paled to see nothing from his window but gray skies and snow-covered roofs.[26] When he approached the front desk to request a room change, the manager confessed ruefully that they had given him their best. For the opera company's November 30 performance, repeated on December 12, conductor Thomas Martin had prepared the German translation, sung by Hans Kiemer (George), Wolfgang Witte (Lennie), Carol Todd (Curley's Wife), and Kurt Meinhardt (Curley). Stephan Mettin directed and Eberhard Bäumler conducted.

For the first time some European critics began to appreciate Floyd for choosing dramatic material so appropriate for musical setting. Despite his reliance on tonality, his illustrative music had "character, substance and dramatic verve . . . magical impressionistic sound . . . rhythmic sharpness. . . . Floyd's music . . . arrives at its own style and dramatic impetus. . . . A mighty success . . . for an opera that contains nothing avant-garde, but a great deal of humanity."[27]

The first weeks of 1974 witnessed new bombs exploding in the Watergate scandal and the first rumblings of Richard Nixon's impeachment. Shreveport Symphony Opera performed *Of Mice and Men* on February 24 and 26; then, at long last, the work had its first outing in the city originally chosen for its world premiere. Bob Holton had sent Kurt Herbert Adler the Seattle tape, and the chagrined maestro swore that he'd never heard *this* opera. Adler later groused to Julius Rudel that he never thought it very good, so rather than include it in the parent company's mainstage repertoire, Adler consigned it to San Francisco Spring Opera, with performances on March 15, 19, 21, and 23. Under the conductor Abraham Kaplan and the director Edward Parone, the cast included William Neill (Lennie), Brent Ellis (George), Harry Danner (Curley), and Alexandra Hunt (Curley's Wife).

The University of Washington and Seattle's Channel 9, KCTS-TV, televised a production of *Markheim* that spring. The project was organized and staged by the school's opera director, Ralph Rosinbum, and conducted by Samuel Krachmalnik, with student singers Robert Julien (Creach), Larry Scali (Stranger), Carol Webber (Tess), and faculty baritone Leon Lishner in the title role. Rosinbum thought *Markheim* ideally suited to television, which could heighten Floyd's suspenseful and supernatural elements through the camera's eye better than a traditional stage frame.[28]

Shot in black and white by KCTS producer Ron Ciro, the resulting film used dynamic special effects and close-ups for Floyd's clocks, mirrors, and characters. Following its local broadcast on June 22, the final product was touted in *Variety* as "a moody Faustian drama . . . a credit to all concerned."[29] The reviewer recommended that the Public Broadcasting System (PBS), itself just four years old, distribute *Markheim* nationally.

On July 25, Floyd and Nikolaidi concertized again in St. Petersburg: Schumann's *Frauenliebe und Leben,* Mahler's *Songs of a Wayfarer,* and the *Flower and Hawk* excerpt they had performed the previous year. Floyd's admirer, the journalist Mary Nik Shenk, enthused about his "mellow rich tone" on a Viennese Bösendorfer grand, and complimented Nikolaidi's histrionic abilities, calling the *Flower and Hawk* excerpt "dramatically explosive.[30]

Two days later, the House Judiciary Committee adopted three articles of impeachment against Richard Nixon, followed in short order by revelations of the smoking gun tape and Nixon's resignation. Around the end of the university summer break, Floyd finished his *Bilby's Doll* libretto. Bob Holton prodded him to follow up with Robert Penn Warren on *All the King's Men,* which had lain dormant for a full year, and the next three months saw an exchange of encouraging but inconclusive letters between Tallahassee and Warren's homes in Vermont and Connecticut.

With their son present, Floyd's parents celebrated their fiftieth wedding anniversary on November 18, and held an enormous reception at their still-new home ten days later. Despite Mrs. Floyd's indisposition, everyone in the family, and Reverend Floyd's parishioners from as far back as 1932, poured into Holly Hill. Family dinner at Ermine's re-created the groaning board of yore: turkey, oyster pie, dressing, followed by a classic southern dessert, ambrosia.[31] Then 126 guests joined the family at the Floyds' to celebrate and reminisce. Miss Alice Mays from Bethune, a prototype for *Susannah*'s church ladies, approached the forty-eight-year-old Floyd with the blunt declaration, "Why Carlisle, you've just grown up to be an old man."

On December 15, 1974, Floyd returned signed contracts to Belwin-Mills for his adaptation of *All the King's Men.* His game was afoot on two boards: he let Warren know that he and Kay would spend Christmas in Great Barrington, Massachusetts, (with Phyllis Curtin and Gene Cook) before proceeding to New York on December 27, "for some production meetings on the new opera I am presently working on" (*Bilby's Doll*).[32]

That fall, Dr. Thomas L. Johnson, the archivist and head librarian of the South Caroliniana Library in Columbia, approached Floyd about acquiring a collection of such a distinguished native son's manuscripts and personal papers. Attached to the University of South Carolina, the library already had much of Floyd's published music; but the composer temporized, replying on December 18 that several institutions had asked him about such a donation, but that he had made no decision.[33]

JONA AND BRUCE CLARKE separated and divorced in 1974. The Floyds immediately invited Jona to visit them in Tallahassee over a long weekend, reaffirming their friendship and offering what comfort they could. Jona found herself the center of attention of the entire Floyd circle: "Look what we have here, Carlisle's college friend, isn't she great?!"[34] The visit proved therapeutic for Floyd too; there were long sessions of what he and Jona had always called "soul splashing." At such moments, Kay slipped discreetly off to read or play the piano; and to the strains of Granados's *Maiden and the Nightingale,* Floyd at last found words to explain why he and Jona had ceased to be a romantic item in 1946.[35]

On February 16, 1975 the opera world reeled to learn of Norman Treigle's death at forty-seven, alone in his New Orleans apartment. The cause was attributed to a gastric ulcer and massive internal bleeding; but many knew that this great artist's decline had lasted several years, fueled by alcohol and prescription drugs. Floyd was simultaneously devastated and furious at the waste of such talent, feeling that Treigle in his downward spiral had ceased to trust anyone and had shut out his closest friends. A round of memorial concerts began in New Orleans on May 30, with Werner Torkanowsky conducting and soprano Nancy Shade and baritone Chester Ludgin singing *Susannah* excerpts. On April 30, 1975, America's involvement in Southeast Asia came to a disastrous end with the fall of Saigon. On a personal level, Floyd spent that whole year caught in his own vortex of change: illness, death, and other traumas of family and friends; working again on two operas simultaneously; accepting positions of national prominence and responsibility; and, in the process of scaling Houston's ramparts, extricating himself from FSU.

That April, thanks to Roger Stevens, Floyd was named to the first of several positions with major arts administrations: the NEA music advisory panel, a position he held until 1980. As long as opera remained part of the music panel, Floyd's specialization made crucial recommendations with regard to grants to producing companies.

His serendipitous forty-ninth birthday present on June 11 was PBS' national broadcast of the University of Washington *Markheim* film. Seattle critic John Voorhees called Floyd one of the only native composers who composed effective English text settings, and praised *Markheim* as "eerie . . . charged with tension . . . wholly compelling.[36]

Four days later, Floyd's spinster maternal aunt Lucile Fenegan, aged sixty-eight, died of a heart attack at a Christian Science service in Southern Pines, North Carolina. Ermine met Floyd's plane from Tallahassee on the afternoon of June 16—Kay stayed at home with the first of a series of respiratory infections later diagnosed as walking pneumonia—and the family convened for the funeral in Laurinburg on June 17. Floyd's mother, Ida, herself just turned sixty, underwent another series of long hospital stays; Reverend Floyd first mentioned Parkinson's disease in his diary on November 14. Then on November 29 the composer's paternal aunt Hazel, aged sixty-six, left Frank Ellerbe a widower.

During Floyd's participation in group therapy in Tallahassee, he met a young woman, Roberta "Bobbi" Martin, whose marriage to artist Daniel Martin[37] was crumbling. Friendship sparked within the group, and, outside, grew to include Kay, with whom Bobbi had much in common, including a dislike of crowds. The Floyds got along well with Bobbi, Daniel, and their children, Flora and Bernard; but their friendship did nothing to alleviate the Martins' marital discord. After spending a weekend with the Floyds, Bobbi became for them "the lady who came to dinner";[38] she moved into the Middlebrook house and her two children gradually became quasi-Floyds. For the composer, the situation was a godsend. Kay now had a close female friend, a kind of second self, while Floyd spent weeks on the road or in his studio with *Bilby's Doll*, with the Houston move looming.

Floyd's last year at FSU began that September with ironically brighter prospects: the school had hired a new provost of the Division of Communication and Arts, also the new director of cultural affairs, Allen Dwight Sapp, a gifted musician who accepted the position in part because he wanted to be on the same faculty as Carlisle Floyd.[39] Despite Floyd's acquisition of this powerful supporter, nothing would keep him from accepting Gockley's offer. Part of the problem, as he told the *Tallahassee Democrat*,[40] was restriction on his creative time owing to a twelve-hour teaching load in piano and composition. And the money: having entered Florida's university system in 1947 as an assistant instructor at an annual base salary of $2,800, he had been dependent for twenty-eight years on commensurately small merit raises. His salary in 1975 was $24,000, well below the national average for schools of FSU's prominence, especially considering his professional accomplishments.

Finally, despite the familiarity of Tallahassee and its importance as the center of his strongest friendships, Houston emerged as a superstar of business and culture. HGO had the fifth largest budget—2.1 million dollars in 1976—of the nation's opera producers, and offered resources that he could not refuse. The only thing left was getting his new opera and contractual commitments all on paper as he rushed to finish composing *Bilby's Doll*. In Houston, Gockley assembled a powerful cast and production staff, and the premiere was set for February 27, 1976.[41] Frank Corsaro would direct, the conducting was entrusted to Christopher Keene,[42] Ming Cho Lee would design sets, and Suzanne Mess the costumes. The large cast, some roles doubled because of the number of performances, included Thomas Page (Deacon Thumb), Alan Titus and Charles P. Long (Jared Bilby), Samuel Ramey and Tom Fox (Mr. Zelley), Nell Evans (Goody Goochy), Joy Davidson and Fredda Rakusin (Hannah), Jack Trussel (Shad), and Catherine Malfitano and Sheri Greenawald in the title role.

But the course of opera, like Shakespeare's characterization of true love, is all but guaranteed not to run smooth. When Corsaro got his copy of the score, he found the piece excellent, and Floyd's treatment of the material strong and effective; but on repeated study, he was troubled by likenesses to Robert Ward's *The Crucible,* with its similar preoccupation with New England witch trials. Then Leonard Bernstein and Alan J. Lerner approached Corsaro to direct their new Broadway extravaganza *1600 Pennsylvania Avenue,* to open in May of 1976. The director loved *that* score, which contained the most music Bernstein had written to date for any musical theater work, but the book remained to be seen.[43]

Corsaro let Floyd know that he had received another very attractive offer—Bernstein was not one to be lightly denied—and asked whether there might be some way to shift *Bilby*'s dates. When this proved impossible, Corsaro found another first-rate director, English-born David Pountney, eager to make an American debut.[44] Yet another friend and trusted colleague had disappointed Floyd.

Gockley responded with a less muted assessment: "Frank dumped us."[45] When the chaotic *1600* script finally arrived, Corsaro realized the enormity of his misstep: "I made the most dreadful boo-boo in our relationship, and as a result, Carlisle kept me at a distance. He understood, but was still hurt by my saying no to him."[46]

Corsaro's temporary estrangement from Bernstein *and* Floyd followed on the heels of the subsequent shipwreck of *1600*.[47]

On October 27, 1975, New York City Opera gave Norman Treigle a grand and somber tribute. Julius Rudel conducted, and Patrick Bakman and Tito Capobianco supervised staging and technical support; Floyd could not be present. Phyllis Curtin had not appeared with the company for eleven years, but Rudel asked her to sing Susannah's first aria; the soprano instead insisted on the second, the more folklike ballad. She and Treigle had sung the opera so many times on that stage; at the end of this aria Floyd's directions called for Blitch to step out of the shadows to compliment and remark her singing such a sad song. On this last night, wearing a simple black velvet dress, Curtin dedicated her aria to Norman. Lighting designer Hans Sondheimer, who always called her his favorite "stage moth" because she could find her light anywhere, surrounded her with a soft pool of light: "I just sang it to Norman, wherever he was. I barely got off the stage before I fell apart."[48]

AS CHRISTMAS APPROACHED, Gockley drew the University of Houston, founded in 1927, into his dream of a world-class advanced opera training program. UH's School of Music had only existed since 1940, and it shared the fine arts building with the Department of Art. As Gockley's codirector, Floyd had all the academic experience in their new partnership; he also had decades of committee work and the innate ability to smooth troubled waters in the stormy interdisciplinary straits of opera, and Gockley urged the school to secure his services. After an interview, Chancellor and President Philip G. Hoffman recommended Floyd's addition to the university faculty and to the M. D. Anderson professorship, citing his international reputation and continued creative output.[49] Floyd would thus be hired and compensated by the university, and would have equal accountability to the school and HGO. The M. D. Anderson endowment guaranteed a full professorship with tenure and an annual salary of $35,000, the 2010 equivalent of about $134,000.

Pressures surrounding the move from Tallahassee began to mount. Friends like the Mastrogiacomos thought Floyd's fall up to Houston predestined; but Dean Wiley Housewright felt betrayed, and treated Floyd with anger and resentment.[50] For years, Floyd had suffered from a variety of stress-related gastric disorders. Visiting his in-laws in Jacksonville, on the night of December 10, 1974 he experienced an esophageal spasm that required a trip to the nearest emergency room. When Kay tapped at the door of her mother's bedroom, Gundy could not be bothered; Guy Reeder was dispatched from his separate sleeping space to drive Floyd to hospital for a Valium injection and a two-night stay for observation and removal of esophageal scar tissue. The condition continued to plague him for much of the next three decades.

Back in Texas, he staged *Susannah* for Fort Worth Opera, with Patricia Wells (Susannah), Robert Moulson (Sam), Michael Devlin (Blitch), and James Atherton

(Little Bat), and conducted by Rudolf Kruger. After the opening on January 16, 1975, he flew to Houston to finish scoring and observe musical rehearsals for *Bilby's Doll,* which had encountered peculiar difficulties. On the cover of the February 7, 1976 *Opera News,* the leads—Ramey, Malfitano, Titus, and Trussel—ringed a natty blazer-clad Floyd. Ramey, whose career had surged after his debut at New York City Opera in 1973, had scored a triumph in Corsaro's HGO production of Handel's *Rinaldo* the previous October, and struck all as a natural choice for Floyd's Zelley; but after appearing at two or three musical rehearsals, to everyone's astonishment he suddenly vanished from sight, one of several in the cast felled by that winter's flu.

Ramey explained, "I got terribly sick and spent a week and a half in my room and going to the doctor. Nobody could figure out what was wrong with me. It was a funny moment: here I was, holed up, but I never got a call from anyone at the opera to check on how I was. After about ten days of the other singers bringing me something to eat, I finally called David [Gockley] and said I was going home. And I didn't have any contact with Carlisle during that period."[51]

Though Ramey still appeared in HGO's program, Tom Fox would sing all performances of Zelley. Early in the rehearsal process, *Opera News* interviewer Ethan Mordden profiled the composer.[52] The writer's definition of Floyd for a large segment of the public unfolded beneath a split-page photo of the impeccably dressed composer in a semirecumbent pose. Mordden viewed Floyd's protagonists, from Susannah to Doll Bilby, as vulnerable and wounded yet exceptional creatures, possessing a unifying bond as outsiders.

During their interview, Floyd let slip a point from his program notes about how societies stunt the arts by discounting their artists. For Mordden, Floyd became the "unprotected poet," and that made the article's three-quarter-inch bold headline. Floyd, always resistant to being typed, was bemused: "Ethan's very decided point of view happened to be basically accurate: that I dealt over and over again with the outsider. But, as I think I pointed out to him, I certainly don't have any monopoly on that, it's a basic theme in so much twentieth-century theater as well as opera. I had to admit that he was right, on the face of it; but I don't know that I ever said anything about a society not protecting its poets. I don't like the role in which that puts the poet, sounding like someone entirely too fragile."

Mordden deserves thanks for bringing Floyd's psychology to the attention of a wider public, with a discussion of ideas rather than a review of events, yet his focus on the composer's portrayal of outsiders self-limits. "Outsiderism" is the symptom of a disease variously interpreted by Floyd as exclusion, devaluation, dependence, or imprisonment, enforced by coercion to conform; and for which the cure, the remedy, is independence. In this, we may rank Floyd with that body of world literature and drama that includes Aeschylus, Shakespeare, Schiller, Goethe, and Beaumarchais: despite elements of outsiderism, all illuminate through protagonists who rise (or fail to rise) above privation, emotional and physical abuse and torment, to a level of freedom and enlightenment.

AMID *BILBY'S* REHEARSALS, arrangements between HGO and UH concretized: on January 29, Floyd called his parents and told them that he was accepting the new professorship.[53] The official letter from Dean John C. Guilds spelled out the advantages: an initial nine-month salary of thirty-five thousand dollars, a discretionary fund of two thousand dollars, and an additional two thousand dollars toward moving expenses. After experiences with Kuersteiner and Housewright at FSU, the rest of the letter offered a real gold ring, a pledge that Floyd could and should devote at least half of his time to research and composition.[54]

Staying at a Holiday Inn, Floyd lost no time in penning his acceptance, longhand, on the hotel's stationery. Collecting more honors, he again made the cover of *Musical America* as "Musician of the Month" for February; and the state of Florida named him one of its "Patriots for the Bicentennial."

Once Christopher Keene began rehearsing the HGO orchestra, Gockley noted what he regarded as the composer's excessive use of percussion. Floyd became famous for his statement, "I'll listen to any criticism, any suggestion you have for improvement;

and I'll agree with you, with the understanding that the solution has to be mine."

Floyd's colleagues knew better than to press when his tight-jawed response was "nonnegotiable," but as collegiality changed to real friendship between Floyd and Gockley, the administrator saw that his confidence in the composer-teacher-administrator was superbly placed. After all, Gockley was still fairly new at this job, especially in collaboration with an academic institution; he was commissioning new works and learning the nuts-and-bolts of "musicking" a libretto.

By the middle of January, now staying at Houston's upscale Warwick Hotel, Floyd pushed overtime to complete *Bilby*'s orchestration, with special attention to those exotic percussion effects he had cultivated since *The Mystery* in 1960. Carl Cunningham conducted an interview in his hotel room while Floyd was enmeshed in work that recalled apocryphal tales of Mozart and Rossini. In this "nouveau-rococo haven . . . racing against time to finish the orchestration of *Bilby's Doll* . . . and armed with a fistful of pencils, an electric eraser and a sizable clothes brush to whisk away the crumbs of ideas that don't work out, Floyd was busily scoring the opera's final scenes, while juggling two other projects the same weekend."[55]

Though left in the lurch, Floyd acknowledged his long-standing gratitude to Frank Corsaro with the dedication of *Bilby's Doll*. He would finish all FSU course work and grading through the end of the spring trimester, and wrote his official resignation on February 12. Provost Allen D. Sapp reminded Floyd that he was an important reason why Sapp was even in Tallahassee; he asked the composer if he could do anything to keep him there, claiming that he could match everything but the city. Floyd confirmed this perception, and on February 20 Sapp wrote Floyd, with a copy to Dean Housewright, that he would be missed, conveying a sense of personal loss but nonetheless congratulating Floyd on his new position.[56] When Floyd sold his house on Middlebrook, it was to Sapp, who stayed just three years at FSU.

On February 25, Kay, his parents, aunts Bunny and Freddie, Ermine and Billy Matheny, their daughters Harriett and Nancy, the Mastrogiacomos and Bob Holton checked into Floyd's latest residence, the Hyatt Regency.

All of his intuitions about the new work proved correct: reaction to the world premiere on February 27 was sharply divided, beginning with his own family. In his parents' hotel room afterward, Reverend Floyd almost reprised his 1959 *Wuthering Heights* tantrum. The prevailing mood in the room was ebullient, with the women all chattering about what a magnificent success *Bilby's Doll* had been, while Reverend Floyd lay on the bed, scowling and surly. At a pause in the conversation, he tossed in a non sequitur, "It was long." In his diary the next day, doubtless aggravated by his son's repeated presentation of the dark side of religious fervor, Reverend Floyd wrote, "We did not sleep much after watching the tragic opera for almost 4 hours."[57]

The press was not quite sure on which side of the fence to land in discussing this strange new work, but the general consensus pointed to a qualified success. The *Houston Post* led the cheerers, describing the work's dissonance as musical metaphor for Doll's progressive derangement, and lauding Floyd's "meaty dramatics and musical sweep . . . broad lyricism . . . soaring arcs of sound and shimmering, instantly affecting orchestral colorations."[58]

The *Houston Chronicle* called the opera "biting but wonderfully luminous," but recommended cuts.[59] Although another critic agreed that both the opera and its production scored "undisputed successes," he too observed that the work could profit by losing at least twenty minutes.[60]

Despite praising the production as "lavish," *The New York Times* critic must have been having a very bad day; he found Floyd's music "rambling and weak" and sounding "more modern than it really wanted to be . . . arbitrary in a slightly perverse way." He thought that cuts of thirty to forty-five minutes might help, but "would not solve all the problems."[61] Yet the worst came with John Ardoin's review for *Opera News*. Ardoin had clearly read and taken issue with Ethan Mordden's piece about society protecting its poets, and Floyd's choice of a witch as a "sympathetic poetic symbol": "If such was Floyd's intention . . . the hysterical figure of Doll he draws . . . is presented in so superficial a fashion that we never truly understand what compels her to act as she does. . . . Symbols aside, I have rarely encountered so confused and confusing a twentieth-century libretto or one couched in such stilted and unevocative language. . . . His sweet-and-sour score wanders about, turns in on itself and takes far too long to say what it sets out to say. Frankly, both text and music struck me as being void of a probing critical sense, of being self-indulgent to the point of tedium."[62]

Floyd made a few nips and tucks by the time Houston's run ended, and Andrew Porter brought encyclopedic knowledge and perspective to his review of the March 2 performance. Like most of his colleagues, after a few quibbles—in particular, Floyd's assertion that Doll symbolized creative imagination—Porter struck to the heart of Floyd's purposes. He pinpointed the center of act 2, the two Shad scenes, as having everything to do with Doll's psychological state, and little with actual witchcraft: "He has most delicately mirrored, and with his music enhanced, the irony of the original novel. . . . Floyd's opera becomes more than a sung play . . . [his music] adds images of the untruths in which both Doll and her accusers believe."[63]

Gockley had assembled a consortium of companies to share productions, and this gave a crucial boost to new works by Floyd and his composer/colleagues at HGO. It guaranteed them not only an opportunity to have their work heard by more than one audience, but also time to absorb criticism and revise accordingly. Opera Omaha booked *Bilby's Doll* into that city's Orpheum Theatre for April 8 and 10. During a few weeks in Tallahassee, Floyd cut at least fifteen minutes, much of it in act 2; completely rewrote act 2, scene 2, omitting the business of Hannah and her suitors; and changed the action to a direct confrontation between Hannah and Doll. He tightened the scenes between Doll and Shad, and the twins' examination by Mather and Kleaver; and eliminated the character of Mrs. Thumb, dividing her lines and stage business between Deacon Thumb, now a widower, and Hannah, strengthening the enmity between Doll and her stepmother. This transformed Hannah into a second female protagonist, and Floyd gave her a seductive moment with Titus in act 2, scene 4.

Before leaving for Omaha, on March 3, 1976, Floyd played one final performance of *The Mystery* for Elena Nikolaidi at FSU, his last public appearance at the keyboard: "As avidly as I approached becoming a pianist, and all the work I put into learning and playing, I retired with respect. I gave it up with so little regret—that's something I'll have to take to my analyst—yet I miss actually making music myself. Despite what many think, you don't do that as a composer, it doesn't engage you in the same ways. Until *Susannah,* I was a pianist who did these little things on the side, but I never took it all that seriously; but *Susannah* I took seriously."

In Omaha, Jonathan Dudley conducted and David Alden directed, having staged Houston's double cast, here pared to Sheri Greenawald (Doll), Tom Fox (Zelley), Fredda Rakusin (Hannah), David Holloway (Titus), Trussel (Shad), and Evans (Goochy). As with most regional post-premiere performances of Floyd's new operas, *Bilby's Doll* was praised more than censured by local press: Omaha's *World-Herald* called the piece "strong, dramatic meat," and Floyd's music "powerfully expressive."[64]

Opera News sent a second critic, who found the opera "a work of psychological and musical subtlety," even defending its length: "The meaning . . . derives from its interlocking scenes. Moments that at first seem nonessential, even trite, help form a pattern whose figuration is unclear until the final curtain. . . . Those who complain about length are insensitive to musical-dramatic cohesion."[65]

By the time *Musical America* appeared that July, the reviewer noticed one facet that had stamped the composer's work increasingly since *Wuthering Heights,* which to some extent explained the hostility of some critics: "Floyd has largely forsaken his formerly direct tonal musical language for an atonalism [*sic*] that has a certain self-conscious sterility and occasionally conflicts with baldly diatonic means."[66]

Bob Holton and Roger Stevens now reminded the composer that he had business to pursue with Robert Penn Warren and a Kennedy Center commission to fulfill; and Floyd and Gockley began to explore ways to involve HGO in that project. But *Bilby's Doll* had earned a special place in Floyd's affections: "The subject matter isn't going to be to everybody's taste. I find it very, very moving, and a wonderful evocation of the period. It's not all that difficult to produce, because it can be done with a very small chorus. But still, the subject matter: maybe I wasn't looking to appeal to an audience, by design. But I love the characters, and it contains some of my favorite music."

16

Synthesizing Opera and Music Theater

Willie Stark, *1970–1981*

As early as January 1970, Floyd told the press that he was considering a piece about an "important person," with contrasting public and private facets.[1] In the weeks following *Of Mice and Men*'s premiere, Floyd crafted a seventy-three-page libretto, *The Man in Shirtsleeves,* of which no copy seems to have survived.[2] Floyd described this effort as the result of a period of wild experimentation in the O'Neill vein, packed with dream sequences. When he had shown it to Treigle, the singer had scratched his head: "Carlisle, I don't have any idea what this thing is about."

Roger Stevens followed through on his intentions to commission Floyd in a contract dated July 20, 1972. Though the work had yet to receive a name, the terms were generous: $2,500 on signing, which Floyd did a few days later; $5,000 on delivery of the first libretto draft, on or about August 30; $1,500 on delivery of the completed libretto; $3,000 on delivery of the completed vocal score; and $3,000 on delivery of the completed full score, for a grand total of $15,000. Bob Holton's hand is evident in an additional $5,000 allocated for extraction of vocal and orchestral scores. Floyd agreed to make every effort to complete the work for fall 1973 performances, and to file a progress report with Stevens on January 1, 1973. Stevens also pledged to pay all of Floyd's travel and living expenses for any meetings, rehearsals, or public appearances that took the composer away from Tallahassee.[3]

By October 1972, Floyd acknowledged the limits of his experimentation, and that Treigle was right. In his *High Fidelity/Musical America* interview,[4] *Shirtsleeves* had crystallized into "a kind of American *Boris [Godunov],*" a complete metamorphosis resulting from consultations with Corsaro and Stevens, and filled with autobiographical overtones. With still-keen memories of Oscar Fenegan, Floyd focused on his protagonist's fixation on his grandfather as the single figure in his life to embody safety, support, and unconditional love. "Mr. Oscar," when queried about family when his son James was still alive, told people, "I have three children and a boy." Floyd wanted something more colloquial than the word "grandson," and his solution was a common southern locution, "grandboy."

Two versions of *Grandboy,* represented by Belwin-Mills, have found their way into Floyd's South Carolina archive. The first, a sixty-seven-page typescript, to which Floyd added a geometrical design for the title page, has three acts of two scenes each. The setting is a generic southern state in the midthirties, opening in the reception room of Governor Purvis Hasty's office at the height of a reelection campaign. Banners and signs bear catchy or corny logos, and various groups mill about, waiting for the populist demagogue. A change in lighting reveals Hasty seated at his desk, abstracted, fixated on a harmonica that his grandfather gave him years ago. A dream sequence unfolds of himself as a boy with his grandfather, who nicknames him Pete. In the outer office, a rally forms around a subgroup of power brokers, Tarbell, Asbell, and Singletary; Hasty's aide, Harvard-educated Thad Endicott; Hasty's wife, Alissa, from a distinguished Chicano family; and the governor's mother Ola, a plain, life-hardened sixty-something little woman fond of quoting scripture and invoking the Almighty. Hasty appears and rallies his troops. Soon the pressures of the campaign begin to show. The elites attempt to manipulate and bend the governor to their will. Alone for a few moments with Alissa, Hasty acknowledges conflicts between his public image and his emotional core.

Scene 2 shifts to the library of the governor's mansion, with Thad bringing an exhausted Hasty back to Alissa. Despite the aphrodisiac of popularity, his marriage is sliding onto the sidelines, and he resolves to quit politics and abandon reelection, to Alissa's relief. Kingmakers Tarbell and company declare that Hasty has lost his mind; but Hasty, supported by Alissa, insists that he quit the race, or at least suspend his campaign. Rocked in Alissa's arms, Hasty invokes his life's dream—and Floyd's boyhood in Bethune—to return home to childhood visions of dragonflies and scuppernong vines.

Act 2 begins five days later in the governor's office. Hasty has his picture taken opening sacks of mail begging him to reconsider running. In the inner room, Thad argues with Alissa about her husband's decision, and she cites increased drinking and its physical symptoms as evidence of his deterioration; but now Hasty's managers ease him back over the fence, thanks to the outpouring of public sentiment. As a joke, Thad apes Hasty's campaign manner to perfection, pointing up the governor's humble origins. When Hasty tries to extract some measure of support from his mother, she falls back on a line much like the one Floyd heard all his life, that she's pleased, without any manifestation of pleasure. When he asks whether his grandfather would have appreciated his accomplishments, her underwhelming response is that she supposes so, as that gentleman respected Purvis. Pressured by a roomful of supporters with wildly different agendas for urging his candidacy, the voices of family dead and alive, and his tortured wife, Hasty cannot decide.

Two days later, at the governor's mansion (act 2, scene 2), Alissa and Ola listen as a radio commentator describes the public's distress that they may lose their advocate; yet Ola refuses to take Alissa's side: after all, the will of heaven rules. Hasty enters with a petition signed by fourteen thousand citizens begging him to run. Alissa tells him that she will leave him if he does, that she cannot stand to watch, much less participate in his ruin. The solution now proposed by the Tarbell-Asbell-Singletary faction is to offer a bright new face in Hasty's place: Thad. Hasty regards this as both a betrayal and goad, and finally commits to continuing the race.

Act 3 drops in on an outdoor political rally, with Thad and Hasty stumping for votes for themselves as now-opposed candidates. After his turn at speaking, Hasty gets a liquor flask from his driver, Tatum, and another dream sequence ensues: his younger "Pete" self lies in a coffin, a knife protruding from his chest, with his mother, grandfather, Tarbell, Thad, and Alissa gathered as mourners. When the tension becomes unbearable, Hasty goes to the coffin, seizes the knife, and plunges it into Thad. The mourners force Hasty into the coffin, press in around him, and raise the knife to make him their victim. When Hasty regains consciousness, he stammers out to Tatum his wish to return to the scuppernong arbor.

The final scene (act 3, scene 2) returns to the reception room and governor's office. A very drunk Hasty forces an argument with Alissa when she appears with a suitcase on her way back to her parents. Ola's only hope for her desperate son is that Alissa will return if God wills it. After reading Bible verses about Jesus in Gethsemane, Hasty attempts to regain command and power with Lorena, a call girl. When this fails dismally, it prompts a long soliloquy about his face on a movie screen, the man who is governor, the stranger that he wants to be. After taking handfuls of sleeping pills, Hasty continues drinking. He reaches for the telephone, calls the police to report the governor's murder at Purvis Hasty's hands. As he slumps to the floor, he draws the harmonica from his pocket, summoning up a final dream sequence: Grandpa pushes Pete in a swing. Outside, voices chant his name while a dream chorus whispers "grandboy." The lights fade on all but the crumpled figure on the floor and the triumphant governor's still-bright face on the screen.

Floyd hinted at musical plans. "It is not a tidy chronological play—more of a dramatic collage. I will use electronic music for the first time in the dream sequence."[5] He had written Hasty for Norman Treigle, with every intention that Corsaro, whom he thought an excellent "play doctor," would direct. They brainstormed a revision of *Grandboy;* the setting was moved to the southwest, making better sense of the Chicano farmers and Alissa's ancestry. Floyd cut most of the dream sequences, leaving shorter, better-focused scenes in an inexorable progression; he treated the initial campaign sequence, among others, as a newsreel projection. Thad and Tarbell converge in a single high-society character, still the governor's assistant; but now he and Alissa have just ended a brief affair, further underscoring rifts in the Hastys' marriage. Thad has kept a pair of her earrings, which he uses as quasi-blackmail for much of the opera, investing them with the significance of the handkerchief in Shakespeare's *Othello* and Verdi's *Otello.* As in *Jonathan Wade* and *Bilby's Doll,* Floyd separated many *Grandboy* scenes with brief interludes. Influenced by Corsaro's multimedia work with designer Ronald Chase, Floyd defined dream areas with multicolored light and pattern projections, to the accompaniment of the grandfatherly harmonica. In the revised denouement, Purvis shoots Thad before consuming the fatal sleeping pills with whiskey, and the governor fades into a last dream sequence of going home to grandpa and the scuppernong vine.

The move to Houston interrupted further progress on *Grandboy* and *Bilby's Doll,* but Floyd never quit on a good idea. In the first months of 1973, he took *Grandboy* back to Roger Stevens and Julius Rudel, the latter still artistic advisor to both the Kennedy Center and the National Opera Institute. In a hallway outside Stevens's office, Rudel cornered Floyd and exercised his usual blend of friendly concern and professional criticism: though he found Floyd's story deficient in motivation and incident, it nonetheless suggested another work about a political demagogue, Robert Penn Warren's *All the King's Men,* and Rudel proposed turning *that* into another Great American Opera.

Far from being offended—*Grandboy* never felt quite right, and Floyd had envisioned Warren's book as an opera for years—he seized on Rudel's idea. Floyd had explored the unique atmosphere of the South and its extreme eccentrics for decades, people who lived outside the norm and still filled their roles within the region's close-knit, formalized society. Warren's model Huey Long was just such a character, whose education and shrewd intelligence took nothing away from his common touch. From this, Floyd began to visualize extraordinary tension attached to the theme of social juxtaposition. His protagonist would be regarded by his upper-crust characters of privilege as a usurper, an intruder, a man who, like his prototype Purvis Hasty in *Grandboy,* would ultimately be destroyed by his own demons of human weakness.

Bob Holton aimed an unsuccessful campaign at Warren's media representatives, William Morris, but here Floyd had a clearer perspective. The Morris Agency knew nothing about opera, and because they saw no financial gain for them in the project, wanted a large chunk of upfront money. With still-fresh memories of inefficient communication with John Steinbeck, Kay reminded Floyd that Paul Engle, whom he had gotten to know in Iowa in 1958, was Warren's personal friend. Engle had cofounded the University of Iowa's international writing program in 1967, and the triumvirate of Floyd, Holton, and Stevens now prevailed on him to initiate an introduction of composer to writer. The ploy succeeded, and Floyd sat down at his typewriter on July 1, 1973 and wrote to Warren. "The Kennedy Center Foundation through Roger Stevens has commissioned me to write an opera . . . for production within the next year or so, the first such commission the Center had made since its opening. Having grappled with an original script [*Grandboy*] for a year, and having finally laid it aside (as Paul may have told you) . . . I re-read your *All the King's Men* with an eye to its possibilities as an opera. . . . Before I proceeded further however, I wanted to determine if the rights for an operatic or musical version were available and if you would consider assigning them to me."[6]

To bolster his profile with the literary lion, Floyd had Holton send biographical information, a copy of his *Of Mice and Men* libretto, the Seattle performance tape, and to express hopes for a meeting. With a canny blend of flattery and modesty, Floyd retold the story of his 1949 paper on Warren's collected poems for Edwin H. Cady's class at Syracuse University: "The poems somehow seemed to elicit the best from me and, as a result, it was the only paper I ever received an A+ for during my college career. I would hope that, if I should end up doing an operatic version of your *All the King's Men,* that particular bit of personal history might repeat itself."[7]

On July 7, Warren responded with crusty grace. "Even to an unmusical barbarian like me your fame has penetrated, and so the introduction by Paul . . . was scarcely necessary. I'd be honored to have you do *All the King's Men,* as you can well imagine."[8]

Yet Warren mentioned "a hitch, for the moment anyway": that February, the Morris Agency had negotiated on Warren's behalf for a Broadway musical adaptation of *All the King's Men* by the lyricist-composer Lee Adams and the producers Herman and Diana Shumlin,[9] envisioned as a country-western version of Warren's classic novella.[10] Notwithstanding, Warren contacted his personal agent, Owen Laster, at William Morris, and signed off to Floyd, "I have told him that I'd love to have you do this."[11]

Floyd got Holton and Stevens to investigate; but in his July 25 letter to Warren, he wrote that he thought this prior commitment "an insuperable obstacle," and wished that "the integrity of the novel is honored and that [Adams'] version is a successful one." Floyd summarized his approach: "Perhaps if Mr. Adams finds the material unworkable for his purposes I may still have an opportunity in the future to attempt a setting suitable for both the opera house and the musical theater; this was in my mind as a goal from the beginning."[12]

In a quick note on August 27, Warren mused to Floyd, "If the Broadway thing blows up—as may well be the case—and if you want to pick up the project again, fine!"[13]

A full year passed without settling rights, and David Gockley pressed Floyd for *Bilby's Doll.* Holton and Stevens, though, with separate but overlapping contacts in New York's theater and music communities, continued to maneuver behind the scenes. Holton prompted Floyd to stir the embers with Warren, and on August 20, 1974, the composer expressed relief since learning from Holton that "Mr. Lee Adams . . . has agreed to relinquish [the rights] to me since he is involved in other projects . . . [and that Stevens] is prepared to reimburse Mr. Adams from his investment thus far."[14]

What Floyd did not mention, but Warren must have known, was that Stevens would spend six thousand dollars of his own money to buy out Adams's option.[15] Before proceeding to a new contract, the William Morris Agency still had to "grant us the kind of agreement we require in order for me to begin work on the opera next year."[16] Floyd underestimated the time it would take to complete *Bilby's Doll,* again imploring Warren to intercede with his agents. He closed with modesty and pluck calculated to appeal to Warren: "While I am by no means sure I can make a successful opera out of your book, I want like hell to try!"[17]

Team Floyd's moves were succeeding, confirmed by Warren's reply on August 25: "If you and Roger and Mr. Rudel *really* want to do this, the thing does sound even more attractive to me than before. I am taking up the matter right away with the William Morris people."[18]

And done it was. A month later Warren, back from his summer home in West Wardsboro, Vermont, dropped Floyd a note, hoping that his mediation had produced results, and sent a new book of his poetry, *Or Else.* Though documents had yet to be signed, by October 7 Floyd could write Warren, "My understanding is that an agreement has been worked out that seems to be to everyone's satisfaction. . . . Legal wheels seem to grind exceeding slow, and I strongly suspect that attorneys, like philosophers (to quote a poet I much admire), tend to 'loll in their disputatious ease. . . .' People continue to feel that the novel and I are ideally mated, while I feel acute trepidation (and excited anticipation) at the prospect of trying to pare your dense, complex book down to libretto proportions."[19]

On December 15, Floyd thanked Warren for "being the prime mover in the lengthy negotiations," and announced his return of signed contracts to Belwin-Mills.[20] He eventually confessed to Stevens his obligation to finish *Bilby's Doll* for Houston before leaping into another grand project, and Stevens graciously agreed, but reminded the composer at every opportunity how long their commission had been cooling.

Less than a month after returning from Houston and Omaha performances of *Bilby's Doll,* Floyd's welter of emotions ran strong: added to the pile of conflicting reviews, he now had to finish lessons, juries, and exams with Florida State University pianists and composers, find a new home in Texas, to say farewell to friends and colleagues, and make the actual move. To local press, Floyd defended himself against allegations that his only reason for moving to Houston was increased salary. He explained the advantages of an endowed chair, a lighter teaching load, and the benefits of an affiliation with the Houston Grand Opera, one of America's fastest-rising and most solvent arts organizations.[21]

Touching on his marital partnership, Floyd credited Kay with being "one of my sternest judges of what I write. . . . I rely on her judgements." Kay added, "Sometimes my criticism meets with resistance. . . . But we work together a great deal." When asked whether Floyd was a "temperamental artist," she responded, "Compared to others I have known . . . he's about as little temperamental as you can get." Kay claimed the study of photography as her current interest, besides the piano and "meeting friends."

Floyd distinguished his works from traditional opera: "The point of view I provide is contemporary"; and he went on to boost opera in English, anything to remove it from "the private preserve of the extremely wealthy." The profile ended with his statement of awareness that *Bilby*'s style had taken him far beyond *Susannah:* "But the fact I don't write the same way any longer is no reason to disclaim the way I wrote then. . . . One continues to develop, to alter attitudes. And *Susannah* as it is, is where I was at that stage. . . . I don't think I should tamper with it on the basis of what I would do now. . . . You just can't go back and reinject yourself into something. If you do, you risk its vitality."

Floyd had moved beyond what had brought him fame and fortune to a more austere and complex manner that had yet to be embraced by majorities of the public or press. He rarely looked back, but that *Susannah* filled his thoughts was logical: FSU had programmed a twentieth anniversary production, staged by Robert J. Murray and conducted by Phillip Spurgeon. During rehearsals, one of Floyd's students approached him, knowing that the composer would care about a planned "inventive" ending: Susannah shooting herself after the curtain fell. This was neither the first nor last time a director forced novelty into an opera that had achieved classic status; but Floyd convinced Murray to rethink his denouement, and performances on May 13, 14, 15, and 16 proceeded without suicide or further alarms.

That spring blossomed with other productions that the composer was unable to attend: Philadelphia's Academy of Vocal Arts presented their *Susannah* on March 31. On May 16, Eau Claire and the Afternoon Music Clubs of Columbia gave a semistaged performance of *Slow Dusk* with a local cast at the University of South Carolina.

A friend coaxed Kay from her resistance to travel, and the two women flew to Houston to investigate a house that Floyd had already seen. On a sizzling May day, they inspected a three-story west-facing townhouse at 4991 Yoakum Boulevard that had an enormous spreading oak in front and was conveniently located just southwest of downtown and equidistant from the University of Houston; Hermann Park and Miller Outdoor Theatre were within a few minutes' walk. Unlike their last property in Tallahassee, there was no yard to speak of, but rather a bricked-over front area behind a spiked iron fence. Kay rang her husband to say, "I don't want to look any more," and she and her friend headed back to the airport.

Houston Grand Opera revived its Miller Theatre *Susannah* on June 3, 5, 7, 9, and 11. Floyd spent some time at the final rehearsals, but he focused on putting together earnest money on the house. He attended the opening of *Susannah,* and on June 5 flew with Ermine and Bob Holton to his latest overseas venture, the Holland Festival's salute to America's bicentennial: *Of Mice and Men* in Scheveningen, Amsterdam, and Rotterdam on June 10, 12, 14, 17, and 20. It was the work's first European performance in English, with Julian Patrick (George), William Neill (Lennie), Thomas McKinney (Curley), and Riki Turovsky (Curley's Wife), and conducted by Michael Charry and staged by Rhoda Levine.

The press attacked; one favorably disposed critic even felt it necessary to remind his readers that despite negative reviews attendance was strong.[22] *Opera News* amplified this assessment: "In spite of personal contact with the Dutch press, Carlisle Floyd could not win the critics over to the noble intentions of his *Of Mice and Men*. . . . Dutch opera fans enjoyed the marvelous libretto and dedicated cast."[23]

Most American and English critics outdid themselves with underhanded compliments, like the finding of the *International Herald Tribune* that Floyd's "expansive lyricism" had diluted the power of Steinbeck's gritty tale.[24] The London *Sunday Times* found the opera "a totally unmemorable score," yet thought that it towered "over more 'original' but still-born novelties by more fashionable contemporaries."[25]

Almost alone in its appreciation was *The Stage*, which compared Floyd's musical idiom favorably to Menotti's and Britten's, praising his lyrical sound craft for its tight bond with dramatic situations and "the stamp of truth and sincerity."[26]

THE COMPOSER flew back to Tallahassee in July's first week to begin moving twenty-nine years of belongings and memories from Florida's dripping summer to Houston's version of the same; yet the month provided another bicentennial observance, even before the movers' boxes could be unpacked. Thanks to the influence of Roger Stevens, one of the last pieces Floyd drew from his Middlebrook mailbox was an invitation to a reception at the British Embassy in Washington, DC, on July 8: Queen Elizabeth II made a six-day state visit honoring the former colony's independence day party, and Floyd would represent American arts. Prince Philip, President Ford, and the likes of Bob Hope, Elizabeth Taylor, Secretary of State Henry Kissinger, Muhammad Ali, Aaron Copland, Mstislav Rostropovich, Supreme Court justices and members of Congress, dined on saddle of lamb in the rose-festooned tents of the embassy gardens.

Kay found such events anathema, so Floyd took Ermine as his date. They watched the royals and President Ford march down into a receiving line; Queen Elizabeth's beautiful skin and Ford's rugged good looks and strength impressed Floyd. The next day he and Ermine rushed back to South Carolina, regaling family and friends with stories of meeting Her Majesty.

Meanwhile, Bobbi Martin had moved with the Floyds and would remain as their Houston guest for about six years. The two women began settling in. In time, Bobbi's daughter Flora also lived with and grew close to the Floyds: the composer drove her to school more days than not. He flew to Jacksonville on July 12 to speak at a dinner meeting of the local opera company, and finally to Houston, where he taught his first and only summer session.

He and Kay furnished the three-tiered Yoakum house, the most elegant they had owned, in an austere manner. Directly inside the foyer lay a wooden staircase with maple railings that soared up to all three floors. The first floor held dining and living rooms, all Mexican-tiled with Philippine mahogany doors opening onto a brick-floored and brick-walled patio. The home piano, unused for composing—Floyd continued to do all creative work at his university studio—sat in the living room. The second level of the house featured a sitting and television room where they entertained informally, a guest bedroom, and Floyd's large master bedroom with floor to ceiling doors; Kay claimed the top floor and its bedroom. She continued to function as businesswoman, tending to day-to-day home management, bill paying, and tax preparation; when personal computers became available, Kay acquired those skills long before Floyd.

Floyd's work and social life underwent a similar sea change. As at FSU, he enjoyed good relations with his university colleagues, especially fellow composer David Ashley White; but a few colleagues resented his celebrity and such privileges as his reduced teaching load. Support arrived in the person of Milton Katims, hired by the university that summer as school director. Following a solid professional career as a violist and conductor, administration proved novel. Floyd observed, "It was like feeding a Christian to the lions, except that he had an absolutely impenetrable ego, the way some conductors do."

Katims took pride in serving as *artistic* director, and resisted assimilation into academia. The school soon hired an executive assistant, and everyone seemed satisfied.[27] Floyd admired Katims's sheer willpower that nonetheless "made life difficult for lots of other people. It was cute for the first two years, everyone indulged him; but after that, it began to wear on the other administrators. He did not change."

Floyd resumed frequent tennis matches at Houston's Metropolitan Club, with Katims and Gockley as partner/opponents, and sometimes played mixed doubles with Kay and a variety of friends, an ideal means of letting off steam from the intersection of their various jobs. Gockley recalled, "Carlisle had great form, and was always serious but pleasant. He was an aggressive player without being a maniac. We just ran around, ran off calories, and enjoyed playing. It was a pretty regular thing, a couple of times a week for a while."[28]

With such staunch allies, Floyd acted on Gockley's plan for a collaborative studio. This met with determined opposition from many music faculty, but Floyd had long known that opera and the academy made strange bedfellows. Still teaching five or six gifted pianists and a few composers at the university, he and Gockley lunched regularly, mapping objectives, courses of study, additional faculty, class schedules, and auditions.

Formulating the Houston Opera Studio's ethos in a paper to the NEA was the easy part. Beginning in the 1977/78 season, the program would offer advanced training and career development for exceptional young singers, conductors, pianist-coaches, and, eventually, designers, directors, and composers. All were chosen for their potential to make noteworthy contributions to opera and musical theater, and identified through auditions in eight regional centers, including Houston, Los Angeles, Chicago, and New York. Most candidates would already have earned bachelor's degrees or artist diplomas, and the studio was designed to bridge the inevitable gap between school and career. Rounding out the experience of candidates took priority not just in opera but also in all genres: they would be immersed in traditional European repertoire, contemporary opera, and the most diverse forms of musical theater. Another of Gockley's goals for the parent Houston Grand Opera was commissioning new works on a level not seen since the Ford Foundation programs of the fifties and sixties; the interface would involve studio workshops and independent performances.

Involvement in HGO's mainstage productions was a cornerstone of the program; students would be cast in supporting roles and would cover principal roles that they might sing in student matinees. Unlike other apprenticeships, though—at times to Gockley's discomfort—the studio would not obligate its singers to "paid slavery" (Floyd's words) in HGO's chorus. On the other hand, studio singers might appear with the company's touring arm, Texas Opera Theater. The studio's own independent, fully-staged productions, utilizing UH students as needed, would apply innovative approaches to standard repertoire and present recitals and concerts with orchestra and master classes with visiting artists in town for HGO's mainstage events. In addition to a physical venue, the university also provided language instructors, who found the studio's career-motivated singers more to their liking than the average undergraduate. The studio's first season, beginning September 1, 1977, lasted forty weeks. Artists might stay for up to three years, with a $7,500 stipend for living expenses, plus full university scholarships. Augmentation of funding developed through patron endowments of singers, as well as supplementary payments to artists for community outreach performances.

Floyd and Gockley functioned as authentic codirectors, conferring on policy matters, the hiring of staff, and scheduling and attending nationwide auditions, at least for the first several years before releasing this last function to junior associates. Though both men shared real friendship and trust, the relationship at times grew strained over institutional priorities, as Floyd made no bones about his allegiance to the university. If he appeared for lunch wearing a foreboding expression, Gockley might begin, "You're gonna pull the plug, right?"[29] As ruler of a mighty empire, Gockley struggled with his lack of absolute control over every aspect of an affiliate program; but Floyd looked out for the best interests of the university--the issuer of his paychecks—and its students.

These were Houston's years as the "Golden Buckle of the Sunbelt," and the university followed through on its promises, including Floyd's discretionary fund. By the time he left Houston twenty years later, that sum had grown from two thousand to almost twenty thousand dollars, and it paid for an office computer, then a second for home, as well as books, music, and photo duplication. In his last months in the city, to assure the continued existence of all his works in clean manuscript, the fund paid copyists' fees.

The first name Floyd threw into the pot for a resident vocal guru was Phyllis Curtin's, but she continued teaching at Yale; the next natural choice fell on Elena Nikolaidi, who proved lure-able from FSU. As with Floyd, the University of Houston paid her entire salary, evenly dividing her teaching load between HGO and UH student singers. Frank Corsaro was named director of dramatic studies. Jean Mallandaine became artistic supervisor and head of the coaching staff, and in years to come the company hired George Darden, Stephen Lord, and Craig Rutenberg. Corsaro had directed at Houston since 1970, and was on hand for *L'incoronazione di Poppea* in the 1976/77 season, as well as the *Of Mice and Men* revival in spring 1977; yet he resisted setting up residence there, and devoted little hands-on time to studio members. Though the company formally announced the appointments of Corsaro and his assistant David Gately, Gerald Freedman was subsequently engaged as codirector of dramatic studies, and Corsaro's formal affiliation with the program ended after 1978.

NEA subsidized the partnership from its inception. Singers from the regional auditions were informed of their selection by May 15, 1977. They were: sopranos Christine Donohue, Sunny Joy Langton, and Erie Mills, mezzo-soprano Constance Fee, tenor Roger Ohlsen, baritone Alberto Garcia, and basses Eric Halfvarson and Richard Vernon, most of whom went on to distinguished performing careers in subsequent decades. Later studio alumni included sopranos Jan Grissom, Mary Mills, and Phyllis Treigle (Norman's daughter).

With Nikolaidi's arrival, rancor spread among entrenched university voice faculty, leading to some retirements; but her presence guaranteed stunning mezzo-sopranos like Beth Clayton, Joyce Di Donato, Denyce Graves, Diane Kesling, Laura Lay, Suzanne Mentzer, and Stella Zambalis.

Male studio graduates included tenors Jason Alexander, David Arlen Bankston, Michael Rees Davis, Bruce Ford, John McVeigh, Chad Shelton, and Mark Thomsen; baritones Robert Galbraith, Greer Grimsley, L. Brad Liebl, Louis Otey, and Eugene Perry; and basses Herbert Perry and Grant Youngblood. Others the program welcomed who now perform and administrate worldwide include pianist-conductors Richard Bado, Craig Bohmler (also a composer), Harold (Hal) France, Ward Holmquist, Peter Pasztor, Robin Stamper; directors Michael Ehrman and Grethe Holby; and composer Michael Ching.

Floyd also acted as the university's liaison with a variety of downtown arts organizations, and Katims placed him on the university-wide governance committee and the dean's advisory committee, of which Floyd became chairman. He appreciated its principal concerns with promotion and tenure, but time-devouring work on two presidential search committees proved disenchanting. Eventually, resistance to the studio ebbed as levels of university student talent and younger faculty increased, and the school grew proud of the association.

Floyd's social life waned with distance from his Tallahassee circle. The friendship with Gockley ripened; Floyd never averted an empathic ear and good advice on staff difficulties, company finances, or personal concerns. Floyd rarely saw his university or studio colleagues outside of school hours; Kay and Bobbi held down the house on Yoakum Boulevard, but there were far fewer parties than in years past. Kay continued reading three or more books at a time, and playing piano, in Floyd's words, "on her own terms. She was a real amateur, in the sense that she truly loved what she pursued." Tennis and movies, mostly take-home videos, filled the rest of their free time.

Gockley saw the Floyds' Houston ménage rarely but perceptively: "When I first met Kay, I found her delightful, witty, intelligent. She'd show up with Carlisle at events, but then I saw less and less of her. I realized that she was agoraphobic, and that he was on his own in his professional life. Everybody knew that he was married, but it got to be that Kay was never around. And they had separate bedrooms; she was always at the computer, or reading, as she withdrew from the world. I knew that Bobbi had been through a divorce, but all of a sudden, there she was, living with them, and Carlisle seemed devoted to her as well. She was just their friend in crisis, and I think it also took some pressure off Carlisle. It became Tweedle Dee and Tweedle Dum: Bobbi and Kay. It gave him more freedom to get out and pursue his own functions. For a while, Bobbi and I played tennis against Carlisle and Kay."[30]

During his involvement with the studio and HGO directing engagements, Frank Corsaro recalled very few visits to the Floyds: "Kay rarely turned up. She was very reclusive, I knew that she was emotionally torn about many things. Quite often we'd make a date, and he'd say, 'She's not coming,' something like that. I never knew what was bothering her, which is really odd."[31]

No Houston clique ever formed, and Gockley recalled only two or three dinners at the Floyds' in their twenty years there, always stand-up parties with groups, hors d'oeuvres, cocktails, wine. The simultaneous long residence of Bobbi's daughter may have contributed to the dearth of social outlets: In Tallahassee, Floyd had a built-in babysitter in his niece Jane Matheny, who was studying voice with Nikolaidi at FSU; but now Floyd's and Kay's roles expanded to surrogate parenthood of Flora Martin.

FLOYD'S TIME AWAY from the university included directing engagements. In 1976, Bob Holton founded Lyra Management, an agency separate from Belwin-Mills, to process such bookings. Toward the beginning of the 1976 fall semester, Floyd directed Seattle Opera's new *Of Mice and Men,* performed on September 16, 18, 22, 24, 25, and 26. Conducted by Henry Holt and Richard Buckley, and with sets and costumes by Charles Allen Klein, the double cast featured many old Floyd hands: Robert Moulson and Dennis Bailey (Lennie), William Chapman (George), William Livingston (Curley), and Kathy Knight (Curley's Wife). During rehearsals, Floyd insisted to an interviewer that he had never been an "opera buff," and that the traditional international presentation of opera held no interest for him. What he instead craved was the unity of musical theater, when the music and the drama served each other. He cited a larger potential audience of well-educated, upper middle-class individuals who, like Kay, would shun operas performed in anything but English.[32]

As ever, Floyd continued to categorize his work with semantic precision. He had called only *The Sojourner and Mollie Sinclair* and *Markheim* operas. *Slow Dusk* was a musical play. *Fugitives, Susannah, Wuthering Heights, The Passion of Jonathan Wade,* and *Of Mice and Men* all bear the Wagnerian rubric musical drama; and *Flower and Hawk* is a monodrama. Belwin-Mills's librettos and scores of *Bilby's Doll* also refer to it as musical drama; but Boosey's current score eschews classification. The next two, *Willie Stark* and *Jonathan Wade II,* are also musical dramas; and the most recent, *Cold Sassy Tree,* closes the circle begun a half-century earlier, as a musical play.

Autumn 1976 brought cross-country trips for studio auditions; in April, he and Gockley submitted a proposal to the university for an annual independent studio production, budgeted at ten thousand dollars for sets and costumes, and professional instrumentalists to augment the university's orchestra, expenses to be shared by the University of Houston and Houston Natural Gas.

At long last, on March 1, 1977 Floyd and Robert Penn Warren updated their 1974 contract[33] and the composer began in earnest to forge a new synthesis of opera and musical theater, drafting his libretto based on *All the King's Men.*

Generations of Warrens had been southerners, and the writer was born in Guthrie, Kentucky, in 1905. From fall 1934 to spring 1938, he taught at Louisiana State University (LSU) in Baton Rouge, and cofounded *The Southern Review,* to which Carlisle Floyd later contributed. Despite subsequent denials, Warren's template for the "King" of *All the King's Men,* with reference to the nursery rhyme "Humpty Dumpty," was Louisiana's demagogue "Kingfish," Governor Huey Long (1893–1935). Long made LSU a force with which to reckon, and blanketed Louisiana with hospitals, highways, and scores of social reform projects during his single term as governor from 1928 to 1932, and during almost four years as United States senator from 1932 until his assassination at the state capitol in Baton Rouge on September 8, 1935.

Warren observed Long firsthand, later singling out his political genius at role-playing: "Vulgarian, buffoon, clown, dude, sentimental dreamer, man of ruthless action, coward, wit, philosopher, orator."[34] Long thus served as the not-so-rough draft of a protagonist too good to be true.[35] Warren, the only writer to win Pulitzer prizes for both fiction and poetry, worked at *All the King's Men* for twenty-two years, from 1937 to 1959. He first shaped the material in 1939 into "a play in verse and prose," *Proud Flesh,* with intimations of Shakespearean tragedy, Greek theater and its eventual stepchild, opera. Warren planned five acts, twelve scenes, with each act introduced by a chorus of highway policemen, football players, construction workers, women on the governor's staff, and surgeons. He assigned all versions of his governor the given name Willie; but in *Proud Flesh,* his surname was "Strong," later modified to "Talos." Summarizing the action for a friend, Warren wrote: "The play is about power, and the various justifications of power. The main character . . . has the talent for gaining power and has never asked himself the question as to its meaning. Its mere exercise has been sufficient. The play is the story of his attempt to give meaning to power, and the only meaning which seems available to him, in our world, is mere humanitarianism."[36]

After a friend convinced him of the play's stage unworthiness, Warren's next version appeared as the novel *All the King's Men,* which occupied him from 1943 to 1946. It was here that Willie finally moved from "Talos" to "Stark." A long list of critics hailed the book as America's best novel and Warren for his virtuosity and drive.[37] The book won a Pulitzer in 1947, and Columbia Pictures paid Warren two hundred thousand dollars for film rights. The result, the first of several cinematic and television versions, won three Academy Awards in 1949, including best picture, best actor (Broderick Crawford as Willie), and best supporting actress (Mercedes McCambridge as Sadie Burke).

Yet Warren still longed to see his story unfold live within a proscenium, and worked on a second play, titled after the novel, between 1947 and 1948, which was produced by New York's New School in 1948, directed by Erwin Piscator. Feeling that this latest version too closely mirrored the novel, he worked on a third drama, *Willie Stark: His Rise and Fall,* from 1956 to 1958, and this was performed in Dallas. Lingering dissatisfaction spurred Warren to create a fourth stage piece, a revision of his 1948 play, also named after the novel, and produced at New York's East 74th Street Theatre in 1959.

After Lee Adams abandoned his country-western setting, no one until Floyd attempted a musical adaptation. Random House and Dramatists Play Service published the play in 1960, and the University of Houston library had a copy, which Floyd read and promptly rejected, regarding it as nondramatic and too imitative of the novel. In the three years it took him to shape his opera, consultations with Warren were infrequent, and the writer never suggested any of his scripts to Floyd, giving the composer unlimited freedom to adapt. A three-year gap in their correspondence ensued.

One of the first things that Floyd winnowed from Warren's dense structure was its web of subplots, such as the saga of Cass Mastern and the patina of Calvinist theology. The composer had also learned not to force abstract philosophical tropes into opera librettos, such as Jack Burden's "great twitch," a nihilistic view of the driving force in men's lives as "the pulse in the blood and the twitch of the nerve."[38] For Floyd's purposes, the characters of Jack Burden and Anne Stanton needed to be created from scratch, but he found Sadie Burke already well defined. After Willie, Jack would become the opera's most important role, with Anne as Sadie's polar opposite. Warren's Willie was also virtually complete, and Floyd wanted him to have "charm, guile, thirst for power . . . at the same time he's a man very true to his roots, charming but ruthless. I see Willie in terms of Greek tragedy. The flaw is his need for vindictive triumph. In grinding under his heel the people who have humiliated him, he is insatiable and brings about a series of circumstances that destroys him."[39]

Floyd's greatest challenge lay in condensing Warren's sprawling time frame into ten days centered on the effort to impeach Governor Stark, the crucible that shapes characters and circumstances. Reworking *Of Mice and Men* had taught Floyd the dangers of basing his libretto too slavishly on a source text, and he charged into the new libretto using only the skeleton of Warren's plot. A nugget from Warren became his idée fixe: "I wonder, if to get the power to do good, a man has to sell his soul."[40]

Floyd's libretto evolved in four stages, all painstakingly detailed variations on the central theme of the plot. His usual handwritten treatment, begun shortly after *Bilby's Doll* in early spring 1976, ran to twenty-three pages. This sketch,[41] had it been fleshed out, would have been far longer than two subsequent typescript versions, one ending midway through act 3, scene 2, and completed around October 1977.[42] To this Floyd added a set of typed addenda and insertions, divided by character: Willie (ten pages), Sugar Boy (one), Jack Burden (two), Sadie (three), Judge Burden and Anne Stanton (one each).[43] The next four years brought clarity through consultations with the director Harold Prince, workshop rehearsals and performances by Houston Opera Studio, mainstage production rehearsals, and television tapings. From *Grandboy,* Floyd carried over the idea of "March of Time" newsreels,[44] with an announcer-cum-Greek chorus to summarize Willie's life and career up to the impeachment proceeding. The constant adjustment that led to the final libretto, hence new composition, is a fascinating study in the sophistication of Floyd's theater of synthesis, in which sung and spoken text alternate without calling awareness to the device.

Act 1, scene 1 reveals a city streetscape adjacent to the state capitol grounds, opening onto Governor Willie Stark's interior office. Willie (baritone) stands alone in shadow at center stage. A wordless chorus of recorded voices underlies a radio announcer's voice, in the typical thirties mix of drama and oration, describing the move to impeach Willie. A chant demanding Willie's vindication begins offstage, and Willie affirms his defiance. Members of a football team rush on, hoist Willie onto their shoulders, and carry him offstage, to ringing support from a ragtag group of the poor, Willie's principal constituency. This theatrical coup becomes a leitmotif throughout the opera.

Inside, Willie's foes exchange predictions with reporters about the impeachment. Willie and his aides—tough secretary Sadie Burke (mezzo-soprano), in love with the Boss; idealistic but ineffectual Jack Burden (tenor); and Lieutenant Governor "Tiny" Duffy (tenor)—threaten the opposition with blackmail unless they change their vote. The enemies relent, but warn that Jack's father, Judge Burden, plans to endorse impeachment. Before leaving for a rally, Willie enlists Duffy and his bodyguard, stuttering Sugar Boy (tenor), to accompany him to confront Judge Burden. Sadie offers a ringing endorsement of Willie, claiming to have taught him everything he knows. Her enthusiasm dissolves when Duffy mentions that Willie has another female admirer. Doing her best to mask shock and jealousy, Sadie proclaims her teamwork with Willie, in words similar to but less grammatical than those Floyd had heard his parents use. She finishes by vowing to kill Willie before surrendering him to another woman.

Scene 2 shifts to the living room, library, and terrace of Judge Burden's home, in the early evening of the same day. A party is in progress, and cocktails are being served as Jack prepares his father for Willie's visit; but the Judge (bass-baritone) refuses to see him, imploring Jack not to let Willie separate them.

When Floyd needed a butler for this social milieu, his mind flew back a quarter-century to Tallahassee parties at the home of the wealthy Hendersons, from whom he appropriated the name of their elderly impeccable butler George Hall. He later softened the name of Judge Burden's trusted retainer to "George William."

Jack's fiancée, Anne Stanton (soprano), bursts into the library, throws her arms around him, and chides him for neglecting her during the impeachment controversy. Jack vows devoted attention once Stark is exonerated. Willie's and Duffy's abrupt arrival shatters everyone's calm, and the judge agrees to give them ten minutes. Anne's discomfort and Willie's aside to her, urging a meeting later that night, make it clear that he and Anne are clandestine lovers. Willie cannot sweet-talk Judge Burden with a campaign-style speech about his humble origins, and the judge curtly excuses himself. Willie orders Duffy to dig up some dirt on the judge. Duffy contends that there is nothing to find, but Willie echoes an evangelistic sentiment Floyd heard at scores of childhood revivals: man is by nature sinful, and inclined to evildoing. As Jack turns to follow Willie and Duffy to the rally, Anne rushes to him, but he closes the door in her face. She touches up her makeup and hair and leaves with Sugar Boy to find Willie.

Scene 3 joins Willie's rally on the courthouse steps in his hometown, Mason City, where he launches into a down-home exhortation, amplified by the radio announcer's report. A young admirer gives Willie a harmonica, another *Grandboy* carryover, with its refrain of return to a safe childhood home. Building to revivalistic heights, Willie basks in the crowd's adulation as the curtain falls.

Act 2 takes us back to the governor's office, filled, as in *Grandboy,* with bags of mail from supporters. Willie poses for photographers, exulting over the populist will. Sugar Boy demonstrates his skill at fast-drawing his pistol to defend the governor, and Willie promises to buy him a target range when they have moved up to the White House. Jack, appalled at the tawdry exhibition and ensuing horseplay, asks Willie why he retains Duffy in his administration. Willie responds that he likes having an urban creature, greedy, realistic, and flexible, working for him. Sadie hands Duffy an envelope, evidence from a Miss Littlepaugh that Judge Burden once took a bribe. Jack, positive of his father's innocence, insists that he be the one to confront him.

Scene 2 moves to the living room of Willie's mother's cell-like house. For distraction, Willie has brought Anne to visit Mrs. Stark (soprano) and his crippled daughter Lucy (soprano). After putting the child to bed, Willie proposes marriage to Anne, to salve his conscience over betraying Jack. Anne struggles, claiming not to know her mind, which Willie takes to mean that he is too crude for a society girl.

In Floyd's treatment and first libretto, act 2, scene 3 took place in Miss Littlepaugh's rented room, with a prolonged confrontation between the spinster, Jack, and Duffy, confirming Judge Burden's bribe; in his revision, Floyd simply had Duffy relate Burden's guilt in scene 2. Willie frets about Jack, who in short order has lost lover and father, voicing Warren's keynote about selling one's soul as a prerequisite for gaining power. Willie leaves to deliver the incriminating letter to Jack, and Anne struggles with her romantic dilemma.

The final scene 3 returns to the split streetscape and library of the governor's mansion, with the football team building a bonfire outside, cheering that Willie is everyone's favorite. Willie sits alone in the library, drinking, watching an old newsreel of himself—Floyd retained this much of his original concept—giving a campaign speech. Sadie enters, and Willie picks a petty quarrel over her appearance, then drunkenly tries to embrace her. Sadie ends this clumsy advance with news about Judge Burden: Jack has given his father the letter. If the judge fails to abandon his support of the impeachment, Willie will send evidence of the bribe to the media. While Sadie goes to her car to get the news release, Sugar Boy brings Anne to Willie. She has just come from breaking off her engagement to Jack, without confessing her involvement with Willie; but now she is eager to marry him. He stammers out his love for her, and they kiss, just as Sadie walks in on them. Willie passes Anne to Sugar Boy for a ride home, and Sadie rages at the object of her affection for his patent ingratitude. An offstage torchlight parade in support of Willie drowns out Sadie's furious rant, as Willie goes out onto a balcony to the intoxication of unqualified popular love.

The first scene of act 3 returns to Judge Burden's study that evening. Jack slumps in dejection, convinced that his father can explain the charges. The judge reads the letter and confesses its accuracy. Jack's coldness makes the judge lash out at Willie's—and Jack's—complicity in such an underhanded smear, and Jack repeats Willie's assertion of man's inherent sinfulness, before rushing out into the night. Judge Burden takes a pistol from his desk drawer and raises it to his temple as the lights fade. (In Floyd's original treatment, the judge turned his back to the audience in his swivel chair and shot himself, to be discovered by Jack, who then called the police.)

Back at the reception room at the governor's office for scene 2, Jack stumbles in, disheveled and dazed. Sadie attempts to console him about his father's suicide, and, unaware of Jack's ignorance of Anne's and

Willie's affair, on his loss of Anne. In another grim reminiscence, Jack mutters that crude Willie was right all along about the alliance of sin and corruption.

Floyd originally planned an additional scene at this point, emphasizing the inherent cynicism of Willie's and Duffy's brand of politics. After deleting this, Floyd moved his last scene to the capitol steps. The crowd, including Jack and Anne, escorted by a state patrolman, swells in frenzied support of Willie, with a gospel hymn adapted to encourage support for the governor as the impeachment vote is tallied within. Willie appears in the main doorway, surrounded by Sugar Boy, Duffy, state legislators, and other officials, exulting in the impeachment's defeat. Jack steps forward from the crowd and fires a pistol at Willie at close range. Willie dies, as his childhood voices summon him back home.

Thus, in October 1977, seven months after beginning his first but far from last libretto on the subject, still titled *All the King's Men,* America's gun culture provided the denouement of a fourth Floyd drama.

After a three-year lacuna in correspondence with Warren, Floyd wrote great apologies for his silence, telling the writer that Belwin-Mills would forward a copy of his draft libretto. With understandable trepidation, he prepared Warren: "As you probably have surmised, a libretto undergoes continued alteration as it is set to music: what you will be seeing now is the version I will be working from as I begin to compose. Needless to say, I'll be anxious to know your reaction to what I've done and would like to talk over the how's and why's of my treatment if it would interest you. Despite the liberties I necessarily took in transferring your material into a very different medium, I hope you will feel that the spirit and atmosphere of your novel have been maintained."[45]

Floyd proposed meeting on November 14 or 15, or during December's first week; he would be in Washington on those dates for NEA meetings, and could easily add a trip to New York or Warren's home in Fairfield, Connecticut. Floyd thought this especially urgent because "aside from the pleasure . . . of finally meeting you . . . [it] would enable me to answer "yes" to people and, in particular, reporters in cities around the country who, when they hear what I'm up to with your novel, invariably want to know if we are acquainted. You might be pleased to know that I have encountered more advance interest already in producing the opera. This . . . is both exhilarating and frightening, especially when the first note of music hasn't been written!"[46]

In the interim, in May 1977 Bob Holton had contacted Ziegler, Diskant, and Roth in Los Angeles, the Steinbeck estate's legal representatives, to secure television rights for Houston's *Of Mice and Men,* scheduled for the Miller Theatre later that spring. Remembering the proposed Broadway run six years earlier, Roger Stevens booked the opera into the Kennedy Center for three weeks that summer, and PBS contemplated televising the production. Unfortunately, Steinbeck had died before settling television rights, and Holton wrote George Diskant on May 12, 1977 that the writer had once told him during a phone conversation that he liked Floyd's libretto better than his own play; Holton also reported Elaine Steinbeck's opinion that there should be no difficulty in obtaining broadcast rights for public television.[47]

Despite further correspondence, the proposal languished in bureaucratic limbo until a year later, when a Ziegler staff member wrote Holton that the firm was not prepared to grant television rights.[48] Floyd was too busy to notice the absence of cameras; he met Frank Corsaro at HGO's spring festival *Of Mice and Men* on June 7, 8, 9, 10, and 11, with Richard Buckley conducting singers Daniel Sullivan and Adib Fazah (George), Robert Moulson and Curtis Rayam (Lennie), William Livingston (Curley), and Sharon Daniels and Judith Haddon (Curley's Wife). After a quick fifty-first birthday party on June 11 with his family in Holly Hill, the composer headed to Washington, DC, where HGO's *Of Mice and Men* played the Kennedy Center Broadway-style between June 21 and July 10: every evening except Mondays, with Saturday and Sunday matinees.

The New York Times, propagating its view of culture in Houston as a cauldron of Texas oil money and space flights, praised Corsaro, Buckley, and the cast. Despite finding that Floyd's libretto established the claustrophobic, doom-laden isolation of ranch life, the critic found the music undistinguished but utilitarian.[49]

At long last, with Wilfred Bain retired from Indiana University since 1973, that school finally gave *Susannah* three performances on August 6, 7, and 8, 1977. Around September 1, Floyd began *Susannah* rehearsals at Lyric Opera of Kansas City, with Sharon Daniels (Susannah), Cary Archer Smith (Blitch), Robert Owen Jones (Sam), and Carroll Freeman (Little Bat), conducted by the company's general director Russell Patterson, with performances on September 21, 24, 29, and October 4 and 7. On September 18, the day of rest before opening, Floyd flew back to Houston for a Houston Opera Studio concert. Introduced by the composer, Richard Vernon sang Blitch's "Prayer" from *Susannah.* On November 1, the National Opera Association honored Floyd with a citation at its annual convention, held at Indiana University. Following the presentation and banquet, a musical tribute included excerpts from *Slow Dusk* and *Bilby's Doll.*

That same day, Warren answered Floyd's most recent letter. Without mentioning the libretto, other than his pleasure that it was finished,[50] he invited Floyd to visit him in Connecticut: "I'm sure that we could talk better at our house than in some hotel lobby or the Century [Club] or something like that. . . . Since I am self-employed (if you want to call writing poems employment—I have just finished a book) hours of the day don't matter much or days of the week."[51]

After giving Floyd his private telephone number, and detailed instructions about getting from La Guardia airport to Fairfield, Warren affirmed that he was anxious for his wife to be present at their meeting: "By the way, though I am an ignoramus about music, music is bread and meat to my wife, and she will be looking forward (as I for not such elegant reasons) to your visit." For the first time in their correspondence, Warren signaled a new tone of intimacy by signing himself "Red Warren," his nickname with family and friends.[52]

After checking in with Roger Stevens in Washington and Bob Holton in New York, within the week Floyd arrived in Fairfield in bitingly cold weather. Warren drove him from the train station to the house, for a single night's stay. Though on tenterhooks to learn the titan's thoughts about his libretto, Floyd did not venture to ask; but outside the house, Warren turned off the engine and said, "Well, I read your libretto, and I like it very much."[53] The composer breathed relief, and the men strolled inside, where Eleanor had cooked an informal supper for three. Talk flowed over whiskey before, wine during, and more whiskey after. Though Floyd held a hand over his postprandial glass, Warren, at his most amiable and agreeable, continued imbibing with gusto. Waving his hands, he got onto a tear about Robert Rossen's 1949 film with Broderick Crawford: "No, no, no, no, that's not my book! Rossen made it into an anti-Fascist tract. Don't you remember the end: 'Tomorrow the world!'? But my Willie and yours are the same. In my book, Jack Burden is the man of inaction; Willie is the man of action."

Floyd, relieved that Warren must after all have glanced at his libretto, raised a point that had nettled him since adding it: "You never see Willie and Anne together in your book." Warren answered, "I know, I was trying to keep to Jack's point of view; but afterward I thought of a way I could have done that: I could have had Jack *imagine* it; but my Willie and yours are the same."

Though bundled tight under covers that night, Floyd could hardly sleep for excitement. The next morning over breakfast, Warren, looking much the worse for wear and drink, began repeating himself. Eleanor joshed, "Oh Red, you told Carlisle that last night." Warren summed up his approval by restating, "I know why you did what you did."

With the master's stamp of approval on his libretto, Floyd could not get back to Houston soon enough to begin composing. Nevertheless, he first took part in the Columbia College (South Carolina) arts gala week on November 17 and 18, speaking the first evening on "Myths and Prejudices in Opera." At eleven the next morning, he and his favorite soprano exchanged views in "A Conversation with Phyllis Curtin and Carlisle Floyd." For the first and only time in their work together, outside of rehearsals, Floyd accompanied Curtin in the first aria of *Susannah.*

Happily back in Houston, his initial impulse was to establish The Sound, beginning with Willie's reminiscence aria at the end of act 1; the resulting thematic material would reappear throughout the piece. In a quasi-Beethovenian torturing of ways and means, he struggled through four versions; only with the fifth did he experience his eureka moment: "I had not to defy that any further, or try to temper it. You can work with it once it's down, but with that fifth try, I had no further doubts. This would be the piece's key dramatic and emotional state."

Unlike such composers as Virgil Thomson, who had a facility for improvising musical sketches, Floyd required the primary layer and filter of a libretto before he knew and understood his characters; after that, the rest fell into place. For Judge Burden, he devised a sound world to convey a rigidly upstanding character, as opposed to the far less resolved Jack, who never truly knows himself, or chameleon Willie.

WHILE FLOYD amassed a stack of new manuscript books, changes in the opera world would soon affect him. In January 1978, at fifty-one, Beverly Sills announced her retirement from singing in order to become Julius Rudel's codirector at City Opera.[54] Rudel had relinquished the company's musical directorship earlier that year after problems with the board; now, despite thirty-five years of fruitful collaboration between the conductor and singer, their administrative pairing proved a mismatch. In December, Rudel abandoned all administrative responsibilities, but, to honor his long association with the company, he was named principal conductor.[55] Finally, the following spring, with decades of future conducting and recording engagements already booked, as well as administrative positions with other companies, Rudel resigned altogether from City Opera.[56]

From the time of the *Julius Caesar* rivalry between Phyllis Curtin and Sills in the sixties, and also Curtin's and Rudel's long-standing championing of Floyd, the composer now suffered collateral damage. He and Sills had known each other socially since 1956, and Floyd never detected animosity or scorn in her attitude; but despite having approached her to sing Curley's Wife in *Of Mice and Men,* Sills neglected the man and his music during her ten-year tenure as City Opera's head. The company revived *Susannah* just once during that period, in 1982, about which Sills commented only on Samuel Ramey's success as Blitch as the reason why "the season wasn't a complete artistic bust."[57] Harold Prince, whom Rudel enticed to direct the spring 1976 world premiere of Josef Tal's *Ashmedai,* did his best to persuade City Opera to program *Of Mice and Men.* Sills parried, "Would *you* direct that?" Prince answered, "Probably; but I will tell you that it is director-proof."[58] *Of Mice and Men*'s company premiere was delayed until 1983, after Christopher Keene's appointment, but went otherwise unremarked in Sills's autobiographies.

Throughout Floyd's composition of *All the King's Men,* a title he retained until the summer of 1979, performances of his works sprang up in unexpected places. In 1977, Belwin-Mills issued its *Flower and Hawk* vocal score with a cover design by the original production's designer, Lloyd Evans. In January 1978, at the National Association of Teachers of Singing conference in Minneapolis, the soprano Bonnie Dirks gave a staged performance of the monodrama. When she repeated the event in Milwaukee on January 29, the *Milwaukee Sentinel* bestowed plaudits for Floyd's welding of pianist, singer, and audience, deeming the piece "an operatic triumph of main stage proportions."[59]

Owing to increases in publishing expenses, and the relative unprofitability of sheet music sales, Belwin-Mills, and later Boosey & Hawkes, put an end to many runs of new scores for public sale. All of Floyd's operas after *Flower and Hawk* would be printed as needed for companies or individuals for contracted performances or productions.

In Houston, Gockley enlisted Floyd, always a strong public speaker, for a Jones Hall series of local PBS telecasts, to attract an audience outside the usual opera-going demographic. On January 19, the subject was Verdi's *Aïda,* and the program included documents, interviews, and still photos detailing the opera's creation. Floyd brought Elena Nikolaidi along to discuss the role of Princess Amneris, which she had sung at the Met and Wiener Staatsoper. On February 16, Floyd discussed comic opera, using Verdi's *Falstaff,* one of his favorites, with baritone Donald Gramm, cast in the title role, and stage director Ande Anderson. Throughout this process, Floyd was bemused by the novelty of conducting rather than giving interviews, learning to relate to the camera, and entertaining as much as possible. He watched a rough cut and final airing of the first program, "through my fingers," but pronounced the product passably good.

That summer, Floyd's busman's holiday took him to Santa Fe, where David Gockley had a summer home. At Santa Fe Opera, Floyd was less than taken with the British composer Stephen Oliver's setting of *The Duchess of Malfi;* but he and Gockley auditioned promising apprentices for Houston's studio. Thus in the midst of his adaptation and composition of *All the King's Men,* Floyd was interested to meet the playwright Peter Shaffer, of *Equus* if not yet *Amadeus* fame, at a cocktail party. Shaffer eased Floyd's concerns over discrepancies between his treatment and Warren's, observing that Warren knew the difference between dramatic and narrative art. As a result, Floyd began to think that he should revisit the new work's title: already identified with *Of Mice and Men,* he began to think that *All the King's Men* might stereotype him as "the man who wrote the 'men operas.'"[60]

Floyd was about to benefit and experience complications from a new kind of workshop, which would test his product at each stage of its development. Just as Roger Stevens ceded his post as chairman of the NEA to Nancy Hanks in 1970 to focus on chairmanship of the Kennedy Center, one of his last-minute innovations was the National Opera Institute (NOI), formally established in July that year. Stevens was its first president, Julius Rudel its first chairman, and the retired bass-baritone George London, whom Stevens had appointed Kennedy Center's first artistic director, was now shifted to NOI's executive directorship.

To encourage the growth and development of opera in the United States, NOI underwrote production expenses for new or as yet unproduced operas; it commissioned composers and librettists for new operas; financed the training, coaching, and living expenses of young singers; and toured performances of opera to far-flung areas of the country. In 1978, NOI's new executive director, John Ludwig, allocated sixty-five thousand dollars to establish a "composer's laboratory," later renamed the "Music Theater Workshop" (MTW). Broadway had long had such processes—everything from the Actor's Studio development program to the so-called backers' auditions; but Houston stood at the head of the line to use this forum for its new operas.

One of MTW's forerunners began at the Eugene O'Neill Theater Center in Waterford, Connecticut. On August 10 and 12, 1978, Floyd saw the culmination of the center's composer-librettist conference, a performance of Edward Thomas's setting of *Desire under the Elms.*[61] Frank Corsaro had nudged Floyd for years to try his hand at O'Neill, and the composer had Bob Holton investigate the rights to *Desire,* only to learn that Thomas had reaped that honor.

At summer's end, while working on *All the King's Men,* Floyd revised his 1964 paper "Society and the Artist" for UH's publication *Forum.*[62] In August's third week, he flew to Washington, DC, to consult with Roger Stevens and John Ludwig about NOI's workshop, which was about to land in Houston, and Stevens's latest brainchild, the Kennedy Center Honors. Stevens appointed Floyd to a ten-year term on the artists' awards committee for the latter, a social function that required the composer's presence at annual ceremonies.

Floyd now visited his aging and increasingly infirm parents in Holly Hill every few months, more often than at any time since his early FSU days. In weeks to come, in addition to her worsening Parkinson's, Mrs. Floyd developed angina and a host of other ailments, but her son's cards and calls were always "the climax," in Reverend Floyd's words.[63] His diary began to include praise that his son could have used in adolescence: "He hasn't changed any, so thoughtful of his mother and me."[64] "He is wonderful."[65]

The Kennedy Center Honors debuted on December 1, 1978, with Marian Anderson, Fred Astaire, George Balanchine, Richard Rodgers, and Artur Rubinstein as its first recipients. Kay continued to shun such jaunts, and Ermine became Floyd's regular partner for this annual event. Honors weekends included Saturday luncheon at the Center, with welcoming speeches. That evening, the secretary of state presided over a reception and dinner at the State Department, to introduce honorees. Sundays packed in an early evening presidential reception at the White House, to deck the celebrities with ceremonial ribbons; and gala performances took place that evening at the Center's Opera House, often taped for delayed broadcast. Honorees and their guests sat in the front of the box tier, and watched onstage performances and film montages of highlights from their careers. For the first several years, Floyd and Ermine attended all events, mixing and mingling with honorees, their guests, and dignitaries, "knee-deep in an entourage of movie and Broadway stars," at luncheons and dinners. Later in Holly Hill, the family—without Floyd—watched the entire delayed telecast: "Ida sat up for it all," hoping for a glimpse of her famous son.[66]

35. Harold Prince, c. 2000. Photograph by Elizabeth Novick. Courtesy of Harold Prince.

FROM THE INCEPTION of *All the King's Men,* Floyd had wanted Corsaro to direct, and the two men discussed the opera throughout its gestation, as far as Corsaro's limited presence in Houston allowed. Yet Corsaro was now aware of a reserve on the composer's part: "Because I had in a sense betrayed him on *Bilby's Doll.* I also questioned many of his choices, so we agreed I was not going to direct it."[67]

Floyd and Gockley saw eye to eye on the intentional blending of classical and popular styles, and around Christmas 1978 they determined to land the country's most brilliant producer-director of musical theater, Harold (Hal) Prince, whose staging of Andrew Lloyd Webber's *Evita* had opened in London the previous June. Prince was now preparing the first production of Stephen Sondheim's *Sweeney Todd.*[68] He had admired *Susannah* for years, and happened to have a slot open in his calendar once *Sweeney* opened. Though Floyd had not gotten beyond composing act 1, he and Gockley flew to New York to meet their new director and to deliver the libretto on February 7, 1979, the day after *Sweeney*'s first preview.

Floyd's play impressed Prince, who was highly musical though not a musician. By that time Floyd had renamed the piece *Willie Stark,* and Prince thought it "a wonderful piece of original material, and very musical." Without hearing a note, he saw exactly what Floyd wanted, and agreed: "It is an opera, and an awfully good one; and a very inviting project for a creative director. And I'm not going to be coy: I'd love to do it!"[69]

Yet even at this early stage, before contracts were inked, Prince suggested reshaping the libretto: "I hesitate pointing out the following, but here goes: You know, I did an opera in the West End [*Evita*], based on Eva Peron, and it opens with a funeral on stage, and stills of hundreds of thousands of weeping mourners. I only point this out because if you can see it, your designer and director can avoid the obvious possibility of visual redundancy. The material is in no way comparable. It's only in the area of stage craft that a problem could arise. Thank you for letting me read it. Bravo and best wishes."[70]

After Jimmy Carter's election to the presidency in November 1977, Livingston Biddle became the NEA's new chairman. Within a year, he established a separate Opera-Musical Theater program (OMT), its goal the elimination of barriers separating all forms of music theater, thus fostering an atmosphere of greater mutual respect and appreciation between practitioners, and the creation, development, and performance of inventive new works.[71]

James (Jim) Ireland, formerly the NEA's budget director, now became OMT's founding director, and one of his first actions was inducting Carlisle Floyd as the program's first chairman. Duties would include guiding panel meetings, coordinating details of business affairs, evaluating productions, and meeting with opera boards as NEA's representative. The position involved a great deal more time and travel away from Houston, but the university's forward-looking chancellor and president, Barry Munitz, surprised him with the not very academic opinion that, in such cases, Floyd could do the school more good away from campus than on it.[72]

OMT's interdisciplinary nature mirrored the conflicts of opera in academia, and was organized over objections from its parent NEA music program and the National Council on the Arts; yet this marked the first time that leading talents from both opera, represented by administrators and musicians of the caliber of Floyd, Kurt Herbert Adler, and David Gockley, and Harold Prince, Stephen Sondheim, and John Kander of the music theater world, sat at the same table to seek effective cooperation from and for their respective disciplines.

When the panel sought to add a creative producer, they turned to Broadway's Stuart Ostrow, who demurred, and Ireland dispatched Floyd to Ostrow's home in Pound Ridge, New York, to persuade him to join.[73] Floyd succeeded, and was rewarded by the presence of a staunch ally when he and Ostrow appeared before the National Council on the Arts to defend and justify OMT's existence against accusations from other NEA factions worried about the effects of splintering programs. On the morning of the hearing, music program director Walter Anderson, opposed to the loss of control of opera in his domain, sat down with Floyd over breakfast and tried to dissuade him from pursuing OMT.[74] Floyd sweat bullets: "It's about the most nervous I have ever been, because I knew that so much rode on it, and that there was much opposition to it. But I felt it was the logical thing to do, to see whether these two art forms could work happily together. And we proved it could be done."

Floyd's and Ostrow's appearance before the council began with the producer declaring that he felt ennobled to have been invited onto the panel, and OMT carried the day. After what Floyd considered "initial sniffing out, like dogs," OMT implemented a training program for new generations of composers and librettists, one group of whom were about to convene in Houston and Minneapolis in the spring of 1979. Two more or less traditional operas were selected for development in Houston: *Conjur Moon,* with libretto by Thomas Lloyd and music by Timothy Lloyd, sons of tenor David Lloyd, who was about to retire as general director of Lake George Opera;[75] and Henry Mollicone's *Starbird,* composed to Kate Pogue's libretto. Each new work was allotted a seven-week rehearsal period, divided into two- or three-week sessions with long breaks for evaluation and revision. Free performances were given on May 17, 18, and 19 for professional and general audiences, who offered feedback to the young creators.

As a librettist and composer, Floyd was one logical reason why Houston had been chosen as an OMT test site, in addition to the available stable of Houston Opera Studio singers. Gockley's first thought about the workshop had been to use it to refine *Willie Stark,* but Floyd stepped back: "I don't know that it's appropriate that they do a work of mine, since I live here and it might look a little incestuous; second, it's a difficult opera to cast."[76]

Gockley acknowledged that no one in that year's studio was vocally suited to Floyd's male protagonist. Thus the Lloyds, Mollicone, and Pogue found themselves in Houston in September 1978, working closely with Floyd, stage directors David Gately and Patrick Bakman, and conductor John DeMain, with preliminary stagings in mid-December.

The Lloyds based *Conjur Moon* on the 1942 play *The Dark of the Moon* by William Berney and Howard

Richardson. Its story was to a point Floydian: set in the Appalachians in the twenties, a "witch boy" craves humanity after falling in love with a mortal girl. In a *New York Times* interview, the composer Timothy Lloyd stated that his proximity to opera had led him to work mostly on instinct, and that the Houston workshop had taught him the economics and expansion required by the operatic medium. Personally, although he had difficulties accepting criticism and felt like a "guinea pig," he deemed the workshop "of incredible value."[77]

But Floyd and colleagues found Lloyd's resistance a fatal component of his participation, and *Conjur Moon* proved unpopular with studio singers and audiences. Mollicone's *Starbird* fared otherwise: the composer, born in 1946, had already written a successful one-act opera, *The Face on the Barroom Floor,* to a libretto by John S. Bowman, based on the historical story of a miner at the Teller House in Central City, Colorado. That work scored a wild success at its Central City premiere in July 1978, and became an annual tradition with company apprentices, who were on-site with the actual painted and preserved "face."

Kate Pogue's *Starbird,* set in New York City, is a young person's space-age fable about three animals whose quarrel is mediated and solved by an alien starbird. Mollicone's setting, influenced by contemporary pop music, Bernstein, Sondheim, Prokofiev, Satie, and Copland, endeared itself on first hearing, and the piece was taken up at once by Houston's touring arm, Texas Opera Theater. Mollicone himself, in a letter from six years later, gives us a glimpse into Floyd's methods. Stumped in his work on a new opera, *Hotel Eden,* Mollicone arrived at Floydian solutions: "It sometimes takes us a long time to realize certain things—nevertheless, I am writing to thank you for some of the wonderful things I learned working with you on *Starbird*—things which I realize have helped me over the past few years. . . . I thought back . . . and remembered your comments about my tendency at the time to overload things musically and how this gets in the way of conveying information. . . . I threw out what I had and rewrote it in a much simpler, more effective version. . . . I am still realizing the value of what I learned. (Keep on teaching!)"[78]

Floyd's summer included staging Cincinnati Opera's *Susannah,* with Patricia Craig (Susannah), James Morris (Blitch), Jon Garrison (Sam), and James Hoback (Little Bat), Christopher Keene conducting, on July 11 and 14. In September, following up on his sons' recent work in the OMT workshop, Lake George Opera's David Lloyd initiated correspondence with Boosey & Hawkes about the *Susannah* he had scheduled for summer 1980. The spoke in this particular wheel was Lloyd's wish for a TV/FM radio simulcast of the production. That October, Boosey's Sylvia Goldstein shared her reservations with Floyd: a company of Lake George's size, despite Floyd's direction, might not present a definitive production; and she wondered how much input Floyd would have.[79] In the meantime, Julius Rudel raised the possibility of a network television taping of City Opera's *Susannah,* and Floyd deferred any decision about Lake George until this was settled. In the event, neither company found a solution, and *Susannah* has yet to be filmed for the general public.

FOLLOWING CLOSE on the heels of the seizure of the American Embassy in Tehran on November 4, and the taking of ninety hostages by Iranian radicals, PBS taped the second annual Kennedy Center Honors on December 2, feting Aaron Copland, Ella Fitzgerald, Henry Fonda, Martha Graham, and Tennessee Williams, with Floyd and Ermine in attendance. At Saturday evening's state department dinner, Floyd found himself sitting beside Fitzgerald. Since their teens, Ermine and Floyd had sparred about his snobbery over popular music, and for decades he knew this great jazz stylist only by reputation; now, doing his diplomatic duty as an artist committee member, he turned to her and asked, "How are you?"

Fitzgerald leaned in close and stammered, "I'm so nervous! I haven't been able to eat for three days!" Entirely charmed, Floyd later listened to a number of her recordings. Sorry that he had missed so much great artistry—like Floyd, Fitzgerald placed supreme importance on musicality and text comprehension—he became an instant admirer of her "scat" style, which he thought was "like singing in tongues."

That fall the Houston Opera Studio welcomed baritone Louis Otey, whom Floyd and Gockley recognized at once as a perfect "baby Willie." With the first two acts complete, the composer no longer needed to be shy about placing the opera into young hands; by December, preliminary stagings began with the director Richard Hudson and the conductor DeMain. Another new studio member, the tenor Carroll Freeman, was given the role of Duffy; David Arlen Bankston sang Jack, Christine Donahue, Anne. Floyd and his colleagues concentrated on act 2, throwing out injunctions right and left: "Too covered . . . too pretty. It's not Sarastro's aria, it's more like musical comedy."[80]

A performance with piano took place before an invited audience on December 15, advertised as a working rehearsal. John Ludwig, representing OMT, and Roger Stevens sat among the crowd. What did not work, Floyd attacked remorselessly: much to Hal Prince's disappointment, the Miss Littlepaugh scene disappeared, and Judge Burden's attack against Anne went to the same circular file. Floyd moved Jack's aria to the beginning of the act; in the scene at Willie's mother's house, he shortened Anne's aria. Nineteen pages of duet in which Willie recounted for Anne his first wife's death and his early involvement in politics also got scissors-and-tape treatment, though portions eventually reappeared in the governor's office scene. In all, more than a half hour of music fell away.

Then, more transpositions: the exposition of Willie's impeachment moved to the beginning of the opera to create a preexisting dramatic situation, the obstacle against which the characters' personal conflicts played out. At the performance, the composer squirmed when a bit of sung chitchat provoked audience giggles, and he changed some previously sung lines to spoken dialogue, thus avoiding setting the prosaic in song:[81] "I tried a great deal of speaking on pitch and in rhythm—anything to . . . ameliorate as much as possible the transition between speaking voice and singing voice and to do it with such consistency that the audience was never consciously aware of how the voice was being employed. . . . That was, I would say, my bow to so-called musical comedy."[82]

At the end of 1979, Jim Ireland tired of the infighting that began to consume OMT, with relentless pressure from the NEA's music program to recapture musical theater. With his background, Ireland longed to rid himself of administrative shackles and involve himself with a producing organization. As it happened, HGO's managing director Robert Buckley had just resigned, and Gockley advertised the position. Ireland wrote to Floyd, inquiring whether the composer thought that Ireland and Gockley would get along. As both men's friend, Floyd found himself in a ticklish situation, because he had no ready answer; but an interview was held, and Ireland served as the organization's managing director for more than twenty years.[83]

A month into the new decade, Floyd attended the Columbia (South Carolina) Lyric Opera's production of *Susannah* on January 31, in cooperation with the University of South Carolina School of Music. The composer's mother was sufficiently ill that neither she nor Reverend Floyd attended; but Ermine represented the family, and drove Floyd to Holly Hill to visit his parents on February 2. Also on this trip, the composer formalized arrangements with Thomas Johnson at the South Caroliniana Library for the university to receive the Carlisle Floyd Archive. The strains of *Willie Stark* workshops showed in the aggressive tone of an interview that appeared in *The State* on February 17. With a stance of defiance, having always been a nonconformist who never accepted the status quo, Floyd deplored "intellectual laziness, that kind of approach which doesn't examine things from the bottom up to see if they work the way they should. . . . I've never followed musical fashions . . . I've never allied myself with any of the so-called schools of modern music and I suppose that's made some people upset. . . . You've got to be true to yourself."[84]

Either a letter from Floyd to "Red" Warren from these weeks never found its way into Beinecke Library's Warren collection, or the composer phoned Warren, but Floyd had clearly informed the writer of

Willie Stark's unveiling on April 24, 1981 in Houston, and that December's workshop had borne results. Warren's letter of February 29 assured Floyd that he had not worried about the composer's silence: "I had laid the matter in your hands, and on the knees of God, and turned my back on it till the time came for you to tell me something. Well, the 'something' sounds very splendid! You must have been in a fury of activity all these months, and I pray that you will not live to think of time wasted. As for opening on April 24—that is my birthday, my seventy-sixth actually in 1981, and I am certainly going to be there, with Eleanor, to inspect the birthday present. I have every reason to expect one of great worth—unless I am painfully misinformed about the giver of the gift."[85]

Warren went on to tell Floyd about his new and revised poetry collections, and repeated his invitation to visit, with a variety of temptations offered by their summer home in Vermont: "We are in deep woods, nearest neighbor a mile off, a large swimming pool at the door, fed by our brook, all forest, and a mountain to watch the sunset over. Also a pretty good tennis court if that appeals to you. I even have some rather good, and well aged, claret in my cellar there."

On March 10, Hal Prince wrote with news that Alex Haley, author of the 1976 novel *Roots*, had visited the producer-director that morning, wanting to know whether Prince might be interested in doing it as a stage play; Prince in turn wondered whether Floyd cared to think of an operatic *Roots*. (He did not.) On March 27, Bob Holton urged Floyd to update the 1972 agreement with Roger Stevens. So much had changed in the interim, not least of all Floyd's move to Houston and the new opera's world premiere date. Floyd was owed his first $1,500 payment from Stevens, as the libretto had long been finished.

A long letter of April 4 arrived from Ernst Bacon, living in Orinda, California, and about to turn eighty-two: "Despite a wake of 81 years, healthy I think, the turbines keep turning, though my navigation appears to be steering into waters more and more remote."[86]

Bacon had just come across a five-year-old letter from Floyd, and, having married Ellen Wendt in 1971, launched into a long chronicle of family news and local and national politics. Bacon's injunction to his former student still touches: "Your continued successes and works are joyful news to me. They probably are demanding enough to keep you from continuing as a pianist. If so, let me remind you that your melodic tone was from early days singularly fine: so let not any of the recent athleticism of so many pianists, not to mention mountainous repertoire, ever deter you from offering what is so far more important and rare, which you have."

FLOYD HAD JUST ENOUGH TIME to fly to Reno, Nevada, in early April to direct *Of Mice and Men*. Nevada Opera's general director Ted Puffer conducted, and the cast of Floyd veterans even included two from Seattle's premiere a decade earlier: Robert Moulson (Lennie) and Archie Drake (Candy). Lawrence Cooper sang George, Carol Gutknecht, Curley's Wife; and Floyd must have twisted an arm to get Houston Opera Studio member Louis Otey cast as Slim.

When New York's Bronx Opera Company presented their *Susannah* at Hunter College Playhouse in Manhattan over the weekend of May 9, Floyd had no chance to attend. *The New York Times* deconstructed the opera's success while seeming to bestow compliments, ranking the "clever simulation" of folklike elements alongside "clumsy orchestration," "banality . . . and the often embarrassing colloquialisms of the text." The critic seemed to begrudge the opera's "healthy if crude vitality," predicting its survival long into the future.[87]

The most important item on Floyd's 1980 agenda thus far was a second OMT workshop on May 25, in Houston's Wortham Theater, a complete *Willie Stark* for an invited audience. Though by now Gockley had signed Hal Prince to direct his mainstage premiere, Richard Hudson again staged the workshop, designed the set, and John DeMain conducted. Rehearsals in April and May resembled a Broadway musical's process more than an opera's, and Floyd continued lopping off old material and adding new. The performers struggled to keep up; but, as Scott Heumann reported, "The singers were excited to be in on the creative end of the project, [John] DeMain explained: 'Diane Kesling *asked* to do Sadie. Carroll Freeman is not interested in small parts like Duffy anymore, but he's right there, because he's such a professional.'"[88]

The singers expressed fears to studio administrators that agents and press might visit the performance and judge them in repertoire of imperfect suitability; and the audience was indeed high-powered enough to justify anyone's trepidation: Roger Stevens; Russell Patterson, the general director of Lyric Opera of Kansas City; Jack O'Brien, artistic director of San Diego's Old Globe Theatre; Robert Holton; and NOI's John Ludwig. Yet Floyd and Gockley adamantly barred the press. When Carl Cunningham of the *Houston Post* asked to attend, he was refused; yet two sometime journalists, John Ardoin, who wrote for *The Dallas Morning News* and numerous national and international opera periodicals, and Scott Heumann, were admitted. Ardoin came not as a critic but as a scout for PBS, planning to televise Kennedy Center performances of the opera; and Heumann came to interview Floyd and observe the workshop for an *Opera News* article.

Before the evening performance on May 25, DeMain offered public disclaimers to calm his performers, but the event triumphed. As with any musical theater piece, the audience burst into frequent spontaneous applause, and gave cast, staff, and Floyd a tumult of "bravos" at the conclusion. As the singers removed makeup and costumes, the public submitted written comments, reviewed first by Gockley and DeMain, then passed to Floyd.

Heumann visited Louis Otey in his dressing room to collect reactions to the event and the title role: "There isn't a role this long in the opera repertory. . . . An hour and twenty minutes. . . . The hardest thing was learning to pace myself. The part pounds at the voice, the top mainly, and it's a difficult acting job." When asked whether Floyd had included cast members in his creative process, Otey explained, "Yes, we felt we were. . . . Sometimes we thought they were more concerned about the project than about the singers, but they did listen to us. It was a group effort. . . . It's a great part. It has everything."[89]

As challenging as the workshop process had been, Floyd felt that it had become an indispensable part of his process as both librettist and composer, in determining the overall shape and pacing of his work. He now had another three months to process and revise, before Belwin-Mills printed its scores and Hal Prince prepared his production. The director had already received a tape of the workshop, yet felt at a disadvantage in one major sense: "I did not have or even want the same impact with Carlisle that I have when I work on a Broadway musical. I have a huge amount of impact on the book and lyrics for a musical; but I don't have the musical competence to offer up that amount of editorial advice for an opera."[90]

After receiving the revised libretto, tape, and stacks of memoranda from the company, Prince responded on June 23 with a four-page play-doctoring letter to both Floyd and Gockley. For set designs he had recommended Eugene Lee,[91] but he worried that the intensely theatrical dynamic of the work they generated might not reflect Floyd's music: "I believe fervently that material must dictate form—not the reverse. The problem at the moment is the material isn't dictating *any* concise form. If you read the libretto you have no such difficulties with the exception of the radio announcer's monologues and the odd sentence. . . . I could stage the play excitingly. It is the lack of character delineating, the sameness with which the characters speak/sing. And it is the lack of theatrical surprise in the transitions which is making it impossible to do anything but a straight forward job."[92]

Floyd felt that the workshop newsreels failed, making the stage look artificial by comparison; and he still doubted the device of the radio announcer. Prince argued back that radio was the period's proper medium, that its very abstraction stimulated the audience's imagination. He hinted, even at this late stage, that he might withdraw: "When I say I believe in the radio announcer as the final image, that is because it's not a gimmick but a true theatrical metaphor. The impact of Willie Stark's life on his times. You tell me it didn't work. Well, as far as I'm concerned it *has* to work. There is no conceivable way it *can't* work, providing I understand your opera and I'm the fellow to direct it. But of course I'm shaken that it didn't work. Indeed I wish to hell it hadn't been tried. . . . And was a workshop really valuable? I keep seeing the letter from Houston telling how well received it was. That causes me to think my involvement might be bad news."

Prince unrolled a list of suggestions: Add pomposity and stylization to the announcer, but give less information. Emphasize the image of Willie the solitary man, expanding on Lee's suggestion of an empty football stadium at the beginning, "a funeral in which the dead man is sitting in the stands;" then wrench Willie out of this fantasy back into the campaign, with something stronger from Floyd than an even-numbers cheer. Floyd needed to modulate Sadie's anger, emphasizing the "buoyancy hiding her insecurity," which in turn masks "her loneliness behind life force."

Prince also found Jack "sanctimonious, priggish," and thought "callow" a better direction; and Judge Burden needed to gain aristocracy: "A Grand Seigneur is less pompous, the power inbred, so that when he falls it's from a hell of a height. These are all victims but it is difficult to warm up to them because they are either complaining at the outset or stern or self-righteous. The difference is you want the judge to get his, you want Jack to lose his idealism."

What Prince missed most in the tape was "a more dynamic, angrier political sound from the crowd . . . there must be an insistent tension-creating rhythm to segue from one scene to another . . . ENERGY. . . . A bomb ticking off." Intuiting Floyd's sensitivity, Prince apologized for this being "a tough letter to take," but, he wrote, "I'm right for me, for what I can provide. . . . I haven't gone into detail about the balance of the piece because my experience indicates [that] if you get the larger thing, the theatrical rhythm right, everything will fall into place."

The relationship that Floyd and Prince developed as cocreators differed from anything in the composer's experience: "He deals with what is and visualizes it on the stage." And revise Floyd did; in the end, Prince maintained, "I didn't find him stubborn about anything, everything I said that he accepted wound up in the next version. I just kept asking a lot of questions, and he's very good to explain why he wrote something the way he did. There were pieces I didn't understand, because I'm not a musician. We disagreed over one scene, between the governor and his daughter [act 2, scene 2] that was pure opera, and I always had problems with it, because I couldn't get my music appreciation teeth into it. And Carlisle said, 'This is probably the best music in the whole piece.' And I thought, 'You don't get an argument, you're the composer, I'm sure you're right.' Very rare, like talking to Bartók or somebody; but we're talking from different places. And 99 percent of the time, that scene was effective. Everything else was totally clear to me, because he writes theatrically. And he's a director's dream. It always occurred to me that Carlisle could have written a very successful musical, he had an amazing gift for picking the right stories. But I didn't pursue it with him, some inner voice told me, 'You can't win this one, he won't do it.' Still, he's so enthusiastic, and I admired him from the first as a composer and learned how good a librettist he is."[93]

Prince loved Eugene Lee's great stairs, the majestic simplicity of the high walls, doorways, and massive staircases that gave Floyd's notion of Greek tragedy three dimensions: "We found metaphors quickly. You have to have a space that represents everything, and that space did for me."

They held New York auditions at the Broadway Theatre, where Prince's *Evita* production had played since 1979. The prospect of getting a Metropolitan Opera star cast in the title role tantalized Floyd: the baritone Sherrill Milnes was contacted, and showed interest; but Prince voiced strong objections, not because of Milnes's high fees, but owing to his limited availability. (Floyd saw that his director was less familiar than he with opera world ways.) Up to this time, Prince's career exposure to the medium had been limited to directing Tal's *Ashmedai* at City Opera in 1976, Puccini's *La fanciulla del West* for Lyric Opera of Chicago in fall 1978, and Weill's *Silverlake* for City Opera in fall 1980. He remained skeptical of "names" like Sherrill Milnes, James Morris (also heard for Willie), or Patricia Craig, a veteran of numerous *Susannah* productions, who auditioned for Anne Stanton.

Judith Dolan designed costumes, Ken Billington, lighting; Timothy Nolen was signed for Willie, and Alan Kays as Jack, Jan Curtis as Sadie, Julia Conwell as Anne, Don Garrard as Judge Burden, and Robert Moulson, by this time a Floydian senior citizen, as Sugar Boy. With the radio announcer now a crucial element, Prince wanted the writer, broadcaster, commentator, and world traveler Lowell Thomas. Gockley scored that major coup, and the company got his immediately recognizable voice—at least to anyone born before 1950—on tape at his home in Pawling, New York.[94]

THE YOUNG ARTISTS selected for Houston's 1980–1981 studio included several destined to be a part of Floyd's present and future: Louis Otey stayed that year, and the program added librettist Kate Pogue, composer Michael Ching, and conductor Harold (Hal) France. In mid-July, Floyd flew to upstate New York to stage *Susannah* for Lake George Opera, where he met Mark Flint, a pianist-conductor playing rehearsals and preparing apprentice artists for a studio production of *Slow Dusk.* Watching from his position at the keyboard as Floyd directed, Flint recalled that "he added cachet to everything he directed. No one knew better how to make it work."[95]

John DeMain conducted a cast that included Karen Hunt (Susannah), Marc Embree (Blitch), Harry Danner (Sam), and Jerry Minster (Little Bat). The production opened on July 31, with repetitions on August 2, 4, 6, and 8, the last a matinee at which Phyllis Curtin joined Floyd in the audience.

Following a two-day visit to Holly Hill—Reverend Floyd wrote, "He is such a prince of a fellow"[96]—and meetings with Stevens and Gockley in Washington, Floyd was Europe bound. The Princes and Harold and Judith Chaplin, daughter of film and theater composer Saul Chaplin, rented a 125-square-meter summer home in an eighteenth-century villa, the Casa Calvario, part of a monastery on a windblown hilltop above the 365 Calvary Steps in Pollença, Majorca. Floyd and Eugene Lee shared guest quarters for three days that August, to process *Willie* revisions. The house came with a staff cook and maid, and meals were served al fresco on the terrace. Arriving after a fifty-kilometer drive from the airport, Floyd handed Prince his list of changes, and the director came outdoors the next morning beaming, "You have made me very happy." The three men compared and coordinated their separate revisions, along with discussing Lee's designs and Prince's production concept in Calvario's unaccustomed tranquility.

When Floyd returned home, Edward Corn of the Opera Company of Philadelphia asked him to direct Offenbach's *Contes d'Hoffmann;* immersed as he was in *Willie Stark*'s world, however, the composer had no interest in Offenbach's supernatural and fantastic elements.[97] On September 1, Robert Penn Warren resumed correspondence with Floyd, wanting a home address to which to send his new book of poems, *Rumor Verified,* as well as confirming the Kennedy Center premiere date.[98] Floyd replied a week later, thanking him for the book and filling him in on all the details of the OMT workshops: "The very modest production . . . turned out to be a sizeable success . . . and I am looking forward more than ever now to seeing the work fully realized next spring. Of course it was extraordinarily valuable for me to be able to see the entire piece on its feet, a luxury I have never before had available in twenty-five years of writing opera, and, as a result, I have spent the summer . . . making changes in the libretto and re-writing music. . . . Your characters emerged as vividly as I had hoped and the audience was completely caught up in the story and consequently I am feeling very optimistic."[99]

The Kennedy Center production would open on May 9, with a run of eleven additional performances through May 29, after which the company would return to Jones Hall in Houston for the PBS taping. After coordinating the year's studio and university activities, Floyd embarked on a change of pace: the direction of revivals of his older works. In Detroit, he staged *Of Mice and Men* for Michigan Opera Theatre's five performances opening on September 16; John DeMain conducted, and the singers included Robert Moulson and Barry Busse (Lennie), Lawrence Cooper (George), James Longacre (Curley), and Elizabeth Wakefield (Curley's Wife).

Like his elder contemporaries Barber and Menotti, Floyd was damned if he did or did not: his music was regularly lambasted in the press as either too contemporary and dissonant, or too tuneful and romantic, and it had taken *Of Mice and Men* ten years to win its deserved place in the canon, with the obvious exceptions of the East Coast and Europe. The *Detroit Free Press* blazoned that Floyd's realization got "Roars of Approval" on September 28 and that it was "no less than brilliant."[100]

During Floyd's weeks in Michigan, Aaron Copland was also in town, for a Detroit Symphony performance, and the two composers met fleetingly. Copland, in the throes of dementia, did not remember Floyd; but when someone mentioned *Of Mice and Men,* Copland told Floyd, repeatedly, "You know I wrote the film score for *Of Mice and Men.*" Floyd praised the work, and when someone else walked into the conversation, Copland looped, "You know I wrote the film score for *Of Mice and Men.*" Floyd left, saddened by this American icon's decline.

He flew directly to Pittsburgh to stage *Susannah* for performances on October 9 and 11. Christopher Keene conducted Patricia Craig (Susannah), James Morris (Blitch), Jon Garrison (Sam), and James Hoback (Little Bat). One local critic observed that, in terms of total theater, Floyd's production surpassed anything the company had done for twenty years.[101]

An even rarer eastern plaudit arrived when *Opera News* editor Robert Jacobson wrote for his December issue:

> It could be that at least with *Of Mice and Men* and *Susannah,* Floyd has arrived at that ultimate accolade, an American classic. Within a single week it was possible to view these two works as produced by Michigan Opera Theatre and the Pittsburgh Opera. . . . Floyd took directorial charge of both, and what a splendid man of the stage he is . . . he gives his work a riveting truth, simplicity and human values, so that big dramatic moments emerge organically from the piece itself and its action, not as theatrical "events" per se. His direction reflects the clarity of his own dramaturgy and composing style. . . . *Of Mice and Men* . . . may be Floyd's finest work, for the orchestra conveys that uniquely American sound of space, land and vision (out of the Copland kitchen) and the score is full of a strange, dark power, strong and lovely in character as it conveys the wells of loneliness, destructiveness and futility of these characters out of Steinbeck . . . [Floyd's score displays] aching lyricism and stabbing emotions.[102]

Floyd met Ermine and his aunt Bunny in New York to fly to Ireland to observe the Wexford Festival *Of Mice and Men* on October 24, 27, 30, and November 2. Curtis Rayam (Lennie), Lawrence Cooper (George), John Winfield (Curley), and Christine Isley (Curley's Wife) sang under John DeMain's baton, directed by Stewart Trotter in sets by John Cervenka. At a company function, Floyd was introduced to the formidable London critic William Mann and his wife.[103] The lady queried, "American opera? Is that not a contradiction in terms?" As Floyd tried to think of a diplomatic answer, Mrs. Mann gave him the perfect opportunity to rescue everyone by adding, "But is it any good?" The composer smiled, "You'll have to answer that for yourself after the performance."

The company housed Floyd in White's Hotel, an eighteenth-century landmark. After a gala opening night reception, Wexford's artistic director, Thomson Smillie, approached the composer with news that another critic, Tom Sutcliffe of the august *Guardian,* wanted to meet him. Remembering Sutcliffe's disparaging *Of Mice and Men* review after the 1976 Holland Festival, Floyd replied, "Well, *I* don't want to meet *him.*" By then it was too late, and there stood Sutcliffe with extended hand. He and Floyd chatted, and the critic made an unusual admission: he had been wrong about the piece on first hearing, and had come to appreciate it after this evening's performance.

At about one a.m., Floyd stepped into the hotel's superannuated lift to go to his room. He pushed the button for his floor, whereupon the contraption sank to the basement. He began pressing alarms, but the revelry above drowned out anything that might have sounded. He tried prying the doors apart, but they parted only a sliver; he began to yell, "Help! Help! Get me out of here!" No one responded. A half hour later, surveying his tiny prison, he was about to curl up for the night on its floor, but emitted one final round of cries. A maintenance worker chanced to hear, and summoned the manager, who appeared with most of his staff and an engineer. Once they managed to wedge open the door, the manager, inclined to understatement, declared, "Oh . . . it's you."

Subsequent events left Floyd with a slightly better taste for Wexford, with a more heartening critical tone than past European assessments. Much to his surprise, William Mann praised the dramaturgy of his condensation of Steinbeck, and the almost draconian economy of his text and highly singable music: "There is not a bit of adipose tissue."[104]

And newly converted Tom Sutcliffe made good on his pledge, admitting his mistake: *Of Mice and Men* deserved "to be taken as seriously as it takes itself." He appreciated Floyd's ability to write music of greater emotional range than most contemporaries, and wrote that the composer articulated and underpinned dramatic situations "in a totally convincing and stirring fashion."[105]

ON NOVEMBER 4, Ronald Reagan won his victory over incumbent President Carter, and the NEA's new director, Frank Hodsoll, would soon be installed. With less than six months to go before *Willie*'s premiere, it was time for Floyd to get down to fine-tuning and orchestration. He dedicated the finished score to Harold Prince.

On Floyd's overnight visit to Holly Hill on November 23, Ermine got their mother to sit up in the living room, combed her hair, and dressed her in "a pretty blue robe." Reverend Floyd, who never got closer to empathy with his suffering wife than to use the words "brave" or "patient" to characterize her attitude, wrote that "Ida's mind was very clear and she talked with much sense."[106]

In the first weeks of 1981, around the time of the release of the Iran hostages after 444 days of captivity, Floyd and Ermine gave Target Methodist Church a set of stained glass windows in honor of their parents. On February 20, all parties signed Floyd's revised contract with Roger Stevens, adding Houston's participation to the twelve Kennedy Center performances of *Willie Stark* in May. Floyd received the balance of his commission, $7,500, on signing, with the figure for parts extraction boosted to $16,000. He would receive round-trip airfare from Houston to Washington, DC, and $75 per diem while in the capital.

Yet one annoying detail preoccupied him: the inclusion of John Ardoin and Scott Heumann in the previous May's workshop had ignited a feud with one of Floyd's erstwhile supporters, the *Houston Post* critic Carl Cunningham. Since May, Cunningham had been particularly critical of Floyd and the Houston Opera Studio. When the two men saw each other at public events, Cunningham refused to speak to Floyd; composer offered to meet critic over lunch to explain the ticklish situation, but Cunningham declined. On February 23, Floyd wrote Cunningham a complete explanation: "Neither [Ardoin nor Heumann] . . . was there 'at the personal invitation of the composer,' as I believe you were told. . . . It was the decision of the management that there be no press invited to the production. . . . I concurred . . . knowing how hastily the production had to be assembled, and having little assurance, even several days before the performance, that my opera would be properly represented. . . . I have appreciated your friendship and support over the years and am very sorry that a good working relationship has been disturbed."[107]

Floyd enclosed a copy of the most recent *Willie Stark* libretto to facilitate Cunningham's preparation for the opening, but healing took some time. One critic had written Floyd before, but this was the only time that he reversed the situation.

With John Ludwig and others, Gockley coordinated an ambitious NOI colloquium around the theme "The Producer and the Composer: A Mutual Need," for April 24 through May 2, 1981. This event would further involve annual meetings of the National Opera Association and Opera America (OA), with representatives from all areas of musical theater: conductors, directors, composers, librettists, translators, and company administrators—and, of course, critics. In addition to the world premiere of *Willie Stark* on April 24, things would receive a jump-start with a Warren symposium at the University of Houston and a press conference. Performances of new works—Philip Glass's *The Panther* and Henry Mollicone's *Starbird*, developed in Houston's NOI workshop and paired with *The Face on the Barroom Floor*—would take place at unusual venues all over Houston.

The Southern Quarterly interviewed Floyd about his recent involvement with Warren, and the resulting sixteen-page piece reflects both *Willie Stark*'s chronology, Floyd's work with Hal Prince, and the composer's vision for the synthesis of opera and musical theater:

> Dealing with musical theater—dealing with opera so to speak—I would like to know that what I do reaches the widest possible audience. That does not mean the same thing to my mind as pandering to the lowest common denominator of public taste, but I feel that the musical theater is a popular art form. . . . I would like to . . . leave as my creation . . . a very good popular art, not elitist art . . . as our very best movies are fine examples of popular art done very, very well. Musical theater and opera have always been popular entertainment. I think that economically for the form to survive that the idea has to be perpetuated. We can't support our opera with small audiences . . . or our musical theater either. It's too costly today.[108]

Dismissing attempts to pigeonhole him as an adherent of any particular school of composition, and scorning musicological approaches to composing, Floyd described his own process as relying "as much as possible on what my inner ear dictates, on the intuitive, to bring it into being and then to develop, mold, and shape it in a highly conscious way. . . . Otherwise composing can become a cerebral exercise. . . . Cerebration comes after the intuitive has had a chance to make its voice heard."[109]

With the cast in town and staging underway, Floyd found in Hal Prince a different kind of director than previous collaborators. Prince suggested a specific time, usually toward the end of each day's work, for the composer to attend rehearsal. At this point or over dinner, Prince might run through corrections that either he or Floyd had to make, or cite particular lines that needed strengthening, which inevitably required quick rewrites. When Gockley attended orchestra rehearsals, he found some of Floyd's writing jarring, "a jagged counterpoint to the vocal line . . . [which] was beautiful, soaring, but the orchestra was making these percussive, sawing sounds, a dissonant commentary. I remember saying, 'You should really have the strings doubling the voice, and emphasize lyricism, rather than compromise it.' I think he threw me a bone once in a while, but that was his particular style and signature. I was always looking to get the arias to be as beautiful and audience-friendly as possible, like Susannah's arias or the final scene in *Of Mice and Men*. There could never be enough of those for me. It became more difficult as he went on to find those moments in his music that broke my heart."[110]

The piece delighted Prince: "Carlisle parsed out the storytelling in a really strong, interesting way. It's so easy to get actors to deliver. And he's an extremely theatrical man; he's a gent, in the real sense of the word, sensitive and kind. Everyone, even the chorus, was so supportive and enthusiastic, and contributory, unlike some of the other choruses with whom I have worked. At the Staatsoper in Vienna, it was horrifying: they were all lazy Socialists. They make music that sounds God-given, but they won't act. And Carlisle doesn't like that, thank God! I was extremely happy with the cast; and the chorus is a huge portion of that show, and they got it, they dug it!"[111]

When grilled by reporters whether he had "directed" Lowell Thomas's readings as the radio announcer, Prince replied, "You think I'm gonna tell Lowell Thomas how to be Lowell Thomas?"

At the beginning of April, Warren, deep into work on a new long poem, "Chief Joseph of the Nez Perce," wrote Floyd a series of quick notes with departure and arrival times, and ticket requests for himself, Eleanor, and other friends. On April 22, Ermine and aunt Bunny arrived, followed soon by the Mastrogiacomos from Tallahassee, and Lowell Thomas and Bob Holton from New York. Warren came the next day, and the huge HGO/NOI/OA machine was up and running. With bevies of press around every corner, separate and joint interviews with Floyd and Warren generated lodes of lead and oceans of ink. At a welcome dinner on April 23, one reporter, seeking to liven her story with a bit of human interest, asked the writer about his consultations with Floyd, which Warren characterized as most informal: "I *hope* we were having bourbon but I can't remember. I hope we didn't waste an afternoon without some."[112]

Kay Floyd would no longer attend anything as crowded and noisy as a Houston premiere, but took in a dress rehearsal. On opening night, April 24, Elena Nikolaidi dropped in on the composer in his dressing room at Jones Hall and handed him a card and Valsa Makis's white pottery amulet that Nikolaidi had found on a recent trip to Greece: a blue eye, to protect against evil influences. The accompanying note explained this token of admiration, love, and devotion to Floyd and his magnificent new work, and all that she expected him to produce in coming years.[113]

The premiere audience gave Floyd heartening cheers and a standing ovation. University Chancellor and President Barry Munitz hosted a dinner at the elegant Plaza Club, which overlooked the city from the forty-ninth floor of the Shell Oil building. Introduced first, Warren enthused about his wonderful seventy-sixth birthday present; in his turn, Lowell Thomas raised a great laugh with his wistful observation, "Oh, to be seventy-six again!"

Beverly Sills, in Houston for NOI week, made no effort to see Floyd, and offered no reaction to *Willie Stark.* But on April 30 the composer made another connection that would affect his future, with the receipt of a warm letter of congratulation from director Jack O'Brien.[114]

The eyes and ears of the southern press were anything but evil: Ann Holmes wrote that Floyd had made great strides in closing the gap between traditional forms of opera and musical theater.[115] David Foit reported for Baton Rouge the birth of a spectacular work that unleashed "American energies with a vitality and a direct strength . . . rare in American opera."[116]

As Floyd was about to relearn, though, independence and resistance to categorization bore a price in the form of heavy brickbats in flight. Donal Henahan thought that Floyd and Prince had retold Warren's complex story as a one-dimensional Broadway show, and experienced Floyd's music as a "strident, prosaic recitative that tears at the listener's patience—and . . . sears the vocal cords," a trivial send-up of Britten and Menotti. He thought it no great loss that the production had overwhelmed the score, which he termed "almost absentminded."[117]

Little better was *Newsweek*'s notice, which described *Willie* as "a slicked-up, Broadway-style show with a severe identity crisis." This critic failed to see the point of Floyd's synthesis between what she termed "highbrow musical and lowbrow opera."[118]

Prince was as stunned as anyone. He had invited representatives from the Shubert theatrical organization, with thoughts of a Broadway run, but his hopes ran into their blank wall. "They didn't get it. I know it's a big cast, but it's not a big set, it's in no way hard to transport or assemble. As for the work, I find it so accessible. You don't have to read a libretto a half hour before the show starts to know what's coming off. And it is a *show,* it plays like that."[119]

The critic-composer Greg Sandow, at the time writing for *The Village Voice,* approached Floyd at a subsequent event, figurative hat in hand, and apologized to the composer on behalf of all his colleagues for Henahan's review. Sandow believed that, had *Willie Stark* premiered in New York instead of Houston, Henahan would not have mounted such an attack; but with Gockley's and Floyd's presumed hubris at stealing New York's thunder for a week, the composer became a convenient sacrificial lamb.

Nonetheless, on May 3, sets and costumes were packed for Washington, DC. In the brief interim, returning to New York after opening, Prince wrote Floyd on April 27, thanking him for his words in the dedication to the work, and fulminating against press abuse. He also had a fair amount of fine-tuning in mind for the Kennedy Center. Perhaps they could end act 1 with Anne's exit, and attach the rally to act 2; change a little staging in the mailbag sequence; have Sugar Boy deliver some lines without the stutter; think of making a larger cut in the encounter of Anne and Sadie in the final scene; and change some lighting and exits after Willie's final aria.[120]

Prince began Washington brushups on May 6. Floyd felt that his function was to make cuts totaling another twenty minutes. Finally, though, when

John DeMain suggested one too many, Floyd balked, and, to his surprise, Prince, the Broadway cut master, applauded. PBS had specified a limit of two hours and twenty-two minutes for the taping, and once they reached that point without the composer sensing damage to his score, he put his foot down.

Houston's premiere had been the only Floyd opening that a substantial family contingent had not attended, owing mainly to Mrs. Floyd's illness; but now Ermine, Billy, and Jane Matheny flew to Washington on May 8, and the reunion with Jona Clarke brought the composer much-needed emotional reinforcement. Eleanor and Red Warren, as well as Stephen Sondheim, sat in the opening night audience at Kennedy Center. As Warren and Floyd walked backstage for their curtain call, the writer repeated what he had told the composer almost three years earlier, "I know why you did what you did."

The Washington press was as good as Houston's had been mixed; The *Washington Post* found the opera "a stunning and evocative visual collaboration."[121] The *New York Daily News* even predicted, "It may be America's answer to *Evita,* and *Willie Stark* has better music."[122] Fellow composer Herman Berlinski wrote as full an appreciation as Floyd had ever received for his willingness to rank communication with an audience before prevailing trends in contemporary music. Finding that the work had kept him "spellbound from the opening to the final curtain," Berlinski pinpointed Floyd's "very carefully selective use" of such devices as "fragmentation of melodic phrases, aphoristic hints of musical ideas" that bound the music to Warren's drama: "This is a truly sophisticated score . . . in essence, eminently American."[123]

Missing only the May 21 performance, Floyd visited his ailing mother for three days in South Carolina. Mrs. Floyd needed to be fed by a nurse-companion, and could tolerate nothing more than baby food. Though emaciated and weakened, she told Floyd that she thought every day of so many things that she wanted to say to him; but his presence apparently made the words lift like mist from her brain. The calamitous tremors, though, did not prevent her from uttering what was, in Floyd's characterization, "about as profane as she ever got": "This is a devil of a way to live."

When the run ended on May 29, the production reassembled in an empty Jones Hall in Houston for three days of PBS taping during June's first week. The Exxon Corporation, together with the Corporation for Public Broadcasting, sponsors of PBS *Great Performances,* had underwritten many of the expenses for *Willie* since the two NOI workshops; and South Carolina ETV and WNET/13 in New York were event producers, with television direction by Brian Large.[124] This project extension added a subplot to the *Willie Stark* experience: Columbia Pictures owned film rights to Warren's story, and the PBS national office waited until forty-eight hours before the broadcast to complete negotiations and give the go-ahead. Because of shortness of time and lingering doubts about the situation, production aired without credits to Warren or the novel; Floyd, whose input at this point involved a few minor nips and tucks, sat with Prince in the hall at taping sessions, with the nationwide broadcast set for September 28.[125]

Despite regional press consensus that the opera had succeeded, dismissal by national journals like *The New York Times* and *Newsweek* poisoned Floyd's emotions. On June 3, Kennedy Center's director of operations, Thomas R. Kendrick, forwarded to the composer the transcript of an on-the-air review by the Washington, DC, media critic Joseph McLellan, also a *Washington Post* reviewer for more than three decades, predicting that *Willie Stark*'s music alone would bring it classic status within a decade.[126]

Before the Houston premiere, Bob Holton had sent a copy of Floyd's libretto and vocal score to the critic Irving Kolodin, charged with profiling the event and the city of Houston for *Saturday Review.* In the quarter-century since he expressed reservations about *Susannah,* Kolodin had come to appreciate Floyd, and he now thought *Willie Stark* "Floyd's best, most mature work," for its "crafty combination of sung and spoken elements," and its interplay of recurring character-defining thematic material.[127]

The Berlinskis, McLellans, and Kolodins wrote for the longer range; in the shorter, Floyd listened to the lying voices of bitterness and depression that repeated the old mantra, "Boy, just go home," now welded to Willie's refrains on that subject. Judy and Hal Prince's redoubt in Majorca became Floyd's home in July's third week. Ermine called almost daily with updates on their mother's condition, and a day earlier than planned, Floyd headed home through London. At the invitation of the Glyndebourne festival director Brian Dickie, whom he had met in Houston, Floyd took the train to Lewes for Peter Hall's production of *Fidelio,* and blanched at seeing the black ties and long gowns of all the other patrons. Critic John Ardoin, who had ridden the same train, cajoled, "Oh don't worry, *you* know who you are."

The curtailment of the Majorcan trip proved providential. On July 18, Ida passed out when Reverend Floyd and Ermine lifted her for bed, and she was sped by ambulance to Trident Hospital in North Charleston. Ermine met Floyd at Charleston airport on July 26, and he spent eight days with the family. Ermine had told him that their mother had been severely depressed for weeks. When they arrived at the hospital the next morning, though Ida was speaking coherently just moments earlier, telling her nurse what an unhappy life she had led, she now acted as though she had no idea who her son was. Floyd recalled: "I don't know whether she was angry at her life, or what; but it was so completely unlike her. She must have known; but I have no idea why she didn't speak to me."

On July 28, Reverend Floyd's sister Doris suffered an asthma attack at a women's club in Dillon, South Carolina. She drove home for her inhaler, but collapsed on her bed, from which she never rose. The next day, Floyd, Ermine, and Billy drove to the hospital to tell Reverend Floyd that Doris had passed in the night. Ida lost consciousness again, resuscitation was attempted, and she was rushed to intensive care. Typical of Parkinson's, the inability to swallow caused her to aspirate bits of food, and she died at 4:15 that afternoon. The family sat in the hospital foyer, with Reverend Floyd eliciting comfort from the nurses. When Ida's body was rolled out on a gurney, he seemed not to notice, and Floyd said, "I think she's left us, Daddy." The minister did not budge for a time. With a nurse on either side, patting his shoulders, it appeared to Ermine and her brother that the focus of attention on their father superseded the loss of his life partner. In days to come, he approached perfect strangers to tell them, "You know, I've lost my wife."

Kay did not join her husband in South Carolina. Ida's funeral and burial were held at Target Church on July 30. Floyd stayed in town until Sunday that week to hear his father preach at Target, after which the entire congregation comforted their minister. Ermine drove her brother to Charleston for his flight back to Houston.

Within the span of a few weeks, death had again scarred Floyd's heart and work. Parkinson's stunted his mother's last six years of life; and now, as the plane winged west, he grieved that he had allowed temporal concerns to interrupt their bond. Her refusal to recognize him at their final encounter seemed proof that she had no idea how much he loved her. He mourned her incapacity for demonstrating affection, and longed to know all that she had not found time or opportunity to say.

17

Falling Down

1981–1986

The journey from *Shirtsleeves* to *Grandboy* to the final version of *Willie Stark* that PBS aired in 1981 took Floyd eleven years. Friends and colleagues had built him up with predictions of a great triumph, but crushing disappointment from its critical reception stole his creative wind. From earliest childhood, his reaction to criticism was never anger, which the family could not tolerate, but rather silent depression, convictions of inadequacy, self-directed anger, and other legacies of his early asthma. He now believed that he had failed Warren, Prince, and Gockley, and this feeling sat atop the slow-burning pyre of incomplete mourning for his mother's death. Not yet alert to the warning signs, he retreated into time-marking and repetition, keeping for the most part to safe activities: teaching, directing, public speaking, receiving honors, visiting his father and Ermine in Holly Hill.

Psychotherapy helped some. He had been involved with Transactional Analysis (TA) at the time he left Tallahassee, and pursued this therapy for a while in Houston. But that old sense of nameless dread had already crept over him with critical assaults on *Bilby's Doll* in 1976. Immersed in her reading on psychiatry, Kay encouraged him to seek out a Jungian therapist in the person of a former Episcopalian rector and frustrated novelist. Self-reflection told Floyd that this healer needed more work than the patient. Floyd had worldwide success on every apparent level, and the new therapist asked repeatedly, "Man, what's the problem? You've got everything!" After no more than six months of this, Floyd left Jung to Kay. More good came from an outpouring of sympathy from friends and colleagues on his mother's death, beginning with Hal Prince's letter from Majorca.[1]

By the end of August, Floyd was in Chicago holding Houston Opera Studio auditions for singers, coaches, accompanists, and composers; and Craig Bohmler combined the latter three skills. The studio needed two mezzo-sopranos that year and had already engaged Stella Zambalis. Susanne Mentzer, working as a receptionist in the Houston Grand Opera offices, heard of the remaining vacancy from a friend. If she could get to Dallas, where Floyd was judging Metropolitan Opera auditions that week, she might stand a chance of doing something for the company besides clerking.[2]

Mentzer did find Floyd in Dallas, and his demeanor toward her was as friendly and courtly as ever. Like all hopeful singers, she expected his response: "We'll let you know." Floyd moved on to Toronto, on NEA/OMT business. The Canadian Opera Company's (COC) general director, Lotfi Mansouri, knew of HGO's success with composer-librettist workshops, and wanted such a program at COC. By August 29, Floyd was hearing singers in New York and wrote Gockley his impressions of Mentzer. When the letter crossed her desk, she stared at the return address, knowing that it most likely held the key to her future. Though in no sense disposed to crime, but acting only as an anxious young artist, she later laughed to recall taking the letter home and steaming it open, finding good and bad news: "I should never have done that, because Floyd had written, 'I guess we'll take her. She's not really what I'd hoped, but we'll take her.'"[3]

THE San Diego Opera performed *Susannah* on September 25, 27, 30, and October 3, with Floyd directing and Christopher Keene conducting Patricia Craig (Susannah), Richard Cassilly (Sam), Melvin Lowery (Little Bat), and Samuel Ramey's first outing with Blitch. Despite the basso's withdrawal from *Bilby's Doll* five years earlier, he now left the composer with overwhelmingly positive impressions. Ramey had first encountered Floyd's music while studying at Wichita State University in the late sixties with Arthur Newman, who in turn had sung Elder McLean in City Opera's 1956 *Susannah;* and any young bass-baritone of the last forty years was bound to be a Norman Treigle fan. After early successes in Metropolitan Opera auditions, at City Opera and HGO, Ramey was a natural for Blitch; but as he began to learn the role for San Diego, he found the revival scene heights and depths more demanding than anything he'd sung: "After all the shouting, you have to come back to that very *cantabile* piece where he tells Susannah of his loneliness. [Floyd] covers the whole bass voice."[4]

Before this, Ramey had never met a working composer, and approached Floyd with trepidation; yet coaching and directing young singers had given Floyd therapeutic insights into his own troubling life and career experiences. Ramey recalled his relief: "He is such a nice, sweet man, he puts you at ease immediately. Before staging, he coached me a little in a studio. He was a joy to work with, he'd reminisce about past productions and singers, and as a director he was terrific! When I told people I was doing my first Blitch with him directing, they looked dubious, but he was so flexible, never fretted, always let singers make suggestions, and listened to any problems we had."

Floyd's time and stamina were tested when he received South Carolina's highest civic honor, the Order of the Palmetto, which required his presence in Columbia the day before *Susannah* opened in San Diego. Governor Richard Wilson Riley would present the award, with officials of South Carolina Educational Television and Exxon attending a reception at the governor's mansion. A limousine gathered Floyd up after dress rehearsal on September 23 and hurtled him to Los Angeles for an overnight flight. After a dawn arrival at Columbia, another car ferried him to the governor's mansion, where he slept from four a.m. until just before the presentation, between 5:30 and 7 on the evening of August 24.

Ermine drove their father from Holly Hill for a tour of the governor's mansion, the award ceremony, and a few words with Floyd. Reverend Floyd's elder brother G. R., the family member capable of puncturing his brother's ministerial facade, had instructed him, "You tell Carlisle that I said you should be proud of him." The composer was whisked back to the airport and flown back to San Diego overnight, to make *Susannah*'s opening on September 25.

The PBS nationwide telecast on September 28 had its own gala aspect, and Floyd took his *Susannah* cast to San Diego's affiliate studio to watch. Perhaps intuiting Floyd's still-raw feelings about this entire experience, Ramey recalled, "It was so much fun to sit there and watch him react. There may have been a few emotional moments, but it was such a fantastic production and great performance. He wanted me to do Willie at some point, there was talk about a Houston revival. He said, 'It's probably on the high side for you, but I'll send you a score. Where it would be a problem, I could rewrite things to make it more possible for you.' But the revival never happened."

Hal Prince's telegram awaited Floyd in Houston: "Dear Pal, I know you don't read reviews, but listen to me: this morning's newspaper reviews are wild raves and you deserve it. Love, Hal."[5]

The *New York Times* staff media critic John J. O'Connor covered the event. Despite the droning arguments of others about Floyd's risky joining of musical theater and opera, O'Connor judged *Willie Stark* a splendid television experience and offered encouragement, in part *because of* Prince at the director's helm, and Warren's and Floyd's quasi-mythical protagonist.[6]

Even rival composers found much to praise, like William Mayer, whose setting of James Agee's *A Death in the Family* had run the gauntlet of OMT's Minneapolis workshop. After thanking Floyd for his role in developing that process, he praised *Willie:* "The poetry is a joy, something you hardly dare hope for in opera! Some of those mystic orchestral clusters were wonderfully evocative, bringing one back through the reaches of time. . . . Things breathed!"[7]

Edward Thomas, composer of *Desire under the Elms,* which Floyd had seen in 1978, wrote that he considered *Willie Stark* "truly a tour de force—a total experience into which one becomes more deeply immersed and involved as the piece progresses to its . . . climactic ending. When it was over, I called Joe Masteroff and we . . . both agreed that this marvelous production could only help opera in general in America. What better composer than you to represent the rest of us in this wonderful showcase?"[8]

ON OCTOBER 19, Floyd wrote Warren, apologizing for not having had a chance to bid him and Eleanor a proper goodbye after the Kennedy Center events. He hoped that the Warrens had seen the opera's telecast and, in a rare burst of self-congratulation, allowed, "I thought it was a superb realization of the opera on film and in many important ways more effective than on the stage. What all of us wanted to achieve was a new look for opera on television, and I think that was brilliantly achieved, thanks to [television director] Brian Large. . . . The response . . . has been remarkable and has made me more than ever aware of the extraordinary power of the medium."[9]

Floyd and Ermine attended Kennedy Center Honors on December 6, saluting the careers of Count Basie, Cary Grant, Helen Hayes, Jerome Robbins, and Rudolf Serkin.

The South Caroliniana librarian Thomas Johnson had secured Floyd's participation in a Warren symposium on the University of South Carolina campus. Warren wrote on January 30 that he would not be attending this event, but repeated his invitation to Floyd to visit at some future date.

The symposium, sponsored by the university's Institute of Southern Studies, took place on February 26 and 27, 1982. Floyd arrived in Columbia with an extra suitcase stuffed with correspondence, family papers, and programs for his South Caroliniana archive, which was being inaugurated with a six-week exhibition on *Willie Stark.* After visits to Holly Hill and North, he returned to Columbia in snow on February 26, and explained to symposium attendees his operatic adaptation of *All the King's Men,* using PBS footage, then flew back to Houston.

New York City Opera revived its 1971 *Susannah* production for single performances in the spring and fall seasons of 1982. On March 30, Bruce Ferden conducted Lou Galterio's restaging of Robert Lewis's production, with Faith Esham (Susannah), Samuel Ramey (Blitch), and John Stewart (Sam). Beverly Sills dug the production out of mothballs for the first-ever presentation of sign language interpretation in a New York opera performance. "*Susannah* is a great choice," she told the press, with signing in mind: "important words, strong plot. . . . And you don't get . . . 45 'addios' before the tenor finally leaves."[10]

Yet the single performance stimulated critic Andrew Porter to write an overdue appreciation of Floyd, whom he deemed the creator of "a national repertory . . . with a commitment that rivals Smetana's in Bohemia or Britten's in Britain." Porter thought Floyd's new *Willie Stark* "a dexterous and accomplished piece," and pondered with elegant understatement how Floyd's operas could excite audiences but leave so many critics cold.[11]

A month later, on April 21, City Opera toured *Susannah* to the Chandler Pavilion in Los Angeles. Donal Henahan took a gratuitous dig at City Opera and, by association, at Floyd and *Susannah,* citing the company's "traditional lower-income audience."[12] From June 3 through 6, Central Opera Service held its national conference in Miami, hosted by Greater Miami Opera and New World Festival of the Arts, with the theme "The Stage Director in the Eighties, The Educator, The Composer."—All of these functions were Floyd strengths, and he directed the company's *Of Mice and Men.* On the afternoon of June 5, he sat on a panel with singers Evelyn Lear and Thomas Stewart and fellow composers John Corigliano and Robert Ward. At Dade County Auditorium on June 15, 17, 19, and 21, *Of Mice and Men* was conducted by Richard Buckley and featured William Neill (Lennie), Brent Ellis (George), Riccardo Calleo (Curley), and Elizabeth Knighton (Curley's Wife). A convention of music critics buzzed at the same time, and the company fretted over the journalist Tim Smith, reputed to hate everything. Floyd thought that days spent with assembled critics sounded like a weekend in hell; and at his interview with Smith, he began by asking whether the latter liked his colleagues. The two men knew at once that they would get along when Smith replied, "No, not really."

Both local newspapers loved the opera and Floyd's direction; but everyone at Greater Miami Opera quailed at the beginning of Tim Smith's review, which opened with a description of Ward's new opera *Minutes till Midnight* as "a lame venture," but proceeded to pronounce *Of Mice and Men* a gratifying total experience. Smith highlighted Floyd's "perfectly constructed libretto," its "musical consistency and dramatic cohesiveness," which had "the intrinsic sense of theater."[13]

SPRING AND SUMMER Houston Opera Studio auditions brought Norman Treigle's daughter Phyllis Susannah into the organization, and she remained until spring 1985. On July 24, Kay's father, Guy Wilton Reeder, died of prostate cancer in Jacksonville, and Floyd, Kay, and her mother attended the funeral in Haynesville, Louisiana. The composer mused about his in-laws as "two very strange people who I cannot imagine having a real relationship with anyone."

That fall Hal Prince became chairman of the National Opera Institute board. He asked Floyd to judge the International American Music Competition for vocalists on September 25, sponsored by the Rockefeller Foundation and held at Carnegie Hall. The conductor Maurice Abravanel, and singers Phyllis Bryn-Julson, Peter Pears, Judith Raskin, Elisabeth Schwarzkopf, and William Warfield comprised the rest of the rather intimidating bank of assessors. The composer Ned Rorem addressed the foundation on the problem of the vanishing recitalist. Eleven aspirants had been whittled down to three finalists: the American sopranos Margaret Cusack and Diana Walker-Leuck, and the Scottish baritone Henry Herford, who eventually took the prize. Afterward, on their way out to the street, Rorem proposed to Floyd that they write librettos for each other; but at that moment such activity was light years removed from Floyd's wish list.

Three days later, Beverly Sills announced that thirty-five-year-old Christopher Keene, an ardent Floyd booster, would become City Opera's artistic supervisor and Sills's second in command. City Opera's single fall *Susannah* on October 28 featured Sharon Daniels (Susannah), Samuel Ramey (Blitch), William Neill (Sam), and William Livingston (Little Bat). The *Times* called the opera "a mixture of implausible bombast and occasional musical insight."[14]

Floyd's renown as a director had spread: from Nebraska came a call from Mary Robert, Opera Omaha's newly appointed administrator, offering him a production of Gounod's *Faust,* to open on February 8, 1983. As with Philadelphia's *Tales of Hoffmann,* he turned it down, in part because of the work's supernatural elements; but even more, the "pants role" of Siébel troubled him. He favored a more realistic production style, and asked whether Robert might cast a young boy to give the opera an earthier feel; she was not interested.

Floyd's 1982 began its final crawl to 1983 with Kennedy Center Honors over the weekend of December 3. Floyd met President Ronald Reagan at the White House, before he and Ermine attended the award ceremony for George Abbott, Lillian Gish, Benny Goodman, Gene Kelly, and Eugene Ormandy.

Floyd shied away from much composing in the eighties, but attracted another level of student through UH and the Houston Opera Studio. He still felt that he knew more about teaching piano than any other musical discipline. Craig Bohmler, who had a bachelor's degree from North Texas State University, entered UH to begin a master's in piano with Floyd. Bohmler played with hand and finger positions that caused him to work much harder than necessary, and at first Floyd made him play nothing but Hanon exercises. After completing his master's degree in 1980, Bohmler took a year off from academics to focus on private piano study with Floyd, who, in the fall of 1981, put in a good word about him with the studio's Jean Mallandaine. Bohmler auditioned with the entire second act of Mozart's *Le nozze di Figaro* and act 1 of Janáček's *Kátya Kabanová,* was hired for the studio, and stayed for three years. His continued lessons with Floyd brought a pianistic epiphany, and he went from playing early Haydn sonatas to the formidable Liszt B-minor Sonata, giving two or three annual recitals. Floyd described Bohmler as "an authentic virtuoso, highly gifted, a real go-getter," and asked him to help edit *Willie Stark*'s vocal score.

Bohmler's interest in composition—musical theater rather than opera—led him to even greater success than the keyboard. In 1989, Floyd called Paulette Haupt-Nolen, wife of Timothy Nolen and musical director at the O'Neill Center, which scheduled a workshop of Bohmler's *Gunmetal Blues.* Contacts generated by that experience led in turn to more than one hundred professional productions in the United States and Canada. His next show, *Enter the Guardsman*—based on the same Molnar play in which Floyd had acted in 1949—scored an even greater success as International Musical of the Year in Denmark in 1996. It played London's West End in the fall of 1998 and received an Olivier Award nomination as best musical. Bohmler testifies, "Carlisle will always be The Man, The Master. I can call him, and do, any time, and he's always there with helpful suggestions, and just to talk through things."[15]

In 1989, another such talent to approach Floyd was the pianist-conductor-composer Robin Stamper, who had already earned his bachelor's at the Eastman School of Music and a master's at Juilliard. Living in Florida and intending to pursue a doctorate, Stamper began work with Edward Kilenyi at Florida State University, and finished ABT (all but treatise) in the 1988–1989 academic year. He accompanied FSU opera productions, including a *Susannah* revival, and Leonard Mastrogiacomo recommended him to Floyd, leading to a Houston Opera Studio audition. Stamper sight-read Ravel's *Gaspard de la nuit* and, another acid test, great chunks of Strauss's *Der Rosenkavalier.*

Stamper's sheer pianism impressed Floyd, but the committee—HGO chorus master Richard Bado, Jim Ireland, John DeMain, and Floyd—judged Stamper unprepared for the studio, though they wanted to give him experience that would guide him there. As a first step, he became the staff pianist for Texas Opera Theater, began lessons with Floyd, and later worked as the coach and accompanist for HGO main stage productions. After advanced study with so many teachers, Stamper's main technical problem was tension, a lethal combination of, as he puts it, "my arms and things going on in my head. . . . Carlisle's technical approach was like doing pushups with the fingers: you use the muscles and tendons, and the underneath part of your hand, the pulling muscles. So I curved my fingers, which are very wide, to stay off the black keys, and learned how to articulate, just by necessity. But Carlisle was so interested in people and personalities. Had I worked with him as a younger person, maybe he could have gotten something into my noggin about why I was so freaked out about playing from memory, and gotten me over it. I learned so much from him about being a person, about self-esteem, which you carry with you wherever you go, including your music. Many teachers approach musicianship based on the style of the time, or what they think the composer thinks; but for me, it was just him helping me figure myself out that freed up other things. If he had wanted to, he could have been a psychiatrist. A man so quiet, genteel, and polite, but so smart, so smart about *me*! His priority was figuring out what made me so nervous and tense, so he went through a layer that nobody had ever gotten to before."[16]

Floyd thought that Stamper may have been the single best keyboard talent to enter his studio, a virtuoso for whom nothing was too difficult. Together they worked through Liszt's B Minor, Beethoven's *Appassionata,* and Chopin's *Ballades.* Stamper recalled, "We actually did work, but there was lots of talk." Both Bohmler and Stamper had interests in composing, but Floyd "only dealt with that in a very offhand manner."[17]

ON JANUARY 4, 1983, Hal Prince telegraphed an invitation to Floyd to the Kennedy Center on February 13 to receive, together with Boris Goldovsky and Leonard Bernstein, the National Opera Institute's highest honor, its Award for Service to American Opera. After Houston Opera Studio auditions in Chicago, New York, Boston, and Dallas, Floyd boarded a plane for New York on February 11, with a transfer through Washington; but New York seemed to have other weekend plans: the "megalopolitan storm," as newspaper headlines called it, dumped 17.6 inches of snow on the city. After checking into a room at the Mayflower, Floyd telephoned a friend, Patrick O'Shea, a producer affiliated with Miami's New World Festival who knew everyone in the culture and media worlds. In Floyd's words, O'Shea was "a sort of gadfly, but very bright, very charming, with a silver tongue." He had just been invited for dinner with Leonard Bernstein, whose latest opera, *A Quiet Place,* was about to begin rehearsing for its world premiere in Houston in June. O'Shea thought the two men might discover they had much in common.

Despite their inevitable pairing as "crossover" composers working to forge an authentically American musical theater, Floyd had avoided meeting Bernstein; but now, stuck in a blizzard, he did not wish to offend his friend. Floyd and O'Shea arrived at Bernstein's apartment at the Dakota, talked to his children, and waited forever. When Bernstein finally emerged, he looked haggard, and, typically, much smaller than Floyd expected. O'Shea introduced his guest, and Bernstein flipped, "Oh yeah, you're like the opera-writing factory."[18]

Floyd bit his tongue. The party headed out to a Chinese restaurant on Broadway, and Bernstein spent most of the meal role-playing the rabbi while discussing Judaism with a friend of his son's who had joined them. When the waiter arrived, Bernstein put his diatribe on hold to declare that he would not accept anything off the menu and that he expected the chef to fix him something special. The menu was fine for Floyd and O'Shea. The rest of the evening proceeded in much the same fashion; Bernstein monopolized the two boys and Floyd and O'Shea conducted their own private conversation. On their way out of the restaurant, Bernstein threw his arms around Floyd, stepped back, rolled his eyes: "Can you *imagine*? I have to be in *Houston* for two or three weeks? By the way, Carlisle, where are you from?"

At least it differed from his encounter with Samuel Barber, whose response had telegraphed the thought, "How soon can you leave?" But Bernstein failed to exude his trademark charm, and Floyd left feeling that he had crossed paths with a world-class egotist. The next morning, February 13, Floyd caught the morning's last flight before snow closed La Guardia, and made it to the Kennedy Center to receive the NOI award.

TWO YEARS HAD PASSED without Floyd feeling the urge to compose again, but Bob Holton was ever an eager godfather. In July 1982 Dickinson College in Carlisle, Pennsylvania, commissioned Floyd, for an honorarium of $7,500 plus transportation and housing, to write a dedication piece for the new Emil R. Weiss Center for the Arts. Signing the contract on October 30 brought a first payment of $2,500. His only other obligation was delivery of the score by March 21, 1983, at which time the balance of $5,000 would be paid. Floyd or Holton/Belwin-Mills were to provide the college with a signed manuscript reproduction for display in the school's archives.[19]

The college requested a song cycle of twenty minutes' duration on a text of Floyd's choosing. He had long admired mezzo-soprano Frederica von Stade, who proved unavailable for the premiere date; but Suzanne Mentzer's talent, charisma, and untiring race to avoid being fired had impressed him, and he now chose her as the new work's first interpreter.

Floyd and Holton had long been devotees of Emily Dickinson's poetry, agreeing that her greatest gift lay in elevating the everyday. In fall 1972 the composer and Kay had driven to New England to see the turning leaves and visit Dickinson's home and grave in Amherst, Massachusetts, where her white dress still hangs in a closet and her writing desk is preserved as she used it. The insights and wit of her poetry have made her a favorite of composers for more than a century, including, besides Floyd, Ernst Bacon, William Bolcom, John Duke, Arthur Farwell, Lee Hoiby, Ned Rorem, Vincent Persichetti, and Aaron Copland. Floyd now set about assembling a forty-minute tapestry of eighteen poems, prose fragments, and excerpts from Dickinson's letters, each focusing on a single theme. The result, *Citizen of Paradise,* is a soul map of poet and composer that touches on autobiographical aspects of both. The cycle's emotional road travels from instinctual brilliance and childlike simplicity to the serenity of age contemplating its inevitable end. Frequent turnouts create opportunities for wry, wistful, heartbreaking observations on the human condition.

Compared to an opera libretto, Dickinson's "concentration . . . forces you to either make your point or get away from it in a hurry."[20] The writing flowed, and Floyd took on average three days to devise each song's scheme, and one for composition. Between a one-line prologue and an epilogue repeating and completing this initial statement excerpted from poem 441—"This Is My Letter to the World That Never Wrote to Me"—Floyd constructed five themed sections.[21] The initial line, preceded by two measures of bell-like unison C, *Andante poco sostenuto,* intimates the C Major triad with passing tones of D and B-flat, leading to a D Major/Minor resolution.

Floyd's section 1, "Self," has two movements, the first drawn from a letter of April 25, 1862 (letter 261) to Dickinson's lifelong friend Thomas Wentworth Higginson, a Unitarian minister, poet-essayist, abolitionist, spiritualist, and early champion of women's rights. Dickinson sketches her upbringing and schooling, with tantalizing clues to her own enigmas.

Beginning and ending on unison D, Floyd uses sophisticated polytonality, *Allegro animato ma non troppo,* with jagged climbing sixteenth notes in a breathless childlike patter, yet cleverly outlining and skirting the D Major triad with amiable dissonance. In a more lyrical coda, "I Would Like to Learn," the tempo slows to *Lento mosso,* and an augmentation of his "climbing" motive in E Major, ending with an abrupt return to the rushed final question, with octaves of D and its high fifth, A.

"I'm Nobody" (poem 288) follows, *Allegro giocoso.* In 6/8, the song gains structure from a hopping sixteenth-eighth syncopation in accompaniment and vocal setting, and, despite unexpected leaps, never veers too far from D Major/Minor.

Floyd's grouping "Friendship and Society" has four parts, beginning with poem 1568, "To See Her Is a Picture," characterizing the notion of a bosom friend. A sedate chordal accompaniment in B Minor/Major, *Andante semplice,* suggests the growth of maturity. With longer, more sustained melodic lines shaped by Dickinson's speech rhythms, each phrase begins with a sixteenth-eighth syncopation, on which the song's seventeen measures are variations. Word painting and emotional high points echo in contrasting stepwise melody, arching upward in intervals of sixths, sevenths, and octaves.

From an 1852 letter to sister-in-law Susan Huntington Dickinson come pungent and poignant memories of a childhood—certainly for Floyd—filled with conflicts over religion. Anchored in E-flat, *Adagio sostenuto,* with frequent changes of meter from 5/4 to 4/4, 6/4, 8/8, 7/4, the setting resembles some of Floyd's earlier songs and dance scores. A solemn churchly feeling emanates from organlike bass pedals, *ostinato* chimes in the treble, alternating with long-limbed interludes inspired by the vocal line's rhythmic elements. Then, at "The Bells Are Ringing," embellished chimes grow urgent.

Next, from a letter of 1880 to Samuel Bowles, the author, social reformer, and owner-editor of the *Springfield Republican,* Dickinson apologizes for giddy behavior. Floyd's teasing romp, *Poco allegro e scherzando,* centers on G Major, 4/4 alternating with 2/4. Intervals of the fourth, major seventh, octaves, and ninths stud the vocal line, with the opening motif repeated in diminution, in B Minor/Major, at "I Am Sorry." Each of the poet's resolutions to behave better are chattery afterthoughts.

"Friendship and Society" closes with poem 401, "What Soft—Cherubic Creatures," again affirming that the world could use a bit more humor and a bit less starch. In C Minor/Major, 6/8, *Allegretto,* Floyd seizes on Dickinson's notion of women as angelic, crafting two stanzas of transparent, delicate syncopation. In the third, rests and *staccati* of the initial melody are filled and smoothed, until "Brittle Lady," which completes the circle with a light heart.

Floyd delineated four phases of "Love," the first from an 1878 letter to Otis P. Lord, instigator and reciprocator of Dickinson's platonic love, and written in both third and second persons. Floyd's treatment, *Andante, appassionato ma largamente,* in 3/4 and 4/4, makes an intense breathless confession in stacked E major/minor, with sixteenth-eighth note syncopations in half tones in accompaniment and vocal line, like catches in the throat.

Floyd's next is his single duplication with Copland's *Twelve Poems,* poem 47, "Heart! We Will Forget Him!" In urgent 3/4, *Allegro poco inquieto ma sostenuto,* Floyd underlines the poem's initial determination—itself a kind of extended oxymoron—with the dark key of C-sharp Minor, and agitated triplets in most vocal measures, set against longer accompanimental note values. At "When you have done," the singer's legato declaration fights an ostinato B-flat in right hand octaves, and D Minor triads in the left, all leading back to a chesty intonation of the final line, leaving no doubt as to the depth of the poet-singer's remembrance.

Poem 587, "Empty My Heart," displays love's third form, global and eternal. Floyd's musical equivalent is a galloping 9/8, *Allegro con slancio* (impetuosity), in A Major/Minor. As introduction, a rushing octuplet figure foreshadows the next measure's vocal entrance. Throughout, the singer's held notes have triplet then duplet underpinning in the accompaniment. Accumulation of volume and tempo calls on the mezzo-soprano's high A for her final word "picked."

"Love" concludes with the swooning, desolate, dark world of Poem 599, "There Is a Pain So Utter." With alternating 3/4 and 4/4, *Largo mosso, ben misurato,* a simple chantlike intonation proceeds in half- and whole-steps, communicating both numbed senses and suspense, until an upward leap of a tenth between "upon it" and "As one within." Subsiding again to emotional torpor, the line descends stepwise and rumbling, taking the mezzo down to low G.

Section Three, "Nature," begins with an 1856 letter to Mrs. J. G. Holland,[22] praising God for creating a world that Dickinson insisted could not be bettered by human notions of heaven, and for "fading things, and things that do *not* fade." In reasonably consistent A Major, Floyd begins in gentle 3/4, *Allegretto e piacevole,* with a folklike legato line. Through ties across bar lines, the accompaniment injects agitation, mirrored by modulation to enharmonic flat keys, and back again to A. "Don't tell him," which Floyd marks *quasi parlando* (almost spoken), is a confidence in short dotted rhythms, preparing a recapitulation and soaring extension, *più largamente,* of the opening melody.

Poem 214, "From Tankards Scooped in Pearl," illuminates different forms of intoxication. The composer tone paints with gentle hiccups, in octaves, in lilting 6/8, *Allegro non troppo e grazioso,* around D Major, mirrored by the singer on a seventh slide down on the word "liquor." As inebriation heightens in the middle section, the accompaniment gathers chromatic density. Just before "Till Seraphs swing," Floyd applies an almost identical restatement of the opening theme to the last stanza.

Poem 1640, "Take All Away from Me," is a kind of artist's credo. Stacking tonic B-flat Major and dominant F, the song begins as straightforward declaration in 3/4, *Allegro poco largamente,* with leaps of a minor seventh and then a ninth up to top space G on the word "ecstasy," Dickinson's sine qua non. The accompaniment throughout has a running nine- or tenfold figure on the first beat, with chordal resolution on beats two and three, to which syncopated sixteenth-eighth figures are added. By the last two lines the piano moves incessantly, with running figures eventually filling all three beats, beneath the sustained voice soaring up to G and F on the word "poverty."

"Death and Solitude" consists of four contemplations, the first, poem 390, "It's Coming—The Postponeless Creature," echoing James Auslander's *Death Came Knocking.* Dickinson centers on death's inevitability, and Floyd's song revolves around C, *Andante mosso, ben misurato,* in 4/4. The basic accompanimental device is an ostinato knocking figure of the lowest octave of C in the left hand, a slur up to D-flat on the offbeat, and a will 'o the wisp thirty-second/sixteenth figuration in the second measure, blurring tonality. The vocal entrance is low, almost whispered, as the piano's repeated figures reveal Death like smoke becoming solid. Melodic half steps and tritones lend a sense of dread, with alternate augmentation, diminution, and fragmentation of melodic "cells" bearing the words forward in inevitable long notes, D-flat/C, "to God."

The climactic song, Dickinson's harrowing narration of her mother's death, comes from an 1882 letter

(779) to Mrs. J. G. Holland. As surely as anything he had done to this point, or would do after, this dramatic scena serves as Ida Fenegan Floyd's epitaph.

An eerie two-bar introduction, *Adagio sostenuto e mesto,* prefigures Floyd's consistent rhythmic device, halves or quarter-notes followed by triplets, or sixteenth/eighth combinations, opening onto a bleak musical plain of wide-spaced half- and whole-note ostinati death knells circling G Minor. As illusory hope for the mother's recovery builds, the rhythm noted above accelerates or slows like a faulty heartbeat, and the tonality shifts to distant regions of E-flat Minor and C-sharp Minor. A description of lifting the elderly patient from bed to chair initiates an increase in tempo, leading to a single low B, a suspension of activity; then a slow downward slide for the mother's penultimate gasps. "Don't leave me" is a sudden outcry over deep bass chords, subsiding into chilly unison octaves and treble chords, with an occasional underpinning of open fifths in the bass. The singer whispers Dickinson's evocation of infinity, pianissimo, on high G-sharp and G. The benediction, "Mother," leaps from high B-flat down a tenth; and for coda, a two-measure augmentation of the introductory theme ends on the open G-D (God?) of the G Minor chord, beneath "What a Name!"

With an increasing sense of resignation and philosophical calm, Floyd next merges three short letter extracts to family and a friend, the combination of which attempts to reconcile fear, resignation, and ecstasy.[23] With accompaniment entirely in bass clef until the final seven measures, and with great rolled chords throughout, Floyd's setting emerges from an abyss of C Minor/Major, *Lento mosso.* Although intervals and harmonies differ from the preceding song, he reuses the long note-triplet or -duplet pattern. Supporting the vocal entrance with half tones and tritone intervals prominent throughout, he writes a final lyrical arioso for "The Small Heart Cannot Break," ecstatic B Minor resolving to C Major.

And, finally, poem 1695, "There Is a Solitude of Space," with Dickinson's exquisite positing of "finite infinity." Flirting with F Major and A Minor in 6/8, 3/8, 4/8, and 5/8, *Lento sostenuto,* Floyd's pianistic scope evokes solitude and space, and leaps from high unison octaves to deep bass fundaments. This supports a fairly straightforward lyrical vocal line, with intervals of sixths, octaves, and tenths yielding to the final statement's repeated middle Cs and As, and gently shifting harmonies beneath.

All that remains is to repeat and complete the Prologue/Epilogue, poem 441. Considering the critical reception of his music for *Willie Stark,* it also serves as the composer's envoi, with its request to the reader/listener to "Judge tenderly—of me." With extremes of life and death things of the past, the Prologue's C-bells greet us like old friends. The device persists throughout the song, accompanying a wide-ranging melody of poignant sixths and octaves. Side trips to A-flat, E-flat, G, and D Minor function as passing backward glimpses, coming to rest in unambiguous C Major—after a sneaky pause on B Major at the word "tenderly," one of the composer's sparse uses of melisma.

Floyd entered and fully inhabited Dickinson's world with *Citizen of Paradise.* The cycle's concentration and sophistication are most reminiscent of his work in the *Episodes* of the sixties, and serve as reliable barometers of his internal world. The Belwin-Mills vocal score—never offered for public sale—bears no dedication; but Floyd later offered this honor to his longtime friend and publisher-agent, Robert Holton. Floyd delivered the songs to Mentzer piecemeal, and she worked through them in private coaching sessions with the composer and Craig Bohmler:

> I'm a better sight reader now than I was then, but I felt so inadequate—and not that he made me feel that way, but I felt this overwhelming responsibility to get it right with the composer. His melodies are the kind that give you goose bumps and make you cry. What else could you want from music? And you can't even explain why that is. The first important thing about his vision was the idea of its being a monodrama, which I really liked, being such a stage creature. The whole thing of writing a letter to herself, to the world, is how it starts and ends; and those are the two hardest things, very exposed and fragile-sounding. He'd come in with song after song, and say, "I thought of this during

> the night." The only thing that made me sad was not always accommodating whatever he wanted, but he was very easy about changing things. These songs are more emotionally draining than anything else; I think the last two are among the most brilliant songs ever written. His whole depiction of relationships, nature, loss, the death song: really intense to work on. I'd stay seated, very contained, just trying to keep a lid on, until the final outburst. I think he really captured that New England propriety—and antipropriety! His priorities were more interpretive than musical. He talked about Emily; her poetry and life meant a lot to him. More than about the text, we'd discuss the time in her life when she wrote a particular poem, in regard to her reclusiveness. It was up to me to work out the texts; and they mean something different to me, now that I'm older. She was a wise soul in a young body, and now I have an older body. I have to play young when I do them, and still keep the wise soul.[24]

Dickinson College planned to award Floyd an honorary doctorate; but before leaving for Pennsylvania, he received the National Opera Institute Award for Service to American Opera, and a citation from the National Federation of Music Clubs, in Columbus, Ohio. He, Mentzer, and Bohmler arrived in Carlisle, Pennsylvania, on May 18 for rehearsals, followed by Ermine and Billy Matheny and Bob Holton. The May 21 premiere in the Rubendall Recital Hall at the Weiss Center delighted the campus audience and invited guests. Mentzer had a white dress made that duplicated Dickinson's own that Floyd had seen, and someone located a writing desk similar to the original in Amherst. Mentzer even wore her hair close to her head and parted in the center, in the style of the two known photographs of the poetess. Floyd devised minimal staging, with a window frame, inkwell, and pen. Mentzer sat at the desk, stood in front of or behind it, or sat in the chair off to one side, making a few crosses and minimal hand gestures; Bohmler and his piano were placed off to one side onstage.

The press seems not to have taken notice of the event. The next day, the chair of the Department of Music, Dr. Truman C. Bullard, and President Banks presented Floyd with his doctorate, *honoris causa,* and the accompanying pink-hooded academic regalia.

ON APRIL 2, Chicago Opera Theatre, directed by Arthur Masella and conducted by Mark Flint, presented the local *Of Mice and Men* premiere, starring Lawrence Cooper (George), William Neill (Lennie), Michael Fiacco (Curley) and Lauren Flanigan (Curley's Wife). A critic for the English periodical *Opera* confessed to being "transported" by Floyd's musical insights "into the heart-breaking, arid world of dispossessed men."[25]

At spring's end, the composer celebrated his fifty-seventh birthday. A cherished gift arrived in the form of a letter from Judith Moore, Catherine Murphy's estranged daughter in Berkeley, California. She confessed that he still felt like family to her. She felt herself somehow "marinated in the broth" of his kindness. Floyd had been the first person to say that he loved her, told her that she had pretty ears, that being intelligent and female were compatible; he had given her Eudora Welty, Robert Penn Warren, Alberto Moravia, Isherwood, innumerable plays, his copies of *The New York Times* and *Theatre Arts.* He had taught her to play two against three rhythms, and to listen to Scriabin. Most important, he taught her the beginnings of trust.[26]

In July Floyd attended *Of Mice and Men,* directed by Cynthia Auerbach, with John DeMain in the pit, at Chautauqua Opera. Lawrence Cooper and William Neill repeated their roles from Chicago, and William Livingstone and Gloria Capone sang the Curleys. Despite the advancing juggernaut of productions, many of which he was asked to direct, and however gratifying the cash flow from Boosey & Hawkes and Belwin-Mills, as well as awards and doctorates, Floyd began to notice a flatness in his emotions, and a vague but pervasive fear and dread. After *Citizen of Paradise,* his desire to write or compose waned and finally withered, and he simply withdrew.

One beacon glimmered from New York's far shore: Christopher Keene, in place as City Opera's music director since January 1, 1983, shoehorned in New York's much-delayed *Of Mice and Men* premiere on October 13. In the parlance of opera professionals

36. Caricature of Floyd, July 29, 1983. By permission of the artist, Patricia Windrow.

responsible for assembling and performing at City Opera, these were still "instant opera" days, with minimal rehearsal, more than two weeks being a luxury. Robert O'Hearn's year-old sets were trucked in from Miami; at least Frank Corsaro directed, and Keene himself conducted. The cast included such stalwarts as Lawrence Cooper (George), William Livingston (Curley), and Carol Gutknecht (Curley's Wife); Corsaro and Robert Moulson as Lennie were Seattle veterans. Unlike his first City Opera experiences, Floyd's function now was only to observe, consult, give interviews, and write an article for the company's *Spotlight;* but he was nervous enough to arrive in the city by October 1 to settle into the Mayflower for the entire rehearsal period; Ermine and Billy Matheny and their daughter Harriett checked in on October 13.

As rehearsals progressed, the psychologically astute Corsaro saw his friend battling old and new demons, many stemming from what the director termed "a typical southern-fried bouillabaisse, something indescribable." Although Floyd spoke of his parents in kindly terms, Corsaro sensed that the composer kept "a very tight hold on their effect and affect."[27] He developed a new theory that fit into any offered thus far: sex is sin, with predictable reflections in the operas. From *Slow Dusk* on—Corsaro might have included *Fugitives'* characters, whom no one knew—Floyd's female protagonists tended to keep sexuality in the shadows and to pay for anything approaching transgression. As Floyd's disaffection and depression accelerated, Corsaro and other close friends saw him racing toward breakdown.

Already in the fallout from *Willie Stark,* Hal Prince also sensed Floyd's internal torture: "You felt that this thing below the skin was very near, that there were demons. Most great artists have them. They're not necessary to creation, but they seem somehow or other to be part of creative life. And southern artists are more likely to have demons than northerners. I don't think the Civil War ever entirely went away. It's that southern gentle sensibility, a part of which is respect for privacy. Carlisle was very sweet, jovial, with not a bitchy bone in his body."[28]

It came as no surprise when the *Times* sent Donal Henahan, who termed the opera "a feeble score" that failed to "do much more than jog along beside the stage action."[29] The critic objected with even greater passion to the presentation of Curley's Wife, the only woman in a work that he thought an antifeminist paean to male bonding, confirming Corsaro's earlier perceptions. A day or so later, Holton asked Floyd whether he'd ever done anything to personally offend Henahan, to which the composer responded with a blank stare and shrug. Yet the barbs drew blood: *Of Mice and Men* had won consistent praise for thirteen years; but now a single poisoned word gained the power to obliterate ten thousand honeyed compliments, and Floyd listened to ancient lying voices.

City Opera performed *Of Mice and Men* just twice more, on October 19 and 27, and never revived the production. Floyd had hoped to meet Elaine Steinbeck, the author's widow, during this Manhattan stay. That she saw a performance is confirmed by her subsequent granting of film rights, should such a venture materialize.

After Floyd returned to Houston on October 18, Henahan remained so exercised that he wrote an editorial using Wagner as a convenient (and conveniently dead) whipping boy, for daring to emphasize drama in opera to the detriment of music (he thought). *Of Mice and Men* underwent a second deconstruction by Henahan, as a species of play with music that he deemed faceless and incidental to the drama. Having devoted more than a thousand words to portraying Floyd as an apostle of opera's impoverishment, Henahan strained credulity with the opening of his penultimate paragraph, "I don't mean to pick on Mr. Floyd."[30]

When asked later whether he was tempted to swear off ever writing again, Floyd responded, "Yes, about once a day." He had grown discouraged at the realization that he had failed to excite others with his personal vision for "a serious American musical theater for our time"; worse, he could not pinpoint why.[31]

Knowing that a new project could generate emotional energy, Frank Corsaro suggested two potential subjects. The first was Harriette Arnow's 1954 novel *The Dollmaker.* Corsaro sensed that it might reawaken Floyd's proven skill at finding melodic musical language for a broad spectrum of human emotion. Arnow set her story in rural Kentucky during World War II, among tobacco farmers and hunters like Sam in *Susannah.* Their lives unfold in rustic cabins without electricity or plumbing, much like the Floyds' in Jordan. Arnow relied heavily on regional dialect and fundamentalist religion, with notes of revival hellfire. In a radically different sense than *Bilby's Doll,* the protagonist Gertie Nevels often feels like a second Susannah: a survivor, also preternaturally skilled at wood carving and whittling. She and daughter Cassie sound much like Lennie and George when they dream of some day owning a neighbor's old house, but are then forced to relocate to Detroit, where life is in most ways far worse.

Corsaro was sanguine enough to call Arnow herself to discuss rights of adaptation; but her final illness had begun, and Corsaro found her "far gone." Floyd gave the book three close readings, thinking it fine, if unsparingly bleak, before realizing that he had already told that story; and David Gockley bestowed the kiss of death on an Arnow project, finding the book "a complete downer."[32]

Corsaro's second temptation came from the pen of Harold Frederic, *The Damnation of Theron Ware,* with its Faustian implications.[33] The protagonist, a Methodist minister in a small upstate New York town, is challenged and ultimately undone by a combination of petty politics and lust in his religious charge. Ware has social and philosophical exchanges with his Catholic counterpart and a local atheist-scientist. Celia, the exotic Irish American organist at the Catholic church, an exponent of Hellenism and free love, seduces Ware emotionally with Chopin. He loses interest in his marriage, and, just short of running away with Celia, is at the last minute rescued by a pair of Methodist fundraisers who convince him to leave the ministry, return to his wife, move with her to Seattle, and take a job in real estate. In any case, Frederic coined his version of illumination with tongue in cheek, coinciding as it does with Ware's downfall and degradation; and the title's damnation is confirmed in the book's final pages: thinking to make a fresh start, Ware fantasizes about winning glory and riches in politics.

Damnation has a curiously modern feel; its realism is expressed in piquant detail. Observations on the Irish, meditations on the nature and uses of religion, incidents of revival meetings and poundings—Frederic calls them "donation parties"—parsonage life, and Ware's regular determinations to leave the ministry, all struck responsive chords in Floyd. Celia's Hellenism—the full realization of potential through pure beauty—bore the imprint of the composer's own quest for independence. Over the next year or so, Floyd read *Theron Ware* six times before putting it aside. He ultimately found Ware unsympathetic, self-congratulatory, and disdainful of his wife. Identification with his own history brought Floyd to equate the tale with his discovery, after *Fugitives,* that even the most intensely personal stories are often unstageworthy.

TOWARD THE END OF 1983, houseguest Bobbi Martin launched a new life and business, but kept an umbilical cord to the Floyds by purchasing a nearby property. Floyd marvels at "that shy creature who would not go anywhere alone, it's a real story of triumph."

Floyd now retreated into something that he knew well and enjoyed when he and Gockley devised a community outreach project with the university, titled "Carlisle Floyd on Opera." This series of lectures on six representative operas featured filmed showings of each. The school was developing a West Houston campus, and, though it meant a fifty-two-mile round trip, Floyd jumped at the chance to introduce others to a medium he knew from the inside out. Previewed on the local Channel 8 "Greenroom" beginning in November, each two-hour lecture occupied one Wednesday evening each month, and on following Thursdays each opera was screened. The first introductory lecture, "The Materials of Opera, A Personal View: The Critical Balance," focused on *Willie Stark.* December brought "How It All Began," with Monteverdi's *L'incoronazione di Poppea.* January 1984 offered "Opera as Comedy: Mozart's *Le nozze di Figaro;* February, "Opera as Tragedy," Verdi's *Otello;* March, Wagner's "Complete Work of Art," *Die Walküre.* The series ended in April with a lecture on "The Realistic Tradition," a discussion of the line from Bizet's *Carmen* to Britten's *Peter Grimes.* The sizeable and enthusiastic audience consisted mainly of adults who could take this as a course for university credit; but attendees were curious and vocal, and Floyd enjoyed the interaction. Many became opera "converts" and HGO season ticket holders.

On December 2, he and Ermine met in Washington for their annual Kennedy Center date; awards this year were presented to Katherine Dunham, Elia Kazan, Frank Sinatra, James Stewart, and Virgil Thomson.

On January 5, the day after his *Figaro* lecture, Floyd took off for Minneapolis–St. Paul. Ed Corn, now Minnesota Opera's executive producer, gave the composer a shot at directing an opera he had not written, and one that actively engaged him, unlike previous offers: Puccini's *Madama Butterfly.* Floyd estimated that he had already directed two dozen productions of *Susannah,* and *Of Mice and Men,* ten.[34]

Frank Corsaro coined a phrase for injecting realism into old stories when he directed *L'incoronazione di Poppea* in Houston: "I'm taking it off the vase." Floyd thought something similar should be done with even as recent an opera as *Butterfly;* remove it from the Hokusai print, so to speak. He would not allow Cio-Cio-San to seem pathetic, and eliminated any display of self-pity on her part. His approach remained nonetheless faithful to the opera's time and setting, and differed by mining each line for maximum content of theatrical gold. By this time, he had seen enough other productions to know what to avoid, and simple logistics glossed over by others had to be addressed. For instance, Puccini anticipated the act 1 entrance of Butterfly's enraged uncle, the Bonze, with four measures of character-driven music, so Floyd devised a positioning of the wedding guests that allowed them to see and react to his approach, thus explaining the music.

Because of the compactness of the rehearsal period, and the premiere set for January 31, he planned his production in far greater detail than with any of his own pieces; and that intricately considered process reveals keys to the overall Floyd ethos. As a writer, he knew that the test of a good libretto lay in its ability to be set to music. He had worked with literary sources from *Susannah* on, always on the lookout for powerful characters in volatile situations that could be externalized. John Luther Long's source novel, David Belasco's dramatic adaptation, and the Italian libretto of Giacosa and Illica did all that and more.

He called his father on the third day of rehearsal to tell him that the temperature was sitting at –23 F.[35] Fortunately, the Radisson Hotel was not much of a sprint to rehearsal, and Minneapolis had installed covered walkways; even so, Floyd made frequent stops to warm nose and ears. In stagings, consistent with his determination to keep the characters unsentimental, honest, and still deeply human and flawed, he differentiated between Butterfly's two distinct faces: the public painted geisha, and the private friend when alone with Suzuki and Pinkerton. He asked his leading lady, Nikki Li Hartliep, to allow the character to be unpleasant, to show irritation.

Floyd's other colleagues included conductor Hal France, tenor Franco Farina (Pinkerton), baritone Lawrence Cooper (Sharpless), mezzo-soprano Stella

Zambalis (Suzuki), and tenor Gary Briggle (Goro). Opening night, January 31, scored a notable success for a company known for its commitment to strong theatrical values; and despite an ambient Minnesota high of 10 degrees, houses were filled. Floyd's press proved that he had accomplished his goals with "a refreshingly direct, unsentimental interpretation."[36]

BACK IN HOUSTON, Floyd gave his *Otello* lecture on February 15. News arrived that Reverend Floyd, after fifty-two years in the ministry, was being gently but firmly retired from his pastorate at Target Methodist. On March 22, Floyd received Houston's award for his outstanding contribution to the performing arts from Mayor Kathryn Whitmire. Ermine again made up for the lack of other family at the ceremony, which was followed by the mayor's ball.

In Tallahassee, FSU had just named its new physics building for the late Harold Richards. His widow Hazel drew up her will with an endowment of fifty thousand dollars for the university's College of Music, in gratitude to Floyd for having brought so much beauty into her life and for having dedicated *Slow Dusk* to her.[37] In Floyd's name, FSU sent Richards a basket of flowers, and in her thank-you note of April 3, she made first contact with the composer since he had moved to Houston eight years earlier.

Though his confidence in new work had dwindled, he had grown restive in the year since *Citizen of Paradise.* At a Houston film festival he saw F. W. Murnau's 1927 silent masterpiece *Sunrise,* and its images thawed enough creative juice to spur tentative research into the film's sources.[38] Floyd tended to business in New York in May's second week: he visited Bob Holton at Belwin-Mills, and Sylvia Goldstein at Boosey & Hawkes, to discuss the possibility of revisiting *The Passion of Jonathan Wade,* and renewing *Susannah* copyright assignment. At the New York Public Library, he also located the literary source of Murnau's *Sunrise,* one of four stories from Hermann Sudermann's *Lithuanian Tales* (1917), "The Journey to Tilsit."[39]

At home in Houston, Floyd nursed a tear in his Achilles tendon, a repeated stress injury from years of tennis, and inactivity sped work on the new subject. "Journey to Tilsit" foreshadowed Theodore Dreiser's *An American Tragedy;* and Murnau's *Sunrise,* subtitled "A Song of Two Humans," echoed it. Novella and film tell the story of a married farmer (Sudermann's fisherman) obsessed with a vampish city woman. The Man, played in the film by George O'Brien, takes the advice of his wicked inamorata, Hollywood's Margaret Livingston, to do away with his wife, played by sweet-natured Janet Gaynor, and run off to the city for a life of carefree debauchery. Man rows Wife across the lake to the nearby village, planning to drown her on the return trip and save himself with a bundle of reeds as a life preserver. He finds, however, that he cannot go through with this dreadful scheme, and in the mad whirl of village festivities, including a church wedding, Man and Wife fall in love again.

Sudermann's original ends in tragedy with the Man himself the drowning victim; but in Murnau's retelling, on the homeward-bound voyage, when a storm comes up, Man wraps Wife in reeds, the boat capsizes, and Man swims to shore. He repudiates his mistress, almost strangles her, and in best cinematic fashion, the wife lives, and the film ends with the rededicated couple embracing at sunrise. Academy Awards were first issued in 1927, and at the 1929 ceremony, *Sunrise* won as best unique and artistic production, and for best cinematography; Janet Gaynor won the first award for best actress in a leading role.

Floyd produced an untitled four-page scenario for a three-act opera, which raised enough encouragement from Gockley for him to begin a complete seventy-two-page libretto. This occupied him for most of a year, with the locale shifted from northern Europe to southern Louisiana between 1890 and 1900.

Unlike anything he had done to date, Floyd wrote the entire draft, its working title *Seth,* in short lines with simple, regular rhyme schemes. Act 1, scene 1 opens in a drawing room with veranda at the Templeton estate, on which Seth Lattimore, Floyd's version of the Man, works as groundskeeper. The property faces an unnamed lake, clearly meant to be Pontchartrain, as the nearby hub of sin and seduction proves to be New Orleans. The house opens onto a lawn, with a family burial plot in the distance, at lake's edge, fringed with clumps of reeds. Floyd situates his plot by employing two theatrical devices, the first a cinematic flashback and flash forward. An old man points out to a group of children a patch of reeds associated with a local legend. Onstage, three men discover a body at the shore, and start to pull it out before the lights fade, indicating that we are about to travel back in time.

Floyd's second device is familiar from the practices of ancient Greek theater, in which characters step outside their assigned roles to comment on or amplify the drama's action. Three new faces rise from darkness: Reverend MacKenzie, Seth's Aunt Madge, and a young worker, Tom, speculate about odd changes in Seth's behavior over the preceding summer. A group gathers around a fresh grave at the burial plot: servants, Seth, and the aristocratic Margot Louviere, who spent the summer attending her dying and just-interred grandfather Templeton. Reverend MacKenzie intones a prayer, and offers condolences, coldly rebuffed by Margot, who declares that she has sold the estate, and that movers will arrive in the morning. Three neighbors gossip about Margot's depravity, living as she does "in sinful New Orleans."[40] With minimal grace, Margot discharges the household staff, but asks Seth to remain behind. She asks him whether her graveside performance was effective, confessing that only her desire to be certain that old Templeton had not changed his will had motivated her recent stay; and he has left everything to her. She spits personal and Catholic disdain for all "those pale, smug Protestant faces," before throwing her rosary across the room, and her arms around Seth's neck, proclaiming, "Pleasure is my religion. . . . And now you and I can be alone!" (7) A passionate if somewhat one-sided love scene develops, as Margot orders Seth to hang portraits of her ancestors, commanding them to watch her lovemaking with Seth. After ordering him to undress and douse the lights, she rhapsodizes about the risen moon's glow: "Let's go outside, Seth, and bathe in the moonlight! Our bodies will be silver in the luminous glow/And our eyes dark jewels in the night!" (10) Floyd's recent *Madama Butterfly* production found ghoulish echoes, as Margot asks him to "bring the flowers from the grave/And cover me with showers of petals!" (12) Seth begs her to stay on at the house; after all, he has a young wife expecting their first child. Margot's reply is an invitation to return with her to New Orleans. Her infatuation with Seth is temporary, but she finds his roughness erotic. She declares that she has no intention of leaving without him in three days; if he refuses, she will expose their affair. Her ultimatum: divorce his wife, or contrive some means to get rid of her, by accident, poison, or some other expedient. Mephisto might be Margot's ventriloquist: "A lifetime with me in exchange/For an act just minutes long. . . . A life of love without measure, A life brimming with pleasure." (16) When Seth's hesitation prompts another burst of her scorn, he assents, proposing an accident: she urges him to drown his wife while he rows across the lake. Margot then suggests that he fashion a vest of reeds to keep him afloat after the boat capsizes. His reticence prompts another withering tirade, and the scene ends as they writhe on a scattered spray of funeral blossoms in the moonlight.

Scene 2 shifts to the interior of Seth's modest house, opening onto a front porch, with Aunt Madge-cum-Greek chorus providing transitional information. The stylized device expands: Seth, his wife Laura, embroidering in silence, and Aunt Madge are revealed apart downstage, as the older woman voices suspicions provoked by Seth's recent behavior. As she begins to quote Seth, he is fixed in a pin-spot, and sings his line, which she mouths. When "real" stage light fades up, it is night outside. Seth is nowhere to be seen, having missed supper for the third time this week. Laura wonders why he has been "so distant, so strange" (22), and launches into a somber meditation on the coldness that has crept into her life and marriage. Aunt Madge compliments Laura on her artistry with the needle—Floyd's memories of mother and aunts—and Laura laments that her depiction of fields at sunrise lacks "a special shade of heliotrope" for the sky (24). Neighbors, a handyman and housekeeper, knock at the door, asking for a word with Laura. The handyman acts as a spokesman, raising issues beginning with Margot's dismissal of the staff, and relaying gossip that something has been going on between that lady and Seth: both he and the housekeeper have seen furtive embraces in half-lit rooms. Laura's response is passionate disbelief unless she hears it from Seth himself, and Aunt Madge shows the group out. Seth trudges onto the porch, hiding a large bundle of reeds in the shadows, before entering and receiving Laura's joyous, loving embrace. He apologizes for neglecting her, and proposes a pleasure trip across the lake to New Orleans to shop and see the latest fair with its circus performers. Aunt Madge interrupts Laura's radiant happiness with her suggestion of a Bible reading, Luke 6: 47–49, on the doom awaiting a house built on inadequate foundations. The act ends quietly as the three sing the Lord's Prayer.

Act 2, scene 1 finds Seth rowing his wife across the lake, reeds stashed behind him. Laura reaffirms her love for Seth in a blissful aria on nature's glories and her excitement at going to New Orleans. In the midst of her giddy chatter, she notices that he has stopped rowing. Seth stands, steps toward her, his hands extended, and Laura realizes that he means her harm. Yet Seth lacks strength to do what is on his mind: he drops his arms and begins to tremble violently. Laura screams, "Get me to land . . . let me out!," and Seth rows quickly again, babbling that she has nothing to fear, that he is not insane (37). When the boat touches the dock, Laura dashes off into the city, sobbing.

The scene changes to a garishly elegant hotel lobby, where Laura sits frozen, huddled alone in a chair. Lights are down on all but Reverend MacKenzie and Seth in their Greek choral function outside the hotel frame. MacKenzie says that he missed Seth in church last Sunday, and that when the two did meet, Seth's behavior seemed erratic.

When the lights come up on scene 2 proper, the hotel clerk asks Laura whether he could assist her, but she needs a while longer to recover strength and composure. A traveling salesman propositions her, but is discouraged by the clerk. A group of three ladies of the evening, April, Mae, and June—"Daughters of Spring"—tease Laura, declaring that no man is worth the grief she feels (42). Upper doors burst open, and circus personnel stream downstairs: clowns, acrobats, trapeze artists, fat lady, midgets, and ringmaster caper about. Seeing Laura still despondent, the clowns launch into a pantomime to cheer her up, before leaving to join the circus parade outside. At the height of mayhem, Seth bursts in. He blurts out concern for Laura's safety, but she tells him to leave her alone, that his sentiment is odd, seeing that he meant to drown her. Competing with the raucous parade outside, Seth sings a passionate aria, confessing that love prevented his harming her, and he begs forgiveness for considering such folly: "Loving you, as I knew then I did,/I could only protect you from harm . . . /Even if the harm was myself." (48) When he asks her to come back home with him, she turns on him in rage, then bursts into tears. The doors to a ballroom open, and a wedding party and Reverend MacKenzie emerge. After a brief recognition scene, Laura turns to the crestfallen Seth, and gently touches him, saying, "It's time we went back home." (50) Now it is Laura who puts an arm around her sobbing husband and leads him out.

Scene 3 finds the couple in the boat at night, Seth rowing in silence, a storm building in the distance. Downstage in their spotlights, the "Greek trio" of Reverend MacKenzie, Aunt Madge, and Tom discuss the situation between Margot and Seth. Seth, whose departure from the boat is concealed by darkness, now joins the trio in its conversation, alternately denying and defending his actions.

Lights fade up on Laura and Seth (in the boat again). He asks whether she will ever be able to forgive him, or even continue to live with him. Laura answers, "Perhaps in time. I don't know now." (54) She tells him of the visit the previous night from the Templeton servants and their revelations about Margot. To her question about whether it was his idea to drown her, Seth humbly admits, "No . . . but I agreed to it." (55) The storm breaks and tosses the boat wildly. Seth hands Laura the bundle of reeds, explaining its use if she falls into the water. An enormous wave capsizes them, and both flounder in the lake, calling out "ever more distantly." (57)

Act 3's single scene returns to the Lattimore house. Seth sits by the fire, soaking wet, with neighbors murmuring in low, anxious voices. Aunt Madge, Reverend MacKenzie, and Tom wonder how Seth could change so drastically, so quickly, and how close he was to death before being dragged from the water. Laura is still missing. Seth, near hysteria, begs the Reverend to hear his prayer, and the others turn their backs to give them privacy for Seth's anguished confession. The handyman enters with news that they have not found Laura, but that there is one final inlet to search. At another knock, Aunt Madge opens to reveal Margot, come to gloat and claim Seth as her prize. His admission that he did not go through with their plan sparks her furious scorn. Seth attacks and begins to strangle her, before Tom and the handyman pull them off each other, and Margot storms out. After more hushed talk, voices call out from the fields that they have found Laura alive. Rescuers carry her in, and Seth kneels to wrap her in a blanket, rocking her in his arms. Laura regains consciousness, and tells of her narrow escape, accomplished only through Seth's risk of his own life to save hers. The two joyously repeat their wedding vows and share a tender kiss. Looking outside at the dawn, Laura asks for her needlework, and locates the very skein of yarn she needs: "Heliotrope is the color of dawn!" (72) Lights dim on Laura and Seth, now silhouetted against the brightening morning sky. We flash forward to the Old Man singing to the children about the reeds at the shore, "so strong . . . watered by tears of remorse." (72) He ends the story with assurances that Seth and Laura went on to lead a happy wedded life.

With its symbolism of light and dark, good and evil, *Seth* became Floyd's paean to marital love. His devotion to the subject recalls the earlier *Passion of Jonathan Wade,* which we have seen as a kind of delayed wedding gift to Kay. *Seth*'s genesis coincided with Bobbi Martin's move from their home, and Floyd had Kay to himself for the first time in almost ten years.

With the libretto revised, polished, and retitled *Reeds,* Floyd showed it to Gockley, who remained enthusiastic; but now Floyd questioned his treatment of the characters and the technical complications posed by the two boat scenes. Another part of the problem lay in the material itself. Although he had made of Margot one of opera's greatest bad girls, he found her so irredeemably and implausibly evil that Seth would never agree to her murderous scheme; and despite ending his second act with the coup de theatre of the suddenly capsizing boat, the characters, *especially* Seth and Laura, seemed reactive and passive. His versification further cast this wholly serious tale into an uneasy limbo between opera, operetta, and musical theater. Despite a nagging sense that this material might bear fruit, by 1984–1985 the composer had reached the point of a clinical depression that generated enough insecurity and dissatisfaction to doom *Seth/Reeds* to a dark, forgotten file.

Meanwhile, Floyd and Gockley worked with the university's music administrators to create a doctorate of musical arts degree program. All parties believed that an upgrading of curriculum would make the synergy of the studio more attractive to older, more experienced students, and would make better use of program staff.[41]

On October 13, aunt Bunny's husband, Yates Gamble, with whom Floyd had such a fraught early relationship, died at home, sitting up in his chair. Ermine and Billy met Floyd's plane in Charleston on October 15, and he, again without Kay, attended the funeral in Laurinburg the next day. Reverend Floyd sent him home on October 18 with a melancholy memento, his "Dutch Boy quilt," which Ida had made for him in Bethune, her fanciful idea of what a Dutch boy might wear: a patchwork outfit of pants, shirt, and cap made from fabric remnants.

At the end of October, the *Houston Post* announced Floyd's "Introduction to Opera" for the university's spring semester, a repackaging of his video series as a music course on the University Park main campus. Floyd and Ermine made their usual Kennedy Center pilgrimage over the weekend of December 1 and 2, and celebrated Lena Horne, Danny Kaye, Gian Carlo Menotti, Arthur Miller, and Isaac Stern. The composer was welcomed home with Houston Symphony performances on December 7, 8, and 10 of his 1970 work, *In Celebration,* conducted by Sergiu Comissiona.

FOR ALMOST THREE YEARS, Floyd had noticed a marked diminution of Robert Holton's effectiveness in his behalf; his first guess why was Bob's never-ending quest to discover and sign the hottest new composers. Holton had been a career builder, forging connections that other publisher-agents could only envy: a network of opera and symphony managers, directors, and conductors, and a stable of the best contemporary composers. Not for nothing had Holton been tapped to serve as an opera and music theater panelist for the NEA, and the NOI bestowed on him its award for service to American opera in 1982.

By the midseventies, it seemed clear that Holton viewed Floyd and his career as self-sustaining, yet their personal friendship suggested an attachment exceeding what Floyd saw between Holton and other clients. The agent had been a quasi-brother just four years Floyd's senior; they had stayed with each other in New York and Florida for decades and had a history of loyal championing and mentoring. Holton now seemed quite different, but the change had been too gradual for Floyd to grasp other probable reasons for its genesis. When Holton returned from a 1981 trip to Mexico, he joked to everyone that he'd contracted some exotic internal parasite, Montezuma's revenge. Almost three years later, his symptoms continued and no doctor had been able to determine its cause or nature.

By the end of 1984, Holton kept to his New York apartment. When Floyd came to the city at the end of January 1985, he looked in on his old friend, finding him bedridden and attended by his mother, Mabel, and a male nurse. Despite obvious pain, Holton launched into one of his ploys to avoid emotional displays: "Don't you have anything better to do than come up here?" Floyd was shocked to see his former paladin emaciated, his face riddled with the dark lesions we now know as Kaposi's sarcoma.

America's first cases of Acquired Immune Deficiency Syndrome (AIDS) had been identified only four years earlier, and few outside the Center for Disease Control knew much about the disease beyond its inevitably fatal presence in the homosexual community. Only in the month of Floyd's last visit to Holton was a diagnostic blood test made available. Floyd was as much in the dark as anyone: knowing only that Holton was seriously ill, he wanted to let him know what his life and work had meant to him, but the man of words now found himself at a complete loss. Holton had no illusions about survival, and asked that "The Dear Mother" from *Citizen of Paradise* be a part of his memorial event. Floyd kissed Holton's forehead before taking his leave.

Soon afterward, panic set in. Could Holton's condition be contagious? Guilt at even formulating the question tormented Floyd as he flew home to Houston. On February 4, he answered a call from Belwin-Mills: Holton had died the day before. Floyd had lost mother and mentor in less than four years, and now Belwin-Mills's uncaptained ship foundered. Rather than replace Holton, the firm was sold to Columbia Pictures, itself a subsidiary of Coca-Cola, whose interest lay in higher profits than those generated by publishing music.

Within Floyd's family circle, other tensions accumulated. On February 2, the day before Holton died, Ermine's daughter Jane, still in Tallahassee, married Daniel Martin, Bobbi's former husband. Now Flora and Bernard lived mostly at the Floyds', except for visits to their father and Jane in Tallahassee.

Within three months after Holton's death, Floyd's emotional symptoms took on dimensions that William Styron, writing about his own plunge into depression, described as "lucidity . . . slipping away from me with terrifying speed . . . a sense of self-hatred . . . a failure of self-esteem . . . so mysteriously painful and elusive . . . as to verge close to being beyond description."[42]

The depression into which Floyd sank lasted from 1985 to 1987. Never portly, he lost an alarming amount of weight. He disappeared from friends' lives and limited social intercourse to the occasional lunch or tennis match with David Gockley. And then, when inner voices began shrieking, he excused himself. Conducting the most mundane conversation brought torture, fear, and wrenching anxiety that siphoned off his final drams of confidence.

Kay, having wanted at the beginning of their relationship to know everything there was to know about Carlisle Floyd, now learned a little too much too fast. Her response took the form not of tenderness or overt compassion, but in getting him to professional care. On the basis of discreet recommendations, he consulted a series of therapists. The first he described as "hopeless," a doctor who offered only sedation with psychotropic drugs like Xanax. Kay thought that one of her TA practitioners, who had also pioneered the medicinal use of lithium to combat bipolar disorders, might help; but no such luck. A third doctor prescribed Ritalin, used to treat attention deficit disorder (ADD) in children, and as a mood and energy booster in adults, which at least got Floyd back to his desk a few hesitant times. More typically, he lay or sat on his bed all day, abstracted or catatonic to observers. At the darkest moments, convinced that he was losing Kay, he shrank into fetal position. When Craig Bohmler stopped by the house, he thought, "I'm afraid we've lost Carlisle"; and when Ermine visited, she realized, "There's nobody there."[43]

One day, shopping at Foley's department store, he lost sight of Kay and panicked: "I knew that I couldn't survive without her." Floyd scheduled a conference with David Tomatz, music director at the university, to discuss his situation. Tomatz displayed warm empathy and encouraged Floyd to take as much time off as he needed; but many social acquaintances not connected with the opera or university were terrified by the manifestations of this depression, and began to drop or shun the Floyds. As ever a great reader on the neurosciences, Kay believed that electroshock therapy offered their only hope. She took Floyd to yet another therapist, who turned out to be neither analyst nor medical doctor. Floyd naturally recalled little about these visits, other than an upscale office with an enormous, surreal fish tank, but he validated Kay's interest in the treatments, which were administered by a fifth practitioner at a local hospital. Ermine made the trip from Holly Hill to be with him overnight in the psychiatric ward after each treatment. He told her repeatedly, "I feel awful, I don't belong here." Yet he experienced no pain during these sessions, which produced remarkable but temporary emotional benefits. Some short- and long-term memories of these years were certainly blunted, or, in cases of minor incidents or social engagements, erased, but at least he felt sporadic bursts of energy, and the ability, if not the desire, to work. Thereafter, however, he never drove past the hospital without feelings of nausea. As long afterward as 1990, when he tried to read Styron's memoir, the feelings and emotions it rekindled of his own return from the brink proved too intense, and he could not force himself get past a few pages.

Professionally, he continued to accept occasional opera directing engagements, but wrote no new music. Gockley noticed differences: "He stayed out of touch for very long time periods. I was working hard, and realized, gosh, I hadn't seen Carlisle in a month, and he lives ten minutes away. That was such a long dry spell; perhaps he felt that he'd lost his muse?"[44]

The rest of the eighties were a blur for Floyd. On March 19, 1985, he appeared before the United States House of Representatives subcommittee on interior appropriations, together with conductor James DePriest, choreographer Eliot Feld, and playwright Marsha Norman, to address the state of the arts in America. Floyd's testimony tells us as much about his inner weather as it clarifies opera world arcana. After remarking that the number of producing companies had grown from three to twenty-five since the launch of his career, he commended the NEA panel review process, and the value of the program's grants as seed money to encourage private philanthropy:

> Even more than dollar amounts is what the Endowment has done about an attitude that has been prevalent throughout American history, an attitude that can be illustrated by an expression from the Henry James novel *The American:* "Women, artists and other impractical people" . . . I now feel a dispiritedness. The term I've heard is "retrenchment." I think that is a polite term. The change is much more serious. . . . We've seen education programs cut or curtailed entirely and touring companies have shortened the length of their tours and their geographical reach. . . . There's no substitute for Federal funding. What the Endowment did was to authenticate the arts as part of our social scheme and bring respect to the Arts.[45]

Joined to Floyd's personal loss of spirit was his growing fear of flying. When Bob Holton's memorial service was held on May 13, Floyd declined to attend. But Ned Rorem went with Sylvia Goldstein and James Kendrick, joining Phyllis Curtin and others in hearing

Frederica von Stade sing Floyd's "The Dear Mother" from *Citizen of Paradise,* which Holton had requested at their last visit. Like Floyd and the rest of "Bob's composers," Rorem claimed that he owed his career to Holton's generosity and sharp personal and professional instincts.[46]

Floyd had been asked to direct a *Willie Stark* revival, coproduced by the Charlotte and Shreveport opera companies. Performances were scheduled for September and October 1985, but he did not attend May production meetings, and he avoided Des Moines Metro Opera's *Of Mice and Men* on June 21. His emotional reluctance to fly was exacerbated by an ischemic stroke of the inner ear that caused sudden and almost total hearing loss on his right side, accompanied by vertigo, which was exaggerated by even a social sip of alcohol.[47] In time he would use a hearing aid, reluctantly and erratically. His inner musical voices were unaffected.

Summer's end coincided with Miami Opera's proposed *Of Mice and Men* filming, with Michael Bronson as executive producer; but the Florida legislature's austerity measures caused Governor Bob Graham to veto the state's enabling grant.[48] Floyd's mood was further darkened by knee surgery on August 12 to repair more stress from years of tennis.[49]

After a two-day mid-September visit to Holly Hill, the composer drove to Charlotte to stage *Willie Stark.*[50] Carey Wong had designed new sets, and Hal France conducted Timothy Nolen, who repeated his Houston and Washington, DC, performances in the title role, and Rosalind Elias (Sadie), Rodney Nolen (Jack), Joan Gibbons (Anne), and Herbert Eckhoff (Judge Burden). Local press thought the result "explosive, ground-breaking . . . accessible without being predictable."[51]

In Shreveport, Floyd welcomed Houston Opera Studio alumnus Louis Otey back as Willie. With the exception of Nancy Elledge as Anne, the cast, conductor, and set all duplicated the Charlotte production.[52] *Opera News* praised Floyd's "exciting theater," and the "intimate, realistic approach" of his staging.[53]

Both productions succeeded, and Floyd soon fell back into his university routine, deriving the greatest enjoyment from teaching piano literature. He illustrated as he discussed, using neglected but never-forgotten keyboard skills in music he loved. On December 6 he met Ermine in Washington, where the Kennedy Center honored Merce Cunningham, Irene Dunne, Bob Hope, Alan Jay Lerner, Frederick Loewe, and Beverly Sills.

With Bob Holton's loss painfully fresh, Floyd's preoccupation during the winter of 1985/86 was another look backward as he orchestrated *Citizen of Paradise.* He consulted representatives of chamber orchestras in Houston, St. Paul, Los Angeles, and Lincoln Center in New York, hoping that added instrumental voices might give the work new life. His orchestra included pairs of flutes, oboes and bassoons, three clarinets, four horns, three each of trumpets and trombones, tuba, and a large but delicately employed percussion battery of timpani, snare drum, tenor drum, bass drum, cymbals, tambourine, gong, xylophone, and piano. The expansion reinforced his conviction that he had written a monodrama; a new (old) chair, desk, and window frame were located and enhanced with modest stage lighting. Susanne Mentzer, asked to sing this premiere, took her white dress out of storage, and Floyd reprised his spare direction. Paired with works of Haydn, Rossini, and Puccini, *Citizen* was given on February 21, 1986 in the sanctuary of Houston's St. John the Divine Episcopal Church, with John DeMain conducting the Texas Chamber Orchestra. Charles Ward found the work's instrumentation and balance "vividly illustrative of that American compositional idiom that roots dissonance in a firm tonal base."[54]

THE WINTER OF 1985/86 brought sweeping change to UH, beginning with the retirement of Milton Katims as director of the School of Music, and his replacement by the cellist David Tomatz. One of Tomatz's priorities, besides continuing the institution's support of celebrity faculty like Floyd and Nikolaidi, was to expand voice and opera by filling retirees' positions with younger singers like soprano Cynthia Clayton, tenor Joseph Evans, bass-baritone Timothy Jones, and baritone Hector Vasquez. In the fall of 1985, the school also welcomed the stage director Buck Ross, codirector of

Des Moines Metro Opera's apprentice program, who was hired by the university to honor its commitment to the opera company, as the studio's director of dramatic studies.[55] After serving on the search committee, Floyd demonstrated graciousness, support, and wisdom; he was ready with advice when asked, but never meddled or intruded as Ross pursued the difficult crossing of disciplines and alliance-building required for an opera program.

The year 1986 began with more unsettling news: thirty-nine-year-old Christopher Keene, after promising beginnings at New York City Opera, announced his resignation as music director effective January 1, 1987. For the press's benefit, Keene and the company invoked the rationale that administrative responsibilities inhibited his artistic development, but it seemed clear that sharing authority with Sills had bred no love between the two.[56]

18

Standing Up

Resurrection and Jonathan *Reborn, 1986–1991*

Despite his depressive spiral and heavy medication, in February 1986 Floyd staged a revival of his 1982 *Of Mice and Men* for the Greater Miami Opera. Using Robert O'Hearn's sets from the earlier production, and conducted by Willie Anthony Waters, the cast reprised William Neill (Lennie), Riccardo Calleo (Curley), and Elizabeth Knighton (Curley's Wife); Timothy Nolen essayed George since making a national impression as Willie Stark.

Just as a constellation of losses had dominated Floyd's life for the last seven years, in 1986 the pendulum's backswing pulled in a flow of allies, and cracks appeared in his inertia. He and Kay devoured works on psychiatry as voraciously as the rest of the world read Stephen King. The writings of the German American Karen Horney made a particular impact with their neo-Freudian slant on neurosis, that is, the view that the condition was an ongoing process rather than a response to time-limited stimuli.[1] Horney believed that parental indifference, ranging from neglect to ridicule, exerted a significant influence on a child's perception of reality; she identified ten sets of neurotic needs that crystallized into a triad of compliance (moving toward people), aggression (moving against people), and detachment (moving away from people).[2] When Floyd sampled Transactional Analysis in the late sixties he remarked the movement's theatricality, its game-playing and scripting, as offering the best hope of any therapy he tried; but although it stimulated his first awareness, it cured nothing for him.

He devoured James F. Masterson's *The Real Self: A Developmental Self and Object Relations Approach* when it first appeared in 1985, before his electroshock treatments, and the book engaged him on second reading.[3] Masterson (1926–2010) enjoyed preeminence in object relations theory. In 1977 he founded the Masterson Institute, a nonprofit organization for teaching and research. The faculty, personally trained and supervised by Masterson, continue to specialize in personality disorders.

In lay terms, object relations theory, a sometimes controversial outgrowth of Freudian theory, and pioneered in the forties and fifties by such prominent British psychologists as Ronald Fairbairn, Melanie Klein, and D. W. Winnicott, approaches the growth of the young mind through relationship to others in its environment. In this sense, the terms "objects" and "others" are synonymous, whether they refer to real people (parents and other primary caregivers) or children's internalized *images* of others. Masterson developed a special focus on borderline and narcissistic disorders, both disorders based on concepts of a false self. He considered that sufferers of borderline disorder had been ignored, misdiagnosed, and mistreated for many years; they were, in his opinion, "sicker than the neurotic but not sick enough to be classified psychotic."[4]

The narcissist, whose exterior self may display aggression, exhibitionism, even confidence—people who "have it all," as Floyd had been told by one therapist—protects an inner self fueled by inadequacy, insecurity, and fear. Many borderlines come to *expect* devastating rejection in their lives (Floyd's lying inner voice, "Why don't you just go on home?"); and the narcissist often falls into deflation—activating abandonment depression at mere hints of criticism, much less the heavy artillery fired in public by the likes of a Donal

Henahan. It is logical that Floyd recognized parts of both types in himself, and *all* of him languished now in depression and creative paralysis.

Both psychic bundles, narcissism and depression, are thought to be rooted in the imperfect separation of mother and child after about one and a half years, and are exacerbated by a fear of abandonment that is caused by either parent's inability to validate the child's emerging real, *independent* self. Abandonment depression carries with it a complex of panic, rage, guilt, helplessness, hopelessness, and emptiness, in response to which the individual develops a false self. Factors like Ida Floyd's parental distancing, or Reverend Floyd's alternating unavailability and emotional abuse, as well as conditioning from a childhood disease like asthma, seep into Carlisle Floyd's rough clinical portrait. His biography is studded with examples of behavior and relationships ranging, as Masterson leads us to expect, from distancing to clinging: the need to stand alone—"I'll listen to any advice, but the final decision will be mine"—or dependence on guides and champions like Robert Holton or Julius Rudel.

Crucial to Masterson's approach—and what Floyd considered the book's greatest value—was his jargon-free description of treatment for each personality type. Masterson based his ideas for treatment on traditional free-associative psychotherapy, with its crucial transference formation between patient and therapist: a bonding of allies, and a projection onto the therapist of both real and unreal aspects of figures from the patient's background, which brings light into the shadows.

In the meantime, David Gockley's concern for his friend grew. Their relationship had blossomed into heartfelt friendship: helping each other through difficult times by lending a sympathetic ear, celebrating successes, mourning failures, collaboration on shared projects like the studio and commissions. Floyd never opened his soul to Gockley about his intimacies with Kay or anyone else past or present. Yet whenever Gockley encountered insuperable personal problems, Floyd listened with keen empathy. He had the ability to step outside his own struggles to help his friend hack through tarry layers of emotional distress by offering his common sense to reassure and validate that Gockley had every reason to feel and respond as he did. Floyd recommended books, and related to Gockley thoughtfully and knowledgeably about the hard-to-determine "whys" that he strove to process in his own life.

After twenty years of professional collaboration, Gockley, like Frank Corsaro, realized that his friend needed the healing that new work could bring, and that a Floyd opera entailed scant risk. Julius Rudel conducted an HGO production of Strauss's *Ariadne auf Naxos* in April 1986, and during the rehearsal period Gockley asked him which works from City Opera's American seasons Rudel thought worthy of revival. The conductor answered at once: *The Passion of Jonathan Wade.*[5] Gockley's initial broaching of the topic provoked Floyd's doubt, then dismissal: after all, almost a quarter century had passed. Yet in the sixties, Sylvia Goldstein had sent Floyd a tape of the City Opera premiere. As early as January 1963 she had reminded Floyd that he needed to submit revisions before the company would publish the opera;[6] and in June 1964, Bob Holton had urged the composer to consider a reworking. Finally, in May 1984, Goldstein jogged his memory on the subject.[7]

As was typical for him, Floyd listened to the tape just once, around 1972, and stashed it away in his memorabilia. He confessed his dissatisfaction with the opera, thinking that it sounded like the work of a gifted student whose lapses he longed to see corrected.[8] Now, twenty-four years later, he had to regain confidence that he *could* in fact compose opera. Plotting his strategy, Gockley showed the score to conductor John DeMain, who found many strengths, but agreed with the boss that it needed serious revision. Gockley asked Floyd to bring the tape for a listening session with DeMain at the HGO offices, and the composer heard his mammoth work through a haze of emotion and memory, feeling more surprise than pleasure that any document had survived. Despite recalling that he *had* had a career, and *had* created a legacy, this hearing provoked such anxiety that he could not sit through the entire opera, and left Gockley and DeMain to complete their discussion.

After tying up loose ends at university and studio, Floyd headed to Knoxville to stage *Susannah,* with performances on April 11 and 13. Robert Lyall conducted the latest generation of interpreters: Faith Esham (Susannah), Jeffrey Wells (Blitch), Joseph Evans (Sam), and Don Bernardini (Little Bat). During her husband's absence, Kay wrote Reverend Floyd to let him know the grief to which his son had come. The minister confided to his diary, "Letter from Kay, which I could not read."[9] Kay *did* have poor penmanship, but if he had meant the statement literally, Ermine was on hand to interpret; and it is rather likely that Reverend Floyd would not or could not respond to his son's plight. On June 9, he sent sixty dollars, one for each year of his namesake's life, but Floyd's sixtieth birthday itself passed without further contact between father and son.

The 1986 fall semester defined ordinariness. The studio shrank from eleven to nine members, of whom just four were new, but Floyd's school load included an exceptional fifteen graduate students. While mulling over *Jonathan Wade,* his sole creative outlet came from the Houston Symphony fanfare project, cosponsored by Citicorp, to celebrate the Texas sesquicentennial. Twenty-one composers received commissions for about $2,500 each to write brief fanfares for HSO's season concerts, beginning on February 15, 1986. The stellar peer group, representing several generations of disparate styles and nationalities, numbered John Adams, Carla Bley, Elliott Carter, Marius Constant, Paul Cooper, Jacob Druckman, John Harbison, Marc Neikrug, Tobias Picker, Steve Reich, Ned Rorem, Christopher Rouse, Poul Ruders, Aulis Sallinen, William Schuman, Josef Tal, Joan Tower, John Williams, Olly Wilson, and Charles Wuorinen.

Floyd tunneled note by note, just far enough out of his psychic paralysis to realize *Flourishes,* one of his most ebullient and straightforward short works. Lasting four minutes, it is a virtuoso turn for full orchestra: his usual complement of woodwinds, four horns, three each of trumpets and trombones, tuba, strings, timpani, and a percussion battery of snare drum, tenor drum, bass drum, suspended cymbals, tambourine, gong, xylophone, and piano. In 3/4, *Poco allegro e marcato,* centered firmly in E Major, an eight-measure timpani solo outlines a jaunty jagged theme of triplets, trills, rolls, and sixteenth-eighth combinations, accompanied by soft polytonal clusters from clarinets, bassoons, and horns. In the ninth bar, a solo trumpet introduces a more lyrical variation on the theme, passed to horns nine measures later, punctuated again by solo timpani. Winds and brasses embellish the material, until, in measure thirty-four, strings take up a diminished rendition of the tune, commented on by horns and trumpets with agitated triplet-sextuplet-sixteenth figures. Gaining volume and weight in passacaglia fashion, with more than a hint of Ravel's *Bolero,* and then a layering of all versions of the rhythmic and melodic material, ornamented with great sweeping glissandi in high winds and strings, *Flourishes* lives up to its title with a brilliant, impudent finish to its ninety-six measures.

In concerts conducted by Sir Neville Marriner on February 14 and 15, 1987, Floyd's piece was sandwiched between Tippett's Concerto for Double String Orchestra, Mozart's Piano Concerto no. 20 in D Minor, and Shostakovich's Symphony no. 1. The *Houston Chronicle* reported *Flourishes* to be "perhaps the most immediately appealing fanfare heard in this series."[10]

Yet this brief toe in the water of composing brought Floyd little satisfaction apart from the paycheck, and Gockley and other colleagues continued to remark on the gravity of his distress. Floyd's principal Houston copyist, James Medvitz, who had prepared the full score of *Flourishes,* sent the composer a list of corrections, with a note, "Take care of yourself—please!"[11] Ned Rorem had been in Houston the previous November, and saw Floyd at some function, noting only that his colleague seemed much out of sorts.[12]

In July, for KUHT, Houston's PBS television affiliate, Floyd participated with the Houston choreographer Ben Stevenson, the sculptor James Surls, the painter John Alexander, and the photographers Ed Hill and Suzanne Bloom in the program "Something Out of Nothing." Directed by Paul Yeager, this showed the artists in their working environments, wrestling their respective materials into shape, and defining the sources of their various arts. Floyd seemed the most reserved of the five subjects, contemplative, composing "in solitude or quiet collaboration in his book-lined living room."[13]

Floyd's mood darkened further when he learned that Phyllis Curtin's husband, Eugene Cook, had died on August 23 within forty-five minutes after his aorta ruptured, before emergency services could reach him. Floyd's emotional outlook continued to be bleak, despite receiving a New Music Theatre award for *Bilby's Doll* in New York on December 1, 1986, presented by baritone Robert Merrill. (Shortly before his death, Bob Holton had nominated Floyd.)

One of the few events to which he looked forward was the annual Washington, DC, jaunt with Ermine, this year over the weekend of December 5, with Kennedy Center Honors for Lucille Ball, Ray Charles, Hume Cronyn, Yehudi Menuhin, Jessica Tandy, and Antony Tudor.

The year 1987 began as Floyd joined fellow composers Paul Cooper, Elsworth Milburn, Paul English, George Burt, and Michael Horvit in forming the Houston Composers Alliance, to promote and encourage the productivity of Houston's creative musicians at home and abroad. The group planned an annual festival concert, the first held on June 25 in Miller Theatre. With the Houston Symphony conducted by Niklaus Wyss and Richard Fletcher, Floyd's *Flourishes* shared the program with works by Ann K. Gebuhr, Samuel Jones, Tobias Picker, Burt, English, Horvit, and Milburn.

Floyd continued going through familiar motions, and in repertoire for which he needed to consult no score. He directed *Susannah* with a student cast at the University of Hartford's Hartt School of Music, conducted by Benton Hess, along with the Floyd/Hendl Susannah Orchestral Suite.[14]

NO PSYCHIATRIC TREATMENT had effected lasting changes in Floyd's depression, yet Ritalin and electroshock left him feeling strong enough to act on impulse and hope, and place a call to the Masterson Institute. He expected to be fobbed off to an assistant, but perhaps the name Carlisle Floyd carried more weight than he knew; at any rate, he was put through to friendly, helpful Dr. James F. Masterson himself. After praising the accuracy and clarity of *The Real Self*, Floyd asked whether Masterson could recommend someone in Houston who offered the sort of treatment his book outlined, and Masterson suggested a former student who was familiar with the institute's research and methodology.

This doctor unfortunately could not fit Floyd into his patient list, but recommended Dr. Jorge de la Torre, who inspired an immediate surge of feeling in Floyd on first meeting. Cuban-born—he confessed to Floyd an awareness that his accent was "all over the place"—he had trained at the Menninger Clinic in Topeka, Kansas. On the faculty of Baylor University College of Medicine in Houston, this elegant, sophisticated man of the world was coincidentally an HGO subscriber. Floyd, having struck emotional bottom, knew after their first session that he had found a healer, and embarked on a nine-year relationship that pulled him back from the brink of the emotional abyss. Despite common interests, however, the two men preserved the formal doctor-patient relationship that was a staple of all Freudian-based therapies. Any such relationship leads to encounters between two people unknown to each other, but only one comes to know the other quite well. Their terms of address were "Dr. de la Torre" and "Dr. Floyd." Floyd knew only that De la Torre was married, and nothing more about the doctor's personal life. At one point during treatment, Floyd ran into the De la Torres at an HGO performance, with predictable results: Mrs. de la Torre, never introduced, literally backed out of the encounter.

When De la Torre, who took no notes, learned the patient's history, he expressed outrage over the shock treatments, and began therapy with a new mix of mood-evening medications, continuing Ritalin and adding Prozac, and Clorazepate to deal with Floyd's anxiety. For three sessions a week for the first two years, later reduced to two, they had face-to-face conversations rather than Freudian couch therapy and its classical model of free-associative talk. Floyd, feeling vulnerable and exposed, always maintained tight control over his emotions, and knew it as a deficiency. De la Torre later told him that it had been "touch and go" at the beginning, with slow, stepwise progress.[15]

Anyone who has undergone psychotherapy will identify with the uncomfortable periods of silence: "De la Torre very much waited for you; and he could wait, and wait. We had some lengthy silences, and I despised them. All you do is get more and more anxious. I think I may have said on a number of occasions, 'I may just as well leave.'"

But he did not. Despite Masterson's focus on borderline and narcissist personalities, De la Torre refused to attach labels to Floyd's condition, to keep him from intellectualizing his actual feelings. Kay wanted diagnoses, but the closest De la Torre came was to give an opinion of clinical depression in remission.

Family issues occupied a surprisingly small portion of their work. De la Torre dealt in the present, with feelings, and the influx of past into present. They certainly touched on the father-son relationship, and Floyd finally expressed angry complaints.

> Daddy always tried to make mama a culprit in my difficulties; and she was, but not deliberately. And he said things deliberately to hurt, or separate himself from me. Mama was always kind to me—not exactly loving, but kind. She never did anything overtly to hurt me. Once in high school I had a photograph taken—I was so thin—and thought I was the world's ugliest thing. I told her, "I feel I'm just so ugly." And instead of saying, "No, no, you're beautiful," or "You're a handsome young man," I got, "Well, son, you can always be pleasant." Taking my side or encouraging me was not in her capacity; but I knew that she wanted the best for me, as she saw the best.

No surprise that he frequently left De la Torre's inner sanctum more depressed than on entering. De la Torre felt that Floyd protected his mother; and Floyd accepted guilt for never accessing emotions that would have helped him fully mourn Ida's death: "I protected her by avoiding my feelings. As a child, I viewed her as the superwoman of the universe. She was so admired in the family. People would say, probably in relation to her dealings with my father, "Ida is a saint." I looked to De la Torre to mediate, or at least show some light in the tunnel. But I felt there wasn't any way of working this out, because you brought all these feelings to the surface without resolution."

When Floyd complained of the therapy's failure, De la Torre offered the abstraction of going to Tiffany's and asking for a ring made of stainless steel. The jeweler says, "I'm sorry, we only have sterling silver." The customer goes back time and again and repeats the process, in other words, asking for something they do not carry; but he keeps going back, hoping to get what he came for. "Of course," recalled Floyd, "every time he said that, it annoyed me. You're still trying to make something right. You're going to the wrong source, and don't know how to get to the right one."

He remained terrified of flying, and this fear revived his childhood sense of incapacity. If in his early years those fears were counterbalanced by bravado, now he could not imagine having flown to such distant places as San Francisco and New York, much less Brussels, London, or Germany.

After four or five years, Floyd suggested that perhaps the couch would bring better results. De la Torre marveled that his patient wanted psychoanalysis at such an advanced stage; but Floyd now found himself straitjacketed by the imprecision of dream work: the burden was all his, with minimal nudges from the therapist. "I found that a total waste of time and money. He tried to get me more to the feeling of each dream, rather than the details. It worked, but I don't think it got us anywhere. I may have expected that I'd understand all the mysterious symbolism, but that seems to me totally arbitrary."

In a few weeks they went back to direct communication. In working through therapeutic transference, Floyd experienced the expected emotions of grief, rage, and resentment. "I probably looked to him to provide solutions, to be the daddy who had deserted me. And I wanted him to like and admire me." Though he craved this "winning over" the therapist, it never happened.

De la Torre kept his distance, and referred to the therapeutic process as admirable and valuable. Floyd felt that they related as inanimate objects and not as people, casting De la Torre in the intellectually abstract role of a "receiver." Floyd always approached sessions with many things on his mind, things he had felt; and yet De la Torre at times seemed to step outside his presumed role. Floyd expressed surprise and consternation: "If I said something he didn't like, or he took issue with, he'd intervene. He'd explode and tell me I was crazy, just that openly."

When blocked, Floyd provoked De la Torre by crediting Ritalin with any measurable progress he experienced, which he knew angered the therapist. After five or six years, Floyd blurted out in anger one day, "This is an absurd relationship! You really are just an abstraction." De la Torre's control did not prevent him from displaying strong reactions to such accusations. Nonetheless, their long relationship saw the transference completed, and Floyd's warm personal attachment was confirmed and even reciprocated in years to come. Yet he found their very success baffling:

> He obviously helped me a great deal, but I don't know how. And I imagine he'd be very happy to hear me say that. At the end, I felt that I'd done most of it myself, and that's probably a good analysis; but that also takes a good technician. Still, I came away from those nine years more convinced than ever of the limitations of psychiatry, in terms of what I thought it could be. And I realized that the fundamental wounds, or WOUND—my father's rejection—remains for the rest of one's life.

At home, the situation with Kay, who felt loved and admired by *her* therapist, changed. Floyd had lived for twenty years with her difficulty in expressing affection, and now had new tools to defuse for himself the tensions in their relationship. "I once told De la Torre about some compliment she'd given me, and he called such moments as valuable as emeralds, because of their scarcity. Kay acted out anger by giving me the silent treatment. Now, rather than respond to her, and beg her to tell me what was wrong, or what I could do to make it up, the work with De la Torre enabled me to just sit in my room and wait until she came around. This would have caused unendurable tension and anxiety before."

On May 20, Floyd saw Michael Ehrman's staging of *Susannah* for Orlando Opera. The title role's interpreter, Elizabeth Holloque, then returned to New York to rehearse Frank Corsaro's *Tosca* at City Opera, and Corsaro asked after Floyd. Holloque's answer prompted a letter to him in which Corsaro reported, "She told me . . . that you seemed to be experiencing some difficulty." The director went on to lament, "American opera has been at such a stand-still—that if it has anything to do with your own personal travail—[it] is certainly endemic to our time and place—and I extend my sympathies and concern to you—one of American opera's super champions. Still there may be light at the end of that particular tunnel too! I'm fishing in the dark—I might be way out of line in your life—but as a friend, it provoked this letter of love and interest—something I've been meaning to do for a long time."[16]

At least Floyd knew that he was not alone through the summer's other crises. In Holly Hill, Reverend Floyd's chronic emphysema had grown worse, and his dependency on others total. By the end of July, he had contracted pneumonia, and Ermine rushed him to Orangeburg Hospital. His high fever and congestion subsided after a few days, and the staff seconded her suggestion that this was the perfect time to effect a long-contemplated move to Orangeburg's Methodist Home.[17]

Floyd visited New York during December's first week to hold auditions for the 1988–1989 studio and to hear Renée Fleming.[18] On December 4, he met with senior staff at Boosey & Hawkes. In a letter from the previous summer, composer Henry Mollicone had observed that matters at Belwin-Mills seemed to be going downhill.[19] Floyd had his fears confirmed in a world without Bob Holton. Opera companies inquiring about rights to any of his newer pieces found themselves unable to secure basic performance materials. In 1986, the firm had assigned *Introduction, Aria, and Dance, Bilby's Doll, Willie Stark, Citizen of Paradise,* and *Flourishes* to Theodore Presser's rental division, and had kept *Of Mice and Men, Flower and Hawk, The Martyr,* and *Overture for Orchestra* (*In Celebration*) for itself. Belwin-Mills had also stopped printing new copies of *any* Floyd works. The composer even received letters from singers who had gone to Patelson's, New York's then-preeminent sheet music store, to buy vocal scores of his four Belwin operas, and found nothing between Flotow's *Martha* and Gay's *Beggar's Opera* on the shop's wall of shelved volumes.

Columbia Pictures, owned by Coca-Cola since 1982, acquired Belwin-Mills in 1985, and the whole bundle, as Columbia Pictures Entertainment Group, was purchased in 1988 by the British firm Filmtrax/Ensign Trust. As early as 1986, Floyd suspected that his best hope lay in returning to Boosey & Hawkes.[20] Stuart Pope had resigned from the firm in November 1984, to be succeeded by James Kendrick; and the continued presence of Floyd's old ally Sylvia Goldstein encouraged him. He reminded Kendrick that his Belwin contract expired on January 8, 1988, and that he had served notice of his intention not to renew.[21] Kendrick and Goldstein welcomed the prodigal son home,[22] but this meant initiating the long, convoluted process of getting all of Floyd's copyrights returned and reassigned. Pursuing conversations with Goldstein and Gockley, Floyd worked with the lawyer Glen Rosenbaum, an HGO subscriber and donor who was on the staff of the prestigious Houston firm Vincent & Elkins, and who donated his services.

BACK IN SOUTH CAROLINA, all was not well with Reverend Floyd. He lived in a small room with another resident, who, as the composer put it, "earned a crown in heaven." The senior Floyd's bullying to deliver mealtime blessings was a chronic offense; and once when a visiting children's group began their pageant with a parade around the home, two youngsters led the procession with Methodist and American flags. Reverend Floyd snatched the former banner away from its surprised bearer, demanding that he, the ordained minister, carry it. The administration had done its best to overlook these faults, but a group of offended ladies now demanded a formal hearing.

Floyd flew from Houston and joined Ermine and Billy at the "trial" to move their father were he "convicted." Floyd tried reasoning with the old man, explaining what he was going through with De la Torre, empathizing with his father's dissatisfaction and unhappiness. Reverend Floyd gave his son looks suggesting that consulting a mental health care professional constituted a character flaw. The "plaintiffs" spoke their pieces. Reverend Floyd "took the stand," denying all charges and asserted without apology the respect and deference due the Reverend C. S. Floyd. Billy Matheny shook his head and declared, "The old man still has lots of spunk," and spunk achieved, if not acquittal, at least postponement of removal.

Five years earlier, Floyd and Ned Rorem had discussed writing librettos for each other; but now Floyd received a serious call to that effect from Hugo Weisgall, whom Terence McEwen of the San Francisco Opera commissioned in 1987 for an opera on the biblical subject of Esther. Flattering as Weisgall's invitation was, Floyd was incapable of considering it; but at least he could finish the year knowing that he had a stable publisher again who held open the door of welcome.[23]

Seeing her husband's progress with De la Torre, Kay undertook a personal, if shorter, odyssey. She had left Tallahassee twelve years earlier convinced that friends thought she had a drinking problem. Houston had never offered anything like the Tallahassee Clique, and the Floyds' infrequent entertaining in Texas was restricted to professional obligations. Floyd's drink of choice had always been Jack Daniels and water, and Kay's, bourbon and something carbonated. Floyd's inner ear condition now ruled out even small amounts of alcohol, and they had renounced it, keeping a well-stocked cabinet just for company. But Kay wanted Tallahassee friends to see her progress. Much to Floyd's surprise, she packed the car, and drove alone, more than seven hundred miles across the Gulf Coast to their old city, where the Mastrogiacomos, her hosts for a few nights, threw a party in her honor.

Relieved and emboldened, and embraced by a community of friends unlike any made in Houston, she reversed the journey back to Texas, and now began working on Floyd to consider moving back to Florida. After all, even though UH offered retirement at age sixty-five, one could choose to withdraw as early as fifty-five with reduced annuity. But Floyd put his foot down; his therapy was working.

He further returned to the world by accepting an invitation from Lotfi Mansouri, the general director of Canadian Opera Company (COC) in Toronto.[24] The two men had known each other for years from various NEA and Opera America functions, as well as from HGO productions. Mansouri had seen the 1976 Amsterdam *Of Mice and Men,* and reassured Floyd that the audience reaction belied press reports. Mansouri sought Floyd's help with a Canadian program similar to the National Opera Institute workshops with which Floyd developed *Willie Stark* in Houston. In 1987, COC inaugurated a composers-in-residence program with commissions to three Canadians for opera or music theater works lasting between thirty and sixty minutes, scored for two to six soloists, and a guarantee of public performances the following spring.[25]

One of the first recipients, Michel-Georges Brégent,[26] devised *Realitillusion,* which featured his own compilation of French and English texts by historical figures, for a cast of six. Brégent outlined his ambition to create a work balanced between intellect, emotion, and spirituality. His peer colleagues, the composer Richard Désilets and the librettist Kim Elaine Gosselin, offered their "lyric fable" *Zoé.* The composer-librettist Timothy Sullivan's *The Dream Play,* based on Strindberg, depicted the God Indra's daughter visiting Earth.[27] When Floyd arrived in Toronto in January 1988 to begin working with this group, Mansouri was away, preparing his transition to the general directorship of San Francisco Opera, and the composers-in-residence program burden fell onto Floyd's shoulders. Ms. Gosselin, though open and receptive, was writing for the theater for the first time; the composers Brégent, Désilets and Sullivan displayed mixed enthusiasm for adapting their idioms to the needs of an opera libretto, an obvious Floyd priority. As days went by, Floyd's frustration at not making demonstrable headway grew; nonetheless, the works of all participants received three performances by the COC studio ensemble that May.[28]

STILL INTRIGUED but conflicted about *Jonathan Wade,* Floyd returned to Houston. Gockley issued a formal commission for a revision of the opera for a ten thousand dollar fee, and set about forging a partnership with the opera companies of Miami and Washington; Floyd thought that three-quarters of the original work might be salvageable.[29]

Already projecting future box office, Boosey had Floyd's assurance that two of the first version's hits, "Free as a Frog" and the spiritual "Down in Galilee," published in separate 1963 choral editions, would be retained. Acting on De la Torre's urging to accept the project, Floyd sighed and plunged in, beginning with a fifty-five-page intermediate revised libretto,[30] with the same characters and episodes. He assigned new historical chronology in act 2, which begins in spring 1866. Act 3 ends in October 1869, the specification of the month the only new element. This version was in fact a little *longer* than the text in Floyd's 1962 full score.

Most other changes were cosmetic. He omitted a second girl's (Miss Blackstock) conversation with Judge Townsend in act 1, scene 2; tightened stage directions; pushed act 3, scene 1 a year forward to October 1869; and Jonathan's Spartan office became a former mansion repurposed as military headquarters now that Jonathan and Celia have begun a family. He halved lines allotted to Enoch (his given name changed back from "Ely") and to Pratt's wife, Amy; and he made one sizeable cut in act 3's escape sequence.

Such tentative adjustment betrayed Floyd's lack of confidence. This draft is almost identical to the 1962 libretto, summarized in chapter 12, but as daunting as revisiting ancient work and history seemed, Floyd's nights gradually became days: as therapy with De la Torre progressed, the composer looked forward to rising each morning, to getting back to work.

Thinking that new research and expert input might give him a fresh perspective, Floyd read a just-published book on the subject, Eric Foner's *Reconstruction: America's Unfinished Revolution, 1863–1877.* A call to the university's history department, to determine whether they had a specialist on Reconstruction, produced another synchronous burst of fortune in the person of Dr. Joseph T. Glatthaar, one of the country's preeminent Civil War scholars.[31] The two men's offices were seventy-five yards apart, and they hit it off on first meeting, phoning or dropping in on each other as needed. Toward the beginning of March, Floyd asked his neighbor-colleague to read and comment on his intermediate revision. Glatthaar's reaction was rapid and enthusiastic: "He had done a magnificent job, and I just made a few minor comments."[32]

The historian observed that the Ku Klux Klan had not formed by April 1865, and Floyd solved this by inventing a precursor organization, which first appears in a five-page "Summary of the Libretto for *The Passion of Jonathan Wade*" for Glatthaar, Gockley, and the HGO board.[33]

In a March 29 memo, Glatthaar enthused:

> Your script is wonderful! . . . suspenseful and very moving. There are only two things that I can suggest. The first one may seem to be a big problem, but I think you can solve it quickly. Celia, because she is a female, would not have to take the oath. You may, however, have her [do so] for symbolic reasons, as a vote for reconciliation of the two sides, which would retain the effectiveness of the scene. The second thing is minor. You may wish to have Jonathan mention that resignation is not an option, because it would take too long for authorities in Washington to accept it, and the confiscation has to take place within twelve hours. Thus, his sole recourse is to flee. This is really great. I am so thrilled that you have asked me to participate . . . and I cannot wait to see it performed."[34]

In weeks to come, as Floyd fine-tuned, he and Glatthaar had three or four more meetings, but the historian thought his contributions insignificant. On the other hand, his opinion of Floyd was glowing: "He was wonderful: impressive, creative, positive, and just so bright. Every time we met, he was so excited to see me. It was such a treat to have somebody of his stature on campus all the time."[35]

Floyd celebrated his progress at the beginning of April with a quick trip to the Chicago Opera Theater, where Mark Flint conducted *Of Mice and Men*'s revival: seven performances with Lawrence Cooper (George), William Neill (Lennie), LeRoy Lehr (Curley), and Lauren Flanigan (Curley's Wife), staged by Arthur Masella.[36] That May, other opera world activity promised to alter Floyd's professional life, when New York City Opera announced that Floyd's champion, the conductor Christopher Keene, would succeed Beverly Sills as general director as of March 15, 1989.

Floyd revisited Toronto in June for a postmortem on Canadian Opera's young composers' works, but his suggestions fell again on deaf ears. Despite his lingering sense that the experience had been anything but happy, Lotfi Mansouri invited him back that December to meet a new triad. Perhaps an earlier start, before the composers had chiseled their ideas in granite, would allow Floyd better feelings about participating.

JULIUS RUDEL spent several weeks of March and April 1988 in Houston, conducting Wagner's *Tannhäuser*, and his conversations with Floyd turned to historical parallels that were on both men's minds. By the time Wagner accepted Paris Opera's 1861 commission to revise his 1842 *Tannhäuser*, his musical language had changed significantly, from *Lohengrin*, *Das Rheingold*, *Die Walküre*, to first attempts at *Siegfried* and *Tristan und Isolde*. Floyd's evolution had been no less dramatic in the thirty-three years since *Susannah*'s birth. He intended to reuse some thematic material from the 1962 *Wade*, but re-creating a nineteen-year-old idiom would result in a blatant pastiche. His evolved characters and dramaturgy needed tightly composed music that was thematically derived and had immediate emotional appeal: "My first obligation as a composer and librettist is simply to absorb an audience, but beyond that I . . . would like people to examine themselves and their feelings . . . beyond an evening of entertainment. Sometimes it is difficult to integrate these elements because we [composers] censor ourselves before we even get it down on the page. . . . I hope the impact . . . will be to stress the terror of losing our humanity. We should always be frightened of that."[37]

The formal commission for the opera first appeared on paper in Gockley's letter to Floyd of June 16, 1988, by which time Gockley had cobbled a partnership with the Opera Company of Greater Miami, and Floyd's compensation grew to twenty-five thousand dollars. Gockley agreed to split expenses of performance materials with Miami, after which they would become either Floyd's or Boosey's property; in exchange, Floyd forwent royalties for any audio recording that might be made by either partner company.[38]

In her June 2 memo, Sylvia Goldstein had suggested that Floyd leave fee negotiations to Boosey. By early December, Seattle and San Diego had joined the partnership, and Goldstein's involvement resulted in another increase in Floyd's fee to thirty thousand dollars, payable in four installments: ten thousand on signing the agreement, ten thousand on presenting a revised piano/vocal score, five thousand on presenting the revised orchestration, and five thousand on opening night in Houston.[39]

In 2002 Floyd explained: "Of all my operas, it is the one that approaches grand opera scale, not by intent, but by what was necessary to get the piece on the stage. It's a very big canvas and there's a lot compressed to its three-and-half-hours. . . . [Reconstruction is] an era . . . that's not too well known in this country. . . . But I didn't want it to be a history lesson. I wanted it to be colorful and authentic, but focus on the central character and the characters around him. I don't think I had the skill as a librettist in 1962 to really bring off a work as complex as that and to make it credible. The whole thing was so hurried. There was not any time for much reflection or to tweak it beforehand, we just had to get it on the stage."[40]

The shift from revising an old work to creating a fundamentally new one came first from the director Jack O'Brien, whom Floyd had known since at least 1976.[41] O'Brien returned to Houston in 1987 for a revival of his *Porgy and Bess* production. Over dinner one evening with Gockley, Floyd showed both men the intermediate *Wade* revision. O'Brien pounced at once on the characters' lack of focus, beginning with the ne'er-do-well Lucas Wardlaw, who needed a sharper point of view, accustomed as he was to privilege. The director also felt that Judge Townsend's exposition should be far more gradual, and that Floyd should develop a tender flirtation between Jonathan and Celia in act 1, scene 3, to show the flowering of the relationship. Floyd remembered, "Once I get prods like that, I can turn them into bigger things than Jack probably intended. But he's a great 'play doctor': he views the word as it is, and shows you where the weaknesses are."

Floyd and Gockley first hoped that O'Brien would direct the unveiling of the new work *Wade,* set for January 18, 1991, but he was tied down with Broadway and Old Globe work. Gockley then jumped at the chance to further involve Floyd, and hired *him* to direct his first world premiere since *Markheim* in New Orleans a quarter-century earlier. Acting on O'Brien's suggestions, Floyd placed his work under the microscope and saw that only a complete rewrite would remedy its weaknesses. He found his original characters two-dimensional and in need of clearer motivation for their actions. Enlisting the audience's identification and involvement became another overriding concern. Revision found its way into most exchanges between Jonathan and Celia, Enoch Pratt, Judge Townsend, and Wardlaw. Elsewhere, subtle cuts, beginning with five lines of atmosphere in the opening chorus, tightened the work's pace. "Generally," remarked Floyd in a 2001 interview, "the most telling scenes are . . . intimate. . . . It's actually an intimate opera, but it's played out against an epic background."[42]

Although Floyd's sprawling tapestry could never adhere to the letter of the ancient Greek unities of time (a single day), place (a single location) or action (a single plot line), his changes channeled the Hellenic spirit into all three areas: a single year, 1865, from May through December; Columbia, South Carolina; and the personal tragedy of Jonathan, Celia, and Judge Townsend. This streamlining even prompted him to overlook historical facts like the bribing of black legislators, who could not have been elected until 1867 at the earliest. Though he ultimately retained his 1962 Blackstock Girl, he telescoped her with another young woman, but with shorter and wider-ranging vocal lines. The meeting of Judge Townsend and Jonathan is more ariose and less "talky." He deleted Amy Pratt from the cast, thereby concentrating Enoch's unpleasantness without a softening influence, and Jonathan and Celia's son Johnny disappeared. A new minor character, Sergeant Branch, appears as a partial replacement for a less sympathetic but infinitely more complex Lieutenant Patrick.[43]

Floyd cut heavily into act 1, scene 2. With new accompaniment, Townsend's aria remains, but shortened and with new melodies. Tension accrues when Celia carries her litany of Yankee injustices too far, and Jonathan gives her a heated piece of his mind before coolly taking leave; but with pitches lowered, the exchange is less hysterical. Celia immediately regrets sending Nicey after him, but the lovers' separation allows for new apologies. Floyd transposed Jonathan's story about his brother in Andersonville prison from its position in the 1962 libretto, in language more graphic and concentrated. Their initial hostility turns first to flirtation, then to deeper attraction: Floyd wanted to suggest "everyone . . . walking on eggshells."[44] After Jonathan bids Celia good night, Floyd changed her aria about doffing her veil of mourning from a series of statements to questions.

The act 1, scene 3 party, extensively recomposed, clarifies the introductions of both Wardlaw and Pratt, as well as Jonathan's intervening trip to Washington, DC, and the return with Pratt. Wardlaw's needling of Wade over the army's relationship with the Freedmen's Bureau grew from Floyd's reading of Foner.[45] Celia's and Jonathan's endearments reveal greater depths, and Pratt's new speeches amplify his intentions for the Bureau. Finally, Nicey gives Pratt a timely comeuppance by specifying that Judge Townsend taught her to write long ago, and that she in fact continues to pass that skill to her black friends. Townsend's dispatch of Lucas and his associates whips up the chorus's defiance, without mention of Lincoln. Virtually the entire act 1 finale has new text, hence vocal settings, with explicit, character-appropriate sentiments for all principals in the drawing of battle lines above the chorus of party guests.

In act 2, scene 1, Floyd eliminated fifteen introductory measures and added a brief aria and other new speeches for Lucas that outline the wastrel's perceptions of changes in the old leisurely ways; far from wanting a new life, he wants his old one restored. Jonathan's ensuing dispute with Pratt incorporates substantial cuts and new music, and Pratt more fully explains his fanatical punitive approach, threatening reprisals should Wade question the commands of his superiors. His arioso about elevating the black race is more of a set piece, almost a marching song; and when Jonathan appeals Pratt's decision, his document goes to Charleston and not Raleigh.

Floyd made good use of Glatthaar's comments on the administration of the loyalty oath to women by strengthening Celia's resolve to let nothing separate her from Jonathan. The composer retained his love themes, but they are only half as long as in the original, and the Ku Klux Klan has given way to the Guardian Knights.

For episode 3, Floyd halved the pardon-seller Riddle's spiel with longer note values to the same melodic shape, and added a *duettino* between Riddle and his Union League cohort. Both changes propel us to the meat of act 2, scene 2, with new music for Lieutenant Patrick and the new order. Throughout his revision, Floyd eliminated most *vuote* (empty measures for dramatic pauses). Jonathan's prosecution of Riddle has mostly new music, and Jonathan's aria urging his conscience to sleep replaces nine lines with six new or rewritten ones.

Jonathan relieves Townsend of his judgeship with sharper new text and music. Celia's subsequent siding with Jonathan strengthened her resolve as she struggled with her decision, which also allowed Floyd to expand what had been a duet into a trio. Though most vocal lines have been written a little lower, Townsend's disowning of Celia rose by a fifth.

The long interlude before the act's concluding wedding is gone. Everything up to the Rector's entrance is new music, and Floyd eliminated the business with the soldier presenting the bouquet. Nicey sings an added verse of her spiritual before the Guardian Knights clash. Their "Thodika, Stevika" has yielded to completely new text, a much more complex, if shorter, interweaving of the music of the two groups, and an extension of the duet between Celia and Jonathan, followed by a hummed recapitulation of Nicey's spiritual.

In act 3, scene 1, with its drastically condensed time frame, Jonathan and Celia have had no time to produce a son, so Celia sings no lullaby. Floyd amplified Pratt's determination to ruin Wade, with a new and showier "vengeance aria," in which he no longer compliments himself on confiscating Townsend's property, but elaborates on a personal hunger for recognition. The scene between Lieutenant Patrick and Pratt is completely new.

The interlude leading to episode 4 is shorter, with most of the music unchanged, up to the carpetbagger speeches, which are cut or shortened; instead, Floyd extended Bell's withdrawal into a real aria with new text.

Tension grows from a new argument between Jonathan and Patrick, lending even greater impetus to Jonathan's decision to desert, and giving Patrick greater definition and depth—and a mini-aria. In the ensuing encounter between Celia and Jonathan, recomposed and shorter, Floyd gets right to the point by telling her about the confiscation order. An argument follows, and a bitter denunciation that her husband is personally responsible for the family's disaster. They bond again in a longer and more complex duet, centered on the wish to live in a better past or brighter future; the scene is made doubly poignant by Jonathan's recomposed reprise of his invocation to sleep.

Floyd preserved the last scene's overall shape, intensifying and condensing action, with new vocal lines, articulations, and accompaniments. He eliminated the Klan song, but Wardlaw threatens Wade directly that the Guardian Knights are out to kill him, and Lieutenant Patrick and Pratt declare their intention to arrest Wade for court martial. After the fatal shot, Celia orders the room cleared and Jonathan's body taken to the mortuary. After bringing Jonathan's dress uniform as funeral garb, and Celia's widow's veil, Nicey sings a new prayer for Jonathan's soul.

Floyd used Gockley as a sounding board for his inspirations, making the new work more collaborative. Both men agreed that act 3 needed a strong visual climax: after Celia pours out her grief, Nicey places the veil over her head, completing the arc of loss, and Nicey has the last word with a reprise of her prayer. As in the final picture of *Susannah,* Floyd creates a powerful image of Celia's future, in this case the isolation of widowhood.

WHILE FLOYD grew daily more absorbed, his lawyer Glen Rosenbaum waged noble war to recover copyrights from Belwin-Mills/Columbia. By the time Floyd spoke to Sylvia Goldstein on June 2, Rosenbaum had learned that Columbia would return *Bilby's Doll, Willie Stark, Fanfare* (*Flourishes*), and *Of Mice and Men.* The chaos that had reigned since Bob Holton's death came fully to light only during the next several months, as negotiations grew ever more baroque over who actually had what. (Theodore Presser's rental division had *Bilby's Doll* and *Willie Stark.*) On October 24, a senior choral editor at Belwin/CPP in Miami informed Rosenbaum that Presser might have *Citizen of Paradise* as well, but his senior instrumental editor was not familiar with *Flourishes,* and thought that Presser had that work as well. In any event, Belwin had printed none of Floyd's works after *The Martyr,* and the firm had no intention of doing so in the future. Because Presser's rental library had physical possession of the works, it appeared that Filmtrax held the copyrights.[46]

Floyd now worked on a third front. His university colleague Buck Ross planned a summer workshop with Des Moines Metro Opera apprentices, to allow Floyd to see his most recent *Bilby's Doll* revisions in action. In the final version that Floyd was preparing for Boosey,[47] most of his changes involved minor nips and tucks in both libretto and music, beginning in act 1, scene 1, in the dialogue between Thumb and Silas. Floyd rewrote text and music in act 1, scene 2, after Doll's folk song, and in her fabrication of poppets for the Thumb twins, as well as in Titus's courtship of Doll. He made more substantial cuts in act 2, scene 1, between Doll and Zelley. He partially replaced lines and music at the point where Zelley verbalizes his longing for a daughter, and at Doll's first confession that she has prayed to both God and Satan.

All but a few lines of act 2, scene 2, the venomous confrontation between Doll and Hannah, are new and recomposed. In scene 3, Floyd cut nine of Doll's lines and four of Shad's after their love night, replacing them with two lines that complete Doll's ballad. He rewrote the first half of the faux marriage business, as well as most of the beginning of scene 4, where the twins claim illness. De la Torre's therapy had sharpened Floyd's objectivity: Already in his 1976 Omaha revisions, he had seen that the conflict of Doll and Hannah served up the meat of the drama, yet he had simply dropped Hannah from sight. Now he assigned all of Mrs. Thumb's lines to Hannah, stoking the fires of her animosity toward Doll.

Everything from Reverend Mather's entrance through his examination of the twins and Titus's renunciation of calling and faith is likewise new. With the exception of a few minor word changes, and Titus's final prayer for mercy for Doll's soul, act 3 remained the same. In all, Floyd and Ross trimmed a half hour. The composer stayed in Indianola, Iowa, for about a week that summer, watching the opera's evolution in rehearsal and critic-free performance.

BY LATE FALL Gockley had signed the German Austrian designer Günther Schneider-Siemssen to recreate South Carolina onstage.[48] Schneider-Siemssen planned to make projections from period photographs of exteriors and monuments in ruined 1865 Columbia, and Floyd enlisted Thomas Johnson at the South Caroliniana Library to provide materials.

During the university holiday break, Ermine met Floyd in Charleston, and drove to the Methodist Home to visit their father. For months, during each of their phone calls, Reverend Floyd asked, "When will you be coming up this way again?" and Floyd obliged, as much as his schedule and aviophobia allowed. Each interaction featured repeated paternal lines, not of apology but of pleas for absolution: "I think about how I treated you as a boy, as a son."

The new Floyd smiled, "I survived, I'm doing fine."

Reverend Floyd might then observe, "Son, you always had a lot of grit." At first, Floyd hoped that the old man was trying to set matters straight between them, but the subject here was neither childhood abuses nor career issues, but rather his father's admiration of Carlisle's stoicism in North with Dr. Truluck's sadistic nasal treatment. Yet this time was different. After a few innocuous remarks, Reverend Floyd hugged him, kissed his cheek, and blurted out, "You are the glory of my life." Floyd had no response. They hugged once more, and Floyd blanked the rest of their conversation, filing the remark away for processing on the anxious flight home.

Early December took Floyd back to Toronto to meet Canadian Opera's new group: composer Andrew MacDonald and his librettist Ken Koebke, at work on *The Unbelievable Glory of Mr. Sharp*, a contemporary murder tale;[49] Peter Paul Koprowski and the librettist Rodney J. Anderson, who collaborated on *Dulcitius: Demise of Innocence*, which unfolds around 300 A.D. during the reign of Rome's Emperor Diocletian; and composer Denis Gougeon and his cocreator Timothy Anderson, at work on *An Expensive Embarrassment*, transposing Chekhov's story "The Marriage Proposal" to present-day New York.[50]

As before, the librettists seemed more amenable than the composers, who ignored most of what Floyd had to say. Lotfi Mansouri, bemused, responded that the participants were all "babes in the woods." Feeling useless, on December 17 Floyd returned to Houston, to find Kay's mother their house guest. Instead of disappearing to his university studio to work on *Jonathan Wade*, he learned that Ermine had just called with news that their father had died. Reverend Floyd, suffering from chronic emphysema, had contracted pneumonia again and had been moved to a hospital in Orangeburg. Four days later he was dead at age eighty-four. At the end, he had risen up in bed and proclaimed, like Olin Blitch entering New Hope Valley, "I am the Reverend C. S. Floyd!" before falling back into peaceful shallow breathing that stopped moments later.

Neither Kay nor Gundy had much to say, having experienced the old man's abuse of Floyd; but as always, Floyd's thoughts anchored on such practical matters as getting to Holly Hill for the funeral. As he packed for a four-day stay, his sadness stopped short of grief, or even relief; yet he felt gratitude that Ermine's enormous burden had lifted, punctuating the end of a family history of moving vans crammed with unfinished business. Kay sent her husband alone to bury his father; but years of therapy had given Floyd the strength to abandon unrealistic expectations of love and support. Though unaware of the "famous family" diary references, he knew that the old man, despite an almost total ignorance of what went into conceiving, writing, and producing operas, had always basked in the glow of his boy's career.

Profound sadness did rise from Floyd's regret that they had never addressed, much less resolved, their differences. In his earliest years, he had loved and admired his father, at the same time fearing his parents too much to express himself. Both elders had lacked the emotional repertoire to overcome their incapacities or his. He could count on the fingers of one hand the number of times his father had treated him as an adult man, rather than from the perspective of the judgmental, punishing minister lurking behind a parental facade.

Floyd, Ermine and her family, and the tiny congregation of Target Methodist ringed the graveside as Reverend Floyd's casket was lowered beside his wife's in South Carolina's December earth. Having packed his *Jonathan Wade* manuscript books, the composer availed himself of the Matheny grand piano to meet his next deadline. Apologizing to Billy and Ermine after breakfast, he disappeared into the living room to complete a set amount of daily work, and his new interest and passion surprised and relieved those who knew him best. He and Ermine discussed the division of Reverend Floyd's estate: their father had left more than ninety thousand dollars in cash and investments in equal shares to son and daughter.[51] Ermine and Billy would soon move into her parents' home and pay Floyd half of its assessed value.

ERMINE'S FREER LIFE now allowed her to attend more Floyd performances and spend more time as a houseguest in Houston. With Floyd's total immersion in *Jonathan Wade,* one such visit opened a window onto his new and more intuitive approach to work. Ermine saw him struggling to get the music teeming in his brain down on paper fast enough. One day as they drove along a Houston freeway, Floyd turned to her with a look half-sheepish, half-surprised, thinking of the uniform/veil sequence at the opera's conclusion, and said: "I feel so funny. I know how I'm going to end it. It came to me while I slept."

In March 1989, Floyd was asked back to Florida State University to stage its *Susannah* revival, with Ward Holmquist conducting a student cast. This sentimental return framed the composer's final meeting with Hazel Richards. Old friend Bill Rogers drove him out to see her for the first time since Floyd had left Tallahassee thirteen years earlier. Floyd sensed that she may have suffered strokes. Any remant of her three-decades-old frostiness was replaced by nostalgia for "those nice times." Hazel had been unable to walk since the early eighties, but, indomitable and imperious as ever, she determined to attend *Susannah*'s April 6 opening. Floyd allowed as how that would be nice, and that was all the encouragement she needed: she rented a private ambulance, and had an attendant wheel her chair into place at the rear of the auditorium. She had exhibited no interest in Floyd's current work, much less his emotional well-being. The two did not speak that night, but Ermine sought her out, only to find that the old woman in her flamboyant caftan preferred to make loud, fanatical declamations to others, proof enough of narcissistic investment in one last celebration of her cherished protégé.[52]

Floyd's return to life accelerated with the coming of spring 1989, first with news that Frank Corsaro had undertaken a project to atone in part for his defection from *Bilby's Doll* in 1976. The Opera/Music Theatre Institute of New Jersey, no relation to the NEA's similarly named program, had been founded by the American basso Jerome Hines in 1987 to provide training and performance opportunities for the most promising young singers on the verge of launching careers but not yet earning a living from music.[53]

As such missions always have, this one spoke to most of the singers in the New York metroplex, attracting commensurately strong talent. Corsaro extracted a one-hour condensation of the opera, without sets or costumes, using his own narration to stitch up plot seams. He oversaw minimal movement, credited in the program as "dramatic supervision," and rehearsed at the Actors Studio in New York in mid-April. For Floyd, it was another opportunity to evaluate the changes he had first seen in Des Moines the previous summer, but with more advanced singers. He spoke with the cast about textual priorities above and beyond vocalism, prompting Corsaro's remark, "You hear that? From a composer?!"

Floyd thought it a pleasant situation, "for an unpolished production," even without seeing the performances on April 27 and 28. Compaction did the work no harm. One critic, while admitting that Floyd's music might strike some as thorny, urged the complete opera's long-overdue reevaluation, and referred to scenes that he found "astonishing even in this trimmed . . . version. . . . [It is a] gripping drama . . . 'frightening' would not be too strong a word."[54]

The National Music Theater Network, which had given Floyd its 1986 award, sponsored a Manhattan performance on May 1. Floyd journeyed to Oklahoma on May 6 for the premiere of Tulsa Opera's *Susannah,* staged by James DeBlasis and conducted by Willie Anthony Waters, with Elizabeth Knighton in the title role, Jeffrey Wells (Blitch), Richard Brunner (Sam), and William Livingston (Little Bat). Tulsa Mayor Rodger A. Randle proclaimed this *Carlisle Floyd Day.*

Back in Houston, Floyd took time out from *Jonathan Wade* to finish an eightieth birthday tribute to Elena Nikolaidi. For the 1989 Lyric Art Festival, a concert was scheduled for June 8, Nikolaidi's actual birthday. A group of present and past students and UH faculty composers—Floyd, Michael Horvit, Robert Nelson, and David Ashley White—wrote songs for the occasion. Floyd culled, adapted, and set three lines of Shakespeare, the first from *Much Ado about Nothing,* spoken in the original by Beatrice: "There was a star danced, and under that was I born."[55]

Floyd's substitution of "*were you* born" tuned the sentiment perfectly to this old friend. The second fragment, from *The Two Noble Kinsmen,* is delivered by two of Shakespeare's three Theban queens to Theseus: "To thee no star be dark! Both heaven and earth/ Friend thee forever!"[56]

Floyd modernized "friend" to "befriend." The manuscript, dated May 10, 1989,[57] is a thirty-two-measure coloratura showpiece, sung at its premiere by soprano Debra Hays,[58] accompanied by Robert Brewer. An ambiguous harmonic introduction concentrates on treble registers of both piano and voice. Alternating 3/4 and 4/4, *Allegro non troppo ma animato,* with two repetitions of a ten-note polytonal run upward, Floyd outlines an F-sharp Major triad, then adds accidentals of C, F, B-flat, D, E, and E-sharp/G-sharp, all blended by pedaling. The vocal line echoes then dances around F-sharp Major, with six, and later another five, repetitions of the word "danced," ending on high C-sharp. Octuplet runs combine E-flat Major and D Major to underscore the line "and under that were you born," leading to a pedal chord grounded in C Major, with a final run up in C Major and accidental F-sharp. The lyrical second section in 6/4, *L'istesso tempo ma più sostenuto, molto espressivo,* wreathes the final verses in warmth and confidence in the piano's rich low and middle registers. Holding mostly to C Major, with related harmonies of A Minor and F Major, a final octuplet uprush of E-flat Major plus D Major resolves definitively in C, combining, and thus reconciling, bass and treble sonorities.

ON MAY 22, Thomas Johnson sent archival illustrations for *Jonathan Wade* set projections. He regretted the lack of interior views of Columbia homes from the 1860s, and wrote that no Confederate monument existed in the city until 1878, and no State House steps until the early twentieth century. Johnson also described the appearance of magnolia leaves in interior photos, remarking that they gave the devastated city's homes modest yet dignified touches of class and beauty. Pine, holly, and camellias provided other touches of living green on mantelpieces and tables amid the bleakness of Reconstruction.[59]

Victory in Floyd's ongoing copyright battle arrived with Glen Rosenbaum's June 8 letter to Sylvia Goldstein that contained an executed assignment of rights and mutual general release instruments for all of the composer's "unpublished" works covered by his 1973 Belwin contract:[60] *Of Mice and Men, Bilby's Doll, Willie Stark, Citizen of Paradise,* and *Flourishes* had all languished out of print, or had never appeared. Boosey's library soon bulged with thirty boxes of Floyd material: printer's tissues and masters of orchestral and vocal scores, chorus and instrumental parts, including reduced orchestrations, and printed scores and promotional materials.

By February 1991, Goldstein, by now promoted to Boosey's senior vice presidency, had discovered the disarray of these materials: copyright renewal dates for Floyd's earlier scores needed to be written into Boosey's calendars, the standard unit of copyright being twenty-eight years. *Of Mice and Men,* for instance, first copyrighted in 1971, had to be renewed before the end of 1999. In addition to substituting Floyd's name for any publisher's in the printed scores, certificates from the United States Copyright Office would have to be secured for all his Belwin works. As Boosey's Linda Golding later said of such transactions, "One of the problems in the industry in general is that details get packed away and reside in people's brains. When those people are no longer able to answer, it's up for grabs. You can only hope that it can be solved in a way that's most beneficial to the composer."[61]

More serious was a February 1990 request from the stage director Malcolm Fraser for a perusal score of *Bilby's Doll* for the University of Cincinnati College-Conservatory of Music. He expressed interest in touring a production in Europe, and pressed Boosey's staff for a quick response. For the time being, however, the boxes of Belwin materials remained unprocessed in Boosey's rental library, and the project never materialized. That March, the film producer Irving Saraf inquired about using a twenty-second segment from Berkeley Opera's 1986 *Of Mice and Men* for a new documentary, *In the Shadow of the Stars,* about members of the San Francisco Opera chorus. Daniel Becker, who played Lennie in Berkeley, was to speak with Floyd's music in the background, but at the top of Saraf's letter, someone wrote that film rights remained unavailable.[62] The film, without Floyd's music, went on to win the 1991 Academy Award for best documentary.

HAVING COME TO RELY ON the workshop process to refine new and old work, Floyd was gratified when his university colleague Buck Ross scheduled another such event at Des Moines Metro Opera for act 1 of *Jonathan Wade* that summer. Floyd had yet to hear the revisions outside his brain. Ross and music director Ward Holmquist began drilling the young artists in May, and gave a public performance of the entire act on July 14. Floyd could not make it to Iowa, but the company sent a videotape of the event on which he based further revisions.

Floyd had not heard from Robert Penn Warren since January 1982, and mourned the great writer's death of prostate cancer on October 14, 1989. The next month, Floyd appeared at the University of Texas–El Paso American Music Week for performances of *Susannah* on November 10 and 12. In addition to attending opening night, that Friday he gave an afternoon lecture, then a master class for composition students. Later that month, Sylvia Goldstein nudged Floyd's memory about how lovely it would be to celebrate the New Year with a Boosey & Hawkes contract.[63]

The eventual document, signed on November 28, addressed the composer's Belwin-Mills issues. He might terminate the contract if, for any two consecutive years after 1990, royalties and other fees did not equal the sum of $1,500.00. The first renewal period would last until December 31, 1994, and guaranteed Floyd slightly different royalties, payable semiannually after June 30 and December 31: 25 percent of sheet music; 66 and 2/3 percent of rentals; 75 percent mechanicals, synchronization, and grand rights; and 50 percent small rights and permissions. Boosey further agreed that Floyd might himself print a reasonable number of copies of his music, in addition to copies generated by the publisher. Floyd agreed to reimburse Boosey for such out of pocket expenses as typesetting, notesetting, printing, and binding, to be deducted from royalties; he would then have possession of all copies once Boosey's expenses had been fully recouped. Henceforth, notices in scores would read that Floyd held all copyrights, with Boosey stipulated as sole agent.

In his December 7 cover letter to Goldstein, Floyd congratulated his friend on her promotion and thanked her and Jim Kendrick for making the negotiation of their new agreement so pleasant, "particularly in light of the Kafkaesque events of the past several years with publishers." He quoted Willie Stark's line about the joy of homecoming.[64]

Toward the end of 1989, Kay's mother, Gundy, accepted the Floyds' invitation to move in with them in Houston. She proved to be no easier a boarder than an in-law. Kay and Floyd trundled her back and forth to doctors and hospitals. Though Floyd spent enough time in his university studio that they rarely saw each other, he knew how much unpleasantness Kay faced, and just after the 1990 winter holidays they moved her to a comfortable retirement community. The end of 1989 had another silver lining; Floyd received a check from Boosey & Hawkes for $5,188.26, the bulk of it for grand rights and sales of sheet music.[65]

In 1990, Ernst Bacon passed away in Orinda, California, just two months short of his ninety-second birthday. Around the same time, negotiations with NPR's *Great Performances* for a film of the new *Jonathan Wade* broke down, as did those for a Corsaro-directed film of Miami Opera's *Of Mice and Men*, a casualty of Florida Governor Bob Martinez's line-item veto.[66] In South Carolina, Thomas Johnson brainstormed having the new *Jonathan Wade* performed in Columbia, the city of its setting, by importing Houston's upcoming production. Floyd and Ermine attended a lunch with a wealthy potential backer, but after HGO finance manager Jim Ireland submitted a budget of $428,000,[67] this too "died a-borning."

In Houston, Floyd sat before a plate full of new libretto and music. In their sessions, De la Torre used the *Wade* project for communicative matching, a technique aimed at eliciting aspects of a patient's personality left stunted by early life experiences.[68] When Floyd completed the text—40 percent of it new—he gave it to De la Torre to read. At their next session, the doctor handed it back with thanks for letting him read it. Still troubled by conversational voids, Floyd asked, "How did you like it?" De la Torre responded crypto-therapeutically that he had agreed to read it, not to say what he thought of it.

Still, buoyed by their progress, and support from HGO, the university, and Boosey, Floyd felt even greater passion for his new *Passion*. He began daily at five a.m., eager to get to his studio. He continued to solicit Glatthaar's input, which arrived in a memo with historical data about the loyalty oath and contradicted nothing that Floyd had written; but Glatthaar also raised the absence of black legislators in South Carolina until 1867–1868, which Floyd let stand.[69] As Schneider-Siemssen's designs progressed, Floyd finished composing 80 percent new material and touched up the libretto. Glatthaar mentioned that the American flag bore thirty-five stars during the last two years of the Civil War; another star was added on July 4, 1865,[70] or three months after the opera's opening scene.

In the winter of 1989/90, as pianist Robin Stamper worked on an artist diploma at the Cincinnati College-Conservatory of Music, HGO's studio coaching staff head Jean Mallandaine called to tell him that none of that year's pianists could handle *Jonathan Wade*. Stamper expressed interest and availability, but withheld commitment until he could inspect Floyd's score. Eleven days later, with the printer's ink barely dry, three volumes arrived via FedEx. Stamper remembers "this gigantic box of opera. I opened it up and almost fainted: sometimes it was three lines, sometimes four. I thought, 'OK, here goes.'"[71] Stamper arrived in Houston ready to work:

> Another pianist told me, "His scores are either hell or whole notes." And I said, "Either hell or Hollywood!" because his music is so Pucciniesque, by way of Americana, but with the big melodic stuff, tumultuous, so intense. *Jonathan Wade* really was pianistically unreasonable: four staves, the whole bit. But he believed so much in the score, he wanted to make sure everything was there. And I was a piano jock, I think that's one of the reasons he liked me: I took great pleasure in playing as many notes as I could, as fast as I could; and as a composer, he liked hearing that."[72]

That Stamper succeeded past all expectation was proven by Floyd's insistence on having him as the coach-accompanist for successive revivals. Floyd and

John DeMain now worked with studio members—sopranos Dana Barrow and Elizabeth (Heidi) Jones, mezzo-soprano Denyce Graves, tenor Eric Perkins, baritone Bruce Brown, and bass-baritone Grant Youngblood—on a May 13 in-house essay of acts 2 and 3. The event proved to Floyd that he had given his characters the breadth and depth they lacked in 1962.

> Things happened too fast in the first version, the characters were too black and white. We knew too much about them too soon, rather than having them evolve over time. For such a complex work, it's necessary to track characters all the way through. If you're dealing with more than one or two, it's very easy to forget that the others have lives of their own that feed into the story and the central characters' lives. You almost had to do a diagram of Jonathan's relationships with surrounding characters, and you had to bring this off within a reasonable amount of time. I'll never take on that many in one opera again, but I think I finally succeeded in making each character real.

He saw that *Wade*'s size and scope would make future productions less likely; it ran for three and a half hours, had fourteen principal roles, a set encompassing projections and solid pieces, and which required quick changes and complex lighting. The company would employ 104 other singers and actors in two adult choruses, children and supernumeraries, and a fifty-seven-piece orchestra. Still, Floyd felt it was one of his best pieces in terms of his personal satisfaction with the result. David Gockley's San Diego counterpart, Ian Campbell, attended the workshop and wrote Floyd on May 15: "From the time I first heard the original version, and read your remarkable libretto, I have felt that this is truly the American opera for the 1990s, and I am even more convinced of this view having seen the workshop and experienced the even finer version which you are putting together."[73]

Floyd's rapport with Campbell was cemented during a visit to San Diego that September. In addition to his usual round of interviews and "informances" for the company, the composer gave a rare performance at a donor party, accompanying a local singer in Jonathan's aria on conscience-sleep. Some of the San Diego patrons puzzled but amused Floyd with their expressions of surprise that a composer could also play the piano.

Gockley spared nothing on Schneider-Siemssen's sets and lighting and engaged the finest singing actors: Dale Duesing (Jonathan), Sheryl Woods (Celia), Debria Brown (Nicey), Harlan Foss (Riddle), Joseph Evans (Lucas), John Duykers (Pratt), and, as a special treat for Floyd, Julian Patrick as Judge Townsend. As Floyd finished one section, he sent manuscript pages directly to Patrick as a favor, but the baritone could not make heads or tails of it. Floyd reassured him, "You're probably remembering that I wrote this for Norman [Treigle], but I've changed it for your voice," and he had Boosey send Patrick one of the first printed complete scores.

Richard McKee as Riddle and Donnie Ray Albert as Judge Bell completed the ensemble. Floyd himself directed, and John DeMain and Ward Holmquist shared conducting duties, with performances on January 18, 20, 23, 26, 29, and February 2, 1991. Floyd eventually changed his original dedication from David Gockley (as in Boosey's scores) to Ian Campbell, not through ill feelings, but to leave Gockley "free" for a later work. During rehearsals, Julian Patrick saw the composer "extraordinarily in love with the piece, and loath to let go of any part of it. The music is beautiful, but I told him that it was too long. Debria Brown's aria is the most wonderful thing in the whole piece: a spiritual, but Carlisle wrote it. He still has an extraordinary ear for writing things that sound like they've been there forever. And what she sang after Jonathan's death: I just stood there with chill bumps."[74]

Patrick, whom Floyd had often directed, offered sharp insights about the composer's stagecraft:

> He talks with you about what you want to do at a given moment, why you're here, and then turns you loose to do what seems to come logically for you, as the person on stage. Occasionally, if that doesn't satisfy him or bring the character to life, he'll help you add some device or idiosyncrasy to change the shape of your performance. He doesn't say 'Do this, do that, go here

> and do that.' He doesn't strive for big pictures—except when the chorus is on stage—but if he trusts you, and you agree about what you want to do, even if it's not quite what he's after, he doesn't interfere.
>
> And he never corrected individuals publically. He'd come to me and say in private, 'You know, you can take a little longer here, or you can take your hat off sooner there.' If you were entering a scene in which something momentous was going to happen that affected your response, he'd say, 'You mustn't bring that idea with you, let the audience see the change.' He was grateful when his plans worked, and would let you know, thank you for getting it right, for making the scene work.

Patrick added, "I've never seen him lay into someone, or be really hard on anyone. I'd see people change, but I didn't know why, I was so busy looking out for myself."

As opening night approached, Floyd took a new measure of Kay's agoraphobia: she refused to attend even the dress rehearsal. With enough worries of his own, he did not pressure her, and the couple hosted a New Year's Eve party for cast and staff.

History now provided a new but familiar obstacle to the opera's success: On January 17, the day before the *Wade* world premiere, President George H. W. Bush ordered the bombardment of Baghdad, and the first Gulf War exploded. *Wade* had always mirrored Floyd's pacifist sentiments, and antiwar tracts have never played well in Texas, or, as the composer observed, "in other parts of the south." Audience mood and enthusiasm were commensurately somber. One critic found the coincidence unfortunate, but appreciated Floyd's latest work as refined and classical: "As librettist, Floyd has crafted a rich, sprawling yet subtly nuanced story. As composer, he has written a work that may be the high point of his career . . . great swaths of emotionally moving music."[75]

Roberto Suro's *New York Times* notice highlighted Floyd's eclectic experimentation, his "movement away from doctrinaire approaches," and his mingling of such traditional ingredients as Nicey's spiritual with "sweeping dissonance and bitonal harmonies."[76]

As often happened, Floyd's best feedback came from his colleagues, past and present. His current leading lady, Sheryl Woods, wrote in her opening night note: "My one and only 'official' acting teacher used to remind us that we could be only as effective as our material. Thank you for giving us so much to work with. This work resonates with such Truth. I love it for its dual vision of what is real and what is ideal; surely we are in dire need of reckoning with both. I am grateful for your spirit and your gifts in expressing it. Thank you for creating a woman of such substance as Celia—such concomitant strength and vulnerability—and for giving me the challenge and privilege of giving her flesh."[77]

Gockley had invited Theodor Uppman and Phyllis Curtin, creators of Jonathan and Celia in 1962, to this latest Houston opening. Uppman wrote Floyd of his hopes that this *Jonathan Wade* might have greater success than the earlier version. He and Curtin agreed that Floyd had preserved the drama's essence and beauty, and that his gift for orchestral color and singable vocal lines had only strengthened.[78]

After closing on February 2, Floyd trimmed another twenty minutes from the score. With the production loaded and shipped to Miami, he began rehearsal with new and old cast members: Carolann Page and Alison England (Celia), Erich Parce double cast with Dale Duesing (Jonathan), James Wood and Julian Patrick (Townsend), Jacque Trussel and Robert Brubaker (Lucas), and William Fleck (Riddle). Debria Brown and John Duykers repeated Nicey and Pratt. Local press welcomed Floyd's return to creation, for the "incredibly moving" opera's theatrical depths: "*Jonathan Wade* resonates with centuries of operatic tradition. . . . Beneath the complexity of the music, there is a lyrical pulse . . . [that] propels and enhances the action."[79] "Within his neo-Romantic style, Floyd writes affectingly and idiomatically for the human voice, orchestrates superbly, and is a seasoned dramatist. . . . *Jonathan Wade* often rivets attention like a good movie."[80]

After performances at Dade County Auditorium on March 18, 19, 20, 23, and 24, conducted by Hal France, the production and personnel sped cross-country to San Diego, where Sheryl Woods rejoined the cast that included Erich Parce and Julian Patrick. Kenneth Montgomery conducted, and Floyd again directed, with performances on April 13, 16, 19, and 21. Despite reservations stemming from the Mideast conflict, critic David Gregson praised the opera's "undeniable audience appeal" and "music and drama of sincerely felt intensity."[81]

JONATHAN WADE had kept Floyd busy enough for the past year that he missed performances of his other works: the *Wuthering Heights* Suite made a rare appearance at Wilfred Laurier University in Waterloo, Ontario, on February 10; Boston's New England Conservatory opened its *Susannah* on April 4; and on April 26 and 28, Duquesne University's School of Music in Pittsburgh performed all of *Wuthering Heights.* On May 26, *Susannah* scored another first, with a production by the obviously advanced music program of New Jersey's Montclair High School.

From Houston that same day, Floyd thanked Ian Campbell for the San Diego production, which he thought "the most fully realized and performed with the greatest polish and conviction" of its three outings to date. But as a man two months away from his sixty-fifth birthday, Floyd needed a break: "As you can imagine, I have felt somewhat in limbo since returning to Houston. My first response after the final performance . . . was overwhelming physical and mental fatigue which had been held at bay during the many months of fueling myself on adrenalin. After several weeks of indulging my need for sleep at all hours . . . and doing only what I was absolutely required to do, I am beginning now to try to balance continuing relaxation with catching up on all those things deferred for so long . . . [but] I really meant it when I said at your Major Donors party last September that I can't imagine agreeing to practice and perform the orchestral accompaniment to [Jonathan's sleep aria] in public for anyone other than Ian Campbell!"[82]

Yet a May 10 interoffice memo between the Boosey employees David Huntley and Linda Golding reveals that the composer in fact overflowed with new plans. Christopher Keene had told Floyd that he planned to import *Jonathan Wade* to City Opera during the 1993–1994 season, and, in an effort to trim its overall length, suggested cutting the episodes. Ardis Krainik, Lyric Opera of Chicago general director, had already committed to a new *Susannah* two years hence, a coproduction with Houston and possibly San Francisco, with either Samuel Ramey or James Morris as Blitch. Hal Prince, whom Floyd had already asked to direct, was unavailable until 1994 at the earliest. Krainik had seen one of the Miami *Wade*s and, according to Floyd, "seemed pleased." During the phone call that sparked a May 10 Boosey memo, Floyd wondered whether Krainik could do both *Susannah* and *Wade,* which Huntley thought unlikely.[83] Boosey and Floyd likewise failed to interest Martin Feinstein of Washington Opera, who also saw the Miami production. Peter Hemmings of Los Angeles Opera, who had been present in San Diego, told Floyd that the story would not interest his audiences.

Floyd also spoke of a *Bilby's Doll* "relaunch" as his next major project, but wished first to identify performing opportunities before committing to a final version.[84] By this time, Seattle Opera had signed on as a cosponsor of *Jonathan Wade,* and Floyd approached Renée Fleming, booked for the Chicago *Susannah,* about learning Celia for those performances in October 1992. After listening to the Houston performance tapes, Fleming responded gratefully but in the negative, feeling that the role's length and intense emotional pitch, which she compared to *Madama Butterfly,* might tax her at this stage of her career.[85]

ON JUNE 11, 1991, Floyd turned sixty-five. He had just learned from Boosey that Decca Records contemplated adding *Susannah* to its American opera series. The producer Michael Haas termed it the opera that Americans, especially marketing people, most wanted, and feared that an untried cast would produce an inadequate recording for Virgin Records. Samuel Ramey had already approached Haas, stating that recording *Susannah* was also his most desired project.[86]

Ermine and Billy Matheny flew to Houston to celebrate the birthday; they brought a stack of cards from South Carolina family and friends, and a filmed retrospective of pictures and recordings by daughter Jane, by now a professional videographer. Its soundtrack began with a solo flute performing the melody of one of the *Episodes,* and continued with a dialogueless compilation of excerpts from various Floyd opera performances. (Ermine was credited as "executive producer," which Floyd took to mean that she had subsidized costs.) Ermine's eldest, Martha, could not attend the Houston celebration, but sent a card depicting a Floyd quite different from his public image: "Watching Jane's video brought back so many memories of waiting for you to drive up in your convertible or one of the T-Birds, or thinking how cool you looked smoking, or shopping & eating & laughing & scratching your dandruff—boy I was a weird kid. But you always loved me and I knew it."[87]

Another present arrived from Ian Campbell, a sheaf of sixteen letters of praise from San Diego Opera patrons. Typical was one from the Los Angeles lawyer Stephen Haworth, who predicted that *Wade* would become America's favorite opera.[88] Along with news that San Diego had added a 1996 *Wade* revival to its calendar, Campbell himself added, "You have created a genuine modern classic of American opera, a work which can hold its own with the best of any nation at any time. It does what only the greatest operas can do: it speaks, it communicates, at a myriad of levels to every hearer, and leaves them touched, moved, and thoughtful. . . . This is your finest achievement in an already remarkable career, and I feel honoured to have been a participant in bringing it to San Diego."

Many of the people who knew Floyd best, who had observed his growth and recent personal and creative resurrection, expressed similar praise. Floyd had discovered a kindred spirit in Boosey's Linda Golding, with her intelligence, broad experience in the opera world, perspective, and humor.[89] Though she had earned a liberal arts degree in music history, she claims her instrument to be "the stereo." Her observations on Floyd offer solid proof that he had corrected his life's course and preserved his independence:

> Carlisle was real, and not some sort of shadow image. I always looked forward to a conversation with him, as a way to ground myself, despite the fact that we were at the time dealing with really complicated copyright contractual issues. In this business, it is rare for an artist to also have a really appealing personality; there is always a concern that they will be taken advantage of. So to have the opportunity to meet and be sociable with a legend that we all grew up with, that's pretty astonishing. And Carlisle is both a legend and much beloved: you scratch the surface of just about any singer, even the newly minted ones, and there is a connection to his music.
>
> Once you establish the relationship, he's extremely generous. I think there is a healthy wariness to him, from growing up in the place that he did; but once we established the relationship, it had an almost familial feel. There was also a trustworthiness about him. I found him very honorable: no coyness, no fooling around about anything.
>
> I always loved being with him. I found his life experiences very appealing, also his willingness to help younger colleagues, which does not happen all that often. He took his work extremely seriously, but not more seriously than the world around him, so there was always a sense of humor about it. He's a great ironist: not a joke teller, but he has a very wry way of looking at things and of expressing himself.
>
> I often found myself wishing that I'd known him as a younger man, because he must have been quite dashing. Just the way he'd always put himself together, just the way he stood, there's a certain flair.[90]

Despite day-to-day stumbles and setbacks, De la Torre had helped Floyd to fall back up into regular, productive work habits. Wishing to somehow personalize and memorialize the circumstances of re-creating *Jonathan Wade,* he inscribed a poster to the therapist: "My gratitude for bringing me back to music, and therefore to myself."

19

Looking Back, Moving On Back

Houston and Tallahassee, 1991–1997

An avid *New York Times* reader, Floyd could only have rejoiced at the paper's announcement on July 10, 1991 that seventy-year-old Donal Henahan would retire later that summer; yet whenever possible, Henahan still filed the occasional column with shots at Floyd. In a review earlier that year, he commented on a soprano's concert performance of an aria from *Susannah* (without specifying which) that straddled popular and classical styles, causing him to ponder a new classification, "popera." "Such minor works," he wrote, "do not transform anything."[1]

Thanks to *Jonathan Wade* productions, Floyd had few financial worries by summer's end. His royalty for the first half of 1991 came to more than $18,000 for grand rights alone.[2] With two *Bilby's Doll* workshops behind him and with performances scheduled at the University of Houston for April 1992 and at Miller Theatre a month later, Floyd left for Kansas City to direct Lyric Opera's *Susannah,* conducted by Russell Patterson. The baritone David Small had sung Jess in the Cincinnati Opera Ensemble touring production of *Slow Dusk* in 1986–1987, and then appeared in the parent company's *Susannah* as Elder McLean in the summer of 1988. Kansas City hired him to repeat this role, as well as to sing Rossini's Figaro, rehearsing both pieces simultaneously and in back-to-back performances; but because of the August 17 death of the baritone Harlan Foss, cast as Blitch, Small found himself on a week's notice shoehorned into the revivalist's part.

With his own memories of childhood hellfire-and-brimstone revivals in Fort Wayne, Indiana, Small had always responded to Floyd's work; but as a higher baritone with a shorter, rounder physique than most Blitches, he began rehearsal feeling awkward and apologetic. For the first week, an assistant gave basic blocking, having taken it from a videotaped production. When the composer arrived, he put Small at ease. "You have exactly the shape of the person I had in mind: a barrel-chested guy, Mack Harrell, who also had a more lyric voice. Norman did it like he did everything, turning it into something else, but just as valid."[3]

The soprano in Kansas City had the same difficulties as Phyllis Curtin in her second aria, and Floyd customized the passage in a manner that kept composer and Susannah happy. He watched an entire run-through, and at the end said, "Very good; but I've never seen any of this staging. Where did you get this?" The assistant produced her tape, and everyone watched a few moments, before Floyd declared, "I have no idea where this came from." He sighed, and began his completely different version.

Small observed, "He understood what we needed as singers, but also how to keep an audience interested: how to time things, when to move forward, when to luxuriate in a moment of passion or humor. And he had such generosity of spirit, such creativity with every aspect of the production. He knew everything from the inside out—not just the piece but also the entire theatrical mechanism—and everything that we needed and *didn't* need."

The production scored a great success, and Small went on to open as Rossini's Figaro the next day, a role with demands diametrically opposed to those of Blitch: "It actually worked brilliantly, and that's a tribute to Carlisle's vocal writing. *Susannah* is a dramatic piece, but so well paced for the singer: a challenging sing, but not brutal. And it's healthy singing. Rossini's the same way, written well for the voice."

By October, memos flew back and forth between Boosey's London and New York offices. The conductor John Mauceri, involved in the Decca series of American opera recordings, had a copy of the recent release of Weill's *Street Scene* sent to Floyd, to demonstrate the product's quality. Mauceri was most insistent on nailing down Samuel Ramey for *Susannah*. Janet Susskind observed to her colleagues that Scottish Opera's managing director—Mauceri worked there as music director from 1987 to 1993—had recently been fired, and Mauceri's employment could soon end.[4]

On October 12, Floyd got a call from Ardis Krainik of Lyric Opera of Chicago, confirming that the new coproduced *Susannah* would open there on October 9, 1993. Two days later, he passed this on to Boosey, adding that he had been favorably impressed by the *Street Scene* recording, and agreed in principle to have Decca undertake *Susannah*, as long as he were granted approval of an American cast with Mauceri at the helm.[5]

IN OCTOBER 1991, change rocked the music program at the university. Computer software magnate John Moores and his wife, Rebecca, both UH alumni, made history by giving the school $51.4 million, a record donation to a public university. Of that sum, $10.2 million—eventually increased by Moores to $18.5 million—was earmarked for a 142,000-square-foot state-of-the-art music facility for the program's 585 undergraduate and graduate students: there would be sixty-two teaching studios, six classrooms, sixty practice rooms, six rehearsal rooms, a library, a central student lounge, and an eight-hundred-seat concert hall, complete with murals by artist Frank Stella. The School of Music became the Moores School of Music; its concert hall, the Moores Opera House, opened on September 23, 1997 with a gala concert by the mezzo-soprano Marilyn Horne.

In November that year, the University of South Carolina appointed Floyd its Robert Evander McNair visiting professor of southern studies. In that capacity, he spent most of March 1992 on the Columbia campus staging *Susannah*, with performances from March 23 to 29, and lecturing on "The Materials of Opera" on March 26.[6]

By year's end, left rotator cuff surgery became the latest legacy of Floyd's tennis playing. Around the same time, despite such overwhelming donations as the Moores' for specific new facilities, UH funding mirrored the collapse of Texas's oil economy, resulting in major cuts for 1992–1993. With opera now a priority in his program, David Tomatz reexamined the music school's partnership with Houston Grand Opera and decided that a better use of his budget lay in an in-house Moores Opera Center directed by Buck Ross. The university had gotten what it needed from the HGO collaboration, and Tomatz finally announced that severing ties with HGO at the end of the school year would save the university between eighty thousand and one hundred thousand dollars over the next twelve months.[7] Now answerable only to the university, Floyd's teaching load naturally increased; and though his name was eventually removed from the HGO studio's masthead as codirector, Gockley continued to include him for auditions and on various panels, for which Floyd donated his time. UH students would still perform in some collaborative ventures with the studio, and Floyd noticed no diminution in the quality of incoming talent.

Regardless of such administrative upheavals, Floyd began rehearsals with combined UH and Houston Opera Studio forces for the sparer *Bilby's Doll*, with performances at Cullen Hall on April 10 and 12, 1992. Robin Stamper worked as one of three musical coaches; the UH faculty conductor Peter Jacoby was musical director, with stage direction by Buck Ross. Constantine Kritikos designed the sets, Sylvia Trybek the costumes, and Christina Giannelli the lighting. UH had a low-voice-poor year in 1991–1992, and the studio provided Chris Owens (Bilby) and Kelly Anderson (Zelley). UH singers included Barbara Divis (Doll), Joseph Consiglio (Deacon Thumb), Nancy Ann Hill and Elizabeth Williams (double cast as Hannah), and Todd Miller and Kerry Kelly (Shad). Carl Cunningham wrote that the revision, in which he especially enjoyed the powerful harmonies and "delicate, exotic percussion effects," was "one of [Floyd's] most sensitive, engrossing pieces of musical theater."[8]

Since the previous fall, Buck Ross had worked on his own libretto for his UH composer/colleague Robert Nelson, adapting E. M. Forster's *A Room With a View*, and the *Bilby's Doll* collaboration provided an opportunity for Ross to submit his work for Floyd's critique: "One of his first and most useful suggestions was reformatting my prose into free verse. It had an immediate effect on seeing what was necessary and what was not, and how to set it."[9]

When Miller Theatre management queried Ross about a suitable work for its outdoor venue, the director wished that he could have offered them *La bohème* or *Die Fledermaus;* but *Bilby's Doll* was the university's current project, and played the Miller on May 22 and 23. The *Chronicle* complimented Floyd's resurrection of both *Jonathan Wade* and *Bilby's Doll,* the latter echoing many of the same strengths as the former.[10]

FLOYD WAS SOON WORKING on two new projects. In the fall of 1991, Gene Brooks, executive director of the American Choral Directors Association (ACDA), had called.[11] The organization had just created its Raymond W. Brock memorial commission series, and the board chose Floyd as its first recipient.[12] Vocal compositions were preferred, and other guidelines stipulated priority to sacred texts, but not necessarily from the Bible; the music had to be substantial yet audience-friendly and of enduring quality.

Still exhausted from *Jonathan Wade,* and preoccupied with *Bilby's Doll,* Floyd met Brooks at Houston Intercontinental Airport to tender a polite refusal; but Brooks persisted, and by mid-June, Floyd's calendar showed open spaces. Linda Golding's memo to Sylvia Goldstein detailed a phone conference with Brooks. This would be ACDA's first major commission since 1976, with a premiere at the organization's national convention in March 1993. After speaking with Brooks again, Floyd chose a themed cycle centered on aspects of mortality, to be called *A Time to Dance.* It did not occur to him until much later that his major choral works—*Death Came Knocking, The Martyr,* and now *A Time to Dance*—all centered on death. Indeed, with the exception of *The Sojourner and Mollie Sinclair,* all of his operas feature on- or offstage deaths. Many if not most serious operas center on the inherent drama of mortality, and Floyd's own triad of personal loss in the last ten years—mother, agent, father—filtered naturally into his choral settings. He saw no stylistic discrepancy between the two media, and likened his choral choices to Verdi's death-centered *Requiem Mass.*[13]

The Brock endowment would fund the $15,000 commission; but the fund had yet to accrue sufficient income, and Brooks added $10,000 of his own money to $5,000 from ACDA budget lines.[14] Floyd received $7,500 on signing. By mid-July, Floyd had devoured *The Oxford Book of Death* (*OBD*)[15] and other anthologies in his personal library, and had chosen ten poems, of which five required Boosey's copyright negotiations. The new work would be his most ambitious choral venture to date, lasting about twenty-five minutes. A solo bass-baritone would act in a variety of quasi-dramatic capacities, juxtaposed with a large SATB chorus. It was also one of his largest orchestras: pairs of flutes, one doubling on piccolo; oboes, one doubling on English horn; clarinets, one doubling on B-flat bass clarinet; bassoons, trumpets, and trombones; four horns, tuba, timpani, percussion (xylophone, suspended and tuned cymbals, vibraphone, glockenspiel, wind chime, snare drum, tenor drum, bass drum, anvil, bells, and gong); piano doubling celesta; harp and strings.

From the *OBD,* Floyd chose as a choral preamble an anonymous two-line verse from an English memento mori medallion from around 1650:[16]

> As soon, as wee, to, bee, begunne:
> We, did, beginne, to, bee, undone.

Floyd announces his chief recurring musical device in the opening bars, the bitonal contrast and conflict of unison half and whole tones, a kind of death-in-life reminder. 6/8 sets the mood of a bleak lullaby *Largo e solenne,* with octaves of E against F in the accompaniment, choral entrances three bars later.

English poet, critic, and playwright John Dryden (1631–1700) devoted much effort to translating and versifying works of such ancient authors as Horace, Ovid, and Lucretius (c. 99–55 B.C.). Floyd adapted from Dryden's translation of Lucretius's *De Rerum Natura:*[17]

> Suppose great Nature's voice should call
> To thee, or me, or any of us all,
> "What dost thou mean, ungrateful wretch, thou vain,
> Thou mortal thing, thus idly to complain,
> And sigh and sob, that thou shalt be no more?"
> Suppose great Nature's voice should call
> To you, or me, or any of us all,
> "For if thy life were pleasant heretofore,
> If all the bounteous blessings, I could give,
> Thou hast enjoyed, if thou hast known to live,
> And pleasure not leaked through thee like a sieve;
> Why dost thou not give thanks as at a plenteous feast,
> Crammed to the throat with life, and rise and take
> thy rest?"
> Suppose great Nature's voice should be heard
> To thee, or me, or any of us all,
> "I would all thy cares and labors end,
> Lay down thy burden and know thy friend."

Here Floyd makes the soloist the voice of nature (mankind's interlocutor in the poem), in response to the framing choral propositions. Set in 4/4 and basic C Major/Minor, with whole-tone E and D Major accents, *Andante con moto, poco maestoso,* the choral entrance establishes a jaunty hornpipe rhythm, with alternating homophonic and contrapuntal echo passages.

Elizabethan, Restoration, and Cavalier poets drew Floyd for the remainder of his public domain offerings. He proceeded with chorus alone, singing the Jacobean dramatist John Webster's "Vanitas Vanitatum" (Vanity of Vanities):[18]

> All the flowers of the spring
> Meet to perfume our burying;
> These have but their growing prime,
> And man doth flourish but his time:
> Survey our progress from our birth—
> We are set, we grow, we turn to earth.
> Sweetest breath and clearest eye
> Like perfumes go out and die,
> And consequently this is done
> As shadows wait upon the sun.
> Vain the ambition of kings
> Who seek by trophies and dead things
> To leave a living name behind,
> And weave but nets to catch the wind.

In E-flat Minor/Major, Floyd initiates another rocking rhythm, *Andante dolente,* in 6/4, with three quarter notes and two eighths, then alternate halves or dotted quarter/eighth/quarter in his accompaniment. The choral entrance in bar three is syllabic, with ties across beat lines, against unison E-flat/D-natural. After progressing through such distant tonalities as E and G-sharp, the chorus whispers the last line tonelessly against open E-flat/B-flat fifths.

From Mark Twain's *Pudd'nhead Wilson* came Floyd's next selection, which he called *Epigram,* for soloist alone:

> All say, "How hard it is that we have to die"—a
> strange complaint
> To come from the mouths of people who have had to
> live.[19]

In 6/8, the tempo indication of *Allegretto alla burla* tells all: it is a joke. Syncopated sixteenth/eighth rhythms and sassy grace notes establish the tone of these fourteen measures in B Major/Minor; the soloist sounds like he may have thrown back a shot or two of whiskey.

Section 4 uses chorus alone, in D Major/Minor, *Allegro risoluto* in 4/4, for lines 1–4 and 9–14 of "Death, Be Not Proud," the tenth of John Donne's *Holy Sonnets,* written around 1610:[20]

> Death, be not proud, though some have called thee
> Mighty and dreadful, for thou art not so:
> For those whom thou thinkest thou dost overthrow
> Die not, poor Death;
> Death, be not proud,
> Thou art slave to Fate, Chance, Kings, and desperate
> men,

And dost with poison, war, and sickness dwell,
And poppies or charms can make us sleep as well
And better than thy stroke, what sellest thou then?
One short sleep past, we wake eternally,
And Death shall be no more: Death, thou shalt die!

The principal theme, a clarion trumpet command, never strays far from the clash of D and E-flat, with vocal doublings working to ensure textual intelligibility.

Floyd chose from Robert Herrick's *Hesperides* the poem "Eternity" for his soloist:[21]

O Years! And Age! Farewell.
Behold I go
Where I do know
Infinity to dwell.
And these mine eyes shall see
All times, how they
Are lost in the sea
Of vast eternity.
Where never moon shall sway
The stars; but she
And [the] night shall be
Drown'd in one endless day.

Floyd's setting, in dreamy 6/4, *Adagio mosso,* lays down an accompaniment with a single high A, soon to clash with G-sharp, against low octaves of D and F, in long note values and ties, contrasting with the soloist's active syllabic proclamation.

Movements six through ten are based on more recent works, and thus excluded from *OBD.* Boosey's biggest chore lay in determining exactly with whom these copyrights resided by 1992, and they reached a more or less industry standard solution by assigning a *pro rata* 50 percent royalty, based on the total number of copyrighted lines. For example, the African American poet Langston Hughes's (1902–1967) "Dear Lovely Death," Floyd's part 6, had been privately printed in 1931 by Troutbeck Press. After a year's search, Boosey discovered that the copyright currently lay with New York's Harold Ober Associates. The poem's ten lines were added to the forty-six *other* lines of copyrighted verse, and, once the formula was applied to Floyd's sheet music royalties, Ober received .833 percent of sheet music sales.[22]

"Dear Lovely Death" dwells on death as change rather than destruction. Floyd set Hughes's poem for chorus alone, as an unaccompanied but intricately chromatic chorale/spiritual that begins and ends in G-sharp Minor/Major.

For part 7, the composer pulled four humorous lines from the British novelist, poet, critic, and teacher Kingsley Amis's longish poem "Delivery Guaranteed," proposing that death, as an end to logistics, makes everything simpler.[23] In rollicking 6/8, *vivo,* around D Major/Minor, with "hiccup" rests, offbeat staccato syncopations, and whimsical text repetitions from soloist and chorus, Floyd establishes a convivial pub atmosphere with his musical figurations, ironic twists complete with hints of tankards of ale and dart tosses. The movement contains his "harmonic stacking" within fixed tonal centers, here another musical equivalent of the coexistence and interdependence of life and death.

Floyd had admired Joseph Auslander's poetry since he had set "Death Came Knocking" in the winter of 1960/61. From Auslander's 1935 collection *No Traveller Returns,* Floyd now chose for his part 8 "Interview with Lazarus." He set this as a dialogue, with the chorus posing questions of the resurrected Lazarus, and the soloist's quizzical, elliptical, or ambiguous answers.[24] Auslander seemed to inspire this kind of intensely dissonant, challenging setting in Floyd. In F Major/Minor, 4/4, *Allegro affrettando,* the agitated and rhythmically complex choral questions employ wide leaps, quick rhythms, and the expected half- and whole-tone juxtapositions between voices. Floyd contrasts nervous treble wavering against open bass fifths in the accompaniment's long note values. The soloist's answers are *Più sostenuto e calmo,* or some variant thereof: he knows, but speaks in riddles. The final two questions become less frantic, and the piece fades out on man's (in)ability to define the infinite, *diminuendo al niente.*

Alice Thomas Ellis's novel *The Birds of the Air* provided four lines of text for Floyd's part 9. Ellis dedicated her book, whose protagonist mother grieves for a dead child, to her own son Joshua, killed as a teenager. The selection is a graceful brief elegy celebrating the bereaved mother's love for the departed.[25] Floyd's twelve measures, 4/4, *Andante con moto,* return to D Major/Minor, with arching choral lines that embrace the poem's longing.

The tenth and final section, and the source of the work's title, is Cecil Day-Lewis's *A Time to Dance,* an altogether positive farewell urging the reader/listener to abandon dirges and move with joy.[26] In a variety of predominantly triple rhythms—6/4, 3/4, 9/8, and 6/8—*Maestoso ed esultato, declamando,* Floyd leaves no doubt that his journey from B Major/Minor to E represents a triumph. After the soloist's confident celebration, the chorus begins timidly, but grows in strength and rhythmic complexity until its final shouts of joy, despite one final clash of A-sharp and B-sharp. Floyd dedicated the entire work to Ermine.

MONTHS BEFORE the premiere of *A Time to Dance,* David Tomatz, representing the university, made an unusual request: would Floyd consider composing something to honor the Cullen Foundation, one of the music school's principal donors since its institution in 1947?[27] The university had booked space at the Wortham Center[28] for a musical tribute to the Cullens. Floyd complied with a fifteen-minute cycle of ten short songs, which he titled *Soul of Heaven,* on the art (and heart) of music. Having woven a tapestry from disparate sources for *A Time to Dance,* the composer continued to find ways of "sustaining interest through diversity of text and mood and at the same time creating a musical structure that built well to the end, not unlike creating an opera libretto. . . . The challenge . . . was to find diverse responses to, and reflections on, music over the centuries and I found the search fascinating and also, for me, illuminating, even startling."[29]

Floyd's sources were without exception in the public domain, eliminating copyright issues. As in *A Time to Dance,* he weighted his content with Renaissance, Elizabethan, and Baroque writers, alternating settings as short as five measures with longer passages. Like the great majority of his songs, none has a key signature, but strong tonalities are outlined by context and melodic contour.

He drew the cycle's title from the first poem, verse 254, from volume 1 of the Cavalier poet Robert Herrick's *The Hesperides and Noble Numbers,* already mined for *A Time to Dance:*[30]

Musick, Thou Soule of Heaven,
Care-charming spell that strikest a stillnesse into
Hell,
Musick, that tamest Tygers and fierce storms that rise
With thy soule-melting Lullabyes,
Fall down, down, down from those chiming spheres
To charm our souls as thou enchantest our ears.

In solemn *Adagio sostenuto,* with a downward sweep like a strummed lute, opposed octaves of F and E-flat introduce the singer at first in sixteenths and then eighths, with E-flat blurred by inclusion of both major and minor thirds. Intervals of fifths, sevenths, and fourths predominate in the melody, with syncopated sixteenth-dotted eighth articulations giving it a jaunty, impudent feeling much in Herrick's Cavalier style. After an excursion to several distant tonalities, Floyd resolves the melody on an enharmonic A-sharp/B-flat, underscored by a progression in the accompaniment from F-sharp Major to E Major/B Major, and finally a low B-flat pedal tone against F and G in treble octaves.

He based the second song on a poem of similar length by the obscure English Aristotelian scholar and physician John Case, from *The Praise of Musicke* (1586), dedicated to Sir Walter Raleigh:[31]

Skarlet is no colour to him who seeth not,
An Emeraul not precious to him that knows it not.
But Musick is no nightbird, God be praised,
She hath flown through the whole world
In the open sight of all men.

Agitated thirty-second note runs—the beating of music's wings?—*energico e marcato,* in various octaves and figurations, outline A Major in the right hand, against low octave D pedals in the left, a restless engine that drives through most of the song's fourteen measures. The singer's entrance in bar two establishes D Major, with sixths and fifths and sevenths, and syncopations imparting an unsettled quality similar to the previous song's. Excursions to B-flat, G-flat, and G in pedal octaves return us firmly to an unambiguous D Major conclusion.

Floyd had already set the Georgia poet Sidney Lanier's "An Evening Song" in the midforties, and now chose a single line, the last, from Lanier's long poem "The Symphony" (1875), a critique of materialism:

> Music is love in search of a word.

The composer's five measures, *Lento mosso,* rarely veer from an A Major core, the vocal line reaching and soaring despite its brevity.

Song four uses a fable of the sixth-century B.C. Greek Aesop, "The Swan and the Goose:"[32]

> A rich man bought a Swan and Goose,
> The Swan for Song,
> The Goose for use.
> It chanced his simple-minded cook
> One night the Swan for the Goose mistook.
> But in the dark about to chop
> The Swan in two above the crop,
> He heard the lyric note
> And stayed the action of the fatal blade.
> And thus we see a proper tune
> Is sometimes very opportune.

Floyd uses fairly consistent, tongue-in-cheek C Major throughout, with grace notes decorating the first and last beats of most measures. *Allegretto* alternates with *Adagio subito,* 6/8 with 3/8. A simple diatonic melody, repeated and varied, illustrates the tale's moral lesson, with a tiny rhythmic hitch just before "and stayed the action of the fatal blade." Even quarter-notes broaden melody and accompaniment on the word "opportune," ending with a diminution of the original melodic germ.

A quotation from Ralph Waldo Emerson reflects the great transcendentalist's appreciation of music's otherworldly dimensions. A lifelong admirer of music, Emerson often apologized for his lack of technical knowledge, but connected his instinctual reception of music with the genesis of love and flowering higher nature:

> So is Music an asylum, [a haven from the world]
> It takes us out of the actual and whispers dim secrets
> that startle our wonder as to who we are, and for
> what,
> whence, and whereto?[33]

Floyd treats this in calm A-flat Major/Minor, *Lento assai,* in 2/4 and 3/4 using sixth and seventh leaps, running eighth notes with ties across beat and bar lines, to mirror Emerson's soul search, traveling as far afield as C Major and A Minor. Brief interludes separate the final sequence of pondering questions, before returning to A-flat.

The six measures of song six, in stately *Largo ben misurato,* treat an aphorism of Friedrich Nietzsche, no. 33, from *Maxims and Arrows,* itself a portion of his 1888–1889 work, *Twilight of the Idols:*[34]

> Without music
> Life would be a mistake.

In a frame suggesting F Major/Minor, Floyd's principal devices are syncopation and staccato accents.

Song seven comes from another relatively obscure English writer, the theater critic, bishop, and theologian Jeremy Collier (1650–1726):[35]

> Have you not observed a Captain at the head of a
> Company,
> How much he is altered by the beat of a drum?
> All of a sudden what a vigorous motion,
> What an erect posture,
> All of a sudden by the beat of a drum.
> His blood, charging through his veins,
> His spirits jump like gunpowder,
> Impatient to attack the enemy.

How strangely does Music awaken the mind
And infuses the body with an unexpected vigor.
The Force of Musick is more wonderful by far
Than the one by whom it be conveyed!

Floyd veers from his usual avoidance of musical literalism, in B-flat Major/Minor, *Andante, risoluto e marcato,* with an ostinato figure of thirty-second note octuplets and sixteenth-note quintuplets, suggesting drumming and trumpet calls, which continue throughout the song, enlivening the vocal line at "all of a sudden." With a shift to C Major at "How strangely," and short phrases interrupted by thirty-second-note "rat-a-tats," the composer leads back to B-flat with an enharmonic progression of drum rolls.

The Renaissance courtier, aûthor, and diplomat Baldassare Castiglione (1478–1529) influenced the spread of humanism into France and England with his treatise on the ideal man of the world. *The Book of the Courtier* was written between 1507 and its first publication in 1528. Castiglione had much to say on the uses of music, and Floyd chose the following for his eighth song:

For proofe that Musick is a very great refreshing
Of all worldly grifes and paines, consider this:
Nature hath taught Musick to all nurses
As a special remedy for wailing babes . . .
Lulla, lulla, lullabye.
The babes at the sound of their nurses soft voices
Fall into a quiet and sweet, deep sleep . . .
Lulla, lulla, lullabye.
The babes then forget the tears so proper to them
And giv'n us by Nature at the tender age,
As a foretaste of the rest of their lives to come.
Lulla, lulla, lullabye.[36]

Floyd sets the first two lines as quasi-recitative, *Andante mosso,* against unison octave E-flats, the song's overall tonality. The line "Nature hath taught Musick," set in a flowing *Adagio commodo,* employs diminution of the E-flat figure, and a lilting *siciliano* with lullaby refrains, ironic comments on an increasingly serious text. The final statement approaches with a delicious progression of A Major to C Minor, E-flat Minor, unison low E-flats, and a final lutelike juxtaposition of E-flat and F in high treble register.

The penultimate song's seven measures derive from the preface to part 4, *Of Human Bondage, or the Strength of the Emotions,* from Baruch Spinoza's (1632–1677) *Ethics,* published posthumously:

Music is good for the melancholy,
Bad for those who mourn,
And neither good nor bad
To the deaf.[37]

In A Major/Minor, *Andante mosso,* Floyd's seven mordant bars feature an ironic triplet figure, mirrored and augmented in the vocal line, then used to comment between phrases, only to return at the end like a final nose thumbing, as the singer speaks the final line.

For the cycle's conclusion, and longest song—fifty-six measures—Floyd drew on, and lightly rephrased, the famous speech of Lorenzo, from act 5, scene 1 of Shakespeare's *The Merchant of Venice:*

Do but note a wild and wanton herd,
Or [a] race of youthful and unhandled colts
Fetching mad bounds, bellowing and neighing loud,
Which is the hot condition of their blood.—
If they perchance hear trumpet sound,
Or any air of music touch their ears,
You shall perceive them make a mutual stand,
Their savage eyes turned to a modest gaze
By the sweet power of music.
That man that hath no music in himself,
Nor is not moved with concord of sweet sounds,
That man is fit for treasons, stratagems and spoils.
Let no such man be trusted. Mark you Music.[38]

In breathless 6/8, *precipitato,* running triplet figures point to F Major, depicting the headlong rush of the "wild and wanton herd." Clarion trumpet calls introduce unaccompanied measures for vocal echoes, "If they perchance hear," and "Or any air of music." With an excursion to D-flat and G-flat, the tempo slows, *Molto meno mosso,* to an attention-getting quasi-tremolo on octave F, above D Major and B-flat Major chords. A brief triplet interlude and repetition of the trumpet call introduce, *Andante largamente,* the final grand statement, which works its way through D Major, B Minor, B-flat Minor, and a soaring piano interlude in C Major, before a triumphant return to F Major with three statements of "Mark you Music."

Floyd's own return to music shines through the dedication of *Soul of Heaven* to Jorge de la Torre. The project had "made me more aware than ever of how music is woven so inextricably into our emotional and psychological makeup as human beings and how barren our lives would be without its limitless variety of stimuli."[39] Floyd had interrupted his work on *A Time to Dance* to complete *Soul of Heaven,* which premiered at the Moores Society dinner concert at Wortham Theater Center on December 1, 1992; Floyd divided the ten songs between the soprano Heidi Jones and the bass-baritone Justin White.

LIKE HIS IDOL VERDI, with one eye on art and the other on the cash box, Floyd had amassed a substantial body of new work between *Bilby's Doll* and *Soul of Heaven.* He reviewed his UH discretionary fund in light of state and university cutbacks and, for the copyist Bill Black, purchased the new software manuscript program Fanfare, to make clean, accurate copies of all his Houston music. The resulting scores were then used by Boosey & Hawkes without deductions from the composer's royalties for score preparation, and Floyd paid minimal sums for print-to-order rental material.

Around the first week of October 1992, he arrived in Seattle to direct *Jonathan Wade,* conducted by Hal France with a mix-and-match cast from the earlier productions: Dale Duesing (Jonathan), Alison England (Celia), Julian Patrick (Townsend), Joseph Evans (Lucas), James Hoback (Pratt), Debria Brown (Nicey), Byron Ellis (Riddle), and Kevin Bell (Judge Bell). On October 30, the Seattle staff conductor Hans Wolf wrote Floyd his appreciation: "It takes a magician to pack into 3 1/2 hours a whole world of American history as well as a wealth of dynamic and imaginative music making—where word and music are one homogenous entity—you can be proud to be that man,"[40] Local press agreed.

By fall 1992, Opéra de Lyon had laid the groundwork for the recording of *Susannah* by Virgin Records, which had been acquired by British EMI a year earlier. Samuel Ramey, signed for Blitch, proved unavailable until August 1993, so taping was slated between August 1 and 6, with preliminary rehearsals from July 7 to 10.[41] Only in February did Virgin name a leading lady for the first commercial recording of any Floyd opera: The Canadian Greek soprano Teresa Stratas. Opéra de Lyon's orchestra and chorus would be conducted by Kent Nagano, who had never considered importing *Susannah* to France.[42] Like most Americans, his first exposure to Floyd came in his student days accompanying peers; only when a soprano auditioned for him in Lyon with Susannah's by-now signature aria had it struck him that "it could speak, in a universal, timeless way. . . . I realized that the melodies were simple, and beautiful in their simplicity, but there's a difference between something simple and something simplistic."[43]

Many of the artists first proposed, like Stratas, were replaced. In months to come, Cheryl Studer was hired for Susannah, a role she had never sung on stage, having specialized in heavier Strauss and Wagner repertoire.[44] In addition to Samuel Ramey as Blitch, Studer's recording colleagues would be Jerry Hadley (Sam), Kenn Chester (Little Bat), Michael Druiett and Anne Howells (Elder and Mrs. McLean), Steven Cole and Della Jones (Gleatons), Stuart Kale and Jean Glennon (Hayeses), and David Pittsinger and Elizabeth Laurence (Otts).

ON FEBRUARY 19, 1993, accompanied by Craig Rutenberg, Susanne Mentzer performed *Citizen of Paradise* in recital at Carnegie Hall's Weill Recital Hall.

The premiere of *A Time to Dance* took place on March 6, 1993 in San Antonio, Texas, with members of the San Antonio Symphony and Westminster Choir, conducted by Joseph Flummerfelt. Floyd had delivered choral scores by October 31, 1992 and the full score by January 1, 1993, for which he received the second half of his commission fee; orchestra parts were delivered by February 1.

Flummerfelt's limited rehearsal time in San Antonio, and the multiple difficulties of "Interview with Lazarus," caused its omission from the premiere. Nonetheless, the packed audience of professional choral directors greeted the new work ecstatically. Mark Gresham, editor of *Chorus! Magazine* noted:

> Floyd's capacity as a word-smith . . . is equal to his skills as a composer, and the cycle of texts chosen shows a wide range of emotional responses to death, yet works beautifully as a unified whole. His musical language—which he himself has described as "conservative"—is at once quite challenging yet ultimately vocally practical, suited to the choral instrument. Floyd's musical language is unabashedly emotive, one of full-blooded expressiveness . . . the piece is a magnificent work; it will prove an audience-moving programming choice for any chorus with the requisite performance skills . . . [as] a viable alternative to the more traditional Requiem text.[45]

The University of Houston choral director Charles Hausmann wrote to Floyd the day after the premiere. "The varied texts are expressive and dramatically represented by your music. . . . I enjoyed the various choral and orchestral sonorities you so masterfully achieved. . . . Joe [Flummerfelt] and the Westminster Choir . . . did a super job presenting this work to an audience who truly understands and appreciates fine choral performance and outstanding literature."[46]

Two decades later, Floyd expressed surprise that choral directors seem to remain ignorant of the work's existence. Since 1993, there have been only two performances, the first conducted by Hausmann at UH on March 16, 1995, with baritone Erich Parce. They too omitted the Auslander setting, and Floyd first heard "Interview with Lazarus" at a concert of the Long Bay Symphony and Carolina Master Chorale in Myrtle Beach, South Carolina, on May 15, 2011.

To attend the premiere of *A Time to Dance,* Floyd stole time from another directing engagement, his first *Wuthering Heights,* at Boston Lyric Opera. Conducted by Stephen Lord, with sets and projections by Clarke Dunham, and costumes by Deborah Newhall, the cast included Jeff Mattsey (Heathcliff), Joan Gibbons (Catherine), Amy Burton (Isabella), Phyllis Pancella (Nelly), Dan Sullivan (Earnshaw), and Patrick Denniston (Edgar). Though the composer had not heard the work since the FSU 1960 production, he found that it "still worked. It's a kind of transitional piece between *Susannah* and the operas that came later. It gave me a chance to write a through-composed opera and it's probably closer to the operas that came later, but there is still enough of *Susannah* to recognize that it is mine. But I liked it and I did not remember that it was as lyrical as it was."[47]

Unfortunately, the performances on March 10, 12, 14, and 16 found little favor with critics. *The New York Times* claimed that "American opera has produced few masterpieces: instead there is an endless litany of obscurities, most of which should rest undisturbed."[48] Perplexed by such animus, Floyd showed a copy of this review to De la Torre at their next session. Emerging from his customary remoteness, the doctor raised his eyebrows and handed the page back to Floyd with a single word: "Suspicious."

At the end of March 1993, Floyd and his publishers reconfirmed his status as a living classic when the soprano Heidi Carter, whose musical journey took her from folk singing to opera, recorded the album *Melodic Mama.* Among her selections she prepared the second aria of *Susannah* with guitar accompaniment. Sylvia Goldstein sent Floyd a demo copy for approval, which he gave. "It sounded like the genuine article, a real folk song. After a work earns its reputation, I feel no qualms about authorizing any number of variations. It's not going to be judged on that basis."

In months to come, a second group named Lark and Spur—soprano Lori Decker and guitarist Jeff Whiteley—released a cassette tape that included a similar version of the same piece, further placing Floyd's inspiration in the context of its Appalachian roots.

With everyone—except Cheryl Studer—in place to record *Susannah,* Floyd grew concerned over achieving uniform, authentic southern diction for the principals and Opéra de Lyon's all-French chorus. He recalled Bob Holton's enthusiasm years earlier for Marni Nixon, a soprano whose unusual combination of skills included accents, impeccable musicianship that furthered her specialty in contemporary music, and overdubbing for a generation of actors with less than perfect singing voices.[49] Floyd got Nixon on the phone and tendered the surprising offer that she be the Appalachian diction coach for *Susannah.* Nixon accepted, but never having done this particular accent, she contacted the speech and dialect expert Sam Chwat. Together they drilled the entire text of Floyd's score, and Nixon made cassette tapes for chorus and for each role, despite trepidation that she might be violating some unspoken "diva code."[50]

From July 7 to 10, Floyd and Ermine found themselves in England for preliminary rehearsals. Hadley and Ramey had been singing in London, and they met Floyd in Manchester, Kent Nagano's home base with the Hallé Orchestra. In rehearsals, with the composer at the piano, Nagano conducted as much of the opera as he could without its title character. On July 31, Floyd, Nixon, and the principals of *Susannah* checked into Le Royal Lyon. Nixon distributed her tapes, and acquired additional responsibilities the next day when the German recording engineer Martin Sauer, unable to understand a word *anyone* sang, implored her not to leave his side.

Nagano introduced Floyd and Nixon to the orchestra, warning that *she* (and *not* the composer) would be the only person allowed to stop the recording for diction errors. Stunned at such empowerment for a function she considered almost menial, Nixon looked over at Floyd, who winked and said, "Go for it, honey," and the session began.

During one day's work, Hadley had trouble finding his note for a difficult entrance. Knowing that Nixon had perfect pitch, Hadley had her stand next to him and sing the pitch softly into his ear, and they became inseparable. The rumor mill worked overtime; every conceivable reason was proposed for Studer's absence: she had just given birth, she was experiencing vocal problems, she was sick with the panoply of upper respiratory infections that terrorize all singers, or she was padding her diva image. Ramey, who had made several recordings without key colleagues present, still found it very strange: "It was hard doing that confrontation scene without her, you very much feed off each other, and I had nothing!"[51]

Detaching herself from Hadley, Nixon, who also sent Studer an "accent cassette," sang Susannah's lines into Ramey's headset. Studer's overdubbing was scheduled for the following spring at Bavaria Music Studios in Munich. By August 6 the entire opera had been taped. Floyd told Nagano that he wanted to thank the orchestra. The conductor offered to translate for him, but Floyd insisted, having written down and practiced his remarks in the silence of his hotel room. "I wanted to say it directly to them. My French was pretty primitive, but when I'm there for any length of time I have a fair accent, which only makes the French infer that I know lots more than I do." The musicians applauded their appreciation.

DAVID GOCKLEY assembled Houston's coproduction team with Lyric Opera of Chicago for *Susannah*'s revival. The stage director Robert Falls and the designer Michael Yeargan collaborated in what had by now become a virtually critic-proof American opera. The strong cast featured Renée Fleming in the title role, Samuel Ramey (Blitch), Michael Myers (Sam), and Richard Markley (Little Bat); and Lyric's fall performances scored a triumph.[52] The critic John van Rhein observed, "Seldom have two hours in the theater whooshed by so fast."[53]

As fall advanced, Floyd's persistent gastrointestinal ailments worsened; a sonogram also revealed kidney cysts that had a 95 percent chance of malignancy. His dread of these conditions was compounded by the death of Kay's mother, Marguerite Reeder, on November 27. While consoling Kay, after Christmas and New Year's, Floyd checked into the hospital for a nephrectomy. Ermine insisted on being there, and when Floyd emerged from anesthesia, she held his hand, stroked his arm: "You're fine, it wasn't cancer." Despite being in the lucky 5 percent, Floyd moaned in depressive relapse, "I don't deserve to live, I don't deserve to be OK." Ermine, again and always the rock in Floyd's life, knew that as long as one kept to the safe ground of work issues her brother remained open and ebullient. Despite years of De la Torre's therapy, a focus on Carlisle the man guaranteed resistance.

Floyd's recovery allowed him to fly to Munich for a single exhausting day of *Susannah* overdubbing sessions with Nagano and Studer on March 31, 1993. At a preliminary keyboard rehearsal with the composer, Studer's timbre struck Floyd as darker than any he had heard in "the old girl's" almost forty years, but Studer was singing with a lighter girlish sound not entirely her own. With his usual tact, Floyd smiled and said, "I think we need to hear the voice we'll hear for the rest of the performance," and all proceeded smoothly. The remainder of his contribution involved supervising the balance between Studer and the existing layers, the communication between the booth and Nagano, or asking the engineer to bring up an internal instrumental line here and there. (He found this process capable of *creating* a performance.) By the end of the day, with twenty separate tracks, one hour and thirty-four minutes of music, they had incorporated Studer into the texture of orchestra, chorus, and soloists.

Once Floyd returned to Houston, he received an urgent phone call from David Tomatz, begging him to take Elena Nikolaidi out to dinner again. (Throughout her tenure at UH, Niki's highly volatile, impulsive temperament prompted her to regularly threaten retirement.) The two of them sipping drinks, Floyd asked, "Have you really thought this through?"

Nikolaidi laughed, declaring in her barely penetrable Greek accent, "Ah, I am so spon-tannous!" After convivial moments, she invariably sighed, "All right, I stay a while." But at the end of this 1993–1994 school year, days short of her eighty-eighth birthday—or eighty-fifth, depending on one's source—Niki knew that angina and high blood pressure precluded further teaching in her high-energy manner. Her husband and former voice teacher Thanos Melos had died in 1992, and she now retired to Tallahassee, where her son lived. Floyd, sad to bid this old friend farewell, thought the move a terrible mistake, as it separated her from teaching, the love of her students, and the opera-related events in which Gockley included her, but she asserted her future devotion to gardening. Her parting thoughts on the art of vocal instruction, another clue to Floyd's admiration for this remarkable woman since her hiring at FSU thirty-four years earlier, appeared in an interview and extolled the joys of making music: "Fine singing requires enormous courage. . . . [W]hen I am successful in drawing out, cajoling, scaring or surprising the best from a singer, it is magic."[54] Though she may have believed that FSU would ask her to teach again, at least part-time, the invitation never came.

Floyd next spent May 11 through 15 at New York's Mayflower Hotel. On May 14, at the Princeton University chapel, he delivered Westminster Choir College's commencement address, a reworking of his 1964 "Society and the Artist" lecture.

Details of *Susannah*'s recording clamored to be addressed: choosing and editing French and German translations for the accompanying libretto, and setting grand rights fees for media plays on commercial and noncommercial radio stations. Virgin Classics released its two-disc *Susannah* on September 5. The accompanying booklet included an appreciation by the media critic and playwright-librettist Jonathan Abarbanel, and a new Floyd essay. Writing of his unsuccessful attempts to peddle the score to NBC Opera, and the negative judgments of the conductor Herbert Grossman, Floyd maintained, forty years later, after worldwide productions, that Grossman's bleak prediction could safely be forgotten, and that *Susannah* had indeed seen what lay beyond the Appalachians' girdle.[55]

The New York Times found that the recording "pulses with the passion and confidence of an artist who has not learned to be intimidated by tradition or contemporary opinion."[56] At 3 a.m. on March 2, 1995, Floyd's phone jangled him awake: Kent Nagano, calling from London at a perfectly reasonable hour there, exulted that "their" opera had won a Grammy for best opera recording at the organization's thirty-seventh awards ceremony.

A DEGREE OF STIMULATION and challenge left Floyd's teaching at the university with the departure of the

Houston Opera Studio in 1992; but instead of retreating into routine, he entered a new period of giving back to the best and brightest of a younger generation of theatrical composers. Mark Adamo, at the time writing music criticism and arts features for the *Washington Post,* flew to Houston to interview Stewart Wallace and Michael Korie, the composer and librettist of *Harvey Milk,* on January 23, 1995.[57] Adamo sandwiched a meeting with Floyd into his hectic schedule. Adamo's first question concerned changes in the American opera scene: the oddly sterile sixties, after City Opera's American seasons and Ford Foundation commissions, but before the Kennedy Center, the National Endowment for the Arts, and the National Opera Institute took up the slack. Floyd was intrigued; in his more than half century of interviews, no one had posed that question. From personal experience, he pointed to the lack of regional infrastructure, and the reluctance of companies outside New York, Chicago, and San Francisco to mount second productions. "Without a revival, a piece doesn't have the opportunity to be known as a piece, rather than as an 'X.'"[58]

According to Adamo, he and Floyd "got along like a house afire. We had already overrun the scheduled half hour or forty-five minutes, so I said, 'You've already given me everything I need, but I'm having a great time, and I'd love to take you to lunch, if you can.' So we went to lunch and talked for an hour and a half."

After the premiere of Adamo's first orchestral piece, the AIDS memorial *Late Victorians,* Summer Opera Theatre, which was resident at Adamo's Washington, DC, alma mater, Catholic University, commissioned him to make an opera of Louisa May Alcott's *Little Women.* He found the material fascinating, but lacking the proper internal theatrical structure. The premiere was proposed for the summer of 1998, only fifteen months away, and Adamo panicked. What did he know about the minutiae of contracts, dealing with copyists, or even how to organize one's life around such an enormous project? Adamo sent Floyd his outline, in which he compared all previous adaptations of Alcott's book, which he described as "the least promising topic for operatic adaptation,"[59] and arrived at his version's general shape. Floyd was enthusiastic about that shape and encouraged its further development. He also generously provided information about copyists, and a contract template showing various deadlines and fee installments. But Summer Opera had by now contracted a librettist who admitted that he was stumped by the novel, and the company declined to consider Adamo as his own librettist. In the winter of 1996 Adamo withdrew, realizing that he had devoted more than a year of his life to a project with no performance in sight. He left a message for Floyd: "This is Mark Adamo and I've just cut my own throat. Please call."

Floyd remained confident of *Little Women*'s potential and suggested that Adamo send him recordings of his music, as well as the opera's proposal, so that he could personally deliver them to David Gockley. Adamo, with nothing more than a bachelor's degree from Catholic University and that single orchestra piece, *Late Victorians,* sent a recording of it to Floyd, who then approached the head of America's most innovative, proactive opera company.

Adamo passed through every stage of euphoria before getting a kindly postcard from Gockley in April 1996, reporting that the company had scheduled its repertoire for the next five years. When Adamo called Floyd to discuss this spoke in the wheel, the latter shrugged, "Oh well, sometimes it happens like that," and *Little Women* assumed a holding pattern.

BY SPRING 1995, while the Moores School of Music had flourished without HGO, the UH School of Theater had exploded with an influx of star talent. Since 1988, Edward Albee had taught advanced playwriting courses and supervised workshops of developing plays. A year later, José Quintero, the director of the Metropolitan Opera National Company 1965 *Susannah,* had been similarly lured to teach advanced acting and directing classes each fall. Since 1993, Floyd's old associate from their NEA days, the producer Stuart Ostrow, had actively sought a place to develop new works away from the glare of Broadway and the often destructive New York press. Floyd's suggestion of contacts led to Ostrow's move to Houston in April 1995. Persuaded to accept the position in part by Floyd's presence, Ostrow immediately launched a new music theater workshop.

Since Kay's 1987 road trip, insistent on a better life in Tallahassee, she had whittled away at Floyd's resistance to moving. His Houston friends all worked at either the university or the opera company. Kay, increasingly distracted and isolated, rarely hosted, much less enjoyed, any associated social events. Retirement was now moot: Floyd would turn seventy the next spring and was already eligible for full benefits. Feeling his age, he began to agree with Kay that moving back to Florida might be good for both of them, yet he dreaded the inevitable termination of his professional life: "I was the only one who thought I should retire. For so many years, my routine had been so fixed, and I was tired of it: day in, day out, I knew when I had to be at school or rehearsal, then go home. It was prescribed. The point was, someone else had bought my time all my life, and now I wanted to decide for myself what I wanted to do, and make my own schedule."

When James Pipkin, his friend and the university's dean of humanities, fine arts, and communication, learned of this decision, he wrote: "Everyone admires your art, but I have also had the opportunity to see your intelligence, eloquence and academic values on a number of occasions. Truman Capote once distinguished artists who create out of their sensibility from artists who create out of their intelligence. (He clearly preferred the latter.) You clearly create out of a wonderful wedding of the two."[60]

The composer David Ashley White served as that year's acting director of music. Without great surprise, but with considerable regret, he received Floyd's October 15, 1995 letter of resignation, effective at the end of the 1995–1996 academic year:[61]

> I am sure you realize that this decision has not been an easy one to arrive at but, after much deliberation, I have concluded that it is the correct one for me at this time of my life. . . . My twenty years at the University . . . have been a time of invaluable professional and personal growth for me, and my gratitude . . . for making much of this possible is unbounded and ongoing. . . . When I came in 1976 I felt that the faculty . . . deserved a student body more able to benefit from what it could offer. Now, thanks to the remarkable increase in the number of highly gifted students attracted to the School in recent years, that situation has happily and very conspicuously been corrected. . . . I will continue to feel a strong connection to the School of Music and follow its fortunes with the keenest interest in the years ahead.[62]

Independence.

KAY MADE IT CLEAR that a tract house or apartment would make her perfectly happy, and in July, Floyd flew back to Tallahassee and purchased a new 4,500-square-foot modern split level house nestled back in heavy woods. They decided to keep the Houston house, with thoughts—on Floyd's part, active *hopes*—that a future move back might be possible.

While the couple began sorting and packing the effects of twenty years in Texas, *Susannah* continued her unchecked progress around the world. That April, New York's DiCapo Opera gave four performances in its intimate space on East 76 Street. In Michael Capasso's production, Lorraine Goodman (Susannah), Marc Embree (Blitch), Jeffrey Ambrosini (Sam), and Thomas Roche (Little Bat), gave "a sheer visceral wallop."[63]

In mid-June, Sweden's Royal Opera announced a single concert performance of "the old girl" at the Kungliga Teatern on November 18; and on July 26, Carolyn Kalett wrote the composer that Boosey's London office would license *Susannah* for at least three performances the following April at the Midlands Arts Centre in Birmingham, England.[64] Interest in Floyd and his operas had reached a new peak since Virgin's CD release the previous fall. *Opera* estimated conservatively that, since its Tallahassee premiere in 1955, the piece had received about 700 performances in 150 separate productions, and clearly felt that foreign audiences deserved an answer to the question "Carlisle who?"

> The figures are mind-boggling for European audiences, used to new operas which appear in a fanfare of publicity before quickly disappearing forever. . . . Floyd has become that rare bird, a contemporary

> composer with a body of operas . . . he has left his mark on the history of modern American music. His operas display a vivid musical language, and a distinctive theatrical imagination.[65]

Longwood Opera in Needham, Massachusetts, scheduled three performances of *Susannah* that September; and in November, negotiations began for a production at Berlin's Deutsche Oper. At year's end, VAI Records released New Orleans Opera's 1962 performance with Curtin, Treigle, and Cassilly.

One of Floyd's sole causes for sorrow that fall was Christopher Keene's death of AIDS-related lymphoma on October 8. The *Times* speculated that David Gockley might be a good choice for the general directorship of City Opera, but Gockley told the paper that he had no interest in moving to New York, and the position was offered to and accepted by Paul Kellogg.

A round of tributes and honors for Floyd began on October 14, 1995, when HGO's guild presented its Bravo award to the composer at a gala brunch at Houston Country Club. In January 1996, Floyd and Kay completed their move to Tallahassee, though loose ends at both the university and HGO kept him shuttling back and forth between Florida and Texas.

Not far into the new year, Floyd gave back again, not to a student, but to old friend Frank Corsaro, whose directing career had branched out into writing. His autobiography *Maverick* had been published to acclaim in 1978, and in 1980 he wrote a libretto for the composer Thomas Pasatieri based on *Before Breakfast,* the same Eugene O'Neill monodrama that Corsaro and Floyd had discussed a decade earlier. In spring 1988, Corsaro succeeded David Lloyd as director of Juilliard's American Opera Center, and commissioned a new opera from the composer Stephen Paulus. This became *Heloise and Abelard,* Corsaro's libretto based on the infamous love scandal of twelfth-century scholar and theologian—*and* priest—Peter Abelard and Heloise Garlande. Before turning his libretto over to Paulus, Corsaro sent it for Floyd's stamp of approval, which was not long in coming, along with the usual astute observations. Floyd also told Gockley that it was the best new opera text he had seen in some time. Corsaro and Paulus went on to finish the piece, which premiered at Juilliard in April 2002.

If there are cosmic or karmic rewards for deeds well and truly done, Floyd experienced an upward soar that February, when he received a letter from Sarah Billinghurst, the Metropolitan Opera's assistant manager: "We're delighted that we are going to perform *Susannah* at the Metropolitan Opera in our 1998/99 season. We will be presenting the opera in the Chicago production directed by Robert Falls and the cast will include Renée Fleming, Jerry Hadley and Sam Ramey, conducted by James Conlon. The opening night will be March 31, 1999."[66]

Between frictions with Kay, and the euphoria of a seal on his career, San Diego Opera's revival of *The Passion of Jonathan Wade* in February/March 1996 came as a centering influence. Floyd again directed, to an even more ecstatic response from the public and press than five years earlier. Fifteen thousand dollars in royalties and grand rights, in addition to his directing fee, came at a most welcome time, with movers' bills to pay. One of Floyd's new San Diego acquaintances was the company's director of marketing and public relations, Todd Schultz, in turn a close friend of the composer Jake Heggie. With Floyd in town and tow, Schultz arranged a lunch at the composer's hotel for March 2, also the production's opening night.[67]

Born in West Palm Beach, Florida, in 1961, Heggie's subsequent family moves brought him to Orinda, California, at age sixteen. Since childhood a gifted pianist, he began composing at eleven, and his mother learned of a local composers' group, the Performing Arts Society, mentored by none other than Ernst Bacon. Heggie recalled: "They were mostly women in their forties, fifties, and sixties, and me. We met once a month with Mr. Bacon. He was very gracious, he listened to what we had to say and went over our music with us in a kind of master class. Once after everyone else had left, I asked if I could take private lessons with him. He said yes, and gave me lots of basic information. Until then, I'd always written from my gut, rather than from any sort of training. And he was so incredibly charismatic, even in his eighties, something about his energy really drew you in."[68]

37. Ian Campbell, Floyd, San Diego, 1996. Permission courtesy of the photographer, M. L. Hart.

By that time, Bacon had become methodical in ways Floyd had never experienced: "He was particularly interested in my setting texts. He gave me exercises, fugues and canons based on people's names, to keep it fun and interesting. I'd bring him the previous week's assignment, we'd talk about it, play with it, see where the missed opportunities were, what I could learn from this or that mistake."

Quite naturally, Bacon mentioned earlier students. Heggie recalled: "He'd tell me about different composers he admired, and people whose music I should pay attention to; and Carlisle was one of those. Bacon said that Carlisle really knew how to capture a character's inner life and psychology, to capture the moment in a way that was right for opera. It was not song writing, but real theater writing. I wasn't a big opera fan, I had not been exposed to really fine singing actors, but later, at UCLA, all my singer friends were doing the arias from *Susannah.* So beautiful and immediate and charismatic. There's such a profile to his music, it struck me right away."

By 1996, Heggie had yet to write anything close to opera, but he knew that his focus would always be on the voice. He concentrated first on chamber works, two- and solo-piano suites, and especially art songs, to the poetry of Emily Dickinson, Rainer Maria Rilke, Philip Littell, and others. Two years later, after negotiations with San Francisco Opera, he was appointed composer in residence and commissioned for a first opera, *Dead Man Walking,* based on Sister Jean Prejean's book, with libretto by playwright Terence McNally. Heggie formulated a list of pressing questions for Floyd, who had always begun with his own libretto: "He told me, 'First and foremost, you have to have a really good working relationship with your librettist, who has to be very flexible. As for your story, clarity in situations and overall plot line is essential; characters can be complex, but situations have to be very clear, so that the musical response can actually be heard and people are not trying to figure out whodunit. They just listen to the musical response to get what's happening.' He said he'd be available to me, if I wanted to fly to see him as I wrote."

Four days later, after seeing *Jonathan Wade*'s opening, his first live experience of a complete Floyd opera, Heggie wrote his thanks. "It was thrilling not only to meet you, but to talk to you in depth about things that have been pressing on my mind. Your words were ringing in my head all weekend. And what a thrill, too, to experience your *Passion of Jonathan Wade.* It is a tremendous, gripping and powerful work. The second act and the finale in particular continue to haunt me. I admire the flesh and blood you gave your characters—and the wonderful *pacing* of the whole work. . . . Meanwhile, please know that you have had a positive influence on yet another composer! It tickles me to tell people that we both studied with Ernst Bacon when we were 17!"[69]

As with Mark Adamo, most of Heggie's subsequent contacts with Floyd took place by phone or letter. As his composition progressed in 1997, he grew concerned about orchestration, having restricted himself mainly to songs with piano accompaniment and chamber works. Floyd's advice again hit the mark: "'When you're orchestrating for singers, the pages should fly by. It's the damned *tutti*[70] that take all the time!' And was he right! What he was saying is that it needed to be very spare."

Floyd's encouragement grew even more important than such technical considerations. Heggie continued: "Confidence is so important in this business. The fact that Carlisle exists is an inspiration: that he had the success he did, and then is so generous and supportive of others who want to pursue it, and is actually excited by that. He doesn't have a jealous bone, he who paved the way for the rest of us. More than anything in life, it's important to have role models, and he's a friend, a mentor, a real hero, and that has given me enormous strength and confidence. He taught me that I don't have to be afraid or ashamed of lyricism, as long as it's in service to the drama."

San Francisco Opera's world premiere of *Dead Man Walking* on October 7, 2000, conducted by Floyd's frequent Houston collaborator Patrick Summers, created a sensation, won further notice through its release on CD the following year,[71] and received more than twenty-four subsequent productions in the United States and abroad. Heggie has written seven other musical theater pieces, and some of the greatest compliments paid him are frequent comparisons to the oeuvre of Carlisle Floyd.[72]

IN 1996, Floyd gave the *Houston Chronicle* a scoop by revealing another motivation for retirement: he was ingesting a new opera source, the Atlanta journalist Olive Ann Burns's novel *Cold Sassy Tree,* a gift from Ermine a year or two earlier. Floyd recalled sitting on planes laughing out loud at the tale, its characters, situations, and language. He described the setting he had in mind as "a comedy drama . . . very southern," and he needed time to "cogitate."[73]

Simultaneous dark undercurrents threatened to undo Floyd's emotional balance. Over the years, Ermine had provided stability in his life and career: his young self's sole emotional mirror, she later offered support by attending as many performances as possible, but family financial crises had kept her from the new *Jonathan Wade.* During a visit to Houston, Ermine asked Floyd to play through the opera's new music, to allow her an impression of the work. Kay naturally refused to participate, so brother and sister drove to his university studio, where Floyd played through *Wade*'s final scene. When they returned home, Ermine enthused, "Kay, how could you have deprived yourself of that?"

Kay took immediate offense, and a rift opened between the two strongest influences in Floyd's life. Kay issued an ultimatum: wife or sister, choose one. When Floyd discussed the situation with De la Torre, the therapist rebuked him in the strongest terms: Ermine could not be his principal confidante. Kay's disorientation grew. Having gotten what she wanted in one area, she felt threatened by Floyd's growing independence, due in large part, ironically, to De la Torre's influence; and their move back to Florida would in any case end that relationship. With the excuse that De la Torre had stopped accepting their health insurance, Floyd terminated their sessions, then wrote Ermine a devastating severance letter that satisfied Kay's demands. Except for occasional correspondence, these soul siblings would not see each other again for the better part of three years, splitting Floyds and Mathenys into bitter factions.

On April 18, 1996, Floyd found better emotional sustenance in Spartanburg, on the stage of Converse

College's Twichell Auditorium, receiving an honorary doctorate of letters at the school's annual founder's day assembly. When asked whether he might care to invite any special guests to the ceremony, Floyd discovered his Bethune teacher Herbert Fincher still alive, in Aiken, South Carolina. Fincher's son drove him to Spartanburg, and Floyd, about to turn seventy, saw his strapping idol transformed into a broken old man of eighty-three. Accepting his award, Floyd shared memories of moving pianos, setting lights, and placing music on this very stage during his Converse years, never thinking that he might receive such an honor fifty-two years later. He reminisced with Fincher over lunch after the presentation, heartened to find the old fellow's mind strong and clear. He thanked Floyd for sharing episodes of his exciting, successful life, from Bethune school days to the present. Fincher treasured those memories and wished Floyd many more years of success and happiness.[74]

Just after *Susannah* played England's Midlands Arts Centre on April 25, 27, 28, and 29, HGO produced the opera as the second installment of its collaboration with Lyric Opera of Chicago. Floyd earned twenty-one thousand dollars from the event, further easing the cost of maintaining two homes.[75] Richard Bado, HGO's chorus master and head of the musical staff, conducted Nancy Gustafson in the title role, with Samuel Ramey (Blitch), Mark Baker (Sam), and Richard Markley (Little Bat), in Marc Verzatt's restaging of Robert Falls's production.[76] A member of that year's studio, tenor John McVeigh, cast as Elder Hayes, would figure prominently in future Floyd performances.

Following a farewell dinner for the composer on May 5, and a benefit lunch for the Moores School of Music Society on May 10, at which David Tomatz presented him with an outstanding faculty award, Floyd flew to Syracuse, where he received his next honorary doctorate at that alma mater, Syracuse University, on May 12.

Floyd's Houston chapter closed with a new accolade on August 14, when university president Glenn Allen Goerke named him professor emeritus. Together with the benefits he continued to receive from his two decades at Florida State University, his UH retirement plan created a bulwark against inflation and the shifting sands of the opera world. The Floyds completed their physical move to Tallahassee, leaving just enough in the Yoakum Boulevard house to make future visits possible, if far from luxurious.

AS IT TURNED OUT, retirement from academia led to situations that may have surprised even Floyd. In August 1996, David Gockley told Mark Adamo that he wanted *Little Women* for two Houston Opera Studio performances in March 1998. It was high time to begin the libretto, and HGO had no problem with Adamo writing his own. He further detailed his slant on the story to Floyd, who expressed admiration but also caution: "Most of our work was by phone. Mark's incredibly bright, and I told him that he had an excellent take on the story. It's very dangerous, even to touch it, but he came up with a clever kind of in, one special phrase that sort of took you into the whole story, and gave it a real narrative thrust throughout."

By spring 1997, Adamo submitted the first draft of his libretto for Floyd's comments. Floyd recalled, "I pointed out some pretty obvious things that I thought expendable, or needed work, and he responded, 'Of course.'" But Adamo balked when Floyd confronted him forcibly with the fundamental lack of clarity of the first scene. Adamo's experience admirably illustrates the workings of Floyd's mind:

> Carlisle said, "You've done all the really difficult things extremely well: all the supporting characters are very sharply drawn. But explain to me this storytelling business." (What is now *Little Women*'s laundry-game scene was originally a series of improvised stories with which the four March sisters entertained each other.) I said, "That's how we learn who the characters are." I was very proud of that sequence; it was quite long and conspicuously rhymed, real virtuoso stuff. And Carlisle said, "Let me get this straight. We're meeting these people for the first time. We have no idea who they are. And we're somehow supposed to identify their characters through subtextual events

in a storytelling game? Don't you think that's subtlety raised to the level of the Japanese?"

He was right. Wistfully, I agreed. But then he continued, "There is also the small problem of your leading lady. What does she want?"

"You know what she wants: to turn things back the way they were."

"Yes, *I* know that because I've been talking to you for a year, but how is the audience going to know that?"

Rather grandly at this point, I replied, "*Surely* the prologue *cabaletta* makes that unmissably clear."

And he said, "No, the prologue *cabaletta* tells us only that she's extremely upset about something to do with time."

In that draft—the end of act 1, scene 1—in the place where now begins Jo's principal scena, "Perfect as we are," there was only Laurie uttering, "You never know, Jo, things change. I'll see you down below," and a cryptic sting from the orchestra before we progressed into act 1, scene 2. I saw a place for a possible second aria, but had no idea what to write. So I stalled: "I realize the prologue aria might be subtler than ideal, but surely the rest of the show fills in the blanks?"

"I wouldn't be so sure."

Somewhat desperately, I asked, "So I have to have her just stroll downstage and explain to the audience what she wants?"

And he said, "Only if you want the audience to understand."

"But how do I make that seem natural, or interesting?"

"I'm afraid that's your problem," he said.[77]

The exchange illustrates what Adamo considers to be Floyd's particular gift as a teacher of the little-understood craft of libretto writing.

He's a brilliant reader of text, but he thinks structurally first. And that method can fill even your first draft with rich detail, because you've considered beforehand the work it has to do. You can rewrite before you write, if you will, which allows you more, not less, spontaneity when it comes to the actual composing. I would never have come up with the rollicking sections of "Perfect as we are" if I hadn't needed to contrast them with the earnest lyrical strophes; but the surprise gift of those sections was how they let me place Jo's writing in the context of her character.

The two men kept in touch for the next year, without Adamo going into any of his musical process with Floyd. The world premiere by the Houston Opera Studio at the Wortham Center's Cullen Theater on March 13 and 15, 1998 scored a mighty hit; there were press echoes of Floyd's insistence on clarifying the central issue of time's passage.[78]

The work caused enough of a sensation that Gockley scheduled an eight-performance revival in March 2000. PBS *Great Performances* broadcast the production on August 29, 2001, and an audio CD in 2001 and a DVD release in 2009 provided further dissemination.[79] From its premiere through August 2011, *Little Women* had already received seventy-five productions in this country and abroad.

Adamo received a subsequent HGO commission, the libretto and music for Aristophanes' *Lysistrata,* premiered in March 2005, with an East Coast debut at New York City Opera in March 2006. Though Adamo sent Floyd that libretto for feedback, the tone of the response was different. "He was a little cool about it. Not unkind, but the abrupt alternation of comic and tragic tones—which, to be fair, he hadn't liked much in *Little Women* either—was much more pronounced in *Lysistrata,* so it didn't interest him as much. But regardless, his generosity and intelligence are givens; and I can't imagine it's unique to me."[80]

Fall 1996 began a round of significant Floyd firsts. On October 14, the Wiener Kammeroper gave *Susannah*'s Austrian premiere, conducted by Christian Arming, and staged by the mezzo-soprano-turned director Brigitte Fassbaender. Ludmila Slepneva sang Susannah; Desmond Byrne, a Canadian from Montreal, Blitch; and Wright Moore, Sam. The articulate Byrne accepted the role because Fassbaender eschewed any trendy "Coca Cola" concepts. In order to help Austrian audiences to better understand *Floyd*'s concept, she set the opera in a puritanical Lutheran community.[81]

The press scorned the opera in familiar slams: "Americanisms . . . film music." "Folkish characteristics frequently cross the borders of banality." "Seldom more than sentimental Kitsch." Vienna's highest compliment proved to be that the opera was "a straightforward, naive, very American tragedy."[82]

THE YEAR 1997 began with the Vancouver Opera's *Susannah,* conducted by David Agler, staged by Morris Panych, and sung by Sally Dibblee (Susannah), David Pittsinger (Blitch), Anthony Dean Griffey (Sam), and Richard Clement (Little Bat). In February, Floyd flew to Berlin for Deutsche Oper's opening night *Susannah* on February 8.[83] In a postcard to Jona Clarke, he wrote, "I have been here since last Saturday [February 1] attending rehearsals for the local premiere . . . and doing the usual interviews with very unusual German journalists—they put their American counterparts to shame in both intelligence and information. This is a remarkable city in so many ways and I've found the people very hospitable."[84]

Floyd considered the English director John Dew's production brilliant. Marie-Jeanne Dufour conducted a cast including Karan Armstrong in the title role, Dean Peterson (Blitch), Stefano Algieri (Sam), and Richard Markley (Little Bat). Even Dew's most radical abstractions contributed to the opera's central thesis. An enormous eye stared out at the audience from two television monitors, opening and closing throughout, an effective metaphor for everything leading to the denouement. Other stylized elements included a monolithic black-clad chorus for the act 1 square-dance scene. For the revival, the group marched into the church with utmost solemnity; when Susannah fled, the sight of eighty heartless judges hurling black hymnals across the stage, a symbolic stoning, invested the ritual with hieratic, mythic qualities.

Desmond Byrne, the role under his belt from the previous fall's Vienna engagement, was called to Berlin to cover Blitch, and sang two performances, after coaching by Floyd during rehearsals. Byrne recalled his awe at encountering a famous living composer whose work he was singing. Though Floyd at seventy appeared frail to Byrne, the singer found him "very elegant and extremely intelligent . . . very alert to what you are doing."[85]

Despite a few detractors, and the usual sniffing at film music influences, the press reflected Berlin's progressive mindset, together with the expression of a little surprise that *Susannah* had become such a fixture of world repertoire.[86]

Despite the Lyon recording three years earlier, *Susannah* had never been staged in France. After another round of transatlantic flights, Floyd attended rehearsals and the first two performances on March 19 and 21 at the Nantes Théâtre Graslin. Jean-Yves Ossonce conducted a polyglot cast, including Régine Nathan (Susannah), Steven Page (Blitch), Marek Torzewsky (Sam), and Michael Preston-Roberts (Little Bat). Floyd thought John Dew's concept conservative compared to Philippe Godefroid's. Though finding the man intelligent and likeable in his position as the company's general director, Floyd wished that Godefroid had consulted him before inserting a wealth of gratuitous "Eurotrash" as his commentary on American pop culture of the 1950s: Elvis Presley's appearance in act 2, sitting down and drinking a beer; Blitch as a flagellant, naked to the waist, scourging himself while Susannah held his coat; and the title character going mad and stabbing Little Bat at the end. "That was a misreading of the entire piece," recalled Floyd. "The last thing Susannah would ever do is wreak violence on another human being. I was willing to go along with many things before that, although I don't think they'd be things I'd ever use in a production."

Reviews were cryptic: "Not a revelatory thunderbolt, but an authentic discovery all the same."[87] At least Floyd could inform Jona Clarke that "the enthusiasm of the audiences both here and Berlin has exceeded my wildest expectations. It has been a very happy time in my life."[88]

ON APRIL 4, his paternal uncle G. R.'s wife, Fredrika (Freddie), died in Tallahassee, where they had settled in an assisted living residence some years earlier. On April 28, Floyd delivered Opera America's twenty-seventh annual conference keynote address in Philadelphia. Considering the theme, opera's four centuries as a medium, he reworked his 1964 "Society and the Artist" paper and lecture, now retitled "A Summing-Up at Seventy." Bearing in mind that he had written his original statements at the age of thirty-five, literally half a lifetime ago, his current perspective had evolved commensurately. His overall regard for the progress of opera, not to mention the progress of Carlisle Floyd, was far more optimistic than his 1985 remarks before the House of Representatives. The burgeoning of resourceful new companies, the improved quality of productions, the possibility of second and third hearings for new works, and the innovation of supertitles all prompted rejoicing. Yet he still had abiding concerns: The predictability of the familiar, tired repertoire warhorses that exerted the "tyranny of the box office; "deconstructive," as opposed to innovative, directorial conceits; and the lack of effective arts education. His most telling concern was, as always, for the relationship of artist and audience: "What redeems artists from the charge of arrogance . . . is a constant awareness that, while it is the artist's unquestioned function to lead . . . it is imperative that he at all times look over his shoulder to be certain that there is someone following. . . . We—the creators of opera and the opera audience—have to find a common language . . . and I am afraid the responsibility is more on our side than on the audience's."

His finish blazed positive, a summation of all that lures audiences into opera houses: "I continue to marvel at the unique expressive power of this art form. The world of opera is the world of the large gesture, the thrilling overstatement. . . . Rendered authentically human and emotionally convincing by passionately committed performers, the kind of artistic experience that results is unmatched anywhere else.[89]

20

Unmatched Experience

Susannah *at the Met, 1997–2000*

The year 1997 brought even more sweeping change to Floyd's career arc, despite and owing to his senior citizenship. This would involve intensified travel, a reappraisal of existing works, and more collecting of the greatest honors bestowed on musicians. It became a time for his unmatched experiences, as he witnessed valedictory productions by highly visible companies new and old. His work had created its niche in the greater world.

That spring, Florida State University asked him to teach an opera literature course, as well as three or four composition students. He enjoyed the former endeavor, the latter not so much, but both kept his hand in academia. He made contact with two enterprising young groups, the New Music-Theater Ensemble of St. Paul and Opera Roanoke, and authorized a smaller orchestration of *Susannah* for performance in alternative venues. He wrote to Craig Fields at Opera Roanoke, "I have felt for some time that performing operas outside the usual theaters designated as opera houses was exciting, and generally unexplored, territory for composers, performers, and audiences alike."[1]

Colorado's Central City Opera performed *Susannah,* with Michael Ehrman's staging, John Moriarty conducting, and Floyd at the opening on July 12.[2] The cast, Diane Alexander (Susannah), Andrew Wenzel (Blitch), and Adam Klein (Sam), generated reviews that caused company management to rejoice over their most glowing press in a decade. Two weeks later, Floyd attended rehearsals and the July 26 opening of Glimmerglass Opera's *Of Mice and Men* in Rhoda Levine's production, conducted by Stewart Robertson, and sets by John Conklin. The cast, including Anthony Dean Griffey (Lennie), Rod Nelman (George), Matthew Lord (Curley), and Juliana Rambaldi and Margaret Lloyd (Curley's Wife), and the production both generated critical raves.[3] Glimmerglass collaborated with the New York State Historical Association, also headquartered in Cooperstown, on a Steinbeck seminar billed as "Portrait of the 30s: Inspiration for an Opera." This event was chaired by Susan Shillinglaw, director of the Center for Steinbeck Studies at San Jose State University, and Floyd and opera staff members presented. The Scottish conductor Robertson spoke amusingly of the opera title's origins in the verse of his countryman Robert Burns, and Professor Shillinglaw aroused unintended hilarity when she referred to that poet as "George" Burns.

Anthony Tommasini wrote of the patronizing attitude that "more intellectually ambitious composers" had shown Floyd: "But this slights his considerable gifts as a composer and dramatist, and *Of Mice and Men* may be his finest score, harmonically gritty . . . tenderly lyrical . . . paced with keen dramatic understanding."[4]

Floyd spent most of that fall in Houston, where on September 23 a gala crowd participated in the official christening of the Moores School of Music, the result of the $70 million gift of John and Rebecca Moores to the University of Houston.

Unbeknownst to Floyd, on November 5, 1997, nominating members of the American Academy of Arts and Letters, including Floyd's colleague Ned Rorem, met in New York to deliberate new candidates. Rorem described the squabbling of the painters and writers over who did and did not deserve membership.

As Floyd's designated nominator was absent, Rorem jumped into the breach and testified that Floyd and Menotti had between them created America's opera tradition; because of the former's age, the academy needed to make a timely decision. The composer Milton Babbitt observed that this was all well and good, but said that he and his fellow members, not Floyd, occupied the power seats.[5]

Elsewhere, the conductor Patrick Summers explained, "Carlisle's music has familiarity and acceptability, combined with an incredible ability to touch the common man. . . . Unfortunately, there is an inherent distrust of that among the music intelligentsia."[6] Nothing further happened on this score in 1997, but the cards lay on the table.

On November 12, Floyd flew from Houston to San Francisco, where he checked into the St. Francis Hotel and proceeded to speak to the City News Service. The next morning, he met the public relations staff of Opera San Jose, about to open *Of Mice and Men.* Former student Craig Bohmler, the production's assistant conductor, volunteered to serve as Floyd's official driver for most of a five-day visit, including a taped interview with the local PBS affiliate, KQED, a full day of interviews in the conference room of Floyd's hotel, a photo shoot, and social and conference time with Jake Heggie, who was in the thick of composing *Dead Man Walking.*

On Opera San Jose's opening night, November 15, Floyd dined with the company's founder and director, the mezzo-soprano Irene Dalis,[7] and company staff, before heading to the Montgomery Theatre for a triumphal opening. But the company had not quite gotten everything they wanted from Floyd. After a matinee on November 16, "An Evening with Carlisle Floyd" also held the stage of the Montgomery, a three-hour round of the composer's responses to audience questions. The next day, he met David Gockley and the two flew back to Houston, discussing the commission that would fill the composer's next two years.

THE YEAR 1997 ended with another family passing, that of his aunt Bunny, née Mary Kate Fenegan, in Arizona on December 11; but 1998 began with a lifetime achievement award from Opera Music Theater International, whose fortunes owed much to Floyd's decades-long participation. James K. McCully, chairman of the National Opera Association's forty-third convention, presented the honor in Washington, DC, on January 17. Distinguished fellow recipients included Seymour Barab, Jack Beeson, Kirke Mechem, Thea Musgrave, and Robert Ward.

As always a popular and astute judge of singers, Floyd, together with Gockley and Richard Bado, judged twenty finalists in HGO's Eleanor McCollum auditions at the Wortham Center on February 13, awarding the six thousand dollar Scott Heumann Memorial Award to the Chinese baritone Chen-Ye Yuan.[8] On February 22, Floyd was back in New York to inaugurate a new lecture, "The Making of an Aria," at the Manhattan School of Music. A joint presentation of the Center for Contemporary Opera, the Manhattan School, and the New York Singing Teachers Association, the event featured commentary on and introduction of eight arias from *Wuthering Heights, Mollie Sinclair, Susannah,* and *Of Mice and Men.*

With Floyd's absorption in his new project, and far-flung productions of his works, in the spring of 1998 Kay lived in the Houston house while Floyd stayed in Tallahassee and attended select performances nationwide. Gockley dispatched him to San Diego during that opera company's *Of Mice and Men* production in January and February, and to confer with Jack O'Brien on the new libretto.[9] Despite missing the Oberlin Conservatory Opera Theater double bill of *Slow Dusk* and Menotti's *The Old Maid and the Thief,* the Chattanooga Opera Association performance of the Floyd/Hendl *Susannah* Suite, and the Springfield (Missouri) Regional Opera *Susannah,* he did make it to Deutsche Oper Berlin's *Susannah* revival in March.[10]

In New York in May, Floyd delivered the Center for Contemporary Opera 1998 lecture on the state of American opera titled "The Materials of Opera: Creating Opera, the Art of Alchemy," a summing-up of his current thinking about the medium:

> The natural habitat of opera is crisis. A good opera is about that day, that moment, when something

> uncommon happened; it is never about everyday occurrences, it is always about the uncommon moment which forces characters to reveal themselves. . . . The strong silent type of the American movie western does not work in opera. Gary Cooper just saying "yep" won't do. . . . Any composer can set the telephone book to music, but it won't be very moving. . . . We are not aware of the individual elements, any more than we are aware of blue and yellow when we see green. It is the fusion of elements which gives opera its great fascination. . . . When it is done well, it is an unmatched experience.[11]

At seventy-two, Floyd's days and nights flew past at breakneck speed. In April he attended an Augusta (Georgia) Opera *Susannah,* helped the company with a number of public relations events, and appeared at the April 30 opening night, conducted by one of his favorites, Mark Flint, and staged by Claudia Zahn. At the celebratory after-party, Floyd told Flint that he had brought out voices in the orchestra that the composer had never heard.[12]

The Opera Festival of New Jersey opened its *Susannah* on July 11, preceded by a day-long symposium at Princeton Theological Seminary. Floyd, usually a willing and effective participant in such events, was back in Houston at work on his new project; but director Rhoda Levine gave him good reports of the production, conducted by Ward Holmquist. Emily Pulley sang Susannah, partnered by Andrew Wenzel (Blitch), Jay Hunter Morris (Sam), and Beau Palmer (Little Bat).[13] One reviewer sneered at the opera as "evidently taken . . . as an important work," and the most frequently performed American opera, "since *The Rake's Progress* [*sic*]."[14] In response to *Susannah*'s upcoming performances at The Metropolitan Opera, another critic asked, "Why?"[15]

If Floyd read such perorations, they did not keep him from *Susannah* at the Opera Theater Center of another city and festival familiar at the remove of forty years, Aspen, Colorado. James Conlon conducted Edward Berkeley's production on August 4, and the company put Floyd up in a guesthouse for about three weeks as he worked on his new opera.

Sharing productions with Glimmerglass and New York City Opera, Paul Kellogg brought Rhoda Levine's *Of Mice and Men* to his Lincoln Center stage. The Met's importation of *Susannah* from Chicago and Houston loomed large across the plaza for April 1999. The first event gave Floyd a chance to finally meet John Steinbeck's widow, Elaine. In their box at the performance, and afterward at dinner, they chatted about possible film versions, which rights she had granted Floyd and Belwin-Mills after City Opera's 1983 production. She told Floyd that she had been a fan of the opera, and confided that her husband preferred those adaptations of his book that centered on its drama of human attachment rather than social polemics. She assured Floyd that Steinbeck would have loved *his* treatment.[16]

The New York Times, which had portrayed Floyd as everything from genius to goose, now began a series of long, thoughtful articles that placed the composer and his two most popular operas in proper context. K. Robert Schwarz credited *Susannah* with more productions (230) and performances (about 750) than any other full-length American opera. He quoted Phyllis Curtin's tongue-in-cheek contention that Floyd's southern background and tonal orientation had excluded him from northeastern and western schools of composition: "He seemed out of the Romantic era, a bit passé and naïve. And slow. . . . You know: He's a southern boy."[17]

Floyd himself addressed this issue of pigeonholing, which he found "irksome," for writing audience-friendly music; but he acknowledged, "I may not have been the outcast, but I certainly was the misfit." Schwarz cited Julius Rudel's characterization of *Susannah* as "a throw of genius, a young man's first explosion," which had attracted "the paying customer [who] tells you what to play." Floyd waxed modest about the Met's production, which had come as an unexpected thunderbolt; but he hoped that this exposure conferred "repertory status" on his "Old Girl."

Floyd's New York weeks satisfied personal and professional needs, as, one by one, most of his oldest friends from every time and place materialized. He met Jona Clarke for dinner at O'Neal's across from Lincoln Center, and they waited for Priscilla Gillette-Perrone.

Seconds after sweeping through the door, before embracing anyone or speaking, she burst into the first line of Floyd's 1946 song "Remember," which they had performed together on his senior recital at Syracuse. "Woo" might have been a matronly seventy-two, but she had not lost an ounce of theatrical flair.

For City Opera's education program, Mark Adamo wrote an essay, "The Father of Us All," which spoke to Floyd's verbal and musical techniques, and explained for the lay listener his polyharmonic language as a reflection of "his characters' emotional patterns," which Adamo felt gave *Of Mice and Men* "momentum of Aeschylean inevitability. . . . In short, *Of Mice and Men* is a serious, richly worked, and emotionally generous opera—among the finest ever composed in this country."[18]

For City Opera, Paul Kellogg engaged a cast mostly new to Levine's production, conducted again by Stewart Robertson: Anthony Dean Griffey (Lennie), Dean Ely (George), Joel Sorensen (Curley), and Nancy Allen Lundy (Curley's Wife).[19] Julian Patrick, the first George, by now in his early seventies, but still singing, delighted Floyd anew as Candy, the old ranch hand whose dog is dispatched. "I was very excited to return to the piece. I love the opera no matter what role I do and I still find that emotional punch. . . . Of course I would love to be singing George still, but there is always going to be some young buck coming along to do it."[20]

During rehearsals, Floyd, always in search of an enterprising and resourceful company to revive *Bilby's Doll*, gave Kellogg a copy of the libretto; but by the time Kellogg ceded his office to Gérard Mortier for a few moments in June 2007, the opera remained unproduced by the company. In *Of Mice and Men*'s wake, the *Times* found little to admire, alluding to its "mildly folksy, Coplandesque melodies."[21] But this proved a minority view. The *New York Post* asserted that this production of the opera placed a seal on Floyd's career, through his persistence in writing singable melodies in the face of prevailing musical fashions.[22]

One of the numerous productions that Floyd could not attend was the Canadian premiere of *Wuthering Heights* by Opera Anonymous in a single concert performance in Toronto.

THE YEAR 1999 unfolded as Carlisle Floyd's annus mirabilis, during which he beheld an astonishing outpouring of his works around the country. On January 6, he gave a preview lecture for Utah Opera in Salt Lake City, and the following day delivered his refurbished "Art of Alchemy" talk from the previous May. The company held a day-long *Of Mice and Men* symposium on January 14, and its opening two nights later. Led by Pamela Berlin (stage director) and Karen Keltner (conductor), Michael Hendrick sang Lennie, alongside Stephen Bryant (George), Michael Myers (Curley), and Diane Alexander (Curley's Wife).

In the course of the year, VAI Records released the North Carolina Public Television audio recording of *The Sojourner and Mollie Sinclair.*[23] The master video had gone missing since its 1963 airings, but a soundtrack tape had turned up in Norman Treigle's personal collection following his death in 1975.

Floyd dropped in on *Of Mice and Men*'s next stop, San Diego, where Karen Keltner and Rhoda Levine led Erich Parce, Anthony Dean Griffey, and Diane Alexander in their accustomed roles on March 6, 9, 12, and 14. Besides participating in the company's public relations efforts, Floyd led a successful reading of completed portions of his new *Cold Sassy Tree.*

March found *Of Mice and Men* at Orlando Opera, staged by Robert Swedberg and conducted by Darryl Oune, with Erich Parce (George), Gary Lakes (Lennie), Dean Anthony (Curley), and Mary Ellen Duncan (Curley's Wife); and at Cleveland Opera, directed by David Bamberger.[24] Anton Coppola, the Seattle conductor in 1970, who turned eighty-two during rehearsals, held down the pit and a young cast featuring Robert McFarland (George), Mark Rehnstrom (Lennie), Matthew Lord (Curley), and Helen Todd (Curley's Wife).

Simultaneously, Toronto's Opera in Concert presented *Susannah* on March 27 and 28, the last thing Floyd saw before he and Kay ensconced themselves in a suite at the Mayflower Hotel in New York for *Susannah*'s Metropolitan Opera bow, and the accompanying round of interviews and other events. A note of welcome from the company's general manager, Joseph Volpe, awaited Floyd. Recalling the National Company *Susannah* in 1965, Volpe enthused that he felt that the Met was greeting an old friend.[25]

Boosey's Linda Golding took charge of Kay, as ever shy of public events. The two women attended dress rehearsal on March 29; then, in Golding's words, "At the performance, all of a sudden, there she wasn't."[26] On March 30, Floyd, Phyllis Curtin, and the journalist Martin Bernheimer gave a Metropolitan lecture series presentation. On March 31, opening night, Mark Adamo dropped off a note of congratulations to his mentor, with regrets that he could not attend the premiere because he was rehearsing a new work, "but I toast you from 10 blocks uptown, and toast the Met as well, for at least recognizing the genius in our midst."[27]

That morning, Anthony Tommasini's thoughtful article appeared in the *Times:* a joint interview with Floyd, Phyllis Curtin, who would join Floyd in the audience, and Renée Fleming, singing the title role that evening. Tommasini marveled that an American composer had joined the elite company of Verdi, Strauss, and Puccini, by living long enough to see his work become part of the permanent repertory with its "unabashedly tonal" score.[28]

April's *Opera News* covered a great deal of ground, devoting eighteen of its hundred pages to Floyd, with articles by Julius Rudel, Barrymore Laurence Scherer, William R. Braun, and Paul Thomason, the last about the work's southern origins. Scherer skillfully repackaged the outsider theme; but Rudel and Curtin contributed personal, eloquent insights into their own involvement with *Susannah.*

The Falls/Yeargan production, conducted by James Conlon, held few surprises, as Floyd had already seen it in Chicago and Houston. For its seven performances,[29] in addition to Renée Fleming as Susannah, the Met had engaged leading Floyd exponents Samuel Ramey (Blitch), Jerry Hadley (Sam), and John McVeigh (Little Bat). The Gleatons were Jane Dutton and Jerold Siena; the Otts, Jane Shaulis and Leroy Lehr; the Hayeses, Jennifer and Jonathan Welch; and the McLeans, Joyce Castle and James Courtney. But to Floyd, the real estate made all the difference. "I was aware that it was the same opera as in 1955, but I knew that its being performed by the Met conferred museum status, as it usually does with American works. But was it any different? I was aware of my surroundings, that's the best way I can put it."

In a way, Floyd's greatest thrill came from the flood of old friends rushing through the Met's doors. Most important, the event provided a rapprochement that ended the almost three-year separation from his sister, which illustrated Lorri Glover's summation of the importance of southern families: "Sibship and kinship simply mattered too much to risk losing over petty differences."[30]

Floyd had made his dissatisfaction about the separation so clear to Kay that she tried reaching Ermine through her eldest daughter Martha, but to no effect. A year earlier, Floyd reported to Jona Clarke that the "Ermine front" remained "painful and baffling."[31] Kay finally picked up the phone and asked Ermine directly to join them for the Met opening.

Former instructors, colleagues, students, and friends turned up from all over the country to cheer their friend and mentor: Alia Ross Lawson, his Converse music theory teacher, now about eighty-five, whose assignment had prompted his first composition, the 1944 Quintet, caught Floyd's eye across orchestra rows. Also there to support and applaud were "the eternal boy"[32] Don Rand, whom Floyd had not seen for almost a half century, and who now taught a large private piano studio in Lake Placid, New York; Peggy Tapp Turman, from Nashville, and Phyllis Curtin, Julius Rudel, Jake Heggie and David Gockley. From Tallahassee came the Mastrogiacomos, the Choppins, Catherine Murphy, Nancy Smith Fichter and husband Robert, Yvon Streetman and others, and, of course, Priscilla, Jona, and Ermine.

Rudel in particular had done his best to atone for the breach resulting from *Of Mice and Men*'s premiere shuffle before 1970. For *Opera News* he wrote:

> It is pure coincidence that my youngest granddaughter and Carlisle Floyd were born under the same Zodiac sign. It is no coincidence that she is named

38. Kay, Floyd, Ermine, Metropolitan Opera, 1999. Courtesy of Carlisle Floyd.

39. Julius Rudel, c. 2000. Courtesy of Julius Rudel.

> Susannah. . . . Ever since I first heard Carlisle's brilliant music-drama . . . it has held an important place in my musical heart . . . it should be thought of as a great opera that has earned a position in the world repertory. . . . Who among us, in any part of the world, has never had to walk through his own valley of New Hope?[33]

During intermission, the playwright Terence McNally interviewed Floyd and his composer colleague Tobias Picker in an American opera roundtable. The performance ended, the audience waited for the composer's appearance with the cast and Conlon, and rose to their feet as one, virtually howling their approval. Jake Heggie confirmed, "The ovation at the end when Carlisle took the stage was thunderous. It surprised even him, you could see it on his face. People were screaming!"[34]

David Gockley exulted that Floyd's reception marked "one of the greatest nights in the history of American opera."[35] The first congratulatory face Floyd saw backstage after bows was Rudel's. A minor glitch in the Met's social mechanism involved a last-minute decision to hold its reception in the second-floor house lobby area, to which Floyd could not invite his out-of-town contingent. After the obligatory appearance with cast and production staff, he rushed across to the Mayflower, where family and friends overflowed the Floyds' suite.

Renée Fleming wrote in her autobiography of identification with Susannah's traumas during the final stages of her divorce. Real tears streamed down her face in the first act, and she found easy access to the character's emotions. Yet when a friend advised her to pay more attention to her acting, she realized that her true mission was not simply to *feel*, but to *express* that feeling in a way that audiences could grasp, and that required a cooler distancing.

In an interview for *USOperaweb*, Anthony Dean Griffey regretted that Yeargan's set had been too small for the Met's enormous stage; yet its clean lines made the Polk siblings appear far too affluent.[36]

A few days later, Phyllis Curtin wrote Floyd congratulations and cautions: "The thrill of the year was seeing you on the Met stage receiving that superb reception . . . [it is] indelibly, joyously in my mind." Although she tasked the cast for various shortcomings, one of Curtin's gravest reservations also concerned the production's focus on "hill billies," particularly Jerry Hadley's presentation of Sam: "[This was] not the piece you wrote. . . . This is not a *Susannah* I will remember.

I SHALL, WILL remember the tearful joy that your presence on the stage brought me."[37]

Floyd always reminded casts that a little regional dialect went a long way, and felt that Hadley had adopted an accent straight out of *The Beverly Hillbillies.* Such approaches he always felt damaged the work by allowing the audience to feel superior to the work's ambience.

The *Times* review surprised everyone with its characterization of *Susannah* as a "small-house opera": "'Susannah, Susannah!' one felt like calling out. 'What's a nice girl like you doing in a place like this?' . . . looking like some lonely tourist lost in the vastness of Grand Central Terminal."[38] And so on.

Peter G. Davis, never a Floyd admirer, expressed the futility of bashing Floyd and *Susannah* at this point, "although many still resent its success." Davis characterized Floyd as an American one-opera Mascagni, who wrote "many other interesting works, but never struck gold again," positing a loss of innocence "as his . . . craft became more sophisticated."[39]

Within days, a flood of personal congratulations began pouring into the composer's mailbox. Priscilla Gillette-Perrone's note elicited smiles with its characterization of performers as ephemeral, compared to Floyd, whom she thought the American Verdi/Schumann, shining on forever.[40]

Ernie Gilbert, president of VAI Records, told Floyd that he had scored a spare ticket to the April 3 performance, and offered it to his house painter, who had never heard, much less attended, an opera. The painter donned jacket and tie, but his shoes still bore spatters betraying his profession; nonetheless, the two were off to the Met. Despite preconceptions about the medium, the painter was utterly carried away: "These are the people whose opinions you have to take very seriously, because they're not predisposed one way or another. I love the challenge of that."[41]

The Met's Sarah Billinghurst wrote, "I wanted to let you know that the complete run of *Susannah* has been a huge success. In fact we sold out the last two performances and last night the cast had a standing ovation! It has given us all such pleasure to have presented your opera here at the Met. Personally I was so delighted it was such a success and it will encourage us all to look at more American operas for future seasons."[42]

THE PROCESSION of *Susannah*s that followed the Met's offered pudding-proof of the opera's appeal and durability, but Floyd was too busy writing a new one to notice. On April 16 and 17, Northern Illinois University in DeKalb gave the opera an outing; and, on April 22, Mark Flint conducted Stanley M. Garner's production at Opéra de Montréal's Théâtre Maisonneuve, with a cast featuring Karen Driscoll (Susannah), Brian Davis (Blitch), Jonathan Boyd (Sam), and Dean Anthony (Little Bat). Flint's experience mirrored Kent Nagano's in Lyon: "For the company, it was a bit of a risk, what with all the Francophile and Anglophile culture wars, but they adored it. Teaching southern dialect to French Canadians was a challenge, but once they got it, no problem."[43]

On Floyd's craft, Flint elaborated, "He's very specific about what he wants dramatically: it's there in the orchestra, everywhere in the music, and there's no reason to fuss with it. Every piece has its flawed moments, and you have to deal with those to make it work, but Carlisle is such a total man of the theater, he knows that medium, what does and does not work. There's not one wasted measure. The only other piece I can say this about is *La bohème*."

On June 3, Stockholm's Royal Philharmonic Orchestra, conducted by Niklas Willen, gave *Susannah* excerpts in concert with soprano Britt-Marie Aruhn. On July 24, 25, 28, and August 6 and 15, the Ashland/Highland Summer Festival, on the grounds of James Monroe's house in Charlottesville, Virginia, performed the opera in an outdoor setting. August 17, 19, 20, and 21 witnessed repetitions of the work at Union Avenue Opera Theatre in St. Louis, with Scott Schoonover conducting Jolly Stewart's production. Washington Opera (Kennedy Center) provided the next home for eight November performances of the Falls/Yeargan production. With Floyd in attendance, John DeMain conducted a new cast: Mary Mills (Susannah), Jeffrey Wells (Blitch), Richard Brunner (Sam), and Beau Palmer (Little Bat). Simultaneously, the University of

Michigan Opera Theatre presented its own *Susannah.*[44] And on November 21, 27, and December 3, the piece rang down the curtain on 1999, again crossing the border, to Canada's Opera Hamilton.

The second half of 1999 also witnessed the passing of the last of his father's generation. On June 15 his eldest uncle, G. R., died in Tallahassee, and his and Freddie's ashes were taken to Mt. Andrew Cemetery near Floydale for interment. Next, on December 11, the youngest Floyd uncle, Sonny (Bascom Lorraine), passed in Arizona.

Floyd, *Susannah,* and the new millennium all found their way to Calgary Opera on January 20; the composer could not attend UCLA Opera Theatre's production on January 21, 22 and 23.

The "old girl" was here to stay; and when Floyd received letters of congratulation from Boosey's licensing manager Sue Klein and from Phyllis Curtin, both emphasized that they could not wait for *Cold Sassy Tree.*[45] Neither, as it turned out, could its composer, who was busy inventing a very different kind of hero and heroine in search of their own forms of independence.

21

Late Fruits

Cold Sassy Tree, *1994–2003*

Aside from his dark period in the eighties, and the resulting hiatus between *Willie Stark* in 1981 and *Jonathan Wade II* in 1991, Floyd had never let more than five years pass without producing a new opera. In the vacuum left by the sundering of the Houston Opera Studio from the University of Houston music program, he was now ready to immerse himself in Olive Ann Burns's novel *Cold Sassy Tree,* which Ermine had recommended as a subject with something for everyone, and as the embodiment of the Old South oral tradition of storytelling. The book has a cast of lovable eccentrics who speak in linguistic tropes that Floyd recognized from his childhood, and he envisioned creating a parable of human growth and transformation by necessity, to be accomplished by grafting a core of reconciliation onto the Burns novel. Death unites people and elicits humankind's best and most generous natures. The character Love Simpson functions as a catalyst and love interest for two generations of male protagonists, and that would form the beating heart of the new opera.

Over the course of eighteen months, during which Floyd attended many productions of earlier works, including the Met's *Susannah,* he read the novel three times, pondering how to craft a libretto from what seemed more a sprawling collection of vignettes than a unified text. He excerpted three pages of unconnected, paraphrased modules that spoke to him most vividly, months later assembling his scenario—which as usual he called a treatment—like a mosaic, making use of some tiles and rejecting others.

Such leisurely pains-taking allowed him to grow a "spine" for his opera,[1] a concept wholly lacking in Burns, and expressed in Floyd's famous twenty-five words or less: "An old man growing young, and a young man growing up, in a relationship that gradually turns out quite differently than it began."

The old man, Rucker, is the river into which young Will's tributary flows. Death constitutes the story's north and south poles, and the South's pragmatic attitude to the end of life plays a leading role in Burns and Floyd: "Based on my parents, I think that southerners are quite objective about death as the ultimate reality. My mother used to say, sounding quite factual and pleasant, 'When I'm a corpse, be sure my hands are covered.' I didn't want to think of anyone as a corpse, but they saw death as a different stage of life: life stops, that's it, without death being a public rite."

Despite initial reservations about how well the book would lend itself to adaptation, Boosey's files show that Floyd set his team, principally the director of business affairs Carolyn Kalett, to investigating rights in the spring of 1994. *Of Mice and Men, Bilby's Doll,* and *Willie Stark* had taught Floyd the importance of settling this labyrinthine task early in his process before investing himself more deeply in any new project.

New York's International Creative Management, Inc. (ICM) represented Burns's stage rights, and, according to the author's sister, Jean Legrand, initially advised against allowing Floyd's adaptation; but after consulting with others in the family, Legrand decided that Burns, in life an enthusiastic church chorister, would have liked the idea, and granted permission. On June 22, 1994, a FAX from Kalett to ICM's Mitch Douglas confirmed that the Burns estate now favored Floyd's operatic treatment. Boosey drafted a preliminary agreement that underwent numerous revisions before all parties signed.[2]

Yet immediate complications arose. In 1986, the film star Faye Dunaway, through her own company, Port Bascom Productions, had purchased the dramatic rights for a television film adaptation in which she starred as Love Simpson, with Richard Widmark as the crusty patriarch Rucker Blakeslee, and Neil Patrick Harris as Will Tweedy. The film's debut on the TNT cable network on October 15, 1989, followed by its release on videocassette and DVD, generated mixed reviews.

On October 14, 1994, Douglas referred Floyd and Boosey to the Port Bascom/Dunaway contract, with assurances that its language constituted no obstacle to securing opera rights; but film and television rights would be excluded.[3] Kalett, knowing that Houston Grand Opera would negotiate with NPR to broadcast the eventual production,[4] replied two weeks later that this exclusion clause posed a substantial problem, explaining that composers needed precisely these rights in order to attract commissions from opera companies. She exerted pressure by stating that if broadcast rights were not granted, she would recommend that Floyd choose a different subject. In any event, she reasoned that Floyd would need at least another four or five years before he had a new opera ready to take the stage.[5]

OLIVE ANN BURNS was born on July 13, 1924, on a farm in Banks County, Georgia. In 1931, the family moved to Commerce, the eventual model for the town in the novel, Cold Sassy. Burns extracted the unusual name from her invented town's foundation myth about a single remaining sassafras tree. Following her 1946 graduation as a journalism major from the University of North Carolina, Chapel Hill, she pursued a distinguished career with the *Atlanta Journal and Constitution Magazine,* writing as "Amy Larkin." Following her mother's cancer diagnosis in 1971, and her own for lymphoma in 1975, Burns compiled her family's recollections of life in Commerce, lightly fictionalized, with the added May-December romance of Love and Rucker, and Will Tweedy's coming of age. Her own great-grandfather served as a model for Rucker, her father for Will Tweedy.[6]

Once rights were settled, Floyd gave the book to Gockley with some trepidation. HGO would have to be an integral part of any such undertaking. Would the Yankee Gockley take to Burns's homespun tale? But the story and its characters drew the administrator utterly in, and he kept the book on his bedside reading table. Floyd pointed out the patch of sandspurs still confronting the project, to which Gockley responded, "Anything you're really attracted to, you can find a way to do." Only such repeated urging—and promise of a commission package—convinced Floyd to jump back into his usual process: treatment, libretto, music.

It would be the twenty-fifth world premiere HGO had developed in as many years. *Cold Sassy Tree* would differ from Floyd's earlier works in that the music would take greater precedence over the details of plot or versification. And the reconciliation between the composer, his wife, and his sister crystallized in harmonic form, in particular in D-flat Major, a key it shared, for example, with the deepest love music in Wagner's *Tristan und Isolde,* to cite just one analogue. "I have private times when I'm composing when I'm very thrilled by sounds, or a particular moment that stirs me. I know I felt that way when I finished the second act of *Cold Sassy Tree.*"

As early as April and May 1995, while Samuel Ramey rehearsed and performed the title role in Verdi's *Attila* in Houston, Floyd approached him with a copy of Burns's book and told the bass, "I have a project in mind, and I'm thinking of you for it."[7] In the meantime, two years passed, with Boosey/ICM negotiations in bureaucratic limbo. On April 24, 1996, four days before the *Houston Chronicle* announced the project, Kalett sent a FAX to Douglas; she asked whether Port Bascom's options were still operative, and if so, whether ICM would object to Boosey negotiating directly with Dunaway's firm.[8]

In April and May, during the HGO installment of the coproduction of *Susannah,* Ramey was back in town singing Blitch; he enthused about the book to Floyd, and reviewed his upcoming engagements with

Gockley. Toward the end of *Susannah*'s run, Gockley told him that he had scheduled the *Cold Sassy Tree* world premiere for April 2000, an unavailable period for Ramey; but Gockley hinted broadly that he would be pleased if Ramey cancelled his other commitment. Ramey could not, would not, did not, and Gockley and Floyd began to cast about for other likely Ruckers a full year before a note of music had been written.

The rights struggle escalated. On June 6, Douglas informed Kalett that Dunaway had assigned her contract to the Turner Broadcasting network TNT. A legal consultant in ICM's Los Angeles office believed that Turner would have the first option to match and thus acquire any opera rights for himself; but owing to the film's seven-year-old status, it seemed likely that Turner would grant a release, and Douglas invited Boosey to submit a formal monetary offer.[9] Despite the lack of resolution by Floyd's seventieth birthday on June 11, 1996, his confidence ran high enough to begin a preliminary treatment that he sent Gockley. "The heart of the story will be the relationship between Rucker Blakely and Love Simpson which begins presumably as a marriage-of-convenience and gradually evolves into a passionately committed love affair."[10]

This document omitted many details of character and setting that Floyd and Gockley already knew from multiple readings of Burns, and these have been inserted in the following plot outlines for greater clarity. In two paragraphs, Floyd outlined his principals, beginning with Rucker Blakely (as opposed to the Burns spelling of the surname, Blakeslee), a fifty-five-year-old Civil War veteran (fifty-nine in Burns), fiercely independent in thought and action. Rucker owns farm lands and a large dry goods store in Cold Sassy, Georgia, in 1900. As a man of property, he indulges his religious nonconformity when the local Baptist church becomes a forum for condemning the private lives of those who have yet to pick up, much less cast, a stone: "A less substantial man would be isolated, ostracized, much more of an outsider; and then nobody would care. They would just say he was uneducated, whatever. But I know, even in Holly Hill, where Ermine lives—even in our twenty-first century—and she is much more religious than I—everyone goes to church at least once or twice a month, or they get talked about."

As Jack O'Brien told Floyd in months to come, "Rucker doesn't have one insecure corpuscle in his body." Floyd responded, "I wish I shared that. But obviously I share his philosophy, and what Will gains in the end: the affirmation of life gained through great pain."

The town's fortunes are bound up with the railroad's, like most of the South Carolina villages in which the Floyds had lived; and the never-comfortable change brought by progress and technology forms a subplot, echoed in Burns and Floyd with trains, motorcars, electricity, and indoor plumbing. (Floyd had lived in houses with neither of the last two.)

Three weeks before the main story begins, Rucker loses his wife of many years, Miss Mattie Lou. To keep his house in the most economical manner, he proposes a marriage of convenience to milliner Love Simpson—a Yankee from Baltimore—beautiful and in her thirties. Rucker's other family consists of two daughters from his first marriage, Mary Willis and Loma, and Loma's husband Campbell Williams, or Camp. (Burns also included Hoyt Tweedy, Mary Willis's spouse, but Floyd eliminated the character, perhaps because, like Jack Floyd, he refused to let Will read the funny papers on Sundays.)

Will Tweedy, Rucker's grandson, plans to become a writer, and narrates the story as a Greek chorus of one. This allowed Floyd to establish a great deal of background and atmosphere in the shortest possible time—which in the theater impacts money and the audience's patience—in a kind of pattering *Sprechstimme* over light orchestration. (Floyd borrowed the idea from Britten's similar practice with Captain Vere in *Billy Budd*.)

Cold Sassy's townspeople fall into two distinct classes: neighbors like busybody Effie Belle Tate (whom Floyd designated as the town operator in these early days of the telephone), and workers at the local cotton mill and their families, contemptuously referred to as "lintheads," like Hosie Roach and Lightfoot McClendon. Floyd eliminated many of Burns's subsidiary characters, and added, or fleshed out, a few of his own, including an anti-Love group, the quintessentially operatic quartet of Effie Belle, Thelma Predmore, and two without surnames in the Burns novel, Lula and Myrtis.

Floyd in fact had a Cottingham cousin named Love;[11] Lula recalled Lula Clyburn, the milk-selling mother of Floyd's best friend from Bethune days; and Myrtis reminded him of a tenth-grade classmate, Myrtiss Beacham, "on whom I imagined I had a crush, for reasons I can't possibly explain, except that she was cool to me." Another autobiographical moment coalesces with Will Tweedy's idyll on the joys of youth in Cold Sassy, invoking the scuppernong arbors that had so enchanted young Carlisle in Bethune.

Yet Burns had written from an even more personal stance, making great capital from residual hostilities between north and south. Floyd found this a kind of red herring. Rucker's Civil War experience, including his profile as an expert marksman and the loss of an arm, fell into the same category. Besides crabbed Loma, Floyd needed a strong villain, and settled on the mill child Hosie Roach. This was another instance of Burns's proximity to her material. Basing Hosie as she did on a real person meant keeping him marginally sympathetic, but Floyd had opposing needs.

As with all of Floyd's adaptations from existing sources, the language of the *Cold Sassy Tree* libretto is almost all his. In his eleven-page plot synopsis, act 1 begins as Rucker (bass-baritone) announces to his family his intention to remarry, arousing predictable dismay.[12]

When Will (tenor) is menaced by a group of lintheads, from the cotton mill, Lightfoot McClendon (soprano) rises to his defense and shames the others away. Jack O'Brien praised Floyd's realization of Lightfoot as a character of real substance, despite her relatively pale presence in Burns. Ignoring the difference in their stations, Will takes a more-than-friendly interest in his classmate.

Love Simpson (soprano) and Rucker return from eloping and confirm their marriage to the family, scandalizing all but Will. Love tries to gain the family's acceptance, explaining her longing for a home of her own, after a life of boarding houses and rented rooms. This aria, destined to become one of the opera's showpieces, had direct origins in Floyd's years of parsonage life, a quarter-century spent sitting in "Aunt Ella chairs," and sleeping in beds that had known many backs. The scandalized response of Rucker's daughters Mary Willis (soprano) and Loma (mezzo-soprano) recalled for Floyd a memory from the life of his maternal great-grandmother, Ida Legette Bennett Cottingham: one day as Daniel Cottingham took his wagon to Marion on business, Ida unpacked clothes of her late first husband for a much-needed airing. When her current spouse returned home earlier than expected, he saw some strange man's clothes hanging on *his* laundry line. In southern parlance, Daniel pitched a jealous fit, and his predecessor's wardrobe disappeared permanently.

A week later, while Love cuts Rucker's hair, a Blakeley family argument ensues over division of the house's furnishings, and Rucker makes himself scarce. When he returns, emulating tales of Floyd's great-great-grandfather James Fenegan, Rucker has shaved off his beard and mustache, eliciting cheers and laughter from Love and Will, but tears from Mary Willis and Loma, convinced that they have lost their father.

Will is chased home again by the mill boys, who warn him away from Lightfoot. He goes to his mother for sympathy, but gets much the same cold comfort Floyd got in parallel situations: find a girl of his own social class. Will storms out.

Will later helps Love rearrange furniture and hang new curtains. Clayton McAllister (baritone), a strapping black-clad Texan in boots and cowboy hat, and carrying an ornamented riding saddle, knocks. Will admits him, while curious locals eavesdrop outside, seeing Clayton hug and kiss Love. He attempts to return his engagement gift from years earlier—the saddle—but asks Love again to marry him. They argue, and Love pushes him out. Effie Belle Tate (mezzo-soprano) arrives at the door with a cake (Floyd's favorite, yellow with coconut frosting), having heard the latest gossip, but Will blocks her entrance. Rucker arrives home from work, and two neighbors tell him what they have seen. After pleasantries with Love—he ignores the saddle—she blurts out the facts about Clayton, whom

Rucker offers her the freedom to marry, which she passionately rejects.

Act 2 opens in the Baptist church with the congregation singing a hymn. Love arrives late, adding her voice to the multitude; but one by one, everyone drops out, until only Love and the minister continue. She proceeds with a fourth verse, alone, before striding out of church.

At home, after explaining the situation to Rucker, he declares that they will hold their own private service. Opening the parlor window for adjacent Baptists to hear the proceedings, he improvises an impassioned sermon against the town's bigotry and narrowness, proposing his own highly idiosyncratic view of religion and man's relation to God. The scene concludes with their hymn booming out in counterpoint to singing from the church.

In Rucker's store, Thelma Predmore (mezzo-soprano) waits for Loma's husband, Camp Williams (tenor), to wrap a package. When Love enters, Camp compliments her as "Mrs. Blakeley." She reminds him that her marriage exists in name only, and leaves. Thelma comments on the shame of Love wearing red during the family's mourning for Miss Mattie Lou, inciting an argument with Rucker. Love returns and overhears Thelma's denunciation of Rucker's indecency at remarrying so soon. Love confronts her, elaborating that her part of the marriage compact consists of cooking and cleaning the house, that she sleeps in the guest room and has no intention of trying to take Mattie Lou's place in either Rucker's heart or bed. Thelma storms out, and Love calls after the departing harpy that she may tattle this tale to everyone she knows, but that she should get the facts right (6).

As Will and Lightfoot sit on the front steps of the Blakely house, she tells him that she has to drop out of school and take a job to earn money to care for her sick father. Will promises to intercede with his grandfather to let her work after school in the store, which prompts her determination to improve her situation (6). Touched, Will kisses her and is observed by his aunt Loma, who scolds, threatening to tell the whole family of this latest breach of class decorum. Will vows to Lightfoot that he will get even with Loma.

Later, Rucker laughs as Loma tells of overhearing Will's gossip about her. Will and two friends arrive, looking sheepish, and Rucker demands to know if the story is true. They have indeed spread Loma tales all over Cold Sassy: that she nursed a pig after giving birth to her baby, that she wore rubber busts under her wedding dress, and that a corsage pin deflated one bust midceremony. Succumbing to Rucker's amusement and general high spirits, even Loma joins the laughter, marveling that Will has such an imagination; and repentant Will embraces his aunt (7).

Floyd's next scene sprang from memories of his grandfather Oscar Fenegan's equivocal relationship with modernity: The twenty-five-mile round-trip from Latta to Marion, which he always made in a wagon before the century's turn, took a whole day. He welcomed the automobile's advent, but getting into an airplane never crossed his mind. Television and even radio represented noise and annoyance, never entertainment. Floyd has Love arrive home exhausted from a buying trip in Atlanta; Rucker, eager for news of her exploits, says that he has a surprise for her, disappearing to the rear of the house. We hear the sound of water rushing through pipes, climaxed by the flush of a toilet: out of consideration for Love, miserly Rucker has invested in modern plumbing. Despite the boundless malice of the town's citizens, he even promises to install electricity and a telephone, out of gratitude for her care of him. The two dance around the room, but when Rucker attempts a more intimate embrace, Love pulls away.

Floyd found Burns's presentation of the tale's most serious moments contrived; Will overhears the couple's intimacies, and Rucker treats Love's soul baring almost humorously, which would kill the opera's turning point. Floyd opted instead for a direct but private confrontation, and has Rucker apologize for his forwardness and launch into a confession: he fell in love with Love long before Miss Mattie Lou's death. Though consumed by guilt, now that he has achieved his heart's desire, he knows that she can never return his feelings because of the difference in their ages. Yet he still longs for her to be a real wife to him, and to move into his bed.

Love offers a parallel confession. Her reticence has nothing to do with age. McAllister had broken off their engagement when he learned that she had been raped as a child by a drunken boarder in an aunt's house (Burns had specified the abuser as her father). Love entered womanhood feeling soiled and damaged; since marrying Rucker, she has fallen in love with him, yet still fears her inadequacies, and breaks into sobbing.

The sexual corruption of innocence here acts as a pole to Susannah's experience with Blitch almost fifty years earlier. Rucker explains that his real love for Mattie Lou had not been a true romance. He and Love kiss. After abandoning any such future formalities as "Mister Blakeley" and "Miss Love," Rucker invites her to abandon her role as guest and to begin sleeping with him (8). They exit, intertwined, into his room, now theirs.

Act 3 begins in the store as Love pulls dresses and hats from boxes of her Atlanta purchases, showing them off to her formerly outspoken critics Mary Willis, Loma, Effie Belle, and Thelma. One by one, they succumb to Love's diplomacy, even outspoken Thelma; and Rucker compliments her sales abilities (9). After sending Love home, he asks Lightfoot to sweep the store, and goes about putting the day's earnings into a nail keg, his version of a safe (9). When Will appears to walk Lightfoot home, he and Rucker argue about his intention to become a writer rather than succeed Rucker as storekeeper. Will stomps off in anger, to wait for Lightfoot by the blacksmith shop, and she and Rucker complete their chores.

Though based directly on Burns's account, Floyd had a parallel incident in his own family history that mirrored the next plot sequence: the murder of his great-great-grandfather, the shopkeeper and postmaster Charles Pinckney Floyd, in 1869. In his opera treatment, Hosie (baritone) and his friend Luther (tenor) now slink in with their mouths covered with kerchiefs and demand Rucker's cash. Rucker empties the keg, the two scramble for the money. Rucker turns the tables, retrieving Hosie's pistol and holding the would-be robbers at bay. He forces Luther to call the sheriff; but Luther, like young Carlisle Floyd in North, has never used a telephone, and treats it like a poisonous serpent. Rucker empties the gun by firing at Hosie's feet, making him dance; but when the ammunition is spent, the younger men throw Rucker to the floor, kick at his head and ribs, and scurry away. Lightfoot finds Will at the blacksmith's, and tells him of the attack. Will sends her for the sheriff and goes for the doctor.

Next morning at the Blakeley house, the uneasy family gathers as Dr. Lomax (bass) examines Rucker, who is unconscious with a concussion, one lung punctured by a broken rib. Outside on the porch, Love confides to Will that she is pregnant, and that she must tell Rucker before his condition worsens, or worse. Will agrees to help raise the child in case his grandfather fails to recover, but the old man comes around, calling for Will. The two reconcile over Will becoming a writer, and Love appears in the doorway. She confesses that she has a secret to tell, but Rucker interrupts with a fresh declaration of love and gratitude. When she finally reveals that she bears his child, he lapses into unconsciousness, then breathes his last.

Later, with the entire family assembled, Will reads a letter outlining Rucker's funeral wishes. He is to be buried in a packing crate kept in the barn for this purpose, and taken to the cemetery in his black tenant farmer's wagon (shades of Baker Campbell). There is to be no preacher at graveside, just a singing of "Blest Be the Tie That Binds," and Will reading Bible verses. Observing that the first three letters of the word "funeral" spell "fun," he has requested a party a week or two after his death for everyone in Cold Sassy—black and white—a celebration of life (12).

The scene dissolves to that festivity in progress; everyone is dressed in their brightest clothing, children run everywhere, there is a hog-calling contest at one side of the stage, and everyone sings Rucker's praises. In his final commentary, Will allows that, though he never married Lightfoot, he still carries a rabbit foot that she gave him for good luck; and he adds that she now teaches third grade at Cold Sassy's grammar school. During a general freeze in action, he reveals that he did in fact help raise Rucker Jr. Miss Love has not lost an ounce of her beauty and style, and now leads the Baptist hymns. Will himself has become a writer, and tends the family store part time (13).

The chorus resumes its eulogy of Rucker and the curtain falls.

FLOYD'S TASTES alerted him to elements in Burns that he needed to eliminate or ignore, such as the suicide of Loma's husband, Camp: "First of all, I don't think suicide is ever funny, and it just comes out of the blue." Finding Burns's description of Love's rape frivolous, he planned to show it as a far more traumatic incident. In focusing on the individuation that Will achieves with his grandfather, Floyd also eliminated the weak character of Will's father, Hoyt Tweedy, transferring some of his functions to Camp, and creating a stronger bond of descent from Rucker to Will.

The scenario bears numerous margin jottings: Gockley's comments and questions, and some of Floyd's answers, suggesting minor amendments and clarifications of motivation. That Gockley was thrilled with Floyd's vision is reflected in his communication to Linda Golding that he would program *Cold Sassy Tree* for spring 2000 in the 2,200-seat Brown Theater. He agreed to leave the dimensions of cast and orchestra entirely to Floyd's discretion, and to give him approval of director, conductor, and principal singers, stipulating only that the piece be about two and a half hours long.[13]

Gockley again based the commission fee on the number of coproducers he hoped to assemble, a team of three or four, in which event Houston's share would be fifty thousand dollars, covering royalties for an initial run of six or seven performances. With just one other company's involvement, Houston would guarantee seventy-five thousand dollars; and with no partners, Houston would pay one hundred thousand dollars; but with four or five partners, Houston's initial fifty thousand (and twenty-five thousand from each coproducer) would be added to 50 percent royalties and other fees stipulated in Floyd's Boosey contract.

The detailed correspondence in the Boosey files tells a fascinating story of the process of generating new operas at the close of the twentieth century. Gockley further agreed to pay for scores, utilizing Floyd's Houston-based copyist Bill Black, and the Fanfare software Floyd had bought with the last of his university discretionary fund.[14] On March 20, Turner Broadcasting confirmed that it had no objection to Floyd's operatic adaptation, and it cleared an eventual television filming of the production.[15]

Linda Golding sent a FAX to Gockley on April 17 that final rights had been granted, and that they could now get down to hammering out details.[16] Floyd's uncomplicated agreement with the Burns estate, dated May 9, 1997, gave him a five-year window in which no other musical adaptation of *Cold Sassy Tree* would be allowed. The estate would receive 25 percent of all royalties and other income, excepting rentals and concert performances; and Floyd, 75 percent, from which Boosey's shares would be deducted. In an undated interoffice memo from around this time, Jack Knudson of Boosey's business staff estimated the expense of preparing the vocal score, conductor's score, and orchestra parts at thirty thousand dollars, which Houston would pay Boosey; and the publisher guaranteed anything exceeding that amount. Only in the event of changes to materials after delivery would Floyd be charged a one-time deduction of 10 percent of the original cost of materials production.[17]

As late as December 2000, ICM's Mitch Douglas inquired about royalties due the Burns estate; but the commissioning agreement's terms gave Boosey the right to withhold such payments until the cost of materials had been recouped. In the meantime, Golding and Gockley maintained a lively exchange about Floyd's fee: she countered Houston's most recent offer with $150,000, at which Gockley bristled that this was triple what Houston had ever paid. The company's value to a composer, he felt, lay in giving new works fully prepared, adequately budgeted launchings and bringing other companies into partnerships, in turn creating built-in revivals.[18]

Gockley requested further clarification about what each cocommissioner would receive in terms of royalty-free performances and rental fees. Golding responded that Boosey considered Houston's $150,000 as lead commissioner fair, giving the company different rights than other partners, but that each cocommissioner should stipulate its guaranteed portion at the signing of the agreement.[19]

With four cocommissioners, Houston would receive seven royalty- and rental-free performances; partners would pay their own royalties, approximately five thousand dollars each, and around five hundred dollars apiece for materials rental. Houston would still cover its own performance material expense, but would recoup this outlay from percentages of partner rental fees. Despite such haggling, it remained clear that Boosey, with Golding and Kalett as tough negotiators, and Gockley, as Floyd's friend and colleague, were all working in the composer's best interests.

By mid-July, Gockley had verbal commitments from Baltimore and San Diego to join the partnership; Charlotte, Austin, New York City Opera, and Miami were nibbling at the edges of the deal. In a memo of July 18, Linda Golding wondered to colleagues at the London office whether Berlin might be tempted; Paul Kellogg indicated interest at Glimmerglass. Golding assured her British associates that Floyd had exercised great freedom in consolidating Burns's book, which she thought an easy read; but, like Gockley, she found Floyd's adaptation even easier.[20]

BEFORE FLOYD COMPLETED HIS LIBRETTO, or wrote a note of music, staffing and casting were well under way. Dean Peterson would create Rucker; Frederica von Stade was approached for Love Simpson, so Floyd's notions of vocal ranges were still fluid. He wanted Jack O'Brien to direct, and Houston's music director, Patrick Summers, to conduct. By August, Boosey's final contract was ready for Floyd's signature: he would receive 10 percent of the retail selling price of all printed copies of the score and 50 percent of all royalties and fees for subpublications; 50 percent of rentals, small rights, and mechanical fees; and 66 2/3 percent of grand rights.[21]

Between *Of Mice and Men* and *Susannah* productions, Floyd spent the remainder of 1997 drafting the libretto. Cold Sassy would speak with the upcountry twang passed down through generations of upcountry Scots-Irish immigrants, who felt blurred *r*s to be a British affectation. This of course differed from the soft planter-Cavalier drawl of low-country Charleston and Savannah, which one tends to regard as the authentic southern accent. Floyd knew both: low-country Latta (his own), and upcountry sandhill Bethune.

The very nature of Burns's storytelling seemed to work against dramatic adaptation, as Floyd told anyone willing to listen, often Linda Golding. But Burns's language took him back to childhood, in particular to expressions that strike today's listener as quaint or archaic, but which he had heard from his parents, and especially his grandfather Oscar Fenegan.

He altered the shape of the work by beginning on Cold Sassy's main street with Will Tweedy's overlaid spoken scene setting, which precedes Rucker's announcement of marrying Love. The new act 1, scene 4 begins with a choral condemnation of Rucker, followed by the competing church services. Floyd ended the act with Rucker's contrarian yet humanistic sermon, and the clash of Baptists clucking away at "Blest Be the Tie That Binds," against the booming Doxology sung by Rucker, Love, and Will. Spiked with orchestral dissonance and rhythmic clashes, this became the composer's witty comment on churches *obstructing* binding ties.

When Floyd's musical thoughts took more definite shape, he changed Rucker's surname a second time, from "Blakeley" to the more singer-friendly open vowels of "Lattimore," a survival from his 1983–1984 *Seth* libretto. He moved Rucker's shave to the first scene of act 2, followed directly by Clayton McAllister's abortive visit. Will and Lightfoot's kiss charged scene 2, and the confrontation and reconciliation with Loma became the meat of scene 3; the act would end with the parallel confessions and love scene of Rucker and Love.

Act 3 kept the scenario's basic shape, with more commentary from Will; but it would be hapless Camp who fumbles with the telephone call to the sheriff. (Gockley questioned Rucker's meanness in tormenting Hosie, and Floyd eventually agreed to cut this business.) Calling for Will, Rucker asks for "my gran'boy," the title of an early version of what became *Willie Stark*.[22] *Cold Sassy Tree* came to Floyd with greater ease than anything he had written to date, and summed up a lifetime in the musical theater. Having worked in the medium for forty years, he "let it happen," and the material made it seem more enjoyable.

He sought out Jack O'Brien for critiques of what he had done. At the end of January 1998, O'Brien offered the former tennis player Floyd "a couple of brief if superficial volleys . . . [to] see if the dialogue that ensues is of any ultimate consequence or assistance."[23] O'Brien stumbled at once over the novel's resistance to stage or musical adaptation:

> As delicious as the characters are, and as original the voice, this is hardly a novel of dramatic tension and consequence of action. . . . I can't help but feel that you are initially revealing perhaps more to the audience in early soliloquies and "confessions" than the stage will bear. This is particularly true in your sketch of act 1 and act 2. Act 3 begins to smack of genuine theatricality. But as I see it, the character of Rucker survives in the book somewhat by *concealing* his intentions and his feelings. . . . He is a snap-mouthed, taciturn old codger who softens only as we are allowed [to] spend time with him—someone who, in fact, keeps people with the exception of Will Tweedy at bay by fear tactics.

O'Brien feared that ending act 1 with Rucker's sermon might dissipate accrued tension, and his criticism of act 2 honed directly in on the parallel confessions: "I didn't buy that part in the book at all, personally. I'm afraid I saw the 'abuse' light flashing yellow long before poor Love got to express herself, but Ms. Burns kept us waiting for it . . . but here we don't have a *release* that produces such a confession, since another confession has immediately preceded it." He found plentiful tension in act 3 "with the robbery and the inevitable death, but I fear we already know too much about these two people to get the most powerful effect of the death-bed confessions."

In the 1992 *New Grove Dictionary of Opera,* Andrew Stiller had written of Floyd's tendency toward economy, beginning with the description of most of his settings as "southern, rural or colonial": "The guiding spirit of Floyd's operas is a studied, almost draconian pragmatism that makes them attractively easy to stage while limiting the heights to which they can aspire."[24]

One of Burns's most impactful moments showed Will Tweedy's near-death experience with a racing train; in another, Will gave Love and Rucker a driving lesson in his grandfather's new Cadillac. Floyd omitted both. In place of the former, he crafted the opera's second scene with character-driven moments from Burns's train scene: Will's encounter with the bullies Hosie and Luther, and the meeting of Will and Lightfoot. O'Brien seized on this, emphasizing that the composer had "simply written off the more powerful scenes—train chases and automobile lessons and such—as initially being not practical for the stage out of kindness to the director, designers, and poor producers, and in doing so, robbed yourself of considerable snap and sass of the original book? I mean, if you just went ahead and did your adaptation as if it were a goddamn film scenario, the collaborators would simply *have* to solve the problems, wouldn't they?"[25]

But as a director, O'Brien admired what Floyd *had* accomplished. "You clearly have an ear for these characters, and you handle . . . elements like the courtship of poor Lightfoot with far more taste and originality than Ms. Burns does . . . although you improve her weakest links, you haven't taken advantage of what broad-shouldered, audacious narrative skill she has that would make this an impolite, impractical, impossible, albeit thrilling evening."

Floyd knew that O'Brien had not calculated the effect of his music, and stuck to his guns on most points. Gockley's insistence that Floyd write a real grand opera duet for Love and Rucker met the same fate; but he saw that O'Brien inspired Floyd's quick, effective, *theatrical* revisions. After the composer's return from the Berlin *Susannah,* Gockley flew him to San Diego in March for two days of face-to-face conferences with O'Brien. All along, with Floyd at the top of his game, the reactions he elicited were overwhelmingly positive. Painful as it was, he appreciated O'Brien's cut to the chase: he had to find more dramatic tension. About Burns, O'Brien fumed that she did not play fair; she led one to expect that certain things would produce a certain result, and then, nothing: "She just drops it, like a candy machine." Floyd agreed.

On characterization, O'Brien counseled Floyd to keep Rucker a secret as long as he could; in other words, to allow him to evolve in surprising ways. Floyd gave Myrtis a line describing the old man's resistance to change, in that he has refused to turn his calendar to the twentieth century. Will has experienced Rucker's penny-pinching for years, so it comes as a seismic shock when the old man springs the news about adding indoor plumbing to surprise Love.

Floyd defended his choices: "Work in the opera house a little longer, let's not create any more problems than we have to." But O'Brien put a button at the end of this argument, "Then come up with a reasonable substitute for the same dramatic point you're trying to make." On the spot, Floyd took the suggestions that caught fire with him and made creative changes. The libretto with which he left San Diego was, with few exceptions, the final version. When Gockley read it, he told Floyd that he had come full circle with the treatment of religious elements, compared to *Susannah* and his other operas. Cold Sassy's Baptist church is structured and tame by comparison to its hell-fixated counterpart in New Hope Valley; and, far from suffering destruction at the hands of church folk for his independence, Rucker towers above his community's pettiness. As far back as *Slow Dusk* and *Fugitives,* protagonists' families concerned themselves with individuation and freedom from restrictive hierarchies, and much the same proved true in Will Tweedy's desire for a life away from the general store, as well as in Love's and Rucker's scandalous yet ultimately triumphant union.

Another of Floyd's favorite moments distills aspects of southern hospitality, as in Rucker's disarming invitation that McAllister stay for a meal. One might suspect that a hot-blooded Civil War veteran—shades of Bethune's Gilliam King—might take justice into his own hands with Clayton's intrusion, but as Floyd observed, "Rucker is too clever for that."

WITH KAY HOLDING DOWN the Yoakum Boulevard residence in Houston, Floyd's welcome back to Tallahassee was the discovery that torrential rains had overtaxed a defective drainage system, inundating his downstairs studio. The joys of home ownership included three weeks of expensive repairs and cleaning. Nonetheless, he reported progress on the opera to Jona Clarke, describing Jack O'Brien as "one of a very few people I've encountered in the business who has a really diagnostic and creative mind and, most importantly, whose reactions I respect and heed. . . . I hope to get down to starting some music before long since the premiere is two years away from this month!"[26]

Yet Floyd again indulged his modesty to the point of disingenuousness. He had already departed from earlier practice by composing music for Will Tweedy's first aria and Lightfoot's aria in act 2 before writing the texts, something he had always disdained as a Tin Pan Alley practice. When he began setting his finished libretto, he confessed to Kay that he felt he had never written *any* opera before, because the demands of comedy were so different from anything he had undertaken; it required a kind of underscoring, rather than the through-composed music of crisis and tragedy.

> As some aesthetician pointed out, opera is a natural habitat for emotion; it doesn't deal with the rational, and it can't. And that's why comedy is so difficult for opera, because it has to be largely visual. It can be *somewhat* verbal, but that's already an intellectual exercise, as opposed to emotional.
>
> This is a curious piece . . . a good seventy-five percent is really quite comic, some of it gently . . . and some of it boisterously. . . . The other twenty-five is extremely serious, even tragic. . . . You know the famous statement, "dying is easy, comedy is hard" . . . I found out that was certainly true . . . writing music for comedy is an entirely different kind of exercise . . . the situational aspect rather than the emotional. So, I felt very comfortable when I got into the heavy emotional scenes because that was what I had been doing for the last forty years. But keeping the comedic aspect . . . buoyant and lively . . . was no easy job.[27]

In May 1998, Lyric Opera of Chicago's general director, William Mason, wrote about the possibility of a Floyd festival: *Susannah,* which Chicago already planned to revive in 2002, and possibly *Of Mice and Men;* and Samuel Ramey's and Frederica von Stade's availability could mean adding *Cold Sassy Tree,* with Chicago possibly coproducing.[28] Already in April, San Diego's Ian Campbell flew to Houston to discuss the opera's casting with Gockley and Floyd. His endorsement of the soprano Patricia Racette for Love Simpson ended consideration of von Stade, had she in fact been free.

After reading Floyd's revised libretto, O'Brien responded, "Congratulations!! You've done a tight, economical and remarkable job of reworking and cutting. The libretto reads smoothly, easily, and most importantly, *dramatically.* It doesn't seem strained or forced in the least, and I had a damned good afternoon with it. I'm immensely impressed. . . . I know how complicated it is to do any serious reworking; but something accomplished on this scale not only does credit to you as a writer, it gives ample proof why you have remained at the very top of your profession."[29]

O'Brien's availability to direct remained unsettled, but Floyd began in the late spring of 1998 to put music to words. He and Kay made another full move back to Yoakum Boulevard, to be on the spot to finish the opera and observe its production. Gockley had turned the commission agreement over to Houston's business manager Jim Ireland, and most of summer 1998 saw an exchange of FAX communications between Ireland and Linda Golding. As usual, score preparation and copying posed sticking points: Ireland proposed that HGO, in an effort to protect eventual partners, might pay as much as thirty thousand dollars toward those costs, reducing Boosey's initial outlay, in exchange for the firm's agreement to eliminate rental fees for cocommissioners.[30]

In the meantime, copyist Bill Black estimated his expense at between $18,000 and $33,000. Boosey's recent hire Holly Mentzer, destined to become Floyd's principal representative for a decade, believed this a gross underestimation, convinced that the full score alone would run to at least $25,000, with another $18,000 to $25,000 for parts, $6,000 for the vocal score, and $7,000 for proofreading, unless Floyd cared to do it himself.[31] Suggestions flew back and forth that Floyd might after all have to bear some of this expense. (When dust settled after the premiere, Boosey discovered that the final cost of score preparation and proofreading had in fact run to $51,245.)[32]

On August 24, Jack O'Brien wrote that his involvement with a musical adaptation of *The Full Monty* would prevent his further involvement in *Cold Sassy Tree,* but that he looked forward to seeing the results.[33]

Floyd's compositional style, with its quartal and quintal harmonies, tone-stacking, cross-pollinating rhythms, and sophisticated orchestration, had progressed from formal designs to a neoromantic flexibility of theme and transformation. In *Cold Sassy Tree,* this takes the shape of rhythmic groupings representing the busybody townspeople like Effie Belle Tate, and the fulminations of Loma and Mary Willis: ostinati of dotted eighths and sixteenths, followed by the second and third notes of a triplet figure, reflecting needling, or rustic character traits. In the encounters between Will and Lightfoot, tritone intervals, melodies that outline a tritone, or chords featuring tritonal harmonies indicate the yearning of two callow youngsters, as opposed to the stylized naïveté, courtesy, and warmth of Love's and Rucker's love music.

In the course of composing, Floyd sent some of Love's part to Patricia Racette, who responded with concerns that the material might not show her to best advantage; the character, she felt, was too much acted on by men. Floyd championed Love's independence as her greatest asset. He asked Racette to contemplate Love's intransigence with Rucker and Clayton, and defied her to find a moment when the character showed the least weakness in the presence of any male. Like most sopranos, Racette sought opportunities to work in her upper register, and thought that Floyd kept Love too much in middle and low voice. Floyd explained that he did not want Love, the more mature, womanly figure, to be vocally confused with the younger lyric Lightfoot. He told Racette, "I'm writing for a character, I don't write for a voice."

By the beginning of 1999, Floyd had composed enough to attend Utah Opera's *Of Mice and Men,* while

Gockley set the *Cold Sassy Tree* premiere for April 14, 2000. His cocommissioners now included Austin, San Diego, Opera Carolina, and Baltimore; Lyric Opera of Kansas City, Utah, and Omaha scheduled productions between 2001 and 2004. Central City Opera expressed interest, and even announced fifteen performances in July and August of 2001, but the company's request for a release from certain partner obligations was denied, and it withdrew; Baltimore Opera cancelled a 2003 production as well, for similar reasons.

Once Gockley cemented San Diego's agreement, he asked Floyd to give the company a kind of musical show-and-tell, allowing Ian Campbell to feel full partnership. At noon on Sunday, February 14, the day after the company's most recent *Of Mice and Men* revival, Floyd presided over a read-through in San Diego's Civic Theatre downstairs rehearsal room. The composer sat at one piano, the staff pianist Andrew Campbell—no relation to Ian—at a second. As members of San Diego's studio sang, staff and visitors like Jake Heggie marveled at Floyd's youthful inspirations.

Floyd recalled a similar event in Houston. On both occasions, "at certain points, I wanted a certain quality and very precise tempo, and probably rooted up the accompanist. I know I did in Houston, at the end of act 2, which to this day I consider the finest thing I've written; and I didn't want it to come off any other way than I knew it could. It was no discredit to the pianist, because he was just reading, but that particular scene goes way beyond what's in the notes."

Two days later, Jake Heggie wrote Floyd, "I am still *reeling* from . . . *Of Mice and Men*—and doubly so from the reading of *Cold Sassy Tree.* I find the new piece inescapably gripping—it flows . . . so naturally—it has great humor and tremendous drama—I was so deeply moved and I really believe it is a work that people *need* to hear. It's powerful, passionate and very beautiful stuff . . . it fills me up, this music. It stays with me—and the drama is *so* touching, *so* moving . . . a great achievement, my friend."[34]

Finally, Nick Reveles, San Diego's director of education and outreach, enthused to Floyd that he and ensemble members felt that *Cold Sassy*'s great moments were destined to join such landmarks as Countess Almaviva's forgiveness of her wayward husband in Mozart's *Le nozze di Figaro,* the death of Madama Butterfly, and the final scene of Berg's *Wozzeck.*[35]

NEARLY FIVE YEARS OF NEGOTIATIONS had taxed Floyd and Gockley, to the extent that the composer feared the abandonment of the project. The continuing—and only partially resolved—struggle over clearances for television and film caused the greatest frustration. Gockley even accused *Floyd* of stalling, and Boosey's London office had to insist that everything possible was being done in this ballet of shadowy entities, but after final revisions to libretto and music, HGO and Boosey at long last managed to put definitive punctuation to the cocommission agreement that Carolyn Kalett sent Floyd on April 8, 1999. Gockley agreed to Floyd's $150,000 fee, but Houston would perform the work without paying initial royalties. Floyd would receive $37,500 on signing, $37,500 on delivery of the vocal score no later than July 1 that year, $37,500 on receipt of full score and orchestral materials no later than January 1, 2000, and $37,500 on opening night in Houston.

Although Houston could not and did not guarantee cocommissioner productions, the agreement still listed four partners: Baltimore, San Diego, Opera Carolina, and Austin. Each company would have royalties for their initial productions waived, up to twenty-five thousand dollars, credited against monies owed Houston. In case of second performance runs or revivals, each company would pay Floyd a royalty of 5 percent of gross box office receipts. The crucial performance material question reached settlement when Houston agreed to pay Boosey thirty thousand dollars for the entire expense of preparing the full orchestral score and parts without charge to cocommissioners, as well as the vocal score, twenty-five of which would be made available without additional charges to HGO, which in turn could make copies for distribution to cocommissioners.

This arrangement covered the initial presentation and one subsequent revival by each cocommissioner. Amazingly, because the actual costs for producing scores exceeded first estimates by twenty-one thousand dollars, all cocommissioners agreed to waive their twenty-five thousand dollar exemptions. They had already agreed to pay Boosey royalties amounting to 5 percent of their box office, but should that figure come to *less* than twenty-five thousand dollars, the company might deduct it and retain the difference.[36]

Unlike previous contracts, Floyd would receive three pairs of complimentary tickets, all between the first and tenth rows of the orchestra section, for each performance by each company. Boosey was also granted one pair of such "comps" during each company's initial run. Floyd might attend however much of each company's rehearsal period as he wished, but companies were required to compensate only his expenses for those rehearsals at which his presence was necessary, as reasonably determined by cocommissioners. In such instances, however, the composer's reimbursement included round-trip coach airfare, a forty dollar per day allowance for meals and other out-of-pocket expenses, and an apartment or first-class hotel for the duration of his stay. Each company further received the right to one live or delayed radio broadcast during each run.

On April 29, 1999, Floyd and the HGO musical staff read through the entire work with piano. Following that year's exhilarating but exhausting round of *Susannah* performances, Floyd returned to Aspen for two weeks in August, and festival management provided a condominium. The succeeding work-throughs and the earlier San Diego and Houston reads replaced the workshops he had enjoyed with *Jonathan Wade* and *Bilby's Doll.* He watched and listened closely as members of Aspen's Opera Theater Center rehearsed selected scenes from *Cold Sassy;* Sylvia Plyler undertook musical preparation, Richard Bado, chorus preparation, and Garnett Bruce devised staging. Floyd arrived thinking that the entire opera would be performed, and went to administrators to express disappointment and annoyance: "I was so tired of this piece living in my head, I wanted to see it out there! I needed to see people embodying these characters, away from me!"

The usual excuses of time and singers' availability were invoked. Floyd's cousin Helen Harris and his sister, Ermine, sat in the audience at one rehearsal and sensed Floyd working hard to suppress agitation and anger. At a pause, Harris asked him, "Do you ever get really upset?" He replied through tight lips, "I've been known to." Worst of all, Aspen's choice to sing Rucker arrived woefully underprepared, and at the next rehearsal the composer's frustration rose. Ermine later told Harris, "You know what you asked him about getting upset? Well, you should have been there the next day! He just went bananas!"[37]

But the young baritone worked most of that evening, drilling the part with a coach, with adequate results. Floyd concocted a narration to connect the dots of selected scenes from the first two acts. For the performance at Wheeler Opera House on August 21, he sat in a box beside the stage to deliver his remarks; the house was packed, and, once he had gotten used to the circumstances, enjoyed the experience.

After entering final revisions into score and libretto, Floyd used his customary orchestra of paired and doubled winds, brass, and strings; piano and celesta would be played by a single performer; and harp. Three percussionists would divide parts for xylophone, vibraphone, glockenspiel, chimes, snare drum, tenor drum, bass drum, gong; suspended, crash, and ancient cymbals; and tambourine, wood block, bell tree, and whip. He had used this basic instrumental complement since *Susannah,* with subtle differences; but in the forty-five intervening years, economy became a challenge rather than an imposition: "Maybe it's a limitation on my part, but I've found this size orchestra to be more practical, and it covers what I need. Sometimes I've wished for three trumpets, but you can do much good 'faking' with oboe, adding that as your third trumpet. And sometimes you wish that the second clarinet and bass clarinet were separate, they provide so much more filler. But then you learn to make do and pull up a bassoon or pull down a flute."

When Patrick Summers later told Floyd he considered *Of Mice and Men* symphonic, and *Cold Sassy Tree* a real singer's opera, Floyd responded: "Of course I treated the orchestras very differently, but I suspect it has more to do with the characters themselves. Like any opera composer worth his salt, I always feel that I'm a victim of the material. I mean,

I can't cut the material to fit my own particular pattern. I think that's where so many composers go off, trying to shoehorn material into their own private idiom. I remember hearing years ago a corny but true statement: 'Opera composers ain't mad with nobody,' referring to our eclecticism. To me, the material dictates, and each of my operas seems very different to me in terms of color."

Another aspect that gave librettist *and* composer fits was strengthening serious elements in light of the comic and maintaining the logical flow of scenic transitions. "Things turn on a dime: in the murder scene, the flushing of the toilet, and the kiss that turns everything upside-down. This required an entirely different kind of music, and virtually no transitions to speak of, but you see it on the stage, and it works. It made me think, what's more lifelike or truthful than abrupt, unprepared change?" His goal remained to show the individual's power to transform, to become a more fully realized being, in the infinite variety that the process implies.

While copyists produced materials, the European premiere of *Flower and Hawk* took place in Vivonne, France, on October 3, staged by Dona Vaughn. Floyd did not attend, but with *Cold Sassy Tree* complete, he spent November 24 through 27 in France, for L'Opéra de Nantes' *Of Mice and Men.*[38] Staged by Rupert Oliver Forbes and conducted by Dominique Trottein, it was given in French as *Des souris et des hommes,* with singers Jeremy Huw Williams (George), Andreas Jäggi (Lennie), Christophe Crapez (Curley), and Magali Léger (Curley's Wife). On November 25, from ten a.m. till noon, Floyd collaborated with local professors at the Université de Nantes Salle du Chateau, in a *débat-rencontre,* or minisymposium, "From Steinbeck to Floyd," reserved for students of English assigned to read Steinbeck's novella.

In contrast to John Dew's *Susannah* there in 1997, Forbes took a surprisingly literal, traditional view of the piece. The company's public relations director, Bénédicte de Vanssay, wrote Floyd in gladdening terms that his music perfectly encapsulated Steinbeck's poetry, tenderness, and tragedy, and that she regretted only that the company had not thought of a lobby concession for handkerchiefs.[39]

GOOD NEWS AWAITED IN HOUSTON: the NEA granted HGO $115,000 to defray *Cold Sassy Tree* world premiere expenses. Floyd and Gockley had assembled a crack production team: the Australian film and stage director Bruce Beresford,[40] the designer Michael Yeargan, and the conductor Patrick Summers. Besides Patricia Racette as Love and Dean Peterson as Rucker, the cast included many old friends: John McVeigh (Will Tweedy), Diane Alexander (Mary Willis), Beth Clayton (Loma), Judith Christin (Effie Belle), Margaret Lloyd (Lightfoot), Joseph Evans (Camp), Christopher Schaldenbrand (Clayton), James C. Holloway (Mayor), Kerri Marcinko (Lula), Jessica Jones (Myrtis), Marie Lenormand (Thelma), Richard Sutliff (Sheriff), Matthew Kreger (Hosie), Scott Scully (Luther), and Oren Gradus (Dr. Lomax).

Gockley and Floyd honored their original Houston Opera Studio commitment by creating high-exposure opportunities for present and past members: Clayton, Gradus, Jones, Lenormand, Marcinko, McVeigh, and Scully, almost half of the cast. Gockley and Opera America's Marc Scorca also finalized plans for the group's 2000 annual conference in Houston, from May 6 to 10; 550 representatives from about eighty North American companies were expected to attend.

Around the same time, bad news came from the dissolution of Gockley's current marriage, and the divorce was finalized in 2000. Having a background and interest in the behavioral sciences, and from his own nine-year process with De la Torre, Floyd placed his sympathetic ear, sage advice, and reading recommendations at Gockley's disposal. Gockley testified to his friend's generosity and resourcefulness.

> He was a great solace. Divorces, separations, personal woes—they're traumatic. Carlisle was my first and deepest level of support. Thank heaven he was there and available to me in those very difficult times. I'm not a great one to talk about my intimate life, and God knows, he isn't, but I could still go to him and say, "I'm

bereft," and bawl, and ask, what do I do? And he always had a keen empathic listening ability; he cut through and made sense of things so that I began to see my way out of what was happening. I always thought he would make a fantastic psychiatrist or therapist. He was always thinking about human behavior, about motivation. *Why* this? *Why* that?[41]

That February, to generate a commercial recording, Boosey staff and Gockley pored over Floyd's contract with the Burns estate and the cocommission agreement. Three firms—Chandos, Naxos, and Koch—expressed interest in issuing the 1991 Houston performance of *The Passion of Jonathan Wade,* and then *Cold Sassy Tree.* Gockley wanted a product in hand in time for the scheduled Austin and San Diego performances of the latter opera, but negotiations bogged down over who would pay and who receive what licensing fees, and contracts were ultimately awarded to a relative newcomer on the American scene, Albany Records.[42]

Floyd needed time off before facing the intensity of staging rehearsals. Astonishing as it may seem, this took the form of a busman's holiday around the country for productions of *Susannah* and *Of Mice and Men.* He sat in the audience at Louisville's Brown Theatre on February 11 for Kentucky Opera's second performance with Jennifer Casey Cabot (Susannah), Mark Delavan (Blitch), Jay Hunter Morris (Sam), and Jon Kolbet (Little Bat), Ward Holmquist conducting Rhoda Levine's production.[43] He next appeared at Phoenix Symphony Hall on February 17 for Arizona Opera's *Of Mice and Men.* Kirk Muspratt conducted Anne Ewers's production, with Michael Hendrick (Lennie), Stephen Bryant (George), Dean Anthony (Curley), and Helen Todd (Curley's Wife).[44] Then, on March 9, Floyd saw Michael Ehrman's *Susannah* at Connecticut Opera in Hartford. Robert Ashens conducted Suzan Hanson (Susannah), Jeffrey Wells (Blitch), Scott Piper (Sam), and Dean Anthony (Little Bat).

MARK ADAMO's *Little Women* held the main stage at Houston's Wortham Center in March, its final performance on March 18 before the company began musical and staging rehearsals for *Cold Sassy Tree.* When Floyd encountered Patricia Racette, she asked whether he remembered their conversations about Love's character and range. He replied good-naturedly, "Absolutely I do." Racette laughed, "That should tell you, don't ever listen to a soprano!"

In the course of rehearsals, Floyd made a number of cuts. With his dread of anything smacking of nineteenth-century melodrama, he and conductor Summers managed to cut almost two pages of music they found extraneous. Summers recalled:

The interesting thing about Carlisle is that, for him, composing is a process of elimination. He has so many ideas . . . an absolute wealth of melodic invention . . . once we were into rehearsal, it was a process of paring it back to decide what story he was going to tell. In the end, there was not anything in *Cold Sassy Tree* that didn't need to be there. Carlisle always had a musical solution to any dramatic problem . . . we had difficulty moving a particular set. I told him . . ."I hate to do this to you because we are in our final weeks, but we need 45 seconds of music here. . . ." Could you tell Verdi you needed 45 more seconds? . . . Carlisle went away overnight and came back with an orchestrated insert for the scene that was exactly 45 seconds long, and it worked. It sounded absolutely organic. . . . Composers are the most gifted people in music.[45]

Bruce Beresford insisted on Floyd's presence beside him in all rehearsals; and like virtually everyone in the opera world, he found that the composer "fit the description southern gentleman to a T. He is at all times softly spoken and courteous. He never needs to raise his voice, as his prestige is such that everyone quiets down and listens when he speaks! At the same time, he has the iron fist in the velvet glove; he knows precisely the dramatic and musical effects he wants and is quick to point out, either to the conductor or director, anything that he thinks could be improved. But he is open to suggestions and quite happy to accept interpretations which are different from his own, provided he can be convinced of their validity."[46]

As Floyd explained in his article on the librettist's craft in the HGO *Playbill* that would greet the audience, his elder colleague Douglas Moore once told him, "Carlisle, I really envy you, you never have to quarrel with your librettist." Easier said than done:

> Compression is the soul of the libretto writer. . . . It's amazing what you can do without! . . . You can't just squirm away from the fact that if it's not necessary to tell the story, then it's best left undone. . . . The important stimuli are . . . rich characters and very dramatic situations or incidents. . . . It's a case of the brain and the heart battling each other. . . . As a librettist the composer part of you is always breathing down your neck . . . asking, is this too talky, is the action carrying the storyline? The forward movement must continue. Good curtains don't just arrive, they have to be built. . . . [But] the composer always [wins]. . . . He's a real tyrant![47]

The tyrant dedicated his latest opera to David Gockley. In rehearsal, Floyd marveled at Beresford's use of storyboarding, a series of quick sketches to previsualize stage pictures, as though through a camera lens. Floyd's most frequent caution to his director, as with *Susannah,* was to keep southern accents within bounds: "Once you start doing these characters, it's easy to get too broad." Beresford arrived believing singing actors incapable of convincing stage laughter, as with Rucker's reaction to Will spreading rumors about Loma. Floyd took Dean Peterson aside and urged him to avoid hollow or false sounds, and the quibble never arose again. Peterson began his laughter as a silent shake, only gradually becoming audible.

The only juncture at which a difference of opinion arose came with the death scene. Floyd had originally composed sung lines for Love to tell Rucker of their child, along with the entire buildup through her dialogue with Will; but Beresford objected to having anything done twice on the stage, that is, duplication in the final moments when Love announces her pregnancy to the community. Despite the emotional gulf between the two utterances and theatrical situations, Floyd compromised by eliminating the disputed lines and had Love bend close to Rucker and whisper her news.

Michael Yeargan, whose *Susannah* set had served Chicago, Houston, and the Met, designed an environment for *Cold Sassy Tree* astounding in size and complexity. Built by R. A. Reed Productions of Portland, Oregon, it had as its centerpiece a thirty-four-foot diameter by foot-high steel turntable, with rolling platforms and flown pieces, enabling Beresford to show the entire town of Cold Sassy in different combinations, from the cityscape painted on the act curtain, to interiors of Rucker's house and store, and a variety of streetscapes. Yeargan even Photoshopped distressed period posters to decorate a seventy-foot-wide forced perspective fence.

In describing the décor of homes in Cold Sassy, Burns emphasized the ubiquity of portraits of Saint Cecilia, patroness of music. Floyd mentioned this to Beresford, adding that, in his grandmother Fenegan's house, the wall above the parlor piano had sported a print of Jean-François Millet's *The Angelus,* which showed a peasant man and woman bowing their heads in prayer at sunset in the fields, another ubiquitous image in many southern homes of the period. Charmed, Beresford added this to his wish list, and there it hung in the Lattimore parlor.

Though no set change took longer than fifty seconds, Floyd was keenly aware of how such long silences filled the theater, but he treasured the almost pre-Raphaelite luminosity of Yeargan's environments. Beresford had cautioned his designer against Disneyfication and prettification; but pretty it was, thanks to Yeargan's assistant, the painter Luke Hegel-Cantarella. In Floyd's words, "You feel that it's all sunlit, you can almost see dust particles in the air, you get heat and humidity with this story. I think Michael was onto something, because, inevitably, it is nostalgic, something from a different time."

Although both Floyd and Kay spent the months before the premiere in Houston, she could not or would not attend a performance, though she still considered dress rehearsal safe. Family and friends again gathered from the four corners, in numbers that equaled the Met experience: Mark Adamo and his partner, the composer John Corigliano; Linda Golding and Jenny Bilfield, representing Boosey & Hawkes; Julian Patrick, wishing that he had been asked to audition for Rucker; Samuel Ramey; the old Tallahassee clique of Mastrogiacomos, Choppins, and Rogerses; and of course, Ermine and Billy Matheny.

The composer took added pleasure from the presence of members of Olive Ann Burns's family from Commerce, Georgia, including her sister and brother-in-law, the estate's executors. They came as HGO's guests of honor, and shared rich memories that reinforced just how autobiographical *Cold Sassy Tree* was. Of Floyd's Rucker, they said, "Aw, that was just like Grandpa." The lightly fictionalized Will Tweedy had been their father (in-law), and they showed Floyd a photograph of the real Miss Love.

Cold Sassy Tree triumphed at its opening on April 14, 2000. A friend approached Floyd, saying, "Isn't it wonderful to see an audience leave a theater all smiles?" which Floyd thought practically unheard of in opera. This one generated by and large the most consistently favorable press of his career, and he released anxiety over his difficulties in crafting a comic opera. The *Houston Chronicle* praised this "exquisite treatment of the basic human emotions of love and loss," and forecast its future as a companion piece to *Susannah:* "He set the texts to an often fascinating idiom: strong, straightforward tonality contrasted by melodies that circled around their central notes with exceptional complexity. His orchestral accompaniment became another character in the story."[48]

The *San Francisco Chronicle* called the opera "[A] minor masterpiece of musical storytelling and assured theatrical know-how . . . [T]he work as a whole moves confidently through its entire arc . . . [its] passages of radiant, lyrical beauty . . . [mark] the culmination of a distinguished operatic career."[49]

The conspicuous absence of *The New York Times* provoked Gockley. "It wasn't that the whole policy of reviewing premieres across the country had changed. It was a dismissal beyond belief. We had major artists, a major director. I wondered how Carlisle took this. I put my arm around him, but all you can say is, it was great, look how the audiences responded. Still, it was a devastating dismissal of an entire genre of American opera."[50]

Opera Now assessed the longer-term impact of *Cold Sassy Tree:* "The first American opera of the 21st century . . . sets a standard that other composers will find hard to meet in years to come. . . . Floyd has given American opera its true voice."[51]

With rights granted in the course of negotiating Floyd's contract,[52] Beresford completed a film of the production, and PBS *Great Performances* approached Gockley with a hard choice: they would air either Mark Adamo's *Little Women* or *Cold Sassy Tree,* but not both. When Gockley broached the topic with Floyd, the elder composer allowed, "I've already had that with *Willie Stark,* so by all means give it to Mark." At the time of this writing, the Floyd/Beresford *Cold Sassy Tree* remains unreleased.

After the world premiere, HGO performed the opera on April 16, 19, 22, 25, 28, 30, and May 6. The eight-performance run sold an astonishing 15,042 tickets, earning $871,720. Considering the hall's run capacity of 18,768, this represented an astonishing tally for a new opera.[53]

The birth of *Cold Sassy Tree* resembled *Of Mice and Men*'s in Seattle thirty years earlier, coinciding as it did with a five-day Opera America conference, and delegates attended the May 6 performance. The next day, a "New Works Sampler" at the Moores School of Music opera house featured a panel of composers—Floyd, William Bolcom, and Jake Heggie—discussing their art, moderated by correspondent Bruce Weber. Bolcom's setting of Arthur Miller's *A View from the Bridge* had scored a hit at its premiere at Lyric Opera of Chicago the previous October; and the world premiere of Heggie's Floyd-assisted *Dead Man Walking* was slated for San Francisco Opera for October 7, 2000.

Samuel Ramey was back in town in April and May to sing Zaccaria in HGO's first production of Verdi's *Nabucco.* Gockley told Floyd that he anticipated reviving *Cold Sassy* before long, and wanted Ramey for Rucker, a role in which the bass could continue to shine as he aged in his career. Floyd took Ramey out to lunch, and the basso was soon on his way to Switzerland to sing Blitch in Opéra de Genève's *Susannah,* the physical production imported from Chicago, with Nancy Gustafson in the title role, and directed by Robert Falls.[54] (Unfortunately, the projected *Cold Sassy Tree* revival never happened.)

Instead of following Ramey to Switzerland, Floyd had replacement surgery on his left knee, more fallout from his tennis-playing years. At the end of June, long before completing his recovery, he and Kay moved out of Yoakum Boulevard and back to Tallahassee. For the remainder of 2000, at seventy-four, he recuperated from surgery and *Cold Sassy Tree,* missing productions of *Susannah* in Fresno, North Carolina, Fort Worth, and again at Indiana University.[55]

Boosey & Hawkes acquired *Cold Sassy Tree* on August 7, 2000; but as of the time of this writing, it is still only available in print "as needed," to performance-licensed companies. On November 16, Floyd appeared at Hofstra University, in Hempstead, Long Island, for a symposium on "Contemporary Opera at the Millennium." After running into Jake Heggie, Floyd delivered the keynote address, "American Opera at the Millennium." That afternoon he joined a panel to address the question "What Is American Opera?"; and that evening, members of Bronx Opera performed scenes from *Susannah.*

No sooner had Christmas 2000 ushered in New Year 2001 than Floyd reappeared for *Cold Sassy Tree*'s progress, first to Austin Lyric Opera, where Garnett Bruce, Aspen's director and Beresford's Houston assistant, staged the revival. Dean Petersen, John McVeigh, and Margaret Lloyd repeated their Houston roles, with Ward Holmquist conducting a mostly new cast, including Marie Plette as Love. Floyd stayed in Austin for rehearsals and the opening on January 12, 2001. A snag arose when Yeargan's set did not fit Bass Hall, and someone eliminated numerous scenic elements. The company's general director was away until final rehearsals, and Floyd approached Bass Hall manager Charles Leslie, as well as the stage manager and crew directly, to set things right: "It may have looked a little crowded, but at least everything was there."[56] The *Austin Chronicle* hailed: "Lines rise and fall, taking us heavenward one moment, into radiant glory, then earthward, into gloom and pain. . . . [I]t reveals this distinguished composer working at the height of his powers, infusing what may be his final work with the lessons of a lifetime."[57]

The company sold 10,255 tickets, earning $485,081, a more than respectable sum for a regional four-performance run.[58]

SINCE NED ROREM'S DISCUSSION of Floyd's candidacy for the American Academy of Arts and Letters, various committees took four years to act. On January 17, 2001, Rorem, that year's academy president, and its secretary John Hollander sent a joint letter: Floyd had been elected to membership in the department of music. Nomination had come from fellow composer Robert Ward, seconded by William Bolcom, Rorem, and David Diamond.

The academy, founded in 1904 by the National Institute of Arts and Letters, functions as the equivalent of France's venerable l'Académie française. Election confers America's highest formal recognition of artistic achievement. Annual membership is set at 250, and by 2001 its music department totaled forty-four persons, a who's who of American composers. Besides the four men listed above, the group included such longtime Floyd colleagues and acquaintances as John Adams, Dominick Argento, Milton Babbitt (who may have been absent, but in any event offered no objection), Jack Beeson, Elliott Carter, John Corigliano, George Crumb, Norman Dello Joio, David Del Tredici, Lukas Foss, John Harbison, Lou Harrison, Leon Kirchner, Steve Reich, George Rochberg, Gunther Schuller, Stephen Sondheim, Joan Tower, Charles Wuorinen, and Ellen Taaffe Zwilich, all of whom voted on new candidates before sending their results on to the entire membership.

Besides Floyd, other new members that year were the composer Samuel Adler, the artists Robert Mangold and Edward Ruschka, and the writers John Irving, Garrison Keillor, and Jane Smiley, all of whom would attend an informal welcoming dinner on April 3, and a formal induction, with the presentation of diplomas, on May 16.

Unfortunately, the Rorem/Hollander letter had been mailed to Floyd's Houston address. During the forwarding process, Floyd landed in Canada for a Calgary Opera *Susannah* dress rehearsal on January 25; the next day, he gave a live television interview with rehearsal clips; and on January 27 he saw and heard Daniel Beckwith conduct Kelly Robinson's production, with Valdine Anderson (Susannah), Andrew Wenzel (Blitch), Steven Harrison (Sam), and Michel Corbeil (Little Bat).

Floyd returned to Tallahassee to find the academy's letter. At the end of March, as the welcome event approached, he received a warm note from his colleague Jack Beeson on election to the august group. Beeson wryly observed that creators of opera are not considered by some as "real" composers, and welcomed Floyd to the academy's exalted precincts.[59]

ON MARCH 24, Helen Harris and ten of her nonoperatic friends witnessed part of the San Diego installment of *Cold Sassy Tree,* Garnett Bruce again whipping Beresford's production into shape, and Karen Keltner in the pit. For this outing, more of the original cast had reassembled: Patricia Racette, Dean Peterson, John McVeigh, Judith Christin, and Beth Clayton. Floyd received another standing ovation. Two of Helen's friends urged her to go backstage and reintroduce herself to her famous relative. Helen responded, "Oh, he doesn't want to bother with his cousin." One of the friends insisted, "If you don't, we'll drag you back there." So Helen complied, and made her way through the line of well-wishers. Floyd reassured her that a three-fourths house was respectable for contemporary opera and then asked her to turn her head to the side. He remarked, "OK, you've got the same profile." When aunt Bunny had moved the family to Arizona, Ermine sent her the portrait the composer had done of Helen almost sixty years earlier, which Floyd remembered precisely.[60]

When San Diego calculated sales data from its other performances (March 27 and 30, and April 1), 13,364 tickets had been sold, an average 118 percent above house capacity, and a gross income of $704,475.

On April 3, Floyd took Linda Golding as his guest to the academy's welcome dinner and cocktails at the organization's landmark headquarters in "upstate Manhattan," Audubon Terrace, at 155 St. and Broadway. Golding recalled: "There's always the question of why it took so long. What were they waiting for? The dinner party was a hoot. There was a sense of professional pride, on Carlisle's behalf, that he's finally getting at least one piece of the formal recognition available to him; and the academy is a piece of that recognition."[61]

In the course of the evening, Floyd had an unexpected reunion with former piano student and actress Polly Holliday, who was in the company of the critic Tim Page. A large group of male admirers surrounded her, among them the writer Reynolds Price, who confessed, "I just love Flo!" After sharing reminiscences of Florida State University, Holliday wrote Floyd, bestowing other late fruits, "I've always wanted to 'explain myself' to you because that year I spent with you at FSU was sort of a nightmare. Not only was the piano driving me bonkers, but I went through a kind of mini-breakdown. . . . That's all over now, of course. (Therapy and God.) But getting into theatre was my salvation and you were so kind to me about everything. I remember your saying to me, 'You look at home on the stage.' It became my home in a very real way. . . . I thought you'd like to know all this since you sat through my excruciating lessons. I am so in love with Bach, I have to make myself remember I have a job at Lincoln Center as an *actress.* Ha."[62]

Floyd's next trip took him to Charlotte for Opera Carolina's *Susannah,* staged by Matthew Lata and conducted by Louis Salemno, with Dean Petersen (Blitch) and Marquita Lister (Susannah). The company believed this to be the opera's first production in which an African American took the title role. Floyd had only positive reactions.

Though Floyd eventually reaped handsome profits from *Cold Sassy Tree,* they did not arrive without birth traumas. On February 9, 2001, ICM hinted at legal action unless Floyd paid ICM a percentage of his commissioning fee, to which ICM believed their agreement entitled them. Carolyn Kalett had explained to ICM the rather different customs of opera commissions, especially the waiver fees granted cocommissioners, and she facilitated a compromise: Floyd retained his entire fee, but conceded $31,250, or 25 percent of the total $125,000 waived for the four cocommissioners, to be deducted from present and future royalties until the entire amount had been paid. When Floyd maintained that Boosey had been very good to him, he meant it. In this instance, they advanced $10,000 against this sum to ICM, keeping everyone out of court.[63]

FLOYD'S NEXT MOMENT IN THE SUN came on May 16, 2001, again in Linda Golding's company, at the American Academy induction ceremony, from noon to postsupper. At table, Floyd sat between Ned Rorem and Jack Beeson, and the three amused each other with an aging composers' version of "back when I was a boy":

> ROREM: "Composers today have it so easy: look at Jake Heggie."
> BEESON: "Oh Ned, you're just jealous."
> ROREM: "I am! I'm *very* jealous."[64]

Floyd's citation praised his melodic gifts and flair for high drama, which with *Cold Sassy Tree* had expanded into high comedy; with both he had captured the south in the medium of opera, as William Faulkner and Tennessee Williams had done in literature and spoken theater. Each new member wrote a statement that was not read, but was made available for others to read during or after the ceremony. Floyd's, "Some Thoughts on the Creative Process," addressed the issue of inspiration with his customary blend of humility, intelligence, and wit.

> People want to know if I have a daily routine or if I only work when spurred by "inspiration." I suspect there are several reasons for this curiosity: one is certainly the way in which the so-called "creative process" has been represented in films or in romantic novels in which the artist is stunned by a single, eye-widening epiphany in which an entire work emerges in its final state. Another may be the layman's sensing that there is in fact an element of genuine mystery in the making of something where nothing existed before. Also, any composer would be hard put to explain in purely rational terms why one particular sound, or combination of sounds, out of so many possibilities, is the only one his inner ear will accept at any given moment.
>
> When I respond that I have a daily routine which I follow fairly strictly I am never sure what the reaction of the audience is: whether people are disappointed that I have shattered some illusion by such a prosaic answer, or relieved that something about writing music is a little less mystifying and therefore slightly closer to their own experience. At this point almost inevitably the question on "inspiration" arises with the questioner's wanting to know if there is actually such a thing, or if "inspiration" is only a lingering Romantic conceit.
>
> I wince uncomfortably when asked this, as do most of my colleagues, I suspect. First of all the creative act is something intensely private and we properly resist subjecting something so personal to possible coarsening through public scrutiny. (I am reminded of Emily Dickinson's incisively categorizing the publication of poems as "the auction of the mind.") Secondly, "inspiration" is a term I rarely use except to say on occasion that certain pages of music strike me as genuinely inspired when I feel a composer has exceeded him or her self. I think also that part of the reason artists distrust the term is that it suggests that he or she has created the work in some sort of trance-like state, virtually without effort, which then seems to diminish it as an expression of its creator. We possibly feel too that ascribing what we create to "inspiration" may trivialize what is an intensely complex effort in which one's entire emotional, psychological, and intellectual make-up participates.
>
> That said, if I feel the questioner is in earnest, even if naïve, I always feel compelled to try to explain "inspiration" as I understand this very real phenomenon, but in as impersonal terms as possible to avoid cheapening the experience. To begin with, a considerable degree of musical experience and compositional skill to draw on are presupposed. Given that, what I would call "inspiration," at least for me, comes only after much work has been done, much groundwork laid, and one has weathered the usual crises

> of self-doubt and discouragement. It arrives at that precise moment when one connects with his or her creative unconscious and some sort of prior knowledge takes over, directing what one writes seemingly without effort. In the case of writing music, one follows unresistingly what the inner ear dictates and the sounds as well as the structure seem to be laid out in advance. The most remarkable aspect, I feel, is that one moment this prior knowledge is not there and the next it's there for the taking. For me, it is the most exhilarating moment in the creative act and one that cannot be summoned by will or by conscious thought. Come to think of it, in those moments the Romantic notion of "inspiration" may not be too far off after all.[65]

While Floyd unwound in Tallahassee, on May 31 and June 1 and 2, Center for Contemporary Opera performed *Markheim* in New York, staged by Charles Maryan, conducted by Richard Marshall, with Blaine Hendsbee as Creach, Salvatore Basile in the title role, Shira Lissek as Tess, and Sam McKelton as the Stranger. The *Times* sent Anne Midgette, who liked the set.[66]

That summer, Floyd also missed a Utah Festival Opera *Susannah,* and *Slow Dusk* at Baltimore Opera,[67] instead saving travel money and energy for the Bregenz Festival *Of Mice and Men.* Conducted by Patrick Summers and transplanted to the fifties by Francesca Zambello, the cast included seasoned Floydians Anthony Dean Griffey (Lennie), Gordon Hawkins (George), Joseph Evans (Curley), and Nancy Allen Lundy (Curley's Wife). As Candy, Julian Patrick again revived memories of the Seattle premiere thirty-one years earlier. Hawkins believed himself the first African American singer to perform George in a major production. "I brought up the issue of how the Austrian audience was going to perceive the piece with a black man and a white man . . . particularly with the anger George has to show towards Lennie. . . . I thought it was fantastic to have two big guys doing this opera. Compared to the others on the stage we seemed more like misfits not because of my color but because of our size. I'm 6'2", 250 pounds, and Tony is even bigger than that. We seemed odd and separate."[68]

Hawkins recalled that Julian Patrick gave him a number of character tips, "some things he had done and if they were really good I stole them."[69] At the premiere on July 18, Austrian President Thomas Klestil gave a preperformance address, expressing hopes that the piece would promote tolerance for Austria's underclass, and the house applauded its sympathy, thrilling to Floyd.

SEPTEMBER 11, 2001 changed everything in America, dramatically so in the performing arts. As the country's youth deployed to distant battlefields, opera organizations began a steady progression of bankruptcies, closures, and cutbacks. Loyal audience members spent less disposable income on performance events, and companies substituted concerts for staged productions and tried-and-true repertoire—meaning eighteenth- and nineteenth-century—for anything new or lesser known, to lure them back. A month later, emotions ran high as Washington Opera imported Bregenz's *Of Mice and Men.* Floyd, Ermine, and Jane Matheny all found their way to the capital, where, despite critical cavils, audiences cheered Karen Keltner's conducting, along with Rod Nelman (George), Michael Hendrick (Lennie), Diane Alexander (Curley's Wife), and Joseph Evans (Curley).[70] At the after-celebration the company's general director, Plácido Domingo, gave Floyd an impromptu tribute. Taping had been forbidden, so no record of Domingo's exact words was preserved, but Ermine and Jane recalled the core of his remarks: Floyd was the incarnation of the American dream, a living maestro in their midst, who through tireless work had perfected his art without fear or compromise, thus realizing his own dreams.

Ermine looked across the table at her brother's placid smile, before realizing that he had neglected to wear his hearing aid and had not heard a word.

In Houston, David Gockley presented the composer with the Houston Grand Opera Artist's Medal on November 12. And in New York, Julius Rudel conducted *Susannah* at the Juilliard School on November 13, 16, and 18. After the two-year disappearance of

40. Plácido Domingo, Floyd, Ermine, Washington (DC) Opera, 2001. Courtesy of Plácido Domingo and Carlisle Floyd.

Flower and Hawk materials in the shuffle from Belwin-Mills, Boosey finally located Floyd's scores and acquired the work. *Susannah* made her official London debut at Opera for All.

Floyd had for some time considered *Cold Sassy Tree* his equivalent of Verdi's *Falstaff,* a valedictory opera: "I figure that's a very good place to stop, unless something really compels me." He now began thinking of writing some form of memoir. From December 2001 through April 2002, with the assistance of James Kendrick and Carolyn Kalett, he made a will and arranged for the disposition of his manuscripts and personal papers. For the former he chose the music division of the Library of Congress; the latter materials, thanks to his ongoing relationship with Thomas Johnson, were already trickling into his native state's South Caroliniana Library.

HGO's turn with *Of Mice and Men* came at the Wortham Center on February 1, 2002, with Gordon Hawkins (George), Anthony Dean Griffey (Lennie), Joseph Evans (Curley), Julian Patrick (Candy), and Elizabeth Futral (Curley's Wife).[71] A commercial recording on the Albany label was in view, and the company planned a composite of three performances, with a "patch session" after one.[72]

Floyd attended the premiere, but returned to Tallahassee immediately. By this time, he no longer had the time, energy, or inclination to take in the growing number of productions of his works: *Susannah* at Shreveport Opera, Western Michigan University, Palm Beach Opera, Eugene Opera, Du Page College Opera, Opera Memphis, Festival Opera of Walnut Creek, Opera Columbus, Baldwin Wallace College, Central Methodist University, Wright State University, and the Amalfi Coast Music Festival presentation in Sorrento, Italy.[73]

Floyd did attend *Susannah* at Knoxville Opera and the Opera Company of Philadelphia, but missed *Of Mice and Men* at New York's Di Capo Opera. Edmonton Opera gave the work its Canadian premiere, barely edging out Vancouver Opera for that record.[74] He took part in a Florentine Opera symposium panel on Steinbeck's novel and his operatic adaptation on March 2, 2003. Two days later, Floyd spoke about the opera at the University of Wisconsin's Peck School of the Arts, and attended the opening on March 7.

He passed on a Clayton College *Slow Dusk* in Morrow, Georgia; *Wuthering Heights* by Atlanta's Capitol City Opera;[75] *The Mystery* at Snow College in Ephraim, Utah, on May 28, 2002; and Tanglewood's "Celebration of American Art Song," a musical tribute to Phyllis Curtin, on July 20. The first half of 2002, with or without Floyd's attendance, earned him more than $140,000 in royalties, rentals, and sales of sheet music.[76]

BEFORE THE LYRIC OPERA OF CHICAGO *Susannah* revival for the 2002–2003 season, the company's education staff asked me to interview Floyd for Lyric's *Season Companion,* which sowed the seeds of this biography. In the first of those conversations, on February 24, 2002, Floyd estimated conservatively that *Susannah* had in its forty-seven years been performed between eight hundred and nine hundred times, in two hundred to three hundred productions. Curtains continue to rise on New Hope Valley in seven to ten worldwide productions every year: "It's like sending your kids off to college. I stayed with it so long, either staging it or being invited to productions, and was thus associated in a very direct way. But in recent years, I've come to feel that she's really on her own; and unless it's a very special production, I really don't need to see this opera again anytime soon."

Another 2002 event that Floyd could not attend was the Converse College reunion weekend, where he became the first male recipient of the Career in Music Achievement Award; Ermine, likewise a Converse alumna, accepted the award in his behalf on April 27. Floyd conserved energy to attend the Lyric Opera of Kansas City *Cold Sassy Tree* on May 4.[77] Yeargan's sets again proved too large for the company's performance space, as they would for venues in Omaha and Utah, and designer Vicki Davis was engaged for the sub-coproduction that Pamela Berlin directed for all three companies. Ward Holmquist, having conducted Austin's performances the year before, brought in Marie Plette as Love. The sole veteran of the world premiere cast, John McVeigh, repeated Will Tweedy, with otherwise new colleagues, including Kristopher Irmiter (Rucker), Amy O'Brien (Lightfoot), and Bradley Garvin (Clayton).

At the Chicago *Susannah,* Floyd had the pleasure of finding Julius Rudel in the pit. Brenda Nuckton restaged Robert Falls's production, and the roles were taken by Samuel Ramey (Blitch), Sondra Radvanovsky (Susannah), Anthony Dean Griffey (Sam), and David Cangelosi (Little Bat).[78]

THE NEA approved a twenty-thousand dollar access grant to Opera Omaha to support a four-week tour of *Cold Sassy Tree* scenes to schools and community centers during 2003–2004, and a ten thousand dollar creativity award to Opera Carolina to subsidize that company's three performances of the opera, expected to reach a local audience of 4,200. Substantial profits from 2002 enabled Floyd to indulge his passion for high-performance automobiles. He had fallen in love with the Ford 2003 Thunderbird hardtop convertible, in an evening black finish: "I wanted it on sight. I didn't care how it drove, how many miles per gallon it got, or anything else. I was just taken by the design, which was unlike anything else I had seen. For that kind of car, I found it understated. There's a moderate amount of chrome, but not too much."

He grieved the loss of friend, ally, and colleague Elena Nikolaidi, who died at ninety-six on November 14, 2002 while visiting her son in Santa Fe. For her *Houston Chronicle* obituary, Floyd eulogized her as one of the most dynamic singers he had encountered, "the kind that you couldn't keep your eyes off. . . . [She had a] fearless commitment to singing."[79]

Opera Carolina gave its *Cold Sassy Tree* performances in February 2003. Garnett Bruce and Karen Keltner rehearsed veterans Dean Peterson, Marie Plette, John McVeigh, and Margaret Lloyd in the four principal roles. Floyd saw the opening night, February 20, 2003,[80] but not before moments of real panic. As a cocommissioner, Opera Carolina had joint custody of Yeargan's set, which would fit its performance venue. Once San Diego completed its run in April 2001, the sets arrived in Charlotte for storage in a local warehouse, and waited there like a time capsule. Opera Carolina's technical director, Ben Howe, periodically cruised by the stand-alone storage building to reassure himself that all was in order.

On a quiet Sunday evening in April 2002, Howe called the general director, James Meena: the warehouse was gone. After realizing that Howe was not joking, Meena tracked the facts. His donor organization had lost its paperwork about the set. The city petitioned to demolish the warehouse, which was a haunt of drug dealers and users. A preliminary inspection revealed Yeargan's enormous apparatus stamped with markings from its builders, Reed Productions, and from the opera companies of Houston and San Diego; but nothing to indicate an Opera Carolina connection. The inspector called the Charlotte Repertory Theater and asked if "this stuff" might be theirs, but of course CRT knew nothing. The entire set was forthwith hauled to dumpsters, and the warehouse razed.

Months of wrangling with insurance companies ensued, during which second-generation sets for *Cold Sassy Tree* were built. When Floyd learned the particulars of this saga, his primary concern was for the quality of the painting. Meena hired Luke Hegel-Cantarella to re-create Yeargan's sun-splashed effects; and with final brush strokes barely dry, Opera Carolina's installment opened on February 20. The local chapter of the stagehands' union produced a t-shirt to commemorate the incident, which was already assuming urban myth proportions around the small world of opera. The garment bore the legend "CST—2003," with a bulldozer poised to knock over a full-grown sassafras tree. Happily, none of this seemed to impact the audience's appreciation of Floyd's work. Opera Carolina's final accounting shows 4,464 tickets sold for their three performances, netting an income of $198,138, and outselling both *The Mikado* and *Carmen* later that season.[81]

AFTER fewer than three years back in Florida, when Floyd was not traveling to Houston or some other performance site, Kay tantalized her husband with Houston's cultural advantages over Tallahassee's and reversed her choice of primary residence. In March 2003, they repacked their entire household and headed back to Yoakum Boulevard, where Floyd lay, exhausted, as Utah Opera prepared the fourth production of *Cold Sassy Tree*. Floyd attended dress rehearsal in Salt Lake City on May 17, 2003. In Pamela Berlin's production conducted by Hal France, Kristopher Irmiter, John McVeigh, and Margaret Lloyd repeated their roles as Rucker, Will, and Lightfoot; but soprano Jessica Jones, who had sung Myrtis in Houston, now debuted as Love Simpson.[82]

On July 3, Houston's American Festival of the Arts, directed by Dr. Michael Remson, gave Floyd's 1987 *Flourishes* a reading session. The program's choral division also performed Floyd's "Long, Long Ago."

While Lake George Opera performed *Susannah* in Saratoga Springs, New York,[83] Ermine and Jane Matheny visited the Floyds at Yoakum Boulevard. One evening, the four watched a rebroadcast of season 5, episode 1 of Inside the Actors Studio, in which Meryl Streep discussed her career with host James Lipton. Of her role as Karen Blixen in the 1985 film *Out of Africa*, the actress related how director Sidney Pollack did not think she was sexy enough to play it, and everyone howled.

The next morning at breakfast, Kay maintained with some heat that they had watched no such program. Ermine, Jane, and Floyd showed their best poker faces, and dropped the subject; but no one could ignore that something serious was happening with Kay, who now decided that they needed to move back to Tallahassee. Floyd repeated farewells to friends and doctors, and asked his primary care physician to examine Kay. At the appointment, in answer to the doctor's structured questions, she looked to Floyd for answers; the doctor asked to see her again in a few weeks, at which time she seemed clearer.

That spring, Floyd chanced to run into Jorge de la Torre at the opera, and the doctor urged his former patient to visit his office. Given Floyd's concerns for Kay, the timing was ideal, but De la Torre offered little encouragement and posited no condition; rather, he cautioned Floyd that such situations do not tend to improve. For the remainder of their conversation, De la Torre opened up about his family for the first time, and spoke warmly about having had the inscribed *Jonathan Wade* poster framed and hung in his home.

Return to Tallahassee the Floyds did, in September. After three complete moves in as many years, Floyd told Kay, "Don't even think about doing this again." From time to time she queried, shouldn't we think of going back? But Floyd's life, to say nothing of his career, had taken another leap; its direction remained to be seen.

22

Twilight in Tallahassee

2003–2012

As Kay retreated into her nest, Floyd at seventy-six found himself a caretaker. He wrote no new music, rationalizing that "you can't subject anyone to listening to you compose at the piano. It's enough to drive you crazy. Kay was remarkably indulgent all those years, it was awful for her to listen to that." He stayed away from the piano altogether; even listening to recorded music, especially his own, became a trial:

> I know everything that's coming. It probably goes back to the same kind of carelessness about taking myself seriously as a composer. I never wanted to be the kind of composer who was always jockeying, self-promoting. I did enough of that in my twenties with *Susannah,* because I was the only one who had any confidence in it, until Phyllis and Mack got involved. Despite the excellent recordings of my operas, there are always musical things that I wish were different. It's kind of atavistic, protective. When Kay and I went to concerts, and not even necessarily of my music, she would say, "Can't you keep a poker face? Anybody can read you if you're displeased with something." And I am not even aware of it.

Yet he thought from time to time about writing a short children's opera. Despite speculating that he might do well directing verismo operas like *Carmen* or *La bohème,* his last exercise of this craft had been the 1996 San Diego *Jonathan Wade* revival. Of his own works, he had yet to direct a production of *Cold Sassy Tree,* but thought that *Mollie Sinclair* might offer a good time. He continued to ponder writing his selected memoirs. If companies invited him to interesting productions, he went, and helped with whatever public relations events they might ask of him; he viewed it as "looking after the children."

Florida State University asked him to teach a few symposia and master classes. The Clique were all alive and well, and great pleasure came from lunches with Lenny Mastrogiacomo, Bill Rogers, or Gregg Choppin; but for the most part he shopped for groceries and prepared most of the meals for himself and Kay. Kay grew increasingly jealous of his time and attention.

In October, Floyd revisited Rhoda Levine's *Of Mice and Men* at City Opera, conducted by Willie Anthony Waters, with Rod Nelman (George) and Anthony Dean Griffey (Lennie).[1] The *Times* conceded that Floyd knew how to write an opera, but that critics tended to dislike his manner of so doing.[2]

He dropped in on an Opera Grand Rapids *Of Mice and Men* on October 17 and 18, gave an informal talk for invited patrons, a master class for students from local colleges and universities, and a preperformance lecture. The Opera Company of Philadelphia mounted a new *Susannah* that October, and the University of Cincinnati College-Conservatory of Music performed *Markheim* in November.[3]

Changes were afoot at Boosey & Hawkes following its acquisition by the venture capital firm HgCapital. In fall 2005, HgCapital offered Boosey for sale for between £60 and £80 million. Interested firms included Elevation Partners, whose partner and managing director was U2 lead singer Bono. Offers came to around £115 million; but this sale eventually fell. The great fear among Boosey's composers concerned the firm's loss of private ownership; but for the moment, "their children" remained safe.

Floyd spent a week that November in Knoxville, coaching University of Tennessee faculty and students on *Susannah,* in a production directed by Carroll Freeman, a veteran Little Bat. Albany Records released the Houston *Of Mice and Men* at the beginning of 2004, to critical acclaim.[4] For *The New York Times,* Anthony Tommasini wrote of this "most powerful, sophisticated and effective" work . . ."finally getting its due."[5]

On November 9 Floyd delivered his lecture on the librettist's craft for the College of Music at FSU. Opera Omaha, the last of the *Cold Sassy Tree* cocommissioners, finally got around to producing it that spring.[6] At the beginning of April, Floyd put in an appearance to boost the company's public relations effort. He saw no rehearsals, but Pamela Berlin and Hal France again took charge of stage and pit, with Kristopher Irmiter, John McVeigh, and Margaret Lloyd in practiced command of Rucker, Will, and Lightfoot; but when Floyd returned to Tallahassee, he found Kay distraught at the thought of his leaving again in two weeks for the opening, and Omaha remained the one he never saw. The composer may have finally been getting his due, but the man encountered serious problems at home. Kay, the couple's financial manager and computer expert, had not filed an income tax return since 1999. Not wanting to embarrass or wound her, Floyd saw the dangerous territory into which they had drifted. He engaged an accountant, the IRS forgave the omission (with substantial penalties), and Kay offered no protest. Her Houston therapist minimized damage by writing a letter outlining her diminished capacities, and Floyd pinpointed these events as the real onset of her problem; yet, incredibly, she resisted an official diagnosis until October 2005.

Floyd visited the memory disorder clinic at Tallahassee Memorial Hospital's neuroscience center to discuss her condition. Kay's neurologist used no more specific a term than dementia; but it was in fact the affliction that at that time could only be conclusively proven by autopsy: Alzheimer's disease. Aricept, Nemenda, and other medications seemed to slow its progress, but, in tandem with Kay's lifelong agoraphobia, the disease resulted in the couple's virtual imprisonment in their new home. By the fall of 2006, Kay's Alzheimer's and her demands on Floyd had reached clinical severity. When he left the room, she called for him at close intervals.

Movie evenings faded too, for the same reasons. At first, Floyd found that Kay's distraction had its advantages: they might watch a particular favorite five times. At the same time, Floyd's passion for reading became a secret vice; if detected, this might send Kay into sudden rages. Yet Floyd, still the most private of men, veiled Kay's condition, referring to it for several years only as "the disease." Even close friends in Tallahassee remained in the dark; *everyone* knew that Kay had receded further into the shadows, but not why. Floyd admitted, "Everything she did before was with the brain, and it amazes me that she can sit for such a long time without speaking. I don't know where her mind is, and I've long since given up asking."

Except for rare family gatherings, when Ermine and Billy or any of their children might visit, entertaining chez Floyd disappeared. Kay even resented his social lunches, or concerts or events in his honor, and they ultimately became impossible unless he could snag Jane or her sister Harriett for a few hours. Except for a weekly housekeeper, only persons Kay knew well were admitted; and even then, if one of the Matheny girls left the dinner table to retrieve something from the downstairs guest room, Kay might whirl in alarm and whisper, "There's a strange woman going to the basement!"[7]

Both still found moments of tenderness, holding onto old nicknames that neither had as children: "Pidge," a shortening of the word "pigeon," had been Floyd's favorite in the early days of their acquaintance, "but I never called her that after we got serious." Now, when in good humor, she might call him "Car," or "Cark": "That's when she likes me, and I know I'm on solid ground."

When interviewers journeyed to Tallahassee, Floyd established a routine. With a sitter in place at home, sessions took place at the interviewer's hotel room or other neutral ground, the composer clutching a can of sugar-free soft drink; all the interviews he gave for this book were conducted thus, or by phone. Throughout, Floyd displayed astounding patience, generosity, and openness; but after an hour, he began to glance at his watch, growing visibly anxious about what might await him at home.

Kay rarely ventured outdoors, except for medical appointments; she spent most of her time in bed, and her formerly trim athlete's shape ballooned. Floyd chose to remain at her side, or at least in the house most of the time, but performances of his works continued unabated. The baritone Donnie Ray Albert and the Meadows Symphony Orchestra, conducted by Paul Phillips, performed *Pilgrimage* at Southern Methodist University in Dallas on February 27.[8] On March 19 and 20, Washington University in St. Louis staged *Susannah,* followed on March 26 and 28 by Dugg McDonough's production with a student cast conducted by John Keene at Louisiana State University in Baton Rouge. Floyd traveled to Rochester, New York, for the Eastman School of Music *Susannah* opening on April 1, before which he gave an informal talk to opera students and a preperformance introduction.

That spring, the Floyds still watched a few DVD movie releases, of which one struck the composer as a promising operatic subject: *The Playboys,* which had been shown briefly in theaters in 1992. This Irish-American-British production starred Robin Wright as Tara, a young woman who has an out-of-wedlock child in a small Irish village. A ramshackle acting troupe, The Playboys, visits on tour, and their inept performance of Shakespeare's *Othello* offers high and low comedy. Despite a meddlesome village priest and a local constable obsessed with Tara, she and the actor Tom fall for each other, and their affair has tragic overtones. The film's blend of the comic and serious paralleled *Cold Sassy Tree,* and Floyd sent David Gockley a copy, but *The Playboys* joined the list of "what if" projects.

He passed on a University of North Carolina *Susannah* in Greensboro, *Of Mice and Men* at Lyric Opera of Kansas City[9] (the company's fifth production of three Floyd operas), and *Slow Dusk* by Yale College Opera Theater that fall. Instead, mid-November found him back in Washington, DC, receiving the National Medal of Arts, the highest award presented

41. National Medal of Arts presentation, 2004: President George W. Bush, Floyd, Laura Bush. Courtesy of Dana Gioia, Chairman, National Endowment for the Arts.

to Americans in the visual, performing, and literary arts, from the hands of President George W. Bush. The year's other recipients were the Andrew W. Mellon Foundation, the writer Ray Bradbury, the choreographer Twyla Tharp, the architectural historian Vincent Scully, and, posthumously, the sculptor Frederick Hart and the poet Anthony Hecht. On November 16, the night before the ceremony, NEA chairman Dana Gioia took the honorees to the Willard Hotel for dinner. Gioia sat with Floyd and Ermine and Billy Matheny, and told them that he had long been the composer's fan. He asked probing questions about contemplated or unfinished projects, reawakening Floyd's interests in Gide's *Symphonie pastorale,* Harold Frederic's *The Damnation of Theron Ware,* and the Sudermann/Murnau *Sunrise.* Gioia astounded with the breadth of his knowledge of all three subjects, and later wrote Floyd, encouraging him to reconsider *Sunrise.* Floyd subsequently reread the first two sources, but again rejected both as unsuited to his operatic purposes.

On Wednesday, November 17, President Bush distributed medals in the Oval Office. Floyd's citation congratulated him for giving American opera its national voice with a series of contemporary classics on American themes. Afterward, Laura Bush and Lynne Cheney held a reception in the foyer and East Room of the White House. Mrs. Bush regaled the group with tales of John Adams's move into an unfinished White House and the hanging of a Gilbert Stuart portrait of George Washington as the first piece of art in the president's residence. She saluted the medalists as important teachers. Floyd soon received a warm note of congratulations from Jorge de la Torre, signed for the first time with the therapist's given name.

FLOYD PERFORMANCES SPANGLED 2005: *Susannah* at Opera Columbus, Hawaii Opera, University of Southern Mississippi, Fargo-Moorhead Opera, Ireland's Wexford Festival, and *The Sojourner and Mollie Sinclair* at the University of North Carolina, Chapel Hill.[10] On May 22, singers on the roster of New York agent Janice Mayer gave a tenth anniversary concert at which John McVeigh premiered Floyd's *Soul of Heaven,* all songs transposed for high voice. Floyd received a tape that led him to believe that the cycle, which he had all but forgotten, was not successful; but the recording contained a great deal of echo: "The space sounds terrible for singing. To tell the truth, I never listened to the whole thing, it didn't charm me a great deal. I remember liking them when they were first done in Houston, but things like that happen."

On August 1, Albany Records released its CD of the Houston *Cold Sassy Tree,* lauded for its "bold colors and unabashed melodicism . . . lively, lovable characters, memorable tunes and magnificent dramatic sequences."[11] Despite brisk sales, David Gockley's gears spun in other directions. "I had promised Carlisle three recordings, and was only able to deliver two. We wanted to issue *Jonathan Wade.* At that time, we were doing fairly sophisticated radio broadcasts that resulted in good tapes, but somebody made off with the master tape of *Jonathan Wade* from our music library, and the others weren't perfect. There was a performance tape from San Diego, but I did not want to issue a recording paid for by Houston Grand Opera that was not from HGO."[12]

On November 4, 2005, FSU awarded Floyd an honorary doctorate of humane letters, to recognize his contributions to music and to the university. That same evening, in Floyd's presence, the College of Music's opera theater opened its fiftieth anniversary production of *Susannah* at the site of its world premiere.[13] Strolling past the composer's old cottage on West Call Street, the stage director Matthew Lata had found the structure in ruins; he picked up a derelict piece of green trim that found its way onto the Polk house set. A week later, the composer also attended Florida State Opera's reprise of the production in Orlando.[14]

IN THE COURSE OF 2006, Stuart Ostrow published a tribute to his old friend and ally, who represented "the genius of our own twentieth-century composers," revoicing the aspirations the two men had shared since their days on NEA panels. Ostrow felt that a synergy of Broadway establishment and conservative elements at NEA shared responsibility for "suppressing quality musical theater today" by insisting on the incompatibility of opera and music theater. Ostrow's solution encompassed precisely the kind of workshops that Floyd had pioneered at HGO and Canadian Opera with crossover works like *Willie Stark,* and his later experiences with Adamo and Heggie with stakes in classical and popular camps. In words that Floyd might have written, Ostrow felt the need for "a new salon . . . a Cradle, a place of origin and continuity where first-time dramatists and songwriters are nurtured, and whose original works are ultimately produced on, and beyond Broadway. We need to teach the student writer to dramatize action, inspire the incipient novelist, poet, and journalist to create insight and humor through lyrics and librettos, and encourage the new composer of MTV, opera, and minimalist music to fuse with the art of telling stories."[15]

Susannah's net again spread worldwide: Cedar Rapids Opera Theatre; Washington University, St. Louis; Opera Vest, in Bergen, Norway; Northwestern State University (Nachitoches, Louisiana); Di Capo Opera Theatre in New York; and Capitol City Opera, Atlanta.[16] That May, niece Jane Matheny, one of the few whose presence Kay tolerated, was between jobs. She moved in with the Floyds, which allowed him to attend a retrospective tribute at Lone Star College in Kingwood, Texas. On May 5, he held a student forum on "How I became a Music Major." On May 6, he participated in a panel discussion on "The Influence of Protestantism on American Culture." And, for a grand finale on May 7, he attended a "Happy Birthday Carlisle Floyd" concert, with the Kingwood Chorale and Chamber Orchestra performing choruses and arias from *Susannah, Cold Sassy Tree, The Passion of Jonathan Wade, Of Mice and Men,* and *Willie Stark.*

Just before his actual eightieth birthday, he came down with an attack of shingles, which he called "the disease everybody else has, and which I knew I would never have." Nonetheless, he and Ermine embarked on a four-day car trip around South Carolina, to the small towns in which they had grown up, a melancholy visitation of the gravesites of peers like MacNeal Clyburn in Bethune, and of vacant or paved-over lots where childhood homes once stood, in Spartanburg, McClellanville, Jordan, and North: "The thing that struck me was how quiet these towns were; almost no one was on the streets. Bethune bustled when I lived there. It may have been the parsonage's proximity to the school, but a great deal more went on commercially. It seemed a lively place, also by contrast to North; but both places struck me like *Die tote Stadt:* buildings without humanity."[17]

Yet Bethune's yellow brick parsonage still stood. At a local garage, Floyd met the grandson of Cecilia King. The lady herself, now ninety-eight, welcomed the composer and Ermine to her home for an astonishing visit, during which King reminisced and gave directions to old sites and acquaintances.

On July 23, Floyd wrote me that he had found Kay "preoccupied and a little morose. After probing, I found out that she was very concerned and unhappy about my going ahead with the plan to work on the book with you. This forced me to consider circumstances I had avoided confronting until now." He went on to share details of the diminishment of their daily lives, and Kay's increased demands on his attention. "Given all this I've regretfully come to the conclusion that it is unwise to proceed with the plans for the book as far as my active participation is concerned."[18]

Fortunately, Jane and other friends and family persuaded him otherwise. I first visited his archive in Columbia, then the man himself in Tallahassee, in mid-August 2006. In the intervening five years, he came to view references to "my biographer" as altogether too pretentious. Lenny Mastrogiacomo finally suggested that Floyd call his chronicler "Bio-Man" or "Bio-Tom."

I never met Kay.

At FSU's September 7 general faculty meeting, Floyd and five former colleagues, including Gregory Choppin, were presented the Torch Award (ARTES), in appreciation for aesthetic and intellectual pursuits that enriched the university's academic programs.

In October, Floyd participated in Virginia Opera's *Susannah* publicity effort.[19] Arriving in Norfolk on October 23, he met the cast—Lillian Sengpiehl (Susannah), Marc Embree (Blitch), Patrick Miller (Sam), Eric W. Johnston (Little Bat)—and held interviews. The next evening, with conductor Joseph Walsh and stage director Dorothy Danner, he grounded an "Opera Insight" program. At dinner afterward, Danner complimented him on his public speaking, "I love the way you use verbs." Floyd realized, "She is the first person who ever said that to me. I thought, 'Thank you God, for Elizabeth Bearden!'"[20]

In its half-century plus, *Susannah* had seen many orchestral variations, but 2007 brought something different. A new company in Minneapolis, Theatre Latté Da, established itself as an experimental presenter, focusing on intimate, untraditional performance venues and instrumental adaptations specific to the time and place of a work's setting. For their *Susannah* in February, artistic director Peter Rothstein and music director Joseph Schlefke proposed an orchestra of piano, violin, guitar, banjo, oboe, and string bass, with performances at the Loring Playhouse, as much a coffeehouse as a theater, in Minneapolis. In the title role, Meghann Schmidt would deliver her two arias—described by the press as "folk songs"[21]—accompanying herself on autoharp.

By the terms of his contract with Boosey & Hawkes, Floyd naturally had the last word on such revisionist approaches. He offered no objection, but wondered how his score would sound with such an ensemble. In the opinion of at least one reviewer, the results failed to satisfy all tastes.

Floyd next learned that Louisiana State University's (LSU) opera theater had scheduled *Willie Stark,* the first production since a Shreveport Opera outing twenty-two years earlier. The choice was logical: LSU had been one of Huey Long's pet projects, and his years as governor saw its size and influence trebled. Of course, the school wanted Floyd on its Baton Rouge campus to promote, instruct, and inspire; and from February 11 to 14 he obliged, finding the staff excellent and, for a student production, the cast eager and competent. His coaching on singing, tempi, instrumental nuances, and props were all implemented. He flew back for the March 22 opening, and participated in an LSU symposium on the opera and its historical sources.[22]

In May's first week, with Jane Matheny holding down the house and Kay, Floyd left for Providence, where Rhode Island College performed another retrospective of his works on May 4. Choral director Teresa Coffman had received her doctorate at the University of Houston, and had written her dissertation on Floyd's choral music. For the event, she scheduled a question-and-answer session with the composer, and assembled, with minimal staging, scenes from *Susannah, Of Mice and Men, Markheim, Willie Stark,* and *The Passion of Jonathan Wade.* (Floyd had requested the last two.) As an extra bonus, the Henry Barnard School fifth-grade chorus sang his *Two Stevenson Songs,* "Rain" and "Where Go the Boats," as well as "Who Has Seen the Wind" and "Long, Long Ago," all but the last of which he had never heard performed since their commissioning by Juilliard forty years earlier.

By June, Floyd's dream of maintaining a second home in Houston had gotten out of hand. Insurers refused to renew policies on an empty house, and inspection revealed that the Yoakum Boulevard property bristled with black mold. Everything from the studs out had to be removed and replaced, and the house was sold within the month.

Reverend Floyd, apart from his difficult character, served as an excellent role model for fiscal responsibility. Floyd strategized with his financial advisers to avoid any investments with risk factors, telling his broker, "I'm the dullest client you'll ever have." Together they consolidated his assets in The Floyd Irrevocable Trust, its initial purpose to ensure Kay's ongoing care. In the wake of the housing, banking, and stock market crises of 2008–2009, that same broker called Floyd to reassure him, "You are absolutely safe. You may have started out as my dullest client, but now you're my sexiest!"

Despite some enforced isolation, the composer never lost touch with much of his past; he maintained contact with old friends like Jona Clarke, Catherine Murphy, or David Gockley. Jake Heggie and Mark Adamo sought him out anew, the latter with a treatment based on *The Gospel of Mary Magdalene.* Gockley, fully engaged in a new position as general director of San Francisco Opera, lamented their physical distance; he contemplated a San Francisco production of *Willie Stark* or *Susannah,* with "recognizable names." By E-mail and telephone, he and Floyd stayed in touch; but when Gockley invited the composer to the West

Coast for a break from his routine, Floyd responded, "I can't, Kay needs me."[23]

On August 4, 2007, the Aston Magna Foundation, celebrating its thirty-fifth anniversary, sold out a tribute for Phyllis Curtin in Great Barrington, Massachusetts, Curtin's home for decades. Following a program of music by Henry Purcell, the soprano's friends and former students contributed memories and appreciations; the bass-baritone David Ripley delivered Floyd's tribute. Paraphrasing the pianist Oscar Levant, Floyd wrote that he could "easily and truthfully say *Susannah, or the Story of Phyllis Curtin,* for without Phyllis, *Susannah* might still be moldering on a shelf in my studio, unheard for these fifty-two years outside the city limits of Tallahassee. . . . [M]any of those offering tributes tonight will properly mention the many facets that make Phyllis unique both as a person and an artist. . . . Her extraordinary musicality and astonishing quickness of learning (aided by sight reading of the highest order) are legendary . . . her singing . . . is always musical and expressive: the line is always beautifully shaded and rhythmically supple, without distortion or loss of pulse or violation of period style. . . . With her the music and the role always came before any considerations of personal ego, and for me this is what made her such a compelling and convincing actress in the huge range of roles she undertook in her career. . . . My admiration and love for this beautiful and elegant lady is undiminished after fifty-odd years of warm friendship and association, and undiminished also is my gratitude."[24]

ON OCTOBER 19, Winthrop University in Rock Hill, South Carolina, awarded Floyd its Medal of Honor in the Arts, to acknowledge his unique contributions to cultural life in the Carolinas; but at home, the Kay situation turned grave. At one point he hired contractors to add a large deck to the back of their house, thinking that she might enjoy spending time outdoors; but she rarely left her bed, and Floyd only appeared on the deck to refill a bird feeder.

Though he remained housebound for the remainder of the year, Floyd's works made the world's rounds: *Susannah* at Indiana University; the Hochschule für Musik und Theater in Hamburg, Germany; *Pilgrimage,* by baritone Kai-Uwe Fahnert and pianist Liana Narubina in Berlin; and *Slow Dusk* at Cornell University.[25]

Floyd now developed new routines to carve personal time from each day to read, answer correspondence, and collect thoughts and breaths of fresh air during shopping errands. Waking at six each morning gave him three or four hours before Kay stirred, and then he waited on her "hand and foot"; but when Jane offered live-in help, he might steal quick lunches with friends, visit a bookstore, or give an hour's interview. Yet even circumscribed independence came with a hefty price tag of guilt and the telltale intestinal problems that resisted a medical solution. After all the years of Floyd's career-enforced unavailability, Kay seemed to want nothing more than for him to watch her breathe.

On November 28, they celebrated their fiftieth wedding anniversary, privately. He brought her a bouquet of red and white roses, with the sentiment, "I hope you're ready for fifty more." The Mathenys turned up the next day, Thanksgiving, with three dozen yellow roses symbolizing the golden anniversary, and Kay beamed thanks.

Floyd's thoughts turned more and more to childhood, and vivid memories of his asthma: "I know how Daddy felt now: you're old, and some days you just don't know if you can get up and go. People don't understand when you take too long in the grocery line, and get impatient with you because you can't move fast."

But after even a minimal emotional feeding, like receiving an award from Winthrop College, he came back, according to Jane, "steppin' high and bright, with it again." His next "fix" came with Atlanta Opera's production of *Cold Sassy Tree* in February 2008. On January 10, though exhausted, he arrived to meet cast and staff and give interviews, advising company administrators to use his time wisely. The first warning bell sounded at a television interview with Pamela Roberts of Georgia Public Broadcasting: for the first time, he felt queasy and uncertain about something he had done routinely for so many years. He was then paraded to a musical run-through, as the cast made one another's acquaintance. Some were Floyd old-timers, like Kristopher Irmiter as Rucker and John McVeigh as Will Tweedy; but the point that disturbed Floyd was that no one had told him that he was expected to make an impromptu presentation. Rehearsal nonetheless stopped, and chairs circled for a question-and-answer session. The cast as a body seemed incapable of untying their tongues in the composer's presence, and McVeigh and Irmiter jumped to the rescue with helpful questions that guided the rest of the session, about topics he had addressed on previous occasions, such as broadness of comedy and accent. But still, remembered Floyd, "I couldn't find words. It may not have been noticeable to others, but it was very much so to me, because of the effort and anxiety it provoked. I didn't feel I did well something I can normally do at two in the morning."

Then the conductor and stage director corralled him, wanting quick solutions to discrepancies in their scores, and proposing last-minute cuts. He approved most, but knew that McVeigh and Irmiter would soon erupt with justified complaints, placing Floyd in a parental triangulation. During supper, he insisted to a company administrator that he needed to return to his room, but his host drove him ten miles to see the Cobb Energy Performing Arts Centre, the company's new performance venue. Floyd had put his hand on the man's arm and said, "I have to get to bed, give me a rain check," but midnight passed before his head touched a pillow.

One cannot help wondering what Floyd might have thought of *Susannah* at Lee University, a small Christian college in Cleveland, Tennessee; but its run on February 1, 2, and 3 overlapped the Atlanta experience. Thanks to Olive Ann Burns's Georgia roots, Georgia Public Broadcasting planned an in-depth look at Floyd's version. For its "State of the Arts" segment, camera crews appeared at rehearsals for interviews with singers, conductor, and director, and a behind-the-curtain look at the company onstage immediately following the opening. Floyd may have thought his earlier interview a disaster, but according to Jane, "Pam Roberts fell madly in love with him."

Ermine and Billy arrived in Atlanta on February 1 for the next night's premiere. Besides McVeigh and Irmiter, the cast included Erin Wall (Love) and Maureen McKay (Lightfoot). The production disappointed Floyd by misreading wistful comedy as farce, which undercut his characters, text, and music, yet the audience rewarded the composer with another standing ovation and long-lasting cheers. Beneath TV lights and flashbulbs, the Georgia Public Broadcasting backstage event came off without a hitch, as Floyd's great-nieces watched. An interviewer asked Floyd about Olive Ann Burns, and the composer gave Ermine credit for alerting him to the book's existence. The camera panned to her for comments, which she handled with aplomb, emphasizing Burns's ability to capture the rhythms and idioms of southern speech and to create characters that were like people they had known all their lives. One of the principals teased Ermine, "If you come up with any more books, give them to him, because we want more operas!" There was laughter and applause.

Floyd returned to Tallahassee with a violent clash of emotions. On the one hand, the support he had drawn from immersion in family and friends brought tears to his eyes. He told Jane, "I haven't had such a feeling of being beloved for so long. I'm not talking about the opera. I had such a wonderful time with my family. I haven't been with people who really know me and love me, and I just basked. I felt so enriched." The opera was another matter. To people's questions, he developed a pat response, "I guess I'm used to the other production." But the reality was otherwise: "It all adds into the annual pool of royalties, but that's no compensation if I don't like the production." His failure receptors vibrated, and within forty-eight hours he spiraled toward the worst depression he had felt in twenty years.

By mid-February, atop gastrointestinal complaints, Floyd's emotional distress had dug up an all-too-familiar stomach pit of dread, impaired self-confidence, and terrible sadness, "a very old and early feeling." It disabled him for days, and he feared he was entering the "one-horse shay" period of life, his memory failing him on points large and small. Kay seemed not to recognize her husband's sufferings, and insisted on constant attention.

Newport Classics asked him to write liner notes for LSU's *Willie Stark* DVD, with a "day before yesterday" deadline. By the beginning of March his distress and anxiety had resulted in sleep deprivation. He suffered his first asthma attack in sixty years.

While he remained immobilized in Florida, on March 14 English Touring Opera gave *Susannah* its much-delayed professional British premiere, directed by John Conway and conducted by Alex Ingram.[26] Other productions of *Susannah* took the stage at Northeastern Illinois University, University of Texas (Austin), Texas Women's University, and Opera Pacific.[27] Amarillo Opera unveiled its single-performance *Cold Sassy Tree* on April 26, sung by Emily Pulley (Love), Timothy Lafontaine (Rucker), Alex Richardson (Will), Nicole Franklin (Lightfoot), and Daniel Collins (Clayton), with Andy Anderson conducting and Paula Homer directing.

By early May, after daunting batteries of tests and scans, and examination by doctors "from knee to face," Floyd had fought his way back from darkness, having "forgotten what it was like to feel so good."

IN ONE OF HIS FINAL ACTS as NEA chairman, Dana Gioia created an annual Opera Honors Awards to acknowledge that opera had arrived for real in America, and to recognize the highest class of opera artists. Besides Floyd, the 2008 recipients were the conductor James Levine, the soprano Leontyne Price, and the administrator Richard Gaddes. Each would leave the ceremony with a check for twenty-five thousand dollars. Floyd immediately felt that he did not deserve such an honor. "What about all those other younger composers, like John Adams? . . . But Dana [Gioia] quickly rattled off all the reasons: I was chosen and so, needless to say, I shut up and didn't protest."[28]

Frank Corsaro, who had written the libretto for Thomas Pasatieri's *Frau Margot* and staged the world premiere at Fort Worth Opera in 2007, enthused to Floyd about the company's gemlike theater, Bass Hall. Floyd thought that Corsaro might have exaggerated, but he made his own trip to Fort Worth, from May 30 to June 3, as *Of Mice and Men* played in repertory with Peter Eotvös's *Angels in America* and Puccini's *Turandot*.[29] Richard Kagey, who had assisted on Atlanta's *Cold Sassy Tree*, directed, with Joseph Illick conducting the Floyd work. Anthony Dean Griffey reprised Lennie, alongside Phillip Addis (George), Matt Morgan (Curley), and Brandi Icard (Curley's Wife). Floyd found everything heartening, from Bass Hall's acoustics to warm press comment.

Between July 5 and August 10, Colorado's Central City Opera gave thirteen performances of Michael Ehrman's *Susannah* production, conducted by Hal France, but logistics kept Floyd penned in Tallahassee. Instead, on July 16 he flew to New York for interviews to be used in a video segment at the NEA ceremony, scheduled for the end of October. As Floyd exited a Manhattan subway onto West 58 Street, a man stopped short in front of him: David Gockley. Both availed themselves of the serendipitous moment and spent three hours catching up. Nonetheless, New York's whirlwind sent him home on July 19 with a complex of maladies that plagued him until that fall.

Early in August, a figure from Floyd's distant past resurfaced in Tallahassee, a fifties-era FSU piano student of Edward Kilenyi's. Five years earlier, this individual had learned that a development firm had purchased the 500 block of West Call Street, and that Floyd's old house, by then a kind of pilgrimage site for the university's music students and staff, faced demolition. Inspired by the move of Frederick Delius's Solano grove cottage to the grounds of Jacksonville University in 1961, Floyd's admirer raised thirty-five thousand dollars to have the structure moved to Millstone Plantation, a two-hundred-acre site about eight miles from Tallahassee, on the shores of Lake McBride. Managed by the Apalachee Land Conservancy, which relocated and restored architectural gems from various periods of Tallahassee's urban past, the site was intended to host seminars and conferences.

After the move in 2003, the Floyd house sat on a bucolic hill at Millstone beneath ancient moss-covered oaks, awaiting restoration expenses estimated at fifty-eight thousand dollars; but the success of this venture emboldened the former Kilenyi student to undertake a different project. Ryan Edwards's performance of Floyd's Sonata in May 1957 convinced the composer's tutee-to-be that it ranked alongside the great parallel works of Copland and Barber. He had snapped up one of the first copies off Boosey's presses, but was daunted by its technical demands; and now, a half-century later, he asked Floyd to help him tackle the work, to be filmed for release on DVD.[30] The Tallahassee Film Festival unveiled the result at All Saints Cinema on April 16, 2009, with Floyd in the audience. (He found the whole event surreal.)

Floyd sifted reams of family photographs for the NEA/Opera America video tribute that would introduce him at the awards ceremony. On Friday afternoon, October 31, recipients attended a lunch in the west conference room of the Supreme Court Building, hosted by opera-loving justices Ruth Bader Ginsburg, Antonin Scalia, Anthony M. Kennedy, and NEA chairman Dana Gioia.

That evening, powers that be in the American opera world, alongside such Floyd supporters as Ermine and Jona Clarke, convened at Washington's Harmon Center for the Arts for a downstairs cocktail party. Santa Fe Opera general director Charles McKay tantalized Floyd with talk of a *Wuthering Heights* revival; Floyd countered by suggesting *Bilby's Doll,* a work even more likely to appeal to Santa Fe audiences. The baritone Sherrill Milnes approached with his own positive reminiscences of his appearance as Heathcliff in *Wuthering Heights* in Chicago in 1961.

After everyone ascended to the theater upstairs, presentations to Floyd and his colleagues proceeded. Justice Ginsburg "called the session to order," and, after remarks from the mezzo-soprano Susan Graham and NEA chairman Gioia, tributes began. Floyd's video introduction featured Phyllis Curtin, Frank Corsaro, Jake Heggie, Mark Adamo, David Gockley, and Denyce Graves. Opera America president and CEO Marc Scorca presented Floyd, who spoke of pride, not so much in his own career as in the progress the medium of opera had made in the country during his lifetime. Aundi Marie Moore,[31] accompanied by the Washington National Opera orchestra conducted by Plácido Domingo, then performed Susannah's most famous aria.

Following her tribute and remarks, Leontyne Price brought all hearts into their respective throats as she

42. Opera America Awards, 2008. Marc Scorca, Opera America; Dana Gioia, Chairman, National Endowment for the Arts; Leontyne Price; Floyd; Richard Gaddes; Wayne Brown, National Endowment for the Arts. Courtesy of Dana Gioia.

announced that she could not express her gratitude in any other way than that for which she had been born. Everyone knew what was coming, and tears flowed as Price began, a cappella, a rendition of "America the Beautiful" that grew stronger with each phrase, utterly belying her eighty-one years.

The next night, November 1, Floyd, never much of a Donizetti fan, attended the first two acts of Washington's season opener, *Lucrezia Borgia,* Renée Fleming singing the title role. After returning to Tallahassee on November 2, Floyd admitted that the entire complex of events was "a little difficult to take in . . . only because it was happening to me. . . . I came home exhausted and it took most of a week for me to recuperate and get some semblance of my normal energy back."[32]

ON NOVEMBER 11, 2008, HgCapital finally disposed of Boosey & Hawkes, selling it for £126 million to Imagem Music.[33] The remainder of the year saw productions of *Flower and Hawk:* at Boston's Goethe Institute, with soprano Dunja Pechstein on November 14; and on November 22 and 30, with soprano Paula Ennis, as part of WordState Vermont's exhibition of history and literature on Eleanor of Aquitaine and the art of courtly love.

Addressing a formidable backlog of correspondence and other business, Floyd at last realized that he could no longer shoulder the responsibility of caring singlehandedly for Kay. She had entered the next phase of Alzheimer's, and he contacted the memory disorder clinic to inquire about nurse-companions. After the holidays, age and frailty settled the matter. On January 3, 2009, she was rushed to an emergency room with a fever of 101. Floyd sat up all night with her, and daybreak found her installed in the hospital, diagnosed with pneumonia and an abnormally high white cell count resulting from another infection. The conditions were resolved with intravenous antibiotics and oxygen, but examining neurologists determined that her Alzheimer's had progressed to the stage at which transfer to a licensed care facility was urged. After a seventeen-day hospital stay, Kay was moved on January 20. Floyd hung pictures from home on the walls of her room, and brought a chair and throw that she particularly liked.

For the first time in half a century, Carlisle Floyd was alone. His first priority had to be to tackle a five-inch layer of bills and other mail, some as old as three or four years, on his kitchen table. For a week or two, he hired three private nurses to attend Kay in shifts. Her outlook brightened; the constant attention and the stimulation of new faces seemed to soothe rather than agitate her. For the most part, her conversations were more lucid and her demeanor pleasant. Floyd assessed her coherency to be about 20 percent. Still, his visits were fraught with the part-and-parcel heartbreak of Alzheimer's: like many sufferers, she obsessed about going home.

He asked, "Where is home?"

"You tell me."

"Is it Houston?"

"Yes."

"Is it Jacksonville?"

"Yes."

Floyd mentioned the old housekeeper, "Wawa," Kay's childish mangling of "Rakestraw," and she brightened at once. Home would always be a place from the distant past where she felt loved and cared for.

Reorganizing his days and nights proceeded slowly. A new cat, Tina, offered good company and slept beside him. Years earlier, he had joined a gym, but his absence agitated Kay; now he reactivated his membership and began working out three days a week, and his energy and general outlook brightened. By summer, he underwent two eye surgeries and reclaimed literal clear vision. Regular lunches with members of the Clique recommenced, and Floyd saw the inside of a bookstore for the first time in months.

On February 27, *Of Mice and Men* opened at Theater Hof in Germany.[34] On March 5 and 7, *Susannah* played the University of Texas (El Paso) and Mobile Opera on March 26 and 28. On March 14, at Weill Recital Hall in Carnegie Hall, the Houston-based tenor Todd Randall Miller, the soprano Marion Russell Dickson, and the pianists Jay Whatley and Shannon Hesse gave a recital of contemporary works with an emphasis on musical theater, including selections from *Susannah, Willie Stark,* and *Soul of Heaven.* England's Hampstead Garden Opera performed *Susannah* on April 4.

Most significantly, a new career-motivated synergy developed, mostly behind Floyd's back. Old friends like Corsaro and Gockley reminded the composer that the word "never" did not always mean never: after all, both Monteverdi and Verdi composed magisterial operas well into their elder years, so why not another Floyd opera? As he reviewed the long sequence of contemplated projects, he fell back onto *Seth/Reeds,* the project based on Sudermann's *Journey to Tilsit,* the subsequent film by F. W. Murnau, and his libretto from 1983–1984.

In the meantime, as an adjunct to the tenth anniversary of its VOX program for composers and librettists, New York City Opera invited Floyd to join the director Anne Bogart and fellow composers Mark Adamo, Eve Beglarian, and Nico Muhly for a discussion of "American Opera: Past, Present, Future," chaired by City Opera's new general manager, George Steele.

He returned to Tallahassee on May 3, with past, present, and future still very much on his mind. With David Gockley's departure for San Francisco Opera in 2006, HGO had a new general director, British-born Anthony Freud, who together with the conductor Patrick Summers invited Floyd to Houston, where André Previn's new opera *Brief Encounter,* based on the 1945 David Lean film, received its world premiere on May 1, 2009. Floyd heard the first act on May 7, and discussed it over a long lunch with Summers two days later. Summers turned the conversation around: had *Floyd* thought about another opera? "Well, kind of," responded Floyd. "Probably not really, but kind of."

Floyd let Summers know his current thoughts about Sudermann/Murnau and *Seth/Reeds.* The baritone Nathan Gunn had whetted the composer's curiosity in *Brief Encounter,* so when Floyd appeared at the Wortham Center to see the entire opera on Saturday evening, Summers took him to Gunn's dressing room for an introduction. Barely had the men shaken hands when Summers effused, "Carlisle's doing a new opera, and it's got a great leading role for you!" Gunn expressed even greater interest when Floyd mentioned Hal Prince's fascination with Murnau; and when the composer worked his way backstage after the performance to congratulate the leads, Gunn whispered, "I'm very interested in what we were talking about earlier."[35]

Back in Tallahassee, Floyd reexamined his libretto:[36]

> I remember it as a short opera, and rhymed, which I would not want to do, but the story has a perfect kind of arc. I picked these pages up with fear and trembling, and prepared to do lots of hacking and rethinking. I quickly found that my fairly reliable memory very much needed the jolt of rereading the script; but it all surprised me, in a good way. I don't think there's much to do to it, the whole story is almost tailor-made for opera, absolutely theatrical from beginning to end. Not having seen it in twenty-five years, I was kind of embarrassed to show it to my friends. I was prepared to do it over, all without rhyme, but it doesn't seem to be mannered, or draw much attention to itself. Still, I'm very reluctant. Interested, but reluctant.

At least the parties were back in touch, daily, by phone or E-mail; but Floyd still fretted about turning eighty-three on June 11, and thought he would need "to go into training" if he undertook another opera.

At the end of 2009, his health was excellent, and Kay well cared for, and, to all appearances, content: "For the first time, she's trusting a human being, and that's me. It's very thrilling, though belated and under the worst possible conditions, and probably more meaningful for those reasons. Of course, I'm the only person she recognizes, but she's confident that I can do for her."

Other Floyd performances took place throughout 2009: New York City Opera presented *Susannah* excerpts at South Street Seaport on June 27, conducted by Steven Mosteller. On November 5, the company reopened its refurbished David H. Koch Theater[37] with an "American Voices" program, including *Susannah*'s revival scene, with Samuel Ramey as Blitch, and Julius Rudel in the pit. On September 11, Taschenoper im Atelier Theater Meilen (Theater Heubühne, Feldmeilen, Switzerland) mounted a complete *Susannah;* on

October 30 and November 1, Kentucky Opera unveiled its new *Of Mice and Men* in Louisville; and Michigan State University performed *Susannah* on November 20, 21, and 22.

In December, Floyd visited the Mayo Clinic's Jacksonville facility for consultation and testing, and returned feeling generally better than he had in some time. Kay was doing as well as might be expected. He visited daily after her long postlunch naps and sat on the bed to chat when she was at her most alert and in the best spirits, but she had lost weight and strength, and had sustained several bad falls. Floyd now experienced an inexplicable return of his eighties depression symptoms. He commiserated over Kay, "She's so fragile at ninety-five pounds, but her eyes are still wonderfully alive, causing me to wonder futilely what still goes on in what remains of that remarkable brain."[38]

Ermine and Billy Matheny drove to Tallahassee to be with Floyd. Together with Jane, they all clustered around Kay on the evening of January 13, 2010. They left shortly after midnight, and "that remarkable brain" whispered into darkness later that morning. Funeral services were held on January 17.

AS OF SUMMER 2009 the forty-four productions of *Susannah* since 1990, and the sixteen *Of Mice and Men*, placed them in the top fifteen most-performed American musical theater works by professional companies in the United States and Canada. Only Menotti's one-act *Amahl and the Night Visitors* (sixty-one) and Gershwin's *Porgy and Bess* (fifty-eight) received more during that period; and these statistics do not include the dozens of colleges, conservatories, or European productions listed in the preceding chapters. Thus Floyd came in substantially ahead of the rest of the competition: *Candide* (Leonard Bernstein, thirty), *Little Women* (Mark Adamo, twenty-three), *My Fair Lady* (Alan Jay Lerner/Frederick Loewe, twenty), *Sweeney Todd* and *A Little Night Music* (Stephen Sondheim, nineteen and eighteen, respectively), *The Ballad of Baby Doe* (Douglas Moore, nineteen), *Vanessa* (Samuel Barber, seventeen), *Street Scene* (Kurt Weill, seventeen), *The Consul* (Menotti, sixteen), *The Crucible* (Robert Ward, fourteen), and *The Tender Land* (Aaron Copland, fourteen).[39]

In 2010, the Mittelsächsiche Philharmonie of Freiberg, Germany, performed the *Wuthering Heights* Suite; and the University of Wisconsin-Milwaukee, *Slow Dusk*. The University of Iowa opened its *Susannah* on April 30, and the Cincinnati College-Conservatory of Music premiered *Of Mice and Men* on May 13. Sarasota Opera, Boston University (at which Floyd enjoyed a reunion with Phyllis Curtin during April 2010), and Des Moines Metro Opera offered other new *Susannahs*.[40] In a workshop setting, the latter's apprentice program finally performed, for the first time anywhere, the double bill of *Markheim* and *The Sojourner and Mollie Sinclair* on July 10.

Baritone Sherrill Milnes, the artistic adviser of Opera Tampa, called early in 2010 to announce that the conductor Anton Coppola would present Floyd with the first Anton Coppola Excellence in the Arts Award in Tampa on May 16. That same day, the Landestheater Salzburg, Austria, gave the European premiere of *The Passion of Jonathan Wade*'s 1991 version, directed by Arila Siegert, accompanied by the Mozarteum-Orchester, conducted by Adrian Kelly, and with sets by Hans Dieter Schall and costumes by Marie-Luise Strandt.[41] The cast included Hubert Wild (Jonathan), Julianne Borg (Celia), Marcell Bakonyi (Judge Townsend), Jeniece Golbourne (Nicey), Eric Fennell (Lucas), and John Zuckerman (Pratt). Audience and press reception indicated increasing enthusiasm for Floyd in Europe, as well as hints that the charms of *Regieoper* (high-concept "director's opera") may have been wearing thin in regions where it began. For European criticism, the reviews amounted to raves for a dramatically thrilling, colorful, effective drama in the grand manner. To these journalists, *Jonathan Wade* aligned itself with the greatest international twentieth-century operas, proof that America had come of operatic age.[42]

Subsequent Opera America statistics demonstrate that Floyd is enjoying a similar groundswell at home. Loyola Opera Theater in North Baltimore performed *Susannah* on February 12, 2011. On March 28, Floyd was inducted into South Carolina's Hall of Fame in Myrtle Beach. The Australian film and opera director Bruce Beresford staged *Of Mice and Men* for Opera Australia in Sydney and Melbourne.[43] Floyd husbanded physical resources to make the long trip, and lent the company assistance with public relations and program notes. His and their success was formidable, beginning with "the dapper, eighty-five-year-old Southern gentleman . . . visibly moved by the standing ovation and thundering applause that greeted him . . . at last, an accessible contemporary opera we can listen to."[44]

BY THE TIME FLOYD flew back to Houston in February 2010 to meet with Freud and Gockley, he had "pretty much concluded that I would not go forward with *Seth,* although we discussed it and I understand what they would like to see changed, even if I don't know how it could be done. . . . I think the production demands are probably too great, and the problem I have always seen for making Seth's actions credible still exist in my mind, although if, as in the original story, he drowns in the last act, that might change the tone somewhat. I talked to Anthony [Freud] about my longtime but futile interest in Gide's *Symphonie pastorale,* and he was very interested in that. However, after rereading it for the fourth or fifth time, I still haven't found a way of dealing successfully with the material."[45]

Thus future composition plans remain far from settled. However, Floyd confirmed in May 2010 that "I've got the itch again," and everything points to a fourteenth Floyd opera. Several months later he wrote that "I am at last aware of and enjoying the fact that after fifty odd years I can do pretty much anything I would like without factoring in another person's welfare or wishes, and this is genuinely exhilarating."[46]

Throughout the first half of 2011, Floyd wrestled with an adaptation of Jeffrey Hatcher's *Stage Beauty,*[47] about the London theater world of the mid-seventeenth century, and the demise of male players of female roles. Floyd described the work as "a stunning exposition on difference." As of summer 2012, after fruitful exchanges with Hatcher, he has drafted a complete libretto, titled *Kynaston* after its male protagonist, and has begun composing his first music in twelve years.

Meanwhile, the world remembers what Floyd has already created. On September 22, 23, and 25, 2011, the Houston Symphony performed *Flourishes;* on September 24, 2011, FSU unveiled its "Celebration of Carlisle Floyd," with excerpts from *Cold Sassy Tree, Of Mice and Men, The Passion of Jonathan Wade,* and *Susannah.* The year 2012 brought new German productions: *Wuthering Heights* at the Mittelsächsiche's Freiburg Theater (February 11, 19; March 3, 4, 6, 27; October 18; November 9, 18, 23) and *Susannah* at Theater Hagen (March 17, 23, 28; April 10, 17). American performances of *Susannah* took place at Milwaukee's Florentine Opera (March 16 and 18), Undercroft Opera in Pittsburgh, Pennsylvania (August 2, 3, 4, 9, 10, 11), Berks Opera Workshop in Reading, Pennsylvania (August 10 and 12); *Of Mice and Men* at Utah Opera (May 5, 7, 9, 11); and *Slow Dusk* at Philadelphia Opera Collective (June 15 and 16). In 2013, Sarasota Opera will present *Of Mice and Men* on March 9, 12, 14, 17, 20 and 23; and Opera Idaho will offer their *Susannah* on May 17 and 19.

Since the 1976 interview with Ethan Mordden, the most prevalent theory about Floyd's priorities and aesthetic predilections proposes his embodiment and ennoblement of the outsider in his operas; but research for this biography suggests that it is rather his ongoing quest for independence in his life, reflected in his works, that defines Carlisle Floyd. However imperfectly, through diligent but painful application he has escaped his childhood. He remains a convinced Deist, in undiminished awe of universal processes. Though he takes genuine pleasure in seeing his operas loved and applauded, somehow he still cannot quite believe in his success. At the same time, he retains a sense of wonder, sweetness, and humor, and a vivid apprehension of life's absurdities amid the sadness behind and before him. Throughout their days and nights, the champion who has never failed him is Ermine. Just as he has fallen up before, it is likely that he will do so again. His least favorite word is "no," his best-beloved is "hope."

Carlisle Floyd is here to stay, even if he is too modest to call it immortality.

> "True independence isn't individuality, which is clinging to self. . . .
> but falling more deeply into life and into . . . true humanity."
>
> —Tracy Cochran

Appendix

Notes

Selected Bibliography

Index

APPENDIX

Mysteries of South Carolina

The Genealogy of Carlisle Floyd

Like Verdi and Britten, the two opera composers he admires most, Carlisle Floyd has roots in a village: Latta, Dillon County, South Carolina.

The likenesses compound. Verdi, born in Le Roncole, a wide spot in the road near Parma, Italy, came on his father's side from farmers, taverners, and grocers; but his mother was descended from the composers Scarlatti, Alessandro, and Domenico. Benjamin Britten's speck on East Anglia's map was Lowestoft. Dad cared for the town's teeth; and Mum, a good amateur musician, sang.

Floyd's Daddy, also Carlisle Sessions Floyd, but called Jack, worked as a farmer, banker, and Methodist minister. Mama, Ida Fenegan, a trained pianist, told the story of troop trains in World War I passing through Latta. Doughboys craned from windows and doors, bawling, where are we? Some helpful local hollered, Latta! Over the huffing and puffing racket, the soldiers fought to clarify their coordinates and asked, Atlanta?—and passed on to their fates.

Circumstances of history, even geography, spread their veils over the edges of Floyd's tale. Genealogical densities complicate the sorting out; and from its inception, South Carolina itself often proves other than it seems. At the very least, its historical realities, much like Carlisle Floyd's life and career, tend to differ from original intentions. Without belaboring the point, every stage of Floyd's journey has its double, every day its night. The south supplies his blood and air, and its ambiguity and mystery form the bedrock and morning mists of his soul and talents.

It is no accident that, of Floyd's thirteen operas (counting the two very different versions of *The Passion of Jonathan Wade* in 1962 and 1991 as separate works), only three[1] have non-American settings; and of the remaining ten, eight unfold in the south.[2]

Latta, just seven miles south of Dillon County's eponymous seat, sits near South Carolina's border with North Carolina. Yet the state only whittled Dillon County from Marion County—as in Francis Marion, the "Swamp Fox" of Revolutionary War fame—in 1910, just sixteen years before Carlisle Floyd entered the world.

Until 1769, the region figured as part of enormous Craven County. From 1769 until 1785, this geography was designated the Georgetown District of Craven County; then, from 1785 until 1798, the unit changed to Liberty County. From 1798 through 1868, it became Liberty County's Marion District, then plain Marion County from 1869 until 1909.

For such a tiny state—the twelfth smallest, at about thirty-two thousand square miles, ahead of West Virginia and behind Maine—South Carolina has an amazingly varied geography. From its Low Country, or coastal counties around Charleston, to the northeastern Pee Dee region of rich farmland where the Floyds and Fenegans settled, to the sandhills—ancient beachfront property dividing the Piedmont region from the coastal plain—to the Blue Ridge, or upstate, South Carolina offers something for almost everyone.

In his first eighteen years, Floyd lived in six different villages in most of these regions, and in one in North Carolina, for periods as short as three months, and never longer than six years. The casual tourist notices similarities in the physical layout of most of these settlements: railroad tracks dictate the main street, which is lined with a modest rank of public buildings and businesses; and one or two perpendicular arteries for homes and churches.

With the exception of cities like Columbia and Charleston, South Carolina appears to owe its existence to the train. Latta originated in 1888, thanks to the Atlantic Coast Line Railroad (ACL), itself an amalgam of a century of mergers and consolidations that determined whether and where communities would sprout.

Two markers will better establish the basis of his identity, character, and activity. The first, South Carolina's quirky history, merits a quick primer. The second is the importance of family within this unusual frame.

BEGINNING IN 1521, from their Caribbean bases the Spanish explored but did not settle present-day South Carolina; yet Spanish Florida proved close enough to harass and prevent anyone else from calling the region to the north home. French Huguenots attempted a short-lived settlement on Parris Island, today the site of a United States Marine Corps training facility.

The English enforced their claim to the area dating from John Cabot's voyages to North America between 1497 and 1498. More than one hundred and fifty years later, King Charles II rewarded his eight most enthusiastic supporters—we would call them venture capitalists—with massive land grants in the New World. According to charters of 1663 and 1665, the original Carolina Colony extended from the Atlantic to the Pacific coast; the colonial separation into North and South Carolina dates from the second and third decades of the eighteenth century.

The eight nobles, or Lords Proprietors, perhaps intuited what summers would be like. None ever set foot in South Carolina, but rather appointed representatives to see to the details of settlement and governance. They disseminated literature depicting Carolina as the New Eden, a fertile bed for olives, wine, figs, and silk, and saw to the abolition of duties on goods exported by the colony. To thin the ranks of French Huguenot refugees in England, and native-born religious dissenters, a policy of religious freedom became another carrot on the lords' stick to persuade settlers to make the arduous voyage the New World.

The first takers proved few and slow in coming. Three ships bearing ninety-two colonists sailed from England in October 1669; the voyage was beset by storms and two ships were lost. Others established a beachhead a year or so later at Albemarle Point, near what became Charles Town in 1680, today's Charleston, in honor of the flamboyant English monarch.

These early English confirmed their southern-climate intolerance with the importation of the first black slaves from Barbados in 1671, earlier experiments with subjugating indigenous natives having proved unsatisfactory. Instead of grapes and figs, what thrived were indigo, rice, cotton, and, later, tobacco. By 1700, historians estimate that more than 40 percent of blacks entering North America came through Charleston.[3] By the 1750s, the colony was populated by about twenty-five thousand whites owning forty thousand blacks, "who endured the most brutal slave system on the mainland."[4]

Those first hardy visionaries of English gardens were doomed to disappointment. The only fresh food available was whatever game could be shot or trapped, fish from the rivers, oysters from coastal beds, and eventual planted crops. A plethora of epidemic diseases like dysentery, malaria, cholera, yellow fever, and whooping cough slashed life expectancy: between 73 and 85 percent of twenty-year-old men, and 55 percent of all women, never lived to see fifty.[5] Skirmishes with twenty-nine Indian tribes promised constant worries, at least until smallpox accomplished what attempts at enslavement could not.

Like most of England's American colonies, Carolina was founded as a for-profit corporation, and the mirage of fabulous wealth to be earned from large plantations induced those with the requisite funds to brave the attendant hardships. This also explains many of the special qualities of the southern family. Kinship often made the literal difference between life and death, and clusters of families tended to bond and intermarry within narrow geographical areas.[6]

Fathers saw to housing and feeding the family, while mothers provided virtually all of their children's nurturing and exposure to religious instruction. Siblings enjoyed special privileges and close bonding within the family. As we will see, these relationships and responsibilities did not alter much between the late seventeenth century and the early twentieth, when the Floyd children entered the world. According to the historian Lorri Glover: "Brothers and sisters frequently had more in common than did other family members, and their connections lasted longer than ties to parents or spouses . . . sibling relationships clearly diverged from the power-based relationships within the patriarchal household."[7]

Ermine Floyd Matheny's indomitable character and unswerving love and support, and her understanding husband, demonstrate why Carlisle Floyd could sustain a career in the face of daunting opposition from within and without, from his own disposition, from the family, and from his various peer groups.

MARION/DILLON COUNTY began acquiring a populace only after 1700. Most English and especially Irish settlers planted corn, peas, potatoes, rye, oats, wheat, and flax, and raised the usual complement of domestic hogs, sheep, goats, and cattle. No towns existed in the region until after 1800. Centers of sparse population arose predictably close to navigable waterways like the Great and Little Pee Dee rivers. One of the area's earlier churches, Catfish Creek Baptist, began ministering in 1802 to the spiritual needs of a congregation of eight men and three women.

Railroad connections expanded across the region. Both Dillon county and its like-named seat received their names from James W. Dillon (1826–1913), a transplanted Irishman who headed the drive to bring the ACL railroad to that part of the state. Thanks to the wildly successful cultivation of tobacco, the railroad built its "Wilson Short Cut" in 1887, from Pee Dee settlement (today Florence, South Carolina) to Wilson, North Carolina, with a loading station for cash crops. This innovation and the town that blossomed around it in 1888 took their name from Captain Robert J. Latta, surveyor of the ACL's right-of-way, and engineer of the original town plan of a half-mile-radius circle. Succeeding years brought a post office, W. W. George's general store, Kornblut's Dry Goods, Gaddy's Drug Company, and two hotels. An early school, the one-room Vidalia Academy, founded in 1877 on a nearby farm, became Latta's first public school in 1898. In 1911, the town got its own library, the last to be built with Carnegie moneys. Today a nucleus of some of these historic buildings stands reassembled in a city park a short stroll from the Floyd house.

Latta numbered 467 inhabitants in 1900; by 1910, the population had ballooned to 1,358. The Floyds, while not the wealthiest of families, had means: cash flow from a tobacco farm, a lovely home, and, soon, the glamour and mobility of a Model A Ford.

FLOYD FAMILY LEGEND had it that "our people"—the quintessential early American olio of English, Irish, and French—came from Virginia. Reverend Floyd always felt bound to add that they were *not* kin to the supposedly horse-thieving North Carolina Floyds. The record shows at least the former legend to have legs, and Carlisle Floyd would discover other dusty corners of his own prehistory, musing, "The south in which I grew up had more in common with Japan than anywhere else, with its reverence for ancestors. The formality was very Japanese, based on pride, honor, faith. I do not think the entrepreneurial north had that; and perhaps they were fortunate. There is a reverse side to everything. I remember one of my aunts, who did not have very much money; she was shabby genteel, but she displayed her coat of arms."

After the New York City Opera tour of *Susannah* to Los Angeles in 1972, Floyd received a letter from fans of Welsh origin who had seen a performance. They asked whether the composer was Welsh, having heard that ethnicity in the opera's folk influences. After Phyllis Curtin had known Floyd for years, and had met Floyd's father and aunts, she said, "I'm convinced that you are all Welsh, by your dark, heavy brows." Finally, at a party following a colleague's recital at Florida State University, the hostess, of Welsh stock, expressed her certainty of Floyd's Welshness. At home he checked dictionaries and encyclopedias and confirmed that "Floyd" was a Welsh name.

He knew the reputation of Wales as a land of song, with its male-voice choirs and the musical "congress," or *Eisteddfod*,[8] of fourth-century origin. From about the sixth century, the region also had a tradition of bards, professional poet-singers who used music to glorify noble patrons, as recorded in the lore of quasi-mythical figures like Aneisin and Taliesin.

The original Celtic pronunciation of *ll,* sometimes rendered as *fl*—its technical name is "voiceless alveolar lateral fricative"[9]—poses difficulties for native English speakers, accounting in part for variants in the name's spelling over the millennia: Flod, Flode, Flood, Floid, Floode, Floyd, Floyde, Fludd, Fludde, Lloit, Lloyd, Loid, Loyd, Loit, Loyt, Tully (an Irish variant), MacTully, Talley, Tally, among others.[10]

The Internet surname database proposes the origins of the name "Floyd" as a nickname connoting a gray-haired person, or a holy person who wore gray garments. "Floyd" appeared in its present spelling around 1509.

By the first years of the seventeenth century, Welsh Floyds had a strong presence in the southeastern county of Brecknockshire, a rural mountainous region of Wales.[11]

43. Floyd coat of arms. Author's collection, courtesy of H. B. Floyd III.

A family coat of arms appeared in the United Kingdom in 1816 with the motto, "Bearing patiently the dust and the sun." Nicholas J. Floyd described it in heraldic language: "Argent, a cross, sable. Crest, A Griffin sejant, azure, holding in dexter paw a garland of laurel."[12] In layman's terms, the coat of arms depicts a silver shield embossed with a black cross. Added to the version that hung in many South Carolina Floyd homes is a knight's helmet, atop which sits a blue dragon or griffin holding a laurel circlet in its right paw. Also diverging from the 1816 emblem, our Floyds' version displays a mantle, representative of a knight's protective cape but with a distinctly botanical aspect, rising from the top of the cross and wreathing the sides.

In the heraldic language of colors, silver connotes peace and sincerity; black, constancy or grief; azure/blue, truth and loyalty. The laurel wreath symbolizes triumph.

JAMESTOWN, a commercial venture of the Virginia Company of London, and named for King James I, became England's first permanent American settlement on May 14, 1607. In the ninety-two years before Virginia's capital moved to Williamsburg, Jamestown witnessed many firsts, including the arrival of Africans as slaves, the first printing press in America, banned by the government, and the first distillation of corn whiskey and cultivation of tobacco as a cash crop.

Jamestown suffered abysmal weather and repeated burning. It was almost abandoned before an infusion of fresh colonists arrived after 1610. In 1622, thanks to a friendly native's timely warning, Jamestown was spared the massacre by indigenous tribes that most Virginia colonists suffered. Two years later, James I assumed personal management of the company, making Virginia the first royal American colony.

Dozens of Floyds eventually made their way to the American south, and to some degree, however distant, many connections exist with the composer's line.[13] Despite the arrival of a John Flood in 1610, Jamestown's first settler with the proper surname was Nathaniel Floyd, born in Brecknockshire, Wales in 1599. At twenty-four, after making his way to London, he took passage on the *Bona Nova,* which plied the Atlantic to Jamestown several times between 1618 and 1623. Records unfortunately do not specify on which trip the man listed as "Nathaniell Floid" arrived, but he first appears in one of the musters, or early censuses, taken after King James I dissolved the Virginia Company in June 1624: "Nathaniel Floyd, aged 24 years, came in the *Nova* and was in 1623–24 included in Edward Blaney's 'muster' over the water opposite James City."[14]

Attempts by genealogists in Carlisle Floyd's family to trace their ancestry to Jamestown presented one of the "brick walls" familiar to researchers. More information, much of it unsourced and fantastic, comes from Nicholas Jackson Floyd's *Biographical Genealogies.* It is included here for the sake of completeness, as well as the fact that these are at the very least Floyd cousins and uncles.

> Nathaniel Floyd and his brother Walter arrived from Wales in Jamestown, VA in 1623 on the vessel "Bona Nova." They likely made frequent trading trips to and from the Old World until they and their offspring settled more permanently in Isle of Wight County and Accomac County. A relative, Richard Floyd, also came to Jamestown in 1653 and moved north to Long Island and is the likely ancestor of William Floyd who signed the Declaration of Independence. Nathaniel is the ancestor of another William Floyd, the progenitor of the Virginia-Kentucky branch of the family. William of VA married Abadiah Davis, a granddaughter of Princess Nicketti who was in turn a granddaughter of Chief Powhatan. Abadiah along with her sisters and brothers are the ancestors of many famous Americans including Governor John Floyd of Virginia, Sgt. Charles Floyd and Sgt. Nathaniel Pryor of the Lewis & Clark expedition, and many more including the Venable, Burke, Cabell, and Shelby families.[15]

Why *Nathaniel* embraced this most uncertain of futures remains a matter for conjecture. His connections are at best tantalizing, on average elusive, and at worst fanciful or misleading. Nathaniel's parents were John Floyd, born in Wales in 1575, and Elizabeth Lady, born in 1574. (Their other children were John, 1601–1687; Walter, born in 1610, who appears to have died without issue; and Richard, 1626–1700, grandfather of General William Floyd, signer of the Declaration of Independence.)[16]

Nathaniel took a wife named Mary, whose birth some family trees show as 1599. Whether she accompanied her husband on the *Bona Nova,* or they found each other in Virginia, is unknown. Nathaniel was granted a patent for 850 acres of land in Northampton and Accomac on November 20, 1637, and Walter, 400 acres at Martin's Hundred, on April 24, 1632; both as so-called headrights for bringing fresh colonists to Virginia.[17]

Such substantial grants suggest that these earliest American Floyds and succeeding generations farmed for the next three hundred years, raising corn, cotton, tobacco, and subsistence crops and livestock for themselves.

Nathaniel's son John settled in Northampton County, Virginia, the southern, remote thirty-five miles of today's Delmarva Peninsula, which separates Chesapeake Bay from the Atlantic Ocean. There he wed Mary Berry in 1625, and the couple had one son, Charles, born in 1628 at Hog Island in Island Bay. John died on July 26, 1687, survived by Mary until her passing in 1690.

In 1705, at age seventy-seven, Charles Floyd married Elizabeth, who was more than fifty years his junior. Her surname has not survived; but their son Samuel, born in 1718, did. (Charles died in Northampton at the recorded age of 118, in November 1746.)

Samuel Floyd married Susan Dixon (1720–1753) in Northampton in 1746, and, apparently jumping the gun, she produced Samuel Jr. in 1745; Samuel Sr. died in Northampton in 1753.

Samuel Jr. married Ann Farrar, born in Fairmont, North Carolina, in 1767. Together they became the first in this Floyd branch to travel the old King's Highway to Marion County, South Carolina, before spawning Samuel III in 1770. Samuel Jr. died there, though the dates of both his and Ann's passings have been lost.

At some point Samuel Jr. acquired substantial farm acreage. The Free State region of Marion County drew the Floyds, but not for the same reasons that spawned the term "free state" in other parts of the nation. Historian Durward T. Stokes maintains that "Free State is the area between Big and Little Reedy Creeks. One traditional accounting for this name is that the area was a neutral ground during the Revolution, agreed upon by Francis [Marion] and the Tories. . . . Another tradition holds that the original settlers . . . were so rowdy and headstrong, they lived without any regard to the rights of others. Be that as it may, but Free State had changed by the latter half of the nineteenth century and was a respectable community."[18]

By this time, the Floyds and collateral Robertses, Stackhouses, and Williamses had grown numerous enough to found a sort of commune in a rough triangle between present-day Latta, eight miles to the west, and Dillon, seven miles north. This happened no later than 1786, when the Buck Swamp Society, one of twenty-two Methodist communities in the area, began worshiping. Meeting at first in a log house, they moved to three subsequent log structures to accommodate larger congregations. In 1844, they constructed a frame building and consecrated it Mount Andrew Methodist Church, in honor of Bishop James Osgood Andrew.

Samuel III married Sarah Ann Lewis, who bore a son, Harmon Floyd, on September 2, 1797; and with him, Carlisle Floyd's paternal great-great-grandfather, the family history passes from one age of obscurity to another of more tangible darkness.

In South Carolina's agrarian economy, wealth meant land and slaves, and Harmon inherited both. He married Ada Williams in 1820, and their son Charles Pinckney Floyd entered the world on September 28, 1823.[19] A fuller accounting seeps from the slave schedules of the 1850 and 1860 censuses. By the latter date, Harmon and Ada owned five black humans: two males, age fifty and two; and three females, age thirty, twenty-two, and four.

Prosperity is further indicated by Harmon's proprietorship of a general store and post office in Free State beginning around 1859. Ada Williams died in 1850, and Harmon remarried another Ada, surnamed Yelverton.

Harmon turned sixty-four shortly after the outbreak of war in 1861, thus age exempted him from service. There is a Charles P. Floyd on record, without dates of service or rank, in Company B of the First South Carolina Artillery, probably Harmon's thirty-seven-year-old son Charles Pinckney. The unit's original members were among those that ignited the war by firing on Fort Sumter in April 1861, and participated thereafter in the state's coastal defense. In February 1865, the Confederate garrison left Charleston to fight William Tecumseh Sherman's troops in various locations in North and South Carolina, finally surrendering the following April.

Having survived warfare, it was in his store that Harmon was robbed and killed, on March 9, 1865. The incident is mirrored in the death of one of Carlisle Floyd's great operatic heroes, Rucker Lattimore, in *Cold Sassy Tree.*

Though Harmon died intestate, the entire estate passed to his only son, Charles Pinckney, who continued to direct family interests. In 1840 he had made a brilliant marriage into the numerous and prosperous family of Reading Roberts (1784–1873)[20] and Penelope Dawson (1783–1847). Their home stood on the site of the future Mt. Andrew Cemetery, which began as the Roberts family graveyard in 1842. In addition to owning around 1,500 acres, Reading's estate included twenty-seven slaves in 1860: seventeen males and ten females between the ages of forty-four and two. In all, Reading himself estimated that he had acquired or "raised" eighty slaves.

In the quaint words of W. W. Sellers, offensive as they are to contemporary sensibilities, "Old man Reddin Roberts was an excellent, quiet citizen; was wealthy before the war, especially in negro property . . . an exemplary man . . . [who] lived at home and kept out of debt."[21]

Reading's and Penelope's progeny totaled twelve, and Charles Pinckney Floyd's choice fell on the youngest daughter, Zilpha (or Zilphia), born in 1823 in Free State/Bucks Swamp. To the union she brought a dowry of nine hundred acres of adjacent Roberts land, adding to the nucleus of subsequent Floyd property.

The 1860 census slave schedules show Charles owning five slaves separate from his father's: three males, age forty-eight, seventeen, and twelve; and two females, age forty-two and fifteen. According to Marion County records, around 1858–1859 Harmon gave his son three hundred acres of land that Charles fenced, cleared, and cultivated.[22]

Ada and young Charles lost no time in immunizing their property against Harmon's intestacy. On October 19, 1865, she petitioned Marion County Probate Court for letters of administration on the "goods and chattels" of Harmon's estate, valued at five thousand dollars.[23]

In his father's footsteps, Charles managed family business with great competence from the nearby village of Nichols. He and Zilpha produced a brood of their own: Charles P. Jr., killed at age eighteen in 1881 in a fight at Campbell's Bridge;[24] Henry Bascom (1858–1942), another second given name that filtered down through generations; three daughters, Nancy Cornelia, Minerva Attelia, and Roberta; and a final son, Giles Roberts (1863–1915), named for Zilpha's brother, who had died at twenty-seven in 1853.

Like his father, Charles Pinckney Floyd met an untimely end. On June 11, 1869, at the age of forty-five, while driving his buggy across the Marion-Wilmington line tracks between Mullins and Nichols, he was struck and killed by a speeding train.

The ensuing saga of Zilpha Roberts Floyd and her late husband's family demonstrates the era's backcountry politics. Soon after Charles Pinckney's funeral, Harmon's widow, Ada Yelverton, reappeared. Marion County probate records state that Ada, "Though not having no [*sic*] minor children . . . insists that under the constitution of S. C. and the laws of the state she is entitled to the right of Homestead in the lands of late Harmon Floyd." This had originally been bequeathed to her now-departed stepson, and on May 10, 1871, the court "set apart to his widow the petitioner the Homestead embracing the family mansion, outhouses and appurtenances such as she may select not to exceed the value of $1000."[25]

Harmon's house and a portion of his lands thus reverted to Ada, and Zilpha was on her own. She and her children returned to the gaunt paternal frame house in Free State. Sellers relates admiringly, "Mrs. Floyd now lives on the homestead of her father, an excellent lady and capital manager; has raised her children in credit and responsibility."[26]

Zilpha turned to religion, worshiping at Mt. Andrew Methodist. When she moved from Nichols to Bucks Swamp after Charles died, she and her children were thrown into the midst (and to a degree mercy) of a large family that had lived in the region since the settlement of South Carolina began. All were dedicated to the church and hard work and were much like Zilpha in their ardent Christianity. In this period of semi-isolation, the U.S. army of occupation prominently on display, almost everyone used the church as the primary social outlet in their lives. Zilpha became extraordinarily zealous in her devotion and demanded the same of her children. H. B. Floyd vividly recalled his grandfather Henry Bascom Floyd Sr., the eldest surviving son of Charles P. and Zilpha, at frequent prayers, usually on his knees and fervently beseeching the Almighty to forgive him for his many sins, though H. B. saw him as the best man in the county, totally without sin. In later years, he observed the same pattern in his own father, Henry Bascom Floyd Jr. (1898–1963), a contemporary of Carlisle's father.

When Zilpha died in 1903, her children's still-rankling feeling of injustice took tangible form in the marker they erected in Mt. Andrew Cemetery that honored her first as "Ma, Zilpha Roberts" in large letters, followed by much smaller characters identifying her as the "wife of C. P. Floyd." Her remaining lands, adjacent to Mt. Andrew Cemetery, were divided between the children, and, according to the Roberts genealogy, the Free State town was henceforth called Floyd Dale, later Floydale.[27]

Sellers relates that Zilpha and C. P.'s youngest son, Giles Roberts, was a fellow sufferer from asthma, the first record of this genetic bequest to future generations.[28]

FLOYD INTERMARRIAGE into the Sessions line gave the composer both a *soupçon* of French ancestry and a middle name. The surname "Sessions" has roots in an Anglo-Saxon prefix, "sass," then "Sasson" (Saxon), both words referring to a tiller of the soil. In France, the cognate "Soissons" is the name of a community in the Aisne district, about sixty miles north of Paris. The name "Sessions" appeared in England as early as 1181 A.D., via emigration to the British Isles following the Norman Conquest of 1066.[29]

The earliest Sessions in the colonies, Samuel, arrived in Massachusetts in 1630. Robert, the first to make his way to South Carolina, received a warrant for 250 acres of land in 1683; the document stated that he had been there since 1678. The Marion County branch began with Benjamin Jenkins Sessions (c. 1750–1810). From this line came Jeremiah Sessions, whose exact dates remain elusive; but he shows up in the 1850 census in Sumter, South Carolina, at age twenty-eight, hence born around 1822.

The legend that reached Ermine and Carlisle Floyd proposes Jeremiah as a possible musical progenitor: "Jeremiah attended a private school. A doctor and a musician, he was in great demand for all the social events."[30]

Jeremiah married Jane Trezevant Wayne, thus intensifying both French and Revolutionary War ingredients in the Floyd gene pool. Both Trezevant sons, Lorraine ("L. T.," 1842–1930) and Percival Wayne (born c. 1846), volunteered for the Confederate Army. The former joined Company B of the Tenth South Carolina Infantry as a private, and saw combat in Tennessee, at Murfreesboro and Chickamauga. He was captured, thinks the family, at Lookout Mountain (Chattanooga), spent fourteen months in a Union prison at Rock Island, Illinois, and returned to South Carolina just before the end of the war in 1865.[31] L. T.'s long life compassed three marriages, the first to Ellen Elizabeth Smith (1868–1932). Their fifth child, Mercer Ermine (1876–1926), through marriage to Giles Roberts Floyd in 1899, provided Carlisle's sister's given name.

Percival's musical inheritance from Jeremiah permeates his war record as a bugler with three different South Carolina units: Company C of Manigault's Light Artillery Brigade, Company H of the First (Orr's) Rifles, and Gregg's Company of the McQueen Light Artillery.[32] Despite losing a limb (it must have been a leg) in action, he subsequently became a dentist.[33] Percy eventually moved to Hillsborough, Florida, where he was listed as sixty-four in the 1910 census, the last such record to show him alive, meaning that he was gone by the time Carlisle Floyd came into the world, though his exploits were family legend.

THE WAYNES, an old English family from Yorkshire, have a blessedly straightforward genealogy. The first to emigrate to America, Anthony (1666–1739), died in Easttown in Chester County, Pennsylvania. His son Isaac's (1699–1774) children included William (1734–1818), who came to South Carolina and in turn produced Francis Asbury Wayne (1787–1870), whose daughter Jane married Jeremiah Sessions.[34]

Isaac's other son Anthony (1745–1796) also blends into Carlisle Floyd's ancestry. A conspicuously dashing Revolutionary War general, he acquired the sobriquet "Mad Anthony" for impulsive behavior that marked his career with dramatic highs and lows. After the colonials suffered a string of crushing defeats, General Washington ordered Wayne to take a British outpost that was protected by a sheer 200-foot cliff at Stony Point, New York.

Wayne and his men attacked at night with only fixed bayonets and captured more than five hundred British soldiers, inspiring patriots to renewed courage. He served with distinction for the remainder of the war and afterward by subduing the Great Lakes Indian tribes, which British authorities in Canada had incited. In 1794, Wayne led his troops to victory in the Battle of Fallen Timbers, and, a year later, accepted the formal surrender of all British-held forts in the region.

At family gatherings, one of Carlisle's many uncles invariably palpated the boy's head, exulting when he found "that Wayne spot." If Floyd ever wanted role models for independence, he needed look no further than Mad Anthony and our next subjects, the Huguenots.

THE TREZEVANTS first snuck into the Floyd line via the Waynes, then the Sessionses. In 1777, William Wayne married Esther Trezevant (b. 1761); but their story requires a digression into the Huguenots' violent history.

French Protestantism began (and almost ended) with the theologian John Calvin (1509–1564), born Jean

Cauvin in Picardy. He established congregations in Switzerland after fleeing France in 1534, and thereafter directed aspects of the French Reformation, such as it was, from safety in Basel, and later Geneva.

Theories of the etymology of the word *Huguenot* abound. The leader of the Confederate Party in Geneva was Besançon Hugues, and some believe that his surname, conflated with the Frankish/German word *eidgenot/eidgenosse* ("confederate"), yields *Huguenot.* Another camp finds the term's origins in France's Flemish region, where groups gathering for secret Bible study were called *Huis Genooten* (housemates); and so on.

After decades of more or less methodical slaughter of French Protestants, hope appeared in the guise of Henry of Navarre, born Huguenot but converted to Catholicism before marrying Marguerite de Valois in 1572. This last-minute switch spared him from the St. Bartholomew Massacre of thousands of Huguenots who had descended on Paris for the wedding festivities on the night of August 23–24, 1572. (The historical event became the subject of one of the nineteenth century's most successful grand operas, Giacomo Meyerbeer's *Les Huguenots,* in 1836.)[35]

The 1598 Edict of Nantes allowed limited Protestant worship in a few specific locations; but Louis XIV abolished this minimal show of tolerance in 1685. Emigration of as many as 161,000 Huguenots to Great Britain and Holland began much earlier,[36] but English authorities were themselves not overly fond of large foreign populations and quickly encouraged their French guests to colonize the New World, especially New York, Massachusetts, and South Carolina. The latter state's Fundamental Constitutions of 1669 guaranteed religious tolerance, and rumors of plantation fortunes to be made circulated widely and wildly.

Most records of the Huguenot diaspora that followed have been lost, but historians estimate that around 1,500 had arrived by 1700, many at present-day Charleston beginning in 1679. Most settled there as a minority nucleus, but a few ventured inland. As the English themselves had experienced, inflation in Charleston guaranteed bare subsistence levels of existence for immigrants; and the warm, humid climate spawned epidemics of malaria, yellow fever, and smallpox. A privately printed tract from around 1685 attempted to dispel prospective settlers' illusions, calling South Carolina the New World's "least agreeable colony. . . . Rains cover the country and drown the cattle. The artificial aristocracy of Landgraves, Cassiques,[37] Cantons, Manors and Baronies make a great show in an empty brain."[38]

Despite the establishment of a few great Huguenot families, like the Manigaults and Horrys—the latter family the inspiration for the Horry District that became part of Marion County—such conditions encouraged these immigrants to move to outlying parts of the colony, like Craven County—the ancestor of Marion and Dillon Counties—along the Santee River.

A thriving Huguenot Society of South Carolina, established in Charleston in 1885, counts more than two thousand members descended from these original settlers. Many Huguenots had specialized as silversmiths and textile manufacturers, with a special focus on the cultivation of silkworms and silk weaving. One of the earlier arrivals, in 1685, was the silversmith Daniel Trezevant (c. 1660–1726), who came with his wife, Suzanne Maulard, daughter Susanna, and son Daniel Jr. Another son, Isaac, born in South Carolina in the 1690s, produced another Daniel (1726–1768), who married Elizabeth Miller in 1753. Their daughter Esther, born in 1761, became the bride of William Wayne in 1777, and the mother of Francis Asbury Wayne in 1789, hence the grandmother of Jane Trezevant Wayne, who crossed the threshold of Carlisle Floyd's paternal ancestry by marrying Jeremiah Sessions.

TRACING THE FLOYD FAMILY GENEALOGY involves a bewildering proliferation of collateral intermarriages in the compactness of Marion/Dillon County. With the maternal line of Fenegan, we encounter the opposite problem of having far less evidence, most information based on family testimony 160-odd years after the fact.

The orthographical variety of the name "Fenegan" is as bizarre as the name "Floyd." Most bearers of these names settled in New York, Pennsylvania, Massachusetts, and Ohio: Faingan, Fanigan, Fannigan, Fannegan, Fenigan, Fenighan, Fennigan, Finegan, Finagin,

Finegin, Finnigen, Finigan, Finngan, Finnegan (the most common), Finnigan, Finnagen, Finnagin, and others. In U.S. censuses, reflecting either a dearth of spelling skills, vagaries of southern accent, or perhaps inebriated census takers in decades past, we even find the isolated Fankan, Fanucam, or, in the case of Carlisle Floyd's maternal great-grandfather, Famgan.[39]

Notwithstanding, the root name is eerily almost synonymous with Floyd: from the Gaelic "O Fionnagáin," "from the line of Fionnagáin," there is a double diminutive of "Fionn," meaning white- or fair-haired.

According to Floyd and Fenegan family sources, the Fenegans came from Ireland's County Cork. On a roll of taxpayers in 1683 and 1685 for County Monaghan—about as far from Cork as one can go and still be in the Republic—we find Finegans, O'Fenigans, and a single O'Fenegan. Four Fenegans, all Irish-born, turn up in 1841 censuses of Lancashire, a county in northwest England on the Irish Sea.

Today's Floyds propose James Fenegan as the first arrival in this country sometime between 1842 and 1846. Ancestry.com immigration records for northeastern as well as southern ports offer numerous candidates; but a James Finnigan, born c. 1819, arrived in New York from Liverpool on the *Columbus* on April 22, 1842, and this is most likely our man.

Although the Irish potato famine, "the Great Hunger," peaked between 1845 and 1847, trouble was already brewing in 1842. Housing and employment shortfalls, bankruptcies, famine, and inequities in landlord-tenant land management all culminated in *An Drochshaol,* "the bad life." Between 1760 and 1815, the potato became a staple rather than supplementary food, and twenty-four failures of that crop occurred between 1728 and 1851. By 1841, the Emerald Isle's population had swollen to more than eight million, of whom two-thirds depended on agriculture for a living; and that year saw a catastrophic potato crop failure, the blight *Phytophthora infestans* wasting an already diseased stock. By 1851, more than two million Irish had either died or emigrated, many in great waves to the United States.

By 1850, we find our candidate as James Fenaghan in Marion, South Carolina, age thirty, hence born around 1820. Additional information below suggests that the record of his true age is an example of one of the many instances when census takers found no one at home and gathered information from neighbors: James's birthplace is listed as Holland, almost certainly a southern drawling of the word "Ireland."

James worked fast. Years before settling in Marion, he married Eliza Douglas, age twenty-six in 1850, in North Carolina;[40] and this southward drift adds weight to New York as his port of entry in 1842, rather than New Orleans or Charleston. For the 1850 census, they listed three small children, Mary (five), Patrick (three), and Joseph (one). Such fecundity is challenging, even with the proposed 1842 arrival, and unthinkable for the two James Finegans who emigrated in 1845.

In 1860, the family still lived in Marion; they had one new child, Anna, age six. Here James's age was given as about forty, which keeps his birth around the year 1820. Records assembled by Carlisle Floyd's aunt Lucile Fenegan, however, based on tombstones in New Holly Cemetery in Dillon County, lists James K. Fenegan (no one living knows what the initial represented), born on March 15, 1813, and his wife, Eliza Douglas, born November 4, 1822. The 1860 census lists six children, curiously omitting their son Michael, born in 1853.

THAT LARGE NUMBERS of recently arrived Irish served in the Confederate army tells a tale both fascinating and heartbreaking. The majority of these immigrants were tenant farmers who could not wait to get back to the land. Like the Huguenots before them, their heads spun with dreams of riches to be made from cotton and later tobacco, and the freedom to practice their chosen religion, whether Catholic or Protestant. America's agricultural south, which felt victimized by the industrial north, offered the newly arrived Irish, who were inherently suspicious of central governments, a striking parallel to the oppression of their Irish homeland by the British north. This in turn provoked ambivalence among the immigrant Irish about slavery. The concept of master and slave tore the scab from the sense of inferiority they had left behind; but the poorest chafed to see many slaves working and living under conditions superior to their own. Southern demagogues encouraged the perception that free blacks would mean stiffer competition for any available work.

That the Irish made splendid fighting machines no one questioned: "At least 40,000 men—an astonishing 90 percent of the able-bodied Irish population in the South—fought for the Confederacy . . . despite the fact that no one compelled them. . . . As non-citizens were exempt from military service, Irish immigrants could have elected not to serve."[41]

In Charleston, the Irish Volunteers formed the bulk of South Carolina's First Infantry, the state's first company to enlist for the war. In other units, conspicuous Irish bravery made them perfect color guards, skirmishers, and sharpshooters, which explained their consistent heavy casualties.

When war broke out in 1861, James Fenegan at age forty-eight (accepting 1813 as his correct birth year; or age forty-one, if 1820 is correct) volunteered as a private and was later promoted to corporal in Company I of South Carolina's Eighth Infantry, also known as "Kershaw's Brigade"[42] and "Conner's Brigade." The roll of names included many Irish, among them Carmichael, Collins, McClenaghan, and Murphy. The company commander for most of the war was the Irish American Colonel John W. Henaghan, until his capture near Winchester, Virginia, in the fall of 1864, when command passed to Lt. Col. Eli Thomas Stackhouse, another of Carlisle Floyd's distant relatives.

James Fenegan's company, traded between the army of Northern Virginia and the army of Tennessee until the war's end, saw action in at least thirty battles. W. W. Sellers tells us that James sustained wounds at Maryland Heights, above Harper's Ferry, West Virginia.[43] The Eighth saw much of the most brutal slaughter of the war: First Manassas, Sharpsburg, Fredericksburg, Chancellorsville, Gettysburg, Chickamauga, The Wilderness, Spotsylvania, Cold Harbor, and Petersburg.

The unit last fought at Bentonville, North Carolina, in the final clash of the armies remaining to Confederate General Joseph E. Johnston and the Union's William Tecumseh Sherman. Fenegan's comrades, of whom only 52 percent were still alive or able by this time, stacked their arms in surrender in Greensboro, and received paroles on April 26, 1865.

James and Eliza's youngest son, Michael James, born on April 9, 1853, duly appears in the 1870 census at age seventeen as part of the "Finnigan" household in Bethea, Marion County. New to the group is Benjamin (nineteen). Joseph seems to have gone missing or died.

After the war, James and family moved to Free State, where, like the Floyds, they farmed, but on a far more modest scale. There is no indication that the two families knew each other at this point. Had they shared a denomination, they might have, but James and his heirs worshipped at Catfish Creek Baptist near Latta, where Michael and Eliza are buried, and the Floyds adhered to Methodism. Baptist congregations existed in Ireland since about 1650 in Dublin, Waterford, and Cork, supervised by the English Baptist Union; and that, plus the dominance of Roman Catholicism, likely influenced James's decision to emigrate.

At family gatherings, James regaled children, grandchildren, and neighbors with tales of how he had single-handedly captured fourteen Yankee soldiers in one action, almost certainly one of the earlier battles like Fredericksburg, when the war was still going well for the Confederacy. Someone always asked, "How'd you do that?" James replied, "Well, sir, I just . . . surrounded them."

When Carlisle Floyd wrote his libretto for *Cold Sassy Tree,* he borrowed another family tale about James for his character Rucker: "James went up to this man he saw every week in church, who had shaved off his beard, and said, 'Oh, you look so much better since you stopped favoring yourself.'"[44]

Like his father, Michael farmed. He married Mary Ann George, born in June 1852, the daughter of John J. George (1825–1868) and Agenora Jackson (1834–1899). Michael inherited his father's lively character and wit, and lived until July 1, 1910, after augmenting, with Mary Ann, the world's Fenegans by six.

The second of these was Oscar James, born January 1, 1877, destined also for farm life. The 1880 census renders the surname "Fennigan" living in Bethea, where they still were in 1900, only now listed as "Famgan," with several more children. Oscar, by now twenty-three, still lived at home; but this changed on December 23, 1903, when he married Katherine Sinclair Cottingham, born in 1881.

"Miss Kate's" family, one of the county's most populous and well-to-do, had been around for a great while. Their arrival in North America went all the way back to George Cottingham (1615–1695), born in Yorkshire, England, before emigrating to Virginia. A Jonathan (1714–1785) made the move to South Carolina, and the family quickly embraced slaveholding as an adjunct to farming, and acquired land in both Carolinas. As we have seen, from South Carolina's beginnings, the application of necronyms—names honoring deceased ancestors or siblings—gave colonists a means of tightening family bonds, and Sinclairs and collateral Legettes ran a close second to Betheas and Cottinghams in turning up in most everyone's family tree in Marion/Dillon County.

Oscar Fenegan's in-laws, Daniel Sinclair Cottingham (1847–1907) and Ida Legette Bennett (1856–1938), expressed pointed displeasure over the family's new member: poor, Irish, a farmer *and* Baptist to boot. (Katherine brought land into the dowry bargain.) But even if their son-in-law attended services at Catfish Baptist—by himself—the Cottinghams knew that Kate would raise her children Methodist.

Oscar and Kate produced three daughters: Ida, born on March 10, 1905, and named for her Grandma Ida Legette Bennett; Lucile, in 1907; Mary Kate, "Bunny," in 1910; and a son, Oscar James Jr., in 1911.

To see Kate through her first pregnancy, Oscar left the farm with tenants and moved to Latta. Along came Grandma Ida, widowed since 1907, and already suffering from dementia. She frequently imagined chickens running loose in the house, and Oscar, another wit and practical joker, humored his mother-in-law by getting down on all fours and "shooing them off."

Young Ida had a nervous, fretful nature. As her granddaughter Jane Matheny saw, "Love meant having someone or something to worry over."

Oscar loved words and music. Besides writing reams of light verse, he played harmonica, danced,

44. Fenegan Family, c. 1907: Katherine Cottingham Fenegan, Ida, Oscar J. Fenegan. Courtesy of Carlisle Floyd.

and sang at family gatherings. The Fenegans kept a musical house: around the piano, played by Ida, the youngest, James, sang bass; and Oscar, a natural low voice, somehow managed to hoist himself up to tenor register for impromptu harmonizing.

IN 1899, GILES ROBERTS FLOYD married Ermine Mercer Sessions (1876–1926). Their first child, Judy, born in 1901, died in infancy of typhoid fever or diphtheria; but Giles proceeded to father, at thoughtful intervals, Giles Roberts Jr. (1902–1999), Carlisle Sessions (1904–1988), Doris Weatherly (1906–1981), Hazel Harriett (1909–1975), and Bascom Lorraine (1913–1999).

This Carlisle, despite inheriting the family asthma gene, showed great and early athletic ability, especially in running and baseball. The Floyd farm's African American foreman, Baker Campbell, shook his head and laughed, "Quick as a jackrabbit," and the name stuck. Only when prey to grandiosity in his ministerial years did he ever use his given name, "Carlisle." On formal occasions, he was "the Reverend C. S. Floyd," but to family and friends he was never anything but "Jack."

Baker Campbell's wife, Laura, was Jack's mammy. His mother, Ermine, homeschooled him at the farm for his first eight years. He later thought he'd been "a mean boy,"[45] and reported frequent dreams in which he strove to make his mama proud.

Around 1909, Giles Sr., approached forty. Taxed by asthma, prosperous enough to live off the farm's income, but eleven years the senior of a wife expecting their fourth child, he entrusted Baker with the tobacco operation in Floydale and commissioned the building of a spacious plantation-style house at 309 North Marion Street in Latta. Construction ended sometime in 1910 and, like Oscar Fenegan, the Floyds moved to town from the country, enhancing the children's educational opportunities. A neighbor child, winsome Ida Fenegan, never stopped talking about when the Floyds moved in to Latta.

"Ermine the First's" home teaching in Floydale bore fruit; Jack was accepted into the Latta school as a third-grader. He began a more structured, formal religious education, which eventually expanded to teaching Sunday school classes at the Methodist church across from their house.

Giles Roberts Sr. departed the world in March 1915, six months shy of his fiftieth birthday, leaving wife Ermine to care for five children between the ages of thirteen and two. His stone in Mt. Andrew Cemetery is engraved, "An honest man is the noblest work of God."

Mama Ermine is reputed to have been the most popular woman in town. Possessing the gift of persuasion, she began selling subscriptions to the *Dillon Herald*. She would head out to the country, make a sale at one farmhouse, and then ask, "Now who lives next door?" Presenting herself to the neighbors and calling the respondent by name usually earned her another subscriber. The *Herald* rewarded her success with a new Buick sedan.

As the genetic dice fell, the transplanted Welsh and English Floyds displayed hardly a note of the bardic strain; but the Irish specialized in bards, and Oscar Fenegan was one, of a kind. And he lived just a few doors up Marion Street from the Floyds on the corner, with a houseful of women, including pretty, delicate, musical Ida, like her sisters also a gifted seamstress and cook. When Jack Floyd played or walked to school, it was usually with Ida. He was her elder by almost a year, but in the same grade.

She was the only girl he ever really loved. Cousin Marjorie Manning recalled, "Ida was just lovely, good, neat as a pin. A friend said that Ida could do more with a scarf than she could do with five hundred dollars!"[46]

On her rambles, Ida saw eccentric "Mr. Giles," Jack's father, sitting on the broad front porch, never doing anything resembling work. He let his hair grow to shoulder-length, believing it an asthma palliative.

At Latta High, Jack succeeded as a pitcher and captain of the baseball team. By the end of senior year, he and Ida were cosalutatorians; he gave the speech, she preferred not to.

Floyd/Manning "brother-cousins," as they were called, traditionally attended Wofford College in Spartanburg. Jack's elder brother, G. R., spent a year there in 1920, but the administration suspended him for a "year of silence" to reflect and mend his ways after he was caught playing cards. G. R.'s characterization in Wofford's yearbook claims that he "took his fun where he found it."[47]

Athletics and academics put Jack in line for a scholarship, and he began at Wofford in 1923, one of 446 students enrolled that year. At that point in the school's history, undergraduates declared no majors. In 1923–1924, Jack fulfilled basic curriculum requirements, weighted to religious content, enough to gain him a license to preach as a first-level ministerial candidate in Methodism, but he did not yet exercise the option. Although he never served in the military, Jack joined the Reserve Officers Training Corps (ROTC), and later recorded his entrance physical height as five feet ten and a half inches.[48]

He stayed for 1923–1924, and part of the next, while Ida entered Coker College in Hartsville. She studied piano with Anne M. Bonnett, who had attended the New England Conservatory and thought highly enough of her pupil to suggest taking her to study in

Paris. But Ida's schooling ended with a family economic crisis in 1924.

The particulars of Oscar Fenegan's financial catastrophe, while the stuff of family legend, have been lost to his descendants. A poet at heart, upstanding and ethical to the core, he had no head for figures; Kate was the shrewd businessperson. While Ida studied at Coker, Oscar raided the trunk in which his wife kept their money and invested in one or more schemes that were in fact too good to be true. When Kate visited the trunk for tuition money, it was gone, along with Ida's college career.

Oscar took a job at the local hardware store for a few weeks, but found either the work or his colleagues uncongenial. Samuel J. Bethea, an officer at Farmers and Merchants Bank and a cousin of Jack Floyd's, offered to write Oscar a personal check to keep his farm from foreclosure until other funds materialized, but Oscar felt that he ought to sell the Floydale property.

Meanwhile, lovesickness prompted Jack to abridge his own education and move back to Latta to become a teller at Farmers and Merchants Bank and to supervise the farm's tobacco production. Just nineteen, he and Ida decided to marry at the Methodist church, and Jack's mother bought them a small white frame bungalow up Marion Street.

The union was almost prevented, however, thanks to Jack's jealousy of other attentions to Ida, real or imagined. Jack confided to his diary that on their wedding day, November 18, 1924, in the presence of the Reverend Mr. Wiggins, "I lived over [that is, "relived"] my courting Ida, almost lost her, and started not to take marriage vows after I saw that she was looking out the window and crying, but she must have wanted me, for she said, 'Say that' [their vows], and I went ahead and repeated them after Mr. Wiggins and I am so glad I did."[49]

The couple spent their wedding night at the Arcade Hotel in Hartsville, and honeymooned in Columbia.[50] Back in their new love nest in Latta, they set about making their own additions to the family tree.

Notes

1. The Cradle: Latta, 1926–1932

1. This and all other unattributed quotes throughout *Falling Up* are drawn from subject interviews between 2002 and 2011.

2. Ida Floyd, *Baby's Record* (1926), 1. Courtesy of Carlisle Floyd.

3. Ibid.

4. Richard Grassby, *Business Community of Seventeenth-Century England* (Cambridge: Cambridge University Press, 1995), 329.

5. Lorraine Trezevant Sessions Jr. (1874–1953).

6. Percival Wayne Sessions Jr. (1879–1954).

7. Abram Stern, *Asthma and Emotion* (New York: Gardner Press, 1981), 10–12.

8. The Cable Company of Chicago, known for progressive technology, was one of the largest piano manufacturing enterprises of its day. In 1880–1881, Cable began producing its Kingsbury line, distinguished for size, durable construction, rich tone, and elegance as both a decorative and functional object.

9. Presser was known for its graded books of repertoire for young pianists, with items like Marie Crosby's *Young Folks at Play* (1909), or Rob Roy Peery's *Tales from Mother Goose, Chapel Echoes: An Album of Sacred and Meditative Music for Pianists Young and Old,* and *First Grade Course for Young Pianists Based on the Music of the Church,* which would have appealed to both elder Floyds.

10. World War I Selective Service System Draft Registration Cards, 1917–1918. National Archives, Washington, DC; and Records Administration, M1509, Roll 1877590, Dillon County, South Carolina.

11. Though Freddie claimed her birthday was December 24, 1908, the Social Security Death Index shows the date as August 7, 1899. She and G.R. married around 1930.

12. Addams (1860–1935) founded the organization in 1889, the first settlement house in the United States to offer various community services, including continuing education, to Chicago's immigrant population. In 1931, Addams became the first woman to receive the Nobel Peace Prize.

13. South Carolina: Race and Hispanic Origin, 1790 to 1990 (Washington, DC: U.S. Census Bureau, 1990).

14. South Carolina Death Index, 1915–1949 (South Carolina Division of Vital Records, Office of Public Health Statistics and Information Services, South Carolina Department of Health and Environmental Control, Columbia, South Carolina).

15. 1920 United States Federal Census, Roll T625_1693, P. 7B, Enumeration District 32, Image 398, Manning, Dillon, South Carolina.

16. Between 1921 and 1929, 5,712 banks across America failed, 79 percent in towns of less than 2,500. Prior to 1933, federal bank deposit insurance was only a dream. In South Carolina, agricultural land values increased over 100 percent between 1912 and 1920, owing to the projection of agricultural futures. The downside of this post—World War I optimism, certainly for banks, was a dramatic rise in farm mortgages to produce extra cash for farmers. Illusory prosperity drifted into reality's cold embrace with soaring real estate taxes and deteriorating wholesale prices. Many farmers used their cash to buy and plant more acreage, flooding the market with crops, driving prices down. See Lee J. Alston, Wayne Grove, and David C. Wheelock, *Structural Causes of Rural Bank Failures in the Twenties: Parallels with the Eighties,* Cliometric Society ASSA Session, August 1990 (http://cliometrics.org/conferences/ASSA/Dec_90/Alston-Grove-Wheelock.shtml). See also W. H. Steiner, "South Carolina Cash Depositories," *Southern Economic Journal* 4, no. 1 (1937): 28–37.

17. Depression studies at North Carolina State University: www.ncsu.edu/ligon/am/ag/depression.htm.

18. Durward T. Stokes, *The History of Dillon County, South Carolina* (Columbia: University of South Carolina Press, 1978), 187.

19. W. H. Ellerbe served as South Carolina's governor from 1897 to 1899. Between 1919 and 1924, Frank Ellerbe played third base for the Washington Senators, St. Louis Browns, and Cleveland Indians.

20. *Baby's Record,* 4.

2. Where's Daddy?: Spartanburg, McClellanville, Jordan, 1932–1936

1. Data from Steve Tuttle, South Carolina Department of History and Archives, E-mail to author, June 21, 2007.

2. Author interview, December 27, 2007.

3. Information on structure, organization, and governance of the Methodist Church is available at www.umc.org. The denomination's *Book of Discipline, 1999* is available online at: www.freemethodistchurch.org.

4. Author interview, January 17, 2007.

5. A situation reflected in Carlisle Floyd's semifictional expositions of parsonage life, "The 'Pounding,'" *The Concept* 43, no. 4 (1944): 24–25, 37–38; and "The Woman and the Romans" (unpublished ms., 1945). Copies of both stories in Box 1, Folder 19, Floyd Archive, South Caroliniana Library, University of South Carolina, Columbia (hereafter FASCL).

6. James Mitchell Graham, born 1926, died 1972 at age forty-six. A member of the Charleston County Council from 1955 to 1972, he served as its chairman for twelve years; and as a founder, officer, and director of the South Carolina Association of Counties from 1967 until his death.

7. Carlisle Floyd, "A Lengthening Shadow," unpublished prose fiction, undated ms. (c. 1946), Box 1, Folder 19, FASCL, and Box 5, Folder 2, FALOC.

8. "The Woman and the Romans."

9. Oscar Fenegan letter, Box 1, Folder 2, FASCL.

10. Carlisle Floyd, *Willie Stark* vocal score, act 1, scene 1 (New York: Boosey & Hawkes, 1980), 76.

11. Carlisle Sessions Floyd Sr. (Reverend C. S. Floyd, "Jack"), August 5, 1964, *Diaries,* 40 vols., 1938–1986, FASCL (hereafter *Diary*).

12. Speech titled "Democracy and Education," September 30, 1896, to the Institute of Arts and Sciences in Brooklyn, New York, later expanded and published in *The Future of the American Negro* (Boston: Small, Maynard, 1899). Washington used the actual line as a tautology, to puncture many of the so-called racial studies: "It has been proven that education unfits the Negro for work, and that education makes him more valuable as a labourer." The speech is given in full at: http://www.edchange.org/multicultural/speeches/booker_t_democracy.htm (accessed July 24, 2012).

13. Mark Twain, "Punch, Brothers, Punch!" in *Punch, Brothers, Punch! and Other Stories* (New York: Slote Woodman, 1878).

14. Incredibly, Sue Richburg, born in 1899, lived until 1997. She too is buried in Jordan's Methodist cemetery.

15. Ermine replied to a question about this, "Not until *Susannah.*"

16. Lorri Glover, *All Our Relations: Blood Ties and Emotional Bonds among the Early South Carolina Gentry* (Baltimore: Johns Hopkins University Press, 2000), 26.

17. *Diary,* June 5, 1975.

3. Golden Days: Bethune, 1936–1939

1. Named for Joseph Kershaw (1727–1791), an ancestor of Civil War General Joseph B. Kershaw, under whom James Fenegan served. See appendix.

2. Tuttle E-mail to author, June 21, 2007.

3. Founded in Alexandria, Virginia, in 1896, the organization spread quickly throughout the South.

4. Written by Walter C. Kittredge (1834–1905), a Yankee and, incidentally, a professional singer from New Hampshire who, when drafted in 1863, wrote the song to express nostalgia at leaving his wife. The song became enormously popular, apparently to soldiers in both blue and gray.

5. Cecelia King interview with author, November 15, 2006. Miss King passed away in 2010.

6. Howard Woody and Davie Beard, *South Carolina Postcards,* vol. 7, *Kershaw County* (Charleston: Arcadia, 2004), 80.

7. Carlisle Floyd, *Cold Sassy Tree* vocal score (New York: Boosey & Hawkes, 2000), act 1, scene 2, 8.

8. Ibid., 167. Coconut cake figures as a special enticement in *Cold Sassy Tree,* act 2, scene 1, when town busybody Effie Belle Tate tries to use the delicacy to shoehorn her way into the Lattimore house at a sensitive moment.

9. For his story "A Lengthening Shadow," Floyd invented the proverb, "Sandspurs ain't scared of a person with a diplomer anymore'n one without one."

10. Floyd's short fiction "Low-Country Town" addresses his father's position in places like Bethune and North. Copy in Box 1, Folder 19, FASCL.

11. Carlisle Floyd interview with author, December 27, 2007.

12. This is the central device of Floyd's fictional account, "The 'Pounding,'" written at Converse College.

13. *Diary,* June 29, 1938.

14. 1850 slave census.

15. *Diary,* November 28, 1938.

16. *Diary,* December 2, 1938.

17. Music by Nacio Herb Brown, from the 1929 film *The Broadway Melody.*

18. Stern, *Asthma and Emotion,* 4–9: "Asthma is a complicated illness which is related to the functioning of the central nervous system and to immunological disorders. It has also become increasingly apparent that asthma is affected . . . by emotional and psychological factors." Stern cites a study conducted by the allergist Aaron Lask, *Asthma: Attitude and Milieu* (Philadelphia: Lippincott, 1966), which asserts, "We found that severely ill asthmatics who do not respond to routine treatment *usually have grave emotional illness, sometimes but not always, at the conscious level.* . . . What is clear, is that successful resolution of the emotional difficulties leads to the virtual disappearance of asthma, and failure to resolve the problem is associated with the persistence of the asthma."

19. Woody and Beard, *Kershaw County,* 81–82.

20. Booth Tarkington, *Penrod* (New York: Penguin, 2007), 179. This would be one of Carlisle's favorite books during his teen years.

21. Bert F. Huennekens, "Headwork," in *The Open Road for Boys* (Boston: Open Road, 1935).

22. Sherman (1898–1987) amassed a daunting catalogue: in addition to sports novels, he wrote a long sequence of self-help books on everything from *Your Key to Happiness* (1935), to *You Live After Death* (1949), to *You Can Stop Drinking* (1950). Late in life, Sherman discovered interests in psychic phenomena, demonic possession, and extraterrestrials.

23. At Syracuse University, 1945–1946. Today's online True-Light Ministries are of course not identical to their *Slow Dusk* counterparts, but a philosophical relationship is evident. See www.ourchurch.com/member/t/TrueLight/.

24. Carlisle Floyd, *Susannah* vocal score (New York: Boosey & Hawkes, 1967), 75.

25. Ibid., 85.

26. Barrymore Laurence Scherer, "Southern Revival," *Opera News*, April 18, 1999, 16–21.

27. Whitcomb (1906–1988) specialized in drawing detailed, idealized men and women in love, to grace the covers and pages of *Cosmopolitan, Good Housekeeping, Collier's, McCall's,* and later *Playboy.*

28. *Diary*, January 17, 1938.

29. *Lum and Abner* aired from 1931 to 1955, in 5,800 daily quarter-hour episodes.

30. The series *Amos and Andy* began airing in 1928, also in fifteen-minute weekday installments. With different actors, it became a successful television program from 1951 to 1953. In the face of mounting criticism of its racial stereotypes by the NAACP and other leaders in the civil rights movement, the radio series ended in 1960.

31. *A Song for Clotilde* aired on February 19, 1939.

32. Book by Clara Louise Burnham (1856–1927), with music by her father, George F. Root (1825–1895). Root was best known for his patriotic Civil War songs, including *The Battle Cry of Freedom,* and Burnham wrote the 1903 best-seller *Jewel.* She provided many texts for her father's songs and dramatic cantatas, like *Snow White* (1888, 1916), and four Christmas shows about Santa Claus. Clara Louise Burnham and George F. Root, *Snow White and the Seven Dwarfs* (Philadelphia: John Church, 1916).

33. Burnham/Root op.cit, 23–24.

34. *Diary*, May 20, 1938.

35. Made with otherwise toxic stramonium leaves; i.e., stinkweed/jimson weed and belladonna.

36. *Social Security Death Index.* National Archives and Records Administration, United States World War II Army Enlistment Records, 1938–1946, Record Group 64, College Park, Maryland.

37. Author interview, September 30, 2006.

38. A character devised by humorist Robert Quillen (1887–1948).

39. Floyd, *Susannah*, 84.

40. Oscar Fenegan poem, Box 1, Folder 2, FASCL.

4. Dark Adolescence: North, 1939–1943

1. *Diary*, November 11, 1939.

2. In 1939, simply North Methodist Church. Methodism's consolidation, of which Reverend Floyd was a lifelong proponent, took until April 1968.

3. "Which Shall Not Perish from the Earth," Box 1, FASCL.

4. Kent Kimes, "Composer Gave Early Hints of Creative Bent," *The Augusta Chronicle,* May 1, 1998, Applause, 4. Floyd appeared in Augusta for a production of *Susannah,* and Mrs. Morgan, living across the river in North Augusta, South Carolina, shared her memories of the now-famous composer. She did, however, misplace him as a seventh-grader.

5. *Diary*, July 9, 1943.

6. *Diary*, February 12, 1940.

7. Shortly after this tour, Iturbi (1895–1980) became a Hollywood fixture, playing himself in movie musicals.

8. Theodosia Paynter and G. A. Grant-Schaefer, *The Adventures of Pinocchio* (Wichita: R. A. Hoffman, 1935).

9. Edward Bliss Jr., ed., *In Search of Light: The Broadcasts of Edward R. Murrow, 1938–1961* (New York: Alfred A. Knopf, 1967), 43–44.

10. *Kings Row* became a Hollywood motion picture in 1942, with an evocative score by Erich Wolfgang Korngold, and featuring future president Ronald Reagan in one of his most acclaimed roles.

11. The piece is a programmatic musical depiction of Robert Burns's 1791 poem of the same name, about a hair-raising horseback ride on the prototypical Gaelic dark and stormy night, the protagonist threatened by witches and warlocks. The most likely piano version available at the time was George William Warren's (c. 1855).

12. *Diary*, May 16, 1941.

13. Richards (1901–2001), who taught at Columbia College for many years, seems to have been one of those pianists gifted foremost as a pedagogue, without an extensive performing career of her own. She died in Camden, South Carolina, at the age of one hundred, in 2001.

14. Anne Coulter Martens, *Don't Darken My Door!* (Chicago: The Dramatic Publishing Company, 1936). Martens ran something of a cottage industry in stage adaptations from other media, like James Hilton's *Lost Horizon*, Betty McDonald's *The Egg and I*, L. Frank Baum's *The Wizard of Oz*, and Lewis Carroll's *Alice in Wonderland.*

15. *Diary*, April 9, 1942.

16. *Diary*, May 1, 1942.

17. *Diary*, October 3, 1942.

18. Author interview, September 30, 2006.

19. The pen name of Mary Ann, or Marian, Evans (1819–1880), who believed that a masculine name would win her writings greater respect.

20. *Diary*, January 9, 1943.

21. *Diary*, March 5, 1943.

22. *Diary*, June 2, 1943.

23. Author interview with Helen Harris, December 27, 2007.

24. Ibid.

25. The source of Elder Gleaton's name in *Susannah.*

5. Escape: Converse College, Spartanburg, 1943–1945

1. These Carlisles were direct descendants of *the* James Carlisle, Civil War hero and president of Wofford College, for whom both Carlisle Floyds were named.

2. Today named the Carroll McDaniel Petrie School of Music.

3. Floyd mentioned the Schillinger system in later correspondence with Bacon. Ukrainian-born Joseph Schillinger (1895–1943) devised a method of composition based on mathematics, with emotional connotations in its application to movie scores. Besides Gerschefski, Schillinger pupils included Glenn Miller—whose orchestration of a theory exercise for his teacher became *Moonlight Serenade*—Benny Goodman, Oscar Levant, Tommy Dorsey, and film composer John Barry. Improbable as it seems, Schillinger's most famous pupil, George Gershwin, composed *Porgy and Bess,* particularly its orchestration, under Schillinger's influence.

4. Following his time at Converse, the pianist-composer Nowak (1911–1995) taught at Syracuse University from 1946 to 1948. His compositions include a Concertino for Piano and Small Orchestra (1944), as well as numerous chamber music works, piano pieces, songs, and modern dance scores.

5. *The Monist,* October 1917; reprinted in Ernst Bacon, *Words on Music* (Syracuse: Syracuse University Press, 1960), 78.

6. The Ernst Bacon Society: www.ernstbacon.org, 1.

7. *New York Times,* May 24, 1942; and *Time,* May 11, 1942. When *Tree* had its New York premiere at Columbia University the next year, critic Olin Downes (*New York Times,* May 6, 1943) was less complimentary, though much impressed with the acting of Douglas Moore, then head of Columbia's Department of Music, and later composer of *The Ballad of Baby Doe. Tree* was performed at least twice more in the 1940s, at the University of Denver in the summer of 1944 and at Syracuse University in May 1947, on both occasions under Bacon's supervision.

8. Bacon's first marriage to Mary Prentice Lillie (or Lilly) lasted from 1927 to 1937. Analee Camp and Bacon married in 1937, and she began teaching as guest artist at Converse in 1939. Her teachers included Emanuel Feuermann and Hans Kindler in cello, and Domenico Brescia in composition.

9. *Diary,* September 15, 1943.

10. Ernst Bacon, *Notes on the Piano* (Seattle: University of Washington Press, 1981), 1.

11. Ibid., 38.

12. Ibid., 76–77.

13. Author interview, May 12, 2007. Bialosky studied with Bacon at Converse (1942–1946) and Syracuse (1946–1949), narrowly missing Floyd at both schools. Bialosky has had a long creative and administrative career. Most of his Bacon-influenced catalogue is represented by the Sanjo Music Company of Palos Verdes Peninsula, California.

14. Bacon, *Notes on the Piano,* 79.

15. Ibid., 80.

16. Floyd later told composer Ellen Taaffe Zwilich that he admired Tchaikovsky's natural melodic gift more than the rigorously developed aesthetic of Brahms, but that he no longer cared to *hear* Tchaikovsky as much as Brahms.

17. Many years later, after winning fame with *Susannah,* Floyd received an unexpected call from Douglas, then in Atlanta, with a brainstorm: Why not make an opera of Margaret Mitchell's *Gone With the Wind*? Floyd thanked him, and promptly dismissed the notion as "another potential *Ring* cycle."

18. *Diary,* November 6, 1943. Reverend Floyd failed to report Carlisle's two As, but the official college transcript shows grades as listed above.

19. In H. T. Lowe-Porter's translation, published by Alfred A. Knopf: *Joseph and His Brothers* (1934), *Young Joseph* (1935), *Joseph in Egypt* (1938); a fourth, *Joseph the Provider,* appeared in 1944.

20. Carlisle Floyd, "Which Shall Not Perish from the Earth," in *We, the Freshmen* (Autumn 1943): 2–3; and *The Concept* 54, no. 1 (November, 9, 1943): 25–26, Spartanburg, Converse College. Copies in Box 1, FASCL.

21. Floyd, "Low-Country Town," *The Concept* 43, no. 3 (1944): 6, 30–32. Copy in Box 1, Folder 19, FASCL.

22. *Strange Fruit* sold over three million copies during Smith's lifetime (1897–1966).

23. Carlisle Floyd, "Tschaikowsky's Sixth" and "The 'Pounding,'" *The Concept* 43, no. 4 (1944): 4, 15, 21, 24–25, 37–38. Copy in Box 1, FASCL.

24. "Tschaikowsky's Sixth," 21.

25. Alia Ross [Lawson) taught music education and theory at Converse from 1943 to 1977. She founded the school's precollege program and remained after retirement its director until 1983; she died in 2006.

26. Comments in Lawson's unpublished memoir. Courtesy of Converse College archivist and the memoir's editor, Dr. Jeffrey R. Willis.

27. Program in Box 1, FASCL.

28. *Diary,* June 6, 1944.

29. Author interview, December 20, 2007.

30. *Diary,* July 21, 1944.

31. Pazmor was born Harriet Horn Pasmore in San Francisco in 1892, but altered the spelling of her name to sound more exotic and European. She championed both early and new music, and gave many first performances of the vocal literature of Charles Ives, Henry Cowell, Ruth Crawford, and Ernst Bacon. Bacon hired her in 1941, and she sang the role of Mom in the 1942 *Tree on the Plains* world premiere. Tall and statuesque, she was inevitably called either "Paz" or "Radiator" by students, who delighted in mimicking her plummy, theatrical speech. She remained on the Converse faculty until 1960, and died in California, at ninety-three, in 1986.

32. Carlisle Floyd to Bacon, July 22, 1945, Box 13, Ernst Bacon Archive, Syracuse University Special Collections (hereafter SUSC).

33. Carl Sandburg, *War Poems,* in *Chicago Poems* (Chicago: Henry Holt, 1916).

34. Carlisle Floyd, "Among the Red Guns" (c. 1945), undated ms., Box 1, Folder 1, Floyd Archive, Library of Congress, Washington, DC (hereafter FALOC).

35. Morse (1912–2004), a graduate of the University of South Carolina, went on to write *The Irrelevant English Teacher* (1974) and *Prejudice and Literature* (1976), both published by Temple University Press, and a number of works on James Joyce, including *The Sympathetic Alien: James Joyce and Catholicism* (New York: New York University Press, 1959).

36. *The Concept* 44, no. 1 (1945): 5, 7. Copy in Box 1, FASCL.

37. Carlisle Floyd, *Ode, The Concept* 44, no. 1 (1945), 5. Copy in Box 1, FASCL.

38. *The Concept* 44, no. 2 (1945): 6–7. Copy in Box 1, FASCL.

39. Carlisle Floyd, "When You Are Old" (1944–1945), unpublished ms. vocal score, Box 10, Folder 5, FALOC.

40. Carlisle Floyd, "Transcendency" and *Too Dear, the Price, The Concept* 44, no. 2 (1945): 11, 16, 34–36. This issue also contains a short nature piece by Ermine, "Enigma." Copy in Box 1, FASCL.

41. With reference to Ibsen's 1881 play *Ghosts,* in which the son, Osvald, suffering from congenital syphilis, falls in love with the family's maid, who turns out to be his half sister.

42. *The Concept* 44, no. 3 (1945): 9. With "Transcendency," Morse echoed his criticism of Carlisle's *Ode:* "It baffles me. There is evidently intense emotion here, but it is not expressed in recognizable symbols and hence is not conveyed to the reader" (9).

43. *Parley Voo,* March 5, 1945 (Spartanburg: Converse College).

44. Judging sheets in Box 1, Folder 32, FASCL.

45. *Diary,* June 1, 1945.

46. *Diary,* July 11, 1945.

47. *Diary,* December 6, 1944.

48. Floyd to Bacon, July 12, 1945, SUSC.

49. Ibid.

50. Floyd to Bacon, July 22, 1945, SUSC.

51. Mozelle (later changed to Moselle) Copeland Shepherd Camp was born on July 23, 1928, the daughter of William A. Camp and Mozelle Copeland.

52. Rossetti (1830–1894) was the sister of the pre-Raphaelite Dante Rossetti, and granddaughter of Lord Byron's physician John Polidori, who first popularized vampire literature in England. "Remember Me" was first published in Christina Rossetti, *Goblin Market and Other Poems* (Cambridge: Macmillan, 1862).

53. Hannah Walker was an upperclasswoman at Converse, several years Floyd's senior, from Auburndale, Florida. No record of her performance of "Remember" has survived.

54. Floyd to Bacon, July 22, 1945, SUSC. Floyd knew that he was on safe ground in mocking the Schillinger system, which Bacon abhorred.

55. Carlisle Floyd, "Remember Me," unpublished ms., 1945, Box 10, Folder 5, FALOC.

56. Floyd to Bacon, August 16, 1945, SUSC.

57. *Diary,* August 29, 1945.

58. Floyd to Bacon, August 16, 1945, SUSC.

59. *Diary,* August 31, 1945.

6. Swimming with Yankees: Syracuse University, New York, 1945–1946

1. Dr. Robin Sellers, "Interview with Carlisle Floyd, September 14, 2006" (Tallahassee: Reichelt Oral History Program, College of Music, Florida State University). Courtesy of Dr. Sellers.

2. Kapell (1922–1953) was widely regarded as America's finest pianist during his short lifetime. Floyd probably heard his Carnegie Hall concert on October 25, 1945, at which he played Rachmaninoff's Rhapsody on a Theme of Paganini.

3. Rainer Maria Rilke, *New Poems* (c. 1907), in *The Poetry of Rainer Maria Rilke,* trans. M. D. Herter Norton (New York: W. W. Norton, 1938, 1966).

4. Priscilla Gillette born in Tenafly, New Jersey, in 1925. She went on from Syracuse to a solid singing, acting, and television career. She starred in first productions of Lerner and Loewe's *Brigadoon* (1947–48), Marc Blitzstein's *Regina* (1949), Cole Porter's *Out of This World* (1950), and Jerome Moross's *The Golden Apple* (1954). She won fame in the television soap opera role of Kate in *The Edge of Night* (1956–1958), and appeared in ten episodes of *Studio One* (1950–1957). She died in New York City on February 2, 2006.

5. Author interview, November 18, 2009.

6. Ibid.

7. *Diary,* December 21, 1945.

8. *Diary,* May 22, 1984.

9. *Diary,* January 8, 1946.

10. Arthur Heacox, *Project Lessons in Orchestration* (Boston: Oliver Ditson, 1928).

11. Elvin Schmitt (1903–1992) had been a student of Alfred Cortot.

12. Curley, born in Massachusetts in 1928, died in the hours before New Year's Day 1989, run down by a car while vacationing in Tallahassee, Florida. After Syracuse, he taught for many years at the University of Illinois at Urbana. His 1985 collection *Living With Snakes* won the Flannery O'Connor Award for short fiction.

13. Glasgow (1873–1945), a native of Richmond, Virginia, wrote twenty novels, most about life in her home state. Her 1941 novel, *In This Our Life,* won a Pulitzer Prize the year after publication, and served as the basis of John Huston's 1942 like-titled film starring Bette Davis and Olivia de Havilland.

14. Barrow (1927–1993) made his career in television soap opera and motion pictures, playing Johnny Ryan in 202 episodes of *Ryan's Hope* between 1975 and 1989. His film credits include Inspector Palmer in *Serpico* (1973). He earned bachelor's and master's degrees in English from Syracuse University and Columbia University, and

a doctorate in theater history from Yale in 1957; he later taught at Brooklyn College, City University of New York.

15. *Diary,* February 2, 1946.

16. Copy in Box 10, Folder 5, FALOC.

17. Floyd inverted these two lines; in Yeats, "Shaking" precedes "Tossing."

18. Carlisle Floyd, "The Fairy's Song," unpublished ms. vocal score, Box 10, Folder 5, FALOC.

19. Floyd to Bacon, June 15, 1946, SUSC.

20. Ibid.

21. Vengerova (1877–1956), one of Curtis's founders in 1924, taught such legendary talents as Samuel Barber, Leonard Bernstein, and her nephew Nicholas Slonimsky.

22. Floyd to Bacon, June 15, 1946, SUSC.

23. Carlisle Floyd, "Who Has Known the Panic," prose fiction, unpublished ms., 1946, Box 1, Folder 19, FASCL. The ms. is dated June 1945, but Floyd informed me that this is a typographical error, that 1946 is the correct date. In June of 1945, he had yet to set eyes on Syracuse, much less *La Gillette.*

24. Carlisle Floyd, "An Evening Song" (1946), unpublished ms. vocal score, Box 10, Folder 5, FALOC.

25. Floyd to Bacon, June 15, 1946, SUSC.

26. *Diary,* August 3, 1946.

27. *Diary,* August 4, 1946.

28. *Diary,* August 6, 1946.

29. *Diary,* August 7, 1946.

30. Carlisle never forgot that Reverend Floyd refused to remarry divorced persons.

31. Author interview with Jona Clarke. March 6, 2007.

32. Floyd to Bacon, January 19, 1947, SUSC.

33. Kuersteiner (1901–1973) had a long career as concert violinist, conductor, and music educator. His tenure as second dean of Florida State University College of Music lasted from 1944 to 1966.

34. Floyd to Kuersteiner, September 19, 1946. Courtesy of the College of Music, Florida State University. The song was "Remember." Carl Deis, a senior editor at Schirmer, and a distinguished arranger and composer in his own right, rejected it. Carlisle had long contemplated writing a piece of chamber music. When he learned that Kuersteiner was a violinist, he felt that this might advantage his job quest, but the piece never materialized.

35. Kuersteiner to Floyd, October 2, 1946. Courtesy of the College of Music, Florida State University.

36. $1,200 in 1946 equals $19,500 in 2010 consumer price index dollars.

37. *Diary,* October 31, 1947.

38. Bacon to Kuersteiner, November 21, 1946. Courtesy of the College of Music, Florida State University.

39. Kuersteiner to Floyd, December 6, 1946. Courtesy of the College of Music, Florida State University.

40. *Diary,* December 26, 1946.

41. *Diary,* December 27, 1946.

42. Rupert Brooke, *Selected Poems* (London: Sidgwick & Jackson, 1917). "The Hill" dates from 1914, the year before Brooke's death.

7. Young Professor Floyd Writes an Opera: Florida State University, Syracuse Again, *Slow Dusk*, 1946–1949

1. Carlisle Floyd to Bacon, January 19, 1947, SUSC.

2. Ibid.

3. Ibid.

4. Floyd called his piece "Phantasm" in homage to Lionel Nowak, whose like-titled work he admired. *Soliloquy and Phantasm* has not survived in a unified manuscript in any collection; but Floyd reused the two pieces as a prelude ("Soliloquy") and interlude ("Phantasm") in his first opera, *Slow Dusk,* in 1948–1949. See Carlisle Floyd, *Slow Dusk* (New York: Boosey & Hawkes, 1957), "Soliloquy," 1–3, and "Phantasm," 32–35.

5. Literally, "utility music," meaning easy enough for anyone to incorporate into personal music making, exhibiting qualities of or about subjects accessible to the common man.

6. Copland had published an autobiographical sketch with this shift in focus in "Composer from Brooklyn," *Magazine of Art* (September 1939): 32. Later reprinted in Aaron Copland, *Our New Music* (New York: Whittlesey House, 1941). The works that demonstrated this manifesto proved his most popular: *Billy the Kid* (1938), *A Lincoln Portrait* (1942), and *Appalachian Spring* (1944).

7. Kuersteiner to Floyd, April 16, 1947. Courtesy of the College of Music, Florida State University.

8. *Diary,* April 27, 1947.

9. *Florida Flambeau,* June 23, 1947.

10. Fosdick (1878–1969), a northeastern Baptist minister, took a controversial liberal stance as champion of modernism versus fundamentalism in religion.

11. Located at what is today the intersection of Appleyard Drive and West Pensacola Street, the campus of Tallahassee Community College. Following Floyd's year there during 1947–1948, Mabry Field served as Tallahassee's principal airport until the city's new facility opened in 1961.

12. Boda (1922–2002) taught theory, composition, and piano at FSU from 1947 to 2001. A Wisconsin native, he had been George Szell's apprentice conductor with the Cleveland Orchestra. His large output includes symphonies, band music, choral work, songs, and chamber music for ensembles of all sizes; but he seems to have never written for the theater.

13. Cowles (1881–1959) studied with Horatio Parker at Yale, and later at the Schola Cantorum in Paris. His compositions include a piano concerto, piano trio, songs, and solo piano works. He was also the father of Broadway producer Chandler Cowles, who figures in Floyd's later story.

14. Martin Bernstein, *An Introduction to Music* (New York: Prentice-Hall, 1937). The book is still in print, appearing in new editions every several years.

15. Edwards (1936–2004) went on to become an accompanist to many star singers. In the sixties and seventies in New York he was the partner of choice for such artists as Phyllis Curtin, Mack Harrell, Teresa Zylis-Gara, Christa Ludwig, and Marni Nixon.

16. World premiere at FSU on December 13, 1956.

17. Carlisle Floyd, *Odyssey* (1947), Box 6, Folder 2, FALOC. Like many of Floyd's early scores, at times only the solo part is completely realized, suggesting both haste and the composer's ability to supply accompaniments ad libitum.

18. Author interview, September 30, 2006.

19. After teaching theory and composition at FSU, Will became department head of music at Boston University and Winthrop University.

20. Floyd to Bacon, February 21, 1948, SUSC.

21. Later made into two different films, in 1942 and 1955, the latter a musical version with score by Jule Styne and Leo Robin. The play also served Leonard Bernstein, Betty Comden, and Adolph Green as the basis of their 1953 Broadway hit *Wonderful Town*.

22. The singer Tourel, born in Vitebsk, Russia, in 1900 with the surname Davidovich, adopted a stage name that was an anagram of her voice teacher, Anna El Tour. Following a distinguished performing and teaching career, Tourel died in New York in 1973.

23. Clarke, son of a much-decorated American general, became an internationally distinguished Mozart scholar. His translations include the first two volumes of Anton Neumayr, *Music and Medicine* (Bloomington: Medi-Ed Press, 1994, 1995). Clarke founded and continues to operate the website www.AproposMozart.com.

24. Floyd to Heimlich, June 7, 1948. Courtesy of Jona Clarke.

25. Ibid.

26. Ibid.

27. Floyd to Bacon, August 7, 1948, SUSC.

28. Ibid.

29. Floyd to Clarkes, August 9, 1948. Courtesy of Jona Clarke. All cited Clarke correspondence and interviews courtesy of Jona Clarke.

30. *Diary*, August 21, 1948.

31. *Diary*, August 31, 1948.

32. "Artists Present Splendid Program," *Orangeburg Observer*. Undated clipping, but probably September 3, 1949. The lack of a printed date reflects the condition of a scrapbook kept by Hazel Moren Richards, Floyd's patroness-to-be, and the volume is stored in Box 14, FASCL. With or without dates or even the name of the newspaper, this scrapbook is the only source for reviews of many early Floyd performances.

33. *Diary*, October 12, 1948.

34. Unpublished poem reprinted here by permission of Joan Kaye Barrow.

35. Carlisle Floyd, "I Am a Beggar on a Lonely Hill" (1948), two unpublished mss. vocal scores, one dated October 1948, both in Box 10, Folder 5, FALOC.

36. Crane (1899–1932) was a hero to many intellectuals of Floyd's generation. As well known for his riotous alcoholism and homosexuality as his brilliant and startling vision of contemporary America, he jumped to his death by drowning near Veracruz, Mexico.

37. Carlisle Floyd, "Old Song," ms. vocal score, 1948, Box 10, Folder 5, FALOC.

38. Owen (1893–1918), one of the great voices silenced in the trenches and battlefields of World War I, died in action a week before the war's end, in the Battle of the Sambre in France. Perhaps the most famous musical use of his poetry is Benjamin Britten's *War Requiem* (1962). "Futility" dates from 1917/18.

39. Carlisle Floyd, "Move Him into the Sun," Box 10, Folder 5, FALOC.

40. Following the final chords Floyd indicates an augmented vocal line without accompaniment.

41. Floyd commented, "It never occurred to me that my poetry needed music; I was operating in a separate sphere. And I think it's quite possible to write poetry you don't fully understand yourself."

42. Floyd, "A Lengthening Shadow," 3–4.

43. Olin Downes, "Opera by Luening Has Its Premiere," *New York Times*, May 6, 1948, 31.

44. *Diary*, December 20, 1948.

45. Fleming (1909–2001), a pianist and theoretician, studied in Europe with Tobias Mathay and Artur Schnabel, and concertized from 1932 to 1940. His SU career began in 1945, and he founded the Department of Fine Arts two years later. Fleming earned his greatest celebrity from studies on the synthesis of music and the visual arts, *Arts and Ideas* (New York: Holt, Rinehart & Winston, 1955) and *Art, Music, and Ideas* (New York: Holt, Rinehart & Winston, 1970), both still in print.

46. M. D. Calvocoressi, *The Principles and Methods of Music Criticism* (London: Oxford University Press, 1923). Eduard Hanslick, *The Beautiful in Music* (London: Novello & Co., 1891).

47. Copy in Box 1, Folder 19, FASCL.

48. Jona Clarke, note to author, May 1, 2007.

49. Bruce Clarke, E-mail to author, April 25, 2007.

50. Thola Tabor Schenck, *Syracuse Post-Standard*, January 12, 1949.

51. Bacon, *Words On Music*, 70.

52. The principal exception was and is the work of Alban Berg. Floyd taught Berg's Piano Sonata, op.1, but, as with his impressions of *Wozzeck*, received this as late Romantic music.

53. Bacon, *Words on Music*, 67.

54. "Motive of prime intention." See Mosco Carner, *Puccini* (New York: Alfred A. Knopf, 1959), 268–73.

55. The reverse of the title of Giambattista Casti's libretto for Salieri's one-act comic opera *Prima la musica, poi le parole*, first

performed on a double bill with Mozart's *Der Schauspieldirektor* in 1786. The phrase had become proverbial for the Italian aesthetic of music's priority over words in opera, also the argument of Richard Strauss's *Capriccio* (1942).

56. Steber (1914–1990) was, like Floyd's future colleague Phyllis Curtin, a southerner, from West Virginia, and one of America's first vocal superstars to base her career in this country.

57. Riegger (1885–1961), a Georgia native, wrote, arranged, and published under nine pseudonyms, including the anagrammatic Gerald Wilfring Gore.

58. *Diary,* March 31, 1949.

59. Wilfred Owen, *Poems by Wilfred Owen* (London: Chatto and Windus, 1921).

60. Mulfinger (1900–1988) had studied piano in Austria with Liszt's pupil Emil von Sauer, and composition and orchestration with Franz Schmidt.

61. "E.V.W.," *Syracuse Herald-Journal,* May 3, 1949.

62. *Diary,* June 3, 1949.

63. Thola Tabor Schenck, *Syracuse Post Standard,* June 4, 1949.

8. Women, and Other *Fugitives*: Tallahassee, 1949–1953

1. Floyd to Clarkes, June 9, 1949.

2. After concertizing in Europe, Zachara (1898–1966) emigrated to the United States in 1928. Before joining FSU's faculty, he had been dean of music at Brenau College in Gainesville, Georgia. His compositions include a piano concerto, a symphony, and band and chamber works.

3. See Ilona Dohnányi, *Ernst von Dohnányi: A Song of Life* (Bloomington: Indiana University Press, 2002).

4. Charles-Louis Hanon (1820–1900) published *The Virtuoso Pianist in Sixty Exercises* in Boulogne, France, in 1873.

5. Czerny's (1791–1857) extensive catalogue included such pedagogical works as *Preparatory School of Finger Dexterity,* op. 636; *School of Velocity,* op. 299; and *Daily Exercises,* op. 337.

6. Rhodes to Floyd, October 27, 1949, Box 1, Folder 3, FASCL. Though Rhodes's letter is dated October 27, Floyd's response dated October 24, 1949, is an obvious error, as only November makes sense, considering the date of Rhodes's notification. Willard Rhodes (1901–1992) won renown as an ethnomusicologist for his pioneering studies of American Indian and African traditional music. A composition student of Nadia Boulanger in 1929, he joined Columbia's faculty in 1937.

7. Ibid.

8. Floyd to Rhodes, October [November] 10, 1949, Willard Rhodes and Robert Penn Warren Archives, Yale Collection of American Literature, Beinecke Rare Book and Manuscript Library, Yale University (hereafter YCAL).

9. E-mails to author from Jocelyn K. Wilk, public services archivist, Columbia University, August 23–27, 2007.

10. The former Bronja Singer, also a pianist and teacher.

11. Foster gave his principal FSU recital on February 24, 1950. The following May 9, he and colleague James M. Gunn shared a composition recital at which Foster's *Three Songs, Suite of Dances,* and *Variations on a Folk Melody for Four Hands* were played. Finally, on May 12, he soloed with the University Symphony Orchestra in Constant Lambert's *The Rio Grande.*

12. Dickinson (1912–2003) studied modern dance with the iconic Martha Graham. During World War II, she served in SPARS, the U.S. Coast Guard Women's Reserve, and taught at FSU from 1935 until 1963. Smith, today Dr. Nancy Smith Fichter, professor emerita of dance, began her FSU study in 1948; she became in turn director of modern dance from 1954 to 1959, and again, after receiving her doctorate, from 1964 until her retirement in 1997.

13. Author interview with Donald Mowrer, February 6, 2007.

14. Harold Richards was retired from his position as department head soon after the Forty-Niners arrived.

15. Author interview with Mowrer.

16. Author interview with Nancy Smith Fichter, January 22, 2006. "Hazel collected people, and was a wonderfully generous spirit. It is in retrospect that one writes the novel; but at the time, I thought of that as a pleasant game on an English stage. She *adored* Carlisle; as far as Hazel was concerned, he was the center of the universe."

17. Kathryn Reece (1899–1994) acted as Grace Carpenter in the Marx Brothers' *Animal Crackers* (1930), and costarred as herself in *Makers of Melody* (1929), a short film about and starring Richard Rodgers and Lorenz Hart. Her final Broadway appearances were in repertory presentations of six Gilbert and Sullivan operettas in 1944. She was married to the conductor-composer Ewald Haun.

18. Molnar (1878–1952), a Hungarian Jew who fled the Nazis, wrote plays frequently adapted for the musical theatre: *Liliom* (1909); Rodgers and Hammerstein's *Carousel* (1945); *The Guardsman* (1910), which was filmed in 1931 with an all-star cast including Alfred Lunt and Lynne Fontanne. In 1941, its plot was used for the movie version of Oscar Straus's *The Chocolate Soldier;* and in 1997 Floyd's student Craig Bohmler converted the play into a musical, *Enter the Guardsman.*

19. Mays, under his theatrical alias, Clay Randolph, served as assistant producer in the Drama Quartet's New York production of Shaw's *Don Juan in Hell* in 1951–1952, and later acted in televised episodes of *Wagon Train* and *Death Valley Days.*

20. "'The Guardsman' Opens 3-Day Run on West Campus Tomorrow," *Tallahassee Democrat,* December 11, 1949, Section 3, 28.

21. Frank F. O'Neill, "The Guardsman Is Applauded," *Tallahassee Democrat,* December 13, 1949, 3.

22. McCalmon (1909–1965) left Florida State to head Cornell University's drama program.

23. "Floyd to Play for FSU Drama," *Tallahassee Democrat,* January 22, 1950, Section 2, 20.

24. "FSU Play Attracts Large Crowd," *Tallahassee Democrat,* February 1, 1950, 5. Four *Iphigenia* performances took place, on January 31 and February 2, 3, and 4, 1950.

25. "Carlisle Floyd Gives Recital," *Tallahassee Democrat,* March 12, 1950, Section 3, 25.

26. Floyd to Clarke, October 28, 1950.

27. The companion piece was *The Romance of the Willow Pattern,* by Ethel Beekman Van Der Ver.

28. "Speech, Music Departments Give 'Experimental Theater,'" *Tallahassee Democrat,* May 11, 1950, 4.

29. *Diary,* May 11, 1950.

30. *Florida Flambeau,* May 11, 1950.

31. Carlisle Floyd, *Fugitives* (1950–1951). All *Fugitives* quotations from the librettos and scores in Box 4, Folders 4 and 5, FALOC. There are differences between these documents, beginning with the score's indication that the original southern city was "small."

32. The middle name of ancestor Charles P. Floyd. See appendix.

33. In *Too Dear, the Price,* chap. 5, note 1.

34. *The Medium* premiered at the Brander Matthews Theater at Columbia University on May 8, 1946, and professionally at the Ethel Barrymore Theatre for six months in 1947. A second Broadway production opened at the Arena Theatre on July 19, 1950, playing until October 14 that year. Even more immediately, as Floyd composed *Fugitives,* FSU's opera theater was in rehearsal for *The Medium,* performed on May 30, 1951.

35. Floyd to Jona Clarke, October 28, 1950.

36. Ibid.

37. One of the theater industry's most prestigious publications from 1916 to 1964.

38. Thomas LeRoy Collins (1909–1991) and Mary Call Darby Collins (1911–2009) became two of Floyd's strongest supporters. Collins governed Florida from 1955 to 1961, served as chairman of the Democratic National Convention in 1960, and was considered as a vice presidential candidate in 1956 and 1960. Coincidentally, Collins had been a pupil in Hazel Richards's history class at Tallahassee's Leon High School.

39. Dates in parentheses indicate the month and year of the appropriate *Theatre Arts Magazine.*

40. *Diary,* March 17, 1951.

41. *Diary,* April 17, 1951.

42. *Florida Flambeau,* April 20, 1951.

43. Letter to Jona Clarke, July 22, 1951.

44. In 1952, Foster became chairman of Indiana University's piano department, and the university named Foster a distinguished professor of music in 1976. He taught there until shortly before his death from pneumonia on February 7, 1977, after the removal, interestingly enough, of his spleen.

45. Lew McSwain Brandes, after earning her bachelor's degree in 1953, followed Sidney Foster to Indiana University to continue her study. She later joined the piano faculty of Butler University in Indianapolis. Author interview, February 23, 2007.

46. Ibid.

47. Ibid.

48. Author interview, February 10, 2008. After two years of army service in Germany, Staples studied for two years at Juilliard. His subsequent teaching career included positions at the State University of New York at Fredonia and Indiana University of Pennsylvania.

49. Ibid.

50. Floyd to Clarke, July 22, 1951.

51. Ibid.

52. Dorothy Madlee, "'Susannah' Composer's Wife 'A Passionate Amateur In Music,'" *Orlando Sentinel,* April 23, 1971, Action/Society, 1D.

53. Author interview, January 22, 2007.

54. Author interview, February 6, 2007.

55. Julie Storm remained in Chicago, eventually committing suicide in the early sixties.

56. Floyd to Jona Clarke, September 7, 1951.

57. Ibid.

58. Ibid.

59. Carlisle Floyd, *Theme and Variations* (c. 1951), Box 11, Folders 4, 5, FALOC.

60. Program from "An Evening of Dance," January 14, 1952, Box 1, FASCL.

61. FSU's department of dance was formally instituted by Smith when she returned from advanced study and teaching in Texas in 1964. She retired from FSU in 1997.

62. Author interview, January 22, 2007. The quotes in the next two paragraphs are from this interview.

63. Becque (1837–1899), a Parisian, was one of the fathers of the Theatre of Cruelty. *La Parisienne,* written in 1882 and first performed in 1885, was his last completed play, a scandalous exposé of both illicit love and a protofeminist tract.

64. Roger Busfield, born into a family of journalists in 1926, in Fort Worth, Texas, earned a PhD at FSU in 1954 in dramatic writing. He is the father of actor Timothy Busfield.

65. *Florida Flambeau,* [January 9,] 1952. The surviving review copy, unattributed and undated, is in Hazel Richards's scrapbook. Box 14, FASCL.

66. Author interview, February 23, 2007.

67. *Florida Flambeau,* [January 15,] 1952. Undated clipping from Hazel Richards's scrapbook, Box 14, FASCL.

68. Author interview, February 6, 2007.

69. Carlisle Floyd, *Nocturne for Voice* (1952). Both unpublished mss. in Box 11, Folder 5, FALOC.

70. An even larger section of Whitman's poem, written in 1859 and first published in the 1860 edition of *Leaves of Grass,* had been set by Frederick Delius in *Sea Drift* (1903–1904), for baritone soloist, chorus, and orchestra, but unknown at the time to Floyd.

71. C. M. Carroll, "Three Musical Works of Floyd Are Featured," *Tallahassee Democrat,* April 6, 1952, Section 4, 35.

72. As of summer 2008, renovated and renamed the Independence Square Lodge, at 404 South Galena Street, a far cry from Floyd's spartan 1952 quarters.

73. Tugboat Annie was a loud, abrasive character first popularized by character actress Marie Dressler in a 1933 film titled for its principal character.

74. Linda J. Noyle, *Pianists on Playing: Interviews with Twelve Concert Pianists* (Metuchen, NJ: Scarecrow Press, 1987), 81.

75. Ibid., 83.

76. Jones (1910–1997), born in Tamworth, Ontario, Canada, built his career in the United States. His compositions, heavily influenced by Milhaud's chromatic neoclassicism, include four symphonies, string quartets, and vocal works in various combinations. He taught in New York, at Juilliard and Mannes College, and as Aspen's composer-in-residence until 1989.

77. *Diary,* September 19, 1952.

78. During our interview, Mowrer reinforced his lack of passion for modern dance as a form or activity, but affirmed that it was a good way to meet attractive women.

79. Donald Mowrer's studies led him to speech therapy. On the faculty of Arizona State University, he has published, with others, such studies as "Analysis of Five Acoustic Correlates of Laughter," *Journal of Nonverbal Behavior* 11, no. 3 (1987); and "Effect of Lisping on Audience Evaluation of Male Speakers," *Journal of Speech and Hearing Disorders* 43 (May 1978).

80. E-mail to author, February 4, 2007.

81. Ibid., February 8, 2007.

82. Graham (1894–1991) had commissioned dance scores by numerous composers, including Aaron Copland (*Appalachian Spring*) and Paul Hindemith (*Hérodiade*), both in 1944; Samuel Barber (*Medea,* 1946), Gian-Carlo Menotti (*Errand into the Maze*), and William Schuman (*Night Journey*) in 1947; and Norman Dello Joio (*Diversion of Angels,* 1949).

83. This could have been either Graham's 1931 ballet *Primitive Mysteries,* the second section of which was *Crucifixion,* with music by Louis Horst; or her 1940 *El penitente,* another Horst score. She periodically revived both works.

9. "The Old Girl," *Susannah*: Tallahassee, 1952–1955

1. In Samuel Johnson's *Dictionary of the English Language* (1755). Like the young Floyd, Johnson was no opera fan.

2. Moore, born Murphy in 1939, died in 2006 of colon cancer in Berkeley, California. She was a senior editor at the weekly *San Diego Reader,* and also published an essay collection, *The Left Coast of Paradise: California and the American Heart* (1987).

3. Judith Moore, *Fat Girl, A True Story* (New York: Hudson Street Press, 2005), 184.

4. Judith Moore, *Never Eat Your Heart Out* (New York: Farrar Straus Giroux), 258–67. Moore wrote an entire chapter, "Eating Peter Rabbit," on the gastronomical history of the species, without reference to the Floyd incident.

5. Edward Kilenyi, Jr., born to Hungarian parents in Philadelphia in 1910, died in Tallahassee in 2000. His father, Edward Sr. (1884–1968), was a violinist, composer, and George Gershwin's teacher for two years.

6. Floyd's childhood idol Robert Taylor appeared prominently among this number.

7. The United States Constitution's Fifth Amendment guarantees indemnity against self-incrimination.

8. Sellers, "Interview with Carlisle Floyd," 12.

9. The Florida legislature withdrew funding for Johns's project in 1964, after its report *Homosexuality and Citizenship in Florida,* nicknamed "The Purple Pamphlet," began circulating as pornography in New York City.

10. *Diary,* June 12, 1953.

11. See Michael D. Coogan, ed., *The New Oxford Annotated Apocrypha,* 3rd ed. (New York: Oxford University Press, 2007), xiii–12. *Susanna* (194–200) was grafted onto canonical stories of the prophet Daniel around 100 B.C., but its setting in the period of the Babylonian captivity of the Hebrews reaches as far back as the sixth century B.C.

12. From Floyd's "credo," in David Ewen, *Composers since 1900* (New York: H. W. Wilson, 1969), 201–2.

13. As did Arthur Miller's play about a literal witch hunt, *The Crucible,* which played on Broadway from January to July 1953, just as Floyd began *Susannah;* and that play's 1961 Pulitzer prize-winning operatic adaptation by Floyd's peer Robert Ward.

14. Rupert Bottenberg, "Definitely not the Beverly Hillbillies," *Montreal Mirror,* April 22, 1999.

15. In an interview with Floyd's cousin Marjorie Manning on January 17, 2007, she told me that her father, Henry Bascom Floyd Jr., the original "Little Bat," accounted this dimwitted character's naming a dubious honor. Floyd was relieved not to be sued.

16. Johnston (1896–1965) served as South Carolina's governor for two terms (1935–1939 and 1943–1945), and as United States senator (1945–1965).

17. *Diary,* April 24, 1978.

18. Floyd, *Susannah* vocal score, 12.

19. Floyd later discovered "Jaybird" in a collection of southern folk humor, but thought that Oscar Fenegan had learned it by osmosis.

20. Libretto copy in Box 11, Folder 1, FALOC.

21. Floyd, *Susannah* vocal score, 4. The plot moments discussed in the next three pages are on 57, 102, and 104.

22. Delmar Jean Hansen (1926–2008) worked on a master's in speech and theater at FSU in 1953. His teaching career ended with thirty-two years at Minnesota State University, Moorhead, where he retired in 1990.

23. Floyd interview with Mark Hinson, *Tallahassee.com*, October 11, 2009.

24. Carlisle Floyd, "Our Hearts Leap Up" (1953–1954), in *F.S.U. Singtime*. A single copy of this seventeen-page paperback volume has been retained in FSU's Strozier Library archives.

25. Floyd, *Susannah* vocal score, 67.

26. *Diary*, December 20, 1953. Mrs. Floyd was typically moody and distant for extended periods when her son left after these visits.

27. Carlisle Floyd, *Susannah* (1953–1955). Notation of date in pencil ms. draft, Box 11, Folder 2, FALOC.

28. Ann E. Lankford, *Florida Flambeau*, [January 14, 1954]. Undated clipping in Richards scrapbook, Box 14, FASCL.

29. Gladys, one of Floyd's adult students, had married George Henderson, vice president of the Lewis State Bank.

30. Lee Rigsby, "Carlisle Floyd Piano Recital Is Gratifying," *Tallahassee Democrat*, February 7, 1954, Section 2, 14.

31. *Diary*, May 21, 1954. Reverend Floyd recorded: "Good letter from Carlisle saying he completed work on his opera and had it sent to New York."

32. 1921 in some sources.

33. Philip D. Curtin, *On the Fringes of History: A Memoir* (Athens: Ohio University Press, 2005), 44–46.

34. Ibid., 65.

35. *Diary*, August 21, 1954.

36. *Diary*, August 27, 1954.

37. See Carlisle Floyd, "Recalling *Susannah*'s Beginnings," Liner notes from 1994 Virgin Classics *Susannah* CD (London: Virgin Classics, 1994), 14–15.

38. *Diary*, September 23, 1954: "Carlisle called to tell us that Pres. Campbell had okayed his opera. He seemed well pleased."

39. Curtin to Floyd, November 26, 1954. All letters from Curtin to Floyd courtesy of Carlisle Floyd and Phyllis Curtain.

40. Floyd to Kay Reeder, December 20, 1954. Courtesy of Carlisle Floyd.

41. Floyd to Clarkes, November 26, 1954.

42. "Eb" was a shortening of Eberle. Later in his career, Thomas became codirector of the Asolo Repertory Theatre in Sarasota, Florida.

43. Floyd, *Susannah* vocal score, 94.

44. Curtin to Floyd, January 21, 1955.

45. Author interview with Curtin, March 3, 2007.

46. "Props Needed," *Tallahassee Democrat*, February 13, 1955, Section 3, 17.

47. Holton, born in Dolgeville, New York, on July 8, 1922, graduated from Wesleyan University and worked as director of serious music at Boosey & Hawkes for eighteen years.

48. Robert Holton, "The Publisher," in *The Opera Journal* (Winter 1971): 31–32.

49. Invitation in Box 1, Folder 12, FASCL.

50. *Diary*, February 23, 1955.

51. Dr. Warren D. Allen, "Thirteen Hundred Witness Premiere Performance of Carlisle Floyd's *Susannah*," *Tallahassee Democrat*, February 25, 1955, 6.

52. *Diary*, February 24, 1955.

53. *Diary*, February 25, 1955.

54. "*Susannah* Has Debut," *New York Times*, February 25, 1955, 18.

55. At least as concerned Floyd: Blount went on to earn a doctorate at the University of Wisconsin–Madison in 1963, whose faculty he joined. For the remainder of his career, he continued to teach and write on various aspects of English pedagogy, gaining a reputation as a pioneer in transformational grammar. He became the longtime partner of abstract painter, pianist, conductor, and scholar Ellsworth Snyder (1931–2005). According to a RootsWeb site listing obituaries from Lee County, Florida (*Fort Myers News-Press*), Blount died on April 30, 1989.

10. The Short, Fast Fall to Fame: *Susannah* in New York, 1955–1956

1. Titled *Music for Dance*, Box 5, Folder 5, FALOC.

2. Author interview, January 22, 2007.

3. Floyd to Clarkes, March 17, 1955. The next two quotes in the text are also from this letter.

4. The firm's history, with roots in the eighteenth century, is told in Helen Wallace, *Boosey & Hawkes: The Publishing Story* (London: Boosey & Hawkes, 2007).

5. Besides Floyd, Holton recruited Stanley Hollingsworth and Dominick Argento the following year.

6. From Holton's piece in the winter 1971 *Opera Journal*. "Down-in-the-Valley" refers to Kurt Weill's 1948 short opera of that name.

7. Born in Cracow, Poland, in 1895, Rosenstock was a child prodigy pianist and student of composer Franz Schreker. He left Nazi Germany in 1933 for, of all places, Japan. He narrowly escaped to America in 1941, began conducting at City Opera in 1948, and was appointed general director in 1952. See Martin M. Sokol, *The New York City Opera: An American Adventure* (New York: Macmillan, 1981), 111–14.

8. Chandler Cowles (1917–1997) had produced all of Menotti's Broadway operas: *The Telephone (1947)*, *The Medium* (1950), *The Consul* (1950), and *The Saint of Bleecker Street* (1954), coproduced with Lincoln Kirstein.

9. The elder Cowles (1881–1959) retired from FSU in 1951.

10. See Martin Duberman, *The Worlds of Lincoln Kirstein* (New York: Alfred A. Knopf, 2007).

11. The pianist-impresario Chotzinoff, born in tsarist Russia in 1889, lured his friend Arturo Toscanini out of retirement in Italy to become the NBC Symphony's conductor in 1937.

12. Grossman married Chotzinoff's daughter Anne. Adler (1899–1990), who was born in a village of Bohemia that today

is a part of the Czech Republic, conducted the Baltimore Symphony from 1959 to 1968. In 1952, his musical adaptations for the Hollywood film *The Great Caruso* won him an Academy Award nomination.

13. Andersen to Floyd, April 21, 1955, Box 1, Folder 14, FASCL. The American Music Center was founded in 1939 by composers Marion Bauer, Aaron Copland, Howard Hanson, Otto Luening, Harrison Kerr, and Quincy Porter, to encourage, publicize, and disseminate American music.

14. Born Diana Rubin in 1905, the much-published Trilling was a founding member of the New York Intellectuals, and married literary and cultural critic Lionel Trilling; she died at ninety-one in 1996.

15. Author interview, February 10, 2008.

16. Floyd to Clarkes, August 30, 1955.

17. Ibid.

18. Floyd to Guggenheim Foundation, September 27, 1955. All cited Guggenheim materials courtesy of the John Simon Guggenheim Memorial Foundation.

19. Floyd to Clarkes, August 30, 1955.

20. Founded in England in 1937 as the Foster Parents Scheme for Children in Spain, the entity provided financial support and hostels for children orphaned or made refugees by the Spanish Civil War. It expanded its focus and altered its name to include all such displaced children in France, England, and Italy.

21. Floyd to Bacon, September 29, 1955, SUSC. The quote in the next paragraph is from the same source.

22. Floyd to Guggenheim Foundation, September 27, 1955. The next two quotes (Harrell and Bacon) are from the same source.

23. "N.B.C. Opera Aide Named," *New York Times*, February 8, 1956, 154.

24. Howard Taubman, "New Company Outgrowth of Television Unit," *New York Times*, December 11, 1955, 157.

25. Rappeport to Floyd, January 16, 1956, Box 1, Folder 33, FASCL.

26. Graham Greene, *The End of the Affair* (New York: Penguin Classics, 1991), 7.

27. Carlisle Floyd, *Frame of Remembrance* (1956). Unpublished pencil piano score in final volume of *Susannah* ms., Box 11, Folder 2, FALOC.

28. Carlisle Floyd, *Be Still, My Soul* (1956). Unpublished pencil piano ms., Box 11, Folder 2, FALOC, together with the six unattributed readings and timings. *Be Still, My Soul* is Jane L. Borthwick's (1813–1897) translation of a sacred hymn by Katherina Schlegel (1697–c. 1768), which appears in most Protestant hymnals set to the principal theme of Jean Sibelius's *Finlandia*. Poem 47 from A. E. Housman's 1896 *A Shropshire Lad* has the same title.

29. Following his City Opera appointment, Leinsdorf (1912–1993) conducted again at the Metropolitan Opera until 1962, later serving as music director of the Boston Symphony for seven years.

30. Erich Leinsdorf, *Cadenza: A Musical Career* (Boston: Houghton-Mifflin, 1976), 154.

31. Svanholm, born in 1904 in Västerås, Sweden, had been one of his generation's great Wagnerian Heldentenors, performing worldwide and on recordings. His presence at *Susannah*'s audition rated an item in the *New York Times* of April 1, 1956. His tenure with the Royal Swedish Opera lasted until the year before his death in 1964.

32. Rappeport taught the 1956–1957 school year at FSU, extended to 1957–1958.

33. Leinsdorf, *Cadenza*, 159.

34. Kerz (1912–1976) worked in Berlin before World War II with theatrical giants Max Reinhardt, Bertolt Brecht, Erwin Piscator, and Caspar Neher. A Jew, he left Germany in 1933, and arrived in the United States in 1941. He worked on Broadway from 1944 to 1971, and he served as a designer and art director for CBS-TV in New York.

35. Cook was born on February 25, 1917. According to a March 16, 1956 profile in *Collier's*, he had initially studied law, then clerked in a legal office. Finding himself enthralled by newsworthy stories, he "fed" them to reporters so successfully that he decided to write them himself. Abandoning law, he worked for newspapers in Camden, Philadelphia, St. Paul, and Chicago; he then served as a Marine combat correspondent for *Time*, *Life*, and *Collier's*, where he oversaw entertainment stories.

36. Curtin to Floyd, May 8, 1956. The following quote is also from this source.

37. *Diary*, June 27, 1956.

38. Curtin to Floyd, July 8, 1956.

39. Floyd to Clarkes, August 16, 1956.

40. Curtin to Floyd, July 8, 1956.

41. McCullers had won her Guggenheim in 1942, Copland and Crane theirs in 1925 and 1931, respectively.

42. Irene Kramarich's career was cut short by her sudden death from a heart ailment at forty-one in 1967.

43. See Floyd's own account in Brian Morgan, *Strange Child of Chaos: Norman Treigle* (New York: iUniverse, 2006), 40–41.

44. *Susannah* vocal score, 81.

45. Phyllis Curtin, "Phyllis Curtin Reminisces about Her Early Productions of Carlisle Floyd's *Susannah*." Liner notes for Video Artists International CD of New Orleans Opera 1962 production, VAI CD (VAIA 1115-2) (Pleasantville, NY, 1995), 9–10.

46. Author interview, March 3, 2007.

47. Morgan, *Strange Child of Chaos*, 39.

48. Ibid.

49. Holton to Floyd, September 18, 1956, Box 1, Folder 39, FASCL.

50. Interview, March 3, 2007.

51. Author interview, February 28, 2007. Rudel, born in Vienna in 1921, emigrated to the United States via Paris, and joined City Opera's staff as coach/pianist in 1943.

52. A copy of this telecast survives at New York's Paley Center for Media, formerly the Museum of Television and Radio.

53. White was born in Vienna in 1910 as Hans Schwarzkopf. Together with Felix Popper and Julius Rudel, this so-called Viennese Triumvirate ran City Opera until the seventies. White died in 2001 at the age of ninety-one.

54. *Diary,* September 26, 1956.

55. *Diary,* September 27, 1956.

56. Ibid.

57. Howard Taubman, "The Opera: 'Susannah,'" *New York Times,* September 28, 1956, 24.

58. Louis Biancolli, "Floyd's 'Susannah' At the City Center," *New York World-Telegram,* September 28, 1956.

59. "Discovery in Manhattan," *Time,* October 8, 1956.

60. Author interview, February 28, 2007.

61. Sokol, *New York City Opera,* 137.

62. Louis Biancolli, "U.S. Opera Shows Way to Europeans," *New York World-Telegram,* October 10, 1956.

63. Sokol, *New York City Opera,* 135–44.

64. Irving Kolodin, "*Susannah* and the Youngers," *Saturday Review,* October 13, 1956, 25.

65. Ronald Eyer, "New York City Opera Begins Ambitious Season," *Musical America,* October 10, 1956, 3. Courtesy of *Musical America.*

66. Collins to Floyd, October 9, 1956, and Barrow to Floyd, October 25, 1956, Box 1, Folder 22, FASCL.

67. Harvey Taylor, "Opera 'Susannah' Superb," *Detroit Times,* November 12, 1956.

68. Winthrop Sargeant, "'Susannah' at City Opera," *The New Yorker,* November 27, 1956, 122–23.

11. The Climb to *Wuthering Heights*:
New Forms, Marriage, 1956–1959

1. Padula and Rogers had just scored a success with *No Time for Sergeants,* which opened on Broadway on October 20, 1955.

2. Dubose Heyward (1885–1940), born in Charleston, won fame for stories and novels set in his native city and state, and their subsequent theatrical adaptations. His greatest fame derived from his *Porgy* book for the Gershwins in 1935.

3. Forbes (1891–1967) was best known for historical novels told through the eyes of unusual observers, as in *Johnny Tremain* (1943), a Revolutionary War tale made into a film by Walt Disney in 1957.

4. *Mirror,* first published in 1928 by Houghton Mifflin, was reprinted in 1985 and 2006. Esther Forbes, *A Mirror for Witches* (Chicago: Academy Publishers, 1985).

5. "Discovery in Manhattan," *Time,* October 8, 1956.

6. Frank Merkling, "New York," *Opera News,* December 5, 1956.

7. Per Floyd's undated Christmas 1956 letter to the Clarkes; and an announcement in the *New York Daily Mirror,* January 1, 1957. Scenario in Box 2, FASCL.

8. Allers and Holm had been members of the original *My Fair Lady* production team.

9. Founded in 1938, the store offered timeless, beautifully tailored classics, far beyond the price range of FSU junior faculty.

10. Barber (1910–1981), who became Menotti's life partner after they met at the Curtis Institute, composed distinguished orchestral, solo, and chamber music, and three operas: *A Hand of Bridge* (1957), *Vanessa* (1958), and *Antony and Cleopatra* (1966), all to Menotti's libretti.

11. Rorem composed his first stage work, *A Childhood Miracle,* in 1951. Based on Nathaniel Hawthorne's *The Snow Image,* and set to Elliott Stein's libretto, it was not premiered until 1955. In the years since, Rorem has written six other operas, the most successful of which are *Miss Julie,* based on Strindberg's play, completed in 1965 and revised in 1978, and Thornton Wilder's *Our Town,* in 2006.

12. Eyer, a pianist and organist born in Grand Rapids, Michigan, in 1910, joined the staff of *Musical America* in 1934, and served as the publication's editor-in-chief until 1960, except for critic Robert Sabin's tenure in that position from 1945 to 1950. Eyer joined the *New York Herald Tribune* staff in 1960, and held various positions with the New York Music Critics Circle.

13. Ronald Eyer and Carlisle Floyd, "Susannah—the New American Opera Reveals a Promising Talent," *Musical America,* February, 3, 1957. Eyer's article, without Floyd's "Credo," also appeared in the winter 1956/57 issue of the British journal *Tempo,* 7–11. Courtesy of *Musical America.*

14. Milton Babbitt, "Who Cares If You Listen?" *High Fidelity,* February 1958. I attended an event in Philadelphia in the early seventies at which a Babbitt student, fueled by a few glasses of cheap wine, proudly announced his master's latest attempt to synthesize the human voice: "Milton's almost got it! Male and low female voices are no problem; and once we figure out sopranos, we won't need singers anymore!" They presumably have yet to do so.

15. Colt (1912–1977), the daughter of financier Russell Colt and actress Ethel Barrymore, was the ninth Barrymore-related generation to go into performing. She sang in New York City Opera's first season (winter 1944), then concentrated on recitals and one-woman shows. She reappeared with the company in the fall of 1975 and spring of 1976, acting rather than singing the Duchess of Krackenthorp in Donizetti's *Daughter of the Regiment.*

16. Emily Brontë, *Wuthering Heights* (Oxford: Oxford University Press, 1985), 79. Randolph Carter's dramatic adaptation was published by the Samuel French Company of New York in 1939 and played for twelve performances on Broadway in April and May that year.

17. Courtesy of Jona Clarke.

18. Author interview, March 3, 2007.

19. Carlisle Floyd, *Bilby's Doll* (1956). Box 2, FASCL; and Box 1, Folder 3, FALOC. Floyd's final version will be considered in chapter 15.

20. Curtin to Floyd, April 27, 1957.

21. Copyright dates in Boosey's published scores, as opposed to dates when they came off the presses, indicate date of initial acquisition.

22. Holton note to Floyd in Box 1, Folder 33, FASCL.

23. Ross Parmenter, "Music: Viennese Chamber Ensemble," *New York Times,* February 25, 1957, 21.

24. Louis Biancolli, "Miss Curtin Gives Town Hall Concert," *New York World-Telegram,* February 25, 1957, 22.

25. Verdi's self-described *anni di galera,* depending on the authority consulted, lasted from 1843 to 1853, during which he produced sixteen new operas, from *I Lombardi* to *La traviata.*

26. Robert Sabin, "Phyllis Curtin, Soprano," *Musical America,* March 7, 1957. Courtesy of *Musical America.*

27. Carlisle Floyd, "Brontë Heroine," *New York Times,* July 13, 1958, X7.

28. Peter Warlock (Philip Heseltine), *Frederick Delius* (Westport, CT: Greenwood Press, 1977), 98, 143; and Christopher Redwood, ed., *A Delius Companion* (New York: Da Capo Press, 1991), 63, 237.

29. Steven C. Smith, *A Heart at Fire's Center: The Life and Music of Bernard Herrmann* (Berkeley and Los Angeles: University of California Press, 1991), 110. Herrmann (1911–1975) is best known for his film scores for Alfred Hitchcock and others. In a piece about Floyd's *Wuthering Heights* commission, the *New York Times* claimed that Herrmann's version was under consideration by the Metropolitan Opera and companies in Philadelphia and Germany. John Briggs, "Santa Fe Commissions Floyd," *New York Times,* October 13, 1957, Arts and Leisure section, 129. San Francisco's Kurt Herbert Adler thought of staging it with George London as Heathcliff, but the baritone's unavailability caused him to abandon the plan.

30. A subsequent CD reissue of the recording is currently out of print.

31. Since Herrmann's score saw publication only in 1965, Floyd could not have known it.

32. Floyd, "Brontë Heroine"; and Floyd, *Wuthering Heights.* Typescript libretto (1957) and act 3 revision for New York City Opera (1959), Box 14, Folder 4, FALOC.

33. Curtin to Floyd, April 22, 1957.

34. William S. Newman, *Notes* 17, no. 4 (1960): 663–64. This is the quarterly journal of the Music Library Association, Middleton, Wisconsin, that reviews new publications of sheet music. Carlisle Floyd, *Sonata for Piano* (1957), pencil ms., Box 10, Folder B, FALOC; published score (New York: Boosey & Hawkes, 1959).

35. Maurice Hinson, *Guide to the Pianist's Repertoire,* 3rd ed. (Bloomington: Indiana University Press, 2000), 293. Hinson describes Sonata thus: "Tonal, clever pianistic figuration with contrapuntal texture, brilliant closing. Large-scale. Demands virtuosity. Difficult."

36. Citation in Box 2, FASCL.

37. USC gave three performances, on April 5, 7, and 10, 1957. One of the sopranos, Maralin Niska, became a leading City Opera singer in the 60s and 70s. The vocal department chairman, William Vennard (1909–1971), sang Blitch, and was already a well-known vocal pedagogue through his text *Singing: The Mechanism and the Technic.*

38. Floyd to Henry Allen Moe, Guggenheim Foundation, November 11, 1957. Courtesy of Guggenheim Foundation.

39. *Diary, August 26, 1957.*

40. *Diary, September 2, 1957.*

41. *Diary, September 24, 1957.*

42. *Diary, September 25, 1957.*

43. John O'Hea Crosby (1926–2002) founded and worked as general director of the Santa Fe Opera beginning in 1957. He became president of the Manhattan School of Music, and of Opera America in 1976, serving four years in the latter position.

44. Cisney (1913–1989) was the first woman director at CBS in the early fifties, having begun her career with off-Broadway and summer stock productions. She staged Thomas's *Mignon* in City Opera's fall 1956 season, but this *Susannah* marked the end of her affiliation with the company.

45. "U.N. Dignitaries To Attend Opera," *New York Times,* October 6, 1957, 12.

46. *Diary,* October 10, 1957.

47. Howard Taubman, "Music: American Opera," *New York Times,* October 11, 1957, 21. There would be two more *Susannah*s that season, on November 8 and 13, without the composer in attendance.

48. Ibid.

49. *Dallas Times Herald,* December 14, 1957.

50. Author interview, January 22, 2007.

51. Curtin to Floyd, November 7, 1957.

52. Author interview, March 3, 2007.

53. E. D., "Composer Group Opens Its Season," *New York Times,* November 24, 1957.

54. *Diary,* November 28, 1957.

55. Quoted in Trilling's obituary: Michael Norman, "Diana Trilling," *New York Times,* October 25, 1996.

56. Julian Jaynes, *The Origin of Consciousness in the Breakdown of the Bicameral Mind* (New York: Houghton Mifflin, 1976).

57. Floyd, "Brontë Heroine."

58. Carlisle Floyd, "Playwriting in the Opera House," *Theatre Arts,* January 1958, 32–33.

59. Curtin to Floyd, January 17, 1958.

60. Ford Foundation archives, L8-476.

61. Following six years' tenure in Chicago, Hendl (1917–2007) went on to the directorship of the Eastman School of Music from 1964 to 1972, and later work at the Juilliard School and Erie Philharmonic.

62. With school and community markets in mind, the *Susannah* Suite was later expanded to a thirty-eight-minute concert presentation with soloists, mixed chorus, and either piano or full orchestra.

63. At the University of Iowa, Engle (1908–1991) headed the famed Iowa Writers' Workshop from 1941 to 1967, and had close

acquaintance with most of the day's great writers. His prolific output included the libretto of a Christmas opera, *Golden Child,* for composer Philip Bezanson, televised on a 1960 Hallmark Hall of Fame program.

64. See Chapter 9 on Floyd's *Susannah* orchestra.

65. The theater, at which Tom Jones and Harvey Schmidt's *The Fantasticks* ran for a record-breaking forty-two years, from 1960 to 2002, was gutted in 2005 and converted to luxury condominiums.

66. Lewis Funke, "From Here to There," *New York Times,* April 24, 1958, 37.

67. Evans Clinchy, "Hartt Opera-Theater Guild Stages 'Susannah,'" *Hartford Times,* April 24, 1958.

68. Corsaro has told his own story with wit and passion in *Maverick* (New York: Vanguard Press, 1978).

69. The Actors Studio and The Method are more talked about than understood, and the studio's history is a dynamic mirror of its times. Some of its more famous alumni were and still are among Floyd's favorite actors: Marlon Brando, Montgomery Clift, James Dean, Tom Ewell, John Garfield, Julie Harris, Kim Hunter, Karl Malden, E. G. Marshall, Marilyn Monroe, Anthony Quinn, Eva Marie Saint, Maureen Stapleton, and Eli Wallach.

70. All Corsaro quotations from author interview, March 5, 2007, except as noted.

71. Julius Rudel interview with author, February 28, 2007.

72. Ross Parmenter, "Opera: New 'Susannah,'" *New York Times,* May 1, 1958, 35.

73. Winthrop Sargeant, "Dawn of a New Day, Maybe," *The New Yorker,* May 10, 1958, 57.

74. Harold C. Schonberg, "The Dean and Da Vinci of the Copyists," *New York Times,* June 4, 1978, D15. Arnstein, born in Budapest in 1898, had his own New York office and staff from 1932 until his death in 1989. Other regular clients included Menotti, Barber, Bernstein, Thomson, and Schuman.

75. Kay (1919–1981), first trained as a cellist, became one of New York's most sought-after arrangers and orchestrators; he was known for numerous works for New York City Ballet, and especially for his collaboration with Leonard Bernstein on *Candide* and *On the Town.*

76. Howard Taubman, "Cold War on the Cultural Front," *New York Times,* April 13, 1958, Magazine section, 12.

77. In addition to directing opera, operetta, pageants, and television dramas, Bill Butler (1919–1998), later better known as Henry, wrote librettos for composers Marvin David Levy (*Mourning Becomes Electra,* 1967), Richard Cumming (*The Picnic,* 1985), and Chester Biscardi (*Tight-Rope,* 1985).

78. Lowry (1913–1993) began in 1953 as the director of the Ford Foundation's education program, out of which grew the arts and humanities initiative, which distributed over $320 million to performing arts organizations and individual artists and $60 million to humanities scholarships.

79. Born George Burnstein in Montreal in 1920, London's family soon moved to Los Angeles. The singer grew up, trained and debuted in the United States, proceeding to a stunning international career before his death in 1985.

80. Corsaro, *Maverick,* 114–15.

81. Howard Taubman, "Opera: 'Susannah' at Fair," *New York Times,* June 26, 1958, 24.

82. "The Brussels All-Stars," *Time,* July 28, 1958, 27.

83. Morgan, *Strange Child of Chaos,* 50. The reference to Canadian-born Raymond Massey (1896–1983) was a great compliment to Treigle's acting. Massey won great fame portraying such monumental historical characters as the abolitionist John Brown and Abraham Lincoln.

84. Born in Chatham, Ontario, in 1928, Guttman led many of Canada's opera-producing organizations, including the Vancouver Opera, Edmonton Opera, Manitoba Opera, Saskatchewan Opera, and Calgary Opera, until retiring in 2001.

85. BCS-0035. This is still the only commercially available film of any portion of *Susannah.*

86. Floyd, "Brontë Heroine."

87. "Brontë in Song," *Time,* July 28, 1958.

88. Santa Fe gave performances on July 18, 19, 22, 1958.

89. Steve Hess, "World Premiere Opens Carlisle Floyd Opera to Santa Fe Audience," *Albuquerque Journal,* July 17, 1958.

90. Levy, born in New Jersey in 1932, went on to receive a commission from the Metropolitan Opera for an operatic adaptation of O'Neill's *Mourning Becomes Electra,* premiered to general critical vilification at its opening at the company's Lincoln Center house in 1967.

91. Martin David Levy, "'Wuthering Heights'—A Drama with Music," *New York Herald Tribune,* July 27, 1958.

92. Author interview, February 28, 2007.

93. Robert Wilder Blue, "The Inseparable Histories of Julius Rudel and New York City Opera: A Reminiscence," US OperaWeb, September 2002.

94. "Brontë in Song," *Time,* July 28, 1958.

95. Mark Huber, "World Premiere," *Musical Courier,* July 1958. From its founding in New York in 1880, the *Courier* was published weekly until 1937, and then bimonthly until its discontinuation in 1962.

96. *Diary,* August 8, 1958.

97. See Francis D. Perkins, "'Wuthering Heights' Now Being Revised," *New York Herald Tribune,* March 29, 1959, as a prelude to City Opera's opening.

98. According to Reverend Floyd's diary for Christmas Eve 1959, the whole family attended services at St. John's Episcopal Church.

99. Clare Conway Jones, *Opera News,* October 27, 1958.

100. *Diary,* October 29, 1958.

101. Harold C. Schonberg, "Two Young Singers Heard in 'Susannah,'" *New York Times,* November 15, 1958, 18.

102. According to the *Springfield Union* for November 12, 1958, Floyd "concocted" the abridgement with conductor Robert Staffanson.

103. Curtin to Floyd, December 20, 1958; and *Diary*, December 25, 1958.

104. Mann (1920–2007) won an Academy Award for his direction of *Marty* in 1955. The film also won awards for best picture, best actor (Ernest Borgnine), and best screenplay (by playwright Paddy Chayefsky).

105. David S. Adams to Floyd, April 13, 1959. Boosey & Hawkes works files.

106. Goldstein to Floyd, April 8, 1959, Box 1, Folder 33, FASCL.

107. *Diary*, April 9, 1959.

108. In Winchell's column in the *New York Daily Mirror.* See Sherman Billingsley, "Things You Never Knew About Winchell," *Herald-Journal,* August 24, 1941.

109. Paul Henry Lang, "Opera: 'Wuthering Heights,'" *New York Herald Tribune,* April 10, 1959. The Lang quotes in the next two paragraphs are from this article.

110. Howard Taubman, "Opera: Floyd's 'Wuthering Heights,'" *New York Times,* April 10, 1959, 22.

111. Miles Kastendieck, "Floyd Captures Force of 'Wuthering Heights,'" *New York Journal American,* April 10, 1959.

112. *Diary,* April 10, 1959.

113. Ibid.

114. *Diary,* April 12, 1959.

12. The Grand One: *The Passion of Jonathan Wade*, 1959–1962

1. Floyd to Adams, April 17, 1959, B & H composer files.

2. Sokol, *New York City Opera,* 159–60.

3. Winthrop Sargeant, "Unscaled Heights," *New Yorker,* April 18, 1959.

4. Irving Kolodin, "Floyd of 'Wuthering Heights,'" *Saturday Review,* April 18, 1959, 24.

5. Robert Sabin, "Floyd's *Wuthering Heights,*" *Musical America,* May 8, 1959. Courtesy of *Musical America.* Sabin (1912–1969) joined the staff of *Musical America* in 1936, and was the publication's editor in chief from 1945 until 1950. In addition to editing the ninth edition of Oscar Thompson's *International Cyclopedia of Music and Musicians,* Sabin also wrote for *Musical Quarterly, Musical Courier, American Record Guide,* and *Tempo.*

6. This and the following quote from author interview, April 20, 2007.

7. Holton note to Floyd about *Wuthering Heights* at City Opera, May 4, 1959, Box 1, Folder 33, FASCL.

8. Founded in 1936 by automotive pioneer Henry Ford (1863–1947) and his only son Edsel (1893–1943), the Ford Foundation had an incalculable impact on America's performing arts. Its grants to companies and individual artists provided substantial assistance to most of the creators of serious music in the fifties, sixties, and beyond.

9. "Ford Unit Grants $130,000 For Music," *New York Times,* March 10, 1959, 8.

10. A healthy infusion to Floyd's FSU salary: $3,000 in 1959 had a Consumer Price Index value of $22,400 in 2010. See www.measuringworth.com/uscompare/.

11. Grant file PA 59-153, Ford Foundation Archives (hereafter FFA).

12. Mistral, born Lucila Godoy Alcaya in 1889, led an extraordinary life as a teacher, poet, and representative to both the League of Nations and United Nations. The first Latin American woman to be awarded the Nobel Prize for literature in 1945, she died in the United States in 1957.

13. Gabriela Mistral, *Poemas de las Madres* (Santiago: Editorial del Pacifico, 1950). Gabriela Mistral, *Desolación* (New York: Columbia University, Instituto de las Españas en los Estados Unidos, 1922).

14. Curtin to Floyd, June 27, 1959.

15. Ibid.

16. Karl Köhler (conductor), Lutz Wenk (sets), Ingeborg Schenk (costumes); the cast included Ditha Sommer (Susannah), Oskar Gernhardt (Sam), Willi Baumeister (Blitch) and Hubert Möhler (Little Bat).

17. Willy Werner Göttig, "Ein Opern-Reisser nach bewährtem Rezept," *Frankfurter Abendpost,* July 2, 1959. Unless otherwise noted, all translations are mine.

18. Alfons Neukirchen, "Amerikanische Susannah im Bade," *Düsseldorfer Nachrichten,* July 2, 1959.

19. Braasch, "Amerikanische Oper stellte sich vor," *Hamburger Abendblatt,* July 7, 1959.

20. Cook to Floyd, July 14, 1959. Like all letters from Cook's wife, Phyllis Curtin, all Cook letters courtesy of Phyllis Curtain and Carlisle Floyd. The lapwing characterization is a humorous reference to Floyd's love duet for Cathy and Heathcliff in *Wuthering Heights.*

21. Chautauqua gave two performances on July 31 and August 3. David Atkinson debuted at NYCO in the spring of 1958 as Sam in Bernstein's *Trouble in Tahiti.*

22. Schiffman, born in Greensboro, North Carolina, in 1928, has composed and been widely performed and recorded in virtually every medium *except* opera, and has a special focus on chamber music.

23. FFA Grant no. 06090118, reel 2463; FFA 60-118.

24. Harold C. Schonberg, "Firkusny Plays Sonata By Floyd," *New York Times,* October 14, 1959, 51.

25. Louis Biancolli, "Firkusny Recital," *New York World-Telegram and Sun,* October 14, 1959, 32.

26. Winthrop Sargeant, *New Yorker,* October 24, 1959.

27. Carlisle Floyd, "Apologia for Composers of Opera," *Central Opera Service Bulletin,* November 1959, 1–2.

28. "Our Young Men Honored," *Tallahassee Democrat,* January 6, 1960, 6.

29. Nixon to Floyd, January 14, 1960, Box 1, Folder 23, FASCL. Smathers to Floyd, February 15, 1960, Box 1, Folder 23, FASCL.

30. *Susannah* played once that spring at NYCO, on February 2, 1960.

31. Cook to Floyd, February 12, 1960. Phyllis Treigle, born May 6, 1960, has had a successful career as an operatic soprano, and currently serves as the assistant department chair of music at the New Orleans Center for Creative Arts, Riverfront.

32. In her review of *The Mystery,* Frances Monachino objected to Floyd's "Ah" at the moment of birth as overly realistic for its context. *Notes* (2nd Series) 25, no. 1 (September 1968).

33. Curtin to Floyd, February 18, 1960.

34. Floyd had met Stokowski at an earlier production of *Susannah.* The conductor's tenure as music director of the Houston Symphony Orchestra ended before the orchestra performed *The Mystery.*

35. Holton to Chester D'Arms, May 5, 1960; bill from Arnstein to Floyd, May 8, 1960; Holton to D'Arms, May 9, 1960; D'Arms to Holton, May 12, 1960. FFA PA 59–153.

36. Thorpe's initial article appeared in the *Washington Star* of February 21, 1960, his review of *Susannah* on February 28, and "John E. Walker's" and Julius Rudel's letters on March 1, 1960.

37. Day Thorpe, "Dull Work Well Sung by City Center Opera," *Washington Star,* February 19, 1960.

38. An Italian dynamic indication, meaning "muted."

39. Doak Campbell held the university's presidency from 1941 until 1957; the more cosmopolitan Strozier, for whom FSU's main library is named, filled the presidency from 1957 until his death in 1960.

40. Claudia Cassidy, "'Susannah' Disappointing Start," *Chicago Tribune,* March 5, 1960.

41. Don Henahan, *Chicago Daily News,* March 5, 1960.

42. *All the King's Men* was first published in 1946, and Floyd read it soon afterward, around the time that he wrote the story "A Lengthening Shadow" in Syracuse.

43. Floyd read Bromfield's book during his high school years in North.

44. Louis Bromfield, *Wild Is the River* (NY: Harper & Bros., 1941), 46, 183.

45. Cook to Floyd, March 13, 1960. Thomas C. Ryan (1924–1986) won later fame for his 1968 screenplay for Carson McCullers's *The Heart Is a Lonely Hunter,* which he also produced; and as writer for *Hurry Sundown* (1967).

46. Cook to Floyd, March 13, 1960. On learning that Preminger had cast Sal Mineo as "Ari Ben Somethingorother," Cook commented, "I wonder what *he* knows about Semitism?"

47. Curtin to Floyd, April 8, 1960.

48. Originally written as incidental music for two pianos for Paul Horgan's play *Death, Mr. President,* about Abraham Lincoln's final weeks of life before his assassination at Ford's Theater, and first performed in 1940 at Converse College.

49. Treigle's 1971 recording of *Pilgrimage* with the New Orleans Philharmonic Symphony Orchestra, conducted by Werner Torkanowsky, included only the first, third, and fifth songs.

50. Sidney Sukoenig, *Syracuse Herald-Journal,* April 25, 1960.

51. William Fleming, "Soprano Joan Aceto Tinkles Like Bells," *Syracuse Post-Standard,* April 25, 1960, 14.

52. FFA 60–118, reel 2463. This is also the source of all Ford Foundation information and correspondence referenced in the next five paragraphs.

53. Following his appointment at Brown, Kunzel (1935–2009) won great fame as principal conductor of the Cincinnati Pops Orchestra for forty-four years beginning in 1965, and won the National Medal of Arts in 2006.

54. Joseph Auslander, *Sunrise Trumpets* (New York: Harper & Row, 1924). Auslander (1897–1965) became America's first poet laureate, serving from 1937 to 1941. *Sunrise Trumpets* was his first published collection, but his best-known works were World War II poems, published as *The Unconquerables* (1943).

55. Goldstein to Floyd, June 7, 1960, B & H works files.

56. Carlisle Floyd, "Death Came Knocking," CMEA program, April 5, 1961, B & H works files.

57. Erich Kunzel, May 16, 1961. In B & H works files, evidently written as promotional material at Robert Holton's behest.

58. Carlisle Floyd, program notes for San Antonio Symphony Orchestra, November 26, 1960. Copies in both B & H work files and Box 3, FASCL.

59. Nikolaidi, born in 1906 (1909 in some sources) in the Greek city of Smyrna in present-day Turkey, sang leading roles at the Vienna Staatsoper from 1936 to 1948, and emigrated to the United States in the latter year. Her well-received Town Hall recital led to appearances with the Metropolitan Opera and a recording contract with Columbia.

60. Floyd to Rudel, Box 8, Folder 1, FALOC.

61. Wade Hampton III (1818–1902) led the Confederate cavalry and later served South Carolina and the reconstituted United States as a state senator, governor, U.S. senator, and federal railroad commissioner. Hundreds of South Carolina streets, schools, and hotels are named for this protean figure, who even appears in Margaret Mitchell's *Gone With the Wind* as Scarlett O'Hara's first husband, Charles Hamilton's, military commander. Reverend Floyd's church in Walterboro stood on Hampton Street.

62. *Diary,* August 22, 1960.

63. Entry for May 25, 1865 in Mary Boykin Chesnut, *A Diary from Dixie,* ed. Ben Ames Williams (Cambridge: Harvard University Press, 1980), 534.

64. Ibid., 535.

65. *Diary,* May 20, 1942.

66. Chesnut, *Diary from Dixie,* 530.

67. Hodding Carter, *The Angry Scar: The Story of Reconstruction* (Garden City: Doubleday, 1959); and James S. Pike, *The Prostrate State: South Carolina under Negro Government* (New York: D.

Appleton, 1974; Harper Torchbooks, 1968); and Harold M. Hyman, *Era of the Oath: Northern Loyalty Oaths during the Civil War and Reconstruction* (Philadelphia: University of Pennsylvania Press, 1954). Carter drew some of his information from Pike's book without attribution.

68. "Rebel Song" and pledge in Carter, *Angry Scar,* 69.

69. Ibid., 210.

70. Georgia slave Nicey Kinney. Ibid., 267.

71. Carlisle Floyd, *The Passion of Jonathan Wade* (1961–1962). Handwritten treatment (scenario) and typed libretto, Box 8, Folder 1, FALOC.

72. Carlisle Floyd, "The Composer as Librettist," *Opera News,* November 10, 1962, 9–12.

73. Robert Wilder Blue, "The Double Life of Jonathan Wade," USOperaWeb, May 2001.

74. Author interview, November 19, 2006.

75. Ibid.

76. Following piano study with Floyd, Polly Holliday (b. 1937) began acting with the Asolo Theatre Company in Sarasota, Florida. During a subsequent decade in New York and numerous Broadway productions, she landed the role of the sassy, uninhibited, man-hungry waitress Florence Jean Castleberry (Flo) on the television sitcom *Alice,* which aired from 1976 to 1980. The character's memorable trademark phrase was "Kiss my grits."

77. Gerald Ashford, *San Antonio Express and News,* November 27, 1960.

78. Bill Richards, *San Antonio Light,* November 27, 1960.

79. The composer thought that allowance should be made in commissions to allow attendance at first performances of commissioned works. Floyd to W. McNeil Lowry, July 8, 1961, FFA 30165002, reel 4197.

80. Reported by Curtin. Despite Steinberg's attitude, Curtin wrote Floyd on January 1, 1962, "*The Mystery* enjoyed a genuine success in Pgh. Steinberg performed it *beautifully.* And I sang it very well. So *many* people told me how moved they were—and about the tears they had. And the two reviews [in the *Press* and *Post Gazette*] were splendid."

81. Ralph Levando, *Christian Science Monitor,* January 20, 1962.

82. Ross Parmenter, "The World of Music," *New York Times,* December 4, 1960, X9.

83. Draper (1884–1956) led a colorful life in Italy in the thirties before displaying outspoken opposition to Mussolini. Many of her pieces from those years, including *The Italian Lesson, Three Women and Mr. Clifford, Doctors and Diets,* and *A Church in Italy,* are still available on recordings.

84. Neway (b. 1919), whom we met in the previous chapter, had gained fame in Menotti's *The Consul* on Broadway in 1950, and as Mother Superior in the first production of Rodgers and Hammerstein's *The Sound of Music* in 1959.

85. Carlisle Floyd, "Monologue" (c. 1961). Two typed versions of this untitled text—including Patricia Neway's penciled annotations on one—are in Box 5, Folder 4, FALOC, together with Floyd's draft musical setting; and in B & H works files.

86. Holton to Floyd, February 8, 1961; and B & H works file.

87. *Diary,* March 2, 1961.

88. Maxwell (1883–1963), a splendid self-invention, excelled as a gossip columnist, writer, and especially as a professional hostess of parties in the highest echelons of society, including international royalty.

89. John Fay, "Top Musical Talent Is Featured at Elsa Maxwell Dinner Party," *Mobile Press-Register,* April 12, 1961.

90. Ibid.

91. John Fay, "Backstage and Studio," *Mobile Press-Register,* April 16, 1961.

92. Ibid.

93. Carl Vollrath studied composition at FSU with Floyd, Ernst von Dohnányi, and John Boda. Vollrath has taught composition and music appreciation at Troy University, Alabama, since 1965. His compositions include six symphonies for band; in addition to his opera, *The Quest,* he composed a body of chamber music. All Vollrath quotes from author interview on August 1, 2008.

94. Ellen Taaffe Zwilich is one of America's most successful composers. Born in Miami in 1939, she has excelled in every musical genre *except* opera. Like Carlisle Floyd, her many honors include a Guggenheim Fellowship and membership in the American Academy of Arts and Letters.

95. Author interview, December 22, 2008.

96. In Lucien Price, *Dialogues of Alfred North Whitehead* (Boston: Little, Brown, 1954).

97. Brown worked as a school band director in Everett, Washington. Besides his compositions for band, his catalogue includes a monodrama, *The Torment of Medea,* based on Euripides; two ballets, *Arthur: King!* and *Ballabile;* and a one-act chamber opera, *The Gift of the Magi.* All Brown quotes from an interview of September 7, 2006 and an E-mail of December 8, 2006.

98. Floyd to W. McNeil Lowry, July 8, 1961, FFA 30652001, reel 2463.

99. *Diary,* June 27, 1961.

100. Curtin to Floyd, January 1, 1962. "Gene is overwhelmingly moved by the new opera, and has talked of it constantly. *Surely* Julius cannot let anybody but me sing it."

101. Ross (1899–1990), born in Langport, Somerset, England, began conducting the Schola Cantorum in 1927, and the group became one of the principal vocal ensembles affiliated with the New York Philharmonic.

102. Paul Henry Lang, *New York Herald Tribune,* March 28, 1962.

103. Miles Kastendieck, "Mixed 'Pilgrimage,'" *New York Journal-American,* March 28, 1962.

104. Carlisle Floyd, Interview in New Orleans *Times-Picayune,* March 18, 1962.

105. The March 31 performance has been preserved on CD by VAI Records as VAI 1115-2, with a booklet containing pieces written by Floyd and Curtin. None of the singers was aware that they were being recorded, and Curtin in particular felt that had been a bad evening; but when VAI's Ernie Gilbert played the tapes for her, she found that Treigle and Cassilly sounded well enough to justify this memento of their work together.

106. Charles L. Dufour, "Original Style Marks 'Susannah' Performance," *New Orleans States-Item,* March 30, 1962.

107. Frank Gagnard, "Cheers Evoked by 'Susannah,'" *Times-Picayune,* March 30, 1962.

108. *Carnival* won Armstrong a 1962 Tony for best set design. He died at age thirty-nine on August 12, 1969.

109. Fletcher (1922–1982) specialized in Shakespeare, directing for five seasons at the San Diego Festival and seven seasons at the Oregon Shakespeare Festival in the fifties and early sixties. He served as artistic director of Seattle Repertory Theater from 1966 to 1970, and as director of the American Conservatory Theater in San Francisco, beginning in 1969.

110. Ernst Bacon, *Syracuse Post-Standard,* May 2, 1962.

111. "City Center Lists New Floyd Opera," *New York Times,* July 25, 1962, X9.

112. Dominick Argento, *Catalogue Raisonné as Memoir: A Composer's Life* (Minneapolis: University of Minnesota Press, 2004).

113. Curtin to Floyd, February 18, 1960.

114. E-mail from Curtin to author, December 7, 2007.

115. Author interview, December 28, 2007.

116. "Composer Urges Opera in English," *New York Times,* June 23, 1962, 23.

117. Rudel quotes from author interview, February 28, 2007.

118. This and the excerpts in the following five paragraphs from Rudel to Floyd, August 25, 1962, Box 1, Folder 23, FASCL.

119. Cook to Floyd, September 3, 1962. The humorous reference is to Curtin's previous Floyd role, Cathy in *Wuthering Heights,* in which the character died *off* her feet.

120. At any rate, before September 25, 1962, when Reverend Floyd's *Diary* has the composer calling his parents *from* New York about tickets to the premiere.

121. Author interview, March 3, 2007.

122. Robert Ward's *Crucible* had won a Pulitzer the previous year.

123. Rorem had negotiated a commission with Rudel and the Ford Foundation for *Mamba's Daughters,* the same subject Floyd had rejected in the fifties, but learned on January 20, 1962 that the *Mamba* project was off. He then wrestled with Jascha Kessler's *Charade,* which he likewise abandoned. See Ned Rorem, *The Later Diaries of Ned Rorem, 1961–1972* (San Francisco: North Point Press, 1983), 49–50.

124. Author interview, April 20, 2007.

125. Cook to Floyd, October 10, 1962.

126. Ross Parmenter, "Music: 'Passion of Jonathan Wade,'" *New York Times,* October 12, 1962, 24.

127. Paul Henry Lang, *New York Herald Tribune,* October 12, 1962.

128. Louis Biancolli, *New York World-Telegram,* October 12, 1962.

129. Moore to Floyd, October 12, 1962, Box 1, Folder 23, FASCL.

130. Frederick M. Winship, "New American Opera By Floyd a Major Work," *The Washington Post,* October 13, 1962, A4.

131. Argento, *Catalogue Raisonné As Memoir,* 32.

132. In 2004, Boosey published a series of American aria volumes, which for soprano includes two examples from *Colonel Jonathan* and one each from four other Argento operas, alongside six Floyd arias from *Cold Sassy Tree, Slow Dusk, The Sojourner and Mollie Sinclair, Susannah,* and *Willie Stark;* and, in 1991, the Metropolitan Opera premiered Argento's *The Ghosts of Versailles,* with libretto by William M. Hoffman.

13. At the Oars: *Mollie Sinclair* to *Markheim,* 1962–1966

1. Rorem, *Later Diaries of Ned Rorem,* 47.

2. Holton to Ribet, October 13, 1962, B & H works files; copy in Box 1, Folder 23, FASCL.

3. Andre Kostalanetz (1901–1980), November 11, 1962, B & H works files. Born in St. Petersburg, Russia, this conductor-arranger married the soprano Lily Pons, and practically invented the genre of "easy listening." He gained great renown through performances and recordings of his arrangements of light classics and popular standards from the forties through the seventies.

4. Cook to Floyd, October 20, 1962, Box 1, Folder 23, FASCL. Ryan's script was directed by Robert Ellis Miller and released in 1968 with a score by Dave Grusin.

5. Sargeant to Floyd, October 17, 1962, Box 1, Folder 23, FASCL.

6. Irving Kolodin, "Carlisle Floyd on the Blue and the Gray," *Saturday Review,* October 27, 1962, 41.

7. Robert Sabin, "America: New York," *Opera,* January 22–27, 1963.

8. Duane Meyer, *The Highland Scots of North Carolina, 1732–1776* (Chapel Hill: University of North Carolina Press, 1957, 1961).

9. England's parliament had passed three earlier stamp acts, but the fourth legislation of 1765 imposed a first direct tax on American colonists, requiring every legal document, permit, commercial contract, newspaper, will, pamphlet, and pack of playing cards to bear a tax stamp.

10. "Carlin" is a Scottish term from Middle English and Norse, meaning an aged woman.

11. Meyer, *Highland Scots,* 163–65.

12. Ibid., 41.

13. Carlisle Floyd, *The Soujourner and Mollie Sinclair,* published vocal score (New York: Boosey & Hawkes, 1968).

14. Beverly Wolter, "Tercentenary Opera," *Winston-Salem Journal,* December 4, 1963, 18.

15. *Diary,* November 21, 1962.

16. Bill Woolsey, *Louisville Times,* February 21, 1963, 18.

17. Curtin to Floyd, February 21, 1963.

18. Bill Woolsey, "Verdi Inspires Young Composer," *Louisville Times,* February 19, 1963.

19. Ibid. Floyd referred to the adaptation by Owen and Donald Davis, which played at New York's National Theater from January to May 1936, starring Ruth Gordon, Raymond Massey, Pauline Lord, and Tom Ewell.

20. Goldstein to Floyd, January 23, 1963, B & H works file. As it turned out, the 1962 *Wade* vocal score (in Arnold Arnstein's master sheets in Box 9, Folders 1 and 3, FALOC) never reached final revised form, and was consequently never published.

21. In 1960, Frank Corsaro took a five-year hiatus from opera, and, more specifically, from City Opera, to direct Broadway productions of Tennessee Williams's *Night of the Iguana* with Bette Davis, which Floyd saw during his *Jonathan Wade* weeks in the city, and a new Actors Studio play, *Baby Want a Kiss,* which opened in April 1964 with a young couple named Joanne Woodward and Paul Newman.

22. *Diary,* January 22, 27, 1963.

23. Roger Sessions's (1896–1985) first completed stage work, the one-act opera *The Trial of Lucullus,* was performed in Berkeley, California, in April 1947. *Montezuma* received its premiere at West Berlin's Deutsche Oper in 1964, and reached the United States only in 1976, under Sarah Caldwell at the Opera Company of Boston. At the time of Sessions's death, he left unfinished a children's opera, *The Emperor's New Clothes,* to a libretto by Andrew Porter.

24. Floyd and Sessions may actually have been distant cousins: the first in Roger's family line to arrive in the colonies was also a Samuel (1614–1706); but no closer connection has appeared.

25. Foss, born in Berlin in 1922, had escaped the Nazis via Paris, around the time of Hitler's rise to power in 1933.

26. Curtin had debuted at the Metropolitan Opera as Fiordiligi in Mozart's *Così fan tutte,* and later sang Salome. Relations grew strained with City Opera. Rudel felt the loss of her talent, and planned a new production of Handel's *Julius Caesar* as a vehicle to celebrate her return, but Beverly Sills employed every wile and connection to be cast in the role, which launched her superstardom in City Opera's 1966 season. In the meantime, Curtin returned to City Opera in the fall of 1964, for *La traviata* and *Salome;* her 1960 performances of *Susannah* were her last of the role with the company.

27. Levine subsequently worked as a stage director with the company.

28. Robert Sabin, "Some Younger Composers," *Tempo* (Spring 1963): 25–26.

29. Howard Klein, "'Susannah' Heard at the City Opera," *New York Times,* May 4, 1963, 35.

30. Floyd to Jona Clarke, June 5, 1963.

31. Ibid.

32. Howard Klein, "State Marks 300 Years," *New York Times,* October 13, 1963, 129.

33. Howard Klein, "Louisville Carries On," *New York Times,* November 10, 1963, Arts & Leisure, X15.

34. Edgar Ray Loessin, born in Texas in 1928, attended the Actors Studio in New York, after which he founded East Carolina's theater arts department in 1963. Since retiring in 1991, he has been an arts critic for WHRO-FM in the Norfolk, Virginia, area.

35. Carlisle Floyd, "The Genesis of *The Sojourner and Mollie Sinclair,*" VAI CD 1172, liner notes (Pleasantville, NY, 1999), 3–5.

36. Floyd to Holton, December 2, 1963, B & H works files. The date is probably Floyd's mistake, as Holton in fact attended the opening.

37. Nell Hirshberg, *Raleigh Observer,* December 3, 1963.

38. "New Music Drama Offered in South," *New York Times,* December 3, 1963, 46.

39. Beverly Wolter, "Tercentenary Opera 'Tis a Bonnie Affair," *Winston-Salem Sentinel,* December 3, 1963.

40. Beverly Wolter, "Opera Writer, Stars Stress Enjoyment," *Winston-Salem Journal,* December 4, 1963.

41. Jane Magrath, *The Pianist's Guide to Standard Teaching and Performance Literature* (Van Nuys, CA: Alfred, c. 1995), 365.

42. Ibid.

43. Weide to Floyd, July 28, 1984, Box 3, FASCL.

44. Floyd to Clarkes, December 21, 1963.

45. "*Sojourner* Is Colorful, Entertaining, Melodious," *Tercentenary News* (Winter 1963): 3–4. Copy in B & H works files.

46. Floyd to Holton, January 21, 1964, B & H works files.

47. Pease (1916–1967) debuted at the Metropolitan Opera in 1942. After serving in World War II, he sang many roles at New York City Opera and later at German opera houses.

48. Floyd to Holton, January 21, 1964, B & H composer files.

49. Holton to Floyd, January 17, 1964, B & H works files.

50. Holton to Floyd, January 31, 1964, B & H works files.

51. *Diary,* February 20, 1964.

52. Minimum wage in 1964 was $1.25 per hour, compared to Arnstein's $4.50.

53. Floyd to Gertrude Smith, March 16, 1964, B & H works files.

54. Goldstein to Floyd, April 3, 1964, B & H works files.

55. 1964 FSU citation in Box 3, FASCL.

56. Carlisle Floyd, "Society and the Artist," typescript, 1964, Box 3, FASCL. Quotes from the next four paragraphs are from this source.

57. Jane Murray, Neway's understudy in the original cast, sang Mollie, and Jerold Teachey, the original Spokesman, sang Dougald; George M. Seymour was the Spokesman.

58. Floyd to Holton, May 9, 1964, B & H works files. The quotes in the next paragraph are from this source.

59. Floyd to Holton, June 8, 1964, B & H works files. The remaining quotes in this paragraph are from this source.

60. Holton to Floyd, June 10, 1964, Box 2, FASCL.

61. "Kennedy Announces a Second Met Company," *New York Times,* October 12, 1963, 43.

62. Manuel (1928–1999) had worked at Covent Garden (Royal Opera and Sadler's Wells Ballet). He became the Met's executive stage manager in 1967, and directed his own productions at the house between 1960 and 1962.

63. Reimueller (1937–1987) was an assistant conductor of the Metropolitan Opera National Company in 1965, and led performances at New York City Opera from the fall of 1970 to spring 1974.

64. Pope to Floyd, September 17, 1964, B & H works files. Once Boosey recouped extraction fees from rentals, they resumed paying Floyd's 33 and 1/3 percent.

65. Pope to Braunagel, June 22, 1964; Braunagel to Pope, June 24, 1964; Floyd to Pope, June 29, 1964, B & H works files.

66. Pope's forty-seven years with Boosey ended in 1984, in a shuffling of personnel remarkably similar to the one that brought him to New York twenty years earlier. See Helen Wallace, *Boosey & Hawkes,* 175.

67. Holton to Floyd, July 21, 1964, B & H works files.

68. Staff, *Central Opera Service Bulletin* (March/April 1967): 11.

69. Floyd to Goldstein August 4, 1964, B & H works files.

70. Author interview with Jane Matheny, February 18, 2008.

71. *Diary,* August 29, 1964.

72. Pope to Floyd, October 28, 1964, B & H works files. The National Company performed *Susannah* twenty-seven times, in Indianapolis, Cleveland, Detroit, Boston, Brooklyn, Newark, Tallahassee, Austin, Los Angeles, Berkeley, Lawrence (KS), Lafayette (IN), Chicago, Washington, DC, Philadelphia, Baltimore, Mexico City, and Guadalajara, Mexico, the opera's first-ever performances south of the border.

73. Sherin (b. 1930) won fame as an actor, director, and producer of television, films, and spoken theater in the sixties. He and actress Jane Alexander married in 1975. In 1993, President Bill Clinton appointed her chairman of the National Endowment for the Arts, in which capacity she served until the end of 1997.

74. The Panamanian Quintero (1924–1999) was best known for his interpretations of the works of Eugene O'Neill.

75. Gertrude Smith to Floyd, March 11, 1965, B & H works files.

76. On March 28 and April 1, 1965.

77. Miles Kastendieck, "Floyd Wearing Well," *New York Journal-American,* March 29, 1965.

78. Reverend Floyd's *Diary* for April 19, 1964 mentions a "new opera," which could have been *Of Mice and Men,* but was more likely *Markheim,* as Steinbeck did not grant approval for the former until November 1965.

79. Robert Louis Stevenson, "The Broken Shaft: Tales of Mid-Ocean," in *Unwin's Christmas Annual* (London: T. Fisher Unwin, 1885). For a modern edition of *Markheim,* see Robert Louis Stevenson, *The Complete Short Stories, with a Selection of the Best Short Novels,* ed. Charles Neider (New York: Da Capo Press, 1998).

80. Carlisle Floyd, *Markheim,* pencil draft vocal score, 1965–1966, Box 5, Folder 3, FALOC; published vocal score (New York: Boosey & Hawkes, 1968).

81. Carlisle Floyd, *Times-Picayune,* December 30, 1965.

82. Floyd to Baxter, April 24, 1965, B & H works files.

83. Floyd to Baxter, May 28, 1965, B & H works files.

84. "FSU's Floyd Is Lauded," *Tallahassee Democrat,* June 24, 1965, Section 2, 17.

85. Ibid.

86. Floyd to Baxter, July 31, 1965, B & H works files. Floyd had "been waiting for a good many days now to hear from you that my two shipments of the *Markheim* full score have arrived safely."

87. Wilfred C. Bain (1908–1997) ruled IU's School of Music as a personal fiefdom until his retirement in 1973. It took IU's opera theater until 1976 to produce *Susannah.*

88. "Off and Running," *Time,* October 1, 1965.

89. Floyd to Goldstein, October 17, 1965, B & H works files.

90. Raymond Ericson, "Met Opera's National Company Gives an Excellent 'Susannah,'" *New York Times,* November 12, 1965, 53. For largely financial reasons, Rudolf Bing got his way with the National Company, which ceased operations at the end of its 1966/67 season. In spirited defense of the enterprise, Risë Stevens maintained to the *New York Times* (August 4, 1968) that *Susannah* proved to be the company's best production.

91. Irving Kolodin, "Music to My Ears," *Saturday Review,* June 26, 1965, 59.

92. T. M. S., "Eileen Farrell Sings First Solo Recital Here in Five Seasons," *New York Times,* December 6, 1965, 50.

93. Theodore Strongin, "Reforms Comparable to New Math," *New York Times,* August 2, 1964, 89. All subsequent JRP citations are filed in the Juilliard School of Music Library, Juilliard Repertory Project Records, Box 2, Folder 1, "F," Miscellaneous, 1964–1969: Richard Felciano-Carlisle Floyd; copies of Floyd's music are in Box 8.

94. Floyd to Fish, January 29, 1966, JRP.

95. Fish to Floyd, February 11, 1966, Box 5, FASCL.

96. Between 1961 and 1963, Diard (1924–2009) sang at the New York City Opera, specializing in lighter roles in the operettas of Gilbert and Sullivan. In the late seventies and eighties, he was chairman of the voice department at the Hartt School of Music. Audrey Schuh, born in New Orleans in 1931, was a hometown favorite, and had other engagements at San Francisco Opera, Houston Grand Opera, and New York City Opera.

97. Crofoot (1929–1979) began his career as an opera and music theater star in 1956 in Canada, England, and the United States. While in Dayton, Ohio in March 1979, directing a production of

Strauss's *Salome,* Crofoot jumped to his death from the fifth floor of the Sheraton Downtown Hotel.

98. Charles Dufour, *New Orleans States-Item,* March 24, 1966.

99. Although he had conceived *Markheim* as a double-bill with *The Sojourner and Mollie Sinclair,* Floyd had no input into the choice of companion piece, but remarked, "Benno Moisievich lived in New Orleans at the time, and it was a curtain-raiser. An odd pairing, but kind of 'New Orleans.' They love their ballet and opera together, it's an old tradition there."

100. Charles L. Dufour, "Premiere of 'Markheim' Here Operatic Success," *New Orleans States-Item,* April 1, 1966.

101. Jack Belsom, "New Orleans," *Opera News,* May 7, 1966, 22.

102. Harry Wells McCraw, "Floyd's Markheim Caps the Season," *High Fidelity,* June 12, 1966, 124–25. Courtesy of *Musical America.* VAI Audio's composite of the two performances is still available on CD as VAIA 1107.

103. Glenn Tucker, "Brief Opera Hailed," *San Antonio Express-News,* November 19, 1966; and Ann Holmes, "'Markheim,' With Strong Score," *Houston Chronicle,* November 21, 1966, 23.

104. Vollrath interview with author, August 1, 2008.

14. Of Mice, Men, Martyrs, Flowers, Hawks, 1963–1972

1. Carlisle Floyd, "The Creation," *The Opera Journal* (Winter 1971): 6.

2. Steinbeck (1902–1968) had already published *Cup of Gold* and *The Pastures of Heaven* (both 1932); *To a God Unknown* (1933) and *In Dubious Battle* (1936) were published subsequently. See also John Steinbeck, *Of Mice and Men* (novella) (New York: Library of America, 1994); and John Steinbeck, *Of Mice and Men* (play) (New York: Dramatists Play Service, 1937, 1964).

3. From Emerson's 1837 address "The American Scholar," to the Cambridge Phi Beta Kappa Society. Jay Parini, *John Steinbeck: A Biography* (New York: Henry Holt, 1995), 27.

4. Steinbeck's banquet speech is available at http://www.subtletea.com/johnsteinbeckspeech.htm (accessed July 30, 2012).

5. George S. Kaufman, "Mice, Men, and Mr. Steinbeck: To Be Continued," *New York Times,* December 5, 1937.

6. Parini, *John Steinbeck,* 170.

7. Holton, "The Publisher," *The Opera Journal* (Winter 1971): 6.

8. Holton to Floyd, December 5, 1963, B & H works files.

9. Floyd to Holton, January 12, 1964, B & H works files.

10. A native of Denison, Texas, Williams (1895–1977) dreamed early of a stage career, but the closest she came was representing the firm's successful writers; she specialized in film and stage rights.

11. Floyd to Holton, June 8, 1964, B & H works files.

12. Contract dated November 19, 1964, B & H works files.

13. Adler to Ford Foundation, December 22, 1964. See also Ford Foundation memos and letters, January 4 and February 9, 1965, FF 60–118.

14. Floyd to Baxter, July 31, 1965, B & H works files.

15. Floyd, "Creation," 6.

16. Carlisle Floyd, *Of Mice and Men* (1965–1966), pencil manuscript draft scores, Box 6, Folder 4, FALOC.

17. Adler to Ford Foundation, March 10, 1965, FF 60–118.

18. Robert Commanday, "New Floyd Opera," *San Francisco Chronicle,* March 10, 1965, 18.

19. *Diary,* April 25, 1966.

20. Memo of a phone conversation between the Ford Foundation's Edward F. D'Arms and Floyd, August 29, 1967 (hereafter D'Arms memo), FF 60–118.

21. Floyd to Arnold Fish, September 16, 1966, JRP. Floyd cited this as a reason for his lateness in submitting his four choral pieces.

22. *Diary,* August 29, 1966.

23. Floyd, "Creation," 8.

24. Both poems in Robert Louis Stevenson, *Penny Whistles* (London: C. J. Clay & Son, at the University Press, 1885).

25. Evaluators' comments in JRP files, Juilliard School of Music Library.

26. Ibid.

27. "Who Has Seen the Wind?" (Rossetti), vocal score transparencies, 1967, Box 4, Folder 6, FALOC.

28. Evaluator comment in JRP files.

29. Floyd believes that he found this traditional ballad in *The Oxford Book of Christmas Poems,* or in another Oxford anthology; either the composer's astounding memory has skipped a beat, or "Long, Long Ago" has since been deleted from more current editions.

30. Evaluator comment in JRP files.

31. Floyd to Arnold Fish, September 19, 1966, JRP files.

32. Torkanowsky (1926–1992), born in Berlin, then raised on an Israeli kibbutz, emigrated to the United States and became music director for Jerome Robbins's Ballet USA. He conducted Menotti's *The Medium* and *The Consul* at the New York City Opera (1959–1962). Following his tenure as music director of the New Orleans Philharmonic Symphony Orchestra (1967–1981), he held a similar position with the Bangor Symphony Orchestra.

33. Carlisle Floyd, *Introduction, Aria, and Dance,* undated full score, c. 1968 (New York: Theodore Presser). As of summer 2012, *Introduction, Aria, and Dance* remains in Presser's rental catalogue. Copy in Box 5, Folder 1, FALOC.

34. Floyd to Pope, January 5, 1967, B & H works files.

35. Bacon to Floyd, January 6, 1967 (mistakenly dated 1966 by Bacon). Courtesy of Carlisle Floyd.

36. Floyd to Bacon, January 19, 1967, Box 13, SUSC. Bacon had moved to Orinda, California, in 1964, and continued to compose prolifically. He was married a fourth and final time in 1971, to Ellen Wendt, who continues to administer the Ernst Bacon Society.

37. Pope to Floyd, January 25, 1967, B & H works files.

38. Floyd to Pope, February 20, 1967, B & H works files.

39. Darden became one of the country's most sought-after accompanists, vocal coaches, and an assistant conductor at the Metropolitan Opera beginning in 1985.

40. D'Arms memo, August 29, 1967.

41. Floyd to D'Arms, September 6, 1967, FF 60–118.

42. No copy of this letter has appeared either in Ford Foundation archives, FASCL, or FALOC.

43. Holton to D'Arms, September 18, 1967, FF 60–118.

44. Floyd, "Creation," 8.

45. Author interview, September 28, 2006.

46. Floyd, "Creation," 9.

47. Capobianco, born in Argentina in 1931, created City Opera's memorable productions of Ginastera's *Don Rodrigo* featuring the young Plácido Domingo (1966), Rimsky-Korsakov's *Le coq d'or* (1967), and Boïto's *Mefistofele* (1969), the last two star vehicles for Beverly Sills and Norman Treigle. In addition to engagements at the Metropolitan, San Diego, and Cincinnati, Capobianco went on to become general director of Pittsburgh Opera in 1983.

48. Floyd, "Creation," 8.

49. See Peter Wynne, "The Best-Laid Plans: Carlisle Floyd Talks about *Of Mice and Men*," New York City Opera *Spotlight* 15, no. 4 (1983): 14–15. Copy in FASCL.

50. Floyd, "Creation," 10.

51. In *Tempo* of May 3, 1970, Treigle claimed that Floyd consulted him about the shapes and ranges of George's lines.

52. Pope to Floyd, March 20, 1968, B & H works files.

53. Floyd to Pope, March 20 and May 21, 1968, B & H works files.

54. Charles Dufour, *New Orleans States-Item*, April 24, 1968.

55. *Diary*, September 14, 1968.

56. Author interview, February 28, 2007.

57. Floyd to Clarkes, undated Christmas note, 1968.

58. Besides working for Boosey from 1966 to 1972, and becoming an award-winning music engraver, Markham served as director of business and finance for New York City Opera from 1980 to 1984, and as managing director of the Opera Company of Boston under Sarah Caldwell.

59. Floyd to Pope, December 20, 1967, B & H works files.

60. Pope to Floyd, January 2, 1969, B & H works files. This would seem to be one of the last, if not *the* last, communications from this period between Floyd and anyone at Boosey.

61. Ross to D'Arms, January 20, 1969, FF 60-118.

62. D'Arms interview with Robert Holton, January 21, 1969, FF 60-118.

63. "Ford Fund to Assist Publishing and Recording of New Music," *New York Times*, January 2, 1970, 77.

64. Ross (1914–2005) served as Seattle's general director until 1983, after which he moved to a similar position with Arizona Opera until 1998.

65. Irving Kolodin, *The Metropolitan Opera, 1883–1966* (New York: Alfred A. Knopf, 1968), 523.

66. See http://www.noa.org/ (accessed July 30, 2012).

67. *Central Opera Service Bulletin* (January-February 1970): 7.

68. Cassilly (1927–1998) went on from Hamburg to sing at such European companies as Berlin's Deutsche Oper, Milan's La Scala, London's Covent Garden, and the Wiener Staatsoper. He sang at the Metropolitan Opera from 1973 to 1990, and taught voice at Boston University.

69. Julian Patrick, "The Performance," *The Opera Journal* (Winter 1971): 19; and author interview with Julian Patrick, December 5, 2007.

70. Robert Moulson, "The Performance," *The Opera Journal* (Winter 1971): 27.

Julian Patrick (1927–2009) began his professional career in New York, with Jerome Moross's *The Golden Apple* (1954). He sang with the Metropolitan Opera National Company for its two seasons, and Floyd had just heard him in *Nine Rivers from Jordan*. Following a City Opera debut in 1958, Robert Moulson (1932–2003), sang widely in Germany, in roles as diverse as Edgardo in *Lucia di Lammermoor*, Don José in *Carmen*, and Radames in *Aïda*. The legendary Anton Coppola, born in 1917, began his career at age eight in the Metropolitan Opera children's chorus. He has since conducted everything from operas and Broadway musicals to his own film scores, including *The Godfather, Part III*. He first conducted at City Opera in 1965, and his opera *Sacco and Vanzetti* premiered in Tampa, Florida, in 2001.

71. Author interview with Leonard Mastrogiacomo, November 19, 2006.

72. Jeffrey sang for four seasons at City Opera, 1964–1967.

73. Sheldon to Ross, February 25, 1969, FF 60-118.

74. Ross to Sheldon, February 28, 1969, FF 60–118.

75. *Central Opera Service Bulletin* (September/October 1969): 12.

76. Author interview with Julian Patrick, December 5, 2007.

77. Carol Bayard, "The Performance," *The Opera Journal* (Winter 1971): 29.

78. Shirley Fleming, "Floyd's New Opera," *Musical America*, February 1970, 10. Courtesy of *Musical America*. The next two quotes are from this source.

79. Patrick, "Performance," 19–20.

80. Ibid., 20.

81. Moulson, "Performance," 28.

82. Ibid., 28.

83. Conversation reported by Corsaro in interview with author, March 5, 2007.

84. Between Santa Fe in 1958 and City Opera's *Wuthering Heights* the next year, Floyd had cut Bonazzi's role of Mrs. Linton.

85. Corsaro, *Maverick*, 116.

86. Frank Corsaro, "The Direction," *The Opera Journal* (Winter 1971): 14.

87. Holton, "Publisher," 32.

88. Raymond Ericson, "His First Love: Theater," *New York Times*, May 28, 1972, D11.

89. Copy of 1970 Belwin-Mills contract on file at Boosey & Hawkes. Subsequent renewals have been either destroyed or lost. Incredibly, the same is true of Floyd's original *Of Mice and Men* manuscript score, as well as correspondence or memoranda pertaining to the genesis, growth, and Belwin's representation of the opera.

90. Patrick interview with author, December 5, 2007.

91. Corsaro, "Direction," 15.

92. Patrick, "Performance," 21.

93. Author interview with Patrick, December 5, 2007.

94. Author interview with Corsaro, March 5, 2007.

95. Wayne Johnson, *Seattle Times,* January 23, 1970.

96. Max Wyman, *The Sun* [Vancouver, Canada], January 23, 1970.

97. Robert Commanday, *San Francisco Chronicle,* January 25, 1970.

98. John Voorhees, "Floyd Talks about Opera," *Seattle Times,* January 29, 1970, B9.

99. Jo Ann Patterson, *Christian Science Monitor,* January 30, 1970.

100. "Threnody for Lost Men," *Time,* February 9, 1970, 51.

101. Ross to Richard C. Shelton, February 6, 1970, FF 60-118.

102. Transactional Analysis (TA) was largely the innovation of the Canadian American psychiatrist Eric Berne in the late fifties; TA is explicated in *Games People Play* (1964) and *What Do You Say After You Say Hello?* (1975).

Berne proposed that the partners in most human transactions could be categorized by three principal ego states: parent (judgmental), adult (rational), and child (usually a weak victim).

103. Eugene N. Zeigler, *When Conscience and Power Meet: A Memoir* (Columbia: University of South Carolina Press, 2008), 230–31.

104. Carlisle Floyd, *In Celebration* (c. 1970), Floyd's ms., Box 5, Folder 4, FALOC, is a version for two pianos. Louisville Orchestra recorded the piece in 1972, conducted by Jorge Mester.

105. John Gruen, *Menotti* (New York: Macmillan, 1978), 200.

106. Virgil Thomson, "A Words-Eye View of the Musical Stage," *New York Times,* October 4, 1970, Arts, 46.

107. The Viennese Martin (1909–1984) and his wife, Ruth, née Kelley, gained considerable fame for English performing versions of much of the standard operatic repertoire. Martin conducted at New York City Opera from 1944 to 1956, and later served as assistant chorus master at the Metropolitan Opera.

108. Thomas Martin, "The Second Production," *The Opera Journal* (Winter 1971): 24.

109. Thomas MacCluskey, "'Of Mice and Men' at Central City," *Rocky Mountain News,* June 28, 1970.

110. Clifton Paisley, "Some Thoughts on Opera by the Composer of *Susannah* and *Of Mice and Men,*" *Research in Review* 1, no. 4 (1970): 1–5.

111. Artistic director Russell Patterson and Ward Holmquist alternated the conducting *Of Mice and Men* on September 22, 26, and October 2, 8, 14, 1970. Stage director Ian Strasfogel's cast included Robert Williams (Lennie), David Holloway (George), Robert Owen Jones (Curley), and Catherine Christensen (Curley's wife).

112. The indefatigable Stevens (1910–1998), after making his fortune in real estate, and chairing the Democratic Party finance committee in 1956, became an equally successful Broadway producer.

113. Igor Stravinsky and Robert Craft, *Conversations with Stravinsky* (Garden City: Doubleday, 1959), 133–34.

114. Carlisle Floyd, "The Composer in Academia," *Journal of the College Music Society* (Geneva, NY: W. F. Humphrey Press, 1970), 78.

115. Allan Holbert, "'Of Mice and Men,'" *Minneapolis Tribune,* October 21, 1970.

116. Curtin sang with the Metropolitan Opera from 1961 to 1973. Fall 1964 marked her last regular season with City Opera, although she made two more guest appearances there in the fall of 1975 and 1976. She taught at Yale University from 1974 to 1983, and then served as dean of the School of the Arts at Boston University until 1992. As of 2012, she continues to be in demand as a teacher of vocal master classes.

117. Chisholm (1904–1965) had settled in South Africa in 1946, and his setting of *Before Breakfast,* titled *Dark Sonnet,* received its premiere in Capetown in 1952. Once O'Neill's text entered the public domain, Corsaro made a libretto of it for Thomas Pasatieri, and that piece was performed at New York City Opera as part of *An American Trilogy* in 1980.

118. Curtin to Floyd, November 7, 1957. See Amy Kelly, *Eleanor of Aquitaine and the Four Kings* (Cambridge: Harvard University Press, 1950). Kelly (1877–1962) retired from Wellesley College in 1943, spent the last twelve years of her life in seclusion, and resisted the college's attempts to entice her back to receive recognition for having written *Eleanor.*

119. The protagonist of Donizetti's 1834 opera, *Rosmonda d'Inghilterra.*

120. Katharine Hepburn won a best actress Academy Award for the 1968 film of Goldman's play; Glenn Close starred as Eleanor in a 2004 television adaptation.

121. Author interview with Phyllis Curtin, March 3, 2007.

122. *Diary,* November 9, 1970.

123. Zeigler, *When Conscience and Power Meet,* 231.

124. David Cook, "'Of Mice and Men,'" *Tallahassee Democrat,* February 5, 1971, 16.

125. Mary Nik Shenk, "Carlisle Floyd Interview," *St. Petersburg Times,* February 10, 1971, 21.

126. Ibid.

127. *Congressional Record,* February 22, 1971, E 1041. Copy in Box 2, FASCL.

128. Corsaro to Floyd, April 8 and May 17, 1971, Box 2, FASCL.

129. Dorothy Madlee, "'Susannah' Composer's Wife 'A Passionate Amateur in Music,'" *Orlando Sentinel,* April 23, 1971, 1D.

130. *Diary,* April 23, 1971.

131. Carlisle Floyd, *Flower and Hawk,* vocal score (New York: Belwin-Mills, 1977), iii. The information on Eleanor and her symbols is taken from Floyd's introduction, "Background and Synopsis."

132. Both versions of *Flower and Hawk* libretto in Box 4, Folder 1, FALOC.

133. Floyd, "Background and Synopsis," iii.

134. Corsaro interview with author, March 5, 2007.

135. Floyd, "Background and Synopsis," iii.

136. July 9 and 11, 1971.

137. John Ardoin, *Dallas Morning News,* July 13, 1971.

138. Gockley interview with author, November 20, 2007. Born in 1943, Gockley became the general director of San Francisco Opera at the beginning of 2006, after thirty-five years in Houston. The quotes in the next two paragraphs are from this source.

139. Herman Melville's poem, whose full title is "The Martyr: Indicative of the Passion of the People on the 15th Day of April, 1865," was first published in *Battle-Pieces and Aspects of the War* (New York, Harper & Bros., 1866).

140. Carlisle Floyd, *'The Martyr' Vocal Score* (New York: Belwin-Mills, 1973), 3.

141. Andrew D. Frank, "The Martyr," *Notes* (2nd Series) 30, no. 3 (1974): 613–14.

142. Carlisle Floyd, *The Martyr,* pencil ms. vocal score, 1970–1971, Box 5, Folder 4, FALOC; published vocal score (New York: Belwin-Mills, 1973).

143. "'Of Mice and Men' Is Gusty [*sic*] Earthy Opera," *Cedar Rapids Gazette,* July 28, 1971. Performances on July 27, 28, 30, and 31, 1971.

144. Donal Henahan, "Treigle 'Preaches' Again in City Opera's 'Susannah,'" *New York Times,* November 2, 1971, 44.

145. Arthur Cohn, "Floyd, Carlisle," *Recorded Classical Music: A Critical Guide to Compositions and Performances* (New York: Schirmer Books, 1981), 48. Orion Records, ORS 7268.

146. Once called the Central Florida Friends of Music, today the Orlando Symphony Orchestra.

147. Gail Stockholm, *Cincinnati Enquirer,* April 12, 1972.

148. Andrew Farkas, "Jacksonville, Florida," *Opera,* September 1972, 838.

149. Paul Hume, *Washington Post,* May 19, 1972.

150. Floyd to Clarkes, undated Christmas card, 1972.

151. Raymond Ericson, "Florida Players Regain Stability," *New York Times,* May 21, 1972, 65.

152. Hoiby to Floyd, May 20, 1972, Box 1, Folder 25, FASCL. Born in the same year as Floyd, 1926, and like Floyd a champion of vocal lyricism, Hoiby excelled at art song and opera. The latter includes settings of Tennessee Williams's *Summer and Smoke* (1971), and Shakespeare's *The Tempest* (1986). After his death in 2011, his 2004 *Romeo and Juliet* awaits a premiere.

15. Completed Circle: Houston and *Bilby's Doll,* 1972–1976

1. Gockley interview with author, November 20, 2007.

2. No *O'Brien* materials have appeared in any Floyd collection.

3. André Gide, *La symphonie pastorale,* trans. Dorothy Bussy (Paris: Éditions de la Nouvelle Revue Française, 1919); published together with *Isabelle* (1911) as *Two Symphonies* (New York: Alfred A. Knopf, 1931).

4. Gide, *La symphonie pastorale,* 172. The Pastor also identifies to Gertrude certain instruments and tonalities in terms of colors, much as Floyd experienced them.

5. "News from Opera Companies: Expansion of Companies," *Central Opera Service Bulletin* 19, no. 1 (1976): 4.

6. Born in Dallas in 1946, Yeargan studied at Yale University with Donald Oenslager and Ming Cho Lee before becoming one of the world's most in-demand designers, for San Francisco, the Met, the Royal Opera (Covent Garden), and dozens of other companies worldwide. The two-time Tony winner currently serves as resident designer for Yale Repertory Theatre.

7. Donal Henahan, "Floyd's Sophisticated 'Of Mice and Men,'" *New York Times,* July 9, 1972, 37.

8. Author interview with Corsaro, March 5, 2007. In a long review of Nadine Hubbs, *The Queer Composition of America's Sound: Gay Modernists, American Music, and National Identity* (Berkeley and Los Angeles: University of California Press, 2004), critic Scott Cantrell wrote in the *Dallas Morning News* of July 10, 2005 that the "softer side of modernism flowered in American operas of the 1950s, in works by gay composers including Barber and his lover Gian Carlo Menotti and the heterosexual Robert Ward and Carlisle Floyd."

9. Holton to Henahan, July 12, 1972, B & H works files.

10. Henahan to Holton, July 13, 1972, B & H works files.

11. Holton to Floyd, July l7 28, 1972, B & H works files.

12. Dorle J. Soria, "Artist Life," *High Fidelity/Musical America,* October 1972, MA-6. Courtesy of *Musical America.*

13. *Diary,* August 24, 1972.

14. "Floyd's *Slow Duck* [sic] at Columbia College," *The State,* November 18, 1972.

15. On January 13, 1973, and on February 10 and 11, 1973, respectively.

16. Carl Cunningham, "'Of Mice and Men' at Houston Grand Opera," *Houston Post,* February 21, 1973.

17. Samuel L. Singe, *The Philadelphia Enquirer,* April 2, 1973.

18. *Central Opera Service Bulletin* 17, no. 1 (Fall 1974): 1, 10.

19. Carlisle Floyd, "*Bilby's Doll:* Origins and Conclusions," Houston Grand Opera program, February-March 1976, 21.

20. Carl Cunningham, "Working Witchcraft," *Houston Post,* February 22, 1976, 28–29.

21. Robert Wilder Blue, "Catherine Malfitano's Brilliant Career," USOperaweb, September 2001.

22. See Carlisle Floyd, *Bilby's Doll, Revised Vocal Score* (New York: Boosey & Hawkes, 1998), 21–22, 123.

23. Floyd, "*Bilby's Doll:* Origins and Conclusions," 21.

24. Ibid., 42.

25. Robert Jacobson, "New York," *Opera News,* December 8, 1973, 46, 49.

26. On his way to Paris in 1777, Mozart and his mother stayed at The White Lamb from October 11 to 26. See Harrison James Wignall, *In Mozart's Footsteps: A Travel Guide for Music Lovers* (New York: Paragon House, 1991). 130–38.

27. Dr. Thea Leitmair, "Das Hohelied der Freundesliebe," *Augsburger Allgemeine,* December 3, 1973, 17.

28. Untitled, undated clipping, *Seattle Times,* [June 8, 1974].

29. "Markheim," *Variety,* June 26, 1974.

30. Mary Nik Shenk, *St. Petersburg Times,* July 27, 1974.

31. *Diary,* November 28, 1974.

32. Floyd to Warren, December 15, 1974, Robert Penn Warren Papers, Box 25, Folder 496, MSS 51, Yale Collection of American Literature, Beinecke Rare Book and Manuscript Library, Yale University (hereafter YCAL).

33. Floyd to Johnson, December 18, 1974, Box 1, Folder 1, FASCL. The university began its South Caroliniana collection in 1906, but only in 1940 did it find a permanent home in the old campus main library building, which was completed in 1840 and was one of Columbia's relatively few buildings left undamaged during General William T. Sherman's occupation of the city in 1865—the period and setting of Floyd's *The Passion of Jonathan Wade.*

34. Jona Clarke interview with author, March 5, 2007.

35. Ibid.

36. John Voorhees, "'Markheim:' A Super Production," *Seattle Times,* June 10, 1975.

37. Of the many individuals approached for interviews for this book, "Bobbi" was one of the few subjects known to be still living who declined. Out of respect for the family's privacy, I have altered their real names.

38. This refers to the 1939 George S. Kaufman and Moss Hart play, *The Man Who Came to Dinner,* and its 1942 film adaptation.

39. Sapp (1922–1999) studied composition at Harvard with Walter Piston and Irving Fine, and later took private lessons from Aaron Copland and Nadia Boulanger. After seven years on Harvard's faculty, three as chairman of music at the University of Buffalo, and three at FSU, he became dean of the University of Cincinnati College-Conservatory of Music.

40. Susan Lykes, "FSU Stars Leaving for Green Paychecks," *Tallahassee Democrat,* April 4, 1976, 3C; and Robert Montgomery, "Floyd Hears the Sound of Freedom," *Tallahassee Democrat,* May 9, 1976, 1E, 4E.

41. With additional performances on February 28 and 29, and March 1, 2, and 5, 1976.

42. Following graduation from the University of California, Berkeley, Keene (1946–1995) worked at Menotti's Spoleto Festival from 1968 to 1980, and at New York City Opera beginning in 1969.

43. Lerner had won fame and fortune with his books and lyrics for *My Fair Lady* (1956) and *Camelot* (1960), both to music by Frederick Loewe; and the superstar composer-conductor Bernstein needs no introduction here.

44. Born in Oxford, England, in 1947, Pountney was the director of productions at the English National Opera from 1982–1993, and staged freelance productions at many of the world's great houses.

45. Author interview with Gockley, November 20, 2007.

46. Author interview with Corsaro, March 5, 2007.

47. When Bernstein's *1600,* under the supervision of its replacement team, finally opened on May 4, the public and press agreed with Corsaro, and the piece entered Broadway's annals of all-time great disasters, closing after seven performances.

48. Author interview with Phyllis Curtin, March 3, 2007.

49. Interoffice memorandum from Hoffman, December 8, 1974, Box 6, FASCL. Monroe D. Anderson (1873–1939), scion of a banking and cotton merchant family, founded the M. D. Anderson Foundation three years before his death, the principal goal being the enrichment of life in the Houston area.

50. Housewright (1913–2003) remained as FSU's dean of music until his retirement in 1979.

51. Samuel Ramey interview with author, August 1, 2008.

52. Mordden, born in Pennsylvania in 1949, has worked as a musical director, librettist, and composer. In the eighties he published books on opera, both fiction and nonfiction, and especially on gay culture in New York City. His books include *Demented: The World of the Opera Diva* (New York: Franklin Watts, 1984). See Ethan Mordden, "Unprotected Poet," *Opera News,* February 7, 1976, 12–15, which repays reading, as do his discussions of Floyd in *Opera in the Twentieth Century: Sacred, Profane, Godot* (New York: Oxford University Press, 1978), 311–13; and *The Splendid Art of Opera: A Concise History* (New York: Methuen, 1982), 377.

53. *Diary,* January 29, 1975.

54. Guilds to Floyd, February 2, Box 1, Folder 24, FASCL.

55. Carl Cunningham, "In a Hotel Monastery," *Houston Post,* February 1, 1976, 19.

56. Sapp to Floyd, February 20, 1976, Box 1, Folder 24, FASCL.

57. *Diary,* February 28, 1976.

58. William Albright, *Houston Post,* February 29, 1976.

59. Ann Holmes, "'Bilby's Doll' Is a Biting, but Luminous New Opera," *Houston Chronicle,* February 29, 1976, Section 2, 4.

60. Donald Dierks, "Bilby's Doll in Houston," *San Diego Union,* March 1, 1976.

61. Allen Hughes, "Opera: Floyd Premiere," *New York Times,* February 29, 1976, 45.

62. John Ardoin, "Houston," *Opera News,* May 1976, 45.

63. Andrew Porter, "Going to the Devil," *The New Yorker,* March 22, 1976, 120–23.

64. Warren Prince, "'Bilby's Doll' Is Compelling Opera," *Omaha World-Herald,* April 9, 1976.

65. Leonard J. Leff, "Omaha," *Opera News,* June 1976, 44.

66. Carl Cunningham, "Holland Festival," *High Fidelity/Musical America,* July 1976, MA-25-26. Courtesy of *Musical America.*

16. Synthesizing Opera and Music Theater: *Willie Stark,* 1970–1981

1. Voorhees, "Floyd Talks about Opera," B9.

2. Since 2009, a copy with the Belwin-Mills imprint listed in the collection of New York's Performing Arts Library at Lincoln Center seems to have vanished.

3. Contract and correspondence in B & H works files.

4. Soria, "Artist Life," MA-6.

5. Ibid.

6. Floyd to Warren, July 2, 1973, MSS 51, YCAL.

7. Ibid.

8. Warren to Floyd, July 7, 1973. All Warren letters to Floyd courtesy of Carlisle Floyd.

9. Adams wrote lyrics for such Broadway successes as *Bye, Bye Birdie* and *Applause.*

10. Floyd to Warren, August 20, 1974, MSS 51, YCAL.

11. Warren to Floyd, July 7, 1973.

12. Floyd to Warren, July 25, 1973, MSS 51, YCAL.

13. Warren to Floyd, August 27, 1973.

14. Floyd to Warren, August 20, 1974, MSS 51, YCAL.

15. Holton to Stevens, August 16, 1974, B & H works files.

16. Floyd to Warren, August 20, 1974, MSS 51, YCAL.

17. Ibid.

18. Warren to Floyd, August 25, 1974.

19. Floyd to Warren, October 7, 1974, MSS 51, YCAL. Floyd cited Warren to himself, from "Monologue at Midnight," the first of his *Eleven Poems on the Same Theme,* first published in the *Virginia Quarterly* 12 (July 1936). See also *The Collected Poems of Robert Penn Warren,* ed. John Burt (Baton Rouge: Louisiana State University Press, 1998), 653.

20. Floyd to Warren, December 15, 1974, MSS 51, YCAL.

21. Montgomery, "Floyd Hears the Sound of Freedom." The quotes in the next two paragraphs are from this source.

22. Klaus Laskowski, "'Of Mice and Men,'" *Orpheus* (September/November 1976): 1–2.

23. Judith Mindszenthy, "Holland," *Opera News,* October 1976, 47.

24. David Stevens, "Plugging into the U.S. Bicentennial," *International Herald Tribune,* June 16, 1976.

25. Felix Aprahamian, "American Week," *London Sunday Times,* June 27, 1976.

26. Edward Mendelsohn, *The Stage,* June 24, 1976.

27. Milton Katims (1909–2006), born in Brooklyn—the family's original name was Katimsky—replaced William Primrose as principal violist of the NBC Symphony Orchestra under Toscanini in 1943, and subsequently performed and recorded much of the viola repertoire. From 1954 to 1976, he served as the Seattle Symphony's music director. His leadership of the University of Houston School of Music lasted from 1976 until 1994, most of Floyd's years with the institution.

28. Author interview with Gockley, November 20, 2007.

29. Ibid.

30. Ibid.

31. Corsaro interview with author, March 5, 2007.

32. Wayne Johnson, "Carlisle Floyd Interview," *Seattle Times,* September 14, 1976.

33. Copy in B & H works files.

34. Warren quote in Thomas W. Cutrer, *Parnassus on the Mississippi: The Southern Review and the Baton Rouge Literary Community, 1935–1942* (Baton Rouge: Louisiana State University Press, 1984), 64–65, 72–73.

35. Joseph Blotner, *Robert Penn Warren: A Biography* (New York: Random House, 1997), 150–230.

36. Ibid., 179.

37. See J. P. Wood, *Saturday Review,* August 17, 1946; and George Mayberry, *New Republic,* September 2, 1946.

38. Robert Penn Warren, *All the King's Men* (New York: Harcourt, Brace, 1946), 310.

39. Scott Heumann, "The Trial of Willie Stark," *Opera News,* April 11, 1981, 11–14.

40. Ibid., 12.

41. Carlisle Floyd, *Willie Stark* (c. 1976–1977), handwritten treatment-scenario, Box 1, Folder 2c, FALOC.

42. Carlisle Floyd, *All the King's Men (Willie Stark),* typescript (1977), Box 1, Folder 2d, FALOC.

43. Floyd, *All the King's Men (Willie Stark),* character addenda (1977), Box 1, Folder 2e, FALOC.

44. "March of Time" newsreels, produced by Time, Inc. between 1935 and 1951, were shown in many theaters before feature movie attractions.

45. Floyd to Warren, October 22, 1977, MSS 51, YCAL.

46. Ibid.

47. Holton to Diskant, May 12, 1977, B & H works files.

48. Richard E. Marks to Holton, June 7, 1978, B & H works files.

49. Allen Hughes, *New York Times,* July 4, 1977, 20.

50. This copy of Floyd's libretto reposes alongside his letters in the Robert Penn Warren archive at Yale's Beinecke Library, but it appears new and untouched, lacking annotations of any kind, indicating at best Warren's cursory appraisal.

51. Warren to Floyd, November 1, 1977.

52. Warren's first marriage to Cinina Brescia, daughter of the Italian American opera composer Domenico Brescia, ended in divorce in 1951. The following year he married Eleanor Clark, a writer of novels, short stories, and nonfiction.

53. Conversations with Warren reported by Floyd.

54. Donal Henahan, "Beverly Sills Will Retire in 1980," *New York Times,* January 10, 1978, 1. Though she surrendered the general directorship of City Opera in 1989, Sills remained on the company's board until 1991, and from 1994 until 2002 served as chairperson of Lincoln Center.

55. Raymond Ericson, "Rudel Resigns as City Opera Director," *New York Times,* December 14, 1978, C17.

56. Donal Henahan, "Rudel Resigns from the City Opera," *New York Times,* April 24, 1980, C19. In any event, Rudel continued to conduct at City Opera until that fall.

57. Beverly Sills, *Bubbles* (Indianapolis: Bobbs-Merrill, 1976), 326.

58. Harold Prince interview with author, February 27, 2007.

59. Lawrence B. Johnson, *Milwaukee Sentinel,* January 30, 1978.

60. Heumann, "Trial of Willie Stark," 12.

61. Broadway playwright Joe Masteroff (*Cabaret, She Loves Me*) wrote the libretto. Cosponsored by the Opera Company of Philadelphia, this was the first operatic venture by both Masteroff and Thomas. The New York premiere of Thomas's *Desire* was given by the New York Opera Repertory Theater at City Center on January 10, 1989, and a CD recording on the Naxos label was released in 2002.

62. Carlisle Floyd, "Society and the Artist," *Forum* 18, no. 3 (1978): 62–65.

63. *Diary,* March 10 and July 21, 1980.

64. *Diary,* May 15, 1979.

65. *Diary,* November 18, 1979.

66. *Diary,* December 5, 1978.

67. Author interview with Corsaro, March 5, 2007.

68. Prince, born in New York in 1928, began his career in theater as assistant to the legendary George Abbott. Prince's credits as a director and producer include Bernstein's *West Side Story* in 1957, and he has collaborated with Stephen Sondheim since 1976.

69. Prince interview with author, February 27, 2007.

70. Prince to Floyd, February 27, 1979, Box 4, FASCL.

71. Mark Bauerlein and Ellen Grantham, *National Endowment for the Arts: A History, 1965–2008* (Washington, DC: National Endowment for the Arts, 2009), 60.

72. Munitz (b. 1941), a true friend of the arts (Floyd's words), is today chancellor of California's state university system and CEO of the J. Paul Getty Trust.

73. Ostrow, born c. 1932 in New York City, had produced, among other shows, *Pippin* and *M. Butterfly.*

74. Anderson (1915–2003), a concert pianist, composer, and educator, was appointed chair of the NEA's music panel in 1968. As head of the music program at Antioch College in 1946, he became one of the first African Americans to chair a department in an integrated college.

75. David Lloyd, born in 1920, headed Lake George Opera as the artistic then general director from 1965 to 1980. As a singer, he was best known for his performances and recordings of Bach, Mozart, and Rossini.

76. Heumann, "Trial of Willie Stark, 12.

77. Raymond Ericson, "Music Notes: A New Way to Make Operas," *New York Times,* July 1, 1979, D19.

78. Mollicone to Floyd, July 9, 1987, Box 4, FASCL.

79. Goldstein to Floyd, October 9, 1979, B & H works files.

80. Heumann, "Trial of Willie Stark," 12.

81. Ibid., 13.

82. Robert Wilder Blue, "Operas We Would Like to See Again: Carlisle Floyd Discusses *Wuthering Heights, The Passion of Jonathan Wade, Bilby's Doll,* and *Willie Stark,*" USOperaWeb, September 2002.

83. The OMT soldiered on in various forms until 1994, chaired successively by Edward Corn, Ann Francis Darling, Patrick J. Smith, and Tomas C. Hernandez, before once more splitting into separate components, that is, opera returned to music, and musical theater to theater.

84. William W. Starr, "The Man behind 'Susannah,'" *The State,* February 17, 1980, magazine section, 2–4.

85. Warren to Floyd, February 29, 1980.

86. Bacon to Floyd, April 4, 1980. Courtesy of Carlisle Floyd.

87. Peter G. Davis, "Opera: Bronx Company Performs in 'Susannah,'" *New York Times,* May 11, 1980, 45.

88. Heumann, "Trial of Willie Stark," 14.

89. Ibid.

90. Prince interview with author, February 27, 2007.

91. Lee (b. 1933) had already worked with Prince on Broadway, creating sets for Bernstein's *Candide* (1974) and Sondheim's *Sweeney Todd* (1979), both of which won him Tony Awards. He went on to design sets for *Wicked* in 2003, and became a staff production designer for NBC's *Saturday Night Live.*

92. Prince to Floyd, June 23, 1980, Box 4, FASCL. All quotes in the next four paragraphs are from this letter.

93. Prince interview with author, February 27, 2007. The quote in the next paragraph is from this interview.

94. Thomas (1892–1981) gained widespread fame between 1918 and 1920 as the journalist who made Lawrence of Arabia famous. Thomas was ubiquitous as a radio news commentator until his retirement in 1976.

95. Mark Flint interview with author, October 26, 2006.

96. *Diary,* August 5, 1980.

97. Corn came to Philadelphia in the seventies, later succeeding James Ireland as OMT's director in spring 1980. In 1981, he was named executive vice president and general director of the Wolf Trap Foundation; and, at the end of 1982, executive producer of Minnesota Opera, where he worked until he died in 1997.

98. Warren to Floyd, September 1, 1980.

99. Floyd to Warren, September 8, 1980, MSS 51, YCAL.

100. Jay Carr, "One of Steinbeck's Best Is Made Even Better," *Detroit Free Press,* September 28, 1980.

101. Robert Croan, *Pittsburgh Post-Gazette,* October 10, 1980.

102. Robert Jacobson, "Detroit/Pittsburgh," *Opera News,* December 20, 1980, 43.

103. Mann is perhaps best known in this country as the author of *The Operas of Mozart* (New York, Oxford University Press, 1977) and *Richard Strauss: A Critical Study of the Operas* (New York, Oxford University Press, 1966).

104. William Mann, "Wexford," *London Times,* October 27, 1980.

105. Tom Sutcliffe, "*Of Mice and Men* at Wexford," *The Guardian,* October 27, 1980.

106. *Diary,* November 23, 1980.

107. Floyd to Cunningham, February 23, 1981, Box 1, Folder 26. FASCL.

108. R. L. Cowser Jr., "Kingfish of American Opera: An Interview with Carlisle Floyd," *The Southern Quarterly* (Spring 1982): 15. Courtesy of *The Southern Quarterly.*

109. Ibid., 15–16.

110. Gockley interview with author, November 20, 2007.

111. Prince interview with author, February 27, 2007.

112. Elizabeth Bennett, "Of Warren and 'Willie Stark,'" *Houston Post,* May 3, 1981, 19A.

113. Card and amulet in Box 1, Folder 33, FASCL.

114. O'Brien to Floyd, April 20, 1981, Box 1, Folder 26, FASCL.

115. Ann Holmes, "Floyd and 'Willie Stark,'" *Houston Chronicle,* April 29, 1981.

116. David Foit, "'Willie Stark' in Houston," *Baton Rouge Sunday Advocate,* April 29, 1981.

117. Donal Henahan, "Opera: Floyd's 'Willie,'" *New York Times,* April 27, 1981 (http://www.nytimes.com/1981/04/27/arts/opera-floyd-s-willie.html).

118. Annalyn Swan, "Grand Opera, Texas-Style," *Newsweek,* May 11, 1981, 96, 99.

119. Author interview with Prince, February 27, 2007.

120. Prince to Floyd, April 27, 1981, Box 4, FASCL.

121. James Lardner, *Washington Post,* May 11, 1981.

122. Bill Zakariasen, *New York Daily News,* May 19, 1981.

123. Herman Berlinski, "A Notable Modern Opera," *The Jewish Week,* May 28, 1981.

124. Jac Venza was executive producer of *Great Performances;* other telecast producers included Sidney J. Palmer and Peter Weinberg. The ETV endowment of South Carolina and the Southern Educational Communication Association provided additional funding.

125. Broadcaster Lowell Thomas died at his home in Pawling, New York, on August 29, 1981; but his voice lived on in the PBS presentation the following September.

126. Joseph McLellan, "McLellan/Week of May 18," WETA-FM transcript, 1981. Copy in Box 4, FASCL.

127. Irving Kolodin, "A Houston World Premiere," *Saturday Review,* April 1981, 35–37.

17. Falling Down, 1981–1986

1. Prince to Floyd, August 20, 1981, Box 5, FASCL.

2. Mentzer, born and raised in Philadelphia, finished her last two years of high school in Santa Fe, New Mexico, where work as an usher at the summer opera persuaded her to pursue a vocal career. Mentzer's year in the HGO studio, 1981–1982, led to a European debut in 1983. She spent four years singing overseas, including in Cologne, West Germany, and made a successful Metropolitan Opera debut in 1988.

3. Mentzer interview with author, April 28, 2009.

4. Ramey interview with author, August 1, 2008. Subsequent quotes from Ramey are from this interview.

5. Prince to Floyd, September 28, 1981, Box 5, FASCL.

6. John J. O'Connor, "TV: Carlisle Floyd's 'Willie Stark' on PBS," *New York Times,* September 28, 1981 (http://www.nytimes.com/1981/09/28/arts/tv-carlisle-floyd-s-willie-stark-on-pbs.html).

7. Mayer to Floyd, October 1, 1981, Box 1, Folder 26, FASCL.

8. Thomas to Floyd, October 8, 1981, Box 1, Folder 26, FASCL. Masteroff wrote the libretto for Thomas's setting of *Desire.*

9. Floyd to Warren, October 19, 1981, MSS 51, YCAL.

10. Laurie Johnston, "City Opera To Be Alive with the Signs Of Music," *New York Times,* March 30, 1982, 14.

11. Andrew Porter, "Down in the Valley," *New Yorker,* April 5, 1982, 172–77.

12. Donal Henahan, "City Opera's Season: The High Hopes Were Its Sopranos," *New York Times,* May 2, 1982.

13. Tim Smith, "Two Worlds Festival," *Fort Lauderdale News,* June 17, 1982. Smith is currently the chief music critic for *The Baltimore Sun,* and the author of *The NPR Curious Listener's Guide to Classical Music.*

14. Edward Rothstein, "City Opera: 'Susannah,'" *New York Times,* October 27, 1982 (http://www.nytimes.com/1982/10/27/arts/city-opera-susannah.html).

15. Author interview with Bohmler, February 13, 2007.

16. Stamper interview with author, March 23, 2007. Subsequent quotes from Stamper are from this interview.

17. Stamper left HGO to become the music director of Kentucky Opera, then the artistic director of Nevada Opera, and finally, the chorus master at Orlando Opera under the general directorship of James Ireland. Floyd described Stamper as "highly overqualified" for this last position.

18. Conversation at this meeting reported by Floyd.

19. President Sam A. Banks to Floyd, July 26 and October 18, 1982. Floyd to Banks, October 31, 1982. Copies of all relevant Dickinson College correspondence courtesy of Dickinson College.

20. Carl Cunningham, *Houston Post,* February 16, 1986.

21. All numbering according to *The Complete Poems of Emily Dickinson,* ed. Thomas H. Johnson (New York: Little Brown, 1961). An incomplete edition of Dickinson's letters is available online at www.emilydickinson.it/letters.html, and this is the source of footnoted letter numbers. Notwithstanding the amazing Dickinson's passing from this world in 1886, Harvard University Press, the copyright holder of Johnson's edition, demanded a reprint fee. Thus I have used only the numbering of poems and dates of letters, which are easily referenced with computer or library tools.

22. Elizabeth Chapin Holland (1823–1896), wife of Josiah Gilbert Holland, coeditor with Samuel Bowles of the *Springfield Republican,* was for three decades Dickinson's most frequent recipient of poems and letters.

23. To Susan Gilbert Dickinson, 1885; to Mrs. James S. Cooper, widow of another Amherst lawyer, spring 1886; and to Susan Gilbert Dickinson, late 1885.

24. Author interview with Mentzer, April 28, 2009.

25. Dorothy Samachson, "Chicago," *Opera,* December 1983, 1432.

26. Moore to Floyd, June 8, 1983, Box 5, FASCL.

27. Author interview with Corsaro, March 5, 2007. Subsequent quotes from Corsaro are from this interview.

28. Author interview with Prince, February 27, 2007.

29. Donal Henahan, "Opera: 'Mice and Men,'" *New York Times,* October 14, 1983 (http://www.nytimes.com/1983/10/14/arts/opera-mice-and-men.html).

30. Donal Henahan, "Music View: Music Has Lost Ground in Modern Opera," *New York Times,* October 23, 1983 (http://nytimes.com/1983/10/23/arts/music-view-music-has-lost-ground-n-modern-opera.html).

31. Roy M. Close, "'Butterfly' Helps Floyd Try His Wings," *St. Paul Pioneer Press,* January 26, 1984.

32. Author interview with Corsaro, November 20, 2007. Arnow (1908–1986) specialized in southern Appalachian subjects. *The Dollmaker* was adapted for an ABC TV movie in 1984 starring Jane Fonda as Gertie.

33. Harold Frederic (1856–1898) made an early career as a London correspondent for *The New York Times.* A champion of naturalism, and a dedicated critic of small-town American life, Frederic is considered a precursor of Sinclair Lewis.

34. Close, "'Butterfly' Helps Floyd." In an interview the next day (Michael Anthony, "Composer-Director Floyd Laments Fact That So Few New Operas Are Performed," *Minneapolis Star & Tribune,* January 27, 16), Floyd paid fellow composer Dominick Argento, still disgruntled over the *Jonathan Wade* situation from 1962, generous compliments, stating that he did not understand why Argento's *The Voyage of Edgar Allan Poe* (1976) had not been given since: "I recommended it last year to Miami. I think it's a good piece."

35. *Diary,* January 8, 1984.

36. Roy M. Close, "'Butterfly' Flight Reasonably Smooth," *St. Paul Dispatch,* February 1, 1984.

37. Postcard from Richards to Floyd, April 3, 1984, Box 5, FASCL.

38. Born Friedrich Wilhelm Plumpe in Bielefeld, Germany, in 1888, Murnau had already made a brilliant career in his native land with such expressionist trailblazers as *Nosferatu* (1922), an adaptation of Bram Stoker's *Dracula (1897).* In 1926, the director emigrated to Hollywood, and joined the staff of Fox Studios, where *Sunrise* was followed by four other films.

39. Sudermann (1857–1928), born in East Prussia (present-day Lithuania) was an influential exponent of naturalism in German literature and theater.

40. Carlisle Floyd, *Seth* libretto (1984–1985), 5. Scenario and libretto courtesy of Carlisle Floyd. All subsequent page numbers of quotes to this libretto will be given parenthetically in the text.

41. Floyd and Gockley to Dr. Michael Williams, UH graduate studies committee, October 15, 1984, Box 5, FASCL.

42. William Styron, *Darkness Visible: A Memoir of Madness* (New York: New Vintage Books, 1992), 4, 5, 7.

43. Author interview with Bohmler, February 13, 2007. Author interview with Ermine, June 21, 2009.

44. Author interview with Gockley, November 20, 2007.

45. "Intercompany Announcements," *Opera America,* April 1985.

46. Ned Rorem, *The Nantucket Diary of Ned Rorem* (San Francisco: North Point Press, 1987), 564.

47. First evidence of this condition was reported by Reverend Floyd in *Diary,* May 24, 1985.

48. Sylvia Goldstein to Floyd, August 3, 1985, B & H works files.

49. *Diary,* August 12, 1985.

50. Performances on October 3 and 5, 1985.

51. LaFleur Payson, "Willie Stark," *Charlotte Observer,* October 4, 1985.

52. Performance on October 26, 1985.

53. Harold Farwell, "Shreveport," *Opera News,* January 18, 1985.

54. Charles Ward, "Texas Chamber Orchestra," *Houston Chronicle,* February 22, 1986, Section 2, 8.

55. Trained in music and theater at Bucknell University, Ross earned an MFA in stage direction from the University of Minnesota, under the supervision of H. Wesley Balk.

56. John Rockwell, "City Opera Official Quits," *New York Times,* January 14, 1986 (http://www.nytimes.com/1986/01/14/arts/city-opera-official-quits.html).

18. Standing Up: Resurrection and *Jonathan* Reborn, 1986–1991

1. Horney (1885–1952) emigrated from Germany to the United States in 1926, and eventually became dean of the American Institute of Psychoanalysis, before teaching at New York Medical College and founding the American Journal of Psychoanalysis.

2. As described in Karen Horney, *Our Inner Conflicts* (New York: Norton, 1945).

3. James F. Masterson, *The Real Self: A Developmental Self and Object Relations Approach* (New York: Brunner/Mazel, 1985). Floyd also read Masterson's revised edition, *The Real Self: Unmasking the Personality Disorders of Our Age* (New York: Collier Macmillan, 1988).

4. Masterson, *Real Self: Unmasking,* viii.

5. Another was Hugo Weisgall's *Six Characters in Search of an Author,* on which Gockley declined to act.

6. Goldstein to Floyd, January 23, 1963, B & H works files.

7. Goldstein to Floyd, May 22, 1984, B & H works files.

8. Raymond Ericson, "His First Love: Theater," *New York Times,* May 28,1972, D11.

9. *Diary,* March 31, 1986.

10. Charles Ward, "Pianist Schiff Delivers Shining Performance," *Houston Chronicle,* February 15, 1987, Section 2, 8.

11. Medvitz to Floyd, c. 1987, B & H works files.

12. Ned Rorem, *Lies: A Diary, 1986–1999* (Cambridge: DaCapo/Perseus, 2002), 40.

13. Patricia C. Johnson, "'Something' Documents Local Artists at Work," *Houston Chronicle,* July 16, 1986, Houston section, 1.

14. Performances on April 9, 10, 11, 12, 1987.

15. Conversations with De la Torre related by Floyd.

16. Corsaro to Floyd, June 8, 1987, Box 6, FASCL.

17. Still in operation, but renamed Methodist Oaks in 1987.

18. Fleming, born in 1959, received her bachelor's degree at the State University of New York at Potsdam in 1981, and a master's at the Eastman School of Music in Rochester, New York, Fleming's childhood home.

19. Mollicone to Floyd, July 29, 1987. Cited in chapter 16, in reference to Floyd's work with Mollicone on *Starbird* in OMT workshops in 1981.

20. The Belwin-Mills catalogue is currently represented by Alfred Music Publishing of Van Nuys, California.

21. Goldstein memo, December 4, 1987, B & H composer file.

22. Interoffice memo from Sylvia Goldstein, December 4, 1987, B & H composer file.

23. Weisgall next turned to the librettist Charles Kondek, and the opera was in due course completed; but McEwen's successor, Lotfi Mansouri, cancelled the production in 1990. *Esther's* successful premiere took place in 1993 at New York City Opera, conducted by Christopher Keene; and a City Opera revival opened in November 2009.

24. Mansouri, born in Teheran in 1929, studied psychology at the University of California, Los Angeles, in the fifties, and soon won fame as an opera stage director and administrator at the Zurich Opera (1960–1966), Geneva Opera (1965–1975), Canadian Opera Company (1976–1988), and San Francisco Opera (1988–2001).

25. *Central Opera Service Bulletin* 20, nos. 1–2 (1987/88): 3.

26. Brégent was born in Montréal, Québec, in 1948, and died there in 1993.

27. Désilets, born in Québec in 1957, and Sullivan, born in Ottawa in 1954, have both gone on to distinguished creative and teaching careers in Canada.

28. *Central Opera Service Bulletin* 29, nos. 1–2 (1988/89): 6.

29. Sylvia Goldstein memo of phone conversation with Floyd, January 17, 1988, B & H works files.

30. Carlisle Floyd, *The Passion of Jonathan Wade* (c. 1988–1989), undated typescript libretto, Box 8, FASCL.

31. Glatthaar's much-awarded books on the period have been used by filmmaker Ken Burns for his 1991 PBS miniseries *The Civil War,* and by novelist E. L. Doctorow for his best-selling *The March* (Westminster, MD: Random House, 2005). Glatthaar left UH in 2005, to become the Stephenson Distinguished Professor of History at the University of North Carolina, Chapel Hill.

32. Author interview with Glatthaar, May 7, 2007.

33. Carlisle Floyd, "Summary of the Libretto for *The Passion of Jonathan Wade*" (1988), Box 5, FASCL.

34. Glatthaar to Floyd, March 29, 1988, Box 1, Folder 26, FASCL.

35. Author interview with Glatthaar, May 7, 2007.

36. April 2, 6, 8, 9, 10, 13, 1988.

37. Blue, "Operas We Would Like to See Again."

38. Gockley to Floyd, June 16, 1988, B & H works files.

39. Gockley to Goldstein, December 2, 1988; Goldstein to Gockley, December 9, 1988; B & H works files.

40. Blue, "Operas We Would Like to See Again."

41. Born in Saginaw, Michigan, in 1939, O'Brien remains one of the world's most successful stage directors. He served as artistic director of San Diego's Old Globe Theatre from 1971 until 2007, and remains the company's artistic director emeritus. Besides his HGO work, he has created productions for Dallas Civic Opera, San Francisco Opera, New York City Opera, and the Metropolitan Opera's *Il Trittico* in 2007. His collaboration with Terrence McNally on the book for a musical version of Steven Spielberg's film *Catch Me If You Can* opened on Broadway on April 10, 2011.

42. Blue, "Double Life of Jonathan Wade."

43. Carlisle Floyd, *The Passion of Jonathan Wade* libretto (New York: Boosey & Hawkes, 1990). See plot synopsis in chap. 12.

44. Blue, "Double Life of Jonathan Wade."

45. Eric Foner, *Reconstruction: America's Unfinished Revolution, 1863–1877* (New York: Harper Collins, 1988), 142–48.

46. Brian Busch to Rosenbaum, October 24, 1988, B & H works files.

47. See plot synopsis in chap. 15.

48. Schneider-Siemssen, born just four days before Floyd, on June 7, 1926, in Augsburg, Germany, has designed for most of the world's great theaters, including for Otto Schenk's 1986 production of *Der Ring des Nibelungen* at the Metropolitan Opera.

49. "Canadian Opera and Music Theater," *Central Opera Service Bulletin* 29, no. 3 (1989): 6–7.

50. MacDonald was born in Guelph, Ontario, in 1958; Koprowski, a naturalized Canadian, was born in Lodz, Poland, in 1947; and Gougeon was born in Granby, Québec, in 1951.

51. In Reverend Floyd's final *Diary,* he listed his assets on November 25, 1986, as $91,743.59.

52. Hazel Richards died in August 1993, a month short of her ninety-second birthday.

53. The program, based at Montclair State College, lasted only a few years.

54. Paul Somers, "Opera/Music Theatre Institute Presents Carlisle Floyd's 'Doll' in Condensed Form," *Newark Star-Ledger,* April 29, 1989.

55. William Shakespeare, *Much Ado About Nothing,* in *The Arden Shakespeare,* 3rd ed. (London: Thomson Learning, 2006), act 2, scene 1, line 309.

56. John Fletcher and William Shakespeare, *The Two Noble Kinsmen,* in *The Arden Shakespeare,* 3rd ed. (London: Thomson Publishing, 1997), act 1, scene 4, line 1.

57. Carlisle Floyd, "A Star Danced," unpublished ms. vocal score, May 10, 1989, Box 12, Folder 1, FALOC.

58. After Hays completed her master's at UH in 1988, she performed roles with HGO and Lyric Opera of Dallas, before moving to Germany, where she sings a variety of lyric and coloratura roles at the Theater Krefeld/Mönchengladbach.

59. Johnson to Floyd, May 22, 1989, Box 5, FASCL.

60. Rosenbaum to Goldstein, June 8, 1989, B & H composer files. The contract of January 10, 1973 to which Rosenbaum referred was apparently the only renewal Floyd signed with Belwin; like his earlier experience with Boosey, the contract agreement "floated" before he returned to the latter publisher in 1987.

61. Author interview with Golding, July 13, 2007.

62. Saraf to Goldstein, March 5, 1990, B & H works files.

63. Goldstein to Floyd, November 14, 1989, B & H composer files.

64. Contract of November 28, 1989; and Floyd to Goldstein, December 7, 1989; B & H composer files.

65. Financial statement, December 31, 1989, B & H composer files.

66. James Kendrick to Floyd, January 19, 1990, B & H works files.

67. Ireland to Johnson, March 29, 1990, Box 1, Folder 1, FASCL.

68. See Masterson, *Real Self: A Developmental Self,* 198–99.

69. Glatthaar to Floyd, "Re: Information on Reconstruction," April 4, 1990, Box 1, Folder 26, FASCL.

70. Ibid. Nevada gained statehood on October 31, 1864.

71. Stamper interview with author, March 23, 2007.

72. Ibid. Following Houston's *Jonathan Wade* run, Stamper accepted the studio's offer of membership for 1991–1992, during which he studied with Floyd and assisted with the revised *Bilby's Doll* in 1992.

73. Campbell to Floyd, May 15, 1990, Box 1, Folder 31, FASCL.

74. Patrick interview with author, December 5, 2007. The quotes in the next three paragraphs are from this source.

75. Charles Ward, "A Sprawling, Timely Tale," *Houston Chronicle,* January 21, 1991, Houston section, 1.

76. Roberto Suro, "1962 Opera's Revision Defines Its Composer," *New York Times,* February 2, 1991 (www.nytimes.com/1991/02/02/arts/opera-s-revision-defines-a-composer.html).

77. Woods to Floyd, January 18, 1991, Box 1, Folder 28, FASCL.

78. Uppman to Floyd, February 14, 1991, Box 1, Folder 28, FASCL.

79. Tim Smith, "Opera Evokes Passions of Civil War Era," *Fort Lauderdale Sun-Sentinel,* March 20, 1991.

80. James Roos, "Floyd's *Wade* an Impressive 'New' Opera," *Miami Herald,* March 20, 1991, 1D, 5D.

81. David Gregson, "'Jonathan Wade' Done with Passion in Civic Premiere," *San Diego Union,* April 15, 1991, 34.

82. Floyd to Campbell, May 26, 1991. Courtesy of Ian Campbell.

83. Huntley to Golding, May 10, 1991, B & H composer files.

84. Ibid.

85. Fleming to Floyd, May 27, 1991, Box 1, Folder 28, FASCL.

86. Interoffice memo from Janis Susskind, B & H London promotional department, to Linda Golding, May 30, 1991, B & H works files.

87. Martha Matheny Solomon to Floyd, June 11, 1991, Box 1, Folder 32, FASCL.

88. Campbell and Haworth to Floyd, June 6, 1991, Box 1, Folder 31, FASCL.

89. Golding, who began at Boosey in public relations in 1991, and worked as president of the New York office until 2001, had headed the rehearsal department and later performed artistic liaison work at the New York City Opera between 1979 and 1990.

90. Linda Golding interview with author, July 13, 2007.

19. Looking Back, Moving On Back: Houston and Tallahassee, 1991–1997

1. Donal Henahan, "Highbrow/Lowbrow and the Area Between," *New York Times,* January 24, 1991 (http://www.nytimes.com/1991/01/24/arts/review-music-highbrow-lowbrow-and-the-area-between.html).

2. Financial statement, June 30, 1991, B & H composer files.

3. David Small interview with author, February 15, 2007. Quotes in the next two paragraphs are from this source.

4. Susskind to Golding, October 7, 1991, B & H interoffice memo, B & H composer files.

5. B & H interoffice memo, October 14, 1991, B & H composer files.

6. Carlisle Floyd, "The Materials of Opera" (1998), typed ms., Box 10, FASCL.

7. Charles Ward, "UH Will End Its Support of Opera Studio," *Houston Chronicle,* February 18, 1992, 1D, 10D. HGO had contributed $320,000 to the studio's budget for 1991–1992.

8. Carl Cunningham, "UH's Opera 'Bilby's Doll' Nicely Done," *Houston Post*, May 26, 1992, 38.

9. Ross interview with author, May 7, 2009. Ross and Nelson won considerable success with their collaboration: Des Moines Metro Opera hosted a workshop of the first act of *A Room With a View* in the summer of 1992, before a complete performance at UH in the fall of 1993. A revival in April 2005 at the Moores Opera Center resulted in its DVD release on Newport Classics, NDV 22001.

10. Charles Ward, "Drama Slows 'Doll's' Music Score," *Houston Chronicle*, May 25,1992, Houston section, 3.

11. Brooks (1936–2007) became ACDA director in 1977.

12. Like Reverend Floyd, Raymond W. Brock served as a Methodist minister around South Carolina before appointment as ACDA development director, in which capacity he established an endowment trust.

13. Teresa Coffman, "Carlisle Floyd's Text Settings in His Works for Chorus," *Choral Journal* (Oklahoma City: American Choral Directors Association) 39, no. 8 (1999): 37–46.

14. Golding to Goldstein, June 16, 1992, B & H works files.

15. D. J. Enright, ed., *The Oxford Book of Death* (Oxford: Oxford University Press, 1987). Hereafter *OBD*.

16. *OBD*, 4. "Memento mori," Latin for "Remember that you die." From ancient times, many cultures used artistic reminders of mortality, including medallions of skulls and skeletons (also painted and sculpted).

17. Written around 50 B.C., the work's usual English title is *On the Nature of Things*. Although *OBD* contains one passage from Dryden's translation, Floyd chose another, from "The Latter Part of the Third Book of Lucretius: Against the Fear of Death," from *The Poetical Works of John Dryden* (London: William Pickering, 1852), 154.

18. Webster (c. 1580–1634) is best known for lurid revenge tragedies like *The White Devil* and *The Duchess of Malfi*. "Vanitas" was written for a later play, *The Devil's Law Case*, first published in 1623. The poem also appeared as no. 220 in *The Oxford Book of English Verse* (Clarendon: Oxford University Press, 1919).

19. *OBD*, 30. Twain's *Pudd'nhead Wilson and the Comedy of the Extraordinary Twins* appeared as a serialization in *The Century Magazine* in 1893/94, before its debut as a novel in 1894.

20. Donne (1572–1631) thought long and hard about his own death. Trained for military and diplomatic service, his appointment to important public offices preceded his ordination as an Anglican priest in 1615. His catalogue spans a gamut from erotic poetry to elegies and finally sermons. Shortly before his death, he commissioned a portrait of himself rising from the grave at the Apocalypse, his own memento mori. *OBD*, 19.

21. *OBD*, 173.

22. B & H contract receipt, September 24, 1993, B & H works files.

23. From Kingsley Amis (1922–1979), *Collected Poems, 1944–1979* (London: Hutchinson, 1979), 154.

24. Auslander's poem is based on the biblical story of Jesus' raising of Lazarus of Bethany from the dead, told in John 11: 41–44. Joseph Auslander, *No Traveller Returns* (New York: Harper & Row, 1935).

25. Alice Thomas Ellis, *The Birds of the Air* (New York: Viking, 1981). Ellis (1932–2005) was born Anna Lindholm in Liverpool and was of Finnish and Welsh ancestry. She married the publisher Colin Haycraft, and after 1977 adopted the Alice Thomas Ellis pseudonym for all of her writing, including novels and nonfiction works on cookery.

26. Day-Lewis (1904–1972), father of the actor Daniel Day-Lewis, was an Irish-born poet, critic, and educator. He was appointed Great Britain's poet laureate in 1968. *A Time to Dance and Other Poems* was published in London by Hogarth in 1935, and in the United States by Random House the following year.

27. Between UH's founding in 1938/39 and the 2009 death of Wilhelmina Daisy Cullen Robertson Smith, the Cullen Foundation gave the UH system approximately $70 million. See *University of Houston Magazine Online* (Spring 2009): 1.

28. Wortham Theater Center houses two separate performance spaces: the 2,200-seat Alice Brown Theater, where HGO plays larger works, and the 1,100-seat Lillie and Roy Cullen Theatre, for more intimate repertoire.

29. Floyd's program notes from the tenth anniversary concert, "New Vistas," of Janice Mayer & Associates, at Dizzy's Club, Frederick P. Rose Hall (Jazz at Lincoln Center), May 22, 2005. Courtesy of Janice Mayer.

30. Herrick's (1591–1674) original title is *Music: A Song*. In the edition cited, the first line is given as "Music, thou queen of heaven."

31. The year of Case's birth is estimated to be between 1539 and 1546; he died in 1600. See John Case, *The Praise of Musicke*, in a hypertext critical edition by Dana F. Sutton (Irvine: University of California, Irvine, 2009). Available online at http://www.philological.bham.ac.uk/music3/ (accessed August 6, 2012).

32. William Ellery Leonard's version, no. 97, in *Aesop and Hyssop* (Chicago: Open Court Publishing, 1912), 97.

33. Floyd lightly adapted a statement from Emerson's 1838 "Journal D." The bracketed words indicate the composer's insertion; Emerson's original had "whispers *to us* dim secrets." Thanks to Heather Cole, assistant curator of modern books and manuscripts at Harvard University Houghton Library, for this information.

34. Nietzsche (1844–1900), himself an amateur composer, became an acolyte, then bitter enemy, of his countryman Richard Wagner. See Friedrich Nietzsche, *Die Götzen-Dämmerung* (the writer's pun on the title of Wagner's fourth music drama in *Der Ring des Nibelungen*). Available online at http://www.handprint.com/SC/NIE/GotDamer.html#sect1 (accessed August 6, 2012).

35. The source of Collier's poem is his "Essay upon Music," in *Essays upon Several Moral Subjects* (London: J. & J. Knapton, 1732), part 2, 30.

36. Baldassare Castiglione, *The Book of the Courtier,* translated by Sir Thomas Hoby in 1561 (London: David Nutt, 1900).

37. Benedict de Spinoza, *The Ethics—Part IV,* translated by R. H. M. Elwes, 1883. Available online at http://www.yesselman.com/e4elwes.htm (accessed August 12, 2012).

38. William Shakespeare, *The Merchant of Venice,* in *Arden Shakespeare,* act 5, scene 1, lines 71–79 and 83–88. Ralph Vaughan Williams set the same last four lines in his 1938 composition *Serenade to Music.* The reader will notice a number of small changes and inversions that Floyd made for his sung text.

39. Floyd, program notes from "New Vistas."

40. Wolf to Floyd, October 39, 1992, Box 9, FASCL.

41. FAX from J. P. Brossmann, Opéra de Lyon, to Linda Golding, September 25, 1992, and FAX with change of dates from Brossmann to Golding, February 1, 1993; B & H works files.

42. The Japanese American conductor Nagano, born in Berkeley, California, in 1951, has occupied a variety of music directorships, including Hallé Orchestra (Manchester, England), Deutsches Symphonie-Orchester (Berlin), Los Angeles Opera, and Bayerische Staatsoper.

43. Nick Kimberley, "Floyd and His *Susannah,*" *Opera,* August 1994, 914.

44. Born in Midland, Michigan, in 1955, Studer studied at Oberlin Conservatory and the University of Tennessee–Knoxville. From 1975 to 1977, she worked with Phyllis Curtin at the Tanglewood Berkshire Music Center.

45. Mark Gresham, "San Antonio, Texas," *Chorus! Magazine* 5, no. 5 (1993): 9. Courtesy of Mark Gresham.

46. Hausmann to Floyd, March 7, 1993, Box 1, Folder 31, FASCL.

47. Blue, "Operas We Would Like to See Again."

48. Alex Ross, "A '58 Opera That Tested Mildly Dissonant Tonality," *New York Times,* March 18, 1993 (http://www.nytimes.com/1993/03/18/arts/review-music-a-58-opera-that-tested-mildly-dissonant-tonality.html).

49. Born in Altadena, California, in 1930, Nixon began singing at fourteen. In opera, concert, recordings, and Broadway and musical theater, she soon earned the sobriquet "the ghostess with the mostess." Her dubbing work provided singing voices for Ingrid Bergman (*Joan of Arc*), Marilyn Monroe (high notes in "Diamonds Are a Girl's Best Friend," in *Gentlemen Prefer Blondes*), and, most famously, Deborah Kerr (*The King and I*), Natalie Wood (*West Side Story*), and Audrey Hepburn (*My Fair Lady*). She received a Peabody Award in 2012 for "outstanding contributions to American music."

50. Marni Nixon, *I Could Have Sung All Night* (New York: Billboard Books, 2006), 255–59.

51. Ramey interview with author, August 1, 2008.

52. October 9, 13, 16, 19, 24, 26, 29, and November 1, 5, 1993.

53. John van Rhein, "'Susannah' at Lyric," *Chicago Tribune,* October 11, 1993.

54. Charles Ward, "Ciao, Niki," *Houston Chronicle,* May 8, 1994, Zest section, 11.

55. See Carlisle Floyd, "Recalling *Susannah*'s Beginnings," Virgin Classics booklet, CD 724354503924, 1994, 13–15.

56. John Rockwell, "A Most American Opera (via France)," *New York Times,* October 30, 1994 (http://www.nytimes.com/1994/10/30/arts/recordings-view-a-most-american-opera-via-France.html).

57. Adamo, born in Philadelphia in 1962, is today best known as the librettist-composer of the operas *Little Women* and *Lysistrata.*

58. Adamo interview with author, May 25, 2007. The quote in the next paragraph is also from this source.

59. Robert Wilder Blue, "From Literary Classic to Hit Opera: Mark Adamo Traces the Journey of *Little Women* to the Stage," USOperaWeb, May 2001. The next Adamo quote is also from this source.

60. Pipkin to Floyd, May 16, 1996, Box 1, Folder 28, FASCL.

61. David Tomatz continued as director of Moores School until 1999. His successor, David Ashley White, is at the time of writing still the school's head.

62. Floyd to White, October 15, 1995. Courtesy of Dr. White.

63. James R. Oestreich, "The Power of Opera in an Intimate Production," *New York Times,* April 5, 1995 (http://www.nytimes.com/1995/04/05/arts/music-review-the-power-of-opera-in-an-intimate-production.html).

64. Kalett to Floyd, July 26, 1995, B & H works files.

65. Nick Kimberley, "Floyd and His 'Susannah,'" *Opera,* August 1994, 911.

66. Billinghurst to Floyd, February 20, 1996, Box 1, Folder 28, FASCL. Billinghurst, a New Zealand native, worked as the artistic administrator at San Francisco Opera for twenty-two years, from 1972 to 1994, after which she undertook the Met's parallel position.

67. Other San Diego *Wade* performances were on March 5, 8, and 10, 1996.

68. Heggie interview with author, April 2, 2007. Quotes in the next three paragraphs are also from this source.

69. Heggie to Floyd, March 6, 1996, Box 9, FASCL. Quotes in the next four paragraphs also from this source.

70. Passages with full orchestra.

71. Erato 86238-2.

72. At the time of writing, Heggie's other operatic works are *Again* (2000), a ten-minute scene to a libretto by Kevin Gregor, and premiered in New York five months before *Dead Man Walking; The End of the Affair,* based on Graham Greene's novel, to a libretto by Heather McDonald, commissioned and premiered by Houston Grand Opera in 2003; *At the Statue of Venus* (2005), commissioned by Opera Colorado for the opening of the Ellie Caulkins Opera House; *To Hell and Back* (2006); *For a Look or a Touch* (2007); *Three Decembers* (2008); *Moby Dick,* libretto by Gene Scheer, based on the classic Herman Melville novel, premiered by Dallas Opera in 2010; and *Another Sunrise,* libretto by Gene Scheer, based on the life of

Holocaust survivor Krystyna Zywulska, and first performed in Seattle in 2012.

73. Charles Ward, "A Revival of Interest," *Houston Chronicle,* April 28, 1996, Zest section, 8. See also Olive Ann Burns, *Cold Sassy Tree* (New York: Delta/Dell, 1994).

74. Fincher to Floyd, April 18, 1996, Box 9, FASCL. Fincher would live another four years, until October 2000.

75. Typed memo from Sue Klein to Carolyn Kalett, Boosey & Hawkes, July 31, 1996. B & H works files.

76. HGO's performances at Wortham Center on May 2, 4, 6, 8, 10, and 12, 1996.

77. Adamo interview with author, May 25, 2007. The next Adamo quote is also from this source.

78. Charles Ward, "'Little Women': A Reality Check," *Houston Chronicle,* March 16, 1998, Houston section, 1.

79. Ondine ODE 988-2D.

80. Adamo interview with author, May 25, 2007.

81. See Wah Keung Chan, "Desmond Byrne on Carlisle Floyd and Susannah," *La Scena Musicale* 2, no. 9 (1997): 92 (http://www.scena.org/lsm/sm2-9/sm2-9Byrne.html).

82. The quotes are from, respectively: Harald Hebling, "Kammeroper," *Wiener Kurier,* October 16, 1996, 12; Walter Dobner, "Amerikanische Opera," *Wiener Presse,* October 16, 1996, 8; Reinhard Kager, "Susannah in Österreich," *Standard,* October 16, 1996, 10; and Karleinz Roschitz, "Floyds 'Susannah,'" *Krone,* October 16, 1996, 8.

83. Other Berlin performances on February 11 and 24, and March 6, 15, 16, 19, and 25, 1997. Its success was reflected in a revival on March 12, 21, and 28, 1998.

84. Floyd to Clarke, February 5, 1997.

85. Keung Chan, "Desmond Byrne."

86. Klaus-Georg Koch, *Berliner Zeitung,* February 10, 1997, 14.

87. Jean Théfaine, *Ouest,* March 22,1997, 8.

88. Floyd to Clarke, March 24, 1996.

89. Carlisle Floyd, "A Summing-Up at Seventy," reprinted in full in Opera America's *Newsline* 6, no. 10 (1997): 20–27.

20. Unmatched Experience: *Susannah* At the Met, 1997–2000

1. Floyd to Craig Fields, Opera Roanoke, June 13, 1997, B & H works files.

2. Central City gave additional performances on July 15, 18, 20, 26, 31, and August 2, 6, 8, 1997.

3. Other Glimmerglass performances were on July 29 and on August 2, 10, 14, 16, 18, 22, 24, 1997.

4. Anthony Tommasini, "Listening for Inner Truths at the Glimmerglass Opera," *New York Times,* August 19, 1997

5. Rorem, *Lies,* 361.

6. Robert Wilder Blue, "Patrick Summers Talks about Carlisle Floyd and American Opera," *USOperaweb,* February 2001.

7. Born in San Jose in 1925, Dalis sang leading roles at most of the world's other great opera houses until her retirement in 1977. She founded Opera San Jose in 1984.

8. After leaving the HGO studio in 2001, Yuan sang leading roles in the company's mainstage productions—including Mark Adamo's *Little Women*—and at numerous American, European, and Asian theaters. We encountered Scott Heumann in 1981, writing about Floyd's *Willie Stark* for *Opera News.* He subsequently became HGO's artistic administrator and dramaturge in 1983, and served the company in numerous other capacities until shortly before his death in May 1993.

9. *Of Mice and Men* performances took place at San Diego Opera on February 14, 17, 20, 22, 1998.

10. Oberlin: March 11, 13, 14, 1998. Chattangooga: March 21, 1998. Springfield: March 27, 1998. Berlin: March 12, 21, 28, 1998.

11. Carlisle Floyd "The Materials of Opera," 1998, typescript, Box 10, FASCL.

12. Flint interview with author, October 26, 2006.

13. Other performances on July 13, 17, 19, 1998.

14. Of the creative team of Russian composer Igor Stravinsky and colibrettists W. H. Auden and Chester Kallman, only Kallman was American-born. *The Rake's Progress* was premiered not in the United States, but in Venice, Italy.

15. Paul Griffiths, "'Susannah' and Its Many Little Mysteries," *New York Times,* July 20, 1998 (http://www.nytimes.com/1998/07/20/arts/opera-review-susannah-and-its-many-little-mysteries.html).

16. Elaine Steinbeck, née Anderson, first married for sixteen years to actor Zachary Scott, outlived her third husband, John Steinbeck, by thirty-five years, dying in April 2003. Born in 1914 in Austin, Texas, she had worked as an actress and became one of the first women to stage manage theatrical and musical productions.

17. K. Robert Schwarz, "A Regional Favorite Gains Prominence," *New York Times,* November 1, 1998 (http://www.nytimes.com/1998/11/01/arts/a-regional-favorite-gains-prominence.html). Quotes in the next paragraph are from this article.

18. Mark Adamo, "The Father of Us All." Courtesy of Mark Adamo.

19. City Opera performances on November 7, 13, 15, 19, 21, 1998.

20. Robert Wilder Blue,"An American Baritone: Julian Patrick Keeps on Singing," US OperaWeb, January 2002.

21. Allan Kozinn, "Steinbeck's Ill-Fated Gathering Of Lost Souls," *New York Times,* November 9, 1998 (http://www.nytimes.com/1998/11/09/arts/opera-review-steinbeck's-ill-fated-gathering-of-lost-souls.htm).

22. Shirley Fleming, "'Of Mice and Men' Melodic, Powerful," *New York Post,* November 9, 1998.

23. VAI 1172.

24. Performances on March 19, 21, 23, 1999.

25. Volpe to Floyd, March 28, 1999, Box 1, Folder 29, FASCL.

26. Golding interview with author, July 13, 2007.

27. Adamo to Floyd, March 31, 1999, Box 1, Folder 29, FASCL.

28. Anthony Tommasini, "Taking a Look into the Soul of 'Susannah,'" *New York Times*, March 31, 1999, E1.

29. March 31 and April 3, 6, 9, 13, 16, 22, 1999.

30. Glover, *All Our Relations*, xiv.

31. Floyd to Clarke, April 7, 1998.

32. Floyd's and Clarke's term for their mutual friend.

33. Julius Rudel, "My Susannah," *Opera News*, April 1999, 22–23.

34. Heggie interview with author, April 2, 2007.

35. Gockley interview with author, November 20, 2007.

36. Robert Wilder Blue, "On the Fast Track: Anthony Dean Griffey," *US Operaweb*, January 2002.

37. Curtin to Floyd, April 9, 1999, Box 1, Folder 30, FASCL.

38. Bernard Holland, "A Petite 'Susannah' in a Great Big House," *New York Times*, April 2, 1999 (http://www.nytimes.com/1999/04/02/arts/music-review-a-petite-susannah-in-a-great-big-house.html).

39. Peter G. Davis, "Witch Hunt," *New York Magazine*, April 19, 1999, 34.

40. Gillette-Perrone to Floyd, April 4, 1999, Box 10, FASCL. Despite subsequent correspondence and calls, this was Floyd's last meeting with his old friend and early interpreter, who died on February 2, 2006.

41. Rupert Bottenberg, "Definitely Not the Beverly Hillbillies," *Montreal Mirror*, April 22, 1999.

42. Billinghurst to Floyd, April 23, 1999, Box 1, Folder 30, FASCL.

43. Mark Flint interview with author, October 26, 2006. Quote in next paragraph also from this source.

44. Washington Opera performances on November 6, 9, 12, 15, 18, 21, 24, 27, 1999. Michigan performances on November 11, 12, 13, 14, 1999.

45. Klein to Floyd, April 7, 1999, Box 10, FASCL. Curtin to Floyd, April 9, 1999, Box 1, Folder 30, FASCL.

21. Late Fruits: *Cold Sassy Tree*, 1994–2003

1. The term "spine" was popularized by the great Russian director and teacher of acting Konstantin Stanislavsky, and by American disciples such as Sanford Meissner and Harold Clurman.

2. Kalett to Douglas, June 22, 1994, B & H works files.

3. Douglas to Kalett, October 14, 1994; and ICM contract with Port Bascom Productions, May 1, 1996, B & H works files.

4. On June 22, 2000, NPR paid Boosey $2,500 for a single nationwide radio broadcast. B & H works files.

5. Kalett to Douglas, October 27, 1994, B & H works files.

6. Published in 1984, *Cold Sassy Tree* became a Book-of-the-Month Club selection. During chemotherapy in 1987, Burns developed congestive heart failure, and, despite beginning a sequel, died on July 4, 1990. The remaining fragments of *Leaving Cold Sassy* were published in 1992.

7. Ramey interview with author, August 1, 2008.

8. Kalett to Douglas, April 24, 1996, B & H works files.

9. Douglas to Kalett, June 6, 1996, B & H works files.

10. Floyd to Gockley, with treatment, February 12, 1997, Box 5, Folder 110, FASCL.

11. *Diary*, June 26, 1945.

12. Carlisle Floyd, *Cold Sassy Tree* scenario, February 17, 1997, Box 5, Folder 110, FASCL. The page numbers of subsequent references to this scenario will be given parenthetically in the text.

13. Gockley FAX to Golding, March 14, 1997, B & H works files.

14. Ibid.

15. Teri Fournier, Turner Broadcasting, to Kalett, March 20, 1997, B & H works files.

16. Golding FAX to Gockley, April 17, 1997, B & H works files.

17. Knudson to B & H staff, undated memo, probably April 1997, B & H works files.

18. Gockley to Golding, May 28, 1997, B & H works files.

19. Golding to Gockley, May 30, 1997, B & H works files.

20. Golding to Winfried Jacobs et al., B & H London, July 18, 1997, B & H works files.

21. Kalett to Floyd, August 13, 1997, and Schedule A of agreement of April 1, 1998; B & H works files.

22. *Grandboy*, see chap. 16.

23. O'Brien to Floyd, January 17, 1998, Box 1, Folder 29, FASCL. The quotes in the next two paragraphs are from this source.

24. Andrew Stiller, "Floyd, Carlisle (Sessions, Jr.)," *New Grove Dictionary of Opera* (London: Macmillan, 1992), 2:246.

25. O'Brien to Floyd, January 27, 1998. Quote in the next paragraph is also from this source.

26. Floyd to Clarke, April 7, 1998.

27. First paragraph quote from Floyd interview with author, July 12, 2002. Second paragraph quote from Robert Wilder Blue, "Carlisle Floyd Continues His Exploration of Southern Life in His First Major Comic Opera," *USOperaweb*, February 2001.

28. Mason to Floyd, May 5, 1998, Box 1, Folder 29, FASCL.

29. O'Brien to Floyd, May 20, 1998, Box 1, Folder 29, FASCL.

30. Ireland to Golding, July 20, 1998, B & H works files.

31. Mentzer to Golding, July 22, 1998, B & H works files.

32. Kalett to Golding, August 28, 1998; Golding to Floyd, September 11, 1998; Golding to Kalett, November 4, 1998; B & H interoffice memo from Carolyn Kalett, August 30, 2000; B & H works files.

33. O'Brien to Floyd, August 24, 1998, Box 1, Folder 29, FASCL.

34. Heggie to Floyd, February 16, 1999, Box 4, FASCL.

35. Reveles to Floyd, February 17, 1999, Box 1, Folder 30, FASCL.

36. Box office tabulation, March 22, 2001, B & H works files.

37. Helen Harris interview with author, December 27, 2007

38. November 27 and 30, 1999.

39. De Vanssay to Floyd, June 25, 1999, Box 3, FASCL.

40. *Cold Sassy Tree* was Beresford's seventh opera production. He had won great acclaim for the films *Breaker Morant* (1980, which he wrote and directed), *Tender Mercies* (1983), *Crimes Of the Heart*

(1986), and *Driving Miss Daisy* (1989), which won him an Academy Award.

41. Author interview, November 20, 2007.

42. Founded in 1987, the Albany Records label specializes in classical music "off the beaten path," with a predictable favoring of American composers.

43. Other Kentucky Opera performances were on February 5 and 13, 2000.

44. Arizona Opera also performed *Of Mice and Men* in Tucson on February 13 and 14; and at Symphony Hall in Phoenix on February 17, 18, 19, and 20, 2000.

45. Blue, "Patrick Summers Talks."

46. Robert Wilder Blue, "Connecting with the Characters: Australian Director Bruce Beresford Brings an American Work to the Opera Stage," USOperaWeb, February 2001.

47. Paul Thomason, "The Words Come First," Houston Grand Opera *Playbill* for *Cold Sassy Tree*, April 2000, 13–15. Copy in FASCL.

48. Charles Ward, "Composer Finds a Hit in Comic Opera," *Houston Chronicle*, April 17, 2000, Houston section, 1.

49. Joshua Kosman, "American Opera Has a New Classic," *San Francisco Chronicle*, April 17, 2000, 34.

50. Author interview with Gockley, November 20, 2007.

51. Wes Blomster, "Houston," *Opera Now*, July 14, 2000.

52. That is, with Turner Broadcasting; a snag remains with restrictions in the contract with ICM.

53. HGO box office performance report in FAX to B & H, March 22, 2001, B & H works files.

54. Performances on June 16, 18, 20, 23, 26, and 28, 2000.

55. Fresno/Kennedy Opera, August 6 and 11, 2000. North Carolina: Longleaf Opera, September 28, 30, and October 1, 2000. Fort Worth: November 2, 3, 4, 2000. Indiana: November 10, 11, 17, 18, 2000.

56. Charles Leslie was the son of one of Floyd's FSU piano students, Robert Leslie. Other Austin performances were on January 13, 14, 15, 2001.

57. Robert Faires, "Final Flowering," *Austin Chronicle*, January 12, 2001, 14.

58. Austin Lyric Opera production sales report, March 22, 2001, B & H works files.

59. Beeson to Floyd, March 23, 2001, Box 3, FASCL.

60. Helen Harris interview with author, December 27, 2007.

61. Author interview with Golding, July 13, 2007.

62. Holliday to Floyd, April 18, 2001, Box 12, FASCL.

63. Kalett to Mitch Douglas and David Schmerler, ICM, April 4, 2001; and Kalett to Floyd, May 31, 2001. B & H works files.

64. Conversation reported by Floyd.

65. Carlisle Floyd, "Some Thoughts on the Creative Process," May 2001. Courtesy of Carlisle Floyd.

66. Anne Midgette, "A Little Chamber Opera Written for Full Orchestra," *New York Times*, June 5, 2001 (http://www.nytimes.com/2001/06/05/arts/music-review-a-little-chamber-opera-written-for-full-orchestra.html).

67. Utah: July 12, 18, 20, 25, 28, and August 2 and 4, 2001. Baltimore: Performances on July 14 and 15, 2001.

68. Robert Wilder Blue, "Verdi Baritone Gordon Hawkins Takes On a Great American Role," USOperaweb, January 2002.

69. Ibid.

70. Performances on October 20, 25, 28, 31, November 3, 6, 9, and 12, 2001.

71. Other HGO performances were on February 3, 6, 9, 12, 15, and 17, 2002.

72. E-mail from Shane Gasbarra, HGO artistic administrator, to Carolyn Kalett, June 2, 2003, B & H works files.

73. Shreveport: January 26, 2002. Michigan: February 23, 24, 28, and March 1 and 2, 2002. Palm Beach: March 1, 3, and 4, 2002. Eugene: March 8 and 10, 2002. Du Page: July 13, 16, 19, and 20, 2002. Memphis: Four performances between August 1 and 20, 2002. Walnut Creek: August 10, 12, and 20, 2002. Columbus: January 30, 31, and February 1 and 2, 2003. Baldwin Wallace: February 12, 13, 14, 15, and 16, 2003. Central Methodist: February 20, 2003. Wright State: February 21, 2003. Amalfi: July 2, 2003.

74. Knoxville and Philadelphia: August 23 and 25, 2002. New York: March 7, 9, and 11, April 25, 26, and 27, and May 2, 3, and 4, 2002. Edmonton: March 9, 12, and 14, 2002. Vancouver: March 23, 26, 28, and 30, 2002.

75. Morrow: February 15 and 16, 2002. Atlanta: February 22 and 23, 2003.

76. B & H composer file.

77. Other performances on May 6, 8, 10, and 12, 2002.

78. Lyric performances were on September 30, and October 4, 6, 9, 12, 16, 19, 22, 25, and 29, 2002.

79. Charles Ward, "Elena Nikolaidi, 96, Opera Star, Teacher," *Houston Chronicle*, November 16, 2002, A39.

80. Other performances were on February 22 and 23, 2003.

81. "Blumenthal Performing Arts Center Total Wraps," B & H works files.

82. Other Utah Opera performances were on May 19, 21, 23 and 25, 2003.

83. July 6, 9, 11, and 13, 2003.

22. Twilight in Tallahassee, 2003–2012

1. Performances on October 4, 14, 18, 23, 26, 29, 31, 2003.

2. Anne Midgette, "The Best Laid Schemes, Set to Music," *New York Times*, October 17, 2003 (http://www.nytimes.com/2003/10/17/arts/opera-review-the-best-laid-schemes-set-to-music.html).

3. Philadelphia: October 11, 14, 17, 19, 22, 24, 25, 2003. Cincinnati: November 14–16, 2003.

4. See Atlanta Audio Society, *Explorations V* (summer 2004): 6–7.

5. Anthony Tommasini, "'Of Mice and Men': It's Not Over till The Slow Guy Sings," *New York Times,* August 22, 2004.

6. April 28, 30, and May 3, 2004.

7. Jane Matheny interviews with author, 2007–2010. Subsequent quotes from Jane Matheny are from these interviews.

8. Albert's performance, from a live recital with the pianist Jo Anne Ritacca on September 6, 2002, was issued on Cinnibar CD CNB 1402.

9. Greensboro: April 2, 2004. Kansas City: November 6, 8, 10, 12, 14, 2004.

10. Columbus: February 4, 5, 6, 2005. Hawaii: February 9, 11, 13, 15, 2005. Mississippi: February 26 and 27, 2005. Fargo: April 8 and 19, 2005. Ireland: October 22, 25, 28, 31, and November 3 and 6, 2005. North Carolina: April 8 and 9, 2005.

11. Wayne Lee Gay, "Floyd: *Cold Sassy Tree,*" *Fort Worth Star-Telegram,* July 31, 2005.

12. Gockley interview with author, November 20, 2007.

13. Other performances on November 12 and 18, 2005.

14. FSU's College of Music outreach arm.

15. Stuart Ostrow, *Present at the Creation: Leaping in the Dark, and Going against the Grain* (New York: Applause Theatre and Cinema Books, 2006), xiii–xvii.

16. Cedar Rapids: February 16 and 18, 2006. St. Louis: March 24 and 25, 2006. Norway: March 22, 24, 25, 26, 31, and April 1, 2006. Louisiana: April 18 and 19, 2006. New York: April 21, 22, 28, 29, 2006. Atlanta: April 28 and 29, 2006.

17. *Die tote Stadt* refers to Erich Wolfgang Korngold's 1920 opera, which was suffused with death and hallucinatory reminiscence. The title's "dead city" is based on Bruges, Belgium.

18. Carlisle Floyd E-mail to author, July 23, 2006.

19. November 10, 12, 15, 17 and 19, 2006, at the Harrison Opera House, Norfolk; on tour November 24 and 25, at the Landmark Theater in Richmond; and December 1 and 3, at the George Mason University Center for the Arts, Fairfax.

20. Bearden was Floyd's creative writing instructor at Converse College in the forties.

21. Graydon Royce, "On Stage: There's Nothing Old about 'Susannah,'" *Minneapolis/St. Paul Star-Tribune,* January 26, 2007, 23. Latté Da gave fifteen *Susannah*s between February 1 and March 18, 2007.

22. Performances were on March 22, 23, and 25, 2007. LSU's production was released on DVD as Newport Classics B0018BDDFO in May 2008.

23. Gockley interview with author, November 20, 2007.

24. Carlisle Floyd, "An Homage to Phyllis," Great Barrington, MA, August 4, 2007. Courtesy of Carlisle Floyd.

25. Indiana: October 19, 20, 26, 27, 2007. Hamburg: December 14, 2007. Berlin: November 16, 2007. Ithaca: November 9 and 10, 2007.

26. London (March 14), Sheffield (March 19), Cheltenham (March 27), Exeter (April 3), Truro (April 9), Buxton (April 26), Cambridge (May 1), The Maltings, Snape (May 9), and Warwick (May 15).

27. Illinois: April 16, 2008. Austin: April 18, 20, 25, 27, 2008. Texas Women's U.: April 26, 2008. Opera Pacific: May 14, 18, 22, 24, 2008.

28. E-mail to author, May 14, 2008. Floyd's modesty proved prophetic: the 2009 recipients were John Adams, Marilyn Horne, and old friends and colleagues Julius Rudel, Frank Corsaro, and Lotfi Mansouri.

29. *Of Mice and Men* on May 31 and June 8, 2008.

30. Available through online marketer *www.arkivmusic.com.*

31. Moore was a member of the WNO Domingo-Cafritz Young Artist Program.

32. E-mail to author, November 12, 2008.

33. Founded in 2008, Imagem currently operates as a licensing and A & R research entity in London, with branch offices in New York and Hilversum (Netherlands), managing publishing rights to more than a hundred thousand songs by such popular stars as Celine Dion, Michael Jackson, Madonna, Britney Spears, and Justin Timberlake.

34. Other performances were on February 28, March 7, 8, 28, 29 (the last two on tour to Bayreuth, a city almost totally consecrated to Richard Wagner), April 4, 28, 29, and May 5 and 15, 2009.

35. Conversations reported by Floyd.

36. For the plot synopsis, see chap. 17.

37. Formerly Lincoln Center's New York State Theatre.

38. E-mail to author, January 3, 2010.

39. Statistics courtesy of Marc A. Scorca and Adam Gustafson, Opera America.

40. Germany: February 7, 2010. Wisconsin: April 1, 2, 3, and 4, 2010. Iowa: Additional performances on May 1 and 2, 2010. Cincinnati: Additional performances on May 14, 15, and 16, 2010. July 3, 7, and 16 at Des Moines Metro Opera.

41. Additional performances on May 18, 21, and June 2, 9, 13, 2010.

42. See, for example, "Die Passion des Jonathan Wade," *Kurier,* May 18, 2010, 18; Karl Herb, "Dramatik swischen den Fronten," *Salzburger Nachrichten,* May 18, 2010; Bernhard Doppler, "Kain und Abel," *DLF Musik-Journal,* May 17, 2010; and Frank Raudszus, "Ein Amerikaner in Salzburg," *Internet-Magazin 'Egotrip',* May 2010.

43. Sydney performances on July 23, 26, and 29, and August 2 and 5, 2011; Melbourne on November 26 and 30, and December 3 and 10, 2011.

44. Melissa Lesnie, "Of Mice and Men: Keeping the American Dream Singing," Limelightmagazine.com, July 25, 2011, http://www.limelightmagazine.com.au/Article/264688,of-mice-and-men-keeping-the-american-dream-singing.aspx.

45. Carlisle Floyd E-mail to author, February 24, 2010.

46. Carlisle Floyd E-mail to author, September 19, 2010.

47. Hatcher, born in Steubenville, Ohio, in 1958, is best known for his adaptations of Stevenson's *Dr. Jekyll and Mr. Hyde* (2008), and

Mitch Albom's *Tuesdays with Morrie* (2002). He adapted his own 1999 play, *Compleat Female Stage Beauty,* as a 2004 screenplay for the film *Stage Beauty,* starring Billy Crudup and Claire Danes.

Appendix. Mysteries of South Carolina: The Genealogy of Carlisle Floyd

1. *Wuthering Heights, Markheim, Flower and Hawk.*

2. *Of Mice and Men* takes place in California, *Bilby's Doll* in New England.

3. Robert M. Weir, *Colonial South Carolina: A History* (Millwood, NY: KTO Press, 1983), 173.

4. Glover, *All Our Relations,* xiv.

5. Ibid., 4.

6. Ibid., 6.

7. Ibid., x.

8. Meaning "sitting" or "session."

9. The sound is made by placing the tip of the tongue against the hard palate and the back of the top teeth, as though pronouncing a regular *l.* But then, one breathes out over the sides of the tongue, making a sound combining elements of *l* and *th,* as in the word "thick." As the letter *y* is a Welsh vowel, the name involves a diphthong of English *oo* followed by a short, unemphasized *ee.* Fortunately, a single *d* is pronounced just as in English, rendering the complete name something like *Hlooeed,* the accent on the *oo.*

10. The surname "Flood" is the family's principal English branch; Old English *flod* means "dweller by the stream." One Wigot de la Flode is documented in Berkshire in 1198, and a Roger Flod in Warwickshire in 1200.

11. Also called Brecknock, Breconshire, and Brecon. Created in 1535, the district was divided into modern Brecknock and Powys in 1974.

12. N. J. Floyd, *Biographical Genealogies of the Virginia-Kentucky Floyd Families* (Baltimore: Williams & Watkins, 1912). Extracted and e-mailed by H. B. Floyd to author.

13. As these Floyds are cousins of the family's South Carolina branch, a resemblance is unmistakable in extant portraits and photographs of William Floyd: www.ushistory.org/declaration/signers/floyd.htm; Col. James John Floyd: http://en.wikipedia.org/wiki/James_John_Floyd; and John Buchanan Floyd: http://en.wikipedia.org/wiki/John_B._Floyd.

14. *Virginia Magazine of History and Biography* 1 (1894): 313. The source is John Camden Hotten, *The Original Lists of Persons of Quality* (New York: G. A. Baker, 1931). Edward Blaney, a man of means who emigrated to Jamestown in April 1620, later served on the Governor's Council.

15. Nicholas Jackson Floyd, *Biographical Genealogies of the Virginia-Kentucky Floyd Families: With Notes of Some Collateral Branches* (Baltimore: Williams and Wilkins, 1912; digitalized 2007). The William/Abadiah branch sired three generations of noteworthy Floyds: Col. James John (1759–1783), a privateer during the Revolution and later a surveyor who spearheaded the settling of Kentucky.

Floyd County, Floyds Fork River, and Floydsburg are all his namesakes. He was ambushed and burned at the stake by Indians three days before the birth of his son, John (1783–1837). John Jr. attended Dickinson College in Carlisle, Pennsylvania, which would have later connections to the composer Carlisle. John Jr. served in the Virginia House of Delegates (1814–1815), as United States Representative (1817–1829), and as Governor of Virginia (1830–1834). In the 1832 presidential election, he ran as a National Republican (precursor of the Whig Party), carrying South Carolina and eleven electoral votes. John Jr.'s son, John Buchanan Floyd (1806–1863), born in Blacksburg, Virginia, and graduated from South Carolina College, served in the Virginia House of Delegates (1847–1849, and 1854). After John served as governor of the state (1849–1852), President James Buchanan appointed him Secretary of War in 1857. He resigned in 1860, serving as a brigadier general in the Confederate Army until 1862, when he lost command of Fort Donelson.

16. Welsh origins and descent from Richard, the other son of John Floyd and Elizabeth Lady, are far clearer: born in 1626, Richard married Susanna Floyd in 1645, and arrived on Long Island in 1656, thus establishing the New York Floyds. They produced another Richard in 1665, and a second Susanna in 1688, before Richard I died in Setauket, Suffolk County, New York, in 1700. Richard II and Margaret Nicoll married in 1685, and had a brood of eight children, the youngest of whom was Nicoll Floyd, born in 1705. With wife Tabitha, he produced William Floyd in 1734, who signed the Declaration of Independence in 1776 and became a general in the Revolution. He served as a delegate to the Constitutional Convention, and later as senator from New York, living until 1821.

17. *Abstracts of Virginia Land Patents and Grants, 1623–1666,* vol. 1 (Baltimore: Genealogical Publishing Co., 1983).

18. Durward T. Stokes, *The History of Dillon County* (Columbia: University of South Carolina Press, 1978), 144.

19. Unlike many surnames passed as given names from one generation to the next, "Pinckney" honors a South Carolina legend with no apparent blood ties to the Floyds: Charles Pinckney (1757–1824) was a notable politician. The Floyds' appropriation of the surname "Pinckney" also appears in Giles Pinckney Floyd of North Carolina (1825–1900).

20. Reading Roberts, born in Davie, North Carolina, on February 2, 1784, appears as "Reddin," "Redden," and "Redin" in various documents. The first Roberts in America, Thomas, settled in North Carolina in the mid-1660s, whether as indentured servant or gentleman is uncertain. Like some Floyds, the Robertses posit descent from the Jamestown line of Pocahontas. The first to make his way to South Carolina, Roger Roberts (1740–c. 1829), worked as supplier to the Continental Army in the Revolution, and in 1797 received a land grant for 288 acres in the Buck Swamp region, i.e., Free State.

See Marylyn M. Roberts, *The Roberts Family History* (Greenville, SC: A Press, 1983).

21. W. W. Sellers, *A History of Marion County, South Carolina* (Columbia, SC: R. L. Bryan, 1902; reissued by Marion Public Library, 1956), 212.

22. *Marion County Probate Records,* vol. 3 (Hemingway, SC: Three Rivers Historical Society, 1985), 36.

23. *Marion County Probate Records,* 3:34. Letters of administration: a legal document that confirms the petitioner's administration of the deceased's estate.

24. W. W. Sellers tells that Zilpha hired him to prosecute the killer, "a man by the name of Anderson . . . who was convicted of manslaughter and sentenced to two years in the State penitentiary" (*History of Marion County,* 211).

25. *Marion County Probate Records,* 3:35–36.

26. Sellers, *History of Marion County,* 211.

27. Roberts, *Roberts Family History,* 17.

28. Sellers, *History of Marion County,* 211.

29. Francis C. Sessions, *Materials for a History of the Sessions Family in America* (Albany: Joel Munsell's Sons, 1890); and genealogy notes from Lucile Fenegan.

30. Author interview with Ermine Floyd Matheny, September 30, 2006.

31. He appears in some roll books as "Laurin T. Sessions."

32. Janet B. Hewett and Joyce Lawrence, eds., *South Carolina Confederate Soldiers,* vol. 1, *Name Register* (Wilmington, NC: Broadfoot, 1991), 435.

33. The 1880 U.S. census locates him at Ridge in Williamsburg, South Carolina, as a dentist and farmer.

34. Edwin Jaquett Sellers, *English Ancestry of the Wayne Family of Pennsylvania* (Philadelphia: Allen, Lane & Scott, 1927), 22–35.

35. Despite her position as Queen of France, Marguerite produced no children, and the marriage to Henri IV was conveniently annulled by the Pope. In 1600, Henri married Marie de Medici in Florence. Their wedding festivities occasioned no massacre, but rather the invention of opera, or at least the first two specimens that have been preserved, Jacopo Peri's (1561–1633) *Euridice,* to a libretto by Ottavio Rinuccini (1562–1621), and Giulio Caccini's (1551–1618) setting of the same text, not performed for the festivities but published earlier that year.

36. Jon Butler, *The Huguenots in America* (Cambridge: Harvard University Press, 1983), 3–63, 91–143.

37. Literally, "mockingbirds," a colonial epithet for braggarts and chatterers.

38. Butler, *Huguenots in America,* 54.

39. 1900 Marion County census.

40. Confirmed by her son Michael's listing in the 1880 U.S. census, by which time he was head of household, living in Bethea, Marion County. In that reporting, Michael told interviewers that his father's birthplace was indeed Ireland.

41. Sean Michael O'Brien, *Irish Americans in the Confederate Army* (Jefferson, NC: McFarland, 2007), 21.

42. Named for Brigadier General Joseph B. Kershaw, born in Camden, South Carolina, near the Floyd's eventual home in Bethune, Kershaw County.

43. Sellers, *History of Marion County,* 591.

44. See Floyd, *Cold Sassy Tree* vocal score, 142.

45. *Diary,* April 15, 1952.

46. Author interview with Marjorie Manning, January 17, 2007.

47. All historical information on Wofford College provided in E-mail to the author from the archivist Dr. Phillip Stone, June 20, 2007.

48. *Diary,* June 18, 1983.

49. *Diary,* April 15, 1952.

50. *Diary,* November 19, 1961, and November 18, 1974.

Selected Bibliography

Archives

Boosey & Hawkes, New York, New York (B & H). Most cited documents are located at the firm's office at 229 West 28 Street, Floor 11, New York City: composer files, works files, promotional files.

Ernst Bacon Archive, Syracuse University Special Collections (SUSC).

Floyd Archive, Library of Congress, Washington, DC (FALOC). Locations as of November 2008: fourteen boxes of original music manuscripts, drafts, typescript librettos, etc.

Floyd Archive, South Caroliniana Library, University of South Carolina, Columbia (FASCL). As of 2011, the collection consists of fifteen boxes of personal papers: programs, reviews, correspondence, family papers, artifacts, and scrapbook. FASCL also has the diaries of Carlisle Sessions Floyd Sr. (Reverend Floyd, "Jack"), 40 vols., 1938–1986 (*Diary*). As of summer 2012, these are still in the cataloguing process.

Ford Foundation, New York, New York (FF). Documentation of grants and commissions to Floyd, New York City Opera, etc.

John Simon Guggenheim Memorial Foundation, New York, New York.

Juilliard Repertory Project Archives, Juilliard School of Music Library, New York, New York (JRP).

Willard Rhodes and Robert Penn Warren Archives, Yale Collection of American Literature, Beinecke Rare Book and Manuscript Library, Yale University (YCAL).

Writings of Carlisle Floyd

"Apologia for Composers of Opera." *Central Opera Service Bulletin* (November 1959): 1–2.

Bilby's Doll, A Musical Drama in Three Acts, part printed, part typed, with composer's handwritten changes, Box 2, FASCL. Printed copy, Melville, NY: Belwin-Mills, 1976. Handwritten and typescript librettos, Box 1, Folders 2–4, FALOC.

"*Bilby's Doll:* Origins and Conclusions." Houston Grand Opera program, February-March 1976. Copy in FASCL.

"Carlisle Floyd on Norman Treigle's Performance as Olin Blitch"; "Carlisle Floyd on New Orleans Opera Performance of *Susannah.*" VAI CD (VAIA 1115-2) liner notes. Pleasantville, NY: 1995.

Cold Sassy Tree. Typed scenario ("Overview and Characters"). February 17, 1997. Copy in FASCL.

"The Composer in Academia." *College Music Symposium 10, Journal of the College Music Society.* Geneva, NY: W. F. Humphrey Press, 1970.

"The Composer as Librettist." *Opera News.* New York: Metropolitan Opera Guild, November 10, 1962.

Flower and Hawk. Handwritten libretto, two versions of typescript libretti, c. 1971, Box 4, Folder 1, FALOC.

Fugitives. Handwritten libretto, 1950–1951, Box 4, Folder 4, FALOC.

"The Genesis of *The Sojourner and Mollie Sinclair.*" VAI CD (VAIA 1172) libretto notes. Pleasantville, NY: 1999.

Grandboy: Text for a Musical Drama in Three Acts. Two undated typed mss., c. 1976–1977. New York: Belwin-Mills. Copies in FASCL.

"An Homage to Phyllis." Typed ms. honoring Phyllis Curtin at celebration in Great Barrington, MA, August 4, 2007. Author's collection, courtesy of Carlisle Floyd.

"A Lengthening Shadow." Unpublished prose fiction, undated ms., c. 1946. Copy in FASCL, and Box 5, Folder 2, FALOC.

"Low-Country Town." Prose fiction, *The Concept* 43, no. 2 (1944): 6, 30–32. [Journal of Converse College, Spartanburg.] Copy in FASCL.

Markheim. Handwritten libretto on legal pad, 1965–1966, Box 5, Folder 3, FALOC.

A Mirror for Witches (handwritten below original typed title *Bilby's Doll*). Unpublished typed scenario and ms. libretto dated December 1956. Copy in FASCL.

Monologue. Two typescripts, one with comments in Patricia Neway's hand in margins, c. 1961, Box 5, Folder 4, FALOC.

"Music Notes." *Parley Voo.* March 5, 1945. [Publication of Converse College, Spartanburg.]

"Ode." Poem, *The Concept* 44, no. 1 (1945): 5. Copy in FASCL.

"The Making of an Opera: Some Considerations." *Creating and Producing Contemporary Opera and Musical Theater: A Series of Fifteen Monographs.* Washington, DC: Opera America, 1983.

"The Materials of Opera" (1998), typed ms., Box 10, FASCL.

Of Mice and Men. Handwritten libretto, version 1, 1964–1967, Box 7, Folder 1, FALOC. Typescript libretto, version 1, Box 6, Folder 5, FALOC.

"On Music Criticism." Unpublished ms., 1945–1946. Copy in FASCL.

The Opera Journal. University, MS: National Opera Association. Winter 1971 issue devoted to the world premiere of *Of Mice and Men:* "The Creation," by C. F.; "The Direction," by Frank Corsaro; "The Premiere," by Henry Holt; "The Performance," by Julian Patrick; "The Second Production," by Thomas Martin; "The Performance," by Robert Moulson and Carol Bayard; "The Publisher," by Robert Holton.

The Passion of Jonathan Wade, 1961–1962. Handwritten treatment/scenario and typed libretto, Box 8, Folder 1, FALOC.

The Passion of Jonathan Wade, 1991. Undated typed scenario, c. 1988/89. Undated typescript libretto, c. 1989, FASCL; and Box 8, Folder 1, FALOC.

"Playwriting in the Opera House" (together with complete *Susannah* libretto). *Theatre Arts Magazine,* January 1958.

"The 'Pounding.'" Prose fiction, *The Concept* 43, no. 4 (1944): 24–25, 37–38. Copy in Box 1, Folder 19, FASCL.

"Recalling *Susannah*'s Beginnings." Virgin Classics *Susannah* CD libretto notes (7 243 5 45039 2). London: Virgin Classics, 1994.

"Resolution." Poem, *Tabard Magazine,* Spring 1946, 20. [Publication of Syracuse University.]

Seth (*Reeds*). Unpublished typed scenario and ms. libretto, 1984–1985. Copy in FASCL.

"Society and the Artist." Typescript, 1964. Copy in FASCL.

"Society and the Artist." University of Houston *Forum,* Summer-Fall 1978. Copy in FASCL.

"Some Thoughts on the Creative Process." Unpublished ms., American Academy of Arts and Letters induction statement, May 16, 2001. Author's collection, courtesy of Carlisle Floyd.

"Some Thoughts on Opera by the Composer of *Susannah* and *Of Mice and Men:* An Interview with Carlisle Floyd." *Research in Review* 1, no. 4 (1970): 1–5. [Publication of Florida State University, Tallahassee.] Copy in FASCL.

"A Summing-Up at Seventy." Keynote address, April 28, 1997, Opera America twenty-seventh annual conference, Philadelphia, PA. *Opera America Newsline* 6, no. 10 (1997): 20–27. [Publication of Opera America, Washington, DC.]

Susannah. Pencil libretto, 1953; typescript libretto, 1953–1954, Box 11, Folder 1, FALOC.

"*Susannah:* An Interview with Carlisle Floyd." *Opera Cues,* Spring 1966. [Publication of Houston Grand Opera Guild.] Copy in FASCL.

"Thought." Poem, *The Concept* 43 no. 4 (1944): 15. Copy in FASCL.

"Too Dear, the Price." One-act play, *The Concept* 44, no. 2 (1945): 11, 34–36. Copy in FASCL.

"Transcendency." Poem, *The Concept* 44, no. 2 (1945): 16. Copy in FASCL.

"Tschaikowsky's Sixth, A Sketch." Prose fiction, *The Concept* 43, no. 4 (1944): 21. Copy in FASCL.

"Which Shall Not Perish from the Earth." Nonfiction prose, *The Concept* 44, no. 1 (1943): 9, 25–26. Copy in FASCL.

"Who Has Known the Panic." Prose fiction, unpublished ms., June 1946. Copy in FASCL.

Willie Stark. Handwritten treatment, c. 1976–1977, Box 1, Folder 2f, FALOC. Two typescript librettos, c. 1977–1979, Box 1, Folder 2d, FALOC. Set of character addenda, 1977–1981, Box 1, Folder 2e, FALOC.

"The Woman and the Romans." Prose fiction, unpublished ms., 1945. Copy in Box 1, Folder 19, FASCL.

Wuthering Heights. Typescript libretto, 1957; also act 3 revisions for New York City Opera, 1959, Box 14, Folder 4, FALOC.

Musical Works of Carlisle Floyd

"Among the Red Guns" (Sandburg). Unpublished ms., c. 1945, Box 1, Folder 1, FALOC.

Be Still, My Soul. Unpublished, untitled pencil two-piano score, texts for readings, in final volume of *Susannah* pencil vocal score, 1956, Box 11, Folder 2, FALOC.

Bilby's Doll. Pencil drafts of vocal score (6 vols.), 1975–1976, Box 2, Folders 1-4, FALOC. Printed vocal score, New York: Boosey & Hawkes, 1998.

Citizen of Paradise (Dickinson). Ms. sketches, inserts, c. 1984, Box 3, Folder 1, FALOC. Printed vocal score, New York: Belwin-Mills, 1983.

Cold Sassy Tree. Pencil draft vocal score (5 vols.), Box 3, Folders 2, 3, FALOC. Printed vocal score, New York: Boosey & Hawkes, 2000.

"Death Came Knocking" (Auslander). SATB chorus score transparencies, c. 1960, Box 3, Folder 4, FALOC. Published score, New York: Boosey & Hawkes, 1964.

"The Dream" (Brontë). Pencil ms., 1956–1957, Box 14, Folder 2, FALOC. Ms. vocal score, New York: Boosey & Hawkes, c. 1956–1957.

Episodes. 2 vols. Published scores, New York: Boosey & Hawkes, 1965.

"Evening Song" (Lanier). Unpublished ms. vocal score (2cc.), 1946, Box 10, Folder 5, FALOC.

"The Fairy's Song" (Yeats). Unpublished ms. vocal score, 1946. Copy in Box 10, Folder 5, FALOC.

Flourishes. Two-piano pencil ms., Box 4, Folder 6, FALOC. Undated published full score, New York: Boosey & Hawkes, c. 1987.

Flower and Hawk. Pencil ms. draft, c. 1971–1972, Box 4, Folder 3, FALOC. Vocal score transparencies, Box 4, Folder 2, FALOC. Published vocal score, New York: Belwin-Mills, 1977.

Frame of Remembrance. Unpublished, untitled pencil piano score in final volume of *Susannah,* 1955, Box 11, Folder 2, FALOC.

Fugitives. Pencil draft vocal score, 1950–1951, Box 4, Folder 5, FALOC. Unpublished vocal score transparencies, 1951, Box 4, Folder 4, FALOC.

"I Am a Beggar on a Lonely Hill" (Barrow). Unpublished ms. vocal score, 1948, Box 10, Folder 5, FALOC.

In Celebration. Two-piano pencil ms., c. 1970; between halves of pencil ms. vocal score of *The Martyr,* Box 5, Folder 4, FALOC.

Introduction, Aria, and Dance. Undated full score, c. 1968, New York: Theodore Presser. Copy in Box 5, Folder 1, FALOC.

"The Jaybird Song" (*Susannah*). Printed scores, New York: Boosey & Hawkes, 1956, 1957, 1964.

"Long, Long Ago." Vocal score transparencies, Box 4, Folder 6, FALOC. Published vocal score, New York: Boosey & Hawkes, 1967.

Lost Eden. Ms. two-piano score, New York: Boosey & Hawkes, c. 1951.

Markheim. Pencil draft vocal score, 1965–1966, Box 5, Folder 3, FALOC. Published vocal score, New York: Boosey & Hawkes, 1968.

The Martyr, Indicative of the Passion of the People on the 15th Day of April, 1865 (Melville). Pencil ms. vocal score, 1970–1971, Box 5, Folder 4, FALOC. Published vocal score, New York: Belwin-Mills, 1973.

Monologue. Unpublished pencil vocal score, c. 1961, Box 5, Folder 4, FALOC.

"Move Him into the Sun" (Owen). Unpublished pencil ms., c. 1948, Box 10, Folder 5, FALOC.

The Mystery (Mistral, trans. Fleet). Pencil draft ms. and vocal score transparencies, 1959–1960, Box 6, Folder 1, FALOC. Published vocal score, New York: Boosey & Hawkes, 1966.

Nocturne (Whitman). Unpublished ms. vocal score and voice part alone, March 5–10, 1952, Box 11, Folder 5, FALOC.

Odyssey for Cello and Piano. Unpublished pencil ms., 1948, Box 6, Folder 2, FALOC.

Of Mice and Men. Version 1 pencil draft scores, 5 vols., 1964–1967, Box 6, Folder 4, and Box 7, Folders 1 and 3, FALOC. Final vocal score transparencies, Version 2, 1967–1970, plus material cut from 1970 premiere and subsequent productions, Box 7, Folder 2, FALOC. Published vocal score, New York: Belwin-Mills, 1971.

"Old Song" (Crane). Ms. vocal score, 1948, Box 10, Folder 5, FALOC.

"Our Hearts Leap Up." *Singtime.* Tallahassee: Florida State University Recreation Association, 1953–1954. Strozier Library archives, M1958.F56.1953.

The Passion of Jonathan Wade (1962). Vocal score transparencies, Box 9, Folder 3, FALOC.

The Passion of Jonathan Wade (1991). Pencil ms. vocal score (6 vols.), Box 8, Folders 1–3, and Box 9, Folders 1–2, FALOC. Vocal score transparencies, Box 9, Folder 3, FALOC. Printed vocal score (3 vols.), New York: Boosey & Hawkes, 1998.

Pilgrimage. Pencil draft ms. vocal score, in volume of *Susannah* pencil ms. vocal score, c. 1955, Box 11, Folder 2, FALOC. Vocal score transparencies, Box 9, Folder 4, FALOC. Published vocal score, New York: Boosey & Hawkes, 1959. Undated full orchestral score, New York: Boosey & Hawkes, c. 1960. Version for baritone soloist and chorus, undated vocal score, c. 1962, New York: Boosey & Hawkes.

"Remember Me" (Rossetti). Unpublished ms. photocopy, 1945, Box 10, Folder 5, FALOC.

Slow Dusk. Ms. vocal score of Sadie's aria (1948), Box 10, Folder 1, FALOC. Published vocal score, New York: Boosey & Hawkes, 1957.

The Sojourner and Mollie Sinclair. Published vocal score, New York: Boosey & Hawkes, 1968.

Sonata for Piano. Pencil ms., c. 1957, Box 10, Folder 3, FALOC. Published score, New York: Boosey & Hawkes, 1959.

Soul of Heaven (texts by various authors). Pencil ms. vocal score, 1992, Box 10, Folder 4, FALOC. Vocal score transparencies, Box 12, Folder 1, FALOC. Printed vocal score, New York: Boosey & Hawkes, 1995.

"A Star Danced" (Shakespeare). Unpublished ms. vocal score, May 10, 1989, Box 12, Folder 1, FALOC.

Susannah. Mixed pencil/ink ms. vocal score, 1953/54, Box 11, Folders 1–2, FALOC. Pencil full score ms., Box 11, Folders 3–4, FALOC. Published vocal score, edited by Ross Reimueller, New York: Boosey & Hawkes, 1956, 1957, 1967.

Susannah Orchestral Suite (Hendl). Full orchestral score, New York: Boosey & Hawkes, 1958.

Theme and Variations. Two-piano score, one with notations for later orchestration, c. 1951, Box 11, Folder 5, FALOC. Pencil ms. full orchestral score, 1951, Box 11, Folder 4, FALOC. Two-piano ms. score, New York: Boosey & Hawkes, 1951.

A Time to Dance: Reflections on Mortality (texts by various authors). Pencil ms. vocal score, vocal score transparencies, Box 12, Folder 1, FALOC. Printed vocal score, New York: Boosey & Hawkes, 1996.

Two Stevenson Songs. "Rain" and "Where Go the Boats?" Vocal score transparencies, 1967, Box 4, Folder 6, FALOC. Published vocal score, New York: Boosey & Hawkes, 1967.

"When You Are Old" (Yeats). Unpublished ms. vocal score, 1944, Box 10, Folder 5, FALOC.

"Who Has Seen the Wind?" (Rossetti). Vocal score transparencies, 1967, Box 4, Folder 6, FALOC.

Willie Stark. Pencil draft vocal score (11 vols.), Box 12, Folders 3, 4, 5; Box 13, Folders 1–3, FALOC. Printed score (3 vols.), Melville, NY: Belwin-Mills, 1980.

A Woman Sings (ballet score). Unpublished pencil ms. piano score, marked *Music for Dance,* 1955, Box 5, Folder 5, FALOC.

Wuthering Heights. Pencil draft vocal score, 1958; revisions for NYCO, 1959, Box 14, Folders 1–3, FALOC. Published vocal score, New York: Boosey & Hawkes, 1961.

Wuthering Heights Symphonic Suite. Full orchestral score, New York: Boosey & Hawkes, 1960.

Books, Articles, and Sheet Music

Abstracts of Virginia Land Patents and Grants, 1623–1666. Vol. 1. Baltimore: Genealogical Publishing Co., 1983.

Alston, Lee J., Wayne Grove, and David C. Wheelock. *Structural Causes of Rural Bank Failures in the Twenties: Parallels with the Eighties.* Cliometric Society ASSA Session, August 1990. Available online: http://cliometrics.org/conferences/ASSA/Dec_90/Alston-Grove-Wheelock.shtml.

Argento, Dominick. *Catalogue Raisonné as Memoir: A Composer's Life.* Minneapolis: University of Minnesota Press, 2004.

Arnow, Harriett Simpson. *The Dollmaker.* New York: Macmillan, 1954.

Auslander, Joseph. *No Traveller Returns.* New York: Harper & Row, 1935.

———. *Sunrise Trumpets.* New York: Harper & Row, 1924.

Babbitt, Milton. "Who Cares If You Listen." *High Fidelity,* February 1958. Available online: http://www.palestrant.com/babbitt.html.

Bacon, Ernst. *Notes on the Piano.* Seattle: University of Washington Press, 1981.

———. *Words on Music.* Syracuse: Syracuse University Press, 1960.

Bauerlein, Mark, and Ellen Grantham. *National Endowment for the Arts: A History, 1965–2008.* Washington, DC: National Endowment for the Arts, 2009.

Bliss, Edward Jr., ed. *In Search of Light: The Broadcasts of Edward R. Murrow, 1938–1961.* New York: Alfred A. Knopf, 1967.

Blotner, Joseph. *Robert Penn Warren: A Biography.* New York: Random House, 1997.

Blue, Robert Wilder. "An American Baritone: Julian Patrick Keeps on Singing." *US OperaWeb,* January 2002.

———. "Carlisle Floyd Continues His Exploration of Southern Life in His First Major Comic Opera." *USOperaWeb,* February 2001.

———. "Catherine Malfitano's Brilliant Career." *USOpera Web,* September 2001.

———. "Connecting with the Characters: Australian Director Bruce Beresford Brings an American Work to the Opera Stage." *US OperaWeb,* February 2001.

———. "The Double Life of Jonathan Wade," *USOperaWeb,* May 2001.

———. "From Literary Classic to Hit Opera: Mark Adamo Traces the Journey of *Little Women* to the Stage." *USOperaWeb,* May 2001.

———. "The Inseparable Histories of Julius Rudel and New York City Opera: A Reminiscence." *USOperaWeb,* September 2002.

———. "On the Fast Track: Anthony Dean Griffey." *USOpera Web,* January 2002.

———. "Operas We Would Like to See Again: Carlisle Floyd Discusses *Wuthering Heights, The Passion of Jonathan Wade, Bilby's Doll,* and *Willie Stark.*" USOperaWeb, September 2002.

———. "Patrick Summers Talks about Carlisle Floyd and American Opera." *US OperaWeb,* February 2001.

———. "Verdi Baritone Gordon Hawkins Takes On a Great American Role," *US OperaWeb,* January 2002.

Bromfield, Louis. *Wild Is the River.* New York: Harper & Brothers, 1941.

Brontë, Emily. *Wuthering Heights.* New York: Oxford University Press, 1985.

Burnham, Clara, and George F. Root. *Snow White and the Seven Dwarfs, An Operetta for Young People.* Philadelphia: John Church, 1916.

Burns, Olive Ann. *Cold Sassy Tree.* New York: Delta/Dell, 1994.

Butler, Jon. *The Huguenots in America: A Refugee People in New World Society.* Cambridge: Harvard University Press, 1983.

Carner, Mosco. *Puccini: A Critical Biography.* New York: Alfred A. Knopf, 1959.

Carter, Hodding. *The Angry Scar: The Story of Reconstruction.* Garden City: Doubleday, 1959.

Chesnut, Mary Boykin. *A Diary from Dixie.* Edited by Ben Ames Williams. Cambridge: Harvard University Press, 1980.

Coffman, Teresa S. "Carlisle Floyd's Text Settings in His Works for Chorus." *Choral Journal* 39, no. 8 (1999): 37–46.

Cohn, Arthur. "Floyd, Carlisle." In *Recorded Classical Music: A Critical Guide to Compositions and Performances.* New York: Schirmer Books, 1981.

Coogan, Michael D., et al., eds. *The New Oxford Annotated Apocrypha.* 3rd ed. Oxford: Oxford University Press, 2007.

Copland, Aaron. "Composer from Brooklyn." *Magazine of Art,* September 1939, 32. Reprinted in Aaron Copland. *Our New Music.* New York: Whittlesey House, 1941.

Corsaro, Frank. *Maverick.* New York: The Vanguard Press, 1978.

Cowser, R. L. Jr. "Kingfish of American Opera: An Interview with Carlisle Floyd." *The Southern Quarterly* (Spring 1982): 5–18.

Curtin, Philip D. *On the Fringes of History: A Memoir.* Athens: Ohio University Press, 2005.

Curtin, Phyllis. "Phyllis Curtin Reminisces about Her Early Productions of Carlisle Floyd's *Susannah.*" Liner notes for Video Artists International CD of New Orleans Opera 1962 production. VAI CD (VAIA 1115-2). Pleasantville, NY: 1995.

Cutrer, Thomas W. *Parnassus on the Mississippi: The Southern Review and the Baton Rouge Literary Community, 1935–1942.* Baton Rouge: Louisiana State University Press, 1984.

Day-Lewis, Cecil. *A Time to Dance and Other Poems.* New York: Random House, 1936.

Dickinson, Emily. *The Complete Poems.* Edited by Thomas H. Johnson. New York: Little Brown, 1961.

Dryden, John. *The Poetical Works of John Dryden.* London: William Pickering, 1852.

Duberman, Martin. *The Worlds of Lincoln Kirstein.* New York: Alfred A. Knopf, 2007.

Ellis, Alice Thomas. *The Birds of the Air.* New York: Viking, 1981.

Enright, D. J., ed. *The Oxford Book of Death.* Oxford: Oxford University Press, 1987.

Ewen, David. *Composers since 1900.* New York: H. W. Wilson, 1969.

Floyd, N. J. *Biographical Genealogies of the Virginia-Kentucky Floyd Families.* Baltimore: Williams & Watkins, 1912.

Foner, Eric. *Reconstruction: America's Unfinished Revolution, 1863–1877.* New York: Harper Collins, 1988.

Forbes, Esther. *A Mirror for Witches.* Chicago: Academy Publishers, 1985.

Gide, André. *Two Symphonies.* New York: Alfred A. Knopf, 1954.

Glasgow, Ellen. *In This Our Life.* New York: Harcourt, Brace, 1941.

Glover, Lorri. *All Our Relations: Blood Ties and Emotional Bonds among the Early South Carolina Gentry.* Baltimore: Johns Hopkins University Press, 2000.

Grassby, Richard. *Business Community of Seventeenth-Century England.* Cambridge: Cambridge University Press, 1995.

Gruen, John. *Menotti.* New York: Macmillan, 1978.

Heumann, Scott. "The Trial of Willie Stark." *Opera News,* April 11, 1981.

Hewett, Janet B., and Joyce Lawrence, eds. *South Carolina Confederate Soldiers, 1861–1865*, vol. 1, *Name Register.* Wilmington, NC: Broadfoot, 1991.

Hinson, Maurice. *Guide to the Pianist's Repertoire.* 3rd ed. Bloomington: Indiana University Press, 2000.

Hubbs, Nadine. *The Queer Composition of America's Sound: Gay Modernists, American Music, and National Identity.* Berkeley and Los Angeles: University of California Press, 2004.

Huennekens, Bert F. "Headwork." *The Open Road for Boys.* Boston: Open Road, 1935.

Hyman, Harold M. *Era of the Oath: Northern Loyalty Oaths during the Civil War and Reconstruction.* Philadelphia: University of Pennsylvania Press, 1954.

Kelly, Amy. *Eleanor of Aquitaine and the Four Kings.* Cambridge: Harvard University Press, 1950.

Kimberley, Nick. "Floyd and His *Susannah.*" *Opera,* August 1994.

Kolodin, Irving. *The Metropolitan Opera, 1883–1966.* New York: Alfred A. Knopf, 1968.

Leinsdorf, Erich. *Cadenza: A Musical Career.* Boston: Houghton Mifflin, 1976.

Magrath, Jane. *The Pianist's Guide to Standard Teaching and Performance Literature.* Van Nuys, CA: Alfred, c. 1995.

Marion County Probate Records. Vol. 3. Hemingway, SC: Three Rivers Historical Society, 1985.

Martens, Anne Coulter. *Don't Darken My Door!* Chicago: Dramatic Publishing Company, 1936.

Masterson, James F. *The Real Self: A Developmental Self and Object Relations Approach.* New York: Brunner/Mazel, 1985.

———. *The Real Self: Unmasking the Personality Disorders of Our Age.* New York: Collier Macmillan, 1988.

Meyer, Duane. *The Highland Scots of North Carolina, 1732–1776.* Chapel Hill: University of North Carolina Press, 1957, 1961.

Moore, Judith. *Fat Girl, A True Story.* New York: Hudson Street Press, 2005.

———. *Never Eat Your Heart Out.* New York: Farrar Straus Giroux, 1997.

Mordden, Ethan. *Opera in the Twentieth Century: Sacred, Profane, Godot.* New York: Oxford University Press, 1978.

———. *The Splendid Art of Opera: A Concise History.* New York: Methuen, 1982.

———. "Unprotected Poet." *Opera News,* February 7, 1976.

Morgan, Brian. *Strange Child of Chaos: Norman Treigle.* New York: iUniverse, 2006.

Nixon, Marni. *I Could Have Sung All Night.* New York: Billboard Books, 2006.

Noyle, Linda J. *Pianists on Playing: Interviews with Twelve Concert Pianists.* Metuchen, NJ: Scarecrow Press, 1987.

O'Brien, Sean Michael. *Irish Americans in the Confederate Army.* Jefferson, NC: McFarland, 2007.

Opera News. Issue devoted in part to broadcast of *Susannah* on April 3, 1999. Articles by William R. Braun, Julius Rudel, Barrymore Laurence Scherer, Paul Thomason. April 1999.

Ostrow, Stuart. *Present at the Creation: Leaping in the Dark, and Going against the Grain.* New York: Applause Theatre and Cinema Books, 2006.

Parini, Jay. *John Steinbeck: A Biography.* New York: Henry Holt, 1995.

Paynter, Theodosia, and G. A. Grant-Schaefer. *The Adventures of Pinocchio* (Wichita: R. A. Hoffman, 1935).

Pike, James S. *The Prostrate State: South Carolina under Negro Government.* New York: D. Appleton Company, 1874; Harper Torchbooks, 1968.

Redwood, Christopher, ed. *A Delius Companion.* New York: Da Capo Press, 1977.

Roberts, Marylyn M. *The Roberts Family History.* Greenville, SC: A Press, 1983.

Rorem, Ned. *The Later Diaries of Ned Rorem, 1961–1972.* San Francisco: North Point Press, 1983.

———. *Lies: A Diary, 1986–1999.* Cambridge: DaCapo/Perseus, 2002.

———. *The Nantucket Diary of Ned Rorem, 1973–1985.* San Francisco: North Point Press, 1987.

Sabin, Robert. "Some Younger Composers." *Tempo* (Spring 1963): 25–26.

Sellers, Edwin Jaquett. *English Ancestry of the Wayne Family of Pennsylvania.* Philadelphia: Allen, Lane & Scott, 1927.

Sellers, W. W. *A History of Marion County, South Carolina.* Columbia, SC: R. L. Bryan, 1902; reissued by Marion Public Library, 1956.

Sessions, Francis C. *Materials for a History of the Sessions Family in America.* Albany: Joel Munsell's Sons, 1890.

Sills, Beverly. *Bubbles.* Indianapolis: Bobbs-Merrill, 1976.

Smith, Lillian. *Strange Fruit.* New York: Harvest, 1944; Harcourt, Brace, 1992.

Smith, Steven C. *A Heart at Fire's Center: The Life and Music of Bernard Herrmann.* Berkeley and Los Angeles: University of California Press, 1991.

Sokol, Martin M. *The New York City Opera: An American Adventure.* New York: Macmillan, 1981.

South Carolina: Race and Hispanic Origin, 1790 to 1990. Washington, DC: U.S. Census Bureau, 1990.

Steinbeck, John. *Of Mice and Men.* New York: Library of America, 1994.

———. *Of Mice and Men.* New York: Dramatists Play Service, 1937, 1964.

Steiner, W. H. "South Carolina Cash Depositories." *Southern Economic Journal* 4, no. 1 (1937): 28–37.

Stern, Abram. *Asthma and Emotion.* New York: Gardner Press, 1981.

Stevenson, Robert Louis. *The Complete Short Stories, with a Selection of the Best Short Novels.* Edited by Charles Neider. New York: Da Capo Press, 1998.

Stiller, Andrew. "Floyd, Carlisle (Sessions, Jr.)." *New Grove Dictionary of Opera.* Vol. 2. London: Macmillan, 1992.

Stokes, Durward T. *The History of Dillon County, South Carolina.* Columbia: University of South Carolina Press, 1978.

Styron, William. *Darkness Visible: A Memoir of Madness.* New York: New Vintage Books, 1992.

Tarkington, Booth. *Penrod.* New York: Penguin, 2007.

Wallace, Helen. *Boosey & Hawkes: The Publishing Story.* London: Boosey & Hawkes, 2007.

Warlock, Peter (Philip Heseltine). *Frederick Delius.* London: Oxford University Press, 1952.

Warren, Robert Penn. *All the King's Men.* New York: Harcourt, Brace, 1946.

———. *The Collected Poems of Robert Penn Warren.* Edited by John Burt. Baton Rouge: Louisiana State University Press, 1998.

Weir, Robert M. *Colonial South Carolina: A History.* Millwood, NY: KTO Press, 1983.

Wignall, Harrison James. *In Mozart's Footsteps: A Travel Guide for Music Lovers.* New York: Paragon House, 1991.

Woody, Howard, and Davie Beard. *South Carolina Postcards,* vol. 7, *Kershaw County.* Charleston: Arcadia, 2004.

Zeigler, Eugene N. Jr. *When Conscience and Power Meet: A Memoir.* Columbia: University of South Carolina Press, 2008.

Index

Italic page number denotes illustration.